Dreamweaver® and Flash™ Bible

Joseph Lowery, Robert Reinhardt, and Jon Warren Lentz

Hungry Minds™

Best-Selling Books • Digital Downloads • e-Books • Answer Networks • e-Newsletters • Branded Web Sites • e-Learning

New York, NY ♦ Cleveland, OH ♦ Indianapolis, IN

Dreamweaver® and Flash™ Bible

Published by
Hungry Minds, Inc.
909 Third Avenue
New York, NY 10022
www.hungryminds.com

Copyright © 2001 Hungry Minds, Inc. All rights reserved. No part of this book, including interior design, cover design, and icons, may be reproduced or transmitted in any form, by any means (electronic, photocopying, recording, or otherwise) without the prior written permission of the publisher.

Library of Congress Catalog No: 2001090746

ISBN: 0-7645-4864-6

Printed in the United States of America

10 9 8 7 6 5 4 3 2 1

1B/RZ/QW/QR/IN

Distributed in the United States by Hungry Minds, Inc.

Distributed by CDG Books Canada Inc. for Canada; by Transworld Publishers Limited in the United Kingdom; by IDG Norge Books for Norway; by IDG Sweden Books for Sweden; by IDG Books Australia Publishing Corporation Pty. Ltd. for Australia and New Zealand; by TransQuest Publishers Pte Ltd. for Singapore, Malaysia, Thailand, Indonesia, and Hong Kong; by Gotop Information Inc. for Taiwan; by ICG Muse, Inc. for Japan; by Intersoft for South Africa; by Eyrolles for France; by International Thomson Publishing for Germany, Austria, and Switzerland; by Distribuidora Cuspide for Argentina; by LR International for Brazil; by Galileo Libros for Chile; by Ediciones ZETA S.C.R. Ltda. for Peru; by WS Computer Publishing Corporation, Inc., for the Philippines; by Contemporanea de Ediciones for Venezuela; by Express Computer Distributors for the Caribbean and West Indies; by Micronesia Media Distributor, Inc. for Micronesia; by Chips Computadoras S.A. de C.V. for Mexico; by Editorial Norma de Panama S.A. for Panama; by American Bookshops for Finland.

For general information on Hungry Minds' products and services please contact our Customer Care department within the U.S. at 800-762-2974, outside the U.S. at 317-572-3993 or fax 317-572-4002.

For sales inquiries and reseller information, including discounts, premium and bulk quantity sales, and foreign-language translations, please contact our Customer Care department at 800-434-3422, fax 317-572-4002 or write to Hungry Minds, Inc., Attn: Customer Care Department, 10475 Crosspoint Boulevard, Indianapolis, IN 46256.

For information on licensing foreign or domestic rights, please contact our Sub-Rights Customer Care department at 212-884-5000.

For information on using Hungry Minds' products and services in the classroom or for ordering examination copies, please contact our Educational Sales department at 800-434-2086 or fax 317-572-4005.

For press review copies, author interviews, or other publicity information, please contact our Public Relations department at 317-572-3168 or fax 317-572-4168.

For authorization to photocopy items for corporate, personal, or educational use, please contact Copyright Clearance Center, 222 Rosewood Drive, Danvers, MA 01923, or fax 978-750-4470.

Credits

Acquisitions Editor
Carol Sheehan

Project Editor
Mildred Sanchez

Technical Editor
Jeffrey Bardzell
Shane Elliot
Derren Whiteman

Copy Editors
Richard H. Adin
Kelly Campbell Hogue
Roxanne Marini
Nancy Rapoport
Laura Stone

Permissions Editors
Carmen Krikorian
Laura Moss

Media Development Specialist
Megan Decraene

Media Development Coordinator
Marisa Pearman

Project Coordinator
Regina Snyder

Graphics and Production Specialists
Amy Adrian
Sean Decker
Joyce Haughey
LeAndra Johnson
Stephanie Jumper
Betty Shulte
Rashell Smith

Quality Control Technicians
Laura Albert
Andy Hollandbeck
Susan Moritz
Carl Pierce
Linda Quigley

Proofreading and Indexing
TECHBOOKS Production Services

About the Authors

Joseph Lowery has been writing about computers and new technology since 1981. He is the author of the previous editions of *Dreamweaver Bible* and *Fireworks Bible* as well as *Buying Online For Dummies* (all from Hungry Minds Inc., formerly IDG Books Worldwide). He has recently co-written a book on Flash with designer Hillman Curtis and has written books on HTML and on using the Internet for business. Joseph is Webmaster for a variety of sites and is a Web-design trainer and consultant. Joseph and his wife, dancer/choreographer Debra Wanner, have a daughter, Margot.

Robert Reinhardt's curiosity and autodidactic energy have carried him from psychology (University of Toronto) to new-media authoring, teaching, and writing. After discovering the Internet while studying in the Image Arts department at Ryerson in Toronto, Robert began the journey of discovery that eventually allowed him to fuse his interest in technology and communication with his background in the visual arts.

Robert has developed and taught workshops and has become increasingly involved with the development of systems for interactive interfaces and data management. Although his head often leads him into the land of scripting and programming, he remains dedicated to the world of images. During their first year in Los Angeles,

Robert and his partner, Snow Dowd, formed a multimedia consulting and design company called the *Makers* (http://www.theMakers.com). They created a broadband Website for "Gossip" with Warner Bros. Online and created graphics for a tie-in video with the band *Tonic*. Recently, the *Makers* have created screen graphics for *The Pledge* and have worked with Outlaw Productions on previsualization graphics for the forthcoming Warner Bros. film *Training Day*. In addition to doing work for entertainment companies, the *Makers* have done work for independent artists and nonprofit organizations.

While establishing the *Makers*, Robert worked as senior art director and program developer with http://www.Rampt.com to create a unique Flash interface and search engine, launched in November 1999. After being recognized as a Macromedia Site of the Day and nominated in the FlashForward film festival in New York, Rampt received the Bandies 2000 award for Best Interface Application, as well as an award of excellence from the New Media Invision Awards 2000. Currently, he develops and teaches Flash workshops with http://Lynda.com and the Moviola Digital Education Center in California, as well as doing on-site training and seminars for clients in the U.S. and Canada. Robert was a speaker at the San Francisco and New York FlashForward 2000 conferences, as well as at the October 2000 DV Web Expo in Long Beach, California.

Jon Warren Lentz is the author of *Flash Bible* and is involved in a number of Flash-related projects, most notably, http://www.Flash-Guru.com. Jon founded Flash-Guru.com because he observed the need for sustained, learner-centered training on a variety of intermediate to advanced Flash topics. Using the *Flash Bible* as a reference, the courses at his Web site are designed to help you implement advanced Flash techniques in your workflow and include in-depth information and developments that occur after publication.

Jon graduated from the Classical Studies program at UCSC, where he received his first notice as a poet and translator. He then metamorphosed into a sculptor and began working with sand-carved glass — a process he helped define as a fine art medium. Following a disabling accident, he reinvented himself as an artist by working with cameras and computers. Jon's images have been featured in the *Graphis Poster Annual*, *Mac Art & Design Magazine* (Sweden), *IdN — The International Designer's Network Magazine* (Hong Kong), and *Shutterbug Magazine*. Jon's abstract fine art and a selection of his glass sculpture may be viewed online at http://www.uncom.com.

Jon is an occasional professor at Palomar College. Although he has taught and lectured on digital art, design, and technology at many venues, he prefers to stay home, work on his own projects, and go to the beach. He resides with his family near San Diego, California.

For the Dreamweaver community — from the program creators to the program users — this book would not exist without your enthusiasm, support, and vision.

JL

To Snow, Stella, and Al. I won't forget the year 2000.

RJR

I dedicate my efforts on this book to the memory of my mother-in-law, Phyllis Rogers.

I also would like to thank my family — near and far — for their unconditional love, support, and encouragement, especially my wife, Roanne, my son, Rob, and my mother and father. In addition, I am thankful for my newfound friends, Jeffrey Bardzell and Nik Schramm, for their wisdom, expertise, and encouragement.

JWL

Foreword

When I first heard that two of the best-selling Bibles — *Dreamweaver 4 Bible* and *Flash 5 Bible* — were going to be combined into one volume, I thought, "Wow, that's product integration!" The more I thought about the concept, the more I realized that the combination was at the forefront of the cutting-edge. Dreamweaver and Flash together embrace the spectrum of Web development: from straight-up professional HTML sites to full-fledged interactive Flash sites to the future of the Web and the marriage of the two technologies. *Dreamweaver and Flash Bible* couldn't come at a more opportune time for savvy Web designers.

Let me back up that statement with a bit of history. Three years ago, when Flash first hit the Web, designers weren't sure how to use Flash or even if they could use it. Despite the relatively small footprint of the Flash Player plugin, its lack of market penetration was a prime concern to many developers and their clients. "Sure, it's quick to install," we'd hear time and again, "but how do we get them to install it to begin with?" Two paths emerged — one forged by Macromedia itself and the other by the community of Flash developers. Macromedia undertook an aggressive and timely push to ensure that the Flash Player was available through many venues. This strategy seems to have been very successful, as the Flash Player is now pre-installed in all Windows 95, 98, and Millennium Edition systems, as well as in all Macintosh systems since version 8.1. Moreover, the Flash Player is part of Internet Explorer 5.5, Netscape Communicator, Netscape 6, and America Online browsers. On the community side of the equation, Flash designers have created a wellspring of interactive, compelling animations and presentations that have made Flash Player a must-have. Together, Macromedia and Flash developers have succeeded beyond our imaginations and, as of this writing, 96% of all Web users have a version of the Flash Player installed.

In the world of HTML, Dreamweaver has taken a different route to success. From its introduction in 1997, Dreamweaver was heralded by serious Web coders and fledgling designers alike. No other tool on the market respected the integrity of the code as much as Dreamweaver did with its Round-Trip HTML editing. For those just entering the world of Web design, Dreamweaver provided a fast on-ramp with its built-in Dynamic HTML behaviors that provided cross-browser compatibility with point-and-click ease. Dreamweaver has continued to innovate with each new release, enhancing its viability to the range of Internet and Intranet developers. Today, Dreamweaver is used by over 1.1 million Web professionals, representing a marketshare of over 70% worldwide.

So, Dreamweaver and Flash are the two most popular Web tools available today, but should they be used together? In a word, yes. Increasingly, we're seeing the age of full-site Flash experimentation evolve into a sophisticated integration of enhanced Flash navigation with fully-searchable HTML content. Likewise, HTML site developers are discovering Flash techniques for creating a better user experience while maintaining their accessibility. Moreover, using the two technologies together seems to further cross-pollination: Dreamweaver designers who begin building a slicker user interface with Flash components such as Flash Buttons and Flash Text might find themselves creating an all-Flash site. Likewise, Flash authors intent on finding new ways to interact with a movie through Dreamweaver hotspots might encounter a client who requires both a Flash and an HTML side. In today's economy, the developer who has a firm grasp on the hottest technologies is in greatest demand.

Look at *Dreamweaver and Flash Bible* as your roadmap to the future of Web development; it's a cutting-edge resource for cutting-edge technologies.

Kevin Lynch
President Products and Office of the President, Macromedia

Preface

Web designers are relentless explorers in the ever-expanding frontier of the World Wide Web. Boundary-pushing is not only the norm; it's practically a job requirement — one of the reasons Dreamweaver and Flash are the leading Web design programs today. Dreamweaver provides the tools you need to build any type of Web site you can imagine. Flash has the astounding ability to generate compact, vector-based graphics and animations for delivery over the Web. Cutting-edge applications require cutting-edge resources — that's the reason *Dreamweaver and Flash Bible* has been written.

Among other accolades, Macromedia's Dreamweaver has one of the most appropriate product names in recent memory. Web-page design is a blend of art and craft; whether you're a deadline-driven professional or a vision-filled amateur, Dreamweaver is the perfect tool for many Web designers. Dreamweaver is not only the first Web-authoring tool to bring the ease of visual editing to an HTML code-oriented world; it brings a point-and-click interface to complex JavaScript coding.

Flash 5 has greatly expanded the interactive and programmatic features of Flash movies. Flash movies can communicate directly with server-side scripts and programs, using standard URL-encoded variables or XML-formatted structures. Sounds can be imported and exported as MP3 audio for high-quality music on the Web at the smallest file sizes. The Flash interface now looks and feels like other Macromedia products, with tool options contained in user-configurable panels. Third-party developers are creating applications that output to the Flash movie format, .SWF files. Flash is poised to be the central application for generating hot, low-bandwidth, interactive content for delivery over the Web.

Who Should Read This Book?

Both Dreamweaver and Flash attract a wide range of Web developers and artists. Because Dreamweaver is the first Web-authoring tool that doesn't rewrite original code, veteran designers are drawn to using Dreamweaver as their first visual editor. Because Dreamweaver automates complicated effects, beginning Web designers are interested in its power and performance. *Dreamweaver and Flash Bible* addresses the spectrum of Web professionals, providing basic information on HTML if you're just starting as well as advanced tips and tricks for seasoned pros. Moreover, this book is a complete reference for everyone working with Dreamweaver and Flash on a daily basis.

Dreamweaver and Flash Bible is a comprehensive and exhaustive reference on Flash. It helps you get started on your first day with the program and remains a valuable resource when you've attained mastery of the program. When you are looking for clues on how to integrate Flash with other programs so that you can deliver unique and compelling content in the Flash format, you know where to turn.

What Hardware and Software Do You Need?

If you don't own a copy of either Dreamweaver 4 or Flash 5, you can use the trial versions on this book's CD-ROM. Written to be platform-independent, this book covers both Macintosh and Windows versions.

Macintosh

Macromedia recommends the following minimum requirements for running Dreamweaver on a Macintosh:

+ Power Macintosh PowerPC (G3 or higher recommended)
+ MacOS 8.6 or 9.*x*
+ 32MB of available RAM
+ 135MB of available disk space
+ Color monitor capable of 800 × 600 resolution
+ CD-ROM drive

Windows

Macromedia recommends the following minimum requirements for running Dreamweaver on a Windows system:

+ Intel Pentium processor, 200MHz or equivalent (Pentium II or higher recommended)
+ Windows 9*x*/ME, NT 4.0 (with Service Pack 3) or Windows 2000
+ 48MB of available RAM
+ 110MB of available disk space
+ 256-color monitor capable of 800 × 600 resolution
+ CD-ROM drive

Note   These are the minimum requirements. As with all graphics-based design tools, more capability is definitely better for using Dreamweaver, especially in terms of memory and processor speed.

How This Book Is Organized

Dreamweaver and Flash Bible can take you from raw beginner to full-fledged professional if you read it cover to cover. However, you're more likely to read each section as needed, taking the necessary information and coming back later. To facilitate this approach, *Dreamweaver and Flash Bible* is divided into 11 major task-oriented parts. Once you're familiar with Dreamweaver and Flash, feel free to skip around the book, using it as a reference guide as you build your own knowledge base. Parts 1 through 6 cover Dreamweaver, and Parts 7 through 11 are Flash-oriented.

The early chapters in the Dreamweaver and Flash sections present the basics, and all chapters contain clearly written steps for the tasks you need to perform. In later chapters, you encounter sections labeled "Dreamweaver Techniques" and "Expert Tutorials in Flash." Both "Dreamweaver Techniques" and the "Flash Expert Tutorials" include step-by-step instructions for accomplishing specific Web-designer tasks — for example, building an image map that uses rollovers or eliminating underlines from hyperlinks through Cascading Style Sheets. Naturally, you can use these sections as stepping stones for your own explorations into Web-page creation and Flash-movie creation.

If you're running Dreamweaver or Flash while reading this book, don't forget to use the CD-ROMs. An integral element of the book, the accompanying CD-ROM offers a vast number of additional Dreamweaver behaviors, objects, commands, browser profiles, and other extensions in addition to relevant code and Flash examples from the book.

Part I: Getting Started with Dreamweaver

Part I begins with an overview of Dreamweaver's philosophy and design. To get the most out of the program, you need to understand the key advantages it offers over other authoring and the deficiencies it addresses. Part I takes you all the way to setting up your first site. In Chapter 2, you get an overview of the Web development process as a quick start to Dreamweaver.

The other opening chapters give you a full reference to the Dreamweaver interface and all of its customizable features. Chapter 6 takes you from the consideration of various Web site design models to publishing your finished site on the Internet, and Chapter 7 shows you how to make the most of Dreamweaver's FTP Site window.

Part II: Using Basic HTML in Dreamweaver

Although Dreamweaver is partly a visual design tool, its roots derive from the language of the Web: HTML. Part II gives you a solid foundation in the basics of HTML, even if you've never seen code. Chapter 8 covers HTML theory, describing how a Web page is constructed and alerting you to some potential pitfalls.

The three fundamentals of Web pages are text, images, and links. You explore how to incorporate these elements to their fullest extent in Chapters 9, 10, and 11, respectively.

Part III: Incorporating Advanced HTML

Part III begins to investigate some of the more advanced structural elements of HTML as implemented in Dreamweaver. Chapter 13 examines the various uses of tables — from a clear presentation of data to organizing entire Web pages. Here you learn to use Dreamweaver 4's greatly enhanced visual-table-editing capabilities to resize and reshape your HTML tables quickly.

Chapter 14 investigates the somewhat complex world of frames and shows how Dreamweaver has greatly simplified the task of building and managing these multi-file creations, particularly with the new Frame objects. In addition, you learn to handle more advanced design tasks, such as updating multiple frames with just one click.

With its own set of objects and behaviors, Dreamweaver complements HTML's extensibility. Chapter 15 offers an in-depth look at the capabilities of Dreamweaver behaviors. Each standard behavior is covered in detail with step-by-step instructions.

Part IV: Adding Multimedia Elements to Dreamweaver

In recent years, the Web has moved from a relatively static display of text and simple images to a full-blown multimedia circus with streaming video, background music, and interactive animations. Part IV contains the power tools for incorporating various media files into your Web site.

Graphics remain the key medium on the Web today, and Macromedia's Fireworks is a top-notch graphics generator. Chapter 16 delves into methods for incorporating Fireworks graphics — with all the requisite rollover and other code intact. Special focus is given to the Dreamweaver-to-Fireworks communication link and how your Web- production efforts can benefit from it.

In addition to Dreamweaver, Macromedia is perhaps best known for one other contribution to Web multimedia: Flash. Chapter 17 explores the possibilities offered by incorporating Flash and Shockwave movies into Dreamweaver-designed Web pages and includes everything you need to know about configuring MIME types. You find step-by-step instructions for building Shockwave inline controls and playing Shockwave movies in frame-based Web pages, as well as instructions for adding Flash buttons, Flash text, and Generator objects.

Part V: Working with Dynamic HTML and Dreamweaver

Dynamic HTML brought a new world of promises to Web designers — promises that went largely unfulfilled until Dreamweaver was released. Part V of *Dreamweaver and Flash Bible* examines this brave new world of pixel-perfect positioning, layers that fly in and then disappear as if by magic, and Web sites that can change their look and feel at the click of a mouse.

Chapter 18 takes a detailed look at the elegance of Cascading Style Sheets and offers techniques for accomplishing the most frequently requested tasks, such as creating an external style sheet. Many of the advantages of Dynamic HTML come from the use of layers, which enable absolute positioning of page elements, visibility control, and a sense of depth. You discover how to handle all these layer capabilities and more in Chapter 19. Chapter 20 focuses on timelines, which have the potential to take your Web page into the fourth dimension. The chapter concludes with a blow-by-blow description of creating a multiscreen slide show, complete with layers that fly in and out on command.

Part VI: Enhancing Website Management and Workflow in Dreamweaver

Although Web-page design gets all the glory, Website management pays the bills. In Part VII, you see how Dreamweaver makes this essential part of any Webmaster's day easier to handle. Chapter 21 starts off the section with a look at the use of Dreamweaver Templates and how they can speed up production while ensuring a unified look and feel across your Web site. Chapter 22 covers the Library, which can significantly reduce any Webmaster's workload by providing reusable and updateable page elements.

Part VII: Mastering the Flash Environment

The first part of this book explores the Flash file format and the interface of Flash 5, explaining the context in which Flash movies interact on the Web (Chapter 23), and working with the new Panels and tools (Chapters 24-28). Specifically, you can read about the new Pen Tool in Chapter 26.

Part VIII: Creating Flash Graphics

After you've learned to work your way through the Flash interface, you can read about the timeline structures (Chapter 30) and the Flash Library (Chapter 31), where you learn about the Symbol types in Flash 5. You can start to learn how to draw with Flash (Chapter 32), animate with Motion and Shape Tweens (Chapter 33), and incorporate external media files such as JPEGs and GIFs (Chapter 34) into your Flash artwork. You see how to structure content on the Main Timeline and create a simple scrolling text interface (Chapter 35).

Part IX: Sound Planning

Because Parts VII and VIII focus mainly on the visual presentation of a Flash movie, you need to start thinking about the effect of sound within a Flash movie. In Chapter 36, you learn the basics of digital sound and see which file formats can be imported into Flash. Chapter 37 shows you how to control the playback of sounds within a Flash movie, and you learn to create interactive buttons with rollover sounds. Chapter 38 explains how to adjust and optimize audio compression in an exported Flash movie.

Part X: Adding Basic Interactivity to Flash Movies

Not everyone wants to use Flash to create animating buttons for HTML documents on the Web. In Part X, you learn to start using Flash actions to create interactive and responsive presentations. You learn the difference between Normal and Expert Modes of the Actions Panel (Chapter 39). Flash 5 has greatly increased the capacity of Flash movies to communicate among its own internal elements like nested Movie Clips (Chapter 40). Properties and methods of the Movie Clip Object are introduced (Chapter 41), and you master the art of preloading and sharing Flash .SWF files (Chapter 42).

Part XI: Distributing Flash Movies

Finally, you need to learn to export (or publish) your Flash presentations to the .SWF file format for use on a Web page or within another presentation such as a floppy disk or CD-ROM project. Chapter 43 details every option in the Publish Settings of Flash 5 and provides tips for optimizing your Flash movies to achieve smaller file sizes for faster download performance. If you prefer to hand-code your HTML, read Chapter 44, which describes how to use the `<EMBED>` and `<OBJECT>` tags, how to load Flash movies into framesets, and how to create plug-in detection systems for your Flash movies.

Conventions Used in This Book

The following conventions are used throughout this book.

Windows and Macintosh conventions

Because *Dreamweaver and Flash Bible* is a cross-platform book, it provides instructions for both Windows and Macintosh users when keystrokes for a particular task differ. Throughout this book, Windows keystrokes are presented first; Macintosh keystrokes are presented second (in parentheses) as follows:

To undo an action, press Ctrl+Z (Command+Z).

The first action instructs Windows users to press the Ctrl and Z keys in combination, and the second action (in parentheses) instructs Macintosh users to press the Command and Z keys together.

Key combinations

When you are instructed to press two or more keys simultaneously, each key in the combination is separated by a plus sign. For example:

Ctrl+Alt+T (Command+Option+T)

The preceding tells you to press the three listed keys for your system at the same time. You can hold down one or more keys and then press the final key. Release all the keys at the same time.

Mouse instructions

When instructed to *click* an item, move the mouse pointer to the specified item, and click the mouse button once. Windows users use the left mouse button unless otherwise instructed. *Double-click* means clicking the mouse button twice in rapid succession.

When instructed to select an item, you may click it once as previously described. If you are selecting text or multiple objects, click the mouse button once, press Shift, move the mouse to a new location, and click again. The color of the selected item or items inverts to indicate the selection. To clear the selection, click once anywhere on the Web page.

Menu commands

When instructed to select a command from a menu, you see the menu and the command separated by an arrow symbol. For example, when instructed to execute the Open command from the File menu, you see the notation File ⇨ Open. Some menus use submenus, in which case you see an arrow for each submenu, as follows: Insert ⇨ Form Object ⇨ Text Field.

Typographical conventions

I use *italic* type for new terms and for emphasis and **boldface** type for text that you need to type directly from the computer keyboard.

Code

A special typeface indicates HTML or other code, as demonstrated in the following example:

```
<html>
<head>
<title>Untitled Document</title>
</head>
<body bgcolor="#FFFFFF">
</body>
</html>
```

This code font is used also within paragraphs to designate HTML tags, attributes, and values such as `<body>`, `bgcolor`, and `#FFFFFF`. All HTML tags are presented in lowercase, as written by Dreamweaver, although browsers are not generally case-sensitive in terms of HTML.

The ¬ character at the end of a code line means you should type the next line of code before pressing the Enter (Return) key.

Navigating Through This Book

Various signposts and icons are located throughout *Dreamweaver and Flash Bible* for your assistance. Each chapter begins with an overview of its information and ends with a quick summary.

Icons appear in the text to indicate important or especially helpful items. Here's a list of the icons and their functions:

 Tips provide you with extra knowledge that separates the novice from the pro.

 Notes provide additional or critical information and technical data on the current topic.

 Sections marked with a New Feature icon detail an innovation introduced in Dreamweaver 4 or Flash 5.

 Cross-Reference icons indicate places where you can find more information on a particular topic.

The Caution icon is your warning of a potential problem or pitfall.

 The On the CD-ROM icon indicates that the accompanying CD-ROM contains a related file in the given folder. See the Appendix for more information about where to locate specific items.

Further Information

You can find more help for specific problems and questions by investigating several Web sites. Macromedia's Web site is the best place to start:

```
www.macromedia.com
```

I heartily recommend that you visit and participate in the official Dreamweaver newsgroup:

```
news://forums.macromedia.com/macromedia.dreamweaver
news://forums.macromedia.com/macromedia.flash
```

You're invited to visit our Web sites for book updates and new developments:

```
http://www.idest.com/dreamweaver
http://www.flash5bible.com
```

Contents at a Glance

Contents

Part III: Incorporating Advanced HTML 365

Part VIII: Creating Flash Graphics — 885

Chapter 30: Exploring the Timeline 887

Chapter 31: Checking Out the Library: Symbols and Instances 913

Part IX: Sound Planning   1073

Getting Started with Dreamweaver

What Is Dreamweaver?

Dreamweaver, by Macromedia, is a professional Web site development program. Among its many distinctions, Dreamweaver·was the first Web development program to take advantage of the capabilities of the latest generation of browsers, making it easy for developers to use advanced features such as Cascading Style Sheets and Dynamic HTML.

Dreamweaver is truly a tool designed by Web developers for Web developers. Designed from the ground up to work the way professional Web designers do, Dreamweaver speeds site construction and streamlines site maintenance. Throughout this chapter, you can see the philosophical underpinnings of the program and get a better sense of how Dreamweaver blends traditional HTML with cutting-edge techniques. You also learn some of the advanced features that Dreamweaver offers to help you manage a Web site.

The Real World of Dreamweaver

Dreamweaver is a program very much rooted in the real world. For example, Dreamweaver recognizes the problem of incompatible browser commands and addresses by producing cross-browser compatible code. Dreamweaver even includes browser-specific HTML validation so you can see how your existing or new code works in a particular browser.

Dreamweaver 4 extends the real-world concept to the workplace. Features such as the Assets panel streamline the production and maintenance process on large Web sites. Dreamweaver's advanced Layout view makes it possible to quickly structure whole pages during the design stage, while keeping your pages backwardly browser-compatible when published. Dreamweaver's commands capability enables Web designers to automate their most difficult Web creations.

Integrated visual and text editors

In the early days of the World Wide Web, most developers "hand-coded" their Web pages using simple text editors such as Notepad and SimpleText. The second generation of Web authoring tools brought visual design or WYSIWYG ("what you see is what you get") editors to market. What these products furnished in ease of layout, they lacked in completeness of code. Professional Web developers found they still needed to hand-code their Web pages, even with the most sophisticated WYSIWYG editor.

Dreamweaver acknowledges this reality and has integrated a superb visual editor — rewritten from the ground up for version 4 — with its browser-like document view. You can work graphically in Design view or programatically in Code view. You even have the option of a split-screen view, which shows the Design and Code views simultaneously. Figure 1-1 shows Dreamweaver's visual editor and code editor working together. Any change made in the Design view is reflected in the Code view and vice versa. If you'd prefer to work with a code editor you're more familiar with, Dreamweaver enables you to work with any text editor. Moreover, the program includes two of the best: a full-version of HomeSite for Microsoft Windows developers and a trial version of BBEdit for Macintosh developers. Dreamweaver enables a natural, dynamic flow between the visual and code editors.

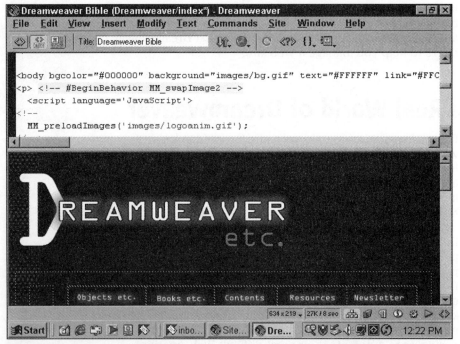

Figure 1-1: Dreamweaver enables you to work with a visual WYSIWYG editor and a code editor simultaneously.

Dreamweaver further tightens the integration between the visual design and the underlying code with the Quick Tag Editor. Web designers frequently need to adjust the HTML code minutely — changing an attribute here or adding a single tag there. The Quick Tag Editor, which appears as a small pop-up window in the Design view, makes these code tweaks quick and easy.

Roundtrip HTML

Most Web authoring programs modify any code that passes through their system — inserting returns, removing indents, adding `<meta>` tags, uppercasing commands, and so forth. Dreamweaver's programmers understand and respect that Web developers all have their own particular coding styles. An underlying concept, Roundtrip HTML, ensures that you can move back and forth between the visual editor and any HTML text editor without your code being rewritten.

Web site maintenance tools

Dreamweaver's creators also understand that creating a site is only a part of the Webmaster's job. Maintaining the Web site can be an ongoing, time-consuming chore. Dreamweaver simplifies the job with a group of site management tools, including a library of repeating elements and a file-locking capability for easy team updates.

In Dreamweaver, Web site maintenance is easier than ever — and very visual. Take note of the Site Map feature that enables you to view your Web site structure at a glance and to access any file for modification. Links are updated automatically, or are under user control, if a file moves from one directory to another. And, you can not only access a library of repeating elements to be inserted in the page, but also define templates to control the entire look and feel of a Web site — and modify a single template to update all the pages sitewide.

Team-oriented site building

Until now, individual Web developers have been stymied when attempting to integrate Dreamweaver into a team development environment. File locking was all too easily subverted, enabling revisions to be inadvertently overwritten, site reports were limited in scope and only output to HTML, and, most notable of all, version control was nonexistent. Dreamweaver 4 addresses all of these concerns while laying a foundation for future connectivity.

New Feature

In a major coup for enterprise Web developers, Dreamweaver 4 supports two source control systems: Visual SourceSafe (VSS) and WebDAV. Connecting to a Visual SourceSafe server is well integrated into Dreamweaver; simply define the VSS server as your remote site and add the necessary connection information. WebDAV, although perhaps less well known than VSS, offers an equally powerful and more available content-management solution. More importantly, Macromedia has developed the source-control solution as a system architecture enabling other third-party content management or version control developers to use Dreamweaver as their front end.

Extensible architecture also underlies Dreamweaver's new site reporting facility. Dreamweaver ships with the ability to generate reports on usability issues such as missing Alt text or documents without an HTML title, or workflow concerns, such as showing who has what files checked out. However, users can also develop custom reports on a project-by-project basis.

The Dreamweaver Interface

When creating a Web page, Webmasters do two things over and over: They insert an element — whether text, image, or layer — and then they modify it. Dreamweaver excels at such Web page creation. The Dreamweaver workspace combines a series of windows, panels, and inspectors to make the process as fluid as possible, thereby speeding up the Webmaster's work.

Easy text entry

Although much of the World Wide Web's glitz comes from multimedia elements such as images and sound, Web pages are primarily a text-based medium. Dreamweaver recognizes this and makes the text cursor the default tool. To add text, just click in Dreamweaver's main workspace — the Document window — and start typing. As shown in Figure 1-2, the Text Property Inspector enables you to change characteristics of the text, such as the size, font, position, or color.

One-stop object modification

You can select Web page elements other than text from the Objects panel. Adding a picture to a Web page is as easy as clicking the Insert Image button from the Objects panel. Dreamweaver asks you to select the file for the image, and your image appears in your current cursor position. Once your graphic is onscreen, selecting it brings up the appropriate Property Inspector to enable you to make modifications. The same technique holds true for any other inserted element — from horizontal rules to Shockwave movies.

Access and manage resources

One standout addition to Dreamweaver's interface is the new Assets panel, shown in Figure 1-3. The Assets panel gathers all the various elements used in an individual site: images, background and text colors, external URLs, included scripts, Flash movies, Shockwave content, and QuickTime media, as well as Dreamweaver templates and library items. Sizeable thumbnails of graphics and media are displayed in the preview pane of the Assets panel — you can even play Flash, Shockwave, and QuickTime elements in preview before dragging them onto the page. Moreover, often-used resources can be listed in a Favorites category, distinguishing them from the rest of the assets found in the sight.

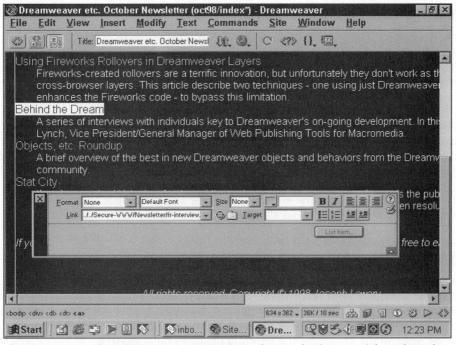

Figure 1-2: Use the Text Property Inspector to change the format of the selected text.

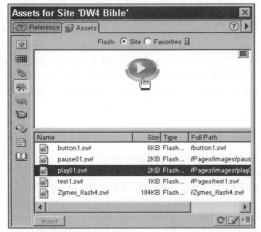

Figure 1-3: Preview a Flash movie with the Assets panel before placing it on the Dreamweaver page.

Complete custom environment

Dreamweaver enables you to customize your workspace to suit you best. A handy Launcher opens and closes various windows, panels, and inspectors, all of which are movable. Just drag them wherever you want them onscreen. Want to see your page by itself? You can hide all windows at the touch of a function button; press it again, and your controls are revealed.

Dreamweaver's customization capabilities extend even further. If you find that you are inserting something over and over, such as a QuickTime video or .wav sound file, you can add that element to your Objects panel. Dreamweaver even enables you to add a specific element — a Home button, for example — to the Objects panel. In fact, you can add entire categories of objects if you like. Moreover, Dreamweaver 4 exposes the entire menu structure for customization — you can not only change keyboard shortcuts, but also add custom menus.

Managing keyboard shortcuts

Keyboard shortcuts are great in theory: just press an easy-to-remember key combination to activate your favorite feature. The problem is that, in reality, there are too many essential features, too few single-purpose keys on the keyboard and, most importantly, too few brain cells to retain all the widely varied keyboard combinations from all the programs the working designer must master.

New Feature

Macromedia has moved to ease keyboard shortcut overload across their entire product line, and Dreamweaver's no exception. Dreamweaver now offers a Keyboard Shortcut Editor that enables you to both standardize and customize the key combinations used in the program. Choose from a Macromedia standard set — common to Dreamweaver, UltraDev, Fireworks, and Flash — or use a set taken from a previous version of Dreamweaver. You can even select a set from an entirely different program such as HomeSite or BBEdit. Best of all, any keyboard shortcut can be personalized to represent a combination that's easy for you to remember.

Simple selection process

As with most modern layout programs, in order to modify anything in Dreamweaver, you must select it first. The usual process for this is to click an object to highlight it or to click and drag over a block of text to select it. Dreamweaver adds another option for this process with the Tag Selector feature. Click anywhere on a Web page under construction and then look at Dreamweaver's status bar. The applicable HTML tags appear on the left side of the status bar.

In the example shown in Figure 1-4, the Tag Selector shows

```
<body> <table> <tr> <td> <div> <p>
```

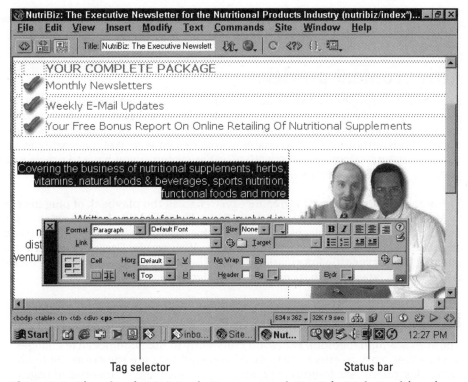

Tag selector   Status bar

Figure 1-4: Choosing the <p> tag in Dreamweaver's Tag Selector is a quick and easy way to highlight the current paragraph on your Web page.

Click one of these tags, and the corresponding elements are selected on your page, ready for modification. The Tag Selector is a terrific time-saver; throughout this book, I point out how you can use it under various circumstances.

Enhanced layout options

Dreamweaver works much more like a desktop publishing program than do many other visual HTML editors. Today's browser capabilities permit images and text to be placed in specific locations on the Web page — a concept known as *absolute positioning*. To enable you to take full advantage of this power, Dreamweaver includes both rulers and grids. You can specify the type of measurement to be used (inches, pixels, or centimeters), as well as the spacing and appearance of the grid lines. You can even have objects snap to the grid for easy alignment.

New Feature

Dreamweaver has always made it easy for designers new to the Web to build nice-looking interactive Web pages without having to know HTML. Dreamweaver 4 expands on that theme with Layout view. Layout view enables designers to draw tables and cells directly on the screen for positioning content. Once drawn, cells can be modified by dragging borders or moving the entire cell. Nested tables may also be included.

Cross-Reference   To find out more about absolute positioning, see Chapter 19; you can learn more about Layout view in Chapter 12.

Active content preview

In order for a browser to display anything beyond standard format graphics, a plug-in is generally required. Plug-ins extend the capability of most browsers to show animations, play music, or even explore 3D worlds. Dreamweaver is one of the first Web authoring tools to enable you to design your Web page with an active plug-in playing the extended file; with all other systems, you have to preview your page in a browser to see the active content.

The active content feature in Dreamweaver enables the playback of plug-ins such as Macromedia Flash, Shockwave, and others. However, this feature extends far beyond that. Many Web pages are coded with server-side includes, which traditionally required the page to be viewed through a Web server. Dreamweaver translates much of the server-side information so that the entire page—server-side includes and all—can be viewed in its entirety at design time.

Extended Find and Replace

The Web is a fluid medium. Pages are constantly in flux, and because changes are relatively easy to effect, corrections and additions are the norm. Quite often a Web designer needs to update or alter an existing page—or series of pages. Dreamweaver's enhanced Find and Replace feature is a real power tool when it comes to making modifications.

Find and Replace works in the Document window, whether in Design View or Code View, as well as in the Code Inspector to alter code and regular content. Moreover, changes are applicable to the current page, the working site, selected Web pages, or an entire folder of pages, regardless of the number. Complex Find and Replace queries can be stored and retrieved later to further automate your work.

Up-to-Date HTML Standards

Most Web pages are created in HyperText Markup Language (HTML). This programming language—really a series of tags that modify a text file—is standardized by an organization known as the World Wide Web Consortium, or W3C (www.w3.org). Each new release of HTML incorporates an enhanced set of commands and features. The current version, HTML 4, is recognized by the majority of browsers in use today. Dreamweaver writes clear, easy-to-follow, real-world browser-compatible HTML 4 code whenever you insert or modify an element in the visual editor.

Straightforward text and graphics support

Text is a basic building block of any Web page, and Dreamweaver makes formatting your text a snap. Once you've inserted your text, either by typing it directly or pasting it from another program, you can change its appearance. You can use the generic HTML formats, such as the H1 through H6 headings and their relative sizes, or you can use font families and exact point sizes.

Cross-Reference Chapter 9 shows you how to work with text in Dreamweaver.

Additional text support in Dreamweaver enables you to add both numbered and bulleted lists to your Web page. The Text Property Inspector gives you buttons for both kinds of lists as well as easy alignment control. Some elements, including lists, offer extended options. In Dreamweaver, clicking the Property Inspector's Expander arrow opens a section from which you can access additional controls.

Graphics are handled in much the same easy-to-use manner. Select the image or its placeholder to enable the Image Property Inspector. From there, you can modify any available attributes, including the image's source, its width or height, and its alignment on the page. Need to touch up your image? Send it to your favorite graphics program with just a click of the Edit button.

Cross-Reference You learn all about adding and modifying Dreamweaver images in Chapter 10.

Enhanced table capabilities

Other features — standard, yet more advanced — are similarly straightforward in Dreamweaver. Tables are a key component in today's Web pages, and Dreamweaver gives you full control over all their functionality. Dreamweaver changes the work of resizing the column or row of a table, previously a tedious hand-coding task, into an easy click-and-drag motion. Likewise, you can delete all the width and height values from a table with the click of a button. Figure 1-5 shows the Table Property Inspector, which centralizes many of these options in Dreamweaver.

Tables are flexible in Dreamweaver. Font changes can be applied to any number of selected cells, rows, or columns. Standard commands enable you to automatically format or sort a table as well.

Easy form entry

Forms, the basic vehicle for Web page data exchange, are just as easy to implement as tables in Dreamweaver. Switch to the Forms category of the Objects panel and insert any of the available elements: text boxes, radio buttons, checkboxes, and even pop-up menus or scrolling lists. With the Validate Form behavior, you can easily specify any field as a required field and even check to ensure that the requested type of information has been entered.

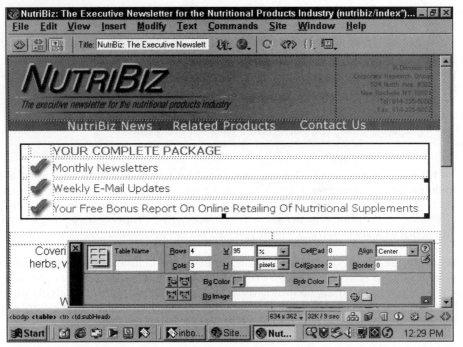

Figure 1-5: The Table Property Inspector is just one of Dreamweaver's paths to a full range of control over the appearance of your table.

Click-and-drag frame setup

Frames, which enable separate Web pages to be viewed on a single screen, are often considered one of the most difficult HTML techniques to master. Dreamweaver employs a click-and-drag method for establishing your frame outlines. After you've set up your frame structure, open the Frames panel (see Figure 1-6) to select any frame and modify it with the Property Inspector. Dreamweaver writes the necessary code for linking all the HTML files in a frameset, no matter how many Web pages are used. Dreamweaver keeps frame creation simple with the Frames category of the Objects panel.

Cross-Reference   For more information on creating frame-based Web pages, see Chapter 14.

Multimedia enhancements

Dreamweaver enables you to drop in any number of multimedia extensions, plug-ins, applets, or controls. Just click the appropriate button on the Objects panel and modify with the Property Inspector. Two multimedia elements, Shockwave movies and Flash files — both from Macromedia — warrant special consideration in Macromedia's Dreamweaver. When you insert either of these objects,

Dreamweaver automatically includes the necessary HTML code to ensure the widest browser acceptance, and you can edit all the respective properties.

Macromedia has formed partnerships with numerous cutting-edge multimedia companies such as RealNetworks, IBM, and Beatnik. Dreamweaver fully supports the fruits of those partnerships: custom objects that enable complex images, audio, and presentations to be easily inserted and displayed in Web pages.

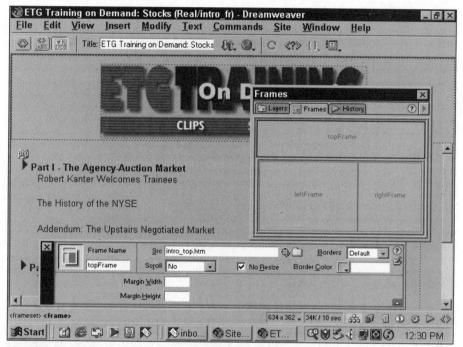

Figure 1-6: In Dreamweaver you use the Frames panel to choose which frame you want to modify through the Property Inspector.

Next-Generation Features

Dreamweaver was among the first Web authoring tools to work with the capabilities brought in by the 4.0 generation of browsers. Both Netscape Communicator 4+ and Microsoft Internet Explorer 4+ include variations of Dynamic HTML (DHTML). Moreover, both of these browsers adhere to the Cascading Style Sheet (CSS) standards to some degree, with support for absolute and relative positioning. Dreamweaver gives Web developers an interface that takes these advanced possibilities and makes them realities.

3D layers

One particular Dynamic HTML feature enables Dreamweaver to be called "the first 3D Web authoring tool." Until Dynamic HTML, Web pages existed on a two-dimensional plane — images and text could only be placed side by side. Dreamweaver supports control of Dynamic HTML layers, meaning that objects can be placed in front of or behind other objects. Layers can contain text, graphics, links, controls — you can even nest one layer inside another.

You create a layer in Dreamweaver by clicking the Draw Layer button on the Objects panel. Once created, layers can be positioned anywhere on the page by clicking and dragging the selection handle. As with other Dreamweaver objects, you can modify a layer through the Property Inspector.

Detailed information on using Dynamic HTML in Dreamweaver is covered in Chapter 18.

Animated objects

Objects in layers can be positioned anywhere on the Web page under construction, and they can also be moved when the page is viewed. Dreamweaver takes this capability and adds its Timelines panel, becoming a 4D Web authoring tool! The Timelines panel, shown in Figure 1-7, is designed along the lines of Macromedia's world-class multimedia creation program, Director. With timelines, you can control a layer's position, size, 3D placement, and even visibility on a frame-by-frame basis. With Dreamweaver, you no longer have to plot a layer's path on a timeline — now you can just draw it using the Record Path of Layer feature.

Dynamic style updates

Dreamweaver completely supports the Cascading Style Sheet (CSS) specification agreed upon by the World Wide Web Consortium. CSS gives Web designers more flexible control over almost every element on their Web pages. Dreamweaver applies CSS capabilities as if they were styles in a word processor. For example, you can make all the <h1> tags blue, italic, and in small caps. If your site's color scheme changes, you can make all the <h1> tags red — and you can do this throughout your Web site with one command. Dreamweaver gives you style control over type, background, blocks, boxes, borders, lists, and positioning.

Dreamweaver enables you to change styles online as well as offline. By linking a CSS change to a user-driven event such as moving the mouse, text can be highlighted or de-emphasized, screen areas can light up, and figures can even be animated. And it can all be done without repeated trips to the server or huge file downloads.

Details on using Cascading Style Sheets are covered in Chapter 18.

Figure 1-7: Use the Timelines panel to animate objects in layers using Dreamweaver's advanced Dynamic HTML features.

JavaScript behaviors

Through the development of JavaScript behaviors, Dreamweaver combines the power of JavaScript with the ease of a drag-and-drop interface. A behavior is defined as a combination of an event and an action — whenever your Web page user does something and then something else happens, that's a behavior. What makes behaviors extremely useful is that they require no programming whatsoever.

Behaviors are JavaScript-based, and this is significant because JavaScript is supported to varying degrees by existing browsers. Dreamweaver has simplified the task of identifying which JavaScript command works with a particular browser. You simply select the Web page element that you want to use to control the action, and open the Behaviors panel from the Launcher. As shown in Figure 1-8, Dreamweaver enables you to pick a JavaScript command that works with all browsers, a subset of browsers, or one browser in particular. Next, you choose from a full list of available actions, such as go to a URL, play a sound, pop up a message, or start an animation. You can assign multiple actions and even determine when they occur.

Cross-Reference For complete details on working with JavaScript behaviors, see Chapter 15.

Figure 1-8: Dreamweaver offers only the JavaScript commands that work with the browser you specify.

Flash and Fireworks integration

Dreamweaver 4 has upped the ante for integration with Macromedia's graphics engine, Fireworks. Now, images derived from Fireworks are identified as such, both in the Property Inspector and in the Assets panel. Graphics may be optimized to alter the file size, cropping, transparency, or many other aspects right from within Fireworks. If more extensive modification is required, selecting the Edit button sends the graphic back to Fireworks. More impressively, sliced images — maintained as a borderless table in HTML — may be edited in their entirety. Fireworks even respects HTML alterations to a degree, such as changes to URLs or converting an image slice to a text block. This degree of integration lends an amazing fluidity to the workflow.

New Feature

Just as Dreamweaver behaviors may add JavaScript interactivity to a page without the developer knowing JavaScript, the new Flash objects offer the potential for including highly attractive navigation elements without mastering that vector-based animation program. Two different types of Flash objects are available: Flash buttons and Flash text. A Flash button (see Figure 1-9) is actually a Macromedia Generator template with full animation and sound capabilities. Because it's a template, the layout artist may customize it with text and a link. Dreamweaver ships with numerous examples, but anyone with Flash 5 can create their own template.

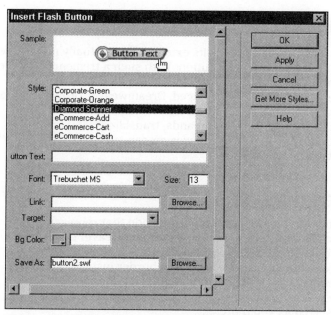

Figure 1-9: Flash buttons make it easy to add animated, sound-capable navigation elements to any page.

Flash text, on the other hand, does not handle any animation other than a simple color rollover. However, it is an effective way to include a heading or other page element in a specific font — a far better solution, with more market penetration, than materializing from Dynamic HTML. Moreover, Flash text weighs far less than an equivalent GIF image.

Roundtrip XML

A new type of markup language has excited a wide cross section of Web designers, intranet developers, and corporate users. XML, which stands for Extensible Markup Language, has piqued the interest of many because of its underlying customizable nature. With XML, tags are created to describe the use of the information, rather than its appearance.

Dreamweaver is capable of exporting and importing XML tags, no matter what the tag definition. As XML grows in popularity, Dreamweaver is ready to handle the work.

Program Extensibility

One of Dreamweaver's primary strengths is its extensibility. Virtually no two Web sites are alike, either in their design or execution. With such a tremendous variety of end results, the more flexible a Web authoring tool, the more useful it is to a wider group of designers. When it was introduced, Dreamweaver broke new ground with objects and behaviors that were easily customizable. Now, Dreamweaver lengthens its lead with custom floaters, commands, translators, and Property Inspectors. The basic underpinnings of Dreamweaver can even be extended with the C-Level Extensibility options.

Objects and behaviors

In Dreamweaver parlance, an *object* is a bit of HTML code that represents a specific image or HTML tag such as a `<table>` or a `<form>`. Dreamweaver's objects are completely open to user customization, or even out-and-out creation. If you'd rather import structured data into a table without a border instead of with the standard 1 pixel border, you can easily make that modification to the Insert Tabular Data object file — right from within Dreamweaver — and every subsequent table is inserted as you'd prefer.

Objects are a terrific time-saving device, essentially enabling you to drop in significant blocks of HTML code at the click of a mouse. Likewise, Dreamweaver behaviors enable even the most novice Web designer to insert complex JavaScript functions designed to propel the pages to the cutting edge. Dreamweaver ships with a full array of standard behaviors — but that's only the tip of the behavior iceberg. Because behaviors, too, are customizable and can be built by anyone with a working knowledge of JavaScript, many Dreamweaver designers have created custom behaviors and made them publicly available.

On the CD-ROM You can find a large assortment of custom objects, behaviors, and commands on the CD-ROM that accompanies this book.

Commands and floating panels

Objects and behaviors are great ways to help build the final result of a Web page, but what about automating the work of producing that page? Dreamweaver employs commands to modify the existing page and streamline production. A great example is the Sort Table command, standard with Dreamweaver. If you've ever had to sort a large table by hand — meticulously moving data, one row at a time — you can appreciate the power of commands the first time you alphabetize or otherwise re-sort a table using this option.

Commands hold a great promise—they are, in effect, more powerful than either objects or behaviors combined. In fact, some of the more complex objects, such as the Rollover Image object, are actually commands. Commands can also extract information sitewide and offer a powerful programmable language within Dreamweaver.

Creating a Dreamweaver command is now easier than ever, thanks to the History panel. Aside from displaying every action you undertake as you build your Web page, the History panel enables you to select any number of those actions and save them as a command. Your new command is instantly available to be called from the menu whenever you need it.

After only a few moments with Dreamweaver, you become accustomed to its use of floating panels. In Dreamweaver 4, custom floating panels can be created. These custom panels can show existing resources or provide a whole new interface for modifying an HTML element.

Custom tags, translators, and Property Inspectors

In Dreamweaver, almost every part of the user interface can be customized—including the tags themselves. Once you've developed your custom third-party tags, you can display and modify their current properties with a custom Property Inspector. Moreover, if your custom tags include content not typically shown in Dreamweaver's Document window, a custom translator can be built, enabling the content to be displayed.

Programs such as Dreamweaver are generally built in the programming language called C or C++, which must be compiled before it is used. Generally, the basic functions of a C program are frozen solid; there's no way you can extend them. This is not the case with Dreamweaver, however. Dreamweaver offers a C-Level Extensibility that permits programmers to create libraries to install new functionality into the program. Translators, for example, generally rely on new C libraries to enable content to be displayed in Dreamweaver that could not be shown otherwise. Companies can use the C-Level Extensibility feature to integrate Dreamweaver into their existing workflow and maximize productivity.

Automation Enhancements

Web site design is the dream job; Web site production is the reality. Once a design has been finalized, its execution can become repetitive and burdensome. Dreamweaver offers a number of ways to automate the production work, keeping the look of the Web pages constant with the minimum work required.

Applying HTML Styles

Designers in every field depend on the consistency and flexibility of styles. Until recently, the only styles available to Web designers came through a Cascading Style Sheet (CSS). While CSS is, for many, an ideal solution, numerous clients are hesitant to authorize its use, for fear of alienating users with older browsers that don't support CSS. The Dreamweaver engineers have come up with a solution that maintains backward-compatibility while simplifying text formatting: HTML Styles.

The HTML Styles panel enables you to define, manage, and apply any combination of text formatting. You can apply your new style to either a selection or an entire paragraph — styles can be defined either to add formatting to the existing tags or to replace them. While redefining an existing HTML Style does not cause text to update, HTML Styles are sitewide and can be used to enforce a consistent look and feel without CSS limitations.

Importing office documents

Much of the Web's content originates from other sources — in-house documents produced by a word processor or spreadsheet program. Dreamweaver bridges the gap between the offline and online world with two useful import features: Import Word HTML and Import Tabular Data.

Microsoft Word, perhaps the premier word processor, is great at creating and storing word processing documents but not so accomplished at outputting standard HTML. An HTML file derived from Word is, to put it mildly, bloated with extraneous and repetitive code. Dreamweaver's Import Word HTML feature strips out the unnecessary code and even permits you to format the code like your other Dreamweaver files. The Import Word HTML command offers a wide range of options for cleaning up the code.

Of course, not all Web content derives from word processing documents — databases and spreadsheets are the other two legs of the modern office software triangle. Dreamweaver includes the capability to incorporate data from any source that can export structured text files through the Import Tabular Data command. Just save your spreadsheet or database as a comma, tab, or otherwise delimited file and bring it directly into Dreamweaver in the table style of your choice.

Reference panel

Even the most advanced coder needs to refer to a reference when including seldom-used HTML tags or arcane JavaScript functions. Dreamweaver now includes a built-in reference with HTML, JavaScript, and Cascading Style Sheet details. Taken from O'Reilly's *Dynamic HTML, The Definitive Reference* by Danny Goodman, Dreamweaver's guide is context-sensitive; highlight a tag or function in Code view and hit Shift+F1 to get a breakdown on syntax and browser compatibility.

History panel

The repetitiveness of building a Web site is often a matter of repeating the same series of commands over and over again. You might, for example, need to add a vertical margin of 10 pixels and a horizontal margin of 5 around most, but not all, of the images on a page. Rather than selecting each image and then entering these values time and again in the Property Inspector, you can now enter the values once and then save that action as a command.

The feature that brings this degree of automation to Dreamweaver is found in the History panel. The History panel shows each step taken by a designer as the page is developed. Although this visual display is great for complex, multilevel undos, the capability to save any number of your steps as an instantly available command is truly time-saving.

Site Management Tools

Long after your killer Web site is launched, you'll find yourself continually updating and revising it. For this reason, site management tools are as important as site creation tools to a Web authoring program. Dreamweaver delivers on both counts.

Object libraries

In addition to site management functions that have become traditional, such as FTP publishing, Dreamweaver adds a whole new class of functionality called *libraries*. One of the truisms of Web page development is that if you repeat an element across your site, you're sure to have to change it — on every page. Dreamweaver libraries eliminate that drudgery. You can define almost anything as a Library element: a paragraph of text, an image, a link, a table, a form, a Java applet, an ActiveX control, and so on. Just choose the item and open the Library panel (see Figure 1-10). Once you've created the Library entry, you can reuse it throughout your Web site. Each Web site can have its own library, and you can copy entries from one library to another.

Being able to include "boilerplate" Web elements is one issue, being able to update them across the site simultaneously is quite another! You can easily change a Library entry through the Library panel. Once the change is complete, Dreamweaver detects the modification and asks if you want to update your site. Imagine updating copyright information across a 400+ page Web site in the wink of an eye, and you start to understand the power of Dreamweaver libraries.

 Cross-Reference   To find out more about making site-wide changes with Library items, see Chapter 22.

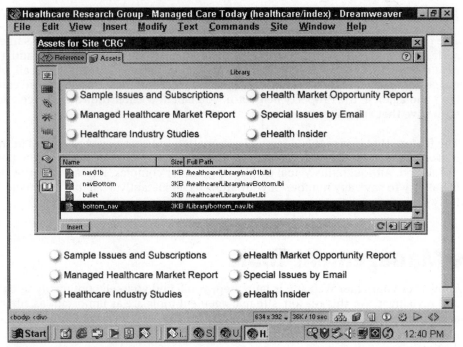

Figure 1-10: Use Dreamweaver's Library feature to simplify the task of updating elements repeated across many Web pages.

Templates

The more your Web site grows, the more you'll find yourself using the same basic format for different pages. Dreamweaver enables the use of Web page templates to standardize the look and feel of a Web site and to cut down on the repetitive work of creating new pages. A Dreamweaver template can hold the basic structure for the page — an image embedded in the background, a navigation bar along the left side, or a set-width table in the center for holding the main text, for example — with as many elements predefined as possible.

But Dreamweaver templates are far more than just molds for creating pages. Basically, templates work with a series of locked and editable regions. To update an entire site based on a template, all you have to do is alter one or more of the template's locked regions. Naturally, Dreamweaver enables you to save any template that you create in the same folder, so that your own templates, too, are accessible through the File ➪ New from Template command. (You can find more about using and creating templates in Chapter 21.)

Browser targeting

Browser targeting is another site management innovation from Dreamweaver. One of the major steps in any site development project is to test the Web pages in various browsers to look for inconsistencies and invalid code. Dreamweaver's Browser Targeting function enables you to check your HTML against any existing browser's profile. Dreamweaver includes predefined profiles for several browsers, and you can create a profile for any browser you'd like to check.

You can also preview your Web page in any number of browsers. Dreamweaver enables you to specify primary and secondary browsers that can display your page at the press of a function key. You can install up to 18 other browsers for previewing your Web page. The entire list of browsers is available through the Preview in Browser command under the File menu.

Converting Web pages

Although Web site designers may have access to the latest HTML tools and browsers, much of the public uses older, more limited versions of browsers. Dreamweaver gives you the power to build Web pages with the high-end capabilities of fourth-generation browsers — and then convert those pages so that older browsers can also read what you've created. Moreover, you can take previously designed Web pages that use tables and "upgrade" them to take advantage of the latest HTML features with the Tables to Layers command. Dreamweaver goes a long way toward helping you bridge the gap between browser versions.

Verifying links

Web sites are ever-evolving entities. Maintaining valid connections and links amid all that diversity is a constant challenge. Dreamweaver includes a built-in link checker so you can verify the links on a page, in a directory, or across your entire site. The Link Checker quickly shows you which files have broken links, which files have links to external sites, and which files may have been "orphaned" (so that no other file connects with them).

FTP publishing

The final step in Web page creation is publishing your page on the Internet. As any Webmaster knows, this final step is one that happens over and over again as the site is continually updated and maintained. Dreamweaver includes an FTP (File Transfer Protocol) publisher that simplifies the work of posting your site. More importantly, Dreamweaver enables you to synchronize your local and remote sites with one command.

You can work with sites originating from a local folder, such as one on your own hard drive. Or, in a collaborative team environment, you can work with sites being developed on a remote server. Dreamweaver enables you to set up an unlimited number of sites to include the source and destination directories, FTP user names and passwords, and more.

The Dreamweaver Site window, shown in Figure 1-11, is a visual interface in which you can click and drag files or select a number of files and transfer them with the Get and Put buttons. You can even set the preferences so the system automatically disconnects after remaining idle for a user-definable period of time.

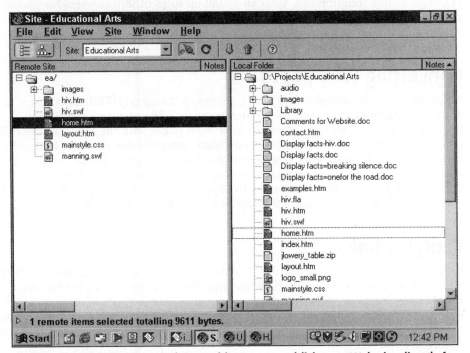

Figure 1-11: The FTP Site window enables you to publish your Web site directly from within Dreamweaver.

Site Map

Web sites can quickly outgrow the stage in which the designer can keep all the linked pages in mind. Dreamweaver includes a visual aid in the Web site management toolbox: the Site Map. With the Site Map, the Web designer can see how the entire Web site is structured. However, you can use the Site Map to do far more than just visualize the Web.

The Site Map, shown in Figure 1-12, can be used to establish the structure of the Web site in addition to viewing it. New pages can be created, and links can be added, modified, or deleted. In fact, the Site Map is so powerful, it becomes a site manager as well.

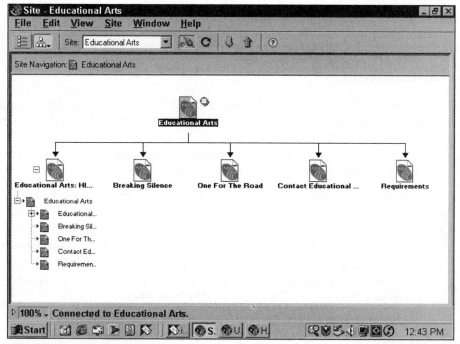

Figure 1-12: Use the Site Map to get an overall picture of your site — and then add new pages or links, right on the map.

File check in/check out

On larger Web projects, more than one person is usually responsible for creation and daily upkeep of the site. An editor may need to include the latest company press release, or a graphic artist may have to upload a photo of the newest product — all on the same page. To avoid conflicts with overlapping updates, Dreamweaver has devised a system under which Web pages can be marked as "checked out" and locked to prevent any other corrections until the file is once again "checked in."

Dreamweaver places a green checkmark over a file's icon in the Site Files window when it has been checked out by you, and a red mark if it has been checked out by another member of your team. And, so you won't have to guess who that team member is, Dreamweaver displays the name of the person next to the filename. You can also keep track of who last checked out a particular Web page (or image) — Dreamweaver keeps an ongoing log listing the file, person, and date and time of the check out.

You can learn all about Dreamweaver's Web publishing capabilities in Chapter 7.

Summary

Building a Web site is half craft and half art, and Dreamweaver is the perfect tool for blending these often dueling disciplines. Dreamweaver's visual editor enables quick and artful page creation, and at the same time, its integrated text editors offer the detail-oriented focus required by programmers. Dreamweaver's key features include the following:

✦ Dreamweaver works the way professional Web developers do, with integrated visual and text editors. Dreamweaver won't convert your HTML code when it's used with preexisting Web pages.

✦ Dreamweaver supports HTML standard commands with easy entry and editing of text, graphics, tables, and multimedia elements.

✦ Dreamweaver makes cutting-edge features, such as Dynamic HTML and Cascading Style Sheets, easy to use.

✦ Dreamweaver offers you a variety of reusable JavaScript behaviors, object libraries, commands, and templates to streamline your Web page creation.

✦ Dreamweaver's wide range of site management tools include FTP publishing with a file-locking capability that encourages team creation and maintenance, as well as a built-in Link Checker and visual Site Map.

In the next chapter, you hit the ground running with a quick-start guide to Dreamweaver.

✦   ✦   ✦

QuickStart for Beginners

Designing a Web site is a big job, and Dreamweaver is a big program; both can be overwhelming when you first approach them. If you're new to Web design in general or to Dreamweaver in particular, the best way to learn about either of them is to build several sample sites. I've found that working on a project helps most people absorb all the little nuances of a program needed to be productive.

This chapter presents an overview of how I use Dreamweaver to begin building a Web site. A hallmark of any world-class software program such as Dreamweaver, is its capability to be used in many ways by many different people. Don't get the idea that what follows is the only way to construct a site; it is, however, the basic methodology that I've used successfully over the years.

If you are totally new to Web-site creation or to Dreamweaver, I recommend reading through the chapter in one sitting. Doing so will give you an overview of both the process and the program. Throughout this chapter, you can find many cross-references to other sections of the book where step-by-step instructions are detailed. As you begin to build your sites, use this chapter as a jumping-off place to delve deeper into each topic.

Setting up a Site

The first phase of designing a Web site involves pure input. You need to gather as much information from your client as possible. Some of this information relates to the overall message of the Web site along with its purpose, intended audience, and goals. Other elements, such as logos, textual content, and prior marketing materials are more tangible. I've found it best to get up front as much information — in both categories — as possible.

Tip
Whenever possible, get your data in digital format; the images ideally should be in a format that your graphics program can read and the content should be in a standard word processing file. Your workflow will be greatly enhanced if you don't have to spend time recreating logos or keying in faxed text.

As you are sketching out design ideas for the look of the site (on paper and in your head), you can begin to set up the structure of the site on your computer. Dreamweaver uses a folder on your hard drive as the local site root; when the site goes live on the Internet, the local site is mirrored on the Web server, also known as the *remote site*. So the very first physical step is to create a folder with the site or client name. All you need is a single folder to define a site in Dreamweaver and to begin building your Web site. Here's one way to start:

1. Using the system file manager, create a folder on your local hard drive and give it a unique name, reflective of the client or site.

2. In Dreamweaver, open the Site window, as shown in Figure 2-1, by choosing the Show Site button from the Launcher. Alternatively, you could select Window ⇨ Site Files or use the keyboard shortcut F8.

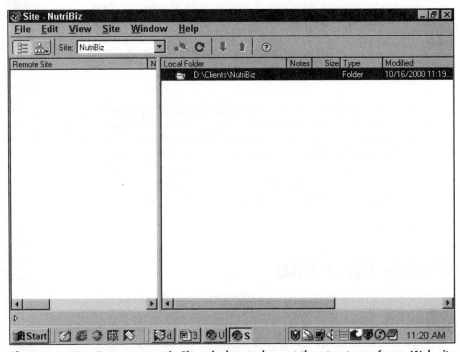

Figure 2-1: Use Dreamweaver's Site window to lay out the structure of your Web site.

3. From the site list, choose Define Sites. The Define Sites dialog box opens, displaying a list of your currently available sites, if any.

4. Select the New button to set the parameters of your new site.

5. In the Site Definition dialog box, enter the name of the new site, its local root folder, its HTTP address, and the name of the home page.

A detailed breakdown of the process of defining a site can be found in Chapter 6.

After the site is initially defined, you have a folder and a single file set up as the home page, as shown in the Site Map view displayed in Figure 2-2. Dreamweaver's Site Map is not just a useful tool for maintaining a Web site; it is also useful when developing the site structure. I recommend that you use it to develop the entire structure of your Web site before you begin adding content.

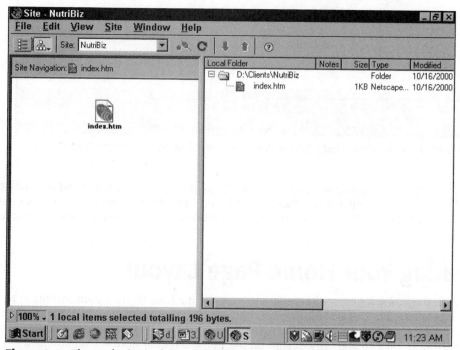

Figure 2-2: The Web site is defined and the home page is created.

Using the techniques outlined in Chapter 6, you can then create new blank files, already linked to your home page. These new pages act as placeholders for content to come. They also help to ease the building of the site by providing existing pages to link to and to preview the navigation of your site. To function properly, many of Dreamweaver's commands depend on a file being saved. So, by prebuilding your site pages, you avoid unnecessary delays and warning dialog boxes. By the time you're finished, your Web site is beginning to take form, as shown in Figure 2-3.

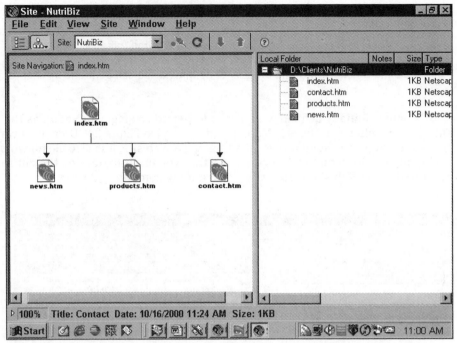

Figure 2-3: Dreamweaver's Site window is a valuable Web-site prototyping tool.

While it's not necessary to create all the pages a site might use, I find it helpful to make the primary ones linked to the home page. Then, when I work on each section, such as Products, I use the Site window to create the pages in that division.

Creating Your Home Page Layout

With the site's structure beginning to emerge, it's time to turn your attention to the page that most visitors' first see at the Web site: the home page. Although any page can act as a doorway to your site, the home page is by far the most commonly used entrance. I like to start my design on the home page for another reason also—I frequently reuse core elements from the home page, such as the logo and navigation system, throughout the site. By setting these designs early—and getting approval for them—I can save myself a fair amount of work down the road while maintaining a consistent look-and-feel to the site.

Starting with the <head>

One of the most important sections of a Web page is also one of those most frequently—and wrongly—ignored: the <head> section. Under normal circumstances, the <head> (as opposed to the <body>) is not seen, but its effect is enormous. The <head> section contains vital information about the page and the site itself, including the page's title, its description, and the keywords used to describe the page for search engines. Much of this information is contained in a page's `<meta>` tags. I like to add this information at the beginning of my Web site development, partly to get the chore out of the way, but primarily so that I don't forget to do it! Dreamweaver offers an easy way to input `<head>` information:

1. Change the Title field in the Toolbar from Unnamed Document to whatever you'd like to appear in the browser title bar. Remember that a page's title is a primary criterion that search engines use to rank a site.

2. Choose View ⇨ Head Content from the main menu or choose Head Content under the View Options button on the Toolbar. The `<head>` section appears at the top of the Document window as shown in Figure 2-4.

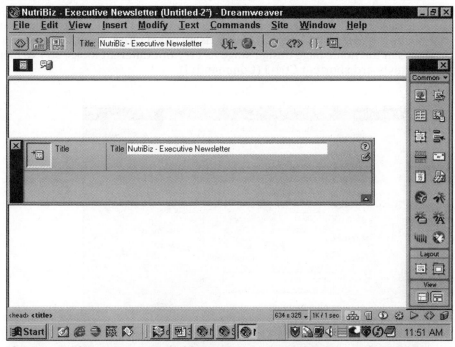

Figure 2-4: The `<head>` area holds important information for search engines.

3. From the Head category of the Objects panel insert both a Keywords and a Description object, and fill them out appropriately. I prefer that my clients supply both the keywords and the description whenever possible. They know their business best and how best to market it.

Cross-Reference For a detailed description of the `<head>` section and its various tags, turn to Chapter 8.

4. Close the Head Content view by deselecting that option under the View Options button of the Toolbar.

Specifying page colors

After the first *Dreamweaver Bible* was published, I received an irate e-mail from a beginning Web designer who was infuriated by one of Macromedia's practices. By default, Dreamweaver pages all specify a white background color — and nothing else. The gentleman who was complaining set his browser colors to have a black background with white lettering — an austere look, but it was his preference. Whenever he previewed default Dreamweaver pages with his browser, his text seemed to disappear. His text was still there, of course, but because it was white text on a white background, it was invisible. The moral of this story is to always specify your background, text, and link colors if you want your Web pages to maintain your designed look.

After entering the `<head>` content, I next define the page's colors and margins through Dreamweaver's Page Properties dialog box, shown in Figure 2-5. Choose Modify ➪ Page Properties to set these parameters. This is also the location for setting up a background image, if you're using one. I often alter these settings several times in the home page design stage as I try out different looks, so I've memorized the keyboard shortcut Ctrl+J (Command+J).

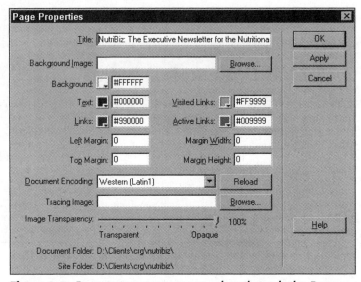

Figure 2-5: Be sure to set your page colors through the Page Properties dialog box.

Tip   Not sure about your color combinations? Dreamweaver has a useful command, Set Color Scheme, which contains background, text, and link color selections that are designed to work together.

Initial graphic layout

Like many small-shop Web designers, I create the majority of the graphics to use on my pages myself, and the Dreamweaver/Fireworks Studio has been a major boon to my productivity. Typically, I create or modify the logo for the home page in Fireworks while Dreamweaver is open, for instant placement and integration. Although the use of layers is always a possibility for placement, I prefer to lay out my pages with tables for most situations. Many designers new to the Web — especially those from a print background — prefer the exact positioning of layers and can use Dreamweaver's excellent layers-to-tables conversion features. The approach that is used is up to you, but remember that many clients still balk at using layers for fear of excluding visitors with older browsers.

Dreamweaver 4 includes a new feature that makes composing the basic layout of a page very straightforward: the Layout View. Here's how a typical home page is developed using this new tool:

1. Start by creating a logo for the Web in your favorite graphics editor. Remember that Web graphics are of a particular format, usually GIF or JPEG with a screen resolution of 72 dpi. Although most Web page visitors' monitors display thousands of colors, it's still good practice to use Web-safe colors wherever possible.

 You can find an explanation of Web graphic formats and Web-safe colors in Chapter 10.

2. In Dreamweaver, choose the Layout View from the bottom of the Objects panel. With Layout View enabled, both the Draw Layout Cell and Draw Layout Table tools, also on the Objects panel, become available.

3. Select Draw Layout Cell and drag out the initial cell for holding the logo. Dreamweaver automatically creates a layout table — a borderless table that is the full width of your window — around the layout cell.

4. Press the Ctrl (Command) key to continue drawing out other layout cells for your navigational elements and any other upfront information such as company name.

   Although your layout is likely to be different from mine, in the example shown in Figure 2-6, I start with a two-row by two-column configuration and modify it as needed.

 Tables are an important layout tool for Web designers. Chapter 12 shows you how to create and modify tables in Dreamweaver.

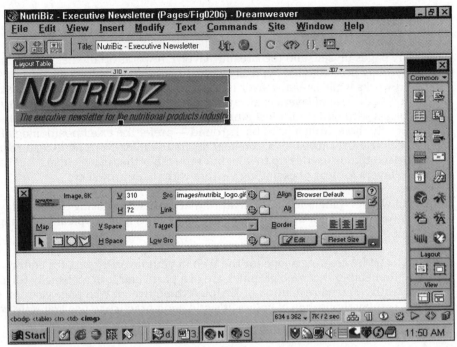

Figure 2-6: Placing the logo in a table to begin laying out the page.

5. Place your logo in the layout cell by choosing Insert Image from the Objects panel or dragging the graphic into place from the Assets panel.

6. Add background color to the table or rows, if desired, by picking a color from the Property Inspector.

   Using a table's background color features is a good, no overhead way to add color to your page. Dreamweaver enables me to sample colors directly from the logo to begin to tie the page together graphically.

7. If desired, adjust the positioning of the logo by using the Align option on the Property Inspector.

I continue to add and modify elements to the logo area until I'm satisfied. In the case of the example site, I added right-justified contact information on one side of the table and then added navigation elements below the logo, as shown in Figure 2-7. I used a contrasting background color for the second smaller row to set off the navigation bar. Initially, the navigation bar is just text and not graphics; this enables me to prototype the page quickly, and I can always replace the text with images at a later date. Cascading Style Sheets or Dreamweaver's HTML Styles control the look of the text.

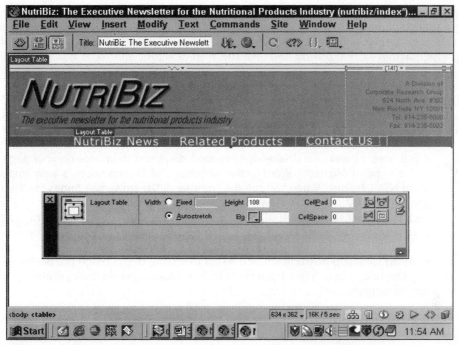

Figure 2-7: All the graphic elements are now in place in the logo area.

Note
One advantage of using tables instead of layers is that tables can adjust in width more consistently across browsers than layers can. Dreamweaver's layout tables are set to 100 percent width. If I use the Page Properties dialog to change the margins to zero, I can be sure the background color will stretch across the page, regardless of the user's browser window size.

Including Client Text

Now that your home page is beginning to attract some eyeballs with its graphic look, it is time to throw in some content to get the message across. Text from a client comes in many forms: from the headings and paragraphs of a marketing brochure to bulleted copy points written especially for the Web, and everything in between. Your job as a Web designer is to make it all flow together in a logical, attractive, understandable fashion.

Many print designers coming to the Internet are appalled at the lack of typographic control on the Web. Particular fonts are, for the most part, suggested rather than specified, with alternatives always available. Sizes are often relative and line spacing — outside of Cascading Style Sheets — is nonexistent. A typical first response is to render blocks of text into graphics to achieve exactly the look desired. In a word, don't. Graphics, unlike text, aren't searchable, and displaying text as graphics defeats much of the purpose of the Web. Moreover, large blocks of graphics can take a long time to download. It's far better to learn the ins and outs of HTML text and take advantage of its universality. Besides, Cascading Style Sheets are increasingly a real option and give the Web designer almost as much control as the print designer.

To facilitate including client-generated text in my Web page designs, I often work with my word processing program and Dreamweaver open simultaneously. This arrangement enables me to quickly cut and paste text from one to the other.

Note   If you have a great deal of already-formatted client text to include on your page — and a copy of Microsoft Word — take advantage of Dreamweaver's new Import Word HTML feature. When you run the command, Dreamweaver brings the Word-generated HTML document into a new page, and you can copy the needed sections (or all of it, if you like) and paste them directly into the home page. Dreamweaver preserves all the coding during the copy-and-paste operation.

I generally adopt a top-down approach when inserting text: I place the headings followed by the body copy. Then I can try different heading sizes, independently of the main paragraphs.

Tip   If you're copying multiple paragraphs from your word processing document, make sure that your paragraphs are separated by two returns. When pasted into Dreamweaver, the paragraph breaks will be preserved. If you just have a single return between paragraphs, Dreamweaver converts the paragraphs to line breaks.

Although it depends on the design, I rarely let the text flow all the way across the page. If my page margins are set at zero — which they often are for the graphics I use — the text then bumps right up against the edge of the browser windows. I frequently use two techniques in combination. First, I place the text in a table that is set at 95 percent width or less and that is centered on the page. This assures me that some "air" or gutter-space is on either side of my text, no matter how the browser window is sized. I'm also fond of the <blockquote> tag, which indents text by a browser-defined amount. You can access the <blockquote> tag by selecting your text and choosing the Indent button on the Property Inspector. The text blocks on the example page shown in Figure 2-8 use both techniques.

I feel that it's important to style your text in some fashion to maintain the desired look. Unless you specify the font, size, and color, you're at the mercy of your visitors' browser preferences — which can totally wreck your layout. You have two methods for defining text formatting: standard HTML tags and Cascading Style Sheets (CSS). Whenever possible, I use CSS because of its greater degree of control and flexibility. With CSS, if a client doesn't like the color of body text I've chosen or its size, I can modify it sitewide with one alteration. HTML tags, on the other hand, offer backward compatibility with 3.0 browsers. However, for most clients, the relatively small percentage of visitors still using the earlier browser versions is a fair trade-off for the power of CSS.

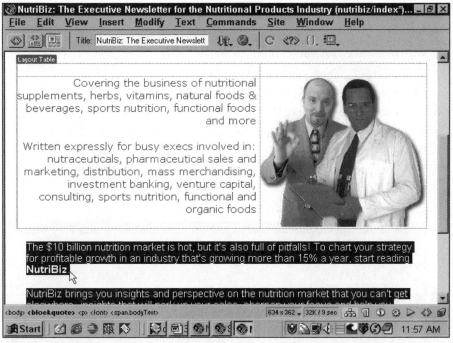

Figure 2-8: The text in the top paragraph (next to the image) is set within a centered table, whereas the text below is indented with the `<blockquote>` tag.

Cross-Reference To get the full scope of what CSS can do for you and your Web sites, see Chapter 18.

Activating the Page

Study after study has proven that an engaged viewer remembers your message better than a passive viewer. One method of grabbing people's attention is to activate your Web page in some fashion, so that some element of the page reacts to the visitor's mouse movements. This reaction could be anything from a simple rollover to the complete rewriting of a frame. Activating a page typically requires a combination of HTML and JavaScript, frequently beyond the programming skill level — or interest — of the Web designer. Luckily, Dreamweaver makes such effects possible through behaviors.

After I have the basic layout of a page done, I go back and activate the page in a fitting manner. As with any effect, too many behaviors can be more distracting than attractive; it's best to use them only when called for. At the very least, I typically use some form of rollover for the navigation bar; this is especially feasible now with Dreamweaver's tighter integration with Fireworks. But even without Fireworks, Dreamweaver enables you to construct a complete multistate navigation bar, or you can just use the Swap Image behavior to create your own.

Here's one method of activating your page:

1. In Fireworks, or another graphics program, create a series of rollover buttons with one image for each state.

   You need at least two states (Up and Over) and as many as four (Up, Over, Down, and Over While Down).

2. In Dreamweaver, remove the temporary text links for the navigation bar.

3. If you've created your rollover buttons in Fireworks, you can just choose Insert Fireworks HTML from the Objects panel.

   Dreamweaver inserts a table of sliced images, such as those in Figure 2-9, complete with all the necessary code.

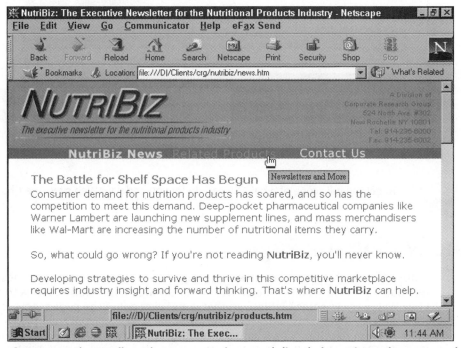

Figure 2-9: These rollover buttons were imported directly from Fireworks-generated HTML.

4. If you're working with separate images for the various rollover states, either use the Swap Image behavior or insert a Navigation Bar object. Either method enables you to select the separate images for your rollover states.

Cross-Reference   All of Dreamweaver's standard behaviors are covered in Chapter 15; information on the Navigation Bar object can be found in Chapter 10.

If I'm using tables for my layouts, I tend to nest the table containing the Navigation Bar inside the cell of another table. This technique gives me a fluid design that resizes and realigns well to match the user's browser window. For instance, in the NutriBiz example site, I merged all the columns in the row beneath the logo and then centered the table containing the navigation buttons.

New Feature Another alternative, sure to give your page some pizzazz, are the new Flash Button objects. A *Flash Button* is a predesigned graphic template with animation and possibly sound that uses your specified text. Flash Buttons are great for quickly turning out a professional quality navigation system. Because the are actually Flash animations, they depend on the user having the Flash Player plugin installed — which, as of this writing, is the case in over 92 percent of the systems running.

After I've completed the initial elements of my page, I take advantage of one of Dreamweaver's key features: Library items. By turning my Navigation Bar into a Library item, I can easily reuse it on the same page (as I do in the example page at the bottom), and on every other page of the site. Not only does this keep consistent elements on every page — an important consideration for design — but if I ever need to update the navigation system by changing a link or adding more buttons, I can do it in one step. Moreover, Dreamweaver's Library items, if activated with behaviors, retain all the necessary code.

Cross-Reference Library items are extremely useful for cutting your production time. Learn more about them in Chapter 22.

Previewing and Posting the Page

No matter how beautiful or spectacular your home page design, it's not a Web page until it's viewed through a Web browser and posted on the Web. Now, "the Web" could just as easily be a company intranet or the Internet. But chances are that if the page is intended to be viewed by numerous people, it will be seen under a number of different circumstances. Different operating systems, browsers, screen sizes, and resolutions are just some of the variables you have to take as a given — which is why previewing and testing your Web page is vitally important.

Here are a few pointers for initially testing your pages in development:

✦ At the very least, you should look at your Web page through versions of both major browsers. Dreamweaver enables you to specify up to 13 browsers with its Preview in Browser feature; I currently have 5 available on my system.

✦ During the initial building phase, my routine is to preview my page with both my primary browser (as of this writing, Netscape 4.7) and secondary browser (Internet Explorer 5.5) whenever I add a major component to the page.

✦ I make it a point to resize the page several times to see how my layout is affected by different screen sizes. If the client has specified maximum browser compatibility as a site requirement, I also look at the page under various screen resolutions.

✦ When a page is largely completed, I run Dreamweaver's Check Target Browsers command to make sure I'm not committing some grievous error. If incompatibilities do appear — as they do especially when checking the earliest browsers as shown in Figure 2-10 — I have to decide whether to keep the offending tag or risk the page being visited by users with those browsers.

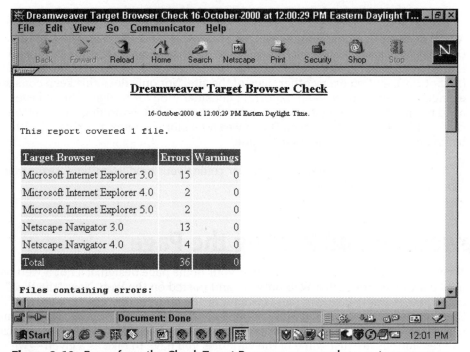

Figure 2-10: Errors from the Check Target Browser command are not uncommon when checking early browser versions.

I also make it a habit to routinely check the Download Stats found in Dreamweaver's status bar. The Download Stats show the "weight" of a page — its file size and the download time at a set speed. By default, the speed is set for a 28.8 Kbps modem, but you can alter that in the Status Bar category of Preferences. Remember that the Download Stats include all the dependent files (images and other media) as well as the size of the page itself.

To be sure that all my ducks are in a row and that all my links are valid, I run Dreamweaver's Check Links Sitewide command. Not only does this give me a report of broken links, but it also displays orphaned files and offers a list of external links that I can verify from its report.

My final testing phase is always conducted online. Here's a procedure that you can use for uploading your site and testing it:

1. Choose Window ⇨ Site Files to open the Site window. By this time you've already established a domain with an Internet host and edited your site definition to include the necessary FTP information.

2. Select the Connect button on the Site window. Dreamweaver logs in to the remote system and displays the remote files in the category opposite the local files.

3. Select the HTML files for the completed Web pages.

4. Choose the Put button.

5. By default, Dreamweaver asks if you'd like to include the dependent files; click Yes.

   Dreamweaver begins to transfer the HTML files and all the dependent files. All necessary subfolders (images, media) are created to replicate the local site structure on the remote site.

Note

If the Include Dependent Files dialog box does not appear, then open Preferences and, on the Site FTP category, select the Dependent Files: Prompt on Put/Check In option.

6. After the file transfer is complete, open a browser and connect to the URL for the site.

7. Navigate to every page and try all links and user actions, including rollovers. Note any "files not found" or other errors.

8. If errors occurred, return to Dreamweaver and verify the links for the problem files.

9. If necessary, repair the links and re-upload the HTML file. In most cases, you will not need to resend the dependent files.

10. Repeat Steps 6 through 9 with all available browsers and systems.

Tip

If the site is publicly viewable on the Internet, be sure to view the pages through an America Online (AOL) browser. Although AOL uses an Internet Explorer-derived browser, it also compresses graphics with its own algorithm and tends to open with smaller-than-normal windows. If you find problems, consult AOL's Webmaster Site at http://webmaster.info.aol.com.

Summary

When people ask me what I like about designing Web sites, I tell them that it appeals to me because it engages both my left and right brain. Web site design is, at turns, both creative and pragmatic, and Dreamweaver balances that equation with grace. Although everyone works differently, these are some of the points I try to keep in mind as I'm working:

✦ The more time spent in planning, the less time spent in revision. Get as much information as possible from the client before you begin designing.

✦ Use Dreamweaver's Site Map to prototype the site; the existing structure saves time as you begin to fill in the content.

✦ Work from the home page out. The home page is primarily used to succinctly express the client's message, and it often sets the tone for the entire site.

✦ Include some interactivity in your Web page. A static page may be beautiful to behold, but an active page enables the visitor to interact and leaves a more lasting impression.

✦ Preview your pages early and often during the development phase. It's far better to discover an incompatibility with the page half done than when you're demoing for the client.

In the next chapter, you get an in-depth tour of all of Dreamweaver's features.

✦   ✦   ✦

Touring Dreamweaver

Dreamweaver's user interface is clean, efficient, and powerful. By offering streamlined tools and controls, Dreamweaver helps you focus on the most important area of the screen: your Web page design. This chapter provides a detailed overview of the Dreamweaver workspace so you know where all the tools are when you need to use them.

Many other Web authoring programs surround your page-in-progress with numerous menu strips, icons, and other interface paraphernalia. Dreamweaver takes a more streamlined approach, however, which enables you to keep the focus on your workspace as your page develops. Dockable panels further reduce onscreen clutter; in Dreamweaver, every panel is dockable, including the Code Inspector.

Viewing the Document Window

Dreamweaver's primary workspace is the Document window. When you first start Dreamweaver, you see what is essentially an empty canvas, as shown in Figure 3-1. This is where you create your Web pages by typing in headlines and paragraphs, inserting images and links, and creating tables, forms, and other HTML elements.

The Web design process consists of creating your page in Dreamweaver and then previewing the results in one or more browsers. As your Web page begins to take shape, Dreamweaver shows you a close representation of how the page looks when viewed through a browser such as Netscape Communicator or Internet Explorer. You can do this as often as you like—Dreamweaver displays the page in your favorite browser with the press of a button. You can even view active elements, such as QuickTime movies or Shockwave and Flash files, in your Web page as you're building it.

Menus   Document window   Objects palette

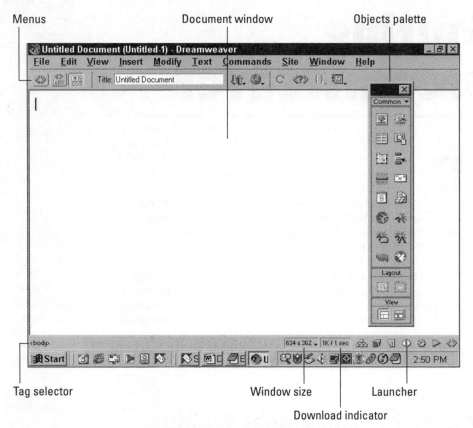

Tag selector   Window size   Launcher

Download indicator

Figure 3-1: Dreamweaver's opening window is designed to maximize your workspace with a minimum of distracting tools and windows.

Dreamweaver surrounds your "empty canvas" with the tools you need to create your Web masterpiece. We start our tour with the first of these: the status bar.

Working with the Status Bar

The status bar is found at the bottom of the Document window. Embedded here are four important tools: the Tag Selector, the Window Size pop-up menu, the Download Indicator, and the Launcher. Beyond displaying useful information such as which windows are open, these status bar tools are extremely helpful and provide the Web designer with several timesaving utilities.

Tip If you don't see the status bar at the bottom of your screen, check the View menu. Make sure there's a checkmark next to the status bar item; if not, select it with your mouse to enable it.

Tag Selector

The Tag Selector is an excellent example of Dreamweaver's elegant design approach. On the left side of the status bar, you see a listing of the current HTML tags. When you first open a blank page in Dreamweaver, you see only the <body> tag. If you type a line of text and then press Enter (Return), the paragraph tag <p> appears. Your cursor's position in the document determines which tags are displayed in the Tag Selector. The Tag Selector constantly keeps track of where you are in the HTML document by displaying the tags surrounding your current cursor position. This becomes especially important when you are building complex Web pages that use such features as nested tables.

As its name implies, the Tag Selector does more than just indicate a position in a document. Using the Tag Selector, you can quickly choose any of the elements surrounding your current cursor. Once an element is selected, you can quickly modify or delete it. If you have the Property Inspector (described later in this chapter) onscreen, choosing a different code from the Tag Selector makes the corresponding options available in the Property Inspector.

Tip If you want to quickly clear most of your HTML page, choose the <body> tag and press Delete. All graphics, text, and other elements you have inserted through the Document window are erased. Left intact is any HTML code in the <head> section, including your title, <meta> tags, and any preliminary JavaScript. The <body> tag is also left intact.

In a more complex Web page section such as the one shown in Figure 3-2, the Tag Selector shows a wider variety of HTML tags. As you move your pointer over individual codes in the Tag Selector, they are highlighted; click one, and the code becomes bold. Tags are displayed from left to right in the Tag Selector, starting on the far left with the most inclusive (in this case the <body> tag) and proceeding to the narrowest selection (here, the italic <i> tag) on the far right.

As a Web page developer, you're constantly selecting elements in order to modify them. Rather than relying on the click-and-drag method to highlight an area — which often grabs unwanted sections of your code, such as <font> tags — use the Tag Selector to unerringly pick just the code you want. Dreamweaver's Tag Selector is a subtle but extremely useful tool that can speed up your work significantly.

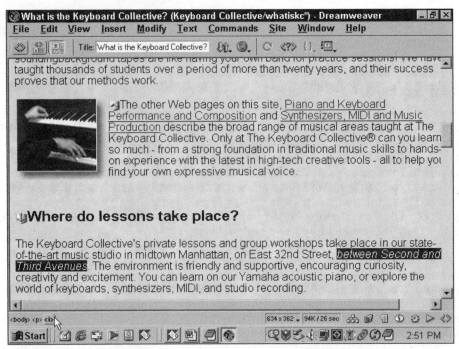

Figure 3-2: The Tag Selector enables you to highlight just the code you want. Here, selecting the <i> tag chooses only the italicized portion of the text.

Window Size pop-up menu

The universality of the Internet enables virtually any type of computer system from anywhere in the world to access publicly available Web pages. Although this accessibility is a boon to global communication, it forces Web designers to be aware of how their creations look under various circumstances — especially different screen sizes.

The Window Size pop-up menu gives designers a sense of how their pages look on different monitors. Located just right of center on the status bar, the Window Size pop-up menu indicates the screen size of the current Document window, in pixels, in *width×height* format. If you resize your Document window, the Window Size indicator updates instantly. This indicator gives you an immediate check on the dimensions of the current page.

But the Window Size pop-up menu goes beyond just telling you the size of your screen — it also enables you to quickly view your page through a wide variety of monitor sizes. Naturally, your monitor must be capable of displaying the larger screen dimensions before they can be selected. To select a different screen size, follow these steps:

1. Click once on the expander arrow to the right of the displayed dimensions. A menu listing the standard sizes, shown in Figure 3-3, pops up.

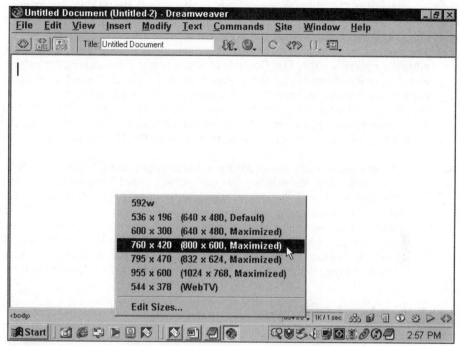

Figure 3-3: You can change your current screen size to any of seven standard sizes — or add your own custom sizes — with the Window Size pop-up menu.

2. Holding down the mouse button, move your mouse over a desired screen size.

3. To select a size, release the mouse button.

The standard sizes, and the machines most commonly using them, are as follows:

✦ 592w

✦ 536×196 (640×480, Default)

✦ 600×300 (640×480, Maximized)

✦ 760×420 (800×600, Maximized)

✦ 795×470 (832×624, Maximized)

✦ 955×600 (1024×768, Maximized)

✦ 544×378 (WebTV)

The first option, 592w, is the only option that does not change the height as well as the width. Instead, this choice uses the current window height and just alters the width.

Tip   You can set up your own custom screen settings by choosing Edit Sizes from the Window Size pop-up menu. This option opens the Status Bar category of the Preferences dialog box. How you modify the pop-up list is described in Chapter 4.

The dimensions offered by the Window Size pop-up menu describe the entire editable area of a page. The Document window has been carefully designed to match specifications set by the primary browsers. Both the left and right margins are the same width as both the Netscape and Microsoft browsers, and the status bar matches the height of the browser's bottom row as well. The height of any given browser environment depends on which toolbars are being used; however, Dreamweaver's menu strip is the same height as the browsers' menu strips.

Tip   If you want to compensate for the other browser user interface elements, such as the toolbar and the Address bar (collectively called "chrome"), you can increase the height of your Document window by approximately 72 pixels. Combined, Navigator's toolbar (44 pixels high) and Address bar (24 pixels) at 68 pixels are slightly narrower than Internet Explorer's total chrome. Microsoft includes an additional bottom separator that adds 6 pixels to its other elements (toolbar, 42 pixels; and Address bar, 24) for a total of 72 pixels. Of course, with so many browser variables, the best design course is to leave some flexibility in your design.

Download Indicator

So you've built your Web masterpiece, and you've just finished uploading the HTML, along with the 23 JPEGs, eight audio files, and three Flash movies that make up the page. You open the page over the Net and — surprise! — it takes five minutes to download. Okay, this example is a tad extreme, but every Web developer knows that opening a page from your hard drive and opening a page over the Internet are two vastly different experiences. Dreamweaver has taken the guesswork out of loading a page from the Web by providing the Download Indicator.

The Download Indicator is located to the right of the Window Size pop-up menu on the status bar. As illustrated in Figure 3-4, Dreamweaver gives you two values, separated by a slash character:

✦ The cumulative size of the page, including all the associated graphics, plug-ins, and multimedia files, measured in kilobytes (K).

✦ The time it takes to download at a particular modem connection speed, measured in seconds (sec).

Tip You can check the download size of any individual graphic by selecting it and looking at the Property Inspector — you can find the file size in kilobytes next to the thumbnail image on the left.

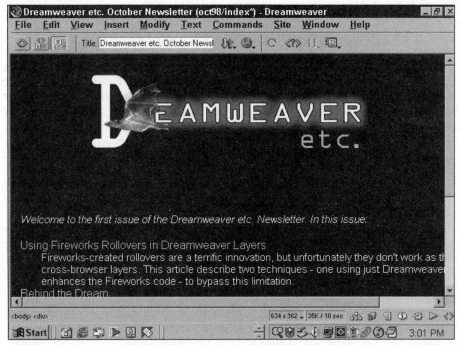

Figure 3-4: Take notice of the Download Indicator whenever you lay out a page with extensive graphics or other large multimedia files.

The Download Indicator is a handy real-world check. As you build your Web pages, it's a good practice to keep an eye on your file's download size — both in kilobytes and seconds. As a Web designer, you ultimately have to decide what your audience will deem is worth the wait and what will have them reaching for that Stop button. For example, the graphic shown in Figure 3-4 is attractive, but at 35K it's on the borderline of an acceptable size. Either the graphic should probably be reduced in size or the number of colors lessened to lower the overall "weight" of the page.

Cross-Reference Not everybody has the same modem connection. If you are working with an intranet or on a broadband site, you can set your connection speed far higher. Likewise, if your site gets a lot of traffic, you can lower the connection speed. You change the anticipated download speed through Dreamweaver's Preferences dialog box, as explained in Chapter 4.

Launcher

On the far right of the status bar, you find the Launcher — or, rather, one of the Launchers. In addition to the one on the status bar (known as the Mini-Launcher), Dreamweaver offers an independent, draggable panel with larger, named buttons that is also known as the Launcher. Both Launchers open and close the same windows by default: Site, Assets, HTML Styles, CSS Styles, Behavior, History, and Code Inspector. A key feature of the Launcher is that it's completely customizable.

As with the Tag Selector, each one of the buttons in the Mini-Launcher lights up when the pointer passes over it and stays lit when selected. You can also use the Launcher to close the windows it has opened — just click the highlighted button. Dreamweaver enables you to keep open any or all of the different windows at the same time.

Clicking a Launcher or Mini-Launcher button when a window is already open has one of two effects. If the window for the button is on top, the window closes. If the window is hidden behind another floating window, the window corresponding to the button is brought forward.

Tip   If you don't want the Mini-Launcher to appear in the status bar, you can turn it off. Choose Edit ⇨ Preferences and then select the Status Bar category. Click Show Launcher in Status Bar to remove its checkmark and then click OK. Naturally, you can turn the Launcher back on by rechecking its box.

The features of the various windows controlled through the Mini-Launcher are discussed in the section "Using the Launcher," later in this chapter.

Accessing the Toolbar

Regardless of the job — whether it's hanging a picture or fixing a faucet — work goes faster when your tools are at your fingertips. The same principle holds true for Web site building: the easier it is to accomplish the most often required tasks, the more productive you'll be as a Web designer. Dreamweaver puts a number of the repetitive tasks, such as previewing your page in a browser, just a function key away. However, there are far more necessary operations than there are function keys. In an effort to put needed functionality right up front, Dreamweaver incorporates the toolbar.

New Feature   The toolbar appears across the top of the Document window, whether in Design or Code view. On the toolbar you'll find some of the most frequently used commands that affect the entire document. The toolbar itself is toggled by choosing View ⇨ Toolbar or by choosing Ctrl+Shift+T (Command+Shift+T). One of the best features of the toolbar is its quick and easy access to changing your Web page's title, as shown in Figure 3-5.

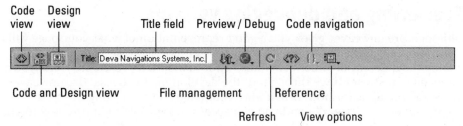

Figure 3-5: The toolbar offers easy access to an important element of a Web page, the title.

The first set of buttons is dedicated to the various views: Code, Code and Design, and Design view. These buttons are mutually exclusive as only one view can be shown at a time. Next to the view buttons is a text field for displaying and altering the title of your document. Dreamweaver, by default, titles every new page "Untitled Document." Not only is it considered bad form to keep this default title, search engines rely on a relevant title to properly index a site. To change a page title, enter the new text in the Title field and press Enter (Return) to confirm your modification.

Managing Files

The File Management button, next to the Title field, contains Web publishing–related commands. While maintaining a Web site, you'll often be required to make small alterations such as changing a bit of text or rescaling an image. I prefer to post these changes as quickly as possible to get the work off my virtual desk. The Get and Put options, along with Check In and Check Out, found on the toolbar under File Management, greatly simplify the process and speed my work. Under the File Management button you'll find:

✦ **Turn off Read Only:** Unlocks the current file for editing.

✦ **Get:** Transfers the remote file to a local site.

✦ **Check Out:** Marks the file as checked out and gets the remote file.

✦ **Put:** Transfers the local file to the remote site.

✦ **Check In:** Marks the file as checked in and puts the file to the remote site.

✦ **Undo Check Out:** Replaces the local version of the page with the remote version effectively undoing any changes made on the local file.

✦ **Design Notes:** Opens the Design Notes dialog box for the current page.

✦ **Locate in Site:** Selects the current page in the file listings of the Site window.

Previewing and debugging your file

Although Dreamweaver gives you a good representation of what your page will look like when rendered in a browser, it's not perfect. There are so many variations among the different browser programs — not to mentions versions — that you absolutely must test your page throughout the development process. Dreamweaver gives you the tools for both previewing your page and debugging it, should JavaScript errors appear — and you can access those tools right from the toolbar.

Selecting the Preview/Debug in Browser button on the toolbar presents a dynamic list of available browsers. All of the browsers entered in Preferences appear first, with the primary and secondary browsers leading the list. After the preview commands, Dreamweaver displays Debug options for all the supported browsers installed on the local system.

Dreamweaver can preview in any browser you assign — however, the debugger only works with specific browsers.

The final entry under the toolbar's Preview/Debug in Browser button is Edit Browser List. When invoked, this command opens the Preview in Browser category of Preferences to enable you to add, remove, or otherwise manage the browsers on your system in relation to Dreamweaver.

Easy Refresh and Reference

The next two options on the toolbar are the Refresh and the Reference buttons. Use the Refresh button when you've altered code directly in the Code view to apply those changes in the Design view; this option is especially useful when the split-screen Code and Design view is in operation. The Reference button, as you might expect, opens the Reference panel. If a tag, attribute, JavaScript object, or CSS style rule is selected, choosing the Reference button causes the Reference panel to open to the pertinent entry.

Straight-away Code Navigation

Dreamweaver's code editor offers a number of key features for programming and debugging Web pages with increasingly complex JavaScript routines. Several of these features are grouped under the Code Navigation button found on the toolbar. One such feature is the ability to set *breakpoints*. Breakpoints are markers that temporarily halt the execution of the code when running the JavaScript Debugger. Once the program execution is stopped, the current values of variables and other information can be retrieved.

While you can set breakpoints directly in the JavaScript Debugger, you can also set them in Dreamweaver's Code view. Position the cursor where you'd like the program to stop during debugging and choose Set Breakpoint from the Code Navigation button. After the first breakpoint is set, two additional commands are dynamically added: Remove Breakpoint and Remove All Breakpoints. Remove Breakpoint is only active when placed on the code line where a breakpoint was previously applied.

The remainder of the menu items under the Code Navigation button display JavaScript functions in the current page. Selecting any of these functions positions the cursor directly on that piece of code in the Code view. This capability makes it easy to quickly move from function to function; it also tells you at a glance which functions are included in a page.

View Options

View Options is a welcome but somewhat schizophrenic button found all the way to the right on the toolbar. The options that it makes available depend on the view mode currently employed. If, for example, you're in Design view and choose View Options, you're given the option to hide the various visual aids, such as table or frame borders, individually or all at once. If, on the other hand, you're in Code view, the View Options button toggles code-oriented functions, such as Word Wrap and Line Numbers. Best of all, if you're in the split-screen Code and Design view, you get both sets of view options!

The view options, all of which act as toggles, under Design view are:

✦ Hide All Visual Aids

✦ Visual Aids ➪ Table Borders, Layer Borders, Frame Borders, Image Maps, and Invisible Elements

✦ Head Content

✦ Rulers

✦ Grid

✦ Tracing Image

✦ Design View on Top

When in Code view, the view options are:

✦ Word Wrap

✦ Line Numbers

✦ Highlight Invalid HTML

✦ Syntax Coloring

✦ Auto Indent

Selecting Items from the Objects Panel

The Objects panel holds the items most often used — the primary colors, as it were — when designing Web pages. Everything from images to ActiveX plug-ins to HTML comments can be selected from the Objects panel. Moreover, the Objects panel is completely customizable — you can add your own favorite items and even set up how the Objects panel is organized.

The Objects panel is divided into seven separate categories of objects: Characters, Common, Forms, Frames, Head, Invisibles, and Special. The initial view is of the Common category. To switch from one category to another, select the small expander arrow at the top of the Objects panel (see Figure 3-6) and then choose an option from the resulting pop-up menu. Each category is described in detail in the following sections.

Drag bar   Close button

Objects   Available panels

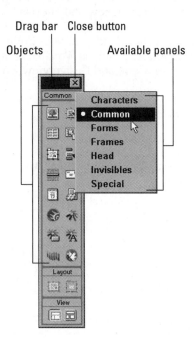

Figure 3-6: The Objects panel acts as a toolbox for holding your most commonly used Web page elements.

New Feature The Objects panel has taken on a new role in Dreamweaver 4. In addition to providing access to the most commonly used elements, the Objects panel also contains the mechanism for switching between Standard view and Layout view. Layout view, itself new in Dreamweaver 4, allows Web designers to quickly structure their page by drawing special tables and cells to hold content. Once the Layout view is selected, two additional tools become available, Draw Layout Cell and Draw Layout Table. Two standard objects (Insert Table and Draw Layer) are not accessible in Layout view. To find out more about how to use Layout view, see Chapter 12.

If the Objects panel is not available when you first start Dreamweaver, you can enable it by choosing Window ⇨ Objects or the keyboard shortcut, Ctrl+F2 (Command+F2). Likewise, choosing Window ⇨ Objects (or the shortcut) again deselects it and closes the Objects panel. You can also remove the Objects panel from your screen by clicking its Close button.

Tip Mac users have the added advantage of being able to windowshade the Objects panel by selecting the Collapse button.

To reposition the Objects panel — or any of the Dreamweaver windows or floating toolbars — just place your cursor over the drag bar at the top of the window and drag it to a new location. The Objects panel can be placed anywhere on the screen, not just inside the Document window. Some Web designers like to size their Document window to a standard width that renders well across a variety of platforms and resolutions, and then place the Objects panel outside of that window so they have a clear canvas with which to work.

Tip You can reshape the Objects panel by positioning your pointer over the panel's border so that a double-headed arrow appears. Click and drag the rectangle into a new size or shape, and the icons within the Objects panel rearrange themselves to fit. If your resized Objects panel is too small to contain all the objects, a small scroll arrow is displayed. Select the arrow, and the Objects panel scrolls to show additional objects; at the same time, another arrow appears at the opposite side of the window to indicate more hidden objects. Mac users can only resize the Objects panel by dragging the lower-right corner.

Common objects

The most often-used HTML elements, aside from text, are accessible through the Common Objects category of the Objects panel. Table 3-1 explains what each of the Common Objects icons represents.

Note   In Dreamweaver 4, the number of objects has increased to the point where, to show them all, the standard Objects panel is widened to two columns. The following tables describe the icons in a left-to-right, top-to-bottom order.

<table>
<tr><td colspan="4" align="center">Table 3-1
Common Objects Category</td></tr>
</table>

Icon	Name	Description	Detailed Information
	Insert Image	Use for including any graphic (including animated GIFs) at the cursor position	See Chapter 10
	Insert Rollover Image	Inserts an image that changes into another image when the user's mouse moves over it	See the section "Inserting Rollover Images" in Chapter 10
	Insert Table	Opens a dialog box for creating a table at the cursor position	See Chapter 12
	Insert Tabular Data	Imports delimited data exported from a spreadsheet or database program	See the section "Importing Tabular Data" in Chapter 12
	Draw Layer	Enables you to drag out a layer of specific size and shape at a specific location	See Chapter 19
	Insert Navigation Bar	Inserts a series of images with links used as buttons for navigation	See Chapter 10
	Insert Horizontal Rule	Draws a line across the page at the cursor position	See the section "Dividing the Web Page with Horizontal Rules" in Chapter 10
	Insert E-mail Link	Inserts a text link that opens an e-mail form when selected	See the section "Adding an E-mail Link" in Chapter 11
	Insert Date	Inserts the current date in a user-selected format	See the section "Incorporating Dates" in Chapter 9
	Insert Server-Side Include	Opens the dialog box for inserting a server-side include	See the section "Applying Server-Side Includes" in Chapter 22

Icon	Name	Description	Detailed Information
	Insert Fireworks HTML	Inserts images and code generated by Fireworks	See Chapter 16
	Insert Flash	Use to include a Flash movie	See Chapter 17
	Insert Flash Button	Creates a Flash button based on a template	See the section "Creating Flash Buttons and Crafting Templates" in Chapter 17
	Insert Flash Text	Makes a Flash headline or other text	See the section "Working with Flash Text" in Chapter 17
	Insert Shockwave	Use to include a Shockwave movie	See Chapter 17
	Insert Generator	Inserts a Generator template file with optional parameters	See the section "Adding Generator Templates" in Chapter 17

All of the common objects except for Insert Horizontal Rule and Draw Layer open a dialog box that enables you to browse for a file or specify parameters.

Tip   If you'd prefer to enter all your information, including the necessary filenames, through the Property Inspector, you can turn off the automatic appearance of the file requester when you insert any object through the Objects panel or the menus. Choose Edit ➪ Preferences and, from the General Category, select Show Dialog When Inserting Objects to uncheck it.

Character objects

Certain special characters — such as © (the copyright symbol) — are represented in HTML by codes called *character entities*. In code, a character entity is either a name (such as © for the copyright symbol) or number (©). Each character entity has its own unique code.

Dreamweaver eases the entry of these complex, hard-to-remember codes with the Characters category. Nine of the most commonly used characters are included as separate objects and a tenth object opens a dialog box with 99 special characters to choose from. Table 3-2 details the new Characters category objects. The Characters category also contains objects for inserting a line break and a non-breaking space.

Table 3-2
Characters Category

Icon	Name	Description	Detailed Information
	Insert Line Break	Puts in a ` ` tag that causes the line to wrap at the cursor position	See the section "Working with Paragraphs" in Chapter 9
	Insert Non-Breaking Space	Inserts a hard space in the current cursor position	See the section "Inserting Symbols and Special Characters" in Chapter 8
	Insert Copyright	Inserts the code for the copyright symbol	See the section "Inserting Symbols and Special Characters" in Chapter 8
	Insert Registered Trademark	Inserts the code for the registered trademark symbol	See "Inserting Symbols and Special Characters" in Chapter 8
	Insert Trademark	Inserts the code for the trademark symbol	See "Inserting Symbols and Special Characters" in Chapter 8
	Insert Pound	Inserts the code for the pound currency symbol	See "Inserting Symbols and Special Characters" in Chapter 8
	Insert Yen	Inserts the code for the yen currency symbol	See "Inserting Symbols and Special Characters" in Chapter 8
	Insert Euro	Inserts the code for the Euro currency symbol	See "Inserting Symbols and Special Characters" in Chapter 8
	Insert Left Quote	Inserts the code for the opening curly quote symbol	See "Inserting Symbols and Special Characters" in Chapter 8
	Insert Right Quote	Inserts the code for the closing curly quote symbol	See "Inserting Symbols and Special Characters" in Chapter 8
	Insert Em Dash	Inserts the code for the em dash symbol	See "Inserting Symbols and Special Characters" in Chapter 8
	Insert Other Character	Opens the dialog box for inserting special characters	See "Inserting Symbols and Special Characters" in Chapter 8

Form objects

The form is the primary method for implementing HTML interactivity. The Forms category of the Objects panel gives you nine basic building blocks for creating your Web-based form. Table 3-3 describes each of the elements found in the Forms category.

	Table 3-3		
	Forms Category		
Icon	**Name**	**Description**	**Detailed Information**
	Insert Form	Creates the overall HTML form structure at the cursor position	See Chapter 13
	Insert Text Field	Places a text box or a text area at the cursor position	See the section "Using Text Boxes" in Chapter 13
	Insert Button	Inserts a Submit, Reset, or user-definable button at the cursor position	See the section "Activating Your Form with Buttons" in Chapter 13
	Insert Check Box	Inserts a checkbox for selecting any number of options at the cursor position	See the section "Providing Checkboxes and Radio Buttons" in Chapter 13
	Insert Radio Button	Inserts a radio button for making a single selection from a set of options at the cursor position	See the section "Providing Checkboxes and Radio Buttons" in Chapter 13
	Insert List/Menu	Enables either a drop-down menu or a scrolling list at the cursor position	See the section "Creating Form Lists and Menus" in Chapter 13
	Insert File Field	Inserts a text box and Browse button for selecting a file to submit	See the section "Using the Hidden Field and the File Field" in Chapter 13
	Insert Image Field	Includes an image that can be used as a button	See the section "Activating Your Form with Buttons" in Chapter 13
	Insert Hidden Field	Inserts an invisible field used for passing variables to a CGI or JavaScript program	See the section "Using the Hidden Field and the File Field" in Chapter 13
	Insert Jump Menu	Opens a dialog box for building a pop-up menu that activates a link	See the section "Navigating with a Jump Menu" in Chapter 13

As demonstrated in Figure 3-7, you can use a table inside a form to get objects to line up properly. All forms return user input via a CGI or JavaScript program. See Chapter 13 for more detailed information.

Form outline   Forms panel

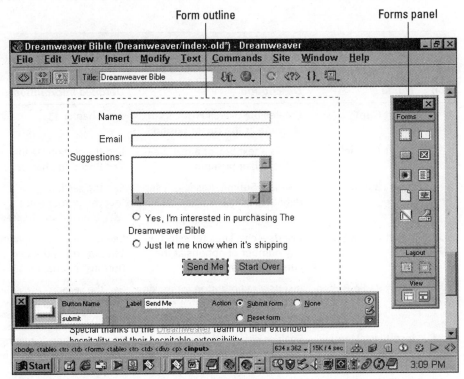

Figure 3-7: Dreamweaver puts a distinctive dashed line around any form if you have View Visual Aids ⇨ Invisible Elements checked.

Frame objects

In HTML terms, a *frame* is a collection of separate pages arranged on a single screen. Frames are contained within framesets, which until Dreamweaver could be created only by dragging frame borders into position or selecting a menu option. Because it involves multiple pages, creating a frameset often proved difficult for the novice designer.

The process for making standard framesets is greatly simplified when using the Frames category objects. Eight of the most commonly used designs are now immediately available. Select any frame object, and that frameset is made, incorporating the existing page.

The blue symbol in the frame object icons indicates which frame on the current page is placed when the frameset is created. For example, if you create a single page with the text "Table of Contents" and then choose the Insert Top Frame object, "Table of Contents" is moved below the newly inserted top frame. All of the Frames category objects are explained in Table 3-4.

	Table 3-4 **Frames Category**		
Icon	**Name**	**Description**	**Detailed Information**
	Insert Left Frame	Inserts a blank frame to the left of the current page	See Chapter 14
	Insert Right Frame	Inserts a blank frame to the right of the current page	See Chapter 14
	Insert Top Frame	Inserts a blank frame above the current page	See Chapter 14
	Insert Bottom Frame	Inserts a blank frame below the current page	See Chapter 14
	Insert Left, Top-Left Corner, and Top Frames	Makes a frameset with four frames where the current page is in the lower right	See Chapter 14
	Insert Left and Nested Top Frames	Makes a frameset where the top spans the lower two frames	See Chapter 14
	Insert Top and Nested Left Frames	Makes a frameset where the left spans the two rightmost frames	See Chapter 14
	Split Frame Center	Creates a frameset with four equal frames	See Chapter 14

Head objects

General document information — such as the title and any descriptive keywords about the page — is written into the `<head>` section of an HTML document. The objects of the Head category enable Web designers to drop in these snippets of code in a handy object format. These objects insert `<meta>` tags with keywords for search engines, specify refresh times, and do many more tasks that impact a Web site's overall performance.

While Dreamweaver enables you to see the `<head>` objects onscreen via the View ➪ Head Content menu option, you don't have to have the `<head>` window open to drop in the objects. Simply click any of the six objects detailed in Table 3-5, and a dialog box opens, prompting you for the needed information.

Table 3-5
Head Objects Category

Icon	Name	Description	Detailed Information
	Insert Meta	Includes document information usable by servers and browsers	See the section "Understanding <meta> and other <head> tags" in Chapter 8
	Insert Keywords	Inserts keywords used by search engines to catalog the Web page	See the section "Understanding <meta> and other <head> tags" in Chapter 8
	Insert Description	Provides a description of the current page	See the section "Understanding <meta> and other <head> tags" in Chapter 8
	Insert Refresh	Sets a tag to refresh the current page or redirect the browser to another URL	See the section "Refreshing the page and redirecting users" in Chapter 8
	Insert Base	Specifies the base address of the current document	See the section "Understanding <meta> and other <head> tags" in Chapter 8
	Insert Link	Declares a relationship between the current document and another object or file	See the section "Linking to other files" in Chapter 8

Invisible objects

As any experienced Web designer knows, what you see onscreen is, increasingly, a small part of the code necessary for the page's generation. Often you need to include an element that Dreamweaver categorizes as an Invisible. The Invisibles category of the Objects panel gives you quick access to the most commonly inserted behind-the-scenes tags, as described in Table 3-6.

Table 3-6
Invisible Objects

Icon	Name	Description	Detailed Information
	Insert Named Anchor	Puts a hyperlink at a particular place on a Web page	See the section "Navigating with Anchors" in Chapter 11

Icon	Name	Description	Detailed Information
◈	Insert Script	Inserts JavaScript or VBScript either directly or from a file	
💬	Insert Comment	Places HTML comment tags inside your script; these comments are ignored by the browser	See the section "Commenting Your Code" in Chapter 9

Tip   Invisible elements can be turned on or off through the Preferences dialog box. Choose Edit ➪ Preferences and then select the Invisible Elements category. A list of 11 options (including the objects listed in the Invisibles category except for Insert Non-breaking Space) is displayed. To turn off an option, click once to remove the checkmark from the option's checkbox. For a complete description of all the Invisible elements and other preferences, see Chapter 4.

Special objects

As noted throughout this book, part of the power of HTML is its ability to go beyond its native capabilities by including special objects. Dreamweaver facilitates the inclusion of these external elements—Java applets, plug-ins, and ActiveX controls—through the objects found in the Special category of the Objects panel. Each of these objects inserts a placeholder on the page to assist with layout; files requiring plug-ins can be played within Dreamweaver while applets and ActiveX controls must be viewed in the browser. Table 3-7 details the three Special objects.

	Table 3-7	
	Special Objects Category	

Icon	Name	Description
♨	Insert Applet	Includes a Java applet at the cursor position
🧩	Insert Plug-in	Use for including a file that requires a plug-in
🔲	Insert ActiveX	Puts a placeholder for an ActiveX control at the cursor position, using the `<object>` tag

Getting the Most out of the Property Inspector

Dreamweaver's Property Inspector is your primary tool for specifying an object's particulars. What exactly those particulars are—in HTML these are known as *attributes*—depends on the object itself. The contents of the Property Inspector change depending on which object is selected. For example, click anywhere on a blank Web page, and the Property Inspector shows text attributes for format, font name and size, and so on. If you click an image, the Property Inspector displays a small thumbnail of the picture, and the image's attributes for height and width, image source, link, and alternative text. Figure 3-8 shows a Property Inspector for a line of text with an attached hyperlink.

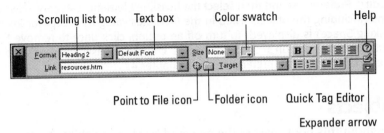

Figure 3-8: The Property Inspector takes many forms, depending on which HTML element you select.

Manipulating the Property Inspector

The Property Inspector is enabled by choosing Window ⇨ Properties or selecting the keyboard shortcut, Ctrl+F3 (Command+F3). As with the Objects panel, the Property Inspector can be closed by selecting the Close button, unchecking Window ⇨ Properties, or choosing the keyboard shortcut again. On the Mac, you can also windowshade the Property Inspector so that only the title bar is left showing by clicking the Collapse button on its window.

You can reposition the Property Inspector in one of two ways. You can click and drag the title bar of the window and move it to a new location, or—unlike the Objects panel—you can click and drag any open gray area in the inspector itself. This is handy for quickly moving the inspector aside, out of your way. However, it only works for Windows.

The Property Inspector initially displays the most typical attributes for a given element. To see additional properties, click the expander arrow in the lower-right corner of the Property Inspector. Virtually all the inserted objects have additional parameters that can be modified. Unless you're tight on screen real estate, it's a good idea to keep the Property Inspector expanded so you can see all your options.

Tip

In addition to using the expander arrow, you can reveal (or hide) the expanded attributes by double-clicking any open gray area of the Property Inspector.

Property Inspector elements

Many of the attributes in the Property Inspector are text boxes; just click in any one and enter the desired value. If a value already appears in the text box, whether number or name, double-click it (or click and drag over it) to highlight the information and then enter your new data — the old value is immediately replaced. You can see the effect your modification has had by pressing the Tab key to move to the next attribute or by clicking outside of the Property Inspector.

Dreamweaver enables you to make small additions to the code without opening up the Code Inspector through the Quick Tag Editor. Located on the right of the Property Inspector just below the Help button, the Quick Tag Editor pops open a small window to display the code for the currently selected tag. You can swiftly change attributes or add special parameters not found in the Property Inspector. The Quick Tag Editor is covered in depth in Chapter 8.

The Property Inspector also uses scrolling list boxes for several attributes that provide a limited number of responses for you to choose. To open the drop-down list of available options, click the arrow button to the right of the list box. Then choose an option by highlighting it.

Tip

Some options on the Property Inspector are a combination drop-down list and text box — you can select from available options or type in your own values. For example, when text is selected, the font name, size, and color options are all combination list/text boxes.

If you see a Folder icon next to a text box (see the Folder icon in the inspector, shown in Figure 3-8), you have the option of browsing for a filename on your local or networked drive, or manually inputting a name. Clicking the folder opens a standard Open File dialog box (called Select File in Dreamweaver); after you've chosen your file and clicked Open, Dreamweaver inputs the name and any necessary path information in the correct attribute.

Dreamweaver enables you to quickly select an onscreen file in either a Document window or a Site window as a link, with its Point to File icon, found next to the Folder icon. Just click and drag the Point to File icon until it touches the file (or the filename from the Site window) you want to reference. The path is automatically written into the Link text box.

Cross-Reference

Dreamweaver can handle all forms of absolute and relative addressing. For more information on specifying HTML pages, be sure to read Chapter 6.

Certain objects such as text, layers, and tables enable you to specify a color attribute. The Property Inspector alerts you to these options with a small color swatch next to the text box. You can type in a color's name (such as "blue") or its six-figure hexadecimal value ("#3366FF") or select the color swatch. Choosing the color swatch displays a color picker, shown in Figure 3-9, with the 212 colors common to both the Netscape and Microsoft browsers — the so-called browser-safe colors. (Some of the 212 Web-safe colors are duplicated to create a more user-friendly interface.) You can go outside of this range by clicking the small painter's palette in the lower-right corner of the color picker. This opens a full-range Color dialog box in which you can choose a color visually or enter its red, green, and blue values or its hue, saturation, and luminance values.

Eyedropper tool

Figure 3-9: Dreamweaver's color picker enables you to choose from a wide selection of colors, right from the palette or right off the desktop, with the Eyedropper tool.

The color picker in Dreamweaver is very flexible. Not only can you choose from a series of color swatches, but you can also select any color onscreen with Dreamweaver's Eyedropper tool. The Eyedropper button has two modes: By default, the Eyedropper snaps the selected color to its nearest Web-safe neighbor; if you deselect Snap to Web Safe from the color picker's context menu, colors are sampled exactly. If you'd like to access the system color picker, the color wheel button opens it up for you. There's also a Default Color tool, which deletes any color choice previously inserted. Finally, you can use the color picker's context menu to change the swatch set shown. By default, the Color Cubes view is shown, but you may also see the swatches in a Continuous Tone configuration as well as restricted to Windows OS, Macintosh OS, or Grayscale colors. While these options may not be used frequently by the Web designer, Macromedia standardized the color picker across its product line to make it easier to switch between applications.

One final aspect of the Property Inspector is worth noting: The circled question mark in the upper-right corner of the Property Inspector is the Help button. Selecting this button invokes online help and displays specific information about the particular Property Inspector you're using. The Help button is also available throughout all of the panels opened by the Launcher, as described in the next section.

Using the Launcher

Dreamweaver's third main control panel, along with the Objects panel and the Property Inspector, is called the Launcher, shown in Figure 3-10.

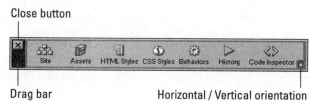

Figure 3-10: The Launcher gives you access to seven different Dreamweaver functions, and up to thirteen if you customize it.

The Launcher opens and closes seven default windows, each of which handles a different aspect of the program:

✦ The Site window handles all elements of publishing to the Web, as well as basic file maintenance such as moving and deleting folders.

✦ The Assets panel puts the resources — images, colors, links, Flash movies, Shockwave movies, QuickTime and MPEG movies, scripts, templates, and Library items — of a site right up front, where they can be dragged and dropped with ease right onto the page.

✦ The HTML Styles panel applies standard HTML formatting to text and paragraph selections.

✦ The CSS Styles panel coordinates the Cascading Style Sheet modifications on each Web page and, if used in conjunction with an external style sheet, throughout your entire Web site.

✦ The Behaviors panel assigns one or more JavaScript actions to a JavaScript event selected from a browser-targeted list.

✦ The History panel shows a list of the user actions that can be replayed, undone, or saved as a command.

✦ The Code Inspector is one view of Dreamweaver's internal code editor, which appears in a separate floating window.

Similar to the other control panels, the Launcher can be started by choosing Window ⇨ Launcher, and closed by either selecting the Close button or choosing Window ⇨ Launcher again. A standard title bar is available on the Launcher for dragging the panel into a new position. The Launcher also includes a small button in the lower-right corner (refer to Figure 3-10) that serves to change the panel's orientation from a horizontal shape to a vertical one, and vice versa.

The free-floating Launcher panel functions identically to the status bar Launcher. Each one of the Launcher buttons is highlighted when the pointer passes over it, and remains highlighted when chosen. As noted, the Launcher can be used to close the windows or bring them to the front as well as open them — just click the highlighted button. Any or all of the windows can be "launched" simultaneously.

Cross-Reference   Both the floating Launcher and status bar Launcher are customizable. You can display the icon for any or all of the 13 standard panels. See the section "Panels Preferences" in Chapter 4.

Site window

The Site window is your gateway to the Web. Through it, you can transfer files from the development folder on your local drive to your online Web server. Any member of your development team can check out a file to work on with no fear that another member is making changes at the same time. The team leader can even check Dreamweaver's log to see who is working on what.

Web sites can become quite complex very quickly, and it's often difficult to remember how pages are linked together. Dreamweaver offers a visual representation of your Web site through its Site Map window. The Site Map window not only enables you to quickly review the structure of a site, you can also use it to add, move, or modify links. You can learn all the details about the Site Map feature in Chapter 7.

Open the Site window by choosing the Site button, on either the Launcher panel or the status bar Launcher, by selecting Window ⇨ Site Files or by pressing F8. As you can see in Figure 3-11, the Site window is two-paned: Local files are shown on the right side, and remote files are displayed on the left. The headings across the top of each pane and the panes themselves can be resized. Position your pointer over a border until a double-headed arrow appears and then click and drag the border to a new position.

Tip   The files of both local and remote folders can be sorted by name, file size, file type, date modified, or checkout status — all the options corresponding to the headings across each pane. For example, to display your files in A-to-Z alphabetical order, click the Name button once. To show them in descending (Z-to-A) order, click the Name button again. If you're constantly updating your site, it's good practice to have your folders sorted in descending date order so that your most recently modified files appear at the top of each pane.

Site Map button   Remote panel   Local panel

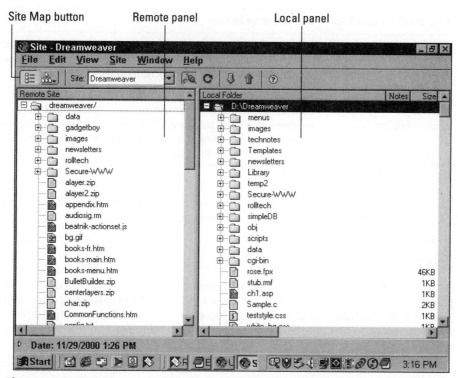

Figure 3-11: Dreamweaver's Site window handles the Webmaster's site management chores.

The major operations performed in the Site window include the following:

Site Window Function	Site Window Action
Connecting to the site	When your site is properly configured, the Connect button automatically calls your remote site and uses whatever login and password are necessary to get you online. After the connection is confirmed, the button changes into a Disconnect button.
Transferring files	To move files between your local drive and the remote server, use the Get and Put buttons. The Get button copies whatever files are highlighted in the Remote pane to the local folder, and the Put button copies files highlighted in the Local pane to the remote directory. To stop a transfer, select the Stop Current Task button — the stop sign in the lower-right corner of the window.

Continued

Site Window Function	Site Window Action
Locking files	When a team of Web designers is working on a site, you have to be able to prevent two people from working on the same file simultaneously. The Checked In/Checked Out indicator not only shows that a file is in use, but who has the file.
Site Map representation	As a site grows in complexity, it is often helpful to get an overview of a site's structure and its links. The Site Map feature gives a visual representation of the complete site and can be chosen by selecting the Site Map button.

Cross-Reference   Maintaining a Web site is a major portion of a Webmaster's responsibility. To learn more about Dreamweaver's site management features, see Part VI.

Assets panel

For most Web pages, an HTML file is just one of the elements necessary for the page's rendering in a browser. In addition to the code, the typical page may require GIFs, JPEGs, Flash movies and other multimedia, external CSS files and added JavaScript files to be complete. Dreamweaver now includes a center for all the resources included in a site: the Assets panel, shown in Figure 3-12.

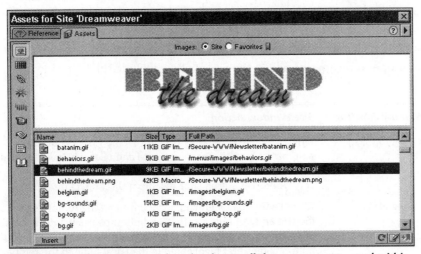

Figure 3-12: The Assets panel tracks almost all the components used within any given site.

New Feature

The Assets panel not only catalogs all the current elements within a site, it makes them extremely easy to include. To add a previously used company logo to a page, just drag it from the Assets panel onto the page. A copy of the image is placed on the page while the logo remains available for further use in the Assets panel. There are nine categories of assets, each represented by an icon on the side of the panel: images, colors, URLs, Flash movies, Shockwave movies, multimedia movies, scripts, templates, and Library items. Each category of the Assets panel accepts a particular file type; Table 3-8 details what you'll find in each category.

Table 3-8
Assets Panel Categories

Category	Types of Elements Cataloged
Images	Standard Web images: GIF, JPEG, and PNG formats
Colors	Colors applied to backgrounds, text, links (including `alink` and `vlink` attributes) in HTML or CSS styles
URLs	Absolute links using any of these protocols: HTTP:, HTTPS:, FTP:, JavaScript:, gopher:, mailto:, or file:
Flash	Flash player movies (.swf)
Shockwave	All Shockwave movie formats
Movies	MPEG or QuickTime
Scripts	External JavaScript and VBScript files included using the `scr` attribute of the `<script>` tag
Templates	Pages saved as a template in Dreamweaver (.dwt files)
Library	Dreamweaver Library items (.lbi files)

There are several ways to display the Assets panel. Select the Show Assets button from the Launcher or choose Window ➪ Assets. You can also use the keyboard shortcut, F11. Once opened, you'll see that the Assets panel is divided into two areas, a preview and a listing. Images and multimedia are shown as a proportionate thumbnail; Flash, Shockwave, and Movie category previews can be played by selecting the Play button that appears in the preview area when a file is selected.

Dreamweaver keeps track of the assets in a site through the use of the site cache, which is enabled when the site is defined. When you open a page in a site and display the Assets panel, the site cache is read and all the available resources are listed. When you add an asset, such as an image or new background color, it appears in the Assets panel automatically the next time a page from the site is opened. You can hasten the process and manually refresh the site cache by selecting the Refresh Site List button on the bottom of the Assets panel. The same procedure holds true for assets removed from your pages.

Tip   If, after selecting Refresh Site List, you still don't see your asset, Ctrl+click (Command+click) Refresh Site List. This action rebuilds the site cache from the ground up so it may take a moment or two, but it ensures that all of your assets are categorized.

Site assets

There are two ways to use an asset on a page, both very straightforward:

✦ Drag the preview of the asset from the Assets panel and drop it in the desired place on the page. You can also drag-and-drop the listing of the asset.

✦ Position the cursor where you'd like the asset to appear, choose the listing from the Assets panel, and then select the Insert or Apply button.

The assets from the media categories — Images, Flash, Shockwave, and Movies — insert the proper code as well as references to specific media files. Colors are applied to selected text via a `<font>` tag; if you drop a color from the Assets panel where no text is selected, the next text you type at that location will take on the specified color. URL assets are similar: Drop a URL asset on selected text to add that link while inserting a URL asset on a cursor position inserts the link using the URL as the text. For example, if you were to drag the URL asset mailto:jlowery@ idest.com on the page, the following code would be inserted:

```
<a href="mailto:jlowery@idest.com">mailto:jlowery@idest.com</a>
```

Dragging either a script or Library asset onto the page inserts the necessary code at the selected position. However, inserting a template from the Assets panel applies that template to the current page.

Cross-Reference   When a template is applied to a page, all the elements on that page must be placed into an editable region of the template or discarded. For more details on working with templates, see Chapter 21.

If you'd like to alter an asset before placing on the page, you can choose to edit any item in all of the categories except for Colors and URLs. Select the Edit button on the Assets panel to invoke the editor, as selected for that file type in Preferences, for the selected asset. After making your modifications and saving the file in the editor, the change is reflected in the Assets panel.

Caution   When editing graphic assets for which Fireworks 4 is the chosen editor, you won't see the Launch and Edit interface as you do when selecting the Edit Image in Fireworks 4 command or choosing the Edit button from the Property Inspector. In Fireworks, choose File ➪ Export to update changed GIFs, JPEGs, and exported PNGs; and File ➪ Save to modify Fireworks source PNGs. You'll have to navigate to the proper file location during export or save to store the image in the same place.

Often designers reuse elements from one site in another. The Assets panel allows you to easily copy any selected asset from one site to any other defined site. To copy an asset from one site to another, follow these steps:

1. Select the desired asset(s) in the Assets panel.

   Ctrl+click (Command+click) additional assets to extend your selection.

2. From the context menu, choose Copy to Site ⇨ Sitename, where Sitename designates the site you want to copy the asset to.

   Dreamweaver informs you that the asset has been placed in the Favorites category of the Assets panel.

3. To view your moved asset, choose Site ⇨ Open Site to switch to the other site and then select Favorites from the Assets panel.

When Dreamweaver copies an asset from one site to another, it moves it to the same relative location. For example, if I were to copy a file with the relative address of /images/logos/mainLogo.gif to another site, Dreamweaver would put the file in the same folders, creating any that did not already exist.

Tip If you have documents open from a number of defined sites, the Assets panel switches to show the assets in the site that the document is from.

To make it easier to find a particular asset, you can sort your entries by any of the headings found in the listings area of the Assets panel. To find all your GIF images, for example, select the Type heading. Select the heading once to sort the files in an ascending order (A–Z) and again to sort in a descending order (Z–A).

Note Unfortunately, the Assets panel is one aspect of Dreamweaver that is not customizable. You can't alter the existing categories to accept additional file types or add new categories.

Favorite Assets view

The Assets panel categories are available in both Site and Favorites views, as controlled by the radio buttons on top of the panel. When the Site view is selected, all the resources within the defined site are visible; on even medium-sized sites, the number of assets can be substantial. To make it easy to locate often-used assets, Dreamweaver provides a Favorites view, which contains only selected assets. Select either the Site or Favorites views at the top of the Assets panel to switch between these two options. To create a Favorite asset, select the asset (or assets) in the Site view and choose the Add to Favorites button found on the bottom of the Assets panel. To delete the entry in the Favorites view, select it and choose Remove From Favorites.

The Favorites view has a number of special properties. First, you can label any asset with an alias or, as it's called in Dreamweaver, a *Nickname*. Giving an asset a Nickname, such as Main Logo, makes retrieval very easy and does not rename the original file. To give a Favorite asset a Nickname, slowly click the filename of the asset twice—do not double-click. The original filename will be highlighted and available for you to enter a new name, as shown in Figure 3-13.

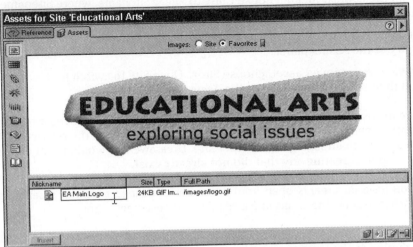

Figure 3-13: In a site with many assets, use the Favorites view to isolate the most frequently used ones; you can give any Favorite asset a Nickname to make it more identifiable.

The Favorites view of the Assets panel gives you another organizational tool with the capability to group assets. In the standard Site view of the Assets panel, all assets are listed equally, one after another. In the Favorites view, you can create a folder by selecting the New Favorites Folder button and then drag any assets into it. Favorites folders can be created in any asset category.

Finally, the Favorites view may be used to create new assets, not just list existing ones. In the Favorites view of the Assets panel, you can create a new:

✦ **Color:** In the Color category, choose the New Color button and select one from the standard color picker.

✦ **URL:** In the URLs category, select the New URL button and enter the desired link and Nickname.

Tip   You can use the New URL option to store relative links in the Assets panel; generally only absolute URLs are treated as assets.

✦ **Template:** In the Templates category, select the New Template button. This creates a blank template; you'll need to choose the Edit button to add content and mark editable regions for the template to be useful.

✦ **Library:** In the Library category, select the New Library Item button; again this creates a blank Library item, which will have to be edited to be made useful. You can also drag any selection from the current document into the Library category of the Assets panel to create a new Library item.

HTML Styles panel

Although Cascading Style Sheets are powerful, they have two major drawbacks: They're not compatible with 3.0 browsers, and they're difficult to master. To offset these disadvantages — and still make it easy to apply formatting to text and paragraphs — Dreamweaver offers HTML styles.

The HTML Styles panel lists all available styles and is used primarily to apply and remove formatting. Two basic types of HTML styles exist: paragraph and selection. A paragraph style is denoted by the ¶ symbol, while styles, which only affect a selection, are marked with an underlined, lowercase *a*, as shown in Figure 3-14. Styles with a plus sign (+) next to them add their formatting to the existing tags; those styles without the plus sign replace the original formatting.

Defined HTML styles

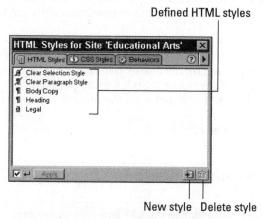

New style   Delete style

Figure 3-14: The HTML Styles panel offers an easy way to apply consistent formatting to any text selection or paragraph.

Features of the HTML Styles panel are listed in the following table:

HTML Styles Panel Function	Document Window Action
Defining styles	New styles can be defined through the Define HTML Style dialog box, which is opened when the New Style button is selected.
Applying styles	All available styles are listed in the panel and applied by selecting one, if the Apply option is enabled. If the Apply option is not selected, you'll have to choose the style and then click the Apply button.
Removing styles	Existing HTML text formatting, whether applied through the HTML Styles panel or another means, can be removed by choosing either Clear Selection Style or Clear Paragraph Style.
Editing styles	Double-clicking an existing HTML style reopens the Define HTML Style dialog box. Styles that are already applied are not affected by any changes.

Cross-Reference HTML styles are explained fully in the section "Using HTML Styles" in Chapter 9.

CSS Styles panel

Through the CSS Styles panel, Dreamweaver makes creating and applying Cascading Style Sheets easy. Style sheets give the Web designer a terrific degree of control over the appearance of text and other elements, throughout the creation stage and when the Web site is live. Styles can be used in conjunction with a single Web page or an entire site.

The CSS Styles panel, shown in Figure 3-15, is accessed by clicking the Show CSS Styles button from either the Launcher panel or the status bar Launcher. You can also open the CSS Styles panel by choosing Window ➪ Styles or by pressing Shift+F11. You can drag or resize the CSS Styles panel with the mouse.

The CSS Styles panel has the following three key uses:

CSS Styles Panel Function	Document Window Action
Defining styles	Through the Style Sheet button on the CSS Styles panel, you can create, modify, and remove CSS formats. CSSs either redefine existing HTML tags or create new user-defined classes.
Applying styles	Once your CSS styles are defined, you can easily apply them to any selected text throughout your Web page. Just click the desired style in the CSS Styles panel, if you have the Apply option selected; otherwise, you'll have to also click the Apply button.
Viewing styled tags	It can be difficult to tell which style has already been applied to which tag. With the CSS Styles panel, pick any text or item on the screen, and the applied style (if any) is highlighted.

Defined CSS Styles

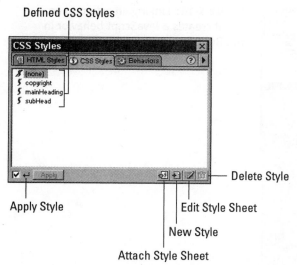

Apply Style

Attach Style Sheet

New Style

Edit Style Sheet

Delete Style

Figure 3-15: The CSS Styles panel displays custom styles and gives you access to Dreamweaver's point-and-click CSS editing capabilities.

Cross-Reference For more detailed information on how to use the CSS Styles panel, see Chapter 18.

Behaviors panel

The Behaviors panel enables nonprogrammers to build cutting-edge Web pages through prebuilt JavaScript actions. Briefly, behaviors are composed of two parts: an action and an event that triggers the action. Dreamweaver includes 25 standard behaviors, and because behaviors can be custom-built, hundreds more are available on the Web — and, of course, on the CD-ROM that accompanies this book. Macromedia also maintains the Dreamweaver Exchange, which is instantly accessible through the Get More Behaviors menu item.

The Behaviors panel is browser-savvy and won't allow you to assign a JavaScript event that only works on 4.0 browsers when you need 3.0 compatibility. With the Behaviors panel, not only can you link several actions to a single event, but you can also specify the order of the actions.

Use the Show Behaviors button on either Launcher (panel or status bar) to open the Behaviors panel. You can also press Shift+F3 or choose Window ⇨ Behaviors. Like the other windows, you can resize or reposition the Behaviors panel with the mouse using the click-and-drag technique. As shown in Figure 3-16, the Behaviors panel displays the events in the left column and the actions in the right column.

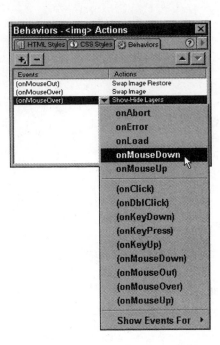

Figure 3-16: Linking an action to an event creates a JavaScript behavior in the Behaviors panel.

Use the Behaviors panel to perform the functions outlined in the following table:

Behaviors Panel Function	Document Window Action
Specifying a browser	The various browsers and browser versions understand specific JavaScript commands. You can target individual browsers by manufacturer or version number, or a combination of the two, by using the Browser pop-up menu.
Picking an action	Behaviors are linked to specific HTML tags; not all HTML tags have behaviors associated with them. Selecting the Behavior pop-up menu (by clicking the + button) displays a list of available actions. Remove an action by highlighting it and clicking the – (minus) button.
Changing an event	The events listed under the Events pop-up menu (the arrow button in between the action and the event) are determined by what's selected in the Browser pop-up menu.
Order the actions	Because you can assign more than one action to an event, Dreamweaver enables you to rearrange the order of the actions. Use the up/down-arrow keys to rearrange the order of your action list for each event.

Behaviors are user-definable. In Chapter 15, you learn how to create your own actions.

On the
CD-ROM

Be sure to check out the Behaviors section of the CD-ROM that accompanies this book to add to your list of Dreamweaver action capabilities.

History panel

Web design is largely a process of experimentation and repetition. You try one approach, and if you're not satisfied, you undo what you've done and try something else. Then, when you find something you like, you do it over and over. In the earliest versions of Dreamweaver, this process was performed rather blindly, if at all: You had little idea of what steps you were undoing, and automation was not an option.

The History panel tracks every action taken by the user — from deleting text to inserting and resizing a layer. A slider, shown in Figure 3-17, points to the last action performed. Dragging the slider up undoes each step in turn; dragging the slider back down redoes the steps. Selected steps can be quickly repeated in the same document by selecting the Replay button. You can save any selection of steps as a Command for application at any other time, in any other document.

Steps

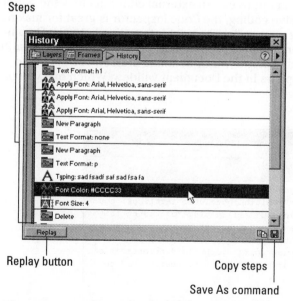

Replay button   Copy steps

Save As command

Figure 3-17: Undo or redo any series of actions by moving the slider in the History panel.

The primary functions of the History panel are covered in the following table:

History Panel Function	Document Window Action
Undo actions	Reverses each action the slider passes over as it is dragged up the History panel.
Redo actions	Reapplies each action the slider passes over as it is dragged down the History panel.
Replay selected steps	Choosing the Replay button repeats selected steps, in sequence.
Save As selected steps as a command	Stores the selected actions under a user-selected name, which is dynamically added to the Command menu.

Code Inspector

The last default window controlled by the Launcher is the Code Inspector (shown in Figure 3-18)—the internal editor designed to complement Dreamweaver's visual layout facility. Although you can opt to use an external editor such as the bundled BBEdit or HomeSite for extensive coding, the Code Inspector is great for making spot edits or quickly checking your code. The tight integration between Dreamweaver's text and visual editors enables simultaneous input and instant updating. The Code Inspector opens in a separate window, unlike the Code or Code and Design view in which code appears in the Document window. Which one you use is a matter of personal preference.

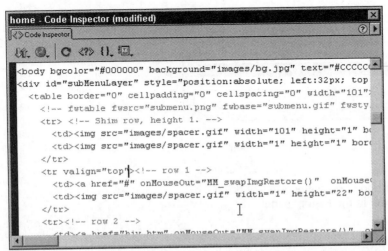

Figure 3-18: The Code Inspector gives you instant access for tweaking your code—or adding entirely new elements by hand.

Tip   You can see the tight integration between the visual editor and the Code Inspector when you have both windows open and you select an object in the Document window. The corresponding code is instantly displayed in the Code Inspector. This feature is useful for quickly finding a specific HTML element for alteration.

Clicking the Code Inspector button on either Launcher opens and closes the Code Inspector, as does choosing Window ➪ Code Inspector or pressing F10. Once the Code Inspector is open, changes made in the Document window are incorporated in real time. However, in order to properly check the code, any changes made in the Code Inspector are not updated in the Document window until the Document window is activated. You can alternate between the two windows by pressing Ctrl+Tab (Option+Tab).

By design, the Code Inspector's layout is simple, to give maximum emphasis to your code. A toolbar along the top of the window replicates the functions found in the Document window's toolbar: File Management, Preview/Debug in Browser, Refresh, Reference, Code Navigation, and View Options.

Tip   You might notice that the code in the Code Inspector is colored. The color coding (no pun intended) is set by the HTML Colors category of the Preferences dialog box—you can even modify the background color of the Inspector.

Customizing Your Workspace with Dockable Panels

Dreamweaver is known for its powerful set of tools: Objects, Behaviors, Layers, Timelines, and so much more. To be truly useful, each tool needs its own panel; but the more tools you use, the more cluttered your workspace can become.

To reduce the amount of screen real estate taken up by the individual windows, but still keep their power, Dreamweaver incorporates dockable panels. All of Dreamweaver's 13 floating panels (including the Code Inspector) can be grouped into a single window—or several windows, if you like. The dockable panel system is completely customizable to give you optimum control over your workflow.

Whenever one panel is docked with another, each becomes accessible by clicking the representative tab. Selecting the tab moves the panel's display to the front of the other docked panels. Grouping panels together is very straightforward. Simply drag one panel by its tab on top of another panel. When you see a border appear inside the stationary panel, release your mouse button. A new tab is created to the right of the existing tab, or tabs. To remove a panel from a docked group, click the tab and drag the panel clear of the others. When you release the mouse button, the panel returns to being an independent floating panel but retains the size and shape of the group it was previously docked with.

Note A couple of restrictions apply when docking panels. First, while you can't dock the Objects panel on another panel, you can combine any other panel in the Objects panel's window. Second, neither the Property Inspector nor the Launcher can be docked.

Dreamweaver displays a symbol for the panel and its name on each tab. When too many panels are combined to fit within the docking window, Dreamweaver shows just the symbols to make room for more tabs. If you add an additional panel to a docking window that is too small, Dreamweaver automatically expands the docking window.

Tip As noted earlier, when you remove a panel from a docked group, the panel retains the size and shape of the group it was docked with. To resize any panel, click and drag its borders. On the Mac, you only resize from the bottom-right corner of a window by dragging the resize handle.

Accessing the Menus

Like many programs, Dreamweaver's menus duplicate most of the features accessible through panels. Certain features, however, are available only through the menus or through a corresponding keyboard shortcut. This section offers a reference guide to the menus when you need a particular feature or command. (Note to Windows users: The menus referred to here are those for the Document window and not the Site window; those menu options particular to the Site window are covered in Chapter 7.)

Tip Almost every element placed in the Document window has a contextual menu associated with it. To access a contextual menu, right-click (Control+click) any area or object. The contextual menus change according to which object or area is selected. Using the contextual menus can enhance your productivity tremendously.

The File menu

The File menu contains commands for file handling and overall site management. Table 3-9 describes the commands and their keyboard shortcuts.

Table 3-9
File Menu Commands

Command	Description	Windows	Macintosh
New	Adds a new Document window	Ctrl+N	Command+N
New from Template	Creates a document based on an existing template	N/A	N/A

Command	Description	Windows	Macintosh
Open	Displays the Open dialog box for opening an existing file	Ctrl+O	Command+O
Open in Frame	Opens an existing file in the selected frame	Ctrl+Shift+O	Command+Shift+O
Close	Closes the current window	Ctrl+W or Ctrl+F4	Command+W
Save	Saves the current document, or displays the Save As dialog box for an unnamed document	Ctrl+S	Command+S
Save As	Displays the Save As dialog box before saving the document	Ctrl+Shift+S	Command+Shift+S
Save As Template	Stores the current document as a template in the Templates folder of the current site	N/A	N/A
Save Frameset	Saves a file describing the current frameset, or displays the Save As dialog box for an unnamed document	N/A	N/A
Save Frameset As	Displays the Save As Frameset before saving the current frameset	N/A	N/A
Save All Frames	Saves all documents in a frameset	N/A	N/A
Revert	Loads the previously saved version of the current page	N/A	N/A
Import ⇨ Import XML into Template	Creates a new document by inserting an XML file into the current template	N/A	N/A
Import ⇨ Import Word HTML	Opens an HTML file saved in Microsoft Word, and optionally, cleans up the code	N/A	N/A
Import ⇨ Import Tabular Data	Inserts a table derived from a file with delimited data	N/A	N/A
Export ⇨ Editable Regions as XML	Saves the current template's editable regions as an XML file	N/A	N/A
Export ⇨ CSS Styles	Creates an external style sheet based on CSS styles in the current document	N/A	N/A

Continued

Table 3-9 *(continued)*			
Command	*Description*	*Windows*	*Macintosh*
Export ⇨ Table	Saves data in the current table as a delimited text file	N/A	N/A
Convert ⇨ 3.0 Browser Compatible	Creates a new Web page, converting all layers to tables	N/A	N/A
Preview in Browser ⇨ Your Browser List	Displays a list of browsers established in Preferences; choose one to preview the current page using that browser	F12 (Primary) Shift+F12 (Secondary)	F12 (Primary) Shift+F12 (Secondary)
Preview in Browser ⇨ Edit Browser List	Displays the Preview in Browser category of Preferences, where the user can add, edit, or delete additional preview browsers	N/A	N/A
Debug in Browser ⇨ Your Browser List	Displays a list of browsers established in Preferences; choose one to debug the current page using JavaScript debugger with that browser	Alt_F12 (Primary) Ctrl+Alt+F12 (Secondary)	Option+F12 (Primary) Command+ Option+F12 (Secondary)
Debug in Browser ⇨ Edit Browser List	Displays the Preview in Browser category of Preferences, where the user can add, edit, or delete additional preview browsers	N/A	N/A
Check Links	Verifies hypertext links for the current document	Shift+F8	Shift+F8
Check Target Browsers	Displays the Check Target Browsers dialog box, where the user can validate the current file against installed browser profiles	N/A	N/A
Design Notes	Displays the Design Notes dialog box for the current document	N/A	N/A
Your Last Opened Files	Displays the last four opened files; select any name to reopen the file	N/A	N/A
Exit (Quit)	Closes all open files and quits	Ctrl+Q or Alt+F4	Command+Q

The Edit menu

The Edit menu gives you the commands necessary to quickly modify your page—or recover from a devastating accident. Many of the commands (Cut, Copy, and Paste) are standard in other programs; others, such as Paste As Text, are unique to Dreamweaver. Table 3-10 lists all of the features found under the Edit menu.

	Table 3-10		
	Edit Menu Commands		
Command	*Description*	*Windows*	*Macintosh*
Undo	Reverses the last action; the number of times you can Undo is determined by a Preferences setting	Ctrl+Z	Command+Z
Redo/Repeat	Repeats the last action	Ctrl+Y	Command+Y
Cut	Places a copy of the current selection on the clipboard, and removes the selection from the current document	Ctrl+X	Command+X
Copy	Places a copy of the current selection on the clipboard, and leaves the selection in the current document.	Ctrl+C	Command+C
Paste	Copies the clipboard to the current cursor position	Ctrl+V	Command+V
Clear	Removes the current selection from the document	Delete or Backspace	Delete
Copy HTML	Copies the current selection onto the clipboard with the HTML codes	Ctrl+Shift+C	Command+Shift+C
Paste HTML	Pastes the current selection from the clipboard as HTML	Ctrl+Shift+V	Command+Shift+V
Select All	Highlights all the elements in the current document or frame	Ctrl+A	Command+A
Select Parent Tag	Chooses the tag surrounding the current selection	Ctrl+Shift+<	Command+Shift+<
Select Child	Chooses the first tag contained within the current selection	Ctrl+Shift+>	Command+Shift+>
Find and Replace	Displays the Find and Replace dialog box for modifying the current document	Ctrl+F	Command+F
Find Next (Find Again)	Repeats the previous Find operation	F3	Command+G

Continued

Table 3-10 *(continued)*			
Command	*Description*	*Windows*	*Macintosh*
Indent Code	Indents selected code (Code view only)	Ctrl+]	Command+]
Outdent Code	Removes indentations for selected code (Code view only)	Ctrl+[	Command+[
Balance Braces	Selects code within the nearest surrounding parentheses or braces (Code view only)	Ctrl+'	Command+'
Set/Remove Breakpoint	Toggles the insertion and removal of a marker that stops the execution of the JavaScript code (Code view only)	Ctrl+Alt+B	Command+ Option+B
Remove All Breakpoints	Eliminates all breakpoints previously set in the code (Code view only)	N/A	N/A
Edit with External Editor (Menu entry specifies external editor when defined)	Opens the External HTML Editor as defined in Preferences ➪ External Editors	Ctrl+E	Command+E
Preferences	Displays the Preferences dialog box	Ctrl+U	Command+U
Keyboard Shortcuts	Opens the Keyboard Shortcuts dialog box to allow customization of the keyboard shortcuts	N/A	N/A

The View menu

As you build your Web pages, you'll find that it's helpful to be able to turn certain features on and off. The View menu centralizes all these commands and switches between the Design and Code views. One of the handiest commands hides all the Visual Aids with a keyboard shortcut, Ctrl+Shift+I (Command+Shift+I). Table 3-11 describes each command under the View menu.

Table 3-11 **View Menu Commands**			
Command	*Description*	*Windows*	*Macintosh*
Code	Displays the code of the current page	N/A	N/A
Design	Displays the browser view of the current page	N/A	N/A

Command	Description	Windows	Macintosh
Code and Design	Splits the view, showing Code and Design views simultaneously; also known as Split view	N/A	N/A
Switch Views	Activates the alternate view in Split view	Ctrl+Tab	Option+Tab
Refresh Design View	Applies changes made in Code view to the Design view	F5	F5
Design View on Top	When selected, shows the Design view above the Code view	N/A	N/A
Head Content	Displays symbols for elements inserted in the `<head>` section of the current document	Ctrl+Shift+W	Command+Shift+W
Table View ⇨ Standard View	Displays the Standard view in the Document window	Ctrl+Shift+F6	Command+Shift+F6
Table View ⇨ Layout View	Engages Layout view for creating layout cells and tables	Ctrl+F6	Ctrl+F6
Table View ⇨ Show Layout Table Tabs	Shows outlines and tabs marking layout cells and tables	N/A	N/A
Visual Aids ⇨ Hide All	Toggles all the visual aids on or off	Ctrl+Shift+I	Command+Shift+I
Visual Aids ⇨ Layer Borders	Toggles the border outlining an unselected layer	N/A	N/A
Visual Aids ⇨ Table Borders	Toggles the border outlining an unselected table	N/A	N/A
Visual Aids ⇨ Frame Borders	Toggles borders in a frameset	N/A	N/A
Visual Aids ⇨ Image Maps	Displays/hides the overlays for defined image maps	N/A	N/A
Visual Aids ⇨ Invisible Elements	Controls whether the symbols for certain HTML tags are shown	N/A	N/A
Code View Options ⇨ Word Wrap	Toggles word wrapping at the window's edge	N/A	N/A
Code View Options ⇨ Line Numbers	Displays a number for every line of code	N/A	N/A
Code View Options ⇨ Highlight Invalid HTML	Shows a yellow highlight for incorrect HTML	N/A	N/A

Continued

Table 3-11 (continued)

Command	Description	Windows	Macintosh
Code View Options ⇨ Syntax Coloring	Toggles code coloring according to function	N/A	N/A
Code View Options ⇨ Auto Indent	Forces the line after a return to indent to the position of the current line	N/A	N/A
Rulers ⇨ Show	Displays the horizontal and vertical rulers	Ctrl+Alt+R	Command+ Option+R
Rulers ⇨ Reset Origin	Resets the rulers' 0,0 coordinates to the upper-left corner of the window	N/A	N/A
Rulers ⇨ Pixels/ Inches/Centimeters	Sets the rulers to a selected measurement system	N/A	N/A
Grid ⇨ Show	Displays a background grid using the current settings	Ctrl+Alt+G	Command+ Option+G
Grid ⇨ Snap To	Forces inserted objects to align with the nearest snap setting	Ctrl+Alt+ Shift+G	Command+ Option+ Shift+G
Grid ⇨ Edit Grid	Displays the Grid Settings dialog box	N/A	N/A
Tracing Image ⇨ Show	Displays the image chosen as the Tracing Image according to the Page Properties settings	N/A	N/A
Tracing Image ⇨ Align with Selection	Aligns the top-left corner of the Tracing Image with the top-left corner of the selected object	N/A	N/A
Tracing Image ⇨ Adjust Position	Enables the Tracing Image to be moved using the cursor keys or numerically	N/A	N/A
Tracing Image ⇨ Reset Position	Resets the position of the Tracing Image to the upper-left corner of the document	N/A	N/A
Tracing Image ⇨ Load	Displays the Open File dialog box for inserting the tracing	N/A	N/A
Plug-ins ⇨ Play	Plays the selected plug-in	Ctrl+Alt+P	Command+ Option+P
Plug-ins ⇨ Stop	Stops the selected plug-in from playing	Ctrl+Alt+X	Command+ Option+X
Plug-ins ⇨ Play All	Plays all plug-ins on the current page.	Ctrl+Alt+ Shift+P	Command+ Option+ Shift+P

Command	Description	Windows	Macintosh
Plug-ins ⇨ Stop All	Stops all plug-ins on the current page from playing	Ctrl+Alt+ Shift+X	Command+ Option+Shift+X
Hide Panels	Closes all open panels	F4	F4
Toolbar	Enables the toolbar to be shown	Ctrl+Shift+T	Command+Shift+T

The Insert menu

The Insert menu contains the same items available through the Objects panel. In fact, if you add additional objects, you can see your objects listed on the Insert menu the next time you start Dreamweaver. All objects are inserted at the current cursor position.

Table 3-12 lists the items available to be inserted in the standard Dreamweaver.

Table 3-12 Insert Menu Commands			
Command	**Description**	**Windows**	**Macintosh**
Image	Opens the Insert Image dialog box that enables you to input or browse for a graphics file	Ctrl+Alt+I	Command+ Option+I
Interactive Images ⇨ Rollover Image	Opens the Rollover dialog box for inserting a Rollover button	N/A	N/A
Interactive Images ⇨ Navigation Bar	Opens the Navigation Bar dialog box for creating a series of Rollover buttons with links	N/A	N/A
Interactive Images ⇨ Flash Button	Inserts an animated button based on a Flash template	N/A	N/A
Interactive Images ⇨ Flash Text	Includes a Flash object for displaying text	N/A	N/A
Interactive Images ⇨ Fireworks HTML	Imports HTML and JavaScript generated by Fireworks	N/A	N/A
Media ⇨ Flash	Opens the Insert Flash Movie dialog box so you can either type in or browse for a movie file	Ctrl+Alt+F	Command+ Option+F

Continued

Table 3-12 *(continued)*

Command	Description	Windows	Macintosh
Media ⇨ Shockwave	Opens the Insert Shockwave dialog box for you to input or browse for a Director file	Ctrl+Alt+D	Command+ Option+D
Media ⇨ Generator	Opens the Insert Generator dialog box to include a Generator template	N/A	N/A
Media ⇨ Applet	Opens the Insert Applet dialog box that permits you to input or browse for a Java class source	N/A	N/A
Media ⇨ Plug-in	Opens the Insert Plug-in dialog box so you can either input or browse for a plug-in.	N/A	N/A
Media ⇨ ActiveX	Inserts an ActiveX placeholder	N/A	N/A
Table	Opens the Insert Table dialog box for establishing a table layout	Ctrl+Alt+T	Command+ Option+T
Layer	Inserts a layer of a preset size	N/A	N/A
Frames ⇨ Left/Right/ Top/Bottom/Left and Top/Left Top/Top Left/Split	Inserts the selected frameset	N/A	N/A
Form	Creates the form structure on your Web page	N/A	N/A
Form Object ⇨ Text Field/Button/Check Box/Radio Button/ List/Menu/File Field/ Image Field/Hidden Field	Inserts the selected form object at the current cursor position	N/A	N/A
Form Object ⇨ Jump Menu	Opens the Jump Menu dialog box for creating a list box with links	N/A	N/A
Server-Side Include	Opens the dialog box for inserting a server-side include	N/A	N/A
E-mail Link	Opens the Insert E-mail Link dialog box to create a mailto: link	N/A	N/A
Date	Opens the Insert Date dialog box for entering the current date	N/A	N/A
Tabular Data	Inserts a table derived from a file with delimited data	N/A	N/A

Command	Description	Windows	Macintosh
Horizontal Rule	Inserts a horizontal line the width of the current window	N/A	N/A
Invisible Tags ⇨ Named Anchor	Displays the Insert Named Anchor dialog box	Ctrl+Alt+A	Command+ Option+A
Invisible Tags ⇨ Script	Displays the Insert Script dialog box	N/A	N/A
Invisible Tags ⇨ Comment	Displays the Insert Comment dialog box	N/A	N/A
Head Tags ⇨ Meta/ Keywords/Description/ Refresh/Base/Link	Displays the appropriate dialog box for inserting the selected HTML tag in the `<head>` section	N/A	N/A
Special Characters ⇨ Line Break	Inserts a line break ` ` tag	Shift+Enter	Shift+Return
Special Characters ⇨ Non-breaking Space	Inserts a hard space	Ctrl+Shift+ spacebar	Command+ Shift+spacebar (or Option+ spacebar)
Special Characters ⇨ Copyright/Registered/ Trademark/Pound/ Yen/Euro/Em-Dash/ Left Quote/ Right Quote	Inserts the HTML code for the selected character entity	N/A	N/A
Special Characters ⇨ Other	Opens the Insert Other Character dialog box to choose a special character	N/A	N/A
Get More Objects	Connects to the Dreamweaver Online Resource Center	N/A	N/A

The Modify menu

Inserting objects is less than half the battle of creating a Web page. Most Web designers spend most of their time adjusting, experimenting with, and tweaking the various elements. The Modify menu lists all the commands for altering existing selections. Table 3-13 lists all the Modify options.

Table 3-13
Modify Menu Commands

Command	Description	Windows	Macintosh
Page Properties	Opens the Page Properties dialog box	Ctrl+J	Command+J
Selection Properties	Displays and hides the Property Inspector	Ctrl+Shift+J	Command+Shift+J
Quick Tag Editor	Displays the Quick Tag Editor for the current selection; repeating the keyboard shortcut toggles between the three Quick Tag Editor modes	Ctrl+T	Command+T
Make Link	Presents the Select HTML File dialog box for picking a linking file	Ctrl+L	Command+L
Remove Link	Deletes the current link	Ctrl+Shift+L	Command+Shift+L
Open Linked Page	Opens the linked page in Dreamweaver	N/A	N/A
Link Target ➪ Default/ _blank/_parent/ _self/_top	Selects the target for the current link	N/A	N/A
Link Target ➪ Set	Enables you to name a target for the link	N/A	N/A
Table ➪ Select Table	Highlights the entire table surrounding the current cursor position	Ctrl+A	Command+A
Table ➪ Merge Cells	Merges selected cells using spans	Ctrl+Alt+M	Command+Option+M
Table ➪ Split Cell	Splits cells into rows or columns	Ctrl+Alt+S	Command+Option+S
Table ➪ Insert Row	Adds a new row above the current row	Ctrl+M	Command+M
Table ➪ Insert Column	Adds a new column before the current column	Ctrl+Shift+A	Command+Shift+A
Table ➪ Insert Rows or Columns	Opens the Insert Rows/Columns dialog box that enables multiple rows or columns to be inserted relative to the cursor position	N/A	N/A
Table ➪ Delete Row	Removes the current row	Ctrl+Shift+M	Command+Shift+M
Table ➪ Delete Column	Removes the current column	Ctrl+Shift + – (minus sign)	Command+Shift+ – (minus sign)

Command	Description	Windows	Macintosh
Table ⇨ Increase Row Span/Decrease Row Span	Increases or decreases by one row the span of the current cell	N/A	N/A
Table ⇨ Increase Column Span/ Decrease Column Span	Increases or decreases the column span of the current cell by one column	Ctrl+Shift+] (Increase Column Span) Command+ Shift+] (Increase Column Span)	Ctrl+Shift+[(Decrease Column Span)\ Command+ Shift+[(Decrease Column Span)
Table ⇨ Clear Cell Heights	Removes specified row height values for the entire selected table	N/A	N/A
Table ⇨ Clear Cell Widths	Removes specified column width values for the entire selected table	N/A	N/A
Table ⇨ Convert Widths to Pixels	Changes column widths from percents to pixels for the entire selected table	N/A	N/A
Table ⇨ Convert Widths to Percent	Changes column widths from pixels to percents for the entire selected table	N/A	N/A
Frameset ⇨ Edit No Frames Content not support frames	Opens a new window for content to be seen by browsers that do	N/A	N/A
Frameset ⇨ Split Frame Left/Split Frame Right/Split Frame Up/Split Frame Down	Moves the current frame in the specified direction, and adds a new frame opposite	N/A	N/A
Navigation Bar	Opens the Navigation Bar dialog box for editing the selected Navigation Bar	N/A	N/A
Arrange ⇨ Bring to Front	Places selected layers or hotspots in front of all other layers or hotspots	N/A	N/A
Arrange ⇨ Send to Back	Places selected layers or hotspots behind all other layers or hotspots	N/A	N/A
Arrange ⇨ Prevent Layer Overlaps	Stops newly created layers from overlapping	N/A	N/A
Align ⇨ Left	Aligns grouped layers or hotspots on the left edge	Ctrl+Shift+1	Command+ Shift+1

Continued

Table 3-13 *(continued)*

Command	Description	Windows	Macintosh
Align ⇨ Right	Aligns grouped layers or hotspots on the right edge	Ctrl+Shift+3	Command+Shift+3
Align ⇨ Top	Aligns grouped layers or hotspots on the top edge	Ctrl+Shift+4	Command+Shift+4
Align ⇨ Bottom	Aligns grouped layers or hotspots on the bottom edge	Ctrl+Shift+6	Command+Shift+6
Align ⇨ Make Same Width	Changes the width of grouped layers or hotspots to that of the last selected layer	Ctrl+Shift+7	Command+Shift+7
Align ⇨ Make Same Height	Changes the height of grouped layers or hotspots to that of the last selected layer.	Ctrl+Shift+9	Command+Shift+9
Convert ⇨ Tables to Layers	Places all content on the page in layers	N/A	N/A
Convert ⇨ Layers to Tables	Places all content in layers in tables	N/A	N/A
Library ⇨ Add Object to Library	Opens the Library category, and adds the selected object	Ctrl+Shift+B	Command+Shift+B
Library ⇨ Update Current Page/Update Pages	Replaces any modified Library items in the current page or current site	N/A	N/A
Templates ⇨ Apply Template to Page	Enables the selection of a template to be overlaid on the current page	N/A	N/A
Templates ⇨ Detach from Template	Breaks the link between the template and the current page	N/A	N/A
Templates ⇨ Open Attached Template	Opens the current template for editing	N/A	N/A
Templates ⇨ Update Current Page	Automatically updates the page with template changes	N/A	N/A
Templates ⇨ Update Pages	Enables the updating of an entire site or of all pages using a particular template	N/A	N/A
Templates ⇨ New Editable Region	Inserts the placeholder for a new editable region	Ctrl+Alt+V	Command+Option+V

Command	Description	Windows	Macintosh
Templates ⇨ Remove Editable Region	Converts the selected region from editable to locked	N/A	N/A
Templates ⇨ No Editable Regions	Displayed in menu until editable regions are created and is then replaced by editable region names	N/A	N/A
Timeline ⇨ Add Object to Timeline	Opens the Timelines panel, and inserts the current image or layer	Ctrl+Alt+ Shift+T	Command+ Option+Shift+T
Timeline ⇨ Add Behavior to Timeline	Opens the Timelines panel, and inserts an onFrame event using the current frame	N/A	N/A
Timeline ⇨ Record Path of Layer	Plots the path of a dragged layer onto a timeline	N/A	N/A
Timeline ⇨ Add Keyframe	Inserts a keyframe at the current Playback Head position	F6	F6
Timeline ⇨ Remove Keyframe	Deletes the currently selected keyframe	Shift+F6	Shift+F6
Timeline ⇨ Change Object	Applies a timeline path to another object	N/A	N/A
Timeline ⇨ Remove Object/Remove Behavior	Deletes the currently selected object or behavior	N/A	N/A
Timeline ⇨ Add Frame/ Remove Frame	Inserts or deletes a frame at the current Playback Head position	N/A	N/A
Timeline ⇨ Add Timeline/Remove Timeline/Rename Timeline	Inserts an additional timeline, deletes the current timeline, or renames the current timeline	N/A	N/A
Translate ⇨ Date	Updates the date and time code inserted by the Date object	N/A	N/A

The Text menu

The Internet was initially an all-text medium, and despite all the multimedia development, the World Wide Web hasn't traveled far from these beginnings. The Text menu, as described in Table 3-14, covers overall formatting as well as text-oriented functions such as spell-checking.

Table 3-14
Text Menu Commands

Command	Description	Windows	Macintosh
Indent	Marks the selected text or the current paragraph with the `<blockquote>` tag to indent it	Ctrl+Alt+]	Command+ Option+]
Outdent	Removes a `<dir>` or `<blockquote>` surrounding the selected text or current indented paragraph	Ctrl+Alt+[	Command+ Option+[
Paragraph Format ⇨ None	Removes all HTML formatting tags surrounding the current selection	Ctrl+0 (zero)	Command+0 (zero)
Paragraph Format ⇨ Paragraph	Converts the selected text to paragraph format	Ctrl+Shift+P	Command+ Shift+P
Paragraph Format ⇨ Heading 1–6	Changes the selected text to the specified heading format	Ctrl+1–6	Command+ 1–6
Paragraph Format ⇨ Preformatted Text	Formats the selected text with a monospaced font	N/A	N/A
Align ⇨ Left	Aligns the selected text to the left of the page, table, or layer	Ctrl+Alt+ Shift+L	Command+ Option+ Shift+L
Align ⇨ Center	Aligns the selected text to the center of the current page, table, or layer	Ctrl+Alt+ Shift+C	Command+ Option+ Shift+C
Align ⇨ Right	Aligns the selected text to the right of the page, table, or layer	Ctrl+Alt+ Shift+R	Command+ Option+ Shift+R
List ⇨ None	Changes a list item into a paragraph	N/A	N/A
List ⇨ Unordered List	Makes the selected text into a bulleted list	N/A	N/A
List ⇨ Ordered List	Makes the selected text into a numbered list	N/A	N/A
List ⇨ Definition List	Converts the selected text into alternating definition terms and items	N/A	N/A
List ⇨ Properties	Opens the List Properties dialog box	N/A	N/A
Font ⇨ Default	Changes the current selection to the default font	N/A	N/A
Font ⇨ Your Font List	Displays fonts in your current font list	N/A	N/A

Command	Description	Windows	Macintosh
Font ⇨ Edit Font List	Opens the Font List dialog box for adding or deleting fonts from the current list	N/A	N/A
Style ⇨ Bold	Makes the selected text bold	Ctrl+B	Command+B
Style ⇨ Italic	Makes the selected text italic	Ctrl+I	Command+I
Style ⇨ Underline	Underlines the selected text	N/A	N/A
Style ⇨ Strikethrough	Surrounds the selected text with the `<s>...</s>` tags for text with a line through it	N/A	N/A
Style ⇨ Teletype	Surrounds the selected text with the `<tt>...</tt>` tags for a monospaced font	N/A	N/A
Style ⇨ Emphasis	Surrounds the selected text with the `<emp>...</emp>` tags for slightly emphasized, usually italic, text	N/A	N/A
Style ⇨ Strong	Surrounds the selected text with the `<strong>...</strong>` tags for more emphasized, usually bold, text	N/A	N/A
Style ⇨ Code	Surrounds the selected text with HTML code for depicting programming code	N/A	N/A
Style ⇨ Variable	Surrounds the selected text with HTML code for depicting a variable in programming, typically in italic	N/A	N/A
Style ⇨ Sample/ Keyboard	Surrounds the selected text with HTML code for depicting monospaced fonts	N/A	N/A
Style ⇨ Citation	Surrounds the selected text with HTML code for depicting cited text, usually in italic	N/A	N/A
Style ⇨ Definition	Surrounds the selected text with HTML code for depicting a definition, usually in italic	N/A	N/A
HTML Styles ⇨ Clear Selection Style	Removes text formatting tags around the current selection	N/A	N/A
HTML Styles ⇨ Clear Paragraph Style	Removes text formatting tags for the paragraph containing the current selection	N/A	N/A

Continued

Table 3-14 *(continued)*

Command	Description	Windows	Macintosh
HTML Styles ⇨ New Style	Displays the HTML Styles dialog box to create a new text style	N/A	N/A
CSS Styles ⇨ None/ Your Style List	Applies a user-defined style to selected text. The None option removes previously applied styles	N/A	N/A
CSS Styles ⇨ New Style	Displays the New Style dialog box for creating a new CSS style	N/A	N/A
CSS Styles ⇨ Edit Style Sheet	Opens the Edit Style Sheet dialog box for adding, deleting, or modifying custom styles	Ctrl+Shift +E	Command+ Shift+E
CSS Styles ⇨ Attach Style Sheet	Displays the Select File dialog box and links the selected CSS file to the current document	N/A	N/A
CSS Styles ⇨ Export CSS Styles	Copies in-document defined CSS styles to an external style sheet	N/A	N/A
Size ⇨ Default ⇨ 1–7	Converts the selected text to the chosen font size	N/A	N/A
Size Change ⇨ +1 through +7	Increases the size of the selected text relative to the defined basefont size (default is 3)	N/A	N/A
Size Change ⇨ +1 through +4 / –1 through –3	Changes the size of the selected text relative to the defined basefont size (default is 3)	N/A	N/A
Color	Opens the operating system's Color dialog box to alter the color of selected or following text	N/A	N/A
Check Spelling	Opens the Spell Check dialog box	Shift+F7	Shift+F7

The Commands menu

Commands are user-definable code capable of affecting almost any tag, attribute, or item on the current page — or even the current site. Commands increase your productivity by automating many of the mundane, repetitive tasks in Web page creation.

Dreamweaver comes with several handy commands, but they are truly just the tip of the iceberg. Commands are written in a combination of HTML and JavaScript and can be created and modified by any capable JavaScript programmer.

Table 3-15 describes the standard Dreamweaver commands.

Table 3-15
Commands Menu

Command	Description	Windows	Macintosh
Start/Stop Recording	Begins remembering the sequence of user commands; toggles with Stop Recording	Ctrl+Shift +X	Command+ Shift+X
Play Recorded Command	Executes the last recorded command	Ctrl+P	Command+P
Edit Command List	Opens the Edit Command List dialog box for arranging and deleting custom items from the Commands menu.	N/A	N/A
Get More Commands	Connects to the Dreamweaver Online Resource Center	N/A	N/A
Manage Extensions	Opens the Extension Manager for installing and removing extensions	N/A	N/A
Apply Source Formatting	Structures the current page according to the Source Format Profile	N/A	N/A
Clean Up HTML	Processes the current page according to various options to remove extraneous HTML	N/A	N/A
Clean Up Word HTML	Processes the current page according to various options to remove extraneous HTML inserted by Microsoft Word	N/A	N/A
Add/Remove Netscape Resize Fix	Inserts or deletes code to compensate for the bug affecting layers in Netscape 4+ browsers	N/A	N/A
Optimize Image in Fireworks	Displays the Optimize Image dialog box for processing images. Requires Fireworks 4	N/A	N/A
Create Web Photo Album	Uses Fireworks to make a thumbnail catalog of a folder of images. Requires Fireworks 4	N/A	N/A
Set Color Scheme	Selects a color scheme for the current page, affecting background color, text color, and the link colors	N/A	N/A
Format Table	Enables a predesigned format to be set on the current table	N/A	N/A

Continued

Table 3-15 *(continued)*			
Command	**Description**	**Windows**	**Macintosh**
Sort Table	Sorts the current table alphabetically or numerically	N/A	N/A
Your Commands	Automatically lists new commands added to the Commands folder	N/A	N/A

The Site menu

Web designers spend a good portion of their day directly interacting with a Web server: putting up new files, getting old ones, and generally maintaining the site. To ease the workflow, Dreamweaver includes the most commonly used commands in the Document window menu as well as the Site window menu.

The Site menus are very different on the Windows and Macintosh platforms. Because of these differences, the commands are listed in two different tables. All the commands found in the Windows Site menu are described in Table 3-16.

Table 3-16 Site Menu Commands (Windows)		
Command	**Description**	**Windows**
Sites Files	Displays the Site window	F8
Site Map	Displays the current site map	Alt+F8
New Site	Presents the Site Definition dialog box for creating a new site	N/A
Open Site ⇨ Your Site List	Displays a user-definable list of sites; when one is selected, the Site window opens pointing to the selected site	N/A
Define Sites	Displays the Site Information dialog box for setting up a new site, or for modifying or deleting an existing site	N/A

Command	Description	Windows
Get	Transfers the selected files from the remote site to the local folder	Ctrl+Shift+D
Check Out	Marks selected files on the remote site as checked out	Ctrl+Alt+Shift+D
Put	Transfers the selected files from the local folder to the remote site	Ctrl+Shift+U
Check In	Marks selected files as checked in	Ctrl+Alt+Shift+U
Undo Check Out	Removes the Check Out designation on selected files	N/A
Reports	Opens the Reports dialog box for running the currently available interactive reports	N/A
Check Links Sitewide ⇨ Selected	Verifies hypertext links for the current or selected documents	Ctrl+F8
Locate in Local Site	Selects the current document in the Site Files list Local pane	N/A
Locate in Remote Site	Selects the current document in the Site Files list Remote pane	N/A

The Macintosh Site menu is set up somewhat differently from the Windows version, although the functionality is the same. Table 3-17 details the Site menu for Macintosh systems.

Table 3-17
Site Menu Commands (Macintosh)

Command	Description	Macintosh
New Site	Presents the Site Definition dialog box for creating a new site	N/A
Open Site ⇨ Your Site List	Displays a user-definable list of sites; when one is selected, the Site Window opens pointing to the selected site	N/A
Define Sites	Displays the Site Information dialog box for setting up a new site, or for modifying or deleting an existing site	N/A

Continued

Table 3-17 *(continued)*

Command	Description	Macintosh
Connect	Connects to the current site online	N/A
Refresh	Refreshes the selected pane in the Site window	F5
Site Files View ➪ New File	Creates a new HTML file in the current site	Command+Shift+N
Site Files View ➪ New Folder	Creates a new folder in the current site	Command+Shift+Option+N
Site Files View ➪ Refresh Local	Rereads and displays the current local folder	Shift+F5
Site Files View ➪ Refresh Remote	Rereads and displays the current remote folder	Option+F5
Site Files View ➪ Select Checked Out Files	Highlights files that have been Checked Out	N/A
Site Files View ➪ Select Newer Local	Highlights files that have been modified locally but not transferred to the remote site	N/A
Site Files View ➪ Select Newer Remote	Highlights files that have been modified remotely but not transferred to the local site	N/A
Site Files View ➪ File View Columns	Opens Preferences to the File View Columns category	N/A
Site Map View ➪ View as Root	Makes the selected file the starting point for the map	Command+Shift+R
Site Map View ➪ Link to New File	Creates a new file and adds a link to the selected page	Command+Shift+N
Site Map View ➪ Link to Existing File	Adds a text link to an existing file to the selected page	Command+Shift+K
Site Map View ➪ Change Link	Selects a new page to use as a link instead of the selected file and updates the link	Command+L
Site Map View ➪ Remove Link	Deletes the selected link	Command+Shift+L
Site Map View ➪ Show/Hide Link	Marks a file and all its dependent files as hidden or displayable	Command+Shift+Y

Command	*Description*	*Macintosh*
Site Map View ⇨ Open Source of Link	Opens the HTML file containing the selected link in Dreamweaver	N/A
Site Map View ⇨ New Home Page	Makes the selected file the starting point for the Site Map	N/A
Site Map View ⇨ Set as Home Page	Presents a Select File dialog box to choose a file that becomes the new starting point for the Site Map	N/A
Site Map View ⇨ Save Site Map ⇨ Save Site Map as PICT | JPEG	Stores the current site map as a graphic file in the chosen format	N/A
Site Map View ⇨ Show Files Marked as Hidden	Displays all hidden files with the filename in italics	N/A
Site Map View ⇨ Show Dependent Files	Shows all the graphic and other additional files associated with the HTML pages	N/A
Site Map View ⇨ Show Page Titles	Displays icons identified by page titles instead of by filenames	Command+Shift+T
Site Map View ⇨ Layout	Opens the Layout dialog box that determines the structure of the Site Map	N/A
Site Map View ⇨ Refresh Local	Redraws the Site Map	Shift+F5
Get	Transfers the selected files from the remote site to the local folder	Command+Shift+D
Check Out	Marks selected files on the remote site as checked out	Command+Option+Shift+D
Put	Transfers the selected files from the local folder to the remote site	Command+Shift+U
Check In	Marks selected files as checked in	Command+Option+Shift+U
Undo Check Out	Removes the Check Out designation on selected files	N/A
Open	Loads a selected file into Dreamweaver	Command+Option+Shift+O
Rename	Renames the selected file	N/A
Unlock	Makes selected read-only files accessible	N/A
Locate in Local Site	Selects the current document in the Site Files list Local pane	N/A

Continued

	Table 3-17 *(continued)*	
Command	**Description**	**Macintosh**
Locate in Remote Site	Selects the current document in the Site Files list Remote pane	N/A
Reports	Opens the Reports dialog box for running the currently available interactive reports	N/A
Check Links Sitewide	Verifies hypertext links for the current or selected documents	Command+F8
Change Link Sitewide	Opens a dialog box to specify a link to change	N/A
Synchronize	Transfers files between the local and remote sites so that the latest version of all selected files are on both sites	N/A
Recreate Site Cache	Rebuilds the Site Cache to enable quicker updates	N/A
FTP Log	Opens the FTP Log window	N/A
Tool Tips	Enables long filenames or page titles to be displayed when passed over by the pointer	N/A

The Window menu

The Window menu manages both program and user-opened windows. Through this menu, described in Table 3-18, you can open, close, arrange, bring to the front, or hide all of the additional Dreamweaver screens.

Table 3-18 Window Menu Commands			
Command	**Description**	**Windows**	**Macintosh**
Objects	Opens the Objects panel	Ctrl+F2	Command+F2
Properties	Shows the Property Inspector for the currently selected item	Ctrl+F3	Command+F3
Launcher	Opens the Launcher panel	N/A	N/A
Sites Files	Displays the Site window	F8	F8
Site Map	Displays the current site map	Alt+F8	Alt+F8

Command	Description	Windows	Macintosh
Assets	Shows the various resources for the current site	F11	F11
Behaviors	Shows the Behaviors panel	Shift+F3	Shift+F3
Code Inspector	Displays the Code Inspector	F10	F10
CSS Styles	Opens the CSS Styles panel	Shift+F11	Shift+F11
Frames	Opens the Frames panel	Shift+F2	Shift+F2
History	Displays the History panel	Shift+F10	Shift+F10
HTML Styles	Opens the HTML Styles panel	Ctrl+F11	Command+F11
Layers	Opens the Layers panel	F2	F2
Library	Opens the Assets panel with the Library category selected	N/A	N/A
Reference	Displays the Reference panel	Ctrl+Shift +F1	Command+ Shift+F1
Templates	Opens the Assets panel with the Templates category selected	N/A	N/A
Timelines	Shows the Timelines panel	Shift+F9	Shift+F9
Arrange Panels	Moves all open panels to their preset positions	N/A	N/A
Show/Hide Panels	Displays/hides all open panels	F4	F4
Minimize All (Windows only)	Reduces all open windows to their smallest size	Shift+F4	N/A
Restore All (Windows only)	Expands all windows to their previous size	Alt+Shift+F4	N/A
Your Open Windows	Displays a list of the currently open document windows	N/A	N/A

Tip All the commands for Dreamweaver's various panels and inspectors are toggles. Select a command once to open the window; select again to close it.

The Help menu

The final menu, the Help menu, offers access to Dreamweaver's excellent online help, as well as special examples and lessons. Table 3-19 explains each of these useful options.

Table 3-19
Help Menu Commands

Command	Description	Windows	Macintosh
Welcome	Opens the Welcome screen	N/A	N/A
Using Dreamweaver	Opens the Dreamweaver online help system in your primary browser	F1	F1
Reference	Opens the Reference panel to the selected code, if any	Shift+F1	Shift+F1
What's New	Displays the What's New section of the Welcome screen	N/A	N/A
Guided Tour	Displays the Guided Tour section of the Welcome screen	N/A	N/A
Lessons	Displays the available Lessons	N/A	N/A
Dreamweaver Exchange	Connects to the Dreamweaver Online Resource Center	N/A	N/A
Manage Extensions	Opens the Extensions Manager	N/A	N/A
Dreamweaver Support Center	Connects to Macromedia's Dreamweaver Support Center	N/A	N/A
Macromedia Online Forums	Connects to Macromedia's Online Forums page	N/A	N/A
Extending Dreamweaver	Opens the Extending Dreamweaver online documentation in your primary browser	N/A	N/A
Creating and Submitting Extensions	Opens the help pages for using the Extension Manager to package extensions	N/A	N/A
Register Dreamweaver	Goes online to register your copy of Dreamweaver	N/A	N/A
About Dreamweaver	Displays the opening splash screen with credits and registration and version information	N/A	N/A

Summary

In this chapter, you've observed Dreamweaver's power and had a look at its well-designed layout. From the Objects panel to the various tools controlled through the Launcher, Dreamweaver offers you an elegant, flexible workspace for creating next-generation Web sites. This chapter covered the following important points:

✦ The Document window is your main canvas for visually designing your Dreamweaver Web pages. This workspace includes simple, powerful tools such as the Tag Selector and the status bar Launcher.

✦ The Objects panel is Dreamweaver's toolbox. Completely customizable, the Objects panel holds the elements you need most often, in seven initial categories: Characters, Common, Forms, Frames, Head, Invisibles, and Special. The Objects panel also switches between Standard view and Layout view.

✦ Dreamweaver's mechanism for assigning details and attributes to an HTML object is the Property Inspector. The Property Inspector is context-sensitive, and its options vary according to the object selected.

✦ The Launcher is the control center for Dreamweaver's specialized functions: the Site window, the Assets panel, the HTML Styles panel, the CSS Styles panel, the Behaviors panel, the History panel, and the Code Inspector. You have two Launchers to choose from: one free-floating panel and the one accessible through the status bar.

✦ Dreamweaver 4 introduces two new panels: the Assets and Reference panels.

✦ Dreamweaver's full-featured menus offer complete file manipulation, a wide range of insertable objects, the tools to modify them, and extensive online — and on-the-Web — help. Many menu items can be invoked through keyboard shortcuts.

In the next chapter, you learn how to customize Dreamweaver to work the way you work by establishing your own preferences for the program and its interface.

✦　　✦　　✦

Setting Your Preferences

Everyone works differently. Whether you need to conform to a corporate style sheet handed down from the powers that be or you think "it just looks better that way," Dreamweaver offers you the flexibility to shape your Web page tools and your code output. This chapter describes the options available in Dreamweaver's Preferences and then details how you can tell Dreamweaver to format your source code your way.

Customizing Your Environment

The vast majority of Dreamweaver's settings are controlled through the Preferences dialog box. You can open Preferences by choosing Edit ➪ Preferences or by using the keyboard shortcut Ctrl+U (Command+U). Within Preferences, you find 16 different categories listed on the left side of the screen. As you switch from one category to another by selecting its name from this Category list, the options available for that category appear in the main area of the dialog box. Although this chapter covers all the options available in each category, the categories are grouped by function, rather than examined in the same order as they appear in the Category list.

Most changes to Preferences take effect immediately after you close the window by clicking OK or the Close button. The following two preferences only are not updated instantly:

✦ The Show Only Site Window on Startup option goes into effect on the next running of Dreamweaver.

✦ If you elect to modify the Source Format, as described in the section "Understanding the Source Format," later in this chapter, you should complete this modification outside of Dreamweaver (in a text editor), save your work, and then start the program.

General Preferences

Dreamweaver's General Preferences, as shown in Figure 4-1, cover program appearance, user operation, and fundamental file settings. The appearance of the program's interface may seem to be a trivial matter, but Dreamweaver is a program for designers — to whom appearance is extremely important. These user-operation options are based purely on how you, the user, work best.

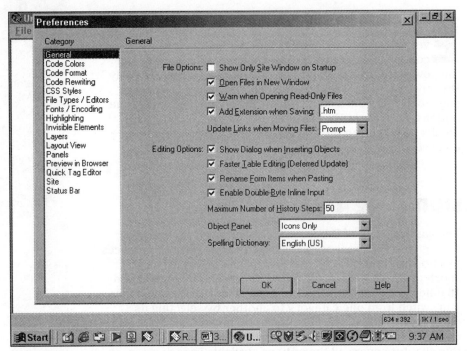

Figure 4-1: Dreamweaver's General Preferences enable you to change your program's appearance and certain overall operations.

File options

The first area of the General category, File Options, determines how you work with HTML and other files.

In choosing all the preferences, including the General ones, you can work in two ways. If you are a seasoned Web designer, you probably want Dreamweaver to work with your established manner to minimize your learning curve. If you're just starting out as a Web page creator, work with the default options for a while and then go back to try other options. You'll want to know right away the styles that work for you.

Show Only Site Window on Startup

Some Web designers prefer to use the Site window as their "base of operations," rather than the Document window. For them, it's easier to construct and maintain their Web pages from the sitewide perspective offered through the Site window. Dreamweaver offers you the option to begin a Web authoring session with the Site window only.

Selecting the Show Only Site Window on Startup option displays the Site window the next time you open Dreamweaver. The Site window is shown in the configuration used the last time you opened it — with or without the Site Map enabled and with the various columns positioned in the same manner. To bring up the Document window, choose File ➪ New Window from the Site window menu.

Open Files in New Window (Windows only)

Select the Open Files in New Window option when you need to have several Web pages open simultaneously. Alternatively, if you want to free up some of your system resources (such as memory) and you need only one Dreamweaver window, you can deselect this option.

If this option is not selected and changes are made to the current file, Dreamweaver asks if you'd like to save the current page when you attempt to load a new file.

Warn when Opening Read-Only Files

Read-only files are locked to prevent accidental overwriting. As an option, Dreamweaver warns you when such a file is opened. The warning is actually more than an alert, however. Dreamweaver provides an option on the warning dialog box to make the file writable. Alternatively, you can just view the file.

Although Dreamweaver enables you to edit the file either way, if the document is still read-only when you save your changes, the Save As dialog box appears, prompting you to store the file under a new name.

Add Extension when Saving

HTML files originally were identified — cleverly enough — by their .html filename extension. When Microsoft jumped on the Internet bandwagon, it reduced the extension to three letters, .htm, to fit its pre-Windows 95 format. But now many different Web file formats and extensions have exploded onto the Internet — .asp, .shtml, .stm, and .phtml, to name just a few. In early versions of Dreamweaver (prior to 2), the .htm extension was not only the default, but a difficult one to change at best. Today, Dreamweaver includes the capability to save your files using any filename extension you specify.

The Add Extension when Saving option is straightforward. Just enter the extension of your choosing in the text box and make sure the option is selected. For example, if you are building nothing but Active Server Pages for a particular Web site, you would change the Add Extension when Saving text box to .asp and select OK in the Preferences dialog box. Now, to save a file, you have to enter only the initial part of the filename, and the appropriate extension is automatically appended.

Update Links when Moving Files

As your site grows in complexity, you'll find that keeping track of the various links is an increasingly difficult task. Dreamweaver has several enhanced features to help you manage links, and the Update Links when Moving Files option is one of them. Dreamweaver can check each link on a page when a file is moved — whether it is the Web page you're working on or one of the support files, such as an image, that goes on the page. The Update Links when Moving Files option determines how Dreamweaver reacts when it notes an altered link.

By default, the Update Links when Moving Files option is set to Prompt, which causes Dreamweaver to alert you to any link changes and requires you to "OK" the code alterations by selecting the Update button. To leave the files as they are, you choose the Don't Update button. You can elect to have Dreamweaver automatically keep your pages up to date by selecting the Always option from the Update Links when Moving Files drop-down list. Finally, you can select the Never option, and Dreamweaver ignores the link changes necessary when you move, rename, or delete a file.

As a general rule, I keep my Update Links when Moving Files option set to Always. It is a very rare circumstance when I intentionally want to maintain a bad link on my Web page. Likewise, I recommend using the Never option with extreme caution.

Editing options

The second main section of the General Preferences screen consists of numerous checkbox options you can turn on or off. Overall, these options fall into the user-interaction category or "What's good for you?" Take the Show Dialog when Inserting Objects option, for example. Some Web creators prefer to enter all their attributes at one time through the Property Inspector and would rather not have the dialog boxes appear for every inserted object. Others want to get their file sources in immediately and modify the rest later. Your selection depends on how you want to work.

The following sections describe the listed options.

Show Dialog when Inserting Objects

By default, almost all the objects that Dreamweaver inserts — via either the Objects panel or the Insert menu — open an initial dialog box to gather needed information. In most cases, the dialog box enables you to input a URL or browse for a source file. Turning off the Show Dialog option causes Dreamweaver to insert a default-sized object, or a placeholder, for the object. You must then enter all attributes through the Property Inspector.

Faster Table Editing (Deferred Update)

When you enter text into a table, the current column width automatically expands while the other columns shrink correspondingly. If you're working with large tables, this updating process can slow your editing. Dreamweaver gives you the choice between faster input or instantaneous feedback.

When the Faster Table Editing preference is turned on, Dreamweaver updates the entire table only when you click outside the table, or if you press Ctrl+spacebar (Command+spacebar). If you prefer to see the table form as you type, turn this option off.

Tip

Two other ways to update tables: Select any tag in the Tag Selector (a useful approach when working with a very large table), or resize the Document window.

Rename Form Items when Pasting

Designing forms can be highly repetitive — and somewhat tedious — work. Moreover, if you do not name each form element uniquely, your efforts will be for thwarted; most form actions require each field to be individually identified. The Rename Form Items when Pasting option is intended to eliminate some of the tedium as well as some of the risks from form design.

New Feature

When the Rename Form Items when Pasting option is selected, as it is by default, any copied form element, such as a text field or checkbox, is automatically renamed, each time it is pasted. This facility allows you to copy a single checkbox once and paste it as many times as necessary. Each time the checkbox is pasted, an incrementing number is added. For example, if I copy a checkbox named beersCB, the first checkbox I pasted is named beersCB2 and the next, beersCB3, and so on. If this option were disabled, each checkbox would be named beersCB, causing problems during processing.

Enable Double-Byte Inline Input

Some computer representations of languages, primarily Asian languages, require more raw descriptive power than others. The ideogram for "snow," for example, is far more complex than a four-letter word. These languages need twice the number of bytes per character and are known as *double-byte languages*. In versions of Dreamweaver before 2, all double-byte characters had to go through a separate text input window instead of directly into the Document window.

Dreamweaver now simplifies the page creation process for double-byte languages with the Enable Double-Byte Inline Input option. Once selected, this option enables double-byte characters to be entered directly into the Document window. To use the old method of inserting such characters, deselect this option.

Maximum Number of History Steps

Before Dreamweaver 3, the number of undo steps was limited by a system's memory — but there was no visual indication of what those steps were. The History panel now shows exactly what actions have been taken. A limit exists, however, to the number of steps that can be tracked. By default, the limit is set to 50.

Although 50 history steps are more than enough for most systems, you can alter this number by changing the Maximum Number of History Steps value. When the maximum number of history steps is exceeded, the oldest actions are wiped from memory and unrecoverable. The history steps are not discarded when a file is saved, unlike the previous undo steps.

Objects panel

Learning a new software program can be tough — simply memorizing which icon means what can increase your learning curve. With Dreamweaver, you don't have to try to remember all of the Object symbols right off the bat. If you like, you can opt to have the name of an Object next to its icon — or even just the name itself. You make this choice in the Objects panel option.

By default, the Objects panel is composed only of icons. When you pass your mouse over each one, a ToolTip appears that names the object. However, if you don't want to hunt for your object, you can select Icons and Text (or Text Only) from the Objects panel option. Whichever option you select, when you exit from Preferences, the Objects panel changes size and shape to accommodate the new format, as shown in Figure 4-2.

Figure 4-2: The Objects panel can display each object's name along with its icon.

Spelling Dictionary

The Spelling Dictionary option enables you to select a spell-checking dictionary from any one of those installed. In addition to the standard English-language version, which has three options — English (US), English (UK-ise), and English (UK-ize) — additional versions of dictionaries exist online. As of this writing, dictionaries in the following languages are also available: German, Spanish, Swedish, French, Italian, Brazilian-Portuguese, and Catalan. You can download these dictionaries from Macromedia's Dreamweaver Object Exchange at www.macromedia.com/support/dreamweaver/dictionary.html. Once downloaded, save the .dat file in the Configuration\Dictionaries folder and restart Dreamweaver.

To select a different dictionary for spell-checking, select the Spelling Dictionary option button and choose an item from the drop-down list. Dreamweaver also maintains a Personal dictionary (although it's not visible on the list) to include those words you wish Dreamweaver to learn during the spell-checking process.

Preferences for invisible elements

By their nature, all HTML markup tags remain unseen to one degree or another when presented for viewing through the browser. You may want to see certain elements while designing a page, however. For example, adjusting line spacing is a common task, and turning on the visibility of the line break tag <BR> can help you understand the layout.

Dreamweaver enables you to control the visibility of 11 different codes — or rather their symbols, as shown in Figure 4-3. When, for example, a named anchor is inserted, Dreamweaver shows you a small gold shield with an anchor emblem. Not only does this shield indicate the anchor's position, but you can also manipulate the code with cut-and-paste or drag-and-drop techniques. Moreover, double-clicking a symbol opens the pertinent Property Inspector and enables quick changes to the tag's attributes.

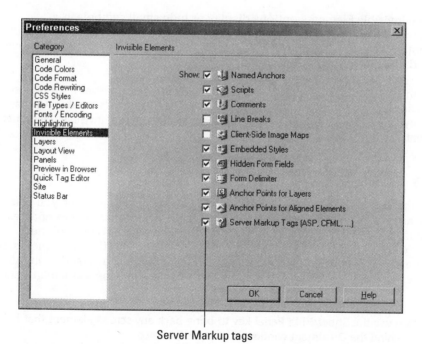

Server Markup tags

Figure 4-3: You can show or hide any or all of the 11 invisible elements listed in the Preferences dialog box.

Tip You can temporarily hide all invisible elements by deselecting View ➪ Visual Aids ➪ Invisible Elements.

The 11 items controlled through the Invisible Elements category are as follows:

✦ Named anchors

✦ Scripts

✦ Comments

✦ Line Breaks

✦ Client-Side Image Maps

✦ Embedded Styles

✦ Hidden Form Fields

✦ Form Delimiter

✦ Anchor Points for Layers

✦ Anchor Points for Aligned Elements

✦ Server markup tags (ASP, CFML, . . .)

Most of the Invisible Elements options display or hide small symbols in Dreamweaver's visual Document window. Several options, however, show an outline or another type of highlight. Turning off Form Delimiter, for example, removes the dashed line that surrounds a form in the Document window.

Tip You may have noticed that the Cold Fusion tags and Active Server Page tags are combined into one symbol, Server markup tags. Dreamweaver's capability to handle dynamic pages generated by databases makes these invisible elements essential.

Panels preferences

Although the various panels and inspectors are convenient, sometimes you just want a clear view of your document. The Panels category of Preferences enables you to choose which of Dreamweaver's accessory screens stay on top of the Document window. As shown in Figure 4-4, you can adjust 14 different elements. By default, they are all set to float above the Document window. The last option, All Other Panels, is used to control the behavior of any custom panels you might end up using.

Tip You can use the Show/Hide Panel key to bring back any screen element that has gone behind the Document window. Just press F4 twice.

Add

Delete

All Other Floaters

Up

Down

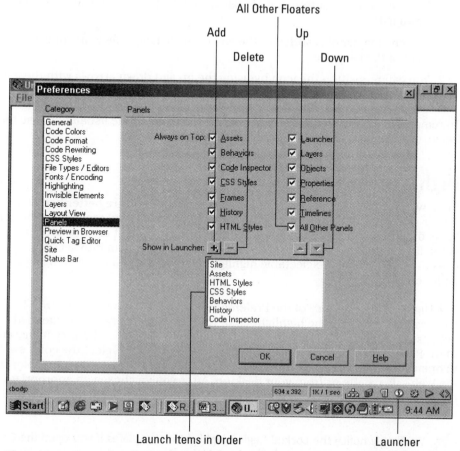

Figure 4-4: If you deselect any of the floating panels, they move behind the Document window.

Launch Items in Order

Launcher

If you prefer to use the Code Inspector rather than the Code view, you might consider taking it off the "always on top" list. Then, after you've made your HTML code edits, click in the Document window. This sequence updates the visual document, incorporating any changes, and simultaneously pushes the Code Inspector behind the Document window. You can switch between the two views of your Web page by using the Ctrl+Tab (Option+Tab) key combination.

The Launcher (both the floating panel and the status bar versions) displays a series of icons for quickly opening and closing various Dreamweaver panels. The Launcher is completely customizable — you can add or remove icons for any of the available panels. Moreover, the order of their appearance is up to you as well.

To add a new icon to the Launcher, follow these steps:

1. Click the Add (+) button and choose an available floating panel from the drop-down list.

   The chosen panel is added to the end of the list, and the icon appears on the right of the Launcher.

2. You can reposition the icon by using the up and down arrows with the panel's name selected.

To remove an icon from the Launcher, select the panel in the list and choose the Delete (-) button.

Highlighting preferences

Dreamweaver is extremely extensible — custom functions are better handled, server-side markup is more acceptable, and more third-party tags are supported. Many of these features depend on "hidden" capabilities that are not noticeable in the final HTML page, but the Web designer must take them into account. Dreamweaver uses user-selectable highlighting to mark areas on a Web page under construction.

The Highlighting category of the Preferences dialog box, shown in Figure 4-5, enables you to choose the highlight color for four different types of extended objects: Editable and Locked Regions, both used in templates; Library Items; and Third-Party Tags. In each case, to choose a highlight color, select the color swatch to open Dreamweaver's color picker. Then use the Eyedropper to pick a color from the Web-safe palette or from your desktop. After you've chosen an appropriate color, make sure to select the related Show checkbox so that the highlighting is displayed.

Note   You'll only notice the Locked Region highlight in Templates if you open the Code view; the Display view only highlights Editable Regions.

Quick Tag Editor preferences

The Quick Tag Editor is designed to bridge the gap between the visual layout and the underlying code. With the Quick Tag Editor, you can quickly edit a tag or wrap the selection in a whole new tag, without opening the Code Inspector. The Quick Tag Editor pops open a small draggable window when invoked, and its preferences, shown in Figure 4-6, control the appearance and behavior of that window.

The Quick Tag Editor has three modes: Edit Tag, Insert HTML, and Wrap Tag. The first option, Apply Changes Immediately While Editing, affects only the Edit Tag mode. When this option is disabled, the Enter (Return) key must be pressed to confirm the edits. In the other two modes, you always must confirm your additions with the Enter (Return) key.

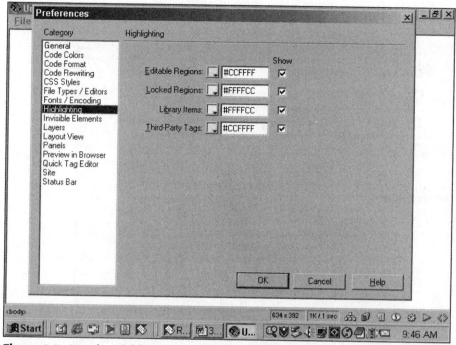

Figure 4-5: Use the Highlighting preferences to control how template regions, library items, and third-party tags appear in the Document window.

The second option, Enable Tag Hint Dropdown, works in all three modes. A short time after the Quick Tag Editor is invoked, a list of possible tags appears. To reduce your typing, when the first letter of the tag is typed, the list scrolls to the tags starting with that letter. For example, if you want to wrap a `<blockquote>` tag around a paragraph, typing a *b* brings the list to the `<b>` (bold) tag; type the next letter, *l*, and the list scrolls to `<blockquote>`—at this point, all you have to do is press Enter (Return) to confirm your choice. The Tag Hint list does not appear at all if Enable Tag Hint Dropdown is unchecked. You can also control the speed at which the Tag Hint list appears by moving the Delay slider; the range is from .5 seconds to 5 seconds.

Tip   If you like using the Tag Hint list, set the Delay slider to .5 second; with that setting, the list pops up almost immediately and speeds your work.

Status bar preferences

The status bar is a handy collection of four different tool sets: the Tag Selector, the Window Size pop-up menu, the Connection Speed Indicator, and the Mini-Launcher. The Status Bar category of the Preferences dialog box, shown in Figure 4-7, controls options for all of these tools except the Tag Selector.

Control the speed of Tag Hints

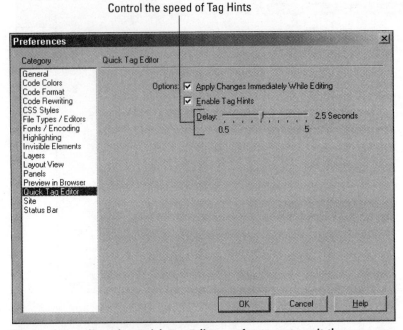

Figure 4-6: Adjust the Quick Tag Editor preferences to suit the way you like to add code to a page.

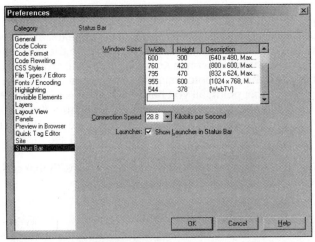

Figure 4-7: Use the Status Bar category to evaluate your real-world download times.

Window Sizes

The Window Sizes list at the top of the Status Bar category shows the current options for the Window Sizes pop-up menu. This list is completely user editable and enables you to add new window sizes, modify existing dimensions, add descriptions, or delete little-used measurements.

As discussed in Chapter 3, the Window Sizes pop-up is a feature in Dreamweaver that enables you to instantly change your screen size so that you may view and build your page under different monitor conditions. To change any of the current dimensions, simply click the measurement you wish to alter and enter a new value. You can also change any description of the existing widths and heights by clicking in the Description column and entering your text. While you can enter as much text as you like, it's not practical to enter more than about 15 to 20 characters.

To enter a new set of dimensions in the Window Sizes list box, follow these steps:

1. From the Status Bar category of the Preferences dialog box, locate the last entry in the current list.

   If the last entry is not immediately available, use the vertical scroll bar to move to the end.

2. Click once in the Width column on the line below the last entry.

3. Enter the desired width of the new window size in pixels.

4. Press Tab to move to the Height column.

5. Enter the desired height for the new window size. Press Tab again.

6. Optionally, you can enter short descriptive text in the Description column. Press Tab when you're finished.

7. To continue adding new sizes, repeat Steps 2 through 6. Click OK when you finish.

Caution You don't have to enter the word *pixels* or the abbreviation *px* after your values in the Width and Height columns of the Window Sizes list box, but you can. If you enter any dimensions under 20, Dreamweaver converts the measurement to its smallest possible window size, 20 pixels.

Connection Speed

Dreamweaver understands that not all access speeds are created equal, so the Connection Speed option enables you to check the download time for your page (or the individual images) at a variety of rates. The Connection Speed setting evaluates the download statistics in the status bar. You can choose from seven preset connection speeds, all in kilobits per second: 14.4, 28.8, 33.6, 56, 64, 128, and 1,500. The lower speeds (14.4 through 33.6) represent older dial-up modem connection rates — if you are building a page for the mass market, you should consider selecting one of these slower rates. Although 56K modems are widespread on the market today, the true 56K connection is a rare occurrence. Use the 128 setting if your audience connects through an ISDN line. If everyone views your page through a direct LAN connection, change the connection speed to 1,500.

You are not limited to these preset settings. You can type any desired speed directly into the Connection Speed text box. You could, for example, specify a connection speed more often experienced in the real world, such as 23.3. If you find yourself designing for an audience using DSL or cable modems, you could change the Connection Speed to 150 or higher.

Show Launcher in Status Bar

The default setting enables the status bar Launcher. When this option is disabled, you always have to access the Launcher by choosing Window ➪ Launcher from the menus.

File Types/Editors preferences

Refinement is often the name of the game in Web design, and giving you quick access to your favorite modification tools — whether you're modifying code, graphics, or other media — is one of Dreamweaver's key features. The File Types/Editors category, shown in Figure 4-8, is where you specify the program you want Dreamweaver to call for any file type you define.

Open in Code View

It's no longer just an HTML world — many other code types may be found on a Web designer's palette. Dreamweaver's internal code is full-featured enough to handle a wide variety of code and, with the Open in Code View option, you can determine which types you'd like it to handle. By default, JavaScript (.js), text (.txt) and Active Server Application (.asa) files are automatically opened in Code view. Dreamweaver attempts to open any other selected file type in the Design view.

If you find yourself hand-editing other file types, such as XML files, you can add their extension to the Open in Code View field. Separate extensions with a space and ensure that you begin each one with a period.

 Note   Although Macintosh systems do not require extensions, you still use them in the Open in Code View feature.

External Code Editor preferences

Dreamweaver recognizes the importance of your choice of a text editor. Although Dreamweaver ships with two extremely robust code editors — as well as its excellent built-in code editor — you can opt to use any other program. To select your editor, enter the path in the External Code Editor text box or select the Browse button to choose the appropriate executable file.

Add   Add

Delete   Delete

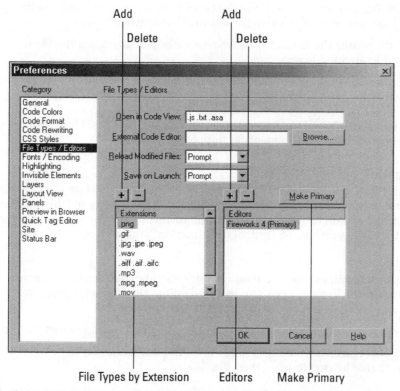

File Types by Extension   Editors   Make Primary

Figure 4-8: Assign your favorite HTML, graphics editors, and more through the newly extended File Types/Editors category of the Preferences dialog box.

The two included editors, BBEdit for Macintosh and HomeSite for Windows, are integrated with Dreamweaver to varying degrees. Both of the editors can be called from within Dreamweaver, and both have "Dreamweaver" buttons for returning to the main program — switching between the editor and Dreamweaver automatically updates the page. Like Dreamweaver's internal HTML editor, BBEdit highlights the corresponding code to a selection made in Dreamweaver; this property does not, however, extend to HomeSite.

You specify and control your external editor selection with the following options.

Enable BBEdit Integration (Macintosh only)

Dreamweaver for Macintosh ships with this option activated. If you prefer to use another editor or an older version of BBEdit that lacks the integration capabilities, deselect this option.

Reload Modified Files

The drop-down list for this setting offers three options for working with an external editor:

✦ **Prompt:** Detects when files are updated by another program and enables you to decide whether to update them within Dreamweaver.

✦ **Always:** Updates the file in Dreamweaver automatically when the file is changed in an outside program.

✦ **Never:** Assumes that you want to make all updates from within Dreamweaver yourself.

Personally, I prefer to have Dreamweaver always update my files. I find it saves a couple of mouse clicks — not to mention time.

Save on Launch

Any external HTML editor — even the integrated HomeSite or BBEdit — opens and reads a previously saved file. Therefore, if you make any changes in Dreamweaver's visual editor and switch to your editor without saving, the editor shows only the most recently saved version. To control this function, you have the following three options:

✦ **Prompt:** Determines that unsaved changes have been made and asks you to save the file. If you do not, the external editor reverts to the last saved version.

✦ **Always:** Saves the file automatically before opening it in the external editor.

✦ **Never:** Disregards any changes made after the last save, and the external editor opens the previously saved file.

Here again, as with Reload Modified Files, I prefer to always save my files when switching back and forth. Keep in mind, however, that saving a file clears Dreamweaver's undo memory and the changes cannot be undone.

Tip   If you try to open a file that has never been saved in an external editor, Dreamweaver prompts you to save it regardless of your preference settings. If you opt not to save the file, the external editor is not opened because it has no saved file to display.

File Types Editor preferences

Dreamweaver has the capability to call an editor for any specified type of file at the touch of a button. For example, when you import a graphic, you often need to modify its color, size, shape, transparency, or another feature to make it work correctly on the Web page. Rather than force you to start your graphics program independently, load the image, make the changes, and resave the image, Dreamweaver enables you to send any selected image directly to your editor. After you've made your modifications and saved the file, the altered image appears automatically in Dreamweaver.

The capability to associate different file types with external editors applies to more than just images in Dreamweaver. You can link one or more editors to any type of media — images, audio, video, even specific kinds of code. The defined external editor is invoked when the file is double-clicked in the Site window. Because the editors are assigned according to file extension as opposed to media type, one editor could be assigned to GIF files and another to JPEGs. The selection is completely customizable.

Note   If you have the same file type defined to Open in Code View and set up in the editor list, the file defaults to opening in Code view.

When a file is double-clicked in the Site window, that file type's primary editor runs. Dreamweaver offers the capability to define multiple editors for any file extension. You might, for instance, prefer to open certain JPEGs in Fireworks and others in Photoshop. To choose an alternative editor, right-click (Control+click) the filename in the Site window and select the desired program from the Open With menu option. The Open With option also enables you to browse for a program.

To assign an editor to an existing file type, follow these steps:

1. Select the file type from the Extensions list.

2. Click the Add (+) button above the Editors list.

   The Add External Editor dialog box opens.

3. Locate the application file of the editor and click Open when you're ready.

   You can also select a shortcut or alias to the application.

4. If you want to select the editor as the primary editor, click Make Primary while the editor is highlighted.

To add a new file type, click the Add button above the Extensions list and enter the file extension — including the period — in the field displayed at the bottom of the list. For multiple file extensions, separate each extension with a space, such as this:

```
.doc .dot .rtf
```

Tip   Looking for a good almost-all-purpose editor? The QuickTime Pro Player makes a great addition to Dreamweaver as the editor for AIFF, AU, WAV, MP3, AVI, MOV, and animated GIF files and others. The Pro Player is wonderful for quick edits and optimization especially with sound files. It's available from the Apple Web site (www.apple.com/quicktime) for both platforms for around $30.

Finally, to remove an editor or a file extension, select it and click the Delete (-) button above the corresponding list. Note that removing a file extension also removes the associated editor.

Cross-Reference Be sure that your graphics program is adept at handling the three graphic formats used on the Web: GIFs, JPEGs, and PNG images. Macromedia makes Fireworks, a graphics editor designed for the Web that integrates nicely with Dreamweaver. In fact, it integrates so nicely, this book includes an entire chapter on it, Chapter 16.

Adjusting Advanced Features

Evolution of the Web and its language, HTML, never ends. New features emerge often from leading browser developers. A competing developer can introduce a similar feature that works in a slightly different way. The HTML standards organization — the World Wide Web Consortium, also known as the W3C — can then endorse one approach or introduce an entirely new method of reaching a similar goal. Eventually, one method usually wins the approval of the marketplace and becomes the accepted coding technique.

To permit the widest range of features, Dreamweaver enables you to designate how your code is written to accommodate the latest Web features: layers and style sheets. The default preferences for these elements offer the highest degree of cross-browser and backward compatibility. If your Web pages are intended for a more specific audience, such as a Netscape-only intranet, Dreamweaver enables you to take advantage of a more specific feature set. Furthermore, Dreamweaver also gives you control over its new Layout view, enabling you to set global options as well as some site-by-site.

Layout View preferences

In Layout view — new in Dreamweaver 4 — a column in a table may be set to automatically match the size of the browser window; if the window is resized, the column is stretched or shrunk accordingly. To maintain the structure of such tables and other complex layout devices, professional designers often include an added row on the top or bottom of the table. This additional row is sized to be one pixel high with the same number of cells as the table itself. Within each cell (except for the resizeable cell) is a transparent GIF image, sized to match the cell's dimensions. This image is sometimes called a *spacer.* One of the major functions of the Layout View category of Preferences is to manage these spacers.

Dreamweaver automatically includes spacers if a column is set to Autostretch and the Autoinsert Spacers When Making Autostretch Tables is selected, as it is by default (see Figure 4-9). If you decide not to include spacers, select Never. Which should you choose? I find that spacers definitely help and, unless you have a compelling reason not to use them — such as a corporate edict — I'd advise you to go with the default option. Because a spacer is an actual graphic image, albeit a small one, you must include such a file in every site. Dreamweaver will create one for you if you like or you can select an existing one. The option for creating or locating a spacer is offered when an autostretch table is designated. However, if you'd prefer not to worry about spacers each time you create an autostretch table, you can pre-select an existing image to use through the Layout View category of Preferences. This option is set on a sitewide basis.

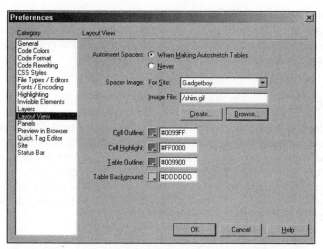

Figure 4-9: Spacer images are used to maintain a table's complex layout; you can set which spacer is used on a site-by-site basis through the Layout View category of Preferences.

To set a spacer image for a site, follow these steps:

1. In the Layout View category of Preferences, choose the site to be affected from the Spacer Image For Site drop-down list.

2. If you do not have a transparent, single pixel GIF image available, select Create.

   Dreamweaver opens the Save Spacer Image File As dialog box.

3. Select a location within your site to store the spacer file.

   If you like, you can also rename the file from spacer.gif to something else.

4. If a graphic on your site is using a transparent, single pixel GIF image, select Browse to locate the graphic.

The remaining options found under the Layout View category are concerned with the various colors used as follows:

✦ **Cell Outline** is the color of the layout cell when it is selected; the default is dark blue.

✦ **Cell Highlight** is the color used to designate an unselected layout cell when the designer's mouse rolls over it, red by default.

✦ **Table Outline** is the color of the outline surrounding the entire table; the outline is initially set to dark green.

✦ **Table Background** is the color of the layout table where no layout cell has been drawn; a light gray is the default background.

Should your site design make any of the colors unusable — if, for example, your page background was the same light gray as the default table background — you can alter the colors by selecting the color swatch and choosing a new color from the standard color picker.

Layers preferences

Aside from helping you control the underlying coding method for producing layers, Dreamweaver enables you to define the default layer. This capability is especially useful during a major production effort in which the Web development team must produce hundreds of layers spread over a Web site. Being able to specify in advance the initial size, color, background, and visibility saves numerous steps — each of which would have to be repeated for every layer. Figure 4-10 shows the layout of the Layers category of the Preferences dialog box.

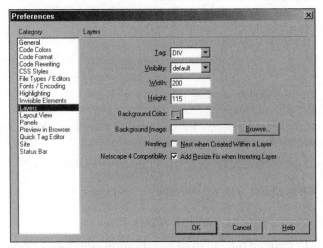

Figure 4-10: In the Layers category, you can predetermine the structure of the default Dreamweaver layer.

The controls accessible through the Layers category include the following:

Tag

Select the arrow button to see the tags for the four HTML code methods for implementing layers: ⟨div⟩, ⟨span⟩, ⟨layer⟩, and ⟨ilayer⟩. The first two, ⟨div⟩ and ⟨span⟩, were developed by the W3C as part of their Cascading Style Sheets recommendation and are supported by version 4.0 (and above) of both Netscape and Internet Explorer. Netscape developed the latter two HTML commands, ⟨layer⟩ and ⟨ilayer⟩; currently only Netscape 4.x supports these tags.

Dreamweaver uses the ⟨div⟩ tag for its default. Supported by both major 4.0 and above browsers, the ⟨div⟩ element offers the widest cross-browser compatibility. You should use only one of the other Tag options if you are building a Web site intended for a specific browser.

Cross-Reference

To learn more about the uses of the various positioning tags, see Chapter 19.

Visibility

Layers can be either visible or hidden when the Web page is first loaded. A layer created using the default visibility option is always displayed initially; however, no specific information is written into the code. Selecting Visible forces Dreamweaver to include a visibility:visible line in your layer code. Likewise, if you select Hidden from the Visibility options, the layer is initially hidden.

Use the Inherit option when creating nested layers. Creating one layer inside another makes the outer layer the parent, and the inner layer the child. If the parent layer is visible and the child layer is set to visibility:inherit, then the child is also visible. This option makes it possible to affect the visibility of many layers with one command — hide the parent layer, and all the inheriting child layers disappear as well.

Width and Height

When you choose Draw Layer from the Objects panel, you drag out the size and shape of your layer. Choosing Insert ⇨ Layer puts a layer of a default size and shape at your current cursor position. The Width and Height options enable you to set these defaults. Select the text boxes and type your new values. Dreamweaver's default is a layer 200 pixels wide by 115 pixels high.

Background Color

Layers can have their own background color independent of the Web page's overall background color (which is set as a ⟨body⟩ attribute). You can define the default background color of any inserted layer through either the Insert menu or the Objects panel. For this preference setting, type a color, either by its standard name or as a hexadecimal triplet, directly into the text box. You can also click the color swatch to display the Dreamweaver browser-safe color picker.

Caution

Note that while you can specify a different background color for the layer, you can't alter the layer's default text and link colors (except on a layer-by-layer basis) as you can with a page. If your page and layer background colors are highly contrasting, be sure your text and links are readable in both environments. A similar caveat applies to the use of a layer's background image, as explained in the next section.

Background Image

Just as you can pick a specific background color for layers, you can select a different background image for layers. You can type a file source directly into the

Background Image text box or select your file from a dialog box by choosing the Browse button. The layer's background image supersedes the layer background color, just as it does with the HTML page. Also, just as the page's background image tiles to fill the page, so does the layer's background image.

Nesting

The two best options about layers seem to be directly opposed: overlapping and nesting layers. You can design layers to appear one on top of another, and you can code layers so that they are within one another. Both techniques are valuable options, and Dreamweaver enables you to decide which one should be the overriding method.

If you are working primarily with nested layers and plan on using the inheritance facility, check the Nest when Created Within a Layer option. If your design entails a number of overlapping but independent layers, make sure this option is turned off. Regardless of your preference, you can reverse it on an individual basis by pressing the Ctrl (Command) key when drawing out your layers.

Netscape 4.x Compatibility

Netscape 4.x has a particularly annoying problem displaying Web pages with layers. When the user resizes the browser, all of the CSS positioning information is lost — in other words, all your layers lose their exact positioning and typically align themselves on the left. The only fix is to force Netscape to reload the page after the browser has been resized.

When the Netscape 4 Compatibility option is enabled, Dreamweaver automatically includes a small JavaScript routine to handle the resizing problem. The code is inserted in the `<head>` section of the page when the first layer is added to the page. If additional layers are added, Dreamweaver is smart enough to realize that the workaround code has already been included and does not add more unnecessary code.

Many Web designers run into this problem as they begin to explore the possibilities of Dynamic HTML. Although the problem has been fixed with the release of Netscape 6, I highly recommend that you enable this option to offset any problems with the large number of Netscape 4.x browsers still in use.

CSS Styles preferences

The CSS Styles category (see Figure 4-11) is entirely devoted to how your code is written. As specified by the W3C, Cascading Style Sheets (CSS) declarations — the specifications of a style — can be written in several ways. One method displays a series of items, separated by semicolons:

```
H1 { font-family: helvetica; font-size: 12pt; line-height: 14pt; ¬
font-weight: bold;}
```

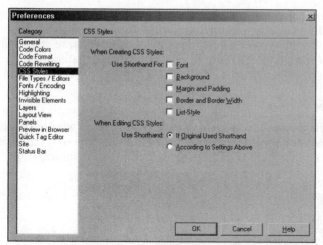

Figure 4-11: The CSS Styles category enables you to code the style sheet sections of your Web pages in a graphics designer–friendly manner.

Certain properties (such as font) have their own grouping shorthand, developed to be more readable to designers coming from a traditional print background. A second, "shorthand" method of rendering the preceding declaration follows:

```
H1 { font: helvetica 12pt/14pt bold }
```

With the CSS Styles category, you can enable the shorthand method for any or all of the five different properties that permit it. Select any of the checkboxes under Use Shorthand For to have Dreamweaver write your style code in this fashion.

The second option in the CSS Styles category determines how Dreamweaver edits styles in previously coded pages. If you want to retain the format of the original page, click Use Shorthand If Original Used Shorthand. If you want Dreamweaver to write new code in the manner that you specify, select Use Shorthand According to Settings Above.

Caution

Although the leading varieties of the 4.0 and above browsers can read the style's shorthand with no difficulty, Internet Explorer 3.0 does not have this capability. IE3 is the only other mainstream browser that can claim support for Cascading Style Sheets, but it doesn't understand the shorthand form. If you want to maintain browser backward-compatibility, don't enable any of the shorthand options.

Making Online Connections

Dreamweaver's visual layout editor offers an approximation of your Web page's appearance in the real world of browsers — offline or online. After you've created the initial draft of your Web page, you should preview it through one or more browsers. And when your project nears completion, you should transfer the files to a server for online, real-time viewing and further testing through a File Transfer Protocol program (FTP). Dreamweaver gives you control over all these stages of Web page development, through the Site and Preview in Browser categories.

Site preferences

As your Web site takes shape, you'll spend more time with the Site window portion of Dreamweaver. The Site category, shown in Figure 4-12, enables you to customize the look and feel of your site, as well as enter essential connection information.

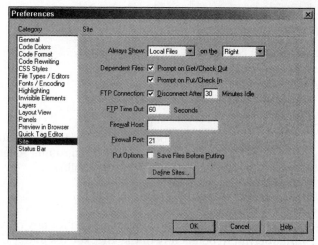

Figure 4-12: Options for Dreamweaver's Site window are handled through the Site category.

The available Site preferences are described in the following sections.

Always Show Local/Remote Files on the Right/Left

The Site window is divided into two panes: one showing local files and one showing remote files on the server. By default, Dreamweaver puts the Local pane on the right and the Remote pane on the left. However, Dreamweaver enables you to customize that option. Like many designers, I'm used to using other FTP programs in which the Remote files are on the right and the Local files on the left; Dreamweaver enables me to work the way I'm used to working.

To switch the layout of your Site window, select the file location you want to change to (Local Files or Remote Files) from the Always Show drop-down list or select the pane you want to change to (Right or Left) from the "on the" drop-down list. Be careful not to switch both options, or you end up where you started!

Dependent files

Web pages are seldom just single HTML files. Any graphic — whether it's in the background, part of your main logo, or used on a navigational button — is uploaded as a separate file. The same is true for any additional multimedia add-ons such as audio or video files. If you've enabled File Check In/Check Out when defining your site, Dreamweaver can also track these so-called dependent files.

Enabling the Prompt checkboxes causes Dreamweaver to ask you if you'd like to move the dependent files when you transfer an HTML file. You can opt to show the dialog box for Get/Check Out, Put/Check In, or both.

Tip   You're not stuck with your Dependent Files choice. If you turn off the Dependent Files prompt, you can make it appear by pressing the Alt (Option) key while clicking the Get or Put button.

FTP Connection: Disconnect After __ Minutes Idle

You can easily forget you're online when you are busy modifying a page. You can set Dreamweaver to automatically disconnect you from an FTP site after a specified interval. The default is 30 minutes; if you want to set a different interval, you can select the FTP Connection value in the Disconnect After text box. Dreamweaver then asks if you want to continue to wait or to disconnect when the time limit is reached, but you can maintain your FTP connection regardless by deselecting this option.

FTP Time Out

Client-server communication is prone to glitches. Rather than hanging up your machine while trying to reach a server that is down or slow, Dreamweaver alerts you to an apparent problem after a set period. You can determine the number of seconds you want Dreamweaver to wait by altering the FTP Time Out value. The default is 60 seconds.

Firewall information

Dreamweaver enables users to access remote FTP servers outside their network firewall. A firewall is a security component that protects the internal network from unauthorized outsiders, while enabling Internet access. To enable firewall access, enter the Firewall Host and External Port numbers in the appropriate text boxes; if you do not know these values, contact your network administrator.

Caution   If you're having trouble transferring files through the firewall via FTP, make sure the Use Firewall (in Preferences) option is enabled in the Site Definition dialog box. You can find the option in the Remote Info category.

Put options

Certain site operations, such as putting a file on the remote site, are now available in the Document window. It's not uncommon to make an edit to your page and then quickly choose the Site ➪ Put command — without saving the file first. In this situation, Dreamweaver prompts you with a dialog box to save your changes. However, you can avoid the dialog box and automatically save the file by choosing the Save Files Before Putting option.

Preview in Browser preferences

Browser testing is an essential stage of Web page development. Previewing your Web page within the environment of a particular browser gives you a more exact representation of how it looks when viewed online. Because each browser renders the HTML slightly differently, you should preview your work in several browsers. Dreamweaver enables you to select both a primary and secondary browser, which can both be called by pressing a function key. You can name up to 18 additional browsers through the Preview in Browser category shown in Figure 4-13. This list of preferences is also called when you choose File ➪ Preview in Browser ➪ Edit Browser List.

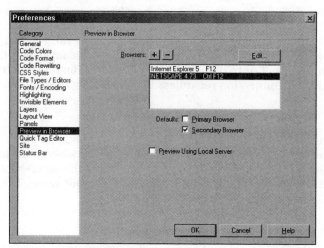

Figure 4-13: The Preview in Browser category lists browsers currently available for preview and enables you modify the list.

If you are developing on Windows, your Web page is using site root relative paths for links, and you have a local server setup, enable the Preview Using Local Server option. This capability ensures that your previews link correctly. The other method to preview sites using site root relative paths places the files on a remote server.

To add a browser to your preview list, follow these steps:

1. Choose Edit ➪ Preferences or press the keyboard shortcut: Ctrl+U (Command+U).

2. Select the Preview in Browser category.

3. Select the Add (+) button.

4. Enter the path to the browser file in the Path text box or click the Browse button to pick the file from the Select Browser dialog box.

5. After you have selected your browser application, Dreamweaver fills in the Name field. You can alter this name if you wish.

6. If you want to designate this browser as your Primary or Secondary browser, select one of those checkboxes in the Defaults section.

7. Click OK when you have finished.

8. You can continue to add browsers (up to a total of 20) by following Steps 3 through 7. Click OK when you have finished.

Once you've added a browser to your list, you can modify your selection by following these steps:

1. Open the Preview in Browser category and highlight the browser you want to alter.

2. Select the Edit button to get the Edit Browser dialog box.

3. After you've made your modifications, click OK to close the dialog box.

Tip

You can quickly make a browser your Primary or Secondary previewing choice without going through the Edit screen. From the Preview in Browser category, select the desired browser and check either Primary Browser or Secondary Browser. Note that if you already have a primary or secondary browser defined, this action overrides your previous choice.

You can also easily remove a browser from your preview list:

1. Open the Preview in Browser category and choose the browser you want to delete from the list.

2. Select the Remove (–) button and click OK.

Customizing Your Code

For all its multimedia flash and visual interactivity, the Web is based on code. The more you code, the more particular about your code you are likely to become. Achieving a consistent look and feel to your code enhances its readability and, thus, your productivity. In Dreamweaver, you can even design the HTML code that underlies a Web page's structure.

Every time you open a new document, the default Web page already has several key elements in place, such as the language the page is to be rendered in. Dreamweaver also enables you to customize your work environment by selecting default fonts and even the colors of your HTML code.

Fonts/Encoding preferences

In the Fonts / Encoding category, shown in Figure 4-14, you can control the basic language of the fonts as seen by a user's browser and the fonts that you see when programming. The Default Encoding section enables you to choose Western-style fonts for Web pages to be rendered in English, one of the Asian languages — Japanese, Traditional Chinese, Simplified Chinese, or Korean — or another language, such as Cyrillic, Greek, or Icelandic Mac.

Dreamweaver 4 has extended the number of encoding options to 10, as well as adding a generic Other category. Many of the encodings have platform-specific configurations, such as Icelandic Mac. Be sure to examine all the choices before you make a selection.

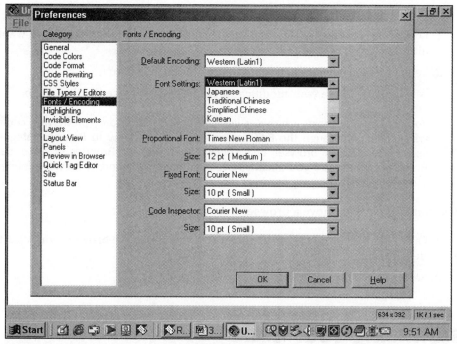

Figure 4-14: Use the Fonts / Encoding category to set both the font encoding for each Web page and the fonts you use when programming.

In the bottom portion of the Fonts / Encoding category, you can alter the default font and size for three different fonts:

✦ **Proportional Font:** This font option sets the default font used in Dreamweaver's Document window to depict paragraphs, headings, and lists.

✦ **Fixed Font:** In a fixed font, every character is allocated the same width. Dreamweaver uses your chosen fixed font to depict preformatted styled text.

✦ **Code Inspector:** The Code Inspector font is used by Dreamweaver's built-in text editor. You should probably use a monospaced font such as Courier or Monaco. A monospaced font makes it easy to count characters, which is often necessary when debugging your code.

Select any one of the three font options by clicking the list and highlighting your choice of font. Change the font size by selecting the value in the Size text box or by typing in a new number.

Don't be misled into thinking that by changing your Proportional Font preference to Arial or another font, all your Web pages are automatically viewed in that type-face. Changing these font preferences affects only the default fonts that you see when developing the Web page; the default font that the user sees is controlled by the user's browser. To ensure that a different font is used, you have to specify it for any selected text through the Text Property Inspector or by choosing Text ➪ Font ➪ Edit Font List from the menus.

Code Rewriting preferences

The exception to Dreamweaver's policy of not altering imported code occurs when HTML or other code is incorrectly structured. Dreamweaver automatically fixes tags that are nested in the wrong order or have additional, unnecessary closing tags — unless you tell Dreamweaver otherwise by setting up the Code Rewriting preferences accordingly (see Figure 4-15).

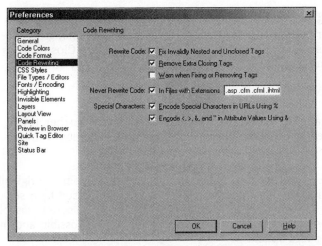

Figure 4-15: The Code Rewriting category can be used to protect nonstandard HTML from being automatically changed by Dreamweaver.

Dreamweaver accommodates many different types of markup languages, not just HTML, through the Never Rewrite Code in Files with Extensions option. Moreover, you can prevent Dreamweaver from encoding special characters, such as spaces, tildes, and ampersands, in URLs or attribute values.

Following are descriptions of the particular controls of the Code Rewriting preferences.

Fix Invalidly Nested and Unclosed Tags

When enabled, this option repairs incorrectly placed tags. For example, if a file contained the following line:

```
<h3><b>Welcome to the Monkey House!</h3></b>
```

Dreamweaver rewrites it as follows:

```
<h3><b>Welcome to the Monkey House!</b></h3>
```

Open that same file while the Fix option is turned off, and Dreamweaver highlights the misplaced code in the Document window. Double-clicking the code brings up a window with a brief explanation.

Caution If a browser encounters nonstandard HTML, the code is probably ignored. Dreamweaver does not follow this protocol, however. Unless Dreamweaver is familiar with the type of code you are using, your code could be altered when the page is opened. If you are using specially formatted database tags or other nonstandard HTML programming, be sure to open a test page first.

Remove Extra Closing Tags

When you're editing your code by hand, it's fairly easy to miss a closing tag. Dreamweaver cleans up such code if you enable the Remove Extra Closing Tags option. You may, for example, have the following line in a previously edited file:

```
<p>And now back to our show...</p></i>
```

Notice that the closing italic tag, </i>, has no matching opening partner. If you open this file in Dreamweaver with the Remove option enabled, Dreamweaver plucks out the offending </i>.

Tip In some circumstances, you want to make sure your pages remain as originally formatted. If you edit pages in Dreamweaver that are preprocessed by a server unknown to Dreamweaver prior to the display of the pages, make sure to disable both the Fix Invalidly Nested and Unclosed Tags option where possible and the Remove Extra Closing Tags option.

Warn When Fixing or Removing Tags

If you're editing a lot of Web pages created on another system, you should enable the Warn when Fixing or Removing Tags option. If this setting is turned on, Dreamweaver displays a list of changes that have been made to your code in the HTML Corrections dialog box. As you can see from Figure 4-16, the changes can be quite extensive when Dreamweaver opens what it regards as a poorly formatted page.

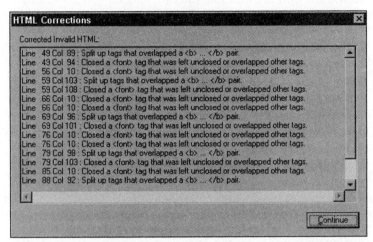

Figure 4-16: Dreamweaver can automatically catch and repair certain HTML errors. You can set Dreamweaver to send a report to the screen in the HTML Corrections dialog box.

Caution Remember that once you've enabled these Rewrite Code options, the fixes occur automatically. If this sequence happens to you by mistake, immediately close the file (without saving it!), disable the Code Rewriting preference options, and reopen the document.

Never Rewrite Code preferences

Many of the database connectivity programs, such as Cold Fusion or Lasso, use proprietary tags embedded in a regular Web page to communicate with their servers. Dreamweaver enables you to explicitly protect file types, identified with a particular file extension.

To enter a new file type in the Never Rewrite Code options, select the In Files with Extensions field. Enter the file extension of the file type, including the period, in the end of the list. Be sure to separate your extensions from the others in the list with a space on either side.

Special Character preferences

In addition to the rewriting of proprietary tags, many middleware vendors faced another problem when trying to integrate with Dreamweaver. By default, earlier versions of Dreamweaver encoded all URLs so that they could be understood by Unix servers. The encoding converted all special characters to their decimal equivalents, preceded by a percent sign. Spaces became %20, tildes (~) became %7E, and ampersands were converted to &. Although this is valid for Unix servers, and helps to make the Dreamweaver code more universal, it can cause problems for many other types of application servers.

Dreamweaver gives you the option to disable the URL encoding, if necessary. Moreover, Dreamweaver also enables you to turn off encoding that is applied to special characters in the attributes of tags. This latter issue can be particularly vexing because, while you can rewrite the attributes in the Code Inspector, if you select the element in the Document window with the Property Inspector open, the attributes are encoded. You can prevent this from happening with the selection of a single checkbox.

In general, however, it's best to leave both of the Special Characters encoding options enabled unless you find your third-party tags being rewritten destructively.

Code Colors preferences

HTML code is a combination of the tags that structure the language and the text that provides the content. A Web page designer often has difficulty distinguishing swiftly between the two — and finding the right code to modify. Dreamweaver enables you to set color preferences for the code as it appears in the Code view or Code Inspector. You can not only alter colors for the background, default tags, and text and general comments, but also specify certain tags to get certain colors.

To modify any of the basic elements (Background, Text, Comments, or Tag Default) or any of the Script colors (Reserved Keywords, Other Keywords, or Strings), select the color swatch next to the corresponding name, as illustrated in Figure 4-17. Select a color from any of the 216 displayed in the color picker or choose the small palette icon to select from the full range of colors available to your system. You can also use the Eyedropper tool to pick a color from the Document window.

To select a different color for a specific tag, first select the tag from the Tag Specific list box. Then choose either the Default option (which assigns the same color as specified for the Tag Default) or a custom color by clicking the color swatch and choosing the color. If you want to set all of the code and text enclosed by the selected tag to the same color, choose the Apply Color to Tag Contents option.

Code Format preferences

Dreamweaver includes two other tools for customizing your HTML. The first is an easy-to-use, point-and-click preferences category called Code Format. The second is a text file called the Source Format (SourceFormat.txt), which must be modified by hand and controls the output of every HTML tag. You can modify your HTML using either or both techniques. All of the options controlled by the Code Format category are written out to the text file.

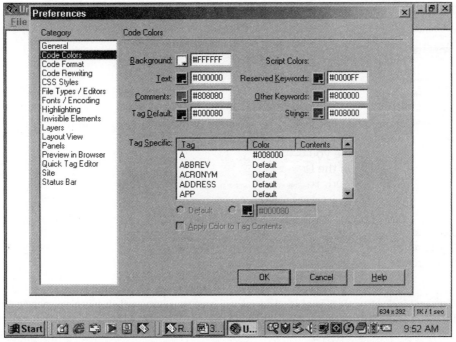

Figure 4-17: Use the Code Colors category to custom color–code the HTML Inspector.

Most of your HTML code parameters can be controlled through the Code Format category. The only reason to alter the SourceFormat.txt text file by hand is if you want to control the appearance of your HTML code at the tag level.

In the Code Format category, you can decide whether to use indentations — if so, whether to use spaces or tabs and how many of each — or to turn off indents for major elements such as tables and frames. You can also globally control the case of your HTML tags and their attributes. As you can see in Figure 4-18, the Code Format category is full featured.

To examine the available options in the Code Format category, let's separate them into four areas: indent control, line control, case control, and centering.

Indent control

Indenting your code generally makes it more readable. Dreamweaver defaults to indenting most HTML tags with two spaces, giving extra indentation grouping to tables and frames. All these parameters can be altered through the Code Format category of the Preferences dialog box.

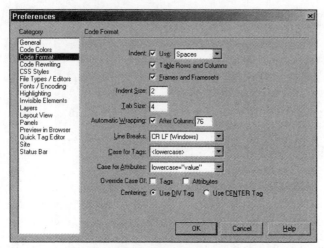

Figure 4-18: The Code Format category enables you to shape your HTML to your own specifications.

The first indent option enables indenting, and you can switch from spaces to tabs. To permit indenting, make sure a checkmark is displayed in the Indent checkbox. Of the 52 separate HTML tags Dreamweaver identifies in its Source Format, 29 tags are designed to be indented. If you prefer your code to be displayed flush left, turn off the Indent option altogether.

To use tabs instead of the default spaces, click the Use arrow button and select tabs from the drop-down list. If you anticipate transferring your code to a word processing program for formatting and printing, you should use tabs; otherwise, stay with the default spaces.

Dreamweaver formats both tables and frames as special indentation groups. Within each of these structural elements, the related tags are indented (or nested) more than the initial two spaces. As you can see in Listing 4-1, each table row (<tr>) is indented within the table tag, and the table data tags (<td>) are nested within the table row.

Listing 4-1: **An Indented Code Sample**

```
<table border="1" width="75%">
 <tr>
 <td>Row 1, Column 1</td>
 <td>Row 1, Column 2</td>
 <td>Row 1, Column 3</td>
 </tr>
 <tr>
 <td>Row 2, Column 1</td>
```

```
<td>Row 2, Column 2 </td>
<td>Row 2, Column 3</td>
</tr>
</table>
```

If you want to disable the special indentation grouping for tables, deselect Table Rows and Columns in the Code Format category. Turn off frame indenting by unchecking Frames and Framesets (this option is selected by default).

The other two items in the indent control section of Code Format preferences are Indent Size and Tab Size. Change the value in Indent Size to establish the size of indents using spaces. To alter the size of tab indents, change the Tab Size value.

Line control

The browser is responsible for ultimately formatting an HTML page for viewing. This formatting includes wrapping text according to each user's screen size and the placement of the paragraph tags (`<p>...</p>`). Therefore, you control how your code wraps in your HTML editor. You can turn off the automatic wrapping feature or set it for a particular column through the line control options of the Code Format category.

To turn off the automatic word-wrapping capability, deselect AutomaticWrapping. When you are trying to debug your code and looking for specific line numbers and character positions, enable this option. You can also set the specific column for the word wrap to take effect. Be sure AutomaticWrapping is enabled and then type your new value in the After Column text box.

Tip If you're using the Code view or Inspector, selecting the Word Wrap option overrides the Automatic Wrapping setting in Code Format.

The Line Breaks setting determines which line break character is appended to each line of the page. Each of the major operating systems employs a different ending character: Macintosh uses a carriage return (CR), Unix uses a line feed (LF), and Windows uses both (CR LF). If you know the operating system for your remote server, choosing the corresponding line break character helps the file to appear correctly when viewed online. Click the arrow button next to Line Breaks and select your system.

Caution The operating system for your local development machine may be different from the operating system of your remote server. If so, using the Line Breaks option may cause your HTML to appear incorrectly when viewed through a simple text editor (such as Notepad or vi). The Dreamweaver Code Inspector, however, does render the code correctly.

Case control

Whether an HTML tag or attribute is in uppercase or lowercase doesn't matter to most browsers — the command is rendered regardless of case. Case is only a personal preference among Web designers. That said, some Webmasters consider case a serious preference and insist on their codes being all uppercase, all lowercase, or a combination of uppercase and lowercase. Dreamweaver gives you control over the tags and attributes it creates, including control over case conversion for files that Dreamweaver imports.

The Dreamweaver default for both tags and attributes is lowercase. Click the arrow button next to Case for Tags and/or Case for Attributes to alter the selection. After you have selected OK from the Code Format category, Dreamweaver changes all the tags in any currently open file. Choose File ➪ Save to write the changes to disk.

Tip   Lowercase tags and attributes are also less fattening, according to the W3C. Files with lowercase tag names and attributes compress better and thus transmit faster.

You can also use Dreamweaver to standardize the letter case in tags of previously saved files. To alter imported files, select the Override Case Of Tags and/or the Override Case Of Attributes options. When enabled, these options enforce your choices made in the Case for Tags and Case for Attributes option boxes in any file Dreamweaver loads. Again, be sure to save your file to keep the changes.

Centering

When an object — whether it's an image or text — is centered on a page, HTML tags are placed around the object (or objects) to indicate the alignment. Since the release of HTML 3.2, the `<center>` tag has been deprecated by the W3C in favor of using a `<div>` tag with an align="center" attribute. By default, Dreamweaver uses the officially preferred method of `<div align="center">`.

Many Web designers are partial to the older `<center>` tag and prefer to use it to align their objects. Dreamweaver offers a choice with the Centering option in the Code Format category. To use the newer method, select the Use DIV Tag option (the default). To switch to the older `<center>` method, select the Use CENTER Tag option. Although use of `<center>` has been officially discouraged, it is so widespread that all browsers continue to support it.

Understanding the Source Format

As noted earlier, Dreamweaver pulls its code configuration guidelines from a text file named SourceFormat.txt. When Dreamweaver is installed, this file is put in the Dreamweaver\Configuration folder. When you make a modification to the Code Format category, the initial profile is renamed as SourceFormat.backup and then Dreamweaver writes a new SourceFormat.txt.

Tip

You can restore the default Source Profile settings at any time. When Dreamweaver is closed, delete SourceFormat.txt and then make a copy of the SourceFormat.original file. Finally, rename the copy as SourceFormat.txt.

Dreamweaver uses a specialized Code Format to create a SourceFormat.txt that can be viewed and edited in any text editor. Three main sections exist, each denoted with a `<?keyword>` format: `<?options>`, `<?elements>`, and `<?attributes>`. Prior to each section, Dreamweaver uses the HTML comment tags to describe them. The file closes with the `<?end>` keyword.

The Source Format (see Listing 4-2) starts with two HTML comments. The first describes the overall document (`Dreamweaver source formatting profile`), followed by the Options section.

Listing 4-2

```
<!-- Dreamweaver source formatting profile -->

<!-- options

        INDENTION    : indention options
            ENABLE       - allows indention
            INDENT       - columns per indention
            TABS         - columns per tab character
            USE          - TABS or SPACES for indention
            ACTIVE       - active indention groups (IGROUP)

        LINES        : end-of-line options
            AUTOWRAP     - enable automatic line wrapping
            BREAK        - CRLF, CR, LF
            COLUMN       - auto wrap lines after column

        OMIT         : element omission options
            OPTIONS      - options

        ELEMENT      : element options
            CASE         - "UPPER" or "lower" case
            ALWAYS       - always use preferred element case
(instead of original case)

        ATTRIBUTE    : attribute options
            CASE         - "UPPER" or "lower" case
            ALWAYS       - always use preferred attribute case
(instead of original case)

-->
<?options>
<indention enable indent="2" tabs="4" use="spaces"
active="1,2">
```

Continued

Listing 4-2 *(continued)*

```
<lines autowrap column="76" break="CRLF">
<omit options="0">
<element case="lower">
<attribute case="lower">
<colors text="0x00000000" tag="0x00000000"
unknowntag="0x00000000" comment="0x00000000"
invalid="0x00000000" object="0x00000000">
<directives break="1,0,0,1">
<directives delimiter="%3C%25=" break="0,0,0,0"> <!-- no line
breaks surrounding a "<%=" script block -->

<!-- element information
    line breaks                 : BREAK  = "before, inside start,
inside end, after"
    indent contents              : INDENT
    indent group                : IGROUP = "indention group
number" (1 through 8)
    specific name case          : NAMECASE = "CustomName"
    prevent formatting          : NOFORMAT
-->
<?elements>
<address break="1,0,0,1">
<applet break="0,1,1,0" indent>
<area break="1,0,0,1">
<base break="1,0,0,1">
<blockquote break="1,0,0,1" indent>
<body break="1,1,1,1">
<br break="0,0,0,1">
<caption break="1,0,0,1">
<center break="1,1,1,1" indent>
<cfabort break="1,0,0,1">
<cfapplet break="1,0,0,1">
<cfapplication break="1,0,0,1">
<cfassociate break="1,0,0,1">
<cfauthenticate break="1,0,0,1">
<cfbreak break="1,0,0,1">
<cfcache break="1,0,0,1">
<cfcatch break="1,1,1,1" indent>
<cfcase break="1,1,1,1">
<cfcol break="1,0,0,1">
<cfcollection break="1,0,0,1">
<cfcontent break="1,0,0,1">
<cfcookie break="1,0,0,1">
<cfdefaultcase break="1,1,1,1">
<cfdirectory break="1,0,0,1">
<cferror break="1,0,0,1">
<cfexit break="1,0,0,1">
<cffile break="1,0,0,1">
<cfform break="1,1,1,1" indent>
<cfftp break="1,0,0,1">
```

```
<cfgrid break="1,1,1,1" indent>
<cfgridcolumn break="1,0,0,1">
<cfgridrow break="1,0,0,1">
<cfgridupdate break="1,0,0,1">
<cfheader break="1,0,0,1">
<cfhtmlhead break="1,0,0,1">
<cfhttp break="1,1,1,1" indent>
<cfhttpparam break="1,0,0,1">
<cfif break="1,1,1,1">
<cfelse break="1,0,0,1">
<cfelseif break="1,1,1,1">
<cfinclude break="1,0,0,1">
<cfindex break="1,0,0,1">
<cfinput break="1,0,0,1">
<cfinsert break="1,0,0,1">
<cfldap break="1,0,0,1">
<cflocation break="1,0,0,1">
<cflock break="1,1,1,1" indent>
<cfloop break="1,1,1,1" indent>
<cfmail break="1,1,1,1" indent>
<cfmodule break="1,0,0,1">
<cfobject break="1,0,0,1">
<cfoutput indent>
<cfparam break="1,0,0,1">
<cfpop break="1,0,0,1">
<cfprocparam break="1,0,0,1">
<cfprocresult break="1,0,0,1">
<cfquery break="1,1,1,1">
<cfregistry break="1,0,0,1">
<cfreport break="1,1,1,1" indent>
<cfscript break="1,1,1,1">
<cfschedule break="1,0,0,1">
<cfsearch break="1,0,0,1">
<cfselect break="1,1,1,1" indent>
<cfset break="1,0,0,1">
<cfsetting break="1,0,0,1">
<cfslider break="1,0,0,1">
<cfstoredproc break="1,1,1,1" indent>
<cfswitch break="1,1,1,1" indent>
<cftable break="1,1,1,1" indent>
<cfthrow break="1,0,0,1">
<cftextinput break="1,0,0,1">
<cftransaction break="1,1,1,1" indent>
<cftree break="1,1,1,1" indent>
<cftreeitem break="1,0,0,1">
<cftry break="1,1,1,1" indent>
<cfupdate break="1,0,0,1">
<dd break="1,0,0,1" indent>
<dir break="1,0,0,1" indent>
<div break="1,0,0,1" indent>
<dl break="1,0,0,1" indent>
<dt break="1,0,0,1" indent>
```

Continued

Listing 4-2 *(continued)*

```
<embed break="0,1,1,0" indent>
<form break="1,1,1,1" indent>
<frame break="1,0,0,1">
<frameset break="1,0,0,1" indent igroup="2">
<h1 break="1,0,0,1" indent>
<h2 break="1,0,0,1" indent>
<h3 break="1,0,0,1" indent>
<h4 break="1,0,0,1" indent>
<h5 break="1,0,0,1" indent>
<h6 break="1,0,0,1" indent>
<head break="1,1,1,1">
<hr break="1,0,0,1">
<html break="1,1,1,1">
<ilayer break="1,0,0,1">
<input break="1,0,0,1">
<isindex break="1,0,0,1">
<layer break="1,0,0,1">
<li break="1,0,0,1" indent>
<link break="1,0,0,1">
<map break="1,0,0,1" indent>
<menu break="1,0,0,1" indent>
<meta break="1,0,0,1">
<object break="0,1,1,0" indent>
<ol break="1,1,1,1" indent>
<option break="1,0,0,1">
<p break="1,0,0,1" indent>
<param break="1,0,0,1">
<pre break="1,0,0,1" noformat>
<script break="1,0,0,1" noformat>
<select break="1,1,1,1" indent>
<mm:treecontrol break="1,1,1,1" indent>
<server break="1,0,0,1" noformat>
<style break="1,0,0,1" noformat>
<table break="1,1,1,1" indent igroup="1">
<td break="1,0,0,1" indent igroup="1">
<textarea break="1,0,0,1" noformat>
<th break="1,0,0,1" indent igroup="1">
<title break="1,0,0,1">
<tr break="1,0,0,1" indent igroup="1">
<ul break="1,1,1,1" indent>
<jsp:getProperty break="1,0,0,1" namecase="jsp:getProperty">
<jsp:setProperty break="1,0,0,1" namecase="jsp:setProperty">
<jsp:useBean break="1,0,0,1" namecase="jsp:useBean">
<jsp:forward break="1,0,0,1">
<jsp:include break="1,0,0,1">
<jsp:plugin break="1,1,1,1">
<jsp:params break="1,1,1,1" indent>
<jsp:param break="1,0,0,1">
<jsp:fallback break="1,0,0,1">
```

```
<!-- attribute information
     specific name case          : NAMECASE = "CustomName"
     values follow attr case     : SAMECASE
-->
<?attributes>
<onAbort namecase="onAbort">
<onBlur namecase="onBlur">
<onChange namecase="onChange">
<onClick namecase="onClick">
<onDragDrop namecase="onDragDrop">
<onError namecase="onError">
<onFocus namecase="onFocus">
<onKeyDown namecase="onKeyDown">
<onKeyPress namecase="onKeyPress">
<onKeyUp namecase="onKeyUp">
<onLoad namecase="onLoad">
<onMouseDown namecase="onMouseDown">
<onMouseMove namecase="onMouseMove">
<onMouseOut namecase="onMouseOut">
<onMouseOver namecase="onMouseOver">
<onMouseUp namecase="onMouseUp">
<onMove namecase="onMove">
<onReset namecase="onReset">
<onResize namecase="onResize">
<onSelect namecase="onSelect">
<onSubmit namecase="onSubmit">
<onUnload namecase="onUnload">
<onDblClick namecase="onDblClick">
<onAfterUpdate namecase="onAfterUpdate">
<onBeforeUpdate namecase="onBeforeUpdate">
<onHelp namecase="onHelp">
<onReadyStateChange namecase="onReadyStateChange">
<onScroll namecase="onScroll">
<onRowEnter namecase="onRowEnter">
<onRowExit namecase="onRowExit">
<align samecase>
<checked samecase>
<codetype samecase>
<compact samecase>
<ismap samecase>
<frame samecase>
<method samecase>
<multiple samecase>
<noresize samecase>
<noshade samecase>
<nowrap samecase>
<selected samecase>
<shape samecase>
<type samecase>
<valign samecase>
<visibility samecase>
<?end>
```

Options

The Options section parallels the options set in the Code Format category. Either you can use Dreamweaver's point-and-click interface by choosing Edit ➪ Preferences and then selecting the Code Format category, or you can edit the `<?options>` section of the SourceFormat.txt file. In the Options description, five parameters are outlined: indention, lines, omit, element, and attribute.

The indention item denotes the indent options:

```
ENABLE - allows indention
INDENT - columns per indention
TABS - columns per tab character
USE - TABS or SPACES for indention
ACTIVE - active indention groups (IGROUP)
```

The final indention option, ACTIVE, relates to the special grouping function that Dreamweaver calls IGROUPS. By default, Dreamweaver assigns IGROUP #1 to Table Rows and Columns and IGROUP #2 to Frames and Framesets.

The line options are detailed as follows:

```
AUTOWRAP - enable automatic line wrapping
BREAK - CRLF, CR, LF
COLUMN - auto wrap lines after column
```

As mentioned earlier, the BREAK options are used to insert the type of line break character recognized by your Web server's operating system. Use CRLF for Windows, CR for Macintosh, and LF for Unix.

The next Options section, OMIT, is reserved by Dreamweaver for further expansion and is not currently used.

The Element and Attribute sections control the case of HTML elements (or tags) and attributes:

```
CASE - "UPPER" or "lower" case
ALWAYS - always use preferred element case (instead of original
case)
```

If the ALWAYS keyword is used, Dreamweaver alters the case of tags and/or attributes when you import a previously saved file.

The following section of the Source Format that starts with `<?options>` contains the actual options read by Dreamweaver at startup. This listing shows the default options from the default SourceFormat.txt file for Dreamweaver 4:

```
<?options>
<indention enable indent="2" tabs="8" use="spaces"
active="1,2">
<lines autowrap column="76">
```

```
<omit options="0">
<element case="lower">
<attribute case="lower">
```

Elements

The Element information in the next section of the Source Format describes the syntax and options for individually controlling each HTML tag.

```
line breaks : BREAK = "before, inside start, inside end, after"
indent contents : INDENT
indent group : IGROUP = "indention group number" (1 through 8)
specific name case : NAMECASE = "CustomName"
prevent formatting : NOFORMAT
```

break

The syntax for break refers to the number of line breaks surrounding the opening and closing HTML tags. For example, the default syntax for the <h1> tag follows:

```
<h1 break="1,0,0,1" indent>
```

The preceding produces code that looks like the following:

```
<h1>Welcome!</h1>
```

If you want to display the opening and closing tags on their own lines, you could change the break value as follows:

```
<h1 break="1,1,1,1" indent>
```

The preceding gives you the following result:

```
<h1>
 Welcome!
</h1>
```

Use zero in the "before" and "after" positions when you want a tag to appear in line with the other code, as in this map tag:

```
<map break="0,1,1,0" indent>
```

The Elements list only contains tags that have opening and closing elements, which are also known as *container tags*. Any single-element tags, such as the image tag, <img>, are presented in line with other elements.

Note For all of the Source Format's comprehensiveness, one type of tag is unavailable: comment tags. While you can't adjust their spacing, you can alter the color of comments through Preferences, in the Code Colors category.

You're not restricted to using 1 and 0 values for `break`. If you want to isolate a tag so that it really stands out, use 2 in the "before" and "after" positions. For example:

```
<p break="2,1,1,2" indent>
```

The preceding produces completely separated paragraphs such as the following:

```
<p>
Synapse Advertising is your first choice for the best in
subliminal advertising.
</p>

<p>
Call Synapse when you want your clients to come a-knockin' at
your door -- ¬
and have no idea why!
</p>
```

indent

The indent keyword ensures that the text contained between the opening and closing tags wraps to the same text column as the tag, rather than appearing flush left. The difference is apparent when you compare almost any text format tag, from paragraph `<p>`, to any heading `<h1>` through `<h6>` tag, to the preformatted tag `<pre>`.

```
<p>Four score and seven years ago our fathers brought forth ¬
on this continent, a new nation, conceived in liberty, and ¬
dedicated to the proposition that all men are created ¬
equal.</p>

<pre>The above speech was offered by President Abraham Lincoln
and is known as ¬
the Gettysburg Address. Now recognized by many as the leading
speech of the ¬
Lincoln presidency, the Gettysburg Address was initially
received to mixed ¬
reviews...</pre>
```

igroup

The igroup keyword is used only when applied to special indentation groups such as tables and frames. For example, all the elements contained in a table have `igroup="1"` as part of their source profile, as shown in the following:

```
<table break="1,1,1,1" indent igroup="1">
<td break="1,0,0,1" indent igroup="1">
<th break="1,0,0,1" indent igroup="1">
<tr break="1,0,0,1" indent igroup="1">
```

The igroup attribute in the indention option activates the indentation set for all the tags in that group. For example, if the indention option read as follows:

```
<indention enable indent="2" tabs="8" use="spaces" active="2">
```

then indenting would be turned off for igroup number 1, tables.

The active igroup causes each element to use the indentation level of the outermost group member as its left margin — and indent from there. Thus, with the indented <table>...</table> pair as the outer igroup member, the <tr>...</tr> pair is indented two more spaces and the <td>...</td> pair is indented another two spaces, so it looks like the following:

```
<table border="2" width="50%">
 <tr>
 <td>Symbol</td>
 <td>Element</td>
 </tr>
 <tr>
 <td>H</td>
 <td>Hydrogen</td>
 </tr>
</table>
```

You can currently define up to six igroups, in addition to the preset tables and frames.

namecase

You can override the general case conventions for any element with the namecase keyword. If you want to use a title case or mixed case for certain tags, you define them in the following way:

```
<applet break="0,1,1,0" indent namecase="Applet">
<blockquote break="1,0,0,1" indent namecase="BlockQuote">
```

You may also use the namecase keyword when defining a custom tag for use in conjunction with a new object. Let's say you've created a series of objects for use with ColdFusion and you want them to stand out in the code. To accentuate your new tag pair, <cfif>...</cfif>, you could add the following line to your Source Format:

```
<cfif break="1,1,1,1" indent namecase="CFIf">
```

This line ensures that a ColdFusion "if" tag is always inserted in the specified mixed case.

Note   In addition to a large number of ColdFusion tags included in the Source Format file, Dreamweaver also supports eight different JavaServer Page tags. You'll find these listed at the end of the <?elements> section with the jsp: prefix.

noformat

As the name implies, the noformat keyword presents the tag-surrounded text without any additional formatting. This keyword is primarily used when the tag is used to reproduce verbatim information, such as when using the preformatted tag `<pre>`. The noformat keyword is also used when the element requires attributes and values in a specific format, such as with `<style>` or `<script>`.

Attributes

The Attributes section has only two options: namecase, which works as previously described in the "Elements" section, and samecase. The namecase option is used to maintain a consistent mixed case approach to JavaScript events, such as `onKeyDown`. The samecase option ensures that an attribute and its value use the same case as its tag. If the `<input>` tag is uppercase, then the named attribute and the value are uppercase.

Caution   Never use the samecase option with any attribute that requires a case-sensitive value. The most common instance of this situation is an attribute such as src that takes a filename as its value — which, in most cases, is case-sensitive.

Case is generally determined for all attributes by the following line found in the Objects section:

```
<attribute case="lower">
```

As with elements, you can alter the case of attributes individually by specifying them in this section. For example, if you always want the source attribute of the image tag to be uppercase, you can include the following line in the Attributes section:

```
<src namecase="SRC">
```

The preceding produces code such as the following:

```
<img SRC="logo.gif>
```

This capability is handy when you are scanning your code and quickly want to find all the source files.

Modifying the Source Format

Because you have to restart Dreamweaver in order for any Source Format modifications to take effect, it's best to edit the file with Dreamweaver closed. You can use any editor capable of saving an ASCII or regular text file. If you want to preserve the previous profile, you can use the Save As feature of your editor to save the file under a different name, such as SourceFormat.backup, prior to making any changes. Then, after you complete your alterations, use Save As again and name it SourceFormat.txt.

Make your changes only to those sections marked with the <?keyword>, such as <?options> or <?elements>. Remember that Dreamweaver is not case-sensitive when it comes to changing commands — other than with the namecase keyword — so you can write lines such as the following:

```
<element case="LOWER">
```

In the preceding example, all your tags are still created, as specified, in lowercase.

Dreamweaver is fairly protective of its Source Format. If you accidentally misspell a keyword (for example, "ident" instead of "indent"), Dreamweaver ignores and then deletes the misspelled keyword. Likewise, misplaced keywords — for instance, using the enable keyword when defining an element instead of an option — are removed from the file when Dreamweaver loads.

One of the Dreamweaver commands enables you to apply the Source Format to an existing page — typically one created outside of Dreamweaver. To use this capability, you first make changes to the Source Format and save it. Then restart Dreamweaver and open the page you want to affect. Finally, choose Commands ➪ Apply Source Formatting. Whatever modifications you made to the Source Format are written to the existing code.

The Source Format is an HTML tinker's paradise. You can shape your code as precisely as necessary, and Dreamweaver outputs it for you. Feel free to experiment and try different code arrangements. Just be sure to have a copy of the original Source Format available as a reference.

Summary

Creating Web pages, like any design job, is easier when the tools fit your hands. Through the Preferences and the Source Format, you can make Dreamweaver work the way you work. The following highlights the basic areas for personalization:

✦ Dreamweaver enables you to customize your Web page design and HTML coding environment through a series of easy-to-use, point-and-click categories.

✦ You can decide how best to use cutting-edge features, such as layers and style sheets, depending on the degree of cross-browser and backward compatibility you need.

✦ Dreamweaver gives you plenty of elbow room for previewing and testing by providing for 20 selections on your browser list.

✦ The Source Format can be modified. You can make alterations, from across-the-board case changes to tag-by-tag presentation, to define the way Dreamweaver writes your HTML code.

In the next chapter, you learn how to get online and offline help from Dreamweaver.

✦   ✦   ✦

Using the Help System

Dreamweaver includes a multifaceted Help system that you can rely on in any number of situations:

✦ To provide quick context-sensitive answers to questions about how to use specific Dreamweaver features

✦ To learn the program using step-by-step instructions presented in a tutorial format

✦ To explain various concepts and capabilities through the hyperlinked Help pages and their embedded Show Me movies

✦ To detail the syntax for specific HTML, JavaScript and Cascading Style Sheet code

✦ To seek specific programming assistance from the peer-to-peer network of the online newsgroups or the Dreamweaver technical support team at Macromedia

Whether you're a novice Web designer or a Dreamweaver master upgrading to the latest version, you'll need the Help system at some point. In this chapter, we'll cover the Help pages, included tutorials and lessons, Dreamweaver 4's new Reference feature, and the online help options.

Navigating the Help Screen

To assist your understanding of Dreamweaver — in both the short term and the long term — Macromedia includes a full electronic manual with the program._To access this searchable guide, choose Help ⇨ Using Dreamweaver or press the keyboard shortcut F1 to open the Dreamweaver HTML Help pages.

If you have defined a primary browser in Dreamweaver through the Preferences, or with File ➪ Preview in Browser ➪ Edit Browser List, that browser opens and the Help pages are loaded. Otherwise, Dreamweaver uses your system's default browser to display the Help pages.

The Dreamweaver Help pages are presented within an HTML frameset as shown in Figure 5-1. The frame on the far left changes according to the current mode (Contents, Index, or Search). The main portion of the frame is reserved for showing the Help pages themselves. Along the top and bottom of each page is a set of navigation arrows for moving from topic to topic within a section.

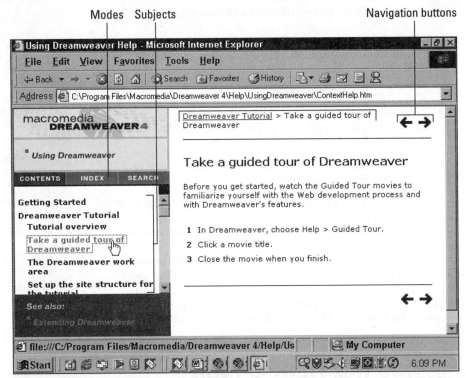

Figure 5-1: The Dreamweaver Help pages comprise a hyperlinked manual that is displayed in your primary or default browser.

Note   Dreamweaver includes a whole other level of online help documentation for the advanced user: Extending Dreamweaver. The Extending Dreamweaver Help pages are the online edition of a second manual that comes with Dreamweaver, and they explain how to customize various aspects of the program. The Extending Dreamweaver Help pages are available from the Help menu or by choosing the Extending Dreamweaver option from the standard Help pages themselves.

Browsing the Help contents

To get the most benefit from the Help pages, maximize your browser window. You can alternate between the Contents and Index by selecting one or the other control button. When you choose Contents, the frame on the left side provides a list of main Dreamweaver subjects and a handy scroll bar for moving through the list.

Selecting any main topic — displayed in bold — in the Help Contents reveals another list of subtopics. You can collapse the main topic by selecting it again or by choosing another main topic. Note that you must click a subtopic to load the information into the main viewing frame. If there is too much information to be displayed on a single screen, another scroll bar appears on the far-right side of the frame. To see the additional text, you can drag the scroll bar or select the frame and use your PgUp and PgDn keys.

Note Dreamweaver takes advantage of your browser's HTML capabilities, and many Help pages contain hyperlinks to other Help screens. If you follow a hyperlink to a new section from the main screen, the Contents updates to reflect your new position.

Using the navigational controls

As you browse through the Help pages, you find you can use your browser's Back and Forward buttons to revisit pages you have already viewed. You can also use the Help pages' own navigational system to move back and forth from topic to topic.

The Next and Previous arrows, shown in Figure 5-2, are tied to the Help pages' content structure and only display current subtopics within each major subject. As you would expect, selecting the Next arrow displays the next topic or subtopic, and Previous arrow displays the prior ones.

If you reach the last subtopic and attempt to use the Next arrow, you get a JavaScript alert saying you are at the end of the section. A similar event occurs when you are looking at the first subtopic and try to view the Previous one. To go to another major subject, you have to select it from the Contents listing and then select one of the subtopics.

Using the Help index

Selecting the Index control button switches to an alphabetical listing of topics covered in the Dreamweaver Help pages. To find the subject you need, select the first letter of the topic you're seeking from the A-B-C . . . letters shown in Figure 5-3; each letter is actually a link that loads the relevant section of the index when selected. For example, if I were looking for information on activating a timeline in Dreamweaver, I would select T. Once the specific letter's index has loaded, scroll down the list by dragging the scroll bar at the near right.

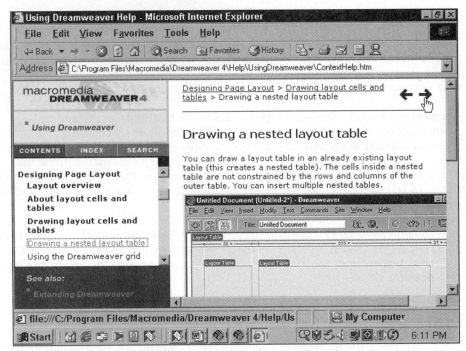

Figure 5-2: Move from topic to topic with the Next and Previous arrows.

Tip   If you'd like to see the entire index, choose the A–Z option. You can also click any-where in the index frame and use your system's PgUp and PgDn keys or wheel-mouse to navigate through the index.

When you find your subject, select it from the list. The corresponding Help page appears in the main frame. Note that when an index listing is divided into a topic and related subtopics, you must choose one of the subtopics to get the related Help page. In this case, the topics themselves are not linked to any specific Help page.

Note   The A–Z index is quite extensive and can take several moments to completely load. Be sure to wait until the browser indicates that the frame is completely loaded before scrolling all the way down.

Searching the Help files

Dreamweaver has included a search function with the Help pages. As designed by Macromedia, the search engine is actually a Java applet that runs within your browser displaying the Help pages. One major advantage to this approach is that it enables you to keep the search window available as you look for the material you need.

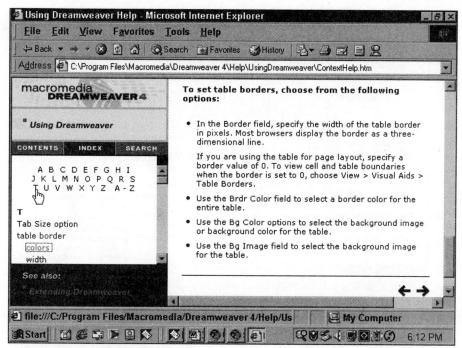

Figure 5-3: Quickly navigate to any index item by choosing its first letter from the A-B-C . . . links visible in Index mode.

To search the Help pages for a particular topic, follow these steps:

1. Select the Search button found at the top of the leftmost frame.

2. In the Search window (see Figure 5-4), enter keywords in the upper text box.

   - To search for a phrase, enter the words as you would normally, for example, "shockwave" (without the quotes).

   - To search for several related keywords that do not have to appear next to each other, enter the words with a plus sign between them, like this: template + behavior

   - By default the search is not case-sensitive. To turn on this feature, select the Case sensitive checkbox.

3. After you've entered your search criteria, select the List Topics button.

   As each page is searched, pages matching your search criteria are displayed in the results window.

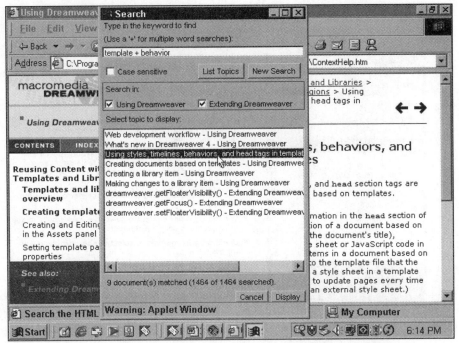

Figure 5-4: Quickly find the topics you're looking for with the Help pages search engine.

4. To see an individual page, double-click its title in the results window. You can also select the title of the page and click the Display button.

   The page linked to the title is displayed in the main frame of the Help pages.

5. Repeat Steps 2 through 4 to continue searching.

6. Click the Cancel button to close the Search window.

To return to either the Contents or the Index listing, select the Contents or Index command buttons, respectively.

Stepping Through the Tutorial

The Dreamweaver Help pages include a step-by-step tutorial that demonstrates how to use the latest Dynamic HTML features to create a Web page. To access the tutorial, choose Help ⇨ Tutorial or, from the Help pages, select the Dreamweaver Tutorial topic.

The Dreamweaver 4 Tutorial takes the form of a complete sample Web site for a fictitious travel company, Compass. In the process of building its Web pages, you get to try your hand at defining a local site, designing a page in Layout view, editing existing pages, working with templates, using the Assets panel, attaching behaviors, and even adding in Flash objects.

To see the sample Web site, in your browser, choose File ➪ Open and locate the Dreamweaver 4\Tutorial\Compass_Site folder. Then select the CompassHome.html file to open it. The example home page, shown in Figure 5-5, should be previewed in a 4.0 or above browser to understand how the various pages link together.

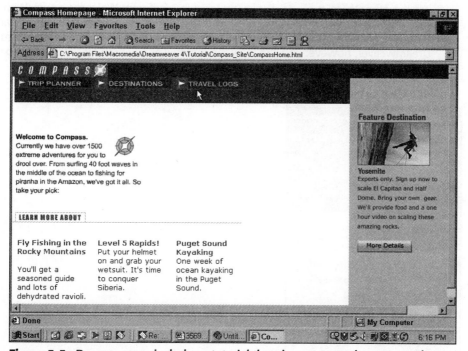

Figure 5-5: Dreamweaver includes a tutorial that demonstrates how to use the program to build an advanced Web page, step by step.

Note

The tutorial folder holds both completed and semicompleted pages. The completed pages are included to give you an idea of how the site should ultimately look. The semicompleted files enable you to work on specific techniques during the tutorial without having to build every page from the ground up each time. For easy identification, the filenames for the pages-in-progress begin with the prefix "DW4," for example, DW4_Destinations.html.

Getting the Guided Tour

Building a Web site is a big job and Dreamweaver is a big program with a large number of features. One of the most common issues faced by newcomers to the field — and the program — is not knowing where to start. To help novices scale the initial learning curve, Dreamweaver offers a series of features that introduce Web building in general and Dreamweaver in particular.

 New Feature

When you run Dreamweaver for the first time, a floating Welcome panel appears displaying four topics (see Figure 5-6): What's New, Guided Tours, Tutorial, and Lessons. The Tutorial link opens the Help Pages section in your default browser but the other three subjects display material in a different Welcome panel. With a combination of text, images, and Flash movies, key concepts and new features are introduced. The Welcome panel appears automatically the first time you run Dreamweaver; however you can view the material at any time by choosing Help ⇨ Welcome.

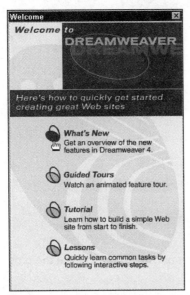

Figure 5-6: Get up-to-speed quickly by exploring Dreamweaver's Welcome panel.

Each of the descriptions shown in the Welcome panel takes a similar approach. Follow these steps to explore a Welcome panel topic:

1. If the Welcome panel is not displayed, choose Help ⇨ Welcome to open it.

 Caution

The Welcome panel is actually a series of Flash movies, so you'll need the Flash Player installed before accessing this feature.

2. Select the primary topic you're interested in:

   - **What's New** examines the new features in Dreamweaver 4.

   - **Guided Tours** offers an overview of the Web-building process in Dreamweaver.

   - **Lessons** describes techniques for accomplishing specific goals in Dreamweaver.

     Subtopics for each category are displayed next for both Guided Tours and Lessons.

3. Unless you've selected What's New, choose the subtopic you'd like to see.

   Each screen of information includes some text along with an image, a movie camera icon, or an image symbol.

4. To view an embedded Flash movie click the movie camera symbol.

Tip

Be sure the sound is turned up on your system when running the movies. All the movies punctuate their actions with sound.

5. To see an image, select the image symbol.

   Some images display helpful screens of information when you move your mouse over them. Along the bottom of the panel, you'll notice that navigational aids have appeared: (from left to right) Home, Rewind, Previous and Next.

6. When you're finished viewing one page, select the Next button.

7. You can review prior screens by selecting the Previous button.

8. To view the topic from the start, select the Rewind button.

9. If you'd like to look at more topics in the current category, select the Home button.

10. To see topics in another category, first select the Home button and then choose the Back button on the lower-left of the Welcome panel.

The lessons found in the Welcome panel — which can be directly accessed by choosing Help ➪ Lessons — includes a couple of additional features, shown in Figure 5-7, not found in the Guided Tours. First, you'll see a step-by-step list of the process covered (for example, Creating an image map) at the start of each lesson. Not only does this give you an overview of the procedure, but the steps themselves are clickable so that you can go directly to the information you need. Within the lessons, a special steps navigation button appears, which, when selected, displays a navigable list of all the steps in that lesson. Select any step to display that screen of information.

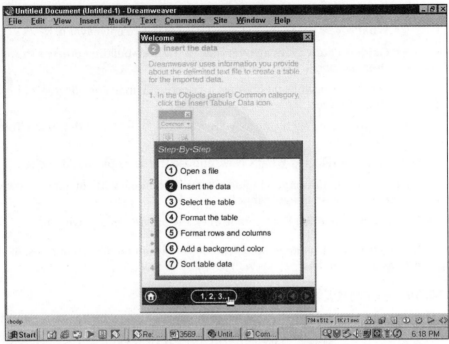

Figure 5-7: Dreamweaver lessons offer step-by-step navigation.

Lessons also offer a tool for trying out the described techniques right away. Dreamweaver comes with a practice page ready for you to work with. On the first page of each lesson, select the Open Practice Page button to load a predesigned HTML page into Dreamweaver. All of the steps in the lesson refer to the practice page and it's a great tool for quickly mastering the concepts described.

Tip   Be sure to use File ⇨ Save As to store your practice page under another name rather than Save so you can revisit the unchanged example page if necessary.

Using the Reference Panel

Pop quiz: What value of a form tag's `enctype` attribute should you use if the user is submitting a file? Is it:

    A. application/x-www-form-urlencoded

    B. multipart/form-data

    C. multipart/data-form

Chances are, unless you've recently had to include such a form in a Web page, you'd have to pull down that well-worn HTML reference book you keep handy and look up the answer to be sure. All code for the Web — including HTML, JavaScript, and Cascading Style Sheets (CSS) — must be precisely written or it will, at best, be ignored; at worst, an error will be generated whenever the user views the page. Even the savviest of Web designers can't remember the syntax of every tag, attribute, and value in HTML or every function in JavaScript or every style rule in CSS. A good reference is a necessity in Web design. (By the way, the answer to the pop quiz is B.)

New Feature

Macromedia has lightened the load on your bookshelf considerably with the addition of the Reference panel in Dreamweaver 4, as shown in Figure 5-8. With the Reference panel, you can quickly look up any HTML tag and its attributes as well as JavaScript objects and CSS style rules. The Reference panel uses content from Danny Goodman's *Dynamic HTML: The Definitive Reference*, published by O'Reilly & Associates, a superb guide to Web technology. Not only does the Reference panel offer the proper syntax for any code in question, it also displays the level of browser support. Moreover, you don't have to dig through the tag lists to find the info you need — just highlight the tag or object in question and press the keyboard shortcut, Shift+F1.

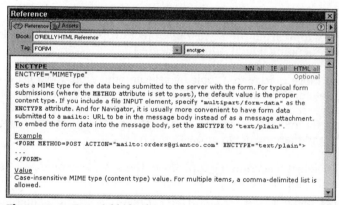

Figure 5-8: To quickly look up a tag, select it in the Tag selector or in Code view and then choose Shift+F1 to open the Reference panel.

There are four different ways to open the Reference panel:

✦ Choose Window ⇨ Reference

✦ Select the Reference button on the toolbar.

✦ Use the Shift+F1 keyboard shortcut.

✦ Use the Ctrl+Shift+F1 (Command+Shift+F1) keyboard shortcut.

What's the difference between the two shortcuts? Shift+F1 is used for context-sensitive help; select any tag (or just place your cursor within text enclosed by the tag) and then choose Shift+F1 to display the entry for the selected tag in the Reference panel. The other shortcut, Ctrl+Shift+F1 (Command+Shift+F1), is not context-sensitive, but rather toggles the Reference panel open and closed — and opens the panel to the last entry viewed.

Tip   To find reference details for the attributes of an HTML tag, a JavaScript object or a CSS style rule included on a Web page, open the Code view and select the code in question prior to choosing Shift+F1 or selecting the Reference button from the toolbar.

To look for information on code not included in the page, follow these steps:

1. Display the Reference panel by choosing Window ➪ Reference or using the keyboard shortcut Ctrl+Shift+F1 (Command+Shift+F1).

2. Select the required guide from the Book drop-down list. The standard options are

   - O'Reilly CSS Reference
   - O'Reilly HTML Reference
   - O'Reilly JavaScript Reference

3. Choose the primary topic from the Style/Tag/Object drop-down list. The list heading changes depending which Book is selected.

Tip   Windows users can move quickly to a topic by selecting the drop-down list and then pressing the key for the first letter of the term being sought. Then they can use the down arrow to move through items that start with that letter. For example, if you were looking for information on the JavaScript regular expressions object, you could press "r" and then the down arrow to reach RegExp.

4. If desired, you can select a secondary topic from the second drop-down list for HTML and JavaScript elements.

   If you've chosen an HTML tag, the secondary list displays all the available attributes for that tag. If you've chosen a JavaScript object, the secondary list shows the available properties for that object.

The information shown depends, naturally, on the book, topic, and subtopic chosen. At the top of each entry, you'll find the name of the subject and details on how it relates to browsers and standards:

✦ The CSS reference shows whether the style is supported in Netscape Navigator (NN) or Internet Explorer (IE). You'll also see which level of the Cascading Style Sheet specification (CSS 1 or CSS 2) the style is derived from and whether it is inherited or not.

✦ The HTML reference tells you which version of Netscape Navigator or Internet Explorer supports the selected tag. The HTML version in which the tag was introduced and information about whether an end tag is required is also displayed.

Note   The book on which the Reference panel is based was published in 1998 and only covers 4.0 browsers and below.

✦ The JavaScript reference details which version of the two main browsers as well as which version of the Document Object Model (DOM) or ECMA (the standard on which JavaScript is based) introduced the selected object.

The Reference panel's context menu allows you to switch between three different font sizes: small, medium, and large. This capability is especially useful when working at resolutions higher than 800×600. You'll also find an option to connect directly to O'Reilly Books Online.

Getting Help Online

Without a doubt, one of the factors that has helped the Web to grow so rapidly is the fact that it is largely self-documenting. Want to learn more about developing Web pages? Find out on the Web! The same holds true for Dreamweaver. An extensive array of information about Dreamweaver is available online — and more is added every day.

Macromedia has done — and continues to do — an excellent job of supporting Dreamweaver on the Web. To that end, Macromedia has developed and continues to sponsor two Web sites: the Dreamweaver Support Center and the Dynamic HTML Zone. The Dreamweaver Support Center is part of the general Macromedia site and focuses exclusively on providing support for Dreamweaver. Let's take a look at this one first.

Note   As with many popular Web sites, the Macromedia sites are constantly in a state of revision. The following information was current when written, but some of the content or structure may have changed by the time you read it. If all else fails, you should always be able to find assistance by starting at www.macromedia.com and looking for the Dreamweaver support area.

Dreamweaver Support Center

Macromedia's primary help center on the Web for Dreamweaver is a terrific resource. Visit the Dreamweaver Support Center at www.macromedia.com/support/dreamweaver/ to find the latest technical data, free downloads, and peer-to-peer connections — and it's all specific to Dreamweaver, naturally. One of the most impressive aspects of the site is its multilevel approach; there's material here for everyone, from rank beginner to the savviest code jockey.

When you visit the Dreamweaver Support Center, you find various areas of help as well as a search facility. Macromedia generally updates the site, shown in Figure 5-9, on a monthly or better basis. It's definitely worth bookmarking in your browser and visiting often.

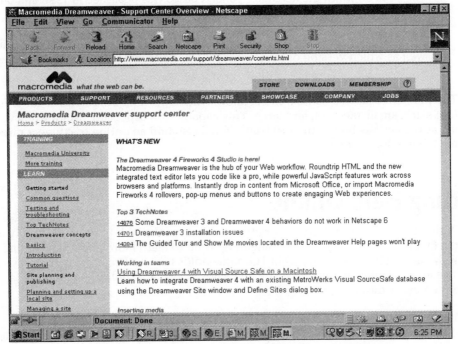

Figure 5-9: The Dreamweaver Support Center Web site is a central resource for gathering the newest information and software related to Dreamweaver.

Dynamic HTML Zone

The Dynamic HTML Zone, at www.dhtmlzone.com, is another extremely valuable online resource center. This site is also hosted by Macromedia, but here the focus is less on Dreamweaver than on implementing Dynamic HTML features in your Web pages. The Dynamic HTML Zone, shown in Figure 5-10, is a great jumping-off place for learning about DHTML through a variety of methods. The following is just some of what you can find at "the DZone."

Articles

The Dynamic HTML Zone contains a collection of some of the finest technical papers about creating DHTML pages on the Web. Both browser-specific and cross-browser features are explained by experts in the field. Sample articles include "Creating Multimedia with Dynamic HTML: An Overview," "Cross-Browser Dynamic HTML," and "Techniques for Building Backward Compatible DHTML."

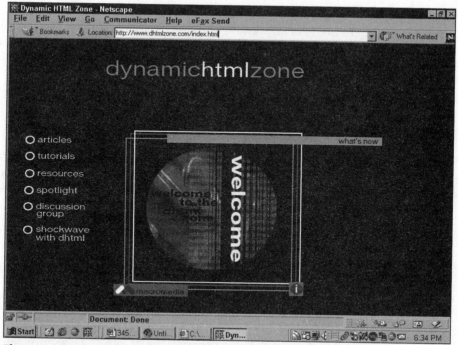

Figure 5-10: Visit the Dynamic HTML Zone for the latest information on building your Web pages with cutting-edge DHTML capabilities.

Tutorials

Learning from tutorials can be dry and tedious — but not at the DZone! Visit SuperFly Fashions and learn helpful general techniques, such as working with CSS layers and initializations. You also find more advanced methods, such as pull-down menus and scrolling text. The tutorials come with an overview as well as a line-by-line analysis of the JavaScript subroutines and other needed HTML code.

Resources

The Resources area is a collection of links to articles, reference guides, demos, various tutorials, and browser data — all related to DHTML. Pulling equally from the Microsoft and Netscape camps, as well as independent organizations such as C|Net and the W3C, these links are a great jumping-off place for all things DHTML.

Spotlight

Want to see what else is being accomplished with Dynamic HTML? Check out the Spotlight area. In addition to the site that's currently "in the spotlight," this page maintains an archive of past sites so honored.

Shockwave in DHTML

Combining the interactivity of Shockwave with the flexibility of Dynamic HTML is an exciting concept, and this area of the DZone gives you all the tools you need to make this marriage happen. You can find both technical white papers and full-featured demos to learn from.

Summary

Dreamweaver is a full-featured program incorporating many new technologies. This chapter describes the substantial alternatives available to you for shortening your learning curve. Key methods include the following:

✦ The expansive electronic manual, Dreamweaver Help pages, which explains how to accomplish specific Web page building tasks through hyperlinked text and embedded multimedia.

✦ Built-in tutorials for learning how to get started with Dreamweaver, by making a Web page with some of the latest effects.

✦ Lessons showing how to use the most popular HTML features as created in Dreamweaver.

✦ The Reference panel offers detailed descriptions of HTML, JavaScript, and CSS syntax.

✦ A wealth of information, online. Constantly updated, always available, Dreamweaver's online resources are a tremendous benefit to any Web designer or developer, no matter what your level of skills.

In the next chapter, you see how to set up your first Dreamweaver site, step by step.

✦   ✦   ✦

Setting Up Your First Site

Web sites — especially those integrating Web applications — are far more than collections of HTML documents. Every image — from the smallest navigational button to the largest image map — is a separate file that must be uploaded with your HTML page. And if you use any additional elements, such as an included script, background sound, digital video, or Java applet, their files must be transferred as well. To preview the Web site locally and view it properly on the Internet, you have to organize your material in a specific manner.

In Dreamweaver, the process of creating a site also involves developing Web applications in a particular server model. Dreamweaver is unique in its ability to author sites for a variety of application servers. While it is feasible to mix pages developed for different server models, it's not really practical. Dreamweaver enables you to select one server model for each site.

Each time you begin developing a new site, you must define several initial parameters, including the chosen server model, as described in this chapter. These steps lay the groundwork for Dreamweaver to properly link your local development site with your remote online site as well as linking properly to your data sources. For those who are just starting to create Web sites, this chapter begins with a brief discussion of approaches to online design. The remainder of the chapter is devoted to the mechanics of setting up your site and basic file manipulation.

Planning Your Site

Planning in Web design, just as in any other design process, is essential. Not only will careful planning cut your development time considerably, but it also makes it far easier to achieve a uniform look and feel for your Web site — and thus make it friendlier and easier to use. This first section briefly covers some of the basics of Web site design: what to focus on, what options to consider, and what pitfalls to avoid. If you are an established Web site developer who has covered this ground before, feel free to skip this section.

Primary considerations

Even before you choose from various models to design your site, you'll need to address the all-important issues of message, audience, and budget.

What do you want to say?

If I had to pick one overriding concern for Web site design, it would be to answer the following question: "What are you trying to say?" The clearer your idea of your message, the more focused your Web site will be. To this end, I find it useful to try to state the purpose of a Web site in one sentence. "I want to create the coolest Web site on the planet" doesn't count. Although it could be regarded as a goal, it's so open-ended that it's almost no concept at all.

Here are some examples of clearly stated Web site concepts:

✦ "To provide the best small-business resource center focused on Microsoft's Office software."

✦ "To chronicle the world's first voyage around the world by hot air balloon."

✦ "To advertise music lessons offered by a collective of keyboard teachers in New York City."

Who is your audience?

Right behind a site's concept — some would say neck-and-neck with it — is the site's audience. Who are you trying to reach? Quite often a site's style is heavily influenced by a clear vision of the site's intended audience. Take, for example, Macromedia's Dynamic HTML Zone (www.dhtmlzone.com). This is an excellent example of a site that is perfectly pitched toward its target; in this case, the intended audience is composed of professional developers and designers. Hence, you'll find the site snazzy but informative and filled with exciting examples of cutting-edge programming techniques.

In contrast, a site that is devoted to mass-market e-commerce must work with a very different group in mind: shoppers. Everyone at one time or another falls into this category, so we're really talking about a state of mind, rather than a profession. Many shopping sites use a very straightforward page design — one that is easily maneuverable and comforting in its repetition, and one that enables visitors to quickly find what they are looking for and, with as few impediments as possible, buy it.

What are your resources?

Unfortunately, Web sites aren't created in a vacuum. Virtually all development work happens under real-world constraints of some kind. A professional Web designer is accustomed to working within a budget. In fact, the term *budget* can apply to several concepts.

First, you have a monetary budget — how much is the client willing to spend? This translates into a combination of development time (for designers and programmers), materials (custom graphics, stock photos, and the like), and ongoing maintenance. You can build a large site with many pages that pulls dynamically from an internal database and requires very little hands-on upkeep. Or you can construct a small, graphics-intensive site that must be updated by hand weekly. Yet it's entirely possible that both sites will end up costing the same.

Second, budget also applies to the amount of time you can afford to spend on any given project. The professional Web designer is quick to realize that time is an essential commodity. The resources needed when undertaking a showcase for yourself with no deadline are very different from contracting on June 30th for a job that must be ready to launch on July 4th.

The third real-world budgetary item to consider is bandwidth. The Web, with faster modems and an improved infrastructure, is slowly shedding its image as the "World Wide Wait." That means today's Webmaster must keep a steady eye on a page's weight — how long it takes to download under typical modem rates. Of course, you can always decide to include that animated video masterpiece that takes 33 minutes to download on a 28.8 modem — you just can't expect anyone to wait to see it.

In conclusion, when you are trying to define your Web page, filter it through these three ideas: message, audience, and the various faces of the budget. The time spent visualizing your Web page in these terms will be time decidedly well spent.

Design options

Many Web professionals borrow a technique used extensively in developing other mass-marketing forms: *storyboarding*. Storyboarding for the Web entails first diagramming the various pages in your site — much like the more traditional storyboarding in videos or filmmaking — and then detailing connections for the separate pages to form the overall site. How you connect the disparate pages determines how your visitors will navigate the completed Web site.

There are several basic navigational models; the modern Web designer should be familiar with them all because each one serves a different purpose and they can be mixed and matched as needed.

The linear approach

Prior to the World Wide Web, most media formats were linear — that is, one image or page followed another in an unalterable sequence. In contrast, the Web and its interactive personality enable the user to jump from topic to topic. Nevertheless, you can still use a linear approach to a Web site and have one page appear after another, like a multimedia book.

The linear navigational model, shown in Figure 6-1, works well for computer-based training applications and other expository scenarios in which you want to tightly control the viewer's experience. Some Web designers use a linear-style entrance or exit from their main site, connected to a multilevel navigational model. One advantage that Dynamic HTML brings is that you can achieve the effects of moving through several pages in a single page through layering.

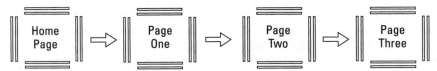

Figure 6-1: The linear navigational model takes the visitor through a series of Web pages.

Caution   Keep in mind that Web search engines can index the content of every page of your site separately. Each page of your site — not just your home page — then becomes a potential independent entrance point. So be sure to include, on every page, navigation buttons back to your home page, especially if you use a linear navigational model.

The hierarchical model

Hierarchical navigational models emerge from top-down designs. These start with one key concept that becomes your home page. From the home page, users branch off to several main pages; if needed, these main pages can, in turn, branch off into many separate pages. Everything flows from the home page; it's very much like a company's organization chart, with the CEO on top followed by the various company divisions.

The hierarchical Web site, shown in Figure 6-2, is best known for maintaining a visitor's sense of place in the site. Some Web designers even depict the treelike structure as a navigation device and include each branch traveled as a link. This enables visitors to quickly retrace their steps, branch by branch, to investigate different routes.

The spoke-and-hub model

Given the Web's flexible hyperlink structure, the spoke-and-hub navigational model works extremely well. The hub is, naturally, the site's home page. The spokes projecting out from the center connect to all the major pages in the site. This layout permits fairly immediate access to any key page in just two jumps — one jump always leading back to the hub/home page and one jump leading off to a new direction. Figure 6-3 shows a typical spoke-and-hub structure for a Web site.

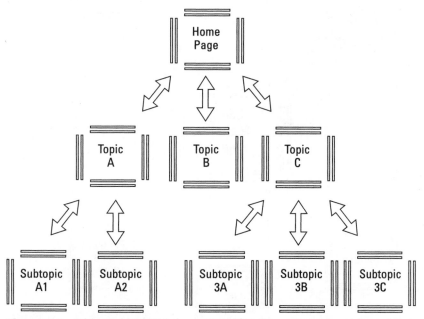

Figure 6-2: A hierarchical Web layout enables the main topics to branch into their own subtopics.

The main drawback to the spoke-and-hub structure is the constant return to the home page. Many Web designers get around this limitation by making the first jump off the hub into a Web page using frames, in which the navigation bars are always available. This design also enables visitors using nonframes-capable browsers to take a different path.

The full Web design

The approach that seems the least structured for a Web site — fullWeb — takes the most advantage of the Web's hyperlink capabilities. This design enables virtually every page to connect to every other page. The full Web design, shown in Figure 6-4, works well for sites that are explorations of a particular topic because the approach encourages visitors to experience the site according to their own needs, not based on the notions of any single designer. The danger in using full Web for your site design is that the visitor can literally get lost. As an escape hatch, many Web designers include a link to a clickable site map, especially for large-scale sites of this design.

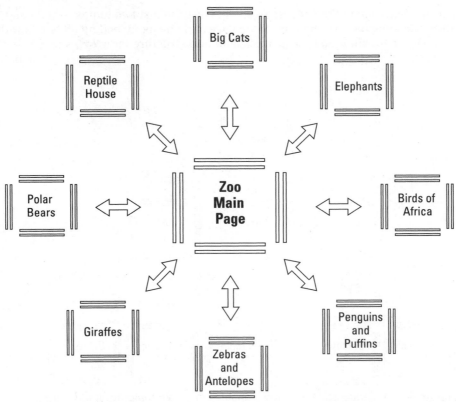

Figure 6-3: This storyboard diagram for a zoo's Web site shows how a spoke-and-hub model might work.

Defining a Site

Now that you've decided on a design and mapped your site, you're ready to set it up in Dreamweaver. When you define a site, you are telling Dreamweaver where to store your Web pages locally, where to transfer them to remotely, as well as the style of code in which to write them. Defining a site is an essential first step.

The Site Definitions dialog box is comprised of five categories of information. Only the first two — Local Info and Remote Info — are essential for site definition and are detailed in the remainder of this section.

Cross-Reference The other categories in the Site Definition dialog box (File View Columns, Site Map Layout, and Design Notes) are helpful for working in a team environment and working visually with Dreamweaver's Site Map. You can find more information on these features in Chapter 7.

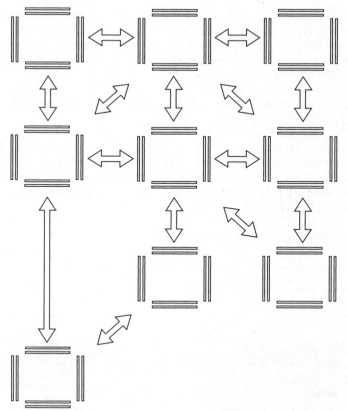

Figure 6-4: In a full Web design, each page can have multiple links to other pages

There are three main steps to defining a site in Dreamweaver:

1. Locate the folder to be used for the local, development site.

2. Enter the remote site information.

3. Specify the application server model to be used for the site.

Establishing local connections

Once your site is on your Web server and fully operational, the site consists of many files — plain HTML, graphics and other media files — that make up the individual Web pages. All of these associated files are kept on the server in one folder, which may use one or more subfolders. This main folder is called the *remote site root*. In order for Dreamweaver to properly display your linked pages and embedded images — just as they are displayed online — the program creates a mirror of your remote site on your local development system. This primary mirror folder on your system is known as the *local site root*.

It's necessary for you to establish the local site root at the beginning of a project. This ensures that Dreamweaver duplicates the complete structure of the Web development site when it comes time to publish your pages to the Web. One of Dreamweaver's key site-management features enables you to select just the HTML pages for publication; Dreamweaver then automatically transfers all the associated files, creating any needed folders in the process. The mirror images of your local and remote site roots are critical to Dreamweaver's ability to expedite your workload in this way.

Tip   If you do decide to transfer an existing Web site to a new Dreamweaver local site root, run Dreamweaver's Link Checker after you've consolidated all your files. Choose File ➪ Check Links or press the keyboard shortcut, Shift+F8. The Link Checker tells you of broken links and orphan files as well. For more information on the Link Checker, see Chapter 7.

To set up a local site root folder in Dreamweaver, follow these steps:

   1. Select Site ➪ New Site from the main Dreamweaver menu.

   The Site window opens, followed shortly by the Site Definition dialog box, as shown in Figure 6-5.

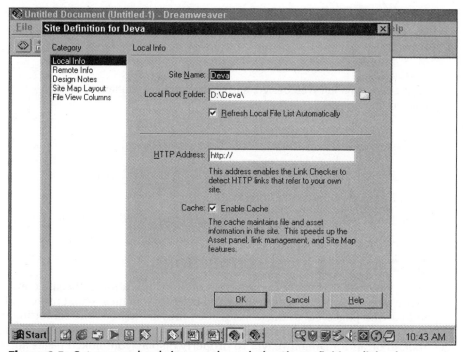

Figure 6-5: Set up your local site root through the Site Definition dialog box.

2. From the Local Info category, type a name for your site in the Site Name text box.

   This name appears in the user-defined site list displayed when you select File ➪ Open Site.

3. Specify the folder to serve as the local site root, by either typing the path name directly into the Local Root Folder text box or clicking the folder button. The Browse button opens the Choose Local Directory dialog box. When you've made your choice there, click the Select button.

4. Leave the Refresh Local File List Automatically option selected. This option ensures that new files are automatically included in the list and relieves you from having to select the Refresh command.

5. Enter the full URL for your site in the HTTP Address text box.

   When checking links for your Web site, Dreamweaver uses the HTTP address to determine whether absolute links, such as `http://www.idest/ Dreamweaver/index.htm`, reference external files or files on your site.

6. For fastest performance, select the Cache option.

   Typically, the use of the cache speeds up link updates.

Specifying the remote site

In addition to defining the local site root, you also need to detail information pertaining to the remote site. The remote site may either be a folder accessed through the local network or via FTP (File Transfer Protocol). If your remote site is located on the local network — in this arrangement the remote site is often said to be on a *staging server* — all you need do is select or create the particular folder to house the remote site. At the appropriate time, the network administrator or other designated person from the Information Technology department, will migrate the files from the staging server to the Web or intranet server.

Note
Many Dreamweaver developers have a Web server located on their development system making it possible to have both the local and remote site on the same machine.

If, on the other hand, you post your material to a remote site via FTP, you'll need various bits of information to complete the connection. In addition to the FTP host's name — used by Dreamweaver to find the server on the Internet — you'll also need, at a minimum, the user name and password to log into the server. The host's technical support staff will provide you with this and any other necessary info.

Caution
Although it's entirely possible to develop your site locally without establishing a remote site root, it's not a recommended practice. Web sites require extensive testing in real-world settings — something that's just not possible with a local development setup. If you don't have the necessary information to establish a remote site root initially, you can still begin development locally; just be sure to transfer your files to your remote site and begin testing as soon as possible.

To enter the remote site information, follow these steps:

1. Continuing in the Site Definition dialog box, select the Remote Info category.

2. From the Remote Info category, as shown in Figure 6-6, choose the type of remote connection that applies to your site:

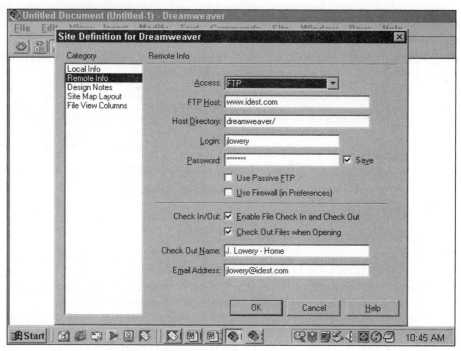

Figure 6-6: Choose whether your remote site is to be accessed via the local network or by FTP in the Web Server Info panel.

- **None:** Choose this option if your site is being developed locally and will not be uploaded to a Web server at this time.

  If you selected None for Server Access, proceed to entering the App Server Info as described in the next section.

- **Local/Network:** Select this option if you are running a local Web server and wish to store your remote site on your local drive or if your Web server is mounted as a network drive.

  If you selected Local/Network for Server Access, enter the name of the remote folder in the Remote Folder text box or click the Browse button to locate the folder. If you wish to automatically update the remote file list (recommended), leave the Refresh Remote File List Automatically option selected. Then proceed to entering the App Server Info as described in the following section.

- **FTP:** Select this option if you connect to your Web server via File Transfer Protocol (FTP).

- **SourceSafe Database:** Choose this option if your site is maintained within a SourceSafe database compatible with Microsoft Visual SourceSafe Client, version 6 on Windows or MetroWerks SourceSave version 1.10 on Macintosh.

- **WebDAV:** Select WebDAV (short for Web-based Distributed Authoring and Versioning) if your site is managed by a collaborative authoring system using WebDAV standards.

3. If FTP is selected, complete the following options:

- **FTP Host:** The host name of the FTP connection for your Web server, usually in the form www.sitename.com. Do not include the full URL, such as ftp://www.sitename.com/index.html.

- **Host Directory:** The directory in which publicly accessible documents are stored on the server. Typical Host Directory names are www/ public/docs/ and public_html/htdoc/. Your remote site root folder will be a subfolder of the Host Directory. If you are unsure of the exact name of the Host Directory, check with your Web server administrator for the proper directory path. Oftentimes the FTP Host connects to the correct directory automatically and this field is left blank.

- **Login:** The login name you have been assigned for access to the Web server.

- **Password:** The password necessary for you to gain access to the Web server. Many servers are case-sensitive when it comes to logins and passwords.

- **Save:** Dreamweaver automatically selects this option after you enter a password. Deselect this box only if you and others access the server from the current system.

- **Use Passive FTP:** Passive FTP establishes the FTP connection through the local software rather than the server. Certain firewall configurations use passive FTP; check with your network administrator to see if you need it.

- **Use Firewall:** This option will be selected for you if you've set the Preferences with the correct host and port information.

4. If SourceSafe Database is selected, choose Settings to display the Open SourceSafe Database dialog box. In the dialog box, complete the following:

- **Database Path:** Enter the path to the SourceSafe database; choose Browse to locate the database in a dialog box.

- **Project:** Enter the name of the project within the SourceSafe database; this will serve as the remote site's root directory.

- **Username:** Enter your login name.

- **Password:** Enter your password.

- **Save:** Keep the Save option enabled, unless you are sharing your system and want to log in into the database each time you access it.

5. If you're building your site with a team and using a WebDAV server, complete the following information:

- **URL:** Enter the absolute URL to the directory of your site on the WebDAV server.

- **Username:** Enter your login name.

- **Password:** Enter your password.

- **Email:** Enter your e-mail address. Unlike with Dreamweaver's own Check In/Check Out feature, an e-mail address is required with WebDAV.

- **Save:** Keep the Save option enabled, unless you are sharing your system and want to log in to the database each time you access it.

Note   Dreamweaver doesn't save the Site Definition information until the program exits. If Dreamweaver should "unexpectedly quit" — the politically correct term for "crash" — any changes made to the Site Definition dialog box in the session will be lost.

Managing Site Info

You can change any of the information associated with your local site roots by selecting File ➪ Open Site ➪ Define Sites (Site ➪ Open Site ➪ Define Sites) from either the main Dreamweaver menu or from the Site Window menu. Choose the site you want to modify from the Site list box at the top of the Site Information dialog box; you'll see the corresponding information for you to edit.

After your participation in a project has ended, you can remove the site from your list. Select File ➪ Open Site ➪ Define Sites (Site ➪ Open Site ➪ Define Sites) to open the Site Information dialog box, choose the site you want to remove in the Site list box, and click the Delete Site button. Note that this action removes the site only from Dreamweaver's internal list; it does not delete any files or folders from your hard drive.

With the local site root folder established, Dreamweaver can properly manage links no matter which address format is used. The various address formats are explained in the following section.

Creating and Saving New Pages

You've considered message, audience, and budget issues. You've chosen a design. You've set up your site and its address. All the preliminary planning is completed, and now you're ready to really rev up Dreamweaver and begin creating pages. This section covers the basic mechanics of opening and saving Web pages in development.

Starting Dreamweaver

Start Dreamweaver as you would any other program. Double-click the Dreamweaver program icon, or single-click if you are using Internet Explorer's Desktop Integration feature in Windows.

Building Placeholder Pages

One technique that I've found helpful over the years — and especially so with the use of document relative addressing in Dreamweaver Web projects — is what I call *placeholder pages.* These placeholder pages can fill the need to include links as you create each Web page in as effortless a manner as possible.

Let's say, for example, you've just finished laying out most of the text and graphics for your home page and you want to put in some navigational buttons. You drop in your button images and align them just so. All that's missing is the link. If you're using document relative addressing, the best way to handle assigning the link would be to click the Browse for File button in the Property Inspector and select your file. But what do you do if you haven't created any other pages yet and there aren't any files to select? That's when you can put placeholder pages to work.

After you've designed the basics of your site and created your local site root, as described elsewhere in this chapter, start with a blank Dreamweaver page. Type a single identifying word on the page and save it in the local site root. Do this for all the Web pages in your plan. When it comes time to make your links, all you have to do is point and click to the appropriate placeholder page. This arrangement also gives you an immediate framework for link testing. When it comes time to work on the next page, just open up the correct placeholder page and start to work.

Another style of working involves using the Site window as your base of operations, rather than the Document window. It's very easy in Dreamweaver to choose File ➪ New File from the Site Window menu several times and create the basic files of your site. You can even create a file and immediately link to it by choosing File ➪ Link to New File; a dialog box opens, allowing you to specify the file name, title of the new document and text for the link. Moreover, any needed subfolders, such as ones for images or other media, can be created by selecting File ➪ New Folder.

Opening Other Types of Files

Dreamweaver defaults to searching for HTML files with an extension of either .html or .htm. To look for other types of files, select the Files of Type arrow button. Dreamweaver allows several other file types, including server-side includes (.shtml, .shtm, or .stm), Active server pages (.asp), and Cold Fusion (.cfm or .cfml). If you need to load a valid HTML file with a different extension, select the All Files option.

If you are working consistently with a different file format, you can add your own extensions and file types to the Dreamweaver Open File dialog box. In the Configuration folder, there is an editable text file called Extensions.txt. Open this file in your favorite text editor to make any additions. If you use Dreamweaver, be sure to edit the file in the HTML Inspector to see the correct format.

The syntax must follow the format of the standard Extensions.txt file:

```
HTM,HTML,ASP,JSP,CFM,CFML,TXT,SHTM,SHTML,STM,LASSO,XML:
All Documents
HTM,HTML:HTML Documents
SHTM,SHTML,STM:Server-Side Includes
XML:XML Files
LBI:Library Files
DWT:Template Files
CSS:Style Sheets
ASP:Active Server Pages
CFM,CFML:Cold Fusion Templates
TXT:Text Files
PHP:PHP Files
LASSO:Lasso Files
JSP:Java Server Pages
```

After the splash screen, Dreamweaver opens with a new blank page. This page is created from the Default.html file found in the Dreamweaver/Configuration/ Templates folder. Of course, it's possible that you'll want to replace the original Default.html file with one of your own — perhaps with your copyright information. All of your blank pages will then be created from a template that you've created.

 Tip If you do decide to create your own Default template, it's probably a good idea to rename the Dreamweaver Default template — as Original-Default.html or something similar — prior to creating your new, personalized Default template.

Opening an existing file

If you're looking to work on a Web page in Dreamweaver that was created in another application, choose File ➪ Open, or the keyboard shortcut Ctrl+O (Command+O). From the standard Open File dialog box, you can browse to your file's location and select it.

If you have just started Dreamweaver or if your current document is blank, your selected file will load into the current window. If, however, you have another Web page open or have begun creating a new one, Dreamweaver opens your file in a new window.

When you first open an existing Web page, Dreamweaver checks the HTML syntax. If it finds any errors, Dreamweaver corrects them and then informs you of the corrections through the HTML Parser Results dialog box. As discussed in Chapter 4, you can turn off this HTML syntax-checking feature. Select Edit ⇨ Preferences and then, from the Code Rewriting category of the Preferences dialog box, deselect one or more of the checkbox options for HTML syntax-checking.

To add an entry, place your cursor at the end of the line above where you want your new file format to be placed, and press Enter (Return). Type in your file extension(s) in capital letters, followed by a colon and then the text description. Save the Extensions.txt file and restart Dreamweaver to see your modifications.

Opening a new window

You can work on as many Dreamweaver documents as your system memory can sustain. When you choose File ⇨ New or one of the keyboard shortcuts (Ctrl+N or Command+N), Dreamweaver opens a new blank page in a separate window. Once the window is open, you can switch among the various windows. To do this in Windows, you select the appropriate icon in the taskbar or use the Alt+Tab method. To switch between Dreamweaver windows on a Macintosh, click on the individual window or use the Window menu.

Opening a new page

After working for a while on a design, you sometimes need to start over or switch entirely to a new project. In either case, choose File ⇨ New or, in Windows, one of the keyboard shortcuts, Ctrl+Shift+N (Command+Shift+N). This closes the current document and opens a new blank page in the same window.

Tip   You can also drag and drop an HTML file onto the Dreamweaver Document window or — if you're just starting a session — onto the Dreamweaver icon on your desktop.

If you've made any modifications to your page, Dreamweaver asks if you would like to save the page. Click the Yes button to save the file or the No button to continue without saving it. To abort the new page opening, click Cancel.

Note   You can easily tell a page has been altered since the last save by looking at the title bar. Dreamweaver places an asterisk after the filename in the title bar for modified pages. Dreamweaver is even smart enough to properly remove the asterisk should you reverse your changes with the Undo command or the History palette.

Each time you open a new page, whether in the existing window or in a new window, Dreamweaver temporarily names the file "Untitled-n," where *n* is the next number in sequence. This prevents you from accidentally overwriting a new file opened in the same session.

Saving your page

Saving your work is very important in any computer-related task, and Dreamweaver is no exception. To initially save the current page, choose File ➪ Save or the keyboard shortcut Ctrl+S (Command+S). The Save dialog box opens; you can enter a filename and, if desired, a different path.

By default, all files are saved with a .htm filename extension for Windows and .html for Macintosh. To save your file with another extension, such as .shtml, change the Files of Type option to the specific file type and then enter your full filename, without the extension.

It seems kind of backward in this day and age of long filenames, but it's still a good idea to choose names for your files without spaces or punctuation other than an underscore or hyphen. Otherwise, not all servers will read the filename correctly and you'll have problems linking your pages.

Closing the page

When you're finished with a page you can close a file without quitting Dreamweaver. To close a page, select File ➪ Close or the keyboard shortcuts, Ctrl+W (Command+W). If you made any changes to the page since you saved it last, Dreamweaver prompts you to save it.

Windows users will note that if you only have one Dreamweaver window open and you close the current page, Dreamweaver asks you if you'd like to quit the program.

Quitting the program

Once you're done for the day — or, more often, the late, late night — you can close Dreamweaver by choosing File ➪ Exit (File ➪ Quit) or one of the standard keyboard shortcuts, Ctrl+Q (Command+Q).

In Windows systems, to make sure you're really ready to shut down the program, Dreamweaver asks you to confirm your desire to quit. If you're confident that you won't quit the program accidentally, select the Don't Warn Me Again option to stop this dialog box from reappearing.

You won't receive an opportunity to confirm your choice if you quit from the Site window in Windows or in Macintosh systems. That's because, on Windows, Dreamweaver's Site window and Document window are really separate applications.

Previewing Your Web Pages

When using Dreamweaver or any other Web authoring tool, it's important to constantly check your progress in one or more browsers. Dreamweaver's Document window offers a near-browser view of your Web page, but because of the variations among the different browsers, it's imperative that you preview your page early and often. Dreamweaver offers you easy access to a maximum of 20 browsers — and they're just a function key away.

Note Don't confuse Dreamweaver's Design view with the Preview in Browser feature. In Design view, Dreamweaver can only show you an approximation of how your page will look on the Web but not all aspects — such as links and rollovers — are active. You need to preview and test your page in a variety of browsers to truly see how your page looks and behaves on the Web.

You add a browser to your preview list by selecting File ➪ Preview in Browser ➪ Edit Browser List or by choosing the Preview in Browser category from the Preferences dialog box. Both actions open the Preview in Browser Preferences panel. The steps for editing your browser list are described in detail in Chapter 4. Here's a brief recap:

1. Select File ➪ Preview in Browser ➪ Edit Browser List.

2. To add a browser (up to 20), click the Add button and fill out the following fields:

   • **Name:** How you want the browser listed.

   • **Application:** Type in the path to the browser program or click the Browse button to locate the browser executable (.EXE) file.

   • **Primary Browser/Secondary Browser:** If desired, select one of these checkboxes to designate the current browser as such.

3. After you've added a browser to your list, you can easily edit or delete it. Choose File ➪ Preview in Browser ➪ Edit Browser List as before, and highlight the browser you want to modify or delete.

4. To alter your selection, click the Edit button. To delete your selection, click the Remove button.

5. After you've completed your modifications, click OK to close the dialog box.

Once you've added one or more browsers to your list, you can preview the current page in these browsers. Select File ➪ Preview in Browser ➪ BrowserName, where BrowserName indicates the particular program. Dreamweaver saves the page to a temporary file, starts the browser, and loads the page.

Note that in order to view any changes you've made to your Web page under construction, you must select the Preview in Browser menu option again (or press one of the function keys for primary/secondary browser previewing, described in the following paragraph). Clicking the Refresh/Reload button in your browser will not load in any modifications. The temporary preview files are deleted when you quit Dreamweaver.

Tip   Dreamweaver saves preview files with a file namelike this: TMP5c34jymi4q.htm; a unique name is generated with each preview to ensure that the browser does not load the page from the cache. If Dreamweaver unexpectedly quits, these TMP files are not deleted. Feel free to delete any TMP files you find in your site.

You can also use keyboard shortcuts to preview two different browsers, by pressing a function key: Press F12 to preview the current Dreamweaver page in your primary browser, and Ctrl+F12 (Command+F12) to preview the same page in your secondary browser. These are the Primary and Secondary Browser settings you establish in the Preferences/Preview in Browser dialog box, explained in Chapter 4.

In fact, with Dreamweaver's Preview in Browser Preferences you can so easily switch the designations of Primary and Secondary browser that you can use that setup for "debugging" a Web page in any browser, simply by changing the preferences. Go to the Preview in Browser Preferences pane, select the browser you want to use for debugging, and check the appropriate checkbox to designate the browser as Primary or Secondary. In the list of browsers in this Preferences pane, you'll see the indicator of F12 or Ctrl+F12 (Command+F12) appear next to the browser's name.

Tip   In addition to checking your Web page output on a variety of browsers on your system, it's also a good idea to preview the page on other platforms. If you're designing on a Macintosh, try to view your pages on a Windows system, and vice versa. Watch out for some not-so-subtle differences between the two environments, in terms of color rendering (colors in Macs tend to be brighter than in PCs) and screen resolution.

Putting Your Pages Online

The final phase of setting up your Dreamweaver site is publishing your pages to the Web. When you begin this publishing process is up to you. Some Web designers wait until everything is absolutely perfect on the local development site and then upload everything at once. Others like to establish an early connection to the remote site and extend the transfer of files over a longer period of time.

I fall into the latter camp. When I start transferring files at the beginning of the process, I find that I catch my mistakes earlier and avoid having to effect massive changes to the site after everything is up. For example, in developing one large site, I started out using filenames with mixed case, as in ELFhome.html. After publishing some early drafts of a few Web pages, however, I discovered that the host had switched servers; on the new server, filenames had to be all lowercase. Had I waited until the last moment to upload everything, I would have been faced with an unexpected and gigantic search-and-replace job.

Once you've established your local site root — and you've included your remote site's FTP information in the setup — the actual publishing of your files to the Web is a very straightforward process. To transfer your local Web pages to an online site, follow these steps:

1. Choose File ⇨ Open Site ⇨ Site Name (Site ⇨ Open Site ⇨ Site Name), where Site Name is the current site.

   The Site window opens, displaying the current site.

2. From the Site window, click the Connect button. (You may need to complete your connection to the Internet prior to choosing the Connect button.)

   Dreamweaver displays a message box showing the progress of the connection.

3. If you didn't enter a password in the Site Information dialog box, or if you entered a password but didn't opt to save it, Dreamweaver asks you to type in your password.

   Once the connection is complete, the directory listing of the remote site appears in the Remote (left-hand by default) pane of the Site window.

4. In the Local (right-hand by default) pane, highlight the HTML files you would like to transfer.

5. Click the Put button at the top of the Site window.

6. Dreamweaver asks if you would like to move the dependent files as well. Select Yes to transfer all embedded graphics and other objects, or No if you'd prefer to move these yourself. You can also select the Don't Ask Me Again box to make transfers of dependent files automatic in the future.

   Dreamweaver displays the progress of the file transfer in the Site window's status bar.

7. When each file transfer is finished, Dreamweaver places a green checkmark next to each file (if File Check In/Out has been enabled in the Site FTP Preferences pane).

8. When you've finished transferring your files, click the Disconnect button.

Remember, the only files you have to highlight for transfer to the remote site are the HTML files. As noted previously, Dreamweaver automatically transfers any dependent files (if you allow it), which means that you'll never forget to move a GIF again! (Nor will you ever move an unnecessary file, such as an earlier version of an image, by mistake.) Moreover, Dreamweaver automatically creates any subfolders necessary to maintain the site's integrity. These two features combined will save you substantial time and worry.

So now your site has been prepped from the planning stages, through the local site root, and onto the Web. Congratulations — all that's left is to fill those pages with insightful content, amazing graphics, and wondrous code. Let's get to it!

Summary

In this chapter, you studied some options for planning your Web site and what you need to do in Dreamweaver to initialize the site. This planning and initialization process is not a detailed one, but there are particular steps to take that can greatly smooth your development path down the road.

✦ Put as much time into planning your site as possible. The more clearly conceived the site, the cleaner the execution.

✦ Set up your local site root in Dreamweaver right away. The local site root is essential for Dreamweaver to properly publish your files to the remote site later.

✦ Preview early, often, and with various browsers. Dreamweaver gives you quick function-key access to a primary and secondary browser. Check your pages frequently in these browsers, and then spend some time checking your pages against other available browsers and browser versions.

✦ Establish an early connection to the Web and use it frequently. You can begin publishing your local site through Dreamweaver's Site window almost immediately.

In the next chapter, you'll learn how to publish your site to the Internet in Dreamweaver.

✦   ✦   ✦

Publishing with the *Site Window*

Site management is an essential part of a Webmaster's job description. Far from static designs, the Web site is not like a magazine advertisement that you're finished with as soon as you send the file to the printer. Publishing your Web site pages on the Internet is really just the first step in an ongoing—often day-to-day—management task.

Dreamweaver includes an integrated but separate window known as the Site window to handle all your Web management needs. With the Site window, you can do the following:

✦ Transfer files to your remote site from your local development site and back again

✦ Issue system commands to enable CGI programs on the server

✦ Monitor your Web site for broken links and orphaned files

✦ Check a file in or out during team Web development

This chapter covers these site management functions and more. However, before you begin exploring the Site window features, it's helpful to know a little more about site management in Dreamweaver.

Site Management with Dreamweaver

At the simplest level, *site management* means transferring your files from the local drive to a publishing server. This is standard File Transfer Protocol (FTP), and many designers are accustomed to working with tools such as WS_FTP and Fetch. These utilities, however, only help you to move files back and forth. In a medium-to-large Web site, other issues must be addressed. For instance, consider the following:

✦ What happens when a large group is working on a single Web site? What prevents the graphics designer from altering the same file the JavaScript programmer is modifying?

✦ How can you tell which version of your logo is the final one among the 15 working versions in your local site root folder?

✦ Do you have to update all your files every time some change is made to a few? Or can you only update those that have changed? How can you tell which ones have changed?

To help the Dreamweaver developer cope with these issues and avoid the type of frustration they can produce, a useful site management tool is included within Dreamweaver: the Site window. Its key features include the following:

✦ A quick, visual view of the elements of your site on your local and remote directories

✦ Fast drag-and-drop functionality for transferring files with dependent file support

✦ Site management check-in and check-out tools for groups working on files within the same Web site

✦ A Link Checker that helps you identify broken or unused objects being posted to your site

✦ A Site Map that enables you to both visualize your Web site structure and alter it

On Windows systems, the Site window runs as a connected but independent process, so that you can close your document window when you're finished designing and then publish your files to the Web through the Site window.

Note The Dreamweaver commands related to the Site window features are in different places on the Windows and Macintosh systems. In Windows, the Site window has its own menu bar; all the Windows-oriented references in this chapter refer to this menu. In addition, Dreamweaver includes a Site menu in the Document window that repeats many commands for easy access. Because Macintosh systems don't have a separate menu for a program's individual windows, Dreamweaver organizes the Site functions in a Site category of the main menu bar.

Setting Up a New Site

The first step in developing an effective site — one that links to other Web pages, uses images and library files, and offers other site root–relative links — is, of course, to establish a site. Dreamweaver has made this very easy to do.

Cross-Reference For complete, detailed information on establishing your initial site, see Chapter 6.

You need to create a folder on your development system that contains the entire HTML, as well as graphics, media, and other files, needed by the site. To create a new site, choose Site ⇨ New Site. The Site Definition dialog box opens with the Local Info category selected, as shown in Figure 7-1. Here you find the information and settings for the current site you are developing. Once you've entered this information, you seldom need to modify it.

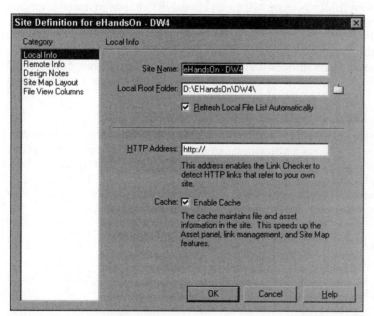

Figure 7-1: The Site Definition dialog box contains settings for the current site you are developing.

The data in the Site Definition dialog box is divided into five categories: Local Info, Remote Info, Design Notes, Site Map Layout, and File View Columns.

Local directory information

The local directory is in a folder on your development system, either on your own hard drive or on a network server.

Site Name

The site name is the name that appears in the Site ⇨ Open Site list. The site name is a reference only you need to know, and it can be as fancy as you want. No hard-and-fast rules exist for creating a site name, except you should keep the name simple so you can easily reference it later. In a large Web design firm, you may need to develop more structured methods for naming various clients' Web sites.

Local Root Folder

The Local Root Folder is the location on your hard drive, or in a network folder, where you place your HTML pages, images, plug-in files, and Library items. Remember, the root folder is essential to an effective Dreamweaver site. As you add links to other Web pages and images, Dreamweaver needs to maintain the relative links between files. The benefit of this becomes apparent when you upload your files to a Web server. By maintaining a root-relative relationship, you ensure that all of the files and associated images can transfer seamlessly together onto any Web site. You won't have to go back and replace the code for any broken images.

Refresh Local File List Automatically

When the Refresh Local File List Automatically option is selected, Dreamweaver updates the list every time Dreamweaver or any other program adds a new file. Although it takes a bit more processing power to constantly watch and update the folder, it's a helpful option and I recommend always selecting it. Without the option checked, you need to choose View ⇨ Refresh Local (Site ⇨ Site Map View ⇨ Refresh Local) or use the keyboard shortcut, Shift+F5, to see the latest files.

HTTP Address

The information entered in the HTTP Address field is used when you access the Link Checker. In this field, you enter the remote URL that corresponds to the local root folder, as if it were a regular Web address.

For example, say you are developing a Web site for My Frozen Custard, Inc. In the HTTP Address field, you would enter the URL for the Web site, as follows:

```
http://www.myfrozencustard.com/
```

With this information, the Link Checker can compare absolute addresses embedded in your Web page to see whether those addresses refer to internal or external files.

Cache

Put a checkmark in the Cache checkbox to speed up Dreamweaver's links and site management tasks.

Remote Info

The Remote Info category contains all of the information required for you to post your files to a remote server. The setup allows for any type of host directory. Typically, though, you upload your files to either a Unix or an NT Web server.

From the Remote Info category (see Figure 7-2), choose Local/Network from the Access drop-down menu to enter or select a folder on your hard drive or on the network from which your files will be served. If you're working on a big site in development with a team of Web-builders, you'll find Dreamweaver 4's new connectivity to SourceSafe databases and WebDAV servers extremely helpful. Should you choose either of these options for remote site access, you'll need to select the Settings button that appears and fill out the required information in the displayed dialog box.

Select FTP from the Access drop-down menu to be presented with a dialog box requesting information needed to access your remote site.

Tip If you don't know the name of your FTP host server or any of the other required host site information (directory, login, password, and firewall preferences), contact your ISP or system administrator. If a hosting server is not yet established, keep Server Access set to None.

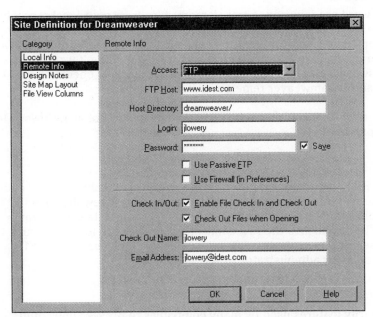

Figure 7-2: Information entered in the Remote Info category is essential for Dreamweaver to connect with your remote site.

FTP Host

The FTP Host is the name of the server on which you will be placing your files. The names for the host will be something like the following:

```
www.yourdomain.com
ftp.yourdomain.com
```

Do not include the protocol information, such as `http://` or `ftp://`, in the FTP host name.

Host Directory

The host directory is the one in which publicly accessible documents are stored on the server. Your remote site root folder will be a subfolder of the host directory. Here's an example of the host directory information:

```
/usr/www/htdocs/jlowery
```

If you don't know the proper directory path, check with your Web server administrator or ISP.

Login and Password

A login and password are required to transfer your files from your local root folder to the host. Your login is a unique name that tells the host who you are. Only you and the host should know your password. Every time you upload or download a file from the host server, you are asked for your password. If you don't want to have to retype your password each time you log on, just select the Save checkbox next to your password, and Dreamweaver remembers it.

Caution   For security reasons, it is highly recommended that you do not allow anyone to know your password.

Use Passive FTP

During a normal FTP process, one computer (the client) establishes a connection with another (the server) and then requests data to be sent. Firewall-protected servers do not allow the initial connection to be made, so no data can be transferred. Passive FTP establishes the FTP connection through the local software rather than the server. The majority of firewall configurations use passive FTP; check with your network administrator to see if you need it.

Use Firewall

Firewalls are security features used by many companies to prevent unwanted access to internal documents. Many different types of firewalls exist, and all have a multitude of security settings. For instance, some firewalls enable people within a company to move documents back and forth through the firewall without any problems. Other companies will not allow Java or ActiveX controls to be moved through the firewall.

If you have a firewall that requires additional security to upload and download files, you should enable the Use Firewall checkbox in the Site Definition window. Selecting this checkbox requires that you go to Dreamweaver Preferences and fill out additional information on proxy servers. A proxy server enables you to navigate files through a firewall.

To make the appropriate proxy server changes, go to Edit ➪ Preferences and choose the Site category from the Preferences dialog box. This category of settings contains selections for firewall information. Enter the firewall host name and port number, which can be provided to you by your ISP or system administrator. By default, most firewalls use port 21.

Check In/Out

You can enable or disable Dreamweaver's file management features by choosing the Check In/Out option. When you select Enable File Check In and Check Out, additional fields become available. You then can select the Check Out Files While Opening option, which automates the check-out process to some degree.

The name you enter in the Check Out Name field is used to inform others in your group when you have downloaded a file from the host server. Because the Check Out Name is one of several columns of information in the Local and Remote panes of the Site window, it's a good idea to keep the name relatively short. (Your initials are an ideal choice for Check Out Name, if that is appropriate.)

New Feature

If you enter your e-mail address in the aptly named field, Dreamweaver presents the check out name as a clickable link that invokes your system's e-mail editor to send a message. The E-mail Address feature enables team members to communicate directly with other team members who may have checked out a particular file.

Integrating Design Notes

Web sites can be complex creations, particularly when worked on by a team of designers, coders, and content providers. Dreamweaver offers a feature aimed at enhancing the communication between various team members: Design Notes. A Design Note can be attached to any Dreamweaver-created page, or any media inserted into a Dreamweaver page, and easily read from within Dreamweaver. Design Notes are also used extensively to facilitate the integration of Flash and Fireworks with Dreamweaver.

To be truly useful, the entire team needs to gain access to the Design Notes. Dreamweaver enables you to maintain the Design Notes on the remote server, as if another dependent file. The preferences in the Define Sites dialog box, shown in Figure 7-3, set up this option, and also give you a simple way to remove all unused Design Notes.

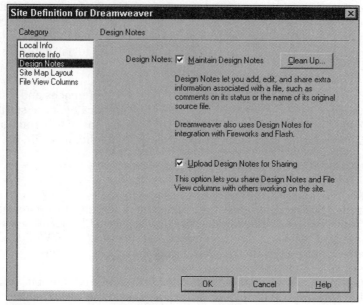

Figure 7-3: Use Design Notes to store information about HTML pages, graphics, or any other Web elements.

Options

Design Notes have only two options. The first option, Maintain Design Notes, enables Design Notes functionality for the site. It must be enabled to add or modify a Design Note for any page within the site. When a file is moved, this option also causes a Design Note to follow its associated file. The second option, Upload Design Notes for Sharing, "gets" or "puts" the Design Note when its associated file is transferred.

Tip   Design note files have an extension of .mno and are stored in a _notes folder. While they physically take up little room, typically under 1K, they greatly enhance your workflow, especially if you're using Fireworks and Flash. I strongly recommend that you keep Maintain Design Notes enabled.

Clean Up

If the Maintain Design Notes option is enabled and a Dreamweaver file is deleted from within Dreamweaver, the associated Design Note is removed also. However, if you delete, move, or rename your HTML files in any other way—with a file manager or other program—the Design Note remains. Select the Clean Up button to remove any Design Notes that no longer have associated HTML files.

Modifying the Site Map

You can control the way that Dreamweaver displays a Site Map in the Site Map Layout category (see Figure 7-4). In the Site Definition dialog box, select Site Map Layout from the Category list to access the Site Map options.

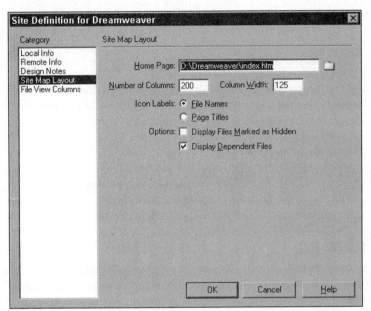

Figure 7-4: You can control what the Site Map shows as well as its overall appearance through the Site Map Layout category.

Home Page

By default, Dreamweaver looks for a file called index.html, index.htm, or default.htm (in that order) in your Local root folder from which to begin creating a Site Map. You can choose another page to appear at the top level of your Site Map by selecting a different file to serve as your home page.

Tip   It's best to include a home page if you plan on using the Site Map feature at all when defining the site. If one is not available, you can just enter the name for the file, like index.htm, in the Home Page field and press Tab; Dreamweaver will create the file for you.

Number of Columns/Column Width

These options (Number of Columns/Column Width) control the way your Site Map is displayed on your screen. You can modify these values in order to make the Site Map fit more easily onto a single page for printing.

By default, the Site Map displays horizontally. You can switch the layout to vertical by changing the Number of Columns field to 1.

Icon Labels

The Icon Labels option enables you to select whether the icons in your Site Map should be displayed using their filenames or their page titles. Page titles are derived from the <title> tag in the <head> section of an HTML document. While this method can be more descriptive, you have to remember to insert the title, either through the Page Properties dialog box — by revealing the Head Content, selecting the Title icon, and entering the desired text in the Title Property Inspector — or entering it into the Title field of the Document window's toolbar. If you don't assign each page a title, Dreamweaver uses "Untitled Document" as the title.

Options

Checking Display Files Marked as Hidden includes hidden HTML files in your Site Map Layout; checking Display Dependent Files includes non-HTML files, such as graphics image files or external JavaScript files, in your Site Map Layout.

File View Columns

Building a major Web site can be an organizational nightmare. Different teams — consisting of graphic artists, coders, and layout designers — are often working on different sections of the site at the same time. While certain pages are finished, others are in process, or have yet to be drafted. Even relatively small Web-design shops need to track the progress of their various clients' sites in order to be productive.

For Web developers, a major organizational advantage, now available in Dreamweaver 4, is the ability to create custom informational columns in the Site window's file view. The File View Columns feature works by storing information in an HTML or other file's Design Note; in essence, with a custom file view column, you can see what's in the Design Note at a glance. File view columns may also be re-ordered to put your project's most important details up front and less necessary built-in columns may be hidden.

Why are custom file view columns important? Let's say your team is working on a large site with a tight deadline. You need to keep track of which pages are completed and which need work. Create a custom file view column called Status, and then list for each file the percentage of completed work, such as 0%, 50%, or 100%. With one click of the Status column header, you can sort all the files, grouping them by the completed percentages, and instantly identifying which files need immediate attention. Add another custom column to include the name of the team member assigned to each page and you've got an instant contact list.

To add a new column in the file view, follow these steps:

1. Choose View ⇨ File View Columns from the Site window on a Windows system or Site ⇨ Site Files View ⇨ File View Columns on a Mac.

   The File View Columns category of the Site Definition dialog box appears.

2. Select the Add button.

   A new entry, initially called untitled, is added to the bottom of the column list.

3. In the Column Name field, enter a unique name to identify your column.

   There are no real restrictions for a column name, but it's best from a practical standpoint to keep them short.

4. In the Associate with Design Note field, enter a custom design note field or choose one of the existing fields from the drop-down list.

5. From the Align option, choose how the information is to be aligned in the column: Left, Center, or Right.

6. Make sure the Show option is selected.

7. To change the order in which your column is displayed on the screen — initially it's the final column, all the way on the right — use the Up and Down buttons to reposition the new column in the list.

   All of the built-in columns, except for Name, can also be moved to a new position. You can also hide a column by selecting it and deselecting the Show option.

8. Click OK when you're done.

With the custom column showing in the file view, enter information for that column in one of the following two ways:

✦ Right-click (control-click) on the filename and choose Design Notes. Then select the All Info tab of the Design Notes dialog box and enter the data in the Value field.

✦ In the file view pane of the Site window, click twice on the custom column for the file in question. The current information in the custom column, if any, will highlight and can be modified directly. Press Enter (Return) when you're done.

Using the Site Window

In Dreamweaver, some site commands, such as Put (which transfers a file from your local to remote site), can be called without using the Site window, but the Site window is "home base" for almost all of Dreamweaver's sitewide functions. You can open the Site window by any of the following methods:

✦ Choose Site ⇨ Open Site ⇨ Your Site.

✦ Select the Site button from the Launcher or Show Site from the Mini Launcher.

✦ Choose Window ⇨ Site Files.

✦ Press the keyboard shortcut F8.

The Site window is your vehicle for moving files back and forth between your local and remote folders. Figure 7-5 illustrates the various parts of the Site window.

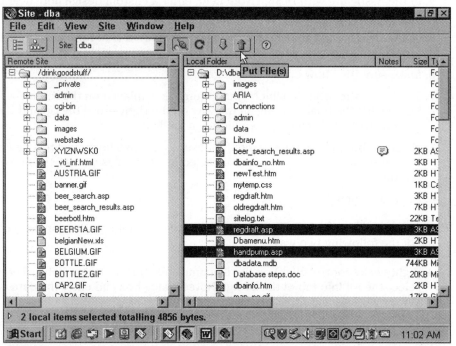

Figure 7-5: The Site window is used for transferring files to and from your remote Web server.

Cross-Reference   For detailed information on the Site Window preferences, see Chapter 4.

Remote Site and Local Root windows

The Site window is arranged in two main windows: By default, the remote site is on the left and the local root directory is on the right. These two windows enable you to view all the files contained within the two directories.

Another helpful view enables you to see which files have been most recently added or modified since the last FTP transfer. Choose either Select Newer Local or Select Newer Remote in the Edit menu (or on a Macintosh, Site ➪ Site Files View ➪ Select Newer Local or Site Files View ➪ Select Newer Remote). Dreamweaver compares the files within the two folders to see which ones have been saved since the last FTP session. The newer files are highlighted and can be easily transferred by selecting the Get or Put button (described in a later section).

Tip   In large sites, the Select Newer Remote operation can take a fairly long time to complete. If possible, selecting individual folders to be checked, while leaving the others unscanned, can speed up the process.

Connect/Disconnect button

The Connect/Disconnect button to the right of the Site drop-down list enables you to begin or end a live session with a remote host server. By clicking the Connect button, you start a new FTP session. You must have a way to connect to the Internet, and you must have a Remote server defined, when you select Connect. You won't see any information in the Remote Site pane until you connect to it.

After Dreamweaver has made the connection to your remote site — as identified in the Site Information dialog box — the Connect button becomes the Disconnect button. To end your FTP session with the host server, click the Disconnect button.

Tip   You can monitor all of your site management transactions by looking at the FTP Log. Select Window ➪ Site FTP Log (Windows) or Site ➪ FTP Log (Macintosh) from within the Site window. A new window pops up and shows you all your transactions as you perform them.

Get and Put buttons

Two of the most useful controls on the Site window are the Get and Put buttons. The Get button retrieves selected files and folders from the host server. The Put button transfers selected files from your local root directory to the host server. Dreamweaver offers several ways to transfer files in the Site window during an active FTP session.

To transfer one or more files from the local directory to the host server, use one of the following methods:

✦ Select the files from the Local Folder pane and drag them over to the Remote Folder pane.

✦ Use the keyboard shortcut — select the files and press Ctrl+Shift+U (Command+Shift+U).

✦ Highlight the files and choose Site ➪ Put.

✦ Select the files in the Local Folder pane and click the Put button.

If the file you are transferring has any dependent files, such as inserted images or Java applets, the Dependent Files dialog box (see Figure 7-6) asks if you want to include dependent files. If you select Yes, all such files are transferred. Select No to move only the file you selected.

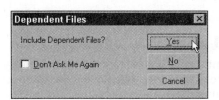

Figure 7-6: After selecting the HTML files, say Yes to the Dependent Files dialog box to transfer all the needed files.

Tip　　The Dependent Files dialog box includes a checkbox that asks if you want to be reminded of this feature again. If you choose this option, but later want the reminder to reappear, you can select either of the Dependent Files options from the Site category of Preferences. To bring up the Dependent Files dialog box on a case-by-case basis, press Alt (Option) when selecting the Get, Put, Check In, or Check Out buttons.

To transfer one or more files from the host server to the local folder, use one of these techniques:

✦ Select the files you want from the Remote Site pane and drag them over to the Local Folder pane.

✦ Use the keyboard shortcut — select the files and press Ctrl+Shift+D (Command+Shift+D).

✦ Highlight the files and select Site ➪ Get.

✦ Select the files in the remote directory and click the Get button.

Caution　　If you select either Site ➪ Get or the Get button without having selected any files in the Remote Site pane, all the files from your host server are moved. Dreamweaver does warn you, however.

Refresh button

As the name implies, the Refresh button re-reads the currently selected directory, whether locally or remotely. This can be useful when other people are working on the same site at the same time — refreshing your screen enables you to see if any additional files have been added or removed during your FTP session. You also need to refresh the Site window if you have modified a file during the FTP session. If you have enabled the Refresh Local Files Automatically option in the Define Site preferences, you only have to use this button to refresh the remote files. The Refresh button is found to the right of the Connect button.

The View (Windows) or Site ⇨ Site Files View (Macintosh) menu options also enable you to refresh the two windows. You can choose from two refresh commands: Refresh Local and Refresh Remote.

Stop Current Task button

Use the Stop Current Task button to halt the current transfer of files in an active FTP session. The Stop Current Task button is the octagonal red X button located in the lower-right corner of the Site window; it appears only while you are actually moving files.

Check Out/Check In buttons

The Check In/Check Out buttons, which are visible to the right of the Get and Put buttons only if you've selected the Check In/Out category in the Site Definition window (as previously shown in Figure 7-2), enable a user to officially check out an item from either the local or host server. The Check Out button provides a visual cue to everyone with access to the server that a file is currently in use. Details on how to use this feature are covered in the next section.

Checking a File In and Out

Your control over the files used for your Web site is very important if you are developing a site with a team. On larger sites, the various Webmaster chores — design, programming, and management — are distributed among several people. Without proper check-in and check-out procedures, it's easy for the same HTML page to get updated by more than one person, and you can wind up with incompatible versions.

Dreamweaver's Check In/Check Out facility solves this file-control problem by permitting only one person at a time to modify a Web page or graphic. Once a file has been checked out — accessed by someone — the file must be checked in again before another person using the Site window can download it and work on it.

Dreamweaver handles the functionality of Check In/Check Out very efficiently. Whenever you establish an active FTP session between your local root folder and the remote server, any files you get or put are displayed with a green checkmark. If other people in your group are also moving files back and forth, their transferred files are marked with a red checkmark. This method provides a quickly recognized, visual representation of the status of files you and your teammates are handling. Files that do not have either a red or green checkmark are not currently checked out by anyone and are available to work on.

If you want to see who is working on what, you can view user names in the Remote Site window. (You may have to scroll the window horizontally to see the column.) The name shown is the Check Out name that they use for logging on to the remote server. The Check Out name is entered through the Site Information dialog box.

Knowing who is working on what, and when, is a good control mechanism, but to really prevent duplication, site file control has to go one step further. Under Dreamweaver's Check In/Check Out system, when you transfer a file from your local root folder to the host server, the file on your local folder becomes read-only. Making the file read-only enables others to see the Web page but prevents anyone else from overwriting the file. The file must be checked in again before others can modify it.

Dreamweaver accomplishes Check In/Check Out by using a set of special files. When a file is checked out, a text file of the same filename but with the extension .lck is placed on the server. The .lck file contains the name of the user who checked out the file, as well as the date and the time that the file was checked out. The .lck files cannot be viewed in the Site window display but can be seen when a third-party FTP program is used.

Caution   Unfortunately, Dreamweaver is not able to make checked-out files in the host server read-only. This means someone in your group using an FTP program other than the Site window could easily overwrite the checked-out file on the server.

To check out one or more files, use any of the following methods:

✦ Select the files you want to transfer and then click the Check Out button at the top of the Site window. All the files are downloaded into your local folder and checked out in your name (denoted by a green checkmark).

✦ Select the files and choose Site ➪ Check Out.

✦ Select the files and use the keyboard shortcut Ctrl+Alt+Shift+D (Command+Option+Shift+D).

To check one or more files back in, do either of the following:

✦ Select the files you want to transfer and then click the Check In button at the top of the Site window. All of the selected files will be uploaded from your local folder to the remote site, and the green checkmark will be removed from their names.

✦ Select the checked-out files and choose Site ➪ Check In.

✦ Select the files and use the keyboard shortcut Ctrl+Alt+Shift+U (Command+Option+Shift+U).

To change the checked-out status of a file, use one of these methods:

✦ Select the file that's checked out and then click the Check In button at the top of the Site window.

✦ Select the file and choose Site ➪ Undo Check Out.

Synchronizing Local and Remote Sites

The necessity of having sets of files stored both locally and remotely often leads to confusion over which file is the most current. The problem is far more likely to occur if you're working in a team situation where numerous people are maintaining the same site.

Dreamweaver includes a one-step command to solve this local-remote dilemma: Synchronize. Found under the Site menu in Windows and on the menu bar in Macintosh systems, the Synchronize command ensures that the most current version of the same files is on both systems. Synchronize can also delete files on one site that do not appear on another. You can apply the Synchronize command sitewide or to selected files or folders.

To synchronize your files, follow these steps:

1. If you want to synchronize only selected files or folders, select those in the local pane of the Site window.

2. Choose Site ➪ Synchronize.

   The Synchronize Files dialog box opens, as shown in Figure 7-7.

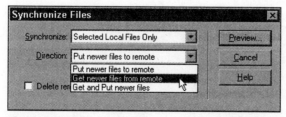

Figure 7-7: The Synchronize command makes sure that both the local and remote sites contain the same files.

3. To synchronize the full site, select Entire *Site Name* Site from the Synchronize list, where *Site Name* is the current site. Otherwise, choose Selected Local Files Only.

4. Set the direction of the synchronization:

   • **Put Newer Files to Remote:** Examines local files and transfers those with more recent modification dates to the remote server.

   • **Get Newer Files from Remote:** Examines remote files and transfers those with more recent modification dates to the local server.

   • **Get and Put Newer Files:** Transfers the most current versions of all files to and from both sites.

5. By selecting the Delete Remote Files Not on Local Drive option, you can remove any local files without a corresponding file on the server side when using the Get Newer Files from Remote direction. If the Put Newer Files to Remote direction is chosen with the Delete option, files on the remote site without a local equivalent are removed.

As with all file deletions, these operations cannot be undone. Use this feature with extreme care.

6. When you're ready, click Preview to begin the process.

   Dreamweaver compares the local and remote sites and begins displaying files in a new Site dialog box for confirmation, as shown in Figure 7-8. If no files are mismatched, Dreamweaver tells you that no synchronization is necessary.

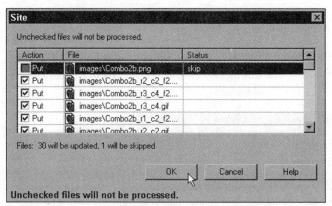

Figure 7-8: Confirm files to get, put, or to be deleted during the Synchronization process in the Site dialog box.

7. Deselect any file for action by removing its checkmark from the Action column.

8. Click OK when you're ready.

   Dreamweaver displays the process of the synchronization in the dialog box and the status bar of the Site window.

9. When the synchronization is complete, you can keep a record of the changes by selecting the Save Log button; if you do, Dreamweaver asks for a file location. When you're done, select the Close button.

Caution On Windows, if you have Dreamweaver windows open other than just the Site window, the Site dialog box may not appear on top of the Site window. Select the other Dreamweaver windows to find the Site dialog box.

Synchronization is a powerful tool in Dreamweaver's site management arsenal. However, care needs to be taken when first using the feature to make sure that team members' system clocks are in sync.

Checking Links

During a Web site's development, hundreds of different files and links are often referenced from within the HTML code. Unfortunately, it's not uncommon for a user to enthusiastically follow a link only to encounter the dreaded Web server error 404: File Not Found. Broken links are one of a Webmaster's most persistent headaches, because a Web page may have not only internal links pointing to other pages on the Web site, but external links as well—over which the Webmaster has no control.

Orphaned files constitute a parallel nightmare for the working Web developer. An orphaned file is one that is included in the local or remote site but is no longer actively referenced by any Web page. Orphaned files take up valuable disk space and can erroneously be transferred from an old site to a new one.

Dreamweaver includes, for the Web designer, a useful feature to ease the labor in solving both of these problems: the Link Checker. The Link Checker command can be used to check a single page, selected pages, a subfolder, or an entire site. Once the Link Checker has completed its survey, you can view broken links, external files (links outside the site, such as absolute references and mailto: links), and orphaned files. You can also repair broken links immediately or save the Link Checker results in a file for later viewing.

To check for links, follow these steps:

1. Make sure that the most current versions of the files have been saved.

2. To check a single document from within Dreamweaver, open the file and then choose File ➪ Check Links, or use the keyboard shortcut Shift+F8.

3. To check for links on an entire site from within Dreamweaver, choose Site ➪ Check Links Sitewide or use the keyboard shortcut Ctrl+F8 (Command+F8).

After Dreamweaver checks all the links on your page or site, it opens the Link Checker dialog box. The Link Checker dialog box, shown in Figure 7-9, provides a summary report of the broken links, external links, and when an entire site is reviewed, orphaned files. You can also use the Save button to store for future reference, in a tab-delimited text file, a report of the problems that the Link Checker has found.

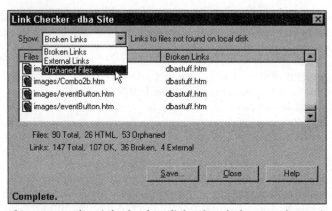

Figure 7-9: The Link Checker dialog box helps you determine which files have broken links and then fix the links directly.

When you list broken links, you can observe any file that is included as a link, inserted as an image, or embedded in the page, but which cannot be located. If you want to fix the broken link, you can do so by double-clicking the highlighted broken-link file. This brings up the file in Dreamweaver, where you can fix any problems using the Property Inspector. You can use the Property Inspector to locate the Src attribute. To open the page from the Link Checker, double-click the Dreamweaver icon next to the broken link.

You can also fix the link directly in the Link Checker window by following these steps:

1. Run the Link Checker command, either for the entire site or a single Web page.

2. In the Link Checker window, select the path and filename of the broken link you want to repair.

3. Enter the correct path for the missing file.

You can also access the Link Checker for both your local and remote folders. After you've selected your files or folders, choose File ➪ Check Links, from the main Dreamweaver menu, to check either the selected files or the entire Web site. Or, you can right-click (Control+click) any of the selected files to display the shortcut menu and choose the Check Link options from there.

Launching External Editors

As Web pages grow in complexity, many different types of media are involved in the creation of a page. Graphic editors, audio editors, word processors, spreadsheet programs, and database systems are all used in the creation and modification of files that can be included on a Web page — and the list grows daily. With Dreamweaver 4's capability to invoke editors for any file type, the workflow has been greatly simplified.

In Dreamweaver, you can assign an editor to any file type — actually you can assign multiple editors to the same file type for maximum flexibility. Because the editors are assigned according to file extension rather than kind of file, you can associate different editors for every different graphic format, if you so choose.

To launch a file's primary editor from the Site window, just double-click the file-name. If you have multiple editors assigned to a file type, you can open the file with an alternative editor by right-clicking (Control+clicking) the filename and choosing the editor from the Open With menu option. There's even a Browse option under the Open With menu to enable you to select an unassigned editor.

To learn how to set up editors for any media type, see the "External Editor Preferences" section in Chapter 4.

You may note that certain editors are preassigned on Windows systems. For example, on my system, if I double-click any .zip file, WinZip loads the archive. Dreamweaver recognizes file extension associations registered on your system. If a file extension has a particular association, it's listed under the Type category in the Site window. My file chap07.zip, for instance, is shown to be a WinZip file.

Macintosh users should check to see if the desired editor opens when the file is double-clicked before assigning new editors in Dreamweaver. On Macintosh, Dreamweaver uses system assignments through creator codes, if available.

Working with the Site Map

A Web site consists primarily of pages linked to other pages, which in turn can be linked to more pages. The more complex the site, the more difficult it becomes to comprehend — or remember — the entire structure when looking at just a directory listing.

With Dreamweaver, you can easily view your entire Web site and its links as a hier-archical tree using the Site Map feature. Not only do problems such as broken links jump out at you — after all, they're depicted in red — but also the Site Map can give you a much needed overview of the entire site. Poor site design can lead to visitors getting "lost" or frustrated with the number of links it takes to get to an important page. Dreamweaver's Site Map gives you a visual reference and enables you to cre-ate the structure for entire sites in a point-and-click environment.

The Site Map is a graphical representation of your site, with all its Web pages symbolized by icons, as shown in Figure 7-10. The Site Map resembles both an organizational chart and a flow chart. The Web site's home page is shown at the top of the chart. A link from one page to another is represented by a connecting line with an arrowhead. Any document, other than the home page, that is linked to additional pages indicates these pages with a plus or minus symbol in Windows systems and a right or down arrow in Macintosh systems. By default, Dreamweaver displays your Site Map only two levels deep. Selecting the plus/minus (arrow) symbols shows and hides the view of the linked pages on deeper levels.

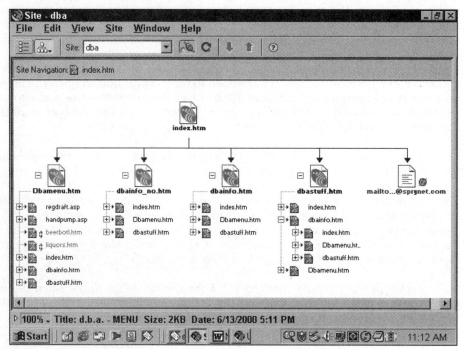

Figure 7-10: Clicking the Site Map icon in the Site window brings up a graphical representation of your site.

To open the Site Map from the Document window, choose Window ➪ Site Map or use the keyboard shortcut Alt+F8 (Option+F8). If the Site window is open, you can select the Site Map button to bring up the Site Map. The Site Map button has two settings, which you can activate by clicking and holding down the corresponding button. The Map Only setting displays just the Site Map. The Map and Files setting shows the Site Map in one pane of the Site window and the Local Files pane in the other.

The Site Map represents internal HTML pages with Dreamweaver page icons. If the link is good, the name is in blue type; if the link is broken, it's red. External files — files on another site — and special links, such as a `mailto:` or `javascript:` link, are indicated with globes. Initially, the Site Map displays only the HTML files, and not any hidden or dependent files, in a site. (Hidden and dependent files are covered later in this section.)

If your site has enabled Dreamweaver's Check In/Check Out features, you see additional symbols on the Site Map. A file checked out by you is indicated by a green checkmark. If someone else has checked out the file, the checkmark is red. It's not uncommon for teams to prevent an important Web page from being altered by making it read-only (Windows) or locking it (Macintosh). Such files are noted with a lock symbol.

To view a Site Map of your site, it must be in a local folder. To view a Site Map of a remote site, you must first download it to a local folder.

Storyboarding with the Site Map

Increasingly, Web designers lay out the structure of their sites in a process called storyboarding before filling in the details with text, image, and media content. This approach is all but essential on larger sites where development is divided among many people. In many ways, laying out the site's structure ahead of the content makes the content phase go much faster. You can, for example, pick an existing page (even if it is empty of content) from the Select File dialog box when building your links, rather than entering a nonexistent page's filename in the Link text box — and then trying to remember to create it later.

All you need to begin building your site with the Site Map is a single file, typically the site's home page. This home page is then defined as such in the Site Map Layout category of the Site Definition dialog box.

To create a Web site structure from the Site Map, follow these steps:

1. Open the Site Map by choosing Window ➪ Site Map or one of the other methods previously described.

2. Select the icon of the site's home page.

3. Choose Site ➪ Link to a New File (Site ➪ Site Map View ➪ Link to a New File). You can also right-click (Ctrl+click) the page's icon and choose Link to New File from the shortcut menu. Or use the key shortcut: Ctrl+Shift+N (Command+Shift+N).

   The Link to New File dialog box appears, as shown in Figure 7-11.

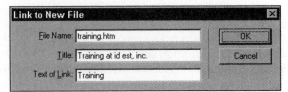

Figure 7-11: Use the Site Map to build the Web site's structure by creating new linked pages in one operation.

4. In the Link to New File dialog box, enter the correct filename, with an extension such as .htm or .html, in the File Name text box. Press Tab to move to the next text box.

5. Enter a title for the new page in the Title text box. Press Tab.

6. Enter the descriptive word or phrase to appear as a link on the original page in the Text of Link text box. Select OK or press Enter (Return) when you're done.

   The HTML page is created, and an icon for the new page appears, with a line connecting it to the original page.

7. To add another link to the home page, select the home page icon again and repeat Steps 3 through 6.

8. To add a new link to the newly created page, select its icon and repeat Steps 3 through 6.

When text links are added to a page, they are placed at the bottom of an existing page, one after another in the same line, like a text-only navigation bar. If the page is new, the text links are naturally the only items on the page.

Connecting to existing pages

Adding existing files to the Site Map is even easier than adding a new file, especially if the file to which you're linking is already in the same site. Part of building a Web-like structure is connecting from one page to another. With the Site Map, this is literally a drag-and-drop affair.

When an HTML icon is selected in the Site Map, a Point to File icon appears. The Point to File feature on the Site Map is basically used the same way it is on the Property Inspectors — just click the symbol and drag your pointer to another file. You can point and link to files in the current site whether or not they're already in the Site Map.

To link to a file that's in the current site but not on the Site Map (in other words, a file that's not linked to the home page or any connected pages), it's best to have both the Site Map and the Local Files panes displayed. To show both panes, select and hold down the Site Map button and then choose Map and Files from the drop-down list. Next, in the Site Map pane, select the file you want to link from — and a Point to File icon appears. Click and drag the Point to File icon from the Site Map to the Local Files pane to select the linking page. A line is drawn from the Point to File icon to the selected file, as shown in Figure 7-12. When your pointer is over the desired file, release the mouse button. The link is added, with a new icon appearing on the Site Map, and a text link is added to the originating page.

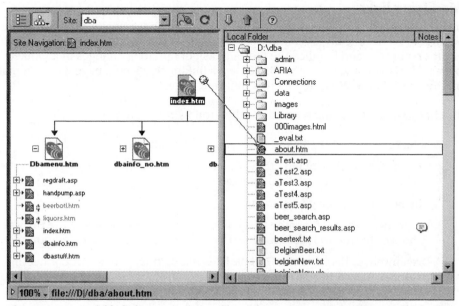

Figure 7-12: Quickly link to an existing file with Dreamweaver's Point to File feature.

If you're linking from one Site Map page to another, the Point to File icon is handy. Just select the originating page's icon and drag its Point to File symbol to the page you want to link to. Rather than draw another line across the screen — which would quickly render the Site Map screen indecipherable with crisscrossing lines — links to existing Site Map files are shown in italics.

Several other methods exist for linking to an existing file. First, you can open a Select File dialog box by selecting the originating file and then choosing Site ➪ Link to Existing File (Site ➪ Site Map View ➪ Link to an Existing File). The keyboard short-cut for this command is Ctrl+Shift+K (Command+Shift+K). You can also invoke the command by choosing Link to an Existing File from the shortcut menu, brought up by right-clicking (Control+clicking) the originating file's Site Map icon. Any of these techniques opens the Select File dialog box to enable you to browse for your file, which is useful for selecting files not in the current site.

If you want to drag and drop external files to create a link, you can use the Site Map in combination with the Windows Explorer or Finder, depending on your operating system. Instead of pointing from the originating file to the linked file, you drag the name or icon representing the external file from Windows Explorer (Finder) and drop it on the Site Map icon of the originating page. To accomplish this, it's best to either have the Site Map and Windows Explorer (Finder) windows side by side or, if they are overlapping, have the Windows Explorer (Finder) window in front.

Modifying links

If you have spent any time in Web site design and management, you know nothing is written in stone. Luckily, Dreamweaver 4 makes changing a link from one page to another a breeze and handles the tedious task of updating changes in all linked pages. Moreover, if you have multiple pages linking to a single page, you can make all the pages in the Web site link to a different page.

To change a link from one page to another, follow these steps:

1. Select the icon of the linked page you want to alter in the Site Map.

2. Choose Site ➪ Change Link (Site ➪ Site Map View ➪ Change Link) or use the keyboard shortcut Ctrl+L (Command+L).

   The Select File dialog box opens.

3. Enter the path and filename in the File Name text box or select the Browse (Choose) button to locate the file. Click OK when you've selected your file.

   Dreamweaver displays the Update Files dialog box with all the connecting pages, as shown in Figure 7-13.

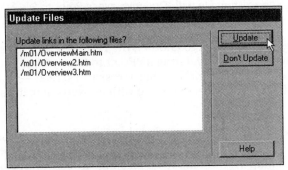

Figure 7-13: Changing a link in the Site Map brings up the Update Files dialog box.

4. To change the link in all the files, choose the Update button.

5. To change the link in some of the files, select the files first, using either the Shift+click or Ctrl+click (Command+click) method, and then choose the Update button.

6. To cancel the link change, choose the Don't Update button.

If you have multiple pages linking to a single page that you want to alter, you can change a link sitewide. Simply select the icon for the linked page you want to modify and choose Site ➪ Change Link Sitewide. As with the Change Link command, the Update Files dialog box opens; the balance of the procedure remains the same.

Tip

I recommend that you enable the Refresh Local File List Automatically option found in the Define Sites dialog box. Dreamweaver picks up changes made inside of its own program and outside of it — even the Site Map view is updated when a change is made on a page.

Deleting links

You can delete a link from one page in several ways. First, select the icon and then do any of the following:

✦ Press the Delete key (Windows only).

✦ Choose Site ➪ Remove Link (Site ➪ Site Map View ➪ Remove Link).

✦ Press Ctrl+Shift+L (Command+Shift+L).

✦ Right-click (Control+click) the icon and, from the shortcut menu, choose Remove Link.

In all cases, the link is deleted without confirmation, and the deletion cannot be undone.

Note

Deleting a link does not delete the file itself, just the link. For the text link, the href attribute is eliminated, but the actual text remains.

Changing titles

Dreamweaver 4 gives you an easy way to change a Web page's title right in the Site Map. Before you can use this feature, however, you must be sure the titles are used to identify the icons, rather than the filenames. Choose View ➪ Show Page Titles (Site ➪ Site Map View ➪ Show Page Titles) or use the keyboard shortcut, Ctrl+Shift+T (Command+Shift+T), to switch to a title view.

To retitle a Web page, click the title twice, slowly — make sure you don't double-click the title, which will open the file. Alternatively, you can select the icon and then click the title. You can also select the icon and then choose File ➪ Rename (Site ➪ Rename) from the menu. In Windows, F2 is the key shortcut. All of these methods make the title an editable field that you can then modify.

Modifying pages through the Site Map

Once you've created and refined your site structure, you're ready to begin adding the content. The Site Map enables you to open a single page or a collection of pages. You can even quickly locate the text or graphic that serves as the source for the link in the connecting page.

Open a page in Dreamweaver's Document window for editing by double-clicking the page's icon in the Site Map. To open more than one page, you must first select all icons. Multiple files can be selected by selecting one file and then Shift+clicking the additional files. Another method of multiple selection is to click into an empty area in the Site Map and then drag a rectangle around the desired files. After all the needed files are selected, choose File ⇨ Open Selection (Site ⇨ Open), and the key shortcut is Ctrl+Alt+Shift+O (Command+Option+Shift+O). Every file opens in a separate Dreamweaver Document window.

Occasionally, you need to go right to the source of a link. Dreamweaver 4 enables you to open the connecting page and instantly select the actual link used to make the connection. To view the actual text or graphic used to make a link, first select the file's icon in the Site Map. Then, choose Site ⇨ Open Source of Link (Site ⇨ Site Map View ⇨ Open Source of Link). Dreamweaver loads the page containing the link, opens the Property Inspector, and selects the link.

Altering the home page

As noted earlier, the Site Map assigns a home page to use as the base for its organization. As with most items in Dreamweaver, this assignation can be changed. But why would you want to change a Web site's home page? One of the primary purposes for the Site Map is to provide a visual representation of a site's structure — one that can easily be presented to a client for discussion. You can set up multiple views of a site, each with its own structure, by just switching the home page.

You can replace the home page with an existing page or a new one. To create a new page and make it the home page, select Site ⇨ New Home Page (Site ⇨ Site Map View ⇨ New Home Page). The New Home Page dialog box opens with two fields to fill out: File Name and Title. After you enter the needed information, the file is created, and the icon appears by itself in the Site Map. Now you can use the Link to Existing File and Link to New features to build your new site organization.

To change the home page to an existing file, choose Site ⇨ Set as Home Page (Site ⇨ Site Map View ⇨ Set as Home Page). The Select File dialog box opens and enables you to choose a new file. Once you've selected a file, the Site Map is recreated using the new file as a base and displaying any existing links.

Viewing the Site Map

The more complex the site, the more important it is to be able to view the Site Map in different ways. To cut down on the number of pages showing, Dreamweaver 4 enables you to hide any pages you choose. For maximum detail, you can also display all the dependent files (such as a page's graphics) in the Site Map. You even have the option of temporarily limiting the view to a particular "branch" of the Site Map. Dreamweaver also enables you to zoom out to get the big picture of a particularly large site or save the Site Map as a graphic.

Tip   If the Site Map columns are too narrow to see the full title or filename, use the ToolTips feature. Enabling View ➪ Tool Tips (Site ➪ Tool Tips) causes Dreamweaver to display the full text of the title or filename in a ToolTip box when your pointer passes over the name.

Working with hidden and dependent files

Web sites are capable of containing several hundred, if not several thousand, pages. In these situations, the Site Map can become overcrowded. Dreamweaver can mark any file (and its associated linked files) as hidden with a single command, View ➪ Show/Hide Link (Site ➪ Site Map View ➪ Show/Hide Link). The key shortcut is Ctrl+Shift+Y (Command+Shift+Y). The Show/Hide Link command is a toggle — applying it a second time to a file removes the "hidden" designation.

To see previously hidden files, choose View ➪ Show Files Marked as Hidden (Site ➪ Site Map View ➪ Show Files Marked as Hidden). Hidden files made visible are displayed in italics.

Dependent files include any image, external style sheet, or media file (such as a Flash movie). By default, dependent files are not displayed in the Site Map; however, you can opt to view them by choosing View ➪ Show Dependent Files (Site ➪ Site Map View ➪ Show Dependent Files). Once visible on the Site Map, you can send any image to its designated image editor by double-clicking its icon. You can also open the Styles panel by double-clicking any external CSS file.

Focusing on part of a Site Map

Most of the time, the overall view, centered on the Web site's home page, is most useful. Sometimes, though, you want to examine a section of the site in greater detail. Dreamweaver enables you to set any page to be treated like a temporary home page or root, ignoring all linking pages above it.

To view just a portion of your Web site, first select the page you wish to choose as the new root. Next, choose View ➪ View As Root (Site ➪ Site Map View ➪ View As Root) or use the keyboard shortcut Ctrl+Shift+R (Command+Shift+R). The Site Map now depicts your selected file as if it were the home page. Notice also that the Site Navigation bar has changed, as shown in Figure 7-14. The Site Navigation bar shows the actual home page and any pages that have been chosen as roots, separated by right-pointing arrows. You can switch from one root to another, or to the actual home page, by clicking its icon in the Site Navigation bar.

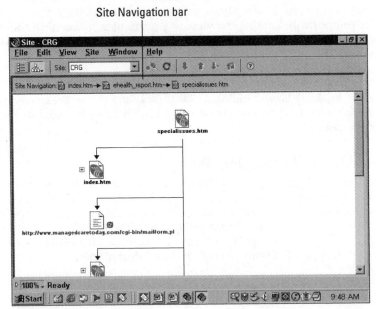

Figure 7-14: To view a section of your Site Map in detail, use the View As Root command.

Zooming out of your Site Map

What do you do when your site is so big that you can't see it all in one screen? Dreamweaver provides a Zoom feature that enables you to pull back for a more encompassing view. The Site Map Zoom button is located on the far left of the Site Window's status bar. Selecting the Zoom button reveals the magnification options to choose from: 100%, 75%, 50%, 25%, and 12%.

Tip　If you find that Dreamweaver is displaying page icons only, with no filenames or titles, you can expand the column width in the layout. Choose View ➪ Layout (Site ➪ Site Map View ➪ Layout) and change the value in the Column Width text box to a higher number. The default column width is 125 pixels.

Converting the Site Map into a graphic

Web designers like to believe that the whole world is wired and on the Web, but in truth, we're not there yet. Sometimes it's necessary to present a client or other interested party with a printout of a site design. Dreamweaver makes it possible to take a snapshot of the current Site Map and save it as a graphic file that can then be inserted into another program for printing—or attached to an e-mail for easy transmission.

To convert the Site Map into a graphic in Windows, choose File ➪ Save Site Map and then choose either BMP or PNG from the drop-down box in the Save box. On the Macintosh, choose Site ➪ Site Map View ➪ Save Site Map, and then the menu flies out to give you two file type options: Save Site Map as PICT or Save Site Map as JPEG.

When you save a Site Map as a graphic, the image is saved at the size necessary to contain all the displayed icons. Figure 7-15 shows a 352@ts1,118 pixel-sized graphic, saved from a Site Map, in Fireworks.

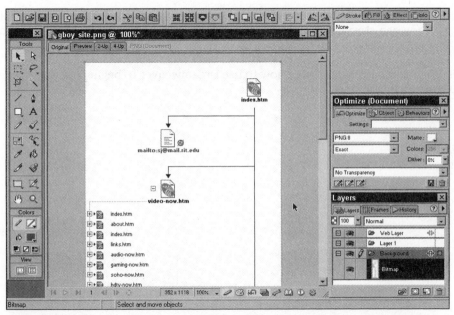

Figure 7-15: This Site Map image, ready for editing in Fireworks, was created in Dreamweaver.

Summary

With the Site window and Dreamweaver's site management tools, a group or an individual Web designer can manage even large and diverse sites.

✦ Setting up a new site is an essential element in managing a Dreamweaver Web site. Without the root directory for the local files, Dreamweaver cannot properly manage the Web pages and associated links.

✦ The Site window enables you to drag and drop files from the host server to the local root folder.

✦ All file check-in and check-out functions for teams can be handled through the Site window.

✦ Broken links can be quickly found and fixed with the Link Checker. You can also find orphaned files and identify external links.

✦ With Dreamweaver's Synchronize command, keeping your local and remote sites in sync is easier than ever.

✦ Dreamweaver's Site Map enables you to quickly visualize your overall site structure.

✦ The Site Map is also useful for creating new pages and their associated links. You can storyboard the entire site structure — links and all — before adding any content.

In the next chapter, you'll see how to use Dreamweaver to begin coding your Web pages.

✦   ✦   ✦

Using Basic HTML in Dreamweaver

Understanding How HTML Works

In a perfect world, you could lay out the most complex Web site with a visual authoring tool and never have to see the HTML, much less code in it. Dreamweaver takes you a long way toward this goal — in fact, you can create many types of Web pages using only Dreamweaver's Document window. As your pages become more complex, however, you will probably need to tweak your HTML just a tad.

This chapter gives you a basic understanding of how HTML works and gives you the specific building blocks you need to begin creating Web pages. Also in this chapter, you get your first look at a Dreamweaver 4 innovation: the new Code view for altering the code, side-by-side with the visual environment. The other Dreamweaver-specific material in this chapter — which primarily describes how Dreamweaver sets and modifies a page's properties — is suitable for even the most accomplished Web designers. Armed with these fundamentals, you are ready to begin your exploration of Web page creation.

The Structure of an HTML Page

The simplest explanation of how HTML works derives from the full expansion of its acronym: HyperText Markup Language. *HyperText* refers to one of the World Wide Web's main properties — the capability to jump from one page to another, no matter where the pages are located on the Web. *Markup Language* means that a Web page is really just a heavily annotated text file. The basic building blocks of HTML, such as `<strong>` and `<p>`, are known as markup elements, or tags. The terms *element* and *tag* are used interchangeably.

An HTML page, then, is a set of instructions (the tags) suggesting to your browser how to display the enclosed text and images. The browser knows what kind of page it is handling based on the tag that opens the page, <html>, and the tag that closes the page, </html>. The great majority of HTML tags come in such pairs, in which the closing tag always has a forward slash before the keyword. Two examples of tag pairs are: <p>...</p> and <title>...</title>. A few important tags are represented by a single element: the image tag <img>, for example.

The HTML page is divided into two primary sections: the <head> and the <body>. Information relating to the entire document goes in the <head> section: the title, description, keywords, and any language subroutines that may be called from within the <body>. The content of the Web page is found in the <body> section. All the text, graphics, embedded animations, Java applets, and other elements of the page are found between the opening <body> and the closing </body> tags.

When you start a new document in Dreamweaver, the basic format is already laid out for you. Listing 8-1 shows the code from a Dreamweaver blank Web page.

Listing 8-1: **The HTML for a New Dreamweaver Page**

```
<html>
<head>
<title>Untitled Document</title>
<meta http-equiv="Content-Type" content="text/html; charset=iso-8859-1">
</head>

<body bgcolor="#FFFFFF" text="#000000">

</body>
</html>
```

Notice how the <head>...</head> pair is separate from the <body>...</body> pair, and that both are contained within the <html>...</html> tags.

Also notice that the <body> tag has two additional elements:

    bgcolor="#FFFFFF"

and

    text="#000000"

These types of elements are known as *attributes*. Attributes modify the basic tag and either can be equal to a value or can stand alone; in this example, the first attribute, bgcolor, is set to a hexadecimal number that represents the color white and the second, text, is set to the hexadecimal value for black. Thus, this attribute sets the background color of the body — the page — to white and the default text color to black. Not every tag has attributes, but when they do, the attributes are specific.

One last note about an HTML page: You are free to use carriage returns, spaces, and tabs as needed to make your code more readable. The interpreting browser ignores all but the included tags and text to create your page. Some minor, browser-specific differences in interpretation of these elements are pointed out throughout the book, but by and large, you can indent or space your code as you desire.

Defining <head> Elements

Information pertaining to the Web page overall is contained in the <head> section of an HTML page. Browsers read the <head> to find out how to render the page — for example, is the page to be displayed using the Western, the Chinese, or some other character set? Search engine spiders also read this section to quickly glean a summary of the page.

When you begin inserting JavaScript (or code from another scripting language such as VBScript) into your Web page, all the subroutines and document-wide declarations go into the <head> area. Dreamweaver uses this format by default when you insert a JavaScript behavior.

Dreamweaver enables you to insert, view, and modify <head> content without opening an HTML editor. Dreamweaver's View Head Content capability enables you to work with <meta> tags and other <head> HTML code as you do with the regular content in the visual editor.

Establishing page properties

When you first start Dreamweaver, your default Web page is untitled, with no background image but a plain white background. You can change all these properties and more through Dreamweaver's Page Properties dialog box.

New Feature You can also change the document title in the Toolbar in Dreamweaver 4. Just enter the information in the Title field and press Enter (Return) to confirm the modification. You'll see the new title appear in the program's title bar and whenever you preview the page in a browser.

As usual, Dreamweaver gives you more than one method for accessing the Page Properties dialog box. You can select Modify ➪ Page Properties, or you can use the keyboard shortcut Ctrl+J (Command+J).

Tip Here's the other way to open the Page Properties dialog box. Right-click (Control+click) any open area in the Document window — that is, any part of the screen not occupied by an image, table, or other object (text outside of tables is okay to click, however). From the bottom of the Shortcut menu, select Page Properties.

The Page Properties dialog box, shown in Figure 8-1, gives you easy control of your HTML page's overall look and feel.

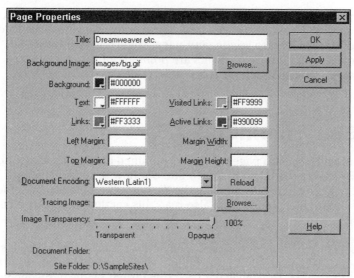

Figure 8-1: Change your Web page's overall appearance through the Page Properties dialog box.

 Note   Technically, some of the values you assign through the Page Properties dialog box are applied to the `<body>` tag; because they affect the overall appearance of a page, however, they are covered in this `<head>` section.

The key areas of the Page Properties dialog box are as follows:

Page Property	Description
Title	The title of your Web page. The name you enter here appears in the browser's title bar when your page is viewed. Search engine spiders also read the title as one of the important indexing clues.
Background Image	The filename of the graphic you want in the page background. Either type in the path directly or pick a file by clicking the Browse (Choose) button. You can embed the graphic of your choice in the background of your page; if the image is smaller than your content requires, the browser tiles the image to fill out the page. Specifying a background image overrides any selection in the Background color field.

Page Property	Description
Background	Click this color swatch to change the background color of the Web page. Select one of the browser-safe colors from the pop-up menu, or enter its name or hexadecimal representation (for example, "#FFFFFF") directly into the text box.
Text	Click this color swatch to control the color of default text.
Links	Click this color swatch to modify the color of any text designated as a link, or the border around an image link.
Visited Links	Click this color swatch to select the color that linked text changes to after a visitor to your Web page has selected that link and then returned to your page.
Active Links	Click this color swatch to choose the color to which linked text changes briefly when a user selects the link.
Left Margin, Top Margin, Margin Width, Margin Height	Enter values here to change the default margin settings used by browsers. The Left and Top Margin settings are used by Microsoft, whereas Margin Width and Margin Height are used by Netscape.
Document Encoding	The character set in which you want your Web page to be displayed. Choose one from the drop-down list. The default is Western (Latin 1).
Tracing Image	Selects an image to use as a layout guide.
Image Transparency	Sets the degree of transparency for the tracing image.

The Page Properties dialog box also displays the document folder if the page has been saved, and the current site root folder if one has been selected.

Cross-Reference The Tracing Image option is a powerful feature for quickly building a Web page based on design comps. For details about this feature and how to use it, see the section "Tracing Your Design with Layers" in Chapter 19.

Choosing a Page palette

Getting the right text and link colors to match your background color has been largely a trial-and-error process. Generally, you'd set the background color, add a contrasting text color, and then add some variations of different colors for the three different link colors — all the while clicking the Apply button and checking your results until you found a satisfactory combination. This is a time-intensive chore, to say the least.

Choosing Colors from an Onscreen Image

One of the features found throughout Dreamweaver, the Eyedropper tool, is especially useful in the Page Properties options. The Eyedropper tool appears whenever you open any of Dreamweaver's color swatches, such as those attached to the Background, Text, and Links colors. You can not only pick a color from the Web-safe palette that appears, but also use the Eyedropper to select any color on any page — including system colors such as those found in dialog boxes and menu strips.

To use the Eyedropper tool to choose a color for the background (or any of the other options) from an onscreen image, follow these steps:

1. Insert your image on the page and, using the vertical scroll bar, position the Document window so that the image and the Page Properties dialog box can be viewed simultaneously.

   If your image is too big to fit both it and the Page Properties dialog box on the same screen, temporarily resize your image by dragging its sizing handles. You can restore the original image size when you're done by selecting the Refresh button on the Image Property Inspector.

2. Open the Page Properties dialog box by choosing Modify ⇨ Page Properties or using the keyboard shortcut Ctrl+J (Command+J).

3. Drag the Page Properties dialog box to a place where the image can be seen.

4. Select the Background color swatch (or whichever one you wish to change).

   The Dreamweaver color picker opens and the pointer becomes an eyedropper.

5. Move the Eyedropper tool over the image until you find the correct color. (On Windows, you must hold the mouse button down as you drag the Eyedropper off the Dreamweaver dialog box to the image.) As you move the Eyedropper over an image, its colors are reflected in the color well and its hex value is shown on the color picker. Click once when you've found the appropriate color.

   The color picker closes.

6. Repeat Steps 4 and 5 to grab other colors from the screen for other color swatches. Click OK when you've finished modifying the page properties.

You don't have to keep the image on your page to get its color. Just insert it temporarily and then delete it after you've used the Eyedropper to grab the shade you want.

However, Dreamweaver ships with a command that enables you to quickly pick an entire palette for your page in one fell swoop. The Set Color Scheme command, shown in Figure 8-2, features palette combinations from noted Web designers Lynda Weinman and Bruce Heavin. The colors available in the command are all Web safe — which means that they will appear the same in the major browsers on all Macintosh and Windows systems without dithering.

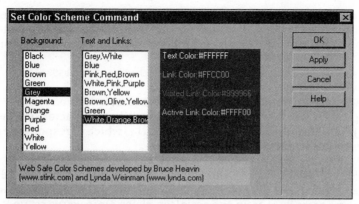

Figure 8-2: Get a Web-safe page palette with one click by using the Set Color Scheme command.

To use the Set Color Scheme command, follow these steps:

1. Choose Commands ➪ Set Color Scheme.

   The Set Color Scheme dialog box opens.

2. Select the background color from the Background column on the left.

   The Text and Links column is updated to show available combinations for the selected background color.

3. Select a color set from the Text and Links column to see various combinations in the Preview pane.

   The color names — such as White, Pink, Brown — refer to the Text, Link, and Visited Link colors, generally. If only one color name is offered, the entire color scheme uses shades of that color. Note that the background color changes slightly for various color combinations to work better with the foreground color choices.

4. Click Apply to see the effect on your current page. Click OK when you finish.

Understanding <meta> and other <head> tags

Summary information about the content of a page — and a lot more — is conveyed through <meta> tags used within the <head> section. The <meta> tag can be read by the server to create a header file, which makes it easier for indexing software used by search engines to catalog sites. Numerous different types of <meta> tags exist, and you can insert them in your document just like other objects.

One <meta> tag is included by default in every Dreamweaver page. The Document Encoding option of the Page Properties dialog box determines the character set used by the current Web page and is displayed in the <head> section as follows:

```
<meta http-equiv="Content-Type" content="text/html; charset=iso-8859-1">
```

The preceding <meta> tag tells the browser that this page is, in fact, an HTML page and that the page should be rendered using the specified character set (the charset attribute). The key attribute here is http-equiv, which is responsible for generating a server response header.

Tip   Once you've determined your <meta> tags for a Web site, the same basic <meta> information can go on every Web page. Dreamweaver gives you a way to avoid having to insert the same lines again and again: templates. Once you've set up the <head> elements the way you'd like them, choose File ➪ Save As Template. If you want to add <meta> or any other <head> tags to an existing template, you can edit the template and then update the affected pages. For more on templates, turn to Chapter 21.

In Dreamweaver, you can insert a <meta> tag or any other tag using the <head> tag objects, which you access via the Head category in the Objects panel or the Insert ➪ Head Tags menu option. The <head> tag objects are described in Table 8-1 and subsequent subsections.

Table 8-1
Head Tag Objects

Head Tag Object	Description
Meta	Inserts information that describes or affects the entire document.
Keywords	Includes a series of words used by the search engine to index the current Web page and/or site.
Description	Includes a text description of the current Web page and/or site.
Refresh	Reloads the current document or loads a new URL within a specified number of seconds.
Base	Establishes a reference for all other URLs in the current Web page.
Link	Inserts a link to an external document, such as a style sheet.

Inserting tags with the Meta object

The Meta object is used to insert tags that provide information for the Web server, through the HTTP-equiv attribute, and other overall data that you want to include in your Web page but not make visible to the casual browser. Some Web pages, for example, have built-in expiration dates after which the content is to be considered outmoded. In Dreamweaver, you can use the Meta object to insert a wide range of descriptive data.

You can access the Meta object in the Head category of the Objects panel or via the Insert menu by choosing Insert ➪ Head Tags ➪ Meta. Like all the Head objects, you don't have to have the Head Content visible to insert the Meta object; although you do have to choose View ➪ Head Content if you wish to edit the object. To insert a Meta object, follow these steps:

1. Select Insert ➪ Head Tags ➪ Meta or select the Meta object from the Head category of the Objects panel. Your current cursor position is irrelevant.

   The Insert Meta dialog box opens, as shown in Figure 8-3.

Figure 8-3: The Meta object enables you to enter a full range of `<meta>` tags in the `<head>` section of your Web page.

2. Choose the desired attribute: Name or an HTTP-equivalent from the Attribute list box. Press Tab.

3. Enter the value for the selected attribute in the Value text box. Press Tab.

4. Enter the value for the content attribute in the Content text box.

5. Click OK when you're done.

Built-in Meta Commands

Although Dreamweaver presents six different Head objects, `<meta>` tags form the basis of four of them: Meta, Keywords, Description, and Refresh. By specifying different `name` attributes, the purpose of the `<meta>` tags changes. For example, a Keywords object uses this format:

```
<meta name="keywords" content="dreamweaver, web, authoring, ¬
HTML, DHTML, CSS, Macromedia">
```

whereas a Description object inserts this type of code:

```
<meta name="description" content="This site is devoted to ¬
extensions made possible by Macromedia's Dreamweaver, the ¬
premier Web authoring tool.">
```

It is possible to create all your `<meta>` tags with the Meta object by specifying the name attribute and giving it the pertinent value, but it's easier to just use the standard Dreamweaver Head objects.

You can add as many Meta objects as you need to by repeating Steps 1 through 4. To edit an existing Meta object, you must first choose View ➪ Head Content to reveal the `<head>` code, indicated by the various icons. Select the Meta tag icon and make your changes in the Property Inspector.

Aiding search engines with the Keywords and Description objects

Let's take a closer look at the tags that convey indexing and descriptive information to search engine spiders. These chores are handled by the Keywords and Description objects. As noted in the sidebar, "Built-in Meta Commands," the Keywords and Description objects output specialized `<meta>` tags.

Both objects are straightforward to use. Choose Insert ➪ Head Tags ➪ Keywords or Insert ➪ Head Tags ➪ Description. You can also choose the corresponding objects from the Head category of the Objects panel. Once selected, these objects open similar dialog boxes with a single entry area, a large text box, as shown in Figure 8-4. Enter the values — whether keywords or a description — in the text box and click OK when you're done. You can edit the Keywords and Description objects, like the Meta object, by selecting their icons in the Head area of the Document window, revealed by choosing View ➪ Head Contents.

Caution   Although you can enter paragraph returns in your Keywords and Description objects, there's no reason to. Browsers ignore all such formatting when processing your code.

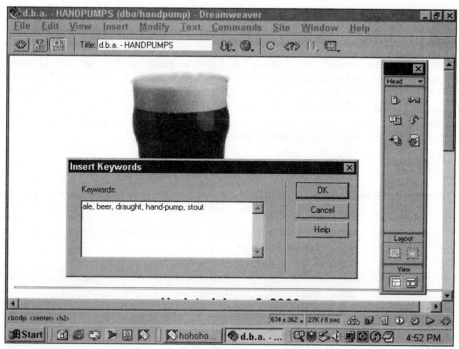

Figure 8-4: Entering information through the Keywords object helps search engines correctly index your Web page.

What you place in the Keywords and Description objects can have a big impact on your Web page's accessibility. If, for example, you want to categorize your Web page as an homage to the music of the early seventies, you could enter the following in the Content area of the Keywords object:

```
music, 70s, 70's, eagles, ronstadt, bee gees, pop, rock
```

In the preceding case, the content list is composed of words or phrases, separated by commas. Use sentences in the Description object, like this:

```
The definitive look back to the power pop rock stylings of early 1970s music, ¬
with special sections devoted to the Eagles, Linda Ronstadt, and the Bee Gees.
```

Keep in mind that the content in the Description should complement and extend both the Keywords and the Web page title. You have more room in both the Description and Keywords objects — really, an unlimited amount — than in the page title, which should be on the short side in order to fit into the browser's title bar.

Caution

When using <meta> tags with the Keywords or Description objects, don't stuff the <meta> tags with the same word repeated over and over again. The search engines are engineered to reject multiple words, and your description will not get the attention it deserves.

Refreshing the page and redirecting users

The Refresh object forces a browser to reload the current page or to load a new page after a user-set interval. The Web page visitor usually controls refreshing a page; if, for some reason, the display has become garbled, the user can choose Reload from the menu to redraw the screen. Impatient Web surfer that I am, I often stop a page from loading to see what text links are available and then — if I don't see what I need — hit Reload to bring in the full page. The code inserted by the Refresh object tells the server, not the browser, to reload the page. This can be a powerful tool but leads to trouble if used improperly.

To insert a Refresh object, follow these steps:

1. Choose Insert ➪ Head Tags ➪ Refresh or select the Insert Refresh object from the Head category of the Objects panel.

   The Insert Refresh dialog box, shown in Figure 8-5, opens.

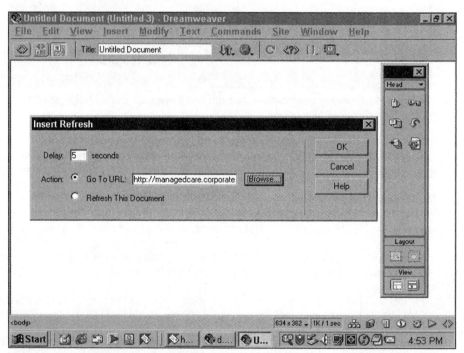

Figure 8-5: Use the Refresh object to redirect visitors from an outdated page.

2. Enter the number of seconds you want to wait before the Refresh command takes effect in the Delay text box.

   The Delay value is calculated from the time the page finishes loading.

3. Select the desired Action:

- Go to URL

- Refresh This Document

4. If you selected Go to URL, enter a path to another page in the text box or select the Browse button to select a file.

5. Click OK when you're done.

The Refresh object is most often used to redirect a visitor to another Web page. The Web is a fluid place, and sites often move from one address to another. Typically, a page at the old address contains the Refresh code that automatically takes the user to the new address. It's good practice to include a link to your new URL on the "change-of-address" page because not all browsers support the Refresh option. One other tip: Keep the number of seconds to a minimum — there's no point in waiting for something to happen automatically when you could click a link.

Caution

If you elect to choose the Refresh This Document option, use extreme caution for several reasons. First, you can easily set up an endless loop for your visitors in which the same page is constantly being refreshed. If you are working with a page that updates often, enter a longer Refresh value, such as 300 or 500. You should be sure to include a link to another page to enable users to exit from the continually refreshed page. You should also be aware that many search engines will not index pages using the meta refresh tag because of wide-spread abuse by certain industries on the Web.

Changing bases

Through the Base object, the `<head>` section enables you to exert fundamental control over the basic HTML element: the link. The code inserted by this object specifies the base URL for the current page. If you use relative addressing (covered in Chapter 6), you can switch all your links to another directory — even another Web site — with one command. The Base object takes two attributes: `Href`, which redirects all the other relative links on your page; and `target`, which specifies where the links will be rendered.

To insert a Base object in your page, follow these steps:

1. Choose Insert ➪ Head Tags ➪ Refresh or select the Insert Base object from the Head category of the Objects panel.

The Insert Base dialog box opens.

2. Input the path that you want all other relative links to be based on in the Href text box or choose the Browse button to pick the path.

3. If desired, enter a default target for all links without a specific target to be rendered in the Target text box.

4. Click OK when you're done.

How does a `<base>` tag affect your page? Let's say you define one link as follows:

```
images/backgnd.gif
```

Normally, the browser looks in the same folder as the current page for a subfolder named images. A different sequence occurs, however, if you set the `<base>` tag to another URL in the following way:

```
<base href="http://www.testsite.com/client-demo01/">
```

With this `<base>` tag, when the same `images/backgnd.gif` link is activated, the browser looks for its file in the following location:

```
http://www.testsite.com/client-demo01/images/backgnd.gif
```

Caution   Because of the all-or-nothing capability of `<base>` tags, many Webmasters use them cautiously, if at all.

Linking to other files

The Link object is used to indicate a relationship between the current page and another page or file. Although many other intended uses exist, the `<link>` tag is most commonly used to apply an external Cascading Style Sheet (CSS) to the current page. This code is entered automatically in Dreamweaver when you create a new linked style sheet (as described in Chapter 18), but to apply an existing style sheet, you need to use the Link object. The Link tag is also used to include TrueDoc dynamic fonts.

To insert a Link object, first choose Insert ➪ Head Tags ➪ Link or select the Insert Link object from the Head category of the Objects panel. This opens the Insert Link dialog box, shown in Figure 8-6.

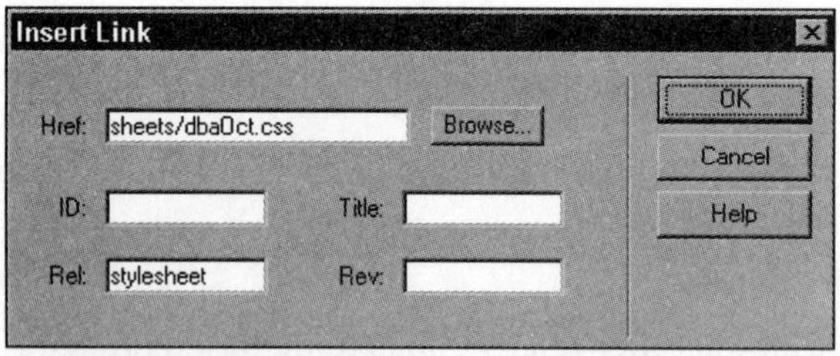

Figure 8-6: The Link object is primarily used to include external style sheets.

Next, enter the necessary attributes:

Attribute	Description
Href	The path to the file being linked. Use the Browse button to open the Select File dialog box.
ID	The ID attribute can be used by scripts to identify this particular object and affect it if need be.
Title	The Title attribute is displayed as a ToolTip by Internet Explorer browsers.
Rel	A keyword that describes the relationship of the linked document to the current page. For example, an external style sheet uses the keyword `stylesheet`.
Rev	Rev, like Rel, also describes a relationship but in the reverse. For example, if home.html contained a link tag with a Rel attribute set to intro.html, intro.html could contain a link tag with a Rev attribute set to home.html.

Note Aside from the style sheet use, there's little browser support for the other link functions. However, the World Wide Web Consortium (W3C) supports an initiative to use the `<link>` tag to address other media, such as speech synthesis and Braille devices, and it's entirely possible that the Link object will be used for this purpose in the future.

Adding to the <body>

The content of a Web page — the text, images, links, and plug-ins — is all contained in the `<body>` section of an HTML document. The great majority of `<body>` tags can be inserted through Dreamweaver's visual layout interface.

To use the `<body>` tags efficiently, you need to understand the distinction between logical styles and physical styles used in HTML. An underlying philosophy of HTML is to keep the Web as universally accessible as possible. Web content is intended to be platform- and resolution-independent, but the content itself can be styled by its intent as well. This philosophy is supported by the existence of logical `<body>` tags (such as `<code>` and `<cite>`), with which a block of text can be rendered according to its meaning, and physical style tags for directly italicizing or underlining text. HTML enables you to choose between logical styles, which are relative to the text, or physical styles, which can be regarded as absolute.

Logical styles

Logical styles are contextual rather than explicit. Choose a logical style when you want to ensure that the meaning, rather than a specific look, is conveyed. Table 8-2 shows a listing of logical style tags and their most common usage. Tags not supported through Dreamweaver's visual interface are noted.

Table 8-2
HTML Logical Style Tags

Tag	Usage
`<big>`	Increases the size of the selected text relative to the surrounding text. Not currently supported by Dreamweaver.
`<cite>`	Citations, titles, and references; usually shown in italic.
`<code>`	Code; for showing programming code, usually displayed in a monospaced font.
`<dfn>`	Defining instance; used to mark the introduction of a new term.
`<em>`	Emphasis; usually depicted as underlined or italicized text.
`<kbd>`	Keyboard; used to render text to be entered exactly.
`<s>`	Strikethrough text; used for showing text that has been deleted.
`<samp>`	Sample; a sequence of literal characters.
`<small>`	Decreases the size of the selected text relative to the surrounding text. Not currently supported by Dreamweaver.
`<strong>`	Strong emphasis; usually rendered as bold text.
`<sub>`	Subscript; the text is shown slightly lowered below the baseline. Not currently supported by Dreamweaver.
`<sup>`	Superscript; the text is shown slightly raised above the baseline. Not currently supported by Dreamweaver.
`<tt>`	Teletype; displayed with a monospaced font such as Courier.
`<var>`	Variable; used to distinguish variables from other programming code.

Logical styles are becoming increasingly important now that more browsers accept Cascading Style Sheets. Style sheets make it possible to combine the best elements of both logical and physical styles. With CSS, you can easily make the text within your `<code>` tags blue, and the variables, denoted with the `<var>` tag, green.

Caution

If a tag is not currently supported by Dreamweaver, you must enter the tag by hand—either through the Code Inspector, the Quick Tag Editor, or another text editor—and preview the result in a browser. For example, you can use the `<sub>` tag to create a formula for water (H20), but you don't see the subscripted 2 in the formula until you view the page through a browser.

Physical styles

HTML picked up the use of physical styles from modern typography and word processing programs. Use a physical style when you want something to be absolutely bold, italic, or underlined (or, as we say in HTML, `<b>`, `<i>`, and `<u>`, respectively).

You can apply the bold and the italic tags to selected text through the Property Inspector or by selecting Text ➪ Style; the underline style is available only through the Text menu.

With HTML version 3.2, a fourth physical style tag was added: `<font>`. Most browsers recognize the size attribute, which enables you to make the selected text larger or smaller, relatively or directly. To change a font size absolutely, select your text and then select Text ➪ Size; Dreamweaver inserts the following tag, where *n* is a number from 1 to 7:

```
<font size=n>
```

To make text larger than the default text, select Text ➪ Size Increase and then choose the value you want. Dreamweaver inserts the following tag:

```
<font size=+n>
```

The plus sign (+) indicates the relative nature of the font. Make text smaller than the default text by selecting Text ➪ Size Decrease; Dreamweaver inserts this tag:

```
<font size=-n>
```

You can also expressly change the type of font used and its color through the face and color attributes. Because you can't be sure what fonts will be on a user's system, common practice and good form dictate that you should list alternatives for a selected font. For instance, rather than just specifying Palatino — a sans serif font common on PCs but relatively unknown on the Mac — you could insert a tag such as the following:

```
<font face=" Palatino, Times New Roman, Times, sans-serif">
```

Caution

In the preceding case, if the browser doesn't find the first font, it looks for the second one (and so forth, as specified). Dreamweaver handles the font face attribute through its Font List dialog box, which is explained fully in Chapter 9.

Working with the Code View and Code Inspector

Although Dreamweaver offers many options for using the visual interface of the Document window, sometimes you just have to tweak the code by hand. Dreamweaver's acceptance by professional coders is due in large part to the easy access of the underlying code. Dreamweaver includes several methods for directly viewing, inputting, and modifying code for your Web page. For large-scale additions and changes, you might consider using an external HTML editor such as BBEdit or Homesite, but for many situations, the built-in Code view and Code Inspector are perfectly suited and much faster to work with.

New Feature

The Code view is the latest addition to Dreamweaver's code-savvy toolbox. With the addition of the Code view, you can either view your code full-screen in the Document Window, split-screen with the Design view, or in a separate panel, the Code Inspector. The underlying engine for all code views is the same — and, for Dreamweaver 4, the code editor has been rewritten from the ground up with significant enhancements to the feature set and performance.

To display the full-screen Code view:

✦ Select View ➪ Code.

✦ Choose the Show Code View button from the Toolbar.

The split-screen Code and Design view is revealed by:

✦ Choose View ➪ Code and Design.

✦ Select the Show Code and Design Views button on the Toolbar.

✦ Press Ctrl+Tab (Option+Tab) when in Design view and the Code Inspector is closed.

To change the relative size of the Code and Design views, drag the splitter bar up or down. In the split-screen Code and Design view, the Code view is shown on top of the Design view. You can reverse that order by choosing View ➪ Design View on Top or selecting Design View on Top from the View Options button on the Toolbar.

You have several ways to open the Code Inspector:

✦ Choose Window ➪ Code Inspector.

✦ Select the Show Code Inspector button in either Launcher.

✦ Use the keyboard shortcut F10.

Tip

To move between Design view and a code view, press Ctrl+Tab (Option+Tab). By default, this shortcut switches to Code view from Design view. However, if you are in the split-screen Code and Design view, this keyboard combination alternates focus between the two windows. If the Code Inspector is open, pressing Ctrl+Tab (Option+Tab) toggles the focus between Design view and the Code Inspector.

Once opened, the Code Inspector (Figure 8-7) behaves like any other floating panel in Dreamweaver: the window can be resized, moved, or hidden, and the inspector can be grouped with any other panel or dragged out onto its own. When the Code Inspector is opened initially, it is automatically selected. If you click in the Document window with the Code Inspector open, the inspector dims but still reflects changes made in the document.

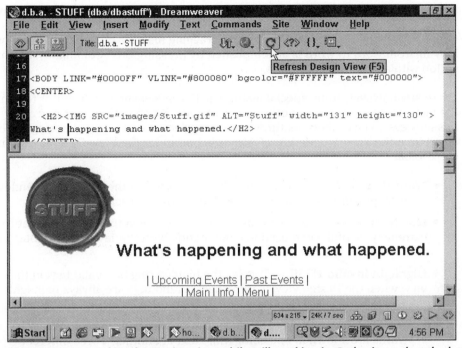

Figure 8-7: To update the Design view while still working in Code view select the handy Refresh button on the Toolbar or choose F5.

In all code views, Dreamweaver does not update the Design view of the document immediately — whereas changes in the Design view are instantly reflected in any open code view. This delay is enforced to enable the code to be completed before being applied. To apply modifications made in the code, switch to the Design view; if the Design view is open, click anywhere in it to give it focus. Should Dreamweaver detect any invalid HTML, such as an improperly closed tag, the offending code is flagged with a yellow highlight in both Design and Code views. Select the marked tag to see an explanation and suggestions for correcting the problem in the Property Inspector.

You can also apply code changes to the Design view by saving the document or by choosing the Refresh button on the Toolbar. The Refresh button becomes active only when modifications are made in any code view. You also have a keyboard and menu alternative: pressing F5 has the same effect as choosing View ➪ Refresh Design View.

By and large, the Code View and Code Inspector acts like a regular text editor. Simply click anywhere in the inspector to add or modify code. Double-click a word to select it. Select an entire line by moving your pointer to the left edge of the code — where the pointer becomes a right-pointing arrow — and clicking once.

Multiple lines can be selected in this same fashion by dragging the right-pointing arrow. Once a section of code is selected, you can drag and drop it into a new location; pressing the Ctrl (Option) key while dragging makes a copy of the selection. Moving from word to word is accomplished by pressing Ctrl (Command) in combination with any of the arrow keys.

There are, however, some special features in Dreamweaver's code editor to simplify the task of writing HTML and other types of code. When in Code or Code and Design view, some of these features can be toggled on and off by choosing the command from the View ➪ Code View Options list or under the View Options button on the Toolbar:

✦ **Word Wrap** — Wraps lines within the boundaries of the Code View window or Code Inspector to eliminate the need for horizontal scrolling.

✦ **Line Numbers** — Displays a number for every line in the code; this feature is extremely helpful when used in combination with the JavaScript Debugger, which reports the line number of an error in the code.

✦ **Highlight Invalid HTML** — Toggles the highlighting of invalid tags in the Code view when the Design view is refreshed. Invalid tags are always highlighted in the Design view.

✦ **Syntax Coloring** — Syntax coloring makes code easier to read. Basic tags and keywords are shown in one color while text in another. Three different types of code are given different colors: Reserved Keywords, Other Keywords, and Strings. These colors are set in the Code Color category of Preferences. You can also set a color for an individual tag to further distinguish it if you like.

Caution   Disabling coloring in the code has a rather unexpected repercussion. With Syntax Coloring disabled, the Reference panel is no longer context-sensitive. In other words, you cannot select a tag, attribute, or CSS style rule in the Code view and then select the Reference button to find that particular entry in the Reference panel.

✦ **Auto Indent** — Auto Indent is another feature intended to improve code readability. With Auto Indent enabled, pressing Enter (Return) at the end of a line causes the new line to start at the same indentation as the preceding line. Press Backspace (Delete) to move the indented line closer to left margin. The number of characters for each indentation is set in the Code Format category of Preferences.

You can also change the indentation — in or out — for selected blocks of code with one command. To further indent a block of code, select it and then choose Edit ➪ Indent Code or use the keyboard shortcut Ctrl+] (Command+]). To decrease the level of indentation for a selected code block, choose Edit ➪ Outdent Code or the keyboard shortcut Ctrl+[(Command+[).

New Feature As a further aid to help you find your way through a maze of code, Dreamweaver 4 includes the Balance Braces command. JavaScript is notorious for using parentheses, brackets, and curly braces to structure its code — and it's easy to lose sight of where one enclosing brace begins and it's closing mate ends. Dreamweaver highlights the content found within the closest pair of braces to the cursor when you select Edit ➪ Balance Braces or use the keyboard shortcut Ctrl-' (Command-'). If you select the command again, the selection expands to the set of surrounding braces. When the selection is not enclosed by parentheses, brackets, or curly braces, Dreamweaver sounds an alert.

Although most Web designers prone to using the code editor in Dreamweaver prefer to handwrite their code, the power of the Objects panel is still at your disposal for rapid code development. Any element available from the Objects panel can be inserted directly into the Code view or inspector. To use the Objects panel, you must first position your cursor where you would like the code for the object to appear and then select the element. You cannot, however, drag-and-drop an element from the Objects panel to the Code view or inspector.

Cross-Reference Keep in mind that the Dreamweaver's code editor is highly customizable. You can change the way the lines wrap, by using indents for certain tag pairs; you can even control the amount of indentation. All the options are outlined for you in Chapter 4.

Rapid Tag Modification with the Quick Tag Editor

I tend to build Web pages in two phases: First, I generally lay out my text and images to create the overall design, and then I go back, adding details and alterations to get the page just right. The second phase of Web page design often requires that I make a small adjustment to the HTML code, typically through the Property Inspector, but occasionally I need to go right to the source — code, that is.

Dreamweaver offers a feature for making minor but essential alterations to the code: the Quick Tag Editor. The Quick Tag Editor is a small pop-up window that appears in the Document window and enables you to edit an existing tag, add a new tag, or wrap the current selection in a tag. One other feature makes the Quick Tag Editor even quicker to use: A handy list of tags or attributes appears to cut down on your typing.

To call up the Quick Tag Editor, use any of the following methods:

✦ Choose Modify ➪ Quick Tag Editor.

✦ Press the keyboard shortcut Ctrl+T (Command+T).

✦ Select the Quick Tag Editor icon on the Property Inspector.

The Quick Tag Editor has three modes: Insert HTML, Wrap Tag, and Edit HTML. Although you can get to all three modes from any situation, which mode appears initially depends on the current selection. The Quick Tag Editor's window (Figure 8-8) appears above the current selection when you use either the menu or keyboard method of opening it, or next to the Property Inspector when you select the icon. In either case, you can move the Quick Tag Editor window to a new location onscreen by dragging its Title bar.

Tip   Regardless of which mode the Quick Tag Editor opens in, you can toggle to the other modes by pressing the keyboard shortcut Ctrl+T (Command+T).

Title bar   Hint list

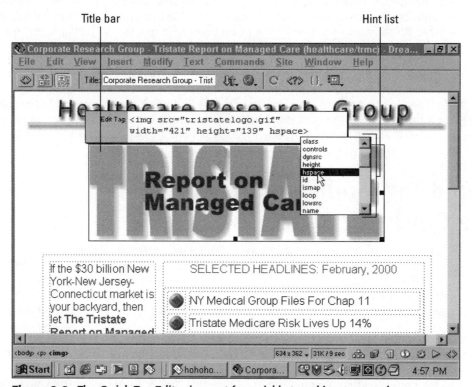

Figure 8-8: The Quick Tag Editor is great for quickly tweaking your code.

See the "Working with the Hint List" sidebar later in this chapter for details about this feature.

Insert HTML mode

The Insert HTML mode of the Quick Tag Editor is used for adding new tags and code at the current cursor position; it is the initial mode when nothing is selected. The Insert HTML mode starts with a pair of angle brackets enclosing a blinking cursor.

You can enter any desired tag—whether standard HTML or custom XML—and any attribute or content within the new tag. When you're done, just press Enter (Return) to confirm your addition.

To add new tags to your page using the Quick Tag Editor Insert HTML mode, follow these steps:

1. Position your cursor where you would like the new code to be inserted.

2. Choose Modify ⇨ Quick Tag Editor or use the keyboard shortcut, Ctrl+T (Command+T), to open the Quick Tag Editor.

   The Quick Tag Editor opens in Insert HTML mode, as shown in Figure 8-9.

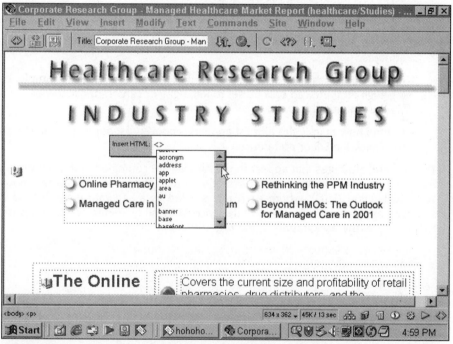

Figure 8-9: Use the Quick Tag Editor's Insert HTML mode to add tags not available through Dreamweaver's visual interface.

3. Enter your HTML or XML code.

Tip

Use the right-arrow key to move quickly past the closing angle bracket and add text after your tag.

4. If you pause while typing, the hint list appears, selecting the first tag that matches what you've typed so far. Use the arrow keys to select another tag in the list and press Enter (Return) to select a tag.

Working with the Hint List

The Quick Tag Editor has a rather nifty feature referred to as the *hint list*. To make it even quicker to use the Quick Tag Editor, a list of tags pops up when you pause in your typing. When you're entering attributes within a tag, a list of appropriate parameters pops up instead of tags. These lists are tied to what, if anything, you've already typed. Say, for instance, you've begun to enter **blockquote** and have only gotten as far typing **b** and **l**. When the hint list appears, it scrolls to "blink"—the first tag in the list starting with those two letters. If you continue typing "o," "blockquote" is selected. All you have to do to insert it into your code is to press Enter (Return).

Here's a few other hint list hints:

✦ Scroll to a tag by using the up- or down-arrow keys.

✦ Double-clicking the selected hint list item also inserts it into the code.

✦ Once the hint list is open, press Esc if you decide not to enter the selected tag or attribute.

✦ If an attribute has a set series of values that can be applied (for example, the `<div>` tag align attribute can only be set to left, right, or center), those values are accessible via the hint list.

✦ Control how quickly the hint list appears—or even if it appears at all—by altering the Quick Tag Editor preferences.

The tags and attributes that appear in the hint list are contained in the TagAttributeList.text file found in the Dreamweaver Configuration folder. The list is in a format known as Data Type Declaration (DTD), where each tag is listed as a separate element and any corresponding attributes are displayed under each of those elements. Here, for example, is the DTD listing for the background sound tag, `<bgsound>`:

```
<!ELEMENT BGSOUND Name="Background sound" >
<!ATTLIST BGSOUND
      Balance
      Loop
      Src
      Volume
>
```

As with almost all other Dreamweaver aspects, the TagAttribute.txt list can be modified to include any special tags and their attributes you might need to include on a regular basis. Just relaunch Dreamweaver after making your changes in a standard text editor and your modifications are included the next time you use the Quick Tag Editor.

    5. Press Enter (Return) when you're done.

The Quick Tag Editor is fairly intelligent and tries to help you write valid HTML. If, for example, you leave off a closing tag, such as `</b>`, the Quick Tag Editor automatically adds it for you.

Wrap Tag mode

Part of the power and flexibility of HTML is the capability to wrap one tag around one or more other tags and content. To make a phrase appear bold and italic, the code is written this way:

```
<b><i>On Sale Now!</i></b>
```

Note how the inner `<i>...</i>` tag pair is enclosed by the `<b>...</b>` pair. The Wrap Tag mode of the Quick Tag Editor surrounds any selection with your entered tag in one easy operation.

The Wrap Tag mode appears initially when you have selected just text (with no surrounding tags) or an incomplete tag (the opening tag and contents but no closing tag). The Wrap Tag mode is visually similar to the Insert HTML mode, as can be seen in Figure 8-10. However, rather than just include exactly what you've entered into the Quick Tag Editor, Wrap Tag mode also inserts a closing tag that corresponds to your entry. For example, let's say I want to apply a tag not available in Dreamweaver's Document window, the subscript or `<sub>` tag. After highlighting the text I want to mark up as subscript (a "2" in the formula, H_2O, for example), I open the Quick Tag Editor and enter **sub**. The resulting code looks like this:

```
H<sub>2</sub>O
```

Caution   You can only enter one tag in Wrap Tag mode; if more than one tag is entered, Dreamweaver displays an alert informing you that the tag you've entered appears to be invalid HTML. The Quick Tag Editor is then closed, and the selection is cleared.

To wrap a tag with the Quick Tag Editor, follow these steps:

1. Select the text or tags you want to enclose in another tag.

2. Choose Modify ➪ Quick Tag Editor or use the keyboard shortcut, Ctrl+T (Command+T), to open the Quick Tag Editor.

   The Quick Tag Editor opens in Wrap Tag mode.

3. If you select a complete tag, the Quick Tag Editor opens in Edit HTML mode; press the keyboard shortcut, Ctrl+T (Command+T), to toggle to Wrap Tag mode.

4. Enter the desired tag.

5. If you pause while typing, the hint list appears, selecting the first tag that matches what you've typed so far. Use the arrow keys to select another tag in the list and press Enter (Return) to select a tag from the hint list.

6. Press Enter (Return) to confirm your tag.

   The Quick Tag Editor closes and Dreamweaver adds your tag before your selection and a corresponding closing tag after it.

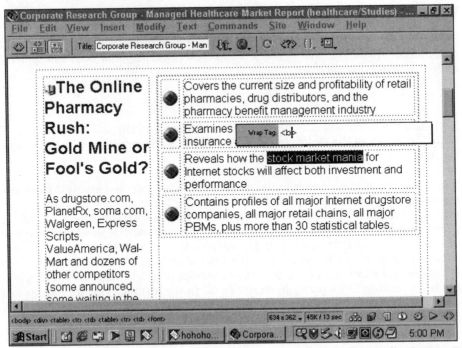

Figure 8-10: Enclose any selection with a tag by using the Quick Tag Editor's Wrap Tag mode.

Edit HTML mode

If a complete tag — either a single tag, such as `<img>`, or a tag pair, such as `<h1>...</h1>` — is selected, the Quick Tag Editor opens in Edit HTML mode. Unlike the other two modes where you are presented with just open and closing angle brackets and a flashing cursor, the Edit HTML mode displays the entire selected tag with all the attributes, if any. The Edit HTML mode is always invoked when you start the Quick Tag Editor by clicking its icon in the Property Inspector.

The Edit HTML mode has many uses. I've found it to be terrific for adding a parameter not found on Dreamweaver's Property Inspector. For example, when building a form that returns the information formatted, you need to declare the enctype attribute to be equal to "text/plain." However, the enctype attribute cannot be assigned from the Property Inspector for the `<form>` tag. So, I just select the tag from the Tag Selector and then click the Quick Tag Editor icon to open the Quick Tag Editor. The `<form>` tag appears with my current parameters, as shown in Figure 8-11.

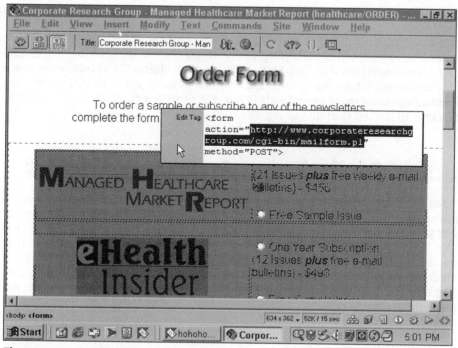

Figure 8-11: In Edit HTML mode, the Quick Tag Editor shows the entire tag with attributes and their values.

To use the Quick Tag Editor in Insert HTML mode, follow these steps:

1. Select an entire tag by clicking its name in the Tag Selector.

2. Choose Modify ➪ Quick Tag Editor.

3. To change an existing attribute, tab to the current value and enter a new one.

4. To add a new attribute, tab and/or use the arrow keys to position the cursor after an existing attribute or after the tag and enter the new parameter and value.

Tip

If you don't close the quotation marks for a parameter's value, Dreamweaver does it for you.

5. If you pause briefly while entering a new attribute, the hint list appears with attributes appropriate for the current tag. If you select an attribute from the hint list, press Enter (Return) to accept the parameter.

6. When you're done editing the tag, press Enter (Return).

In addition to this capability to edit complete tags, Dreamweaver has a couple of navigational commands to help select just the right tag. The Select Parent Tag command—keyboard shortcut Ctrl+Shift+< (Command+Shift+<)—highlights the tag immediately surrounding the present tag. Going the other direction, Select Child Tag—keyboard shortcut Ctrl+Shift+> (Command+Shift+>)—chooses the next tag, if any, contained within the current tag. Both commands are available under the Edit menu. Exercising these commands is equivalent to selecting the next tag in the Tag Selector to the left (parent) or right (child).

Inserting Symbols and Special Characters

When working with Dreamweaver, you're usually entering text directly from your keyboard, one keystroke at a time, with each keystroke representing a letter, number, or other keyboard character. Some situations, however, require special letters that have diacritics or common symbols, such as the copyright mark, which are outside of the regular, standard character set represented on your keyboard. HTML enables you to insert a full range of such character entities through two systems. The more familiar special characters have been assigned a mnemonic code name to make them easy to remember; these are called *named characters*. Less typical characters must be inserted by entering a numeric code; these are known as *decimal characters*. For the sake of completeness, named characters also have a corresponding decimal character code.

Both named and decimal character codes begin with an ampersand (&) symbol and end with a semicolon (;). For example, the HTML code for an ampersand symbol follows:

    &

Its decimal character equivalent follows:

    &

Caution   If, during the browser-testing phase of creating your Web page, you suddenly see an HTML code onscreen rather than a symbol, double-check your HTML. The code could be just a typo; you may have left off the closing semicolon, for instance. If the code is correct and you're using a named character, however, switch to its decimal equivalent. Some of the earlier browser versions are not perfect in rendering named characters.

Named characters

HTML coding conventions require that certain characters, including the angle brackets that surround tags, be entered as character entities. Table 8-3 lists the most common named characters.

Table 8-3 Common Named Characters		
Named Entity	**Symbol**	**Description**
&lt;	<	A left angle bracket or the less-than symbol
&gt;	>	A right angle bracket or the greater-than symbol
&amp;	&	An ampersand
&quot;	"	A double quotation mark
	°	A nonbreaking space
&copy;	(c)	A copyright symbol
&reg;	(r)	A registered mark
&trade;	(tm)	A trademark symbol, which cannot be previewed in Dreamweaver but is supported in Internet Explorer

Tip

Those characters that you can type directly into Dreamweaver's Document window, including the brackets and the ampersand, are automatically translated into the correct named characters in HTML. Try this with the Code Inspector open. Also, you can enter a nonbreaking space in Dreamweaver by typing Ctrl+Shift+spacebar (Command+Shift+spacebar) or by choosing the Non-breaking Space object.

Decimal characters

To enter almost any character that has a diacritic — such as á, ñ, or â — in Dreamweaver, you must explicitly enter the corresponding decimal character into your HTML page. As mentioned in the preceding section, decimal characters take the form of &#number;, where the number can range from 00 to 255. Not all numbers have matching symbols; the sequence from 14 through 31 is currently unused and the upper range (127 through 159) is only partially supported by Internet Explorer and Netscape Navigator. Also, not all fonts have characters for every entity.

Using the Character objects

Not only is it difficult to remember the various name or number codes for the specific character entity you need, it's also a bit of a process to enter the code by hand. The Dreamweaver engineers recognized this need and created a series of Character objects on their own category of the Objects panel.

Ease-of-use is the guiding principal for the new Character objects. Nine of the most commonly used symbols, such as © and ™ are instantly available as separate objects. And a single object exists offering access to 99 different character entities. Inserting the single Character objects is a straightforward point-and-click affair. Either drag the desired symbol to a place in the Document window or position your cursor and select the object.

The nine individual Character objects are detailed in Table 8-4.

Table 8-4		
Character Objects		
Icon	*Name*	*HTML Code Inserted*
©	**Insert Copyright**	`&copy;`
®	**Insert Registered Trademark**	`&reg;`
™	**Insert Trademark**	`&#153;`
£	**Insert Pound**	`&pound;`
¥	**Insert Yen**	`&yen;`
€	**Insert Euro**	`&euro;`
—	**Insert Em-Dash**	`&#151;`
"	**Insert Left Quote**	`&#147;`
"	**Insert Right Quote**	`&#148;`

Note You may notice that the Character objects insert a mix of named and number character entities. Not all browsers recognize the easier-to-identify named entities, so for the widest compatibility, Dreamweaver uses the number codes for a few objects.

The final object on the Characters category is used for inserting these or any other character entity. The Other Characters object displays a large table with symbols for 99 different characters, as shown in Figure 8-12. Simply select the desired symbol and Dreamweaver inserts the appropriate HTML code into the current cursor position. By the way, the very first character — which appears to be blank — actually inserts the code for a nonbreaking space, also accessible via a keyboard shortcut, Ctrl+Shift+spacebar (Command+Shift+spacebar). The nonbreaking space is also available on the Characters category of the Objects panel.

Note Keep in mind that the user's browser must support the character entity for it to be visible to the user. In the case of the Euro symbol, that support is still very haphazard.

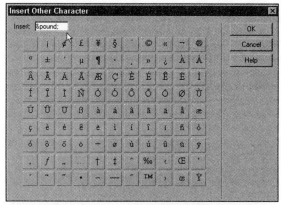

Figure 8-12: Use the Other Character objects to insert the character entity code for any of 99 different symbols.

Summary

Creating Web pages with Dreamweaver is a special blend of using visual layout tools and HTML coding. Regardless, you need to understand the basics of HTML so that you have the knowledge and the tools to modify your code when necessary. This chapter covered these key areas:

✦ An HTML page is divided into two main sections: the `<head>` and the `<body>`. Information pertaining to the entire page is kept in the `<head>` section; all the actual content of the Web page goes in the `<body>` section.

✦ You can change the color and background of your entire page, as well as set its title, through the Page Properties dialog box.

✦ Use `<meta>` tags to summarize your Web page so that search engines can properly catalog it. In Dreamweaver, you can use the View Head Contents feature to easily alter these and other `<head>` tags.

✦ When possible, use logical style tags, such as `<strong>` and `<cite>`, rather than hard-coding your page with physical style tags. Style sheets bring a great deal of control and flexibility to logical style tags.

✦ Special extended characters such as symbols and accented letters require the use of HTML character entities, which can either be named (as in ") or in decimal format (as in ").

In the next chapter, you learn how to insert and format text in Dreamweaver.

✦   ✦   ✦

Adding Text to Your Web Page

If content is king on the Web, then certainly style is queen—together they rule hand in hand. Entering, editing, and formatting text on a Web page is a major part of a Webmaster's job. Dreamweaver gives you the tools to make the task as clear-cut as possible. From headlines to comments, this chapter covers the essentials of working with basic text.

At first, Web designers didn't have many options for manipulating text. However, now the majority of browsers understand a number of text-related commands, and the designer can specify the font as well as its color and size. Dreamweaver includes a range of text manipulation tools. These topics are covered in this chapter, along with an important discussion of manipulating whitespace on the Web page.

Starting with Headings

Text in Hypertext Markup Language (HTML) is primarily composed of headings and paragraphs. Headings separate and introduce major sections of the document, just as a newspaper uses headlines to announce a story and subheads to provide essential details. HTML has six levels of headings; the syntax for the heading tags is ⟨h*n*⟩, where *n* is a number from 1 to 6. The largest heading is ⟨h1⟩ and the smallest is ⟨h6⟩.

Remember that HTML headings are not linked to any specific point size, unlike type produced in a page layout or word processing program. Headings in an HTML document are sized relative to one another, and their final, exact size depends on the browser used. The sample headlines in Figure 9-1 depict the basic headings as rendered through Dreamweaver and as compared to the default paragraph font size. As you can see, some headings are rendered in type smaller than that used for the default paragraph. Headings are usually displayed with a boldface attribute.

Figure 9-1: Standard HTML enables you to use up to six different size headings.

Two methods set text as a particular heading size in Dreamweaver. In both cases, you first need to select the text you want to affect. If you are styling a single line or paragraph as a heading, just position the cursor anywhere in the paragraph to select it. If you want to convert more than one paragraph, click and drag out your selection.

Tip   You can't mix heading levels in a single paragraph. That is, you can't have in the same line a word with an <h1> heading next to a word styled with an <h4> heading. Furthermore, headings belong to a group of HTML text tags called *block elements*. All block elements are rendered with a paragraph return both above and below, which isolates ("blocks") the text. To work around both of these restrictions, you can use <font size=n> tags to achieve the effect of varying sizes for words within the same line or for lines of different sizes close to one another. The <font size=n> tag is covered later in this chapter, in the section "Styling Your Text."

Once the text for the heading is selected, you can choose your heading level by selecting Text ➪ Paragraph Format and then one of the Headings 1 through 6 from the submenu. Alternatively, you can make your selection from the Text Property Inspector. (If it's not already open, display the Property Inspector by selecting Window ➪ Properties.) In the Text Property Inspector, open the Format drop-down list (see Figure 9-2) and choose one of the six headings.

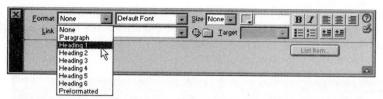

Figure 9-2: You can convert any paragraph or line into a heading by using the Format options in the Text Property Inspector.

Headings are often used in a hierarchical fashion, largest to smallest — but you don't have to do it that way. You can have an ⟨h3⟩ line followed by an ⟨h1⟩ paragraph, if that's what your design needs. Be careful using the smallest headings, ⟨h4⟩–⟨h6⟩; they are likely to be difficult to read on any resolution higher than 800×600.

Working with Paragraphs

Usually the bulk of text on any Web page is composed of paragraphs. Paragraphs in HTML are denoted by the ⟨p⟩ and ⟨/p⟩ pair of tags. When your Web page is processed, the browser formats everything between those two tags as one paragraph and renders it to fit the user's screen, word wrapping as needed at the margins. Any additional line breaks and unnecessary whitespace (beyond one space between words and between sentences) in the HTML code are ignored.

Tip   In the early version of HTML, paragraphs used just the opening ⟨p⟩ tag, and browsers rendered everything between ⟨p⟩ tags as one paragraph; the closing tag was optional. As of HTML 3.2, however, an optional closing ⟨/p⟩ tag was added. Because so many Web pages have been created with just the opening paragraph tag, most browsers still recognize the single-tag format. To be on the safe side in terms of future compatibility, enclose your paragraphs within both opening and closing tags when you do any hand-coding.

Dreamweaver starts a new paragraph every time you press Enter (Return) when composing text in the Document window. If you have the Code view or the Code Inspector open when you work, you can see that Dreamweaver inserts the following code with each new paragraph:

```
<p> </p>
```

The code between the tags creates a nonbreaking space that enables the new line to be visible. You won't see the new line if you have just the paragraph tags with nothing (neither a character nor a character entity, such as) in between:

```
<p></p>
```

When you continue typing, Dreamweaver replaces the nonbreaking space with your input, unless you press Enter (Return) again. Figure 9-3 illustrates two paragraphs with text and a third paragraph with the nonbreaking space still in place.

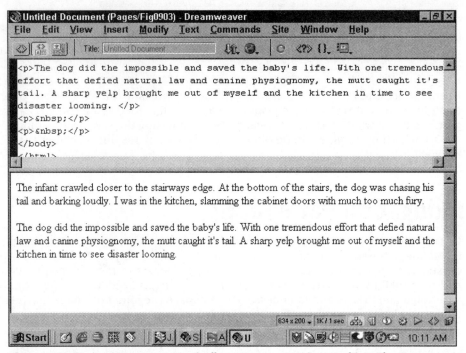

Figure 9-3: Dreamweaver automatically wraps any text inserted into the Document window. If you press Enter (Return) without entering text, Dreamweaver enters paragraph tags surrounding a nonbreaking space.

You can easily change text from most other formats, such as a heading, to paragraph format. First, select the text you want to alter. Then, in the Property Inspector, open the Format options drop-down list and choose Paragraph. You can also choose Text ➪ Paragraph Format ➪ Paragraph from the menu or use the keyboard shortcut Ctrl+Shift+P (Command+Shift+P).

All paragraphs are initially rendered on the page in the default font at the default size. The user can designate these defaults through the browser preferences, although most people don't bother to alter them. If you want to change the font name or the font size for selected paragraphs explicitly, use the techniques described in the upcoming section, "Styling Your Text."

Tip

Remember, you can always use the Tag Selector on the status bar to select and highlight any tag surrounding your current cursor position. This method makes it easy to see exactly what a particular tag is affecting.

Editing paragraphs

By and large, the editing features of Dreamweaver are similar to other modern word processing programs — with one or two Web-oriented twists. Dreamweaver has Cut, Copy, and Paste options, as well as Undo and Redo commands. You can search for and replace any text on your Web page under construction and even check its spelling.

The "twists" come from the relationship between the Design and Code views of the Document window, which give Dreamweaver special functionality for copying and pasting text and code. Let's see how that works.

Inserting text

You've already seen how you can position the cursor on the page and directly enter text. In this sense, Dreamweaver acts like a word processing program, rather than a page layout program. On a blank page, the cursor starts at the top-left corner of the page. Words automatically wrap to the next line when the text exceeds the right margin. Press Enter (Return) to end the current paragraph and start the next one.

Indenting text

In Dreamweaver, you cannot indent text as you can with a word processor. Tabs normally have no effect in HTML. To indent a paragraph's first line, one method uses nonbreaking spaces, which can be inserted with the keyboard shortcut Ctrl+Shift+spacebar (Command+Shift+spacebar). Nonbreaking spaces are an essential part of any Web designer's palette because they provide single-character spacing — often necessary to nudge an image or other object into alignment. You've already seen the code for a nonbreaking space —   — that Dreamweaver inserts between the <p>...</p> tag pair to make the line visible.

Aside from the keyboard shortcut, two other methods involve inserting a nonbreaking space. You can enter its character code —   — directly into the HTML code. You can also style your text as *preformatted*; this technique is discussed later in this chapter.

Tip

Another method exists for indenting the first line of a paragraph: Cascading Style Sheets. You can set an existing HTML tag, such as <p>, to any indent amount using the Text Indent option found on the Block panel of the Style Sheet dialog box. Be aware, however, that the various browsers support style sheets differently and to a different extent. A full discussion of text indent and other style sheet controls is in Chapter 18.

Inserting Text from Other Applications

The Paste command can also insert text from another program into Dreamweaver. If you cut or copy text from a file in any other program — whether it is a word processor, spreadsheet, or database program — Dreamweaver inserts it at the cursor position. The results of this Paste operation vary, however.

Dreamweaver can paste only plain, unformatted text — any bold, italic, or other styling in the original document are not retained in Dreamweaver. Paragraph breaks, however, are retained and reproduced in two different ways. A single paragraph return becomes a line break (a <br> tag) in Dreamweaver, whereas text separated by two returns is formatted into two HTML paragraphs, using the <p>... </p> tag pair.

If you need to import a great deal of text and want to retain as much formatting as possible, you can use another application, such as Microsoft Word, to save your text as an HTML file. Then open that file in Dreamweaver with the Import Word HTML command.

Cutting, copying, and pasting

Text can be moved from one place to another — or from one Web document to another — using the standard cut-and-paste techniques. No surprises here: Before you can cut or copy anything, you must select it. Select by clicking the mouse at the beginning of the text you want to cut or copy, drag the highlight to the end of your selection, and then release the mouse button.

Here are some other selection methods:

✦ Double-click a word to select it.

✦ Move the pointer to the left margin of the text until the pointer changes to a right-facing arrow. Click once to highlight a single line. Click and drag down the margin to select a group of lines.

✦ Position the cursor at the beginning of your selection. Hold down the Shift key and then click once at the end of the selection.

✦ You can select everything in the body of your document by using Edit ➪ Select All or the keyboard shortcut Ctrl+A (Command+A).

✦ Use the Tag Selector to select text or other objects contained within specific tags.

✦ You can also select text by holding down Shift and using the right- or left-arrow key to select one character at a time. If you hold down Ctrl+Shift (Command+Shift), you can press the right- or left-arrow key to select a word at a time.

When you want to move a block of text, first select it and then use Edit ➪ Cut or the keyboard shortcut Ctrl+X (Command+X). This sequence removes the text from the document and places it on your system's clipboard. To paste the text, move the pointer to the new location and click once to place the cursor. Then select Edit ➪ Paste or the keyboard shortcut Ctrl+V (Command+V). The text is copied from the clipboard to its new location. You can continue pasting this same text from the clipboard until another block of text is copied or cut.

To copy text, the procedure is much the same. Select the text using one of the preceding methods and then use Edit ➪ Copy or Ctrl+C (Command+C). The selected text is copied to the clipboard, and the original text is left in place. Then position the cursor in a new location and select Edit ➪ Paste (or use the keyboard shortcut).

Using drag-and-drop

The other, quicker method for moving or copying text is the drag-and-drop technique. Once you've selected your text, release the mouse button and move the cursor over the highlighted area. The cursor changes from an I-beam to an arrow. To move the text, click the selected area with the arrow cursor and drag your mouse to a new location. The arrow cursor now has a box attached to it, indicating that it is carrying something. As you move your cursor, a bar (the insertion point) moves with you, indicating where the text will be positioned. Release the mouse button to drop the text. You can copy text in the same manner by holding down the Ctrl (Option) key as you drag and drop your selected text. When copying this way, the box attached to the cursor is marked with a plus sign (on Macintosh computers the box is the same size as the text selection and no plus sign appears).

To remove text completely, select it and then choose Edit ➪ Clear or press Delete. The only way to recover deleted text is to use the Undo feature described in the following section.

Copying and Pasting Code

The "Editing paragraphs," section earlier in this chapter mentioned that Dreamweaver includes a couple of "twists" to the standard Cut, Copy, and Paste options. The combination of Dreamweaver's Design and Code views enables you to copy and paste both text and code. Previous versions of Dreamweaver used a couple of additional commands — Copy Text Only and Paste As Text — to accomplish what Dreamweaver 4 now does with the dual page views.

Put simply, to copy just text from Dreamweaver to another application, use the Design view; to copy both text and code, use the Code view. To understand how two views interact, let's examine how they are used. Table 9-1 explains the variations.

Table 9-1			
Results of Copy/Paste from Design and Code views			
Selected Text	*Copy From*	*Paste To*	*Result*
Example Text	Design view	Other program	Example Text
Example Text	Design view	Design view	**Example Text**
\<b>Example Text\</b>	Code view or other program	Code view	**Example Text**
			(Design view)
			\<b>Example Text\</b> (Code view)
\<b>Example Text\</b>	Code view or other program	Design view	\<b>Example Text\</b> (Design view)
			<b>Example Text</b>
			(Code view)

Notice that in the final row of Table 9-1, if you copy formatted text such as the bold-face "Example Text" sample and insert it in the Design view, you get the following:

```
&lt;b&gt;Example Text&lt;/b&gt;
```

If you remember the section on named character entities in Chapter 8, you may recognize < as the code for the less-than symbol (<) and > as the code for the greater-than symbol (>). These symbols are used to represent tags such as \<b> and \</b> to prevent a browser from interpreting them as tag delimiters.

So what possible real-life uses could there be for Dreamweaver's implementation of the regular Copy and Paste commands in the different views? First, these options are a major benefit for programmers, teachers, and writers who constantly have to communicate in both HTML code and regular text. If an instructor is attempting to demonstrate a coding technique on a Web page, for example, she can just copy the code in the Code view and Paste it into the Design view — instantly transforming the code into something readable online.

Undo, Redo, and the History panel

The Undo command has to be one of the greatest inventions of the twentieth century. Make a mistake? Undo! Want to experiment with two different options? Undo! Change your mind again? Redo! The Undo command reverses your last action, whether you changed a link, added a graphic, or deleted the entire page. The Redo command enables you to reverse your Undo actions.

Dreamweaver displays all of your previous actions on the History panel, so you can easily see what steps you took. To use the Undo command, you can either choose Edit ➪ Undo or press the keyboard shortcut Ctrl+Z (Command+Z); either command undoes a single action at a time. To undo multiple actions, drag the slider in the History panel to the last action you want to keep or just click the slider track at that action.

The complement to Undo is the Redo command. To reverse an Undo command, choose Edit ➪ Redo or Ctrl+Y (Command+Y). To reverse several Undo commands, drag the slider in the History panel back over the grayed-out steps; alternately, you can click the slider track once at the step up to which you'd like to redo.

Tip The best use I've found for the Redo command is in concert with Undo. When I'm trying to decide between two alternatives, such as two different images, I'll replace one choice with another and then use the Undo/Redo combination to go back and forth between them. Because Dreamweaver replaces any selected object with the current object from the clipboard — even if one is a block of text and the other is a layer — you can easily view two separate options with this trick. The History panel enables you to apply this procedure over any number of steps.

Dreamweaver's implementation of the Undo command enables you to back up as many steps as set in the Maximum Number of History Steps found in Preferences. The History steps can even undo actions that had taken place before a document was saved. Note that the History panel has additional features besides multiple undos.

On the CD-ROM Although the History panel lets you replay any series of selected steps at the press of a button, you have to press that button every time you want to replay the steps. I developed a custom extension called Repeat History with which you can repeat any selected steps any number of times. You'll find Repeat History in the Additional Extensions folder on the CD-ROM.

Checking your spelling

A typo can make a significant impression. Not many things are more embarrassing than showing a new Web site to a client and having that client point out a spelling error. Dreamweaver includes an easy-to-use Spell Checker to help you avoid such awkward moments. I make it a practice to spell-check every Web page before it's posted online.

You start the process by choosing Text ➪ Check Spelling or you can press the keyboard shortcut Shift+F7. This sequence opens the Check Spelling dialog box, as seen in Figure 9-4.

Spell-Checking in Non-English Languages

Macromedia has made additional language dictionaries available. As of this writing, dictionaries in these other languages are also available: German, Spanish, French, Italian, Brazilian-Portuguese, Catalan, and Swedish. You can download these dictionaries from Macromedia's Dreamweaver Object Exchange at `www.macromedia.com/support/dreamweaver/dictionary.html`.

To use the dictionaries, download the compressed file to your system. After uncompressing them, store the file with the .dat extension in the Configuration\Dictionaries folder and restart Dreamweaver. Finally, open Preferences (Edit ➪ Preferences) and, from the General panel, select the Dictionary option button. Choose the new language from the drop-down list, and you're ready to spell correctly in another tongue.

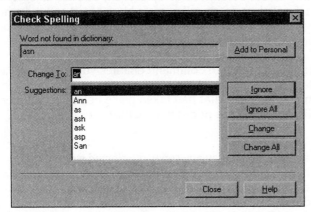

Figure 9-4: Dreamweaver's Spell Checker double-checks your spelling and can find the typos on any Web page.

Once you've opened the Check Spelling dialog box, Dreamweaver begins searching your text for errors. Unless you have selected a portion of your document, Dreamweaver checks the full document regardless of where your cursor is placed. When text is selected, Dreamweaver checks the selection first and then asks if you'd like to do the entire document.

Dreamweaver checks your Web page text against two dictionaries: a standard English (or your chosen language) dictionary and a personal dictionary, to which you can add words. If the Spell Checker finds any text not in either of the program's dictionaries, the text is highlighted in the Document window and appears in the Word not found in dictionary field of the dialog box. A list of suggested corrections appears in the Suggestions list box, with the topmost one highlighted and also displayed in the Change To box. If Dreamweaver cannot find any suggestions, the Change To box is left blank. At this point, you have the following options:

✦ **Add to Personal:** Select this button to include the highlighted word in your personal dictionary and prevent Dreamweaver from tagging it as an error in the future.

✦ **Ignore:** Select this button when you want Dreamweaver to leave the currently highlighted word alone and continue searching the text.

✦ **Ignore All:** Select this button when you want Dreamweaver to disregard all occurrences of this word in the current document.

✦ **Change:** If you see the correct replacement among the list of suggestions, highlight it and select the Change button. If no suggestion is appropriate, you can type the correct word into the Change To text box and then select this button.

✦ **Change All:** Choosing this button causes all instances of the current word to be replaced with the word in the Change To text box.

Tip

Have you ever accidentally added a misspelled word to your personal dictionary and then been stuck with the error for all eternity? Dreamweaver enables you to recover from your mistake by giving you access to the dictionary itself. The personal dictionary, stored in the Dreamweaver\Configuration\Dictionaries\personal.dat file, can be opened and modified in any text editor.

Using Find and Replace

Dreamweaver's Find and Replace features are both timesaving and lifesaving (well, almost). You can use Find and Replace to cut your input time substantially by searching for abbreviations and expanding them to their full state. You can also find a client's incorrectly spelled name and replace it with the correctly spelled version — that's a lifesaver! However, that's just the tip of the iceberg when it comes to what Find and Replace can really do. The Find and Replace engine should be considered a key power tool for any Web developer. You can not only search multiple files but also easily check the code separately from the content.

Here's a short list of what the Find and Replace feature makes possible:

✦ Search the Document window to find any type of text.

✦ Search the underlying HTML to find tags, attributes, or text within tags.

✦ Look for text within specific tags with specific attributes — or look for text that's outside of a specific tag with specific attributes.

✦ Find and replace patterns of text, using wildcard characters called *regular expressions*.

✦ Apply any of the preceding Find and Replace operations to the current document, the current site, any folder, or any group of selected files.

The basic command, Find and Replace is found, with it's companion, Find Next (Find Again, on the Macintosh), under the Edit menu. You can use both commands in either Dreamweaver's Design or Code view, and — in Windows systems — the Site window. Although invoked by a single command, you can use the Find feature independently or in conjunction with Replace.

Find and Replace operations can be applied to one or a series of documents. In addition to searching the current document, you can also apply Find and Replace to all of the files in a folder or a site. Furthermore, individual files selected in the Site window are also searchable.

Finding and replacing text on the visual page

The most basic method of using Find and Replace takes place in the Document window. Whenever you need to search for any text that can be seen by the public on your Web page — whether it's to correct a spelling or change a name — Dreamweaver makes it fast and simple.

Tip   The Find and Replace dialog box, unlike most of Dreamweaver's dialog boxes, is actually a *nonmodal window*. This technical term just means that you can easily move back and forth between your Document window and the Find and Replace dialog box without having to close the dialog box first, as you do with the other Dreamweaver windows.

To find some text on your Web page, follow these steps:

1. From the Document window, choose Edit ➪ Find and Replace or use the keyboard shortcut Ctrl+F (Command+F).

2. In the Find and Replace dialog box, shown in Figure 9-5, make sure that Text is the selected Search For option.

3. In the text box next to the Search For option, type the word or phrase you're looking for.

Tip   If you select your text *before* launching the Find dialog box, it automatically appears in the Search For text box.

4. Select the appropriate search options, if any:

   • If you want to find an exact replica of the word as you entered it, select the Match Case checkbox; otherwise, Dreamweaver searches for all variations of your text, regardless of case.

   • To force Dreamweaver to disregard any whitespace variations, such as additional spaces, hard spaces or tabs, select the Ignore Whitespace Differences option. For most situations, it's a good idea to leave this default option enabled.

   • Selecting Use Regular Expressions enables you to work with Dreamweaver's wildcard characters (discussed later in this section). Use Regular Expressions and Ignore Whitespace Differences are mutually exclusive options.

Search For Options list   Search For Text box

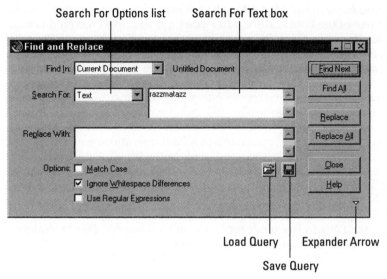

Load Query | Expander Arrow

Save Query

Figure 9-5: The Find and Replace dialog box.

5. Select the Find Next button to begin the search from the cursor's current position.

   • If Dreamweaver finds the desired text, it highlights the text in the Document window.

   • If Dreamweaver doesn't find the text in the remaining portion of the document, it asks if you want to continue searching from the beginning. Select Yes to continue or No to exit.

6. If you want to look for the next occurrence of your selected text, click the Find Next button again.

7. To look for all occurrences of your text, choose Find All.

   The Find dialog box expands to display the List window. Dreamweaver lists each found occurrence on a separate line in the List window.

Tip   You can quickly move from one found selection to another by double-clicking the line in the List window. Dreamweaver highlights the selection, scrolling the Document window, if necessary.

After searching the page, Dreamweaver tells you how many occurrences of your selection, if any, were found.

8. You can enter other text to search or exit the Find dialog box by clicking the Close button.

The text you enter in the Find dialog box is kept in memory until it's replaced by your next use of the Find feature. After you have executed the Find command once, you can continue to search for your text without redisplaying the Find dialog box, by selecting Edit ⇨ Find Next (Find Again) or the keyboard shortcut F3 (Command+G). If Dreamweaver finds your text, it is highlighted — in fact, Dreamweaver acts exactly the same as when the Find dialog box is open. The Find Next (Find Again) command gives you a quick way to search through a long document — especially when you put the F3 (Command+G) key to work.

When you add the Replace command to a Find operation, you can search your text for a word or phrase and, if it's found, replace it with another word or phrase of your choice. As mentioned earlier, the Replace feature is a handy way to correct mistakes and expand abbreviations. Figure 9-6 shows an example of the latter operation. This example intentionally uses the abbreviation DW throughout the input text of a Web page article. Then the example uses the Replace All function to expand all the DWs to Dreamweaver — in one fell swoop. This technique is much faster than typing "Dreamweaver" nine times.

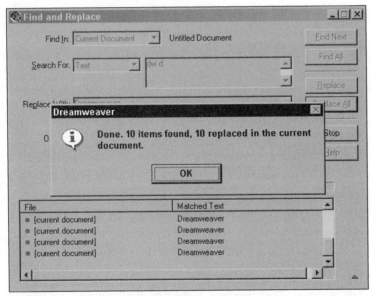

Figure 9-6: Use the Edit ⇨ Replace command to correct your text one item at a time or all at once.

When you replace text in the Document window, it is replaced regardless of its formatting. For example, suppose you had the following paragraph:

Mary's accusation reminded Jon of studying synchrones in high school. *Synchrones*, he recalled, were graphs in which the lines constantly approached zero, but never made it. "Yeah," he thought, "That's me, all right. I'm one big **synchrone**."

Upon discovering that "synchrone" should actually be "asymptote," you could use the Find and Replace feature to replace all the plain, italic, and bold versions of the "synchrone" text simultaneously.

Tip   It's possible to alter formatting as well — to change all the formatting to just under-lining for example — but for that, you need to perform your Find and Replace oper-ations in the Code Inspector, as discussed in the following section.

Follow these steps to use Dreamweaver's Replace feature in the Document window:

1. Choose Edit ⇨ Find and Replace, or the keyboard shortcut Ctrl+F (Command+F).

2. In the Find and Replace dialog box, make sure that Text is the selected Search For option and then, in the text box next to the Search For option, type the word or phrase you're looking for.

3. In the Replace With text box, type the substitute word.

4. Click the Find Next button. Dreamweaver begins searching from the current cursor position. If Dreamweaver finds the text, it is highlighted.

   If the text is not found, Dreamweaver asks if you want to continue searching from the top of the document. Select Yes to continue or No to exit.

5. To replace the highlighted occurrence of your text, select the Replace button. Dreamweaver replaces the found text with the substitute text and then auto-matically searches for the next occurrence.

6. If you want to replace all instances of the Find text, select the Replace All button.

   When Dreamweaver has found all the occurrences of your Find text, it dis-plays the number of replacement operations and a line for each in the List window.

   Double-clicking a line in the List window highlights the changed text in the Document window.

7. When you've finished using the Replace dialog box, click the Close button to exit.

Tip   You can also rerun Find and Replace operations by highlighting the appropriate step in the History panel and choosing the Replay button.

Searching the code

The power curve ramps up significantly when you start to explore Dreamweaver's HTML Find and Replace capabilities. Should your client decide that he wants the company's name to appear in blue, bold, 18-point type throughout the 300-page site, you can accommodate him with a few keystrokes — instead of hours of mind-numbing grunt work.

Storing and Retrieving Queries

Dreamweaver enables you to develop extremely complex queries. Rather than forcing you to reenter queries over and over again, Dreamweaver enables you to save and load them when needed. You can store and retrieve Find and Replace queries; Dreamweaver saves them with .dwr file extensions, respectively.

To save a query, select the diskette icon on the Find and Replace dialog box. The standard Save Query (Save Query to file) dialog box appears for you to enter a file name; the appropriate file extension is appended automatically. To load a previously saved query, select the folder icon on the Find and Replace dialog box to open the Load Query dialog box. Although only queries with a .dwr extension are being saved in the current version, you can still load both .dwq and .dwr files saved from previous Dreamweaver versions.

Although saving and opening queries is an obvious advantage when working with complex wildcard operations, you can also make it work for you in an every day situation. If, for example, you have a set series of acronyms or abbreviations that you must convert repeatedly, you can save your simple text queries and use them as needed without having to remember all the details.

You can perform three different types of searches that use the HTML in your Web page:

✦ You can search for text anywhere in the HTML code. With this capability, you can look for text within Alt or any other attribute — and change it.

✦ You can search for text relative to specific tags. Sometimes you need to change just the text contained within the `<b>` tag and leave all other matching text alone.

✦ You can search for specific HTML tags and/or their attributes. Dreamweaver's Find and Replace feature gives you the capability to insert, delete, or modify tags and attributes.

Looking for text in the Code

Text that appears onscreen is often replicated in various sections of your off-screen HTML code. It's not uncommon, for example, to use the Alt attribute in an `<img>` tag that repeats the caption under the picture. What do you think would happen under those circumstances if you replaced the wording with the standard Find and Replace features in the Design view of the Document window? You're still left with the task of tracking down the Alt attribute and making that change as well. Dreamweaver enables you to act on both content and programming text in one operation — a major savings in time and effort, not to mention aggravation.

To find and replace text in both the content and the code, follow these steps:

1. Choose Edit ⇨ Find and Replace to open the dialog box.

2. Select the parameters of your search from the Find In option: Current Document, Current Site, or Folder.

   Remember, you can also search specific files if you launch the Find and Replace dialog box from the Site window.

3. Choose the Search For option button and select the Source Code option from the drop-down list.

4. Enter the text you're searching for in the text box next to the Search For option.

5. If you are replacing, enter the new text in the Replace With text box.

6. Select any options desired: Match Case, Ignore Whitespace Differences, or Use Regular Expressions.

7. Choose your Find/Replace option: Find Next, Find All, Replace, or Replace All

8. Select Close when finished.

Caution As with all Find and Replace operations—especially those in which you decide to Replace All—you need to exercise extreme caution when replacing text throughout your code. If you're unsure about what's going to be affected, choose Find All first and, with your Code view or Inspector open, step through all the selections to be positive no unwanted surprises exist. Should you replace some code in error, you can always undo the operation — but only if the document is open. Replacing text or code in a closed file, as is done when the operation is performed on a folder, the current site, or selected files in the Site window, is not undoable.

Using advanced text options in Find and Replace

In Find and Replace operations, the global Replace All isn't appropriate for every situation; sometimes you need a more precise approach. Dreamweaver enables you to fine-tune your searches to pinpoint accuracy. You can look for text within particular tags — and even within particular tags with specific attributes. Moreover, you can find (and replace) text that is outside of particular tags with specific attributes.

Dreamweaver assists you by providing a drop-down list of every standard HTML tag, as well as numerous special function tags such as those used for Cold Fusion applications. You can also search for your own custom tags. You don't have to try to remember which attributes go with which tag either. Dreamweaver also supplies you with a context-sensitive list of attributes that changes according to the tag selected.

In addition to using the tag's attributes as a search filter, Dreamweaver can also search within the tag for text or another tag. Most HTML tags are so-called container tags that consist of an opening tag and a closing tag, such as <b> and </b>. You can set up a filter to look for text within a specific tag — or text outside of a specific tag. For example, if you were searching for the word *big*:

```
The big, red boat was a <b>big</b> waste of money.
```

you could build a Find and Replace operation that changed one instance of the one word (big, red) but not the other (big) — or vice versa.

To look for text in or out of specific tags and attributes, follow these steps:

1. Choose Edit ➪ Find and Replace to open the Find and Replace dialog box.

2. Select the parameters of your search from the Find In option: Current Document, Current Site, or Folder.

3. Choose the Search For option button and select the Text (Advanced) option from the drop-down list.

   The Add and Remove (+ and –) tag options are made available, as shown in Figure 9-7.

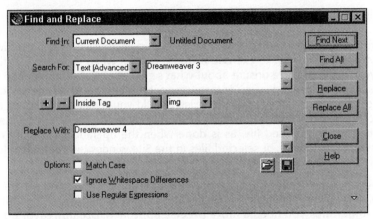

Figure 9-7: The advanced text features of Find and Replace enable you to manipulate text and code simultaneously.

4. Enter the text you're searching for in the text box next to the Search For option.

5. Select either Inside Tag or Not Inside Tag from the option list.

6. Select the tag to include or exclude from the adjacent option list.

7. To add a further restriction on the search, click the Add button (the plus sign).

   Another line of search options is added to the dialog box.

8. Select the additional search filter. The available options include the following:

Filter	Description
With Attribute	Enables you to select any attribute from the adjacent option list. You can set this attribute to be equal to, less than, greater than, or not equal to any given value by choosing from the available drop-down lists.
Without Attribute	Finds text within a particular tag that does not include a specific attribute. Choose the attribute to be equal to, less than, greater than, or not equal to any given value by choosing from the available drop-down lists.
Containing	Searches the tag for either specified text or another user-selectable tag found within the initial tag pair.
Not Containing	Searches the tag for either text or a tag not found within the initial tag pair.
Inside Tag	Enables you to look for text that is within two (or more) sets of specific tags.
Not Inside Tag	Enables you to look for text that is in one tag, but not in another tag, or vice versa.

9. To continue adding filter conditions, select the Add button (the plus sign) and repeat Steps 7 and 8.

10. To remove a filter condition, select the Remove button (the minus sign).

11. If you are replacing, enter the new text in the Replace With text box.

12. Select any options desired: Match Case, Ignore Whitespace Differences, or Use Regular Expressions.

13. Choose your Find/Replace option: Find Next, Find All, Replace, or Replace All.

14. Select Close when finished.

Tip You can continue to add conditions by clicking the Add (+) button. In fact, I was able to add so many conditions, the Find/Replace dialog box began to disappear off the screen! To erase all conditions, change the Search For option to Text or Source Code and then change it back to Text (Advanced).

Replacing HTML tags and attributes

Let's say a new edict has come down from the HTML gurus of your company: No longer is the `<strong>` tag to be used to indicate emphasis; from now on; use only the `<b>` tag. Oh, and by the way, change all the existing pages — all 3,000+ Web and intranet pages — so that they're compliant. Dreamweaver makes short work out of nightmare situations such as these by giving you the power to search and replace HTML tags and their attributes.

But Dreamweaver doesn't stop there. Not only can you replace one tag with another, you can also perform the following:

✦ Change or delete the tag (with or without its contents)

✦ Set an attribute in the tag to another value

✦ Remove any or all attributes

✦ Add text and/or code before or after the starting or the ending tag

To alter your code using Dreamweaver's Find and Replace feature, follow these steps:

1. As with other Find and Replace operations, choose Edit ⇨ Find and Replace to open the dialog box.

2. Select the parameters of your search from the Find In option: Current Page, Current Site, or Folder.

3. Choose the Search For option button and select the tag option from the drop-down list.

   The dialog box changes to include the tag functions.

4. Select the desired tag from the option list next to the Search For option.

Tip   You can either scroll down the list box to find the tag or you can type the first let-ter of the tag in the box. Dreamweaver scrolls to the group of tags that begin with that letter when the list is visible (Windows only).

5. If desired, you can limit the search by specifying an attribute and value, or with other conditions, as discussed in detail in the previous section.

Note   If you want to search for just a tag, select the Remove button (the minus key) to eliminate the additional condition.

6. Make a selection from the Action list, shown in Figure 9-8. The options are as follows:

Action	Description
Replace Tag & Contents	Substitutes the selected tag and all included content with a text string. The text string can include HTML code.
Replace Contents Only	Changes the content between the specified tag to a given text string, which can also include HTML code.
Remove Tag & Contents	Deletes the tag and all contents.
Strip Tag	Removes the tag but leaves the previously enclosed content.

Action	Description
Change Tag	Substitutes one tag for another.
Set Attribute	Sets an existing attribute to a new value or inserts a new attribute set to a specific value.
Remove Attribute	Deletes a specified attribute.
Add Before Start Tag	Inserts a text string (with or without HTML) before the opening tag.
Add After End Tag	Inserts a text string (with or without HTML) after the end tag.
Add After Start Tag	Inserts a text string (with or without HTML) after the opening tag.
Add Before End Tag	Inserts a text string (with or without HTML) before the end tag.

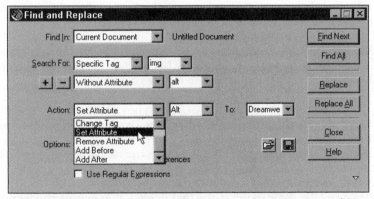

Figure 9-8: The Action list enables you to replace tags or modify them by setting the existing attributes or adding new ones.

Note

Not all the options listed in the preceding table are available for all tags. Some so-called empty tags, such as <img>, consist of a single tag and not tag pairs. Empty tags have only Add Before and Add After options instead of Add Before Start Tag, Add After Start Tag, Add Before End Tag, and Add After End Tag.

7. Select any options desired: Match Case, Ignore Whitespace Differences, or Use Regular Expressions.

8. Choose your Find/Replace option: Find Next, Find All, Replace, or Replace All.

9. Select Close when finished.

Tip   You don't have to apply a single action to all the instances Dreamweaver locates if you choose Find All. In the list of found expressions, select a single item and then choose Replace. Dreamweaver makes the revision and places a green dot next to the item so you can tell it has been altered. If you want, you can then select another item from the list, choose a different action, and then select Replace.

Concentrating your search with regular expressions

As powerful as all the other Find and Replace features are, they are boosted to a higher level of flexibility with the addition of regular expressions. I've referred to regular expressions as being similar to wildcards in other programs, but their capabilities are really far more extensive.

Regular expressions are best described as a *text pattern matching system*. If you can identify any pattern in your text, you can manipulate it with regular expressions. What kind of pattern? Let's say you have a spreadsheet-like table with lots of numbers, showing both dollars and cents, mixed with explanatory text. With regular expressions, you can match the pattern formed by the dollar sign and the decimal point and reformat the entire table, turning all the figures deep blue with a new font — all in one Find and Replace operation.

Note   If you're into Unix, you recognize regular expressions as being very close to the grep utility — *grep*, by the way, stands for Get Regular Expressions and Print. The Find and Replace feature in BBEdit also features a grep-like syntax.

You can apply regular expressions to any of the types of Find and Replace operations previously discussed, with just a click of the Use Regular Expressions checkbox. Note that when you select Use Regular Expressions, the Ignore Unnecessary Whitespace option is deselected. This is because the two options are mutually exclusive and cannot be used together.

The most basic regular expression is the text itself. If you enable the feature and then enter **th** in the Search For text box, Dreamweaver locates every example of "th" in the text and/or source. Although this capability by itself has little use beyond what you can also achieve with standard Find and Replace operations, it's important to remember this functionality as you begin to build your patterns.

Using wildcard characters

Initially, it's helpful to be able to use what traditionally are know as *wildcards* — characters that match different types of characters. The wildcards in regular expressions represent single characters and are described in Table 9-2. In other words, no single regular expression represents all the characters, as the asterisk does when used in PC file searches (such as *.*). However, such a condition can be represented with a slightly more complex regular expression (described later in the "Matching character positions and repeating characters" section).

Table 9-2
Regular Expression Wildcard Characters

Character	Matches	Example
.	Any single character	**w.d** matches **wid**e but not world.
\w	Any alphanumeric character, including the underscore	**w\wd** matches **wid**e and **world**.
\W	Any nonalphanumeric character	**jboy\Widest.com** matches **jboy@idest.com**.
\d	Any numeric character 0–9	**y\dk** matches **Y2K**.
\D	Any nonnumeric character	**\D2\D** matches **Y2K** and **H2O**.
\s	Any whitespace character, including space, tab, form feed, or line feed	**\smedia** matches **media** but not Macromedia.
\S	Any nonwhitespace character	**\Smedia** matches Macro**media** but not media.
\t	A tab	Matches any single tab character in the HTML source.
\f	Form feed	Matches any single form-feed character in the HTML source.
\n	Line feed	Matches any single line-feed character in the HTML source.
\r	Carriage return	Matches any single carriage-return character in the HTML source.

Tip   The backslash character (\) is used to escape special characters so that they can be included in a search. For example, if you want to look for an asterisk, you need to specify it in this way: *. Likewise, when trying to find the backslash character, precede it with another backslash character, as follows: \\.

Matching character positions and repeating characters

With regular expressions, not only can you match the type of character, but you can also match its position in the text. This feature enables you to perform operations on characters at the beginning, end, or middle of the word or line. Regular expressions also enable you to find instances in which a character is repeated an unspecified number of times or a specific number of times. Combined, these features broaden the scope of the patterns that can be found.

Table 9-3 details the options available for matching by text placement and character repetition.

	Table 9-3 Regular Expression Character Positions and Repeating Characters	
Character	**Matches**	**Example**
^	Beginning of a line	**^c** matches the first c in "**C**all me Ishmael."
$	End of a line	**d$** matches the final "d" in "Be afraid. Be very afrai**d**."
\b	A word boundary, such as a space or carriage return	**\btext** matches **text**book but not SimpleText.
\B	A nonword boundary inside a word	**\Btext** matches Simple**Text** but not textbook.
*	The preceding character zero or more times	**b*c** matches **BBC** and **c**old.
+	The preceding character one or more times	**b+c** matches **BBC** but not cold.
?	The preceding character zero or one time	**st?un** matches **stun** and **sun** but not strung.
{n}	Exactly *n* instances of the preceding character	**e{2}** matches reed and each pair of two e's in "Ai**ee**eeeeee!" but nothing in Dreamweaver.
{n,m}	At least *n* and *m* instances of the preceding character	**C{2,4}** matches #**CC**00FF and #**CCCC**00 but not the full string #CCCCCC.

Matching character ranges

Beyond single characters, or repetitions of single characters, regular expressions incorporate the capability of finding or excluding ranges of characters. This feature is particularly useful when you're working with groups of names or titles. Ranges are specified in set brackets. A match is made when any one of the characters, not necessarily all of the characters, within the set brackets is found.

Descriptions of how to match character ranges with regular expressions can be found in Table 9-4.

Table 9-4
Regular Expression Character Ranges

Character	Matches	Example
[abc]	Any one of the characters a, b, or c	**[lmrt]** matches the l and m's in **lemm**ings and the r and t in **r**oad**t**rip.
[^abc]	Any character except a, b, or c	**[^etc]** matches **GIFs** but not etc in the phrase "GIFs etc."
[a-z]	Any character in the range from a to z	**[l-p]** matches l and o in **lo**wery and m, n, o an p in **p**oint**m**an.
x|y	Either x or y	**boy|girl** matches both **boy** and **girl**.

Grouping with regular expressions

Grouping is perhaps the single most powerful concept in regular expressions. With it, any matched text pattern is easily manipulated — for example, the following list of names:

✦ John Jacob Jingleheimer Schmidt

✦ James T. Kirk

✦ Cara Fishman

could be rearranged so that the last name is first, separated by a comma, like this:

✦ Schmidt, John Jacob Jingleheimer

✦ Kirk, James T.

✦ Fishman, Cara

Grouping is handled primarily with parentheses. To indicate a group, enclose it in parentheses in the Find text field. Regular expressions can manage up to nine grouped patterns. Each grouped patterned is designated by a dollar sign ($) in front of a number (1–9), in the Replace text field, like this: **$3**.

Caution   Remember that the dollar sign is also used after a character or pattern to indicate the last character in a line.

Table 9-5 shows how regular expressions use grouping.

Table 9-5
Regular Expressions Grouping

Character	Matches	Example
(p)	Any pattern p	**(\b\w*)\.(\w*\b)** matches two patterns, the first before a period and the second, after — such as in a file name with an extension. The backslash before the period escapes it so that it is not interpreted as a regular expression.
$1, $2 . . . $9	The *n*th pattern noted with parentheses	The replacement pattern **$1's extension is ".$2"** would manipulate the pattern **(\b\w*)\.(\w*\b)** so that Chapter09.txt and Image12.gif would become **Chapter09's extension is ".txt"** and **Image12's extension is ".gif."**

The <br> tag

As with headings, the paragraph tag falls among the class of HTML objects called *block elements*. As such, any text marked with the <p>...</p> tag pair is always rendered with an extra line above and below the text, often called whitespace. To have a series of blank lines appear one after the other, use the break tag <br>. Multiple break tags may also be used to provide whitespace between elements.

Break tags are used within block elements, such as headings and paragraphs, to provide a line break where the <br> is inserted. Dreamweaver provides two ways to insert a <br> tag: You can choose the Enter Line Break button from the Characters panel of the Objects panel or you can use the keyboard shortcut Shift+Enter (Shift+Return).

Figure 9-9 demonstrates the effect of the <br> tag. The menu items in Column A on the left are the result of using the <br> tag within a paragraph. In Column B on the right, paragraph tags alone are used. The <h1> heading is also split at the top (modified through style sheet selections) with a break tag to avoid the insertion of an unwanted line.

By default, Dreamweaver marks <br> tags with a symbol: A gold shield with the letters BR and the standard Enter/Return symbol. You can turn off this display feature by choosing Preferences ⇨ Invisible Elements and deselecting the Line Breaks checkbox.

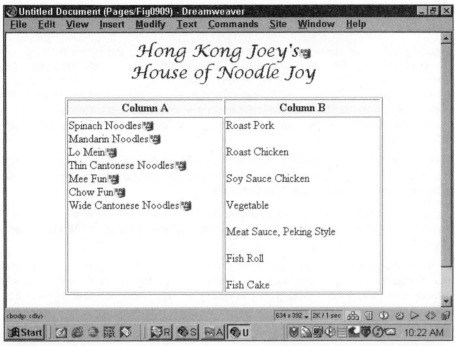

Figure 9-9: Use break tags to wrap your lines without the additional line spacing brought about by <p> tags.

Other whitespace tags

If you can't get the alignment effect you want through the regular text options available in Dreamweaver, two other HTML tags can affect whitespace: <nobr> and <wbr>. Although a tad on the obscure side, these tags can be just the ticket in certain circumstances. Let's see how they work.

The <nobr> tag

Most of the time, you want the user's browser to handle word-wrapping chores automatically. Occasionally, however, you may need to make sure that a particular string of text is rendered in one piece. For these situations, you can use the no break tag <nobr>. Any text that comes in between the opening and closing tag pair—<nobr>...</nobr>—is displayed in one continuous line. If the line of text is wider than the current browser window, a horizontal scroll bar automatically appears along the bottom of the browser.

The <nobr> tag is supported only through the Netscape and Microsoft browsers and must be entered by hand into your HTML code. Use the <nobr> tag under very special circumstances.

Overcoming Line-Spacing Difficulties

Line spacing is a major issue and a common problem for Web designers. A design often calls for lines to be tightly spaced, and also of various sizes. If you use the break tag to separate your lines, you get the tight spacing required, but you won't be able to make each line a different heading size. As far as HTML and your browser are concerned, the text is still one block element, no matter how many line breaks are inserted. If, on the other hand, you make each line a separate paragraph or heading, the line spacing will be unattractively "open."

You can use one of several workarounds for this problem. First, if you're using line breaks, you can alter the size of each line by selecting it and choosing a different font size, either from the Property Inspector or the Text ⇨ Size menu.

A second option renders all the text as a graphics object and inserts it as an image. This gives you total control over the font's appearance and line spacing, at the cost of added download time.

For a third possible solution, take a look at the section on preformatted text later in this chapter. Because you can apply styles to a preformatted text block (which can include line breaks and extra whitespace), you can alter the size, color, and font of each line, if necessary.

Ultimately the best solution is to use Cascading Style Sheets (CSS). The majority of browsers now in use support line spacing through CSS; however, if 3.0 browser compatability is a site requirement, you'll have to use one of the other methods outlined here.

The <wbr> tag

The companion to the <nobr> tag is the word break tag <wbr>. Similar to a soft hyphen in a word processing program, the <wbr> tag tells the browser where to break a word, if necessary. When used within <nobr> tags, <wbr> is the equivalent of telling a browser, "Keep all this text in one line, but if you have to break it, break it here."

As with the <nobr> tag, <wbr> is supported only by Netscape and Microsoft browsers and must be entered by hand via the Quick Tag Editor, Code view, Code Inspector, or your external editor.

Importing Word HTML

Microsoft Word has offered an option to save its documents as HTML since the release of Word 97. Unfortunately, Microsoft's version of HTML output is, at best, highly idiosyncratic. Although you could always open a Word HTML file in

Dreamweaver, if you ever had to modify the page—which you almost always do—it took so long to find your way through the convoluted code that you were almost better off building the page from scratch. Fortunately, that's no longer the case with Dreamweaver.

The capability to Import Word HTML is a key workflow enhancement for Dreamweaver. Dreamweaver can successfully import and automatically clean up files from Microsoft Word 97, Word 98, or Word 2000. The cleanup takes place automatically upon import, but you can also finely tune the modifications that Dreamweaver makes to the file. Moreover, you can even apply the current Source Format profile so that the HTML is styled to look like native Dreamweaver code.

Naturally, before you can import a Word HTML file, you have to have created one. To export a document in HTML format in Word 97/98, choose File ➪ Save as HTML; in Word 2000, the command has changed to File ➪ Save as Web Page. Although the wording change may seem to be a move toward less jargon, what Word actually exports is significant. With Word 2000 (and all the Office 2000 products), Microsoft heartily embraced the XML standard and uses a combination of standard HTML and custom XML code throughout their exported Web pages. For example, here's the opening tag from a Word 2000 document, saved as a Web page:

```
<html xmlns:o="urn:schemas-microsoft-com:office:office"
xmlns:w="urn:schemas-microsoft-com:office:word"
xmlns:dt="uuid:C2F41010-65B3-11d1-A29F-00AA00C14882"
xmlns="http://www.w3.org/TR/REC-html40">
```

which Dreamweaver alters to:

```
<html>
```

If you accept the defaults, importing a Word HTML file is a two-step affair:

1. Choose File ➪ Import ➪ Import Word HTML.

The Import Word HTML dialog box opens and Dreamweaver detects whether the HTML file was exported from Word 97/98 or 2000. The interface options change accordingly.

Caution If Dreamweaver can't determine what version of Word generated the file, an alert appears. Although Dreamweaver will still try to clean up the code, it may not function correctly. The same alert appears if you inadvertently select a standard nonHTML Word document.

2. Click OK to confirm the import operation.

Dreamweaver creates a new HTML document, imports the file, and cleans up the code. If the Show Log on Completion option is selected, Dreamweaver informs you of the modifications made.

For most purposes, accepting the defaults is the best way to quickly bring in your Word HTML files. However, because Web designers have a wide range of code requirements, Dreamweaver provides a full set of options so you can tailor the Word-to-Dreamweaver transformation to your liking. Two different sets of options exist — one for documents saved from Word 97/98 and one for those saved from Word 2000. The different sets of options can be seen on the Detailed tab of the Import Word HTML dialog box; the Basic tab is the same for both file types. Table 9-6 details the Basic tab options, the Word 97/98 options, and the Word 2000 options.

Table 9-6
Import Word HTML Options

Option	Description
Basic	
Remove all Word-specific markup	Deletes all Word-specific tags, including Word XML, conditional tags, empty paragraphs, and margins in `<style>` tags.
Clean up CSS	Deletes all Word-specific CSS code, including inline CSS styles where styles are nested, "mso" designated styles, non-CSS style declarations, CSS style attributes from tables and orphaned (unused) style definitions.
Clean up `<font>` tags	Deletes `<font>` tags that set the default body text to an absolute font size 2.
Fix invalidly nested tags	Deletes tags surrounding paragraph and block-level tags.
Set background color	Adds a background color to the page. Word does not supply one. The default added color is white (#ffffff). Colors can be entered as hexadecimal triplets with a leading hash mark or as a valid color name — that is, red.
Apply source formatting	Formats the imported code according to the guidelines of the current Source Format profile used by Dreamweaver.
Show log on completion	Displays a dialog box that lists all alterations when the process is complete.
Detailed Options for Word 97/98	
Remove Word specific markup	Enables the general clean up of Word-inserted tags.
Word meta and link tags from `<head>`	Specifically enables Dreamweaver to remove Word-specific `<meta>` and `<link>` tags from the `<head>` section of a document.
Clean up `<font>` tags	Enables the general clean up of `<font>` tags.

Option	*Description*
Convert size [7-1] to	Specifies which tag, if any, is substituted for a `<font size=n>` tag. Options are: * `<h1>` through `<h6>` * `<font size=1>` through `<font size=7>` * Default size * Don't change

Detailed Options for Word 2000

Remove Word specific markup	Enables the general clean up of Word-inserted tags.
XML from `<html>` tag	Deletes the Word-generated XML from the `<html>` tag.
Word meta and link tags from `<head>`	Specifically enables Dreamweaver to remove Word-specific `<meta>` and `<link>` tags from the `<head>` section of a document.
Word XML markup	Enables the general clean up of Word-inserted XML tags.
`<![if...]>` `<![endif]>` conditional tags and their contents	Removes all conditional statements.
Remove empty paragraphs and margins from styles	Deletes `<p>` tags without a closing `</p>` and styles tags including margin attributes—for example, `style='margin-top:0in'`.
Clean up CSS	Enables the general clean up of Word inserted CSS tags.
Remove inline CSS styles when possible	Deletes redundant information in nested styles.
Remove any style attribute that starts with "mso"	Eliminates all Microsoft Office (mso) specific attributes.
Remove any non-CSS style declaration	Deletes nonstandard style declarations.
Remove all CSS styles from table rows and cells	Eliminates style information from `<table>`, `<tr>`, and `<td>` tags.
Remove all unused style definitions	Deletes any declared styles that are not referenced in the page.

You don't have to remember to run the Import Word HTML command to take advantage of Dreamweaver's cleanup features. If you've already opened a document saved as Word HTML, you can choose Commands ⇨ Clean Up Word HTML and gain access to the exact same dialog box for the existing page.

Styling Your Text

When the Internet was founded, its intended focus was to make scientific data widely accessible. Soon it became apparent that even raw data could benefit from being styled contextually, without detracting from the Internet's openness and universality. Over the short history of HTML, text styles have become increasingly important, and the World Wide Web Consortium (W3C) has sought to keep a balance between substance and style.

Dreamweaver enables the Web designer to apply the most popular HTML styles directly through the program's menus and Property Inspector. Less prevalent styles can be inserted through the integrated text editors or by hand.

Working with preformatted text

Browsers ignore formatting niceties considered irrelevant to page content: tabs, extra line feeds, indents, and added whitespace. However, you can force browsers to read all the text, including whitespace, exactly as you have entered it. By applying the preformatted tag, <pre>, you tell the browser that it should keep any additional whitespace encountered within the text. By default, the <pre> tag also renders its content with a monospace font such as Courier. For these reasons, the <pre> tag was used to lay out text in columns in the early days of HTML, before tables were widely available.

You can apply the preformatted tag either through the Property Inspector or the menus. Before you use either technique, however, be sure to select the text or position the cursor where you want the preformatted text to begin. To use the Property Inspector, open the Format list box and choose Preformatted. To use the menus, choose Text ⇨ Paragraph Format ⇨ Preformatted.

The <pre> tag is a block element format, like the paragraph or the headings tags, rather than a style. This designation as a block element format has two important implications. First, you can't apply the <pre> tag to part of a line; when you use this tag, the entire paragraph is altered. Second, you can apply styles to preformatted text — this enables you to increase the size or alter the font, but at the same time maintain the whitespace feature made possible with the <pre> tag. All text in Figure 9-10 uses the <pre> tag; the column on the left is the standard output with monospaced font; the column on the right uses a different font in a larger size.

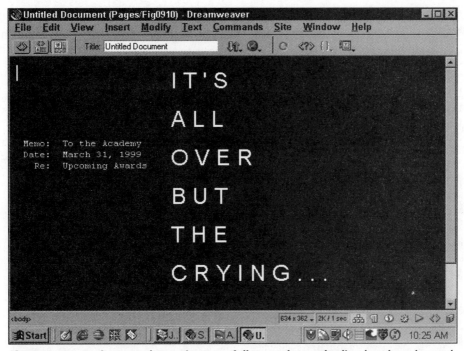

Figure 9-10: Preformatted text gives you full control over the line breaks, tabs, and other whitespace in your Web page.

Depicting various styles

As explained in Chapter 8, HTML's logical styles are used to mark text relatively or within a particular context, rather than with a specific look. The eventual displayed appearance of logical styles is completely up to the viewer's browser. This is useful when you are working with documents from different sources — reports from different research laboratories around the country, for instance — and you want certain conformity of style. Logical styles are utilitarian; physical styles such as boldface and italic are decorative. Both types of styles have their uses in material published on today's Web.

All of Dreamweaver's styles are accessed by choosing Text ⇨ Style and selecting from the 13 available style name options. A checkmark appears next to the selected tags. Style tags can be nested (put inside one another), and you can mix logical and physical tags within a word, line, or document. You can have a bold, strikethrough, variable style; or you can have an underlined, cited style. (Both variable and cite are particular logical styles covered later in this section.) If, however, you are trying to achieve a particular look using logical styles, you should probably use the Cascading Style Sheets feature.

The styles that can be applied through regular HTML are just the tip of the iceberg compared to the possibilities with Cascading Style Sheets. For details on using this feature, see Chapter 18.

Take a look at Figure 9-11 for a comparison of how the styles are rendered in Dreamweaver, Internet Explorer 5.0, and Netscape Communicator 4.7. While the various renderings are mostly the same, notice the browser differences in the Definition styles and the difference in how the Keyboard style is rendered in Dreamweaver and either browser.

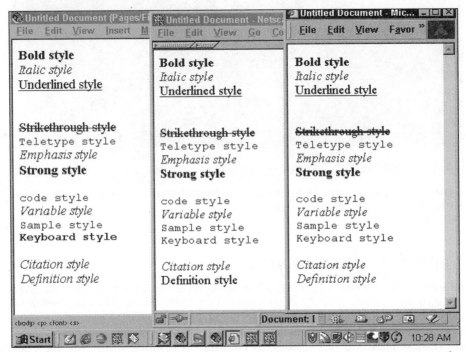

Figure 9-11: In this comparison chart, the various renderings of Dreamweaver style tags are from Dreamweaver, Netscape Communicator 4.7, and Internet Explorer 5.0 (from left to right).

Two of the three physical style tags — bold and italic — are both available from the Text Property Inspector and through keyboard shortcuts (Ctrl+B or Command+B, and Ctrl+I or Command+I, respectively). The Underline tag, <u>, is available only through the Text ⇨ Style menu. Underlining text on a Web page is generally discouraged in order to avoid confusion with links, which are typically displayed underlined.

Both physical and logical style tags are described, with examples, in Table 9-7.

	Table 9-7 **Dreamweaver Style Tags**	
Style	**Tag**	**Description**
Bold	`<b>`	Text is rendered with a bold style.
Italic	`<i>`	Text is rendered with an italic style.
Underline	`<u>`	Text is rendered underlined.
Strikethrough	`<s>`	Used primarily in edited documents to depict edited text. Usually rendered with a line through the text.
Teletype	`<tt>`	Used to represent an old-style typewriter. Rendered in a monospace font such as Courier.
Emphasis	`<em>`	Used to accentuate certain words relative to the surrounding text. Most often rendered in italic.
Strong Emphasis	`<strong>`	Used to strongly accentuate certain words relative to the surrounding text. Most often rendered in boldface.
Code	`<code>`	Used to depict programming code, usually in a monospaced font.
Sample	`<samp>`	Used to display characters in a literal sequence, usually in a monospaced font.
Variables	`<var>`	Used to mark variables in programming code. Most often displayed in italics.
Keyboard	`<kbd>`	Used to indicate what should be user input. Often shown in a monospaced font, sometimes in boldface.
Citation	`<cite>`	Used to mark citations, references, and titles. Most often displayed in italic.
Definition	`<dfn>`	Used to denote the first, defining instance of a term. Usually displayed in italic.

Using the <address> tag

Currently, Dreamweaver does not support one useful style tag: the `<address>` tag. Rendered as italic text by browsers, the `<address>...</address>` tag pair often marks the signature and e-mail address of a Web page's creator. The `<address>` tags should go around a paragraph tag pair; otherwise, Dreamweaver flags the closing `</p>` as invalid.

The easiest way to do this in Dreamweaver is to use the Quick Tag Editor. Select your text and press Ctrl+T (Command T) to automatically enter Wrap Tag mode. If Tag Hints is enabled, all you'll have to type is **ad** and press Enter (Return) twice to accept the hint and confirm the tag.

If you're applying the ⟨address⟩ tag to multiple lines, use ⟨br⟩ tags to form line breaks. The following example shows the proper use of the ⟨address⟩ tags:

```
<address><p>The President<br>
 1600 Pennsylvania Avenue<br>
 Washington, DC 20001</p></address>
```

This preceding code is shown on a Web browser as follows:

The President
1600 Pennsylvania Avenue
Washington, DC 20001

Tip   To remove a standard style, highlight the styled text, choose Text ⇨ Style, and select the name of the style you want to remove. The checkmark disappears from the style name. To remove a nonstandard tag such as ⟨address⟩, choose the tag in the Tag Selector and right-click (Control+click) to open the shortcut menu and select Remove Tag.

Using HTML Styles

In the world of Web design, consistency is a good thing. A site where headings, subheads, and body text are consistent from page to page is far easier for the visitor to quickly grasp than one where each page has its own style. Although the best approach for a consistently designed site may be the use of Cascading Style Sheets, that approach requires 4.0 and later browsers, and many clients are not willing to write off those potential Web visitors using older software.

To bridge the gap between old and new—and to make it easier to apply the same set of tags over and over again—Dreamweaver includes HTML Styles. HTML Styles are similar to CSS in that you define a custom style for text and give it any attributes you want: font name, size, color, format, and so on. Then you apply that style to either a selection or an entire block of text. The primary difference is that, with HTML Styles, Dreamweaver adds the necessary standard HTML tags, instead of CSS style declarations, to recreate your style. In other words, if you always set your legal disclaimers in Verdana at a –1 size in a deep red color, you can define your "legal" style once and apply it over and over again with one step, anywhere on the site.

HTML Styles, however, are not a replacement for CSS styles, and you should keep in mind some important differences:

✦ Modifying a HTML Style definition affects only subsequent applications of the style. When a CSS style is altered, the change is immediately seen wherever the style has been applied on the current page as well as in all future applications.

✦ HTML Styles use standard text tags and cannot, therefore, create some of the special effects possible in CSS. For example, you could not create a HTML Style that eliminates the underline from a link or changes the leading of a paragraph.

✦ Although defined HTML Styles are accessible from anywhere within a site, they are applied on a document-to-document basis, whereas with CSS, an external style sheet could be defined and linked to pages anywhere on your site.

Even with these differences, however, HTML Styles are an enhancement to a designer's workflow and extremely easy to use.

Note   In the remainder of this section, when I refer to a style or styles, I'm referring to HTML Styles. CSS Style references are designated as such.

Applying HTML Styles

The HTML Styles panel, shown in Figure 9-12, displays all currently available styles as well as options for removing style formatting, editing existing styles, adding new styles, or removing styles from the panel.

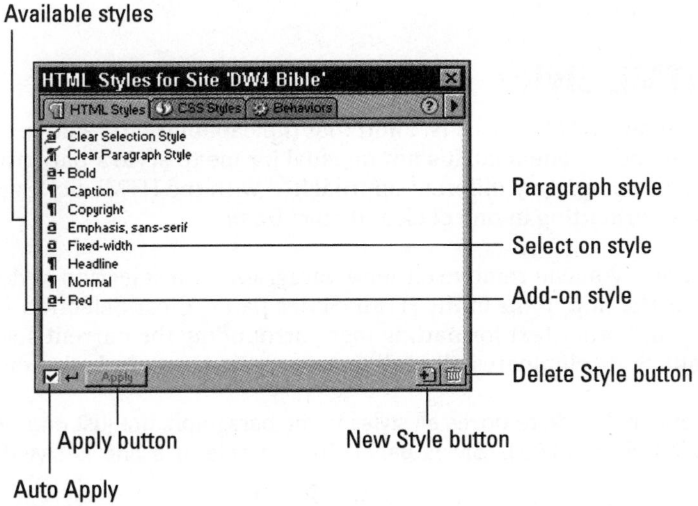

Available styles

HTML Styles for Site 'DW4 Bible'
HTML Styles CSS Styles Behaviors
Clear Selection Style
Clear Paragraph Style
Bold
Caption ————————————————— Paragraph style
Copyright
Emphasis, sans-serif
Fixed-width ————————————————— Select on style
Headline
Normal
Red ————————————————— Add-on style
————————————————— Delete Style button
Apply

Apply button   New Style button

Auto Apply

Figure 9-12: Manage your standard formatting through the HTML Styles panel.

HTML Styles are divided into two distinct types: paragraph and selection styles. A paragraph style affects an entire block element, whether it is a single heading, a paragraph, or another block element such as a block quote. Paragraph styles are designated with a ¶ symbol in the HTML Styles panel. A paragraph style is applied to the entire current block element, whether the cursor has selected the text or is just within the block. A selection style, on the other hand, applies formatting only to selected text. Selection styles are marked in the HTML Styles panel with an underlined lowercased *a*, like this (a̲).

It's possible for both paragraph and selection styles to either clear the existing style before adding the new formatting or add the new formatting to the existing style. The default behavior is for existing formatting to be removed; if the style is to be added, a small plus sign (+) is shown in front of the style name.

To apply an HTML Style, follow these steps:

1. Open the HTML Styles panel in one of the following ways:
   - Select Window ➪ HTML Styles.
   - Choose the HTML Styles button from either Launcher.
   - Press the keyboard shortcut, Ctrl+F11 (Command+F11).

2. To apply a style to the currently selected text, choose any designated (a̲) HTML Style.

Tip   It's easiest to always have the Auto Apply option selected, so that your choices immediately are applied; if this option is not selected, click the Apply button.

3. To apply a style to the current block element, choose any so-designated (¶) HTML Style.

Removing HTML Styles

As useful as applying new HTML Styles is, I find that the capability to remove all such formatting even more beneficial. It's not unusual for me to style a paragraph and then want to try a completely different approach — with the HTML Styles panel, I can wipe out all the formatting in one click and start fresh.

As with applying styles, you can remove either a paragraph or a selection style. Both are available as the first items in the HTML Styles panel. Clear Selection Style removes all <font> and other text formatting tags surrounding the current selection. Clear Paragraph Style eliminates all such tags from the current block element.

Caution   Removing a paragraph style removes all styles to the paragraph, not just ones you may have added via the HTML Styles panel. For example, if a line is styled in this way:

```
<h1><font color="#FFFF00">Welcome</font></h2>
```

Moving HTML Styles from Site to Site

Custom HTML styles are available from any page in your site. But what happens if you start a new site? Do you have to recreate your custom styles again? Every new site starts with the same set of default styles standard in Dreamweaver. (The next section describes how to alter even those defaults.) But you can easily transfer styles you've created for one site to another, just by copying the right file.

The information describing the custom HTML styles is stored in each site's Library folder in a file named styles.xml. To transfer the HTML styles, just copy the styles.xml file from one site's Library folder to the Library folder for another site. Library folders are created within a site when they are first needed, so if you've just defined your site, the Library folder may not exist yet. You can, however, safely create it within the local site root and move your styles.xml file into the folder.

Selecting Clear Paragraph Style converts the line to this:

```
<p>Welcome</p>
```

The Clear Selection Style command does not require that the formatting tags be adjacent to the selection. If you select some text in the middle of a paragraph styled in a particular color and font, choosing Clear Selection Style inserts appropriate tags before and after the selection so that the selection has no style whatsoever, but the surrounding text remains styled. A before and after view of the process is shown in Figure 9-13.

If you no longer wish to have a defined style displayed in the HTML Styles panel, select that style and choose the Delete Style button. Alternatively, you could select the style and choose Delete Style from the context-sensitive menu on the panel.

Defining HTML Styles

Naturally, the standard list of styles is just a jumping-off place for the HTML Styles panel. To get the most out the feature, you should design your own custom styles. Dreamweaver gives you a number of methods to define a style:

✦ **Style by Example** — Create a new style from formatted text onscreen.

✦ **Modify an Existing Style** — Edit a standard or custom style to your liking. You can even duplicate the style first, so both old and new versions are available.

✦ **Build a New Style** — Select all the desired attributes for your selection or paragraph style and try it out right away on selected text.

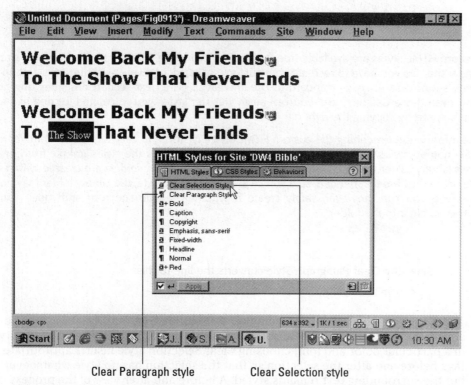

Clear Paragraph style   Clear Selection style

Figure 9-13: You can remove all styling from a bit of text and keep the surrounding styling with the Clear Selection Style command.

All style definitions are managed in the Define HTML Style dialog box, shown in Figure 9-14. How the dialog box is opened depends on which method you're using to create or modify your style.

✦ To create a style from example, select tags you want to include in the style from the Document window or the Tag Selector and then choose the New Style button from the HTML Styles panel.

✦ To modify an existing style, double-click its name in the HTML Styles panel list.

✦ To create a new style built on an existing one, select the style and then, from the context-sensitive menu of the HTML Styles panel, select Duplicate.

✦ To create a style from the ground up, choose the New Style button on the HTML Styles panel.

To define an HTML Style, follow these steps:

1. Open the Define HTML Style dialog box using one of the previously described methods.

2. Enter a unique name for your style, if creating a new one.

3. Choose whether your style is to apply to a selection or a paragraph.

4. Select whether your style will add to the existing style or clear existing style.

5. Choose the desired font attributes:

- Font

- Size

- Color

- Style: Bold, Italic, or Bold-Italic

- Other . . . (Additional Optional Styles): Underline, Strikethrough, Teletype, Emphasis, Strong, Code, Variable, Sample, Keyboard, Citation, Definition

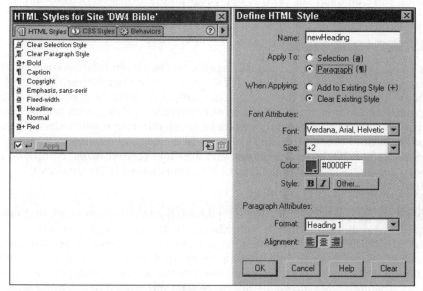

Figure 9-14: Build or modify styles in the Define HTML Style dialog box.

6. If defining a paragraph style, select from the following attribute options:

- Format: None, Heading 1 through Heading 6, or Preformatted

- Alignment: Right, Center, Left.

7. Click OK when you're done.

Tip

To start over at any time, select the Clear button.

Modifying Text Format

As a Web designer, you easily spend at least as much time adjusting your text as you do getting it into your Web pages. Luckily, Dreamweaver puts most of the tools you need for this task right at your fingertips. All the text-formatting options are available through the Text Property Inspector. Instead of hand-coding `<font>`, `<blockquote>`, and alignment tags, just select your text and click a button.

Note   In HTML text formatting today, programmers are moving toward using Cascading Style Sheets and away from hard-coding text with `<font>` and other tags. Both 4.0+ versions of the major Web browsers support Cascading Style Sheets to some extent, and Internet Explorer has had some support since the 3.0 version. The current realities of browser competition, however, dictate that to take advantage of the widest support range, Web designers must continue to use the character-specific tags. Even after Cascading Style Sheets gain widespread acceptance, you'll probably still need to apply tags on the local level occasionally.

Adjusting font size

The six HTML heading types (H1 to H6) enable you to assign relative sizes to a line or to an entire paragraph. In addition, HTML gives you a finer degree of control through the size attribute of the font tag. In contrast to publishing environments, both traditional and desktop, font size is not specified in HTML with points. Rather, the `<font>` tag enables you to choose one of seven different explicit sizes that the browser can render (absolute sizing), or you can select one relative to the page's basic font. Figure 9-15 shows the default absolute and relative sizes, compared to a more page designer–friendly point chart (accomplished with Dreamweaver's Cascading Style Sheets features).

Which way should you go—absolute or relative? Some designers think that relative sizing gives them more options. As you can see by the chart in Figure 9-15, browsers are limited to displaying seven different sizes no matter what—unless you're using Cascading Style Sheets. Relative sizing does give you additional flexibility, though, because you can resize all the fonts in an entire Web page with one command. Absolute sizes, however, are more straightforward to use and can be coded in Dreamweaver without any additional HTML programming. Once again, it's the designer's choice.

Absolute size

You can assign an absolute font size through either the Property Inspector or the menus. In both cases, you choose a value, 1 (smallest) through 7 (largest), to which you want to resize your text; you might note that this order is the reverse of the heading sizes, which range from H1 to H6, largest to smallest.

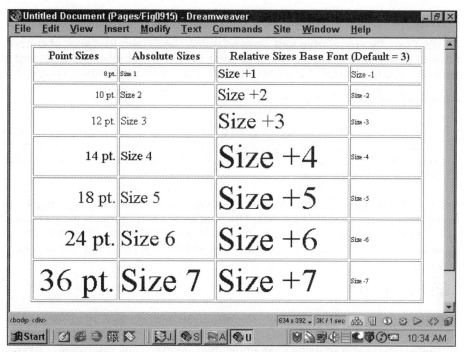

Figure 9-15: In this chart, you can see the relationships between the various font sizes in an HTML browser and as compared to "real-world" point sizes.

To use the Property Inspector to pick an absolute font size, follow these steps:

1. Select your text.

2. In the Property Inspector, open the Font Size drop-down list of options.

3. Choose a value from 1 to 7.

To pick an absolute font size from the menu, follow these steps:

1. Select your text.

2. Choose Text ⇨ Size and pick a value from 1 to 7, or Default (which is 3).

Tip   You can also use the keyboard shortcuts for changing absolute font sizes. Headings 1 through 6 correspond to Ctrl+1 through Ctrl+6 (Command+1 through Command+6). The Paragraph option is rendered with a Ctrl+Shift+P (Command+Shift+P); you can remove all formatting with Ctrl+0 (Command+0).

Relative size

To what exactly are relative font sizes relative? The default font size, of course. The advantage of relative font sizes is that you can alter a Web page's default font size with one command, the `<basefont>` tag. The tag takes the following form:

```
<basefont size=value>
```

where value is a number from 1 to 7. The `<basefont>` tag is usually placed immediately following the opening `<body>` tag. Dreamweaver does not support previewing the results of altering the `<basefont>` tag and the tag has to be entered by hand or through the external editor.

You can distinguish a relative font size from an absolute font size by the plus or minus sign that precedes the value. The relative sizes are plus or minus the current `<basefont>` size. Thus, a `<font size=+1>` is normally rendered with a size 4 font because the default `<basefont>` is 3. If you include the following line in your Web page:

```
<basefont size=5>
```

text marked with a `<font size=+1>` is displayed with a size 6 font. Because browsers display only seven different size fonts with a `<basefont size=5>` setting — unless you're using Cascading Style Sheets — any relative size over `<font size=+2>` won't display differently when previewed in a browser.

Relative font sizes can also be selected from either the Property Inspector or the menus. To use the Property Inspector to pick a relative font size, follow these steps:

1. Select your text or position the cursor where you want the new text size to begin.

2. In the Property Inspector, open the Font Size drop-down list of options.

3. To increase the size of your text, choose a value from +1 through +7.

   To decrease the size of your text, choose a value from –1 to –7.

To pick a relative font size from the menus, follow these steps:

1. Select your text or position the cursor where you want the new text size to begin.

2. To increase the size of your text, choose Text ⇨ Size Increase and pick a value from +1 to +7.

   To reduce the size of your text, choose Text ⇨ Size Decrease and pick a value from –1 to –7.

Dreamweaver's Color Pickers

Dreamweaver includes a color picker for selecting colors for all manner of HTML elements: text, table cells, and page background. Dreamweaver's color picker—in keeping with the Macromedia common user interface—offers a number of palettes from the context menu to choose your colors: Color Cubes, Continuous Tone, Windows OS, Mac OS, and Grayscale. The most common choices for Web designers are Color Cubes and Continuous Tone, both of which display the 216 Web safe colors common to the Macintosh and Windows palettes. By default, the Snap to Web Safe option, also found in the context menu, is chosen.

Once you've opened the text color picker by selecting the color swatch on the Property Inspector, the cursor changes shape into an eye-dropper. This eye-dropper can sample colors from any of the displayed swatches or from any color on-screen. Simply click the color swatch and drag the eye-dropper over any graphic to choose a color.

If you choose a color outside of the "safe" range, you have no assurances of how the color is rendered on a viewer's browser. Some systems select the closest color in RGB values; some use dithering (positioning two or more colors next to each other to simulate another color) to try to overcome the limitations of the current screen color depth. So be forewarned: If at all possible, stick with the browser-safe colors, especially when coloring text.

Mac Users: The system color picker—brought up when the Palette icon on the color picker menu is selected—for Macintosh is far more elaborate than the one available for Windows. The Mac version has several color schemes to use: CMYK (for print-related colors), RGB (for screen-based colors), HTML (for Web-based colors), and Crayon (for kid-like colors). The CMYK, HTML, and RGB systems offer you color swatches and three or four sliders with text entry boxes, and accept percentage values for RGB and CMYK, and hex values for HTML. Both RGB and HTML also have a snap-to-Web color option for matching your chosen color to the closest browser-safe color. The Hue, Saturation, and Value (or Lightness) sliders also have color wheels.

Adding font color

Unless you assign a color to text on your Web page, the browser uses its own default, typically black. As noted in "Establishing Page Properties" in Chapter 8, you can change the font color for the entire page by choosing Modify ⇨ Page Properties and selecting a new color from the Text Color swatch. You can also color any specific headings, words, or paragraphs that you have selected in Dreamweaver.

Tip When adding a new font color, size, or name to text that already has one `<font>` tag applied to it, it's best to use the Tag Selector to highlight the text by selecting that `<font>` tag. If you select your text by clicking and dragging, you're likely to not select the entire contents of the tag, which results in multiple `<font>` tags being applied.

The <font> tag goes to work again when you add color to selected elements of the page — this time, with the color attribute set to a particular value. HTML color is expressed in either a hexadecimal color number or a color name. The hexadecimal color number is based on the color's red-green-blue value and is written as follows:

```
#FFFFFF
```

The preceding represents the color white. You can also use standard color names instead of the hexadecimal color numbers. A sample color code line follows:

```
I'm <font color="green">GREEN</font> with envy.
```

Dreamweaver understands both color names and hexadecimal color numbers, but its HTML code output is in hexadecimal color numbers only.

Again, you have two ways to add color to your text in Dreamweaver. The Property Inspector displays a drop-down list of the browser-safe colors and also gives you an option to choose from a full-spectrum Color dialog box. If you approach your coloring task via the menus, the Text ⇨ Color command takes you immediately to the Color dialog box.

To use the Property Inspector to color a range of text in Dreamweaver, follow these steps:

1. Select the text you want to color or position the cursor where you want the new text color to begin.

2. From the Property Inspector, you can

   • Type a hexadecimal color number directly into the Font Color text box.

   • Type a color name directly into the Font Color text box.

   • Select the Font Color swatch to open the browser-safe color picker.

3. If you chose to type a color name or number directly into the Font Color text box, press Tab or click the Document window to see the color applied.

4. If you clicked the Font Color swatch, select your color from the browser-safe colors available. As you move your pointer over the color swatches, Dreamweaver displays the color in the corner and the color's hexadecimal number below.

5. For a wider color selection from the Color dialog box, select the Palette icon in the lower-right corner of the color swatch.

To access the full-spectrum color picker in Windows, follow these steps:

1. Select your text or position your cursor where you want the new text color to begin.

2. Choose Text ⇨ Color to open the Color dialog box, as shown in Figure 9-16.

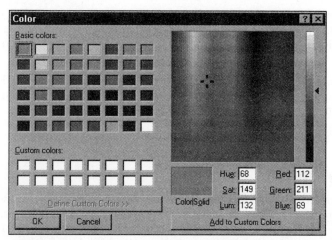

Figure 9-16: Use the Color dialog box in Windows to choose a color for your font outside of the browser-safe palette.

3. Select one of the 48 preset standard colors from the color swatches on the left of the Color dialog box, or use either of the following methods:

   • Select a color by moving the Hue/Saturation pointer and the Luminance pointer.

   • Enter decimal values directly into either the Red, Green, and Blue boxes or the Hue, Saturation, and Luminance boxes.

4. If you create a custom color, you can add it to your palette by selecting Add to Custom Colors. You can add up to 16 custom colors.

5. Click OK when you are finished.

Caution

When you add a custom color to your palette in Windows, the new color swatch goes into the currently selected swatch or, if no swatch is selected, the next available swatch. Make sure you have selected an empty or replaceable swatch before selecting the Add to Custom Color button. To clear the custom colors, first set the palette to white by bringing the Luminance slider all the way to the top. Then, select the Add to Custom Color button until all the color swatch text boxes are empty.

To access the full-spectrum color picker in Macintosh systems, follow these steps:

1. Select the text or position your cursor where you want the new text color to begin.

2. Choose Text ➪ Color to open the Color dialog box.

3. From the Color dialog box, select the Color Palette icon.

   The Macintosh color picker opens.

4. In the Macintosh color picker, the list of available pickers is displayed in the left pane, and each particular interface is shown in the right. Choose the specific color picker icon from the left pane and create the color desired in the right.

   The number and type of color pickers vary from system to system, depending on the version of the operating system and whether you've added any third-party color pickers.

5. When you've found the desired color, click OK.

Assigning a specific font

Along with size and color, you can also specify the typeface in which you want particular text to be rendered. Dreamweaver uses a special method for choosing font names for a range of selected text, due to HTML's unique way of handling fonts. Before you learn how to change a typeface in Dreamweaver, let's further examine how fonts in HTML work.

About HTML fonts

Page layout designers can incorporate as many different fonts as available to their own systems. Web layout designers, on the other hand, can use only those fonts on their viewers' systems. If you designate a paragraph to be in Bodoni Bold Condensed, for instance, and put it on the Web, the paragraph is displayed with that font only if that exact font name is on the user's system. Otherwise, the browser uses the default system font, which is often Times or Times New Roman.

Fonts are specified with the `<font>` tag, aided by the `name` attribute. Because a designer can never be certain of which fonts are on visitors' computers, HTML enables you to offer a number of options to the browser, as follows:

```
<font name="Arial, Helvetica, sans-serif">Swiss Maid Foundry</font>
```

The browser encountering the preceding tag first looks for the Arial font to render the enclosed text. If Arial isn't there, the browser looks for the next font in the list, which in this case is Helvetica. Failing to find any of the specified fonts listed, the browser uses whichever font has been assigned to the category for the font — sans-serif in this case.

The W3C and some Web browsers recognize five main categories of fonts: serif, sans-serif, monospace, cursive, and fantasy. Internet Explorer has a higher compliance rating on this issue than Netscape Communicator.

Selecting a font

The process for assigning a font name to a range of text is similar to that of assigning a font size or color. Instead of selecting one font name, however, you're usually selecting one font series. That series could contain three or more fonts, as previously explained. Font series are chosen from the Property Inspector or through a menu item. Dreamweaver enables you to assign any font on your system — or even any font you can name — to a font series, as covered in the section "Editing the Font List," later in this chapter.

To assign a specific font series to your text, follow these steps:

1. Select the text or position your cursor where you want the new text font to begin.

2. From the Property Inspector, open the drop-down list of font names. You can also choose Text ➪ Font from the menu bar. Your font list is displayed.

3. Select a font from the Font List. To return to the system font, choose Default Font from the list.

It's also possible to enter the font name or font series directly in the Property Inspector's Font drop-down list.

Tip
Font peculiarities are one of the key reasons to always test your Web pages on several platforms. Macintosh and Windows have different names for the same basic fonts (Arial in Windows is almost identical to Helvetica in Macintosh, for instance), and even the standard font sizes vary between the platforms. On the plus side, standard Microsoft fonts (Arial, Verdana for example) are more common on the Macintosh since Mac OS 8.1, but differences still exist. Overall, PC fonts are larger than fonts on a Macintosh. Be sure to check out your page on as many systems as possible before finalizing your design.

Editing the Font List

With the Edit Font List dialog box, Dreamweaver gives you a point-and-click interface for building your font lists. Once the Edit Font List dialog box is open, you can delete an existing font series, add a new one, or change the order of the list so your favorite ones are on top. Take a look at Figure 9-17 to see the sections of the Edit Font List dialog box: the current Font List, the Available Fonts on your system, and the Chosen Fonts. The Chosen Fonts are the individual fonts that you've selected to be incorporated into a font series.

Let's step through the process of constructing a new font series and adding it to the Font List:

1. To open the Edit Font List dialog box, either choose Edit Font List through the Font Name option arrow in the Property Inspector, or select Text ➪ Font ➪ Edit Font List.

2. If the Chosen Fonts box is not empty, clear the Chosen Fonts box by selecting the plus (+) button at the top of the dialog box. You can also scroll down to the bottom of the current Font List and select "(Add fonts in list below)."

3. Select a font from the Available Fonts list.

4. Click the << button to transfer the selected font to the Chosen Fonts list.

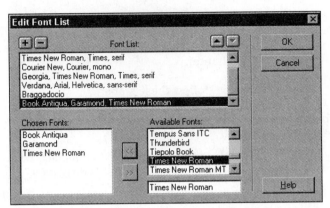

Figure 9-17: Dreamweaver's Edit Font List dialog box gives you considerable control over the fonts that you can add to your Web page.

5. To remove a font you no longer want or have chosen in error, highlight it in the Chosen Fonts list and select the >> button.

6. Repeat Steps 3 through 5 until the Chosen Fonts list contains the alternative fonts desired.

7. If you want to add another, separate font series, repeat Steps 2 through 5.

8. Click OK when you are finished adding fonts.

To change the order in which font series are listed in the Font List, follow these steps:

1. In the Font List dialog box, select the font series that you want to move.

2. If you want to move the series higher up the list, select the up-arrow button at the top-right of the Font List. If you want to move the series lower down the list, select the down-arrow button.

To remove a font series from the current Font List, highlight it and select the minus (–) button at the top-left of the list.

Remember, you need to have the fonts on your system to make them a part of your Font List. To add a font that's unavailable on your computer, type the name of the font into the text box below the Available Fonts list and press Enter (Return).

Aligning text

You can easily align text in Dreamweaver, just like in a traditional word processing program. HTML supports the alignment of text to the left or right margin, or in the center of the browser window. Like a word processing program, Dreamweaver aligns text one paragraph at a time. You can't left-align one word, center the next, and then right-align the third word in the same paragraph.

To align text, you can use one of three methods: a menu command, the Property Inspector, or a keyboard shortcut. To use the menus, choose Text ⇨ Alignment and then pick the alignment you prefer (Left, Right, or Center). Table 9-8 explains the Text Property Inspector's Alignment buttons and the associated keyboard shortcuts.

Table 9-8 Text Alignment Options in the Property Inspector		
Button	**Alignment**	**Keyboard Shortcut**
	Left	Ctrl+Alt+L (Command+Option+L)
	Center	Ctrl+Alt+C (Command+Option+C)
	Right	Ctrl+Alt+R (Command+Option+R)

Note A fourth way to align text is through the Cascading Style Sheets. Any style can be set to align your text. Moreover, not only are Left, Right, and Center supported – so is Justify, which causes text to be flush against both left and right margins, creating a block-like appearance. The Justify value is supported in browsers 4.0 and later.

Cross-Reference Traditional HTML alignment options are limited. For a finer degree of control, be sure to investigate precise positioning with layers in Chapter 19.

Indenting entire paragraphs

HTML offers a tag that enables you to indent whole paragraphs, such as inset quotations or name-and-address blocks. Not too surprisingly, the tag used is called the `<blockquote>` tag. Dreamweaver gives you instant access to the `<blockquote>` tag through the Indent and Outdent buttons located on the Text Property Inspector, as shown in Figure 9-18.

Outdent— ⎣Indent

Figure 9-18: Indent paragraphs and blocks of text with the Indent and the Outdent buttons.

To indent one or more paragraphs, select them and click the Indent button in the Property Inspector. Paragraphs can be indented multiple times; each time you click the Indent button, another `<blockquote>...</blockquote>` tag pair is added.

Note   You can't control how much space a single `<blockquote>` indents a paragraph — that characteristic is determined by the browser.

If you find that you have over-indented, you can use the Outdent button, which is also located on the Property Inspector. The Outdent button has no effect if your text is already at the left edge.

You also have the option of indenting your paragraphs through the menus; choose Text ➪ Indent or Text ➪ Outdent.

Tip   You can tell how many `<blockquote>` tags are being used to create a particular look by placing your cursor in the text and looking at the Tag Selector.

Incorporating Dates

With the Web constantly changing, keeping track of when information is updated is important. Dreamweaver includes a new command that enables you to insert today's date in your page, in almost any format imaginable. Moreover, you can set the inserted date to be automatically updated every time the page is saved. This means every time you make a modification to a page and save it, the current date is added.

The Insert Date command uses your system clock to get the current date. In addition, you can elect to add a day name (for example, Thursday) and time to the basic date information. Once the date text is inserted, it can be formatted in the same way as any other text — adding color or a specific font type or changing the date's size.

To insert the current date, follow these steps:

1. Choose Insert ➪ Date or select the Insert Date object from the Common panel of the Objects panel.

    The Insert Date dialog box, shown in Figure 9-19, is displayed.

2. If desired, select a Day Format to include in the date from the drop-down list. The options are:

    [No Day]   Thu

    Thursday,   thu,

    Thursday   thu

    Thu,

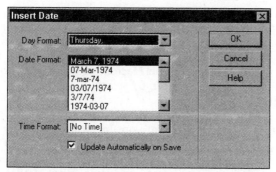

Figure 9-19: Keep track of when a file is updated by using the Insert Date command.

3. Select the desired date format from the drop-down list. The example formats are:

March 7, 1974	7./03/7.4
07.-Mar-1974	07.03.1974
7.-mar-7.4	07.03.74
03./07/1994	7.-03-197.4
3./7/747.	March, 197.4
1974.-03-07	74.-03-07
7./3/7.4	

Tip

If you are creating Web pages for the global market, consider using the format designated by the 1974-03-07 example. This year-month-day format is an ISO (International Organization for Standardization) standard and is computer sortable.

4. Select the desired time format, if any, from the drop-down list. The two example time formats are:

[No Time]

10.:18 PM

22.:18

5. If you want the date modified to include the current date every time the file is saved, select the Update Automatically on Save option.

6. Click OK when you're done.

It's no problem at all to format an inserted date when the Update Automatically on Save option is *not* selected — then it's just plain text and the formatting can be added easily through the Text Property Inspector. However, if the date is to be automatically updated, it's inserted as a special Macromedia datatype with its own Property Inspector. You can style it, however, by selecting options from the Text menu or applying an HTML or CSS style.

If your date object includes the Automatic Update option, you can modify the format. Select the date and, in the Property Inspector, choose the Edit Date Format button. The Edit Date Format dialog box opens and is identical to the Insert Date dialog box, except the Update Automatically on Save option is not available.

Commenting Your Code

When will you know to start inserting comments into your HTML code? The first time you go back to an earlier Web page, look at the code and say, "What on earth was I thinking?" You should plan ahead and develop the habit of commenting your code now.

Browsers run fine without your comments, but for any continued development — of the Web page or of yourself as a Webmaster — commenting your code is extremely beneficial. Sometimes, as in a corporate setting, Web pages are codeveloped by teams of designers and programmers. In this situation, commenting your code may not just be a good idea; it may be required.

An HTML comment looks like the following:

```
<!-- Created by Hummer Associates, Inc. -->
```

You're not restricted to any particular line length or number of lines for comments. The text included between the opening of the comment, `<!--`, and the closing, `-->`, can span regular paragraphs or HTML code. In fact, one of the most common uses for comments during the testing and debugging phase of page design is to "comment out" sections of code as a means of tracking down an elusive bug.

To insert a comment in Dreamweaver, first place your cursor in Code View, Design View, or in the Code Inspector where you want the comment to appear. Then select the Insert Comment button from the Invisibles panel of the Objects panel. This sequence opens the Insert Comment dialog box, where you can insert the desired text; click OK when you've finished. Figure 9-20 shows the Insert Comment dialog box, with the corresponding completed comment in the split Design/Code View.

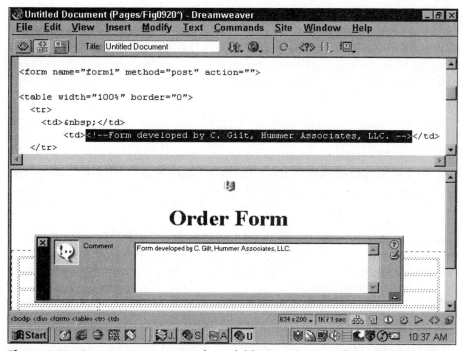

Figure 9-20: Comments are extremely useful for inserting into the code information not visible on the rendered Web page.

By default, Dreamweaver inserts a Comment symbol in the Document window. As with the other Invisibles, you can hide the Comment symbol by choosing Edit ➪ Preferences and then deselecting the Comments checkbox in the Invisible Elements panel. You can also hide any displayed Invisibles by selecting View ➪ Invisible Elements or using the keyboard shortcut, Ctrl+Shift+I (Command+Shift+I).

When you need to edit a comment, double-click the Comment symbol to display the current comment in an editable window. After you've finished making your changes to the comment, select the Close button of the Comment window. A comment can be moved or duplicated by selecting its symbol and using the Cut, Copy, and Paste commands under the Edit menu. You can also right-click (Command+click) the Comment symbol to bring up the shortcut menu. Finally, you can click and drag Comment symbols to move the corresponding comment to a new location.

Summary

Learning to manipulate text is an essential design skill for creating Web pages. Dreamweaver gives you all the tools you need to insert and modify the full range of HTML text quickly and easily. This chapter covered the following topics related to adding text to your Web page:

✦ HTML headings are available in six different sizes: $\langle h1 \rangle$ through $\langle h6 \rangle$. Headings are used primarily as headlines and subheads to separate divisions of the Web page.

✦ Blocks of text are formatted with the paragraph tag $\langle p \rangle$. Each paragraph is separated from the other paragraphs by a line of whitespace above and below. Use the line break tag, $\langle br \rangle$, to make lines appear directly above or below one another.

✦ Dreamweaver offers a full complement of text-editing tools — everything from Cut and Paste to Find and Replace. Two commands, Copy Text Only and Paste As Text, are unique to Dreamweaver and make short work of switching between text and code.

✦ Dreamweaver's Find and Replace feature goes a long way toward automating your work on the current page as well as throughout the Web site. Both content and code can be searched in a basic or very advanced fashion.

✦ Where possible, text in HTML is formatted according to its meaning. Dreamweaver applies the styles selected through the Text ⇨ Style menu. For most styles, the browser determines what the user views.

✦ You can format Web page text much as you can text in a word processing program. Within certain limitations, you can select a font's size and color, as well as the font itself.

✦ Dreamweaver's HTML Styles feature enables you to consistently and quickly format your text.

✦ HTML comments are a useful (and often requisite) vehicle for embedding information into a Web page that remains unseen by the casual viewer. Comments can annotate program code or insert copyright information.

In the next chapter, you learn how to insert and work with graphics.

✦   ✦   ✦

Inserting Images

The Internet started as a text-based medium primarily used for sharing data among research scientists and among U.S. military commanders. Today, the Web is as visually appealing as any mass medium. Dreamweaver's power becomes even more apparent as you use its visual layout tools to incorporate background and foreground images into your Web page designs.

Completely baffled by all the various image formats out there? This chapter opens with an overview of the key Web-oriented graphics formats, including PNG. Also, this chapter covers techniques for incorporating both background and foreground images — and modifying them using new methods available in Dreamweaver 4. Animation graphics and how you can use them in your Web pages are also covered here, as are techniques for creating rollover buttons. Finally, this chapter introduces integration with Fireworks, Macromedia's award-winning Web graphics tool; Dreamweaver and Fireworks make a potent team for creating and publishing Web graphics.

Web Graphic Formats

If you've worked in the computer graphics field, you know that virtually every platform — as well as every paint and graphics program — has its own proprietary file format for images. One of the critical factors in the Web's rapid, expansive growth is the use of cross-platform graphics. Regardless of the system you use to create your images, these versatile files ensure that the graphics can be viewed by all platforms.

The trade-off for universal acceptance of image files is a restricted field: just two file formats, with a possible third just coming into view. Currently, only GIF and JPEG formats are fully supported by browsers. A third alternative, the PNG graphics format, is experiencing a limited but growing acceptance.

You need to understand the uses and limitations of each of the formats so you can apply them successfully in Dreamweaver. Let's look at the fundamentals.

GIF

GIF, the Graphics Interchange Format, was developed by CompuServe in the late 1980s to address the problem of cross-platform compatibility. With GIF viewers available for every system from PC and Macintosh to Amiga and NeXT, the format became a natural choice for an inline (adjacent to text) image graphic. GIFs are bitmapped images, which means that each pixel is given or mapped to a specific color. You can have up to 256 colors for a GIF graphic. These images are generally used for illustrations, logos, or cartoons — anything that doesn't require thousands of colors for a smooth color blend, such as a photograph. With a proper graphics tool, you can reduce the number of colors in a GIF image to a minimum, thereby compressing the file and reducing download time.

The GIF87a and GIF89a varieties

The GIF format has two varieties: "regular" (technically, GIF87a) and an enhanced version known as GIF89a. This improved GIF file brings three important attributes to the format. First, GIF89a supports transparency, in which one or more of the colors can become invisible. This property is necessary for creating nonrectangular-appearing images. Whenever you see a round or irregularly shaped logo or illustration on the Web, a rectangular frame is displayed as the image is loading — this is the actual size and shape of the graphic. The colors surrounding the irregularly shaped central image are set to transparent in a graphics-editing program (such as Fireworks or Adobe Photoshop) before the image is saved in GIF89a format.

Note   Most of the latest versions of the popular graphic tools default to using GIF89a, so unless you're working with older, legacy images, you're not too likely to encounter the less flexible GIF87a format.

Although the outer area of a graphic seems to disappear with GIF89a, you won't be able to overlap your Web images using this format without using layers. Figure 10-1 demonstrates this situation. In this figure, the same image is presented twice — one lacks transparency, and one has transparency applied. The image on the left is saved as a standard GIF without transparency, and you can plainly see the shape of the full image. The image on the right was saved with the white background color made transparent, so the central figure seems to float on the background.

Interlacing capabilities of GIF89a

The second valuable attribute contributed by GIF89a format is *interlacing*. One of the most common complaints about graphics on the Web is lengthy download times. Interlacing won't speed up your GIF downloads, but it gives your Web page visitors something to view other than a blank screen. A graphic saved with the interlace feature turned on gives the appearance of "developing," like an instant picture, as the file is downloading. Use of this design option is up to you and your clients. Some folks swear by it; others can't abide it.

Figure 10-1: The same image, saved without GIF transparency (left) and with GIF transparency (right)

Animation capabilities of GIF89a

Animation is the final advantage offered by the GIF89a format. Certain software programs enable you to group your GIF files together into one large page-flipping file. With this capability, you can bring simple animation to your page without additional plug-ins or helper applications. Unfortunately, the trade-off is that the files get very big, very fast. For more on animated GIFs in Dreamweaver, see the section "Applying Simple Web Animation" later in this chapter.

JPEG

The JPEG format was developed by the Joint Photographic Experts Group specifically to handle photographic images. JPEGs offer millions of colors at 24 bits of color information available per pixel, as opposed to the GIF format's 8-bit and 256 colors. To make JPEGs usable, the large amount of color information must be compressed, which is accomplished by removing what the algorithm considers redundant information. This is often referred to as *lossy* compression—in which pixels are lost—as opposed to *lossless* compression, a characteristic of GIF images.

The more compressed your JPEG file, the more degraded the image. When you first save a JPEG image, your graphics program asks you for the desired level of compression. As an example, take a look at the three pictures in Figure 10-2. Here you can compare the effects of JPEG compression ratios and resulting file sizes to the original image itself. As you can probably tell, JPEG does an excellent job of compression, with even the highest degree of compression having only a little visible impact. Keep in mind that each picture has its own reaction to compression.

| 100% JPEG - 48K | 50% JPEG - 7K | 10% JPEG - 2K |

Figure 10-2: JPEG compression can save your Web visitors substantial download time, with little loss of image quality.

Tip   With the JPEG image-compression algorithm, the initial elements of an image "compressed away" are least noticeable. Subtle variations in brightness and hue are the first to disappear. When possible, preview your image in your graphics program while adjusting the compression level to observe the changes. With additional compression, the image grows darker and less varied in its color range.

With JPEGs, what is compressed for storage must be uncompressed for viewing. When a JPEG picture on your Web page is accessed by a visitor's browser, the image must first be downloaded to the browser and then uncompressed before it can be viewed. This dual process adds additional time to the Web-browsing process, but it is time well spent for photographic images.

JPEGs, unlike GIFs, have neither transparency nor animation features. A newer strand of JPEG called Progressive JPEG gives you the interlace option of the GIF format, however. Although not all browsers support the interlace feature of Progressive JPEG, they render the image regardless.

PNG

The latest entry into the Web graphics arena is the Portable Network Graphics format, or PNG. Combining the best of both worlds, PNG has lossless compression, like GIF, and is capable of millions of colors, like JPEG. Moreover, PNG offers an interlace scheme that appears much more quickly than either GIF or JPEG, as well as transparency support that is far superior to both the other formats.

One valuable aspect of the PNG format enables the display of PNG pictures to appear more uniform across various computer platforms. Generally, graphics made on a PC look brighter on a Macintosh, and Mac-made images seem darker on a PC. PNG includes gamma correction capabilities that alter the image depending on the computer used by the viewer.

Before the 4.0 versions, the various browsers supported PNG only through plug-ins. After PNG was endorsed as a new Web graphic format by the W3C, both 4.0 versions of Netscape and Microsoft browsers added native, inline support of the new format. Perhaps most important, however, Dreamweaver was among the first Web authoring tools to offer native PNG support. Inserted PNG images preview in the Document window just like GIFs and JPEGs. Browser support is currently not widespread enough to warrant a total switch to the PNG format (it's still lacking in Internet Explorer for Macintosh, for example), but its growing acceptance certainly bears watching.

Tip   If you're really excited about the potential of PNG, check out Macromedia's Fireworks, the first Web graphics tool to use PNG as its native format. Fireworks takes full advantage of PNG's alpha transparency features and enhanced palette.

Two excellent resources for more on the PNG format is the PNG home page at `www.freesoftware.com/pub/png/` and the W3C's PNG page at `www.w3.org/Graphics/PNG`.

Using Inline Images

An *inline image* can appear directly next to text — literally in the same line. The capability to render inline images is one of the major innovations of the World Wide Web's transition from the Internet. This section covers all the basics of inserting inline images into Dreamweaver and modifying their attributes.

Inserting inline images

Dreamweaver can open and preview any graphic in a GIF, JPEG, or PNG format. With Dreamweaver, you have six methods for placing a graphic on your Web page:

✦ From the Objects panel, select the Insert Image button.

✦ From the menu bar, choose Insert ➪ Image.

✦ From the keyboard, press Ctrl+Alt+I (Command+Option+I).

✦ Point to an image file in the Site window using Dreamweaver's Point to File feature.

✦ Drag either the Insert Image button or an icon from your file manager (Explorer or Finder) to your page.

✦ Drag a *thumbnail* (a small version of an image) or filename from the Images category of the Assets panel onto your page. This capability is new in Dreamweaver 4 and is covered in detail in a following section.

The first four methods require that you first position the cursor at the point where you want the image to appear on the page; the drag-and-drop method enables you to place the image inline with any existing element.

For all but the method using the Assets panel, Dreamweaver opens the Select Image Source dialog box (shown in Figure 10-3) and asks you for the path or address to your image file. Remember that in HTML, all graphics are stored in separate files linked from your Web page. The image's address can be just a filename, a directory path and filename on your system, a directory path and filename on your remote system, or a full URL to a graphic on a completely separate Web server. You don't have to have the file immediately available to insert the code into your HTML.

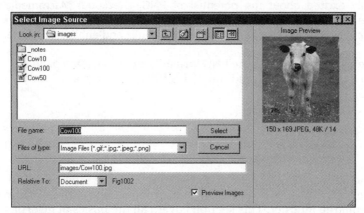

Figure 10-3: In this Select Image Source dialog box, you can keep track of your image's location relative to your current Web page.

From the Select Image Source dialog box, you can browse to your image folder, and preview images before you load them. To enable this feature, make sure the Preview Images option is selected. Dreamweaver can preview GIF, JPEG, or PNG files.

In the lower portion of the dialog box, the URL text box displays the format of the address Dreamweaver inserts into your code. Below the URL text box is the Relative To list box. Here you can choose to declare an image to be relative to the document you're working on (the default) or relative to the site root. (After you've saved your document, you see its name displayed beside the Relative To box.)

To take full advantage of Dreamweaver's site management features, you must open a site, establish a local site root, and save the current Web page before beginning to insert images. For more on how to begin a Dreamweaver project, and about document-relative and site root–relative addressing, see Chapter 6.

Relative to Document

Once you've saved your Web page and chosen Relative to Document, Dreamweaver displays the address in the URL text box. If the image is located in a folder on the same level as, or within, your current site root folder, the address is formatted with just a path and filename. For instance, if you're inserting a graphic from the sub-folder named images, Dreamweaver inserts an address like the following:

```
images/men10.jpg
```

If you try to insert an image currently stored outside of the local site root folder, Dreamweaver temporarily appends a prefix that tells the browser to look on your local system for the file. For instance, the file listing would look like the following in Windows:

```
file:///C|/Dreamweaver/Figs/men10.jpg
```

while on the Macintosh, the same file is listed as follows:

```
file:///Macintosh HD/Dreamweaver/Figs/men10.jpg
```

Dreamweaver also appends the `file:///C|` prefix (or just `file:///Macintosh HD` in Macintosh) if you haven't yet saved your document. It is strongly recommended that you save your file before you begin developing the Web page. You can easily upload Web pages with this `file:///C|` (`file:///Macintosh HD`) prefix in place—and miss the error completely. Because your local browser can find the referenced image on your system, even when you are browsing the remote site, the Web page appears perfect. However, anyone else browsing your Web site only sees placeholders for broken links. Saving your page before you begin enables Dreamweaver to help you avoid these errors. To this end, do not check the Don't show me this message again checkbox that appears when you're reminded to save your file the first time. This message can save you an enormous amount of grief!

After you select your image file, you see the prompt window shown in Figure 10-4. Dreamweaver asks if you want to copy this image to your local site root folder. Whenever possible, keep all of your images within the local site root folder so that Dreamweaver can handle site management efficiently. Click Yes, and you next see the Save Copy As dialog box, which points to the local site root folder. If you select No, the file is inserted with the src attribute pointing to the path of the file.

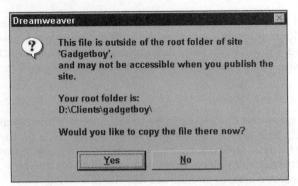

Figure 10-4: Dreamweaver reminds you to keep all your graphics in the local site root folder for easy site management.

Relative to Site Root

Should you select Site Root in the Relative To field of the Select Image Source dialog box, and you are within your site root folder, Dreamweaver appends a leading forward slash to the directory in the path so the browser can correctly read the address. Thus, the same men10.jpg file appears in both the URL box and the HTML code as follows:

```
/images/men10.jpg
```

When you use site root–relative addressing and you select a file outside of the site root, you get the same reminder from Dreamweaver about copying the file into your local site root folder — just as with document-relative addressing.

Dragging images from the Assets panel

Quite often, a Web designer works from a collection of images, much like a painter uses a palette of colors. Reusing images builds consistency in the site look and feel and makes it easier for a visitor to navigate through the site. However, trying to remember the differences between two versions of a logo — one named logo03.gif and another named logo03b.gif — often required inserting them both to find the correct image. Dreamweaver 4 eliminates the visual guesswork and simplifies the reuse of graphics with the new Assets panel.

New Feature

The Images category is key to the Assets panel. Not only does the Assets panel list all the GIF, JPEG, and PNG files found in your site — whether or not they are embedded in a Web page — selecting any graphic from the list instantly displays a thumbnail. Previewing the images makes it easy to select the proper one. Moreover, once you've found the correct image, all you need do it drag it from the Assets panel to the page.

Before you can use graphics from the Assets panel, you must catalog the site by choosing the Refresh Site List button, as shown in Figure 10-5. When you click the Refresh button (or choose Refresh Site List from the context menu on the Assets panel), Dreamweaver examines the current site and creates a list of the graphics, their sizes, file types, and full paths. To see an image, just click its name and a thumbnail appears in the preview area of the panel.

Thumbnail

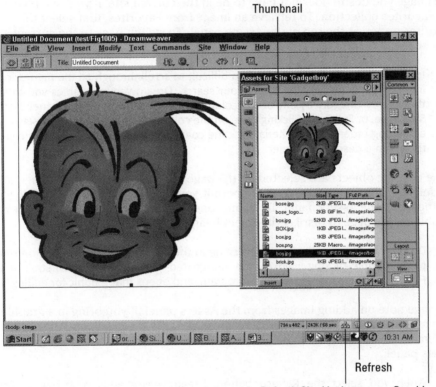

Refresh

Refresh Site List button   Graphics list

Figure 10-5: Reuse any graphic in your site or from your Favorites collection by dragging it out from the Assets panel.

Tip

To increase the size of the thumbnail, make the preview area larger by dragging open the border between the preview and list areas. You can also expand the size of the entire panel by dragging its corner. Dreamweaver increases the size of the thumbnail while maintaining the width:height ratio so if you just move the border or resize the panel a little bit you may not see a significant change. Thumbnails are never displayed larger than their actual size.

You can insert an image from the Assets panel onto your Web page in two ways:

✦ Drag the image or the file listing onto the page.

✦ Place your cursor where you'd like the image to appear, and — once the listing of the desired image is highlighted in the Assets panel — select the Insert button.

The image you desire does not have to be in the current site, if you've added it to the Favorites collection. To retrieve an image from Favorites, first select the Favorites option at the top of the Assets panel. To switch back to the current site, choose the Site option.

Tip   In sites with many images, it's often difficult to scroll through all the names looking for a particular image. To aid your search, Dreamweaver enables you to sort the Images category by any of the columns displayed in the Assets panel: Name, Size, Type, or Full Path. Clicking once on the column heading sorts the assets in an ascending order by that criteria; click the column again to sort by that same criteria, but in a descending order.

If one or more objects are selected on the page, the inserted image is placed after the selection; Dreamweaver does not permit you to replace a selected image with another from the Assets panel. To change one image into another, double-click the graphic on the page to display the Select Image Source dialog box.

Caution   Do not double-click the image or listing in the Assets panel to insert it onto the page. Double-clicking invokes the designated graphics editor, whether it be Fireworks, Photoshop, or another program, and opens that graphic for editing.

One final note on adding images from the Assets panel: If you bring in a graphic from a location outside of the site, Dreamweaver asks that you copy the file to the current site. You must select the Refresh button to display this new image in the Assets panel.

Tip   When you select the Refresh button, Dreamweaver adds new images (and other assets) to the cache of current assets. If you add assets from outside of Dreamweaver, using, for example, a file manager, you might need to completely re-create the Assets panel by Ctrl-clicking (Command-clicking) the Refresh button.

Modifying images

When you insert an image in Dreamweaver, the image tag, `<img>`, is inserted into your HTML code. The `<img>` tag takes several attributes, all of which can be entered through the Property Inspector. Code for a basic image looks like the following:

```
<img src="images/Collection01.gif" width="172" height="180">
```

Dreamweaver centralizes all of its image functions in the Property Inspector. The Image Property Inspector, shown in Figure 10-6, displays a small thumbnail of the image as well as its file size. Dreamweaver automatically inserts the image filename in the Src text box (as the `src` attribute). To replace a currently selected image with another, click the folder icon next to the Src text box, or double-click the image itself. This sequence opens the Select Image Source dialog box. When you've selected the desired file, Dreamweaver automatically refreshes the page and corrects the code.

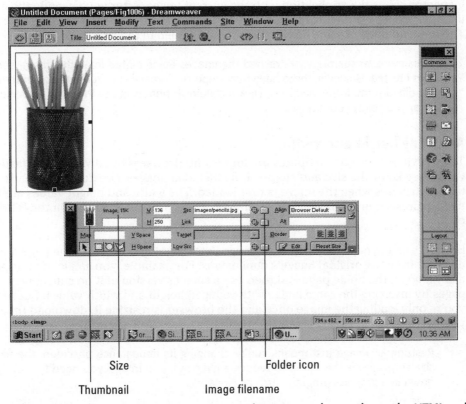

Size

Folder icon

Thumbnail

Image filename

Figure 10-6: The Image Property Inspector gives you total control over the HTML code for every image.

With the Property Inspector open when you insert your image, you can begin to modify it immediately.

Editing the image

Dreamweaver is a terrific Web authoring tool, but it's not a graphics editor. Quite often, after you've inserted an image into your Web page, you find that the picture needs to be altered in some way. Perhaps you need to crop part of the image or make the background transparent. Dreamweaver enables you to specify your primary graphics editor for each type of graphic in the File Types/Editors category of the Preferences.

Once you've picked an image editor, clicking the Edit button in the Property Inspector opens the application with the current image. After you've made the modifications, just save the file in your image editor and switch back to Dreamweaver. The new, modified graphic has already been included in the Web page.

Note　Dreamweaver seamlessly refreshed the images being edited in all the image editors I tested. However, there have been reports of images not reappearing in their modified form. If this happens, click the Refresh button in the Property Inspector after you select your image.

Adjusting height and width

The `width` and `height` attributes are important: Browsers build Web pages faster when they know the size and shape of the included images. Dreamweaver reads these attributes when the image is first loaded. The width and height values are initially expressed in pixels and are automatically inserted as attributes in the HTML code.

Browsers can dynamically resize an image if its height and width on the page are different from the original image's dimensions. For example, you can load your primary logo on the home page and then use a smaller version of it on subsequent pages by inserting the same image with reduced height and width values. Because you're only loading the image once and the browser is resizing it, download time for your Web page can be significantly reduced.

Note　Resizing an image just means you're changing its appearance onscreen; the file size stays exactly the same. To reduce a file size for an image, you need to scale it down in a graphics program such as Fireworks.

You don't have to use pixels to enter your resizing measurements into Dreamweaver's Property Inspector. You can also use inches (in), picas (pc), points (pt), millimeters (mm), or centimeters (cm). The values must be entered without spaces between the number and the measurement abbreviation, as follows:

```
72pt
```

You can also combine measurement systems. Suppose, for example, you want to resize a picture's height to 2 inches and 5 centimeters. In the Property Inspector, you enter the following value in the H text box:

```
2in+5cm
```

Dreamweaver translates both inches and centimeters to their equivalent in pixels and then adds them together. The measurements are system-dependent; on the Macintosh, an inch equals 72 pixels and on Windows, an inch is 96 pixels.

When you use values with a combined measurement system, you can only add values — you can't subtract them. When you press the Tab key or click outside of the height and width boxes, Dreamweaver converts your value to pixels.

Tip
> With Dreamweaver, you can visually resize your graphics by using the click-and-drag method. A selected image has three sizing handles located on the right, bottom, and lower-right corners of its bounding box. Click any of these handles and drag it out to a new location — when you release the mouse, Dreamweaver resizes the image. Hold down the Shift key after dragging the corner sizing handle, and Dreamweaver maintains the current height/width aspect ratio.

If you alter either the height or the width of an image in the Property Inspector, Dreamweaver displays the values in bold in their respective fields. You can restore an image's default measurements by selecting the H or the W independently — or you can choose the Refresh button to restore both values.

Caution
> If you elect to enable your viewer's browser to resize your image on the fly using the height/width values you specify, keep in mind that the browser is not a graphics-editing program and that its resizing algorithms are not sophisticated. View your resized images through several browsers to make sure that the results are acceptable.

Using margins

You can offset images with surrounding whitespace by using the margin attributes. The amount of whitespace around your image can be designated both vertically and horizontally through the vspace and hspace attributes, respectively. These margin values are entered, in pixels, into the V Space and H Space text boxes in the Image Property Inspector.

The V Space value adds the same amount of whitespace along the top and bottom of your image; the H Space value increases the whitespace along the left and right sides of the image. These values must be positive; HTML doesn't allow images to overlap text or other images (outside of layers). Unlike in page layout, "negative whitespace" does not exist.

Titling your image

When you first insert a graphic into the page, the Image Property Inspector displays a blank text box next to the thumbnail and file size. Fill in this box with a unique name for the image, to be used in JavaScript and other applications.

As a page is loading over the Web, the image is first displayed as an empty rectangle if the <img> tag contains the width and height information. Sometimes these rectangles include a brief title to describe the coming image. You can enter this alternative text in the Alt text box of the Image Property Inspector.

> **Tip**
>
> Good coding practice associates an Alt title with all of your graphics. Aside from giving the user some clue as to what's coming, these mini-titles are also used to display the screen tips that pop up in some browsers when the user's pointer passes over the graphic. The real benefit of mini-titles, however, is providing input for browsers not displaying graphics. Text-only browsers are still in use, and some users, interested only in content, turn off the graphics to speed up the text display. Moreover, the W3C is working toward standards for browsers for the visually impaired, and the Alt text can be used to describe the page.

Bordering a graphic

When you're working with thumbnails (a series of small versions of images) on your Web page, you may need a quick way to distinguish one from another. (Refer to Figure 10-5 for an example of a thumbnail.) The border attribute enables you to place a one-color rectangular border around any graphic. The width of the border is measured in pixels, and the color is the same as the default for the page's text color as specified in the Page Properties dialog box. To turn on the border, enter a value in the Border text box located on the lower half of the Image Property Inspector. Entering a value of zero explicitly turns off the border.

One of the most frequent cries for help among beginning Web designers (using Dreamweaver or another program) results from the sudden appearance of a bright blue border around their image. Whenever you assign a link to an image, HTML automatically places a border around that image; the color is determined by the Page Properties' Link color, where the default is bright blue. Dreamweaver intelligently assigns a zero to the border attribute whenever you enter a URL in the Link text box. If you've already declared a border value and enter a link, Dreamweaver won't zero-out the border. You can, of course, override the no-border option by entering a value in the Border text box.

Specifying a lowsrc

Another option for loading Web page images, the lowsrc attribute, displays a smaller version of a large graphic file while the larger file is loading. The lowsrc file can be a grayscale version of the original, or a version that is physically smaller or reduced in color or resolution. This option is designed to reduce the file size significantly for quick loading.

Select your `lowsrc` file by choosing the File icon next to the Low text box in the Image Property Inspector. The same criteria that applies to inserting your original image also applies to the `lowsrc` picture.

Tip

One handy `lowsrc` technique first proportionately scales down a large file in a graphics-processing program. This file becomes your `lowsrc` file. Because browsers use the final image's height and width information for both the `lowsrc` and the final image, your visitors immediately see a "blocky" version of your graphic, which is replaced by the final version when the picture is fully loaded.

Working with alignment options

Just like text, images can be aligned to the left, right, or center. In fact, images have much more flexibility than text in terms of alignment. In addition to the same horizontal alignment options, you can align your images vertically in nine different ways. You can even turn a picture into a floating image type, enabling text to wrap around it.

Horizontal alignment

When you change the horizontal alignment of a line — from left to center or from center to right — the entire paragraph moves. Any inline images that are part of that paragraph also move. Likewise, selecting one of a series of inline images in a row and realigning it horizontally causes all the images in the row to shift.

In Dreamweaver, the horizontal alignment of an inline image is changed in exactly the same way you realign text, with alignment buttons found on the Property Inspector. As with text, buttons exist for Left, Center, and Right. Although these are very conveniently placed on the lower portion of the Graphics Property Inspector, the alignment attribute is actually written to the `<p>` or other block element enclosing the image.

Vertical alignment

Because you can place text next to an image — and images vary so greatly in size — HTML includes a variety of options for specifying just how image and text line up. As you can see from the chart in Figure 10-7, a wide range of possibilities is available.

To change the vertical alignment of any graphic in Dreamweaver, open the Align drop-down list in the Image Property Inspector and choose one of the options. Dreamweaver writes your choice into the `align` attribute of the `<img>` tag.

The various vertical alignment options are listed in the following table, and you can see examples of each type of alignment in Figure 10-7.

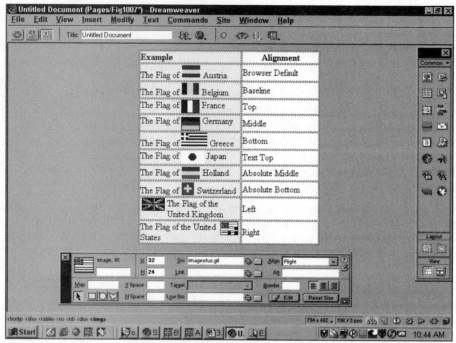

Figure 10-7: You can align text and images in one of nine different ways using the Align option box on the Image Property Inspector.

Vertical Alignment Option	Result
Browser Default	No alignment attribute is included in the `<img>` tag. Most browsers use the baseline as the alignment default.
Baseline	The bottom of the image is aligned with the baseline of the surrounding text.
Top	The top of the image is aligned with the top of the tallest object in the current line.
Middle	The middle of the image is aligned with the baseline of the current line.
Bottom	The bottom of the image is aligned with the baseline of the surrounding text.
Text Top	The top of the image is aligned with the tallest letter in the current line.
Absolute Middle	The middle of the image is aligned with the middle of the text or object in the current line.

Vertical Alignment Option	Result
Absolute Bottom	The bottom of the image is aligned with the descenders (as in y, g, p, and so forth) that fall below the current line.
Left	The image is aligned to the left edge of the browser or table cell, and all text in the current line flows around the right side of the image.
Right	The image is aligned to the right edge of the browser or table cell, and all text in the current line flows around the left side of the image.

The final two alignment options, Left and Right, are special cases; details about how to use their features are covered in the following section.

Wrapping text

Long a popular design option in conventional publishing, wrapping text around an image on a Web page is also supported by most, but not all, browsers. As noted in the preceding section, the Left and Right alignment options turn a picture into a floating image type, so called because the image can move depending on the amount of text and the size of the browser window.

Tip
Using both floating image types (Left and Right) in combination, you can actually position images flush-left and flush-right, with text in the middle. Insert both images side by side and then set the leftmost image to align left and the rightmost one to align right. Insert your text immediately following the second image. Unless you place a <p> or <br> at the top, this arrangement does not render correctly in Dreamweaver (the first line overlaps the left image), but it does display as expected in most browsers.

Your text wraps around the image depending on where the floating image is placed (or anchored). If you have the feature enabled in the Invisibles pane of Preferences, Dreamweaver inserts a Floating Image Anchor symbol to mark the floating image's place. Figure 10-8 shows two examples of text wrapping. In the top case, the Floating Image Anchor symbol is placed in the midst of the first paragraph, which causes the three paragraphs to flow around the right-aligned image. In the bottom case, the image is left-aligned.

The Floating Image Anchor is not just a static symbol. You can click and drag the anchor to a new location and cause the paragraph to wrap in a different fashion. Be careful though — if you delete the anchor, you also delete the image it represents.

You can also wrap a portion of the text around your left- or right-aligned picture and then force the remaining text to appear below the floating image. However, the HTML necessary to do this task cannot currently be inserted by Dreamweaver and must be coded by hand. You have to force an opening to appear by inserting a break tag, with a special clear attribute, where you want the text to break. This special <br> tag has three forms:

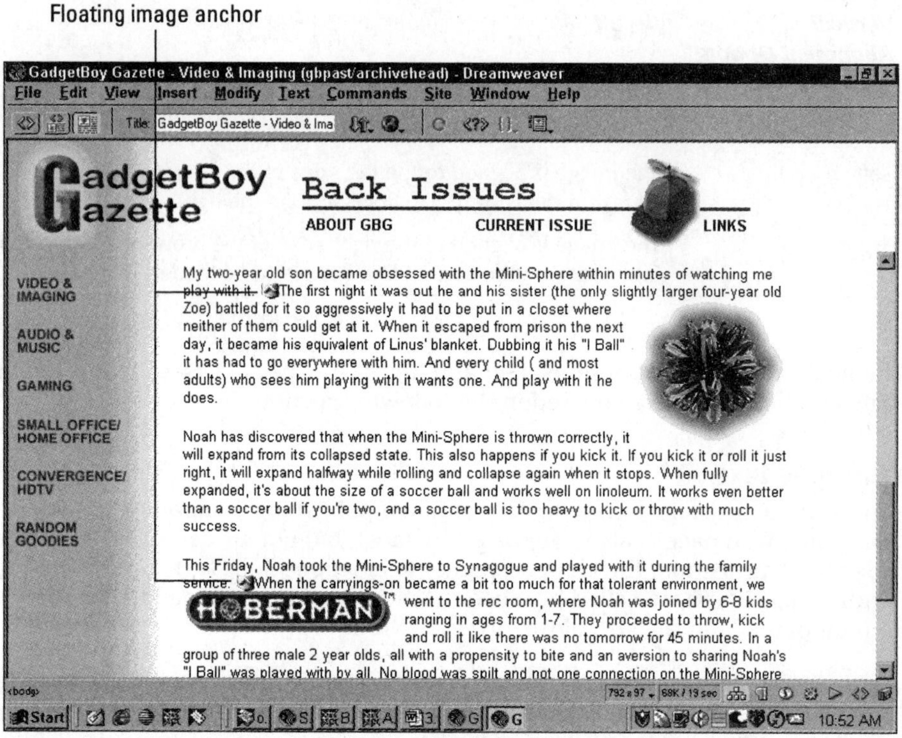

Floating image anchor

Figure 10-8: Aligning an image left or right enables text to wrap around your images.

`<br clear=left>`   Causes the line to break, and the following text moves down vertically until no floating images are on the left.

`<br clear=right>`   Causes the line to break, and the following text moves down vertically until no floating images are on the right.

`<br clear=all>`   Moves the text following the image down until no floating images are on either the left or the right.

On the CD-ROM

One of the Dreamweaver objects included on CD-ROM that accompanies this book is an enhanced break tag that enables you to include any version of the `clear` attribute. To access these objects, copy the new_break.htm and new_break.gif files from the Dreamweaver\Configuration\Objects\Invisibles folder into the same folder on your system, and then restart Dreamweaver.

Putting Pictures in the Background

In this chapter, you've learned about working with the surface graphics on a Web page. As seen in Chapter 8, you can also have an image in the background of an HTML page. This section covers some of the basic techniques for incorporating a background image in your Dreamweaver page.

Note   Remember, you add an image to your background in Dreamweaver by modifying the Page Properties. Either choose Modify ⇨ Page Properties or select Page Properties from the contextual menu that pops up when you right-click (Command+click) any open area on the Web page. In the Page Properties dialog box, select a graphic by choosing the Browse (Choose) button next to the Background Image text box. You can use any file format supported by Dreamweaver — GIF, JPEG, or PNG.

Two key differences exist between background images and the foreground inline images discussed in the preceding sections of this chapter. First and most obvious, all other text and graphics on the Web page are superimposed over your chosen background image. This capability can bring extra depth and texture to your work; unfortunately, you have to make sure the foreground text and images work well with the background.

Cross-Reference   You can quickly try out a number of professionally designed background and fore-ground color combinations with the Set Color Scheme command. For more information on how to use this Dreamweaver command, see Chapter 8.

Basically, you want to ascertain that enough contrast exists between foreground and background. You can set the default text and the various link colors through the Page Properties dialog box. When trying out a new background pattern, you should set up some dummy text and links. Then use the Apply button on the Page Properties dialog box to test different color combinations. See Figure 10-9 for an example of this test at work.

The second distinguishing feature of background images is that the viewing browser completely fills either the browser window or the area behind the content of your Web page, whichever is larger. So, if you've created a splash page with only a 200×200 foreground logo, and you've incorporated an amazing 1,024×768 background that took you weeks to compose, no one can see the fruits of your labor in the background — unless they resize their browser window to 1,024×768. On the other hand, if your background image is smaller than either the browser window or what the Web page content needs to display, the browser and Dreamweaver repeat (or tile) your image to make up the difference.

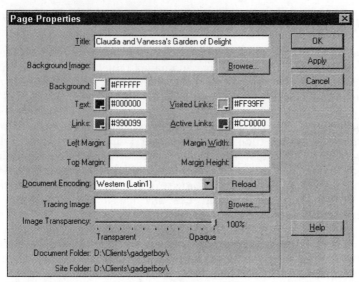

Figure 10-9: If you're using a background image, be sure to check the default colors for text and links to make sure enough contrast exists between background and foreground.

Dividing the Web Page with Horizontal Rules

HTML includes a standard horizontal line that can divide your Web page into specific sections. The horizontal rule tag, <hr>, is a good tool for adding a little diversion to your page without adding download time. You can control the width (either absolutely or relative to the browser window), the height, the alignment, and the shading property of the rule. These horizontal rules appear on a line by themselves; you cannot place text or images on the same line as a horizontal rule.

To insert a horizontal rule in your Web page in Dreamweaver, follow these steps:

1. Place your cursor where you want the horizontal rule to appear.

2. From the Common pane of the Objects panel, select the Insert Horizontal Rule button or choose the Insert ➪ Horizontal Rule command.

   Dreamweaver inserts the horizontal rule and opens the Horizontal Rule Property Inspector, as shown in Figure 10-10.

3. To change the width of the line, enter a value in the width (W) text box. You can insert either an absolute width in pixels or a relative value as a percentage of the screen.

Tiling Images

Web designers use the tiling property of background images to create a variety of effects with very low file-size overhead. The columns typically found on one side of Web pages are a good example of tiling. Columns are popular because they enable the designer to place navigational buttons in a visual context. An easy way to create a column that runs the full length of your Web page uses a long, narrow background image.

Take a look at the following figure:

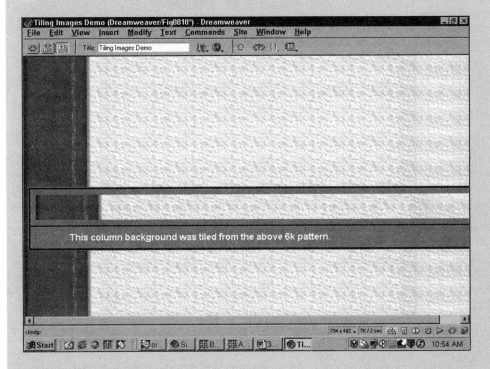

The background image is 45 pixels high, 800 pixels wide, and only 6K in size. When the browser window is set at 640×480 or 800×600, the image is tiled down the page to create the vertical column effect. You could just as easily create an image 1,000 pixels high by 40 pixels wide to create a horizontal column.

- To set a horizontal rule to an exact width, enter the measurement in pixels in the width (W) text box and press the Tab key. Then select pixels in the drop-down list.

- To set a horizontal rule to a width relative to the browser window, enter the percentage amount in the width (W) text box and press Tab. Then select the percent sign (%) in the drop-down list.

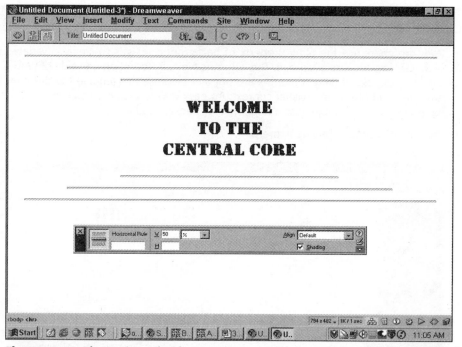

Figure 10-10: The Horizontal Rule Property Inspector controls the width, height, and alignment for these HTML lines.

4. To change the height of the horizontal rule, type a pixel measurement in the height (H) text box.

   For both the width and height values, you can also enter a value in inches (in), picas (pc), points (pt), millimeters (mm), or centimeters (cm), just as with images. When you press Tab to leave the text box, Dreamweaver converts your entry to pixels.

5. To change the alignment from the default (centered), open the Align drop-down list and choose another alignment.

6. To disable the default "embossed" look for the rule, deselect the Shading checkbox.

7. If you intend to address (call) your horizontal rule in JavaScript or another application, you can give it a unique name. Type it into the unlabeled name text box located directly to the left of the H text box.

To modify any inserted horizontal rule, simply click it. (If the Property Inspector is not already open, you have to double-click the rule.) As a general practice, size your horizontal rules using the percentage option if you are using them to separate items on a full screen. If the horizontal rules are being used to divide items in a specifically sized table column or cell, use the pixel method.

Tip

To use the Shading property of the horizontal rule properly, your background should be a shade of gray. The default shading is black along the top and left, and white along the bottom and right. The center line is generally transparent (although Internet Explorer enables you to assign a color attribute). If you use a different background color or image, be sure to check the appearance of your horizontal rules in that context.

Many designers prefer to create more elaborate horizontal rules; in fact, these rules are an active area of clip art design. These types of horizontal rules are regular graphics and are inserted and modified as such.

Applying Simple Web Animation

Why include a section on animation in a chapter on inline images? On the Web, animations are, for the most part, inline images that move. Outside of the possibilities offered by Dynamic HTML (covered in Part VI), Web animations typically either are animated GIF files or are created with a program such as Flash that requires a plug-in. This section takes a brief look at the capabilities and uses of GIF animations.

A GIF *animation* is a series of still GIF images flipped rapidly to create the illusion of motion. Because animation-creation programs compress all the frames of your animation into one file, a GIF animation is placed on a Web page in the same manner as a still graphic.

In Dreamweaver, click the Insert Image button in the Objects panel or choose Insert ➪ Image and then select the file. Dreamweaver shows the first frame of your animation in the Document window. To play the animation, preview your Web page in any graphics-capable browser.

As you can imagine, GIF animations can quickly grow to be very large. The key to controlling file size is to think small: Keep your images as small as possible with a low bit-depth (number of colors) and use as few frames as possible.

To create your animation, use any graphics program to produce the separate frames. One excellent technique uses an image-processing program such as Adobe Photoshop and progressively applies a filter to the same image over a series of frames. Figure 10-11 shows the individual frames created with Photoshop's Lighting Effects filter. When animated, a spotlight appears to move across the word.

You need an animation program to compress the separate frames and build your animated GIF file. Many commercial programs, including Macromedia's Fireworks, can handle GIF animation. QuickTime Pro can turn individual files or any other kind of movie into an animated GIF, too. Most animation programs enable you to control the number of times an animation loops, the delay between frames, and how transparency is handled within each frame.

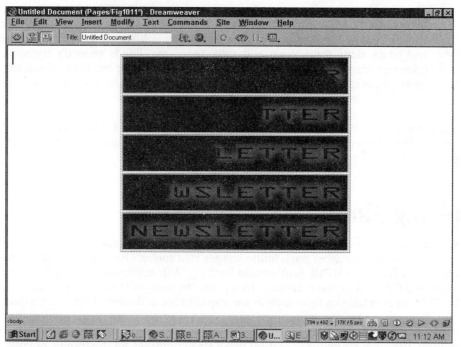

Figure 10-11: Five of twelve frames are compressed into one animated file.

Tip

If you want to use an advanced animation tool but still have full backward compatibility, check out Flash, from Macromedia. Flash is best known for outputting small vector-based animations that require a plug-in to view, but it can also save animations as GIFs or AVIs. See Chapter 23 and 33 for more details.

Dreamweaver Technique: Including Banner Ads

Banner ads have become an essential aspect of the World Wide Web; for the Web to remain, for the most part, freely accessible, advertising is needed to support the costs. Banner ads have evolved into the de facto standard. Although numerous variations exist, a banner ad is typically an animated GIF of a particular width and height and under a specified file size.

Two organizations, the Standards and Practices Committee of the Internet Advertising Bureau (IAB) and the Coalition for Advertising Supported Information and Entertainment (CASIE), established a series of standard sizes for banner ads. Although no law dictates that their guidelines have to be followed, the vast majority of commercial sites adhere to the suggested dimensions. The most common banner sizes (in pixels) and their official names are listed in Table 10-1.

Table 10-1
IAB/CASIE Advertising Banner Sizes

Dimensions	Name
468×60	Full Banner
392×72	Full Banner with Vertical Navigation Bar
234×60	Half Banner
125×125	Square Button
88×31	Micro Button
120×90	Button 1
120×60	Button 2
120×240	Vertical Banner

File size for a banner ad is not as clearly determined, but it's just as important. The last thing a hosting site wants is for a large, too heavy banner to slow down the loading of its page. Usually a commercial site has an established maximum file size for a particular banner ad size. Generally banner ads are around 10K and no more than 12K. The lighter your banner ad, the faster it loads and — as a direct result — the more likely Web page visitors stick around to see it.

Inserting a banner ad on a Web page is very straightforward. As with any other GIF file, animated or not, all you have to do is insert the image and assign the link. As any advertiser can tell you, the link is as important as the image itself, and you should take special care to ensure that it is correct when inserted. Advertising links are often quite complex as they not only link to a specific page, but may also carry information about the referring site. Several companies monitor how many times an ad is selected — the *clickthru rate* — and often a CGI program is used to communicate with these companies and handle the link. Here's a sample URL from CNet's News.com site:

```
http://home.cnet.com/cgi-acc/clickthru.acc?¬
clickid=00001e145ea7d80f00000000&adt=003:10:100&edt=cnet&cat=1:1002:&site=CN
```

Obviously, copying and pasting such URLs is highly preferable to entering them by hand.

It's not unusual for an advertisement to come from an outside source, so a Web page designer often has to allow space for the ad without incorporating the actual ad. Some Web designers use special placeholder images. In Dreamweaver, placeholder ads can easily be maintained as a Library item and placed as needed from the Assets panel, as shown in Figure 10-12. If you'd prefer not to use placeholder graphics such as these, you could also just insert a plain `<img>` tag—with no `src` parameter—using the Quick Tag Editor. When an `<img>` tag without a `src` is in the code, Dreamweaver displays a broken image icon that could then be resized to the proper banner ad dimensions in the Property Inspector.

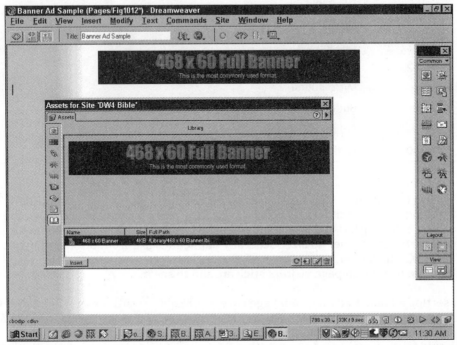

Figure 10-12: Use the Library to store standard banner ad images for use as placeholders.

Inserting Rollover Images

Rollovers are among the most popular of all Web page effects. A *rollover* (also known as a *mouseover*) occurs when the user's pointer passes over an image and the image changes in some way. It may appear to glow or change color and/or shape; when the pointer moves away from the graphic, the image returns to its original form. The rollover indicates interactivity and attempts to engage the user with a little bit of flare.

Rollovers are usually accomplished with a combination of HTML and JavaScript. Dreamweaver was among the first Web authoring tools to automate the production of rollovers through its Swap Image and Swap Image Restore behaviors. Later versions of Dreamweaver make rollovers even easier with the Rollover Image object. With the Rollover Image object, if you can pick two images, you can make a rollover.

Technically speaking, a rollover is accomplished by manipulating an <img> tag's
src attribute. You'll recall that the src attribute is responsible for providing the
actual file name of the graphic to be displayed; it is, quite literally, the source of the
image. A rollover changes the value of src from one image file to another. Swapping
the src value is analogous to having a picture within a frame and changing the picture while keeping the frame.

Caution The picture frame analogy is appropriate on one other level: It serves as a
reminder of the size barrier inherent in rollovers. A rollover changes only one property of an <img> tag, the source — it cannot change any other property such as the
height or width. For this reason, both your original image and the image that is displayed during the rollover should be the same size. If they are not, the alternate
image is resized to match the dimensions of the original image.

Dreamweaver's Rollover Image object automatically changes the image back to its
original source when the user moves the pointer off the image. Optionally, you can
elect to preload the images with the selection of a checkbox. Preloading is a Web
page technique that reads the intended file or files into the browser's memory
before they are displayed. With preloading, the images appear on demand, without
any download delay.

Rollovers are typically used for buttons that, when clicked, open another Web page.
In fact, JavaScript requires that an image include a link before it can detect when a
user's pointer moves over it. Dreamweaver automatically includes the minimum
link necessary: the #target link. Although JavaScript recognizes this symbol as indicating a link, no action is taken if the image is clicked by the user; the #, by itself, is
an empty link. You can, naturally, supply whatever link you want in the Rollover
Image object.

To include a Rollover Image object in your Web page, follow these steps:

1. Place your cursor where you want the rollover image to appear and choose
   Insert ⇨ Rollover Image or select Insert Rollover Image from the Common
   panel of the Objects panel. You can also drag the Insert Rollover Image button
   to any existing location on the Web page.

   Dreamweaver opens the Insert Rollover Image dialog box shown in
   Figure 10-13.

2. If desired, you can enter a unique name for the image in the Image Name text
   box, or you can leave the name automatically generated by Dreamweaver.

3. In the Original Image text box, enter the path and name of the graphic you
   want displayed when the user's mouse is not over the graphic. You can also
   choose the Browse (Choose) button to select the file. Press Tab when you're
   done.

4. In the Rollover Image text box, enter the path and name of the graphic you
   want displayed when the user's pointer is over the graphic. You can also
   choose the Browse (Choose) button to select the file.

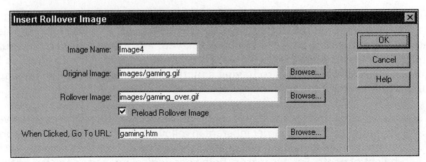

Figure 10-13: The Rollover Image object makes rollover graphics quick and easy.

5. If desired, specify a link for the image by entering it in the When Clicked, Go To URL text box. If you are entering a path and file by hand, be sure to delete the initial target link, #. If you use the Browse (Choose) button to select your file, the target link is deleted for you.

6. To enable images to load only when they are required, deselect the Preload Images option. Generally, it is best to leave this option selected (the default) so that no delay occurs in the rollover appearing.

7. Click OK when you're finished.

Tip   Keep in mind that the Rollover Image object inserts both the original image and its alternate, whereas the Swap Image technique is applied to an existing image in the Web page. If you prefer to use the Rollover Image object rather than the Swap Image behavior, nothing prevents you from deleting an existing image from the Web page and inserting it again through the Rollover Image object. Just make sure that you note the path and name of the image before you delete it so you can find it again.

Adding a Navigation Bar

Rollovers are nice effects, but a single button does not make a navigation system for a Web site. Typically, several buttons with a similar look and feel are placed next to each other to form a *navigation bar*. To make touring a site as intuitive as possible, the same navigation bar is usually repeated on each page or used once, as a frame element. Consistency of design and repetitive use of the navigation bar simplifies getting around a site — even for a first-time user.

Some designers build their navigation bars in a separate graphics program and then import them into Dreamweaver. Fireworks, with its capability to export both images and code, makes this a strong option. Other Web designers, however, prefer to build separate rollover images in a graphics program and then assemble all the pieces at the HTML layout stage. Dreamweaver now automates such a process with its Navigation Bar object.

The Navigation Bar object incorporates rollovers — and more. A Navigation Bar element can use up to four different images, each reflecting a different user action:

✦ Up — The user's pointer is away from the image.

✦ Over — The pointer is over the image.

✦ Down — The user has clicked the image.

✦ Over While Down — The user's pointer is over the image after it has been clicked.

You don't have to use all four states — it's up to you whether you use just the first two, like a standard rollover, or add the third and possibly the fourth. You can even skip the Over state and just use Up and Down. While it's possible to display an Over While Down state without a Down state, it doesn't make much sense to do so.

One key difference separates a fully functioning navigation bar from a group of unrelated rollovers. When the Down state is available, if the user clicks one of the buttons, any other Down button is changed to the Up state. The effect is like a series of mutually exclusive radio buttons: You can show only one selected in a group. The Down state is often used to indicate the current selection.

Tip

While you can use the Navigation Bar object on any type of Web design, it works best in a frameset situation with a frame for navigation and one for content. If you insert a navigation bar with Up, Over, Down, and Over While Down states for each button in the navigation frame, you can target the content frame and gain the full effect of the mutually exclusive Down states.

Before you can use Dreamweaver's Navigation Bar object, you have to create a series of images for each button — one for each state you plan to use. It's completely up to the designer how the buttons appear, but it's important that a consistent look and feel be applied for all the buttons. For example, if rolling over Button A reveals a green glow, rolling over Buttons B, C, and D should also cause the same green glow, as demonstrated in Figure 10-14.

To insert a navigation bar, follow these steps:

1. From the Objects panel, select the Insert Navigation Bar object.

   The Insert Navigation Bar dialog box appears, as shown in Figure 10-15.

2. Enter a unique name for the first button in the Element Name field and press Tab.

Caution

Be sure to use Tab rather than Enter (Return) when moving from field to field. When Enter (Return) is pressed, Dreamweaver attempts to build the navigation bar. If you have not completed the initial two steps (providing an Element Name and a source for the Up Image), an alert is displayed; otherwise, the navigation bar is built.

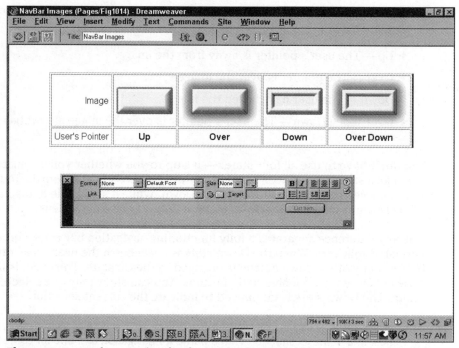

Figure 10-14: Before you invoke the Navigation Bar object, create a series of buttons with a separate image for each state to be used.

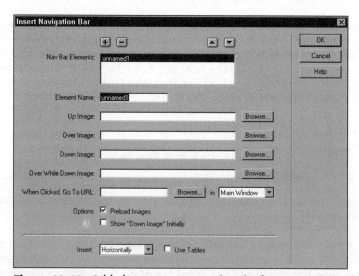

Figure 10-15: Add elements one at a time in the Insert Navigation Bar dialog box.

3. In the Up Image field, enter a path and filename or browse to a graphic file to use.

4. Select files for each of the remaining states you wish to use: Over, Down, and Over While Down.

5. Enter a URL or browse to a file in the When Clicked, Go To URL field.

6. If you're using a frameset, select a target for the URL from the drop-down list.

7. Enable or disable the Preload Images option as desired.

   For a multistate button to be effective, the reaction has to be immediate, and the images must be preloaded. It is highly recommended that the Preload Images option be enabled.

8. If you want the current button to display the Down state first, select the Show "Down Image" Initially option.

   When this option is chosen, an asterisk appears next to the current button in the Nav Bar Element list. Generally, you don't want more than one Down state showing at a time.

9. To set the orientation of the navigation bar, select either Horizontally or Vertically from the Insert drop-down list.

10. If you want to contain your images in a table, keep the Use Table option selected.

    If you decide not to use tables in a horizontal configuration, images are presented side by side; when a vertical navigation bar is built without tables, Dreamweaver inserts a line break (
 tag) between each element.

11. Select the add (plus) button and repeat Steps 2 through 8 to add the next element.

12. To reorder the elements in the navigation bar, select an element in the Nav Bar Elements list and use the up and down buttons to reposition it in the Element list.

13. To remove an element, select it and click the delete (minus) button.

Each page can have only one Dreamweaver-built navigation bar. If you try to insert a second, Dreamweaver asks if you'd like to modify the existing series. Clicking OK opens the Modify Navigation Bar dialog box, shown in Figure 10-16, which is identical to the Insert Navigation Bar dialog box, except you can no longer change the orientation or table settings. You can also alter the inserted navigation bar by choosing Modify ⇨ Navigation Bar.

Cross-Reference If you're looking for even more control over your navigation bar, Dreamweaver also includes the Set Navigation Bar behavior, which is fully covered in Chapter 15.

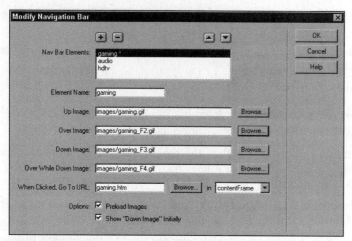

Figure 10-16: Once you've inserted your navigation bar, you can adjust it through the Modify Navigation Bar dialog box.

Summary

In this chapter, you learned how to include both foreground and background images in Dreamweaver. Understanding how images are handled in HTML is an absolute necessity for the Web designer. Some of the key points follow:

✦ Web pages are restricted to using specific graphic formats. Virtually all browsers support GIF and JPEG files. PNG is also gaining acceptance. Dreamweaver can preview all three image types.

✦ Images are inserted in the foreground in Dreamweaver through the Insert Image command of the Objects panel or from the Assets panel. Once the graphic is inserted, almost all modifications can be handled through the Property Inspector.

✦ You can use HTML's background image function to lay a full-frame image or a tiled series of the same image underneath your text and graphics. Tiled images can be employed to create columns and other designs with small files.

✦ The simplest HTML graphic is the built-in horizontal rule. Useful for dividing your Web page into separate sections, the horizontal rule can be sized either absolutely or relatively.

✦ With the Rollover Image object, you can easily insert simple rollovers that use two different images. To build a rollover that uses more than two images, you have to use the Swap Image behavior.

✦ Animated images can be inserted alongside, and in the same manner as, still graphics. The individual frames of a GIF animation must be created in a graphics program and then combined in an animation program.

✦ When used in conjunction with Fireworks, images can now be optimized from within Dreamweaver. Moreover, it's easier to integrate code generated from Fireworks — and you can even specify Dreamweaver-style HTML.

✦ You can add a series of interrelated buttons — complete with four-state rollovers — by using the Navigation Bar object.

In the next chapter, you learn how to use hyperlinks in Dreamweaver.

✦   ✦   ✦

Establishing Web Links

To me, links are the Web. Everything else about the
medium can be replicated in another form, but without
links, there would be no World Wide Web. As your Web design
work becomes more sophisticated, you'll find more enhanced
uses for links: sending mail, connecting to an FTP site — even
downloading software. In this chapter, you learn how
Dreamweaver helps you manage the various types of links, set
anchors within documents to get smooth and accurate navigation, and establish targets for your URLs. But first, let's begin
with an overview on Internet addresses to give you the full
picture of the possibilities.

Understanding URLs

URL stands for Uniform Resource Locator. An awkward
phrase, it nonetheless describes itself well — the URL's function is to provide a standard method for finding anything on
the Internet. From Web pages to newsgroups to the smallest
graphic on the most esoteric of pages, everything can be referenced through the URL system.

The URL can use up to six different parts, although all parts
are not necessary for the URL to be read. Each part is separated by some combination of a slash, colon, and hash mark
delimiter. When entered as an attribute's value, the entire URL
is generally enclosed within quotes to ensure that the address
is read as one unit. A generic URL using all the parts looks like
the following:

```
method://server:port/path/file#anchor
```

Here's a real-world example that also uses every section:

```
http://www.idest.com:80/dreamweaver/index.htm#
bible
```

In order of appearance in the body of an Internet address, left to right, the parts denote the following:

✦ **The method used to access the resource.** The method to address Web servers is the HyperText Transport Protocol (HTTP). Other methods are discussed later in this section.

✦ **The name of the server providing the resource.** The server can either be a domain name (with or without the "www" prefix) or an Internet Protocol (IP) address, such as 199.227.52.143.

✦ **The port number to be used on the server.** Most URLs do not include a port number, which is analogous to a telephone extension number on the server, because most servers use the defaults.

✦ **The directory path to the resource.** Depending on where the resource (for example, the Web page) is located on the server, the following paths can be specified: no path (indicating that the resource is in the public root of the server), a single folder name, or a number of folders and subfolders.

✦ **The filename of the resource.** If the filename is omitted, the Web browser looks for a default page, often named index.html or index.htm. The browser reacts differently depending on the type of file. For example, GIFs and JPEGs are displayed by themselves; executable files and archives (Zip, StuffIt, and so on) are downloaded.

✦ **The named anchor in the HTML document.** This part is another optional section. The named anchor enables the Web designer to send the viewer to a particular section of an HTML page.

Because it is used to communicate with servers, the HTTP access method is far and away the most prevalent method on today's World Wide Web. In addition to the HTTP access method, other methods connect with other types of servers. Table 11-1 discusses some of these options.

Table 11-1
Various Internet Access Methods and Protocols

Name	Syntax	Usage
File Transfer Protocol	ftp://	Links to an FTP server that is generally used for uploading and downloading files. The server can be accessed anonymously, or it may require a user name and password.
Gopher	gopher://as	Connects to a directory tree structure primarily used for disseminating all-text documents.
HyperText Transfer Protocol	http://	Used for connecting to a document available on a World Wide Web server.

Name	Syntax	Usage
JavaScript	javascript://	Executes a JavaScript function.
Mailto	mailto:	Opens an e-mail form with the recipient's address already filled in. These links are useful when embedded in your Web pages to provide visitors with an easy feedback method.
News	news://	Connects to the specified Usenet newsgroup. Newsgroups are public, theme-oriented message boards where anyone can post or reply to a message.
Telnet	telnet://	Enables users to log directly onto remote host computers and interact directly with the operating system software.

Part of the richness of today's Web browsers stems from their capability to connect with all the preceding (and additional) services.

Note The mailto: access method enables you not only to open up a preaddressed e-mail form but also to specify the topic, with a little extra work. For example, if Joe Lowery wants to include a link to his e-mail address with the subject heading "Dreamweaver Bible," he can insert a link such as the following:

```
mailto:jlowery@idest.com?subject=Dreamweaver Bible
```

The question mark acts as a delimiter that enables a variable and a value to be passed to the browser. When you're trying to encourage feedback from your Web page visitors, every little bit helps. A note of caution: This method is not standardized HTML, and while it works with most browsers and mail programs, you could get unexpected results with some systems.

Surfing the Web with Hypertext

Most often, you assign a link to a word or phrase on your page, an image such as a navigational button, or a section of graphic for an image map (a large graphic in which various parts are links). Once you have created the link, you have to preview it in a browser; links are not active in Dreamweaver's Document window.

Designate links in HTML through the anchor tag pair: `<a>` and `</a>`. The anchor tag generally takes one main attribute—the hypertext reference, which is written as follows:

```
href="link name"
```

When you create a link in Dreamweaver, the anchor pair surrounds the text or object that is being linked. For example, if you link the phrase "Back to Home Page," it may look like the following:

```
<a href="index.html">Back to Home Page</a>
```

When you attach a link to an image, logo.gif, your code looks as follows:

```
<a href="home.html"><img src="images/logo.gif"></a>
```

Creating a basic link in Dreamweaver is easy. Simply follow these steps:

1. Select the text, image, or object you want to establish as a link.

2. In the Property Inspector, enter the URL in the Link text box as shown in Figure 11-1. You can use one of the following methods to do so:

   • Type the URL directly into the Link text box.

   • Select the folder icon to the right of the Link text box to open the Select File dialog box, where you can browse for the file.

   • Select the Point to File icon and drag your mouse to an existing page or link. This feature is explained later in this section.

   • Drag a link from the Assets panel onto a text or image selection.

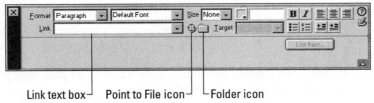

Link text box┘   Point to File icon┘   └Folder icon

Figure 11-1: You can enter your link directly into the Link text box, point to it directly with the Point to File icon, or select the folder icon to browse for a file.

Only a few restrictions exist for specifying linked URLs. Dreamweaver does not support any letters from the extended character set (also known as High ASCII), such as ¡, à, or ñ. Complete URLs must have fewer than a total of 255 characters. You should be cautious about using spaces in path names and, thus, URLs. Although most browsers can interpret the address, spaces are changed to a %20 symbol for proper Unix usage, which can make your URLs difficult to read.

Note   Whitespace in your HTML usually doesn't have an adverse effect. However, Netscape browsers are sensitive to whitespace when assigning a link to an image. If you isolate your image tag from the anchor tags as in the following example:

Links Without Underscores

To remove the underlined aspect of a link, you can use one of two methods. The classic method—which works for all graphics-capable browsers—uses an image rather than text as the link. You must make sure the `border` attribute of your image is set to 0 because a linked image usually displays a blue border if a `border` attribute exists. Dreamweaver adds border="0" to all image links now, as a default.

The second, newer method uses Cascading Style Sheets. While this is an excellent one-stop solution for 4.0 and later browsers, the links will still be seen with underlines on the earlier browser versions. Refer to the Dreamweaver Technique for eliminating the underlines in links in Chapter 18.

```
<a href="index.htm">
<img src="images/Austria.gif" width="34" height="24">
</a>
```

Netscape browsers attach a small blue underscore—a tail, really—to your image. Because Dreamweaver codes the anchor tag properly, without any additional whitespace, this odd case applies only to hand-coded or previously coded HTML.

Text links are most often rendered with a blue color and underlined. You can specify the document link color by choosing Modify ➪ Page Properties and selecting the Link Color swatch. In Page Properties, you can also alter the color to which the links change after being selected (the Visited Link Color) and the color flashed when the link is clicked (the Active Link Color).

Note   Want to add a little variety to your text links? You can actually change the color of the link on an individual basis. To do this, you have to enter the link in the Property Inspector before you apply the color. Be sure to exercise a little discretion though—you don't want to use so many different colors that your Web page visitors can't figure out the navigation.

Inserting URLs from the Assets panel

Internet addresses get more complicated every day. Trying to remember them all correctly and avoid typos makes the Web designer's job unnecessarily difficult. At least, it's unnecessary if you make use of the URLs category of Dreamweaver 4's new Assets panel. With the Assets panel, you can drag-and-drop the trickiest URLs with a flick of the mouse tail.

New Feature   As with other Assets panel categories, you'll need to select the Refresh Site List button to make available all the possible URLs in a site. Alternatively, you could choose Refresh Site List from the context menu on the panel. Either action causes

Dreamweaver to scan all the Web pages within the site and extract all the complete Internet addresses found. Only full Internet addresses — whether to files (such as www.idest.com/dreamweaver) or to e-mail addresses (for example, mailto:jlowery@idest.com) — are visible in the Assets panel. Document or site relative links are not listed as an Asset. To assign a link to a document or site relative page, use one of the other methods, such as pointing to a file, discussed in this chapter.

To assign a URL from the Assets panel, follow these steps:

1. If it's not already visible, select Window ⇨ Assets or click the Assets icon on the Launcher to display the Assets panel. Alternatively, you show the Assets panel by pressing the keyboard shortcut, F11.

2. Select the URLs icon on the side of the Assets panel to show that category, as seen in Figure 11-2.

URLs icon

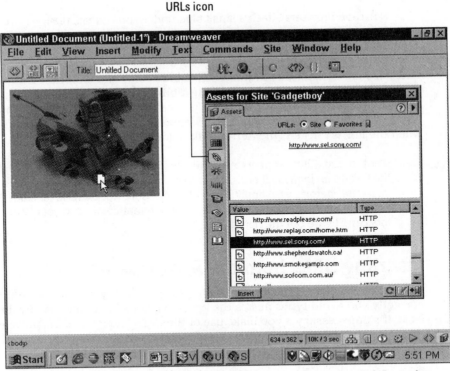

Figure 11-2: Banish typos from your absolute URLs by dragging a link from the Assets panel to any selected text or graphic.

3. If necessary, select the Refresh button on the Assets panel to list the most current links found in the site.

4. In the Document window, select the text or image you want the link assigned to.

5. Drag the desired link from the Assets panel onto the selected text or image; alternatively, highlight the link in the panel and then choose the Apply button.

You'll notice that the Edit button on the Assets panel is unavailable for the URLs category. Links cannot be edited; they can only be applied as shown in the preview area.

Pointing to a file

Dreamweaver has an alternative method of identifying a link—pointing to it. By using the Point to File icon on the Property Inspector, you can quickly fill in the Link text box by dragging your mouse to any existing named anchor or file visible in the Dreamweaver environment. The Point to File feature saves you from having to browse through folder after folder as you search for a file you can clearly see onscreen.

You can point to a file in another open Dreamweaver window or one in another frame in the same window. If your desired link is a named anchor located further down the page, Dreamweaver automatically scrolls to find it. You can even point to a named anchor in another page, and Dreamweaver enters the full syntax correctly. Named anchors are covered in detail later in this chapter.

Perhaps one of the slickest applications of the Point to File icon is when it is used in tandem with the Site window. The Site window lists all the existing files in any given Web site, and when both it and the Document window are onscreen, you can quickly point to any file.

Cross-Reference   For more details about using the Site window in this fashion, see Chapter 7.

Pointing to a file uses what could be called a "drag-and-release" mouse technique, as opposed to the more ordinary point-and-click or drag-and-drop method. To select a new link using the Point to File icon, follow these steps:

1. Select the text or the graphic that you'd want to make into a link.

2. In the Property Inspector, click and hold the Point to File icon located to the right of the Link text box.

3. Holding down the mouse button, drag the mouse until it is over an existing link or named anchor in the Document window or a file in the Site window.

   As you drag the mouse, a line extends from the Point to File icon, and the reminder "Point to a file to make a link" appears in the Link text box.

4. When you locate the file you want to link to, release the mouse button. The filename with the accompanying path information is written into the Link text box as shown in Figure 11-3.

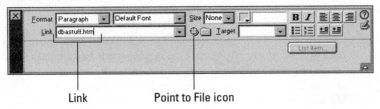

Link   Point to File icon

Figure 11-3: The Point to File capability enables you to quickly insert a link to any onscreen page.

Addressing types

As you learned in Chapter 6, three types of URLs are used as links: absolute addresses, document-relative addresses, and site root–relative addresses. Let's briefly recap these address types.

✦ **Absolute addresses** require the full URL, as follows:

```
http://www.macromedia.com/software/dreamweaver/
```

This type is most often used for referencing links on another Web server.

✦ **Document-relative addresses** know the method, server, and path aspects of the URL. You need to include only additional path information if the link is outside of the current Web page's folder. Links in the current document's folder can be addressed with their filename only. To reference an item in a subfolder, just name the folder, enter a forward slash, and then enter the item's filename, as follows:

```
images/background.gif
```

✦ **Site root–relative addresses** are indicated with a leading forward slash. For example:

```
/navigation/upndown.html
```

The preceding address links to a file named upndown.html stored in the navigation directory at the current site root. Dreamweaver translates site-relative to document-relative links when the Preview in Browser feature is used.

A Webmaster often must perform the tedious but necessary task of verifying the links on all the Web pages in a site. Because of the Web's fluid nature, links can work one day and then be broken the next. Dreamweaver has enhanced its powerful link-checking capabilities with link-updating features.

Cross-Reference To find out how to keep your site up to date with a minimum of effort, see Chapter 7.

Adding an E-Mail Link

E-mail links are very common on the Web. Rather than opening a new Web page like a regular link, when an e-mail link is clicked, a window for sending a new e-mail message is displayed. The message window is already preaddressed to the recipient, making it convenient to use. All the user has to do is add a subject, enter a message, and select Send.

E-mail links no longer need be added by hand. Dreamweaver includes an object that streamlines the process. Just enter the text of the line, and the e-mail address and the link is ready. E-mail links, like other links, do not work in Dreamweaver when clicked and must be previewed in the browser.

To enter an e-mail link with the new object, follow these steps:

1. Position your cursor where you want the e-mail link to appear.

2. From the Common category of the Objects panel, select the Insert E-Mail Link button.

   The Insert E-Mail Link dialog box, shown in Figure 11-4, appears.

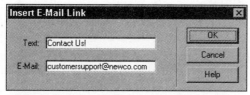

Figure 11-4: The Insert E-Mail Link object creates links that make it simple for your Web page visitors to send an e-mail.

3. In the Insert E-Mail Link dialog box, enter the visible text for the link in the Text field.

4. Enter the e-mail address in the E-Mail field.

Caution The e-mail address must be in the format name@company.com. Dreamweaver does not check to make sure you've entered the proper format.

5. Click OK when you're done.

Note   If you already have the text for the e-mail link in the document, you can also use the Property Inspector to insert an e-mail link. Just highlight the text and in the Link field of the Property Inspector, enter the URL in this format:

```
mailto:name@company.com
```

Make sure that the URL is a valid e-mail address with the @ sign properly placed.

Here's a bit of the frustration that Web designers sometimes face: On some browsers, notably Internet Explorer, the user may see a dialog box when the e-mail link is first selected. The dialog box informs them that they are about to send an e-mail over the Internet. The user has an option to not see these warnings, but there's no way for the Web designer to prevent them from appearing.

Navigating with Anchors

Whenever you normally link to an HTML page, through absolute or relative address-ing, the browser displays the page from the top. Your Web visitors must scroll to any information rendered below the current screen. One HTML technique, however, links to a specific point anywhere on your page regardless of the display window's contents. This technique uses *named anchors*.

Using named anchors is a two-step process. First you place a named anchor some-where on your Web page. This placement is coded in HTML as an anchor tag using the name attribute, with nothing in between the opening and closing tags. In HTML, named anchors look like the following:

```
<a name="bible"></a>
```

The second step includes a link to that named anchor from somewhere else on your Web page. If used, a named anchor is referenced in the final possible portion of an Internet address, designated by the hash mark (#), as follows:

```
<a href="http://www.idest.com/dreamweaver/index.htm#bible>
```

You can include any number of named anchors on the current page or another page. Named anchors are commonly used with a table of contents or index.

To insert a named anchor in Dreamweaver, follow these steps:

1. Place the cursor where you want the named anchor to appear.

2. Choose Insert ➪ Named Anchor. You can also select the Insert Named Anchor button from the Invisibles category of the Objects panel. Or use the key short-cut Ctrl+Alt+A (Command+Option+A).

3. The Named Anchor dialog box opens. Type the anchor name into the text box.

Caution

Named anchors are case-sensitive and must be unique within the page.

When you press Enter (Return), Dreamweaver places a named anchor symbol in the current cursor location and opens the Named Anchor Property Inspector (shown in Figure 11-5).

Named Anchor symbol

Insert Named Anchor button

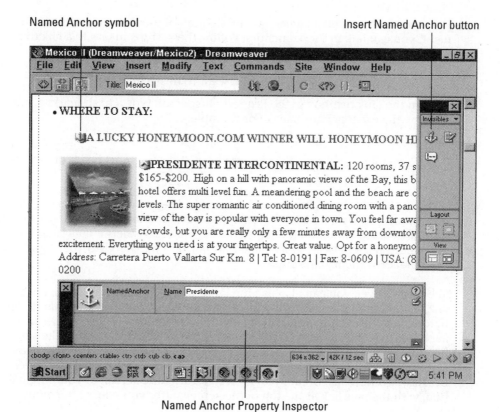

Named Anchor Property Inspector

Figure 11-5: The Named Anchor tag enables you to link to specific areas of a Web page.

4. To change an anchor's name, click the named anchor symbol within the page and alter the text in the Property Inspector.

As with other invisible symbols, the named anchor symbol can be cut and pasted or moved using the drag-and-drop method.

Moving within the same document

One of the major advantages of using named anchors is the almost instantaneous response the viewer receives when they click them. The browser only needs to scroll to the particular place in the document because the entire page is loaded. For long text documents, this capability is an invaluable time-saver.

Once you have placed a named anchor — or all of them at once — in your document, you can link to these anchors. Follow these steps to create a link to a named anchor in the same document:

1. Select the text or image that you want to designate as a link.

2. In the Link text box of the Property Inspector, type a hash mark, #, followed by the exact anchor name. For example:

   #top

   Remember, anchor names are case-sensitive and must be unique in each document.

Note   You should place the named anchor one line above the heading or image to which you want to link the viewer. Browsers tend to be quite literal. If you place the named anchor on the same line, the browser renders it up against the top of the window. Placing your named anchor up one line gives your topic a bit of breathing room in the display.

In Dreamweaver, you can also use the Point to File icon to choose a named anchor link. If your named anchor is in the same document, just drag the Point to File icon to the named anchor symbol. When you release the mouse, the proper named anchor is inserted into the Link text box. If the named anchor is on the same page but offscreen, Dreamweaver automatically scrolls the Document window as you approach the edge. In Windows, the closer you move to the edge, the faster Dreamweaver scrolls. Dreamweaver even returns the screen to your original location, with the new link at the top of the screen, after you release the mouse button.

In long documents with a table of contents or index linking to a number of named anchors, it's common practice — and a good idea — to place a link back to the top of the page after every screen or every topic. This technique enables your users to return to the menu quickly and pick another topic without having to manually scroll all the way back.

Using named anchors in a different page

If your table of contents is on a separate page from the topics of your site, you can use named anchors to send the viewer anywhere on a new page. The technique is exactly the same as already explained for placing named anchors, but one minor difference exists when it comes to linking. Instead of placing a hash mark and name to denote the named anchor, you must first include the URL of the linked page.

Let's say you want to call the disclaimer section of a legal page from your table of contents. You could insert something like the following in the Link text box of the Property Inspector:

```
legal.htm#disclaimer
```

This link, when activated, first loads the referenced Web page (legal.htm) and then goes directly to the named anchor place (#disclaimer). Figure 11-6 shows how you would enter this in the Property Inspector. Keep in mind, you can use any form of addressing prior to the hash mark and named anchor.

Figure 11-6: You can also link to any part of a separate Web page using named anchors.

Note   One of the more obscure uses for named anchors comes into play when you are trying to use Dreamweaver's JavaScript Behavior feature. Because JavaScript needs to work with a particular type of tag to perform `onMouseOver` and other events, one trick marks some text or image with a link to #nowhere. You can use any name for the nonexistent named anchor. In fact, you don't even have to use a name—you can just use a hash mark by itself (#). One problem area: Netscape browsers have a tendency to send the page to the top if a link of this type is used. Many programmers have begun to substitute a JavaScript function instead, such as `javascript:;`. Dreamweaver itself now uses `javascript:;` instead of # when a new behavior is attached to an image.

Targeting Your Links

Thus far, all of this chapter's links have had a similar effect: They open another Web page or section in your browser's window. What if you want to force the browser to open another window and load that new URL in the new window? HTML enables you to specify the target for your links.

Targets are most often used in conjunction with frames — that is, you can make a link in one frame open a file in another. (Chapter 14 covers the subject of frames in depth.) Here, though, let's take a look at one of the HTML predefined targets useful in a situation where you want to load another URL into a new window.

To specify a new browser window as the target for a link in Dreamweaver, follow these steps:

1. Select the text or image you want to designate as your new link.

2. In the Property Inspector, enter the URL into the Link text box.

   After you've entered a link, the target option becomes active.

3. Choose the option button next to the Target list box and select _blank from the drop-down list. You can also type it in the list box.

   Dreamweaver inserts a _blank option in the Target list box, as shown in Figure 11-7. Now, when your link is activated, the browser spawns a new window and loads the referenced link into it. The user has both windows available.

Figure 11-7: You can force a user's browser to open a separate window to display a specific link with the Target command.

The _blank target is most often used when the originating Web page is acting as a jump station and has numerous links available. By keeping the original Web page open, the user can check out one site without losing the origin point.

Note Three other system-wide targets exist: _top, _parent, and _self. Both _top and _parent are primarily used with framesets: _top target replaces the outermost frameset and _parent replaces the frameset containing the current page. These two have the same effect, except in the case of nested framesets. The _self target is the default behavior and only the current page is replaced.

You can even use the _blank target technique on named anchors in the same document, thereby emulating frames to some degree.

Caution Some key online services, such as America Online and WebTV, don't enable their built-in browsers to open new windows. Every link that is accessed is displayed in the same browser window.

Summary

Whether they are links for Web site navigation or jumps to other related sites, hypertext links are an essential part of any Web page. Dreamweaver gives you full control over your inserted anchors.

✦ Through a unique URL, you can access virtually any Web page, graphic, or other item available on the Internet.

✦ The HyperText Transfer Protocol (HTTP) is the most common method of Web connection, but Web pages can link to other formats, including FTP, e-mail, and newsgroups.

✦ Any of the three basic address formats — absolute, document relative, or site root relative — can be inserted in the Link text box of Dreamweaver's Property Inspector to create a link.

✦ Dreamweaver has a quick linking capability through its Point to File feature.

✦ The Assets panel tracks all of your absolute and mailto: URLs and makes it easy to apply any of them to your pages. Document or site relative URLs are not displayed in the Assets panel, however.

✦ Named anchors give you the power to jump to specific parts of any Web page, whether the page is the current one or located on another server.

✦ With the _blank target attribute, you can force a link to open in a new browser window, leaving your original window available to the user.

In the next chapter, you learn how to use various types of lists in Dreamweaver.

✦   ✦   ✦

Incorporating Advanced HTML

Setting Up Tables

Tables bring structure to a Web page. Whether used to align numbers in a spreadsheet or to arrange columns of text on a page, an HTML table brings a bit of order to otherwise free-flowing content. Initially, tables were implemented to present raw data in a more readable format. But it didn't take long for Web designers to take up tables as the most capable tool to control page layout.

Dreamweaver's implementation of tables reflects this current trend in Web page design. Drag-and-drop table sizing, easy organization of rows and columns, and instant table reformatting all help get the job done in the shortest time possible. Table editing features enable you to select and modify anything in a table from a single cell to multiple columns. Moreover, using Dreamweaver commands, you can sort your table in a variety of ways or completely reformat it.

Dreamweaver 4 introduces a new feature that takes table layout to the next level of ease-of-use and power. With the Layout view, designers are able to draw individual cells with a stroke of the mouse and Dreamweaver automatically creates a borderless, content-ready table. You can even add nested tables to maintain design integrity. While you still need to know the basics of table functionality to make the most out of this new tool, Layout view offers a fully backward-compatible technique for visually structuring your Web page.

Although the absolute positioning capabilities offered by Dynamic HTML give Web designers another route to precise layout control, many Web designers use a combination of tools to get desired effects and maintain wide browser compatibility. In other words, HTML tables are going to be around for a long time.

HTML Table Fundamentals

A table is basically a grid that expands as you add text or images. Tables consist of three main components: rows, columns, and cells. *Rows* go across a table from left to right, and *columns* go up and down. A *cell* is the intersection of a row and a column; it's where you enter your information. Cells expand to fit whatever they hold. If you have enabled the table border, your browser shows the outline of the table and all its cells.

In HTML, all the structure and all the data of a table are contained between the table tag pair, `<table>` and `</table>`. The `<table>` tag can take numerous attributes, determining a table's width and height (which can be given in absolute measurement or as a percentage of the screen) as well as the border, alignment on the page, and background color. You can also control the size of the spacing between cells and the amount of padding within cells.

HTML uses a strict hierarchy when describing a table. You can see this clearly in Listing 12-1, which shows the HTML generated from a default table in Dreamweaver.

Listing 12-1: **Code for an HTML Table**

```
<table border="1" width="75%">
  <tr>
    <td> </td>
    <td> </td>
    <td> </td>
  </tr>
  <tr>
    <td> </td>
    <td> </td>
    <td> </td>
  </tr>
  <tr>
    <td> </td>
    <td> </td>
    <td> </td>
  </tr>
</table>
```

Note   The   seen in the table code is HTML for a nonbreaking space. Dreamweaver inserts the code in each empty table cell because some browsers collapse the cell without it. Enter any text or image in the cell, and Dreamweaver automatically removes the   code.

Rows

After the opening `<table>` tag comes the first row tag `<tr>`. Within the current row, you can specify attributes for horizontal alignment or vertical alignment. In addition, browsers recognize row color as an added option.

Cells

Cells are marked in HTML with the `<td>...</td>` tag pair. No specific code exists for a column; rather, columns are seen as the number of cells within a row. For example, in Listing 12-1, notice the three sets of `<td>` tags between each `<tr>` pair. This means the table has three columns. A cell can span more than one row or column — in these cases, you see a `rowspan=value` or `colspan=value` attribute in the `<td>` tag.

Cells can also be given horizontal or vertical alignment attributes; these attributes override any similar attributes specified by the table row. When you give a cell a particular width, all the cells in that column are affected. Width can be specified in either an absolute pixel measurement or as a percentage of the overall table.

Tip   After the initial `<table>` tag, you can place an optional caption for the table. In Dreamweaver, you have to enter the `<caption>` tag by hand in the Code view or inspector. Here's an example to show how the tag works:

```
<caption align="center" valign="bottom">Table of
Periodic Elements</caption>
```

Column/row headings

A special type of cell called a *table header* is used for column and row headings. Information in these cells is marked with a `<th>` tag and is generally rendered in boldface, centered within the cell.

Inserting Tables in Dreamweaver

You can control almost all of a table's HTML features through Dreamweaver's point-and-click interface. To insert a Dreamweaver table in the current cursor position, use one of the following three methods:

✦ Select the Insert Table button on the Objects panel.

✦ Choose Insert ➪ Table from the menus.

✦ Use the keyboard shortcut: Ctrl+Alt+T (Command+Option+T).

The Insert Table dialog box, shown in Figure 12-1, contains the following default values when it is first displayed:

Attribute	Default	Description
Rows	3	The number of horizontal rows.
Columns	3	The number of vertical columns.
Width	75%	Sets the preset width of the table. Available in a percentage of the containing element (screen, layer, or another table) or an absolute pixel size.
Border	1 pixel	The width of the border around each cell and the entire table.
Cell Padding	(Empty)	The space between a cell's border and its contents. Although not shown, Dreamweaver displays 1 pixel of cell padding unless a different value is entered.
Cell Spacing	(Empty)	The number of pixels between each cell. Although not shown, Dreamweaver displays 2 pixels of cell spacing unless a different value is entered.

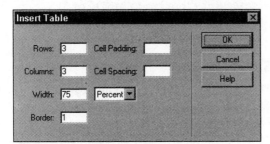

Figure 12-1: The Insert Table dialog box starts out with a default of three columns and three rows; you can adjust as needed.

If you aren't sure of the number of rows and/or columns you need, put in your best guess — you can add or delete rows or columns as necessary.

The default table is sized to take up 75 percent of the browser window. You can alter this percentage by changing the value in the Width text box. The table maintains this proportion as you add text or images, except in two situations:

✦ When an image is larger than the specified percentage

✦ When the nowrap attribute is used for the cell or table row and there is too much text to fit

In either case, the percentage set for the table is ignored, and the cell and table expand to accommodate the text or image. (For further information on the nowrap attribute, see the section "Cell wrap," later in this chapter.)

Note

The Insert Table dialog box uses what are called *sticky* settings and displays your previously used settings the next time you open the dialog box. This handy feature enables you to set the border width to zero and forget about resetting it each time.

If you prefer to enter the table width as an absolute pixel value, as opposed to the relative percentage, type the number of pixels in the Width text box and select pixels in the drop-down list of width options.

Figure 12-2 shows three tables: At the top is the default table with the width set to 75 percent. The middle table, set to 100 percent, will take up the full width of the browser window. The third table is fixed at 300 pixels — approximately half of a 640×480 window.

Tip

You don't have to declare a width for your table at all. If you delete the value in the Width text box of the Insert Table dialog box, your table starts out as small as possible and only expands to accommodate inserted text or images. However, this can make it difficult to position your cursor inside a cell to enter content. You can always delete any set size — pixel or percentage — later.

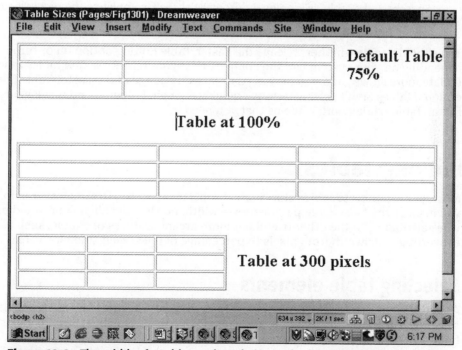

Figure 12-2: The width of a table can be relative to the browser window or set to an absolute width in pixels.

Setting Table Preferences

Two preferences directly affect tables. Both can be set by choosing Edit ⇨ Preferences and looking in the General category.

The first pertinent option is the Show Dialog when Inserting Objects checkbox. If this option is turned off, Dreamweaver always inserts a default table (3 rows by 3 columns at 75 percent width of the screen with a 1-pixel border), without displaying a dialog box and asking for your input. Should you wish to change these values, you can adjust them from the Table Property Inspector once the table has been inserted.

The second notable preference is labeled Faster Table Editing (Deferred Update). Because tables expand and contract dynamically depending on their contents, Dreamweaver gives you the option of turning off the continual updating. (Depending on the speed of your system, the updating can slow down your table input.) If the Faster Table Editing option is enabled, the table is updated whenever you click outside of it or when you press the keyboard shortcut, Ctrl+Space (Command+Spacebar).

Note   If you have enabled Faster Table Editing and begin typing in one cell of your table, notice that the text wraps within the cell, and the table expands vertically. However, when you click outside of the table or press Ctrl+Space (Command+ Spacebar), the table cells adjust horizontally as well, completing the redrawing of the table.

You should decide whether to leave the Faster Table Editing option on or turn it off, depending on your system and the complexity of your tables. Nested tables tend to update more slowly, and you may need to take advantage of the Faster Table Editing option if tables aren't getting redrawn quickly enough. I recommend turning off Faster Table Editing until it seems that you need it.

Modifying Tables

Most modifications to tables start in the Property Inspector. Dreamweaver helps you manage the basic table parameters — width, border, and alignment — and provides attributes for the other useful but more arcane features of a table, such as converting table width from pixels to percentage of the screen, and vice versa.

Selecting table elements

As with text or images, the first step in altering a table (or any of its elements) is selection. Dreamweaver simplifies the selection process, making it easy to change both the properties and the contents of entire tables, selected rows or columns, and even nonadjacent cells. You can change the font size and color of a row with a click or two of the mouse — instead of highlighting and modifying each individual cell.

Note   All of the following discussions about table selections pertain only to the Standard view and are not applicable in Layout view.

In Dreamweaver, you can select the following elements of a table:

+ The entire table

+ A single row

+ Multiple rows, either adjacent or separate

+ A single column

+ Multiple columns, either adjacent or separate

+ A single cell

+ Multiple cells, either adjacent or separate

Once a table element is selected, you can modify its contents.

Selecting an entire table

Several methods are available for selecting the entire table, whether you're a menu- or mouse-oriented designer. To select the table via a menu, do one of the following:

+ Choose Modify ⇨ Table ⇨ Select Table.

+ With the cursor positioned in the table, choose Edit ⇨ Select All or use the keyboard shortcut, Ctrl+A (Command+A).

+ Right-click (Control+click) inside a table to display the shortcut menu and choose Table ⇨ Select Table.

To select an entire table with the mouse, use one of these techniques:

+ Click the bottom or right border of the table. You can also click anywhere along the table border when the pointer becomes a four-sided arrow.

+ Select the <table> tag in the Tag Selector.

+ Click immediately to one side of the table and drag the mouse over the table.

However you select the table, the selected table is surrounded by a black border with sizing handles on the right, bottom, and bottom-right corner (as shown in Figure 12-3), just as a selected graphic.

Selecting a row or column

Altering rows or columns of table text without Dreamweaver is a major time-consuming chore. Each cell has to be individually selected, and the changes applied. Dreamweaver has an intuitive method for selecting single or multiple columns and rows, comparable — and in some ways, superior — to major word processing programs.

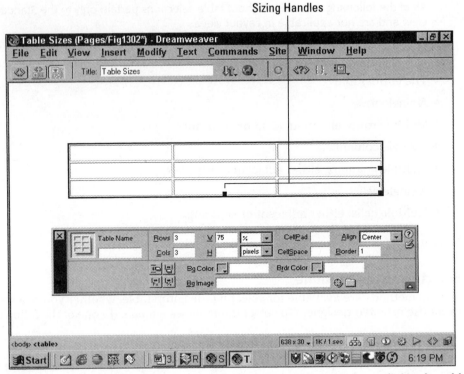

Figure 12-3: A selected table can be identified by the black border outlining the table and the three sizing handles.

As with entire tables, you have several methods for selecting columns or rows. None of the techniques, however, use the menus; row and column selection is handled primarily with the mouse. In fact, you can select an entire row or column with one click.

The one-click method for selecting a single column or row requires that you position your pointer directly over the column or to the left of the row you want to choose. Move the pointer slowly toward the table — when the pointer becomes a single arrow, with the arrowhead pointing down for columns and to the right for rows, click the mouse. All the cells in the selected column or row are bounded with a black border. Any changes now made in the Property Inspector, such as a change in font size or color, affect the selected column or row.

You can select multiple, contiguous columns or rows by dragging the single arrow pointer across several columns or rows. To select a number of columns or rows that are not next to one another, use the Ctrl (Command) key. Press the Ctrl (Command) key while selecting each individual column, using the one-click method. (Not even Word 2000 can handle this degree of complex table selection.)

Tip

If you have trouble positioning the mouse so that the single arrow pointer appears, you can use two other methods for selecting columns or rows. With the first method, you can click and drag across all the cells in a column or row. The second method uses another keyboard modifier, the Shift key. With this technique, click once in the first cell of the column or row. Then, hold down the Shift key while you click in the final cell of the column or row. You can also use this technique to select multiple adjacent columns or rows; just click in another column's or row's last cell.

Selecting cells

Sometimes you need to change the background color of just a few cells in a table, but not the entire row — or you might need to merge several cells to form one wide column span. In these situations, and many others, you can use Dreamweaver's cell selection capabilities. As with columns and rows, you can select multiple cells, whether they are adjacent to one another or separate.

Individual cells are generally selected by dragging the mouse across one or more cell boundaries. To select a single cell, click anywhere in the cell and drag the mouse into another cell. As you pass the border between the two cells, the initial cell is highlighted. If you continue dragging the mouse across another cell boundary, the second cell is selected, and so on. Note that you have to drag the mouse into another cell and not cross the table border onto the page; for example, to highlight the lower-right cell of a table, you need to drag the mouse up or to the left.

Tip

You can also select a single cell by pressing the Ctrl (Command) key and clicking once in the cell, or you can select the rightmost <td> tag in the Tag Selector.

Extended cell selection in Dreamweaver is handled identically to extended text selection in most word processing programs. To select adjacent cells, click in the first desired cell, press and hold the Shift key, and click in the final desired cell. Dreamweaver selects all in a rectangular area, using the first cell as the upper-left corner of the rectangle and the last cell as the lower-right corner. You could, for instance, select an entire table by clicking in the upper-left cell and then Shift+clicking the lower-right cell.

Just as the Shift key is used to make adjacent cell selections, the Ctrl (Command) key is used for all nonadjacent cell selections. You can highlight any number of individual cells — whether or not they are next to one another — by pressing the Ctrl (Command) key while you click in the cell.

Tip

If you Ctrl+click (Command+click) a cell that is already selected, that cell is deselected — regardless of the method you used to select the cell initially.

Editing a table's contents

Before you learn how to change a table's attributes, let's look at basic editing techniques. Editing text in Dreamweaver tables is slightly different from editing text outside of tables. When you begin to enter text into a table cell, the table borders
expand to accommodate your new data, assuming no width has been set. The other
cells appear to shrink, but they, too, expand once you start typing in text or inserting an image. Unless a cell's width is specified, the cell currently being edited
expands or contracts, and the other cells are forced to adjust their width. Figure
12-4 shows the same table (with one row and three columns) in three different
states. In the top table, only the first cell contains text; notice how the other cells
have contracted. In the middle table, text has been entered into the second cell as
well, and you can see how the first cell is now smaller. Finally, in the bottom table,
all three cells contain text, and the other two cells have adjusted their width to
compensate for the expanding third cell.

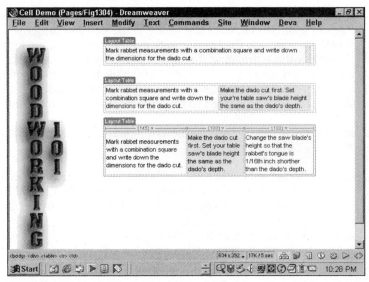

Figure 12-4: As text is entered into a cell, the cell expands; other
cells contract, even if they already contain text.

If you look closely at the bottom table in Figure 12-4, you can also see that the
text doesn't line up vertically. That's because the default vertical alignment in
Dreamweaver, as in most browsers, provides for entries to be positioned in the
middle of the cell. (Later in this section, you learn how to adjust the vertical
alignment.)

Moving through a table

When you've finished entering your text in the first cell, you can move to the next cell in the row by pressing the Tab key. When you reach the end of a row, pressing Tab takes your cursor to the first cell of the next row. To go backward, cell to cell, press Shift+Tab.

> **Tip** Pressing Tab has a special function when you're in the last cell of a row — it adds a new row, with the same column configuration as the current one.

The Home and End keys take you to the beginning and end, respectively, of the cursor's current line. If a cell's contents are large enough for the text to wrap in the cell, move to the top of the current cell by pressing Ctrl+Home (Command+up arrow or Command+Home). To get the bottom of the current cell in such a circumstance, press Ctrl+End (Command+down arrow).

When you're at the beginning or end of the contents in a cell, the arrow keys can also be used to navigate from cell to cell. Use the left and right arrows to move from cell to cell in a row, and the up and down arrows to move down a column. When you come to the end of a row or column, the arrow keys move to the first cell in the next row or column. If you're moving left to right horizontally, the cursor goes from the end of one row to the beginning of the next row — and vice-versa, if you move from right to left. When moving from top to bottom vertically, the cursor goes from the end of one column to the start of the next, and vice-versa when moving bottom to top.

Cutting, copying, and pasting in tables

In the early days of Web design (about four years ago), woe if you should accidentally leave out a cell of information. It was often almost faster to redo the entire table than to make room by meticulously cutting and pasting everything, one cell at a time. Dreamweaver ends that painstaking work forever with its advanced cutting and pasting features. You can copy a range of cells from one table to another and maintain all the attributes, such as color and alignment as well as the content — text or images — or you can copy just the contents and ignore the attributes.

Dreamweaver has one basic restriction to table cut-and-paste operations: Your selected cells must form a rectangle. In other words, although you can select nonadjacent cells, columns, or rows and modify their properties, you can't cut or copy them. Should you try, you get a message from Dreamweaver such as the one shown in Figure 12-5; the table above the notification in the figure illustrates an incorrect cell selection.

Copying attributes and contents

When you copy or cut a cell using the regular commands, Dreamweaver automatically copies everything — content, formatting, and cell format — in the selected cell. Then, pasting the cell reproduces it all — however, you can get different results depending on where the cell (or column or row) is pasted.

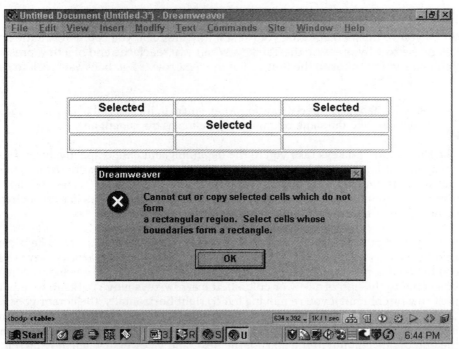

Figure 12-5: Dreamweaver enables you to cut or copy selected cells only when they form a rectangle, unlike the cells in the table depicted here.

To cut or copy both the contents and the attributes of any cell, row, or column, follow these steps:

1. Select the cells you wish to cut or copy.

   Remember that to cut or copy a range of cells in Dreamweaver, they must form a solid rectangular region.

2. To copy cells, choose Edit ➪ Copy or use the keyboard shortcut, Ctrl+C (Command+C).

3. To cut cells, choose Edit ➪ Cut or use the keyboard shortcut, Ctrl+X (Command+X).

   If you cut an individual cell, the contents are removed, but the cell remains. If, however, you cut an entire row or column, the cells are removed.

4. Position your cursor to paste the cells in the desired location:

   - To replace a cell with a cell on the clipboard, click anywhere in the cell to be replaced. If you cut or copied multiple cells that do not make up a full column or row, click in the upper-left corner of the cells you wish to replace. For example, a range of six cells in a 2×3 configuration replaces the same configuration when pasted.

Dreamweaver alerts you to the differences if you try to paste one configuration of cells into a different cell configuration.

- To insert a new row with the row on the clipboard, click anywhere in the row below where you'd like the new row to appear.

- To insert a new column with the column on the clipboard, click anywhere in the column to the right of where you'd like the new column to appear.

- To replace an existing row or column in a table, select the row or column. If you've cut or copied multiple rows or columns, you must select an equivalent size and shape of cells to replace.

- To insert a new table based on the copied or cut cells, click anywhere outside of the table.

5. Paste the copied or cut cells by choosing Edit ➪ Paste or pressing Ctrl+V (Command+V).

Tip

To move a row or column that you've cut from the interior of a table to the exterior (the right or bottom), you have to first expand the number of cells in the table. To do this, first select the table by choosing Modify ➪ Table ➪ Select Table or using one of the other techniques previously described. Next, in the Table Property Inspector, increase the number of rows or columns by altering the values in the Rows or Cols text boxes. Finally, select the newly added rows or columns and choose Edit ➪ Paste.

Copying contents only

It's not uncommon to need to move data from one cell to another, while keeping the destination cell's attributes, such as its background color or border, intact. For this, you need to use Dreamweaver's facility for copying just the contents of a cell.

To copy only the contents, select a cell as previously described and then choose Edit ➪ Copy or use the keyboard shortcut, Ctrl+C (Command+C). Then put your cursor in the destination cell and, instead of choosing Edit ➪ Paste, choose Edit ➪ Paste HTML, or use the keyboard shortcut, Ctrl+Shift+V (Command+Shift+V). Instead of selecting the entire cell to copy, you can also just select the text, or a portion of the text, and use the standard Edit ➪ Copy and Edit ➪ Paste commands to avoid pasting in the format of the copied text.

Unlike the copying of both contents and attributes described in the previous section, content-only copying has a couple of limitations:

- ✦ First, you can copy only the contents of one cell at a time. You can't copy contents only across multiple cells.

- ✦ Second, you can't replace the entire contents of one cell with another and maintain all the text attributes (font, color, and size) of the destination cell. If you select all the text to be replaced, Dreamweaver also selects the `<font>` tag that holds the attributes and replaces those as well. The workaround is to select all but one letter or word, paste the contents, and then delete the unwanted text.

Working with table properties

The <table> tag has a large number of attributes, and most of them can be modified through Dreamweaver's Property Inspector. As with all objects, the table must be selected before it can be altered. Choose Modify ➪ Table ➪ Select Table or use one of the other selection techniques previously described.

Once you've selected the table, if the Property Inspector is open, it presents the table properties as shown in Figure 12-6. Otherwise, you can open the Table Property Inspector by choosing Window ➪ Properties Inspector.

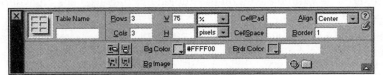

Figure 12-6: The expanded Table Property Inspector gives you control over all the tablewide attributes.

Setting alignment

Aligning a table in Dreamweaver goes beyond the expected left, right, and center options — you can also make a table into a free-floating object around which text can wrap to the left or right.

With HTML, you can align a table using two different methods, and each gives you a different effect. Using the text alignment method (Text ➪ Align) results in the conventional positioning (left, right, and center), and using the Table Property Inspector method enables you to wrap text around your realigned table. Figure 12-7 compares some of the different results you get from aligning your table with the two methods.

To align your table without text wrapping, follow these steps:

1. Select your table using one of the methods described earlier.

2. In the Property Inspector, make sure the Align option is set to Default.

3. Select the Text ➪ Align command and then choose one of the three options: Left, Center, or Right.

   Dreamweaver surrounds your table code with a division tag pair, <div>...</div>, with an align attribute set to your chosen value.

To align your table with text wrapping, making your table into a floating object, follow these steps:

1. Select the table.

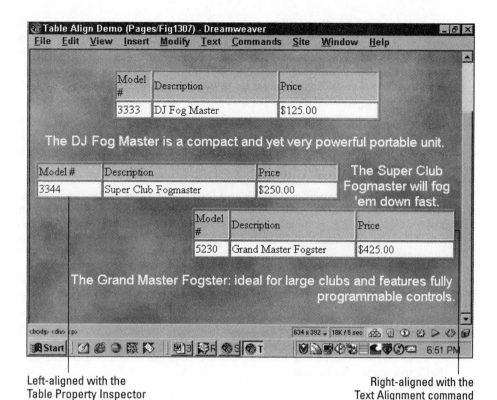

Left-aligned with the
Table Property Inspector

Right-aligned with the
Text Alignment command

Figure 12-7: Tables can be centered, as well as aligned left or right—with or without text wrapping.

2. In the Table Property Inspector, open the Align drop-down list and choose one of the four options:

Alignment Option	Result
Default	No alignment is written. Table aligns to the browser's default, usually left, with no text wrapping.
Left	Aligns the table to the left side of the browser window and wraps text around the right side.
Right	Aligns the table to the right side of the browser window and wraps text around the left side.
Center	The table aligns to the center of the browser window. Text does not wrap around either side. Note: This alignment option works only with 4.0 and above browsers.

Dreamweaver codes these alignment attributes in the `<table>` tag. As with floating images, Dreamweaver places an anchor point for floating elements on the Web page. However, you cannot drag-and-drop or cut-and-paste the anchor point, unlike most other Invisible symbols, for a floating table.

Resizing a table

The primary sizing control on the Table Property Inspector is the Width text box. You can enter a new width value for the entire table in either a screen percentage or pixels. Just enter your value in the Width text box and then select % or pixels in the drop-down list of options.

Dreamweaver also provides a quick and intuitive way to resize the overall table width, column widths, or row height. Pass your pointer over any of the table's borders, and the pointer becomes a two-headed arrow; this is the resizing pointer. When you see the resizing pointer, you can click and drag any border to new dimensions.

As noted earlier, tables are initially sized according to their contents. Once you move a table border in Dreamweaver, however, the new sizes are written directly into the HTML code, and the column width or row height is fixed — unless the contents cannot fit. If, for example, an inserted image is 115 pixels wide and the cell has a width of only 90 pixels, the cell expands to fit the image. The same is true if you try to fit an extremely long, unbroken text string, such as a complex URL, in a cell that's too narrow to hold it.

Dreamweaver enables you to set the height of a table using the Height text box in much the same way as the Width box. However, the height of a table — whether in pixels or a percentage — is maintained only as long as the contents do not require a larger size. A table's width, though, takes precedence over its height, and a table expands vertically before it expands horizontally.

Changes to a cell or column's width are shown in the `<td>` tags, as are changes to a row's height and width, using the `width` and `height` attribute, respectively. You can see these changes by selecting the table, cell, column, or row affected and looking at the W (Width) and H (Height) text box values.

For an overall view of what happens when you resize a cell, row, or column, it's best to look at the HTML. Here's the HTML for an empty table, resized:

```
<table border="1" width="70%">
  <tr>
    <td width="21%"> </td>
    <td width="34%"> </td>
    <td width="45%"> </td>
  </tr>
  <tr>
    <td width="21%" height="42"> </td>
```

```
        <td width="34%" height="42"> </td>
        <td width="45%" height="42"> </td>
      </tr>
      <tr>
        <td width="21%" height="42"> </td>
        <td width="34%" height="42"> </td>
        <td width="45%" height="42"> </td>
      </tr>
    </table>
```

Notice how the width for each cell and the entire table is expressed as percentages. If the table width were initially set at a pixel value, the cell widths would have been, too. The row height values, on the other hand, are shown as an absolute measurement in pixels.

You can switch from percentages to pixels in all the table measurements, and even clear all the values at once — with the click of the right button. Four measurement controls appear in the lower-left portion of the expanded Table Property Inspector, as shown in Figure 12-8.

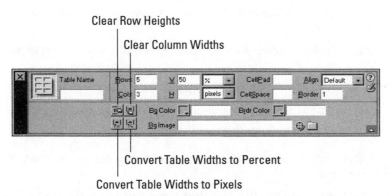

Figure 12-8: You can make tablewide changes with the four control buttons in the Table Property Inspector.

From left to right, the measurement controls are as follows:

Measurement Control Button	Description
Clear Row Heights	Erases all the `height` attributes in the current table
Clear Column Widths	Deletes all the `width` attributes found in the `<td>` tags
Convert Table Widths to Pixels	Translates the current widths of all cells and for the entire table from percentages to pixels
Convert Table Widths to Percent	Translates the current widths of all cells and for the entire table from pixels to percentages

Note Selecting Clear Row Heights doesn't affect the table height value.

If you clear both row heights and column widths, the table goes back to its "grow as needed" format and, if empty, shrinks to its smallest possible size.

Caution When converting width percentages to pixels, and vice versa, keep in mind that the percentages are relative to the size of the browser window — and in the development phase that browser window is Dreamweaver. Use the Window Size option on the status bar to expand Dreamweaver's Document window to the same sizes as what you expect to be seen in various browser settings.

Inserting rows and columns

The default Dreamweaver table configuration of three columns and three rows can be changed at any time. You can add rows or columns almost anywhere in a table, using various methods.

You have three methods for adding a single row:

✦ Position the cursor in the last cell of the last row and press Tab to add a new row below the present one.

✦ Choose Modify ⇨ Table ⇨ Insert Row to insert a new row above the current row.

✦ Right-click (Control+click) to open the shortcut menu and select Table ⇨ Insert Row. Rows added in this way are inserted above the current row.

You have two ways to add a new column to your table:

✦ Choose Modify ⇨ Table ⇨ Insert Column to insert a new column to the left of the current column.

✦ Right-click (Control+click) to open the shortcut menu and select Table ⇨ Insert Column from the shortcut menu. The column is inserted to the left of the current column.

You can add multiple rows and columns in one of two different ways:

✦ Increase the number of rows indicated in the Rows text box of the Table Property Inspector. All new rows added in this manner appear below the last table row. Similarly, you can increase the number of columns indicated in the Cols text box of the Table Property Inspector. Columns added in this way appear to the right of the last column.

✦ Use the Insert Rows or Columns dialog box.

The Insert Rows or Columns feature enables you to include any number of rows or columns anywhere relative to your current cursor position.

To add multiple columns using the Insert Rows or Columns dialog box, follow these steps:

1. Open the Insert Rows or Columns dialog box (shown in Figure 12-9) by selecting Modify ⇨ Table ⇨ Insert Rows or Columns or by choosing Table ⇨ Insert Rows or Columns from the shortcut menu.

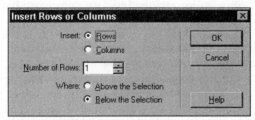

Figure 12-9: Use the Insert Rows or Columns feature to add several columns or rows simultaneously.

2. Select either Rows or Columns.

3. Enter the number of rows or columns you wish to insert — you can either type in a value or use the arrows to increase or decrease the number.

4. Select where you want the rows or columns to be inserted.

   • If you have selected the Rows option, you can insert the rows either Above or Below the Selection (the current row).

   • If you have selected the Columns options, you can insert the columns either Before or After the Current Column.

5. Click OK when you're finished.

Deleting rows and columns

When you want to delete a column or row, you can use either the shortcut menu or the Table Property Inspector. On the shortcut menu, you can remove the current column or row by choosing Delete Column or Delete Row, respectively. Using the Table Property Inspector, you can delete multiple columns and rows by reducing the numbers in the Cols or Rows text boxes. Columns are deleted from the right side of the table, and rows are removed from the bottom.

Caution — Watch out — exercise extreme caution when deleting columns or rows. Dreamweaver does not ask for confirmation and removes these columns and/or rows whether or not data exists in them. You can, of course, undo the operation, if necessary.

Setting table borders and backgrounds

Borders are the solid outlines of the table itself. A border's width is measured in pixels; the default width is one pixel. This width can be altered in the Border field of the Table Property Inspector.

You can make the border invisible by specifying a border of 0 width. You can still resize your table by clicking and dragging the borders, even when the border is set to 0. When the View ➪ Table Borders option is selected, Dreamweaver displays a thin dashed line to represent the border.

When the border is visible, you can also see each cell outlined. The width of the outline around the cells stays constant, regardless of the width of the border. However, you can control the amount of space between each cell with the CellSpace value in the Table Property Inspector, covered later in this chapter.

To change the width of a border in Dreamweaver, select your table and enter a new value in the Border text box. With a wider border, you can see the default shading: The top and left side are a lighter shade, and the bottom and right sides are darker. This gives the table border a pseudo-3D appearance. Figure 12-10 shows single-cell tables with borders of various widths.

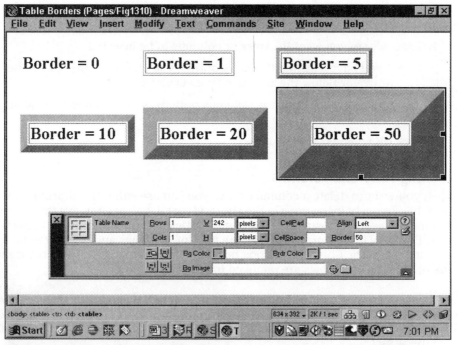

Figure 12-10: Changing the width of the border can give your table a 3D look.

In Dreamweaver, you can directly assign colors to the border. To choose a color for the border, select the Border color swatch or enter a color name in the adjacent text box.

In addition to colored borders, a table can also have a colored background. (By default, the table is initially transparent.) Choose the background color in the Table Property Inspector by selecting a color in the Bg Color swatch or entering a color name in the adjacent text box. As you see later in the chapter, you can also assign background colors to rows, columns, and individual cells — if used, these specific colors all override the background color of the overall entire table.

Working with cell spacing and cell padding

HTML gives you two methods to add white space in tables. *Cell spacing* controls the width between each cell, and *cell padding* controls the margins within each cell. These values can be set independently through the Table Property Inspector.

Tip   Although not indicated in the Table Property Inspector, the default value is 2 pixels for cell spacing and 1 pixel for cell padding. Some Web page designs call for a close arrangement of cells and are better served by changing either (or both) the CellSpace or CellPad values to 1 or 0.

To change the amount of white space between each cell in a table, enter a new value in the CellSpace text box of the Table Property Inspector. If you want to adjust the amount of white space between the borders of the cell and the actual cell data, alter the value in the CellPad text box of the Table Property Inspector. Figure 12-11 shows an example of a table with wide (10 pixels) cell spacing and cell padding values.

Merging and splitting cells

You have seen how cells in HTML tables can extend across (span) multiple columns or rows. By default, a cell spans one column or one row. Increasing a cell's span enables you to group any number of topics under one heading. You are effectively merging one cell with another to create a larger cell. Likewise, a cell can be split into multiple rows or columns.

Dreamweaver enables you to combine and divide cells in two different ways. If you're more comfortable with the concept of merging and splitting cells, you can use two handy buttons on the Property Inspector. If, on the other hand, you prefer the older method of increasing and decreasing row or column span, you can still access these commands through the main and shortcut menus.

To combine two or more cells, first select the cells you want to merge. Then, from the Property Inspector, select the Merge Cells button or press the keyboard short-cut Ctrl+Alt+M (Command+Option+M); Windows users also have the option of just pressing M. If the Merge button is not available, multiple cells have not been selected.

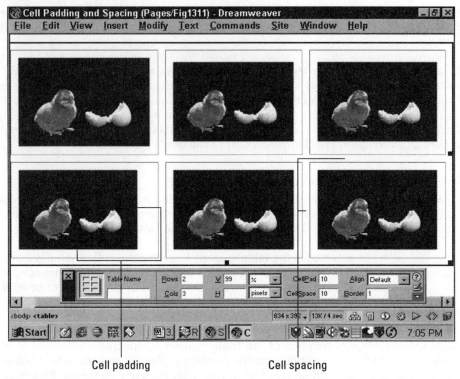

Cell padding   Cell spacing

Figure 12-11: You can add additional white space between each cell (cell spacing) or within each cell (cell padding).

To divide a cell, follow these steps:

1. Position your cursor in the cell to split.

2. From the Property Inspector, select the Split Cell button or press the keyboard shortcut, Ctrl+Alt+S (Command+Option+S).

   The Split Cell dialog box (shown in Figure 12-12) appears.

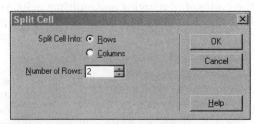

Figure 12-12: Use the Split Cell dialog box to divide cells horizontally or vertically.

3. Select either the Rows or Columns option to decide whether the cell will be split horizontally or vertically.

4. Enter the Number of Rows or Columns in the text box or use the arrows to change the value.

5. Select OK when you're done.

The same effect can be achieved by using the menus. To do so, first position the cursor in the cell to be affected and then choose one of the following commands from the Modify ➪ Table menu:

Command	Description
Increase Row Span	Joins the current cell with the cell below it
Decrease Row Span	Separates two or more previously spanned cells from the bottom cell
Increase Column Span	Joins the current cell with the cell immediately to its right
Decrease Column Span	Separates two or more previously spanned cells from the right edge

Existing text or images are put in the same cell if the cells containing them are joined to span rows or columns. Figure 12-13 shows a table containing both row and column spanning.

Tip
When you need to build a complex table such as this one, it's best to map out your table before you begin constructing it, and complete it prior to entering your data.

Setting cell, column, and row properties

In addition to the overall table controls, Dreamweaver helps you set numerous properties for individual cells one at a time, by the column or by the row. When attributes overlap or conflict, such as different background colors for a cell in the same row and column, the more specific target wins out. The hierarchy, from most general to most specific, is as follows: tables, rows, columns, and cells.

You can call up the specific Property Inspector by selecting the cell, row, or column you want to modify. The Cell, Row, and Column Property Inspectors each affect similar attributes. The following sections explain how the attributes work in general and — if any differences exist — specifically in regard to the cell, column, or row.

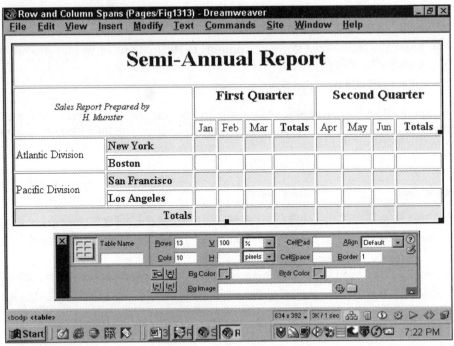

Figure 12-13: This spreadsheet-like report was built using Dreamweaver's row- and column-spanning features.

Horizontal alignment

You can set the Horizontal Alignment attribute, `align`, to specify the default alignment, or Left, Right, or Center alignment, for the element in the cell, column, or row. This attribute can be overridden by setting the alignment for the individual line or image. Generally, Left is the default horizontal alignment for cells.

Vertical alignment

The HTML `valign` attribute determines whether the cell's contents are vertically aligned to the cell's top, middle, bottom, or along the baseline. Typically, browsers align cells vertically in the middle by default. Select the Vertical Alignment option arrow in the Cell, Column, or Row Properties dialog box to specify a different alignment.

Top, Middle, and Bottom vertical alignments work pretty much as you would expect. A Baseline vertical alignment displays text near the top of the cell and positions the text—regardless of font size—so that the baselines of all the text in the affected row, column, or cell are the same. You can see how images and text of various sizes are displayed under the various vertical alignment options in Figure 12-14.

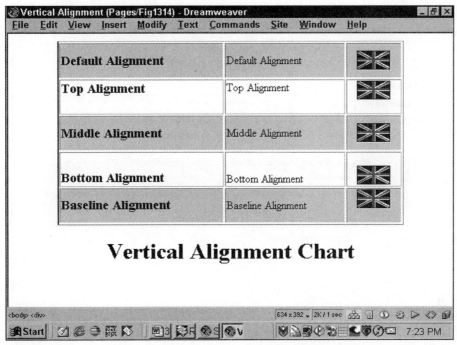

Figure 12-14: You can vertically align text and images in several arrangements in a table cell, row, or column.

Cell wrap

Normal behavior for any cell is to automatically wrap text or a series of images within the cell's borders. You can turn off this automatic feature by selecting the No Wrap option in the Property Inspector for cell, column, or row.

 Note   I've had occasion to use this option when I absolutely needed three images to appear side by side in one cell. In analyzing the results, I found that on some lower-resolution browsers, the last image wrapped to the next line.

Table header cells

Quite often in tables, a column or a row functions as the heading for that section of the table, labeling all the information in that particular section. Dreamweaver has an option for designating these cells: the Header option. Table header cells are usually rendered in boldface and centered in each cell. Figure 12-15 shows an example of a table in which both the first row and first column are marked as table header cells.

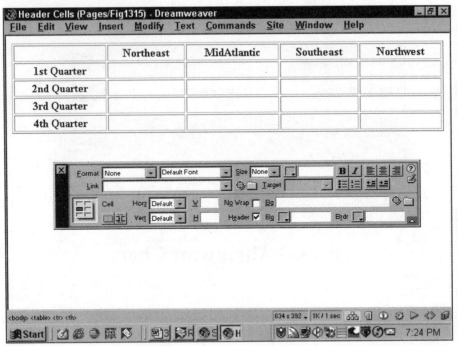

Figure 12-15: Table header cells are a good way to note a category's label — either for a row or a column, or both.

Width and height

The gridlike structure of a table makes it impossible to resize only one cell in a multicolumn table. Therefore, the only way you can enter exact values for a cell's width is through the Width section available only in the Column Properties dialog box. In this section of the dialog box, you can enter values in pixels or as a percentage of the table. The default enables cells to automatically resize with no restrictions outside of the overall dimensions of the table.

Similarly, whenever you change a cell's height, the entire row is altered. If you drag the row to a new height, the value is written into the H (Height) text box for all cells in the row. On the other hand, if you specify a single cell's height, the row resizes, but you can see the value only in the cell you've changed.

Color elements

Just as you can specify color backgrounds and borders for the overall table, you can do the same for columns, rows, or individual cells. Corresponding color swatches and text boxes are available in all dialog boxes for the following categories:

✦ **Background Color:** Specifies the color for the selected cell, row, or column. Selecting the color swatch opens the standard color picker.

✦ **Border Color:** Controls the color of the single-pixel border surrounding each cell.

As with all Dreamweaver color pickers, you can use the Eyedropper tool to select a color from the Web-safe palette or from any item on a page. You can also select the Eraser tool to delete any previously selected color. Finally, choose the Palette tool to open the Color dialog box and select any available color.

Working with Table Formats

Tables keep data organized and generally make it easier to find information quickly. Large tables with many rows, however, tend to become difficult to read unless they are formatted with alternating rows of color or some other device. Formatting a large table is often an afterthought as well as a time-consuming affair. Unless, of course, you're using Dreamweaver's Format Table command.

The Format Table command enables you to choose from 17 preset formats or customize your own. This versatile command can style the top row, alternating rows in the body of the table, the left column, and the border. It's best to completely build the structure of your table — although you don't have to fill it with data — before formatting it; otherwise, you might have to reformat it when new rows or columns are added.

To apply one of the preset table formats, follow these steps:

1. Select your table by choosing Modify ⇨ Table ⇨ Select Table or by using one of the other techniques.

2. Choose Commands ⇨ Format Table.

   The Format Table dialog box (shown in Figure 12-16) opens.

3. Select any of the options from the scrolling list box on the left side of the Format Table dialog box.

   As you select an option, a representation of the table appears to the right, and the attribute values used are displayed below.

4. When you've found a table format that's appropriate, select OK to close the dialog box, and the format is applied.

The preset formats are divided into three groups: Simple, AltRows, and DblRows. The Simple formats maintain the same background color for all rows in the body of the table but change the top row and the left column. The AltRows formats alternate the background color of each row in the body of the table; you have eight different color combinations from which to choose. The final category, DblRows, alternates the background color of every two rows in the body of the table.

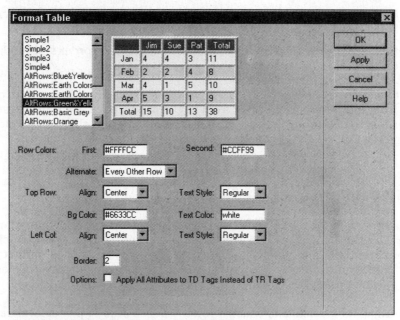

Figure 12-16: Select any one of 17 different preset formats from the Format Table dialog box or customize your own.

Although 17 different formats may seem as if there are plenty of choices, it's really just the jumping-off place for what's possible with the Format Table command. Each variable applied to create the preset formats can be customized. Moreover, you don't have to apply the changes to your selected table to see the effect — you can preview the results directly in the Table Format dialog box. Following are the variable attributes in the Table Format dialog box:

Attribute	Description
Row Colors: First	Enter a color (in color name or hexadecimal format) for the background colors of the first row in the body of a table. The Row Colors do not affect the top row of a table.
Row Colors: Second	Enter a color (in color name or hexadecimal format) for the background colors of the second row in the body of a table. The Row Colors do not affect the top row of a table.
Row Colors: Alternate	Establishes the pattern for using the specified Row Colors. Options are `<do not alternate>`, Every Other Row, Every Two Rows, Every Three Rows, and Every Four Rows.
Top Row: Align	Sets the alignment of the text in the top row of the table to left, right, or center.

Attribute	Description
Top Row: Text Style	Sets the style of the text in the top row of the table to Regular, Bold, Italic, or Bold Italic.
Top Row: Bg Color	Sets the background color of the top row of the selected table. Use either color names or hexadecimal values.
Top Row: Text Color	Sets the color of the text in the top row of the selected table. Use either color names or hexadecimal values.
Left Col: Align	Sets the alignment of the text in the left column of the table to Left, Right, or Center.
Left Col: Text Style	Sets the style of the text in the left column of the table to Regular, Bold, Italic, or Bold Italic.
Border	Determines the width of the table's border in pixels.
Options: Apply All Attributes to TD Tags Instead of TR Tags	Writes attribute changes at the cell level, `<td>`, rather than the default, the row level, `<tr>`.

The final option in the Format Table dialog box, Apply All Attributes to TD Tags Instead of TR Tags, should be used in only one of two situations: One, the selected table is nested inside another table and you want to override the outer table's `<tr>` format; or two, you anticipate moving cells from one table to another and want to maintain the formatting. Generally, the code produced by selecting this option is bulkier and could impact a page's overall download size, if the table is sufficiently large.

Caution Currently, there's no way to save your custom format without editing the tableFormats.js JavaScript file in the Commands folder. Otherwise, you need to reenter the selections each time you apply them.

Sorting Tables

Have you ever painstakingly built a table, alphabetizing every last entry by last name and first name, only to have the client call up with a list of 13 additional names that just have to go in? "Oh, and could you sort them by zip code instead of last name?" Dreamweaver contains a Table Sort command designed to make short work of such requests. All you need to do is select your table, and you're ready to do a two-level-deep sort, either alphabetically or numerically.

The Table Sort command can rearrange any size table; more important, it's HTML savvy and gives you the option of keeping the formatting of your table rows. This capability enables you to maintain a table with alternating row colors and still sort the data—something not even the most powerful word processors can handle. The Table Sort command is useful for generating different views of the same data, without having to use a database.

The Table Sort command is straightforward to use; just follow these steps:

1. Select your table by choosing Modify ➪ Table ➪ Select Table or by using one of the other techniques.

2. Choose Commands ➪ Sort Table.

   The Sort Table dialog box (shown in Figure 12-17) opens.

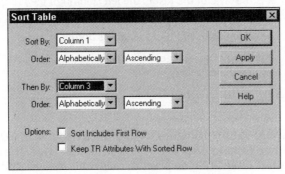

Figure 12-17: Sort your tables numerically or alphabetically with the Sort Table command.

3. Choose the primary sort column from the Sort By option list.

   Dreamweaver automatically lists the number of columns in the selected table in the option list.

4. Set the type of the primary sort by choosing either Alphabetically or Numerically from the first Order option list.

5. Choose the direction of the sort by selecting either Ascending or Descending from the second Order option list.

6. If you wish to add a second level of sorting, repeat Steps 3 through 5 in the Then By section.

7. If your selected table does not include a header row, select the Sort Includes First Row option.

8. If you have formatted your table with alternating row colors, choose the Keep TR Attributes with Sorted Row option.

9. Click OK when you're finished.

Tip　As with any sorting program, if you leave blank cells in the column you're basing the sort on, those rows appear as a group on top of the table for an ascending sort and at the end for a descending sort. Be sure that all the cells in your sort criteria column are filled correctly.

Importing Tabular Data

In the computer age, there's nothing much more frustrating than having information in a digital format and still having to enter it manually — either typing it in or cutting and pasting — to get on the Web. This frustration is multiplied when it comes to table data, whether created in a spreadsheet or database program. You have to transfer lots of small pieces of data, and it all has to be properly related and positioned.

Dreamweaver's Import Tabular Data goes a long way toward alleviating the tedium — not to mention the frustration — of dealing with tabular information. The Import Tabular Data command reads any delimited text file and inserts the information in a series of rows and columns. You can even set most characteristics for the table to be created, including the width, cell padding, cell spacing, and border.

Quite often, the first step in the process of importing table data into Dreamweaver is to export it from your other program. Most spreadsheet and database programs have some capability of outputting information in a text file; each bit of data (whether it's from a cell of a spreadsheet or field of a database) is separated — or *delimited* — from every other data by a special character, typically a tab or comma. In Dreamweaver, you can choose which delimiter is used in the Import Tabular Data dialog box to ensure a clean transfer with no loss of data.

Tip　Although you have many types of delimiters to choose from, I generally default to exporting tab-delimited files. With a tab-delimited file, you usually don't have to worry if any of your data contains the delimiter — which would throw off the import. However, testing shows that Dreamweaver correctly handles comma-delimited files with and without quotes, so you could also use that format safely.

To import a tabular data file, follow these steps:

1. Be sure the data you wish to import has been saved or exported in the proper format: a delimited text file.

2. Choose File ➪ Import ➪ Import Tabular Data.

   The Import Table Data dialog box, shown in Figure 12-18, is displayed.

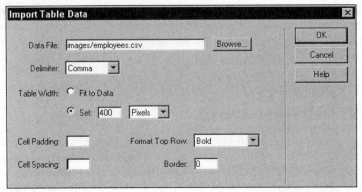

Figure 12-18: Any external data, saved in a delimited text file, can be brought into Dreamweaver through the Import Tabular Data command.

3. Select the Data File Browse button to find the desired file.

4. Choose the delimiter used to separate the fields or cells of data from the Delimiter option list. The choices are Tab, Comma, Semicolon, Colon, and Other.

Tip　If you select a file with a .csv extension, the Comma delimiter is automatically chosen. CSV is short for Comma Separated Values.

5. If you choose Other from the Delimiter list, a blank field appears to the right of the list. Enter the special character, such as a pipe (|), used as the delimiter in the exported file.

   Now that the imported file characteristics are set, you can predefine the table the information will be imported into, if desired.

6. If you want to set a particular table width, enter a value in the Set field and choose either Pixels or % from the option list. If you want the imported file to determine the size of the table, keep the Fit to Data option selected.

7. Enter any Cell Padding or Cell Spacing values desired, in their respective fields.

   As with standard tables, by default Cell Padding is set to 2 pixels and Cell Spacing to 1 if no specific values are entered.

8. If you'd like to style the first row, choose Bold, Italic, or Bold Italic from the Format Top Row option list.

   This option is typically used when the imported file contains a header row.

9. Set the Border field to the desired width, if any. If you don't want a border displayed at all, set the Border field to 0.

10. Click OK when you're done.

Even though the Import Tabular Data option is under the File menu, it doesn't open a new file — the new table is created at the current cursor position.

Caution If your data comes in wrong, double-check the delimiter used by opening the file in a text editor. If Dreamweaver is expecting a comma delimiter and your file uses tabs, data is not separated properly.

Designing with Layout Mode

As discussed earlier in this chapter, experienced Web designers regard tables as one of their primary layout tools because, outside of Dynamic HTML's layers, tables are the only way for you to get close to positioning your page elements the way you want them to appear. It's a lot of work to do this with raw tables, but designers are a persistent group — and for good reason: Persistence has a big payoff.

New Feature Thanks to the introduction of the Layout view in Dreamweaver 4, structuring your page with tables just got a whole lot easier. When you're in Layout view, you simply draw out separate areas to hold your content and Dreamweaver automatically converts these areas to cells and tables. The layout cells are very pliable and can be moved easily about the page, resized, and reshaped. Moreover, Layout view gives you professional design power with options such as tables that stretch to fit the browser window and transparent spacer images that maintain the structural integrity of tables across all browsers.

Although they share the same underlying HTML structure, tables and cells created in Layout view differ from those created in Standard view in the following ways:

✦ Borders are set to zero and, thus, turned off.

✦ Cell padding and cell spacing are also set to zero to enable content to appear directly next to each other.

✦ Layout tables optionally include a row for each column that holds a one pixel high transparent GIF image called a spacer.

✦ Columns in a layout table are set to either a fixed pixel width or designed to automatically stretch to the full width of the page.

In addition to these physical differences, Layout view has a different appearance. Each layout table is marked with a tab and the column width is identified at the top of each column as shown in Figure 12-19.

Dreamweaver puts the entrance to Layout view right up front on the Objects panel. At the bottom of the panel, two new areas have been added for Dreamweaver 4. To switch modes, click the Layout View button; to return to the traditional mode, select the Standard View button. If the Objects panel is not open, use the menu by choosing View ➪ Table View ➪ Layout View or the keyboard shortcut Ctrl+F6 (Command+F6). Once Layout view has been enabled, two buttons above the view modes become active: Draw Cell and Draw Table.

Layout Table tabs   Column widths

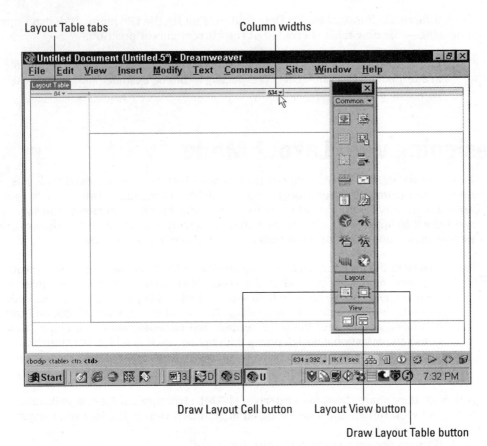

Draw Layout Cell button   Layout View button

Draw Layout Table button

Figure 12-19: In Layout view, tables and columns are immediately identifiable and extremely flexible.

By the way, don't fret about your existing pages: they'll show up just fine in Layout view. In fact, looking at a well-designed legacy page in Layout view is very helpful to understanding how the pages of a professional Web designer are built.

Drawing cells and tables

Although you can use the Layout view to modify the structure of existing pages, this mode is best when designing Web pages from the ground-up. The Draw Cell and Draw Table commands enable you to quickly layout the basic structure of your page by defining the key document areas. For example, with just four mouse moves in Layout view, I could design a page with sections for a logo, a navigation bar, a copyright notice, and a primary content area. Now I'm ready to fill out the design with graphics, text, and other assets.

Here's how it works:

1. On a blank page, choose the Layout View button from the bottom of the Objects panel.

   When you first enter Layout view, Dreamweaver displays a help screen to explain how the new feature works. After you get the hang of working in Layout view, feel free to select the Don't Show Me This Message Again option to prevent further appearances of the dialog box.

2. Select the Draw Cell button, directly above the View modes. The cursor changes to a plus (+) sign.

   Although it may seem backwards, it's best to initially use the Draw Cells rather than Draw Table. Dreamweaver automatically creates the HTML table necessary to hold any cells you draw, resulting in less tables and tighter code. The Draw Table command is best used to make a nested table.

3. Move your cursor anywhere on the page and drag out a layout cell, as shown in Figure 12-20.

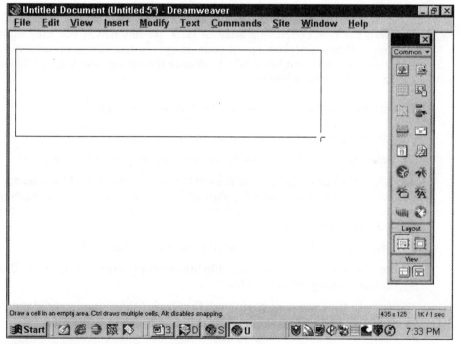

Figure 12-20: Use the Draw Cell command to define the basic page structure in Layout view.

Dreamweaver creates a table around the cell; the cell is drawn in the current background color with the surrounding table shown in white. When the mouse moves over it, the outline of a layout cell highlights in red, and turns blue when selected; likewise a Layout table's outline is green. These colors can be user-defined in Preferences.

Tip　If you're within eight pixels of the edge of the Document window or another layout cell, the border of the new layout cell snaps to that edge. Press the Alt (Option) key when drawing a layout cell to temporarily disable snapping.

4. Repeat Step 3 until your layout is complete.

   Dreamweaver drops out of Draw Cell mode after your first cell is created to prevent unintentional cells. To create several layout cells in a row, hold down Ctrl (Command) while dragging.

As indicated earlier, the Draw Table command is best suited for creating nested tables. A table is said to be nested when it is placed within an existing table. Nested tables are useful when a design requires that a number of elements, for example, a picture and a related caption, remain stationary in relation to one another while text on the page flows according to the size of the browser window.

Tip　While the tabs designating a layout table are very handy, you may want to turn them off at a certain stage of your design. To hide them, choose View ➪ Table View ➪ Show Layout Table Tabs to disable the option. Select the command again to bring them back into view.

To create a nested table in Layout view, follow these steps:

1. Choose the Layout View button on the Objects panel.

2. Select the Draw Layout Table button, also from the Objects panel.

3. When the cursor is over an area of the table unoccupied by a layout cell, the cursor changes to a plus (+) sign and a layout table can be dragged out. When not over a valid area, the cursor is shown as a slashed circle — the universal sign for "not allowed."

   The new layout table is inserted as shown in Figure 12-21.

4. To divide the nested layout table into multiple areas, choose the Draw Cell button to drag out new cells.

5. As with the Draw Cell command, the Draw Table command defaults to dragging one table at a time. To draw several tables in a row, select Ctrl (Command) while dragging out a layout table.

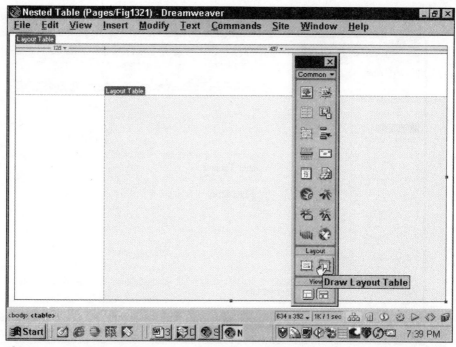

Figure 12-21: Nested tables are easily added with the Draw Layout Table command.

While the Layout view is an excellent method for quickly structuring a page, there are some limitations you should be aware of:

✦ Layout tables and cells can only be drawn in the area of the Document window that does not have any code associated with it. In other words, you need to draw cells and tables below the apparent end of the document. The result is that the new table code is placed right before the closing body tag.

✦ Two objects are disabled in Layout view: the Standard Table and the Layer objects. To add either of these objects to the page, you need to return to Standard view.

✦ Layout cells and tables cannot be copied, cut, or pasted. These operations are available from the Standard view, however.

It's worthwhile to note that the Layout view works exceedingly well with Dreamweaver's Grid feature. With the Grid showing (View ➪ Grid ➪ Show Grid) and Snap to Grid enabled (View ➪ Grid ➪ Snap to Grid), precisely laying out cells and tables is quite literally a snap. With Dreamweaver's Layout view, complex but useful designs, such as the one shown in Figure 12-22, are within reach.

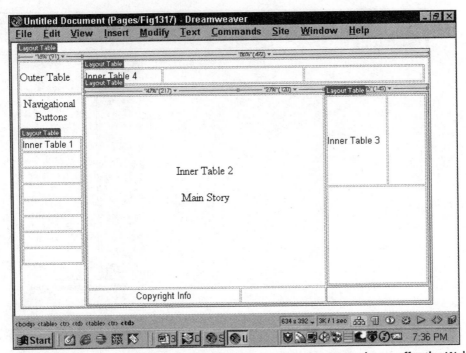

Figure 12-22: Nested tables — created in Dreamweaver's Layout view — offer the Web designer tighter command of Web page elements.

Modifying layouts

Layout view is not only a boon for creating the initial page design, but it also makes the inevitable modifications more straightforward. Cells are positionable within a layout table much the same as layers on a page. However, one difference exists; cells, unlike layers, cannot overlap. Resizing layout cells and tables is also easier. Unlike in Standard view where any table or cell border is draggable, in Layout view cells and tables have sizing handles — much the same as a selected image.

To easily manipulate layout and cells, they have to be easily selectable. Dreamweaver handles that chore with colorful flair. Pass your cursor over any layout cell, when you pass the border of a cell it changes from blue to red. Click once on the red highlight and the cell is selected. A selected cell is notable by the eight sizing handles placed on its perimeter. Once a cell is selected, the Property Inspector displays the available attributes.

Tip   To select a cell without moving the cursor over the border, Ctrl+click (Command+click) anywhere in the cell.

The Layout Cell Property Inspector (see Figure 12-23) offers six key attributes:

✦ **Width:** Enter a pixel value for a Fixed cell width or select the Autostretch option to enable the cell to grow as needed. (Autostretch is covered in the next section.) The width of each cell is shown on top of each column in Layout view. The column width property is an important one and is explained in greater detail later in this section.

✦ **Height:** Enter a pixel value for cell height. Percentages cannot be entered in Layout view.

✦ **Horz:** Select a horizontal alignment for the cell's content; the options are Default, Left, Center, and Right.

✦ **No Wrap:** When enabled, this option keeps content — text and images — from wrapping to the next line, which, if the column is in Autostretch mode, may alter the width of the cell.

✦ **Bg:** Choose a background color for the cell.

✦ **Vert:** Choose a vertical alignment for the cell's content; the options are Default, Top, Middle, Bottom, and Baseline.

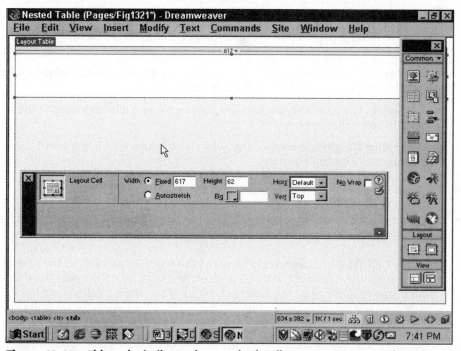

Figure 12-23: Although similar to the standard Cell Property Inspector, the Layout Cell Property Inspector offers a different set of options.

Note   Not all the attributes of a table cell are available through the Layout cell Property Inspector. To add a background image, specify a border color, designate it as a header cell or split the cell, you need to switch to Standard view.

To reshape or resize a layout cell, drag any one of the sizing handles on the cell's border into the unused area of a table. Likewise, you can drag a cell into any open table area, for example, any area of the table unoccupied by another cell.

Tip   To maintain the width-height ratio of a cell, press Shift when resizing.

Tables may be similarly selected and resized. Layout tables are selected by clicking the title bar marking the table, or by clicking inside an open, gray-colored area within the table or on the table border. If the layout table is nested within another table, it can be dragged to a new location within the outer table. Non-nested tables cannot be dragged to a new location on the page, however.

Once a layout table is selected, the attributes in the Property Inspector become available as shown in Figure 12-24. These attributes include:

✦ **Width:** Enter a pixel value for a Fixed table width or select the Autostretch option to enable the table to grow as needed. (Autostretch is discussed in the next section.)

✦ **Height:** Enter a pixel value for table height. Percentages cannot be entered in Layout view.

✦ **CellPad:** Controls the amount of space between the content and the cell border throughout the table. The default value is zero.

✦ **CellSpace:** Controls the amount of space between cells throughout the table. The default value is zero.

✦ **Clear Row Heights:** Removes any set height values for all rows and reduces the table to existing content.

Caution   When the Clear Row Heights option is used with nested tables, Dreamweaver doesn't redraw the cell border to match the table border — in other words, the cell height is not cleared. To correct, drag the bottom cell border to match that of the table.

✦ **Make Cell Widths Consistent:** Reduces the width of all cells to the size of their respective content. If a cell is stretched beyond its original fixed size by an image or some text, the column header of the layout cell shows the fixed size next to the actual size in parenthesis. Choosing Make Cell Widths Consistent adjusts the fixed size to match the actual size.

✦ **Remove All Spacers:** Choosing this option deletes all single pixel images used to ensure browser compatibility for layout tables and their corresponding rows. Spacers are discussed in detail in a later section.

✦ **Remove Nesting:** Converts a nested table to rows and cells of the outer table.

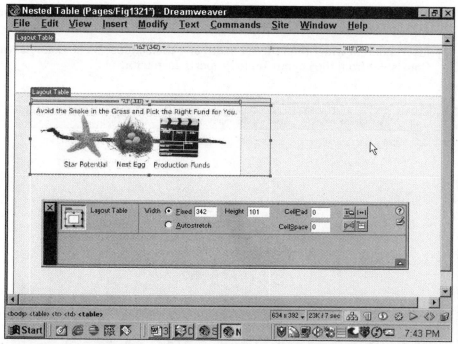

Figure 12-24: The Layout Table Property Inspector includes important options for converting nested tables and sizing cells to fit existing content.

Altering column widths

The table elements in Layout view borrow a couple of pages from the professional Web designer's playbook. First, any column can easily be converted from a fixed width to a flexible width — in Dreamweaver this is known as *autostretch*. Second, when the Autostretch option is chosen for a layout table, Dreamweaver inserts a spacer (a single-pixel high transparent GIF) in a new row along the bottom of the table. The spacer is sized to match the fixed width of each of the columns except for one — which is designated as an autostretch column. For a table to use the Autostretch option, one column must be flexible.

You can alter the width of a column in a number of ways:

✦ Visually, select the cell and then drag a sizing handle to a new position.

✦ For pixel precise width, use the Layout Cell Property Inspector and enter the desired size in the Width field. If the cell is currently in Autostretch mode, select the Fixed Width option to enable the value field.

✦ To convert an Autostretch column to its current on-screen pixel width, choose Make Column Fixed Width from the column header menu as shown in Figure 12-25.

✦ To make a fixed width column automatically stretch, choose Make Column Autostretch from the column header menu.

✦ Insert content wider than the set width and then choose Make Column Width Consistent from the Layout Table Property Inspector.

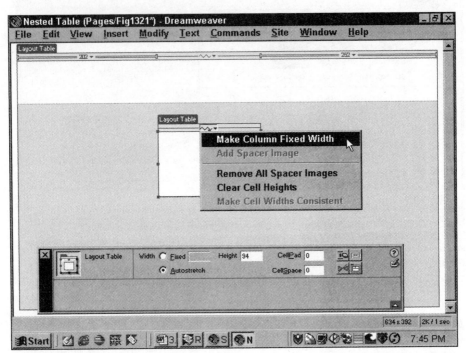

Figure 12-25: The switch between fixed width and autostretch through the column header menu.

Working with the spacer image

If you've ever painstakingly created a complex table only to find that it looks great in one browser but collapses into an unidentifiable mess in another, you're going to love spacer images. Long used by Web site designers as a method of ensuring a table's stability, a spacer image is simply an image — usually a single-pixel transparent GIF — that is resized to match the width of a column. Because no browser collapses a column smaller than the size of the largest image it contains, spacer images retain a table's design under any circumstance.

Dreamweaver gives you several options when working with spacer images:

✦ You can have Dreamweaver create a spacer image for you.

✦ You can use an existing image as a spacer image.

✦ You can opt to never include spacer images.

The first time Autostretch is applied as an option in a table, Dreamweaver displays a dialog box (see Figure 12-26) that enables you to create or locate a spacer image. If you choose to create a new spacer image, you are then asked to select a location in the current site to store it. Generally you would save such a file in an images, assets, or media folder.

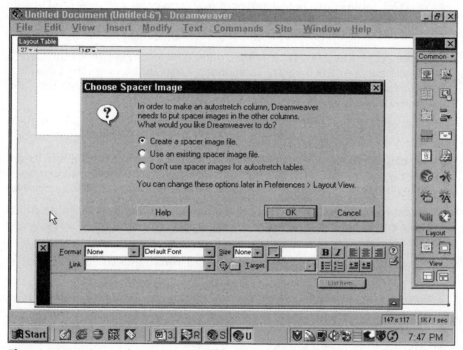

Figure 12-26: Spacer images essentially make layout tables browser-proof and Dreamweaver can either create one for you or enable you to use an existing image.

This image is then automatically inserted whenever an autostretch table or cell is created. One reason to use an existing image rather than a new one is if you work with sliced tables from Fireworks. Fireworks creates a single-pixel GIF image titled spacer.gif. The choice of a spacer image is a sitewide preference that can be viewed or changed by selecting the Layout View category of Preferences. Although it's not a commonly recommended practice, the Layout View category is also where you can disable spacer images.

Summary

Tables are an extremely powerful Web page design tool. Dreamweaver enables you to modify both the appearance and the structure of your HTML tables through a combination of Property Inspectors, dialog boxes, and click-and-drag mouse movements. Mastering tables is an essential task for any modern Web designer and worth the somewhat challenging learning curve. The key elements to keep in mind are as follows:

✦ An HTML table consists of a series of rows and columns presented in a grid-like arrangement. Tables can be sized absolutely, in pixels, or relative to the width of the browser's window, in a percentage.

✦ Dreamweaver inserts a table whose dimensions can be altered through the Objects panel or the Insert ⇨ Table menu. Once in the page, the table needs to be selected before any of its properties can be modified through the Table Property Inspector.

✦ Table editing is greatly simplified in Dreamweaver. You can select multiple cells, columns, or rows — and modify all their contents in one fell swoop.

✦ You can assign certain properties — such as background color, border color, and alignment — for a table's columns, rows, or cells through their respective dialog boxes. A cell's properties override those set for its column or row.

✦ Dreamweaver brings power to table building with the Format Table and Sort Table commands as well as a connection to the outside world with its Import Tabular Data option.

✦ Dreamweaver 4's new Layout view enables you to quickly prepare the basic structure of a page by drawing out layout cells and tables.

✦ Putting a table within another table — also known as *nesting tables* — is a powerful (and legal) design option in HTML. Nested tables are easily accomplished in Dreamweaver's Layout view by inserting a layout table.

✦　　✦　　✦

Interactive Forms

A form, in the everyday world as well as on the Web, is a type of structured communication. When you apply for a driver's license, you're not told to just write down all your personal information, you're asked to fill out a form that asks for specific parts of that information, one at a time, in a specific manner. Web-based forms are just as precise, if not more so.

Dreamweaver has a robust and superior implementation of HTML forms — from the dedicated Forms category in the Objects panel to various form-specific Property Inspectors. In addition to their importance as a tool for communication between the browsing public and Web site administrators, forms are integral to building some of Dreamweaver's own objects.

In this chapter, you learn how forms are structured and then created within Dreamweaver. Each form object is explored in detail — text fields, radio buttons, checkboxes, menus, list boxes, command buttons, hidden fields, and password fields.

How HTML Forms Work

Forms have a special function in HTML: They support interaction. Virtually all HTML elements apart from forms are concerned with design and presentation — delivering the content to the user, if you will. Forms, on the other hand, give the user the ability to pass information back to Web site creators and administrators. Without forms, the Web would be a one-way street.

Forms have many, many uses on the Web, such as for surveys, electronic commerce, guest books, polls, and even real-time custom graphics creation. For such feedback to be possible, forms require an additional component to what's seen onscreen so that each form can complete its function. Every form needs some type of connection to a Web server, and usually this connection uses a *common gateway interface (CGI)* script, although JavaScript and Java can also be used. This means that, in addition to designing your forms onscreen, you or someone who works with you must implement a program that collects and manages the information from the form.

Forms, like HTML tables, can be thought of as self-contained units within a Web page. All the elements of a form are contained within the form tag pair <form> and </form>. Unlike tables, you cannot nest forms, although there's nothing to stop you from having multiple forms on a page.

The <form> tag has three attributes, only two of which (method and action) are commonly used:

✦ The method attribute tells the server how the contents of the form should be presented to the CGI program. The two possible method values are get and post. Get passes the attached information to a URL; it is rarely used these days because it places limitations on the amount of data that can be passed to the gateway program. Post causes the server to present the information as standard input and imposes no limits on the amount of passed data.

✦ The second <form> attribute is action. The action attribute determines what should be done with the form content. Most commonly, action is set to a URL for running a specific CGI program or for sending e-mail.

✦ The third attribute for <form> is enctype, which specifies the MIME media type. It is used infrequently.

Typical HTML for a <form> tag looks something like this:

```
<form method="post" action="http://www.idest.com/_cgi-bin/mailcall.pl">
```

 Tip   The .pl extension in the preceding example form tag stands for *Perl* — a scripting language often used to create CGI programs. Perl can be edited in any regular text editor.

Within each form is a series of input devices — text boxes, radio buttons, checkboxes, and so on. Each type handles a particular sort of input; in fact, the main tag for these elements is the <input> tag. With one exception, the <textarea> tag, all form input types are called by specifying the type attribute. The text box tag, for example, is written as follows:

```
<input type=text value="lastname">
```

All form input tags have value attributes. Information input by the user is assigned to the given value. Thus, if I were to fill out a form with a text box asking for my last name, such as the one produced by the foregoing tag, part of the message sent would include the following string:

```
lastname=Lowery
```

Web servers send all the information from a form in one long text string to whatever program or address is specified in the `action` attribute. It's up to the program or the recipient of the form message to parse the string. For instance, if I were to fill out a small form with my name, e-mail address, and a quick comment such as "Good work!" the server would send a text string similar to the following:

```
name=Joseph+Lowery&address=jlowery@idest.com&comment=Good+work%21
```

As you can see, the various fields are separated by ampersands, and the individual words within the responses are separated by plus signs. Characters outside of the lower end of the ASCII set — like the exclamation mark in the example — are represented by their hexadecimal values. Decoding this text string is called *parsing the response.*

Tip If you're not using the mailto method for getting your Web feedback, don't despair. Most CGI programs parse the text string as part of their basic functionality before sending it on its way.

Inserting a Form in Dreamweaver

A form is inserted just like any other object in Dreamweaver. Place the cursor where you want your form to start and then either select the Insert Form button from the Forms category of the Objects panel or choose Insert ⇨ Form from the menus. Dreamweaver inserts a red dashed outline stretching across the Document window to indicate the form.

If you have the Property Inspector open, the Form Property Inspector appears when you insert a form. As you can see from Figure 13-1, you can specify only three values regarding forms: the Form Name, the Action, and the Method.

Specifying a form name enables the form to be directly referenced by JavaScript or other languages. Because of the interactive nature of forms, Web programmers often use this feature to gather information from the user.

In the Action text box, you can directly enter a URL or mailto address, or you can select the folder icon and browse for a file.

Note Sending your form data via a mailto address is not without its problems. Some browsers, most notably Internet Explorer, are set to warn the user whenever a form button using mailto is selected. While many users let the mail go through, they do have the option to stop it from being sent.

The Method defaults to POST, the most commonly used option. You can also choose GET or DEFAULT, which leaves the method up to the browser. In most cases, you should leave the method set to POST.

Form outline   Insert Form button

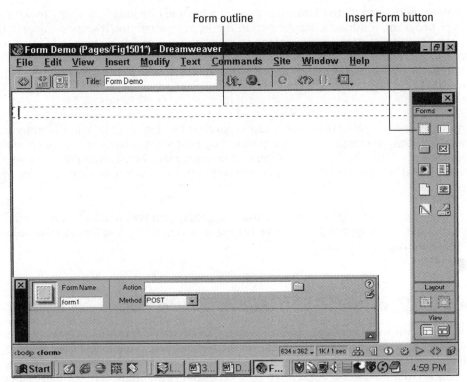

Figure 13-1: Inserting a form creates a dashed red outline of the form and displays the Form Property Inspector, if available.

Note   Forms cannot be placed inline with any other element such as text or graphics.

Keep in mind a few considerations when it comes to mixing forms and other Web page elements:

✦ Forms expand as objects are inserted into them; you can't resize a form by dragging its boundaries.

✦ The outline of a form is invisible; there is no border to turn on or off.

✦ Forms and tables can be used together only if the form either completely encloses or is completely enclosed inside the table. In other words, you can't have a form spanning part of a table.

✦ Forms can be inserted within layers, and multiple forms can be in multiple layers. However, the layer must completely enclose the form. As with forms spanning tables, you can't have a form spanning two or more layers. (A workaround for this limitation is discussed in Chapter 19.)

Declaring the Enctype

The `<form>` attribute `enctype` is helpful in formatting material returned via a form. Enctype can have three possible values. By default `enctype` is set to `application/x-www-form-urlencoded`, which is responsible for encoding the form response with ampersands between entries, equal signs linking form element names to their values, spaces as plus signs, and all nonalphanumeric characters in hexadecimal, such as `%3F` (a question mark).

The second `enctype` value, `text/plain`, is useful for e-mail replies. Instead of one long string, your form data is transmitted in a more readable format with each form element and its value on a separate line as in this example:

```
fname=Joseph
lname=Lowery
email=jlowery@idest.com
comment=Please send me the information on your new products!
```

The final `enctype` value, `multipart/form-data`, is used only when a file is being uploaded as part of the form. There's a further restriction: The Method should be set to POST, instead of GET.

Dreamweaver doesn't include a space on the Form Property Inspector for the `enctype` attribute, so you have to add it manually either through the HTML Source Inspector or the Quick Tag Editor. To use the Quick Tag Editor, select the `<form>` tag in the Tag Selector and press Ctrl+T (Command+T). Tab to the end of the tag and enter `enctype="value"`, substituting one of the three possible values.

Tip You can turn off the red dashed form outline in Dreamweaver's preview, if you like. Choose Edit ⇨ Preferences and, in the Invisible Elements category, deselect the Form Delimiter option.

Using Text Boxes

Anytime you use a form to gather text information typed in by a user, you use a form object called a *text field*. Text fields can hold any number of alphanumeric characters. The Web designer can decide whether the text field is displayed in one line or several. When the HTML is written, a multiple-line text field uses a `<textarea>` tag, and a single-line text field is coded with `<input type=text>`.

Text fields

To insert a single-line text field in Dreamweaver, you can use any of the following methods:

✦ From the Forms category of the Objects panel, select the Insert Text Field button to place a text field at your current cursor position.

✦ Choose Insert ➪ Form Objects ➪ Text Field from the menu, which inserts a text field at the current cursor position.

✦ Drag the Insert Text Field button from the Objects panel to any existing location in the Document window and release the mouse button to position the text field.

When you insert a text field, the Property Inspector, when displayed, shows you the attributes that can be changed (see Figure 13-2). The size of a text field is measured by the number of characters it can display at one time. You can change the length of a text field by inserting a value in the Char Width text box. By default, Dreamweaver inserts a text field approximately 20 characters wide. The *approximately* is important here because the *final* size of the text field is ultimately controlled by the browser used to view the page. Unless you limit the number of possible characters by entering a value in the Max Chars text box, the user can enter as many characters as desired, and the text box scrolls to display them.

Note that the value in Char Width determines the visible width of the field, whereas the value in Max Chars actually determines the number of characters that can be entered.

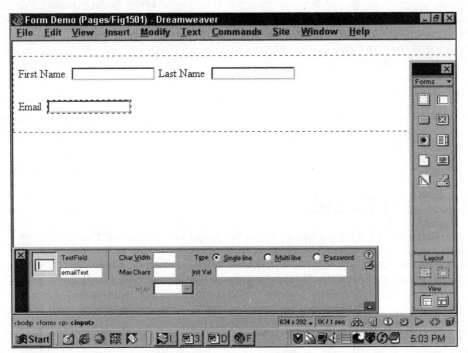

Figure 13-2: The text field of a form is used to enable the user to type in any required information.

Neat Forms

Text field width is measured in a monospaced character width. Because regular fonts are not monospaced, however, lining up text fields and other form objects can be problematic at best. The two general workarounds are preformatted text and tables.

Switching the labels on the form to preformatted text enables you to insert any amount of white space to properly space (or *kern*) your text and other input fields. Previously, Web designers were stuck with the default preformatted text format—the rather plain-looking Courier monospaced font. Now, however, newer browsers (3.0 and later) can read the `face=fontname` attribute. So you can combine a regular font with the preformatted text option and get the best of both worlds.

Going the preformatted text route requires you to insert a lot of spaces. So when you are working on a larger, complex form, using tables is probably a better way to go. Besides the speed of layout, the other advantage that tables offer is the capability to right-align text labels next to your text fields. The top form in the following figure gives an example of using preformatted text to get different-sized form fields to line up properly, while the bottom form in the figure uses a table.

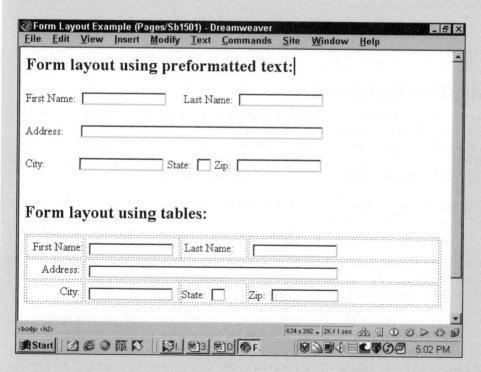

Combining differently sized text fields on a single row—for example, when you're asking for a city, state, and zip code combination—can make the task of lining up your form even more difficult. Most often, you'll spend a fair amount of time in a trial-and-error effort to make the text fields match. Be sure to check your results in the various browsers as you build your form.

The Init Value text box on the Text Field Property Inspector is used to insert a default text string. The user can overwrite this value, if desired.

Password fields

Generally, all text entered into text fields displays as you expect — programmers refer to this process as *echoing*. You can turn off the echoing by selecting the Password option in the Text Field Property Inspector. When a text field is designated as a password field, all text entered by the user shows up as asterisks in Windows systems or as dots on Macintoshes.

Use the password field when you want to protect the user's input from prying eyes (as your PIN number is hidden when you enter it at an ATM, for instance). The information entered in a password field is not encrypted or scrambled in any way, and when sent to the Web administrator, it displays as regular text.

Only single-line text fields can be set as password fields. You cannot make a multi-line `<textarea>` tag act as a password field without employing JavaScript or some other programming language.

Cross-Reference   Making sure that your user fills out the form properly is called validating the input. Dreamweaver includes a standard form validation behavior, covered in Chapter 15.

Multiline text areas

When you want to give your users a generous amount of room to write, set the text field to the Multiline option on the Text Field Property Inspector. This converts the default 20-character width for single-line text fields to a text area approximately 18 characters wide and 3 lines high, with a horizontal and vertical scroll bar. Figure 13-3 shows a typical multiline text field embedded in a form.

You control the width of a multiline text area by entering a value in the Char Width text box of the Text Field Property Inspector, just as you do for single-line text fields. The height of the text area is set equal to the value in the Num Lines text box. As with the default single-line text field, the user can enter any amount of text desired. Unlike the single-line text field, which can restrict the number of characters that can be input through the Max Chars text box, you cannot restrict the number of characters the user enters into a multiline text area.

By default, text entered into a multiline text field does not wrap when it reaches the right edge of the text area; rather, it keeps scrolling until the user presses Enter (Return). Dreamweaver 4 enables you to force the text to wrap by selecting Virtual or Physical from the Wrap drop-down list. The Virtual option wraps text on the screen but not when the response is submitted. To wrap text in both situations, use the Physical wrap option.

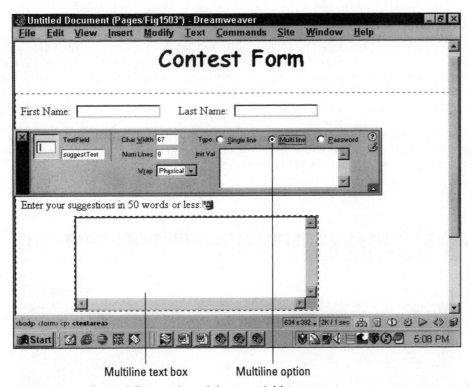

Figure 13-3: The Multiline option of the Text Field Property Inspector opens up a text box for more user information.

One other option is to preload the text area with any default text you like. Enter this text in the Init Val text box of the Text Field Property Inspector. When Dreamweaver writes the HTML code, this text is not entered as a value, as for the single-line text field, but rather goes in between the `<textarea>...</textarea>` tag pair.

Providing Checkboxes and Radio Buttons

When you want your Web page reader to choose between a specific set of options in your form, you can use either checkboxes or radio buttons. Checkboxes enable you to offer a series of options from which the user can pick as many as desired. Radio buttons, on the other hand, enable your user to choose only one selection from a number of options.

Tip   You can achieve the same functionality as checkboxes and radio buttons with a different look by using the drop-down list and menu boxes. These options for presenting choices to the user are described shortly.

Checkboxes

Checkboxes are often used in a "Select All That Apply" type of section, when you want to enable the user to choose as many of the listed options as desired. You insert a checkbox in much the same way you do a text box: Select or drag the Insert Check Box object from the Objects panel or choose Insert ➪ Form Objects ➪ Check Box.

Like other form objects, checkboxes can be given a unique name in the text box provided in the Check Box Property Inspector (see Figure 13-4). If you don't provide one, Dreamweaver inserts a generic one, such as checkbox4.

Insert Check Box button

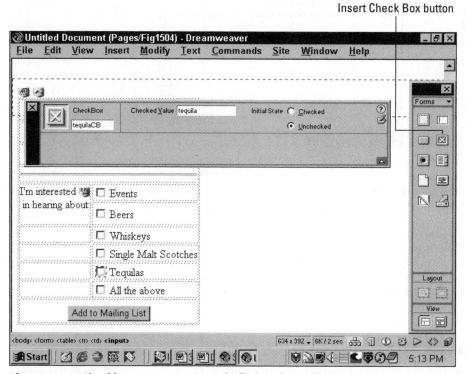

Figure 13-4: Checkboxes are one way of offering the Web page visitor any number of options to choose.

In the Checked Value text box, fill in the information you want passed to a program when the user selects the checkbox. By default, a checkbox starts out unchecked, but you can change that by changing the Initial State option to Checked.

Radio buttons

Radio buttons on a form provide a set of options from which the user can choose only one. If users change their minds after choosing one radio button, selecting another one automatically deselects the first choice. You insert radio buttons in the same manner as checkboxes. Choose or drag Insert Radio Button from the Forms category of the Objects panel, or choose Insert ⇨ Form Objects ⇨ Radio Button.

Unlike checkboxes and text fields, each radio button in the set does not have a unique name — instead, each *group* of radio buttons does. Giving the entire set of radio buttons the same name enables browsers to assign one value to the radio button set. That value is determined by the contents of the Checked Value text box. Figure 13-5 shows two different sets of radio buttons. One is named computersRadio and the other, osRadio.

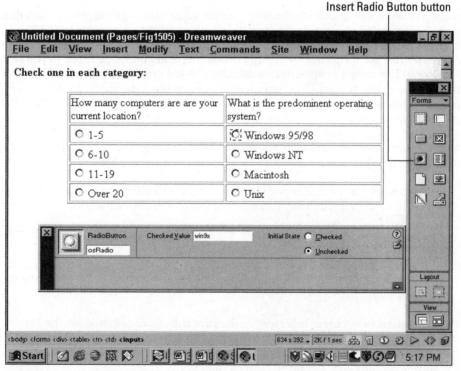

Figure 13-5: Radio buttons enable a user to make just one selection from a group of options.

To designate the default selection for each radio button group, you select the particular radio button and make the Initial State option Checked instead of Unchecked.

Tip Because you must give radio buttons in the same set the same name, you can speed up your work a bit by creating one button, copying it, and then pasting the others. Don't forget to change the Checked Value for each button, though.

Creating Form Lists and Menus

Another way to offer your user options, in a more compact form than radio buttons and checkboxes, is with form lists and menus. Both objects can create single-line entries in your form that expand or scroll to reveal all the available options. You can also determine how deep you want the scrolling list to be; that is, how many options you want displayed at a time.

Drop-down menus

A drop-down menu should be familiar to everyday users of computers: The menu is initially displayed as a single-line text box with an option arrow button at the right end; when the button is clicked, the other options are revealed in a list or menu. (Whether the list "pops up" or "drops down" depends on its position in the browser window at the time it is selected. Generally, the list drops down, unless it is close to the bottom of the screen.) The user selects one of the listed options, and when the mouse is released, the list closes up and the selected value remains displayed in the text box.

Insert a drop-down menu in Dreamweaver as you would any other form object, with one of these actions:

✦ From the Forms category of the Objects panel, select the Insert List/Menu button to place a drop-down menu at the current cursor position.

✦ Choose Insert ➪ Form Objects ➪ List/Menu from the menu to insert a drop-down menu at the current cursor position.

✦ Drag the Insert List/Menu button from the Property Inspector to any location in the Document window and release the mouse button to position the drop-down menu.

With the List/Menu object inserted, make sure the Menu option (not the List option) is selected in the Property Inspector, as shown in Figure 13-6. You can also name the drop-down menu by typing a name in the Name text box; if you don't, Dreamweaver supplies a generic "select" name.

The HTML code for a drop-down menu uses the `<select>...</select>` tag pair surrounding a number of `<option>...</option>` tag pairs. Dreamweaver gives you a straightforward user interface for entering labels and values for the options on your menu. The menu item's *label* is what is displayed on the drop-down list; its *value* is what is sent to the server-side processor when this particular option is selected.

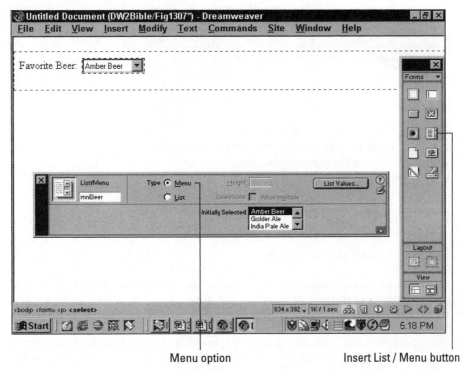

Menu option   Insert List / Menu button

Figure 13-6: Drop-down menus are created by inserting a List/Menu object and then selecting the Menu option in the List/Menu Property Inspector.

To enter the labels and values for a drop-down menu — or for a scrolling list — follow these steps:

1. Select the menu for which you want to enter values.

2. From the List/Menu Property Inspector, select the List Values button. The List Values dialog box appears (see Figure 13-7).

3. In the Item Label column, enter the label for the first item. Press the Tab key to move to the Value column.

4. Enter the value to be associated with this item. Press the Tab key.

5. Continue entering items and values by repeating Steps 3 and 4.

6. To delete an item's label *and* value in the List Values dialog box, highlight it and select the Remove button at the top of the list. To delete either the item's label or value, but not both, highlight either the label or the value and press the Delete or Backspace key.

7. To continue adding items, select the Add button or continue using the Tab key.

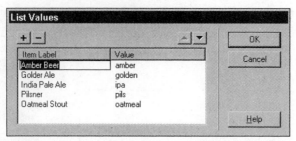

Figure 13-7: Use the List Values dialog box to enter and modify the items in a drop-down menu or scrolling list.

8. To rearrange the order of items in the list, select an item and then press the up- or down-arrow keys to reposition it.

9. Click OK when you've finished.

If you haven't entered a value for every item, the server-side application receives the label instead. Generally, however, it is a good idea to specify a value for all items.

You can preselect any item in a drop-down menu so that it appears in the list box initially and is highlighted when the full list is displayed. Dreamweaver enables you to pick your selection from the Initially Selected menu in the Property Inspector. The Initially Selected menu is empty until you enter items through the List Values dialog box. You can preselect only one item for a drop-down menu.

Scrolling lists

A scrolling list differs from a drop-down menu in three respects. First, and most obviously, the scrolling list field has up- and down-arrow buttons, rather than an option arrow button, and the user can scroll the list, showing as little as one item at a time, instead of the entire list. Second, you can control the height of the scrolling list, enabling it to display more than one item — or all available items — simultaneously. Third, you can enable the user to select more than one item at a time, as with checkboxes.

A scrolling list is inserted in the same manner as a drop-down menu — through the Objects panel or the Insert ➪ Form Objects menu. Once the object is inserted, select the List option in the List/Menu Property Inspector.

You enter items for your scrolling list just as you do with a drop-down menu, by starting with the List Values button and filling in the List Values dialog box.

As it does for drop-down menus, Dreamweaver automatically shows the first list item in the scrolling list's single-line text box. However, all the list items are displayed in the Document window, as shown in Figure 13-8.

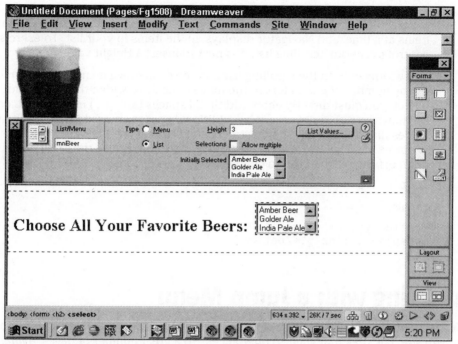

Figure 13-8: Scrolling lists enable multiple selections.

By default, the Selections checkbox for Allow multiple selections is enabled in the List/Menu Property Inspector, and the Height box (which controls the number of items visible at one time) is empty.

When multiple selections are enabled (by selecting the Allow multiple selections checkbox), the user can then make multiple selections by using two keyboard modifiers, the Shift and Control keys:

> ✦ To select several adjacent items in the list, the user must click the first item in the list, press the Shift key, and select the last item in the list.

> ✦ To select several nonadjacent items, the user must hold down the Control (Command) key while selecting the items.

Other than the highlighted text, no other acknowledgment (such as a checkmark) appears in the list. As with drop-down menus, the Web designer can preselect options by highlighting them in the Initially Selected menu. Use the same techniques with the Shift and Control (Command) keys as a user would.

Keep in mind several factors as you are working with scrolling lists:

> ✦ If you disable the Allow multiple selections box and do not set a Height value greater than 1, the list appears as a drop-down menu.

✦ If you do not set a Height value at all, the number of items that appear onscreen is left up to the browser. Internet Explorer, by default, shows four items at a time, and Navigator displays all the items in your list. To exercise control over your scrolling list, it is best to insert a Height value.

✦ The widths of both the scrolling list and the drop-down menu are determined by the number of characters in the longest label. To widen the List/Menu object, you must directly enter additional spaces ( ) in the HTML code; Dreamweaver does not recognize additional spaces entered through the List Values dialog box. For example, to expand the Favorite Beer List/Menu object in our example, you'd need to switch to Code view, or use the Code Inspector or an external text editor, to change the following code:

```
<option value="oatmeal">Oatmeal Stout</option>
```

to this:

```
<option value="oatmeal">Oatmeal Stout ¬
   </option>
```

Navigating with a Jump Menu

It's not always practical to use a series of buttons as the primary navigation tool on a Web site. For sites that want to offer access to a great number of pages, a *jump menu* can be a better way to go. A jump menu uses the menu form element to list the various options; when one of the options is chosen, the browser loads — or jumps to — a new page. In addition to providing a single mechanism for navigation, a jump menu is easy to update because it doesn't require relaying out the page. Because they are JavaScript-driven, jump menus can even be updated dynamically.

Dreamweaver includes a jump menu object that handles all the JavaScript coding for you — all you have to provide is a list of item names and associated URLs. Dreamweaver even drops in a Go button for you, if you choose. The Jump Menu object is easily used in a frame-based layout for targeting specific frames. Once inserted, the Jump Menu object is modified like any other list object, through the List/Menu Property Inspector.

To insert a jump menu, follow these steps:

1. Position your cursor in the current form, if one exists, where you'd like the jump menu to appear.

   If you haven't already inserted a form, don't worry. Dreamweaver automatically inserts one for you.

2. From the Forms category of the Objects panel, choose the Insert Jump Menu button.

   The Insert Jump Menu dialog box, shown in Figure 13-9, is displayed.

3. In the Insert Jump Menu dialog box, enter the label for the first item in the Text field.

When you confirm your entry by tabbing out of the field, Dreamweaver updates the Menu Items list.

4. Enter the path and filename of the page you want opened for the current item in the When Selected, Go To URL field; alternatively, you can select the Browse (Choose) button to select your file.

5. To add additional jump menu items, select the add (+) button and repeat Steps 3 and 4.

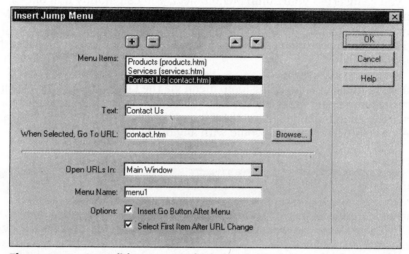

Figure 13-9: Consolidate your Web site navigation through a jump menu.

6. You can adjust the positioning of the items in the jump menu by selecting an item in the Menu List and using the up and down arrows to move it higher or lower.

7. Pick the destination target for the page from the Open URLs In list.

Unless you're working in a frameset, you have only one option — Main Window. When a Jump Menu object is added in a frameset, Dreamweaver displays all frame names as well as Main Window as options.

Tip The Main Window option always replaces your current page with the new page. If you want to have your new page open in a separate window, and keep your current page active, you'll have to edit the HTML. Select the jump menu object on the page and open the Quick Tag Editor. In the code, locate the onChange event and change "parent" to "_blank." If you're working with a Go button, you need to follow the same procedure with the `onClick` event of the tag.

8. If desired, enter a unique name for the jump menu in the Menu Name field.

9. To add a button that activates the jump menu choice, select the Insert Go Button After Menu option.

10. To reset the menu selection to the top item after every jump, choose the Select First Item After URL Change.

11. Click OK when you're done.

Dreamweaver inserts the new jump menu with the appropriate linking code.

Modifying a jump menu

Once you've inserted your Jump Menu object, you can modify it in one of two ways: through the standard List/Menu Property Inspector or through the Jump Menu behavior. While the List Property Inspector uses a List Value dialog box, editing the Jump Menu behavior opens a dialog box similar to the one used to insert the jump menu object.

To alter the items in an existing jump menu via the List/Menu Property Inspector, select the jump menu and click the List Values button. In the List Values dialog box, you see the jump menu labels on the left and the URLs on the right. You can add, move, or delete items as you would with any other list.

Wrapping Graphics Around a Jump Menu

Jump menus are useful in many circumstances, but as a raw form element, they often stick out of a Web page design like a sore thumb. Some designers solve this dilemma by including their jump menu within a specially constructed graphic. The easiest way to create such a graphic is to use a program like Fireworks, which enables a single image to be sliced up into separate parts. The slices are then exported to an HTML file and reassembled in a table.

When you create your graphic, you need to leave room for the jump menu to be inserted in Dreamweaver. This usually entails designating one slice as a nongraphic or text-only slice in your graphics program. Fireworks uses a transparent GIF—called a *spacer image*—as a placeholder. Once you bring the HTML into Dreamweaver, delete the spacer image and insert the Jump Menu object in its place. The figure below shows a jump menu wrapped in a graphic.

Here are a few pointers for wrapping a graphic around a jump menu:

✦ Use a flat color—not a gradient—as the background for the menu.

✦ Select the background color of the graphic to be the background color of the cell of the table holding your jump menu.

✦ Make sure you leave enough height in your graphic to accommodate the jump menu in all browsers. Netscape displays a standard list/menu form element approximately 24 pixels high on a PC; I typically leave about 30 pixels in my graphic.

✦ Form elements are drawn by the user's operating system and are vastly different on each platform. Test your designs extensively.

✦ Integrate your Go button, if you're using one, right in the graphic. Be sure to set it as its own slice, so it comes in as a separate image and can be activated with a Jump Menu Go behavior.

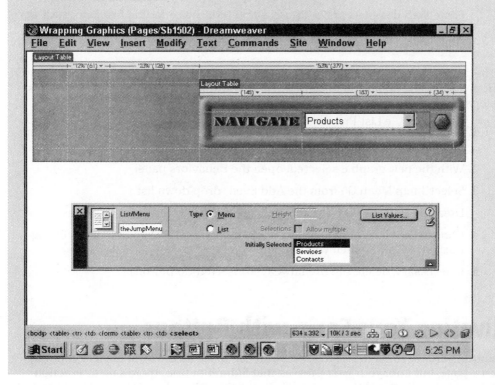

Caution Note one caveat for adding new URLs to the jump menu through the Property Inspector: Any filenames with spaces or special characters should be URL-encoded. In other words, if one of your filenames is `about us.htm`, it should be entered using the hexadecimal equivalent for a space (%20): `about%20us.htm`.

If you'd prefer to work in the same environment as you did when creating the Jump Menu object, go the Behaviors panel route. Select the jump menu and from the Behaviors panel double-click the Jump Menu event. The Jump Menu dialog box opens — it is identical to the Insert Jump Menu dialog box except the Go button option is not available.

Activating Go buttons

The Dreamweaver jump menu is activated immediately whenever a user makes a choice from the list. So why would you want a Go button? The Go button, as implemented in Dreamweaver, is useful for selecting the first item in a jump menu list. To ensure that the Go button is the sole means for activating a jump selection, you need to remove an attached behavior. Select the jump menu item and then open the Behaviors panel. From the Behaviors panel, delete the Jump Menu event.

Tip Some Web designers prefer to use a non-URL choice for the first item, such as "Please Select A Department." When entering such a non-URL option, set the Go to URL (or the Value in the List Value Properties) to #.

The generic Go button is a nice convenience, but it's a little, well, generic. To switch from a standard Go button to a graphical Go button of your choosing, follow these steps:

1. Insert the image that you want to use as your new Go button next to the jump menu.

2. With the new graphic selected, open the Behaviors panel.

3. Select Jump Menu Go from the Add Event drop-down list.

   Dreamweaver displays a dialog box showing all available jump menus.

4. Choose the name of the current jump menu from the Jump Menu Go dialog box list; click OK when you're done.

5. If necessary, delete the Dreamweaver-inserted Go button.

Activating Your Form with Buttons

Buttons are essential to HTML forms. You can place all the form objects you want on a page, but until your user presses that Submit button, there's no interaction between the client and the server. HTML provides three basic types of buttons: Submit, Reset, and Command buttons.

Submit, Reset, and Command buttons

A Submit button sends the form to the specified Action (generally the URL of a server-side program or a mailto address) using the noted Method (generally post). A Reset button clears all the fields in the form. Submit and Reset are both reserved HTML terms used to invoke specific actions.

A Command button permits the execution of functions defined by the Web designer, as programmed in JavaScript or other languages.

To insert a button in Dreamweaver, follow these steps:

1. Position the cursor where you want the button to appear. Then either select the Insert Button icon from the Form category of the Objects panel, or choose Insert ➪ Form Objects ➪ Button from the menu. Or you can simply drag the

Insert Button icon from the Objects panel and drop it into place on an existing form.

2. Choose the button Action type. As shown in Figure 13-10, the Button Property Inspector indicates that the Submit form button action is selected. (This is the default.) To make a Reset button, select the Reset form option. To make a Command button, select the None option.

3. To change the name of any button as you want it to appear on the Web page, enter the new name in the Label text box.

Tip   When working with Command buttons, it's not enough to just insert the button and give it a name. You have to link the button to a specific function. A common technique is to use JavaScript's onClick event to call a function detailed in the <script> section of the document:

```
<input type="BUTTON" name="submit2" value="yes" ¬
onClick="doFunction()">
```

Insert Button button

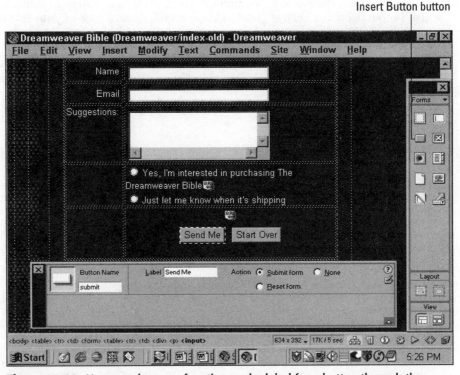

Figure 13-10: You can choose a function and a label for a button through the Button Property Inspector.

Graphical buttons

HTML doesn't limit you to the browser-style default buttons. You can also use an image as a Submit, Reset, or Command button. Dreamweaver has the capability to add an image field just like other form elements: Place the cursor in the desired position and choose Insert ➪ Form Objects ➪ Image Field, or select the Image Field icon from the Forms category of the Objects panel. You can use multiple image fields in a form to give the user a graphical choice, as shown in Figure 13-11.

When the user clicks the picture that you've designated as an image field for a Submit button, the form is submitted. Any other functionality, such as resetting the fields, must be coded in JavaScript or another language and triggered by attaching an onClick event to the button. This can be handled through the Dreamweaver behaviors, covered in Chapter 15 or by hand-coding the script and inserting the onClick code.

In fact, when the user clicks a graphical button, not only does it submit your form, but also it passes along the x, y coordinates of the image. The x coordinate is submitted using the name of the field and an .x attached; likewise, the y coordinate is submitted with the name of the field and a .y attached. Although this latter feature isn't often used, it's always good to know all the capabilities of your HTML tools.

Figure 13-11: Each flag in this page is not just an image; it's an image field that also acts as a Submit button.

Using the Hidden Field and the File Field

You should also be aware of a couple of other special-purpose form fields. The *hidden field* and the *file field* are supported through all major browsers. The hidden field is extremely useful for passing variables to your gateway programs, and the file field enables the user to attach a file to the form being submitted.

The hidden input type

When passing information from a form to a CGI program, the programmer often needs to send data that should not be made visible to the user. The data could be a variable needed by the CGI program to set information on the recipient of the form, or it could be a URL to which the CGI program will redirect the user after the form is submitted. To send this sort of information unseen by the form user, you must use a hidden form object.

The hidden field is inserted in a form much like the other form elements. To insert a hidden field, place your cursor in the desired position and choose Insert ⇨ Form Objects ⇨ Hidden Field or choose the Insert Hidden Field icon from the Forms category of the Objects panel.

The hidden object is another input type, just like the text, radio button, and checkbox types. A hidden variable looks like this in HTML:

```
<input type="hidden" name="recipient" value="jlowery@idest.com">
```

As you would expect, this tag has no representation when it's viewed though a browser. However, Dreamweaver does display a Hidden Form Element Invisible symbol in the Document window. You can turn off the display of this symbol by deselecting the Hidden Form Element option from the Invisible Elements category of Preferences.

The file input type

Much more rarely used is the file input type, which enables any stored computer file to be attached to the form and sent with the other data. Used primarily to enable the easy sharing of data, the file input type has been largely supplanted by modern e-mail methods, which also enable files to be attached to messages.

The file field is inserted in a form much like the other form elements. To insert a file field, place your cursor in the desired position and choose Insert ⇨ Form Objects ⇨ File Field or choose the Insert File Field icon from the Forms category of the Objects panel. Dreamweaver automatically inserts a text box for the filename to be input, with a Browse (Choose) button on the right. In a browser, the user's selection of the Browse (Choose) button displays a standard Open File dialog box from which a file can be selected to go with the form.

Summary

HTML forms provide a basic line of communication from Web page visitor to Web page administrator. With Dreamweaver, you can enter and modify most varieties of form inputs, including text fields and checkboxes. This chapter covered the following important points:

✦ For the most part, a complete form requires two working parts: the form object inserted in your Web page and a CGI program stored on your Web server.

✦ To avoid using a server-side script, you can use a mailto address rather than a URL pointing to a program in a form's action attribute. However, you still have to parse the form reply to convert it to a usable format.

✦ The basic types of form input are text fields, text areas, radio buttons, checkboxes, drop-down menus, and scrolling lists.

✦ Dreamweaver includes a Jump Menu object, which uses a drop-down list as a navigational system.

✦ Once a form is completed, it must be sent to the server-side application. This is usually done through a Submit button on the form. Dreamweaver also supports Reset and user-definable Command buttons.

In the next chapter, you learn how to use Dreamweaver to develop frames and framesets.

✦   ✦   ✦

Using Frames and Framesets

Frames constitute one of the Webmaster's major design tools. A *frame* is a Web page that is subdivided into both static and changing HTML pages. Not too long ago, the evolution of frames was right where Dynamic HTML is today in terms of general acceptance. The use of frames and framesets has become even more widespread over the last year or so, and the technology is now supported through every major browser version. It's safe to say that every Web designer today needs a working knowledge of frames to stay competitive.

The first time I fully appreciated the power of frames, I was visiting a site that displayed examples of what the Webmaster considered "bad" Web pages. The site was essentially a jump-station with a series of links. The author used a frameset with three frames: one that ran all the way across the top of the page, displaying a logo and other basic information; one narrow panel on the left with a scrolling set of links to the sites themselves; and the main viewing area, which took up two-thirds of the center screen. Selecting any of the links caused the site to appear in the main viewing frame.

I was astounded when I finally realized that each frame was truly an independent Web page and that you didn't have to use only Web pages on your own site — you could link to any page on the Internet. That was when I also realized the amount of work involved in establishing a frame Web site: Every page displayed on that site used multiple HTML pages.

Dreamweaver takes the head-pounding complexity out of coding and managing frames with a point-and-click interface. You get easy access to the commands for modifying the properties of the overall frame structure as well as each individual frame. This chapter gives you an overview of frames, as well as all the specifics you need for inserting and modifying frames and framesets. Special attention is given to defining the unique look of frames through borders, scroll bars, and margins.

Frames and Framesets: The Basics

It's best to think of frames in two major parts: the frameset, and the frames themselves. The frameset is the HTML document that defines the framing structure — the number of individual frames that make up a page, their initial size, and the shared attributes among all the frames. A frameset by itself is never displayed. Frames, on the other hand, are complete HTML documents that can be viewed and edited separately or together in the organization described by the frameset.

A frameset takes the place of the <body> tags in an HTML document, where the content of a Web page is found. Here's what the HTML for a basic frameset looks like:

```
<frameset rows="50%,50%">
  <frame src="top.html">
  <frame src="bottom.html">
</frameset>
```

Notice that the content of a <frameset> tag consists entirely of <frame> tags, each one referring to a different Web page. The only other element that can be used inside of a <frameset> tag is another <frameset> tag.

Columns and rows

Framesets, much like tables, are made up of columns and rows. The columns and rows attributes (cols and rows) are lists of comma-separated values. The number of values indicates the number of either columns or rows, and the values themselves establish the size of the columns or rows. Thus, a <frameset> tag that looks like this:

```
<frameset cols="67,355,68">
```

denotes three columns of widths, 67, 355, and 68, respectively. And this frameset tag:

```
<frameset cols="270,232" rows="384,400">
```

declares that two columns exist with the specified widths (270 and 232) and two rows with the specified heights (384 and 400).

Sizing frames

Column widths and row heights can be set as absolute measurements in pixels, or expressed as a percentage of the entire screen. HTML frames also support an attribute that assigns the size relative to the other columns or rows. In other words, the relative attribute (designated with an asterisk) assigns the balance of the remaining available screen space to a column or row. For example, the following frameset:

```
<frameset cols="80,*">
```

sets up two frames, one 80 pixels wide and the other as large as the browser window allows. This ensures that the first column will always be a constant size — making it perfect for a set of navigational buttons — while the second is as wide as possible.

The relative attribute can also be used proportionally. When preceded by an integer, as in n*, this attribute specifies that the frame is allocated *n* times the space it would have received otherwise. So frameset code like this:

```
<frameset rows="4*,*">
```

ensures that one row is proportionately four times the size of the other.

Creating a Frameset and Frames

Dreamweaver offers several ways to divide your Web page into frames and make your frameset. The first method uses the menus. Choose Modify ⇨ Frameset and, from the submenu, select the direction in which you would like to split the frame: left, right, up, or down. Left or right splits the frame in half vertically; up or down splits it horizontally in half.

You can also create a frameset visually, using the mouse. To create frames with this method, follow these steps:

1. Turn on the frame borders in your Dreamweaver Document window by selecting View ⇨ Visual Aids ⇨ Frame Borders.

   A 3-pixel-wide inner border appears along the edges of your Document window.

2. Position the cursor over any of the frame borders.

3. Press Alt (Option).

   If your pointer is over a frame border, the pointer changes into a two-headed arrow when over an edge and a four-headed arrow (or a drag-hand on the Mac) when over a corner.

4. Drag the frame border into the Document window. Figure 14-1 shows a four-frame frameset being created.

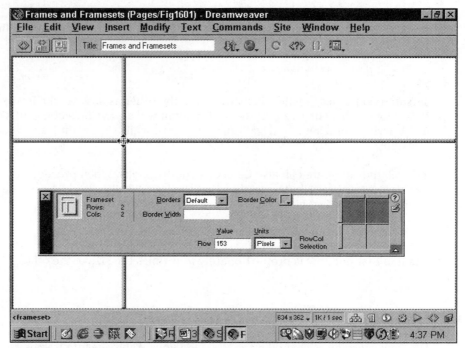

Figure 14-1: After you've enabled the frame borders, you can drag out your frameset structure with the mouse.

Dreamweaver initially assigns a temporary filename and an absolute pixel value to your HTML frameset code. Both can be modified later, if you wish.

Tip

With the menu method of frameset creation, you can initially create only a two-way frame split. To further split the frame using the menu commands, you must first select each frame. However, by Alt+dragging (Option+dragging) the corner of the frame border, you can quickly create a four-frame frameset.

When the frameset is selected, Dreamweaver displays a black, dotted line along all the frame borders and within every frame. You can easily reposition any frameset border by clicking and dragging it. If you just want to move the border, make sure you don't press the Alt or Option key while dragging the border; this action creates additional frames.

Adding more frames

You're not at all limited to your initial frame choices. In addition to being able to move them visually, you can also set the size through the Frameset Property Inspector, as described in the next section. Furthermore, you can continue to split either the entire frame or each column or row as needed. When you divide a column or row into one or more frames, you are actually nesting one frameset inside another.

Tip

Once you've created the basic frame structure, you can select View ⇨ Frame Borders again (it's a toggle) to turn the borders off and create a more accurate preview of your page.

Using the menus

To split an existing frame using the menus, position the cursor in the frame you want to alter and choose Modify ⇨ Frameset ⇨ Split Frame Left, Right, Up, or Down. Figure 14-2 shows a two-row frameset in which the bottom row was split into two columns and then repositioned. The Frameset Property Inspector indicates that the inner frameset (2 columns, 1 row) is selected. The direction in the command (Left, Right, Up, and Down) indicates the frame the existing page will be placed in. For example, I selected Split Frame Right for Figure 14-2, and the current page is placed in the right frame.

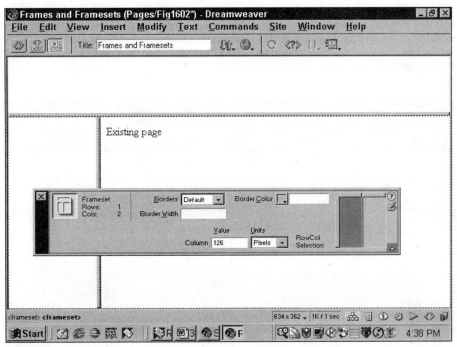

Figure 14-2: Use the Modify ⇨ Frameset menu option to split an existing frame into additional columns or rows and create a nested frameset.

You can clearly see the "nested" nature of the code in this HTML fragment describing the frameset in Figure 14-2:

```
<frameset rows="163,333" cols="784">
  <frame src="file://Dev/UntitledFrame-34">
  <frameset cols="115,663" rows="*">
    <frame src="file://Dev/UntitledFrame-57">
    <frame src="file://Dev/UntitledFrame-35">
  </frameset>
</frameset>
```

Tip You can also split an existing frame by Alt+dragging (Option+dragging) the current frame's border, but you have to choose an inner border that does not extend across the page.

Using the mouse

When you need to create additional columns or rows that span the entire Web page, use the mouse method instead of the menus. Alt+drag (Option+drag) any of the current frame's borders that go across the entire page, such as one of the outer borders. Figure 14-3 shows a new row added along the bottom of our previous frame structure.

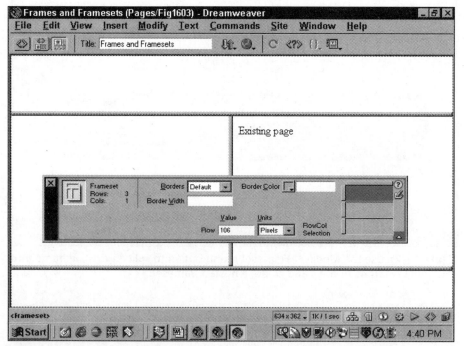

Figure 14-3: An additional frame row was added using the Alt+drag (Option+drag) method.

Tip You can also split a smaller frame by first selecting it and then Alt+dragging or Option+dragging one of its borders. As you can see in this chapter, you select a frame by Alt+clicking (Windows) or Option+Shift+clicking (Macintosh) inside the frame.

Quick Framesets with the Frames Objects

Dragging out your frameset in Dreamweaver is a clear-cut method of setting up the various frames. However, now matter how easy it is, it can still be a bit of a chore to create even simple framesets by clicking and dragging. To hasten the development workflow, Dreamweaver uses Frame objects, which can build a frameset with a single click.

Although a frame-based Web design could potentially be quite complex with numerous nested framesets, most of the sites using frames follow a more simple, general pattern. Dreamweaver offers eight of the most common frameset configurations in the Frames category of the Objects panel, shown in Figure 14-4. Choose one of the basic designs, and you're ready to tweak the frame sizes and begin filling in the content. It's a great combination of ease-of-use mixed with design flexibility.

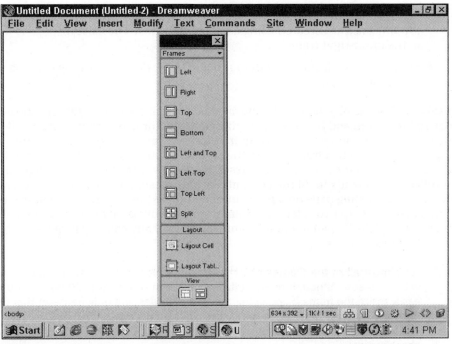

Figure 14-4: The Frames category of the Objects panel holds eight of the most commonly used frameset configurations.

The Frames category is roughly organized from simplest framesets to most complex. You might notice that each of the icons on the panel shows an example frameset with one blue section. The placement of the color is quite significant. The blue indicates in which frame the current page will appear when the frameset is constructed. For example, if I had begun to construct my main content page, and then decided to turn it into a frameset with a separate navigation strip frame beneath it, I would choose the Bottom Frames object. Figure 14-5 provides a before-and-after example with the preframe content on the left and the same content after a Bottom Frame object has been applied.

The eight different framesets available from the Frames category are:

✦ **Left:** Inserts a blank frame to the left of the current page.

✦ **Right:** Inserts a blank frame to the right of the current page.

✦ **Top:** Inserts a blank frame above the current page.

✦ **Bottom:** Inserts a blank frame below the current page.

✦ **Left and Top:** Makes a frameset with four frames where the current page is in the lower right.

✦ **Left Top:** Makes a frameset where the left spans the two rightmost frames; a nested frameset is used to create the right frames. The existing page is placed in the lower-right frame.

✦ **Top Left:** Makes a frameset where the top spans the lower two frames; the lower frames are created using a nested frameset. The existing page is placed in the lower-right frame.

✦ **Split:** Creates a frameset with four equal frames and moves the existing page to the lower right.

Using the Frames objects is quite literally a one-click operation. Just select the desired frameset, and Dreamweaver automatically turns on Frame Borders, if necessary, and creates and names the required frames. For all Frames objects, the existing page is moved to a frame where the scrolling option is set at Default, and the size is relative to the rest of the frameset. In other words, the existing page can be scrolled and expands to fill the content. For this reason, it's best to apply a Frames object to an existing page only if it is intended to be the primary content frame. Otherwise, it's better to select the Frames object while a blank page is open and then use the File ➪ Open in Frame command to load any existing pages into the individual frames.

Note

For almost all of the Frames objects, Dreamweaver creates one or more frames with a set size. Although by default, the set width or height is 80 pixels, you can easily resize the frame by dragging the frame border. The only frameset that does not have at least one set frame is the Split object where the four frames are divided equally. Dreamweaver also sets the Scroll option to No for frames with absolute sizes.

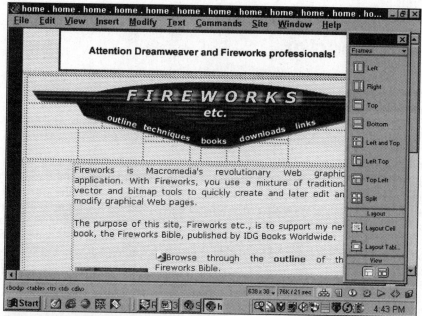

Before Bottom Frame object has been applied.

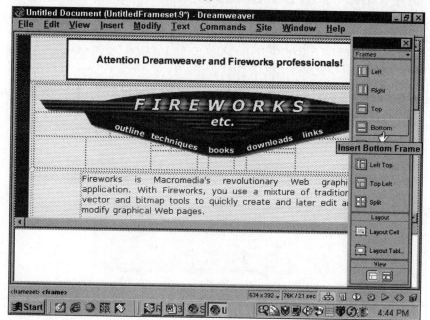

After Bottom Frame Object has been applied.

Figure 14-5: Existing content is incorporated in a new frameset when a Frames object is chosen.

Working with the Frameset Property Inspector

The Frameset Property Inspector manages those elements, such as the borders, that are common to all the frames within a frameset; it also offers more precise sizing control over individual rows and columns than you can do visually. To access the Frameset Property Inspector, choose Window ⇨ Properties, if the Property Inspector is not already open, and then select any of the frame borders.

Tip　When a browser visits a Web page that uses frames, it displays the title found in the frameset HTML document for the entire frame. The easiest method to set that title is to select the frameset and then enter the name directly in the Title field of the toolbar, if visible. You can also set the title by selecting the frameset and then choosing Modify ⇨ Page Properties. In the Page Properties dialog box, enter your choice of title in the Title text box, as you would for any other Web page. All the other options in the Page Properties dialog box — including background color and text color — apply to the `<noframes>` content, covered in the section "Handling Frameless Browsers," later in this chapter.

Resizing frames in a frameset

With HTML, when you want to specify the size of a frame, you work with the row or column in which the frame resides. Dreamweaver gives you two ways to alter a frame's size: by dragging the border or, to be more precise, by specifying a value in the Frameset Property Inspector.

As shown in Figure 14-6, Dreamweaver's Frameset Property Inspector contains a Row/Column selector to display the structure of the selected frameset. For each frameset, you select the tab along the top or left side of the Row/Column selector to choose the column or row you want to modify.

Row/Column selector tabs

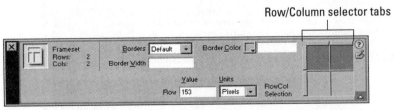

Figure 14-6: In the Frameset Property Inspector, you use the Row/Column Selector tabs to choose which frame you are going to resize.

Tip　The Row/Column Selector shows only one frameset at a time. So if your design uses nested framesets, you won't see an exact duplicate of your entire Web page in the Row/Column Selector.

Whether you need to modify just a row, a column, or both a row and a column depends on the location of the frame.

✦ If your frame spans the width of an entire page, like the top or bottom row in Figure 14-3, select the corresponding tab on the left side of the Row/Column Selector.

✦ If your frame spans the height of an entire page, select the equivalent tab along the top of the Row/Column Selector.

✦ If your frame does not span either height or width, like the middle row in Figure 14-3, you need to select both its column and its row and modify the size of each in turn.

Once you have selected the row or column, follow these steps to specify its size:

1. To specify the size in pixels, enter a number in the Frameset Property Inspector's Value text box and select Pixels as the Units option.

2. To specify the size as a percentage of the screen, enter a number from 1 to 100 in the Value text box and select Percent as the Units option.

3. To specify a size relative to the other columns or rows, first select Relative as the Units option. Now you have two options:

   • To set the size to occupy the remainder of the screen, delete any number that may be entered in the Value text box; optionally, you can enter 1.

   • To scale the frame relative to the other rows or columns, type the scale factor in the Value text box. For example, if you want the frame to be twice the size of another relative frame, put a 2 in the Value text box.

Tip   The Relative size operator is generally used to indicate that you want the current frame to take up the balance of the frameset column or row. This makes it easy to specify a size without having to calculate pixel widths and ensures that the frame has the largest possible size.

Manipulating frameset borders

By default, Dreamweaver sets up your framesets so all the frames have gray borders that are 6 pixels wide. You can alter the border color, change the width, or eliminate the borders altogether. All of the border controls are handled through the Frameset Property Inspector.

Tip   Border controls for individual frames also exist. Just as table cell settings can override options set for the entire table, the individual frame options override those determined for the entire frameset, as described in the section "Working with the Frame Property Inspector," later in this chapter. Use the frameset border controls when you want to make a global change to the borders, such as turning them all off.

If you are working with nested framesets, it's important that you select the outermost frameset before you begin making any modifications to the borders. You can tell that you've selected the outermost frameset by looking at the Dreamweaver Tag Selector; it shows only one <frameset> in bold. If you select an inner nested frameset, you see more than one <frameset> in the Tag Selector.

Eliminating borders

When a frameset is first created, Dreamweaver leaves the borders display up to the browser's discretion. You can expressly turn the frameset borders on or off through the Frameset Property Inspector.

To eliminate borders completely, enter a zero in the Border Width text box. Even if no width value is displayed, the default is a border 6 pixels wide. If you turn off the borders for your frameset, you can still work in Dreamweaver with View ➪ Visual Aids ➪ Frame Borders enabled, which gives you quick access to modifying the frameset. The borders are not displayed, however, when your Web page is previewed in a browser.

Border appearance options

You can control the appearance of your borders to a limited degree. In the Borders drop-down list of options, choosing Yes causes browsers to draw the borders with a 3D appearance. Select No, and the frameset borders are drawn as a single color. Browsers generally interpret the three-dimensional look as the default option.

Border color options

To change the frameset border color, select the Border Color text box and then enter either a color name or a hexadecimal color value. You can also select the color swatch and choose a new border color from the browser-safe color picker. Clicking the Palette icon on the color picker opens the extended color selector, just as for other color swatches in Dreamweaver.

 Caution   If you have nested framesets on your Web page, make sure you've selected the correct frameset before you make any modifications through the Frameset Property Inspector. You can move from a nested frameset to its "parent" by using the keyboard shortcut Alt+up arrow (Command+up arrow). Likewise, you can move from a parent frameset to its "child" by pressing Alt+down arrow (Command+down arrow).

Saving a frameset and frames

As mentioned earlier, when you're working with frames, you're working with multiple HTML files. You must be careful to save not only all the individual frames that make up your Web page but also the frameset itself.

Dreamweaver makes it easy to save framesets and included frames by providing several special commands. To save a frameset, choose File ⇨ Save Frameset to open the standard Save File dialog box. You can also save a copy of the current frameset by choosing File ⇨ Save Frameset As. You don't have to select the frameset border or position your cursor in any special place to activate these functions.

Saving each frame in the frameset can be a chore unless you choose File ⇨ Save All Frames. The first time this command is invoked, Dreamweaver cycles through each of the open frames and displays the Save File dialog box. Each subsequent time you choose File ⇨ Save All Frames, Dreamweaver automatically saves every updated file in the frameset.

To copy an individual frame, you must use the regular File ⇨ Save As command.

Closing a frameset

There's no real trick to closing a Dreamweaver frameset: just choose File ⇨ Close. If the frameset is your last open file, Dreamweaver asks if you'd like to quit the program (unless you've previously selected the Don't Ask Me Again option).

Modifying a Frame

What makes the whole concept of a Web page frameset work so well is the flexibility of each frame.

✦ You can design your page so that some frames are fixed in size while others are expandable.

✦ You can attach scroll bars to some frames and not others.

✦ Any frame can have its own background image, and yet all frames can appear as one seamless picture.

✦ Borders can be enabled — and colored — for one set of frames but left off for another set.

Dreamweaver uses a Frame Property Inspector to specify most of a frame's attributes. Others are handled through devices already familiar to you, such as the Page Properties dialog box.

Page properties

Each frame is its own HTML document, and as such, each frame can have independent page properties. To alter the page properties of a frame, position the cursor in the frame and then choose Modify ⇨ Page Properties. You can also use the keyboard shortcuts, Ctrl+J or Command+J. Or you can select Page Properties from the shortcut menu by right-clicking (Control+clicking) any open space on the frame's page.

Joining Background Images in Frames

One popular technique is to insert background images into separate frames so they blend into a seamless single image. This takes careful planning and coordination between the author of the graphic and the designer of the Web page.

To accomplish this image consolidation operation, you must first "slice" the image in an image-processing program, such as Fireworks or Adobe Photoshop. Then save each part as a separate graphic, making sure that no border is around these image sections — each cut-up piece becomes the background image for a particular frame. Next, set the background image of each frame to the matching graphic. Be sure to turn off the borders for the frame-set and set the Border Width to zero.

You can find a command on the CD-ROM that accompanies this book to help you eliminate your borders. Look for the Zero Page Borders Command in Andrew Wooldridge's folder.

Correct sizing of each piece is important to ensure that no gaps appear in your joined background. A good technique is to use absolute pixel measurements for images that fill the frame and, where the background images tile, set the frame to Relative spacing. In the following figure, the corner frame has the same measurement as the background image (107×126 pixels), and all the other frames are set to Relative.

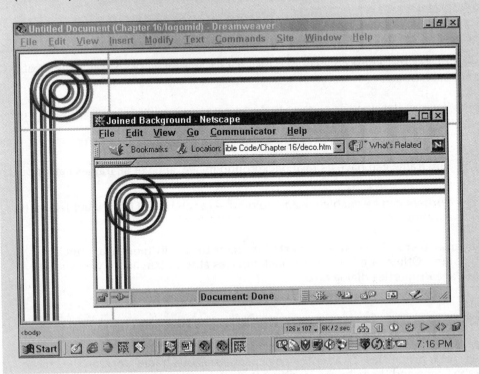

From the Page Properties dialog box, you can assign a title, although it is not visible to the user unless the frame is viewed as a separate page. If you plan on using the individual frames as separate pages in your <noframes> content (see "Handling Frameless Browsers" at the end of this chapter), it's good practice to title every page. You can also assign a background and the various link colors by selecting the appropriate color swatch or entering a color name into the correct text box.

Working with the Frame Property Inspector

To access the Frame Property Inspector, you must first select a frame. Selecting a frame is different from just positioning the cursor in the frame. You have two ways to properly select a frame: using the Frames panel or using the mouse in the Document window.

The Frames panel shows an accurate representation of all the frames in your Web page. Open the Frames panel by choosing Window ➪ Frames. As you can see in Figure 14-7, the Frames panel displays names, if assigned, in the individual frames, and (no name) if not. Nested framesets are shown with a heavier border.

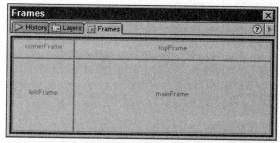

Figure 14-7: Use the Frames panel to visually select a frame to modify.

To select a frame, click directly on its represented image in the Frames panel. If the Frame Property Inspector is open, it reflects the selected frame's options. For more complex Web pages, you can resize the Frames panel to get a better sense of the page layout. To close the Frames panel, select the Close button or choose Window ➪ Frames again.

Tip   When you are working with multiple framesets, use the Tag Selector together with the Frames panel to identify the correct nested frameset. Selecting a frameset in the Tag Selector causes it to be identified in the Frames panel with a heavy black border.

To select a frame with the mouse, press Alt (Option+Shift) and click in the desired frame. Once the frame is selected, you can move from one frame to another by pressing Alt (Command) and then using the arrow keys.

Naming your frames

Naming each frame is essential to getting the most power from a frame-structured Web page. The frame's name is used to make the content inserted from a hyperlink appear in that particular frame. For more information about targeting a link, see the section "Targeting Frame Content," later in this chapter.

Frame names must follow specific guidelines, as explained in the following steps:

1. Select the frame you want to name. You can either use the Frames panel or Alt+click (Option+Shift+click) inside the frame.

2. If necessary, open the Property Inspector by choosing Window ➪ Properties.

3. In the Frame Property Inspector, shown in Figure 14-8, add the frame's name in the text box next to the frame logo. Frame names have the following restrictions:

   - You must use one word, with no spaces.

   - You may not use special characters such as quotation marks, question marks, and hyphens.

   - You may use the underscore character.

   - You may not use certain frame names: `_blank`, `_parent`, `_self`, and `_top`.

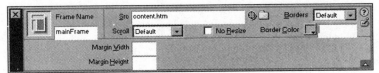

Figure 14-8: The Frame Property Inspector enables you to name your frame and control all of a frame's attributes.

Opening a Web page into a frame

You don't have to build all Web pages in frames from scratch. You can load an existing Web page into any frame. If you've selected a frame and the Frame Property Inspector is open, just type the link directly into the Src text box or choose the folder icon to browse for your file. Or you can position your cursor in a frame (without selecting the frame) and choose File ➪ Open in Frame.

Setting borders

You can generally set most border options adequately in the Frameset Property Inspector; you can also override some of those options, such as color, for each frame. These possibilities have practical limitations, however.

To set borders from the Frame Property Inspector for a selected frame, you can make the borders three-dimensional by choosing Yes in the Borders drop-down option list, or use the monochrome setting by choosing No. Leaving the Borders option at Default gives control to the frameset settings. You can also change a frame's border color by choosing the Border Color swatch in a selected frame's Property Inspector.

Now, about those limitations: They come into play when you try to implement one of your border modifications. Because frames share common borders, it is difficult to isolate an individual frame and have the change affect just the selected frame. As an example, Figure 14-9 shows a frameset in which the borders are set to No for all frames except the one on the lower right. Notice how the left border of the lower-right frame extends to the top, all the way over the upper frame. You have two possible workarounds for this problem. First, you can design your frames so that their borders do not touch, as in a multi-row frameset. Second, you can create a background image for a frame that includes a border design.

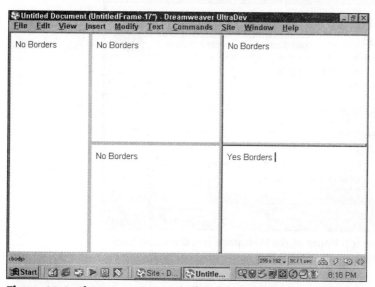

Figure 14-9: If you want to use isolated frame borders, you have to carefully plan your Web page frameset to avoid overlapping borders.

Adding scroll bars

One of the features that has given frames the wide use they enjoy is the capability to enable or disable scroll bars for each frame. Scroll bars are used when the browser window is too small to display all the information in the Web page frame. The browser window size is completely user controlled, so the Web designer must apply the various scroll bar options on a frame-by-frame basis, depending on the look desired and the frame's content.

Four options are selectable from the Scroll drop-down list on the Frame Property Inspector:

✦ **Default:** Leaves the use of scroll bars up to the browser.

✦ **Yes:** Forces scroll bars to appear regardless of the amount of content.

✦ **No:** Disables scroll bars.

✦ **Auto:** Turns scroll bars on if the content of the frame extends horizontally or vertically beyond what the browser window can display.

Figure 14-10 uses an automatic vertical scroll bar in the lower frame; you can see it on the far right.

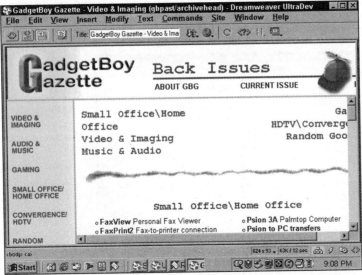

Figure 14-10: The top frame of the Web page has the scroll bars turned off, and the bottom-right frame has scroll bars enabled.

Resizing

By default, all frames are resizable by the user; that is, a visitor to your Web site can widen, narrow, lengthen, or shorten a frame by dragging the border to a new position. You can disable this resizing capability, however, on a frame-by-frame basis. In the Frame Property Inspector, select the No Resize option to turn off the resizing feature.

Tip   Although it might be tempting to select No Resize for every frame, it's best to enable resizing, except in frames that require a set size to maintain their functionality (for instance, a frame containing navigational controls).

Setting margins

Just as you can pad table cells with additional space to separate text and graphics, you can offset content in frames. Dreamweaver enables you to control the left/right margins and the top/bottom margins independently. By default, about 6 pixels of space are between the content and the left or right frame borders, and about 15 pixels of space are between the content and the top or bottom frame borders. You can increase or decrease these margins, but even if you set the values to zero, some room still exists between the borders and the content.

To alter the left and right margins, change the value in the Frame Property Inspector's Margin Width text box; to change the top and bottom margins, enter a new value in the Margin Height text box. If you don't see the Margin Width and Height text boxes, select the Property Inspector expander arrow.

Modifying content

You can update a frame's content in any way you see fit. Sometimes, it's necessary to keep an eye on how altering a single frame's content affects the entire frameset. Other times, it is easier — and faster — to work on each frame individually and later load them into the frameset to see the final result.

With Dreamweaver's multiwindow structure, you can have it both ways. Work on the individual frames in one or more windows and the frameset in yet another.

Although switching back to the frameset window won't automatically update it to show your changed frames, you can use one shortcut. After saving changes in the full frame windows, go to the frameset window. In any window you've altered elsewhere, make another small change, such as inserting a space. Then, choose File ⇨ Revert. This command is normally used to revert to the previously saved version, but in this case, you're using it to update your frames.

Caution   To preview changes made to a Web page using frames, you must first save the changed files. Currently, Dreamweaver creates a temporary file of the frameset, but not any of the included frames.

Deleting frames

As you're building your Web page frameset, you inevitably try a frame design that does not work. How do you delete a frame once you've created it? Click the frame border and drag it into the border of the enclosing, or parent, frame. When no parent frame is present, drag the frame border to the edge of the page. If the frame being deleted contains any unsaved content, Dreamweaver asks if you'd like to save the file before closing it.

Tip   Because the enclosing frameset and each individual frame are all discrete HTML pages, each keeps track of its own edits and other changes — and therefore each has its own Undo memory. If you are in a particular frame and try to undo a frameset alteration, such as adding a new frame to the set, it won't work. To reverse an edit to the frameset, you have to select the frameset and then choose File ⇨ Undo, or use one of the keyboard shortcuts (Ctrl+Z or Command+Z). To reverse the creation of a frameset, you must select Undo twice.

Targeting Frame Content

One of the major uses of frames is for navigational control. One frame acts as the navigation center, offering links to various Web pages in a site. When the user selects one of the links, the Web page appears in another frame on the page; and that frame, if necessary, can scroll independently of the navigation frame. This technique keeps the navigation links always visible and accessible.

When you assign a link to appear in a particular frame of your Web page, you are said to be assigning a target for the link. You can target specific frames in your Web page, and you can target structural parts of a frameset. In Dreamweaver, targets are assigned through the Text and Image Property Inspectors.

Targeting sections of your frameset

In the earlier section on naming frames, you learned that certain names are reserved. These are the four special names HTML reserves for the parts of a frameset that are used in targeting: _blank, _parent, _self, and _top. With them, you can cause content from a link to overwrite the current frame or to appear in an entirely new browser window.

To target a link to a section of your frameset, follow these steps:

1. Select the text or image you want to use as your link.

2. In the Text (or Image) Property Inspector, enter the URL and/or named anchor in the Link text box. Alternatively, you can select the folder icon to browse for the file.

3. Select the Target text box. You may need to expand the Image Property Inspector to see the Target text box.

4. Select one of the following reserved target names from the drop-down list of Target options (see Figure 14-11) or type an entry into the text box:

   • **_blank:** Opens the link into a new browser window and keeps the current window available.

   • **_parent:** Opens the link into the parent frameset of the current frame, if any.

- **_self:** Opens the link into the current frame, replacing its contents (the default).

- **_top:** Opens the link into the outermost frameset of the current Web page, replacing all frames.

Figure 14-11: Choose your frame target from the Property Inspector's Target drop-down list.

The generic nature of these reserved target names enables them to be used repeatedly on different Web pages, without your having to code a particular reference each time.

For an example of structural targeting, look at the code for the Dreamweaver Help system. The Index frame, for example, uses the implied _self target whenever a major Help topic is selected to open an HTML document that shows all the subtopics.

Caution

A phenomenon known as *recursive frames* can be dangerous to your site setup. Let's say you have a frameset named index_frame.html. If you include in any frame on your current page a link to index_frame.html and set the target as _self, when the user selects that link, the entire frameset loads into the current frame—including another link to index_frame.html. Browsers can handle about three or four iterations of this recursion before they crash. To avoid the problem, set your frameset target to _top.

Targeting specific frames in your frameset

Earlier I stressed the importance of naming each frame in your frameset. Once you have entered a name in the Name text box of the Frame Property Inspector, Dreamweaver dynamically updates the Target list to include that name. This feature enables you to target specific frames in your frameset in the same manner that you target the reserved names noted previously.

Although you can always type the frame name directly in the Name text box, the drop-down option list comes in handy for this task. You avoid not only having to keep track of the various frame names in your Web page, but you avoid typing errors as well. Targets are case-sensitive, and names must match exactly or the browser won't be able to find the target.

Updating two frames or more at once

Sooner or later, most Web designers using frames have the need to update more than one frame with a single click. The problem is, you can't group two or more URLs together in an anchor tag. Here is an easy-to-implement solution, thanks to Dreamweaver's behaviors.

Cross-Reference   If you're not familiar with Dreamweaver's JavaScript behaviors, you might want to look over Chapter 15. before continuing.

To update more than one frame target from a single link, follow these steps:

1. Select your link in the frame.

2. Open the Behaviors panel from the Launcher or by choosing Window ⇨ Behaviors.

3. Make sure that 4.0 Browsers is selected in the Show Events For category of the add behavior button on the Behaviors panel.

4. Select the + (add behavior) button to display the list of available behaviors.

5. Choose Go To URL from the drop-down option list.

6. Dreamweaver displays the Go To URL dialog box (Figure 14-12) and scans your document for all named frames. Select a target frame from the list of windows or frames.

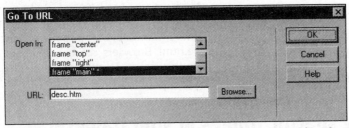

Figure 14-12: You can cause two or more frames to update from a single link by using Dreamweaver's Go To URL behavior.

Caution   You won't be able to use this behavior until you name your frames as detailed in the section "Naming your frames" earlier in this chapter.

7. Enter a URL or choose the Browse (Choose) button to select one.

Dreamweaver places an asterisk after the targeted frame to indicate that a URL has been selected for it. You can see this in Figure 14-12.

8. Repeat Steps 6 and 7 for any additional frames you want to target.

9. Click OK when you're finished.

   Dreamweaver automatically selects the `onClick` event for the Go To URL behavior.

Now, whenever you click your one link, the browser opens the URLs in the targeted frames in the order specified.

Handling Frameless Browsers

Not all of today's browsers support frames. Netscape began supporting frames in Navigator version 2.0; Microsoft didn't start until IE version 3.0 — and a few of the earlier versions for both browsers are still in use, particularly among AOL users. Some less prevalent browsers also don't support frames. HTML has a built-in mechanism for working with browsers that are not frame-enabled: the `<noframes>`...`</noframes>` tag pair.

When you begin to construct any frameset, Dreamweaver automatically inserts a `<noframes>` area just below the closing `</frameset>` tag. If a browser is not frames-capable, it ignores the frameset and frame information and renders what is found in the `<noframes>` section.

What should you put into the `<noframes>` section? To ensure the widest possible audience, Webmasters typically insert links to a nonframe version of the site. The links can be as obvious or as discreet as you care to make them. Perhaps a more vital reason is that most of the search engine indexing systems (called *spiders*) don't work with frames. If your frameset is index.html and you want the spider to find the rest of your site, you need to have a descriptive text from your home page as well as a link to each page in the noframes content. Many Webmasters also include links to current versions of Netscape or Internet Explorer, to encourage their nonframe-capable visitors to upgrade.

Dreamweaver includes a facility for easily adding and modifying the `<noframes>` content. Choose Modify ➪ Frameset ➪ Edit NoFrames Content to open the NoFrames Content window. As you can see in Figure 14-13, this window is identical to the regular Dreamweaver Document window, with the exception of the "NoFrames Content" in the title bar. In this window, you have access to all the same objects and panels that you normally do. When you have finished editing your `<noframe>` content, choose Modify ➪ Frameset ➪ Edit NoFrames Content again to deselect the option and return to the frameset.

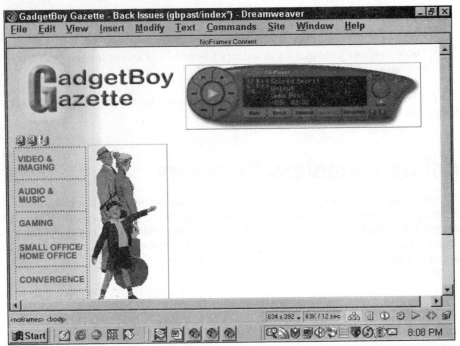

Figure 14-13: Through the Edit NoFrames Content command, Dreamweaver enables you to specify what's seen by visitors whose browsers are not frame-capable.

Here are some pointers to keep in mind when working in the NoFrames Content window:

✦ The page properties of the `<noframes>` content are the same as the page properties of the frameset. You can select the frameset and then choose Modify ⇨ Page Properties to open the Page Properties dialog box. While in the NoFrames Content window, you can also right-click (Control+click) in any open space to access the Page Properties command.

✦ Dreamweaver disables the File ⇨ Open commands when the NoFrames Content window is onscreen. To move existing content into the `<noframes>` section, use Dreamweaver's Copy and Paste features.

✦ The `<noframes>` section is located in the frameset page, which is the primary page examined by search engine spiders. It's a good idea to enter `<meta>` tag information detailing the site, as described in Chapter 8, in the frameset page. While you're in the NoFrames Content window, you can switch to Code view, or open the Code Inspector, and add the `<meta>` tags.

Investigating Iframes

Iframes (short for inline frames) are an HTML 4.0 specification worth noting. An iframe is used to include one HTML document inside another — without building a frameset. What makes iframes visually arresting and extremely useful is their ability to display scroll bars automatically, as shown in Figure 14-14. While iframes are supported by Internet Explorer 4 and above and Netscape 6, you'll have to hand-code or use an extension to insert the tags into Dreamweaver; currently, no menu or object option exists within the standard configuration of Dreamweaver.

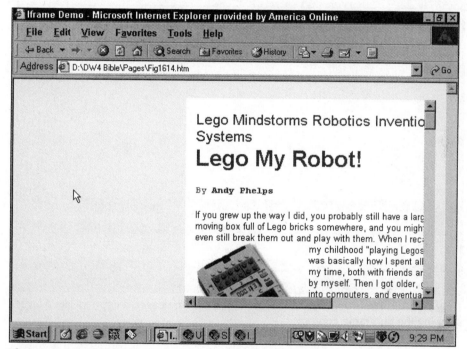

Figure 14-14: The iframe — also known as an inline frame — is a cutting-edge technique for including one HTML page within another.

The `iframe` tag uses the `src` attribute to specify which HTML file is to be included. Any content — whether text, images or whatever — found between the opening and closing `iframe` tags is displayed only if the browser does *not* support iframes. In other words, it's the no-iframe content. Here's an iframe code example:

```
<iframe src="/includes/salespromo.htm" name="promoFrame"
style="position:absolute; width:200px; height:300px; top:139px;
left:530px">Iframes are not supported by this browser.</iframe>
```

If you're familiar with Cascading Style Sheet layers, you'll notice that the style attribute is identical in iframes. This has an interesting effect in Dreamweaver: iframe code is displayed like a layer with the "no-iframe content" visible as shown in Figure 14-15. This makes positioning and resizing the iframe very straightforward. To see the actual iframe content, you'll need to preview the page in a compatible browser.

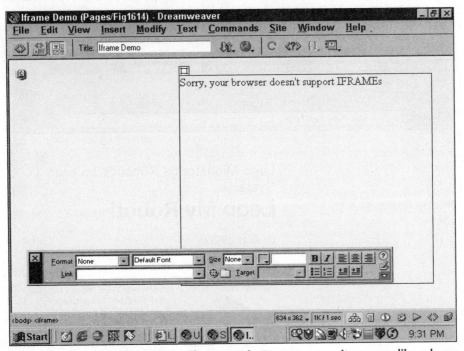

Figure 14-15: When you view an iframe tag in Dreamweaver, it appears like a layer showing the no-iframe content.

On the CD-ROM

Can't wait to start using iframes but don't want to hand-code? Be sure to check out Massimo Foti's Iframe object, which takes advantage of Dreamweaver's interpretation of iframes as a layer. You'll find it under his name on the CD-ROM under Additional Extensions.

Summary

Frames are a significant Webmaster design tool. With frames and framesets, you can divide a single Web page into multiple, independent areas. Dreamweaver gives Web designers quick and easy access to frame design through the program's drag-and-drop interface.

✦ A framed Web page consists of a separate HTML document for each frame and one additional file that describes the frame structure, called the *frameset*.

✦ A frameset comprises columns and rows, which can be sized absolutely in pixels, as a percentage of the browser window, or relative to the other columns or rows.

✦ Dreamweaver enables you to reposition the frame borders by dragging them to a new location. You can also add new frames by Alt+dragging (Option+dragging) any existing frame border.

✦ Framesets can be nested to create more complex column and row arrangements. Selecting the frame border displays the Frameset Property Inspector.

✦ Select any individual frame through the Frames panel or by Alt+clicking (Option+Shift+clicking) within any frame. Once the frame is selected, the Frame Property Inspector can be displayed.

✦ You make your links appear in a specific frame by assigning targets to the links. Dreamweaver supports both structured and named targets. You can update two or more frames with one link by using a Dreamweaver JavaScript behavior.

✦ You should include information and/or links for browsers that are not frame-capable, through Dreamweaver's Edit NoFrames Content feature.

✦   ✦   ✦

Using Behaviors

Behaviors are truly the power tools of Dreamweaver. With Dreamweaver behaviors, any Web designer can make layers appear and disappear, execute any number of rollovers, or control a Shockwave movie — all without knowing even a snippet of JavaScript. In the hands of an accomplished JavaScript programmer, Dreamweaver behaviors can be customized or created from scratch to automate the most difficult Web effect.

Creating behaviors is one of the more challenging Dreamweaver features to master. Implementing these gems, however, is a piece of cake. This chapter examines the concepts behind and the reality of using behaviors — detailing the use of all the behaviors included with Dreamweaver and some from other notable third-party sources. This chapter also contains tips on managing your ever-increasing library of behaviors.

Here's a guarantee for you: Once you get the hang of using Dreamweaver behaviors, your Web pages will never be the same.

Understanding Behaviors, Events, and Actions

A *behavior*, in Macromedia parlance, is the combination of an event and an action. In the electronic age, one pushes a button (the event), and something (the action) occurs — such as changing the channel on the TV. In Dreamweaver, events can be anything as interactive as a user's click of a link or something as automatic as the loading of a Web page. Behaviors are said to be *attached* to a specific element on your page, whether it's a text link, an image, or even the ⟨body⟩ tag.

Dreamweaver has simplified the process of working with behaviors by including default events in every possible object on the Web page. Instead of having to think about both *how* you want to do something and *what* you want to do, you only have to focus on the *what* — the action.

To help you understand conceptually how behaviors are structured, let's examine the four essential steps for adding a behavior to your Web page:

✦ **Step 1: Pick a tag.** All behaviors are connected to a specific HTML element. You can attach a behavior to everything from the `<body>` to the `<textarea>` of a form. If a certain behavior is unavailable, it's because the necessary element isn't present on the page.

✦ **Step 2: Choose your target browser.** Different browsers — and the various browser versions — support different events. Dreamweaver enables you to choose either a specific browser, such as Internet Explorer 4, or a browser range, such as version 3 and 4 browsers.

✦ **Step 3: Select an action.** Dreamweaver makes active only those actions available to your specific page. You can't, for instance, choose the Show-Hide Layer action until you insert one or more layers. Behaviors guide you to the workable options.

✦ **Step 4: Enter the parameters.** Behaviors get their power from their flexibility. Each action comes with a specific parameter form (which represents the dialog box that the user sees) designed to customize the JavaScript code output. Depending on the action, you can choose source files, set attributes, and enable features. The parameter form can even dynamically update to reflect your current Web page.

Dreamweaver 4 comes with 25 cross browser–compatible actions, and both Macromedia and third-party developers have made many additional actions available, with even more in the works. Behaviors greatly extend the range of possibilities for the modern Web designer — without learning to program JavaScript. All you need to know about attaching behaviors is presented in the following section.

Attaching a Behavior

When you see the code generated by Dreamweaver, you understand why setting up a behavior is also referred to as *attaching* a behavior. As previously noted, Dreamweaver needs a specific HTML tag in order to assign the behavior (Step 1). The link tag `<a>` is often used because, in JavaScript, links can respond to several different events, including `onClick`. Here's an example:

```
<a href="#" onClick="MM_popupMsg('Thanks for coming!')">Exit Here</a>
```

You're not restricted to one event per tag or even one action per event. Multiple events can be attached to a tag to handle various user actions. For example, you may have an image that does all of the following things:

✦ Highlights when the user's pointer moves over the image

✦ Reveals a hidden layer in another area of the page when the user clicks the mouse button on the image

✦ Makes a sound when the user releases the mouse button over the image

✦ Starts a Flash movie when the user's pointer moves away from the image

Likewise, a single event can trigger several actions. Updating multiple frames through a single link used to be difficult — but no more. Dreamweaver makes it easy by enabling you to attach several Go to URL actions to the same event, onMouseClick. In addition, you are not restricted to attaching multiple instances of the same action to a single event. For example, in a site that uses a lot of multimedia, you could tie all of the following actions to a single onClick event:

✦ Begin playing an audio file (with the Play Sound action).

✦ Move a layer across the screen (with the Play Timeline action).

✦ Display a second graphic in place of the first (with the Swap Image action).

✦ Show the copyright information for the audio piece in the status bar (with the Set Text of Status Bar action).

You can even determine the order in which the actions connected to a single event are executed.

With Dreamweaver behaviors, hours of complex JavaScript coding is reduced to a handful of mouse clicks and a minimum of data entry. All behavior assigning and modification is handled through the Behaviors panel.

Using the Behaviors panel

The Behaviors panel is a two-columned window (see Figure 15-1) that neatly sums up the behaviors concept in general. After attaching a behavior, the triggering event (onClick, onMouseOver, and so on) is shown on the left and its associated action — what exactly is triggered — is on the right. A down arrow between the event and action, when clicked, displays other available events for the current browser model. Double-click the action to open the associated parameter window, where you can modify the action's attributes.

As typical in Dreamweaver, you have your choice of methods for opening the Behaviors panel:

✦ Choose Window ➪ Behaviors.

✦ Select the Show Behaviors button from either Launcher.

✦ Use the keyboard shortcut Shift+F3 (an on/off toggle).

Expert Tip The Behaviors panel can be closed by toggling it off with Shift+F3 or hidden with the other floating panels by pressing F4.

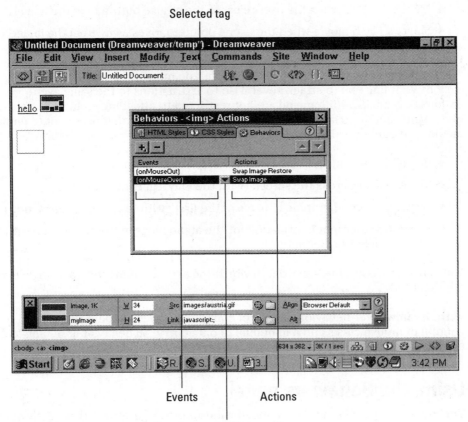

Figure 15-1: You can handle everything about a behavior through the Behaviors panel.

After you have attached a behavior to a tag and closed the associated action's parameter form, Dreamweaver writes the necessary HTML and JavaScript code into your document. Because it involves functions that can be called from anywhere in the document, the JavaScript code is placed in the <head> section of the page, and the code that links the selected tag to the functions is written in the <body> section. A few actions, including Play Sound, place additional HTML code at the bottom of the <body>, but most of the code—there can be a lot of code to handle all the cross-browser contingencies—is placed in the <head> HTML section.

Adding a behavior

Now let's look more closely at the procedure for adding (or attaching) a behavior. As noted earlier, you can assign only certain events to particular tags, and those options are further defined by the type of selected browser.

Note   Even in the latest browsers, key events such as onMouseDown, onMouseOver, and onMouseOut work only with anchor tags. To circumvent this limitation, Dreamweaver can enclose an element, such as <img>, with an anchor tag that links to nowhere — src="javascript:;". Events that use the anchor tag in this fashion are seen in parentheses in the pop-up menu of events.

To add a behavior to your Web page, follow these steps:

1. Select an object in the Document window.

Expert Tip   If you want to assign a behavior to the entire page, select the <body> tag from the Tag Selector.

2. Open the Behaviors panel by choosing Window ➪ Behaviors or selecting the Show Behaviors button from either Launcher. You can see the selected tag at the top of the Behaviors panel.

3. Select the + (add action) button to reveal the available options, as shown in Figure 15-2. Choose one from the pop-up menu.

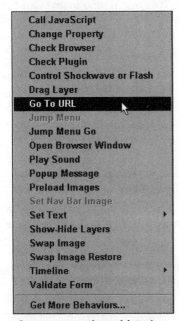

Figure 15-2: The Add Action pop-up menu dynamically changes according to what's on the current page and which tag is selected.

4. Enter the necessary parameters in the Action's dialog box.

5. Click OK when you're finished to close the dialog box.

Dreamweaver adds a line to the Behaviors panel displaying the added action and its default action.

A trigger — whether it's an image or a text link — may have multiple behaviors attached to it. One graphical navigation element could, for instance, perform a Swap Image when the user's mouse moves over it, a Swap Image Restore when the mouse moves away and, when clicked, show another Web page in an additional smaller window with the Open Browser Window behavior.

Dreamweaver includes a menu item at the bottom of the Add Action list: Get More Behaviors. To use this feature, go online and then choose the option. You will be connected with the Dreamweaver Exchange, a service from Macromedia with a huge selection of extensions of all flavors, including behaviors.

Managing events

Every time Dreamweaver attaches a behavior to a tag, it also inserts an event for you. The default event that is chosen is based on two selections: the browser type and the tag selected. The different browsers in use have widely different capabilities, notably when it comes to understanding the various event handlers and associated tags.

For every browser and browser combination shown in the Browser drop-down list, Dreamweaver has a corresponding file in the Configuration\Behaviors\Events folder. Each of the tags listed in each file, such as I.E. 4.0.htm, has at least one event associated with it. The entries look like this:

```
<INPUT TYPE="Text" onBlur="*" onChange="" onFocus="" onSelect="">
```

The default event for each tag is marked with an asterisk; in the example, `onBlur` is the default event. After you've selected an action and completed the dialog box, the default event appears in the Events column alongside the action in the Actions column.

If you find yourself changing a particular default event over and over again to some other event, you might want to modify the Event file to pick your alternative as the default. To do this, open the relevant browser file found in the Configuration\Behaviors\Events folder in a regular text editor (not Dreamweaver) and move the asterisk to a different event for that particular tag. Resave the file and restart Dreamweaver to try out your new default behavior.

Should the default event not be the one you prefer to use, you can easily choose another. Choose a different event by selecting the down arrow next to the displayed default event in the Behaviors panel and select any event in the drop-down list (see Figure 15-3).

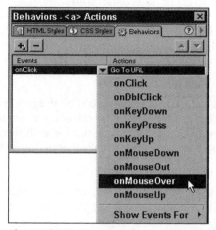

Figure 15-3: You can change the event by selecting the Events arrow button.

Which events are available depends on the browser model selected. By default, 3.0 and Later Browsers is chosen. To change browser models, choose Show Events For from the Events list and select one of the following:

✦ 3.0 and Later Browsers

✦ 4.0 and Later Browsers

✦ IE 3.0

✦ IE 4.0

✦ IE 5.0

✦ Netscape 3.0

✦ Netscape 4.0

The Dreamweaver\Configuration\Behaviors\Events folder contains HTML files corresponding to the six browsers offered in the Show Events For submenu. You can open these files in Dreamweaver, but Macromedia asks that you not edit them—with one exception. Each file contains the list of tags that have supported *event handlers* (the JavaScript term for events) in that browser.

The older the browser, the fewer event handlers are included—unfortunately, this also means that if you want to reach the broadest Internet audience, your event options are limited. In the broadest category, 3.0 and Later Browsers, only 13 different tags can receive any sort of event handler. This is one of the reasons why, for example, Internet Explorer 3 can't handle rollovers: the browser doesn't understand what an onMouseOut event is, and so the image can't revert to its original state.

If you do open and examine an event file in Dreamweaver, notice a group of yellow tags and a few form objects (see Figure 15-4). The yellow tags identify what Dreamweaver sees as invalid HTML. Those form objects—the buttons, checkbox, radio button, and text—render normally but aren't active.

Caution It's far better to use a standard text editor such as HomeSite or BBEdit to open and modify an event file than to use Dreamweaver. By default, Dreamweaver attempts to correct the invalid HTML it finds in the file, and if you save the file with these unwanted corrections in place, your file will be corrupted, and you'll lose access to certain events.

In this case, viewing the HTML is far more instructive than the Document window, as you can see by looking at Listing 15-1. This example gives the event handler definitions for the 3.0 and Later Browsers category.

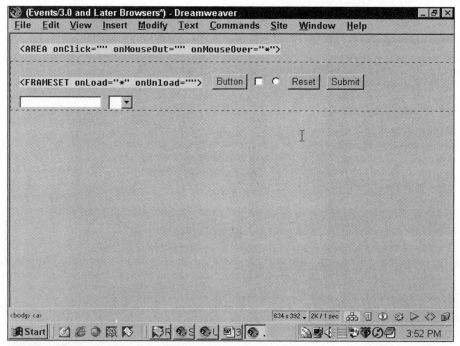

Figure 15-4: The event files define the tags that support particular event handlers in a selected browser.

Listing 15-1: The Events File for 3.0 and Later Browsers

```
<A onMouseOver="*">
<AREA onClick="" onMouseOut="" onMouseOver="*">
<BODY onLoad="*" onUnload="">
<FORM onReset="" onSubmit="*">
<FRAMESET onLoad="*" onUnload="">
<INPUT TYPE="Button" onClick="*">
<INPUT TYPE="Checkbox" onClick="*">
<INPUT TYPE="Radio" onClick="*">
<INPUT TYPE="Reset" onClick="*">
<INPUT TYPE="Submit" onClick="*">
<INPUT TYPE="Text" onBlur="*" onChange="" onFocus=""
onSelect="">
<SELECT onBlur="" onChange="*" onFocus="">
<TEXTAREA onBlur="" onChange="*" onFocus="" onSelect="">
```

By contrast, the events file for Internet Explorer 5.0 shows support for every tag under the HTML sun — 92 in all — with almost every tag able to handle any type of event.

Expert Tip Although any HTML tag could potentially be used to attach a behavior, the most commonly used by far are the <body> tag (for entire-page events such as onLoad), the <img> tag when used as a button, and the link tag, <a>.

To locate the default events for any tag as used by a particular browser, consult Table 15-1. The table also shows, at a glance, which browsers support which tags to receive events.

Standard actions

The following 25 standard actions ship with Dreamweaver 4:

Call JavaScript	Open Browser Window	Show-Hide Layers
Change Property	Play Sound	Swap Image
Check Browser	Popup Message	Swap Image Restore
Check Plugin	Preload Images	Play Timeline
Control Shockwave or Flash	Set Nav Bar Image	Stop Timeline
Drag Layer	Set Text of Frame	Go to Timeline Frame
Go to URL	Set Text of Layer	Validate Form
Jump Menu	Set Text of Status Bar	
Jump Menu Go	Set Text of Text Field	

Table 15-1
Default Events by Browser

Tag	3.0 and Later Browsers	4.0 and Later Browsers	IE 3.0	IE 4.0	IE 5.0	Netscape 3.0	Netscape 4.0
<a>	onMouseOver	onClick	OnMouseOver	onClick	onClick	onClick	onClick
<acronym>					onClick		
<address>				onClick	onClick		
<applet>				onLoad	onLoad		
<area>	onMouseOver	onMouseOver		onClick	onClick	onMouseOver	onMouseOver
<b>				onMouseOver	onMouseOver		
<bdo>					onClick		
<big>				onMouseOver	onMouseOver		
<blink>				onMouseOver	onMouseOver		
<body>	onLoad	onLoad	OnLoad	onLoad	onLoad	onLoad	onLoad
<button>				onClick	onClick		
<caption>				onMouseOver	onMouseOver		
<center>				onMouseOver	onMouseOver		
<cite>				onMouseOver	onMouseOver		
<code>				onMouseOver	onMouseOver		
<col>				onMouseOver	onLoseCapture		
<colgroup>					onLoseCapture		
<dd>				onMouseOver	onMouseOver		
<del>					onMouseOver		
<dfn>				onMouseOver	onMouseOver		
<dir>				onMouseOver	onMouseOver		
<div>				onClick	onClick		
<dl>				onMouseOver	onMouseOver		
<dt>				onMouseOver	onMouseOver		
<em>				onMouseOver	onMouseOver		
<embed>				onLoad	onLoad		
<fieldset>				onClick	onClick		
<font>				onMouseOver	onMouseOver		
<form>	onSubmit	onSubmit	OnSubmit	onSubmit	onSubmit	onSubmit	onSubmit
<frame>	onLoad	onLoad	OnLoad	onLoad	onLoad	onLoad	onLoad
<frameset>				onLoad	onLoad		
<h1>...<h6>				onMouseOver	onMouseOver		
<hr>				onMouseOver	onMouseOver		
<i>				onMouseOver	onMouseOver		
<iframe>				onFocus	onFocus		
<ilayer>		onMouseDown					onLoad
<img>	onClick	onClick	OnClick	onClick	onClick	(None selected)	onMouseDown
<input type=button | checkbox | image | radio | reset | submit>				onClick	onClick	onClick	onClick

Tag	3.0 and Later Browsers	4.0 and Later Browsers	IE 3.0	IE 4.0	IE 5.0	Netscape 3.0	Netscape 4.0
`<input type=file | password>`		onChange		onChange	onChange	onChange	onChange
`<input type=text>`	onBlur	onBlur	OnBlur	onBlur	onBlur	onBlur	onBlur
`<ins>`				onMouseOver	onMouseOver		
`<kbd>`				onClick	onClick		
`<label>`				onClick	onClick		
`<layer>`							onMouseOver
`<legend>`					onClick		
`<li>`				onMouseOver	onMouseOver		
`<listing>`				onMouseOver	onMouseOver		
`<map>`				onClick	onClick		
`<marquee>`				onMouseOver	onMouseOver		
`<menu>`				onMouseOver	onMouseOver		
`<nobr>`				onMouseOver	onMouseOver		
`<object>`				onLoad	onLoad		
`<ol>`				onMouseOver	onMouseOver		
`<p>`				onMouseOver	onMouseOver		
`<plaintext>`				onMouseOver	onMouseOver		
`<pre>`				onMouseOver	onMouseOver		
`<q>`					onClick		
`<rt>`							
`<s>`				onMouseOver	onMouseOver		
`<samp>`				onMouseOver	onMouseOver		
`<select>`	onChange	onChange	OnChange	onChange	onChange	onChange	onChange
`<small>`				onMouseOver	onMouseOver		
`<span>`				onMouseOver	onMouseOver		
`<strike>`				onMouseOver	onMouseOver		
`<strong>`				onMouseOver	onMouseOver		
`<sub>`				onMouseOver	onMouseOver		
`<sup>`				onMouseOver	onMouseOver		
`<table>`				onMouseOver	onMouseOver		
`<tbody>`				onMouseOver	onMouseOver		
`<td>`				onMouseOver	onMouseOver		
`<textarea>`	onChange	onChange	onChange	onChange	onChange	onChange	onChange
`<tfoot>`				onMouseOver	onMouseOver		
`<th>`				onMouseOver	onMouseOver		
`<thead>`				onMouseOver	onMouseOver		
`<tr>`				onMouseOver	onMouseOver		
`<tt>`				onMouseOver	onMouseOver		
`<u>`				onMouseOver	onMouseOver		
`<ul>`				onMouseOver	onMouseOver		
`<var>`				onMouseOver	onMouseOver		
`<xmp>`				onMouseOver	onMouseOver		

Each action operates independently and differently from the others, although many share common functions. Each action is associated with a different dialog box or parameter form to enable easy attribute entry.

The following sections describe each of the standard actions: what the action does, what requirements must be met for it to be activated, what options are available, and most important of all, how to use it. Each action is written to work with all browser versions 4 and above; however, some actions do not work as designed in the older browsers. The charts included with every action show the action's compatibility with older browsers. (The information in these charts was adapted from the Dreamweaver Help pages and is used with permission.)

Note   The following descriptions assume that you understand the basics of assigning behaviors and that you know how to open the Behaviors panel.

Call JavaScript

With Call JavaScript, you can execute any JavaScript function — standard or custom — with a single mouse click or other event. As your JavaScript savvy grows, you'll find yourself using this behavior again and again.

Call JavaScript is straightforward to use; simply type in the JavaScript code or the name of the function you want to trigger into the dialog box. If, for example, you wanted to get some input from a visitor, you could use JavaScript's built-in prompt() method, like this:

```
result=prompt("Whom shall I say is calling?","")
```

When this code is triggered, a small dialog box appears with your query (here, "Whom shall I say is calling?") and a space for an input string. The second argument in the prompt() method enables you to include a default answer — to leave it blank, just use two quotes.

Note   You can use either single or double quotes in your Call JavaScript behavior; Dreamweaver automatically adjusts for whichever you choose. However, I find it easier to use single quotes because Dreamweaver translates double quotes into character entities; that is, " becomes ".

Naturally, you could use Call JavaScript to handle much more complex chores as well. To call a specific custom function that is already in the <head> section of your page, just enter its name — along with any necessary arguments — in the Call JavaScript dialog box, shown in Figure 15-5.

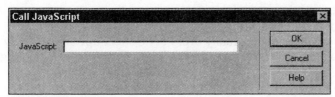

Figure 15-5: Trigger any JavaScript function by attaching a Call JavaScript behavior to an image or text.

To use the Call JavaScript behavior, follow these steps:

1. Select the object to trigger the action.

2. From the Behaviors panel, select the add action button and choose Call JavaScript.

3. In the Call JavaScript dialog box, enter your code in the text box.

4. Click OK when you're done.

Note
In the following charts that detail action behaviors for both newer and older browsers, the phrase "Fails without error" means that the action won't work in the older browser, but that it doesn't generate an error message for the user to see. Where the table indicates "error," it means the user receives a JavaScript alert message.

Here's the browser compatibility chart for the Call JavaScript behavior:

Call JavaScript	Netscape 3.x	Internet Explorer 3.0	Internet Explorer 3.01
Macintosh	Okay	Fails without error	
Windows	Okay		Okay

Change Property

The Change Property action enables you to dynamically alter a property of one of the following tags:

`<layer>`	`<div>`	`<form>`	`<textarea>`
`<span>`	`<img>`	`<select>`	

You can also alter the following `<input>` types:

radio	checkbox	text	password

Exactly which properties can be altered depends on the tag as well as on the browser being targeted. For example, the <div> tag and Internet Explorer 4.0 combination enables you to change virtually every style sheet option on the fly. The Change Property dialog box (see Figure 15-6) offers a list of the selected tags in the current page.

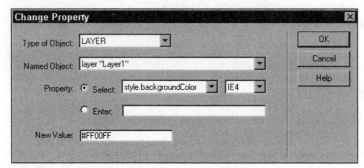

Figure 15-6: The Change Property action enables you to alter attributes of certain tags dynamically.

Caution It's important that you name the objects you want to alter so that Dreamweaver can properly identify them. Remember to use unique names that begin with a letter and contain no spaces or special characters.

This behavior is especially useful for changing the properties of forms and form elements. Be sure to name the form if you wish to use Change Property in this manner.

To use the Change Property action, follow these steps:

1. Select the object to trigger the action.

2. From the Behaviors panel, select the add action button and choose Change Property.

3. In the Change Property dialog box, choose an object type, such as FORM or SELECT, from the Type of Object drop-down list.

4. In the dynamic Named Object drop-down list, choose the object on your page you wish to affect.

5. Click the Select radio button. Select the target browser in the small list box on the far right and then choose the property to change. If you don't find the property in the drop-down list box, you can type it yourself into the Enter text box.

Note Many properties in the various browsers are read-only and cannot be dynamically altered. Those properties listed in the option list are always dynamic.

6. In the New Value text box, type the property's new value to be inserted when the event is fired.

7. Click OK when you're done.

Here's the browser compatibility chart for the Change Property behavior:

Change Property	*Netscape 3.x*	*Internet Explorer 3.0*	*Internet Explorer 3.01*
Macintosh	Okay	Fails without error	
Windows	Okay		Okay

Check Browser

Some Web sites are increasingly split into multilevel versions of themselves to gracefully handle the variety of browsers in operation. The Check Browser action acts as a type of browser "router" capable of sending browsers to appropriate URLs, or just letting them stay on the current page. The Check Browser action is generally assigned to the <body> tag and uses the onLoad event. If used in this fashion, it's a good idea to keep the basic page accessible to all browsers, even those with JavaScript disabled.

The Check Browser parameter form (see Figure 15-7) is quite flexible and enables you to specify decimal version numbers for the two main browsers. For instance, you may want to let all users of Navigator 4.04 or later stay on the current page and send everyone else to an alternative URL. The URLs can be either relative, such as alt/index.html, or absolute, such as www.idest.com/alt/index.html.

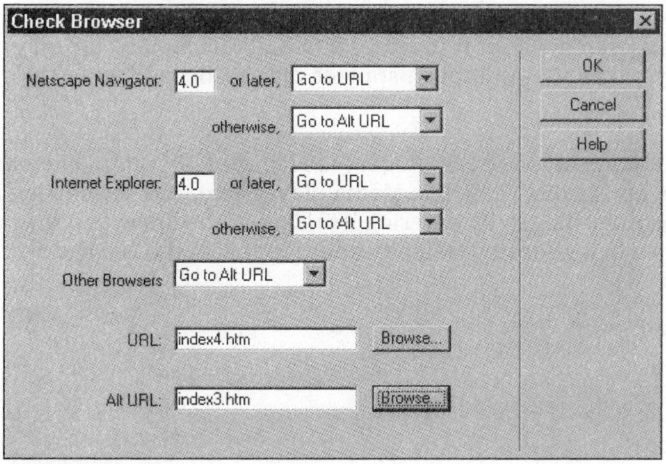

Figure 15-7: The Check Browser action is a great tool for segregating old and new browsers.

To use the Check Browser action, follow these steps:

1. Select the object to trigger the action.

2. From the Behaviors panel, select the add action button and choose Check Browser.

3. Specify the Netscape Navigator and Internet Explorer versions and whether you want the browser to stay on the current page, go to another URL, or proceed to a third alternative URL.

Note   With both major browsers, you can specify the URL that the lower version numbers should visit.

4. Set the same options for all other browsers, such as Opera or OMNIWeb.

5. Enter the URL and alternative URL options in their respective text boxes or select the Browse (Choose) button to locate the files.

Here's the browser compatibility chart for the Check Browser behavior:

Check Browser	Netscape 3.x	Internet Explorer 3.0	Internet Explorer 3.01
Macintosh	Okay	Fails without error	
Windows	Okay		Okay

Check Plugin

If certain pages on your Web site require the use of one or more plug-ins, you can use the Check Plugin action to see if a visitor has the necessary plug-in installed. Once this has been examined, Check Plugin can route users with the appropriate plug-in to one URL, and users without it to another URL. You can look for only one plug-in at a time, but you can use multiple instances of the Check Plugin action, if needed.

By default, the parameter form for Check Plugin (see Figure 15-8) offers five plug-ins: Flash, Shockwave, LiveAudio, Netscape Media Player, and QuickTime Plug-in. You can check for any other plug-in by entering its name in the Enter text box; use the name that appears when choosing Help ⇨ About Plugins in the Navigator menus.

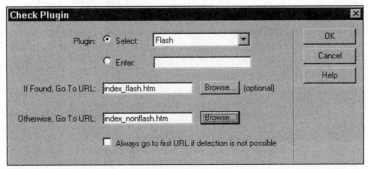

Figure 15-8: Running a media-intensive site? Use the Check Plugin action to divert visitors without plug-ins to alternate pages.

Expert Tip If you use a particular plug-in regularly, you may want to also modify the Check Plugin.js file found in your Actions folder. Add your new plug-in name to the PLUGIN_NAMES array and the corresponding PLUGIN_VALUES array in the initGlobal function.

Although Check Plugin cannot check for specific ActiveX controls, this action can route the Internet Explorer user to the same page as users who have plug-ins. The best way to handle both browsers is to use both ActiveX controls and plug-ins, through the <object> and <embed> methods.

On the CD-ROM Another method for determining whether a plug-in or other player is available is to use the Check MIME action included on the CD-ROM that accompanies this book. This action works in the same way as the Check Plugin action, except you enter the MIME type.

To use the Check Plugin action, follow these steps:

1. Select the object to trigger the action.

2. From the Behaviors panel, select the add action button and choose Check Browser.

3. Select a plug-in from the drop-down list. You can also type another plug-in name in the Enter text box.

Note The names presented in the drop-down list are abbreviated, more recognizable names, and not the formal names inserted into the code. For example, when the option Shockwave is selected, the phrase Shockwave for Director is actually input into the code. On the other hand, any plug-in name you enter manually into the Enter field is inserted verbatim.

4. If you want to send users who are confirmed to have the plug-in to a different page, enter that URL (absolute or relative) in the If Found, Go To URL text box or use the Browse (Choose) button to locate the file. If you want them to stay on the current page, leave the text box empty.

5. In the Otherwise, Go To URL text box, enter the URL for users who do not have the required plug-in.

6. Should the browser detection method fail — as with certain browsers, such as some versions of Internet Explorer on the Macintosh — you can keep the user on the initial page by enabling the "Always go to first URL if detection is not possible" option. Otherwise, if the detection fails, for any reason, the users are sent to the URL listed in the Otherwise field.

Here's the browser compatibility chart for the Check Plugin behavior:

Check Browser	Netscape 3.x	Internet Explorer 3.0	Internet Explorer 3.01
Macintosh	Okay	Fails without error	
Windows	Okay		Okay

Control Shockwave or Flash

The Control Shockwave or Flash action enables you to command your Shockwave and Flash movies through external controls. With Control Shockwave or Flash, you can build your own interface for your Shockwave or Flash material. This action can be used in conjunction with the `autostart=true` attribute (entered through the Property Inspector's Parameter dialog box for the Shockwave or Flash file) to enable a replaying of the movie.

You must have a Shockwave or Flash movie inserted in your Web page in order for the Control Shockwave or Flash action to be available. The parameter form for this action (see Figure 15-9) lists all the Shockwave or Flash movies by name that are found in either an `<embed>` or `<object>` tag. You can set the action to control the movie in one of four ways: Play, Stop, Rewind, or Go to Frame. You can choose only one option each time you attach an action to an event. If you choose the last option, you need to specify the frame number in the text box. Note that specifying a Go to Frame number does not start the movie there; you need to attach a second Control Shockwave or Flash action to the same event to play the file.

Figure 15-9: Build your own interface and then control a Shockwave and Flash movie externally with the Control Shockwave or Flash action.

Be sure to name your Shockwave or Flash movie. Otherwise, the Control Shockwave or Flash action lists both unnamed <embed> **and** unnamed <object> for each file, and you cannot write to both tags as you can with a named movie.

To use the Control Shockwave or Flash action, follow these steps:

1. Select the object to trigger the action.

2. From the Behaviors panel, select the add action button and choose Control Shockwave or Flash.

3. In the Control Shockwave or Flash dialog box, select a movie from the Named Shockwave Object drop-down list.

4. Select a control by choosing its radio button:

   • **Play:** Begins playing the movie at the current frame location.

   • **Stop:** Stops playing the movie.

   • **Rewind:** Returns the movie to its first frame.

   • **Go to Frame:** Displays a specific frame in the movie. Note: For this option, you must enter a frame number in the text box.

5. Click OK when you're done.

Here's the browser compatibility chart for the Control Shockwave or Flash behavior:

Control Shockwave or Flash	Netscape 3.x	Internet Explorer 3.0	Internet Explorer 3.01
Macintosh	Okay	Fails without error	
Windows	Okay		Fails without error

Drag Layer

The Drag Layer action provides some spectacular — and interactive — effects with little effort on the part of the designer. Drag Layer enables your Web page visitors to move layers — and all that they contain — around the screen with the drag-and-drop technique. With the Drag Layer action, you can easily set up the following capabilities for the user:

✦ Enable layers to be dragged anywhere on the screen.

✦ Restrict the dragging to a particular direction or combination of directions — a horizontal sliding layer can be restricted to left and right movement, for instance.

✦ Limit the drag handle to a portion of the layer such as the upper bar or enable the whole layer to be used.

✦ Provide an alternative clipping method by enabling only a portion of the layer to be dragged.

✦ Enable changing of the layers' stacking order while dragging or on mouse release.

✦ Set a snap-to target area on your Web page for layers that the user releases within a defined radius.

✦ Program a JavaScript command to be executed when the snap-to target is hit or every time the layer is released.

Cross-Reference   Layers are one of the more powerful features of Dreamweaver. To get the most out of the layer-oriented behaviors, familiarize yourself with layers by examining Chapter 19.

Layers must be inserted in your Web page before the Drag Layer action becomes available for selection from the Add Action pop-up menu. You must attach the action to the <body> — you can, however, attach separate versions of Drag Layer to different layers for different effects.

Drag Layer's parameter form (see Figure 15-10) includes a Get Current Position button that puts the left and top coordinates of a selected layer into the appropriate boxes for the Drop Target parameters. If you plan on using targeting, place your layer at the target location before attaching the behavior.

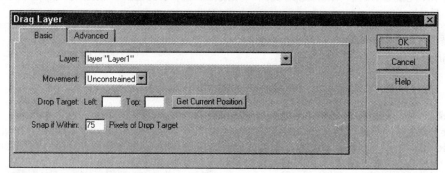

Figure 15-10: With the Drag Layer action, you can set up your layers to be repositioned by the user.

To use the Drag Layer action, follow these steps:

1. Select the <body> tag.

2. From the Behaviors panel, select the add action button and choose Drag Layer.

3. In the Layer drop-down list of the parameter form in the Basic tabbed panel, select the layer you want to make draggable.

4. To limit the movement of the layer, change the Movement option from Unconstrained to Constrained. Text boxes for Up, Down, Left, and Right appear. Enter pixel values in the text boxes to control the range of motion:

   • To constrain movement vertically, enter positive numbers in the Up and Down text boxes and zeros in the Left and Right text boxes.

   • To constrain movement horizontally, enter positive numbers in the Left and Right text boxes and zeros in the Up and Down text boxes.

   • To enable movement in a rectangular region, enter positive values in all four text boxes.

5. To establish a location for a target for the dragged layer, enter coordinates in the Drop Target: Left and Top text boxes. Select the Get Current Position button to fill these text boxes with the layer's present location.

6. To set a snap-to area around the target coordinates where the layer falls, if released in the target location, enter a pixel value in the Snap if Within text box.

7. For additional options, select the Advanced tab.

8. If you want to limit the area to be used as a drag handle, select the radio button for Drag Handle: Area Within Layer. Left, Top, Width, and Height text boxes appear. In the appropriate text boxes, enter the Left and Top coordinates of the drag handle in pixels, as well as the Width and Height dimensions.

Note   If you want to enable the whole layer to act as a drag handle, make sure the Drag Handle: Entire Layer radio button is selected.

9. To control the positioning of the dragged layer, set the following While Dragging options:

   • To keep the layer in its current depth and not bring it to the front when it is dragged, deselect the checkbox for While Dragging: Bring Layer to the Front.

   • To change the stacking order of the layer when it is released, select either Leave on Top or Restore z-order from the drop-down list.

10. To execute a JavaScript command while the layer is being dragged, enter the command or function in the Call JavaScript text box.

11. To execute a JavaScript command when the layer is dropped on the target, enter the code in the When Dropped: Call JavaScript text box. If you want the JavaScript to execute only when the layer is snapped to its target, select the Only if snapped option — this option requires that a value be entered in the Snap if Within text box.

12. Click OK when you're done.

Note   If you—or someone on your team—has the JavaScript programming skills, you can gather information output from the Drag Layer behavior to enhance your pages. Dreamweaver declares three variables for each draggable layer: MM_UPDOWN (the y coordinate), MM_LEFTRIGHT (the x coordinate), and MM_SNAPPED (true, if the layer has reached the specified target). Before you can get any of these properties, you must get an object reference for the proper layer. Another function, MM_findObj (layername), handles this chore.

Here's the browser compatibility chart for the Drag Layer behavior:

Drag Layer	*Netscape 3.x*	*Internet Explorer 3.0*	*Internet Explorer 3.01*
Macintosh	Fails without error	Fails without error	
Windows	Fails without error		Fails without error

Go to URL

Dreamweaver brings the same power of links—with a lot more flexibility—to any event with the Go to URL action. One of the trickier tasks in using frames on a Web page is updating two or more frames simultaneously with a single button click. The Go to URL action handily streamlines this process for the Web designer. Go to URL can also be used as a preload router that sends the user to another Web page once the onLoad event has finished.

The dialog box for Go to URL (see Figure 15-11) displays any existing anchors or frames in the current page or frameset. To load multiple URLs at the same time, open the drop-down list and select the first frame that you want to alter; then enter the desired page or location in the URL text box. Select the second frame from the list and enter the next URL (or Browse/Choose to find it). If you select a frame to which you have previously assigned a URL, that address appears in the URL text box.

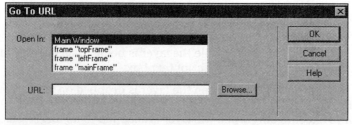

Figure 15-11: Update two or more frames at the same time with the Go to URL action.

To use the Go to URL action, follow these steps:

1. Select the object to trigger the action.

2. From the Behaviors panel, select the add action button and choose Go to URL.

3. From the Go to URL dialog box, select the target for your link from the list in the Open In window.

4. Enter the path of the file to open in the URL text box or click the Browse (Choose) button to locate a file.

   An asterisk appears next to the frame name to indicate that a URL has been chosen.

5. To select another target to load a different URL, repeat Steps 3 and 4.

6. Click OK when you're done.

Here's the browser compatibility chart for the Go to URL behavior:

Go to URL	Netscape 3.x	Internet Explorer 3.0	Internet Explorer 3.01
Macintosh	Okay	Fails without error	
Windows	Okay		Okay

Jump Menu and Jump Menu Go

Although most behaviors insert original code to activate an element of the Web page, several behaviors are included to edit code inserted by a Dreamweaver object. The Jump Menu and Jump Menu Go behaviors both require a previously inserted Jump Menu object before they become active. The Jump Menu behavior is used to edit an existing Jump Menu object, while the Jump Menu Go behavior adds a graphic image as a "Go" button.

To use the Jump Menu behavior to edit an existing Jump Menu object, follow these steps:

1. Select the Jump Menu object previously inserted into the page.

2. In the Behaviors panel, double-click the listed Jump Menu behavior.

3. Make your modifications in the Jump Menu dialog box, as shown in Figure 15-12.

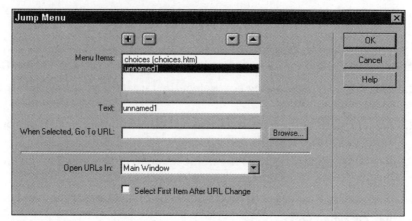

Figure 15-12: The Jump Menu behavior is used to modify a previously inserted Jump Menu object.

You can alter the existing menu item names or their associated URLs, add new menu items, or reorder the list through the Jump Menu dialog box.

4. Click OK when you're done.

To add a button to activate the Jump Menu object, follow these steps:

1. Select the image or form button you'd like to make into a Go button.

A Jump Menu object must be on the current page for the Jump Menu Go behavior to be available.

2. From the Behaviors panel, select Jump Menu Go from the Add behavior list.

The Jump Menu Go dialog box, shown in Figure 15-13, is displayed.

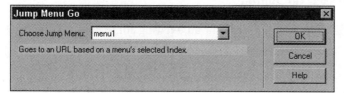

Figure 15-13: Add a graphic or standard button as a Go button with the Jump Menu Go behavior.

3. Select the name of the Jump Menu object you want to activate from the option list.

4. Click OK when you're done.

Here's the browser compatibility chart for both Jump Menu behavior:

Jump Menu	Netscape 3.x	Internet Explorer 3.0	Internet Explorer 3.01
Macintosh	Okay	Fails without error	
Windows	Okay		Fails without error

Open Browser Window

Want to display your latest design in a borderless, nonresizable browser window that's exactly the size of your image? With the Open Browser Window action, you can open a new browser window and specify its exact size and attributes. You can even set it up to receive JavaScript events.

You can also open a new browser window with a regular link by specifying target="_blank", but you can't control any of the window's attributes with that method. You do get this control with the parameter form of the Open Browser Window action (see Figure 15-14); here you can set the window width and height, and whether or not to display the Navigation Toolbar, Location Toolbar, Status Bar, Menu Bar, Scrollbars, and Resize Handles. You can also name your new window, a necessary step for advanced JavaScript control.

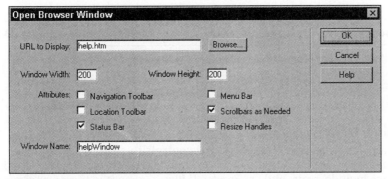

Figure 15-14: Use the Open Browser Window action to program in a pop-up advertisement or remote control.

You have to explicitly select any of the attributes you want to appear in your new window. Your new browser window contains only the attributes you've checked, plus basic window elements such as a title bar and a Close button.

To use the Open Browser Window action, follow these steps:

1. Select the object to trigger the action.

2. From the Behaviors panel, select the add action button and choose Open Browser Window.

3. In the URL to Display text box, enter the address of the Web page you want to display in the new window. You can also select the Browse (Choose) button to locate the file.

4. To specify the window's size and shape, enter the width and height values in the appropriate text boxes.

   You must enter both a width and height measurement, or the new browser window opens to its default size.

5. Check the appropriate Attributes checkboxes to enable the parameters you want.

6. If you plan on using JavaScript to address or control the window, type a unique name in the Window Name text box. This name cannot contain spaces or special characters. Dreamweaver alerts you if the name you've entered is unacceptable.

7. Click OK when you're done.

Here's the browser compatibility chart for the Open Browser Window behavior:

Open Browser Window	Netscape 3.x	Internet Explorer 3.0	Internet Explorer 3.01
Macintosh	Okay	Fails without error	
Windows	Okay		Okay

Play Sound

The Play Sound action is used to add external controls to an audio file that normally uses the Netscape LiveAudio plug-in or the Windows Media Player. Supported audio file types include .wav, .mid, .au, and .aiff files — generally to add background music with a hidden sound file. The Play Sound action inserts an `<embed>` tag with the following attributes set:

✦ loop=false

✦ autostart=false

✦ mastersound

✦ hidden=true

✦ width=0

✦ height=0

Instead of automatically detecting which sound files have been inserted in the current Web page, Play Sound looks for the sound file to be inserted though the action's dialog box (see Figure 15-15).

Figure 15-15: Give your Web page background music and control it with the Play Sound action.

Note   Dreamweaver can detect if a visitor's browser has the Windows Media Player installed and, if so, issue the appropriate commands.

To use the Play Sound action, follow these steps:

1. Select the object to trigger the action.

2. From the Behaviors panel, select the add action button and choose Play Sound.

3. To play a sound, enter the path to the audio file in the Play Sound text box or select the Browse (Choose) button to locate the file.

4. Click OK when you're done.

Here's the browser compatibility chart for the Play Sound behavior:

Play Sound	Netscape 3.x	Internet Explorer 3.0	Internet Explorer 3.01
Macintosh	Okay	Fails without error	
Windows	Okay		Fails without error

Popup Message

You can send a quick message to your users with the Popup Message action. When triggered, this action opens a JavaScript Application Alert with your message. You enter your message in the Message text box on the action's parameter form (see Figure 15-16).

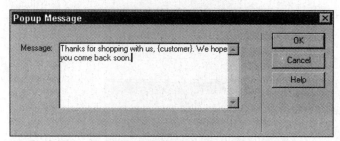

Figure 15-16: Send a message to your users with the Popup Message action.

To use the Popup Message action, follow these steps:

1. Select the object to trigger the action.

2. From the Behaviors panel, select the add action button and choose Popup Message.

3. Enter your text in the Message text box.

4. Click OK when you're done.

Expert Tip   You can include JavaScript functions or references in your text messages by surrounding the JavaScript with curly braces. For example, today's date could be incorporated in a message like this:

```
Welcome to our site on {new Date()}!
```

You could also pull data entered into a form to incorporate into a message, as in this example:

```
Thanks for filling out our form, ¬
{document.theForm.firstname.value}.
```

If you need to display a curly brace in a message, you must precede it with a back-slash character, \.

Here's the browser compatibility chart for the Popup Message behavior:

Popup Message	Netscape 3.x	Internet Explorer 3.0	Internet Explorer 3.01
Macintosh	Okay	Fails without error	
Windows	Okay		Okay

Preload Images

Designs commonly require a particular image or images to be displayed immediately when called by an action or a timeline. Because of the nature of HTML, all graphics are separate files that normally are downloaded when needed. To get the snappy response required for certain designs, graphics need to be preloaded or cached so that they will be available. The Preload Images action performs this important service. You designate the images you want to cache for later use through the Preload Images parameter form (see Figure 15-17).

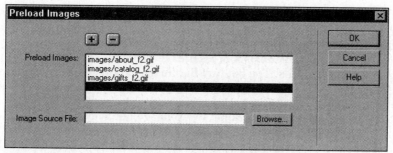

Figure 15-17: Media-rich Web sites respond much faster when images have been cached with the Preload Images action.

Note   You don't need to use the Preload Images action if you're creating rollovers. Both the Rollover object and the Swap Image action enable you to preload images from their dialog boxes.

To use the Preload Images action, follow these steps:

1. Select the object to trigger the action.

2. From the Behaviors panel, select the add action button and Preload Images.

3. In the action's parameter form, enter the path to the image file in the Image Source File text box or select the Browse (Choose) button to locate the file.

4. To add another file, click the + (add) button and repeat Step 2.

Caution   After you've specified your first file to be preloaded, be sure to press the + (add) button for each successive file you want to add to the list. Otherwise, the highlighted file is replaced by the next entry.

5. To remove a file from the Preload Images list, select it and click the – (delete) button.

6. Click OK when you're done.

Here's the browser compatibility chart for the Preload Images behavior:

Preload Image	Netscape 3.x	Internet Explorer 3.0	Internet Explorer 3.01
Macintosh	Okay	Fails without error	
Windows	Okay		Fails without error

Set Nav Bar Image

The Set Nav Bar Image action, like the Jump Menu actions, enables you to edit an existing Dreamweaver object. The Nav Bar object, inserted from the Common category of the Objects panel, consists of a series of user-specified images acting as a group of navigational buttons. The Set Nav Bar Image action enables you to modify the current Nav Bar object, adding, reordering, or deleting images as buttons as well as setting up advanced rollover techniques. In fact, the Set Nav Bar Image action could be thought of as a superduper Swap Image behavior.

Cross-Reference   To refresh your memory about the capabilities of the Nav Bar Image, see Chapter 10.

The main aspect that sets a nav bar apart from any other similar series of rollover images is that the nav bar elements relate to one another. When you select one element of a nav bar, by default, all the other elements are swapped to their up state. The Set Nav Bar Image action enables you to modify that default behavior to a rollover in another area or any other image swap desired. You can also use the Set Nav Bar Image to include another image button in the nav bar.

To modify an existing Nav Bar object, follow these steps:

1. Choose any image in a Nav Bar object.

2. From the Behaviors panel, double-click any of the Set Nav Bar Image actions displayed for the image.

   The same Set Nav Bar Image dialog box (see Figure 15-18) opens regardless of whether you select an action associated with the onClick, onMouseOver, or onMouseOut event.

3. Make any desired edits — changing the Up, Over, Down, or Over While Down state images or their respective URLs or targets — from the Basic tab of the dialog box.

4. To change any other images when the current image is interacted with, select the Advanced tab.

5. On the Advanced tab of the dialog box, choose which state you want to trigger any changes from the drop-down list:

   • Over Image or Over While Down

   • Down State

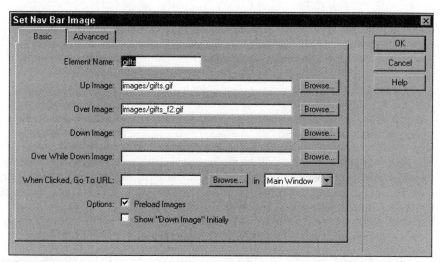

Figure 15-18: Modify an existing Nav Bar element through the Set Nav Bar Image action.

6. Select the image you wish to change from the Also Set Image list.

Dreamweaver lists all the named images on the current page, not just those in the nav bar.

7. Select the path of the new image to be displayed in the To Image Field text field.

An asterisk appears after the current image in the list box, signifying that a swap image has been chosen.

8. If you chose Over Image or Over While Down as the triggering event, an optional field, If Down, enables you to specify another graphic to swap the image of the down state image as well.

9. To alter other images with the same triggering event, repeat Steps 6 through 8.

Here's the browser compatibility chart for the Set Nav Bar Image behavior:

Set Nav Bar Image	Netscape 3.x	Internet Explorer 3.0	Internet Explorer 3.01
Macintosh	Okay	Fails without error	
Windows	Okay		Fails without error

Set Text of Frame

Dreamweaver has grouped together four similar behaviors under the Set Text heading:

✦ Set Text of Frame

✦ Set Text of Layer

✦ Set Text of Status Bar

✦ Set Text of Text Field

Set Text of Frame enables you to do much more than change a word or two — you can dynamically rewrite the entire code for any frame. You can even incorporate JavaScript functions or interactive information into the new frame content.

The Set Text of Frame action replaces all the contents of the <body> tag of a frame. Dreamweaver supplies a handy "Get Current HTML" button that enables you to easily keep everything you want to retain and change only a heading or other element. Naturally, you must be within a frameset to use this behavior, and the frames must be named correctly — that is, uniquely without special characters or spaces.

To change the content of a frame dynamically, follow these steps:

1. Select the triggering object.

2. In the Behaviors panel, choose Set Text ⇨ Set Text of Frame from the Add Behavior list.

The Set Text of Frame dialog box opens as shown in Figure 15-19.

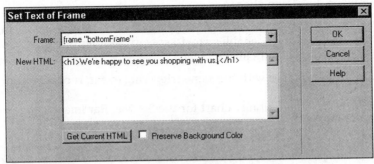

Figure 15-19: The Set Text of Frame behavior enables you to interactively update the contents of any frame in the current frameset.

3. Choose the frame you wish to alter from the Frame option list.

4. Enter the code for the changing frame in the New HTML text area.

Keep in mind that you're changing not just a word or phrase, but all the HTML contained in the <body> section of the frame.

5. If you want to keep the majority of the code, select the Get Current HTML button and change only those portions necessary.

Expert Tip The same JavaScript capabilities outlined in the Popup Message section are available in the Set Text of Frame behavior.

6. To maintain the frames `<body>` attributes, such as the background and text colors, select the Preserve Background Color option.

   If this option is not selected, the frames background and text colors are replaced by the default values (a white background and black text).

7. Click OK when you're done.

Here's the browser compatibility chart for the Set Text of Frame behavior:

Set Text of Frame	Netscape 3.x	Internet Explorer 3.0	Internet Explorer 3.01
Macintosh	Okay	Fails without error	
Windows	Okay		Okay

Set Text of Layer

The Set Text of Layer behavior is similar to the previously described Set Text of Frame behavior in that it replaces the entire HTML contents of the target. The major difference, of course, is that with one you're replacing the code of a layer and with the other, the `<body>` tag of a frame. You're also able to include any valid JavaScript functions within a pair of curly braces, { }, in the HTML code as with other Set Text behaviors. You should also note that, unlike Set Text of Frame, no button exists for getting the current HTML in Set Text of Layer.

To set the text of a layer dynamically, follow these steps:

1. Make sure that the layer you want to change has been created and named properly.

2. Select the tag, link, or image you want to trigger the behavior.

3. From the Behaviors panel, select the add action button and choose Set Text ⇨ Set Text of Layer from the option list.

   The Set Text of Layer dialog box opens, as shown in Figure 15-20.

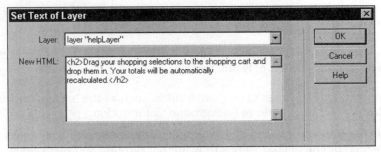

Figure 15-20: Replace all the HTML in a layer with the Set Text of Layer behavior.

4. Select the layer to modify from the Layer option list.

5. Enter the replacement code in the New HTML text area.

Expert Tip   Although no "Get Current HTML" button exists here as with the Set Text of Frame behavior, a workaround does exist. Before invoking the behavior, select and copy all the elements inside the layer. Because Dreamweaver copies tags as well as text in the Document window, you can then just paste the clipboard into the New HTML text area. Be careful not to select the layer tag, <div>, or the layer's contents — if you do, you are pasting a layer in a layer.

6. Click OK when you're done.

Here's the browser compatibility chart for the Set Text of Layer behavior:

Set Text of Layer	Netscape 3.x	Internet Explorer 3.0	Internet Explorer 3.01
Macintosh	Fails without error	Fails without error	
Windows	Fails without error		Fails without error

Set Text of Status Bar

Use the Set Text of Status Bar action to show your choice of text in a browser's status bar, based on a user's action such as moving the pointer over an image. The message stays displayed in the status bar until another message replaces it. System messages, such as URLs, tend to be temporary and visible only when the user's mouse is over a link.

The only limit to the length of the message is the size of the browser's status bar; you should test your message in various browsers to make sure that it is completely visible.

To display a message only when a user's pointer is over an image, use one Set Text of Status Bar action, attached to an `onMouseOver` event, with your associated text. Use another Set Text of Status Bar action, attached to an `onMouseOut` event, that has a null string (a couple of spaces) as the text.

All text is entered in the Set Text of Status Bar parameter form (see Figure 15-21) in the Message text box.

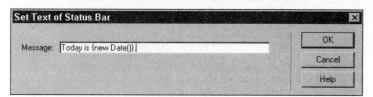

Figure 15-21: Use the Set Text of Status Bar action to guide your users with instructions in the browser window's status bar.

To use the Set Text of Status Bar action, follow these steps:

1. Select the object to trigger the action.

2. From the Behaviors panel, select the add action button and choose Set Text of Status Bar.

 As with the other Set Text behaviors, you can include valid JavaScript functions and variables in the Set Text of Status Bar behavior by offsetting them with curly braces.

3. Enter your text in the Message text box.

4. Click OK when you're done.

Here's the browser compatibility chart for the Set Text of Status Bar behavior:

Set Text of Status Bar	Netscape 3.x	Internet Explorer 3.0	Internet Explorer 3.01
Macintosh	Okay	Fails without error	
Windows	Okay		Okay

Set Text of Text Field

The final Set Text behavior enables you to update any text or textarea field, dynamically. The Set Text of Text Field behavior accepts any text or JavaScript input. (JavaScript functions and variables must be enclosed in a set of curly braces.) A text field must be present on the page for the behavior to be available.

To change the displayed text of a text field, follow these steps:

1. From the Behaviors panel, choose Set Text ⇨ Set Text of Text Field from the Add Action list.

   The Set Text of Text Field dialog box is displayed, as shown in Figure 15-22.

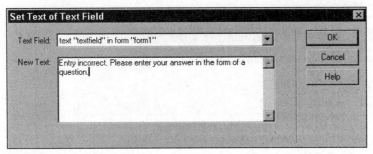

Figure 15-22: Dynamically update text form elements with the Set Text of Text Field behavior.

2. Choose the desired text field from the drop-down list.

3. Enter the new text and/or JavaScript in the New Text area.

4. Click OK when you're done.

Here's the browser compatibility chart for the Set Text of Text Field behavior:

Set Text of Text Field	Netscape 3.x	Internet Explorer 3.0	Internet Explorer 3.01
Macintosh	Okay	Fails without error	
Windows	Okay		Okay

Show-Hide Layers

One of the key features of Dynamic HTML layers is their capability to appear and disappear on command. The Show-Hide Layer action gives you easy control over the visibility attribute for all layers in the current Web page. In addition to explicitly showing or hiding layers, this action can also restore layers to the default visibility setting.

The Show-Hide Layers action typically reveals one layer while concealing another; however, you are not restricted to hiding or showing just one layer at a time. The action's parameter form (see Figure 15-23) shows you a list of all the layers in the current Web page, from which you can choose as many as you want to show or hide.

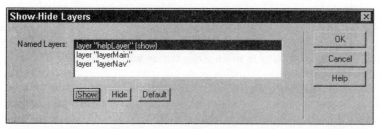

Figure 15-23: The Show-Hide Layers action can make any number of hidden layers visible, hide any number of visible layers, or both.

To use the Show-Hide Layers action, follow these steps:

1. Select the object to trigger the action.

2. From the Behaviors panel, select the add action button and choose Show-Hide Layer.

   When the dialog box opens, the parameter form shows a list of the available layers in the open Web page.

3. To reveal a hidden layer, from the Show-Hide Layer dialog box, select the layer from the Named Layers list and click the Show button.

4. To hide a visible layer, select its name from the list and click the Hide button.

5. To restore a layer's default visibility value, select the layer in the list and click the Default button.

Here's the browser compatibility chart for the Show-Hide Layers behavior:

Show-Hide Layer	*Netscape 3.x*	*Internet Explorer 3.0*	*Internet Explorer 3.01*
Macintosh	Fails without error	Fails without error	
Windows	Fails without error		Fails without error

Swap Image and Swap Image Restore

Button rollovers are one of the most commonly used techniques in Web design today. In a typical button rollover, a user's pointer moves over one image, and the graphic appears to change in some way, seeming to glow or change color. Actually, the onMouseOver event triggers the almost instantaneous swapping of one image for another. Dreamweaver automates this difficult coding task with the Swap Image action and its companion, the Swap Image Restore action.

In recognition of how rollovers most commonly work in the real world, Dreamweaver makes it possible to combine Swap Image and Swap Image Restore in one easy operation—as well as to preload all the images. Moreover, you can use a link in one frame to trigger a rollover in another frame without having to tweak the code as you did in early versions.

When the parameters form for the Swap Image action opens, it automatically loads all the images it finds in the current Web page (see Figure 15-24). You select the image you want to change—which could be the same image to which you are attaching the behavior—and enter the address for the file you want to replace the rolled-over image. You can swap more than one image with each Swap Image action. For example, if you want an entire submenu to change when a user rolls over a particular option, you can use a single Swap Image action to switch all of the sub-menu button images.

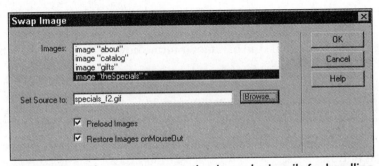

Figure 15-24: The Swap Image action is used primarily for handling button rollovers.

If you choose not to enable the Restore Images `onMouseOut` option, which changes the image back to the original, you need to attach the Swap Image Restore action to another event. The Swap Image Restore action can be used only after a Swap Image action. No parameter form exists for the Swap Image Restore action—just a dialog box confirming your selection.

Note   If the swapped-in image has different dimensions than the image it replaces, the swapped-in image is resized to the height and width of the first image.

To use the Swap Image action, follow these steps:

1. Select the object to trigger the action.

2. From the Behaviors panel, select the add action button and choose Swap Image.

3. In the parameter form, choose an available image from the Named Images list of graphics on the current page.

4. In the Set Source To text box, enter the path to the image that you want to swap in. You can also select the Browse (Choose) button to locate the file.

   An asterisk appears at the end of the selected image name to indicate an alternate image has been selected.

5. To swap additional images using the same event, repeat Steps 3 and 4.

6. To preload all images involved in the Swap Image action when the page loads, make sure the Preload Images option is checked.

7. To cause the selected images to revert to their original source, make sure that the Restore Images onMouseOut option is selected.

8. Click OK when you're done.

Here's the browser compatibility chart for the Swap Image and Swap Image Restore behaviors:

Swap Image and Swap Image Restore	Netscape 3.x	Internet Explorer 3.0	Internet Explorer 3.01
Macintosh	Okay	Fails without error	
Windows	Okay		Fails without error

Timelines: Play Timeline, Stop Timeline, and Go to Timeline Frame

Any Dynamic HTML animation in Dreamweaver happens with timelines, but a timeline can't do anything without the actions written to control it. The three actions in the timeline set — Play Timeline, Stop Timeline, and Go to Timeline Frame — are all you need to set your Web page in motion.

Before the Timeline actions become available, at least one timeline must be on the current page. All three of these related actions are located in the Timeline pop-up menu. Generally, when you are establishing controls for playing a timeline, you first attach the Go to Timeline Frame action to an event and then attach the Play Timeline action to the same event. By setting a specific frame before you enable the timeline to start, you ensure that the timeline always begins at the same point.

Cross-Reference For more detailed information on using timelines, see Chapter 20.

The Play Timeline and Stop Timeline actions have only one element on their parameter form: a drop-down list box offering all timelines in the current page.

The Go to Timeline Frame action's parameter form (see Figure 15-25), aside from enabling you to pick a timeline and enter a specific go-to frame, also gives you the option to loop the timeline a set number of times.

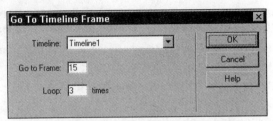

Figure 15-25: Control your timelines through the three Timeline actions. The Go to Timeline Frame parameter form enables you to choose a go-to frame and designate the number of loops for the timeline.

Expert Tip   If you want the timeline to loop an infinite number of times, leave the Loop text box empty and turn on the Loop option in the Timelines panel.

To use the Go to Timeline Frame action, follow these steps:

1. Select the object to trigger the action.

2. From the Behaviors panel, select the add action button and choose Go to Frame.

3. In the dialog box Timeline list, choose the timeline for which you want to set the start frame.

4. Enter the frame number in the Go to Frame text box.

5. If you want the timeline to loop a set number of times, enter a value in the Loop text box.

6. Click OK when you're done.

To use the Play Timeline action, follow these steps:

1. Select an object to trigger the action and then choose Timeline ⇨ Play Timeline from the Add Action pop-up menu in the Behaviors panel.

2. In the parameter form's Timeline list, choose the timeline that you want to play.

To use the Stop Timeline action, follow these steps:

1. Select an object to trigger the action and then choose Timeline ⇨ Stop Timeline from the Add Action pop-up menu in the Behaviors panel.

2. In the parameter form's Timeline list, choose the timeline that you want to stop.

Note   You can also choose All Timelines to stop every timeline on the current Web page from playing.

Here's the browser compatibility chart for the Timeline behaviors:

Timelines: Play Timeline, Stop Timeline, and Go to Timeline Frame	Netscape 3.x	Internet Explorer 3.0	Internet Explorer 3.01
Macintosh	Image source animation and invoking behaviors work, but layer animation fails without error.	Fails without error	
Windows	Image source animation and invoking behaviors work, but layer animation fails without error.		Fails without error

Validate Form

When you set up a form for user input, each field is established with a purpose. The name field, the e-mail address field, the zip code field — each has its own requirements for input. Unless the CGI program is specifically written to check the user's input, forms usually take input of any type. Even if the CGI program can handle it, this server-side method ties up server time and is relatively slow. The Validate Form action checks any text field's input and returns the form to the user if any of the entries are unacceptable. You can also use this action to designate any text field as a required field.

The Validate Form action can be used to check either individual fields or multiple fields for the entire form. Attaching a Validate Form action to an individual text box alerts the user to any errors as the form is being filled out. To check the entire form, the Validate Form action must be linked to the form's Submit button.

The Validate Form dialog box (see Figure 15-26) enables you to designate any text field as required, and you can evaluate its contents. You can require the input of a text field to be a number, an e-mail address (for instance, jdoe@anywhere.com), or a number within a range. The number range you specify can include positive whole numbers, negative numbers, or decimals.

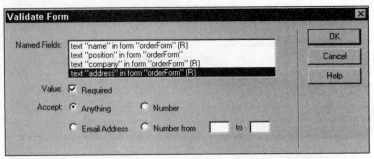

Figure 15-26: The Validate Form action can check your form's entries without CGI programming.

To use the Validate Form action, follow these steps:

1. Select the form object, such as a Submit button or text field, to trigger the action.

Expert Tip You can also attach the Validate Form to a checkbox or radio button, but it's really useful only if you want to require the field.

2. From the Behaviors panel, select the add action button and choose Validate Form.

3. If validating an entire form, select a text field from the Named Fields list.

   If you are validating a single field, the selected form object is chosen for you and appears in the Named Fields list.

4. To make the field required, select the Value: Required checkbox.

5. To set the kind of input expected, choose from one of the following Accept options:

   - **Anything:** Accepts any input.
   - **Number:** Enables any sort of numeric input. You cannot mix text and numbers, however, as in a telephone number such as (212) 555-1212.
   - **Email Address:** Looks for an e-mail address with the @ sign.
   - **Number from:** Enables you to enter two numbers, one in each text box, to define the number range.

6. Click OK when you're done.

Date validation is currently problematic when attempted with Dreamweaver's Validate Form action—you can't enter a date such as "011200" and have it recognize the entry as a number because of the leading zero. For easy date validation, use the Validate Form Plus action included on this book's CD-ROM. If you need more detailed validation, check out the JavaScript Integration Kit for Flash 5, also on the CD-ROM. One of the key components of this extension is a set of 17 validation behaviors that can be used to check form entries in Flash or in a regular HTML page.

Here's the browser compatibility chart for the Validate Form behavior:

Validate Form	Netscape 3.x	Internet Explorer 3.0	Internet Explorer 3.01
Macintosh	Okay	Fails without error	
Windows	Okay		Okay

Managing and Modifying Your Behaviors

The standard behaviors that come with Dreamweaver are indeed impressive, but they're really just the beginning. Because existing behaviors can be modified and new ones created from scratch, you can continue to add behaviors as you need them.

The process of adding a behavior is simplicity itself. Just copy the HTML file to the Configuration\Behaviors\Actions folder and restart Dreamweaver.

If you find that your Add Action pop-up list is starting to get a little unwieldy, you can create subfolders to organize the actions better. When you create a folder within the Actions folder, that subfolder appears on the Add Action pop-up menu as a submenu, as you saw when you worked with the Timelines actions in the preceding section. Figure 15-27 shows a sample arrangement. This example has a subfolder called Beatnik - Advanced and another called Tracks to organize these diverse behaviors from Beatnik. You can even create sub-subfolders to maintain several levels of nested menus.

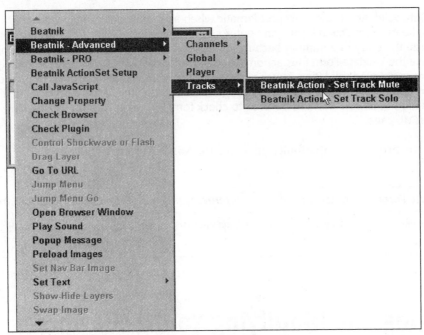

Figure 15-27: To create a new submenu in the Actions pop-up menu, just create a folder in the Actions directory.

Altering the parameters of a behavior

You can alter any of the attributes for your inserted behaviors at any time. To modify a behavior you have already attached, follow these steps:

1. Open the Behaviors panel (go to Window ⇨ Behaviors or click the Show Behaviors button in either Launcher, or press Shift+F3).

2. Select the object in the Document window or the tag in the Tag Selector to which your behavior is attached.

3. Double-click the action that you want to alter. The appropriate dialog box opens, with the previously selected parameters.

4. Make any modifications to the existing settings for the action.

5. Click OK when you are finished.

Sequencing your behaviors

When you have more than one action attached to a particular event, the order of the actions is often important. For example, you should generally implement the Go to Timeline Frame action ahead of the Play Timeline action. To specify the sequence in which Dreamweaver triggers the actions, reposition as necessary in the Actions page by highlighting one and using the up and down arrow buttons to reposition it in the list.

Deleting behaviors

To remove a behavior from your list of actions attached to a particular event, simply highlight the behavior and select the – (delete) button. If the removed behavior is the last action added, the event is also removed from the list; this process occurs after you select any other tag or click anywhere in the Document window.

Summary

Dreamweaver behaviors can greatly extend the Web designer's palette of possibilities — even a Web designer who is an accomplished JavaScript programmer. Behaviors simplify and automate the process of incorporating common, and not so common, JavaScript functions. The versatility of the behavior format enables anyone proficient in JavaScript to create custom actions that can be attached to any event. When considering behaviors, keep the following points in mind:

✦ Behaviors are a combination of events and actions.

✦ Behaviors are written in HTML and are completely customizable from within Dreamweaver.

✦ Different browsers support different events. Dreamweaver enables you to select a specific browser or a browser range, such as all 4.0 browsers, on which to base your event choice.

✦ Dreamweaver includes 25 standard actions. Some actions are not available unless a particular object is included on the current page.

✦   ✦   ✦

Adding Multimedia Elements to Dreamweaver

Fireworks Integration

Imagine demonstrating a newly completed Web site to a client who *didn't* ask for an image to be a little bigger, or the text on a button to be reworded, or the colors for the background to be revised. In the real world, Web sites — particularly the images — are constantly being tweaked and modified. This fact of Web life explains why Fireworks, Macromedia's premier Web graphics tool, is so popular. One of Fireworks' main claims to fame is that everything is editable all the time. If that were all that Fireworks did, the program would have already earned a place on every Web designer's shelf just for its sheer expediency. But Fireworks is far more capable a tool — and now, that power can be tapped directly in Dreamweaver.

With the release of Dreamweaver 4 and Fireworks 4, an even greater level of integration between the two Macromedia products has been achieved. You can optimize your images — reduce the file size, crop the graphic, and make colors transparent — within Dreamweaver using the Fireworks inter-face. Moreover, you can edit your image in any fashion in Fireworks and, with one click of the Update command, auto-matically export the graphic with its original export settings. Perhaps most importantly, now Dreamweaver can control Fireworks — creating graphics on the fly — and then insert the results in Dreamweaver.

A key Fireworks feature is its capability to output HTML and JavaScript for easy creation of rollovers, sliced images, and image maps with behaviors. With Fireworks, you can specify Dreamweaver-style code, so that all your Web pages are consistent. Once HTML is generated within Fireworks, Dreamweaver's Insert Fireworks HTML object makes code insertion effortless. Dreamweaver now recognizes images — whether whole or sliced — as coming from Fireworks and dis-plays a special Property Inspector.

Web pages and Web graphics are closely tied to one another. With the tight integration between Dreamweaver and Fireworks, the Web designer's world is moving toward a single design environment.

Easy Graphics Modification

It's not uncommon for graphics to need some alteration before they fully integrate into a Web design. In fact, I'd say it's far more the rule than the exception. The traditional workflow generally goes like this:

1. Create the image in one or more graphics-editing programs.

2. Place the new graphic on a Web page via your Web authoring tool.

3. Note where the problems lie — perhaps the image is too big or too small, maybe the drop shadow doesn't blend into the background properly, or maybe the whole image needs to be flipped.

4. Reopen the graphics program, make the modifications, and save the file again.

5. Return to the Web page layout to view the results.

6. Repeat Steps 3 through 5 ad infinitum until you get it right.

Although you're still using two different programs even with Dreamweaver and Fireworks integration, there is a feature that enables you to open a Fireworks window on the Dreamweaver screen: Optimize Image in Fireworks. Now you can make your alterations with the Web page noticeable in the background. I've found that this small advantage cuts my trial-and-error to a bare minimum and streamlines my workflow.

If you're not familiar with Fireworks, you're missing an extremely powerful graphics program made for the Web. Fireworks combines the best of both vector and bitmap technologies and was one of the first graphics programs to use PNG as its native format. Exceptional export capabilities are available in Fireworks with which images can be optimized for file size, color, and scale. Moreover, Fireworks is terrific at generating GIF animations, rollovers, image maps, and sliced images.

With the latest versions of Dreamweaver and Fireworks, you have two ways to alter your inserted graphics: the Optimize Image in Fireworks command and the Edit button in the Image Property Inspector.

Note
The full integration described in this chapter requires that Fireworks 4 be installed after Dreamweaver 4. Certain features, such as the Optimize Image in Fireworks command, work with Dreamweaver 4 and Fireworks 2 and above, but any others requiring direct communication between the two programs work only with Fireworks 4.

Optimizing an image in Fireworks

Although you can design the most beautiful, compelling image possible in your graphics program, if it's intended for the Internet, you need to view it in a Web page. Not only must the graphic work in the context of the entire page, but the file size of the Web graphic must also be taken into account. All these factors mean that most, if not all, images need to undergo some degree of modification once they're included in a Web page. Fireworks makes these alterations as straightforward as possible by including a command for Dreamweaver during its installation.

The Optimize Image in Fireworks command opens the Export module of Fireworks, as shown in Figure 16-1, right in Dreamweaver's Document window.

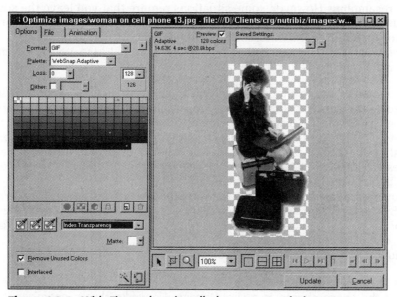

Figure 26-1: With Fireworks 4 installed, you can optimize your images from within Dreamweaver.

The Export module consists of three tabbed panels: Options, File, and Animation. Although a complete description of all of its features is beyond the scope of this book, here's a breakdown of the major uses of each area:

✦ **Options:** The Options panel is primarily used to try different export options and preview them. You can switch file formats from GIF to JPEG (or Animated GIF or PNG) as well as alter the palette, color depth, and dithering. Transparency for GIF and PNG images is set in the Options panel. Fireworks also has an Export to Size wizard that enables you to target a particular file size for your graphic.

✦ **File:** An image's dimensions are defined in the File panel. Images can be rescaled by a selected percentage or pixel size. Moreover, you can crop your image either numerically — by defining the export area — or visually with the Cropping tool.

✦ **Animation:** Frame-by-frame control for animated GIFs is available on the Animation panel. Each frame's *delay* (how long it is onscreen) is capable of being defined independently, and the entire animation can be set to either play once or loop a user-determined number of times.

Note If you crop or rescale an inserted image in Fireworks, you need to update the height and width in Dreamweaver. The easiest way to accomplish this is to select the Refresh button in the image's Property Inspector.

Fireworks saves its source files in an expanded PNG format to maintain full editability of the images. Graphics for the Web must be exported from Fireworks in GIF, JPEG, or standard PNG format. Dreamweaver's Optimize Image in Fireworks command can modify either the source or exported file. In most situations, better results are achieved from using the source file, especially when optimizing includes rescaling or resampling. However, some situations require that you leave the source file as is and modify only the exported files. Let's say, for example, that one source file is used to generate several different export files, each with different backgrounds (or *canvases*, as they are called in Fireworks). In that case, you'd be better off modifying the specific exported file rather than the general source image.

Dreamweaver enables you to choose which type of image you'd like to modify. When you first execute the Optimize Image in Fireworks or the Edit Image command, a Find Source dialog box (Figure 16-2) appears. If you want to locate and use the source file, choose Yes; to use the exported image that is inserted in Dreamweaver, select No. If you opt for the source file — and the image was created in Fireworks — Dreamweaver reads the Design Note associated with the image to find the location of the source file and open it. If the image was created with an earlier version of Fireworks or the image has been moved, Dreamweaver asks you to locate the file with a standard Open File dialog box. By setting the Fireworks Source Files option, you can always open the same type of file: source or exported. Should you change your mind about how you'd like to work, open Fireworks and select Edit ➪ Preferences, and then choose the desired option from the Launch and Edit category.

Note There's one exception to Fireworks always following your Launch and Edit preferences. If the image chosen is a sliced image, Fireworks always optimizes the exported file rather than the source, regardless of your settings.

```
┌─ Find Source ────────────────────────────────────────── ☒ ┐
│ Optimizing '"'woman on cell phone 13.jpg'"'.        ┌─────────┐│
│                                                     │   Yes   ││
│ Do you wish to use an existing Fireworks document   └─────────┘│
│ as the source of                                    ┌─────────┐│
│ '"'woman on cell phone 13.jpg'"'?                   │   No    ││
│                                                     └─────────┘│
│ To skip the dialog, choose from the popup below.  This setting can also be │
│ found in the Preferences dialog                               │
│                                                               │
│ Fireworks Source Files:                                       │
│ ┌───────────────────────────────────────────────────┬───┐    │
│ │ Ask When Launching                                │ ▼ │    │
│ └───────────────────────────────────────────────────┴───┘    │
└───────────────────────────────────────────────────────────────┘
```

Figure 16-2: Set the Find Source dialog box to always use the source graphics image or the exported image, or to choose from a popup menu for each optimization.

Exploring Fireworks Source and Export Files

The separate source file is an important concept in Fireworks, and its use is strongly advised. Generally, when working in Fireworks, there is a minimum of two files for every image output to the Web: your source file and your exported Web image. Whenever major alterations are made, it's best to make them to the source file and then update the export files. Not only is this an easier method of working, but also you get a better image this way.

Source files are always Fireworks-style PNG files. Fireworks-style PNG files differ slightly from regular PNG format because they include additional information, such as paths and effects used that can be read only by Fireworks. The exported file is usually in GIF or JPEG format, although it could be in standard PNG format. Many Web designers keep their source files in a separate folder from their exported Web images so the two don't get confused. This source-and-export file combination also prevents you from inadvertently re-editing a lossy compressed file such as a JPEG image and reapplying the compression.

To use the Optimize Image in Fireworks command, follow these steps:

1. In Dreamweaver, select the image that you'd like to modify.

Note You must save the current page at least once before running the Optimize Image in Fireworks command. The current state of the page doesn't have to have been saved, but a valid file must exist for the command to work properly. If you haven't saved the file, Dreamweaver alerts you to this fact when you call the command.

2. Choose Commands ⇨ Optimize Image in Fireworks.

Tip You can also invoke the Optimize Image in Fireworks command from the context menu—just right-click (Control+click) on the image.

3. If your Fireworks Preferences are set to ask whether a source file should be used in editing, the Find Source dialog box opens. Choose Yes to use the PNG format source file and No to work with the exported file.

   The Optimize Images dialog box appears.

4. Make whatever modifications are desired from the Options, File, or Animation tabs of the Optimize Images dialog box.

5. When you're finished, select the Update button.

Note If you're working with a Fireworks source file, the changes are saved to both your source file and exported file; otherwise, only the exported file is altered.

Editing an image in Fireworks

Optimizing an image is great when all you need to do is tweak the file size or to rescale the image. Other images require more detailed modification — as when a client requests that the wording or order of a series of navigational buttons be changed. Dreamweaver enables you to specify Fireworks as your graphics editor; and if you've done so, you can take advantage of Fireworks' capability to keep every element of your graphic always editable. And believe me, this is a major advantage.

In Dreamweaver, external editors can be set for any file format; you can even assign more than one editor to a file type. When installing the Dreamweaver/Fireworks Studio, Fireworks is preset as the primary external editor for GIF, JPEG, and PNG files. If Fireworks is installed outside of the Studio setup, the external editor assignment is handled through Dreamweaver Preferences.

To assign Fireworks to an existing file type, follow these steps:

1. Choose Edit ⇨ Preferences.

2. Select the External Editors category.

3. Select the file type (GIF, JPEG, or PNG) from the Extensions list as shown in Figure 16-3.

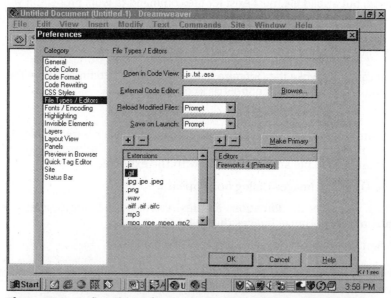

Figure 16-3: Define Fireworks as your External Editor for GIF, JPEG, and PNG files to enable the back-and-forth interaction between Dreamweaver and Fireworks.

4. Click the Add (+) button above the Editors list. The Add External Editor dialog box opens.

5. Locate the editor application and click Open when you're ready.

Note The default location in Windows systems is in C:\Program Files\Macromedia\ Fireworks 4\Fireworks 4.exe; on the Macintosh it's Macintosh HD:Applications: Fireworks 4:Fireworks 4. (The .exe extension may or may not be visible in your Windows system.)

6. Click Make Primary while the editor is highlighted.

Now, whenever you want to edit a graphic, select the image and click the Edit button in the Property Inspector. You can also right-click (Control+click) the image and select Edit Image to start editing it. Fireworks starts up, if it's not already open. As with the Optimize Image in Fireworks command, if the inserted image is a GIF or a JPEG and not a PNG format, Fireworks asks if you'd like to work with a separate source file, if that option in Fireworks Preferences is set. If so, Fireworks automatically loads the source file.

When the image opens in Fireworks, the graphic's window indicates that this particular graphic is being edited from Dreamweaver in Fireworks as shown in Figure 16-4. In the same title bar, a Done button is available for completing the operation after you've made your alterations to your file in Fireworks. Alternatively, you can choose File⇨ Update or use the keyboard shortcut Ctrl+S (Command+S). If you're working with a Fireworks source file, both the source file and the exported file are updated and saved.

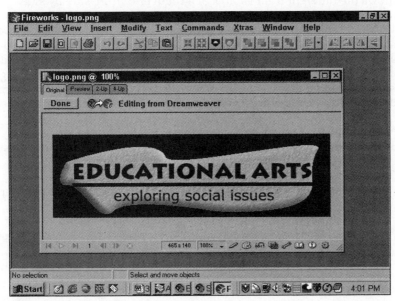

Figure 16-4: Fireworks now graphically depicts where the current image being edited is from.

Inserting Rollovers

The rollover is a fairly common, but effective, Web technique that you can use to indicate interactivity. Named after the user action of "rolling the mouse pointer over" the graphic, this technique uses from two to four different images per button. With Fireworks, you can both create the graphics and output the necessary HTML and JavaScript code from the same program. Moreover, Fireworks has some sophisticated twists to the standard "on/off" rollovers to further easily enhance your Web page.

Rollovers created in Fireworks can be inserted into Dreamweaver through several methods. First, you can use Fireworks to just build the images and then export them and attach the behaviors in Dreamweaver. This technique works well for graphics going into layers or images with other attached behaviors. The second method of integrating Fireworks-created rollovers involves transferring the actual code generated by Fireworks into Dreamweaver — a procedure that can be handled with one command: Insert Fireworks HTML.

Using Dreamweaver's behaviors

With its full-spectrum editability, Fireworks excels at building consistent rollover graphics simply. The different possible states of an image in a rollover — Up, Over, Down, and Over While Down — are handled in Fireworks as separate frames. As with an animated GIF, each frame has the same dimensions as the document, but the content is slightly altered to indicate the separate user actions. For example, Figure 16-5 shows the different frame states of a rollover button, side by side.

Note   Many Web designers use just the initial two states — Up and Over — in their rollover buttons. The third state, Down, takes place when the user clicks the button, and it is useful if you want to indicate that moment to the user. The Down state also indicates which button has been selected (which is "down") when a new page appears, but the same navigation bar is used, notably with frames. The fourth state, Over While Down, is called when the previously selected button is rolled over by the user's pointer.

To insert Fireworks-created graphics using Dreamweaver behaviors, follow these steps:

1. Create your graphics in Fireworks, using a different frame for each rollover state.

Caution   You cannot use Fireworks's Insert ➪ New Button command to build your button for this technique because the separate states are now stored as frames.

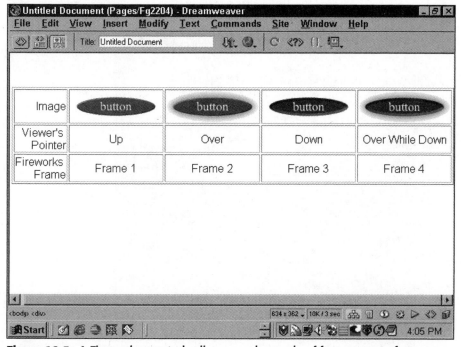

Figure 16-5: A Fireworks-created rollover can be made of four separate frames.

2. In Fireworks, choose File ⇨ Export. The Export dialog box opens (see Figure 16-6).

3. Enter a new filename in the Base Name text box, if desired.

   In this operation, Fireworks uses the filename as a base name to identify multiple images exported from a single file. When exporting frames, the default settings append "_fn", where n is the number of the frame. Frame numbers 1 to 9 are listed with a leading zero (for example, MainButton_f01).

4. In the Save As Type list box, select Frames to Files.

5. If desired, select the Trim Images option. I recommend that the default practice be to trim your images when exporting frames as files. This option results in smaller, more flexible files.

6. Select the Save button to store your frames as separate files.

Note You can attach the rollover behaviors to your images in several ways in Dreamweaver. The following technique uses Dreamweaver's Rollover object.

Figure 16-6: From Fireworks, you can export each frame as a separate file to be used in Dreamweaver rollovers.

7. From the Common panel of the Objects palette, choose the Insert Rollover Image object.

8. In the Insert Rollover Image dialog box, choose the Original Image Browse (Choose) button to locate the image stored with the first frame designation, _f01.

9. If desired, give your image a different unique name than the one automatically assigned in the Image Name text box.

10. Choose the Rollover Image Browse button to locate the image stored with the second frame designation, _f02.

11. Click OK when you're done.

12. If you'd like to use the Down (_F03) and Over While Down (_F04) images, attach additional swap image behaviors by opening the Swap Image behavior and following the steps outlined in Chapter 15.

Note Many Web designers build their entire navigation bar — complete with rollovers — in Fireworks. Rather than create and export one button at a time, all the navigation buttons are created as one graphic, and slices or hotspots are used to make the different objects or areas interact differently. You learn more about slices and hotspots later in this chapter under "Using Fireworks' Code."

Using Fireworks' code

In some ways, Fireworks is a hybrid program, capable of simultaneously outputting terrific graphics and sophisticated code. You can even select the type of code you want generated in Fireworks 4: Dreamweaver; Dreamweaver Library compatible; or code compatible with other programs such as GoLive and FrontPage. You'll also find a Generic code option. You can choose these options during the Export procedure.

For rollovers, Fireworks generally outputs to two different sections of the HTML document, the <head> and the <body>; only the FrontPage style keeps all the code together. The <head> section contains the JavaScript code for activating the rollovers and preloading the images; <body> contains the HTML references to the images themselves, their links, and the event triggers (onClick or onMouseOver) used.

The general procedure is to first create your graphics in Fireworks and then export them, simultaneously generating a page of code. Now, the just-generated Fireworks HTML page can be incorporated in Dreamweaver. Dreamweaver includes two slick methods for including your Fireworks-output code and images. The Insert Fireworks HTML object places the code — and the linked images — right at your current cursor position. You also have the option of exporting your Fireworks HTML directly to the clipboard and pasting it, verbatim, into Dreamweaver.Just as an image requires a link to create a rollover in Dreamweaver, Fireworks images need to be designated as either a *slice* or a *hotspot*. Slices are rectangular areas that permit different areas of the same graphic to be saved as separate formats — the entire graphic is formatted as an HTML table. Each slice can also be given its own URL; Fireworks requires either slices or hotspots to attach behaviors.

A Fireworks *hotspot* is a region defined for an image map. Hotspots can be rectangular, elliptical, or polygonal — just like those created by Dreamweaver by using the Image Map tools. Because Fireworks is an object-oriented graphics program, any selected image (or part of an image) can be automatically converted to a hotspot. Like slices, hotspots can have both URLs and behaviors assigned to them.

The Fireworks program describes slices and hotspots as being part of the graphic's Web layer. The Web layer can be hidden or locked, but not deleted. Figure 16-7 shows the same button with both a slice and a hotspot attached.

Figure 16-7: The Fireworks image on the left uses a slice object, whereas the image on the right uses a polygon hotspot.

Note   In addition to the technique outlined in the text that follows, you could also use Fireworks's Button Editor (available by choosing Insert ➪ New Button) to create your rollover images and behaviors.

To include Fireworks-generated code in your Dreamweaver document, first follow these steps in Fireworks:

1. Create your graphics in Fireworks, placing the image for each interactive state on its own frame.

2. When the object is selected, choose Insert ➪ Hotspot or Insert ➪ Slice to add the item to your Web layer for attaching behaviors. Alternatively, you can use any of the Hotspot or Slice tools found in the Fireworks toolbox.

3. Select the hotspot or slice and use Fireworks' Object Inspector to assign an Internet address to the selected graphic.

4. Click the target symbol displayed in the center of the hotspot or hotspot to display a menu of available behaviors. Alternatively, you could open Fireworks' Behavior Inspector and choose the Add Behavior button (the + sign).

5. Select Simple Rollover.

Tip

The Simple Rollover behavior is used to create single-button or multiple-button rollovers in which one image is replaced by another image in the same location; only two frames are used for a Simple Rollover. Use Swap Image to create more complex rollovers such as those in which the rollover triggers an image change in another location. A third alternative, Nav Bar, should be used in situations where the navigation system is to be placed in a frameset; Nav Bar can hold all four states (Up, Over, Down, and Over While Down).

6. Export the object by choosing File ⇨ Export.

7. From the Export dialog box, enter a name in the filename text box and make sure HTML and Images is displayed in the Save as Type drop-down list.

   If you intend to use the graphics in several places on your site, choose Dreamweaver Library (*.lbi) from the Save as Type list.

8. To change the type of HTML code generated, choose the Options button and make a choice from the Style drop-down list.

   Dreamweaver code is the default Style; other options include GoLive, FrontPage, and Generic.

9. Choose the location to store your HTML code by navigating to the desired folder. Note that Dreamweaver 4 Library code must be saved in a site's Library folder.

   If you'd prefer to not save your HTML, choose Copy to Clipboard from the HTML drop-down list.

10. To save your graphics in a separate folder, select the Put Images in Subfolder option.

Caution

Fireworks defaults to placing the graphics in the images subfolder, even if one does not exist. Select a folder by choosing Browse.

11. Click Export when you're done.

When Fireworks completes the exporting, you have one HTML file (unless you've chosen the Copy to Clipboard option) and one object file for each slice and frame. Now you're ready to integrate these images and the code into your Dreamweaver page. Which method you use depends on the HTML style selected when the graphics were exported from Fireworks:

✦ If you chose Dreamweaver, use the Insert Fireworks HTML object.

✦ If you chose Dreamweaver Library, open the Library palette in Dreamweaver and insert the corresponding Library item.

✦ If you chose Copy to Clipboard, position your cursor where you'd like the graphics to appear and select Edit ⇨ Paste or press Ctrl+V (Command+V).

Both the Library and Clipboard methods are one-step, self-explanatory techniques — and the Insert Fireworks HTML is hardly more complex. To insert the

Fireworks code and images into your Dreamweaver page using the Insert Fireworks HTML object, follow these steps:

1. Make sure that you've exported your graphics and HTML from Fireworks with Dreamweaver HTML Style selected.

2. Select the Insert Fireworks HTML object from the Common panel of the Objects palette or choose Insert ⇨ Interactive Media ⇨ Fireworks HTML.

   The Insert Fireworks HTML dialog box, shown in Figure 16-8, appears.

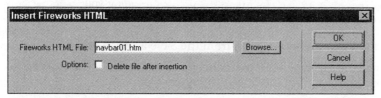

Figure 16-8: Import Fireworks code directly into Dreamweaver with the Insert Fireworks HTML object.

3. If you want to remove the Fireworks-generated HTML file after the code is inserted, select the Delete file after insertion option.

4. Enter the path to the Fireworks HTML file or select the Browse button to locate the file.

5. Click OK when you're done. Dreamweaver inserts the Fireworks HTML and graphics at the current cursor location.

Note   If you're a hands-on kind of Web designer, you can also use the HTML Inspector to copy and paste the JavaScript and HTML code. If you do, you can find helpful comments in the Fireworks file such as "Begin copying here" and "Stop copying here."

All the methods for inserting Fireworks HTML work with images with either hotspots or sliced objects (or both), with or without behaviors attached.

Modifying sliced images

Placing sliced images on your Web page couldn't be simpler, thanks to the Insert Fireworks HTML command. But, like standard nonsliced graphics, sliced images often need to be modified. One technique that many designers use is to create a framing graphic that encompasses HTML text; in Fireworks, a sliced area designated as a text slice can hold any HTML content. Text is often modified, and if it's in a framing graphic, that could mean that the images need to be changed or the table will separate making the separate slices apparent.

New Feature   In Dreamweaver 4, sliced images from Fireworks are recognized as a Fireworks Table and may be modified through a dedicated Property Inspector.

The Fireworks Table Property Inspector shown in Figure 16-9 displays the PNG source file and an Edit button for sending the entire table back to Fireworks for alterations. As with nonsliced graphics, select Done from the document title bar in Fireworks when your modifications are complete to update the source and exported files. The newly exported images are then reloaded into Dreamweaver.

Caution   While Fireworks attempts to honor any changes that you make to the HTML table, certain alterations may result in Fireworks overwriting your table. If, for example, you add or remove one or more cells from the table in Dreamweaver, Fireworks recognizes that the tables no longer match. An alert is displayed indicating that Fireworks will replace the table in Dreamweaver. To keep your table the same in Dreamweaver, make no changes in Fireworks and select Done.

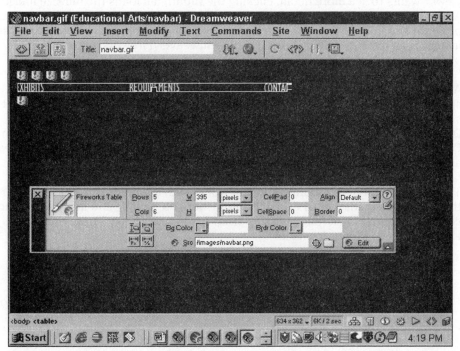

Figure 16-9: Modify sliced graphics by first selecting the surrounding table and then choosing Edit from the Fireworks Table Property Inspector.

Controlling Fireworks with Dreamweaver

Dreamweaver and Fireworks integration extends deeper than just the simplified insertion of code and graphics. Dreamweaver can communicate directly with Fireworks, driving it to execute commands and return custom-generated graphics. This facility enables Web designers to build their Web page images based on the existing content. This interprogram communication promises to streamline the work of the Webmaster — and that promise is already beginning to come through with existing Dreamweaver commands.

Web photo album

Online catalogs and other sites often depend on imagery to sell their products. Full-scale product shots can be large and time-consuming to download, so it's not uncommon for Web designers to display a thumbnail of the images instead. If the viewer wants to see more detail, clicking the thumbnail loads the full-size image. Although it's not difficult to save a scaled-down version of an image in a graphics program and link the two in a Web layout program, creating page after page of such images is an overwhelming chore. The Dreamweaver/Fireworks interoperability offers a way to automate this tedious task.

A new Dreamweaver command, Create Web Photo Album, examines any user-specified folder of images and then uses Fireworks to scale the graphics to a set size. When the scaling is completed, the thumbnail graphics are brought into a Dreamweaver table, complete with links to a series of pages with the full-size image. Create Web Photo Album is an excellent example of the potential that Dreamweaver and Fireworks intercommunication offers.

The Create Web Photo Album command works with a folder of images in any format that Fireworks reads: GIF, JPEG, TIFF, Photoshop, PICT, BMP, and more. The images can be scaled to fit in a range of sizes, from 36×36 to 200×200. These thumbnails are exported in one of four formats:

- ✦ **GIF WebSnap 128:** Uses the WebSnap Adaptive palette, which is limited to 128 colors or fewer
- ✦ **GIF WebSnap 256:** Same as preceding format but with as many as 256 colors available
- ✦ **JPEG Better Quality:** Sets the JPEG quality setting at 80 percent with no smoothing
- ✦ **JPEG Smaller File:** Sets the JPEG quality setting at 60 percent with a smoothing value of 2

The images are also exported in one of the same four settings, at a user-selected scale; the default scale is 100 percent.

To create a thumbnail gallery using Create Web Photo Album, follow these steps:

1. Choose Commands ⇨ Create Web Photo Album.

   The Create Web Photo Album dialog box appears, as shown in Figure 16-10.

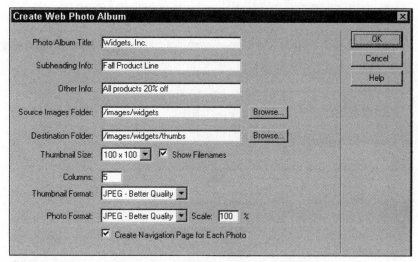

Figure 16-10: Use the Creat Web Photo Album dialog box to build a thumbnail gallery page, linked to full-size orignals.

2. Enter the Photo Album Title, Subheading Info, and Other Info into their respective text fields, if desired.

3. Enter the path to the folder of source images or select the Browse (Choose) button to locate the folder in the Source Images Folder field.

4. Enter the path to the Destination Folder or select the Browse (Choose) button to locate the folder in its field.

   Dreamweaver creates up to three subfolders in the Destination Folder: one for the original, rescaled images, another for the thumbnail images, and a third for the HTML pages created.

5. Select the desired thumbnail size from the drop-down list with the following options: 36×36, 72×72, 100×100, 144×144, and 200×200.

6. Select the Show Filenames option if you want the file name to appear below the image.

7. Choose the number of Columns for the table.

8. Select the export settings for the thumbnail images from the Thumbnail Format option list.

9. Select the export settings for the linked large-sized images from the Photo Format option list.

10. Choose the size of the linked large-sized images in the Scale field.

11. Select the Create Navigation Page for Each Photo option, if desired. Each photo's navigation page includes links to the Next and Previous images as well as the Home (main thumbnail) page, as shown in Figure 16-11.

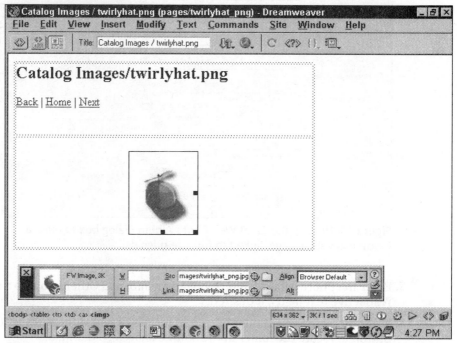

Figure 16-11: You can add simple, clear navigation options to your Web Photo Album.

12. Click OK when you're done.

If Fireworks is not open, the program launches and begins processing the images. When all the images are created and exported, Fireworks returns control to Dreamweaver. Dreamweaver then creates a single HTML page with the title, sub-heading, and other information at the top, followed by a borderless table. As shown in Figure 16-12, each image is rescaled proportionately to fit within the limits set in the dialog box.

Custom Graphic Makers: Convert Text to Graphics and Convert Bullets to Graphics

Excited by the potential of Dreamweaver and Fireworks communication, I built two custom extensions that I originally called StyleBuilder and BulletBuilder. Macromedia took these extensions, enhanced them, and then released them as two-thirds of the InstaGraphics Extensions. StyleBuilder — now called Convert Text to Graphics — enables you to convert any standard text in your Dreamweaver Web page to a graphic. The command converts all text in a standard HTML tag, such as <h1> or <b>, any custom XML tag, or any selection. The graphics are based on Fireworks styles, displayed in a small swatch in the dialog box; you can specify a font on your system as well as a text size to be used. Fireworks styles can be updated at any time, and the swatch set recreated on the fly in Fireworks.

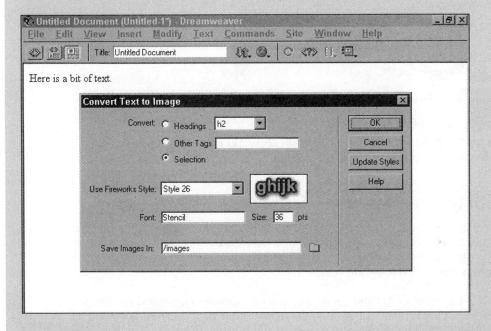

Convert Bullets to Graphics (nee BulletBuilder) is similar to Convert Text to Graphics, but instead of changing text to graphics, this command converts the bullets of an unordered list to different graphic shapes. Choose from 10 different shapes, including diamonds, stars, starbursts, and 4 different triangles. The chosen shape is rendered in any available Fireworks style at a user-selected size. You have the option to convert the current bullet list or all such lists on the page.

You can find both commands in the Additional Extensions folder on the CD-ROM that accompanies this book or online at the Dreamweaver Exchange.

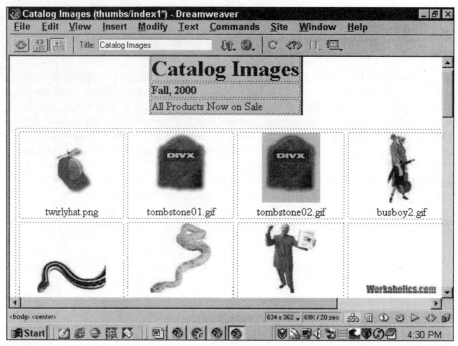

Figure 16-12: Build a thumbnail gallery with Fireworks right from Dreamweaver with the Create Web Photo Album command.

Building Dreamweaver/Fireworks extensions

To make communication between Dreamweaver and Fireworks viable, two conditions had to be met. First, Fireworks had to be scriptable. Second, a link between the two programs needed to be forged. The Dreamweaver 4/Fireworks 4 combination meets both criteria — and then some.

As with Dreamweaver 4, almost every operation is under command control in Fireworks 4. This is most apparent when using either program's History palette. If your action appears as a repeatable item in the History palette, a corresponding JavaScript function controls it. Fireworks' wealth of JavaScript functions also serves to expose its control to Dreamweaver — and the first condition for interoperability is handled. To create a strong link between programs, Dreamweaver engineers expanded on the Fireworks API used in the Optimize Image in Fireworks command, where Dreamweaver actually launches a streamlined version of Fireworks. This operation is controlled by a C-level extension called FWLaunch.

Here's a step-by-step description of how Dreamweaver is typically used to communicate with Fireworks:

1. The user selects a command in Dreamweaver.

2. Dreamweaver opens a dialog box, as with other extensions.

3. After the user has filled in the dialog box and clicked OK, the command begins to execute.

4. All user-supplied parameters are read and used to create a JavaScript scriptlet or function, which serve as instructions for Fireworks.

5. If used, the scriptlet is stored on the disk.

6. Fireworks is launched with a command to run the Dreamweaver-created scriptlet or function.

7. Fireworks processes the scriptlet or function, while Dreamweaver tracks its progress via a cookie on the user's machine.

8. Once Fireworks is finished, a positive result is returned. The Fireworks API includes several error codes if problems such as a full disk are encountered.

9. While tracking the Fireworks progress, Dreamweaver sees the positive result and integrates the graphics by rewriting the DOM of the current page.

10. The dialog box is closed, and the current page is refreshed to correctly present the finished product.

To successfully control Fireworks, you need a complete understanding of the Fireworks DOM and its extension capabilities. Macromedia provides documentation for extending Fireworks at its support site: www.macromedia.com/support/fireworks.

Tip   I've also found the History palette in Fireworks to be useful — especially the Copy Command to Clipboard function. To see the underlying JavaScript used to create an object in Fireworks, first make the object. Then highlight the History palette steps and select the Copy to Clipboard button. Paste the clipboard contents in a text editor to see the exact steps Fireworks used; you can then begin to generalize the statements with variables and other functions.

On the Dreamweaver side, six useful methods are in the FWLaunch C Library. Table 16-1 details the methods.

Table 16-1
FWLaunch Methods

Method	Returns	Use
bringDWToFront()	N/A	Brings the Dreamweaver window in front of any other application running.
bringFWToFront()	N/A	Brings the Fireworks window in front of any other application running.
execJsInFireworks (javascriptOrFileURL)	Result from running the scriptlet in Fireworks. If the operation fails, returns an error code: 1: The argument proves invalid 2: File I/O error 3: Improper version of Dreamweaver 4: Improper version of Fireworks 5: User canceled operation	Executes the supplied JavaScript function or scriptlet.
mayLaunchFireworks()	Boolean	Determines whether Fireworks may be launched.
optimizeInFireworks (fileURL, docURL, {targetWidth}, {targetHeight})	Result from running the scriptlet in Fireworks. If the operation fails, returns an error code: 1: The argument proves invalid 2: File I/O error 3: Improper version of Dreamweaver 4: Improper version of Fireworks 5: User canceled operation	Performs an Optimize in Fireworks operation, opening the Fireworks Export Preview dialog box.
validateFireworks (versionNumber)	Boolean	Determines if the user has a specific version of Fireworks.

Summary

Creating Web pages is almost never done with a single application: In addition to a Web layout program, you need a program capable of outputting Web graphics — and Fireworks is a world-class Web graphics generator and optimizer. Macromedia has integrated several functions with Dreamweaver and Fireworks to streamline production and ease modification. Here are some of the key features of the integration:

✦ You can update images placed in Dreamweaver with Fireworks in two ways: Optimize or Edit. With the Optimize Image in Fireworks command, just the Export Preview portion of Fireworks opens; with the Edit Image command, the full version of Fireworks is run.

✦ Graphics and HTML exported from Fireworks can be incorporated into a Dreamweaver page in numerous ways: as a Library item, an HTML file (complete with behavior code), or just pasted from the clipboard.

✦ New interapplication communication between Dreamweaver and Fireworks makes commands such as Create Web Photo Album possible.

✦ Dreamweaver includes a special C-level extension called FWLaunch, which provides the primary link to Fireworks.

In the next chapter, you see how you can add downloaded or streaming video to your Dreamweaver-created Web pages.

✦　　✦　　✦

Inserting Flash and Shockwave Elements

Animated splash screens, sound-enabled banners, button bars with special fonts, and other exciting Web elements are often built with Macromedia's Flash. Flash combines vector graphics and streaming audio into great-looking, super–low bandwidth files that can be viewed in a browser using the Flash player plug-in. Flash's vector graphics have also turned out to be just the thing for Web-based cartoons. Beginning with version 4, Flash gained its own scripting language, ActionScript, and added MP3 compression to its streaming audio. With a huge base of installed players — as of this writing, well over 90 percent of browsers can view basic Flash content — Flash is an excellent way to liven up a Web page.

But Flash is not Macromedia's only solution for building interactive presentations for the Web. To many Web designers, Shockwave has represented the state of the art in Web interactivity since Macromedia first created the format in 1995. With Shockwave, multimedia files created in Macromedia's flagship authoring package, Director, can be compiled to run in a browser window. This gives Web designers the capability to build just about anything — from interactive Web interfaces with buttons that look indented when pushed, to arcade-style games, multimedia Web front-ends, and complete Web sites built entirely in Director — bringing a CD-ROM "look and feel" to the Web. Today, Shockwave continues to be an important force on the Web, as the enormous success of Macromedia's Shockwave.com amply demonstrates.

The final component in Macromedia's vector-graphic tool chest is a server-side technology called Generator. Generator works with templates built in Flash to display customized graphics, built on-demand. In its initial release, Generator was available only to designers working on big-budget, high-end sites and did not gain a sizeable foothold in the market.

However, Macromedia has recently changed its pricing policy on Generator and made the technology much more accessible to developers.

As you might expect, Macromedia makes it easy to incorporate Shockwave, Flash and Generator files into your Dreamweaver projects. All of these formats have special objects that provide control over virtually all of their parameters through the Property Inspector — and each format is cross-browser compatible by default. In Dreamweaver 4, Macromedia has moved to capitalize on the popularity of Flash and the flexibility of Generator with the introduction of two new tools: Flash Buttons and Flash Text. Now, it's easier than ever to incorporate customized, well-crafted Flash elements in your Web page without knowing a bit of Flash.

To take full advantage of the enhanced graphics potential of Flash and Shockwave's multimedia capabilities, you need to understand the differences between Director and Flash, as well as the various parameters available to each format. In addition to covering this material, this chapter also shows you how to use independent controls — both inline and with frames — for your Shockwave and Flash movies.

Shockwave and Flash: What's the Difference?

Director and Flash share many features: interactivity, streaming audio, support for both bitmaps and vector graphics, and "shocked fonts." Both can save their movies in formats suitable for viewing on the Web. So how do you choose which program to use? Each has its own special functions, and each excels at producing particular types of effects. Director is more full featured, with a complete programming language called Lingo that enables incredible interactivity. And Director movies can include Flash animations. Director also has a much steeper learning curve than does Flash. Flash is terrific for short, low-bandwidth animations with or without a synchronized audio track; however, the interactive capabilities in Flash are limited compared to Director.

Director is really a multimedia production program used for combining various elements: backgrounds, foreground elements called *sprites*, and various media such as digital audio and video (see Figure 17-1). With Director's Lingo programming language, you can build extraordinarily elaborate demos and games, with Internet-specific commands. When you need to include a high degree of interactivity, build your movie with Shockwave.

One of the primary differences between Director and Flash is the supported graphic formats. Director is generally better for bitmap graphics, in which each pixel is mapped to a specific color; both GIF and JPEG formats use bitmap graphics. Flash, on the other hand, uses primarily vector graphics, which are drawing elements described mathematically. Because vector graphics use a description of a drawing — a blue circle with a radius of 2.5 centimeters, for instance — rather than a bitmap, the resulting files are much smaller. A fairly complex animation produced with Flash might be only 10K or 20K, whereas a comparable digital video clip could easily be 10 times that size.

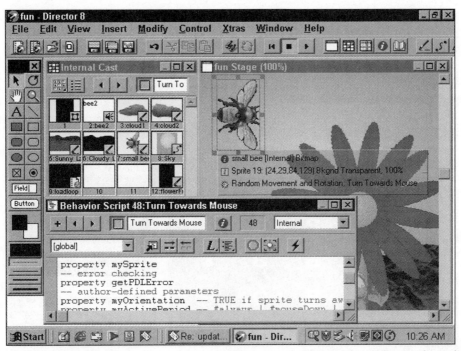

Figure 17-1: Director works mainly with bitmaps and video, and enables "multimedia programming" using Lingo.

Aside from file size, the other feature that distinguishes vector graphics from bitmap graphics is the smoothness of the line. When viewed with sufficient magnification, bitmap graphics always display telltale "stair-steps" or "jaggies," especially around curves. Vector graphics, on the other hand, are almost smooth. In fact, Flash takes special advantage of this characteristic and enables users to zoom into any movie — an important effect that saves a lot of bandwidth when used correctly.

However, these differences were significantly blurred with the release of Director 7, which incorporates its own native vector graphics and introduces the capability to include Flash movies within Director movies. Flash 4 blurred the line the other way by incorporating streaming MP3-encoded audio and QuickTime integration, both things that were traditionally the province of Director. In Flash 5, Flash's scripting capabilities have been significantly beefed up with the expansion of ActionScript into a JavaScript-based programming language.

Flash animations can be used as special effects, cartoons, and navigation bars within (or without) frames (see Figure 17-2). Although Flash isn't the best choice for games and other complex interactive elements, you can use Flash to animate your navigation system — complete with sound effects for button-pushing feedback.

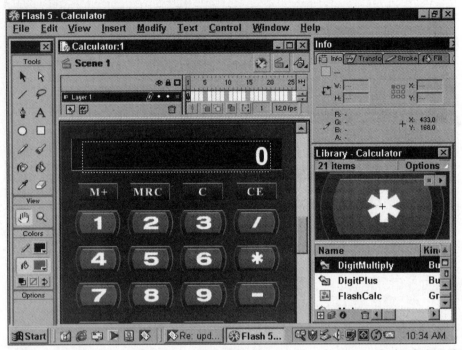

Figure 17-2: Flash movies tend to look more cartoon-like, thanks to Flash's lightweight vector graphics.

If Flash is a power tool, Director is a bulldozer. Director has been significantly expanded to handle a wide variety of file types, such as QuickTime and MP3, with advanced streaming capabilities. Supporting multimedia interactivity is Director's own programming language, Lingo, which has also been enhanced. Furthermore, Director now includes multiplayer support for network game play and chat rooms, XML parsing, embedded compressed fonts, up to 1,000 sprite channels, and a potential frame rate of 999 frames per second. Luckily, Dreamweaver enables you to pack all that power into a Web page with its Shockwave object.

Including Flash and Shockwave Movies in Dreamweaver Projects

Dreamweaver makes it easy to bring Shockwave and Flash files into your Web pages. The Objects panel provides an object for each type of movie, both located in the Common category.

Because Shockwave and Flash objects insert both an ActiveX control and a plug-in, Dreamweaver enables you to play the movie in the Document window. First it displays a plug-in placeholder icon (see Figure 17-3).

Flash placeholder   Insert Flash object

Insert Shockwave object

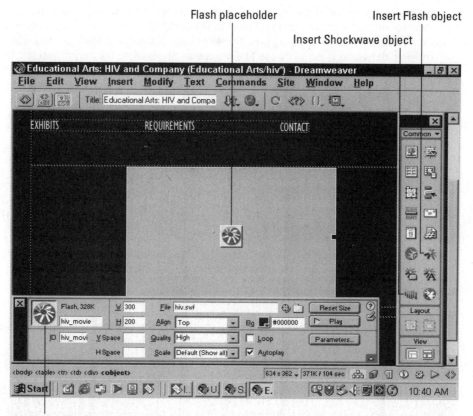

Flash property inspector

Figure 17-3: Dreamweaver includes many interface elements for working with Shockwave and Flash.

Before you can successfully include a Shockwave file, you need to know one small bit of information — the dimensions of your movie. Dreamweaver automatically reads the dimensions of your Flash file when you use the Insert Flash Movie object. Unfortunately, if you're incorporating a Shockwave movie, you still need to enter the dimensions by hand in the Shockwave Property Inspector.

To check the width and height of your movie in Director, load your file and then choose Modify ➪ Movie ➪ Properties to open the Movie Properties dialog box.

Note

It is essential to know the movie's height and width before you can include it successfully in Dreamweaver-built Web pages. During the development phase of a Dreamweaver project, I often include the movie dimensions in a file name, as an instant reminder to take care of this detail. For example, if I'm working with two different Shockwave movies, I can give them names such as navbar125x241.dcr and navbar400x50.dcr. (The .dcr extension is automatically appended by Director when you save a movie as a Shockwave file.) Because I consistently put width before height in the filename, this trick saves me the time it would take to reopen Director, load the movie, and choose Modify ⇨ Movie to check the measurements in the Movie Properties dialog box. The alternative to keeping track of the Director movie's dimensions is to choose File ⇨ Save as Shockwave Movie in Director; this creates an HTML file with all the necessary parameters—including width and height—that can be inserted into Dreamweaver. You'll find a detailed description of this process later in this chapter.

To include either a Shockwave or Flash file in your Web page, follow these steps:

1. Position the cursor in the Document window at the point where you'd like the movie to appear.

2. Insert the movie using any of these methods:

   • Choose Insert ⇨ Media ⇨ Shockwave or Insert ⇨ Media ⇨ Flash from the menus.

   • In the Common category of the Objects panel, select either the Insert Shockwave or Insert Flash button.

   • Drag the movie object from the Objects panel to any location in the Document window.

3. In the Select File dialog box, enter the path and the filename in the File Name text box or select the Browse (Choose) button to locate the file. Click OK.

   Dreamweaver inserts a small plug-in placeholder in the current cursor position, and the Property Inspector displays the appropriate information for Shockwave or Flash.

4. Preview the Flash or Shockwave movie in the Document window by selecting the Play button found in the Property Inspector. You can also choose View ⇨ Plugins ⇨ Play.

5. End the preview of your file by selecting the Stop button in the Property Inspector or selecting View ⇨ Plugins ⇨ Stop.

Tip   If you have more than one Flash or Shockwave movie on your page, you can control them all by choosing View ⇨ Plugins ⇨ Play All and View ⇨ Plugins ⇨ Stop All. If your files appear in different pages in a frameset, you have to repeat the Play All command for each page.

As noted earlier, you must specify the dimensions of your file in the Property Inspector before you can preview the movie in a browser; again, Dreamweaver supplies this information automatically for Flash files, but you have to enter it yourself for Shockwave movies. Shockwave and Flash have some different features in the Dreamweaver Property Inspector. These differences are covered separately in the following sections.

Specifying Shockwave Properties

Once you've inserted your Shockwave file, you're ready to begin entering the specific parameters in the Property Inspector. The Property Inspector takes care of all but one Shockwave attribute, the palette parameter. Some of the information, including the ActiveX Class ID, is automatically set in the Property Inspector when you insert the movie.

 You can find a custom command called Insert Shockwave HTML that automates the process of inserting a Shockwave movie and its Director-generated HTML. Look in the Configuration\Commands folder on the CD-ROM that accompanies this book. If you'd prefer a version developed by Macromedia that does the same job, visit the Dreamweaver Exchange to download the Insert Shockwave extension.

To set or modify the parameters for a Shockwave file, follow these steps:

1. Select the Shockwave placeholder icon.

2. In the Shockwave Property Inspector, enter the width and the height values in the W and H text boxes, respectively, as shown in Figure 17-4. Alternatively, you can click and drag any of the three resizing handles on the placeholder icon.

Generating HTML Within Director

In Director, you can generate a file with all the appropriate HTML code at the same time that you save your Shockwave movie, with just the selection of a checkbox. When you choose File ➪ Save as Shockwave Movie in Director, the dialog box contains a Generate HTML option. Selecting this option causes Director to save an HTML file with the same name as your Shockwave movie but with an appropriate file extension (.html for Macintosh and .htm for Windows). You can easily copy and paste this HTML code directly into Dreamweaver.

When you open the Director-generated HTML file, you see the name of your file and the Shockwave placeholder, correctly sized and ready to preview. To move this object into another Web page in progress, just select the Shockwave object and choose Edit ➪ Copy. Then switch to your other page and choose Edit ➪ Paste. Naturally, you can also use the keyboard shortcuts or, if both pages are accessible, just drag and drop the object from one page to another.

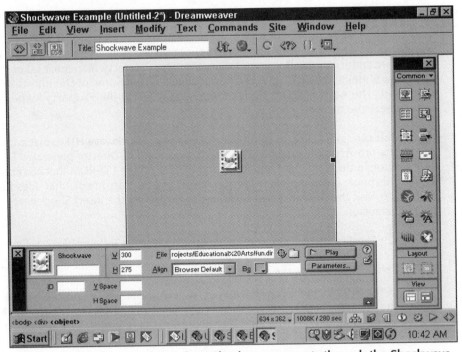

Figure 17-4: Modify parameters for a Shockwave property through the Shockwave Property Inspector.

Tip

Pressing the Shift key while dragging the corner resizing handle maintains the current aspect ratio.

3. To designate how the Shockwave HTML code is written, select one of these three options from the Tag drop-down list:

- **Object and Embed:** This is the default option and ensures that code is written for both Internet Explorer and Netscape. Use this option unless your page is on an intranet where only one browser is used.

- **Object only:** Select this option to enable your movie to be viewed by Internet Explorer–compatible browsers.

- **Embed only:** Select this option to enable your movie to be viewed by Netscape-compatible browsers.

4. Set and modify other object attributes as needed; see Table 17-1 for a list.

Table 17-1
Property Inspector Options for Shockwave Objects

Shockwave Property	Description
Align	Choose an option to alter the alignment of the movie. In addition to the browser default, your options include Baseline, Top, Middle, Bottom, Texttop, Absolute Middle, Absolute Bottom, Left, and Right.
Alt Image	The Alt Image file is displayed in browsers that do not support the `<embed>` tag and is available if you select Embed Only. This image does not display in Dreamweaver. Enter the path to the alternative image, or select the Folder icon to open a Select Image Source dialog box.
BgColor	The background color is visible only if the width and height of the plug-in are larger than the movie. To alter the background color of your plug-in, choose the color swatch and select a new color from the pop-up menu; or enter a valid color name in the BgColor text box.
Border	To place a border around your movie, enter a number in the Border text box. The number determines the width of the border in pixels. The default is zero or no border.
H Space	You can increase the space to the left and right of the movie by entering a value in the H (Horizontal) Space text box. The default is zero.
ID	The ID field is used to define the optional ActiveX ID parameter, most often used to pass data between ActiveX controls.
(Name)	If desired, you can enter a unique name in this unlabeled field on the far left of the Property Inspector. The name is used by JavaScript and other languages to identify the movie.
V Space	To increase the amount of space between other elements on the page and the top and bottom of the movie plug-in, enter a pixel value in the V (Vertical) Space text box. Again, the default is zero.

Additional parameters for Shockwave

As you can with other plug-ins, you can pass other attributes to the Shockwave movie via the Parameters dialog box — available by clicking the Parameters button on the Property Inspector. Press the add (+) button to begin inserting additional parameters. Enter the attributes in the left column and their respective values in the right. To remove an attribute, highlight it and select the delete (–) button.

Automatic settings for Shockwave files

When you insert a Shockwave or Flash file, Dreamweaver writes a number of parameters that are constant and necessary. In the `<object>` portion of the code, Dreamweaver includes the ActiveX Class ID number as well as the `codebase` number; the former calls the specific ActiveX control, and the latter enables users who don't have the control installed to receive it automatically. Likewise, in the `<embed>` section, Dreamweaver fills in the `pluginspage` attribute, designating the location where Navigator users can find the necessary plug-in. Be sure you don't accidentally remove any of this information — however, if you should, all you have to do is delete and reinsert the object.

Only one other general attribute is usually assigned to a Shockwave file, the `palette` parameter. This parameter takes a value of either foreground or background.

✦ If `palette` is set to background, the movie's color scheme does not override that of the system; this is the default.

✦ When `palette` is set to foreground, the colors of the selected movie are applied to the user's system, which includes the desktop and scroll bars.

Note that `palette` is not supported by Internet Explorer.

Caution   Web designers should take care when specifying the `palette=foreground` parameter. This effect is likely to prove startling to the user; moreover, if your color scheme is sufficiently different, the change may render the user's system unusable. If you do use the `palette` parameter, be sure to include a Director command to restore the original system color scheme in the final frame of the movie.

Designating Flash Attributes

Flash movies require the same basic parameters as their Shockwave counterparts — and Flash movies have a few additional optional ones as well. As it does for Shockwave files, Dreamweaver sets almost all the attributes for Flash movies through the Property Inspector. The major difference is that several more parameters are available.

To set or modify the attributes for a Flash file, follow these steps:

1. After your Flash movie has been inserted in the Document window, make sure it's selected. Dreamweaver automatically inserts the correct dimensions for your Flash movie.

2. Set any attributes in the Property Inspector as needed for your Flash movie. (Refer to the previous descriptions of these attributes in the section "Specifying Shockwave Properties.") In addition, you can also set the parameters described in Table 17-2.

Table 17-2
Property Inspector Options for Flash Objects

Flash Parameter	Possible Values	Description
Autoplay	Checked (default)	Enables the Flash movie to begin playing as soon as possible.
Loop	Checked (default)	If Loop is checked, the movie plays continuously; otherwise, it plays once.
Quality		Controls antialiasing during playback.
	High	Antialiasing is turned on. This can slow the playback frame rate considerably on slower computers.
	Low	No antialiasing is used; this setting is best for animations that must be played quickly.
	AutoHigh (default)	The animation begins in High (with antialiasing) and switches to Low if the host computer is too slow.
	AutoLow	Starts the animation in Low (no antialiasing) and then switches to High if the host machine is fast enough.
Scale		Scale determines how the movie fits into the dimensions as specified in the width and height text boxes
	ShowAll (default)	Displays the entire movie in the given dimensions while maintaining the file's original aspect ratio. Some of the background may be visible with this setting.
	ExactFit	Scales the movie precisely into the dimensions without regard for the aspect ratio. It is possible that the image could be distorted with this setting.
	NoBorder	Fits the movie into the given dimensions so that no borders are showing and maintains the original aspect ratio. Some of the movie may be cut off with this setting.

Setting the scale in Flash movies

Be careful with your setting for the Scale parameter, in order to avoid unexpected results. If you have to size a Flash movie out of its aspect ratio, the Flash player needs to know what to do with any extra room it has to fill. Figure 17-5 demonstrates the different results that the Scale attribute can provide. Only the figure in the lower right is at its proper dimensions. The gray box is the actual size of the authoring canvas.

Show All   No Border (note cut off figure)

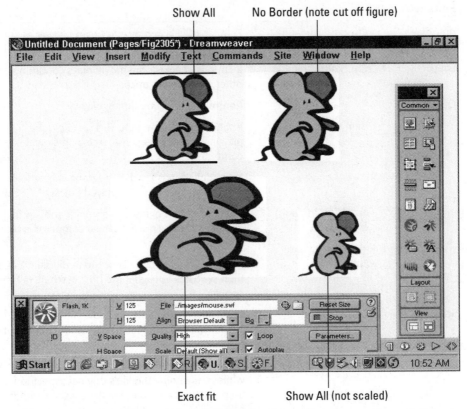

Exact fit   Show All (not scaled)

Figure 17-5: Your setting for the Scale attribute determines how your movie is resized within the plug-in width and height measurements.

Tip

Dreamweaver makes it easy to rescale a Flash movie. First, from the Property Inspector, enter the precise width and height of your file in the W and H text boxes. Then, while holding down the Shift key, click and drag the corner resizing handle of the Flash placeholder icon to the new size for the movie. By Shift+dragging, you retain the aspect ratio set in the Property Inspector. This enables you to quickly enlarge or reduce your movie without distortion.

Additional parameters for Flash

Flash has two additional attributes that can be entered through the Parameters dialog box (click the Parameters button on the Property Inspector): salign and swliveconnect. The salign attribute determines how the movie aligns itself to the surrounding frame when the Scale attribute is set to ShowAll. In addition, `salign` determines which portion of the image gets cut off when the Scale attribute is set to NoBorder. The alignment can be set to L (left), R (right), T (top), or B (bottom). You can also use these values in combination. For example, if you set `salign=RB`, the movie aligns with the right-bottom edge or the lower-right corner of the frame.

The `swliveconnect` attribute comes into play when you're using FSCommands or JavaScripting in your Flash movies. FSCommands are interactive commands, such as Go to URL, issued from inside the Flash movie. The latest versions of the Netscape browser initialize Java when first called — and if your Flash movie uses FSCommands or JavaScript, it uses Java to communicate with the Netscape plug-in interface, LiveConnect. Because not all Flash movies need the LiveConnect connection, you can prevent Java from being initialized by entering the `swliveconnect` attribute in the Parameters dialog box and setting its value to false. When the `swliveconnect=false` parameter is found by the browser, the Java is not initialized as part of the loading process — and your movie loads more quickly.

Creating Flash Buttons and Crafting Templates

The primary argument against using Flash has always been, "Not everyone has the Flash plug-in, so not everyone can see Flash movies." When Macromedia began promoting the 96.4 percent and above market penetration of the Flash Player, that argument started to fade. True, this almost universally installed base applies to the Flash 2 player — as of this writing, over 88 percent of browsers have Flash 4 players and almost 40 percent, Flash 5 — but the basic ability to play back .swf files is all that's necessary to display simple animations and enable sounds.

While Flash is often used to create standalone movies, cartoons, and interactive games, it is also capable of making excellent navigation aids. One feature of traditional user interfaces — audio feedback, the "click" that one hears when a button has been chosen onscreen — has been long missing on the Web because of the lack of a universally available sound engine. With navigation buttons created in Flash, sound is very easy to incorporate, as are animation effects and smooth blends. Best of all, these effects are extremely low bandwidth and often weigh less on a page than a comparable animated GIF file, even without the sound.

New Feature

Dreamweaver designers may now add the power and beauty of Flash objects to their Web page design palette. Both animated Flash Buttons and static Flash Text (covered later in this chapter) may now be created directly within Dreamweaver. Flash Buttons are based on template designs created in Flash and customized in Dreamweaver. This separation of design and implementation allows Flash graphic designers to create the overall look for a navigational button or button series and

Dreamweaver layout artists to incorporate them into the proper page design, adding the appropriate button text, links, and background color where needed. Flash Buttons, like any Flash movie, may be previewed in Dreamweaver and resized as needed.

Dreamweaver comes with 44 different Flash Button templates with additional styles available at the Macromedia Exchange. The buttons are primarily intended to be used as links to other Web pages although some are designed as VCR-like player controls. To insert a Flash Button, follow these steps:

1. Make sure that the current document has been previously saved.

   If you're working on a new document, Dreamweaver requires that you save it before adding a Flash Button.

2. Choose Insert Flash Button from the Common category of the Objects panel or select Insert ⇨ Interactive Images ⇨ Flash Button.

   The Insert Flash Button dialog box, shown in Figure 17-6, is displayed.

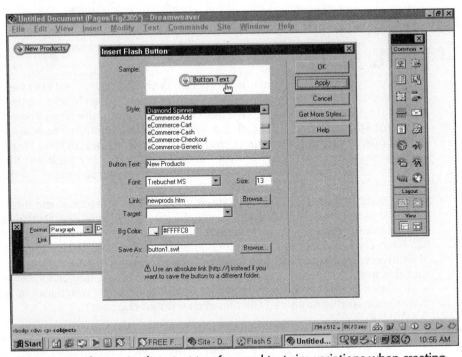

Figure 17-6: Choose Apply to test typeface and text size variations when creating your Flash Button.

3. Select a button type from the Style list.

   The previews shown in the Sample area are live demonstrations and will play as designed when moused-over and/or clicked. There is, however, one exception: no sound is heard in preview; you'll have to preview the Flash Button in the browser to get the full effect.

4. If it's a navigation button, enter the custom text desired in the Button Text field.

   The Button Text field is physically limited to 50 characters, although for most practical purposes, your text will be shorter. Certain symbols, such as those in the Control group, ignore the text and font settings.

5. Select a typeface from the Font drop-down list.

   The fonts listed are TrueType fonts found on your system. Most of the button templates have a preselected font and text size. If the preselected font is not found on your system, a small alert appears at the bottom of the dialog box.

6. Enter the desired font size, in points, in the Size field.

7. If the button is to link to another page, enter the absolute or document relative URL in the Link field. Alternatively, you can choose the Browse button to locate the file.

   Flash movies don't handle site root–relative links correctly, so your link needs to either be absolute, such as `www.idest.com/contact.htm`, or document relative. Use document relative links only if the Flash Button is to be stored in the same folder as the page referenced.

8. If working in a frame-based site or you want the link to open in another page, select an option from the Target drop-down list.

   The standard system targets — _blank, _self, _parent, and _top — are always available. Additional frame names appear if the Flash Button is inserted in an existing frameset.

9. If the Flash Button is to be placed on a page or in a table with a background color other than white, select the Bg Color swatch to choose an appropriate background. Alternatively, the hexadecimal color number or standard color name may be entered directly into the Bg Color text field.

10. Enter a path and filename for the Flash Button file. If you like, you can use the suggested default name in the site root or select the Browse button to choose a different location.

11. Choose Apply to insert the button in the cursor location on the page.

12. Click OK when you're done.

Tip

If you'd like to see what other styles are available, open the Insert Flash Button dialog box and choose Get More Styles. Your primary browser will launch and go to the Dreamweaver Exchange where you can search for new styles. Once you've installed the additional extensions using the Extension Manager, you'll need to relaunch Dreamweaver to see the new styles. One word of caution: selecting Get More Styles immediately closes the dialog box without creating a button.

Once your Flash Button is inserted, it can be modified on the page. Choose the Flash Button to activate the specific Property Inspector that, along with standard Flash object parameters, offers a couple of new controls: Edit and Reset Size. Selecting Edit reopens the Insert Flash Button dialog box and allows you to modify any of the settings. Use Reset Size if you have altered the dimensions of the Flash Button — by dragging one of the sizing handles or entering new values in the Width and/or Height fields — and want to return to the preset size.

Tip　If you've moved an existing Flash Button to a frame-based design, select the button and choose Edit from the Property Inspector. Under Target, you'll find names for all the frames in your new frameset to make it easy to position your content.

The Flash Button samples that ship with Dreamweaver are nice, but to be truly useful, you — or someone on your team — must be able to create your own templates that fit the design of your site. The Flash Button templates you see previewed in Dreamweaver are actually Generator templates, created in Flash.

To create the Generator templates, you'll need Flash, of course, and the free Generator authoring extensions from Macromedia. The authoring extensions are included in Flash 5 or can be downloaded from the Macromedia site at `www.macromedia.com/software/generator/trial`. Additionally, you'll need to copy two Generator object files from the *Dreamweaver and Flash Bible* CD-ROM to their proper place in the Flash and Generator installations. From the Dreamweaver 4/More Extensions/Flash Objects/Generator Text Object folder, copy these files:

✦ InsertText.def to Flash 5/generator/template folder

✦ InsertText.class to Generator 2/extras

If you don't have the CD-ROM, you can download these files from the same Macromedia site listed previously.

Once you have the Generator Text object files in place, the next step is to create your button in Flash. As with other Flash Buttons, your graphic should be converted to a button-type symbol and it may use all four keyframes: Up, Over, Down, and Hit. Once you've built the button, follow these steps to add the Generator functionality:

1. In Flash, choose Window ➪ Generator Objects.

2. From the Generator Objects panel, drag the Insert Text object over the previously built button.

   Position the Insert Text object so that its center is over where you'd like your button text to appear.

3. When the Insert Text object is in place and selected, the Generator Insert Text panel displaying the appropriate properties appears. Double-click the Insert Text object to bring the panel to the front if necessary.

   Within the panel, you'll need to set several parameters to placeholder values so that the Insert Flash Button dialog box in Dreamweaver can function properly. In each case, enter the value in the right column.

4. Enter the following values in the Generator Insert Text panel:

- **Text:** Enter {Button Text}
- **Font:** Enter {Button Font}
- **Font Size:** Enter {Button Size}
- **Alignment:** Enter either left, right, center or justified.
- **Vertical Alignment:** Enter either top, center or bottom.
- **URL:** Enter {Button URL}
- **Window:** Enter {Button Target}

5. Shrink the movie to the size of your button by dragging the button to the upper-left corner of the stage and choosing Modify ➪ Movie. In the Movie Properties dialog box, select the Match Contents option.

6. Save the movie as a .fla file so that you may adjust it later.

7. Choose File ➪ Export Movie and select Generator Template as the file type. Save the template in the Dreamweaver/Configuration/Flash Objects/Flash Buttons folder.

Now your Flash Button is almost ready to use. If you like, you can choose the Insert Flash Button object in Dreamweaver and see your button; however, no sample text will be displayed. There's one last procedure that's required if you want to preview your Flash Button with example text. Interestingly enough, you use the Insert Flash Button object to create the preview:

1. Open Dreamweaver and save a blank page.

2. Choose the Insert Flash Button object.

3. Select your newly inserted button from the Style list.

New buttons are found at the end of the list.

4. Enter desired default values in the Text, Font, and Size fields.

These values will be preset whenever this particular Flash Button is chosen.

5. In the Save As field, store the file under the same name as your style in the Dreamweaver/Configuration/Flash Objects/Flash Buttons Preview folder.

6. Click OK when you're done.

The next time you access the Flash Button object, your custom template will display a full preview, with text.

Working with Flash Text

The addition of Flash Text to Dreamweaver goes a long way toward solving one of the Web designer's most perplexing problems: how to achieve good-looking text that uses non-standard fonts. While standard HTML text allows font families — a series of fonts offered in hopes that one of them is installed on the user's system — few designers stray outside of tried and true options such as Arial, Helvetica, and Times New Roman for the majority of their content. This is especially grating to print designers coming to the Web who rely on typography as a primary design tool. The advent of Dynamic HTML promised to bring a wider selection of typefaces with so-called dynamic font technology, but lack of built-in cross-browser support for any one system dashed those hopes.

New Feature   The new Flash Text feature allows the designer to use any TrueType font to create low-weight, jaggie-free headings, right from within Dreamweaver itself. The ubiquitous nature of the Flash Player ensures cross-browser support without resorting to GIF images, which are often not as crisp as required. Moreover, with Flash Text, you can easily declare a second color for automatically enabled rollovers — you don't even have to attach a Dreamweaver behavior.

The Flash Text feature is especially useful for creating headings in a corporate-approved typeface. Because it doesn't involve downloading a font resource as dynamic font technologies do, there is no concern about the misuse of copyrighted fonts. The only downside to Flash Text over a dynamic font technology is that unlike dynamically created fonts, Flash Text cannot be searched on a page. To overcome this limitation, Web designers can include key phrases in <meta> tags.

To use the Flash Text object, follow these steps:

1. Make sure your page has been saved before proceeding.

2. Choose Insert Flash Text from the Common category of the Objects panel or select Insert ⇨ Interactive Images ⇨ Flash Text.

   The Insert Flash Text dialog box appears, as shown in Figure 17-7.

3. Select the desired typeface from the Font drop-down list.

4. Enter the font size desired in the Size field.

5. Choose Bold and/or Italic styles for your text.

6. Select the alignment on the page: left, center, or right.

7. Select a basic color from the color swatch or enter a hexadecimal value or valid color name in the Color field.

8. If desired, choose a secondary color for the text to change to when the user moves his or her mouse over the Flash Text from the Rollover Color swatch.

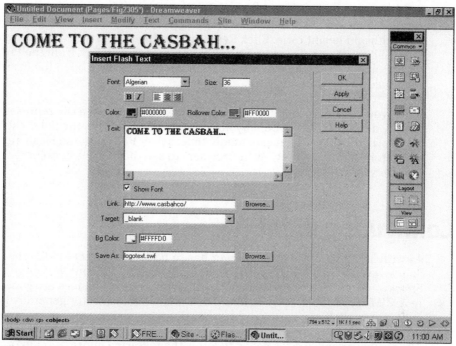

Figure 17-7: Use the Insert Flash Text object to create headlines with a non-standard or custom font.

9. Enter the desired text in the Text field.

There's no real limit to the amount of text that can be entered other than practical considerations, and line returns are acceptable.

10. If you want to see the text in the default font in the Text field, disable the Show Font option.

11. If desired, enter an absolute or document relative URL in the Link field.

As with Flash Buttons, site relative links are not available in Flash Text objects.

12. If you're working in a frame-based site or want the link to open in a new browser window, choose the appropriate Target from the drop-down list.

13. Optionally, choose a background color from the Bg Color swatch.

14. Enter a filename and path to store the object in the Save As field. Alternatively, select the Browse button to locate a folder.

If you're using document relative links in the Flash Text object, be sure to store the object in the same folder as the current document.

15. Click Apply to preview what your button will look like in your document and then click OK when you're done.

As with Flash Buttons, you can resize a Flash Text object by dragging the resizing handles; press the Shift key while dragging to constrain the dimensions to their initial width and height ratio. Click Reset Size on the Property Inspector to restore the original dimensions. To edit a Flash Text object, choose Edit from the Property Inspector; alternatively, you can double-click the object to open the Insert Flash Text dialog box again.

When you create a Flash Text object, Dreamweaver makes a GIF representation for display during layout — you may notice some roughness in the lines, especially if you resize the object. You can, at any time, select Play from the Flash Text Property Inspector (or choose Preview in Browser) to see the true Flash object with its smooth vector shape.

Configuring MIME Types

As with any plug-in, your Web server has to have the correct MIME types set before Shockwave files can be properly served to your users. If your Web page plays Shockwave and Flash movies locally, but not remotely, chances are good the correct MIME types need to be added. The system administrator generally handles configuring MIME types.

The system administrator needs to know the following information in order to correctly configure the MIME types:

✦ **Shockwave:** application/x-director (.dcr, .dir, .dxr)

✦ **Flash:** application/x-shockwave-flash (.swf)

Both Shockwave and Flash are popular plug-ins, and it's likely that the Web server is already configured to recognize the appropriate file types.

Tip   Movies made by an earlier version of Flash, called FutureSplash, can also be played by the Flash plug-in — but only if the correct MIME type is added: `application/futuresplash` with the file extension .spl.

Adding Generator Objects

Generator is Macromedia's tool for personalizing and delivering Flash content. While developers create Flash movies on their own systems, Generator graphics are built on-demand, by the server. Generator works with a series of variables in each template, which is filled in when the page containing the Generator object is requested by the browser. Think of Generator as a graphic mail-merge system in which the basic letter is the animation and the form fields can be anything from a user's name to data returned from a database. Although Generator is largely used to customize Flash content on the fly, it can also output other formats including GIF, JPEG, PNG, and QuickTime.

Inserting a Generator template into a Web page is very straightforward in Dreamweaver. Most of the work comes from providing values for the variables through a name/value pair interface. To add a Generator template, follow these steps:

1. Position your cursor where you'd like the Generator object to appear and choose Insert Generator from the Common category of the Objects panel or select Insert ⇨ Media ⇨ Generator.

   The Insert Generator dialog box, shown in Figure 17-8, appears.

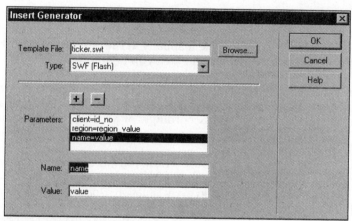

Figure 17-8: Generator templates allow Flash movies and other graphics to be personalized by the server.

2. Enter the path to the Generator template file or choose the Browse button to locate the file.

   Generator templates have a .swt file extension.

3. Choose the kind of media to be created by Generator from the Type drop-down list: SWF (Flash), GIF, JPEG, MOV (QuickTime), or PNG.

4. To enter parameters for the object, first select the Add button.

   In the Parameters list, the temporary name=value listing appears.

5. Enter the name for your parameter in the Name field.

6. Enter the value of your parameter in the Value field.

7. Repeat Steps 4 through 6 for each parameter.

8. To remove a parameter, highlight it in the Parameters list and choose the Remove button.

9. Click OK when you're done.

Managing Links in Flash Movies with Dreamweaver

Many Web sites rely heavily on Flash movies, substituting movies for entire pages that would otherwise be created with HTML. Others take advantage of Flash's interactivity in their main navigation buttons. Adding links to buttons in Flash is easy, but embedding multiple URLs into multiple SWF files can make modifying a site's structure a nightmare, forcing you to re-create every SWF file in your site. Luckily, Dreamweaver comes to the rescue, with link management features that are SWF-savvy.

Dreamweaver extends its link management to include the links contained in Flash SWF movies. Edit links within a SWF file manually in the Site Map, or move SWF files in the Site Files view and let Dreamweaver clean up behind you.

Within the Site window, you can drag SWF files to new folders just as you would an HTML file. Unless your Update Links preference is set to Never, Dreamweaver will either modify the links in the SWF file accordingly or prompt you for permission to do so.

Caution   Be careful with the type of links you use — Flash (or, more accurately, browser playback of Flash) can't handle them all. Absolute URLs are very common in Flash movies because they can be used in every situation. Document relative links may be used successfully in all cases if the Web page and the Flash file are stored in the same folder. Site root relative links, such as `/products/widgets.htm`, should not be used in Flash movies.

To modify the links in a SWF file manually, follow these steps:

1. Choose Window ⇨ Site Map to view the Site Map.

2. Choose View ⇨ Show Dependent Files (Site ⇨ Site Map View ⇨ Show Dependent Files) to include dependent files such as Flash movies in the Site Map.

3. Locate the SWF file that you want to modify. If it contains any links, a plus sign is shown next to its icon. Click the plus sign to expand a branch of links from the SWF file, as shown in Figure 17-9.

4. To change a link, select it and choose Site ⇨ Change Link (Site ⇨ Site Map View ⇨ Change Link) or use the key shortcut Ctrl+L (Command+L). Alternatively, you can right-click (Control+click) the link and choose Change Link from the contextual menu. Dreamweaver displays a Select HTML File dialog box.

5. Select a new file by navigating to an HTML file or entering an URL. Click OK when you're done.

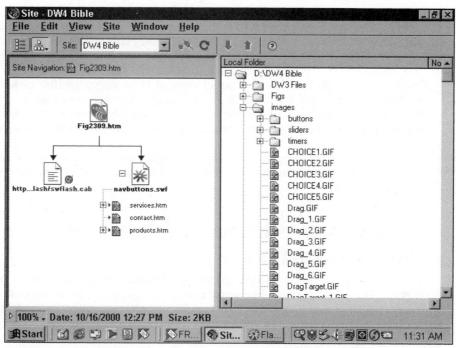

Figure 17-9: Dreamweaver's Site Map displays links contained in Flash SWF movies.

Note If your preferences call for Dreamweaver to prompt you before updating links, Dreamweaver will ask you to confirm that you want this link changed.

The link in your SWF file is changed.

Just as with HTML files, you can also remove links from a SWF file by selecting the link and choosing Site ➪ Remove Link (Site ➪ Site Map View ➪ Remove Link) or use the keyboard shortcut Ctrl+Shift+L (Command+Shift+L).

Caution Dreamweaver changes links within SWF files, but the links in the original Flash document that you edit in Flash itself will remain unchanged. Make sure to update your Flash document before exporting a revised SWF file.

Providing User Interaction with Shockwave Movies

What happens once you've installed your Director or Flash Shockwave files? Many movies are set to play automatically or upon some action from the user, such as a mouse click of a particular hotspot within the page. The Show Me movies used in

Dreamweaver are good examples of the kind of interactivity you can program within a Director Shockwave movie. But what if you want the user to be able to start or stop a movie in one part of the page, using controls in another part? How can controls in one frame affect a movie in a different frame?

Dreamweaver includes a Control Shockwave or Flash behavior that makes inline controls — controls on the same Web page as the movie — very easy to set up. However, establishing frame-to-frame control is slightly more complex in Dreamweaver and requires a minor modification to the program-generated code.

Both of the following step-by-step techniques rely on Dreamweaver behaviors. If you're unfamiliar with using behaviors, you should review Chapter 15 before proceeding.

Dreamweaver technique: Creating inline Shockwave controls

Certainly it's perfectly acceptable to make your Director or Flash movies with built-in controls for interactivity, but sometimes you want to separate the controls from the movie. Dreamweaver includes a JavaScript behavior called Control Shockwave or Flash. With this behavior, you can set up external controls to start, stop, and rewind Shockwave and Flash movies.

To create inline Shockwave or Flash controls:

1. Insert your Shockwave or Flash file by choosing either the Insert Shockwave or Insert Flash button from the Objects panel.

2. From the Select File dialog box, enter the path to your file in the File Name text box or select the Browse (Choose) button to locate your file.

3. For Shockwave, enter the width and height of your movie in the W and H text boxes, respectively, in the Property Inspector. The dimensions for Flash movies are entered automatically.

4. Enter a unique name for your movie in the text box provided.

5. If you are inserting a Flash movie, deselect the Autoplay and Loop options.

6. To insert the first control, position the cursor where you'd like the control to appear on the page.

7. Select Insert Image from the Objects panel or select some text.

8. In the Link box of the Property Inspector, enter a dummy link or just a hash symbol, #, to create an empty target.

9. Open the Behaviors panel by selecting the Show Behaviors button from the Launcher or by pressing Shift+F3.

10. If necessary, change the selected browser to 4.0 Browsers; you can do this by selecting an option from the Show Events For submenu of the Add Behavior menu.

11. Select the + (Add Action) button and choose Control Shockwave or Flash from the drop-down list.

12. In the Control Shockwave or Flash dialog box (see Figure 17-10), select the movie you want to affect from the Movie drop-down list.

Figure 17-10: In the Control Shockwave or Flash dialog box, you assign a control action to an image button or link.

13. Now select the desired action for your control. Choose from the four options: Play, Stop, Rewind, and Go to Frame. If you choose the Go to Frame option, enter a frame number in the text box.

14. Click OK to close the Control Shockwave or Flash dialog box.

15. Repeat Steps 6 through 14 for each movie control you'd like to add. Figure 17-11 shows a sample Web page with Play and Stop controls.

Dreamweaver technique: Playing Shockwave movies in frames

Framesets and frames are great for Web sites in which you want your navigation and other controls kept in one frame and the freedom to vary the content in another frame. It's entirely possible to set up your movie's playback buttons in one frame and the Shockwave movie in another. The method and the tools used are similar to those used in the preceding technique for adding same-page controls to a Shockwave movie. For this technique using frames, some HTML hand-coding is necessary, but it is relatively minor — only one additional line per control!

As you saw in the previous section, Dreamweaver's Control Shockwave or Flash behavior lists all the Shockwave and Flash movies in the page and enables you to choose the one you want to affect (as previously shown in Figure 17-11). Unfortunately, the behavior looks on only one page and not through an entire frameset. However, with a little sleight-of-hand and a bit of JavaScript, you can get the effect you want.

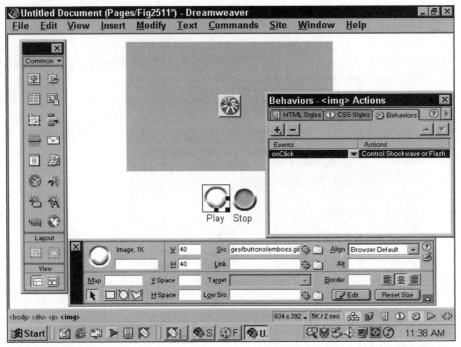

Figure 17-11: This Web page contains Play and Stop controls using the Control Shockwave or Flash behavior.

Note Before you begin applying this technique, you should construct (and save) your frameset and individual frames. Be sure to name each frame uniquely, because you have to provide the names in order to address the correct frames.

To place Shockwave controls in frames:

1. In one frame, insert the images or links that are going to act as the Shockwave controls. (For this demonstration, the control frame is named frControl.)

2. In another frame, insert the Shockwave file (either Shockwave or Flash) by choosing the appropriate object from the Objects panel. (For this demonstration, the movie frame is named frMovie.)

3. Be sure to modify the Shockwave Property Inspector with the necessary parameters: name, width, height, and source; and, if you're inserting a Flash file, deselect the Autoplay and Loop checkboxes.

4. Copy the Shockwave placeholder by selecting it and choosing Edit ➪ Copy.

5. Position the cursor in the frControl frame and paste the placeholder in a temporary position by choosing Edit ➪ Paste. At this point, the placement for the placeholder is not critical, as long as it is in the same frame as the images or links you are going to use as controls. The placeholder will be deleted shortly.

Instead of using the Copy and Paste commands, you can hold down Ctrl (Command) and click and drag the placeholder to its new temporary position.

6. Now select the first image or link you want to use as a control. As described in the preceding technique, attach the Control Shockwave or Flash behavior to the selected object. As you learned in the preceding exercise, this entails the following actions:

   • With the image or link selected, open the Behaviors panel.

   • Add the Control Shockwave or Flash action.

   • In the Control Shockwave or Flash dialog box, specify the movie and select the required action (Play, Rewind, Stop, or Go to Frame).

7. The major work is finished now. All you still need to do is add a little HTML. Switch to Code view, open the Code Inspector, or use your favorite external editor to edit the file.

8. Locate the image or link controls in the code. Each JavaScript routine is called from within an `<a>` tag and reads something like the following, where `fMovie` is the name of the Flash movie:

```
<a href="#" onClick="MM_controlShockwave ¬
('document.fMovie', 'document.fMovie','Play')">
```

9. Wherever you see the JavaScript reference to document, change it to

```
parent.frameName.document
```

where `frameName` is the unique name you gave to the frame in which your movie appears. In our example, `frameName` is `frMovie`, so after the replacement is made, the tag reads as follows:

```
<a href="#" onClick="MM_controlShockwave('parent.ù
frMovie.document.fMovie','document.fMovie','Play')">
```

By making this substitution, you've pointed the JavaScript function first to the "parent" of the current document — and the parent of a frame is the entire frameset. Now that we're looking at the entire frameset, the next word (which is the unique frame name) points the JavaScript function directly to the desired frame within the frameset.

Tip   If you have a number of controls, you might want to use Dreamweaver's Find and Replace features to ensure that you've updated all the code.

10. Finally, delete the temporary Shockwave movie that was inserted into the frame containing the controls.

Test the frameset by pressing F12 (primary browser) or Shift+F12 (secondary browser). If you haven't changed the Property Inspector's default Tag attribute (the default is Object and Embed), the Shockwave movie should work in both Netscape and Internet Explorer.

Dreamweaver technique: Triggering behaviors from Flash movies

Flash includes a number of its own behaviors for creating interactivity, but Flash behaviors don't do JavaScript as Dreamweaver behaviors do. A Flash-heavy project might benefit from Dreamweaver's Open Browser Window or Pop-up Message behaviors as much as the next site. The technique in this section shows you how to trigger Dreamweaver behaviors from buttons in a Flash movie.

What Flash buttons do is specified in the Flash authoring environment, not in Dreamweaver. Dreamweaver can attach behaviors to HTML elements such as anchor tags and body tags but not to plug-ins. The solution lies in creating dummy "buttons" in Dreamweaver and copying the JavaScript code from those links into the actions attached to Flash buttons, within Flash itself.

Note
The following technique can be used for any Dreamweaver behavior. The JavaScript Integration Kit for Flash 5 (JIK) extension, covered later in this chapter, has several built-in functions including Open Browser Window and Swap Image. Use the following procedure if you don't want to use the JIK extension or need to incorporate a behavior not included in that extension.

To trigger Dreamweaver behaviors from Flash buttons, follow these steps:

1. Create a new Dreamweaver document or open an existing one.

2. Create a dummy link that represents a button in your Flash movie. If you want a Flash button to open a new browser window, attach the Open Browser Window behavior to your dummy link, as in Figure 17-12.

3. Place your cursor within the dummy link and choose the <a> tag from the Tag Chooser in Dreamweaver's status bar to completely select the link.

4. Click the Show Code and Design views button on the toolbar or choose View ➪ Code and Design from the menus. Note that the dummy link is selected in both the Code and Design portions of the document window and looks something like this:

```
<a href="#"
onClick="MM_openBrWindow('myBuddy.htm','','scrollbars=yes','w
idth=250,height=200')">popup copywrite message</a>
```

5. Select everything between the quotes in the `onClick` attribute — including the parentheses — as shown in Figure 17-13, and copy it to the clipboard. This is the actual JavaScript that we want the Flash button to execute.

6. In Flash, double-click the button you want to add the Dreamweaver behavior to. The Instance Properties dialog box opens. Select the Object Actions tab, as shown in Figure 17-14.

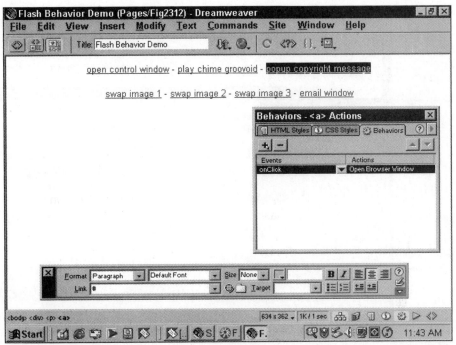

Figure 17-12: Attach a behavior you want to trigger from Flash to a dummy link in Dreamweaver.

7. Click the + (add) button and choose Get URL from the Basic Actions category to add a Flash Get URL behavior to your Flash button. In the URL box, type:

```
javascript:
```

and then paste the contents of the clipboard — your JavaScript code — so that you have something like this (refer back to Figure 17-14):

```
javascript:MM_openBrWindow('myBuddy.htm','','scrollbars=yes',
'width=250,height=200')
```

Click OK when you're done.

8. Repeat Steps 2 through 7 for each additional button or behavior you'd like to use.

9. Export your Flash movie as a SWF file and place it into the same page in Dreamweaver where you built your dummy links. Note that the <head> tag of this page contains JavaScript functions that match your dummy links and the JavaScript inside your Flash movie, as shown in Figure 17-15.

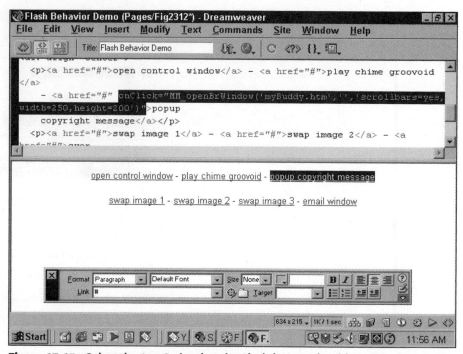

Figure 17-13: Select the JavaScript that the Flash button should execute from within the `onClick` attribute of your anchor tag.

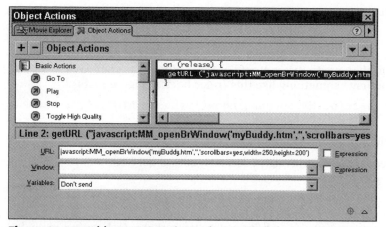

Figure 17-14: Add your JavaScript code to a Flash button Get URL behavior in the Instance Properties dialog box in Flash.

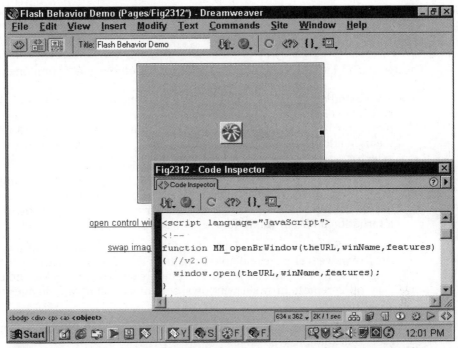

Figure 17-15: The JavaScript in your Flash movie relies on the same JavaScript functions that Dreamweaver inserted in the ⟨head⟩ tag as you built your dummy links.

10. Delete your dummy links — but not the JavaScript functions in the ⟨head⟩ tag — and publish your page.

When users click the buttons in your Flash movie, javascript: URL sends the commands to the browser, executing the JavaScript functions in your Web page. Flash buttons open new browser windows, pop-up messages, and so on. This works in Netscape and in Internet Explorer.

Tip

Shockwave authors can also use JavaScript URLs from Lingo to trigger Dreamweaver behaviors in a manner similar to the preceding. The JavaScript-savvy can also reference their own JavaScript functions using this method.

Dreamweaver Technique: Using the JavaScript Integration Kit for Flash 5

With an eye toward smoothing the integration between Flash and Dreamweaver, Macromedia released the JavaScript Integration Kit for Flash 5 (JIK). The JIK is a suite of commands and behaviors installable in Dreamweaver — versions 3 and above — via the Extension Manager. You can download the current version from the Macromedia Exchange; choose Commands ➪ Get More Commands to go directly online.

The JavaScript Integration Kit for Flash 5 consists of four main components:

✦ **Macromedia Flash Player Controls:** Allows the designer to include interactive control over Flash movies in a Web page. New Dreamweaver behaviors assign play, stop, rewind, fast-forward, pan, and zoom actions to any graphic element. In addition, an HTML drop-down menu can be turned into a Flash movie selector.

✦ **Advanced Form Validations:** Ensures that your visitors are entering the proper type of information in your Flash form. You can apply any of 18 client-side form validations — everything from a required, non-blank to an International Phone Validation.

✦ **Browser Scripts for Flash:** Embeds up to 10 different JavaScript functions in the Dreamweaver page, callable from any Flash 5 movie. With these functions, your Flash movie can control form elements such as text fields and select lists, open remote browser windows, set cookies, and swap images on the Web page.

✦ **Flash Dispatcher Behavior:** Detects the visitor's Flash Player version and redirects to a suitable Web page.

The beauty of the JIK is that its various components can be mixed and matched to achieve a wide range of effects and control. The resulting Web page offers a greater degree of interactivity for the visitor as well as for the Flash designer.

Macromedia Flash Player Controls

One method of engaging your Web page visitors is to give them more control over their viewing experience. Rather than just displaying a movie from beginning to end, allow the viewer to pause, rewind, and play the animation at will. Flash's vector-based nature even allows you to zoom in and out, without loss of image clarity. While all of this functionality is available through Flash ActionScripting, not all designs require the controls to be maintained within a Flash movie. The Flash Player Controls allow all of the common VCR-like functionality — and then some — to be assigned to HTML elements such as images or hotspots.

When the JavaScript Integration Kit is installed, 10 different behaviors are grouped under the MM Flash Player Controls:

✦ Fast Forward Flash

✦ Go To Flash Frame

✦ Go To Flash Frame Based on Cookie

✦ Load Flash Movie

✦ Pan Flash

✦ Play Flash

✦ Rewind Flash

✦ Set Flash by List

✦ Stop Flash

✦ Zoom Flash

As with any other Dreamweaver behavior, the player controls must be assigned to a target: a text link, an image map hotspot, or a graphic with a link attached. Typically, such a graphic button would use a false link, such as # or javascript:; so that it may act as a trigger but not actually open a URL.

You must have at least one Flash movie in the page before the Flash Player Controls become available, as shown in Figure 17-16. Once activated, the user interfaces for the Flash Player Controls vary according to their function as detailed below. With the Play, Stop, Rewind Flash behaviors, you just pick the Flash movie you want to control from the drop-down list. All the other behaviors include this option as well so you can affect any movie on the page.

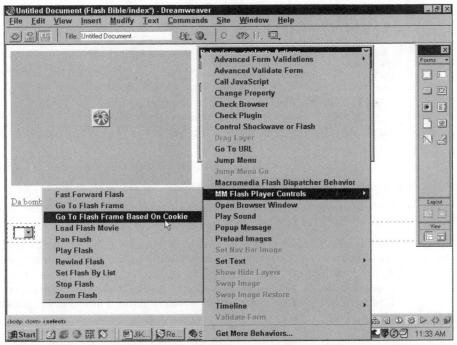

Figure 17-16: The Flash Player Controls become active once a Flash movie is present in the current Dreamweaver document.

To use the Flash Player Controls, follow these steps:

1. Insert at least one Flash movie by choosing an animation from the Assets panel or applying the Insert Flash object.

2. Enter a unique name in the ID field of the Flash Property Inspector for each movie. A distinct ID avoids browser compatibility problems; if one is not initially supplied, Dreamweaver offers to make one for you when any of the behaviors are applied.

3. Select the text link, hotspot, or image to trigger the behavior.

   If you'd like to apply the Set Flash by List behavior, select a form list object.

4. Choose Window ➪ Behaviors to open the Behaviors panel, if necessary. Alternatively, you can select the Show Behavior icon from the Launcher or use the keyboard shortcut, Shift+F3.

5. Choose the Add button from the Behaviors panel and select the desired behavior under the MM Flash Player Controls heading.

   The chosen behavior's dialog box appears, similar to the one shown in Figure 17-17.

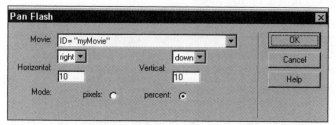

Figure 17-17: With the Pan Flash behavior, your viewer can move around a Flash movie in any direction. As shown, this behavior pans in a diagonal direction, down and to the right, every time it is triggered.

6. Select the parameters for your behavior.

   • For the Play Flash, Rewind Flash, and Stop Flash behaviors, select the desired animation to affect from the Movie drop-down list.

   • For the Fast Forward Flash behavior, select the desired animation to affect from the Movie drop-down list. In the first blank field, enter the desired value you want the movie to advance by. Select either Frames or Percent from the drop-down list. For example, to advance the movie by 5 percent each time the behavior is called, enter 5 in the first field and choose Percent from the list.

   • For the Go To Flash Frame behavior, select the desired animation to affect from the Movie drop-down list and then enter the frame number to move to in the Go To Frame field.

- For the Go To Flash Frame Based on Cookie behavior, select the desired animation to affect from the Movie drop-down list, enter the name of the cookie to read in the Cookie Name field, enter the value to look for in the Cookie Value field, and then enter the frame number to advance to when the cookie name and value are read in the Go To Frame field.

- For the Load Flash Movie behavior, select the desired animation to you want to replace from the Replace Movie drop-down list. Enter the file-name for the movie to load in the With Movie field or locate the movie by selecting the Browse button. Input the level to load the movie into in the Level field.

  To replace an existing movie with the loaded movie, enter a level number that is currently occupied by another movie. To replace the original movie and unload every level, choose 0 for the Level. To begin playing the movie immediately, set the Play option to Yes; otherwise, set Play to No.

Caution   As Dreamweaver warns you, the Load Flash Movie behavior is not supported for Netscape browsers.

- For the Pan Flash behavior, select the desired animation to affect from the Movie drop-down list, choose the Horizontal and/or Vertical direction — up, down, right, or left — to pan to from the drop-down lists, and then select the degree of the pan by entering a value in the fields below each direction. You can pan diagonally by entering non-zero values for both the Horizontal and Vertical direction. Choose whether you'd like the pan values to operate in either Pixel or Percent mode.

- For the Set Flash by List behavior, select the desired animation to affect from the Movie drop-down list, choose the list object from the Select Box drop-down list, and input the level to load the movie into in the Level field. To replace an existing movie with the loaded movie, enter a level number that is currently occupied by another movie. To replace the original movie and unload every level, choose 0 for the Level.

  To begin playing the movie immediately, set the Play option to Yes; otherwise, set Play to No. For the Set Flash by List behavior to work properly, you'll also need to set the values of each of the list items to a relative or absolute file URL pointing to a .swf file. Click the Parameters button on the List/Menu Property Inspector to enter new labels and their corresponding values.

Caution   As Dreamweaver warns you, the Set Flash by List behavior is not supported for Netscape browsers.

- For the Zoom Flash behavior, select the desired animation to affect from the Movie drop-down list. Enter the value desired in the Zoom field. To zoom in, enter a number greater than 100; to zoom out, enter a number below 100. To reset the movie to the original zoom level, enter 0.

7. After you've chosen all the desired parameters from the dialog box, select OK to close it.

    The Behaviors panel displays the event and action for the behavior just applied.

8. By default, onClick is the selected event. To change the triggering event to onMouseOver or onMouseOut, select the down arrow between the event and the action and choose the desired event from the list.

Advanced Form Validations

HTML forms can be tricky: The more you use forms to gather information from your visitors, the greater the possibility for user error. In a sense, forms are a classic double-edged sword and a few people taking advantage of Flash's increased interactivity are getting nicked by them. If, for example, your online form includes two fields for a telephone number, one for the U.S. and one for international visitors, you'll want to be sure that the proper data is entered in the correct field. To ensure that a user enters the type of information you're expecting in your Flash form, that information needs to be validated. The JavaScript Integration Kit includes methods for validating 18 different types of data.

For the Advanced Form Validations to work, you'll need to work both with your Flash movie and with the Dreamweaver page the movie is embedded in. Here's an overview of the process:

On the Dreamweaver side:

1. Create a form with hidden fields — one for each of the Flash fields you want to validate.

2. Attach the Advanced Validate Form behavior to the form itself.

3. Add one of the Browser Scripts for Flash functions, FDK_setFormText, to the page.

4. Attach the desired validation behavior to the <body> tag of the current document.

On the Flash side:

1. Make sure every form field has a unique variable name assigned to it.

2. Add a getURL action to the on (press) event of the submit button, calling the FDK_setFormText function inserted into the Dreamweaver page.

3. Add another getURL action to the on (release) event of the submit button, which invokes the FDK_Validate function — which was put on the Dreamweaver document by the Advanced Validate Form behavior.

You'll need to keep track of the names of the Hidden field inputs inserted in Dreamweaver, as well as the name of the form itself; they both are referenced when the functions are added in Flash.

Now that you have an overview, let's go through the process with a little more detail. Again, we'll start with the Dreamweaver page:

1. Choose Insert ➪ Form to add a form to your document.

   In Dreamweaver, the form is automatically named.

2. Within the form, add a Hidden form field for every Flash field you'd like to validate. Give each Hidden field a unique name and leave the Value blank.

3. Select the ⟨form⟩ tag in the Tag Selector and, from the Behaviors panel, choose the Advanced Validate Form behavior.

   The Advanced Validate Form dialog box appears, as shown in Figure 17-18.

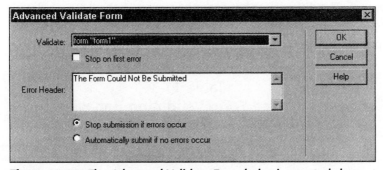

Figure 17-18: The Advanced Validate Form behavior controls how validations overall are applied.

4. In the Advanced Validate Form dialog box:

   - Select the form containing the Hidden elements you want to use from the Validate drop-down list.

   - To stop validating when an incorrect entry is encountered, check the Stop on First Error option.

   - Enter any desired message in the Error Header text area. The Error Header is displayed in addition to any validation-specific error messages.

   - If your behavior is assigned to an onSubmit event (the default) choose the Stop Submission If Errors Occur option; otherwise, select the Automatically Submit If No Errors Occur option.

   - Select OK to close the dialog box when you're done.

5. Choose Commands ➪ Browser Scripts for Flash.

The Browser Scripts for Flash command, discussed in more detail later in this section, embeds functions in the Dreamweaver page for communicating with Flash.

6. When the Browser Scripts for Flash dialog box opens, select the `FDK_setFormText` option; close the dialog box when you're done.

Our final preparation in Dreamweaver is to add the individual validation behaviors required.

7. Select the `<body>` tag from the Tag Selector and choose the Add (+) button in the Behaviors panel. From the drop-down list, select a validation behavior from the Advanced Form Validations category.

Most of the Advanced Form Validation behaviors have similar dialog boxes in which you can choose the particular form element (the Hidden field relating to the Flash form field) affected, make the field required, and set the error message. The differences between the various behaviors are detailed in Table 17-3.

8. Repeat Step 7 for every validation you'd like to apply in the form.

Table 17-3
Advanced Form Validation Behaviors

Behavior	Description
Alphanumeric Validation	Displays an error if non-alphanumeric characters are entered.
Credit Card Validation	Removes any spaces or hyphens and then displays an error message if the card number is not valid. This behavior does not authorize credit card purchases.
Date Validation	Optionally allows dates in the future, past, or in a particular range and specific format.
E-mail Validation	Makes sure that the entry contains an @ and a period.
Entry Length Validation	Accepts a defined number range of characters — for example, from 5 to 10.
Floating Point Validation	Displays an error if a non-number is entered; floating point numbers can contain decimals.
Integer Validation	Displays the message if a non-number or a number with decimals is entered. You can also set an acceptable number range.
International Phone Validation	Removes parentheses, spaces, and hyphens and then makes sure at least six digits are entered.
Like Entry Validation	Checks one form field entry against another; typically used for password verification.

Behavior	Description
Mask Validation	Allows the designer to require a specific pattern of text, and numbers to be entered. Use A to indicate a letter, # for numbers and ? if the entry could be either a letter or a number. For example, the mask A###?? would require a letter followed by three numbers, followed by two other alphanumeric characters.
Nonblank Validation	Displays a message if the field is left empty.
Radio Button Validation	Ensures that at least one option in a specified radio button group is selected. Note: This behavior is only used with HTML form elements.
Selection Made in List Validation	Displays an error if the user does not make a selection from a specific drop-down list. Note: This behavior is only used with HTML form elements.
Social Security Validation	Removes any hyphens, checks for a proper length and then reformats the number into a 3-2-4 configuration, as in 123-45-6789.
Time Validation	Displays an error if a valid time with minutes within a certain range is not entered. Military time and most variations of a.m. and p.m. are accepted.
URL Validation	Looks for valid URL protocols and displays an error message if one is not found at the start of the entry. Accepted URLs include: `ftp://`, `http://`, `javascript:`, `file://`, `gopher://`, `https://`, `mailto:`, `rlogin://`, `shttp://`, `snews://`, `telnet://`, `tn3270://`, `swais://`
US Phone Validation	Verifies that the entered information is either 7 or 10 digits after removing any parentheses and hyphens.
Zip Code Validation	Requires the entry to be either 5 or 9 digits.

Now that the Dreamweaver page is prepped, you're ready to prepare the Flash movie:

1. In Flash, add the required form fields as text input fields
2. In the Text Options panel, enter a unique name in the Variable field.
3. Make sure your form has a graphic that acts as a submit button.
4. Select the submit button graphic and open the Object Actions panel.
5. Add an `on (press)` event and attach a `getURL` function to the event.
6. In the `getURL` function, call the `FDK_setFormText` function that was embedded into the Dreamweaver page. The `FDK_setForm Text` function takes three arguments: the name of the form, the name of the field to be validated, and the variable name assigned to the corresponding field in Flash.

   For example, let's say the form is named `theForm` and you've created a field for gathering an e-mail address and given it a name in Dreamweaver such as emailHidden. In Flash, the variable assigned to the corresponding text field might be called emailField. In this case, the getURL function would read:

```
getURL("javascript:FDK_setFormText('theForm','emailHidden','"
add emailField add "')";)
```

Note the addition of the word add on either side of the variable name, as shown in the code and Figure 17-19. This syntax is required for the parameters to be passed correctly.

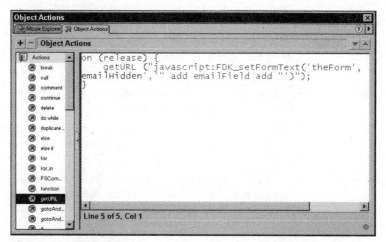

Figure 17-19: Enter a FDK_setFormText function for every Flash field you need to qualify.

7. Continue adding as many FDK_setFormText functions as you have fields to validate to the same getURL action. Separate each function with a semicolon.

   After you've entered all the required FDK_setFormText functions, you'll need to add one last event and function.

8. In the Object Actions panel for the submit button graphic, add an on (release) event and attach a getURL action to it.

9. In the getURL action, insert the FDK_Validate function. This function takes four arguments, which correspond to the options available in Dreamweaver's Advanced Validate Form dialog box: FormName, stopOnFailure, AutoSubmit, and ErrorHeader. Both stopOnFailure and AutoSubmit are Booleans and accept either true or false.

   As an example, suppose the form is again called theForm, that you'd like the form to stop processing when an error is encountered as well as automatically be submitted, and that your general error message reads, "Attention!! I found an error on the form!" Here, the getURL function would look like this:

```
getURL("javascript:FDK_Validate('theForm',true,true,'Attentio
n!! I found an error on the form!\\n\\n');");
```

The \n\n after the function call acts as a hard return in the alert box to separate the generic message header and the specific validation error.

The final step is to cross the bridge again from Flash to Dreamweaver, bringing your exported Flash movie into the Dreamweaver page. Be sure to give it both a name and ID (both of which can be the same) in the Property Inspector.

Browser Scripts for Flash

With the JavaScript Integration Kit, integration is a two-way street: not only is it easier to control Flash movies, the Flash movies can also affect the HTML page. The JIK includes one overall command called Browser Scripts for Flash, which offers over 5 different types of control:

✦ Setting a form element's value

✦ Setting a cookie

✦ Opening a remote browser window

✦ Swapping images for rollovers

✦ Setting list menu items

Implementing these functions in Dreamweaver is simplicity itself: Just choose Commands ➪ Browser Scripts for Flash and check off the desired options you see in Figure 17-20. The various functions are grouped into five different categories. If you open a page with these functions already in place, you'll find the option already selected; deselecting the checkbox removes the function from the page when the dialog box is closed.

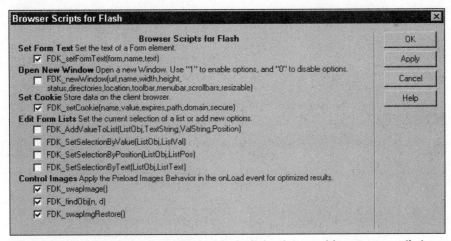

Figure 17-20: The Browser Scripts for Flash dialog box enables you to easily insert or remove functions that you can call from Flash.

Like the form validations, using the Browser Scripts is a two-program process. Once you've installed them in Dreamweaver you need call the function in a Flash action. Each of the functions takes its own series of parameters and typically, each one is invoked using an action such as getURL. The functions and their arguments are explained in Table 17-4.

Table 17-4 Browser Scripts for Flash Functions		
Function	*Arguments*	*Description*
FDK_setFormText elementName variableName	FormName	Sets the value of a form element.
FDK_newWindow windowName width height status directories location toolbar menubar scrollbars resizable	URL	Opens a remote browser window. The width and height values are entered in pixels; for all other parameters (except URL and windowName) enter a 0 to disallow the element and a 1 to include it.
FDK_setCookie cookieValue expiresWhen path domain secureBoolean	CookieName	Sets a cookie from within a Flash movie and can be used in conjunction with the Go To Flash Frame Based on Cookie behavior.
FDK_swapImage [blank] replacementPath 1	ImageName	Performs an image swap in the HTML document. The second parameter is intentionally left blank.
FDK_swapImgRestore	n/a	Restores a previously executed image swap. For complex pages using multiple image swaps, it's best to explicitly swap the image from its replacement to its original source rather than use the FDK_SwapImgRestore behavior.
FDK_findObj	n/a	Used in conjunction with the FDK_SwapImage behavior.

Function	Arguments	Description
FDK_AddValueToList TextString ValString Position	ListObj	Inserts a new value into a form list element.
FDK_SetSelection ByValue ListValue	ListObj	Determines the selection of a list item with a given value.
FDK_SetSelection ByPosition ListPos	ListObj	Determines the selection of a list item in a particular list position.
FDK_SetSelection ByText ListText	ListObj	Determines the selection of a list item with a given label.

Flash Dispatcher Behavior

The final component of the JavaScript Integration Kit, the Flash Dispatcher Behavior, is designed to smooth visitor access to your Web-based Flash content. The Flash Dispatcher checks to see if the visitor to your site already has the Flash player and, if so, what version. If the proper version — or no player at all — is found, this behavior gives you several options. The visitor's browser can be redirected to a Flash-less page or to a site for downloading an appropriate version, if an automatically downloaded version is not possible.

To apply this behavior, select the <body> tag from the Tag Selector and, from the Behaviors panel, choose Macromedia Flash Dispatcher Behavior. In the dialog box (see Figure 17-21), you have the following options:

- ✦ **Macromedia Flash Content URL:** Enter or locate the path to the page containing the Flash movie.

- ✦ **Alternate URL:** Enter or locate the path to a Web page the visitor should go to if the proper Flash player is not found.

- ✦ **Macromedia Flash Version:** Choose the lowest permissible version from 2.0, 3.0, 4.0, or 5.0

- ✦ **Require Latest Plugin:** Select this option to require the latest version of the Flash Player.

- ✦ **No Player Options:** Any visitors who do not have the Flash Player installed are sent to a selectable download page or are directed to use the Alternate URL.

- ✦ **Improper Version Options:** Any visitors who do not have the required version of the Flash Player installed will be sent to a selectable upgrade page or are directed to use the Alternate URL.

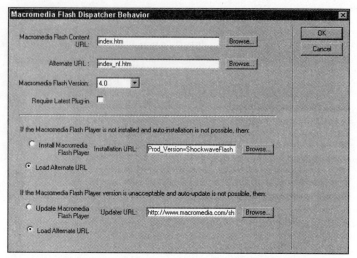

Figure 17-21: Make sure that only visitors with the proper Flash player can see your movies with the Flash Dispatcher Behavior.

The Flash Content URL can be the same page that the behavior is applied to or, in the case of what is referred to as a gateway script, another page.

Summary

Together, the interactive power of Shockwave and the speedy glitz of Flash can enliven Web content like nothing else. Dreamweaver is extremely well-suited for integrating and displaying Shockwave and Flash movies. Here are some key pointers to keep in mind:

✦ Saving your Director movies as Shockwave enables them to be played on the Web with the help of a plug-in or ActiveX control.

✦ Flash movies are a way to enhance your Web pages with vector animations, interactivity, and streaming audio. Flash movies require the Flash player plug-in or ActiveX Control.

✦ Dreamweaver has built-in objects for both Director and Flash movies. All the important parameters are accessible directly through the Property Inspector.

✦ You need only three parameters to incorporate a Shockwave movie: the file's location, height, and width. Dreamweaver automatically imports a Flash movie's dimensions. You can get the exact measurements of a Shockwave movie from within Director.

✦ Dreamweaver comes with a JavaScript behavior for controlling Shockwave and Flash movies. This Control Shockwave or Flash behavior can be used as-is for adding external controls to the same Web page or — with a minor modification — for adding the controls to another frame in the same frameset.

✦ Dreamweaver behaviors can be triggered from a Shockwave or Flash movie.

✦ The JavaScript Integration Kit for Flash 5 is a powerful set of extensions that enable Flash movies to control Dreamweaver behaviors and for HTML elements to activate Flash movies.

✦   ✦   ✦

Working with Dynamic HTML and Dreamweaver

Building Style Sheet Web Pages

All publications, whether on paper or the Web, need a balance of style and content to be effective. Style without content is all flash with no real information. Content with no style is flat and uninteresting, thus losing the substance. Traditionally, HTML has tied style to content wherever possible, preferring logical tags such as `<strong>` to indicate emphasis to physical tags such as `<b>` for bold. Although this emphasis on the logical worked for many single documents, its imprecision made it unrealistic, if not impossible, to achieve style consistency across a broad range of Web pages.

The Cascading Style Sheets specification has changed this situation — and much more. As support for Cascading Style Sheets (CSS) grows, more Web designers can alter font faces, type size and spacing, and many other page elements with a single command — and have the effect ripple not only throughout the page, but also throughout a Web site. Moreover, an enhancement of CSS called CSS-P (for positioning) is the foundation for what has become commonly known as *layers*.

Dreamweaver was one of the first Web authoring tools to make the application of Cascading Style Sheets user friendly. Through Dreamweaver's intuitive interface, the Web designer can access over 70 different CSS settings, affecting everything from type specs to multimedia-like transitions. Dreamweaver enables you to work the way you want: Create your style sheet all at once and then link it when you're ready, or make up your styles one-by-one as you build your Web page.

In this chapter, you find out how CSS works and why you need it. A Dreamweaver Technique for removing underlines from links walks you through a typical style sheet session. With that experience under your belt, you're ready for the sections with detailed information on the current CSS commands and how to apply them to your Web page and site. Also, the section on defining styles helps you understand what's what in the Style Definition dialog box. Finally, you learn how you can create external style sheets to create — and maintain — the look and feel of an entire Web site with a single document.

Understanding Cascading Style Sheets

The Cascading Style Sheets system significantly increases the design capabilities for a Web site. If you are a designer used to working with desktop publishing tools, you will recognize many familiar features in CSS, including the following:

✦ Commands for specifying and applying font characteristics

✦ Traditional layout measurement systems and terminology

✦ Pinpoint precision for page layout

Cascading Style Sheets are able to apply many features with a simple syntax that is easy to understand. If you're familiar with the concept of using styles in a word processing program, you'll have no trouble grasping style sheets.

Here's how the process works: CSS instructions are given in rules; a style sheet is a collection of these rules. A rule is a statement made up of an HTML or custom tag, called a *selector*, and its defined properties, referred to as a *declaration*. For example, a CSS rule that makes the contents of all <h1> tags (the selector) red in color (the declaration) looks like the following:

```
h1 {color:red}
```

In the following sections, you see the various characteristics of CSS — grouping, inheritance, and cascading — working together to give style sheets their flexibility and power.

Grouping properties

A Web designer often needs to change several style properties at once. CSS enables declarations to be grouped by separating them with semicolons. For example:

```
h1 {color:red; font-family:Arial,Helvetica,sans-serif; font-size:18pt}
```

The Dreamweaver interface provides a wide range of options for styles. Should you ever need to look at the code, you'll find that Dreamweaver groups your selections exactly as shown in the preceding example. Although Dreamweaver keeps each selector in its own rule, when you are hand-coding your style sheets, you can group selectors as well as declarations. Separate grouped selectors with commas, rather than semicolons. For example:

```
h1, h2, p, em {color:green; text-align:left}
```

Inheritance of properties

CSS rules can also be applied to more than one tag through inheritance: the ability of a parent or outer tag to pass on characteristics to the child or inner tags. Most, but not all, CSS declarations can be inherited by the HTML tags enclosed within the CSS selector. Suppose you set all <p> tags to the color red. Any tags included within a <p>...</p> tag pair then inherit that property and are also colored red.

Inheritance is also at work within HTML tags that involve a parent-child relationship, as with a list. Whether numbered (ordered, <ol>) or bulleted (unordered, <ul>), a list comprises any number of list items, designated by <li> tags. Each list item is considered a child of the parent tag, <ol> or <ul>. Take a look at the following example:

```
ol {color:red}
ul {color:blue}
```

With the preceding example, all ordered list items appear in red, whereas all unordered list items appear in blue. One major benefit to this parent-child relationship is that you can change the font for an entire page with one CSS rule. The following statement accomplishes this change:

```
body {font-family: Arial}
```

The change is possible in the previous example because the <body> tag is considered the parent of every HTML element on a page.

Tip

There's one exception to the preceding rule: tables. Netscape browsers (through version 4.75) treat tables differently than the rest of the HTML <body> when it comes to style sheets. To change the font of a table, you'd have to specify something such as the following:

```
td {font-family: Arial}
```

Because every cell in a table uses the <td> tag, this style sheet declaration affects the entire table. Dreamweaver is uneven in its application of this treatment. Setting the entire <body> to a particular font family is displayed correctly in the Document window, with even tables being affected. However, changing the color of a font in the <body> style sheet declaration does not alter the font color of text in a table in the Document window.

Cascading characteristics

The term *cascading* describes the capability of a local style to override a general style. Think of a stream flowing down a mountain; each ledge encountered by the stream has the potential to change its direction. The last ledge determines the final direction of the stream. In the same manner, one CSS rule applying generally to a block of text can be overridden by another rule applied to a more specific part of the same text.

For example, let's say you've defined, using style sheets, all normal paragraphs — <p> tags — as a particular font in a standard color, but you mark one section of the text using a little-used tag such as <samp>. If you make a CSS rule altering both the font and color of the <samp> tag, the section takes on the characteristics of that rule.

The cascading aspect of style sheets also works on a larger scale. One of the key features of CSS is the capability to define external style sheets that can be linked to individual Web pages, acting on their overall look and feel. Indeed, you can use the cascading behavior to fine-tune the overall Web site style based on a particular page or range of pages. Your company may, for instance, define an external style sheet for the entire company intranet, and each division could then build upon that overall model for its individual Web pages. For example, let's say that the company style sheet dictates that all <h2> headings are in Arial and black. One department could output their Web pages with <h2> tags in Arial, but colored red rather than black, while another department could make them blue.

Defining new classes for extended design control

Redefining existing HTML tags is a step in the right direction toward consistent design, but the real power of CSS comes into play when you define custom tags. In CSS-speak, a custom tag is called a *class*, and the selector name always begins with a period. Here's a simple example: To style all copyright notices at the bottom of all pages of a Web site to display in 8-point Helvetica all caps, you could define a tag as follows:

```
.cnote {font-family:Helvetica; font-size:8pt; font-transform:uppercase}
```

If you define this style in an external style sheet and apply it to all 999 pages of your Web site, you have to alter only one line of code (instead of all 999 pages) when the edict comes down from management to make all the copyright notices a touch larger. Once a new class has been defined, you can apply it to any range of text, from one word to an entire page.

How styles are applied

CSS applies style formatting to your page in one of three ways:

- ✦ Via an external, linked style sheet
- ✦ Via an internal style sheet
- ✦ Via embedded style rules

External style sheets

An *external* style sheet is a file containing the CSS rules; it links one or more Web pages. One benefit of linking to an external style sheet is that you can customize and change the appearance of a Web site quickly and easily from one file.

Two different methods exist for working with an external style sheet: the `link` method and the `import` method. Dreamweaver defaults to the link method, but you can also choose import if you prefer.

For the `link` method, a line of code is added outside of the `<style>` tags, as follows:

```
<link rel="stylesheet" href="mainstyle.css">
```

The `import` method writes code within the style tags, as follows:

```
<style type="text/css">
@import "newstyles.css";
</style>
```

Between the `link` and the `import` methods, the `link` method is better supported among browsers.

Internal style sheets

An *internal* style sheet is a list of all the CSS styles for a page.

Dreamweaver inserts all the style sheets at the top of a Web page within a `<style>...</style>` tag pair. Placing style sheets within the header tags has become a convention that many designers use, although you can also apply a style sheet anywhere on a page.

The `<style>` tag for a Cascading Style Sheet identifies the type attribute as `text/css`. The following is a sample internal style sheet:

```
<style type="text/css">
<!--
p {  font-family: "Arial, Helvetica, sans-serif"; color: #000000}
.cnote {  font: 8pt "Arial, Helvetica, sans-serif"; text-transform: uppercase}
h1 {  font: bold 18pt Arial, Helvetica, sans-serif; color: #FF0000}
-->
</style>
```

The HTML comment tags `<!--` and `-->` prevent older browsers that can't read style sheets from displaying the CSS rules.

Embedded style rules

The final method of applying a style inserts it within HTML tags using the `style` attribute. This method is the most "local" of all the techniques; that is, it is closest to the tag it is affecting and therefore has the ultimate control — because of the cascading nature of style sheets as previously discussed.

When you create a layer within Dreamweaver, you notice that the positioning attribute is a Cascading Style Sheet embedded within a `<div>` tag such as the following:

```
<div id="Layer1" style="position:absolute; visibility:inherit; left:314px; ¬
top:62px; width:194px; height:128px; z-index:1">
</div>
```

For all its apparent complexity, the Cascading Style Sheets system becomes straightforward in Dreamweaver. You often won't have to write a single line of code. But even if you don't have to write code, you should understand the CSS fundamentals of grouping, inheritance, and cascading.

Creating and Applying a Style Sheet in Dreamweaver

Dreamweaver uses three primary tools to implement Cascading Style Sheets: the CSS Styles panel, the Edit Style Sheet dialog box, and the Style Definition dialog box. Specifically, the CSS Styles panel is used to apply styles created in the Edit Style Sheet dialog box and specified with the Style Definition dialog box. With these three interfaces, you can accomplish the following:

✦ Link or import all your styles from an external style sheet

✦ View and edit most of the attributes included in the official release of CSS Level 1

✦ Modify any styles you have created

✦ Apply styles to selected text or to a particular tag surrounding that text

Caution

The fourth-generation browsers (and above) support many of the attributes from the first draft of the Cascading Style Sheets standard. Neither Netscape Navigator 4.0 nor Microsoft Internet Explorer 4.0 fully supports CSS Level 1, however. Of the earlier browsers, only Internet Explorer 3.0 supports a limited set of the CSS Level 1 features: font attributes, indents, and color. However, this support is rendered differently in Internet Explorer 3.0 and 4.0. Netscape Navigator 3.0 does not support any of the features of CSS Level 1. On the brighter side, Netscape Navigator 6.0 offers virtually complete compliance of CSS 1 and quite a lot of CSS 2. The current version of Internet Explorer for Windows (5.5 for Windows and 5.0 for Macintosh) is not as complete, but better than the 4.x versions.

Dreamweaver technique: Eliminating underlines from links

Because Dreamweaver's interface for CSS has so many controls, initially creating and applying a style can be a little confusing. Before delving into the details of the various panels, dialog boxes, and floating windows, let's quickly step through a typical style sheet session. Then, you can have an overall understanding of how all the pieces fit together.

Note   Don't panic if you encounter unfamiliar elements of Dreamweaver's interface in this introductory technique. You see them at work again and again as you work through the chapter.

Disabling the underline for the anchor tag, <a>, which is normally associated with hyperlinked text, is one modification commonly included in style sheets. To accomplish this task, follow these steps:

1. Open the CSS Styles panel by choosing Windows ➪ CSS Styles or selecting the Show CSS Styles button from either Launcher.

2. In the CSS Styles panel, select the New Style button. This sequence opens the New Styles dialog box.

3. In the New Styles dialog box, select Redefine HTML Tag and choose the anchor tag, a, from the drop-down list. Finally select Define In This Document Only to create an internal CSS style sheet. Click OK, and the Style Definition window opens.

Tip   You can also select the Use CSS Selector option and choose a:link from the drop-down list. You can even employ the a:hover style, which enables text to change color or style on rollover. You must, however, define the four CSS Selector styles in a particular order for them to work correctly. Start by defining the a:link class and then proceed to define a:active, a:visited, and a:hover, in that order. Note that these altered styles do not preview in Dreamweaver.

4. In the Style Definition window, select Type from the list of categories.

5. In the Decoration section of the Type category, select the option none. You can also make any other modifications to the anchor tag style, such as color or font size. Click OK when you're done.

Tip   Many designers, myself included, like to make the link apparent by styling it bold and in a different color.

The Style Definition window closes, and any style changes instantly take effect on your page. If you have any previously defined links, the underline disappears from them.

Now, any links that you insert on your page still function as links — the user's pointer still changes into a pointing hand, and the links are active — but no underline appears.

Tip   This technique works for any text used as a link. To eliminate the border around an image designated as a link, the image's border must be set to zero in the Image Property Inspector. Dreamweaver handles this automatically when a graphic is made into a link.

Using the CSS Styles panel to apply styles

The CSS Styles panel, shown in Figure 18-1, is a flexible and easy-to-use interface with straightforward command buttons listing all available style items. As with all of Dreamweaver's primary panels, you can open the CSS Styles panel in several ways:

✦ Choose Windows ⇨ CSS Styles.

✦ Select the New Style button from either Launcher.

✦ Press Shift+F11.

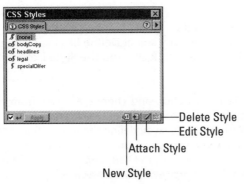

Figure 18-1: The Dreamweaver CSS Styles panel helps you apply consistent styles to a Web page.

The main part of the CSS Styles panel is the list of defined custom styles or classes. Every custom tag you create is listed alphabetically in this window. Once you've chosen the portion of your HTML document that you're stylizing, you can choose one of the custom styles listed here by simply selecting it, if the Apply option is selected. If the option is not checked, select the desired style and choose the Apply button.

At the bottom right-hand corner of the CSS Styles panel are four buttons. The first of these, Attach Style Sheet is a new addition in Dreamweaver 4 and is used for quickly linking the current Web page to an existing style sheet. Clicking the second — the New Style button — begins the process of defining a new CSS style, either in an external or internal style sheet. The third button, Edit Style Sheet, opens the multifaceted Edit Style Sheet dialog box, in which you can create a new style, link a style sheet, edit or remove an existing style, or duplicate a style that you can then alter. Before you can begin applying styles to a Web page or site, the styles must be defined, and using the Edit Style Sheet dialog box is the pain-free method of accomplishing this task. You can, of course, switch to Code view or open the Code Inspector and add the style by hand, but you can avoid this process with the Edit Style Sheet dialog box. You get a close look at this tool in the upcoming section "Editing and managing style sheets." The final button is for deleting styles once they are defined.

Attaching an external style sheet

As CSS-enabled browsers begin to become predominant, more Web designers are encountering clients with existing external style sheets. To apply the site's design specifications to a new page, all the designer need do is link the current page to the CSS document. Dreamweaver 4 provides a streamlined method for doing just that.

New Feature

The Attach Style Sheet button, found on the CSS Styles panel, is a one-step solution for linking external style sheets to the current document. When Attach Style Sheet is selected, a standard Select File dialog box appears with the *.css filter set. Simply locate the desired style sheet and select it: Dreamweaver inserts the necessary code into the ⟨head⟩ of your document. If any HTML tags — such as ⟨p⟩ or any of the heading tags — on your page are defined in the style sheet, you'll see an immediate change in your document.

When the Attach Style Sheet feature is applied, Dreamweaver uses the link attribute to connect style sheet to Web page. The link attribute is much more widely used by professional designers than the import attribute; however, if you'd prefer to use import instead, you can still attach a style sheet with this method as described in a section later in this chapter, "Importing an External Style Sheet."

Applying, changing, and removing a style

As noted above, any HTML tags redefined as CSS styles in an attached style sheet will automatically be applied to your document. However, any custom CSS styles must be applied on a case-by-case basis. Most Web designers use a combination of HTML and custom CSS styles. Only custom CSS styles appear in the CSS Styles panel.

New Feature

Dreamweaver 4 enables you to tell where a custom style is from — whether it's from a linked external style sheet or included in the current document — at a glance. The CSS Styles panel now displays a small chain-link symbol next to the listing if the style can be found on a separate style sheet. In larger sites, it's often important to differentiate between two similarly named custom styles.

To apply an existing custom style, follow these steps:

1. Choose Windows ⇨ CSS Styles or select the Show CSS Styles button from either Launcher to open the CSS Styles panel.

2. To apply the style to a section of the page enclosed by an HTML tag, select the tag from the Tag Selector.

   To apply the style to a section that is not enclosed by a single HTML tag, use your mouse to select that section in the Document window.

3. Select the desired custom style from the CSS Styles panel.

   Dreamweaver applies the custom style either by setting the `class` attribute of the selected tag to the custom style or — if just text is selected, not an enclosing tag — to a `<span>` tag which wraps around the text.

As you might expect, Dreamweaver offers a second way of applying a style to your pages. The following method, using the menus, does not employ the CSS Styles panel:

1. Highlight the text to which you're applying the style, either through the Tag Selector or by using the mouse.

2. Select Text ⇨ CSS Styles ⇨ Your Style.

   The same dynamic CSS Styles list is maintained in the context menu, accessible through a right-click (Ctrl+click) on the selected text.

Changing styles

In prior versions of Dreamweaver, multiple `<span>` tags were a common phenomenon as designers tried out different styles without properly selecting the `<span>` tag. It was not unusual to see this type of code:

```
<span class="head1"><span class="head2"><span
class="head3">News of the Moment</span></span></span>
```

In situations such as these, the CSS style in the span tag closest to the text, in this example head3, is rendered. The other span tags are just so much cluttered code. Dreamweaver 4 now strives to prevent nested `<span>` tags, automatically.

New Feature

Changing from applied custom style to another is extremely straightforward in Dreamweaver4. No longer do you have to be sure to select the enclosing tag — whether it's a `<span>` or other tag — to replace the style. In fact, you don't have to select anything: just place your cursor anywhere within the styled text and select a different custom style from the CSS Styles panel. Dreamweaver changes the old style to the new without adding additional `<span>` tags.

But what if you want to apply a new style to a text range within an existing `<span>` tag? Again, Dreamweaver's default is to avoid nested span tags. Here's how it works. Let's say you're working with the following code:

```
<span class="bodyCopy">Developing strategies to survive
requires industry insight and forward thinking in this
competitive marketplace.</span>
```

If you apply a custom style called hype to the phrases industry insight and forward thinking by first selecting those phrases and then choosing hype from the CSS Styles panel, the code looks like this:

```
<span class="bodyCopy">Developing strategies to survive
requires </span><span class="hype">industry insight</span> and
<span class="hype">forward thinking</span><span
class="bodyCopy"> in this competitive marketplace.</span>
```

Dreamweaver wraps each phrase in a distinct `<span>` tag so that nesting is entirely avoided. This behavior enables the style of each phrase to be altered more easily.

 Tip　If you positively, absolutely would prefer to nest your `<span>` tags, you can do so by Shift+clicking on the desired style in the CSS Styles panel.

If your cursor is positioned within a tag without an existing style, you can still quickly apply the custom CSS style. Dreamweaver now automatically applies the chosen style to the following tags:

- ✦ `<p>`
- ✦ `<h1>`-`<h6>`
- ✦ `<td>`
- ✦ `<th>`
- ✦ `<caption>`
- ✦ `<li>`
- ✦ `<ul>`
- ✦ `<ol>`
- ✦ `<pre>`
- ✦ `<blockquote>` or `<bq>`

 Caution　In most cases, this new functionality means that it's far easier to apply—and change—CSS styles than ever before. However, should your cursor be in a tag other than those listed above, such as an `<address>` tag, Dreamweaver wraps the text in a paragraph tag and assigns the style to the `<p>` tag. If your text is not within a span or one of the tags listed above, be sure to select the tag you want to apply the style to from the Tag Selector.

Removing applied styles

Getting rid of an applied style also gets a whole lot simpler in Dreamweaver 4. Now, just position your cursor anywhere in the stylized text and select (none) from the

CSS Styles panel. Dreamweaver removes the class attribute if the style was attached to a tag other than `<span>` while surrounding `<span>` tags are completely deleted. Naturally, if you choose the tag containing the style through the Tag Selector, selecting (none) also eliminates the style from the tag.

Note Be sure your cursor is just positioned within styled text and not selecting any. Selecting (none) from the CSS Styles panel when text alone — no tags — is highlighted, has no effect.

Defining new styles

Selecting the New Style button in the CSS Styles panel brings up a new dialog box (see Figure 18-2) where you specify the type of style you're defining. You can opt to create the new styles in an external style sheet or in the current document. After you've chosen the type of style desired, select the Define In This Document Only option to create an internal style sheet. Any style sheets already linked to (or imported into) the current document appear in the drop-down list along with the New Style Sheet File option. If you choose Define In New Style Sheet File, a standard file dialog box opens for you to name and store your new .css file.

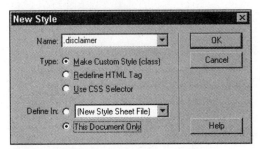

Figure 18-2: The first step in defining a new style is to select a style type and enter a name for the style, if it's a custom one.

The following sections explain the three style types in depth:

✦ Make Custom Style (class)

✦ Redefine HTML Tag

✦ Use CSS Selector

Make Custom Style (class)

Making a custom style is the most flexible way to define a style on a page. The first step in creating a custom style is to give it a name; this name is used in the `class` attribute. The name for your class must start with a period and must be alphanumeric without punctuation or special characters. If you do not begin the name of your custom style with a period, Dreamweaver inserts one for you.

Following are typical names you can use:

```
.master
.pagetitle
.bodytext
```

Caution

Although you can use names such as body, title, or any other HTML tag, this approach is not a good idea. Dreamweaver warns you of the conflict if you try this method.

Redefine HTML Tags

The second radio button in the New Style dialog box is Redefine HTML Tag. This type of style is an excellent tool for making quick, global changes to existing Web pages. Essentially, the Redefine HTML Tag style enables you to modify the features of your existing HTML tags. When you select this option, the drop-down list displays over 40 HTML tags in alphabetical order. Select a tag from the drop-down list and click OK.

Use CSS Selector

When you use the third style type, Use CSS Selector, you define what are known as *pseudo-classes* and *pseudo-elements*. A pseudo-class represents dynamic states of a tag that may change under user action or over time. Several standard pseudo-classes associated with the <a> tag are used to style hypertext links.

When you choose Use CSS Selector, the drop-down list box contains four customization options, which can all be categorized as pseudo-classes:

✦ a:active customizes the style of a link when the user selects it.

✦ a:hover customizes the style of a link while the user's mouse is over it.

Note

The a:hover pseudo-class is a CSS Level 2 specification and is currently supported only by Internet Explorer 4.0 and above as well as Netscape 6.

✦ a:link customizes the style of a link that has not been visited recently.

✦ a:visited customizes the style of a link to a page that has been recently visited.

Tip

Dreamweaver does not preview pseudo-class styles, although they can be previewed through a supported browser.

A pseudo-element, on the other hand, enables control over contextually defined page elements: for example, pseudo-elements enable you to style paragraphs within a table differently than paragraphs outside of a table. Similarly, text that is nested within two blockquotes (giving the appearance of being indented two levels) can be given a different color, font, and so on than text in a single blockquote.

Because of their specific nature, Dreamweaver does not display any pseudo-elements in the Use CSS Selector list. You can, however, enter your own. For example, to style text within nested blockquotes, enter the following in the Use CSS Selector field of the New Style dialog box:

```
blockquote blockquote
```

Basically, you are creating a custom style for a set of HTML tags used in your document. This type of CSS selector acts like an HTML tag that has a CSS style applied to it; that is, all page elements fitting the criteria are automatically styled.

Editing and managing style sheets

The Edit Style Sheet dialog box, shown in Figure 18-3, displays all your current styles — including HTML tags and custom styles — and provides various controls to link a style sheet and edit, create, duplicate, or remove a style. To access the Edit Style Sheet dialog box, choose the Edit Style Sheet button on the CSS Styles panel.

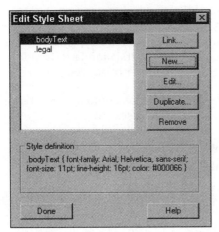

Figure 18-3: The Edit Style Sheet dialog box lists and defines any given style, in addition to presenting several command buttons for creating and managing styles.

Tip   To start editing one of your styles immediately, double-click the style in the list window of the Edit Style Sheet dialog box. This sequence takes you to the Style Definition dialog box, in which you redefine your selected style.

Use the following five command buttons along the right side of the Edit Style Sheet dialog box to create new external sheets or manage your existing style sheets:

✦ **Link:** Enables you to create an external style sheet or link to (or import) an existing external style sheet.

✦ **New:** Begins the creation of a new style by first opening the New Style dialog box, described in the following section.

✦ **Edit:** Modifies any existing style.

✦ **Duplicate:** Makes a copy of the selected style as a basis for creating a new style.

✦ **Remove:** Deletes an existing style.

Importing an external style sheet

As noted earlier, most Web designers prefer the link method of including an external style sheet to the import method. However, Dreamweaver offers both options, albeit in a slightly more difficult to get to place.

To import a separate style sheet, follow these steps:

1. Open the CSS Styles panel by choosing Windows ➪ CSS Styles or selecting the Show CSS Styles button from either Launcher.

2. Select the Edit Style Sheet button.

3. In the Edit Style dialog box, select the Link command button.

   The Link External Style Sheet dialog box pops up, where you can access all your style sheets, by browsing and linking.

4. Either type in the File/URL path or select the Browse button to locate a style sheet; the Cascading Style Sheet file has the .css file name extension on your hard drive. If you have not already created a style sheet, you can do so by locating the place you want the style sheet and then creating a name for it. Useful names for style sheets can be master.css, contents.css, or body.css.

5. Choose the Import option.

   Naturally, you could also, at this point, choose the Link option

When you go back to the Edit Style Sheet dialog box, you see a link file referenced in the listing above all the styles, followed by (link) or (import). You can double-click the file listing to open a new Edit Style Sheet dialog box for your external style sheet file. The defined styles within the style sheet then appear in the CSS Styles panel.

Tip

Once you've defined your external style sheet, a couple of shortcuts exist for the Edit Style Sheet dialog box. First, you can press the Ctrl (Option) key and click the Edit Style Sheet button in the CSS Styles panel. Rather than displaying the Edit Style Sheet dialog box with a link to your external style sheet (which you'd have to double-click or highlight and select Edit to modify), you'll see the dialog box for the external style sheet immediately.

The second method is useful if you have the Site window open. Just double-click any .css file, and the Edit Style Sheet dialog box for that file opens instantly.

If you've already defined styles in the current document and you want to convert them to an external style sheet, Dreamweaver has you covered. Just choose File ➪ Export ➪ Export CSS Styles and enter a file name in the Export Styles as CSS File dialog box. Follow the directions in this section for linking this newly created file to your other Web pages as a style sheet.

Tip

You can also export internal styles to an external style sheet by pressing Ctrl (Option) while clicking the Done button in the Edit Style Sheet dialog box.

Styles and Their Attributes

After you've selected a type and name for a new style or chosen to edit an existing style, the Style Definition dialog box opens. A Category list from which you select a style category (just as you select a category in Dreamweaver's Preferences dialog box) is located on the left side of this dialog box.

Dreamweaver offers you eight categories of CSS Level 1 styles to help you define your style sheet:

- ✦ Type
- ✦ Background
- ✦ Block
- ✦ Box
- ✦ Border
- ✦ List
- ✦ Positioning
- ✦ Extensions

You can apply styles from one or all categories. The following sections describe each style category and its available settings.

Note Dreamweaver doesn't preview all the possible CSS attributes. Those attributes that can't be seen in the Document window are marked with an asterisk in the Style Definition dialog box.

Type options

The Type category (see Figure 18-4) specifies the appearance and layout of the typeface for the page in the browser window. The Type category is one of the most widely used and supported categories — it can be rendered in Internet Explorer 3.0 and above and Netscape Navigator 4.0 and above. Table 18-1 explains the settings available in this category.

Table 18-1
CSS Type Attributes

Type Setting	Description
Font	Specifies the font or a collection of fonts, known as a *font family*. You can edit the font list by selecting Edit Font List from the drop-down list. (This sequence opens the Edit Font List dialog box, as described in Chapter 9.)
Size	Selects a size for the selected font. If you enter a value, you can then select the measurement system in the adjacent text box (the default is points). The relative sizes, such as small, medium, and large, are set relative to the parent element.
Style	Specifies a normal, oblique, or italic attribute for the font. An oblique font may have been generated in the browser by electronically slanting a normal font.
Line Height	Sets the line height of the line (known as *leading* in traditional layout). Typically, line height is a point or two more than the font size, although you can set the line height to be the same as or smaller than the font size, for an overlapping effect.
Decoration	Changes the decoration for text. Options include underline, overline, line-through, blink, and none. The blink decoration is displayed only in Netscape browsers.
Weight	Sets the boldness of the text. You can use the relative settings (light, bold, bolder, and boldest) or apply a numeric value. Normal is around 400; bold is 700.
Variant	Switches between normal and small caps. Small caps is a font style that displays text as uppercase, but the capital letters are a slightly larger size. The Variant option is not currently fully supported by either primary browser.
Case	Forces a browser to render the text as uppercase, lowercase, or capitalized.
Color	Sets a color for the selected font. Enter a color name or select the color swatch to choose a browser-safe color from the pop-up menu.

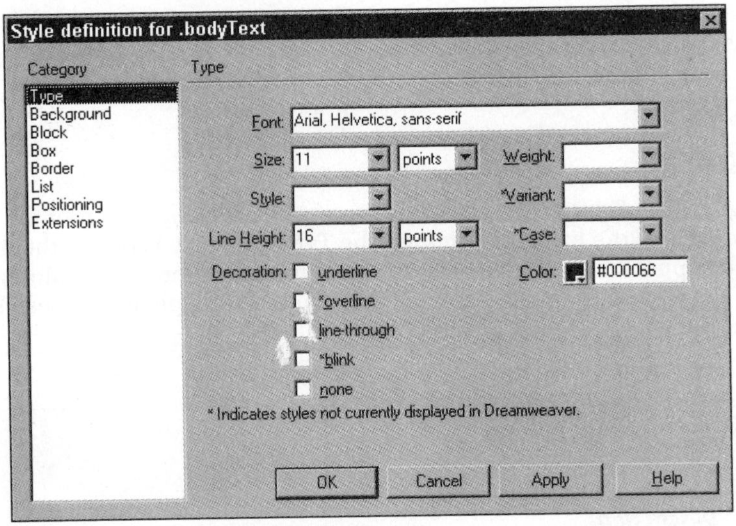

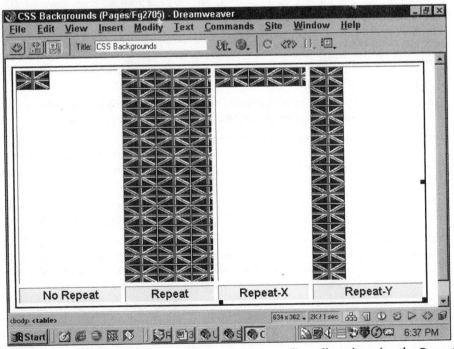

Figure 18-4: Type settings for your style

Figure 18-5: You can achieve a number of different tiling effects by using the Repeat attribute of the CSS Background category.

Background options

Since Netscape Navigator 2.0, Web designers have been able to use background images and color. Thanks to CSS Background attributes, designers can now use background images and color with increased control. Whereas traditional HTML background images are restricted to a single image for the entire browser window, CSS backgrounds can be specified for a single paragraph or any other CSS selector. (To set a background for the entire page, apply the style to the <body> tag.) Moreover, instead of an image automatically tiling to fill the browser window, CSS backgrounds can be made to tile horizontally, vertically, or not at all (see Figure 18-5). You can even position the image relative to the selected element.

Currently only Netscape 6 fully supports the CSS Background attributes shown in Figure 18-6 and listed in Table 18-2. The Repeat attribute enjoys full support across 4.x browsers and above, but Positioning and Attachment are rendered only in Internet Explorer 4.0 and above and Netscape 6.

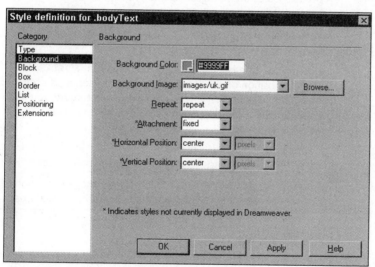

Figure 18-6: The CSS Background options enable a much wider range of control over background images and color.

Table 18-2
CSS Background Attributes

Background Setting	Description
Background Color	Sets the background color for a particular style. Note that this setting enables you to set background colors for individual paragraphs or other elements.
Background Image	Specifies a background image.
Repeat	Determines the tiling options for a graphic:
	no repeat displays the image in the upper-left corner of the applied style
	repeat tiles the background image horizontally and vertically across the applied style
	repeat-x tiles the background image horizontally across the applied style
	repeat-y tiles the background image vertically down the applied style
Attachment	Determines whether the background image remains fixed in its original position or scrolls with the page. This setting is useful for positioned elements. If you use the overflow attribute, you often want the background image to scroll in order to maintain layout control.
Horizontal Position	Controls the positioning of the background image in relation to the style sheet elements (text or graphics) along the horizontal axis.
Vertical Position	Controls the positioning of the background image in relation to the style sheet elements (text or graphics) along the vertical axis.

Block options

One of the most common formatting effects in traditional publishing long absent from Web publishing is justified text — text that appears as a solid block. Justified text is possible with the Text Align attribute, one of the six options available in the CSS Block category, as shown in Figure 18-7. Indented paragraphs are also a possibility. Table 18-3 lists the CSS Block options.

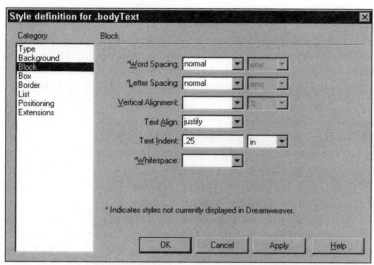

Figure 18-7: The Block options give the Web designer enhanced text control.

Table 18-3
CSS Block Attributes

Block Setting	Description
Word Spacing	Defines the spacing between words. You can increase or decrease the spacing with positive and negative values, set in ems.
Letter Spacing	Defines the spacing between the letters of a word. You can increase or decrease the spacing with positive and negative values, set in ems.
Vertical Alignment	Sets the vertical alignment of the style. Choose from baseline, sub, super, top, text-top, middle, bottom, or text-bottom, or add your own value.
Text Align	Sets text alignment (left, right, center, and justified).
Text Indent	Indents the first line of text on a style by the amount specified.
Whitespace	Controls display of spaces and tabs. The normal option causes all whitespace to collapse. The pre option behaves similarly to the `<pre>` tag; all white space is preserved. The nowrap option enables text to wrap if a ` ` tag is detected.

Box options

The Box attribute defines the placement and settings for elements (primarily images) on a page. Many of the controls (shown in Figure 18-8) emulate spacing behavior similar to that found in `<table>` attributes. If you are already comfortable using HTML tables with cell padding, border colors, and width/height controls, you can quickly learn how to use these Box features, which are described in Table 18-4.

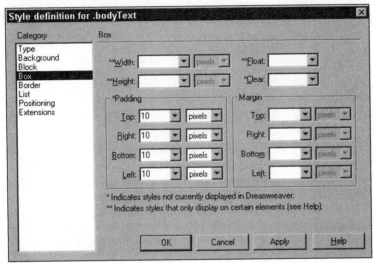

Figure 18-8: The CSS Box attributes define the placement of HTML elements on the Web page.

Table 18-4
CSS Box Attributes

Box Setting	Description
Width	Sets the width of the element.
Height	Defines the height of the element.
Float	Places the element at the left or right page margin. Any text that encounters the element wraps around it.
Clear	Sets the side on which layers cannot be displayed next to the element. If a layer is encountered, the element with the Clear attribute places itself beneath the layer.
Padding	Sets the amount of space between the element and the border or margin, if no border is specified. You can control the padding for the left, right, top, and bottom independently.
Margin	Defines the amount of space between the borders of the element and other elements in the page.

Dreamweaver imposes some specific restrictions on which Box attributes can and cannot be previewed in the Document window. For example, the Float and Clear attributes can be previewed only when applied to an image. The Margin attributes can be previewed when applied to block-level elements, such as any of the <h1> through <h6> tags or the <p> tag. Padding is not displayed within Dreamweaver.

Border options

With Cascading Style Sheets, you can specify many parameters for borders surrounding text, images, and other elements such as Java applets. In addition to specifying separate colors for any of the four box sides, you can also choose the width of each side's border, as shown in the CSS Border category (see Figure 18-9). You can use eight different types of border lines, including solid, dashed, inset, and ridge. Table 18-5 lists the Border options.

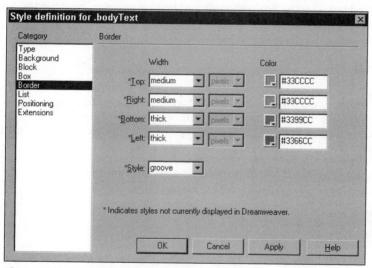

Figure 18-9: Borders are useful when you need to highlight a section of text or a graphic.

Table 18-5
CSS Border Attributes

Border Setting	Description
Top	Sets the color and settings for a border along the top of an element.
Right	Sets the color and settings for a border along the right side of an element.
Bottom	Sets the color and settings for a border along the bottom of an element.
Left	Sets the color and settings for a border along the left side of an element.
Style	Sets the style of the border. You can use any of the following as a border: Dotted, Dashed, Solid, Double, Groove, Ridge, Inset, and Outset.

Tip   CSS Border attributes are especially useful for highlighting paragraphs of text with a surrounding box. Use the Box category's Padding attributes to inset the text from the border.

List options

CSS gives you greater control over bulleted points. With Cascading Style Sheets, you can now display a specific bulleted point based on a graphic image, or you can choose from the standard built-in bullets, including disc, circle, and square. The List category also enables you to specify the type of ordered list, including decimal, Roman numerals, or A-B-C order.

Figure 18-10 shows, and Table 18-6 describes, the settings for lists.

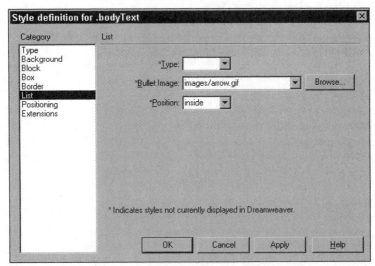

Figure 18-10: Specify a graphic to use as a bullet through the List category.

Table 18-6
List Category for Styles

List Setting	Description
Type	Selects a built-in bullet type. The options include disc, circle, square, decimal, lowercase roman, uppercase roman, lowercase alpha, and uppercase alpha.
Bullet Image	Sets an image to be used as a custom bullet. Enter the path to the image in the text box.
Position	Determines if the list item wraps to an indent (the default) or to the margin.

Positioning options

For many designers, positioning has increased creativity in page layout design. With positioning, you have exact control over where an element is placed on a page. Figure 18-11 shows the various attributes that provide this pinpoint control of your page elements. The options are described in Table 18-7.

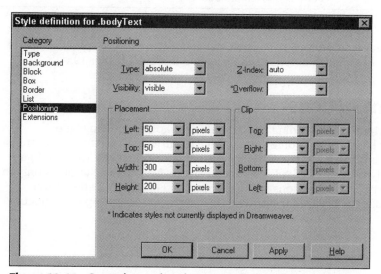

Figure 18-11: Control over the placement of elements on a page frees the Web designer from the restrictions imposed with HTML tables and other old-style formats.

	Table 18-7 CSS Positioning Attributes	
Positioning Setting	**Description**
Type	Determines whether an element can be positioned absolutely or relatively on a page. The third option, static, does not enable positioning.
Visibility	Determines whether the element is visible or hidden, or inherits the property from its parent.
Z-Index	Sets the apparent depth of a positioned element. Higher values are closer to the top.
Overflow	Specifies how the element is displayed when it's larger than the dimensions of the element. Options include the following: Clip, where the element is partially hidden; none, where the element is displayed and the dimensions are disregarded; and Scroll, which inserts scroll bars to display the overflowing portion of the element.
Placement	Sets the styled element's placement with the left and top attributes, and the dimensions with the width and height attributes.
Clip	Sets the visible portion of the element through the top, right, bottom, and left attributes.

Cross-Reference   Dreamweaver layers are built upon the foundation of CSS positioning. For a complete explanation of layers and their attributes, see Chapter 19.

Extensions options

The specifications for Cascading Style Sheets are rapidly evolving, and Dreamweaver has grouped some cutting-edge features in the Extensions category. As of this writing, the majority of the Extensions attributes (see Table 18-8) are supported only by Internet Explorer 4.0 and above; Netscape 6 supports only the cursor property. The Extensions settings shown in Figure 18-12 affect three different areas: page breaks for printing, the user's cursor, and special effects called *filters*.

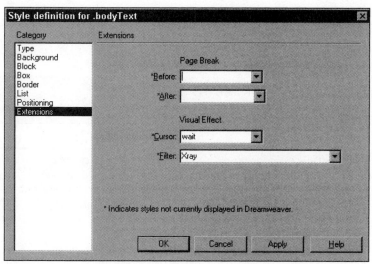

Figure 18-12: The Extensions category is currently supported only by Internet Explorer 4 and above, as well as Netscape 6.

Table 18-8
CSS Extensions Attributes

Extensions Setting	Description
Pagebreak	Inserts a point on a page where a printer sees a page break. Not supported by any current browser.
Cursor	Defines the type of cursor that appears when the user moves the cursor over an element. Currently supported only by Internet Explorer 4.0 and above, as well as Netscape 6.
Filter	Filters enable you to customize the look and transition of an element without having to use graphic or animation files. Currently supported only by Internet Explorer 4.0 and above.

Note One of the problems with the Web's never-ending evolution of page design is evident when you begin to print the page. The Pagebreak attribute alleviates this problem by enabling the designer to designate a style that forces a page break when printing; the break can occur either before or after the element is attached to the style. Although no browser currently supports this feature, it's a good candidate for support by future browsers.

The Filter attribute offers 16 different special effects that can be applied to an element. Many of these effects, such as wave and xray, are quite stunning. Several effects involve transitions, as well. Table 18-9 details all these effects.

	Table 18-9 CSS Filters	
Filter	**Syntax**	**Description**
Alpha	alpha(Opacity=*opacity*, FinishOpacity=*finishopacity*, Style=*style*, StartX=*startX*, StartY=*startY*, FinishX=*finishX*, FinishY=*finishY*)	Sets the opacity of a specified gradient region. This can have the effect of creating a burst of light in an image.
	Opacity is a value from 0 to 100, where 0 is transparent and 100 is fully opaque.	
	Style can be 0 (uniform), 1 (linear), 2 (radial), or 3 (rectangular).	
BlendTrans*	blendtrans(duration=*duration*)	Causes an image to fade in or out over a specified time.
	Duration is a time value for the length of the transition, in the format of *seconds.milliseconds*.	
Blur	blur(Add=*add*, Direction=*direction*, Strength=*strength*)	Emulates motion blur for images.
	Add is any integer other than 0.	
	Direction is any value from 0 to 315 in increments of 45.	
	Strength is any positive integer representing the number of pixels. affected.	
Chroma	chroma(Color= *color*)	Makes a specific color in an image transparent.
	Color must be given in hexadecimal form, for example, #rrggbb.	
DropShadow	dropshadow(Color=*color*, OffX=*offX*, OffY=*offY*, Positive=*positive*)	Creates a drop shadow of the applied element, either image or text, in the specified color.
	Color is a hexadecimal triplet.	

Filter	Syntax	Description
	OffX and *OffY* are pixel offsets for the shadow.	
	Positive is a Boolean switch; use 1 to create shadow for nontransparent pixels and 0 to create shadow for transparent pixels.	
FlipH	FlipH	Flips an image or text horizontally.
FlipV	FlipV	Flips an image or text vertically.
Glow	Glow(Color=*color*, Strength=*strength*)	Adds radiance to an image in the specified color.
	Color is a hexadecimal triplet.	
	Strength is a value from 0 to 100.	
Gray	Gray	Converts an image in grayscale.
Invert	Invert	Reverses the hue, saturation, and luminance of an image.
Light*	Light	Creates the illusion that an object is illuminated by one or more light sources.
Mask	Mask(Color=*color*)	Sets all the transparent pixels to the specified color and converts the nontransparent pixels to the background color.
	Color is a hexadecimal triplet.	
RevealTrans*	RevealTrans(duration=*duration*, transition=*style*)	Reveals an image using a specified type of transition over a set period of time.
	Duration is a time value that the transition takes, in the format of *seconds.milliseconds*.	
	Style is one of 23 different transitions.	
Shadow	Shadow(Color=*color*, Direction=*direction*)	Creates a gradient shadow in the specified color and direction for images or text.
	Color is a hexadecimal triplet.	

Continued

Table 18-9 (continued)		
Filter	**Syntax**	**Description**
	Direction is any value from 0 to 315 in increments of 45.	
Wave	Wave(Add=*add*, Freq=*freq*, LightStrength=*lightstrength*, Phase=*phase*, Strength=*strength*)	Adds sine wave distortion to the selected image or text.
	Add is a Boolean value, where 1 adds the original object to the filtered object and 0 does not.	
	Freq is an integer specifying the number of waves.	
	LightStrength is a percentage value.	
	Phase specifies the angular offset of the wave, in percentage (for example, 0% or 100% = 360 degrees, 25% = 90 degrees).	
	Strength is an integer value specifying the intensity of the wave effect.	
Xray	Xray	Converts an image to inverse grayscale for an X-rayed appearance.

* These three filters require extensive documentation beyond the scope of this book.

Note   Although only Internet Explorer uses the filters described here, Netscape 6 does have the capability to control opacity. The MozOpacity property of the style command may be set programmatically to a percentage value as in this code:

```
document.myImage.style.MozOpacity = '50%';
```

You can also declare the MozOpacity property as part of a CSS style. The following code example shows a CSS style that changes the opacity to 77% to whatever it's applied for both Internet Explorer 4 (and above) and Netscape 6.

```
.myOpacity { filter: alpha(opacity=77); -moz-opacity:
77% }
```

Summary

In this chapter, you discovered how you can easily and effectively add and modify Cascading Style Sheets. You can now accomplish all of the following:

✦ Update and change styles easily with the CSS Styles panel.

✦ Easily apply generated styles to an element on a page.

✦ Apply a consistent look and feel with linked style sheets.

✦ Position fonts and elements, such as images, with pinpoint accuracy.

✦ Exercise control over the layout, size, and display of fonts on a page.

✦ Define external style sheets to control the look and feel of an entire site.

In the next chapter, you learn how to position elements on a page in Dreamweaver using layers.

✦   ✦   ✦

Working with Layers

For many years, page designers have taken for granted the capability to place text and graphics anywhere on a printed page—even enabling graphics, type, and other elements to "bleed" off a page. This flexibility in design has eluded Web designers until recently. Lack of absolute control over layout has been a high price to pay for the universality of HTML, which makes any Web page viewable by any system, regardless of the computer or the screen resolution.

Lately, however, the integration of positioned layers within the Cascading Style Sheets specification has brought true absolute positioning to the Web. Page designers with a yen for more control can move to the precision offered with Cascading Style Sheets-Positioning (CSS-P).

Dreamweaver's implementation of layers turns the promise of CSS-P into an intuitive, designer-friendly, layout-compatible reality. As the name implies, layers offer more than pixel-perfect positioning. You can stack one layer on another, hide some layers while showing others, move a layer across the screen—and even move several layers around the screen simultaneously. Layers add an entirely new dimension to the Web designer's palette. Dreamweaver enables you to create page layouts using layers and then convert those layers to tables that are viewable by earlier browsers.

This chapter explores every aspect of how layers work in HTML—except for animation with timelines, which is saved for Chapter 20. With the fundamentals under your belt, you learn how to create, modify, populate, and activate layers on your Web page.

Layers 101

When the World Wide Web first made its debut in 1989, few people were concerned about the aesthetic layout of a page. In fact, because the Web was a descendant of SGML — a multiplatform text document and information markup specification — layout was trivialized. Content and the capability to use hypertext to jump from one page to another were emphasized. After the first graphical Web browser software (Mosaic) was released, it quickly became clear that a page's graphics and layout could enhance a Web site's accessibility and marketability. Content was still king, but design was moving up quickly.

The first attempt at Web page layout was the server-side image map. This item was a typically large graphic (usually too hefty to be downloaded comfortably) with hotspots. Clicking a hotspot sent a message to the server, which returned a link to the browser. The download time for these files was horrendous, and the performance varied from acceptable to awful, based on the server's load.

The widespread adoption of tables, released with HTML 2.0 and enhanced for versions 3.2 and 4.0, radically changed layout control. Designers gained the capability to align objects and text — but a lot of graphical eye candy was still left to graphic files strategically located within the tables. The harder designers worked at precisely laying out their Web pages, the more they had to resort to workarounds such as nested tables and 1-pixel-wide GIFs used as spacers. To relieve the woes of Web designers everywhere, the W3C included a feature within the new Cascading Styles Sheet specifications that allows for absolute positioning of an element upon a page. Absolute positioning enables an element, such as an image or block of text, to be placed anywhere on the Web page. Both Microsoft Internet Explorer 4.0 (and above) and Netscape Navigator 4.0 (and above) support layers under the Cascading Style Sheets–Positioning specification.

The addition of the third dimension, depth, truly turned the positioning specs into layers. Now objects can be positioned side-by-side, and they have a *z-index* property as well. The z-index gets its name from the practice in geometry of describing three-dimensional space with x, y, and z coordinates; z-index is also called the *stacking order* because objects can be stacked upon one another.

A single layer in HTML looks like the following:

```
<div id="Layer1" style="position:absolute; visibility:inherit; width:200px; ¬
height:115px; z-index:1"></div>
```

Positioned layers are most commonly placed within the `<div>` tag. Another popular location is the `<span>` tag. These tags were chosen because they are seldom used in the HTML 3.2 specification (Dreamweaver supports both tags). Both Microsoft and Netscape encourage users to employ either of these tags, because the two primary browsers are designed to credit full CSS-P features to either the `<div>` or `<span>` tag. You should generally use these tags when anything but specific Navigator 4.*x* compatibility is desired.

Positioning Measurement

The positioning of layers is determined by aligning elements on an x-axis and a y-axis. In CSS, the x-axis (defined as "Left" in CSS syntax) begins at the left side of the page, and the y-axis (defined as "Top" in CSS syntax) is measured from the top of the page down. As with many of the other CSS features, you have your choice of measurement systems for Left and Top positioning. All measurements are given in Dreamweaver as a number followed by the abbreviation of the measurement system (without any intervening spaces). The measurement system options follow:

Unit	Abbreviation	Measurement
Pixels	px	Relative to the screen
Points	pt	1 pt = $\frac{1}{72}$ in
Inches	in	1 in = 2.54 cm
Centimeters	cm	1 cm = 0.3937 in
Millimeters	mm	1 mm = 0.03937 in
Picas	pc	1 pc = 12 pt
EMS	em	The height of the element's font
Percentage	%	Relative to the browser window

If you don't define a unit of measurement for layer positioning, Dreamweaver defaults to pixels. If you decide to edit out the unit of measurement, the Web browser defaults to pixels.

Note Netscape has developed two additional proprietary tags for using layers in its 4.x browser: `<layer>` and `<ilayer>`. The primary difference between the two tags has to do with positioning: the `<layer>` tag is used for absolute positioning, and the `<ilayer>` tag for relative positioning. Unfortunately, layers created by the `<div>` tag and the `<layer>` tag have different feature sets. These tags are no longer supported in Navigator 6.0; instead Netscape's latest browser fully supports the CSS standard tags, `<div>` and `<span>`.

Creating Layers with Dreamweaver

Dreamweaver enables you to create layers creatively and precisely. You can drag out a layer, placing and sizing it by eye, or choose to do it by the numbers — it's up to you. Moreover, you can combine the methods, quickly eyeballing and roughing out a layer layout and then aligning the edges precisely. For Web design that approaches conventional page layout, Dreamweaver even includes rulers and a grid to which you can snap your layers.

You can handle the creation of layers in Dreamweaver in one of three ways:

✦ You can drag out a layer, after selecting the Draw Layer button from the Objects panel.

✦ You can put a layer in a predetermined size by choosing Insert ➪ Layer.

✦ You can create a layer with mathematical precision through the CSS Styles panel.

The first two methods are quite intuitive and are explained in the following section. The CSS Styles panel method is examined later in this chapter in the section "Embedding a layer with style sheets."

Inserting a layer object

When you want to draw out your layer quickly, use the object approach. If you come from a traditional page-designer background and are accustomed to using a program such as QuarkXPress or PageMaker, you're already familiar with drawing out frames or text boxes with the click-and-drag technique. Dreamweaver uses the same method for placing and sizing new layer objects.

To draw out a layer as an object, follow these steps:

1. From the Common category of the Objects panel, select the Draw Layer button. Your pointer becomes a crosshair cursor. (If you decide not to draw out a layer, you can press Shift+Esc at this point or just click once without dragging to abort the process.)

2. Click anywhere in your document to position the layer and drag out a rectangle. Release the mouse button when you have an approximate size and shape with which you're satisfied (see Figure 19-1).

After you've dragged out your layer, notice several changes to the screen. First, the layer now has a small box on the outside of the upper-left corner. This box, shown in Figure 19-2, is the selection handle, which you can use to move an existing layer around the Web page. When you click the selection handle, eight sizing handles appear around the perimeter of the layer.

Layer icon   Selected layer   Draw Layer button

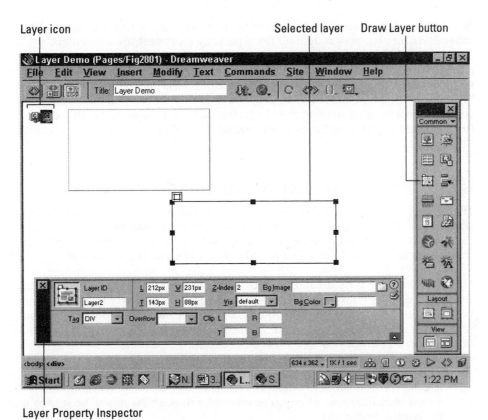

Layer Property Inspector

Figure 19-1: After selecting the Drag Layer object in the Objects panel (Common), the pointer becomes crosshairs when you are working on the page. Click and drag to create the layer.

Selection handle

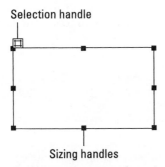

Sizing handles

Figure 19-2: Once a layer is created, you can move it by dragging the selection handle and size it with the sizing handles.

Another subtle but important addition to the screen is the Layer icon. Like the other Invisibles icons — so named because they represent the unseen code — the Layer icon can be cut, copied, pasted, and repositioned. When you move the Layer icon, however, its corresponding layer does not move — you are actually only moving the code for the layer to a different place in the HTML source. Generally, the layer code's position in the HTML is immaterial — however, you may want to locate your layer source in a specific area to be backwardly compatible with 3.0 browsers. Dragging and positioning Layer icons one after another is a quick way to achieve this task.

Using the Insert ⇨ Layer command

The second method to create a layer is through the menus. Instead of selecting an object from the Objects panel, choose Insert ⇨ Layer. Unlike the click-and-drag method, inserting a layer through the menu automatically creates a layer in the upper-left corner; the default size is 200 pixels wide and 115 pixels high.

Although the layer is by default positioned in the upper-left corner of the Document window, it does not have any coordinates listed in the Property Inspector. The position coordinates are added when you drag the layer into a new position. If you repeatedly add new layers through the menus without moving them to new positions, each layer stacks directly on top of one another, with no offset.

Caution   It's important for every layer to have a specific position (left and top) assigned to it. Otherwise, the browser displays all layers directly on top of one another. To give a layer measurements, after you've inserted it through the menu, be sure to drag the layer, even slightly.

Setting default characteristics of a layer

You can designate the default size — as well as other features — of the layer that is inserted with Insert ⇨ Layer. Choose Edit ⇨ Preferences or use the keyboard shortcut Ctrl+U (Command+U) to open the Preferences dialog box. Select the Layers category. The Layers Preferences category (see Figure 19-3) helps you to set the layer attributes listed in Table 19-1.

Table 19-1 Layer Preferences	
Layer Preference	*Description*
Tag	Sets the HTML code to use when creating layers. The options are `<div>` (the default), `<span>`, `<layer>`, and `<ilayer>`.
Visibility	Determines the initial state of visibility for a layer. The options are default, inherit, visible, and hidden.

Layer Preference	Description
Width	Sets the width of the layer in the measurement system of your choice. The default is 200 pixels.
Height	Sets the height of the layer in the measurement system of your choice. The default is 115 pixels.
Background Color	Sets a color for the layer background. Select the color from the pop-up menu of Web-safe colors.
Background Image	Sets an image for the layer background. In the text box, enter the path to the graphics file or click the Browse (Choose) button to locate the file.
Nesting Option	If you want to nest layers when one layer is placed in the other automatically, check the Nest when Created Within a Layer checkbox.
Netscape 4 Compatibility	To add code for a workaround to a known problem in Navigator 4.x browsers, which causes layers to lose their positioning coordinates when the user resizes the browser window, select this option.

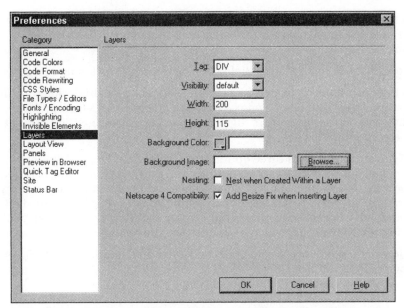

Figure 19-3: If you're building layers to a certain specification, use the Layers Preferences category to designate your options.

Embedding a layer with style sheets

In addition to laying out your layer by eye, or inserting a default layer with Insert ⇨ Layer, you can also specify your layers precisely through style sheets. Although this method is not as intuitive as either of the preceding methods, creating layers through style sheets has notable advantages:

✦ You can enter precise dimensions and other positioning attributes.

✦ The placement and shape of a layer can be combined with other style factors such as font family, font size, color, and line spacing.

✦ Layer styles can be saved in an external style sheet, which enables similar elements on every Web page in a site to be controlled from one source.

 If you haven't yet read Chapter 18, which discusses building style sheet Web pages, you may want to look it over before continuing here.

To create a layer with style sheets, follow these steps:

1. Choose Window ⇨ CSS Styles or select the Show CSS Styles button from the Launcher. This selection opens the CSS Styles panel.

2. From the CSS Styles panel, select the New Style button. This selection opens the New Style dialog box.

3. From the New Style dialog box, set the Type option set to Make Custom Style (class). Enter a name for your new style and then choose Define In This Document Only. Click OK.

4. This opens the Style definition dialog box. Select the Positioning category.

5. From the Positioning category (see Figure 19-4), enter desired values for these attributes: Type, Visibility, Z-Index, Overflow, Placement (Left, Top, Width, and Height), and Clip settings (Top, Right, Bottom, Left). Overflow and Clip settings are optional.

   The Type attribute offers three options: Absolute, Relative, and Static. While you are familiar with the first two options, the third option, Static, is probably new to you. Use Static when you don't want to add content to a layer, but you still want to specify a rectangular block. Static <div> types ignore the Left and Top attributes. Dreamweaver does not display a static <div> type, so you'll have to preview your page in a browser to see the results.

6. If appropriate, select other categories and enter any additional style sheet attributes desired. Click OK when you're done.

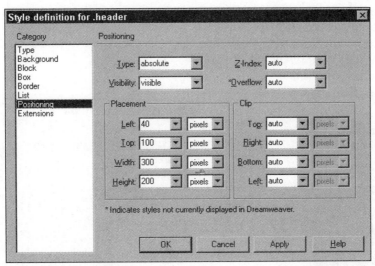

Figure 19-4: Use the Positioning category of the Style definition dialog box to set layer attributes in an internal or external style sheet.

Keep in mind that layers are part of the overall Cascading Style Sheet specification and can benefit from all of the features of style sheets. You may decide that a specific area of text — a header, for instance — must always be rendered in a bold, red, 18-point Arial font with a green background, and that it should always be placed 35 pixels from the left margin and 25 pixels from the top of the page. You can place the style sheet within a .css file, link your Web pages to this file, and receive a result similar to what's shown (in black and white) in Figure 19-5. Within one component — the Cascading Style Sheet file — you can contain all of your positioning features for a page's headers, titles, and other text, graphics, or objects. This capability gives you the benefit of controlling the position and look of every title linked to one style sheet.

Choosing relative instead of absolute positioning

In most cases, absolute positioning uses the top-left corner of the Web page or the position where the `<body>` tag begins as the point of origin from which the Web browser determines the position of the text, image, or object. You can also specify measurements relative to objects. Dreamweaver offers two methods to accomplish relative positioning: the relative attribute and nested layers.

Using the relative attribute

In the first method, you select Relative as the Type attribute in the Style Sheet Positioning category. Relative positioning does not force a fixed position; instead, the HTML tags around it guide the positioning. For example, you may place a list of some items within a table and set the positioning relative to the table. You can see the effect of this sequence in Figure 19-6. In this illustration's Positioning category, the Type attribute is set to Relative and the Placement/Left value is set to 0.5 inch for a style applied to the listed items.

Figure 19-5: You can apply the layer style to any element on any Web page linked to the style sheet.

Note Dreamweaver 4 doesn't preview relative positioning unless you're working with a nested layer, so you should check your placement by previewing the page in a browser, as shown in Figure 19-6.

Relative attributes can be useful, particularly if you want to place the positioned objects within free-flowing HTML. Free-flowing HTML repositions itself if the browser window is larger or smaller than the designer is aware. When you're using this technique, remember to place your relative layers within absolutely positioned layers. Otherwise, when the end user resizes the browser, the relative layers position themselves relative to the browser and not to the absolutely positioned layers. This situation can produce messy results — use relative positioning with caution when mixed with absolute layers.

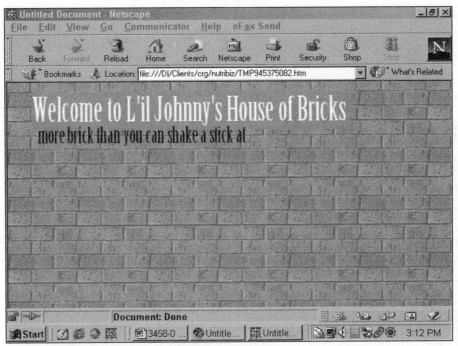

Figure 19-6: Relative positioning through styles can give your document a clean look, although the effect is not previewed in Dreamweaver.

Using nested layers

The second technique for positioning layers relatively uses nested layers. Once you nest one layer inside another, the inner layer uses the upper-left corner of the outer layer as its orientation point. For more details about nesting layers, refer to the section "Nesting with the Layers panel," later in this chapter.

Modifying a Layer

Dreamweaver helps you deftly alter layers once you have created them. Because of the complexity of managing layers, Dreamweaver offers an additional tool to the usual Property Inspector: the Layers panel. This tool enables you to select any of the layers on the current page quickly, change layer relationships, modify their visibility, and adjust their stacking order. You can also alter the visibility and stacking order of a selected layer in the Property Inspector, along with many other attributes. Before any modifications can be accomplished, however, you have to select the layer.

Selecting a layer

You can choose from several methods to select a layer for alteration (see Figure 19-7).

Layers Palette

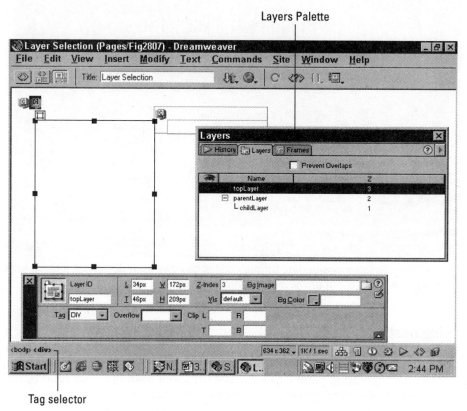

Tag selector

Figure 19-7: You have four different methods for selecting a layer to modify.

Your method of choosing a layer most likely depends on the complexity of your page layout:

✦ When you have only a few layers that are not overlapping, just click the selection handle of the layer with which you want to work.

✦ When you have layers placed in specific places in the HTML code (for example, a layer embedded in a table using relative positioning), choose the Layer icon.

✦ When you have many overlapping layers that are being addressed by one or more JavaScript functions, use the Layers panel to choose the desired layer by name.

✦ When you're working with invisible layers, click the `<div>` (or `<span>`) tag in the Tag Selector to reveal the outline of the layer.

Resizing a layer

To resize a layer, position the pointer over one of the eight sizing handles surrounding the selected layer. When over the handles, the pointer changes shape to a two- or four-headed arrow. Now click and drag the layer to a new size and shape.

You can also use the arrow keys to resize your layer with more precision. The following keyboard shortcuts change the width and height dimensions while the layer remains anchored by the upper-left corner:

✦ When the layer is selected, press Ctrl+arrow (Command+arrow) to expand or contract the layer by one pixel.

✦ Press Shift+Ctrl+arrow (Shift+Command+arrow) to increase or decrease the selected layer by the current grid increment. The default grid increment is five pixels.

Tip You can quickly preview the position of a layer on a Web page without leaving Dreamweaver. Deselecting the View ⇨ Visual Aids ⇨ Layer Borders option leaves the layer outline displayed only when the layer is selected, but otherwise it is not shown.

Moving a layer

The easiest way to reposition a layer is to drag the selection handle. If you don't see the handle on a layer, click anywhere in the layer. You can drag the layer anywhere on the screen — or off the bottom or right side of the screen. To move the layer off the left side or top of the screen, enter a negative value in the left and top (L and T) text boxes of the Layer Property Inspector.

Tip To hide the layer completely, match the negative value with the width or height of the layer. For example, if your layer is 220 pixels wide and you want to position it offscreen to the left (so that the layer can slide on at the click of a mouse), set the Left position at −220 pixels.

As with resizing layers, you can also use the arrow keys to move the layer more precisely:

✦ Press any arrow key to move the selected layer one pixel in any direction.

✦ Use Shift+arrow to move the selected layer by the current grid increment.

Using the Layer Property Inspector

You can modify almost all the CSS-P attributes for your layer right from the Layer Property Inspector (see Figure 19-8). Certain attributes, such as width, height, and background image and color are self-explanatory or recognizable from other objects. Other layers-only attributes such as visibility and inheritance require further explanation. Table 19-2 describes all the Layer properties, and the following sections discuss the features unique to layers.

Figure 19-8: The Layer Property Inspector makes it easy to move, resize, hide, and manipulate all of the visual elements of a layer.

Table 19-2
Layer Property Inspector Options

Layer Attribute	Possible Values	Description
BgColor	Any hexadecimal or valid color name	Background color for the layer.
BgImage	Any valid graphic file	Background image for the layer.
Clip (Top, Bottom, Left, Right)	Any positive integer region of the layer. If the values are not specified, the entire layer is visible.	Measurements for the displayable
H (Height)	Any integer measurement in pixels, centimeters, millimeters, inches, points, percentage, ems, or picas	Vertical measurement of the layer.
L (Left)	Any integer measurement in pixels, centimeters, millimeters, inches, points, percentage, ems, or picas	Distance measured from the origin point on the left.
Name	Any unique name without spaces or special characters	Labels the layer so that it can be addressed by style sheets or JavaScript functions.
Overflow	visible, scroll, hidden, or auto	Determines how text or images larger than the layer should be handled.
T (Top)	Any integer measurement in pixels, centimeters, millimeters, inches, points, percentage, ems, or picas	The distance measured from the origin point on the top.

Layer Attribute	Possible Values	Description
Tag	span, div, layer, or ilayer	Type of HTML tag to use for the layer.
Vis (Visibility)	default, inherit, visible, or hidden	Determines whether a layer is displayed. If visibility is set to inherit, then the layer takes on the characteristic of the parent layer.
W (Width)	Any integer measurement in pixels, centimeters, millimeters, inches, points, percentage, ems, or picas	The horizontal measurement of the layer.
Z-Index	Any integer	Stacking order of the layer in relation to other layers on the Web page. Higher numbers are closer to the top.

Name

Names are important when working with layers. To refer to them properly for both CSS and JavaScript purposes, each layer must have a unique name: unique among the layers and unique among every other object on the Web page. Dreamweaver automatically names each layer as it is created in sequence: Layer1, Layer2, and so forth. You can enter a name that is easier for you to remember by replacing the provided name in the text box on the far left of the Property Inspector.

Caution

Netscape Note: Netscape Navigator 4.x is strict with its use of the ID attribute. You must ensure that you call the layer with an alphanumeric name that does not use spacing or special characters such as the underscore or percentage sign. Moreover, make sure your layer name begins with a letter and not a number — in other words, layer9 works but 9layer can cause problems.

Tag attribute

The Tag drop-down list contains the HTML tags that can be associated with the layer. By default, the positioned layer has <div> as the tag, but you can also choose <span>, <layer>, or <ilayer>. As previously noted, the <div> and <span> tags are endorsed by the World Wide Web Consortium group as part of their CSS standards. The <layer> and <ilayer> tags are Netscape Navigator 4.x proprietary tags, although Netscape also supports the CSS tags.

Indeed, if you are working on a Navigator 4.x-based intranet, you may want to change the default layer tag. Choose Edit ➪ Preferences and then, from the Layers category, select either <layer> or <ilayer> from the Tag drop-down list.

Visibility

Visibility (Vis in the Property Inspector) defines whether or not you can see a layer on a Web page. The following four values are available:

✦ **Default:** Enables the browser to set the visibility attribute. Most browsers use the inherit value as their default.

✦ **Inherit:** Sets the visibility to the same value as that of the parent layer, which enables a series of layers to be hidden or made visible by changing only one layer.

✦ **Visible:** Causes the layer and all of its contents to be displayed.

✦ **Hidden:** Makes the current layer and all of its contents invisible.

Remember the following when you're specifying visibility:

✦ Whether or not you can see a layer, you must remember that the layer still occupies space on the page and demands some of the page loading time. Hiding a layer does not affect the layout of the page, and invisible graphics take just as long to download as visible graphics.

✦ When you are defining the visibility of a positioned object or layer, you should not use default as the visibility value. A designer does not necessarily know whether the site's end user has set the default visibility to visible or hidden. Designing an effective Web page can be difficult without this knowledge. The common browser default is for visibility to be inherited, if not specifically shown or hidden.

Overflow

Normally, a layer expands to fit the text or graphics inserted into it. You can, however, restrict the size of a layer by changing the height and width values in the Property Inspector. What happens when you define a layer to be too small for an image, or when an amount of text depends on the setting of the layer's overflow attribute? CSS layers (the <div> and <span> tags) support four different overflow settings:

✦ **Visible (Default):** All of the overflowing text or image is displayed, and the height and width settings established for the layer are ignored.

✦ **Hidden:** The portion of the text or graphic that overflows the dimensions is not visible.

✦ **Scroll:** Horizontal and vertical scroll bars are added to the layer regardless of the content size or amount, and regardless of the layer measurements.

✦ **Auto:** When the content of the layer exceeds the width and/or height values, horizontal and vertical scroll bars appear.

Currently, support for the overflow attribute is spotty at best. Dreamweaver doesn't display the result in the Document window; it must be previewed in a browser to be seen. Navigator offers limited support: Only the attribute's hidden value works correctly and, even then, just for text. Only Internet Explorer 4.0 or above and Netscape 6 render the overflow attribute correctly, as shown in Figure 19-9.

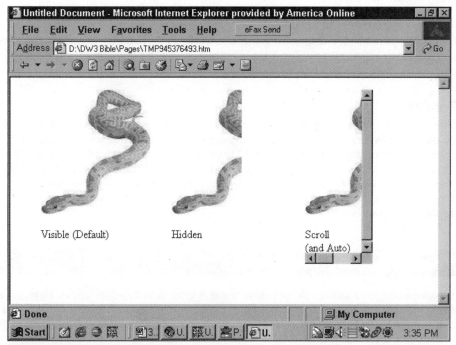

Figure 19-9: When your contents are larger than the dimensions of your layer, you can regulate the results with the overflow attribute.

Netscape Note: The Overflow property is not recognized by the Netscape Navigator 4.x proprietary layer tags, `<layer>` and `<ilayer>`.

Clipping

If you're familiar with the process of cropping an image, you'll quickly grasp the concept of clipping layers. Just as desktop publishing software hides but doesn't delete the portion of the picture outside of the crop marks, layers can mask the area outside the clipping region defined by the Left, Top, Right, and Bottom values in the Clip section of the Layer Property Inspector.

All clipping values are measured from the upper-left corner of the layer. You can use any CSS standard measurement system: pixels (the default), inches, centimeters, millimeters, ems, or picas.

The current implementation of CSS only supports rectangular clipping. When you look at the code for a clipped layer, you see the values you inserted in the Layer Property Inspector in parentheses following the clip attribute, with the `rect` (for rectangular) keyword, as follows:

```
<div id="Layer1" style="position:absolute; left:54px; top:24px; ¬
width:400px; height:115px; z-index:1; visibility:inherit; ¬
clip:rect(10 100 100 10)">
```

Generally, you specify values for all four criteria: Left, Top, Right, and Bottom. You can also leave the Left and Top values empty or use the keyword `auto` — which causes the Left and Top values to be set at the origin point: 0,0.

Z-index

One of a layer's most powerful features is its capability to appear above or below other layers. You can change this order, known as the *z-index*, dynamically. Whenever a new layer is added, Dreamweaver automatically increments the z-index — layers with higher z-index values are positioned above layers with lower z-index values. The z-index can be adjusted manually in either the Layer Property Inspector or the Layers panel. The z-index must be an integer, either negative or positive.

A Visual Clipping Technique

In Dreamweaver, you cannot draw the clipping region visually — the values have to be explicitly input in the Clip section of the Layer Property Inspector. That said, a trick using a second temporary layer makes it easier to position your clipping. Follow these steps to get accurate clipping values:

1. Insert your original layer and image.

2. Nest a second, temporary layer inside the first, original layer (select the Draw Layer button in the Objects panel and draw out the second layer inside the first).

   If you have your Layer Preferences set so that a layer does not automatically nest when created inside another layer, press the Ctrl (Command) key while you draw your layer, to override the preference.

3. Position the second layer over the area you want to clip. Use the layer's sizing handles to alter the size and shape, if necessary.

4. Note the position and dimensions of the second layer (the Left, Top, Width, and Height values).

5. Delete the second layer.

6. In the Property Inspector for the original layer, enter the Clip values as follows:

- **L:** Enter the Left value for the second layer.
- **T:** Enter the Top value for the second layer.
- **R:** Add the second layer's Left value to its Width value.
- **B:** Add the second layer's Top value to its Height value.

Dreamweaver displays the clipped layer after you enter the final value. The following figure shows the original layer and the temporary layer on the left, and the final clipped version of the original layer on the right.

Tip   Although some Web designers use high values for the z-index, such as 3,000, the z-index is completely relative. The only reason to increase a z-index to an extremely high number is to ensure that that particular layer remains on top.

The z-index is valid for the CSS layer tags as well as the Netscape 4.*x* proprietary layer tags. Netscape 4.*x* also has two additional attributes that can affect the apparent depth of either the `<layer>`- or `<ilayer>`-based content: above and below. With above and below, you can specify which existing layer is to appear directly on top of or beneath the current layer. You can only set one of the depth attributes, the z-index, or above or below.

Caution Certain types of objects — including Java applets, plug-ins, and ActiveX controls — ignore the z-index setting when included in a layer and appear as the uppermost layer. However, certain ActiveX Controls — most notably Flash — can be made to respect the z-index.

When you designate the layer's tag attribute to be either `<layer>` or `<ilayer>`, the Property Inspector displays an additional field: the A/B attribute for setting the above or below value, as shown in Figure 19-10. Choose either attribute from the A/B drop-down list and then select the layer from the adjacent list. The layer you choose must be set up in the code before the current layer. You can achieve this condition in the Document window by moving the icon for the current layer to a position after the other layers. Although you must use either `<layer>` or `<ilayer>` to specify the above or below attribute, the layer specified can be either a CSS or Netscape type.

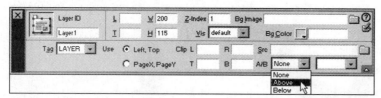

Figure 19-10: Choosing the Netscape-specific tags LAYER or ILAYER from the Property Inspector causes several new options to appear, including the A/B switch for the above/below depth position.

Caution Working with the above and below attributes can be confusing. Notice that they determine which layer is to appear on top of or underneath the current layer, and not which layer the present layer is above or below.

Background image or color

Inserting a background image or color with the Layer Property Inspector works in a similar manner to changing the background image or color for a table (as explained in Chapter 12). To insert an image, enter the path to the file in the Bg Image text box or select the Folder icon to locate the image file on your system or network. If the layer is larger than the image, the image is tiled, just as it would in the background of a Web page or table.

To give a layer a background color, enter the color name (either in its hexadecimal or nominal form) in the Bg Color text box. You can also select the color swatch to pick your color from the color picker.

Additional Netscape 4.x properties

In addition to the above and below values for the z-index attribute, two other Netscape 4.x variations must be noted for the sake of completeness — both of which appear as options in the Property Inspector when either `<layer>` or `<ilayer>` is selected as the layer tag.

When either `<layer>` or `<ilayer>` is selected, the Page X, Page Y option becomes available as a radio button in the Property Inspector in addition to Left, Top. With Netscape 4.x layers, Left, Top places the layer relative to the top-left corner of its parent (whether that's the page or another layer if the layer is nested). Page X, Page Y positions the layer based on the top-left corner of the page, regardless of whether the layer is nested.

The other additional Netscape 4.x layer attribute is the source property. You can specify another HTML document to appear within a `<layer>` or `<ilayer>` — much like placing other Web pages in frames. To specify a source for a Netscape 4.x layer, enter the path to the file in the Src text box or select the Folder icon to locate the file.

Caution   Although these properties are available in Dreamweaver, they should really only be used if your Web site is used as a Netscape 4.x intranet. Neither of these properties is supported by Internet Explorer or Netscape 6.

The Layers panel

Dreamweaver offers another tool to help manage the layers in your Web page: the Layers panel. Although this tool doesn't display as many properties about each element as the Property Inspector, the Layers panel gives you a good overview of all the layers on your page. It also provides a quick method of selecting a layer — even when it's offscreen — as well as enabling you to change the z-index and the nesting order.

The Layers panel, shown in Figure 19-11, can be opened either through the Window menu (Window ➪ Layers) or by pressing the keyboard shortcut F2.

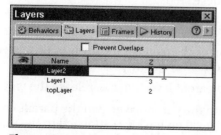

Figure 19-11: Use the Layers panel to select quickly or alter the visibility or relationships of all the layers on your page.

Modifying properties with the Layers panel

The Layers panel lists the visibility, name, and z-index settings for each layer. All of these properties can be modified directly through the Layers panel.

The visibility of a particular layer is noted by the eye symbol in column one of the Layers panel. Selecting the eye symbol cycles you through three different visibility states as follows:

✦ **Eye closed:** Indicates that the layer is hidden.

✦ **Eye open:** Indicates that the layer is visible.

✦ **No eye:** Indicates that the visibility attribute is set to the default (which, for both Navigator and Internet Explorer, means inherit).

Tip To change all of your layers to a single state simultaneously, select the eye symbol in the column header. Unlike the individual eyes in front of each layer name, the overall eye toggles between open and shut.

You can also change a layer's name (in the second column of the Layers panel). Just double-click the current layer name in the Layers Property Inspector; the name is highlighted. Type in the new name and press Enter (Return) to complete the change.

The z-index (stacking order) in the third column can be altered in the same manner. Double-click the z-index value; then type in the new value and press Enter (Return). You can enter any positive or negative integer. If you're working with the Netscape proprietary layer tags, you can also alter the above or below values previously set for the z-index through the Property Inspector. Use A for above and B for below.

Tip To change a layer's z-index interactively, you can drag one layer above or below another in the Layers panel.

Nesting with the Layers panel

Another task managed by the Layers panel is nesting or unnesting layers. This process is also referred to as *creating parent-child layers*. To nest one layer inside another through the Layers panel, follow these steps:

1. Choose Window ⇨ Layers or press F2 to open the Layers panel.

2. Press the Ctrl (Command) key, then click the name of the layer to be nested (the child), and drag it on top of the other layer (the parent).

3. When you see a rectangle around the parent layer's name, release the mouse.

   The child layer is indented underneath the parent layer, and the parent layer has a minus sign (a down-pointing triangle on the Mac) attached to the front of its name.

4. To hide the child layer from view, select the minus sign (down-pointing triangle) in front of the parent layer's name. Once the child layer is hidden, the minus sign turns into a plus sign (a right-pointing triangle on the Mac).

5. To reveal the child layer, select the plus sign (right-pointing triangle on the Mac).

6. To undo a nested layer, select the child layer and drag it to a new position in the Layers panel.

Caution   When it comes to nested layers, Netscape 4.x does not "play well with others." In fact, the expected results are so rarely achieved that it's best to avoid nested layers in cross-browser sites for the time being.

You can use the nesting features of the Layers panel to hide many layers quickly. If the visibility of all child layers is set to default — with no eye displayed — then by hiding the parent layer, you cause all the child layers to inherit that visibility setting and also disappear from view.

Tip   You can also delete a layer from the Layers panel. Just highlight the layer to be removed and press Delete. Dreamweaver does not enable you to delete nested layers as a group, however — you have to remove each one individually.

Aligning layers with the ruler and grid

With the capability to position layers anywhere on a page comes additional responsibility and potential problems. In anything that involves animation, correct alignment of moving parts is crucial. As you begin to set up your layers, their exact placement and alignment becomes critical. Dreamweaver includes two tools to simplify layered Web page design: the ruler and the grid.

Rulers and grids are familiar concepts in traditional desktop publishing. Dreamweaver's ruler shows the x-axis and y-axis in pixels, inches, or centimeters along the outer edge of the Document window. The grid crisscrosses the page with lines to support a visual guideline when you're placing objects. You can even enable a snap-to-grid feature to ensure easy, absolute alignment.

Using the ruler

With traditional Web design, "eyeballing it" was the only option available for Web page layout. The absolute positioning capability of layers filled this deficiency. Now online designers have a more precise and familiar system of alignment: the ruler. Dreamweaver's ruler can be displayed in several different measurement units and with your choice of origin point.

To enable the ruler in Dreamweaver, choose View ⇨ Rulers ⇨ Show or use the keyboard shortcut Ctrl+Alt+R (Command+Option+R). Horizontal and vertical rulers appear along the top and the left sides of the Document window, as shown in Figure 19-12. As you move the pointer, a light-gray line indicates the position on both rulers.

Figure 19-12: Use the horizontal and vertical rulers to assist your layer placement and overall Web page layout.

By default, the ruler uses pixels as its measurement system. You can change the default by selecting View ➪ Rulers and choosing either inches or centimeters.

Dreamweaver also enables you to move the ruler origin to a new position. Normally, the upper-left corner of the page acts as the origin point for the ruler. On some occasions, it's helpful to start the measurement at a different location—at the bottom-right edge of an advertisement, for example. To move the origin point, select the intersection of the horizontal and the vertical rulers and drag the crosshairs to a new location. When you release the mouse button, both rulers are adjusted to show negative values above and to the right of the new origin point. To return the origin point to its default setting, choose View ➪ Rulers ➪ Reset Origin, or you can simply double-click the intersection of the rulers.

Tip

You can access a ruler shortcut menu by right-clicking (Command+clicking) the ruler itself. The shortcut menu enables you to change the system of measurement, reset the origin point, or hide the rulers.

Lining up with the grid

Rulers are generally good for positioning single objects, but a grid is extremely helpful when aligning one object to another. With Dreamweaver's grid facility, you can align elements visually or snap them to the grid. You can set many of the grid's other features, including grid spacing, color, and type.

To turn on the grid, choose View ⇨ Grid ⇨ Show Grid or press Ctrl+Alt+G (Command+Option+G). By default, the grid is displayed with mustard-yellow (#CCCC99) lines set at 50-pixel increments.

The snap-to-grid feature is enabled by choosing View ⇨ Grid ⇨ Snap To Grid or with the keyboard shortcut Ctrl+Alt+Shift+G (Command+Option+Shift+G). When activated, Snap to Grid causes the upper-left corner of a layer to be placed at the nearest grid intersection when the layer is moved.

Like most of Dreamweaver's tools, the grid can be customized. To alter the grid settings, choose View ⇨ Grid ⇨ Edit Grid. In the Grid Settings dialog box, shown in Figure 19-13, you can change any of the following settings (just click OK when you're done):

Grid Setting	Description
Color	Change the default color by selecting the color swatch to open the Dreamweaver color picker where you can click on a new swatch, or type a new value in the text box.
Show Grid	Show or hide the grid with this checkbox toggle.
Snap to Grid	Checkbox toggle to enable or disable the Snap to Grid feature.
Spacing	Adjust the distance between grid points by entering a numeric value in the text box.
Spacing Unit of Measure	Select Pixels, Inches, or Centimeters from the Spacing drop-down list.
Display	Choose either solid lines or dots for the gridlines.

Adding elements to a layer

Once you have created and initially positioned your layers, you can begin to fill them with content. Inserting objects in a layer is just like inserting objects in a Web page. The same insertion methods are available to you:

✦ Position the cursor inside a layer, choose Insert in the menu bar, and select an object to insert.

✦ With the cursor inside a layer, select any object from the Objects panel. Note: you cannot select the Draw Layer object.

✦ Drag an object from the Objects panel and drop it inside the layer.

A known problem exists with Netscape Navigator 4.*x* browsers and nested layers — and layers in general — using the `<div>` tag. Whenever the browser window is resized, the layers lose their left and top position and are displayed along the left edge of the browser window or parent layer. Dreamweaver includes the capability to insert code that serves as a workaround for this problem. With this code in place, if the browser is resized, the page reloads, repositioning the layers. If you want the code to be automatically inserted the first time you add a layer to your page, select the Add Resize Fix When Inserting Layers option found on the Layers category of Preferences. You can also insert it on a case-by-case basis by choosing Commands ➪ Add/Remove Netscape Resize Fix. As the name implies, this command also deletes the Netscape Resize Fix code.

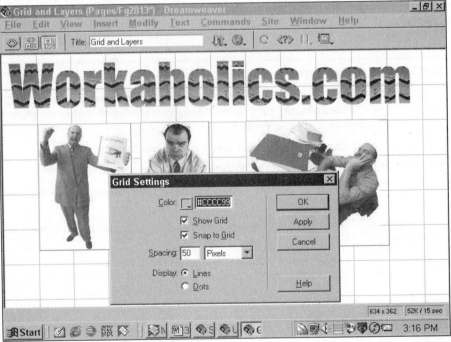

Figure 19-13: Dreamweaver's grid feature is extremely handy for aligning a series of objects.

Forms and layers

When you're mixing forms and layers, follow only one rule: Always put the form completely inside the layer. If you place the layer within the form, all form elements after the layer tags are ignored. With the form completely enclosed in the layer, the form can safely be positioned anywhere on the page and all form elements still remain completely active.

Although this rule means you can't split one form onto separate layers, you can set up multiple forms on multiple layers — and still have them all communicate to one final CGI or other program. This technique uses JavaScript to send the user-input values in the separate forms to hidden fields in the form with the Submit button. Let's say, for example, that you have three separate forms gathering information in three separate layers on a Web page. Call them formA, formB, and formC on layer1, layer2, and layer3, respectively. When the Submit button in formC on layer3 is selected, a JavaScript function is first called by means of an `onClick` event in the button's `<input>` tag. The function, in part, looks like the following:

```
function gatherData() {
   document.formC.hidden1.value = document.formA.text1.value
   document.formC.hidden2.value = document.formB.text2.value
}
```

Notice how every value from the various forms gets sent to a hidden field in formC, the form with the Submit button. Now, when the form is submitted, all the hidden information gathered from the various forms is submitted along with formC's own information.

Note

Netscape Note: The code for this separate-forms approach, as written in the preceding listing, works in Internet Explorer. Netscape 4.x, however, uses a different syntax to address forms in layers. To work properly in Netscape 4.x, the code must look like the following:

```
document.layers["layer3"].document.formC.hidden1.value=¬
document.layers["layer1"].document.formA.text1.value
```

To make the code cross-browser compatible, you can use an initialization function that allows for the differences, or you can build it into the `onClick` function.

Creating Your Page Design with Layers

While the advantage to designing with layers is the greater flexibility it affords, one of the greatest disadvantages of using layers is that they are viewable in only the most recent generation of browsers. Dreamweaver enables you to get the best of both worlds by making it possible for you to use layers to design complex page layouts, and then to transform those layers into tables that can be viewed in earlier browsers. Designing this way has some limitations — you can't, for example, actually layer items on top of each other. Nevertheless, Dreamweaver's capability to convert layers to tables (and tables to layers) enables you to create complex layouts with ease.

Using the Tracing Image

Page-layout artists are often confronted with Web-page designs that have been mocked up in a graphics program. Dreamweaver's Tracing Image function enables you to use such images to guide the precise placement of graphics, text, tables, and forms in your Web page, enabling you to match the original design as closely as possible.

In order to use a Tracing Image, the graphic must be saved in either JPG, GIF, or PNG format. Once the Tracing Image has been placed in your page, it is viewable only in Dreamweaver — it will never appear in a browser. A placed Tracing Image hides any background color or background graphic in your Web page. Preview your page in a browser, or hide the tracing layer, to view your page without the Tracing Image.

Adding the Tracing Image to your page

To add a Tracing Image to your Dreamweaver page, select View ⇨ Tracing Image ⇨ Load. This brings up a Select Image Source dialog box that enables you to select the graphic you would like to use as a Tracing Image. Clicking Select brings up the Page Properties dialog box, shown in Figure 19-14, where you may specify the opacity of the Tracing Image, from Transparent (0%) to Opaque (100%). You can change the Tracing Image or its transparency at any point by selecting Modify ⇨ Page Properties to bring up the Page Properties dialog box. You can toggle between hiding and showing the Tracing Image by selecting View ⇨ Tracing Image ⇨ Show. The Tracing Image can also be inserted directly in the Page Properties dialog box by entering its path in the Tracing Image text box or selecting the Browse button to locate the image.

Moving the Tracing Image

The Tracing Image cannot be selected and moved the same way as other objects on your page. Instead, you must move the Tracing Image using menu commands. You have several options for adjusting the Tracing Image's position to better fit your design. First, you can align the Tracing Image with any object on your page by first selecting the object and then choosing View ⇨ Tracing Image ⇨ Align with Selection. This lines up the upper-left corner of the Tracing Image with the upper-left corner of the bounding box of the object you've selected.

To precisely or visually move the Tracing Image to a specific location, select View ⇨ Tracing Image ⇨ Adjust Position. Then enter the x and y coordinates into the boxes in the Adjust Tracing Image Position dialog box, shown in Figure 19-15. For more hands-on positioning, use the arrow keys to nudge the tracing layer up, down, left, or right one pixel at a time. Holding down the Shift key while pressing the arrow keys moves the Tracing Image in five-pixel increments. Finally, you can return the Tracing Image to its default location of 9 pixels down from the top and 11 pixels in from the left by selecting View ⇨ Tracing Image ⇨ Reset Position.

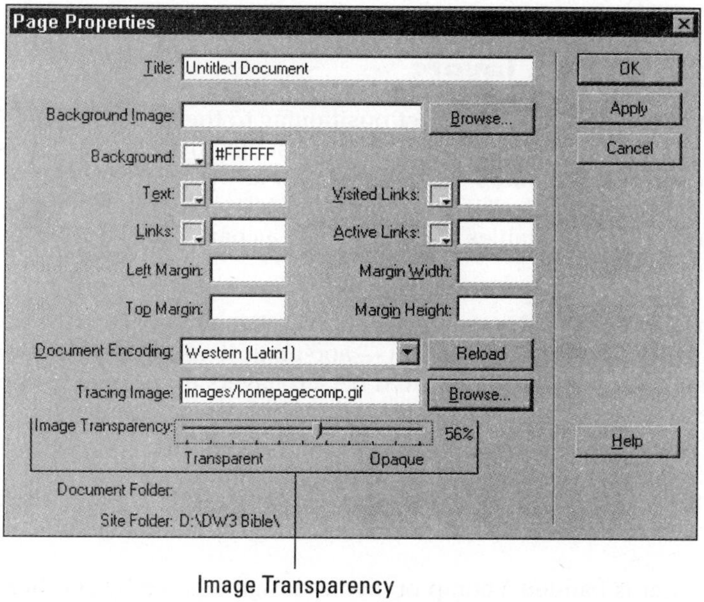

Image Transparency

Figure 19-14: Setting the transparency of the Tracing Image to a setting such as 51 percent can help you differentiate between it and the content layers you are positioning.

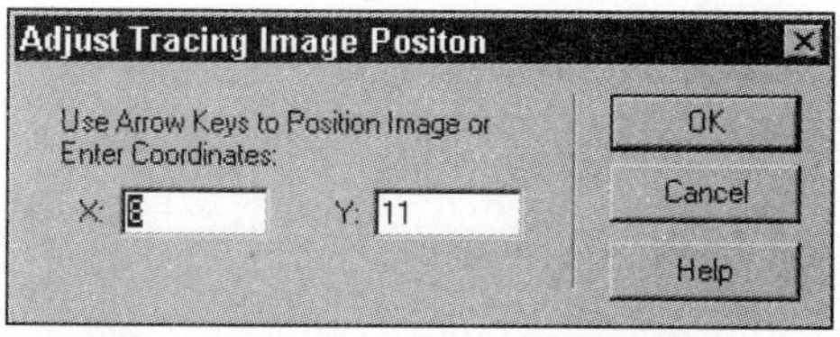

Figure 19-15: Use the Adjust Tracing Image Position dialog box to precisely place your graphic template.

Preventing overlaps

In order to place layers on your page that can later be converted to a table, the layers must not overlap. Before you begin drawing out your layers, open the Layers panel — either by selecting Windows ⇨ Layers or pressing F2 — and put a checkmark in the Prevent Overlap box at the top of the Inspector window. You can also select Modify ⇨ Arrange ⇨ Prevent Layer Overlaps to toggle overlap protection on and off.

Designing precision layouts and converting content to layers

As noted earlier, layers brought pixel-perfect positioning to the Internet. Now, Web designers can enjoy some of the layout capabilities assumed by print designers. Unfortunately, you need a 4.0 browser or better to view any page created with layers, and a portion of the Web audience is still using 3.0 or older browsers. Dreamweaver includes layers-to-tables and back again as part of its round-trip repertoire.

Web designers can freely design their page and then lock it into position for posting. Moreover, if the design needs adjustment — and all designs need adjustment — the posted page can be temporarily converted back to layers for easy repositioning. The Convert Tables to Layers and Convert Layers to Table menu commands work together terrifically and greatly enhance the designer's workflow.

The two commands are described in detail in the following sections, but let's examine a typical Dreamweaver layout session to see how they function together:

1. The Web designer is handed a comp or layout design created by another member of the company or a third-party designer.

2. After creating the graphic and type elements, the Web designer is ready to compose the page in Dreamweaver.

3. Ideally, the comp is converted to an electronic graphic format and brought into Dreamweaver as a Tracing Image.

4. If at all possible, it's best for conversion purposes not to overlap any layers, so the Web designer enables the Prevent Overlap option.

5. Each element is placed in a separate layer and placed in position, following the Tracing Image, if any.

6. With one command (Convert Layers to Table), the layout is restructured from appearing in layers to being in tables for backward browser compatibility.

7. After the client has viewed the page — and made the inevitable changes — the page is converted from tables to layers. Again, in Dreamweaver, this process is triggered by one command (Convert Tables to Layers) and takes seconds to complete.

8. The trip from tables to layers and back again is made as many times as necessary to get the layout pixel-perfect.

Convert Tables to Layers and Convert Layers to Table is a one-two combination that cuts layout time tremendously and frees the designer to create visually instead of programmatically.

Dreamweaver enables you to take any page and enclose all the contents in layers for easy design layout with drag-and-drop ease. Convert Tables to Layers is very flexible and enables the designer to convert pages previously constructed either partially or totally with tables or ones that already have layers in place. You can even quickly convert an all-text page into a layer.

Tip One valuable use for this command is to better prepare a page to use another Dreamweaver feature: Convert to 3.0 Browser Compatible. While you no longer have to have every page element in a layer to use this feature, if you use the Convert Tables to Layers command first, you get better results.

With the page open in Dreamweaver, select Modify ⇨ Convert ⇨ Tables to Layers to view the command's dialog box, shown in Figure 19-16.

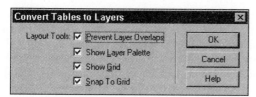

Figure 19-16: Choose the appropriate Layout Tools to help you reposition your content using layers.

By default, each of the following Layout Tools options are enabled:

✦ **Prevent Layer Overlaps:** You want this option turned on if you plan to convert the layers back to a table.

✦ **Show Layer Palette:** This automatically opens the Layers panel for you with each layer given a default name by Dreamweaver.

✦ **Show Grid:** This option reveals the grid overlay that can help with precision layout.

✦ **Snap to Grid:** With this turned on, layers snap to the nearest gridlines as they are moved onscreen.

You can uncheck any of these options before you convert the page.

Tip Turn off Show Grid and Snap to Grid if you are laying out objects on top of a Tracing Image, as they may interfere with the absolute positions that you are trying to achieve.

Converting layers to tables

To convert a Web page that has been designed with layers into a table for viewing in older browsers, simply select Modify ➪ Convert ➪ Layers to Table. This opens the Convert Layers to Table dialog box, shown in Figure 19-17, with the following options:

✦ **Most Accurate:** This creates as complex a table as is necessary to guarantee that the elements on your Web page appear in the exact locations that you've specified. This is the default setting.

✦ **Smallest:** Collapse empty cells less than *n* pixels wide: Selecting this option simplifies your table layouts by joining cells that are less than the number of pixels wide that you specify. This may result in a table that takes less time to load; however, it also means that the elements on your page may not appear in the precise locations where you've placed them.

✦ **Use Transparent GIFs:** When you select this option, Dreamweaver fills all empty cells with a transparent spacer graphic to ensure that the table looks the same across a variety of browsers. When Dreamweaver creates the table layout, it places a file called transparent.gif in the same folder as your Web page. You must make sure to include this file when you upload your page to your server in order for it to display correctly.

✦ **Center on Page:** Selecting this option puts `<div align=center>` tags around your table so that it displays in the middle of a browser window. Deselecting this option leaves out those tags so that the table starts from its default position in the upper-left corner of a browser.

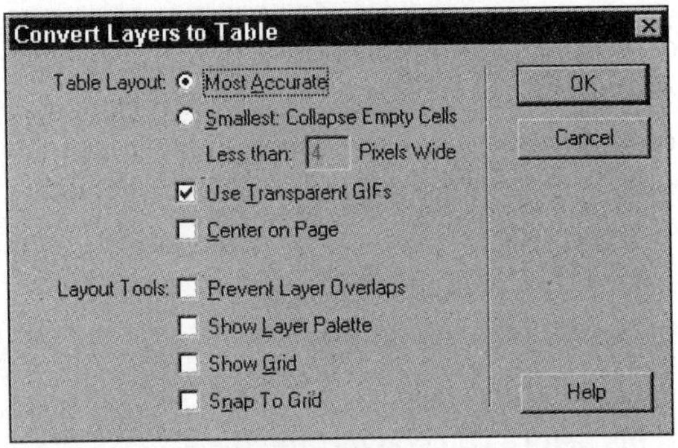

Figure 19-17: Check off the right Layout Tools options to help reposition your content as a table.

Once you have converted your layout into a table, as shown in Figure 19-18, you should preview it in your browser. If you aren't happy with the way your layout looks, or if you wish to do further modifications, you can convert the table back into layers by selecting Modify ➪ Convert ➪ Tables to Layers as described previously, selecting the layers to drag and drop the contents into new positions. Finally, transform your layout back into a table and preview it again.

Figure 19-18: The results of transforming layers into a table, using the default settings.

Tip

It's worth pointing out that the two Modify ➪ Convert commands can be easily reversed by choosing Edit ➪ Undo, whereas the effectively similar File ➪ Convert ➪ 3.0 Browser Compatible command cannot.

Activating Layers with Behaviors

While absolute positioning is a major reason to use layers, you may have other motives for using this capability. All the properties of a layer — the coordinates, size and shape, depth, visibility, and clipping — can be altered dynamically and interactively as well. Normally, dynamically resetting a layer's properties entails some fairly daunting JavaScript programming. Now, with one of Dreamweaver's hallmarks — those illustrious behaviors — activating layers is possible for nonprogrammers as well.

Cross-Reference

In case you missed it, Chapter 15 describes Dreamweaver's rich behaviors feature.

Behaviors consist of two parts, the event and the action. In Dreamweaver, three standard actions are designed specifically for working with layers:

- ✦ **Drag Layer:** Enables the user to move the layer and get a response to that movement.

- ✦ **Set Text of Layer:** Interactively alter the content of any layer to include any HTML, not just text.

- ✦ **Show-Hide Layers:** Controls the visibility of layers, either interactively or through some preprogrammed action on the page.

You can find detailed information about these actions in their respective sections in Chapter 15. The following sections outline how to use these behaviors to activate your layers.

Note   Netscape 6 was released just before Dreamweaver 4; consequently some of the layer-oriented behaviors do not work properly with that version of Netscape's browser. As of this writing, there are third-party replacements for the Drag Layer behavior, written by Jaro von Flocken; and the Set Text of Layer and Show-Hide Layers behavior, both contributed by Al Sparber. You can find these extensions on the CD-ROM that accompanies this book or on the Macromedia Exchange.

Drag Layer

For the Web designer, positioning a layer is easy: click the selection handle and drag the layer to a new location. For the readers of your pages, moving a layer is next to impossible — unless you incorporate the Drag Layer action into the page's design.

With the Drag Layer action, you can set up interactive pages in which the user can rearrange elements of the design to achieve an effect or make a selection. Drag Layer includes an option that enables you to execute a JavaScript command if the user drops the layer on a specific target. In the example shown in Figure 19-19, each pair of shoes is in its own layer. When the user drops a pair in the bag, a one-line JavaScript command opens the desired catalog page and order form.

After you've created all your layers, you're ready to attach the behavior. Because Drag Layer initializes the script to make the interaction possible, you should always associate this behavior with the <body> tag and the onLoad event.

Follow these steps to use the Drag Layer action, and to designate the settings for the drag operation:

1. Choose the <body> tag from the Tag Selector in the status bar.

2. Choose Window ➪ Behaviors or select the Show Behaviors button from either Launcher. The Behaviors panel opens.

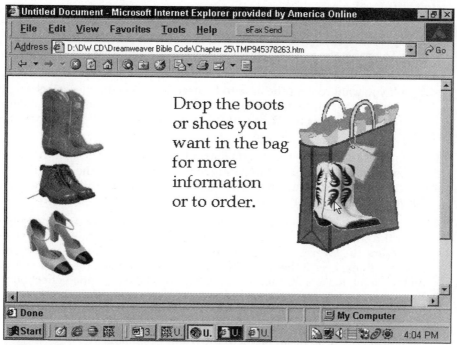

Figure 19-19: On this interactive page, visitors can drop merchandise into the shopping bag; this feature is made possible with the Drag Layer action.

3. In the Behaviors panel, make sure that 4.0 and Later Browsers is displayed in the Show Events For Submenu of the Add Behavior pop-up menu.

4. Click the + (add) action button and choose Drag Layer from the Add Behavior pop-up menu.

5. In the Drag Layer dialog box, select the layer you want to make available for dragging.

6. To limit the movement of the dragged layer, select Constrained from the Movement drop-down list. Then enter the coordinates to specify the direction to which you want to limit the movement in the Up, Down, Left, and/or Right text boxes.

7. To establish a location for a target, enter coordinates in the Drop Target: Left and Top text boxes. You can fill these text boxes with the selected layer's present location by clicking the Get Current Position button.

8. You can also set a snap-to area around the target's coordinates. When released in the target's location, the dragged layer snaps to this area. Enter a pixel value in the Snap if Within text box.

9. Click the Advanced tab.

10. Designate the drag handle:

    - To enable the whole layer to act as a drag handle, select Entire Layer from the drop-down menu.

    - If you want to limit the area to be used as a drag handle, select Area within Layer from the drop-down menu. Enter the Left and Top coordinates as well as the Width and Height dimensions in the appropriate text boxes.

11. If you want to keep the layer in its current depth and not bring it to the front, deselect the checkbox for While Dragging: Bring Layer to the Front. To change the stacking order of the layer when it is released after dragging, select either Leave on Top or Restore z-index from the drop-down list.

12. To execute a JavaScript command when the layer is dropped on the target, enter the code in the Call JavaScript text box. If you want the script to execute every time the layer is dropped, enter the code in the When Dropped: Call JavaScript text box. If the code should execute only when the layer is dropped on the target, make sure there's a check in the Only if Snapped checkbox.

13. Click OK.

14. To change the event that triggers the action (the default is onLoad), select an event from the drop-down menu in the Events column.

Set Text of Layer

We've seen how layers can dynamically move, change their visibility, and their depth — but did you know that you could also change a layer's *content* dynamically? With Dreamweaver, you can do it easily. A standard behavior, Set Text of Layer, enables you to swap the entire contents of one layer for whatever you'd like. You're not limited to exchanging just text either. Anything you can put into HTML, you can swap — which, is pretty much everything!

This behavior is extremely useful for putting up context-sensitive help and other information. Rather than construct a series of layers which you show and hide, a single layer is used, and just the contents change. To use Set Text of Layer, follow these steps:

1. Insert and name your layers as desired.

2. Select the graphic, button, or text link you'd like to act as the trigger for your changing the content of the layer.

3. Choose Window ➪ Behaviors or select the Show Behaviors button from either Launcher to open the Behaviors panel.

4. Choose Set Text ➪ Set Text of Layer from the + (add) action pop-up menu.

    The dialog box (see Figure 19-20) shows a list of the available layers in the current Web page as well as providing a space for the new content.

Targeted JavaScript Commands

The following simple yet useful JavaScript commands can be entered in the Snap JavaScript text box of the Drag Layer dialog box:

✦ To display a brief message to the user after the layer is dropped, use the `alert()` function:

```
alert("You hit the target")
```

✦ To send the user to another Web page when the layer is dropped in the right location, use the JavaScript location object:

```
location = "http://www.yourdomain.com/yourpage.html"
```

The location object can also be used with relative URLs.

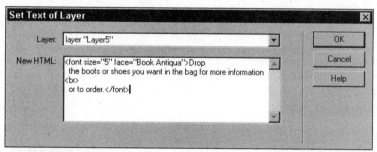

Figure 19-20: Swap out all the contents of a layer using the Set Text of Layer behavior.

5. Select the layer you want to alter from the Layer option list.

6. Enter the text or code in the New HTML text area.

You can enter either plain text, which is rendered in the default paragraph style, or any amount of HTML code, including `<img>`, `<table>`, or other tags.

Tip   If you're entering a large amount of HTML, don't bother doing so by hand—Dreamweaver can do it for you. On a blank page, create your HTML content and then select and copy it. Then, in the Set Text of Layer dialog box, paste the code using Ctrl+V (Command+V).

7. Click OK when you're done.

If you want several layers to change when a single event is triggered, just add more Set Text of Layer behaviors to the same object.

Note You may need to change the behavior event from its default; to do so select the down arrow in between the Event and Action columns on the Behaviors panel and choose a new event from the list.

Show-Hide Layers

The capability to implement interactive control of a layer's visibility offers tremendous potential to the Web designer. The Show-Hide Layers action makes this implementation straightforward and simple to set up. With the Show-Hide Layers action, you can simultaneously show one or more layers while hiding as many other layers as necessary. Create your layers and give them a unique name before invoking the Show-Hide Layers action.

To use Show-Hide Layers, follow these steps:

1. Select an image, link, or other HTML tag to which to attach the behavior.

2. Choose Window ➪ Behaviors or select the Show Behaviors button from either Launcher to open the Behaviors panel.

3. Choose Show-Hide Layers from the + (add) action pop-up menu. The parameters form (see Figure 19-21) shows a list of the available layers in the open Web page.

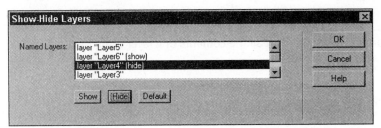

Figure 19-21: With the Show-Hide Layers behavior attached, you can easily program the visibility of all the layers in your Web page.

4. To cause a hidden layer to be revealed when this event is fired, select the layer from the list and click the Show button.

5. To hide a visible layer when this event is fired, select its name from the list and click the Hide button.

6. To restore a layer's default visibility value when this event is fired, select the layer and click the Default button.

7. Click OK when you are done.

8. If the default event is not suitable, use the drop-down menu in the Events column to select a different one.

Dreamweaver Technique: Creating a Loading Layer

As Web creations become more complex, most designers want their layers to zip on and off screen or appear and disappear as quickly as possible for the viewer of the page. A layer can act only when it has finished loading its content — the text and images. Rather than have the user see each layer loading in, some designers use a loading layer to mask the process until everything is downloaded and ready to go.

A loading layer is fairly easy to create. Dreamweaver supplies all the JavaScript necessary in one behavior, Show-Hide Layers. Keep in mind that because this technique uses layers, it's good only for 4.0 browsers and above. Use the following steps to create a loading layer:

1. Create all of your layers with the contents in place and the visibility property set as normal.

2. Create the loading layer. (Choose Insert ⇨ Layer or select the Draw Layer button from the Objects panel.)

3. Enter and position whatever contents you want displayed in the loading layer while all the other layers are loading.

4. Open the Layers panel (F2).

5. Turn off the visibility for all layers except the loading layer. In essence, you're hiding every other layer.

6. Select the <body> tag from the Tag Selector.

7. Choose Window ⇨ Behaviors or select Show Behaviors from either Launcher to open the Behaviors panel.

8. Select the + (add) action button and choose Show-Hide Layers from the pop-up menu.

9. In the Show-Hide Layers dialog box, select the loading layer and then click the Hide button.

10. Select all the other layers and set them to Show. Click OK when you are done.

11. Leave onLoad (the default) as the event to trigger this action.

Now, when you test your Web page, you should see only your loading layer until everything else is loaded, then the loading layer disappears, and all the other layers are made visible.

Note

A loading layer may be the last bastion of the <blink> tag. Created by Netscape fairly early in the history of the Web, the <blink>...</blink> tag pair was grossly overused and is today generally shunned. However, if you apply it (by switching to Code view, using the Code Inspector or through the Quick Tag Editor) just to the ellipse following the term "Loading . . ." like this:

```
<h2>Loading<blink>...</blink></h2>
```

you get a small bit of movement on the page, similar to a blinking cursor. Only Netscape Navigator supports the `<blink>` tag. You could also use an animated GIF to create the pulsing image for a cross-browser effect.

Summary

Layers are effective placement tools for developing the layout of a page. Anyone used to designing with desktop publishing tools can quickly learn to work layers effectively. The following points will help guide your way:

✦ Layers are visible only on fourth-generation and above browsers.

✦ Layers can be used to place HTML content anywhere on a Web page.

✦ You can stack layers on top of one another. This depth control is referred to as the *stacking order* or the *z-index*.

✦ Dreamweaver can convert layers to tables for viewing in earlier browsers, and back again for straightforward repositioning.

✦ Layers can be constructed so that the end user can display or hide them interactively, or alter their position, size, and depth dynamically.

✦ Dreamweaver gives you rulers and grids to help with layer placement and alignment.

✦ Layers can easily be activated by using Dreamweaver's built-in JavaScript behaviors.

In the next chapter, you learn how to develop timelines, which enable layers and their contents to move around the Web page.

✦   ✦   ✦

Working with Timelines

Motion implies time. A static object, such as an ordinary HTML Web page, can exist either in a single moment or over a period of time. Conversely, moving objects (such as Dynamic HTML layers flying across the screen) need a few seconds to complete their path. All of Dreamweaver's Dynamic HTML animation effects use the Timeline feature to manage this conjunction of movement and time.

Timelines can do much more than move a layer across a Web page, however. A timeline can coordinate an entire presentation: starting the background music, scrolling the opening credits, and cueing the voice-over narration on top of a slideshow. These actions are all possible with Dreamweaver because, in addition to controlling a layer's position, timelines can also trigger any of Dreamweaver's JavaScript behaviors on a specific frame.

This chapter explores the full and varied world of timelines. After an introductory section brings you up to speed on the underlying concepts of timelines, you learn how to insert and modify timelines to achieve cutting-edge effects. A Dreamweaver Technique shows you, step by step, how to create a multiscreen slideshow complete with fly-in and fly-out graphics. From complex multilayer animations to slideshow presentations, you can do it all with Dreamweaver timelines.

Cross-Reference Because timelines are so intricately intertwined with behaviors and layers, you need to have a good grasp of these concepts. Before examining the topic of timelines, make sure to read Chapter 15 and Chapter 19.

Entering the Fourth Dimension with Timelines

Web designers in the early days had little control over the fourth dimension and their Web pages. Only animated GIFs, Java, or animation programs such as Macromedia's Flash could create the illusion of motion events. Unfortunately, all of these technologies have some limitations.

The general problem with animated GIF images is related to file size. An animated GIF starts out as an image for every frame. Therefore, if you incorporate a three-second, 15-frames-per-second animation, you are asking the user to download the compressed equivalent of 45 separate images. Even though an animated GIF is an index color file with a limited 256 colors and uses the format's built-in compression, the GIF file is still a relatively large graphic file. Moreover, for all their apparent animated qualities, GIFs enable no true interaction other than as a link to another URL. Animations created with Dynamic HTML and Dreamweaver's timelines, on the other hand, do not significantly increase the overall size of the Web page and are completely interactive. DHTML is not the only low-bandwidth approach to animations with interactive content for the Web. You can create animations, complete with user-driven interactions, with Java — as long as you're a Java programmer. Certainly Java development tools are making the language easier to use, but you still must deal with the rather long load time of any Java applet and the increasing variety of Java versions. As another option, Macromedia Director movies can be compressed or "shocked" to provide animation and interactivity in your pages. As with Java, the Director approach requires a bit of a learning curve. Shockwave movies can also have long load times and require the user to have a plug-in application.

Macromedia's Flash might be the best alternative to GIF images, even though Flash has its own set of caveats to keep in mind. On the plus side, Flash files are small and can be streamed through their own player. This arrangement is tempting, and if you just want animation on a page, Flash is probably a superior choice to any of the approaches previously described. On the minus side, Flash is limited to its own proprietary features and functions, and every user must have the Flash plug-in or ActiveX control installed — although Flash player is rapidly becoming ubiquitous, making this point moot. However, you cannot layer Flash animation on top of other layers on a page. Moreover, once you, or another designer, have created a Flash animation, the animation must be edited with the same animation package.

Cross-Reference   See Chapter 17 for a discussion of Flash.

Timeline capabilities

Dreamweaver timelines are part of the HTML code. For the movement of one layer straight across a Web page, Dreamweaver generates about 70 lines of code devoted to initializing and playing the timeline. But just what is a timeline? A timeline is composed of a series of frames. A frame is a snapshot of what the Web page, more specifically, the objects on the timeline, look like at a particular moment. You probably know that a movie is made up of a series of still pictures; when viewed quickly, the pictures create the illusion of movement. Each individual picture is a frame; movies show 24 frames per second, and video uses about 30 frames per second. Web animation, on the other hand, generally displays about 15 frames per second (fps). Not surprisingly, Dreamweaver's timeline is similar to the one used in Macromedia's timeline-based, multimedia authoring tool and animation package, Director.

If you have to draw each frame of a 30-second animation, even at 15 fps, you won't have time for other work. Dreamweaver uses the concept of *keyframes* to make a simple layer movement workable. Each keyframe contains a change in the timeline object's properties, such as position. For example, let's say you want your layer to start at the upper left (represented by the coordinates 0,0) and travel to the lower right (at 750,550). To accomplish this task, you need only specify the layer's position for the two keyframes — the start and the finish — and Dreamweaver generates all the frames in between.

Timelines have the following three primary roles:

✦ A timeline can alter a layer's position, dimensions, visibility, and depth.

✦ Timelines can change the source for any image on a Web page and cause another graphic of the same height and width to appear in the same location.

✦ Any of Dreamweaver's JavaScript behaviors can be triggered on any frame of a timeline.

A few ground rules

Keep the following basic guidelines in mind when you're using timelines in the Web pages you create with Dreamweaver:

✦ Timelines require a 4.0 browser or later.

✦ For a timeline to be able to animate an object, such as text, the object must be within a layer. If you try to create a timeline with an element that is not in a layer, Dreamweaver warns you and prevents you from adding the object to the timeline.

✦ Events don't have to start on the beginning of a timeline. If you want to have an action begin five seconds after a page has loaded, you can set the behavior on frame 60 of the timeline, with a frame rate of 15 frames per second.

✦ The selected frame rate is a "best-case scenario" because the actual frame rate depends on the user's system. A slower system or one that is simultaneously running numerous other programs can easily degrade the frame rate.

✦ You can include multiple animations on one timeline. The only restriction? You can't have two animations affecting the same layer at the same time. Dreamweaver prevents you from making this error.

✦ You can have multiple timelines that animate different layers simultaneously or the same layer at different times. Although you can set two or more timelines to animate the same layer at the same time, the results are difficult to predict and generally unintended.

Creating Animations with Timelines

Dreamweaver provides an excellent tool for managing timelines — the Timelines panel. Open this tool by choosing Window ➪ Timelines or using the keyboard shortcut Shift+F9.

The Timelines panel uses VCR-style controls combined with a playback head, which is a visual representation showing which frame is the current one. As shown in Figure 20-1, the Timelines panel gives you full control over any of the timeline functions.

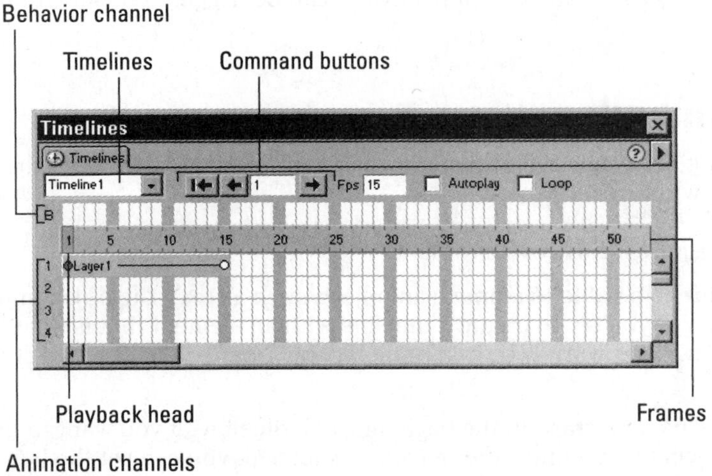

Figure 20-1: Dreamweaver's Timelines panel enables you to quickly and easily master animation control.

The Timelines panel has four major areas:

✦ **Timeline Controls:** Includes the Timeline pop-up menu for selecting the current timeline; the Rewind, Back, and Play buttons; the Fps (frame rate) text box; and the Autoplay and Loop checkboxes.

✦ **Behavior Channel:** Shows the placement of any behaviors attached to specific frames of the timeline.

✦ **Frames:** Displays the frame numbers for all timelines and the playback head showing the current frame number.

✦ **Animation Channels:** Represents the animations for any included layers and images.

Adding Layers to the Timelines Panel

As with many of Dreamweaver's functions, you can add a layer or an image to the Timelines panel in more than one way. You can either insert a layer into a timeline through the menus (Modify ➪ Timeline ➪ Add Object to Timeline), or you can drag and drop an object into a timeline or use the keyboard shortcut, Ctrl+Alt+Shift+T (Command+Option+Shift+T). The default timeline is set at a frame rate of 15 fps. When you add an object to a timeline, Dreamweaver inserts an animation bar of 15 frames in length, labeled with the object's name. The animation bar shows the duration (the number of frames) for the timeline's effect on the object. An animation bar is initially created with two initial keyframes: the start and the end.

To add a layer or image to the Timelines panel through the menus, follow these steps:

1. Choose Window ➪ Timelines or use the keyboard shortcut, Shift+F9, to open the Timelines panel.

2. In the Document window, select the layer or image you want to add to the timeline.

3. Choose Modify ➪ Timeline ➪ Add Object to Timeline. An animation bar appears in the first frame of the timeline, as shown in Figure 20-2.

4. To add another object, repeat Steps 2 and 3. Each additional animation bar is inserted beneath the preceding bar.

Tip

The first time you add an image or layer to the Timelines panel, Dreamweaver displays an alert message that details the limitations of timelines. If you don't want to see this alert, turn it off by checking the Don't Show Me This Message Again checkbox.

As previously noted, you can add as many objects to a timeline as you desire. If necessary, increase the size of the Timelines panel by dragging any border of its window.

You have a little more flexibility when you add an object by dragging it into the timeline. Instead of the animation bar always beginning at frame one, you may drop the object in to begin on any frame. This approach is useful, especially if you are putting more than one object into the same animation channel.

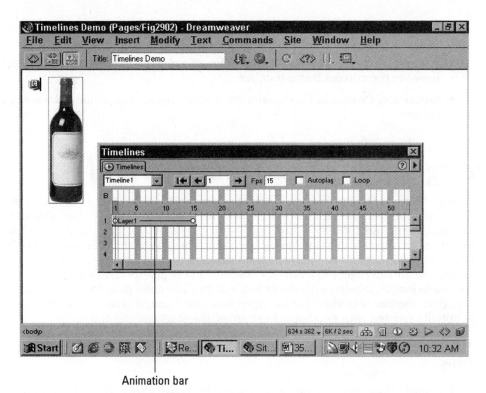

Animation bar

Figure 20-2: The default animation bar is set at 15 frames, but can be easily modified.

To place an object in a timeline with the drag-and-drop method, follow these steps:

1. Open the Timelines panel by choosing Window ➪ Timelines or using the keyboard shortcut, Shift+F9.

2. In the Document window, select the object — layer or image — you want to add to the timeline and drag it to the Timelines panel. As soon as the object is over the Timelines panel, a 15-frame animation bar appears.

3. Holding the mouse button down, position the animation bar so that the animation begins in the desired frame. Release the mouse button to drop the object into the timeline.

Note   Your placement does not have to be exact; you can modify it later.

Placing a layer or image on a timeline is just the beginning. To begin using your timeline in depth, you have to make changes to the object for the keyframes and customize the timeline.

Modifying a Timeline

When you add an object—either an image or a layer—to a timeline, notice that the animation bar has an open circle at its beginning and end. An open circle marks a keyframe. As previously explained, the designer specifies a change in the state of the timeline object in a keyframe. For example, when you first insert a layer, the two generated keyframes have identical properties—the layer's position, size, visibility, and depth are unchanged. For any animation to occur, you have to change one of the layer's properties for one of the keyframes.

For example, let's move a layer quickly across the screen. Follow these steps:

1. Create a layer. If you like, add an image or a background color so that the layer is more noticeable.

2. Open the Timelines panel.

3. Drag the layer into the Timelines panel and release the mouse button.

4. Select the ending keyframe of the layer's animation bar.

   The playback head moves to the new frame.

5. In the Document window, grab the layer's selection handle and drag the layer to a new location. A thin line connects the starting position of the layer to the ending position, as shown in Figure 20-3. This line is the animation path.

6. To play your animation, first click the Rewind button in the Timelines panel and then click and hold down the Play button.

If you want to change the beginning position of your layer's movement, select the starting keyframe and then move the layer in the Document window. To alter the final position of your layer's movement, select the ending keyframe and then move the layer.

Tip   For more precise control of your layer's position in a timeline, select a keyframe and then, in the layer's Property Inspector, change the Left and/or Top values. You can also select the layer and use the arrow keys to move it.

Altering the animation bars

A Web designer can easily stretch or alter the range of frames occupied by a layer or image in an animation bar. You can make an animation longer or smoother, or have it start at an entirely different time. You can also move the layer to a different animation channel so it runs before or after another animation.

Use the mouse to drag an animation bar around the timeline. Click any part of the bar except on the keyframe indicators and move it as needed. To change the length of an animation, select the first or final keyframe and drag it forward or backward to a new frame.

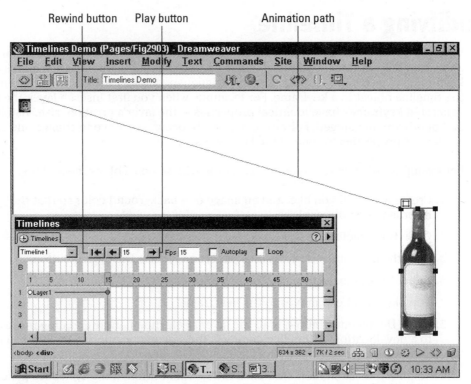

Figure 20-3: When you move a layer on a timeline, Dreamweaver displays an animation path.

You can remove an animation bar in two ways: select it and press Delete, or choose Modify ➪ Timeline ➪ Remove Object.

Using the Timeline controls

As you probably noticed if you worked through the example in the preceding section, you don't have to use a browser to preview a timeline. The Timeline controls shown in Figure 20-4 enable you to fine-tune your animations before you view them through a browser.

At the top-left corner is the Timeline pop-up menu, which is used to indicate the current timeline. By default, every new timeline is given the name Timeline*n*, where *n* indicates how many timelines have been created. You can rename the timeline by selecting it and typing in the new name. As you accumulate and use more timelines, you should give them recognizable names.

Tip   If you change the timeline name, you must enter a one-word name using alphanumeric characters that always begin with a letter. Netscape Navigator 4.*x* cannot read spaces or special characters in JavaScript.

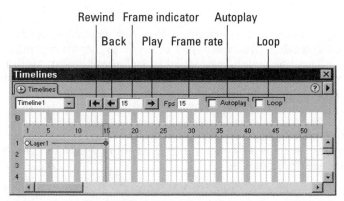

Figure 20-4: The Timeline controls enable you to move back and forth in your timeline, easily and precisely.

The next three buttons in the control bar enable you to move through the frames of a timeline. From left to right:

✦ **Rewind:** Moves the playback head to the first frame of the current timeline.

✦ **Back:** Moves the playback head to the previous frame. You can hold down the Back button to play the timeline in reverse.

✦ **Play:** Moves the timeline forward one frame at a time; hold down the Play button to play the timeline normally. When the last frame is reached, the playback head moves to the first frame of the current timeline and continues playing it.

The field between the Back and Play buttons is the frame indicator text box. To jump to any specific frame, enter the frame number in this box.

The next item in the control bar is the Fps (frames per second) text box. To change the frame rate, enter a new value in the Fps text box and press Tab or Enter (Return). The frame rate you set is an ideal number that a user's browser attempts to reach. The default rate of 15 frames per second is a good balance for both Macintosh and Windows systems.

Tip   Because browsers play every frame regardless of the frame rate setting, increasing the frame rate does not necessarily make your animations smoother. A better method for creating smooth animations is to drag the end keyframe farther out and therefore increase the number of frames used by your animation.

The next two checkboxes, Autoplay and Loop, affect how the animation is played.

Autoplay

If you mark the Autoplay checkbox, the current timeline begins playing as soon as the Web page is fully downloaded. Dreamweaver alerts you to this arrangement by telling you that the Play Timeline action is attached to an `onLoad` event. Autoplay is achieved by inserting code into the `<body>` tag that looks similar to the following:

```
<body bgcolor="#FFFFFF" onload="MM_timelinePlay('timeline1')">
```

Caution　If you don't use the Autoplay feature, you must attach the Play Timeline action to another event and tag, such as an `onMouseClick` event and a button graphic. Otherwise, the timeline does not play.

Looping

Mark the Loop checkbox if you want an animation to repeat once it has reached the final frame. When Loop is enabled, the default setting causes the layer to replay itself an infinite numbers of times; however, you can change this setting.

When you first enable the Loop checkbox, Dreamweaver alerts you that it is placing a Go to Frame action after the last frame of your current timeline. To set the number of repetitions for a timeline, follow these steps:

1. In the Timelines panel, check the Loop checkbox.

2. Dreamweaver displays an alert informing you that the Go to Timeline Frame action is being added one frame past your current final frame. To disable these alerts, select the Don't Show Me This Message Again option.

3. In the Behavior channel (above the Frame numbers and playback head), double-click the behavior you just added.

Note　When you first add a behavior to a timeline, Dreamweaver presents a dialog box reminding you how to perform this action. Select the Don't Show Me This Message Again option when you've mastered the technique.

The Behaviors panel opens, with an `onFrame` event in the Events column and a Go To Timeline Frame action showing in the Actions column.

4. Double-click the `onFrame` event. The Go to Timeline Frame dialog box opens (see Figure 20-5).

5. Enter a positive number in the Loop text box to set the number of times you want your timeline to repeat. To keep the animation repeating continuously, leave the Loop text box blank.

6. Click OK when you are finished.

Tip　Your animations don't have to loop back to the beginning each time. By entering a different frame number in the Go to Frame text box of the Go to Timeline Frame dialog box, you can repeat just a segment of the animation.

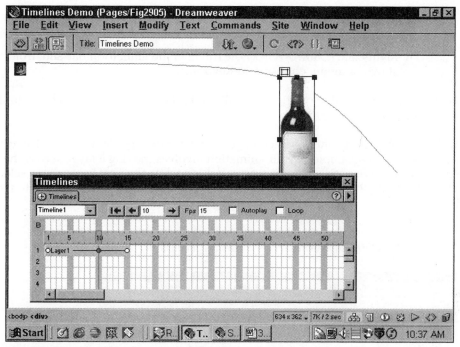

Figure 20-5: Selecting the Loop option on the Timelines panel adds a Go to Timeline Frame action, which you can customize.

Adding keyframes

Animating a timeline can go far beyond moving your layer from point A to point B. Layers (and the content within them) can dip, swirl, zigzag, and generally move in any fashion — all made possible by keyframes in which you have entered some change for the object. Dreamweaver calculates the differences between each keyframe, whether the change is in a layer's position or size. Each timeline starts with two keyframes, the beginning and the end; you have to add other keyframes before you can insert the desired changes.

You can add a keyframe to your established timeline in a couple of different ways. The first method uses the Add Keyframe command, and the second method uses the mouse to click a keyframe into place.

Adding keyframes with the Add Keyframe command

To add a keyframe with the Add Keyframe command, follow these steps:

1. In the Timelines panel, select the animation bar for the object with which you are working.

2. Select the frame in which you want to add a keyframe.

3. Add your keyframe by either of the following methods:

  a. Choose Modify ⇨ Timeline ⇨ Add Keyframe.

  b. Right-click (Control+click) the frame in the animation bar and, from the shortcut menu, choose Add Keyframe.

A new keyframe is added on the selected frame, signified by the open circle in the animation bar.

While your new keyframe is selected, you can alter the layer's position, size, visibility, or depth. For example, if your animation involves moving a layer across the screen, you can drag the layer to a new position while the new keyframe is selected. The animation path is redrawn to incorporate this new position, as illustrated in Figure 20-6.

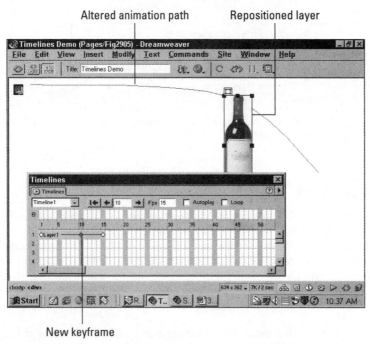

Figure 20-6: Repositioning a layer while a keyframe is selected can redirect your animation path.

Adding a keyframe with the mouse

The second method for adding a keyframe is quicker. To add a keyframe using the mouse, simply hold down the Ctrl (Command) key. Then click anywhere in the animation bar to add a keyframe. Your cursor turns into a small open circle when it is over the Timeline window to show that it is ready to add a new keyframe.

What if you want to move the keyframe? Simply click and drag the keyframe to a new frame, sliding it along the animation bar in the Timelines panel.

> **Tip** If, after plotting out an elaborate animation with a layer, you discover that you need to shift the entire animation — say, six pixels to the right — you don't have to redo all your work. Just select the animation bar in the Timelines panel and then, in the Document window, move the layer in question. Dreamweaver shifts the entire animation to your new location.

Removing timeline elements

The easiest way to remove an object, keyframe, or behavior from the Timelines panel is to select the element and press Delete. You cannot use this technique to delete individual frames or entire timelines, however. For these situations, you must use the menus as follows:

✦ To remove the whole timeline, choose Modify ➪ Timeline ➪ Remove Timeline.

✦ To remove an individual frame, choose Modify ➪ Timeline ➪ Remove Frame.

The Timelines panel's shortcut menu also contains all the removal commands. Right-click (Control+click) the Timelines panel anywhere below the control bar and, in the shortcut menu (see Figure 20-7), choose the removal command you need: Remove Keyframe, Remove Behavior, Remove Object, Remove Frame, or Remove Timeline.

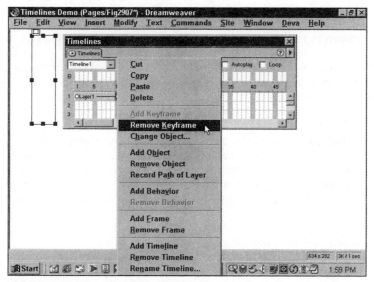

Figure 20-7: The Timelines panel's shortcut menu is extremely handy for doing quick edits.

You can also Cut, Copy and Paste Timelines between documents. The Delete command in the shortcut menu is the same as Remove Timeline.

Changing animation speed

You can alter your Dynamic HTML animation speed with two different methods that can be used separately or together.

✦ Drag the final keyframe in the animation bar out to cover additional frames, or back to cover fewer frames. Any keyframes within the animation bar are kept proportional to their original settings. This method works well when altering the speed of an individual animation bar.

✦ Change the frames per second value in the Fps text box of the Timelines panel. Increasing the number of frames per second accelerates the animation, and vice versa. Adjusting the Fps value affects every layer contained within the timeline; you cannot use this method for individual layers.

Caution

Browsers play every frame of a Dynamic HTML animation, regardless of the system resources. Some systems, therefore, play the same animation faster or slower than others. Don't depend on every system to have the same timing.

Recording a layer's path

Plotting keyframes and repositioning your layers works well when you need to follow a pixel-precise path, but it can be extremely tedious when you're trying to move a layer more freely on the screen. Luckily, another, easier method exists for defining a movement path for a layer. In Dreamweaver, you can simply drag your layer around the screen to create a path and refine the path or its timing afterward.

The Record Path of Layer command automatically creates the necessary series of keyframes, calculated from your dragging of the layer. To fine-tune your work, you can select any keyframes and reposition the layer or even delete it entirely. This feature is a definite time-saver for quickly inserting your DHTML animation.

Keep in mind that a timeline represents not only positions but also positions over time, and thus, movement. The Record Path of Layer command is very smart when it comes to time; the slower you drag the layer, the more keyframes are plotted. You can vary the positioning of the keyframes by changing the tempo of your dragging. Moreover, the duration of the recorded timeline reflects the length of time spent dragging the layer.

To record a layer's path, do the following:

1. In the Document window, select the layer you are going to move.

Caution

Make sure that you've selected the layer itself and not its contents. If you've correctly selected the layer, it has eight selection boxes around it.

2. Drag the layer to the location in the document where you want it to be at the start of the movement.

3. From the menu bar, select Modify ➪ Timeline ➪ Record Path of Layer. You can also right-click (Control+click) the selected layer and choose Record Path from the shortcut menu.

If it's not already open, the Timelines panel appears.

4. Click the layer and drag it around onscreen to define the movement. As you drag the layer, Dreamweaver draws a gray dotted line that shows you the path it is creating (see Figure 20-8).

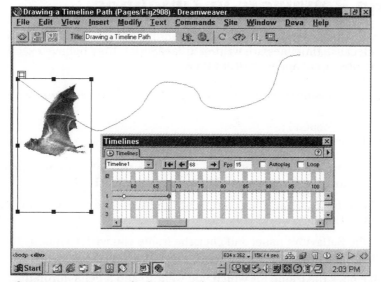

Figure 20-8: To record a layer's path, Select Modify ➪ Timeline ➪ Record Path of Layer and then drag your layer in the Document window.

Each dot represents a keyframe. The slower you draw, the closer the keyframes are placed; moving quickly across the Document window causes Dreamweaver to space out the keyframes.

5. Release the mouse. This ends the recording.

Unless Dreamweaver is instructed not to, Dreamweaver displays an alert reminding you of the capabilities of the Timelines panel. If the alert dialog box does appear, you can select the Don't Show Me This Message Again option to prevent this dialog box from reappearing.

After you've finished recording a layer's movement, you see a new animation bar in the Timelines panel, representing the motion you just recorded. The duration of the new timeline matches the duration of your dragging of the layer. A number of keyframes that define your layer's movement already are inserted in this animation bar. You can use any of the procedures described earlier in this chapter to modify the timeline or its keyframes. If you select the same layer at the end of the generated timeline and perform the Record Path operation again, another animation bar is added at the end of the current timeline.

Caution   Any new paths recorded with the same layer are added after the last animation bar. You can't select a keyframe in the middle of a path and then record a path from that point; the starting keyframe of the newly recorded path corresponds to the position of the layer in the last keyframe.

Triggering Behaviors in Timelines

Adding a behavior to a timeline is similar to adding behaviors to any object on a Web page. Because timelines are written in JavaScript, they behave exactly the same as any object enhanced with JavaScript.

Use the Behavior channel section of the Timelines panel to work with behaviors in timelines.

You can attach a behavior to a timeline in four ways:

✦ Highlight the frame in which you wish to have the behavior and then right-click (Control+click). Select Add Behavior from the shortcut menu.

✦ Highlight the frame in which you want to activate the behavior and choose Modify ➪ Timeline ➪ Add Behavior to Timeline.

✦ Open the Behaviors panel and click the frame you wish to modify in the Behavior channel.

✦ Double-click the frame for which you want to add a behavior in the Behavior channel.

After a behavior is attached to a frame and you open the Behaviors panel, you see that the event inserted in the Events pane is related to a frame number — for example, onFrame20. Each frame can trigger multiple actions.

Cross-Reference   For more specifics about Dreamweaver behaviors, see Chapter 13.

Behaviors are essential to timelines. Without these elements, you cannot play or stop your timeline-based animations. Even when you select the Autoplay or Loop options in the Timelines panel, you are enabling a behavior. The three behaviors always deployed for timelines are Play Timeline, Stop Timeline, and Go to Timeline Frame.

If you are not using the Autoplay feature for your timeline, you must explicitly attach a Play Timeline behavior to an interactive or another event on your Web page. For example, a timeline is typically set to start playing once a specific picture has loaded, if the user enters a value in a form's text box or — more frequently — when the user selects a Play button. You could use the Stop Timeline behavior to pause an animation temporarily.

Caution   If you find your Behaviors panel locked on the timeline and you're unable to attach a behavior to any other object, you've encountered a known Dreamweaver issue. Click on any other frame in your timeline — besides the one with the attached behavior — to free up the Behaviors panel.

To use the Play Timeline or Stop Timeline behavior, follow these steps:

1. In the Document window, select a tag, link, or image that you want to trigger the event.

2. Choose Window ⇨ Behaviors or select the Show Behavior button from the Launcher to open the Behaviors panel.

3. In the Behaviors panel, click the + (add) Action button, and from the pop-up menu choose either of the following methods:

    a. Timeline ⇨ Play Timeline to start a timeline.

    b. Timeline ⇨ Stop Timeline to end a timeline.

4. In the Play Timeline or Stop Timeline dialog box (see Figure 20-9), choose the timeline that you want to play (or stop) from the appropriate Timeline drop-down list.

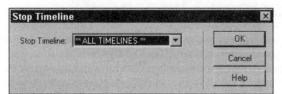

Figure 20-9: You can use the Stop Timeline behavior to stop all timelines or a specific timeline.

5. Click OK when you are finished.

6. Select an event to trigger the behavior from the drop-down menu in the Events column.

When you select the option to loop your timeline, Dreamweaver automatically inserts a Go to Frame behavior — with the first frame set as the target. You can display any frame on your timeline by inserting the Go to Frame behavior manually. To use the Go to Frame behavior, follow these steps:

1. In the Document window, select a tag, link, or image that you want to have trigger the event.

2. Choose Window ➪ Behaviors or select the Show Behavior button from the Launcher to open the Behaviors panel.

3. In the Behaviors panel, select the + (add) Action button and choose Timeline ➪ Go to Timeline Frame from the drop-down list.

4. Choose the timeline you want to affect from the Timeline drop-down menu.

5. Enter the frame number in the Go to Frame text box.

6. If you'd like the timeline to loop a set number of times, enter a value in the Loop text box. Click OK when you are finished.

   Remember, if you don't enter a value, the timeline loops endlessly.

Tip   Depending on the type of effect desired, you may want to use two of the Timeline behaviors together. To ensure that your timeline always starts from the same point, first attach a Go to Timeline Frame behavior to the event and then attach the Play Timeline behavior to the same event.

Dreamweaver Technique: Creating a Multiscreen Slideshow

Moving layers around the screen is pretty cool, but you've probably already figured out that you can do a lot more with timelines. One of the possibilities is a graphics slideshow displaying a rotating series of pictures. To demonstrate the range of potential available to timelines, the following sample project shows you how to construct a slideshow with more than one screen, complete with moving layers and triggered behaviors.

This technique has four steps:

1. **Prepare the graphic elements.** The process is easier if you have most (if not all) of your images for the slideshow — as well as the control interface — ready to go.

2. **Create the slideshow timeline.** In this project, one timeline is devoted to rotating images on four different "screens."

3. **Create the moving layers timeline.** The slideshow begins and ends with a bit of flair, as the screens fly in and fly out.

4. **Add the behaviors.** The slideshow includes controls for playing, pausing, restarting, and ending the slideshow, which then takes the user to another Web page.

This technique is intended to act as a basis for your own creations, not as an end in itself. You can add many variations and refinements; for example, you can preload images, make rollover buttons, and add music to the background. Following is a fundamental structure focused on the use of timelines, which you can expand with additional objects as needed.

Note   The end result of this Dreamweaver Technique can be viewed only by 4.0 browsers or later.

Step 1: Preparing the graphic elements

Using a timeline for a slideshow presentation has only one restriction, but this qualification is significant — all the graphics in one "screen" must have the same dimensions. The timeline doesn't actually change the image tag; it only changes the file source for the tag. Thus, the height and width of the last image inserted overrides all the values for the foregoing graphics.

Luckily, all major image-processing software can resize and extend the canvas of a picture with little effort. When creating a slideshow, you may find it useful to do all of the resizing work at one time. Load in your images with the greatest width and height — they may or may not be the same picture — and use these measurements as your common denominators for all graphics.

Go ahead and create your interface buttons earlier rather than later. Experience shows that the more design elements you prepare ahead of time, the less adjusting you have to do later. Also, activating a timeline with a behavior is a straightforward process, and a finished interface enables you to incorporate the buttons quickly.

Finally, you should create and place the layers you want to use. The sample Web page in this technique is built of four screens, all of the same dimensions. The four different layers are uniquely named, but they all have the same size.

Tip   If you are making multiple versions of the same layer, consider changing the default layer size to fit your design. Choose Edit ⇨ Preferences and select the Layers category. Once you've customized the height and width values, all the layers incorporated in the Web page with the Insert ⇨ Layer command automatically size correctly. You only have to position those layers once they are created.

To recap, use the following steps to prepare your graphics:

1. Create all the images to be used as slides. All the slides must be the same height and width.

2. Prepare and place your interface buttons.

3. Create the number of layers that you need for the different screens in the slideshow.

4. Position your layers so that each can hold a different slide. The preceding example has four layers, centered on the screen in two rows.

5. Insert your opening slides into each of the layers.

Note   Your opening slide doesn't have to be a graphic image. You could also use a solid-colored GIF or a slide with text.

Try to work backward from a final design whenever layer positioning is involved. At this stage, all of the elements are in their final placement, ready for the slideshow to begin (see Figure 20-10). Next, you can activate the slideshow.

Figure 20-10: Before activating any layers or setting up the slideshow, design the layout.

Step 2: Creating the slideshow timeline

For all the attention that timelines and layers receive, you may be surprised that one of the best features of Dreamweaver timelines has nothing to do with layers. You can use timelines to change images anywhere on your Web page—whether or not they are in layers. As explained in Step 1, the timeline doesn't actually replace one <img> tag with another, but rather alters an image by swapping the src attribute value. The src attribute changes just as changes in a layer's position, shape, or depth must happen at a keyframe.

In planning your slideshow, you need to decide how often a new slide appears, because you need to set keyframes at each of these points. If you are changing your slides every few seconds, you can change the frame rate to 1 fps. This setting helps you easily keep track of how many seconds occur between each slide change (and because no animation is involved with this timeline, a rapid frame rate is irrelevant). Note, however, that on the timeline described previously in this chapter that involved moving layers, the frame rate should be maintained at around 15 fps. Each timeline can have its own frame rate.

The only other choices involve the Autoplay and Loop options. As with frame rate, you can set each timeline to its own options without interfering with another timeline. This example has the slideshow loop but does not start automatically. Use the Play button to enable the user to start the show. But first, let's add the images to the slides.

To put images into a slideshow on a timeline, follow these steps:

1. Choose Window ⇨ Timelines to open the Timelines panel.

2. If desired, rename Timeline1 by selecting the name and typing your own unique name.

3. Select one image from those onscreen in the positioned layers and drag the graphic to the Timelines panel.

Be sure to grab the image, not the layer.

4. Release the animation bar at the beginning of the timeline.

5. Repeat Steps 3 and 4 for each image until all images are represented on the timeline.

6. Change the frame rate by entering a new value in the Fps text box. This example changes the frame rate to 1.

7. Select the Loop or Autoplay options, if desired.

8. On one of the animation bars representing images, select the frame for a keyframe.

9. Choose Modify ➪ Timeline ➪ Add Keyframe, or right-click (Control+click) the frame on the timeline and choose Add Keyframe from the shortcut menu.

10. In the Image Property Inspector, select the Src folder to locate the graphic file for the next slide image.

11. Repeat Steps 9 and 10 until every animation bar has keyframes for every slide change and each keyframe has a new or different image assigned.

This example changes slides every five seconds, as you can see in Figure 20-11 by looking at the keyframe placement. Although the slideshow has all four images changing simultaneously, you can also stagger the timing of the image changes. Simply drag one or more of the animation bars a few frames forward or backward after the keyframes have been set.

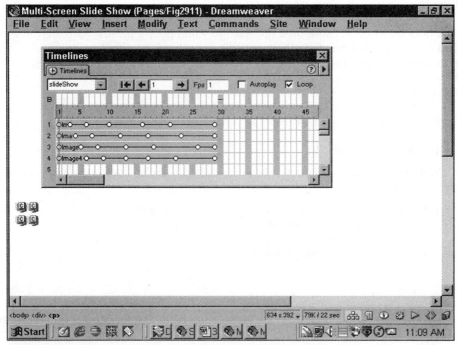

Figure 20-11: Each keyframe on each animation bar signals a change of the slide image.

Tip   To preview your slide changes, you don't have to go outside of Dreamweaver. Just click and hold down the Play button on the Timelines panel.

Step 3: Creating the moving layers timeline

At this stage, the slideshow is functional but a little dull. To add a bit of showmanship, you can "fly in" the layers from different areas of the Web page to their final destination. This task is easy — to complete the effect, the layers "fly out" when the user is ready to leave.

You can achieve these fly-in/fly-out effects in several ways. You can put the opening fly-in on one timeline and the ending fly-out on another. A more concise method combines the fly-in and fly-out for each layer on one timeline — separating them with a Stop Timeline behavior. After the fly-in portion happens when the page has loaded (because the example selects the Autoplay option for this timeline), the fly-out section does not begin to play until signaled to continue with the Play Timeline behavior.

To create the moving layers' opening and closing for the slideshow, follow these steps:

1. Choose Modify ➪ Timeline ➪ Add Timeline, or right-click (Ctrl+click) the Timelines panel and choose Add Timeline from the shortcut menu.

2. Rename your new timeline if desired.

3. Select the Autoplay checkbox so that this timeline begins playing automatically when the Web page is loaded.

4. Select any one of the layers surrounding your images and drag it onto the Timelines panel.

Caution   This time, make sure you move the layers — not the images.

5. To set the amount of time for the fly-in section to span, drag the final keyframe of the animation bar to a new frame. The example sets the end at 30 frames, which at 15 fps lasts two seconds.

6. From the Document window, select the same layer again and drag it to the Timelines panel. Place it directly after the first animation bar. This animation bar becomes the fly-out portion.

7. Drag the final keyframe to extend the time, if desired.

8. At this point, all four keyframes — two for each animation bar — have exactly the same information. Now change the positions for two keyframes to enable the layer to move. Select the first keyframe in the opening animation bar.

9. Reposition the layer so that it is offscreen. Although you can complete this task manually to the right or bottom of the screen by dragging the layer to a new location, you can also use the Layer Property Inspector to input new values directly for the Left and Top attributes.

Tip   Use negative numbers to move a layer offscreen to the left or top of the browser window.

10. From the Timelines panel, select the last keyframe of the closing animation bar.

11. Reposition the layer offscreen. If you want the layer to return in the same manner as it arrived, enter the same values for the Left and Top attributes as in the first keyframe of the opening animation bar.

12. Repeat Steps 4 through 11 for every layer.

Now, when you preview this timeline, the layers fly in and immediately fly out again. Figure 20-12 shows the layers in the example in mid-animation. In the final phase of the technique, you add behaviors to put the action under user control.

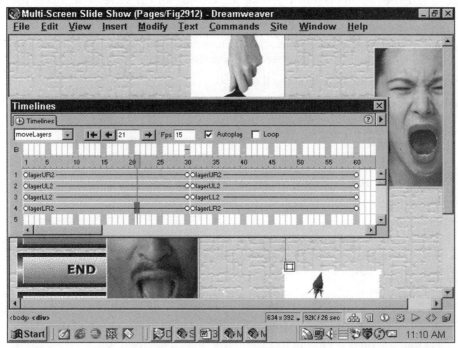

Figure 20-12: You can use two animation bars side by side to achieve a back-and-forth effect.

Step 4: Adding the behaviors

Although it may be fun to watch an unexpected effect take place, giving the user control over aspects of a presentation is much more involving—for the designer as well as the user. The example is ready to incorporate the user-interaction aspect by attaching Dreamweaver behaviors to the user interface and to the Behavior channel of the Timelines panel.

Two timeline behaviors have already been attached to the example. When the Loop option is selected in Step 2 for the slideshow timeline, Dreamweaver automatically includes a Go to Timeline Frame behavior after the final frame that sends the timeline back to the first frame. In the moving layers timeline, enabling the Autostart option causes Dreamweaver to attach a Play Timeline behavior to the onLoad event of the Web page's <body> tag. To complete the project, five behaviors need to be added.

First, you need a behavior to stop the moving layers from proceeding after the fly-in portion of the animation:

1. From the Timelines panel, double-click the final frame of the first animation bar in the Behavior channel.

2. In the Behaviors panel, select Timeline ➪ Stop Timeline from the + (add) Actions pull-down menu.

3. From the Stop Timeline dialog box, select the timeline that contains the moving layers.

4. Click OK. An onFrame event is set for the Stop Timeline action by default.

Second, you need a behavior to enable the user to begin playing the slideshow:

1. In the Document window, select the Play button.

2. In the Behaviors panel, select the Timeline ➪ Play Timeline action from the + (add) Action drop-down list.

3. In the Play Timeline dialog box, choose the timeline representing the slideshow.

4. Click OK. An onMouseDown event is set to trigger the action by default.

The next behavior enables the user to stop the slideshow temporarily:

1. In the Document window, select the Pause button.

2. In the Behaviors panel, select Timeline ➪ Stop Timeline from the + (add) Actions drop-down list.

3. Choose the layer representing the slideshow in the Stop Timeline dialog box.

4. Click OK. An onMouseDown event is set to trigger the action by default.

To enable the user to begin the slideshow from the beginning, follow these steps:

1. In the Document window, select the Restart button.
2. In the Behaviors panel, add the Timeline ⇨ Go to Timeline Frame action.
3. In the Go to Timeline Frame dialog box, choose the layer representing the slideshow.
4. Enter a 1 in the Frame text box.
5. Click OK. An onMouseDown event is set to trigger the action by default.
6. Add the next action. In the Behaviors panel, select Timeline ⇨ Play Timeline from the + (add) Action drop-down list.
7. In the Play Timeline dialog box, choose the layer representing the slideshow.
8. Click OK. An onMouseDown event is attached to the action by default.

To end the presentation and move the user on to the next Web page, follow these steps:

1. In the Document window, select the End button.
2. In the Behaviors panel, select the Timeline ⇨ Play Timeline action from the + (add) Action drop-down list.
3. Choose the timeline representing the moving layers in the Play Timeline dialog box and click OK. The timeline begins playing where it last stopped — just before the layers are about to fly out. An onMouseDown event is set to trigger the action by default.
4. Add the next behavior. Select the Go to URL action from the + (add) drop-down list.
5. In the Go to URL dialog box, enter the path to the new page in the URL text box or select the Browse button to locate the file. Click OK when you are finished.

The project is complete and ready to test. Feel free to experiment, trying out different timings to achieve different effects.

On the CD-ROM You can test the final working version by using your browser to view the Multiscreen Slideshow Demo in the Code section of the CD-ROM that accompanies this book.

Summary

Timelines are effective tools for developing pages in which events need to be triggered at specific points in time.

✦ Timelines can affect particular attributes of layers and images, or they can start any Dreamweaver behavior.

✦ Use the Timelines panel to set an animation to play automatically, to have it loop indefinitely, and to change the frames-per-second display rate of the timeline.

✦ You must use one of the timeline behaviors to activate your timeline if you don't use the Autoplay feature.

In the next chapter, you learn how you can use Dreamweaver to explore the brave new world of XML, the Extensible Markup Language.

✦　　✦　　✦

Enhancing Web Site Management and Workflow in Dreamweaver

Utilizing Dreamweaver Templates

Let's face it: Web design is a combination of glory and grunt work. Creating the initial design for a Web site can be fun and exciting, but when you have to implement your wonderful new design on 200 or more pages, the excitement fades as you try to figure out the quickest way to finish the work. Enter templates. Properly using templates can be a tremendous time-saver. Moreover, a template ensures that your Web site has a consistent look and feel, which, in turn, generally means that it's easier for users to navigate.

In Dreamweaver, new documents can be produced from a standard design saved as a template, as in a word processing program. Furthermore, you can alter a template and update all the files that were created from it earlier; this capability extends the power of the repeating element Libraries to overall page design. Templates also form the bridge to one of the hottest technologies shaping the Web — XML (Extensible Markup Language).

Dreamweaver makes it easy to access all kinds of templates — everything from your own creations to the default blank page. This chapter demonstrates the mechanism behind Dreamweaver templates and shows you strategies for getting the most out of them.

Understanding Templates

Templates exist in many forms. Furniture makers use master patterns as templates to create the same basic design repeatedly, using new wood stains or upholstery to differentiate the end results. A stencil, in which the inside of a letter, word, or design is cut out, is a type of template as well. With computers, templates form the basic document into which specific details are added to create new, distinct documents.

Dreamweaver templates, in terms of functionality, are a combination of traditional templates and updateable Library elements. Once a new page is created from a template, the new document remains attached to the original template unless specifically separated or detached. Because the new document maintains a connection to previous pages in a site, if the original template is altered, all the documents created from it can be automatically updated. This relationship is also true of Dreamweaver's repeating elements Libraries. In fact, templates can even include Library elements.

Cross-Reference   Library items can work hand-in-hand with templates. See Chapter 22 for a detailed discussion of Library items.

Templates are composed of two types of regions: *locked* and *editable*. Every element on the Web page template falls into one category or the other. When a template is first created, all the areas are locked. Part of the process of defining a template is to designate and name the editable regions. Then, when a document is created from that template, the editable regions are the only ones that can be modified.

Naturally, templates can be altered to mark additional editable areas or to relock editable areas. Moreover, you can detach a document created from a template at any point and edit anything in the document — you cannot, however, reattach the document to the template without losing newly inserted content. On the other hand, a document based on one template can be changed to a completely different look but with the same content, if another template with identical editable regions is applied.

Dreamweaver ships with a tutorial that illustrates the power of templates. The tutorial, found in the Dreamweaver/Tutorial folder, is based on an example Web site for a travel company called Compass. Previewing the site in a browser shows that all the sample pages for the different trips in the Destinations section are basically the same — only the destination title, description, and Flash movie vary. The layout, background, and navigation controls are identical on every page. Each of these pages was created from the template page shown in Figure 21-1. Notice the highlighting surrounding certain areas; in a template, the editable regions are highlighted, and the locked areas are not. A tab further identifies each editable region to make it easier to add the right content in the right area.

Creating Your Own Templates

You can use any design that you like for your own template. Perhaps the best course to take is to finalize a single page that has all the elements that you want to include in your template. Then, convert that document to a template and proceed to mark all the changeable areas — whether text or image — as editable regions.

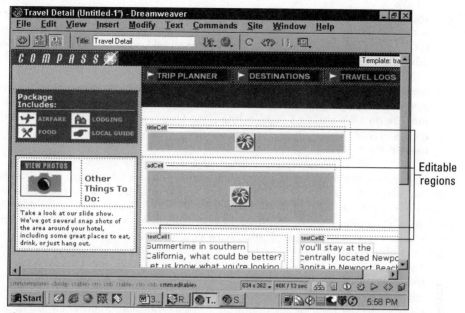

Figure 21-1: In this sample template from the Dreamweaver tutorial, editable regions are highlighted.

Before saving your file as a template, consider these points when designing your basic page:

✦ **Use placeholders where you can.** Whether it's dummy text or a temporary graphic, placeholders give shape to your page. They also make it easier to remember which elements to include. If you are using an image placeholder, set a temporary height and width through the Property Inspector or by dragging the image placeholder's sizing handles; of course, you can also just insert a sample graphic.

✦ **Finalize and incorporate as much content as possible in the template.** If you find yourself repeatedly adding the same information or objects to a page, add them to your template. The more structured elements you can include, the faster your pages can be produced.

✦ **Use sample objects on the template.** Often you have to enter the same basic object, such as a plug-in for a digital movie, on every page, with only the filename changing. Enter your repeating object with all the preset parameters possible on your template page as an editable region, and you only have to select a new filename for each page.

✦ **Include your** `<meta>` **information.** Search engines rely on `<meta>` tags to get the overview of a page and then scan the balance of the page to get the details. You can enter a Keyword or Description object from the Head panel of the Objects palette so that all the Web pages in your site have the same basic information for cataloging.

Note You cannot enter separate `<meta>` tag information into template-derived pages without inserting it directly into the code. Dreamweaver defines one editable area for the title—your hand-entered `<meta>` tags should go in this region. This procedure is described in detail later in this chapter.

✦ **Apply all needed behaviors and styles to the template.** When a document is saved as a template, all the code in the `<head>` section is locked. Because most behaviors and CSS (Cascading Style Sheet) styles insert code here, documents created from templates cannot easily apply new behaviors or create new styles.

You can create a template from a Web document with one command: File ➪ Save As Template. Dreamweaver stores all templates in a Templates folder created for each defined site, with a special file extension, .dwt. After you've created your page and saved it as a template, notice that Dreamweaver inserts `<<Template>>` in the title bar to remind you of the page's status. Now you're ready to begin defining the template's editable regions.

Note You can also create a template from an entirely blank page if you like. To do so, open the Assets panel and select the Templates category. From the Templates category, select the New Template button. You can find more information on how to use the Assets panel's Templates category later in this chapter.

Using Editable Regions

As noted earlier, when you convert an existing page into a template via the Save As Template command, the entire document is initially locked. If you attempt to create a document from a template at this stage, Dreamweaver alerts you that the template doesn't have any editable regions, and you cannot change anything on the page. Editable regions are essential to any template.

Marking existing content as editable

Two techniques exist for marking editable regions. First, you can designate any existing content as an editable region. Second, you can insert a new editable region anywhere you can place your cursor. In both cases, you must give the region a unique name. Dreamweaver uses the unique name to identify the editable region when entering new content, applying the template, and exporting or importing XML.

Note As noted, each editable region must have a unique name, but the names need only be different from any other editable region on the same page. The name could be used for objects or JavaScript functions, or for editable regions on a different template.

To mark an existing area as an editable region, follow these steps:

1. Select the text or object that you wish to convert to an editable region.

> **Tip**
>
> The general rule of thumb with editable regions is that you need to select a complete tag pair, such as `<table>...</table>`. This has several implications. For instance, while you can mark an entire table or a single cell as editable, you can't select multiple cells, a row, or a column to be so marked. You have to select each cell individually (`<td>...</td>`). Also, you can select the content of a layer to be editable and keep the layer itself locked (so that its position and other properties cannot be altered), but if you select the layer to be editable, you can't lock the content.

2. Choose Modify ➪ Templates ➪ New Editable Region. You can also use the keyboard shortcut Ctrl+Alt+W (Command+Option+W), or right-click (Control+click) the selection and choose Editable Regions ➪ New Editable Region from the shortcut menu. Dreamweaver displays the New Editable Region dialog box.

> **Tip**
>
> If you want the flexibility of adding returns to your editable region, make sure it includes at least one return. The easiest method is to select the `<p>` tag in the Tag Selector. If just text is selected, Dreamweaver does not allow any returns, although line breaks are accepted.

3. Enter a unique name for the selected area. Click OK when you're done or Cancel to abort the operation.

> **Caution**
>
> While you can use spaces in editable region names, some characters are not permitted. The illegal characters are the ampersand (&), double quote ("), single quote ('), and left and right angle brackets (< and >).

Dreamweaver outlines the selection with the color picked in Preferences on the Highlighting panel. The name for your newly designated region is displayed on a tab marking the area; the region is also listed in the Modify ➪ Templates submenu. If still selected, the region name has a checkmark next to it in the Templates submenu. You can jump to any other editable region by selecting its name from this dynamic list.

> **Tip**
>
> Make sure you apply any formatting to your text — either by using HTML codes such as `<font>`, or by using CSS styles — before you select it to be an editable region. Generally, you want to keep the defined look of the content while altering just the text, so make just the text an editable region and exclude the formatting tags. It's helpful to have the HTML Inspector open for this detailed work.

Inserting a new editable region

Sometimes it's helpful to create a new editable region where no content currently exists. In these situations, the editable region name doubles as a label identifying the type of content expected, such as {CatalogPrice}. Dreamweaver always puts new region names in curly braces as just shown and highlights the entry in the template.

To insert a new editable region, follow these steps:

1. Place your cursor anywhere on the template page.

2. Choose Modify ➪ Templates ➪ New Editable Region. You can also use the keyboard shortcut Ctrl+Alt+V (Command+Option+V), or right-click (Control+click) the selection and choose New Editable Region from the shortcut menu.

   Dreamweaver displays the New Editable Region dialog box.

3. Enter a unique name for the new region. Click OK when you're done or Cancel to abort the operation.

Dreamweaver inserts the new region name in the document, surrounded by curly braces, marks it with a named tab and adds the name to the dynamic region list (which you can display by choosing Modify ➪ Templates).

Tip   One editable region, the Web page's title, is automatically created when you save a document as a template. The title is stored in a special editable region called doctitle. To change the title (which initially takes the same title as the template), enter the new text in the Title field of the Toolbar. You can also use the keyboard shortcut Ctrl+J (Command+J) to open the Page Properties dialog box. Finally, you can select View ➪ Head Elements and choose the Title icon to enter the new text in the Property Inspector.

Locking an editable region

Inevitably, you'll mark a region as editable that you'd prefer to keep locked, or you may discover that every page constructed to date has required inputting the same content, so it should be entered on the template and locked. In either event, converting an editable region to a locked one is a simple operation.

To lock an editable region, follow these steps:

1. Place your cursor in the editable region you want to lock.

2. Choose Modify ➪ Templates ➪ Remove Editable Region. The Unmark Editable Region dialog box, shown in Figure 21-2, appears with the selected region highlighted.

Note   You don't have to preselect the editable region to unmark it. If you don't, the Unmark Editable Region dialog box opens but doesn't highlight any selection; you have to choose it by name.

Creating Links in Templates

A common problem that designers encounter with Dreamweaver templates centers on links. People often add a link to their template and discover that it doesn't work when the new page is derived from the template. The main cause of this error stems from linking to a nonexistent page or element by hand—that is, typing in the link rather than using the Select File dialog box to choose it. Designers tend to set the link according to their final site structure without taking into account how templates are stored in Dreamweaver.

For example, when creating a template, let's say that you have links to three pages, products.htm, services.htm, and about.htm, all in the root of your site. Both products.htm and services.htm have been created, so you select the folder icon in the Property Inspector and select those files in turn. Dreamweaver inserts those links like this: `../products.htm` and `../services.htm`. The `../` indicates the directory above the current directory—which makes sense only when you remember that all templates are stored in a subfolder of the site root called Templates. These links are correctly resolved when a document is derived from this template to reflect the stored location of the new file.

Let's assume that the third file, about.htm, has not yet been created, and so that link is entered by hand. The common mistake is to enter it as it should be when it's used: about.htm. However, because the page is saved in the Template folder, Dreamweaver converts that link to /Templates/about.htm for any page derived from the template—and the link will fail. This type of error also applies to dependent files, such as graphics or other media.

The best solution is to always use the folder icon to link to an existing file when building your templates. If the file does not exist, and if you don't want to create a placeholder page for it, link to another existing file in the same folder and modify the link manually.

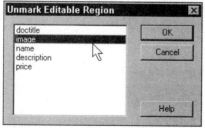

Figure 21-2: Convert an editable region to a locked one with the Unmark Editable Region command.

3. Click OK in the Unmark Editable Region dialog box to confirm your choice.

   The editable region highlight is removed, and the area is now a locked region of the template.

Caution   If you are removing a newly inserted editable region that is labeled with the region name in curly braces, then the label is not removed and must be deleted by hand on the template. Otherwise, it appears as part of the document created from a template and won't be accessible.

Adding Content to Template Documents

Constructing a template is only half the job—using it to create new pages is the other half. Because your basic layout is complete and you're only dropping in new images and entering new text, pages based on templates take a fraction of the time needed to create regular Web pages. Dreamweaver makes it easy to enter new content as well—you can even move from one editable region to the next, much like filling out a form (which, of course, is exactly what you're doing).

To create a new document based on a template, follow these steps:

1. In the Template category of the Assets panel, select the desired template and choose the New from Template from the panel's context menu. Alternatively, choose File ⇨ New from Template.

   If you chose the command from the File menu, the Select Template dialog box, shown in Figure 21-3, appears.

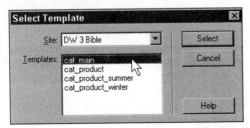

Figure 21-3: Create a new document based on any template listed in the Select Template dialog box.

2. If you wish to create a template from a local site other than the current one, select it from the Site drop-down list.

3. Select the desired template from those in the Templates list box.

4. Click OK when you're done.

When your new page opens, the editable regions are again highlighted; furthermore, the cursor is only active when it is over an unlocked region. If you have the Code view open, you also will see that the locked region is highlighted in a different color as shown in Figure 21-4. The highlighting makes it easy to differentiate the two types of regions.

Locked areas

Editable regions

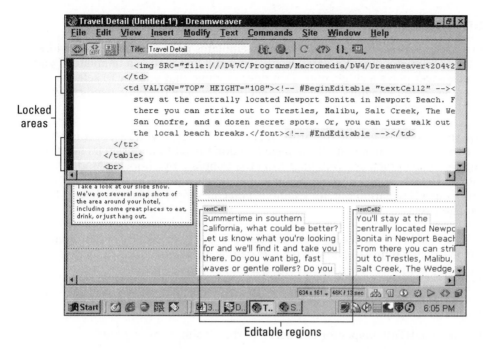

Figure 21-4: In a document based on a template, the editable regions are clearly marked, as are the locked portions in the Code view.

Generally, it is easiest to select the editable region name or placeholder first and then enter the new content. Selecting the editable regions can be handled in several ways:

✦ Highlight each editable region name or placeholder with the mouse.

✦ Position your cursor inside any editable region and then select the `<mm:editable>` tag in the Tag Selector.

✦ Choose Modify ➪ Templates and then select the name of your editable region from the dynamic list.

Note

If all your editable regions are separate cells in a table, you can tab forward and Shift+Tab backward through the cells. With each press of the Tab key, all the content in the cell is selected, whether it is an editable region name or a placeholder.

Naturally, you should save your document to retain all the new content that's been added.

Adding behaviors to template-derived documents

The current implementation of Dreamweaver templates does not enable behaviors to be added to any document created from — and still linked to — a template. If you try, Dreamweaver plays a single note, as it does anytime that you try to select a locked region. With behaviors, the `<head>` section — where the code needs to go — is locked in a template.

You have three ways to handle the problem, however. First, if you're just using the template to get the basic layout of the page and don't need to maintain its link for updating, you can detach the Web page from the template by choosing Modify ⇨ Templates ⇨ Detach from Template. Second, if all your pages require the same behavior, as in a Navigation Bar, for example, you can simply add the behavior to the template itself.

The final method is the most involved, but also the most flexible. By adding some code to the original template, new behaviors can be attached, either to the template or to any template-based document. Here are the steps required for the modification:

1. Open the template for editing.

2. Display the HTML Inspector and scroll to the closing `</head>` tag.

   If you select the `<body>` tag from the Tag Selector, the closing `</head>` tag is just above the selected region.

3. Enter this code above the `</head>` tag:

```
<mm:editable>
<script>
</script>
</mm:editable>

<mm:editable>
<!-- Dummy comment, to be deleted by Dreamweaver -->
</mm:editable>
```

4. Choose File ⇨ Save and update any documents linked to the template.

When a document is derived from this modified template, Dreamweaver removes the dummy comment but maintains the `<script>...</script>` pair, enabling behaviors to be added.

Inserting meta tags in documents based on templates

With the exception of the `<title>` tag, Dreamweaver locks the entire head section when a template is made. Therefore, a special procedure must be used to add page-specific `<meta>` tags to a document derived from a template. While it is considered a best practice to include as many `<meta>` tags as possible in the general template, often special keyword or description `<meta>` tags must be included on a page-by-page basis. If you try to add any item from the Head category of the Objects panel, Dreamweaver notifies you with a beep that the insertion is not allowed.

To work around the locked `<head>` region, the `<meta>` tag is added within the editable region surrounding the title. Here's the most direct method for accomplishing this task:

1. Choose Show Code and Design Views or Show Code View from the Toolbar.

   You also have the option of selecting the Code Inspector button from the Launcher or pressing the keyboard shortcut F10.

2. In the Code view, scroll up to the top of the document until the `<!-- #BeginEditable -->` ... `<!-- #EndEditable -->` tags surrounding the `<title>` tag are visible.

3. Place the cursor behind the closing `</title>` tag.

4. From the Head category of the Objects panel, choose the desired `<meta>` tag: Insert Meta, Insert Keywords, Insert Description, or Insert Refresh.

   The appropriate dialog box opens.

5. Enter the desired attributes for the `<meta>` tag in the dialog box and select OK when you're done.

   Dreamweaver inserts the completed `<meta>` tag behind the `<title>` tag, but within the editable region.

By using this technique, any updates to the general template will still be reflected in the derived document and you'll have the added advantage of unique `<meta>` tags where necessary.

Working with Templates in the Assets Panel

As a site grows, so does the number of templates it employs. Overall management of your templates is conducted through the Templates category of the Assets panel. You can open the Templates palette by choosing Windows ➪ Templates or by pressing the keyboard shortcut Ctrl+F11 (Command+F11). The Templates category, shown in Figure 21-5, displays a list of the current site's available templates in the lower pane and a preview of the selected template in the upper pane.

The Templates palette has five buttons along the bottom of its window:

✦ **Apply** — Creates a document derived from the currently selected template if the current document is blank, or, if the current document is based on a template, changes the locked regions of the document to match the selected template.

✦ **Refresh Site List** — Displays the list of all the templates currently in the site.

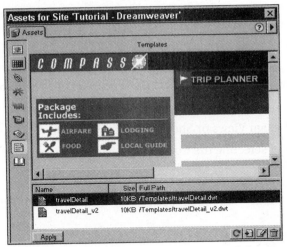

Figure 21-5: Use the Templates category of the Assets panel to preview, delete, open, create, or apply your current site's templates.

✦ **New Template**—Creates a new blank template.

✦ **Edit**—Loads the selected template for modification.

✦ **Delete**—Removes the selected template.

The Assets panel's context menu offers all of these options and more as explained in Table 21-1:

<table>
<tr><td colspan="2">Table 21-1
Template Category Context Menu</td></tr>
<tr><td>*Command*</td><td>*Description*</td></tr>
<tr><td>Refresh Site List</td><td>Displays the list of all the templates currently in the site.</td></tr>
<tr><td>New Template</td><td>Starts a new blank template.</td></tr>
<tr><td>New from Template</td><td>Creates a new document based on the currently selected template.</td></tr>
<tr><td>Edit</td><td>Opens the current template for modifying.</td></tr>
<tr><td>Apply</td><td>Creates a document derived from the currently selected template if the current document is blank or, if the current document is based on a template, changes the locked regions of the document to match the selected template. The same effects can also be achieved by dragging the template from the Assets panel to the current document.</td></tr>
</table>

Command	Description
Rename	Renames the selected template.
Delete	Removes the selected template.
Update Current Page	Applies any changes made in the template to the current page, if the current page is derived from a template.
Update Site	Applies any changes made in any templates to all template-based documents in the site.
Copy to Site	Copies the highlighted template, but none of the dependent files, to the selected site.
Locate in Site	Opens the Site window and highlights the selected template.

Creating a blank template

Not all templates are created from existing documents. Some Web designers prefer to create their templates from scratch. To create a blank template, follow these steps:

1. Open the Templates category of the Assets panel by selecting its symbol or by choosing Window ⇨ Templates.

2. From the Templates category, select New Template. A new, untitled template is created.

3. Enter a title for your new template and press Enter (Return).

4. While the new template is selected, press the Edit button. The blank template opens in a new Dreamweaver window.

5. Insert your page elements.

6. Mark any elements or areas as editable regions using one of the methods previously described.

7. Save your template.

Deleting and opening templates

As with any set of files, there comes a time to clean house and remove files that are no longer in use. To remove a template, first open the Templates category of the Assets panel. Next, select the file you want to remove and choose the Delete button.

Caution   Be forewarned: Dreamweaver does not alert you if files exist that were created from the template that you're about to delete. Deleting the template, in effect, "orphans" those documents, and they can no longer be updated via a template.

You can edit a template—to change the locked or editable regions—in several ways. To use the first method, choose File ⇨ Open and, in the Select File dialog box, change the Files of Type to Template Files (*.dwt) on Window systems and choose Template Files from the Show drop-down list on Macintosh systems. Then, locate the Templates folder in your defined site to select the template to open.

The second method of opening a template for modification uses the Templates category of the Assets panel. Select a template to modify and choose the Edit button. You can also double-click your template to open it for editing.

Finally, if you're working in the Site window, open a template by selecting the Templates folder for your site and open any of the files found there.

Tip   After you've made your modifications to the template, you don't have to use the Save As Template command to store the file—you can use the regular File ⇨ Save command or the keyboard shortcut Ctrl+S (Command+S). Likewise, if you want to save your template under another name, use the Save As command.

Applying templates

Dreamweaver makes it easy to try a variety of different looks for your document while maintaining the same content. Once you've created a document from a template, you can apply any other template to it. The only requirement is that the two templates have editable regions with the same names. When might this feature come in handy? In one scenario, you might develop a number of possible Web site designs for a client and create templates for each different approach, which are then applied to the identical content. Or, in an ongoing site, you could completely change the look of a catalog seasonally but retain all the content. Figure 21-6 shows two radically different schemes for a Web site with the same content.

To apply a template to a document, follow these steps:

1. Open the Templates category of the Assets panel.

2. Make sure the Web page you want to apply the style to is the active document.

3. From the Templates category, select the template you want to use and click the Apply button.

Tip   You can also drag onto the current page the template you'd like to apply or choose Modify ⇨ Templates ⇨ Apply Template to Page from the menus.

4. If content exists without a matching editable region, Dreamweaver displays the Choose Editable Region for Orphaned Content dialog box. To receive the content, select one of the listed editable regions from the template being applied and click OK.

The new template is applied to the document, and all the new locked areas replace all the old locked areas.

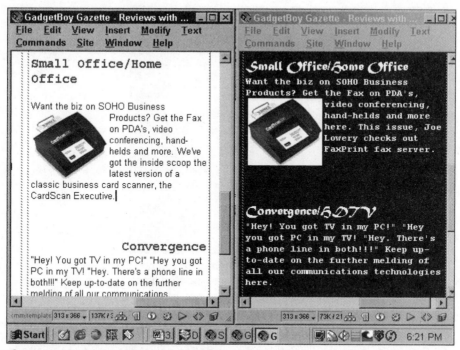

Figure 21-6: You can apply a template to a document created from another template to achieve different designs with identical content.

Updating Templates

Anytime you save a change to an existing template — whether or not any documents have been created from it — Dreamweaver asks if you'd like to update all the documents in the local site attached to the template. As with Library elements, you can also update the current page or the entire site at any time. Updating documents based on a template can save you an enormous amount of time — especially when numerous changes are involved.

To update a single page, open the page and choose Modify ⇨ Templates ⇨ Update Current Page or select the same command from the context menu of the Assets panel. Either way, the update is instantly applied.

To update a series of pages or an entire site, follow these steps:

1. Choose Modify ⇨ Templates ⇨ Update Pages.

The Update Pages dialog box, shown in Figure 21-7, appears.

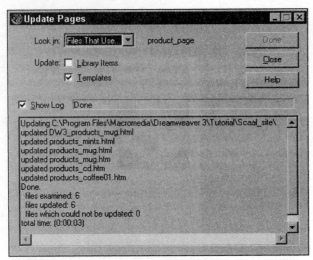

Figure 21-7: Any changes made to a template can be automatically applied to the template's associated files by using the Update Pages command.

2. To update all the documents using all the templates for an entire site, choose Entire Site from the Look In option and then select the name of the site from the accompanying drop-down list.

3. To update pages using a particular template, choose Pages Using from the Look In option and then select the name of the template.

4. To view a report of the progress of the update, make sure that the Show Log option is enabled.

5. Click Start to begin the update process.

The log window displays a list of the files examined and updated, the total number of files that could not be updated, and the elapsed time.

Changing the Default Document

Each time you open a new document in Dreamweaver — or even just start Dreamweaver — a blank page is created. This blank page is based on an HTML file called Default.html that is stored in the Configuration\Templates folder. The default page works in a similar fashion to the templates in that you can create new documents from it, but no editable or locked regions exist — everything in the page can always be altered.

The basic blank-page document is an HTML structure with only a few properties specified — a document type, character set, and white background for the body:

```
<html>
<head>
<title>Untitled Document</title>
<meta http-equiv="Content-Type" content="text/html; charset=iso-8859-1">
</head>

<body bgcolor="#FFFFFF">

</body>
</html>
```

Naturally, you can change any of these elements — and add many, many more — after you've opened a page. But what if you want to have a <meta> tag with creator information in every page that comes out of your Web design company? You can do it in Dreamweaver manually, but it's a bother, and chances are that you'll forget. Luckily, Dreamweaver provides a more efficient solution.

In keeping with its overall design philosophy of extensibility, Dreamweaver enables you to modify the Default.htm file as you would any other file. Just choose File ➪ Open and select the Configuration\Templates\Default.htm file. As you make your changes, save the file as you would normally. Now, to test your modifications, choose File ➪ New — your modifications should appear in your new document.

Summary

Much of a Web designer's responsibility is related to document production, and Dreamweaver offers a comprehensive template solution to reduce the workload. When planning your strategy for building an entire Web site, remember that templates provide these advantages:

✦ Templates can be created from any Web page.

✦ Dreamweaver templates combine locked and editable regions. Editable regions must be defined individually.

✦ After a template is declared, new documents can be created from it.

✦ If a template is altered, pages built from that template can be automatically updated.

✦ The default template that Dreamweaver uses can be modified so that every time you select File ➪ New, a new version of your customized template is created.

In the next chapter, you learn how to streamline production and site maintenance with repeating page elements from the Dreamweaver Library.

✦   ✦   ✦

Using the Repeating Elements Library

One of the challenges of designing a Web site is ensuring that buttons, copyright notices, and other cross-site features always remain consistent. Fortunately, Dreamweaver offers a useful feature called *Library items* that helps you insert repeating elements, such as a navigation bar or a company logo, into every Web page you create. With one command, you can update and maintain Library items efficiently and productively.

In this chapter, you examine the nature and the importance of repeating elements and learn how to effectively use the Dreamweaver Library feature for all your sites.

Dreamweaver Libraries

Library items within Dreamweaver are another means for you, as a designer, to maintain consistency throughout your site. Suppose you have a navigation bar on every page that contains links to all the other pages on your site. It's highly likely that you'll eventually (and probably more than once) need to make changes to the navigation bar. In a traditional Web development environment, you must modify every single page. This creates lots of opportunities for making mistakes, missing pages, and adding code to the wrong place. Moreover, the whole process is tedious — ask anyone who has had to modify the copyright notice at the bottom of every Web page for a site with over 200 pages.

One traditional method of updating repeating elements is to use *server-side includes*. A server-side include causes the server to place a component, such as a copyright notice, in a specified area of a Web page when it's sent to the user. This arrangement, however, increases the strain on your already overworked Web server and many hosting companies do not permit server-side includes for this reason. To add to the designer's frustrations, you can't lay out a Web page in a WYSIWYG format and simultaneously see the server-side scripts (unless you're using a Dreamweaver translator). So you either take the time to calculate that a server-side script will take up a specific space on the Web page, or you cross your fingers and guess.

A better way in Dreamweaver is to use an important innovation called the *Library*. The Library is designed to make repetitive updating quick, easy, and as error-free as possible. The Library's key features include the following:

✦ Any item — whether text or graphic — that goes into the body of your Web page can be designated as a Library item.

✦ Once created, Library items can be placed instantly in any Web page in your site, without your having to retype, reinsert, or reformat text and graphics.

✦ Library items can be altered at any time. After the editing is complete, Dreamweaver gives you the option to update the Web site immediately or postpone the update until later.

✦ If you are making a number of alterations to your Library items, you can wait until you're finished with all the updates and then make the changes across the board in one operation.

✦ You can update one page at a time, or you can update the entire site all at once.

✦ A Library item can be converted back to a regular non-Library element of a Web page at any time.

✦ Library items can be copied from one site to another.

✦ Library items can combine Dreamweaver behaviors — and their underlying JavaScript code — with onscreen elements, so you don't have to rebuild the same navigation bar every time, reapplying the behaviors over and over again.

Using the Library Assets Panel

Dreamweaver's Library control center is located on the Assets panel in the Library category. There you find the tools for creating, modifying, updating, and managing your Library items. Shown in Figure 22-1, the Library category is as flexible and easy to use as all of Dreamweaver's primary panels, with straightforward command buttons, a listing of all available Library items, and a handy Preview pane.

Insert Library item   Library item preview   New Library button

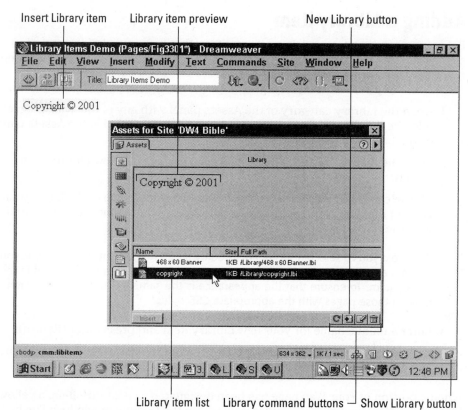

Library item list   Library command buttons ⏗ Show Library button

Figure 22-1: With the Dreamweaver Library feature, you can easily add and modify consistent objects on an entire Web site.

As usual, you can open the Library panel in several ways:

✦ Choose Window ⇨ Library.

✦ Select the Library symbol on the Assets panel.

✦ Select the Library button from the Launcher.

Cross-Reference

To use Library items, you must first create a site root folder for Dreamweaver, as explained in Chapter 6. A separate Library folder is automatically created to hold the individual Library items and is used by Dreamweaver during the updating process.

Ideally, you could save the most time by creating all your Library items before you begin constructing your Web pages, but most Web designers don't work that way. Feel free to include, modify, and update your Library items as much as you need to as your Web site evolves — that's part of the power and flexibility you gain through Dreamweaver's Library.

Adding a Library item

Before you can insert or update a Library item, that item must be designated as such within the Web page. To add an item to your site's Library, follow these steps:

1. Select any part of the Web page that you want to make into a Library item.

2. Open the Library category of the Assets panel with any of the available methods: the Window ⇨ Library command, the Library symbol in the Assets panel or the Library button in the Launcher.

3. From the Library category (see Figure 22-1), select the New Library Item button.

   The selected page element is displayed in the upper pane of the Library category. In the lower pane — the Library item list — a new entry is highlighted with the default name "Untitled."

Note   If the text you've selected has been styled by a CSS rule, Dreamweaver warns you that the appearance may be different because the style rule is not included in the Library item. To ensure that the appearance is the same, include the Library item only on those pages with the appropriate CSS styles.

4. Enter a unique name for your new Library item and press Enter (Return).

   The Library item list is resorted alphabetically, if necessary, and the new item is included.

When a portion of your Web page has been designated as a Library item, a yellow highlight is displayed over the entire item within the Document window. The highlight helps you to quickly recognize what is a Library item and what is not. If you find the yellow highlight distracting, you can disable it. Go to Edit ⇨ Preferences and, from the Highlighting category of the Preferences dialog box, deselect Show check box for Library Items. Alternatively, deselecting View ⇨ Visual Aids ⇨ Invisible Elements hides Library Item highlighting, along with any other invisible items on your page.

Note   Dreamweaver can include Library items only in the `<body>` section of an HTML document. You cannot, for instance, create a series of `<meta>` tags for your pages that must go in the `<head>` section.

Moving Library items to a new site

Although Library items are specific to each site, they can be used in more than one site. When you make your first Library item, Dreamweaver creates a folder called Library in the local root folder for the current site. To use a particular Library item in another site, simply open the Library folder from your system's desktop and copy the item to the new site's Library folder.

Drag-and-Drop Creation of Library Items

A second option for creating Library items is the drag-and-drop method. Simply select an object or several objects on a page and drag them to the Library category (either the top or bottom pane); release the mouse button to drop them in.

You can drag any object into the Library category: text, tables, images, Java applets, plug-ins, and/or ActiveX controls. Essentially anything in the Document window that can be HTML code can be dragged to the Library. And, as you might suspect, the reverse is true: Library items can be placed in your Web page by dragging them from the Library category and dropping them anywhere in the Document window.

Note   Be sure to also move any dependent files or other assets such as images and media files associated with the Library items.

Inserting a Library item in your Web page

When you create a Web site, you always need to incorporate certain features, including a standard set of link buttons along the top, a consistent banner on various pages, and a copyright notice along the bottom. Adding these items to a page from the Library can be as easy as dragging and dropping them.

You must first create a Web site and then designate Library items (as explained in the preceding section). Once these items exist, you can add the items to any page created within your site.

To add Library items to a document, use the following steps:

1. Position the cursor where you want the Library item to appear.

2. From the Library category, select the item you wish to use.

3. Select the Insert button. The highlighted Library item appears on the Web page.

Tip   As noted earlier, you can also use the drag-and-drop method to place Library items in the Document window.

When you add a Library item to a page, you notice a number of immediate changes. As mentioned, the added Library item is highlighted. If you click anywhere on the item, the entire Library item is selected.

It's important to understand that Dreamweaver treats the entire Library item entry as an external object being linked to the current page. You cannot modify Library items directly on a page. For information on editing Library entries, see the section "Editing a Library Item," later in this chapter.

While the Library item is highlighted, notice also that the Property Inspector changes. Instead of displaying the properties for the HTML object that is selected, the item is identified as a Library item, as shown in Figure 22-2.

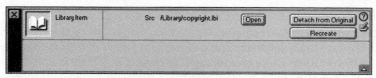

Figure 22-2: The Library Item Property Inspector identifies the source file for any selected Library entry.

You can also see evidence of Library items in the HTML for the current page. Open the Code Inspector, and you see that several lines of code have been added. The following code example indicates one Library item:

```
<!-- #BeginLibraryItem "/Library/title.lbi" -->
<font color="#FF6633" face="Verdana, Arial, Helvetica, sans-serif" ¬
size="-4">
<b>Copyright &copy; 2000</b></font>
<!-- #EndLibraryItem -->
```

In this case, the Library item happens to be a phrase: "Copyright (c) 2000." (The character entity © is used to represent the c-in-a-circle copyright mark in HTML.) In addition to the code that specifies the font face, color, and size, notice the text before and after the HTML code. These are commands within the comments that tell Dreamweaver it is looking at a Library item. One line marks the beginning of the Library item:

```
<!-- #BeginLibraryItem "/Library/title.lbi" -->
```

and another marks the end:

```
<!-- #EndLibraryItem -->
```

Two items are of interest here. First, notice how the Library demarcation surrounds not just the text ("Copyright (c) 2000") but all of its formatting attributes. Library items can do far more than just cut and paste raw text. The second thing to note is that the Library markers are placed discreetly within HTML comments. Web browsers ignore the Library markers and render the code in between them.

The value in the opening Library code, "/Library/title.lbi", is the source file for the Library entry. This file is located in the Library folder, inside of the current site root folder. Library source (.lbi) files can be opened with a text editor or in Dreamweaver; they consist of plain HTML code without the <html> and <body> tags.

The .lbi file for our title example would contain the following:

```
<font color="#FF6633" face="Verdana, Arial, Helvetica, sans-serif" ¬
size="-4">
<b>Copyright &copy; 2000</b></font>
```

The power of repeating elements is that they are simply HTML. There is no need to learn proprietary languages to customize Library items. Anything, except for information found in the header of a Web page, can be included in a Library file.

The importance of the `<!-- #BeginLibraryItem>` and `<!-- #EndLibraryItem>` tags becomes evident when you start to update Library items for a site. You examine how Dreamweaver can be used to automatically update your entire Web site in the section "Updating Your Web Sites with Libraries," later in this chapter.

Deleting an item from the Library

Removing an entry from your site's Library is a two-step process. First, you must delete the item from the Library category. Then, if you want to keep the item on your page, you must make it editable again. Without completing the second step, Dreamweaver maintains the Library highlight and, more importantly, prevents you from modifying the element.

To delete an item from the Library, follow these steps:

1. Open the Web page containing the Library item you want to delete.

2. Open the Library category by choosing Window ➪ Library or by selecting the Library button from the Launcher.

3. Select the Library item in the list and click the Delete button.

4. Dreamweaver asks if you are sure you want to delete the item. Select Yes, and the entry is removed from the Library item list. (Or select No to cancel.)

5. In the Document window, select the element you are removing from the Library.

6. In the Property Inspector, click Detach from Original.

7. As shown in Figure 22-3, Dreamweaver warns you that if you proceed, the item cannot be automatically updated (as a Library element). Select OK to proceed. The Library highlighting vanishes, and the element can now be modified individually.

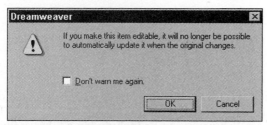

Figure 22-3: When making an item editable from the Library, Dreamweaver alerts you that, if you proceed, you won't be able to update the item automatically using the Library function.

Should you unintentionally delete a Library item in the Library category, you can restore it if you still have the entry included in a Web page. Select the element within the page and, in the Property Inspector, choose the Recreate button. Dreamweaver restores the item to the Library item list, with the original Library name.

Renaming a Library item

It's easy to rename a Library item, both in the Assets panel and across your site. Dreamweaver automatically updates the name for any embedded Library item. To give an existing Library entry a new name, open the Library category and click the name of the item twice, slowly — do not double-click. Alternatively, you could choose Rename from the context menu of the Assets panel. The name is highlighted, and a small box appears around it. Enter the new name and press Enter (Return).

Dreamweaver then displays the Update Files dialog box with a list of files in which the renamed Library item is contained. Select Update to rename the Library item across the site. If you select Don't Update, the Library item will be renamed only in the Library category. Furthermore, your embedded Library items will be orphaned — that is, no master Library item will be associated with them and they will not be updateable.

Editing a Library Item

Rarely do you create a Library item that is perfect from the beginning and never needs to be changed. Whether it is due to site redesign or the addition of new sections to a site, you'll find yourself going back to Library items and modifying them, sometimes over and over again. You can use the full power of Dreamweaver's design capabilities to alter your Library items, within the restraints of Library items in general. In other words, you can modify an image, reformat a body of text, add new material to a boilerplate paragraph, and have the resulting changes reflected across your Web site. However, you cannot add anything to a Library item that is not contained in the HTML <body> tags.

To modify Library items, Dreamweaver uses a special editing window identifiable by the double angle brackets surrounding the phrase "Library Item" in the title bar. You access this editing window through the Library category or the Property Inspector. Follow these steps to modify an existing Library item:

1. In the Library category, select the item you wish to modify from the list of available entries.

2. Click the Open Library Item button. The Library editing window opens with the selected entry, as shown in Figure 22-4.

3. Make any necessary modifications to the Library entry.

4. When you are finished with your changes, choose File ⇨ Save or press Ctrl+S (Command+S).

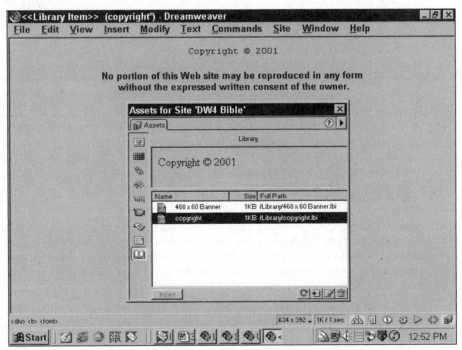

Figure 22-4: Use the Library editing window to modify existing Library items.

5. Dreamweaver notes that your Library item has been modified and asks if you would like to update all of the Web pages in your site that contain the item. Select Yes to update all of the Library items, including the one just modified, or select No to postpone the update. (See the next section, "Updating Your Web Sites with Libraries.")

6. Close the editing window by selecting the Close button or choosing File ➪ Close.

Once you've completed the editing operation and closed the editing window, you can open any Web page containing the modified Library item to view the changes.

Cross-Reference

You cannot use some features to their fullest when editing Library items. These include timelines, behaviors, and styles. Each of these modifications requires a JavaScript function to be placed in the <head> tags of a page — a task that the Dreamweaver Library function cannot handle. If you add a behavior to a Library item while editing it, the JavaScript function will be copied to your page next to the Library item itself. While this will work in some instances — a pop-up message for example — other behaviors will perform erratically. One workaround is to use a Dreamweaver template to add entire pages with JavaScript functions included, as described in Chapter 21. You could, of course, also add behaviors to a page element before converting it to a Library item.

Updating Your Web Sites with Libraries

The effectiveness of the Dreamweaver Library feature becomes more significant when it comes time to update an entire multipage site. Dreamweaver offers two opportunities for you to update your site:

✦ Immediately after modifying a Library item, as explained in the preceding steps for editing a Library item

✦ At a time of your choosing, through the Modify ➪ Library command

An immediate update to every page on your site can be accomplished when you edit a Library item. After you save the alterations, Dreamweaver asks if you'd like to apply the update to Web pages in your site. If you click Yes, Dreamweaver not only applies the current modification to all pages in the site, but it also applies any other alterations that you have made previously in this Library.

The second way to modify a Library item is by using the Modify ➪ Library command, and when you use this method, you can choose to update the current page or the entire site.

To update just the current page, choose Modify ➪ Library ➪ Update Current Page. Dreamweaver makes a quick check to see what Library items you are managing on the current page and then compares them to the site's Library items. If any differences exist, Dreamweaver modifies the page accordingly.

To update an entire Web site, follow these steps:

1. Choose Modify ➪ Library ➪ Update Pages. The Update Pages dialog box opens (see Figure 22-5).

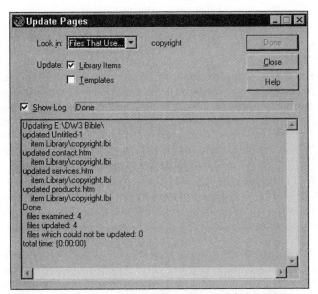

Figure 22-5: The Update Pages dialog box enables you to apply any changes to your Library items across an entire site and informs you of the progress.

2. If you want Dreamweaver to update all of the Library items in all of the Web pages in your site, select Entire Site from the Look In drop-down list and choose the name of your site in the drop-down list on the right. You can also have Dreamweaver update only the pages in your site that contain a specific Library item. Select the Files That Use option from the Look In drop-down list and then select the Library item that you would like to have updated across your site from the drop-down list on the right.

3. If you want to see the results from the update process, leave the Show Log checkbox selected. (Turning off the Log reduces the size of the Site Update dialog box.)

4. Choose the Start button. Dreamweaver processes the entire site for Library updates. Any Library items contained are modified to reflect the changes.

Note Although Dreamweaver does modify Library items on currently open pages during an Update Site operation, you have to save the pages to accept the changes.

The Update Pages log displays any errors encountered in the update operation. A log containing the notation

```
item Library\Untitled2.lbi -- not updated, library item not found
```

indicates that one Web page contains a reference to a Library item that has been removed. Though this is not a critical error, you might want to use Dreamweaver's Find and Replace feature to search your Web site for the code and remove it.

Applying Server-Side Includes

In some ways, the server-side include (SSI) is the predecessor of the Dreamweaver Library item. The difference is that with Library items, Dreamweaver updates the Web pages at design time, whereas with server-side includes, the server handles the updating at runtime (when the files are actually served to the user). Server-side includes can also include server variables, such as the current date and time (both locally and Greenwich mean time) or the date the current file was last saved.

Because server-side includes are integrated in the standard HTML code, a special file extension is used to identify pages using them. Any page with server-side includes is most often saved with either the .shtml or .shtm extension. When a server encounters such a file, the file is read and processed by the server.

Note   Not all servers support server-side includes. Some Web hosting companies disable the function because of potential security risks and performance issues. Each .shtml page requires additional processing time, and if a site uses many SSI pages, the server can slow down significantly. Be sure to check your Web host's policy before including SSIs in your Web pages.

Server-side includes are often used to insert header or footer items into the <body> of an HTML page. Typically, the server-side include itself is just a file with HTML. To insert a file, the SSI code looks like the following:

```
<!-- #include file="footer.html" -->
```

Note how the HTML comment structure is used to wrap around the SSI directive. This ensures that browsers ignore the code, but servers do not. The file attribute defines the path name of the file to be included, relative to the current page. To include a file relative to the current site root, use the virtual attribute, as follows:

```
<!-- #include virtual="/main/images/spaceman.jpg" -->
```

As evident in this example, you can use SSIs to include more than just HTML files — you can also include graphics.

With Dreamweaver's translator mechanism, server-side includes can be visible in the Document window during the design process. All you need to do is make sure that the Translation preferences are set correctly, as described in the section "Modifying Translators," later in this chapter.

One of the major benefits of SSIs is inserting information from the server itself, such as the current file size or time. One tag, `<!-- #echo -->`, is used to define a custom variable that is returned when the SSI is called, as well as numerous *environmental variables*. An environmental variable is information available to the server, such as the date a file was last modified or its URL.

Table 22-1 details the possible server tags and their attributes.

<table>
<tr><td colspan="3" align="center">Table 22-1
Server-Side Include Variables</td></tr>
<tr><td>*Tag*</td><td>*Attribute*</td><td>*Description*</td></tr>
<tr><td>`<!-- #config -->`</td><td>`errmsg`, `sizefmt`, or `timefmt`</td><td>Used to customize error messages, file size, or time and date displays</td></tr>
<tr><td>`<!-- #echo -->`</td><td>`var` **or environmental variables, such as** `last_modified`, `document_name`, `document_url`, `date_local`, **or** `date_gmt`</td><td>Returns the specified variable</td></tr>
<tr><td>`<!-- #exec -->`</td><td>`cmd` **or** `cgi`</td><td>Executes a system command or CGI program</td></tr>
<tr><td>`<!-- #flastmod -->`</td><td>`file` **or** `virtual`</td><td>Displays the last modified date of a file other than the current one</td></tr>
<tr><td>`<!-- #fsize -->`</td><td>`file` **or** `virtual`</td><td>Displays the size of a file other than the current one</td></tr>
<tr><td>`<!-- #include -->`</td><td>`file` **or** `virtual`</td><td>Inserts the contents of the specified file to the current one</td></tr>
</table>

Adding server-side includes

Dreamweaver has made inserting a server-side include in your Web page very straightforward. You can use a Dreamweaver object to easily select and bring in the files to be included. Any other type of SSI, such as declaring a variable, must be entered in by hand, but you can use the Comment object to do so without switching to Code View, or opening the Code Inspector.

To use server-side includes to incorporate a file, follow these steps:

  1. In the Document window, place your cursor in the location where you would like to add the server-side include.

2. Select Insert ➪ Server-Side Include or choose Insert Server-Side Include from the Common category of the Objects panel.

   The standard Select File dialog box appears.

3. In the Select File dialog box, type in the URL of the HTML page you would like to include in the File Name text box or use the folder icon to locate the file. Click OK when you're done.

   Dreamweaver displays the contents of the HTML file at the desired location in your page. Should the Property Inspector be available, the SSI Property Inspector is displayed (see Figure 22-6).

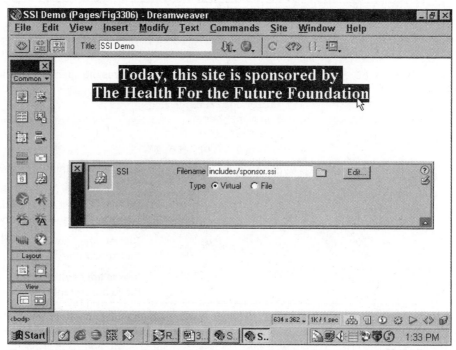

Figure 22-6: The selected text is actually a server-side include automatically translated by Dreamweaver, as is evident from the SSI Property Inspector.

4. In the Property Inspector, if the server-side include calls a file-relative document path, select the Type File option. Or, if the SSI calls a site root-relative file, choose the Type Virtual option.

Tip   Because server-side includes can be placed only within the body of a Dreamweaver file, the contents of the HTML page that you wish to include should not have any tags that are not readable within the body section of a document, such as `<head>`, `<title>`, or `<meta>` — or the `<body>` tag itself. You can, however, design your HTML page in Dreamweaver, and then use Code View, or the Code Inspector, to remove any such tags before inserting the page into your document with a server-side include.

Editing server-side includes

As is the case with Library items, it is not possible to directly edit files that have been inserted into a Web page using server-side includes. In fact, should you try, the entire text block highlights as one. The text for a server-side included file is not editable through Dreamweaver's Code View, or Code Inspector, although the SSI code is.

To edit the contents of the server-side included file, follow these steps:

1. Select the server-side include in the Document window.
2. Select the Edit button from the SSI Property Inspector.

   The file opens in a new Dreamweaver window for editing.
3. When you've finished altering the file, select File ⇨ Save or use the keyboard shortcut Ctrl+S (Command+S).
4. Close the file editing window by choosing File ⇨ Close.

Dreamweaver automatically reflects the changes in your currently open document.

Unlike when editing Library items, Dreamweaver does not ask if any other linked files should be updated because all blending of regular HTML and SSIs happens at runtime or when the file is open in Dreamweaver and the SSI translator is engaged.

Extending Dreamweaver with XSSI

Both Dreamweaver Library items and server-side includes are useful for easily updating a range of pages when changing one item. But what if you have to change that one item several times a day—or based on which domain the user is coming from? To handle these tasks automatically, a system must support some form of conditional tags, such as if-then statements. Such a system is now available through Apache servers and XSSI, extended server-side includes. Most importantly, a full set of XSSI objects, translators, and Property Inspectors for Dreamweaver have been built by the wonderful programmers at Webmonkey (www.webmonkey.com). You can find the XSSI extensions on the CD-ROM that comes with this book.

In addition to handling standard server-side includes, the XSSI extensions offer a series of conditional statements: if, elif (else-if), else, and endif. The beauty of the Webmonkey objects is that you can construct or edit these conditional statements through their graphical user interface. The basic syntax of the conditional statements is as follows:

Continued

Continued

```
<!--#if expr="text_expression" -->
If the above is true, perform this action
<!--#elif expr="text_expression" -->
Else if the above is true, do this
<!--#else -->
Otherwise, do this
<!--#endif -->
```

The XSSI extensions also have the capability of setting an environmental variable so that you can view your page under various conditions. For example, let's say you've written a script that includes a particular file that greets the visitor in a proper way, depending on which browser is being used. Your conditional script would look to the HTTP_USER_AGENT variable to see which message to serve. With the XSSI Set Env Variables command, you could test your script during the design phase without having to visit the server at different times of the day. The following figure displays the Set XSSI Environment Variables dialog box.

Inserted Library item   Library item preview

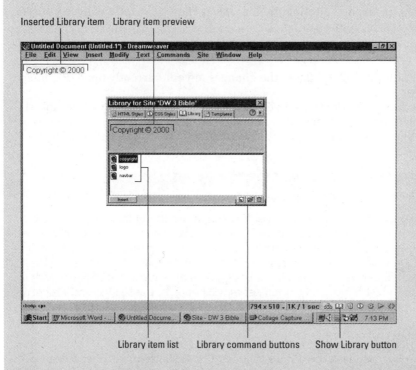

Library item list   Library command buttons   Show Library button

One note of caution: Due to a potential conflict between the two translators, installing the XSSI extensions disables the standard SSI translator. Make sure your system is XSSI compatible (it uses Apache server software) before incorporating the XSSI extensions.

Summary

In this chapter, you learned how you can easily and effectively create Library items that can be repeated throughout an entire site to help maintain consistency.

✦ Library items can consist of any text, object, or HTML code contained in the <body> of a Web page.

✦ The quickest method to create a Library item is to drag the code from the Dreamweaver Document window into the Library category's list area.

✦ Editing Library items is also easy: just click the Edit button in the Assets panel or choose Open from the Property Inspector, and you can swiftly make all of your changes in a separate Dreamweaver Library Item window.

✦ The Modify ➪ Library ➪ Update Pages command enables easy maintenance of your Web site.

✦ Server-side includes enable files to be inserted into the final HTML at runtime by the server. Dreamweaver's translation feature enables you to preview these effects.

✦   ✦   ✦

Mastering the Flash Environment

Understanding the Flash Framework

In this chapter, we introduce Flash. We discuss the nature of the Flash application and why it is so unique and powerful. We discuss both its similarity and dissimilarity to other programs with which you may be familiar. Then, to wrap up, we talk about the capabilities of Flash. Let's get started.

Introducing the Flash 5 Framework

Flash is a hybrid application that is like no other application. On the immediate surface, it may seem (to some) to be a simple hybrid between a Web-oriented bitmap handler, and a vector-drawing program, such as Macromedia Freehand or Adobe Illustrator. But while Flash is indeed such a hybrid, it's also capable of much, much more. It's also an interactive multimedia-authoring program. Also, it's a sophisticated animation program suitable for creating a range of animations — from simple Web ornaments to broadcast-quality cartoons. As if that weren't enough, it's also the host of a scripting language — Flash now supports a robust, fully featured ActionScript language, grounded in the JavaScript standard. This language enables Flash 5 to couple with XML (Extensible Markup Language), HTML (Hypertext Markup Language), and other content in many ways. So it's also a scripting language that's capable of communication with other parts of the Web. Furthermore, in alliance with Macromedia Generator, Flash 5 is also capable of serving as the front end and graphics engine for the premiere, robust solution for the delivery of dynamic Web content (graphics, charts, sounds, personalized

Flash movies) from databases and other back-end resources. A final note to our list of Flash capabilities: Just as this manuscript was going to press, we learned that Macromedia has collaborated with the makers of ColdFusion to create a toolkit that will enable dynamic data-driven Flash interfaces that are based on CFML (ColdFusion Markup Language) or JSP (JavaServer Pages).

So, what's this hybrid we call *Flash* capable of? That's a question that remains to be answered by developers such as you. In fact, we're hoping that you will master this application and show us a thing or two. That's why we've written this book: to point out the facets of the tool, hoping that you will take the tool in your hands and amaze us — and the world!

So, if Flash is a hybrid application, and if this application is capable of just about anything, a good place to start working with this powerhouse is to inquire: What are the components of this hybrid? And if they were separated out, how might their capabilities be described? Those are the questions that we answer in this chapter.

Bitmap handler

In truth, Flash has limited capabilities as an image-editing program. It is more accurate to describe this part of the Flash application as a bitmap handler. Bitmap images are composed of dots on a grid of individual pixels. The location (and color) of each dot must be stored in memory, which makes this a memory-intensive application and leads to large file sizes. However, for photographic-quality images, bitmap formats are indispensable. One more drawback to bitmap images is that they cannot be scaled without adversely affecting the quality (clarity and sharpness). The adverse effects of scaling an image up are more pronounced than when scaling down. Because of these two drawbacks — file sizes and scaling limitations — bitmaps images are not ideal for Web use.

Vector program

Much of the Flash application is a vector-based drawing program, with capabilities similar to either Macromedia Freehand or Adobe Illustrator. A vector-based drawing program doesn't rely upon individual pixels to compose an image. Instead, it draws shapes by defining points that are described by coordinates. Lines that connect these points are called *paths,* and vectors at each point describe the curvature of the path. Because this scheme is mathematical, there are two distinct advantages: Vector content is significantly more compact, and it's thoroughly scalable without image degradation. These advantages are especially significant for Web use.

Vector animator

The vector animation component of the Flash application is unlike any other program that preceded it. Although Flash is capable of handling bitmaps, its native file format is vector-based. So, unlike all other animation and media programs, Flash relies on the slim and trim vector format for transmission of your final work. Instead of storing megabytes of pixel information for each frame, Flash stores compact vector descriptions of each frame. Whereas a bitmap-based animation program (such as Apple's QuickTime) struggles to display each bitmap in rapid succession, Flash quickly renders the vector descriptions as needed and with far less strain on either the bandwidth or the recipient's machine. This is a huge advantage when transmitting Flash animations and Flash content over the Web.

Authoring program

You might say that the body of Flash is a multimedia-authoring program, or multimedia-authoring environment. It authors movies that can contain multiple kinds of media, such as sound, still graphics, and moving graphics. Yet it is also an interactive multimedia program because it has the capability to assign action commands to the movies that it authors.

Animation sequencer

Most multimedia-authoring programs have a component for sequencing content as animation, and Flash is no exception. But in Flash, the animation sequencer is the core of the application. The organization of sequences, also known as movies, is as follows:

✦ The Movie may have any number of *scenes*, which may be arranged (or rearranged) into a sequence to create a playing order. Scenes play through from first to last (unless Flash's interactive commands, known as "actions," dictate otherwise).

✦ Each scene may contain an unlimited number of *layers*, which are viewed from front-to-back in the scene. The stacking order of these layers is arranged in the timeline: The topmost layer in the timeline appears at the front of the scene, while the bottom layer is at the back.

✦ Furthermore, each layer may also have a stacking order of the objects within it. Always at the *bottom* level are ungrouped vector lines and shapes. Above, in the *overlay* level, are bitmaps, text, groups, grouped items, and symbol instances. *Groups* are one or more items that have been selected and "grouped." *Symbol instances* may be one or more references to an item that resides in the Library. Any of these items may be moved in front or behind others on that layer without moving them to another layer.

Groups and grouping are covered in Chapter 30, "Exploring the Timeline," while symbols and symbol instances are covered in Chapter 31, "Checking Out the Library: Symbols and Instances."

✦ The units that are responsible for the illusion of time in an animation are *frames*. Each layer may be composed of a sequence of one or more frames that are controlled by the timeline.

✦ Finally, there are two basic kinds of frames: *static frames* and *keyframes*. Each layer must begin with a keyframe, which may be empty. Static frames simply repeat the content of the prior frame. Keyframes are where content or emptiness is either placed or changed. (Emptiness, or an empty keyframe, functions as a *stop frame*.) Animation is achieved either by changing the contents on a frame-by-frame basis—which is called *frame-by-frame animation*—or by establishing two keyframes and instructing Flash to interpolate the change between them—which is called *tweening*.

With the upgrade to Flash 5, the timeline has seen considerable changes to both its terminology and functionality, as well to the options for controlling various timeline behaviors. For detailed coverage of all this and more, please refer to Chapter 30, "Exploring the Timeline."

Programming interface and database front end

With Flash 4, Macromedia expanded the capabilities of Flash to include limited—but powerful—programming capabilities that were capable of controlling the nature and quality of Flash interactivity. Furthermore, these capabilities—augmented with Generator 2—gave Flash the ability to work as the database front end for sophisticated interactive applications such as online shopping, forms, and other activities not normally associated with an animation program. In fact, there were many ingenious creations that melded code with vector content in ways that no one could have imagined! But that was Flash 4.

Flash 5 has changed all of that in ways that we cannot begin to describe—simply because there is little, if any, limitation to what Flash 5 is now capable of. All one need add is a dash of genius, and genius is in good supply among Flash aficionados. What are we talking about? Well, with Flash 5:

✦ ActionScript matured from a limited quasi-scripting vocabulary to a robust scripting language that's backward compatible with Flash 4, yet based in JavaScript. To be accurate, Macromedia developed Flash 5 ActionScript from the ECMA-262 specification. (The ECMA is the European Computers Manufacturers Association—www.ecma.ch.) This ECMA-262 specification was derived from JavaScript to establish an international standard for the JavaScript language. (Thus, *technically*, Flash ActionScript is not 100 percent compliant with JavaScript.)

✦ Support for XML was added. You can now send and receive XML data from Flash movies. You can also open live sockets for a constant XML data feed.

✦ Math operations have been greatly expanded with the Math Object, including common sine, cosine, and tangent methods.

✦ The color and sound properties of Flash symbols can be controlled with scripting.

✦ Using Symbol Linkage, Sounds and Movie Clips are now directly accessible from the Library without appearing on the authoring timeline.

Viewing Flash movies

Generally, Flash movies are played back in one of three ways. The most common implementation is for Flash movies to be played back within Web browsers — either as part of an HTML page, or as a 100-percent Flash Web page that contains no visible content other than the Flash Movie. Flash movies can also be played through a separate application called the *Flash Player*. In addition to the Flash Player, Flash movies can also be created as Stand Alone Projectors that facilitate playback without the need for either the player or the browser.

There are several other ways in which Flash movies, or their parts, can be played back or displayed. Since Flash 4, the Publish feature has offered provisions for the export of movies, or sections of movies, to either the QuickTime digital video format, the QuickTime Flash layer vector format, or to the Animated GIF format. Parts of movies can also be exported as a series of individual bitmaps or as vector files. Single frames can also be exported to these formats. Recently, methods were developed that enable Flash content to be used as screensavers.

Finding Applications for Flash 5 Movies

A Flash movie can be many things, depending on the function and design of a project. Because Flash has only just hit its adolescence, things are definitely getting interesting. Already Flash has unforeseen relationships with all forms of communication, around the world. And Flash's popularity continues to grow, unabated. But that's all based on Flash 4!

If you were to compare the functionality of a Flash 4 movie to that of a Flash 5 movie, you'd agree that, yet again, Flash movies have come a long way—but in an even shorter time than when we last said that. There's already an impressive legacy of Flash movies and we don't usually refer to youths as having a legacy. Here's a short list of the (known) possibilities for Flash 5:

✦ A splash page animation for a Web site

✦ An interactive map

✦ An interactive form on a Web page

✦ An interactive database that sends and retrieves information with server-side scripts; this has been a function since Flash 4

✦ A live, multiuser game or chat with XML sockets that allows real-time communication between Internet users

✦ An online jukebox that can play MP3 audio that is delivered dynamically via Macromedia's Generator 2 application

✦ Stand-alone Web applications—check out the calculator sample in the Flash Samples menu

✦ Entire Web sites, presented without *any* HTML-based graphics or textual content—which means absolute control over scaling and placement of items, including fonts

✦ Interactive art presentations that involve 3D transformations and multiuser experiences (check out www.yugop.com)

✦ Web installation art that offers access to high-quality bitmapped artwork and rich audio experiences

✦ Interactive QuickTime Flash movie trailers that allow user feedback while watching

✦ Stand-alone Presentations or Slide Shows on either CD-ROM or floppy disk

✦ With the help of third-party tools, screensavers for both Windows and Macintosh made from Flash movies

✦ Web cartoons—in the last 18 months, there has been an explosion of Flash cartooning

✦ Broadcast-quality cartoons—of which Turnertoons' *Weber*, *The Murkeys* and Richard Bazley's *Journal of Edwin Carp* are groundbreaking examples

✦ As a platform for QuickTime editing and enhancements—there's a world of possibilities in the synergy of QuickTime and Flash 5 (We've developed workflows about which even Macromedia said, "It can't be done.")

✦ Flash movies can be integrated into a larger Shockwave Director movie that can play QuickTime movies, MIDI audio, and other media formats that Flash doesn't support

As you can probably tell from this list, if you can imagine a use for Flash, it can probably be accomplished.

Planning interactive Flash projects

Before you attempt to construct interactive projects in Flash, you should be familiar with the structure of the authoring environment. Even if you already know Flash 4, this is advisable. That's because with the release of Flash 5, Macromedia has again added many new features to the interface, and either moved or improved other features and functionalities. So, to get a firm footing with the new interface, we strongly suggest that you work your way through this book—from the beginning.

Moreover, you need to proactively plan your interactive projects before you attempt to author them in Flash. An ounce of preplanning goes a long way during the production process. Don't fool yourself—the better your plan looks on paper, the better it will perform when it comes to the final execution.

Interactive planning is discussed in Eric Jordan's Expert Tutorial, "Interface Design," which is located in Chapter 35.

In general, you can teach yourself how to organize interactive elements by creating simple flowcharts, such as Figure 23-1, that describe the Flash-authoring environment.

Figure 23-1 shows how Flash movies are made up of individual scenes that, in turn, contain keyframes to describe changes on the Stage. What you can't see in the figure is the efficiency created (or time saved) by being able to share Flash Libraries between Flash projects (.FLA files) and by linking other Flash movies to a parent Flash movie using the `Load Movie` action, as well as other scripting methods. Before you start to try to do that level of interactivity, though, you need to know the difference between Flash movies and .SWF movies.

Looking at Flash movie file types

Flash movie (.FLA) files are geared to work in an efficient authoring environment. Within this environment, content can be organized into scenes, and the ordering of scenes can be rearranged throughout the production cycle. Layers provide easy separation of graphics within each scene, and, as guide or mask layers, they can also aid drawing or even provide special effects. The timeline shows keyframes, motion and shape tweens, labels, and comments. All imported bitmaps and sounds are stored in the Flash Library (which can be shared with other Flash movie files). The quality of these Library files (or symbols) is identical to that of the originals.

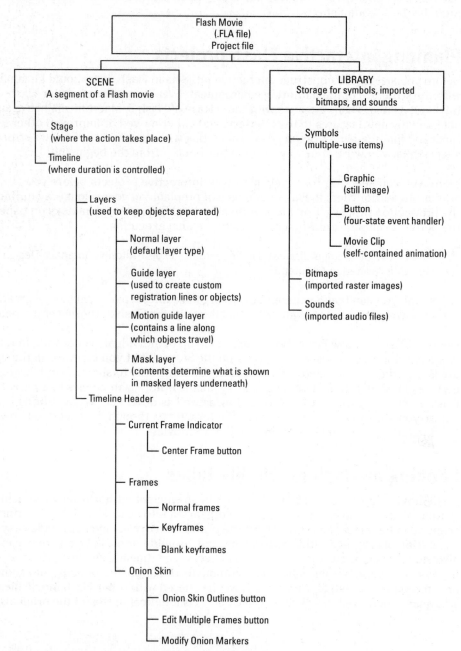

Figure 23-1: Elements of the Flash Environment

However, when a Flash movie (.FLA) is exported to a Small Web Format file (.SWF), much of this information is discarded in order to create small .SWF files (or as small as possible) for network delivery (for example, the Internet or intranets). In fact, just about everything that's stored in the original FLA file will be transformed in some way. The elements in the Library are loaded and stored on the first frame of their use — while unused Library elements are simply discarded. (They are *not* exported to the .SWF file.) Thus, for maximum efficiency, elements that are reused are saved into the .SWF file only once because they are referenced from one location in the SWF file. Layers and scenes are "flattened" in the order that is established in the .FLA file. In other words, the .SWF file contains the all the elements from the original .FLA in one layer, controlled by a single timeline. Technically, .SWF files are not compressed like ZIP or SIT/HQX files — only individual bitmaps and sounds are compressed according to the settings specified for each element in the Library and/or during the export process.

Refer to Figure 23-2 for a graphic explanation of the characteristics of the Shockwave Flash movie (.SWF) Format.

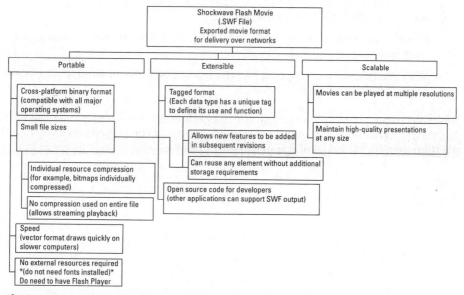

Figure 23-2: How a Shockwave Flash movie works

Note Flash movie (.FLA) files are referred to as *Flash editor documents* by some documentation included with the software. Also, the term "Shockwave Flash" no longer exists in the Macromedia Flash documentation — Flash movies for the Web are simply called .SWF files. Originally, SWF stood for Shockwave Flash but later, according to one source, Macromedia revisited the acronym and tweened it to mean, Small Web File. (Because "Shockwave" originally referred to Shockwave Director movies, perhaps Macromedia is trying to avoid confusion between the two?) Still, to the general public, it appears that Flash movies are still considered to be Shockwave movies; our position is to simply refer to Flash movies, when distributed for download, as .SWFs (and avoid the unimportant controversy).

Summary

✦ Flash is a hybrid program that has combined many of the most powerful features of various other types of programs, and then mixed them with some unique capabilities.

✦ Flash is recognized as one of the most robust and capable programs available for the creation of content for the Web.

✦ Flash is not limited to the Web. In fact, Flash is the software of choice in numerous other niches.

✦ With Flash 5, ActionScripting has risen to a new level of robust capability, modeled on JavaScript.

Now that we've given you a taste of the capabilities and distinctions of the Flash Authoring Environment, and shown you how some of the larger pieces fit together; it's time for you to look at some of the particulars.

✦   ✦   ✦

Exploring the Interface: Panels, Settings, and More

This chapter tours all Flash menus and panels. In some cases, the basic function of a panel or menu item is discussed, while the deeper explanation is deferred to another chapter or area of the book that's dedicated to that particular function — or group of functions. In most cases, however, we've tried to deliver a full explanation right here in this chapter. We hope you use it as both a learning device and as a reference tool.

Learning Flash Tool Basics

Terminology: A book about a software program must be clear and consistent in the terms and names that are used to describe the various thingamajigs and doohickeys that make the program work. We considered carefully before we settled upon the terminology that has — we hope — been applied consistently throughout this book. So, here's our logic: Wherever possible, we use terms derived from the Flash interface and Macromedia's documentation. When we've discovered inconsistencies, we've tried to choose terminology that's most consistent with other Macromedia products.

The Toolbox

The default location for the Flash Drawing Toolbox is in the upper-left corner of the Flash Program window. However, if you haven't just installed Flash, or if someone else has changed the defaults in Flash, you may not be able to find the Drawing Toolbox.

The Toolbox consists of four main sections. The top section contains all 14 Flash Tools, from left to right and top to bottom: Arrow, Subselect, Line, Lasso, Pen, Text, Oval, Rectangle, Pencil, Brush, Ink Bottle, Paint Bucket, Dropper, and Eraser. The second section contains the Flash View Tools: the Hand and Magnifier. Beneath the View Tools is the Color Tray, and beneath that is the Options Tray.

Using Tool options

Depending on the tool selected, the Options Tray may display some of the options, or properties, that control the functionality of each particular tool — while other controls may appear in the new Flash 5 panels. Of the options that are located in the Options Tray, some appear as a pop up or drop-down menus with multiple options, while others are simple buttons that toggle a property on or off. Thus, if an option turns a property on or off, then it's a button. (For example, if the Lasso is selected, the Magic Wand option can be turned on or off by clicking its button in the Options Tray.) But if an option has more than two options, then it's a menu.

 With the release of Flash 5, Macromedia has introduced an extensive panels system for the comprehensive control of many operations. These panels are introduced and discussed in general within this chapter. Their functionality will be discussed in relationship with specific tools, both in the subsequent chapters of Part VII.

Most of the options that appear within the Options Tray of the Toolbox can also be accessed from menus on the Menu Bar, or with keyboard combinations. However, all of the controls for the Line, Pen, Text, Oval, Rectangle, Pencil, and Ink Bottle Tools are now located in the new panels system. The new Subselect Tool has no options or controls. All of the controls and options for each tool are described in detail in subsequent chapters of Part VII.

Making the Drawing Toolbox visible

If the Drawing Toolbox is not visible on the PC Flash screen, it can be opened from the Flash Menu Bar by choosing Window ⇨ Tools. Conversely, when the Toolbox is visible, unchecking the Tool menu item hides it. On the Mac, the Drawing Toolbox is always a floating panel that can be dragged anywhere in the screen.

Docking the Flash Drawing Toolbox on the PC

On the PC only, the Drawing Toolbox can be deployed as either a floating panel or as a panel that's docked to either edge of the Flash program window. *Docking* means that a floating panel is dragged to the edge of the program window, where it then melds to the border of the window. It remains docked there until it is either moved to another docked position, floated off to resume usage as a panel, or is closed. You can drag the panel anywhere around the screen, or you can drag it to the edge of the Flash program window, which docks it there.

 Tip   On the PC, to drag the Drawing Toolbox to the edge of the program window, yet prevent it from docking, press the Control key while dragging.

Quick work with keyboard shortcuts

All of the tools that are accessed from the Drawing Toolbox have keyboard equivalents, or shortcuts, that are single keystrokes (see Figure 24-1). For example, to access the Arrow Tool—which is the tool with the black arrow icon, located in the upper-left corner of the Drawing Toolbox—you can simply press the V key when the Stage or timeline is in focus. *Thus, the V key is the keyboard shortcut for the Arrow Tool on both the Mac and the PC.* This is easier than moving the mouse up to the Drawing Toolbox to click the Arrow Tool, and it saves mouse miles, besides. Henceforth, throughout this book, when we mention a new tool, the keyboard shortcut for that tool follows in parentheses, as follows: Arrow (V).

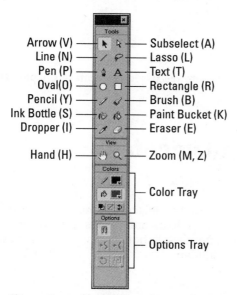

Figure 24-1: The PC Drawing Toolbox is shown here with the keyboard shortcuts for each tool. With the release of Flash 5, the Toolbox is now identical on both the Mac and the PC.

Using tooltips

On both PC and Mac platforms, each tool has a cursor icon that resembles the tool's icon in the Toolbox. For example, when you select the Brush by clicking the Brush button on the Toolbox, the cursor (or mouse pointer) turns into an icon similar to the Brush icon in the Toolbox. In most other programs, these cursor icons are referred to as *tooltips*: When you are working with a particular tool, the cursor icon for that tool appears on screen. In Flash, this kind of tooltip cannot be turned off. That's because Flash uses the term tooltip to refer to a text label that appears onscreen, adjacent to the cursor, when the cursor is paused over a tool button in the Toolbox. These text labels—Flash Tooltips—tell you the name of the tool and its keyboard shortcut. You can personalize Flash so that these Flash Tooltips are either visible or hidden.

✦ To change the Tooltips setting on the PC, choose Edit ⇨ Preferences to open the Preferences dialog; then, on the General Tab, in the Selection Options area, either check or uncheck Show Tooltips.

✦ To change the Tooltips setting on the Mac, choose Edit ⇨ Preferences to open the Preferences dialog; then, on the General Tab, in the Selection area, either check or uncheck Show Tooltips.

Note   Tooltips display information only about the tools that are part of the actual Flash program itself, and not about buttons that are part of a scene in a Flash movie. (If you are familiar with Macromedia Director, then you know that Sprites—which can be similar to buttons in Flash—can show or hide information about their properties. Flash does not offer this type of "tip.")

Color and Flash tools

Cross-Reference   The Color Tray and other colorful matters are discussed in depth in Chapter 28, "Applying Color."

Getting to Know the Fundamental Flash Interface

Before discussing the Flash menu items, panels, and miscellaneous dialogs, we take a look at the interface and its default array of toolbars and panels. We look at the way the program looks when first opened after installation, and some of the basic possibilities for arranging these and other fundamental panels and toolbars.

Cross-platform consistency

There's much to celebrate in this new version of Flash, and one improvement that really shows is the consistency between the Mac and PC versions of Flash 5. Although there are a few inconsistencies, many of them are attributable to the nature of the divergent operating systems, and none of them are even remotely as bothersome as with prior versions.

Figure 24-2 shows how Flash looks on the Mac. Note the Launcher Bar at the bottom right, which can be used to invoke the default groupings of Flash panels. These are, from left to right: Instance, Mixer, Character, Info, Explorer, Frame Actions, and the Library.

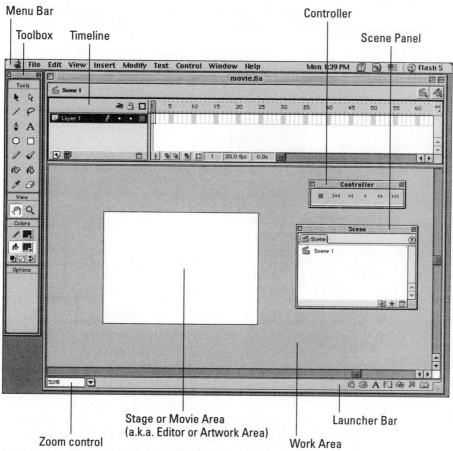

Figure 24-2: Flash on the Mac with most of the panels closed

Figure 24-3 shows Flash on the PC with the panels closed. There are three optional features that are absent from the Mac version. These include the Main Toolbar, the dockable Controller, and the Status Bar. However, note the consistency especially as regards the Toolbox (Tools), timeline, Launcher Bar, and the overall feel of the interface.

Main Toolbar

Toolbox   Menu Bar   Timeline   Controller

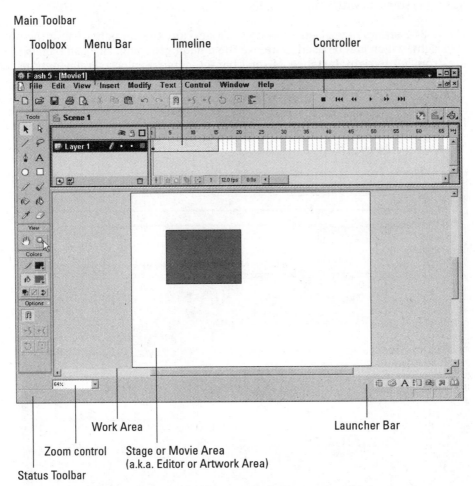

Work Area   Launcher Bar

Zoom control   Stage or Movie Area
                (a.k.a. Editor or Artwork Area)

Status Toolbar

Figure 24-3: Flash on the PC with the panels closed

Note

One of the minor ways in which the PC version differs from the Mac version is that the Toolbox and the Controller can be docked (or undocked) to the program window. As in Figure 24-3, the Toolbox and Controller were dragged to the edge of the program window, where they're docked seamlessly to the interface. Note that the Toolbox docks only to the sides, while the Controller can also dock to the top and bottom, as well as mesh with other toolbars. To move either the Toolbox or Controller, yet prevent docking, press the Control key while dragging.

With Flash 5, Macromedia significantly altered the look and feel of Flash by replacing the inspectors and palettes of Flash 4 with a comprehensive system of panels. As was mentioned previously with regard to the Toolbox, some tool options have also migrated to the panels system. The implementation of panels is consistent across both the Mac and the PC. Throughout the book, we discuss each panel in context with the tools and operations where it is used. As shown in the following figures, there are many ways to arrange these panels for a customized workflow. For examples of panels viewed simultaneously, see Figure 24-4 for the Mac version and 24-5 for the PC version.

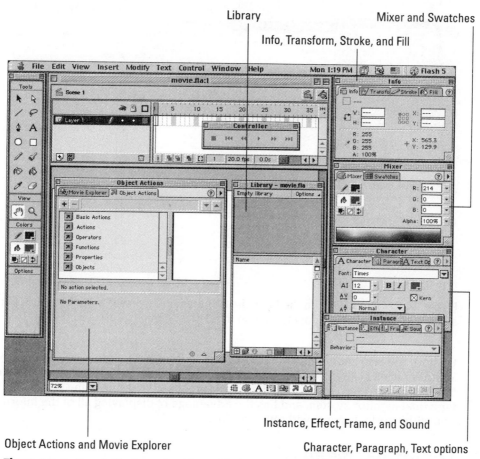

Figure 24-4: Here's Flash on the Mac with the panels viewed simultaneously.

Instance, Effect, Frame, and Sound

Info, Transform, Stroke, and Fill

Mixer and Swatches

Align and Scene

Library

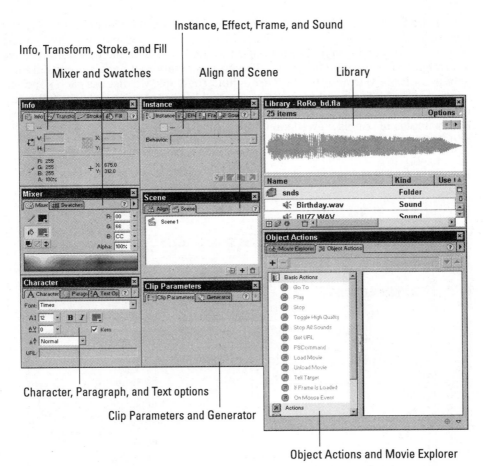

Character, Paragraph, and Text options

Clip Parameters and Generator

Object Actions and Movie Explorer

Figure 24-5: Here's Flash on the PC with all of the panels viewed simultaneously. Four additional panels that are not included in the default groupings are also displayed.

On both the Mac and the PC, you can drag the panel tabs off the panels or onto another panel. Figure 24-6 shows an alternative mega-panel grouping in which all of the Flash panels have been joined using this method. This grouping is most suited for a dual-monitor system, and has the advantage of displaying all of the information within a single panel without scrolling.

Contextual menus

Flash contextual menus pop-up in response to a right-click (Control+click for the Mac) on a selected item in the timeline, Library window, or on the Stage. Contextual menus duplicate most functions and commands that are accessible either through the drop-down menus of the Menu Bar, or through the many panels and dialogs, which are discussed in this chapter.

Movie Explorer   Library

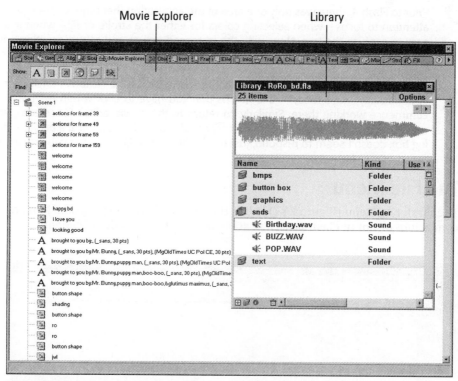

Figure 24-6: Here's an alternative mega-panel grouping in which all of the Flash panels have been dragged together.

Cross-Reference

Although the Flash timeline is a central axis of the Flash interface, we defer discussion of the timeline for two reasons. First, the timeline has changed considerably since Flash 4 and, as such, deserves more attention. Second, the Flash drawing tools and most of the menus and panels can be introduced more clearly (at first) without the complication of the timeline. If you must check out the timeline, see Chapter 30, "Exploring the Timeline."

Using the Menu Bar

Now that we've introduced most of the *major* elements of the Flash interface, we begin at the far left of the Menu Bar and work through the major points of all the drop-down menus, submenus, and panels. It's a gruesome, tedious job, but someone has to dive in and make sense of all these interrelated and (sometimes) seemingly duplicate or parallel operations.

Note   Prior to Flash 4, there was only one area of the application that required users to pay attention to focus—when selecting colors for either the stroke or fill—when it was easy to confuse the two. Now, with the increased power and robust scripting environment of Flash 5, focus has become an important aspect of the program. What is focus? *Focus* is a term used to describe which part of the application has priority, or focus, at a given time. For example, all panels, such as the Actions Panel, do not automatically "have focus"—this means that you have to click within the panel to commence working there. Similarly, to return to the movie editor (or screen), you must click there to return focus to that aspect of the application. So, if a panel or dialog box doesn't seem to respond, just remember to FOCUS on what you are doing.

The File Menu

The Flash File Menu (Figure 24-7) is like the front door of the program. Most of what comes into or out of Flash passes in some fashion through the File Menu.

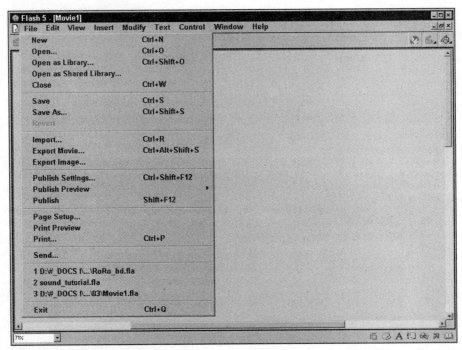

Figure 24-7: File Menu on the PC

> ✦ **New:** By default, Flash opens a new Flash document whenever the program is launched (unless Flash is launched from an extant movie). But once the program is open, File ➪ New generates all new documents.

✦ **Open:** File ➪ Open launches the Open dialog, which is used to browse and locate a Flash-compatible file. Compatible formats are:

- Flash Movie — .FLA

Caution   As of this writing, a number of lingering issues impact reverse compatibility between Flash 5 and legacy Flash movies that were authored in earlier versions of Flash. Although we anticipate that there will be a fix for this, it would be *impossible* for us to stress the following too strongly: ALWAYS (*always!*) make a copy of any legacy Flash movie *before* opening it in Flash 5. Otherwise, if there is a problem with the file in Flash 5 and you have saved it as a Flash 5 .FLA, and you don't have a copy in the legacy flavor . . ., you will be stuck (and there will be no alternative but to start over, from zero).

- Futuresplash Movie — .SPA

- SmartSketch Drawing — .SSK

- Flash Player Movie — .SWF

✦ **Open as Library:** Use File ➪ Open as Library to launch the Open as Library Dialog and browse for the Flash Movie whose Library you want to open. This makes the components of that Movie available for use within another movie. For more about working with the Flash Library, refer to Chapter 31, "Checking Out the Library: Symbols and Instances."

✦ **Open as Shared Library:** Use File ➪ Open as Shared Library to launch the Open as Shared Library dialog and browse for the Flash Movie that you want to open as a Shared Library, which is a powerful new functionality of Flash 5. For more about working with the Flash Library, refer to Chapter 31, "Checking Out the Library: Symbols and Instances."

✦ **Close:** Close any open movie with File ➪ Close.

✦ **Save:** Save an open movie with File ➪ Save.

✦ **Save As:** To save an open movie to another location or with another name, use File ➪ Save As.

Tip   To make saving a quickly accomplished task, File ➪ Save appends any changes to the end of the .FLA file. So, if you delete a handful of bitmaps from your project and then save, your file size may actually increase. By doing a File ➪ Save As, Flash restructures and writes a new file from scratch, resulting in a cleaner, smaller file. Consequently, File ➪ Save As takes a little longer to complete.

✦ **Revert:** Made a big goof that Edit ➪ Undo can't undo? Use File ➪ Revert to revert to the previously saved version of the current movie. Of course, this won't spare you much grief unless you *save often and incrementally*.

✦ **Import:** Many compatible formats can be opened directly into Flash. Use File ➪ Import to launch the Import dialog for these formats:

- Adobe Illustrator — .EPS, .AI

- AIFF Sound — .AIF

- AutoCAD DXF — .DXF
- Bitmap — .BMP, .DIB (Mac with QuickTime 4 installed)
- Enhanced Metafile — .EMF
- Flash Player — .SWF, .SPL
- FreeHand — .FH7, .FH8, .FH9, .FT7, .FT8, .FT9
- GIF Image — .GIF
- JPEG Image — .JPG
- Macintosh PICT Image — .PCT (Windows with QuickTime 4 installed)
- MacPaint Image — .PNTG (only with QuickTime 4 installed)
- MP3 Sound — .MP3
- Photoshop 2.5, 3 Image — .PSD (only with QuickTime 4 installed)
- PNG Image — .PNG
- QuickTime Image — .QTIF (only with QuickTime 4 installed)
- QuickTime Movie — .MOV
- Silicon Graphics Image — .SGI (only with QuickTime 4 installed)
- Sun AU — .AU
- TGA Image — .TGA (only with QuickTime 4 installed)
- Tiff Image — .TIFF (only with QuickTime 4 installed)
- WAV Sound — .WAV
- Windows Metafile — .WMF

✦ **Export Movie:** Flash can also directly export to several compatible formats. Use File ➪ Export to write your movie to any of these formats:

- Adobe Illustrator Sequence — .AI
- Animated GIF — .GIF
- Bitmap Sequence — .BMP
- DXF Sequence — .DXF
- EMF Sequence — .EMF
- EPS 3.0 Sequence — .EPS
- Flash Player — .SWF
- Futuresplash Player — .SPL
- Generator Template — .SWT

- GIF Sequence — .GIF
- JPEG Sequence — .JPG
- PNG Sequence — .PNG
- QuickTime — .MOV
- WAV Audio — .WAV
- Windows AVI — .AVI
- WMF Sequence — .WMF

✦ **Export Image**

- Adobe Illustrator — .AI
- AutoCAD DXF — .DXF
- Bitmap — .BMP
- Enhanced Metafile — .EMF
- EPS 3.0 — .EPS
- Flash Player — .SWF
- FutureSplash Player — .SPL
- Generator Template — .SWT
- GIF Image — .GIF
- JPEG Image — .JPG
- PNG Image — .PNG
- Windows Metafile — .WMF

Publishing

One of the most celebrated features of Flash 4 was the Publish feature, which replaced Aftershock. This is a powerful, robust aspect of Flash that required no changes in this upgrade to Flash 5. So if you're familiar with Flash 4, you'll be thoroughly at home with the Publish workflow, which is covered in depth in Chapter 44, "Integrating Flash Content with HTML." The areas of the File Menu which pertain to the Publish feature are:

✦ Publish Settings

✦ Publish Preview

✦ Publish

Printing

Although Flash is considered a Web and animation program, it fully supports printed output. The functionality and specific dialogs vary slightly from the Mac to the PC — while other variations are subject to which printers and printer drivers are installed on your machine. The Flash Page Setup dialog is the most standard aspect of the program and the choices for paper size, margins, center positioning, and orientation are pretty intuitive. However, the Layout area of the PC Page Setup Dialog deserves a little more attention. The options here are:

✦ **Frames:** Use this drop-down menu to choose to print either **All Frames** of the animation or the ecological default, which is to print the **First Frame Only.**

✦ **Layout:** There are three basic options:

• **Actual Size:** This prints the Frame at full size, subject to the accompanying Scale setting: At what scale do you want to print your frames? Enter a percentage.

• **Fit on One Page:** This automatically reduces or enlarges the Frame so that it fills the maximum printable area, without distortion.

• **Storyboard:** This enables you to print several thumbnails per page in the following arrangements: Boxes, Grid, or Blank. There are accompanying settings for Frames Across, Frame Margin, and Label Frames. This is a great tool for circulating comps and promotional materials.

Tip   When printing Storyboard Layouts, use File ⇨ Print Preview to ensure optimal results.

✦ **Print Margins (Mac Only):** Refer to the prior discussion (immediately preceding) of Frames, Layout, and Actual Size for an explanation of these equivalent options on the Mac. Note the **Disable PostScript** check box.

Note   When printing single large areas of color surrounded by complex borders, problems may occur on PostScript Printers. If you encounter such problems, try using the Disable PostScript check box in the Mac Print Margins dialog (Edit ⇨ Print Margins) or in the PC Preferences dialog (Edit ⇨ Preferences ⇨ General ⇨ Printing Options). Otherwise, divide the complex area into several simpler areas and use the Modify commands (Modify ⇨ Smooth / Straighten / Optimize) to reduce the complexity of these areas (which may, however, drastically alter your artwork — so save first!).

✦ **Print Preview:** Use Print Preview to see an onscreen preview of how the printed output looks, based upon the options you've chosen in the Page Setup and Print Margins (Mac Only) dialogs.

✦ **Print:** Just print it!

✦ **Send** (PC only): This is a new command that invokes the default e-mail client so that that you can readily send the Flash file as an attachment.

✦ **Exit/Quit:** Finally, at the very bottom of the File Menu is the command to close Flash. On the PC, it's File ⇨ Exit; the Mac equivalent is File ⇨ Quit.

The Edit Menu

The Edit Menu (Figure 24-8) isn't nearly as complex as the File Menu. Still, it's an important menu because many of these commands are central to so many Flash operations.

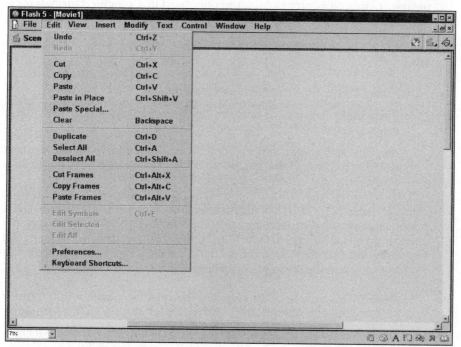

Figure 24-8: Edit Menu on the PC with the Equivalent Mac Menu Inset

✦ **Undo:** When you make a mistake, before you do anything else — Do the Undo.

Note

Flash generates an Undo stack for several different parts of the interface: Each timeline (Main Timeline and Movie Clip timelines) has its own undo stack, as does the ActionScript Panel. Furthermore, Undo does not transcend Focus: You cannot Undo work on the Stage from the ActionScript Panel — you must first return focus to the Stage to exercise Undo.

✦ **Redo:** The anti-Undo, this undoes what you just undid.

✦ **Cut:** This removes any selected item(s) and places it on the clipboard.

✦ **Copy:** This copies any selected item(s) and places it on the clipboard, without removing it.

✦ **Paste:** Disabled if nothing has been copied or cut, this pastes items from the clipboard into the currently active frame on the currently active layer. You can also paste into panel controls.

✦ **Paste in Place:** This is like Paste, except that it pastes the object precisely in the same place (with regards to X and Y coordinates) from which it was copied.

✦ **Paste Special (PC only):** This is like Paste on steroids, with version control. It pastes or embeds contents from the Clipboard in a specified format; it can also paste and simultaneously generate a link to information in another movie. The Paste Special Dialog has these fields:

  • **Source:** This displays the local path to the source of the item that is on the clipboard.

  • **Paste:** This pastes the data on the clipboard.

  • **Paste Link:** This pastes data on the clipboard, maintaining a link to the original document, but is generally not available.

  • **As:** This field may have several choices, depending both on the nature of the item (including the application that created it) that is on the clipboard, and also on which radio button is activated.

Tip

In the *As* section: (1) Flash Drawing pastes a portion of a Flash drawing. (2) Object pastes an object together with the information needed to edit it. (You convert the object to an editable Flash element with Modify ➪ Break Apart.) (3) Picture (Metafile) pastes in a form that Flash can edit. (4) Text (ASCII) pastes unformatted text. (5) Text (Native) pastes text with formatting intact.

  • **Result:** This indicates the result of the selected combination of the Paste / Paste Link and As options.

  • **Display as Icon:** This check box is enabled when any combination of the options permits the selected item to be pasted as an Icon.

  • **Change Icon:** This button is evoked when Display as Icon is enabled. Click this button to open the Change Icon dialog (complete with browse capability), which facilitates selection of an alternate icon.

  • **OK:** Once these settings have been determined, click OK.

✦ **Clear:** This removes a selected item(s) from the Stage *without* copying it to the Clipboard.

✦ **Duplicate:** This command duplicates a selected item or items, without burdening the Clipboard. The duplicated item appears adjacent to the original.

✦ **Select All:** Does what it says.

✦ **Deselect All:** Does what it says.

✦ **Cut Frames:** Cut a selected Frame or Frames with this command.

✦ **Copy Frames:** Copy a selected Frame or Frames with this command.

✦ **Paste Frames:** Pastes the Frame(s).

✦ **Edit Symbols:** Select an instance of a symbol and choose this command to edit in symbol-editing mode. For more about symbols and editing symbols, refer to Chapter 31, "Checking Out the Library: Symbols and Instances."

✦ **Edit Selected:** This is only enabled if a group or symbol is selected on the Stage. It opens a group or symbol for editing in a separate *tab* while dimming the rest of the Flash Stage — similar to Edit in Place with symbols.

✦ **Edit All:** When editing a group, Edit All is used to go back to editing the normal Flash scene.

✦ **Preferences:** The Preferences item of the Edit Menu invokes a tabbed dialog. A full explanation of this dialog follows.

Preferences

The Preferences dialog is one of the places where you get to tell Flash how you want it to behave. After you've established your preferences, this is how the program will be configured for every movie that you make. Nearly all options are identical on both platforms — with the exception of the clipboard settings, which are a reflection of the different ways that the two platforms handle their clipboards.

As shown in Figure 24-9, options for the General tab of the Preferences dialog are:

✦ **Undo Levels:** This sets the number of undos that Flash holds in memory to cover your mistakes. The maximum combined number of undos is 200. The default is 100. Undo levels devour system memory, so if you work smart and save incrementally, you can set your undos between 10 and 25. The only limitation here is the RAM on your machine.

✦ **Printing Options (PC only):** As discussed previously in this chapter, in context with the Printing commands of the File Menu, when printing single large areas of color surrounded by complex borders, problems may occur on PostScript Printers. If you encounter such problems, try checking this option to Disable PostScript. The equivalent option is available on the Mac by choosing File ➪ Print Margins.

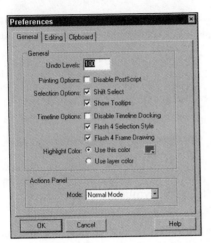

Figure 24-9: The General tab of the Preferences dialog for the PC

✦ **Selection Options:**

- **Shift Select:** Shift Select controls how Flash accumulates multiple selections. When Shift Select is **ON**, Flash behaves normally: Hold down the Shift key to select and acquire additional elements. When **OFF**, simply click, click, click to continue adding elements to the selection. (Veteran users of Flash may recall that this is also how Flash implemented Select when it was Futuresplash and Flash 2.)

- **Show Tooltips:** Tooltips are little labels that appear adjacent to the cursor when the cursor is held over a tool, prior to clicking the tool. These labels tell the name of the tool and related keyboard shortcut. Deselect this option to turn this feature off.

✦ **Timeline Options:**

- **Disable Timeline Docking:** This option prevents the timeline from attaching to the application window once it's been deployed as a floating panel.

- **Flash 4 Selection Style:** Flash 5 introduced a new methodology for selecting frames in the timeline. This option toggles that functionality back to Flash 4 Selection Style. For in-depth coverage of the timeline, refer to Chapter 30, "Exploring the Timeline."

- **Flash 4 Frame Drawing:** Flash 5 also introduced a new methodology for drawing frames in the timeline. This option toggles that functionality back to the Flash 4 style. For in-depth coverage of the timeline, refer to Chapter 30, "Exploring the Timeline."

✦ **Highlight Color:** This preference controls the highlight color for selected objects: groups, symbols, or text — but not shapes.

- **Use this color:** Check this option to choose a highlight color for selections from the Swatches pop-up.

- **Use layer color:** Check this option to use the layer color as the highlight color for selections. This option enables you to distinguish selected items according to their associated layer color. For a more detailed explanation of the advantages of this option, refer to Chapter 30, "Exploring the Timeline."

✦ **Actions Panel:** This drop-down menu has two options that configure the Frame Actions Panel each time you launch Flash. The options are Normal or Expert Mode. For a detailed explanation of the Actions Panel, refer to Chapter 39, "Understanding Actions and Event Handlers."

As shown in Figure 24-10, options for the Editing tab of the Preferences dialog are:

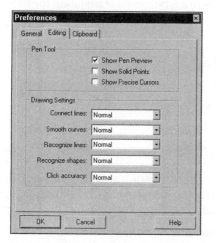

Figure 24-10: The Editing tab of the Preferences dialog for the PC

✦ **Pen Tool:** With the release of Flash 5, Macromedia added a robust Pen Tool to the Flash Toolbox. Three preferences to control the performance of the Pen Tool are located here. Because fine, accurate use of the Pen Tool often involves the use of selection tools in order to move and adjust control points, we've chosen to introduce the Pen Tool at the end of the chapter on selections, immediately prior to the chapter on drawing tools. For a detailed discussion of the Pen Tool in context, refer to Chapter 26, "Working with Selections and the Pen Tool."

- **Show Pen Preview:** With this option checked, Flash will display a preview of the next line segment, in response to moving the pointer, prior to clicking to make the next end point and create the line segment.

- **Show Solid Points:** Check this option to display selected anchor points as solid points, and unselected points as hollow points. The default, which is unchecked, displays anchor points in the opposite manner: The default is for selected points to be hollow and for unselected points to be solid.

- **Show Precise Cursors:** This option toggles the Pen tool cursor between the default Pen Tool icon and a precision crosshair cursor. We advise that you check this option to use the precision cursor.

✦ **Drawing Settings:** Previous versions of Flash had a drawing control that was referred to as the Assistant. It controlled the performance of one of Flash's most celebrated features, the "automated helpers" that aid drawing, which include Line Processing and Shape Recognition. With Flash 5, these controls have been relocated — intact — here as the Drawing Settings. For more about the principles of Line Processing and Shape Recognition, please refer to Chapter 27, "Working with the Drawing and Painting Tools." In all cases, the Assistant controls the degree of "automatic help" for each of six categories of assistance. For all assistants, the options range from off, to lax, to moderately aggressive, to aggressive. Only one assistant has an option that's equivalent to always on. Regardless of the particular assistant, here's a universal translation for these somewhat quirky settings:

  Off = OFF

  Must be close / Rough / Strict = Lax

  Normal = Moderately Aggressive

  Can be distant / Smooth / Tolerant = Aggressive

  Always snap = Always ON

  - **Connect lines:** Controls snapping between an extant line and a line that's being drawn. If the line that's being drawn is within the threshold, it snaps to the nearest point of the other line. This setting also controls vertical and horizontal line recognition, which is the aspect of Line Processing that makes nearly vertical or horizontal lines absolutely vertical or horizontal.

  - **Smooth curves:** When drawing with the Pencil Tool, with the mode set to either Straighten or Smooth, this setting controls how much smoothing will be applied to curved lines.

  - **Recognize lines:** This setting determines how nearly straight a line segment needs to be in order for Flash to make it perfectly straight.

  - **Recognize shapes:** In Flash, roughly drawn circles, ovals, squares, rectangles, and arcs of either 90 or 180 degrees can be recognized as geometric shapes and automatically redrawn with absolute precision. This is called *Shape Recognition*, and this setting controls the degree of what is "permissible."

  - **Click accuracy:** This setting controls how close the cursor must be to an item before Flash recognizes the item. A tolerant setting means that you either inadvertently select an item, which is a bother, or that you can be close and easily select an item, which may be cool. We think Normal is the best setting for this.

As shown in Figure 24-11, options for the Clipboard tab of the Preferences dialog are:

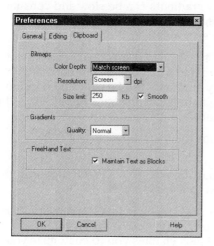

Figure 24-11: The Clipboard tab of the Preferences dialog for the PC

✦ **Bitmaps (PC) / PICT Settings (Mac):**

  • **Color Depth (PC):** Choose **None** if you are only pasting back into Flash. This only copies the Flash vector format, which is faster and conserves system memory. Otherwise, if you want to copy bitmaps to the clipboard (in addition to the default Windows Metafile), choose a bitmap format — which is only useful when pasting to and from bitmap applications, such as Photoshop. In which case, choose the appropriate bit depth for your use.

  • **Type (Mac):** As with the PC, choose **Objects** if you are only pasting back into Flash. This only copies the Flash vector format, which is faster and conserves system memory. Otherwise, choose a bitmap format if you want to copy bitmaps (in the PICT format) to the clipboard — which is only useful when pasting into bitmap applications, such as Photoshop. As with the equivalent setting for the PC, chose the appropriate bit depth for your use.

  • **Resolution:** Choose the resolution at which you want to capture bitmaps.

  • **Size Limit (PC):** Use this entry box to limit the amount of RAM (memory) that will be gobbled up by bitmaps on the clipboard.

  • **Smooth (PC):** Smooth is antialiasing, which means that the edges of shapes and lines are dithered to look smooth on screen. Check Smooth to turn antialiasing on.

  • **Include PostScript (Mac):** Although mostly unused now, the original Pict format had the capability to include postscript items.

- **Gradients on Clipboard (PC):** The Quality drop-down controls the quality of the gradient fills that are created when copying to the Windows Clipboard. Copying higher quality gradients can be slow and consumes system RAM. If you're only pasting back into Flash, choose **None,** because full gradient quality is preserved regardless.

- **Gradients (Mac):** As with the PC, the Quality drop-down controls the quality of gradient fills that are created when copying to the Mac Clipboard. Copying higher quality gradients can be slow and consumes system RAM. Choose **None** if you're only pasting back into Flash, as full gradient quality is preserved regardless.

✦ **FreeHand Text:** This command confirms the marriage between Flash and FreeHand.

- **Maintain Text as Blocks:** When pasting text from a FreeHand file, if this option is checked, the pasted text remains editable.

✦ **Keyboard Shortcuts:** This final item of the Edit Menu invokes the Keyboard Shortcuts dialog, which is a powerful new feature of Flash 5. As shown in Figure 24-12, the Keyboard Shortcuts dialog enables you to customize your Flash keyboard shortcuts to maintain consistency with other applications or to develop a personalized workflow. Not only can you choose keyboard shortcuts developed from other applications, you can also save your modifications and custom settings. A full explanation of this dialog follows.

Keyboard shortcuts

There is one major reason to applaud the inclusion of this feature in Flash 5: It enables the disabled. Imagine how wonderful this facility might be for someone who has lost the use of one of his or her hands. For other disabilities, this feature could make the difference between the ability to work effectively in Flash or not. We have a friend who is a quadriplegic; having the use of neither his hands nor his feet, this intrepid fellow accomplishes amazing feats in Flash — with a mouth stick! These keyboard commands enable him, and others with disabilities, to use the program with a little more ease.

Another reason to celebrate this feature is that it facilitates the development of a custom workflow — for example, drawing tablet with one hand, keyboard with the other. The disadvantage of this feature is that, in a busy studio where artists are swapping seats like musical chairs, irresponsible keyboard changes can lead to team grief. In a studio, Keyboard Shortcuts must be implemented with regard for others working in the same environment. But this is a small detraction from the greater value of this feature. We hope that Macromedia will build upon their example and continue to lead the way, and will offer greater accessibility for the disabled with subsequent releases.

Delete set buttons

Rename set button

Duplicate set button

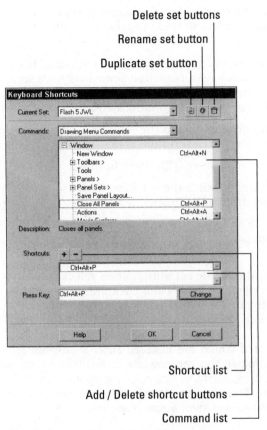

Shortcut list

Add / Delete shortcut buttons

Command list

Figure 24-12: The Keyboard Shortcuts dialog

To create a new keyboard shortcut, you must first duplicate an existing set, from which you can then add or subtract existing shortcuts to form your custom short-cut set. Here's the process:

1. Select a shortcut set from the Current Set pop-up menu. This is now the active set.

2. Duplicate the active set by clicking the Duplicate Set button. The Duplicate dialog appears. Enter a new name for this set in the Duplicate Name field and click OK.

   A similar procedure is employed to rename a shortcut set. Simply click the Rename Set button and enter the new name in the ensuing dialog. (But you cannot rename the built-in sets that ship with the program.)

3. Select a commands list from the Command pop-up menu (Drawing Menu Commands, Drawing Tools, or Test Movie Menu Commands) either to add a command or to modify it.

4. Next, in the Command list, choose either a grouping or a command from one of the previously chosen commands lists. Note that some lists have sublists. Click the Plus sign (or small arrow on the Mac) to expand a particular category. Figure 24-13 shows commands for the Window Menu.

5. Now choose a command that you want to add (or subtract) — a description of the selected command appears in the Description area.

6. To delete the existing shortcut, click the (–) Shortcut button.

7. To add a shortcut for this command, click the (+) Shortcut button, and then enter the shortcut key combination in the Press Key entry box. Click Change, and then OK to close the dialog.

8. Or, to change an existing command, select the command and click the Change button.

9. To delete a shortcut set, click the Delete set button, then select the set to be deleted from the ensuing Delete Set dialog and click the Delete button. (Because you cannot delete the built-in sets that ship with the program, they do not appear in the Delete Set dialog.)

Tip

Keyboard Shortcut sets are stored within the installed Flash 5 program folder, within the Keyboard Shortcuts folder. You can navigate to this location on your hard drive and copy, backup, restore, delete, or otherwise manipulate any of these files from this folder. Keyboard Shortcuts are transferable between machines, although we had no success transferring them across platforms.

The View Menu

As shown in Figure 24-13, the View Menu is dedicated to controlling how movies — and some tools — are viewed in Flash. There are also a few controls that toggle functionality.

✦ **Goto:** The Goto command leads to a Pop-up menu of scenes in the current movie, including four handy shortcuts to the First, Previous, Next and Last scenes.

Cross-Reference

The next three commands — Zoom In, Zoom Out, and Magnification — are covered in greater detail in Chapter 25, "Using Tools for Navigation and Viewing."

✦ **Zoom In:** This increases the view by 50 percent.

✦ **Zoom Out:** This decreases the view by 50 percent.

✦ **Magnification:** This command leads to eight preset magnification levels. See Chapter 25, "Using Tools for Navigation and Viewing," for more detail.

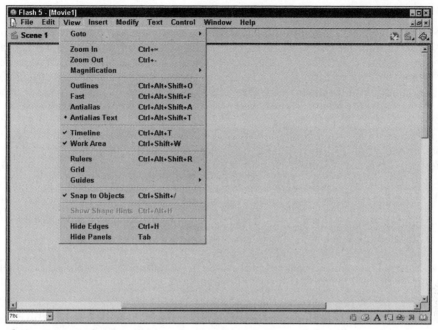

Figure 24-13: View Menu

Note   The next four commands: Outlines, Fast, Antialias, and Antialias Text have *no* effect on the way in which Flash exports your movie. Quality decisions are made in the Publish Settings, which are covered in Chapter 43, "Publishing Flash Movies." These settings only affect screen quality and screen speed — meaning, "How much longer until this picture appears?"

✦ **Outlines:** Use this command to display all shapes as outlines, and to show all lines as thin lines. This command is useful for reshaping graphic elements, and for getting the general timing and sense of a movie. It also speeds up the display of complex scenes. It is a global equivalent of the outlines toggle of individual frames.

✦ **Fast:** This command also speeds up display. It turns off both antialiasing and dithering. Although the default is Off, the recommended setting is On. Unfortunately, this setting is *not* saved as a preference — it must be set for every movie.

✦ **Antialias:** Not to be confused with the wife of your outlaw cowboy uncle, antialiasing dithers the edges of shapes and lines so that they look smoother on screen. It also slows the display. It works best with fast, 24-bit video cards. This is really a toggle in opposition with the *Fast* command: turn this On and *Fast* goes Off. The setting we recommend for Antialias is Off.

✦ **Antialias Text:** As with Antialias, this is also a toggle in opposition to the *Fast* command. It smoothes the edges of text *only* and works best with large font sizes — it can be dreadfully slow when there's a lot of text.

✦ **Timeline:** Use this toggle to show or hide the timeline.

✦ **Work Area:** This command makes the light-gray area that surrounds the Stage (or Movie Area) visible. This can be useful when your movie has items that are either partially or completely off stage — as, for example, when you have something move into or out of a scene. To work with these items (to place or manipulate them) off stage, use View ➪ Work Area. To see the maximum Stage/Work Area, use View ➪ Work Area, and then use View ➪ Show All.

A good example of the utility of the Work Area feature can be seen in both the Weber movie, and the Journal of Edwin Carp. Cartoonists such as Turner and Bazley rely upon this capability of Flash for creating effects (such as long pans) in which very large background artwork hangs off the Stage (or view area) until called upon or tweened through.

Caution   You cannot deselect items that are selected and offstage when View ➪ Work Area is toggled off. This can lead to inadvertent deletions, so be careful!

✦ **Rulers:** This command toggles the Rulers (which display at the top and left edges of the Work Area) on or off — use Modify ➪ Movie to change units of measurement.

✦ **Grid:** Click this command to access three commands that control the parameters and use of both Snapping and the Flash Grid.

   • **Show Grid:** This command toggles the Drawing Grid on or off.

   • **Snap to Grid:** This command toggles the Snap to Grid function on or off. Snap to Grid works regardless of whether the Grid has been made visible with View ➪ Grid ➪ Show Grid — if the Grid has not been made visible, it just snaps to the *invisible* Grid.

   • **Edit Grid:** Use this command to invoke the Grid dialog, where you can change Grid Color, Spacing, and the settings for Snap accuracy. Snap accuracy controls how close an item, symbol, or — while drawing — the end of a line must be to a Grid intersection before the item, symbol, or line endpoint snaps to the Grid. Both Show Grid and Snap to Grid check boxes are also included in this dialog. Edited Grid settings can be saved as the default by clicking the Save Default button, which enables you to have these setting as presets for all subsequent Flash movies.

Note   The default Grid size of 18 pixels is inherited from the origins of Flash in the SmartSketch program — it's because 18 pixels equals 0.25 inch! But you aren't stuck with that. Grid units can be changed by entering the appropriate abbreviation (for example: 25 pt., .5", .5 in, 2 cm, and so on) in the Grid Spacing entry boxes. Although the specified units *will* be applied to the grid, they will be translated into the current unit of measurement for the Ruler. Thus, if the Ruler is set to pixels, and the Grid units are changed to .5 in, then, on reopening the Grid dialog, the Grid units will be displayed as 36 pix (because pixels are allocated at 72 pix = 1"). Changing Ruler Units via Modify ➪ Movie also changes Grid Units.

✦ **Guides:** When Rulers are turned on, Guides, a new feature for Flash 5, can be dragged onto the Stage from either ruler. These four commands control the parameters of these Guides.

- **Show Guides:** This is a simple toggle to either show or hide the Guides.

- **Lock Guides:** This is a toggle that either locks or unlocks all current Guides.

- **Snap to Guides:** This is a toggle that extends Snap behavior to Guides. It works independently of the other Snap toggles — so, if Snap to Grid is turned off in the Edit Grid dialog, and Snap to Objects is also turned off, Snap to Guides is still active, unless, of course, it, too, is toggled off.

- **Edit Guides:** This command invokes the Guides dialog box, where Guide Color and Guide-specific Snap accuracy can be adjusted. Also included are check boxes for the other three Guide commands: Show Guides, Snap to Guides, and Lock Guides. This enables you to establish Guide settings and then click the Save Default button to have these setting as presets for all subsequent Flash movies.

✦ **Snap to Objects:** Due to the recent trend among high-end Flash developers to structure their Flash authoring as *Object-Oriented Flash,* it's advisable — for the sake of future clarity — to think of this command as a Snap to Items command. Snap to Items means that, when moving or manipulating an item, the item snaps into alignment with items already placed on the stage.

✦ **Show Shape Hints:** This toggles Shape Hints to make them visible or invisible. It does not disable shape hinting. Shape Hints are used when tweening shapes. For more about Shape Tweens (or Shape Morphing) refer to Chapter 33, "Animating in Flash."

✦ **Hide Edges:** Use this command to hide selection highlights, so that you can edit items without the added confusion of their selection highlights.

Tip If you want to Hide Edges permanently, in every movie you make, a similar, more permanent effect can be obtained by first creating a Color Swatch with a Zero Alpha, and then setting the Highlight Color to that color in the General tab of the Edit ⇨ Preferences dialog. For more about Color Swatches, refer to Chapter 28, "Applying Color."

✦ **Hide Panels:** This command hides all visible panels. However, it is not a toggle because repeating the command does not return the panels to visibility. To return the panels to visibility, you must invoke them from either the Launcher Bar or the Window Menu. However, pressing Tab hides and returns your currently visible set of panels.

The Insert Menu

As shown in Figure 24-14, the Insert Menu is used to insert Symbols, Layers, Guides, Frames, and Scenes into the current Movie.

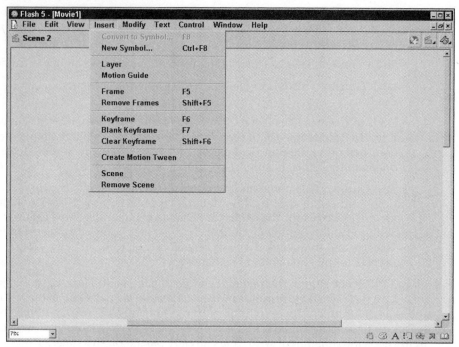

Figure 24-14: Insert Menu

✦ **Convert to Symbol:** Use this command to convert a selected item (or items) on stage into a new Symbol and evoke the Symbol Properties Dialog. Refer to Chapter 31, "Checking Out the Library: Symbols and Instances," for a full explanation of symbols.

✦ **New Symbol:** Use this command to create a new symbol in Symbol-editing Mode. To use this command, first make sure that nothing is selected by using Edit ⇨ Deselect All. Refer to Chapter 31, "Checking Out the Library: Symbols and Instances," for a full discussion of symbols.

✦ **Layer:** This command creates a new layer directly above the currently active layer. The new layer becomes the active layer.

✦ **Motion Guide:** Use this command to add a Motion Guide layer (also referred to as a Motion Path). The Motion Guide layer appears above the selected layer. For more information about using Motion Guides to tween along a path, refer to Chapter 30, "Exploring the Timeline."

✦ **Frame:** Use this command to insert a new frame at any selected point on the timeline. If a frame is selected, then that selected frame (together with all frames to the right on that layer) are shifted to the right to accommodate the new frame — other layers are left alone. But if no layers (or frames) are selected, then all layers get a new frame at the current position of the Playhead (indicating the active frame) and preexisting frames on all layers shift right.

✦ **Remove Frame:** This command deletes the selected Frame.

✦ **Keyframe:** Use this command to convert a selected Frame into a Keyframe.

✦ **Blank Keyframe:** This command inserts a new Keyframe at a selected point on the timeline. If a frame is selected, then that selected frame (together with all frames to the right on that layer) shift to the right to accommodate the new frame — other layers are left alone. If no layers (or frames) are selected, then all layers get a new frame at the current frame marker's position and pre-existing frames on all layers shift right.

✦ **Clear Keyframe:** This command changes a Keyframe back into a simple Frame, whereupon the contents of the former Keyframe are replaced with copies of the Keyframe immediately previous in the timeline.

✦ **Create Motion Tween:** This command is one step in the process of creating a tweened animation. Refer to Chapter 30, "Exploring the Timeline," for the full scoop on tweened animation.

✦ **Scene:** This command inserts a new, empty Scene immediately following the currently active Scene. By default, new Scenes are numbered — use the Scene panel to rename and to organize Scenes.

✦ **Remove Scene:** This command deletes the currently active Scene.

The Modify Menu

As shown in Figure 24-15, the Modify menu is thick with commands that invoke pop-ups, submenus, and panels. Not shown are the pop-ups for the first five items on the menu: Instance, Frame, Layer, Scene, and Movie. Although all of these are introduced here, substantial discussion of these items has been deferred until they can be handled in context with the Flash workflow.

✦ **Instance:** The Modify ⇨ Instance command evokes the Instance Panel, which is used to control independent behaviors of Symbol Instances. In its default configuration, the Instance Panel is accompanied by the Effect Panel. Together, they have fields for Instance Behavior, Options, Name, and Color Effect. These topics are introduced in greater depth in Chapter 31, "Checking Out the Library: Symbols and Instances."

✦ **Frame:** The Modify ⇨ Frame command, opens the Frame Panel. In its default configuration, the Sound Panel accompanies the Frame Panel. Together, they have fields for the control of frame labels, tweening, and sound. These topics are introduced in greater depth in Chapter 33, "Animating in Flash," and in Part IX, "Sound Planning."

✦ **Layer:** The Modify ⇨ Layer invokes the Layer Properties dialog, which is used to control and edit the properties of the active layer of the timeline. The timeline is discussed fully in Chapter 30, "Exploring the Timeline."

✦ **Scene:** Modify ⇨ Scene opens the Scene Properties panel, which has only one function: to rename the current scene.

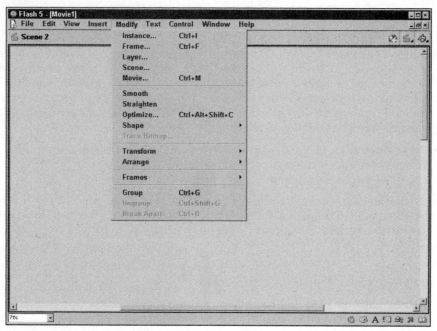

Figure 24-15: The Modify Menu

✦ **Movie:** Modify ⇨ Movie leads to the Movie Properties dialog, which is used to change Frame Rate, Movie Dimensions, Background Color, and Ruler Units.

• **Frame Rate:** Changes the Frame Rate.

• **Dimensions:** Establishes the Dimensions of the Movie.

• **Match:** The Match Printer button matches the Movie Dimensions to the currently selected printer's maximum printable dimensions. The Match Contents button adjusts the Movie Dimensions to include all active items, from the upper left-hand corner to the lower right-hand corner of the entire movie (including animation, and the space it may cover during such movements). The expanse includes a narrow zone of white (stage) around it.

• **Background Color:** Click the chip to choose a color from the Swatches pop-up.

Tip

The Background Color can be changed at any time during an animation by adding a new layer at the bottom of the layer stack, and then creating a Keyframe at the point where you want the color to change. Next, draw a rectangle the size of the stage (or larger) position it to cover the stage, and fill with the new color. Subsequent changes of background color can be accomplished with the insertion of another Keyframe and changing the color of the rectangle at that point. For more information, see Chapter 31, "Checking Out the Library: Symbols and Instances."

- **Ruler Units:** Use this drop-down menu to specify units for the movie. Remember, Ruler Units also changes Grid Units — and impacts Snap to Grid behavior.

- **OK:** Applies changes to the current movie only.

- **Save Default:** Click this button to add these settings to the preferences. They become the default for all subsequent movies created with File ⇨ New.

The next group of commands replaces the prior grouping of commands that were located within the Curves submenu. These commands aren't only for manipulating curves — they're useful for manipulating other things, too. See Chapter 32, "Drawing in Flash," for detailed explanations in context. These commands are as follows:

✦ **Smooth:** Reduces curves and bumps.

✦ **Straighten:** Straightens out lines and curves.

✦ **Optimize:** Lessens the number of curves in a shape. Use this command to reduce the size of Flash files.

✦ **Shape:** Lets you convert lines to fills, expand and shrink fills, and soften the edges of fills.

✦ **Trace Bitmap:** Use this command to convert an imported bitmap into a vector graphic with editable, discrete areas of color. Please refer to Chapter 34, "Using Bitmaps and Other Media with Flash," for a full treatment of the use of various media — including bitmaps — within the Flash vector environment.

✦ **Transform:** Use Modify ⇨ Transform to access the Transform submenu, home to the following commands: *Scale, Rotate, Scale and Rotate, Rotate 90 ° CW, Rotate 90 ° CCW, Flip Vertical, Flip Horizontal, Remove Transform,* and *Edit Center.* These are explained in context in Chapter 32, "Drawing in Flash." As for the remaining commands, *Add Shape Hint* and *Remove All Hints* are explained in Chapter 33, "Animating in Flash."

✦ **Arrange:** Use Modify ⇨ Arrange to open the Arrange submenu, which is used to move selected items, symbols, and groups either forward or backward in the stack of items that are layered in the currently active Layer. The options — which are intuitive — are:

  - **Bring to Front:** This moves the selected item to the absolute front of the active layer's stack.

  - **Bring Forward:** This moves the selected item one step forward in the stack.

  - **Send Backward:** This moves the selected item one step backward in the stack.

- **Send to Back:** This moves the selected item all the way back to the hinterlands of the stack.

- **Lock:** Use this to lock the selected item in its current position in the stack.

- **Unlock:** Use this to release the selected item from its locked status in the stack.

✦ **Frames:** Modify ➪ Frames yields the Frames submenu, with four commands:

- **Reverse:** To reverse an animation sequence, first check that there's a keyframe at the beginning and end of the sequence. Next, select the entire sequence — keyframe to keyframe — and choose Modify ➪ Frames ➪ Reverse.

- **Synchronize Symbols:** Sometimes an animation sequence is encapsulated as a symbol and used as a graphic instance in a movie. If the number of frames occupied by this graphic instance doesn't jive with the number of frames in the original sequence, erratic looping occurs. Although this command is supposed to adjust timing and ensure synchronous looping, it rarely works. The optimal solution is to synchronize the animations manually.

- **Convert to Keyframes:** Use this command to convert a range of selected frames into keyframes. This command is an obvious candidate for a custom keyboard shortcut.

- **Convert to Blank Keyframes:** Use this command to downgrade a range of selected keyframes to blank keyframes. This command is another obvious candidate for a custom keyboard shortcut.

✦ **Group:** Use this command to Group two or more selected items. Details and advantages of grouping are discussed in Chapter 28, "Applying Color," and Chapter 29, "Working with Text."

✦ **Ungroup:** This command ungroups items that have been grouped — it's also discussed in Chapter 28, "Applying Color," and Chapter 29, "Working with Text."

✦ **Break Apart:** This command is used to separate groups, blocks of type, instances, bitmaps, and OLE items. It can be used to reduce the file size of imported graphics. However, it may not be reversible, and it also has some unintuitive effects, so refer to the discussion of this command in Chapter 29, "Working with Text," before using! Furthermore, because this command turns blocks of type into graphics, applying it to type increases file size — sometimes significantly.

The Text Menu

This menu (see Figure 24-16) contains duplicate commands for text controls that are available in one of the three Text Panels.

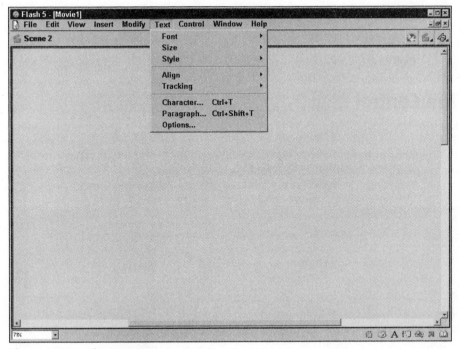

Figure 24-16: The Text Menu

These commands are:

✦ **Font:** Although this command duplicates the Font drop-down menu located at the top of the Character Panel, it's much easier to work with — if you know your fonts. That's because Text ➪ Font invokes a scrolling pop-up menu that extends from top to bottom of your screen. The only disadvantage of this menu is that it lacks the additional display that the Text Panel offers, which shows the font name in the character set of the highlighted font.

✦ **Size:** This command offers 13 preset sizes ranging from 8 points to 120 points. Although it's quick and easy, it lacks the infinite precision of the Size control located on the Text Panel, which presents both a numeric entry field and a slider bar for the selection of point size.

✦ **Style:** This command gives you the easiest access for changing the style of selected text. The options are Plain, Bold, Italic, Subscript, and Superscript.

✦ **Align:** This command duplicates the function of the upper pane of the Paragraph Panel. Here the options are Align Left, Align Center, Align Right, and Justify.

✦ **Tracking:** This command offers abbreviated control of text tracking. It isn't nearly as robust or as precise as the lower pane of the Paragraph Panel. That's because the options are limited to Increase, Decrease, and Reset.

✦ **Character:** This command invokes the Character Panel.

✦ **Paragraph:** This command invokes the Paragraph Panel.

✦ **Options:** This command invokes the Text Options Panel.

The Control Menu

Despite the Control Menu's alluring title (see Figure 24-17), this is not the menu for Type A personalities. Rather, like the VCR controller, which Type A's always seem to finagle onto their armrest, the Control Menu displays buttons that control the movie playback features within Flash.

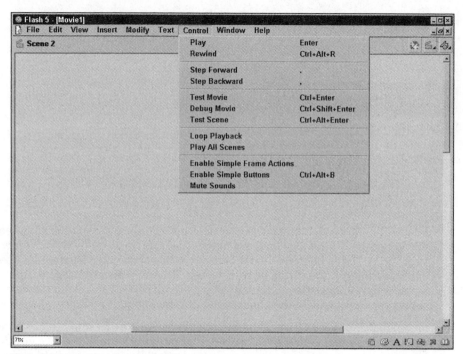

Figure 24-17: The Control Menu

✦ **Play:** This command plays the movie in the authoring environment.

✦ **Rewind:** This command returns the movie back to frame 1.

✦ **Step Forward:** Use this command to step the movie forward one frame.

✦ **Step Backward:** Use this command to step the movie one frame backward.

✦ **Test Movie:** Some interactive functions will not work when the movie is played within the Flash playback environment. This command uses the settings established in the Publish Settings dialog to export the current movie and instantly play it within a new Flash Player window. The exported movie is *not* a temporary file; it is saved to the same folder as the parent .FLA file. The Keyboard Shortcut for this command is Ctrl+Enter/Command+Return.

Tip

If you're doing a lot of coding and are accustomed to using the default keyboard shortcut to do Test Movie, you must first return focus from the Actions Panel to the Editor. But that's a pain! The easy fix is to use the Keyboard Shortcuts dialog to assign a custom key for Control ➪ Test Movie.

✦ **Debug Movie:** This is a new feature of Flash 5 that enables developers to debug a Flash movie for problems in their code. It launches the Debugger Panel.

✦ **Test Scene:** This command is similar to the Test Movie command; the only exception is that it tests the current scene only, whereas Test Movie runs the whole shebang.

✦ **Loop Playback:** This command is a toggle that enables looping with all subsequent implementations of the *Play, Test Movie,* and *Test Scene* commands.

✦ **Play All Scenes:** The default within the Flash Movie Controller is to play the current scene only. So, like *Loop Playback,* this is another toggle — it overrides the default single-scene playback and enables all scenes to be played with subsequent implementations of the *Play, Test Movie,* and *Test Scene* commands.

✦ **Enable Frame Actions:** This is a toggle that controls whether Frame Actions are enabled. Use *Enable Frame Actions* only during tests and playback within Flash; otherwise, it may be difficult to edit a movie.

✦ **Enable Simple Buttons:** Like *Enable Frame Actions,* this toggle controls whether buttons are enabled. It would be impossible to edit, move, or manipulate buttons if they were continually enabled. So, enable buttons only during tests and playback within Flash. This is limited to simple buttons because complex buttons cannot be effectively tested within the Flash Editor environment.

✦ **Mute Sounds:** This command toggles sound on or off, within the Flash Editor environment.

The Window Menu

The Window Menu, shown in Figure 24-18, is the launch pad for a number of key panels and dialogs. It has several commands that are used to arrange the display of multiple movies.

✦ **New Window:** This command opens the currently active movie in a new window.

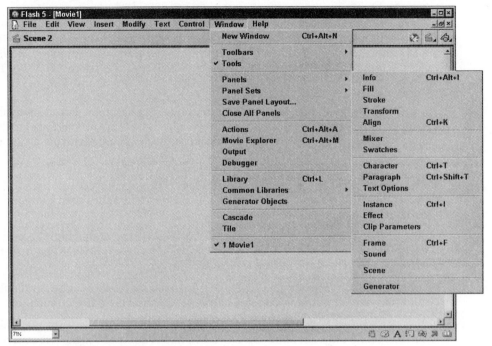

Figure 24-18: The Window Menu

✦ **Toolbars (PC Only):** This command opens the Toolbars subpanel, which
contains the following commands.

- **Main:** The Main Toolbar is the just the Standard Toolbar from Flash
  4, with a different name. As shown earlier in Figure 24-3, this toolbar is similar to the production toolbars of many programs. It
  duplicates commonly used tools for easier access, and is generally
  for those who are unfamiliar with the program. Because it devours
  precious screen space, we urge that it be disabled.

- **Status:** The Status Toolbar, shown in Figure 24-3, gives text read-
  outs that may explain the use of tools, buttons, and many interface
  elements. Generally, the text is too limited to be much help. Leave
  this option disabled; it, too, devours precious screen space and
  retards learning.

✦ **Controller (PC placement):** This command toggles the display of the
Controller Toolbar. With buttons similar to a VCR, the Controller is used
to test animations within the Flash Movie Editor. (It can be used instead
of the commands on the Control Menu to play a movie within Flash.)
From right to left, the buttons are: *Stop*, *Rewind*, *Step Back One Frame*,
Play, *Step Forward One Frame*, and *Fast Forward*.

✦ **Tools:** On both the Mac and the PC, this command toggles display of the Toolbox, which was shown earlier in Figure 24-1.

✦ **Controller (Mac placement):** On the Mac, this command, which toggles display of the Controller Toolbar, is in the front lineup of the Window Menu commands.

Note   Experienced users usually disable these additional toolbars: Main Toolbar and Status Toolbar.

✦ **Panels:** This command opens the Panels submenu, which leads to groupings of most of the primary panels of Flash 5, which are:

• **Info:** The top pane of this panel has a readout for the width and height of a selected item, as well as the x and y coordinates. These readouts are also, numeric entry fields, permitting a numeric transformation of both the dimensions and position of the selected item. There's also an alignment grid that's used to toggle the x,y coordinates between the item's center and the top-left corner of the item. The bottom pane delivers the information about the (pixel precise) current mouse location: R, G, B, and Alpha values as well as x,y coordinates. The Info Panel is discussed in context in Chapter 32, "Drawing in Flash."

• **Fill:** This panel is used to select or create fills — Solid, Gradient, or Bitmap — that are applied with the Paint Bucket (K) Tool. Fills are discussed in context in Chapter 27, "Working with the Drawing and Painting Tools," and in Chapter 28, "Applying Color."

• **Stroke:** Strokes are lines created by the Pen (P) or Pencil Tool (Y), as well as the outlines of filled shapes. Three controls handle the qualities that define a stroke: Stroke Style, Thickness, and Color. Like fills, strokes are first discussed in context in Chapter 27, "Working with the Drawing and Painting Tools," and Chapter 28, "Applying Color."

• **Transform:** This panel is a complement to the numeric transformation capabilities of the Info Panel. The Transform Panel facilitates changing the dimensions of a selected item according to percentage, with a check box to constrain transformations to the original aspect ratio of the item. Controls for Skew and Rotate are also located here. The Transform Panel is discussed, in concert with the Info Panel, in Chapter 32, "Drawing in Flash."

Tip   With the default panel layout, you can use the Info Panel button on the Launcher Bar to invoke the default Info/Transform/Stroke/Fill cluster.

• **Align:** The Align Panel is used to align multiple selected items according to various criteria. This panel has intuitive, visual buttons that can be used to align, resize, and evenly distribute two or more selected items. These options can be used separately or in combinations. This panel is discussed in context in Chapter 32, "Drawing in Flash."

- **Mixer:** The Mixer Panel is used to mix colors and save them as color swatches. Colors may be assigned to either the Stroke or Fill Color Chips of the Color Tray. Additionally, the readout for the color space can be chosen from RGB (Red, Green, Blue), HSB (Hue, Saturation, Brightness), or hex (hexadecimal) color specification types. The Mixer Panel is discussed in concert with the Swatches Panel in Chapter 28, "Applying Color."

- **Swatches:** The Swatches Panel is used to load, organize, save, and remove both individual Color Swatches and Color Sets. See Chapter 28, "Applying Color."

Tip   With the default panel layout, use the Mixer Panel button on the Launcher Bar to invoke the default Mixer/Swatches cluster.

- **Character:** The Character Panel offers control over the following aspects of text in Flash. Controls include font; point size; bold and italic; color; tracking; kerning; character position; and URL entry. The Character Panel is discussed — in concert with the Paragraph and Text Option Panels — in Chapter 29, "Working with Text."

- **Paragraph:** The Paragraph Panel controls the alignment and placement of text in Flash. The controls include Align (Left, Center, Right, or Full Justification), Left Margin, Right Margin, Indentation, and Line Spacing. The Paragraph Panel is discussed in context in Chapter 29, "Working with Text."

- **Text Options:** The Text Options Panel is used to select the type of text that you will be using in Flash. The choices are Static, Dynamic, or Input Text. There are other choices as well, subject to the type of text you will be using. These details are introduced in Chapter 29, "Working with Text."

Tip   With the default panel layout, use the Character Panel button on the Launcher Bar to invoke the default Character/Paragraph/Text Options cluster.

- **Instance:** The Instance Panel is used to control various fundamental properties of Symbol Instances. These properties vary according to whether the instance Behavior is as a Movie Clip, Button, or Graphic. The Instance Panel is first discussed in context in Chapter 31, "Checking Out the Library: Symbols and Instances."

- **Effect:** The Effect Panel controls color effects for symbol instances. The choices are Brightness, Tint, Alpha, and Advanced, which is a combination of the preceding three choices. These controls are first introduced in Chapter 31, "Checking Out the Library: Symbols and Instances."

- **Clip Parameters:** The Clip Parameter Panel is where Smart Clips are made. Smart Clips are a new feature of Flash 5, whereby Clip Parameters can be defined for each movie clip in the Library. By defining attributes (and default values for each attribute), a developer can create templates for interactivity, for ease of use by designers, and other purposes yet to be discovered by the indefatigable legions of Flash genius. The Clip Parameter Panel is discussed in context in Chapter 43, "Publishing Flash Movies."

- **Frame:** The Frame Panel has two functions: It is used to add labels and comments to individual frames, and to hold the controls that manage the finer aspects of Motion and Shape Tweening. The labeling aspect of the Frame Panel is discussed in Chapter 30, "Exploring the Timeline," while the Tweening controls are discussed in Chapter 33, "Animating in Flash."

- **Sound:** Controls for Flash sound are located in the Sound Panel, the Library, and the Publish Settings. The Sound Panel controls are used to set the Effect, Sync, and Loop for each sound, while the Edit button launches the Edit Envelope. Sound is covered in depth in the three chapters of Part IX, "Sound Planning."

Tip   With the default panel layout, use the Instance Panel button on the Launcher Bar to invoke the default Instance/Effect/Frame/Sound cluster. (For better workflow, we suggest that you consider adding Clip Parameters to this cluster. The procedure for accomplishing this feat is discussed later.)

- **Scene:** The Scene Panel duplicates the function of the Edit Scene button, which is located at the right side of the Timeline Header. When working with Flash Movies that have two or more scenes, the Scene Panel facilitates switching from one scene to another, as well as duplicating, adding, and deleting them.

- **Generator:** If you have Generator installed, the Generator Panel displays common (as well as any custom) Generator Objects that have been installed.

✦ **Panel Sets:** This command invokes the Panel Sets submenu, which displays the command for the Default Layout, as well as any custom panel layout that may have been saved.

✦ **Save Panel Layout:** Select this command to launch the Save Panel Layout dialog, which has a Name field and rudimentary buttons. Enter a name with which to save the current arrangement of panels. If you enter a name that's been saved previously, Flash queries whether you want to overwrite it.

✦ **Close All Panels:** This command closes all open panels. However, repeating this command does not reopen those same panels — so it is *not* a toggle.

Tip   There is a toggle that closes and then reopens all open panels. On both platforms, the shortcut key for this toggle is the Tab key.

✦ **Actions:** The Actions panel is used for assigning and authoring ActionScript. Although excluded from the Panels submenu, both the Actions Panel and the Movie Explorer Panel, which follows, can be arranged together with the other panels and saved into a panel set.

✦ **Movie Explorer:** The Movie Explorer is a powerful new feature of Flash 5. It's like the helpmate of the Library because it provides an asset overview (in a file menu environment, analogous to the Mac Finder or the Windows Explorer) of the current Flash Movie, and offers many shortcuts for editing, updating, and troubleshooting many of the same items that would be much more difficult to sleuth out from the Library. A good example of the utility of the Movie Explorer is changing text and font choice. Doing operations like this from the Movie Explorer can be a *serious* time-saver. The Movie Explorer is introduced in Chapter 31, "Checking Out the Library: Symbols and Instances."

Working with Panels

Depending upon your point of view, the proliferation of panels in Flash 5 can be either an enhancement to or the bane of your workflow. Even if you have dual 21" monitors, or a cinema display, here are some tips that can make your work with panels a lot more productive:

✦ Double-click the title bar of any panel to collapse it upward into just a title bar with the panel tab(s) showing. Unfortunately, collapsed status is not retained when closing the program, nor when saving a panel set.

✦ Use the Launcher Bar. As shown at the beginning of this chapter, in Figures 24-2 and 24-3, the Launcher Bar is located at the lower-right corner of the Flash Editor. It's a default that cannot be excluded from your working environment. It is very handy for launching specific panels as needed, and then closing them.

✦ Alt/Option+Click the close box of any panel to close all panels simultaneously.

✦ Just because you open a panel doesn't mean that it has focus. You have to click in the field where you want to start typing, even if there is only one field.

✦ After you've typed text in a panel field (whether in the Actions Normal mode or other panel), either hit Tab or Enter to make the change take. This is especially useful when entering Frame Labels or Comments, or when entering a number of Instance Names for Movie Clip instances. However, you still must have the field selected or else hitting Tab just toggles all the panels on and off.

 • If a panel isn't open, choosing it from the Panels submenu, tapping the keyboard shortcut, or clicking its Launcher button opens it.

 • If a panel is open and is at the back in the stacking order of other panels, then choosing it from the Panels submenu, tapping the keyboard shortcut, or clicking its Launcher button brings it to the front.

 • If a panel is open and is at the top of the stacking order of other panels, then choosing it from the Panels submenu, tapping the keyboard shortcut, or clicking its Launcher button closes that panel.

 • You can rearrange panels into new panel groups by dragging the panel of choice by its tab. Because panels cannot be regrouped within an existing set, you must plan the order for a panel group before you assemble the group.

 • Alt/Option+double-click any item brings up all relevant panels.

Tip   Both the Actions Panel and the Movie Explorer have buttons on the Launcher Bar to access them without hesitation.

✦ **Output:** Unlike so many of the commands available from the Windows menu, this one isn't a panel—it really is a window, and cannot be ganged together with the panels. After export to .SWF, this opens the Output Window, which shows precise file-size reports on every scene, symbol, text, and so on. It's very helpful for analyzing download problems and testing the effectiveness of preloaders.

✦ **Debugger:** Another new addition to Flash 5, the Debugger Panel is used for troubleshooting Flash ActionScript code, and/or to monitor the properties of Flash movies and symbols. The debugger can be enabled within Flash using Control ⇨ Debug Movie, or it can be evoked from a Web page in a browser. By using the latter method, the Flash application gets focus and the Debugger Panel becomes active (meaning that you don't get a Debugger window/Panel in the browser). This is intended for advanced authoring and can get complex, quickly.

✦ **Library:** The Library is also a true window and not a panel. As was shown earlier in Figures 24-4 and 24-5, the Library is the repository of all recurring elements, known as Symbols, that are placed as Instances within a Flash movie. Imported sounds and bitmaps are automatically placed in the Library. Upon creation, both buttons and Movie Clips (which are symbols) are stored in the Library. It's a smart practice to make a Symbol for nearly *every* item within a Flash movie. The Library is covered in depth in Chapter 31, "Checking Out the Library: Symbols and Instances." Although it differs from the Common Libraries discussed next, they are related. The Windows ⇨ Library is specific to the current movie, whereas Common Libraries are available whenever Flash is open.

✦ **Common Libraries:** The Libraries Menu is the one menu over which the user has real control. That's because—in addition to the Library items that are placed there in the process of a default installation of Flash—you have the option of placing your own items there, too. The default Libraries contain a selection of buttons and symbols to get you started. These are located in the Libraries folder of the Flash application folder. (And when you're tired of them, you can remove them!) To add your own buttons, symbols, or libraries for specific projects, first save them in a Flash file with a descriptive name, then place that Flash file in the Libraries folder within the Flash Program folder on your hard drive. Because these default Common Libraries have such obvious names, we won't waste valuable pages to describe them. They are **Buttons, Graphics, Learning Interactions, Movie Clips, Smart Clips,** and **Sounds.**

✦ **Generator Objects:** This is another true window, and not a panel. This command is disabled, unless you have Generator installed. Generator is a separate program, with a database engine that melds to the Flash's pictorial and animation engine.

    ✦ **Cascade:** This command cascades all open windows so that they overlap in a cascade descending from the top left to the bottom right, like fanned out playing cards.

    ✦ **Tile:** This command tiles all open movie windows so that they are arranged, side-by-side like an eclectic tile job. (Panels and application windows are not tiled.)

The Help Menu

There are so many varied forms of Flash help that it's astounding. In this chapter, we look at a few of the sources for help. The Flash Help Menu, shown in Figure 24-19, directs users to two kinds of help, offline and online. Unless you've opted for a custom install or have removed the help files from your Flash installation, there are a number of offline Help resources directly accessible from the Help Menu. First, beginners may benefit from the lessons and samples. In addition, there are four Flash Help Topics, a sophisticated help system that's viewed offline in your Web browser. Finally, a vast array of online resources are available on the Web — some of which are also linked directly from the Help Menu.

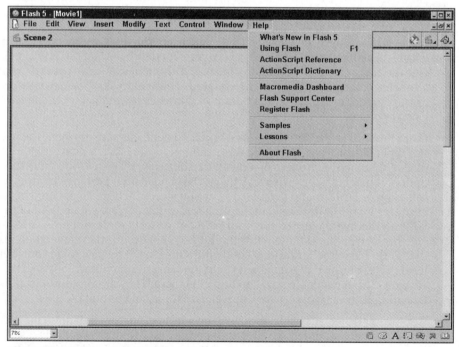

Figure 24-19: The Help Menu

Offline learning resources

Aside from the normal Help files, Flash offers a beginner's course with eight lessons, sample movies, and ActionScript resources.

Lessons and samples

If you accepted the default installation, these are available to you from the Help Menu. (Note, however, that you may not have the Lessons or Samples installed if you chose to do a custom install. In this case, you'll probably want to reinstall Flash in order to have access to these terrific resources.) These excellent, free Lessons and Samples are near the bottom of the Help Menu and are highly recommended for all new Flash users.

Help resources

From the Menu Bar, any of the following four resource topics launch your Web browser and open an offline Web page. Like the Lessons and Samples, these are installed as a default with the program. (If you don't have Flash Help Topics installed, you have to reinstall Flash if you want to access this resource.) The four main topics offer help and instruction in the following areas:

✦ **What's New in Flash 5:** This is an overview of new features and tools. The topics are linked to the relevant areas of the offline manual Using Flash.

✦ **Using Flash:** This is the offline manual, presented as a series of self-paced seminars on the principal tools and methods of working with Flash.

✦ **ActionScript Reference:** This is a reference to the new, robust, Flash 5 ActionScript language.

✦ **ActionScript Dictionary:** This is a dictionary of the new Flash 5 ActionScript language.

Online learning resources

The Flash Help Menu also leads to three resources that are viewed online through a Web browser; these are the new Macromedia Dashboard and the Flash Developers Center.

✦ **Macromedia Dashboard:** This resource is like a mini-browser, built in Flash. The menu has the following Flash-related items: News, Community, Support, Resources, Training, Feedback, and Flash Player. The Dashboard is designed to include a current featured site and a featured community. It also provides an Auto-Update feature, to help you stay current on all features. Technically, the Dashboard is another panel, so it can be grouped with any panel set.

Tip   If you have your monitor set to a high resolution (or if you happen to be getting on in years) you may find the text at Dashboard a bit difficult to read. If so, remember that this is scalable vector content: Simply grab any corner of the panel with your mouse and drag out the Dashboard to a more legible size.

✦ **Flash Support Center:** This is Macromedia's original online resource, the Flash Support Center, sometimes also referred to as the Developer's Resource Center. This is Macromedia's primary vehicle for the distribution of up-to-date information about Flash and Flash related topics, so check here regularly for the latest developments. This is a searchable area with current (and archived) articles on many Flash topics. There are also links to downloads, documentation, forums, and many other gems.

✦ **Register Flash:** Although this isn't exactly a resource for help, Macromedia isn't going to give you direct help unless you register your copy of Flash — enough said?

Summary

✦ Flash 5 is the most consistent, cross-platform version yet.

✦ Flash 5 had many enhancements to the interface, preferences, and sundry settings that help to make the program clearer and more powerful.

✦ Some of the most obvious changes are the addition of panels and the inclusion of the new Movie Explorer, while keyboard shortcuts enable users to personalize Flash to facilitate their workflow.

✦ There's not much to be done in Flash that doesn't rely on these menus, panels, settings, and preferences to get it accomplished. So, use this chapter as a reference.

✦ Now that you've toured the Flash menus, panels, settings, and preferences, you're ready to step on out into Flashland and start *creating*.

✦   ✦   ✦

Using Tools for Navigation and Viewing

Before you embark on a project in Flash, you need to know how to get to the action—in a scene, a symbol, or any other element in the movie. You need to know how to change the size of your viewing area (not everyone has 21" monitors). You also need to know how to move efficiently and quickly to areas of the scene that might be off-screen. That's because (surprise!) scrollbars aren't necessarily the easiest way to shift among the contents of the screen. Flash offers familiar navigation and viewing tools for changing the viewable area of a scene and for moving to different areas of a scene.

The Magnifier Tool

The Flash Magnifier Tool (Z) is similar to the zoom tool of many other programs. It has two options, Zoom In and Zoom Out. The Z key is the keyboard shortcut for the Magnifier Tool on both the Mac and the PC. Although this may seem counter-intuitive, the Magnifier Tool is nearly synonymous with the Zoom Tool—furthermore, this keyboard shortcut brings Flash into alignment with usage established in other major software. Keyboard shortcuts for tools located in the Drawing Toolbar are single keystrokes. For example, simply press the Z key to activate the Magnifier Tool. Throughout this book, we indicate keyboard shortcuts with the following notation: Magnifier Tool (Z).

Note Due to the redesign of Flash 5, keyboard shortcuts are now subordinate to what is called *focus,* the active part of the Flash interface. When the Main Timeline and Stage have focus, then the keyboard shortcuts work as they did previously: Simply tap the appropriate key and the related tool is invoked. However, if you are working in any of the various new panels, because that panel has focus, the keyboard shortcuts will not respond — in this case, Flash is not broken. Simply click anywhere on the Stage to switch focus and reenable the function of the keyboard shortcuts.

Zoom In/Zoom Out

Zoom In brings you closer to the drawing so that you're viewing it at a higher level of magnification, whereas *Zoom Out* pulls you away from the drawing by showing it at a lower level of magnification. Each level of *Zoom In* brings you in twice as close, and each level of *Zoom Out* pulls you away in increments of one-half. In addition, here's a less obvious use of the Zoom Tool: If you double-click the Magnifier Tool (see Figure 25-1), it forces the movie to display at 100 percent.

Magnifier Tool (Z)

Zoom Out
Zoom In

Figure 25-1: The Magnifier Tool's options are Zoom In and Zoom Out.

To toggle the Magnifier Tool between the Zoom In and the Zoom Out options on the PC, press Alt+click. On the Mac, press Option+click.

New Feature

Flash 5 has added these keyboard zoom commands that bring Flash further into alignment with other Macromedia programs. To Zoom In, press Ctrl/Command with the plus (+) key. To Zoom Out, press Ctrl/Command with the minus (–) key.

Another way of working with the Zoom Tool, which is useful when you want to zoom in on a specific area of your work, is to activate the Magnifier Tool either by clicking it in the Drawing Toolbar or by pressing the (Z) key and then dragging out a rectangle with the Magnifier Tool in the Flash work space. Flash opens the rectangular area at the highest level of magnification that includes the entire area of the rectangle.

The Hand Tool

When you're zoomed in close on the screen, you have two methods for moving around the stage. You can use the scroll bars, or you can use the Hand Tool, which looks like a little gloved hand. Although the scroll bars might be more familiar, especially if you are unfamiliar with drawing and graphics applications, you'll probably find that you can navigate the Flash workspace contents more accurately and intuitively by using the Hand Tool (H). Use this tool by clicking and dragging (while holding down the mouse) in the direction that you want to move the screen. It's important to note that the Hand Tool does not move items in a scene to a new location — the Arrow Tool does that. Rather, the Hand Tool shifts the viewable portion of a scene to reveal another section that may be positioned awkwardly or somewhere off-screen. In addition to this functionality, there's a less obvious use of the Hand Tool — it will fit the Stage in the frame.

Tip

The Hand Tool can also be activated temporarily by pressing the space bar; this is a toggle that causes the Hand Tool mouse pointer (the little gloved hand) to appear, regardless of what tool is currently selected in the Tool Palette.

Zoom Control and View Commands

In addition to the use of the Magnifier Tool, similar operations of magnification can also be accomplished with either the Zoom Control (PC only) or with the View Command. The only real difference between these tools and the Magnifier Tool is where they are located within the program and the manner in which they are used to control the level of magnification.

Note

With the release of Flash 5, the Zoom Control has changed considerably. Although it has been retained as an integral part of the PC version of Flash, it's been moved to the bottom left of the Stage, where it resides as part of the Launcher Bar. It has been removed entirely from the Mac version.

The Zoom Control

On the PC, the Zoom Control is a numeric entry box and pop-up menu, located at the bottom-left corner of the Stage, as part of the Launcher Bar (see Figure 25-2). The Zoom Control can be used as either a pop-up menu or a numerical entry box. Click the pop-up to display a series of preset Zoom levels, or enter a number in the numerical entry box and press Enter to view the Flash workspace at any other zoom percentage that you desire.

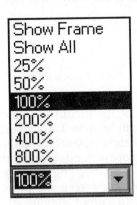

Figure 25-2: The Zoom Control and Zoom Control pop-up menu on the PC

The following preset Zoom levels can be selected from the Zoom Control drop-down menu: Show Frame, Show All, 25%, 50%, 100%, 200%, 400% and 800%. Also, a specific zoom level, such as 122%, can be obtained by typing the exact value in the entry box. Selecting Show Frame or Show All often results in a zoom level other than the evenly incremented zoom percentages available in the Zoom Control drop-down menu. That's because these selections are determined by two factors: the pixel size of a given movie and the pixel area available to the scene on a given computer monitor.

The Magnification commands

In addition to the Magnifier Tool, the new keyboard shortcuts, and the Zoom Control (PC only), the Magnification commands, shown in Figure 25-3, are also available to adjust your screen view. On both the Mac and PC, the Magnification commands are accessed from the Menu Bar, View ➪ Magnification.

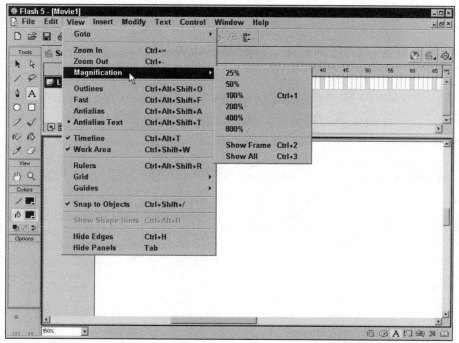

Figure 25-3: The Magnification commands include three presets with keyboard shortcuts. Also, note that the Work Area command is accessed from the View Menu.

The Magnification menu contains the following preset commands: 25%, 50%, 100%, 200%, 400%, 800%, Show Frame, and Show All. (For those of you on the PC, three of these Magnification commands are equivalent to settings available through the Zoom Control drop-down menu.) Three view commands also have corresponding keyboard shortcuts:

✦ **100% (Ctrl/Command+1):** Depending on your monitor resolution and video card, this setting shows your work at actual size. For example, if your movie size is 500 pixels × 400 pixels and your screen size is 800 × 600, then your movie will occupy roughly 40 percent of your total screen area in Flash.

✦ **Show Frame (Ctrl/Cmnd+2):** This setting adjusts the zoom to show everything within the frame boundary, as defined by the movie properties.

✦ **Show All (Ctrl/Cmnd+3):** This setting adjusts the zoom to fit the contents of the current frame. If the frame is empty, the entire scene is displayed.

How Zoom Affects Tool Size

Zoom has a counterintuitive effect on brush sizes and other tools. For example, identical brush sizes draw at different sizes, depending on the Zoom level that you have set! Similarly, the Paint Bucket's interpretation of *gap* (meaning, is that a big gap or a small gap?) is entirely dependent on the zoom setting. It's best to think of brush size and gap size as a fixed *screen image* size. (Caution: This is *unlike* Photoshop and many other programs with fixed *image pixel* size.) Whatever size the brush appears to be on the screen or Work Area *is the effective size of that brush*. Its size is not measured in fixed pixels.

Other tools and functions that are affected by the Zoom setting are those that modify shapes, such as the Smooth option and the functions available by choosing Modify ➪ Curves.

For optimum accuracy when manually placing or aligning items on Stage, use a consistent Zoom setting. For example, if you are arranging several items around a particular point, unless you use the same Zoom setting when you place each item, the accuracy of your positioning may be compromised, which may result in an unwanted jitter in your animation. (Gap is discussed at length in Chapter 26, "Working with Selections and the Pen Tool.")

Another related command, also accessible from the View Menu, View ➪ Work Area, is the Work Area command. (On prior versions of Flash, this command was included with the Magnification commands.) This command adjusts the view to include the work area displayed in gray outside the Stage. It's useful when you're working with items that are completely or partially out of the scene (or out of view). This command enables you to work with items positioned off-screen.

Tip To see the broadest possible Work Area and Stage, choose View ➪ Work Area, and then select either 50% or 100%, depending on your screen size and movie size.

Figure 25-4 compares two brush strokes made with the same exact brush at two different levels of Zoom. Using the third largest brush, the stroke on the left was painted at a Zoom level of 100%, while the stroke on the right was painted at a Zoom of 200%.

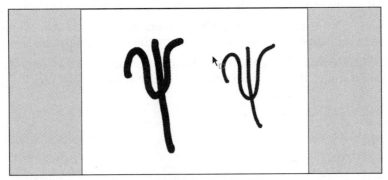

Figure 25-4: How Zoom affects effective Tool Size

Summary

✦ Two basic tools that are common to many other programs, the Magnifier Tool and the Hand Tool, facilitate moving around in Flash.

✦ The Magnifier Tool enables you to either zoom in or zoom out of the Flash Stage. Similar functionality is also offered by the Magnification and Work Area commands, which are accessed from the View menu.

✦ The Hand (or Grabber) Tool enables you to scoot areas of the Flash Stage in or out of the viewable area of zoom.

✦ The level of zoom has a direct, counterintuitive effect upon both the apparent Tool size and also the accuracy of positioning and aligning of items on stage.

✦   ✦   ✦

Working with Selections and the Pen Tool

Flash has a pair of tools — the Lasso Tool and the Arrow Tool — that can be used to select lines, shapes, groups, symbols, buttons, and other items. The Lasso Tool is primarily used to make free-form selections and to select odd-shaped sections of a drawing. The Arrow Tool is used primarily to select discrete lines, shapes, groups, symbols, buttons, and other items. In combination with the Magnet option and the Shape Recognition options, the Arrow Tool has many unique capabilities not found in any other program. In addition to these tools, the new Subselect Tool, which also looks like an arrow, can be used (in a limited way) to select these items. However, the Subselect Tool is primarily a companion for the Pen Tool, which is introduced at the end of this chapter. We've chosen to address the Pen Tool among the selection tools because the Pen Tool draws lines by laying down editable points. Additionally, both the Pen Tool and the Subselect Tool are used to manipulate those points, and, thereby, edit lines. Nevertheless, both the Pen Tool and the Subselect Tool are equally useful for selecting and editing all lines and shape, so they're selection tools, too.

The Lasso Tool

The Lasso Tool (L) is used to group-select odd or irregular-shaped areas of your drawing. After areas are selected, they can be moved, scaled, rotated, or reshaped as a single unit. The Lasso Tool can also be used to split shapes, or select portions of a line or a shape. As shown in Figure 26-1, it has three options in the Options Tray: the Polygon Lasso, the Magic Wand, and the Magic Wand properties.

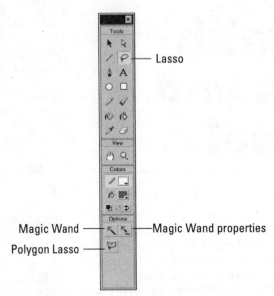

Magic Wand ———— ————Magic Wand properties

Polygon Lasso ————

Figure 26-1: The Lasso Tool and options

The Lasso Tool works best if you drag a loop around the area you wish to select. (Hence the tool name Lasso!) But if you slip or if you don't end the loop near where you started, Flash closes the loop with a straight line between your starting point and the end point. Because you can use the Lasso Tool to define an area of *any* shape—limited only by your ability to draw and use the multiple selection capabilities of Flash—the Lasso Tool gives you more control over selections than the Arrow Tool.

Tip   To add to a previously selected area, hold down the Shift key before initiating additional selections.

Using the Polygon option with the Lasso Tool

The Polygon Lasso affords greater precision when making straight-edge selections, or—in mixed mode—selections that combine freeform areas with straight edges. To describe a simple polygon selection, click the Polygon option to toggle the Lasso Tool *on* and commence Polygon selection mode. In Polygon Mode, selection points are created by a mouse click, causing a straight selection line to extend between mouse clicks. To complete the selection, double click.

Mixed mode usage, which includes Polygon functionality, is available when the Lasso Tool is in Freeform Mode. To work in Freeform Mode, the Polygon option must be in the *off* position. While drawing with the Freeform Lasso, press the Alt (Option) key to temporarily invoke Polygon Mode. (Polygon Mode continues only as long as the Alt (Option) key is pressed.) Now, straight polygonal lines can be described between selection points that are created by a mouse click. That is, *as long as the Alt (Option) key is pressed, a straight selection line extends between mouse clicks*. To return to Freeform Mode, simply sneeze — or release the Alt (Option) key. Release the mouse to close the selection.

Note
Sometimes aberrant selections — selections that seem inside out, or that have a weird, unwanted straight line bisecting the intended selection — result from Lasso selections. That's usually because the point of origination of a Lasso selection is the point to which the Lasso will snap when the selection is closed. It usually takes a little practice to learn how to *plan* the point of origin so that the desired selection will be obtained when the selection is closed.

Using the Magic Wand option with the Lasso Tool

The Magic Wand option of the Lasso Tool is used to select ranges of a similar color in a bitmap that has been broken apart. After you select areas of the bitmap, you can change their fill color or delete them. Breaking apart a bitmap means that the bitmap image is subsequently seen by Flash as a collection of individual areas of color. (This is not the same as *tracing* a bitmap, which reduces the vast number of colors in a continuous-tone bitmap to areas of solid color.) After an image is broken apart, you can select individual areas of the image with any of the selection tools, including the Magic Wand option of the Lasso Tool. You can restore a broken bitmap by selecting the entire image (this causes it to look like a negative relief), and then choosing Modify ➪ Group from the Menu Bar. The equivalent shortcut is Ctrl (Command)+G.

Cross-Reference
Techniques and settings for using the Magic Wand when working with Bitmaps, as well as Tracing Bitmaps, are covered in Chapter 34, "Using Bitmaps and Other Media with Flash."

Using Magic Wand properties

The Magic Wand properties option has two modifiable settings: Threshold and Smoothing. To set them, click the Magic Wand properties button while the Lasso Tool is active.

The Threshold setting of the Magic Wand option

The Threshold setting defines the breadth of adjacent color values that the Magic Wand option includes in a selection. Values for the Threshold setting range from 0 to 200: The higher the setting, the broader the selection of adjacent colors. Conversely, a smaller number results in the Magic Wand making a narrower selection of adjacent colors.

Note   A value of zero results in a selection of contiguous pixels that are all the same color as the target pixel. With a value of 20, clicking on a red target pixel with a value of 55 selects all contiguous pixels in a range of values extending from red 35 to red 75. (For those of you who are familiar with Photoshop, it is important to note that the Flash Threshold is unlike Photoshop in which a Threshold setting of 20 selects all contiguous pixels in a range of values extending from red 45 to red 65.)

The Smoothing setting of the Magic Wand option

The Smoothing setting of the Magic Wand option determines to what degree the edge of the selection should be smoothed. This is similar to antialiasing. (Antialiasing dithers the edges of shapes and lines so that they look smoother on screen.) The options are Smooth, Pixels, Rough, and Normal.

The Arrow Tool

The Arrow Tool is used to select and move an item — or multiple items — on the Stage. The Arrow Tool is also used to reshape lines and shapes, as those users familiar with prior versions of Flash may remember. The Arrow Tool's new neighbor, which is also an arrow, but a white one, is the Subselect Tool. Its debut in Flash was occasioned by the addition of the Pen Tool. Thus, it is most useful for moving and editing anchor points and tangents on Bézier curves, as well as *single* items.

New Feature   Now, with the addition of a new Pen Tool, Flash 5 enables you to draw and manipulate lines and shapes using Bézier curves (or Bézier handles), much like other vector-based programs. Often, this manipulation is accomplished with the Subselect Tool. Because the Subselect Tool is technically a selection tool, and because it is used in concert with the Pen Tool, which can also be used to select and edit points on lines created by any of the other drawing tools, we present a full discussion of both tools at the end of this chapter.

Use the Arrow Tool to reshape a line or shape by pulling on any unselected line (or shape), or on its end points, curves, or corners. The Arrow Tool is also used to select and move Flash elements, including lines, shapes, groups, symbols, buttons, and other items. Five options appear in the Option Tray when the Arrow Tool (A) is selected (see Figure 26-2): Magnet (or Snap), Smooth, Straighten, Rotate, and Scale.

Tip   When you are busy with another tool, you can temporarily toggle to the Arrow Tool by pressing and holding down the Ctrl (Command) key.

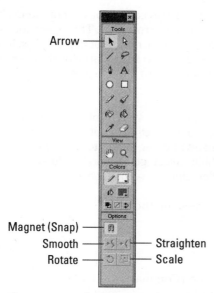

Arrow

Magnet (Snap)
Smooth ———— Straighten
Rotate ———— Scale

Figure 26-2: The Arrow Tool and its five options

Using the Arrow Tool to select items

The Arrow Tool is the primary selection tool in Flash. When you click a line or shape, a checkered pattern appears, covering it, to indicate that the line or shape has been selected. If the item is either a Symbol or a Group, a thin, colored border (called the Highlight) indicates selection status. This Highlight Color may be set in the Preferences dialog by choosing Edit ⇨ Preferences ⇨ General.

Figure 26-3 shows a shape, a group, and a symbol as they look both when unselected (the top items) and selected (the bottom items). The hatched pattern covers and surrounds the square indicating that it is a selected graphic, while the thin borders that surround the group and the symbol indicates that they have been selected.

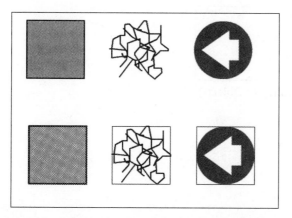

Figure 26-3: Using the Arrow Tool to select items

In addition to clicking on a line to select it, you can also select one or more items by dragging a rectangular marquee over them using the Arrow Tool. This operation is called *drag-select*. Additional items can be added to a current selection by pressing the Shift key and clicking the items. When you drag-select to select, previously selected items are deselected and excluded from the selection. To include previously selected items, press the Shift key as you drag-select.

> **Note**   Prior to Flash 4, the implementation of Shift Select was unlike other graphics applications: Additional lines were added to a selection simply by clicking them. Since Flash 4, the Shift key must be pressed in order to add to the current selection. To change this default setting for Shift Select, go to Edit ➪ Preferences, and click the General tab. Then, in the Selection Options section, uncheck Shift Select.

Deselect one or more items by using any of these methods:

✦ Pressing the Escape key

✦ Choosing Edit ➪ Deselect All

✦ Using the keyboard shortcut Ctrl+Shift+A (Command+Shift+A)

✦ Clicking anywhere outside all the selected items

Using the Magnet option of the Arrow Tool

The Magnet (or Snap to Objects) option button is a toggle that causes items being drawn or moved on screen to snap to existing items on the Stage. Click the option button to toggle snapping on or off, or choose View ➪ Grid ➪ Snap to Objects.

As shown in Figure 26-4, the rectangular shape is being moved to the right with the Arrow Tool and is snapping to the invisible grid. When snap is turned on, Flash snaps the item to existing items. You can tell that an item is snapping by the presence of an o icon beside the Arrow mouse pointer. For some shapes, the icon or snap function will not work unless, when clicking to grab the shape before moving, the shape is clicked either at the center, corner, or side.

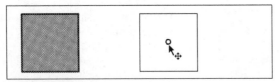

Figure 26-4: Using the Magnet (Snap to Objects) option of the Arrow Tool

Even if the Magnet option is turned on, you can temporarily override the Snap function by holding down the Shift key as you drag or move an item.

The functionality and degree of precision of the Magnet (or Snap) button are controlled by settings that can be customized in the Grid field of the Grid dialog, which can be accessed by choosing View ⇨ Grid ⇨ Edit Grid. The settings are measured in pixels, relative to the movie size (*not* the screen size).

Understanding shape recognition

Shape recognition is the general term for a set of options that can be set to assist accurate drawing and manipulation of basic shapes. These options are the Smooth and Straighten options, which are used in conjunction with the Arrow Tool to clean up drawings by clicking their respective buttons to invoke their smoothing or straightening action. This is fully explained in the sections that follow.

When used in conjunction with the Pencil Tool, more powerful shape recognition can be invoked — the only real difference is that, with respect to the Pencil Tool, shape recognition processes the lines automatically. For example, a crude lumpy oval will be automatically recognized and processed into a true oval. Using shape recognition with the Pencil Tool is explained in greater detail in the first section of Chapter 27, "Working with the Drawing and Painting Tools."

For the Arrow and the Pencil Tools, both the degree to which shape recognition processes your drawings and also the strength with which the Smooth and Straighten options interact with your drawings may be adjusted with the Drawing Settings pane of the Editing tab of the Preferences dialog: Edit ⇨ Preferences ⇨ Editing.

Here's how shape recognition works with the Arrow Tool: Sketch something spontaneously (but not too wildly!). Then use shape recognition to transform your sketch into precision geometric forms. Start by sketching a rough circle, square, or rectangle. Then click the Arrow Tool and select the item you've just sketched. Then click either the Straighten or Smooth button to begin shape recognition. For hard-edged items such as a polygon, click the Straighten option button repeatedly until your rough sketch is a recognizable and precise geometric form. For smooth-edged items that approximate an oval, click the Smooth option button repeatedly until your rough sketch becomes an exact circle.

In addition to the treatment here in this chapter, shape recognition is detailed elsewhere in the book. The settings that control shape recognition are first explained in Chapter 24, "Exploring the Interface: Panels, Settings, and More." Shape recognition is also discussed further, in context with drawing processes, in Chapter 32, "Drawing in Flash."

Using the Smooth option with the Arrow Tool

The Smooth option is a button that simplifies selected curves, as shown in Figure 26-5. Smoothing reduces the number of bumps and variations (or points of transition) along the span of a complex curve so that the curve spans the same distance with fewer points. Repeated use of the Smooth button on a line results in a curve with only two points, one at either end. To use this option, a line must first be selected with the Arrow Tool, and then the Smooth button can be used to reduce the points in the selected line (or line segment). Action similar to the Smooth button can also be accessed by choosing Modify ➪ Smooth.

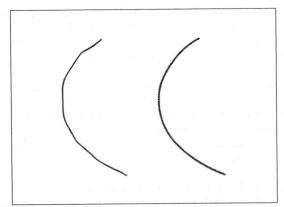

Figure 26-5: Using the Smooth option with the Arrow Tool: The curve on the left was drawn with the Pencil Tool (in Ink Mode). Then the curve was selected by clicking it with the Arrow Tool and smoothed by hitting the Smooth option button twice. That result is shown on the right.

Using the Straighten option with the Arrow Tool

The Straighten option is a button that is used to make selected line segments less curved. The Straighten button operates on the same principle as the Smooth button, except that it's used for straightening (instead of smoothing) a selected line segment. Repeated use of the Straighten button turns a curvy line into a series of angled lines. Action similar to the Straighten button can also be accessed by choosing Modify ➪ Straighten.

In Figure 26-6, the Pencil Tool (in Ink Mode) was used to draw the rough, freehand T on the left. After selecting this rough T by clicking with the Arrow, the Straighten option button was clicked once to create the refined T shown on the right.

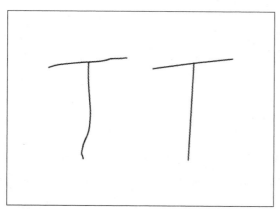

Figure 26-6: Using the Straighten option with the Arrow Tool

Note The degree of the Smoothing or Straightening adjustments that can be made with the Smooth or Straighten button is regulated by the number of times that the button is clicked. Although it may appear that the degree of automatic Smoothing or Straightening can be adjusted by choosing Edit ➪ Preferences ➪ Editing and then selecting one of the four choices (Off, Rough, Normal, or Smooth), these options *only* affect smoothing or straightening done *during* the drawing process (with shape recognition turned on), *not* adjustments made with the Smooth or Straighten buttons.

Using the Rotate option with the Arrow Tool

The Rotate option enables you to rotate, skew, or slant a selected line, group, symbol, or item. With the graphic element selected, click the Rotate option to put it into Rotation Mode. Eight circular handles appear. Drag a corner handle to rotate the item. Drag either a middle or side handle to skew or slant. You can also rotate items by choosing Modify ➪ Transform ➪ Rotate.

In Figure 26-7, the Rectangle Tool was used to draw the square shown at the upper left. After it was selected by clicking with the Arrow Tool, the Rotate button was clicked, resulting in the superimposed checker pattern and bounding box with eight *circular,* draggable handles, as shown at the upper right. Then, the square was rotated counterclockwise by click-dragging one of the four circular handles located at the corners of the square, as shown at the bottom left. Click-dragging any of the four internal handles (the handles not on the corners) results in a skewing of the shape, as shown at the bottom right.

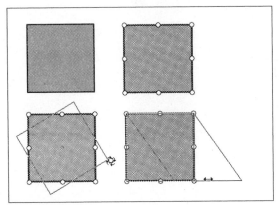

Figure 26-7: Using the Rotate option with the Arrow Tool

Tip   When reshaping, scaling, or rotating a solid item with fills, Flash handles the filled area as if a line of zero thickness enclosed it. As you readjust such an item to a new shape, the fill either expands or contracts accordingly.

Using the Scale option with the Arrow Tool

The Scale option button enables you to scale or stretch a selected line, shape, group, symbol, button, or other item. With the graphic element selected, click the Scale button. Eight square handles appear around the selected graphic element. Click and drag a corner handle to scale the item. Click and drag either a middle or side handle to stretch the item. You can also scale by choosing Modify ➪ Transform ➪ Scale.

As shown in Figure 26-8, after drawing the square on the upper left with the Rectangle Tool, the square is first selected with the Arrow Tool and then the Scale button is clicked, resulting in the superimposed checker pattern and bounding box with eight square, draggable handles, as shown at the upper right. Clicking and dragging on any corner handle, as shown at the lower left, symmetrically resizes the square. Asymmetrical scaling is accomplished by clicking and dragging on any of the side handles, as shown at the lower right.

Using the Scale and Rotate dialog

Choosing Modify ➪ Transform ➪ Scale and Rotate elicits a dialog that combines the properties of both the Rotate and Scale option buttons in one dialog, enabling you to input numeric values for the amount of scale and transformation. (It's very much like the Photoshop Numeric Transform Tool.) The keyboard shortcut for this hybrid is Ctrl+Alt+S (Command+Option+S). This functionality is further duplicated in the Transform Panel (Window ➪ Panels ➪ Transform). Although using either numeric transform dialog may seem unintuitive and hard to use unless you already know what you want to accomplish, they are *extremely* valuable for repetitive production tasks.

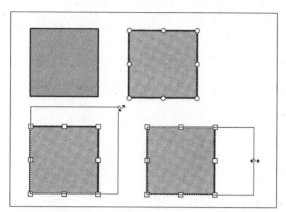

Figure 26-8: Using the Scale option with the Arrow Tool

Using arrow states to reshape and reposition drawings

In addition to the actions accomplished by selecting a line (or line section) and clicking an option, three arrow states — Move Selected Element, Reshape Curve or Line, and Reshape Endpoint or Corner — enable you to reshape and move parts of your drawings. It works like this: As you move the Arrow Tool over the Flash Stage, the Arrow Tool changes the state of its cursor to indicate what tasks it can perform in context with various items (the line or fill) closest to the Arrow Tool's current position.

Tip   When reshaping brush strokes and similar items with the Arrow Tool, make sure that you don't select the entire brush stroke before trying to reshape the outline. If you do, you'll only be able to move the entire brush stroke — you won't be able to reshape it.

Figure 26-9 shows a series of images that demonstrate the various Arrow states in context with several kinds of shapes. These shapes are a filled shape, a brush stroke, and a brush stroke with an outline applied. In the upper left, the *Move Selected Element* Arrow state appears when the Arrow is passed over either one of these shapes. In the upper right, the *Reshape Curve or Line* Arrow state appears when the Arrow is hovered over any line or over the perimeter of a brush stroke. At the lower left, the *Reshape Endpoint or Corner* Arrow state appears when the Arrow is hovered over a corner. At the lower right, an Arrow state cursor is being used to reshape each item.

Figure 26-10 shows the completion of the reshape operations indicated in Figure 26-9.

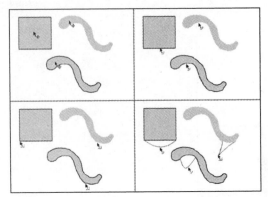

Figure 26-9: Using Arrow states to reshape and reposition items

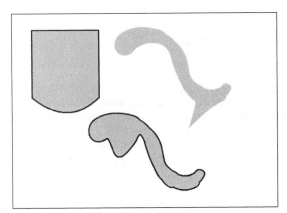

Figure 26-10: The changes resulting from the reshaping shown in Figure 26-9

To make your reshaping go even easier, try these techniques:

✦ Press the Ctrl+Alt (Command+Option) keys, click a line or segment of a line, and drag to create a new corner point.

✦ Selected lines cannot be reshaped. Click anywhere (outside all selected items) to deselect, and then reshape the line by clicking it with one of the different states of the Arrow Tool.

✦ Smooth complex lines to make reshaping easier.

✦ Increase magnification to make your reshaping easier and more accurate.

✦ Prior to reshaping, select any group of elements (as a multiple selection, using Shift+select) that you want to change in unison.

Moving grouped and ungrouped elements with the Arrow Tool

Text and Groups are selected as single elements and move as a single unit. After you create text in a given frame (text functions are discussed in Chapter 29, "Working with Text"), Flash treats the text as one block, or group, meaning that all the individual letters move together when the box is selected. Similarly, a group of graphic elements — such as lines, outlines, fills, or shapes — can be grouped and moved or manipulated as a single element. However, when you move an item that is not grouped, only the selected part is moved. This can be tricky when you have ungrouped fills and outlines, because selecting one without the other could result in detaching the fill from the outline or vice versa. To move separate elements (such as a rectangular line and its colored fill area) in the same direction simultaneously, group them first. To group separate elements, first select them all, and then group them with Modify ➪ Group. If necessary, they can be ungrouped later. Grouping is further discussed in Chapter 32, "Drawing in Flash."

Duplicating items with the Arrow Tool

The Arrow Tool can also be used for duplicating items. Simply press the Alt (Option) key while dragging a selected item (or line segment) with the Arrow Tool. The original item remains in place, and a new item is deposited at the end of your drag stroke.

Introducing the Pen Tool

Finally, Flash has a Pen Tool. Some developers groused over the addition of this new feature, saying that the original drawing set was fine and that this was only being added to attract new users who might be more familiar with FreeHand or other drawing programs. Frankly, these people sounded like members of a child's club, comfortable in their tree fort, as they haul up the rope ladder. The inclusion of the Pen Tool and its close associate, the Subselect Arrow, shown in Figure 26-11, has made the Flash drawing tools far more robust and gives artists more options for creating, editing, and optimizing their art.

For example, previously, when trying to the reduce file size of a movie, an artist might resort to one of the Optimize commands, hoping to reduce the number of points in a drawing. But this had the disadvantage of being both unpredictable and uncontrollable. Now, with the Pen Tool, an artist can select individual points and delete them one by one, resulting in aesthetic precision and reduced file size!

Figure 26-11: Neither the Pen Tool nor the Subselect Tool has options in the Options Tray.

Using the Pen Tool

The Pen Tool (P) is used to draw precision paths that define straight lines and smooth curves. These paths define adjustable line segments, which may be straight or curved—the angle and length of straight segments is completely adjustable, as is the slope and length of curved segments. To draw a series of straight-line segments with the Pen Tool, simply move the cursor and click successively: Each subsequent click defines the end point of the line. To draw curved line segments with the Pen Tool, simply click *and drag*: The length and direction of the drag determines the depth and shape of the current segment. Both straight- and curved-line segments can be modified and edited by adjusting their points. In addition, any lines or shapes that have been created by other Flash drawing tools can also be displayed as paths (points on lines) and edited with either the Pen Tool or the Subselect Tool.

Cross-Reference

The Preferences for the Pen Tool are located in the Pen Tool section of the Preferences dialog. (Choose Edit ➪ Preferences ➪ Editing.) There are three settings: Pen Preview, Point display, and Cursor style. These settings are covered in detail in Chapter 24, "Exploring the Interface: Panels, Settings, and More." As regards your preference for Cursor style, although you can choose between a precise crosshair cursor and a tool icon cursor, you can also use a keyboard shortcut to toggle between the two: Caps Lock toggles Pen Tool cursors between the precise crosshair and the Pen icon.

As Figure 26-12 shows, the Pen Tool cursor displays a number of tiny icons to the lower right of the Pen Tool. These are the Pen states. Four of these Pen states are shown in this composite image, which is a detail of a path describing a white line over a light-gray background, shown at a zoom of 1600.

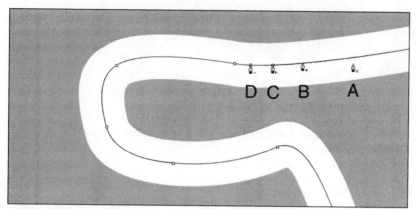

Figure 26-12: In addition to the choice between the cursor icon and crosshair, the Pen Tool displays seven Pen states that indicate the Pen's function under various circumstances.

✦ The Pen displays a small (x) when it's simply over the stage (A).

✦ When the Pen is over a path, it displays a (+) to indicate that clicking there will add a point to the path (B).

✦ When the Pen hovers over an existing point, it displays a (^) to indicate that clicking that point will turn it into a corner point (C).

✦ When the Pen hovers over a corner point, it displays a (–) sign to indicate that clicking this corner point will delete it (D).

Tip Working with the Pen Tool in a movie whose background color is set to black can seem to be nearly impossible — if your Layer Outline Color is set to black! Change the Layer Outline Color to contrast with your background and Pen away! This same principle applies if your background is red (or any other color) and the Layer Outline Color is set to that same color.

As shown in Figure 26-13, there are three more Pen states and a number of details to be defined about the Pen Tool.

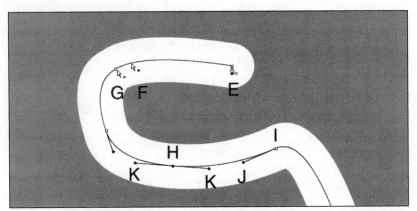

Figure 26-13: More Pen states are shown in this composite image, together with other functions of the Pen Tool.

- ✦ When the Pen is hovered over an end point, it displays an (o) to indicate that this is an end point (E). Click this point to connect a continuation of this path or, when making a closed shape, to close the path.

- ✦ With the Ctrl (Command) key pressed, when the Pen hovers over a path or line, it displays as a hollow arrow with a filled black box (F). In this manner, the Pen Tool is mimicking the Subselect Tool.

- ✦ With the Ctrl/Command key pressed, when the Pen hovers over a point, it displays the same hollow arrow, but with a hollow box (G). In this manner, too, the Pen Tool is mimicking the Subselect Tool.

- ✦ When adjusting a path with either the Pen Tool or the Subselect Tool, the default for selected points is a filled circle (H), while unselected points display as a hollow squares (I). Note that the unselected points display a single tangent handle (J), bound toward the selected point, which displays two tangent handles (K).

Now that we've toured the various Pen Tool icons and Pen states, and have defined the fine details, points, and tangent handles, it's time to start drawing with the Pen Tool. To draw and adjust a straight-line segment with the Pen Tool, follow these steps:

1. Click to initiate the beginning of your line.

2. Then, click to create subsequent points and define individual line segments.

3. Each subsequent click creates a *corner* point on the line that determines the length of individual line segments.

4. To adjust straight segments, press the Ctrl (Command) key and click a point to select it. Continue pressing the Ctrl (Command) key as you drag and move the point to change the angle or length of the segment.

5. Or, with the Ctrl (Command) key pressed, click and drag on the tangent handles of the point to adjust the line. Remember that corner points occur on a straight segment or at the juncture of a straight segment and a curved segment.

Tip   When drawing with the Pen Tool, press the Shift key to force constrain drawing to either 45-degree or 90-degree angle.

To draw and adjust a curved line segment with the Pen Tool, follow these steps:

1. In one continuous motion, click to create the first anchor point.

2. Then, drag the Pen Tool in the direction you want the curve to go.

3. Repeat this process to create subsequent *curve* points for curved segments.

4. Or simply click elsewhere to change to make the subsequent segment a straight line with a *corner* point.

5. As with adjusting straight segments, press the Ctrl (Command) key and click a point to select it, continue pressing the Ctrl (Command) key as you drag and move the point to change the angle or length of the segment.

6. Or, with the Ctrl (Command) key pressed, click and drag on the tangent handles of the point to adjust the depth and shape of the curve.

Although both corner points and curve points may be adjusted, they behave differently:

✦ Because a corner point defines a corner, adjusting the tangent handle of a corner point only modifies the curve that occurs on the same side as the tangent handle that is being adjusted.

✦ Because a curve point defines a curve, moving the tangent handle of a curve point modifies the curves on both sides of the point.

✦ You can also use the arrow keys, located on your keyboard, to nudge corner and curve points into position. Press the Shift key to augment the arrow keys and to make them nudge 10 pixels with each click.

Note   You can also reshape any lines or shapes created with the Pen, Pencil, Brush, Line, Oval, or Rectangle Tools by dragging with the Arrow Tool, or by optimizing their curves with Modify ⇨ Optimize.

Using the Subselect (Arrow) Tool

The Subselect Tool (A) has two purposes:

1. **To either move or edit individual anchor points and tangents.** (You can use the Subselect Tool to display points on both lines and shape outlines and modify them by adjusting their points.)

2. **To move individual objects.** When moving the Subselect Tool over a line or point, the hollow arrow cursor displays one of two states: When over a line it displays a small, filled square next to it; when over a point, it displays a small, hollow square. When either cursor appears, the item can be clicked and moved about the stage.

Note If you use the Subselect Tool to drag a selection rectangle around two items, you'll find that although both may be selected, you can only move one of them.

Figure 26-14 shows the use of the Subselect Tool to move a path (A), to move a single point (B), to select a tangent handle (C), and to modify a curve by adjusting its tangent handle (D). Note that both the before and after are shown before releasing the handle.

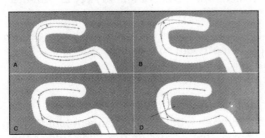

Figure 26-14: Using the Subselect Tool

The Subselect Tool is most useful for modifying and adjusting paths. To display anchor points on a line or shape outline created with the Pencil, Brush, Line, Oval, or Rectangle Tools, simply click the line or shape outline with the Subselect Tool. This reveals the points that define the line or shape. Click any point to cause its tangent handles to appear. If you have a shape that is all fill, without any stroke, you'll need to position the Subselect Tool precisely at the edge of the shape in order to select or move it with the Subselect Tool.

To convert a corner point into a curve point, follow these steps:

1. Click to select the point with the Subselect Tool.

2. While pressing the Alt (Option) key, click and drag the point.

3. A curve point with tangent handles appears, replacing the original corner point.

Note   By holding down the Ctrl (Command) key, the Pen Tool can also be used to mimic the function of the Subselect Tool—except when converting a corner point.

An important use of the Pen Tool/Subselect Tool combo is editing lines for optimal file size. The simpler your shapes, the smaller your file size and the faster your movie downloads. Most often, this involves deleting extraneous points. There are a couple of ways to delete points:

✦ Choose the Subselect Tool from the Toolbox, and then click to select the line with the Subselect Tool, which causes the individual points to appear as hollow circles along the line. Select the point that you wish to delete. Click the delete key.

✦ Choose the Pen Tool from the Toolbox, which causes all paths on the current layer to be selected. Bring the Pen Tool over the point that you want to delete. The cursor updates and displays a small inverted v (^) to the lower right, which is the Corner Point cursor. Click the point with the Corner Point cursor, and continue to hover over the point. After clicking with the Corner Point cursor, the cursor updates and displays a small minus sign (–) to the lower right, which is the Delete Point cursor. Click the point with the Delete Point cursor to delete it.

✦ When deleting more than one point from a closed shape, such as an oval or polygon, use the Subselect Tool to drag and select any number of points. Press Delete to eliminate the selected points. The path heals itself, closing the shape with a smooth arc or line.

Tip   If you used the Subselect Tool to select a path and then Shift+select several points on it, those points will show handles, turning from solid squares to hollow circles, which indicates that they are now moveable. However, if you attempt to move all of the points simultaneously with the Subselect Tool, only one point will move. However, all the points *can* be moved in unison by tapping the arrow keys.

Stroke and color

You may have noticed that we've been discussing the Pen Tool and the Subselect Tool in a relative vacuum—that is, there's been no mention yet of either stroke or color. Well that's easy enough to do, because both *those* controls are sequestered off in the Stroke Panel. But that's not why we've refrained from discussing the more colorful aspects of the Pen Tool. Rather, in this chapter, we focused on the aspects of the Pen Tool that are most closely related to selecting. We begin the next chapter, "Working with the Drawing and Painting Tools," with a rudimentary discussion of color as it applies to all Drawing Tools. This is a discussion of the settings for the Stroke and Fill Panels, which involve Stroke Height and Stroke Color—the color settings for the Pen Tool. See you there.

Shifting Points? Too Many Points?

We've heard reports of perceived problems with the new Pen Tool. Some users noted that Pen paths seemed to "add points" when adding keyframes, or between sessions. Naturally, this seemed very odd, so we did some research through a contact at Macromedia—and here's what we found out.

The Macromedia Flash Player is driven by quadratic curves, which differ from Bézier curves in two ways: They are faster drawing and they result in a more compact file. This is partially because they employ a single tangent handle for each node, rather than the two tangent handles per node in a Bézier format.

The Flash Editor is also driven by quadratics, and even when drawing with the Pen Tool, the internal curve descriptions are still in quadratics—so, you can always push and pull on those Pen Tool curves, and do many other things in the customary *Flash* manner. Therefore, each time you choose the Pen Tool, Flash converts selected lines to an onscreen Bézier representation in order to support Bézier-style curve editing. When the editing is done, Flash converts the curve back to quadratics for storage and display—the Bézier nodes aren't stored.

At the next Pen Tool editing session, the Bézier representation is created, on the fly from the stored quadratic definition. This can lead to some confusion, because it may appear as though the number of points has increased. However, there's no worry about too many points, or changed points, because—in the strict Flash sense—those points don't really exist in the file. What is important is the overall shape complexity that is stored in the saved quadratic representation. When you optimize a line by reducing points with the Pen Tool, this reduces complexity and that is retained when the file is saved. Summary: You will see your shapes accurately retained, but because the Bézier nodes are calculated on demand and only appear while editing, the points may display differently between sessions.

Summary

✦ Flash provides a range of tools that are used to select and modify items on the Stage.

✦ The Lasso Tool is useful for making free-form selections, while the Magic Wand option is a powerful tool for selecting a range of colors — particularly when working with imported bitmaps that you break apart.

✦ The Arrow Tool has multiple uses. With its shape-recognition features, it can be used to smooth or straighten selected drawings — which simplifies their forms to create smaller file sizes.

✦ The Arrow Tool is also used to rotate, scale, and skew selected items.

✦ The Arrow states enable you to simply click lines, fills, and corners to reshape items with rapid ease.

✦ The new Flash Pen Tool and its companion, the Subselect Tool, enhance the Toolbox with their precision path-drawing and point-editing capabilities.

✦   ✦   ✦

Working with the Drawing and Painting Tools

Flash 5 significantly revamped the former Toolbar and renamed it the *Toolbox*. Flash 5 also added two new tools: the *Pen Tool* and the *Subselect (Arrow) Tool*. Both of these new tools were described in detail in Chapter 26, "Working with Selections and the Pen Tool." In this chapter, we look at the rest of the drawing tools — the Pencil, Line, Oval, Rectangle, Brush, Dropper, Ink Bottle, Paint Bucket, and Eraser Tools.

Perhaps the most significant renovation of the Toolbox is in the area formerly referred to as the Modifier Tray. This is now called the *Options Tray*. Although that, in itself, is not a big deal, *this* is: For most tools, many of the former modifiers (or options) have been relocated to individual panels. General routines for accessing and managing panels were discussed in the Window menu section of Chapter 24, "Exploring the Interface: Panels, Settings, and More."

Choosing Colors

Whenever any Flash Drawing or Painting Tool is used, the stroke and fill colors are determined by the current settings of the color controls located in the Flash Toolbox. These controls are present regardless of which tool is being used. Although these controls operate like color chips that indicate the current color, they're really buttons: Click either Color button to open the current Swatches pop-up, shown in Figure 27-1, and select a new stroke or fill color.

In addition to the basic reorganization of the Toolbox, the color controls include three new buttons, arrayed across the bottom of the Color Tray. These are, from left to right, buttons for Default Stroke and Fill, None, and Swap. The Default button sets the stroke to black and the fill to white. The None button (only active with the Pen, Oval, and Rectangle Tools) sets the active control to apply no color. The Swap button swaps the current colors between the Stroke and Fill controls.

Figure 27-1: This is the current Swatches pop-up for the Pencil Tool.

Clicking either the Stroke or Fill Color buttons invokes the current Swatches pop-up. This pop-up displays the same Swatch that is currently loaded in the Swatches Panel. It includes a hexadecimal color entry box, another iteration of the None button, and a button that launches the Color Picker. For all drawing tools, elementary color selection is accomplished by clicking either the Stroke or Fill Color buttons and then choosing a color from the Swatches pop-up. More advanced color usage is detailed in the next chapter.

We've devoted Chapter 28, "Applying Color," to an explanation of Flash Color. It includes not only the details of working with Flash Color, but also a little primer on color theory, computer color, and Web color.

The Stroke and Fill Panels

Users of prior versions of Flash, when beginning to use the Drawing and Painting Tools, might well inquire about the disappearance of the controls for Line Thickness and Line Style, as well as the Fill Color control. But that's because these controls now reside in the Stroke and the Fill Panels, where they are now referred to as the Stroke Height, Stroke Style, and Fill Style controls. These panels, and the controls they contain, are consistently available regardless of which tool is being used. Panels are accessed from the Window menu, by choosing Window ⟳ Panels and then choosing the individual panel from the submenu.

Stroke Color

To select a color for a stroke that you are about to draw, click the Stroke Color button of the Stroke Panel (see Figure 27-2) to invoke the Swatches pop-up and then select a color. To change the color of a stroke that's already drawn, first select the item with the Arrow Tool, click the Stroke Color button of the Stroke Panel, and then select a new color from the Swatches pop-up.

Note Selecting stroke color and changing stroke color can be accomplished with either the Stroke Color button in the Toolbox or in the Stroke Panel. This same procedure can also be applied to paths drawn with the Pen Tool.

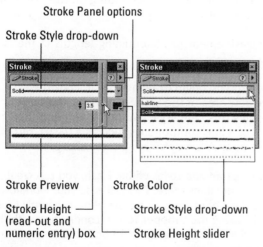

Figure 27-2: The Stroke Panel and Stroke Style drop-down

Stroke Height

In Flash 5, for all tools that draw or display a line or outline, the thickness of the line — or *stroke* — is controlled by either dragging the Stroke Height slider or by entering a value in the Stroke Height numeric entry box. When dragging the slider, the numeric entry box updates and displays a height readout analogous to the current position of the slider. This also functions as a precise numeric entry field. Simply enter a value to create a stroke with a specific height, or thickness. Permissible values range from 0 to 10, with fractions expressed in decimals.

Note   Depending upon the level of zoom, some lines may not be visible on screen — even though they will print correctly on a high-resolution printer.

Stroke Style

The Stroke Style drop-down offers seven stroke, or line, styles: Hairline, Solid, Dashed, Dotted, Ragged, Stippled, and Hatched.

Using the custom stroke styles

Click the Stroke Panel options (the triangular button at the upper right of the Stroke Panel) and then choose Custom (the only option) to access the Line Style dialog. The Line Style dialog, which remains unchanged from Flash 4, is used to generate custom line styles by selecting from a range of properties for each preset line. Basic properties include Stroke Weight and Sharp Corners. Depending on the preset line style, additional properties are available for each style.

Note   Points are the default unit of measurement for determining lengths in the Line Style dialog.

To closely examine a custom line before you begin drawing with it, click the Zoom 4× check box beneath the preview area of the Line Style dialog. Note the Sharp Corners check box, which toggles this Line Style feature on and off. The Sharp Corners feature ensures that the end of a line component (such as a dash), rather than a space, extends to each corner, so that the corners appears sharp.

Tip   Although there is no way to save custom line styles within Flash, you can create a separate .FLA file and save your favorite lines there. This will ease your workflow if you want to make more extensive use of Custom Line Styles. You can apply these styles quite easily to other lines by using the Dropper Tool in conjunction with the Ink Bottle Tool. For more information, see the sections on both the Dropper and the Ink Bottle Tools in this chapter.

Hairline line style

If you need a line that always appears one pixel wide, and does not scale subject to zoom, choose Hairline from the Stroke Style drop-down.

Solid Line Style

The Solid Line Style draws a solid, unbroken line. The customization variables for the Solid Line Style are limited to Thickness and Sharp Corners. These two variables are always available in the Line Style dialog, regardless of which Line Style is being customized.

> **Note**   The Solid Line Style is the optimal Line Style for Web viewing because it requires fewer points to describe it and, consequently, is less file intensive. The smaller file sizes theoretically translate into faster download times when the artwork is transmitted over the Web. However, the difference in file size may be so nominal that the difference in download time that it saves is negligible.

Dashed Line Style

The Dashed Line Style draws a solid line with regularly spaced gaps. Customization variables that appear in the Line Style dialog for the Dashed Line Style are Line Thickness, Sharp Corners, Dash Length, and Gap Length. Both Dash Length and Gap Length are precisely adjustable by changing the numeric entries in their respective fields.

Dotted Line Style

The Dotted Line Style draws a dotted line with evenly spaced gaps. At first glance, the Dotted Line Style appears to have only one variable — Dot Spacing. Change the numeric entry in this field to control the quality of the custom dashed line. But don't overlook the Thickness drop down, which offers a range of settings for Dot Thickness.

Ragged Line Style

The Ragged Line Style draws a ragged line with various gaps between the dots. The quality of both the raggedness and the gaps are adjustable. The Ragged Line Style has three parameters unique to ragged lines: Pattern, Wave Height, and Wave Length. Each has a drop-down menu with multiple variables that, in combination, afford myriad possibilities.

Stippled Line Style

The Stippled Line Style draws a stippled line that goes a long way toward mimicking an artist's hand-stippling technique. The qualities of stippling are adjustable with three variables unique to the nature of stippled lines: Dot Size, Dot Variation, and Density. Each variable has a drop-down with multiple settings that can be combined to generate a staggering array of line effects.

Hatched Line Style

The Hatched Line Style draws a hatched line of amazing complexity that can be used to accurately mimic an artist's hand-drawn hatched-line technique. As shown in Figure 27-3, the numerous hatching qualities are highly adjustable, making this perhaps the most complex of all the Flash drawing tools. The Line Style dialog has six parameters unique to hatched lines: Thickness (hatch-specific), Space, Jiggle, Rotate, Curve, and Length.

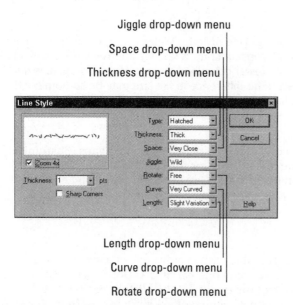

Figure 27-3: The Hatched Line Style wins the prize for the most variables. With these six drop-down lists, a plethora of unique line effects can be hatched.

Note   The Hatched Line Style thickness settings are in addition to the usual Thickness settings that are available as a default with the Line Style dialog. Combined, they offer a much higher level of adjustment. The default thickness (measured in points) defines the thickness of the overall hatched line, while this additional thickness setting defines the thickness of the individual scrawls that comprise the aggregate hatched line.

Applying and changing fills with the Fill Panel

The Oval, Rectangle, Brush, and Paint Bucket Tools all rely on the Fill Panel (shown in Figure 27-4) to set or customize the type and color of fill applied to a new shape that is about to be drawn, or to change the color of a selected shape (or shapes).

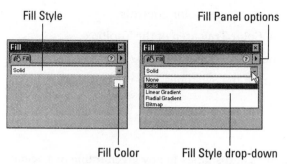

Fill Style

Fill Panel options

Fill Color

Fill Style drop-down

Figure 27-4: The Fill Panel and the Fill Style drop-down, which offers five kinds of fills: None, Solid, Linear Gradient, Radial Gradient, and Bitmap.

The Fill Style can be changed as follows: Choose a Fill Style from the drop-down of the Fill Panel. Then click the Fill Color button on the Toolbox to invoke the Swatches pop-up. If you've chosen a Solid Fill Style, then select a color for your fill. If you've chosen either gradient, clicking the Fill Color button causes a row of gradient color chips to appear at the bottom of the Swatches pop-up. Choose a gradient for your fill. For a more exhaustive discussion of color, including working with swatches, and creating and selecting gradients, please refer to Chapter 28, "Applying Color."

Adjusting Stroke and Color

Changes in stroke and color apply to lines or curves drawn with the Pen, Line, Pencil, Oval, and Rectangle Tools. For ovals and rectangles, the changes apply only to the outline, not to the fill.

Changing Stroke Height

To change the Stroke Height, or Thickness, of a line, follow these steps:

1. Use the Arrow Tool to select the line.

2. If it's not already open, access the Stroke Panel from the Window menu by choosing Window ⇨ Panels ⇨ Stroke.

3. Choose a new Stroke Height either by using the Stroke Height slider or by entering a new Stroke Height in the numeric entry field and pressing Enter.

Changing Stroke Color

To change the Stroke Color of a line, follow these steps:

1. Select the line with the Arrow Tool.

2. Then, locate either one of these Stroke Color controls:

- The Stroke Color in the Color Tray area of the Toolbox
- The Stroke Color on the Stroke Panel (Window ⇨ Panels ⇨ Stroke)

3. Finally, choose a new color from the Swatches pop-up.

The Pencil Tool

The Pencil Tool is used to draw lines and shapes in any given frame of a scene and — at first glance — operates much like a real pencil. (A frame is the basic unit of a Flash creation. Frames and scenes are described in Chapter 30, "Exploring the Timeline.") But a deeper examination reveals that — unlike a real pencil — the Flash Pencil Tool can be set to straighten lines and smooth curves as you draw. It can also be set to recognize or correct basic geometric shapes. Or, you can use the Pencil Tool options to create specific shapes. In addition, you can modify lines and shapes manually.

When the Pencil Tool is active, one option appears in the Options Tray. This is the Pencil Mode pop-up menu, shown in Figure 27-5, which sets the Pencil Tool's current drawing mode. Users of prior versions of Flash might inquire about the disappearance of the controls for Stroke Weight and Line Style — these now reside in the Stroke Panel, where they are referred to as the Line Style and Stroke Height controls.

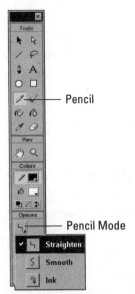

Figure 27-5: The Pencil Tool and the Pencil Mode option are shown here with pop-up, which reveals the Straighten, Smooth, and Ink processing options.

Using the Pencil Mode pop-up options

The Pencil Mode pop-up menu has options that control how Flash processes the lines that you draw. That's right, unlike any other program we know of, Flash can p-r-o-c-e-s-s the lines that you draw, as you draw them! We call this *line processing* — it's a kind of shape recognition specific to the Pencil Tool that may make drawing easier for artists who are draftsmanship-challenged. It also has the benefit of generating drawings that are simpler and less complex (meaning that they are described by fewer points). As a result, the drawings transmit across the Web at greater speed because they require less data, which means a smaller file size, to describe them. The Pencil Tool has three processing options. Two are Straighten and Smooth; the third, for those who prefer the characteristics of hand drawing, is Ink Mode. Working in Ink Mode lets you turn off all line processing.

Understanding line processing

So, what is meant by processing the lines? Processing differs from shape recognition in that it is automatic and occurs while the line is *in the process of being drawn*. This differs from shape recognition with the Arrow Tool because that occurs after the line is drawn — in fact, it can be done at any time after the line is drawn. (For more information on shape recognition, refer to the section on the Arrow Tool, in Chapter 26, "Working with Selections and the Pen Tool.") The Straighten, Smooth, and Ink processing options of the Pencil Tool control the degree to which automatic processing occurs. Each of these options is detailed in subsequent sections of this discussion of the Pencil Tool. These options are also affected by the settings in the Drawing Settings Panel of the Editing tab of the Preferences dialog (choose Edit ⇨ Preferences and click the Editing tab).

 Cross-Reference In addition to the treatment here, the settings that control line processing and shape recognition are explained in Chapter 24, "Exploring the Interface: Panels, Settings, and More."

Straighten option

Drawing with the Straighten option processes your drawings while taking into account line and shape recognition. This means that separate lines are automatically connected, lines that approximately straight are straightened, and wobbly curves are smoothed. In short, approximate shapes are recognized and automatically adjusted.

Smooth option

Drawing with the Smooth option reduces the zeal with which Flash automatically processes your drawings. With Smooth option, line straightening and shape recognition are disabled. You can draw curved lines, and they will be smoothed slightly. Additionally, a line that ends near another line will be joined to it.

Ink option

Drawing with the Ink option turns off all Flash processing. You're left with the lines as you've drawn them. Your lines are *not* smoothed, straightened, or joined.

Caution   For Web deployment, lines drawn with the Ink option can become unnecessarily complex. If this happens to you, these lines can be selected with the Arrow Tool and then slightly optimized by choosing either Modify ⇨ Smooth or Modify ⇨ Optimize from the menu.

You can also choose to smooth, straighten, or join lines and shapes that have been drawn with the Ink option simply by using the Arrow Tool to select what you've drawn and then using either the Arrow Tool's Smooth or Straighten options. Or, for maximum control, manually edit extraneous points with either the Pen or the Subselect Tool.

The Line Tool

Drawing with the Line Tool creates a perfectly straight line that extends straight from the starting point to the end point, simply choose the tool and start drawing. As shown in Figure 27-6, the Line Tool has no options on the Options Tray. Line Thickness is chosen from the Stroke Height control of the Stroke Panel, while the basic Line Style may be chosen from the Stroke Style drop-down. As shown in Figures 27-2 and 27-3, Custom Line Styles may be created with the Line Style dialog, which is accessed from the Stroke Panel options.

Figure 27-6: The Line Tool has no options.

Depress the Shift key while drawing to constrain the Line Tool to angles of 45 degrees or 90 degrees.

The Oval Tool

Drawing with the Oval Tool creates a perfectly smooth oval. Ovals are drawn by dragging diagonally from one "corner" of the oval to the other. Press the Shift key at any time while the shape is being drawn to constrain the shape to a perfect circle. As shown in Figure 27-7, the Oval Tool has no options.

— Oval

Figure 27-7: The Oval Tool
has no options.

To either choose or change the Stroke Height or Style, use the Stroke Panel. To choose or change the fill of an oval, use the Fill Panel.

The Rectangle Tool

Drawing with the Rectangle Tool creates a perfect rectangle, which means that all four of the corners are at 90-degree angles. Rectangles are drawn by dragging from one corner of the rectangle to the other. Pressing the Shift key at any time while the shape is being drawn creates a perfect square. As shown in Figure 27-8, the Rectangle Tool has one option—Rounded Rectangle Radius.

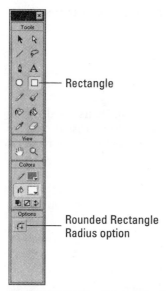

Figure 27-8: The Rectangle Tool
has one option in the Options Tray:
Rounded Rectangle Radius.

As with the Oval Tool, to choose or change the Stroke Height or Style of a
Rectangle, use the Stroke Panel. To choose or change the fill, use the Fill Panel.

The Rounded Rectangle Radius Tool is useful for making rounded rectangles —
a.k.a. interactive button shapes. Click this option to elicit the Rectangle Settings
dialog (shown in Figure 27-9), which accepts numeric values between 0 and 999.
Subsequent rectangles will be drawn with this value applied to the corner radius,
until the value entered in this dialog is either changed or returned to zero. Note
that this button is *not* a toggle; to turn off rounded rectangle drawing, click the
option and enter a value of zero.

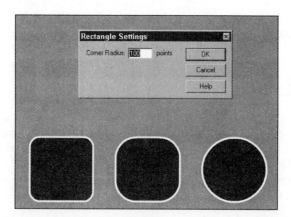

Figure 27-9: The Rectangle
Settings dialog with three
shapes drawn with the following
Corner Radius settings: (from
right to left) 25, 50, and 100.

Using the (Paint) Brush Tool

The Brush Tool is used to paint with brushlike strokes and to fill enclosed areas. Unlike the Pencil Tool, which creates a single, solid line, the Brush Tool creates filled shapes with outlines of zero thickness. (This is easily demonstrated by painting a stroke with the Brush, then choosing a new color for the Ink Bottle, and then clicking that brushed line with the Ink Bottle. The Brush line of zero thickness will acquire the line thickness and color from the Ink Bottle—if there were no line, the Ink Bottle would be unable to alter the stroke in this manner.) The fills can be solid colors, gradients, or fills derived from bitmaps. Additionally, the Brush Tool options permit you to paint in unusual ways: You can choose to paint in front of or behind an element, or you can apply paint only within a specific filled area, or within a selection. The Brush Mode option drop-down reveals five painting modes that are amazingly useful for a wide range of effects when applying brush strokes: Paint Normal, Paint Fills, Paint Behind, Paint Selection, and Paint Inside, as shown in Figure 27-10.

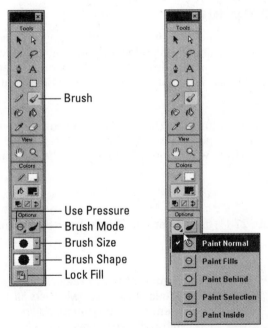

Figure 27-10: The Brush Tool and options (left); the Brush Mode drop-down (right)

Depending on whether you have a pressure-sensitive tablet connected to your computer, four or five options appear in the Options Tray when the Brush Tool is active. The Use Pressure option—which only appears if you have a pressure-sensitive tablet attached to your computer—and the Brush Mode are both unique to the Brush Tool. The Lock Fill option is common to both the Brush Tool and the Paint

Bucket (which is discussed subsequently in this chapter). Although similar to Stroke Weight and Line Style, the Brush Size and Brush Shape drop-downs are also fairly unique to the Brush Tool. In the following sections, we run through all of the Brush options — just to make certain that we're clear on all points, even if there is some review.

> **Note**   Painting with the background color (such as white) is not the same as erasing. Painting with the background color may appear to accomplish something similar to erasing. However, you are, in fact, creating a filled item that can be selected, moved, deleted, or reshaped. Only erasing erases!

To choose or change the Brush Color, either click the Fill Color button on the Toolbox, or use the Fill Panel. Because the Brush Tool creates filled shapes with outlines of zero thickness, the Stroke Color button is defunct when the Brush Tool is active.

Using the Brush Mode option

The Brush Mode option is a drop-down menu with five modes for applying brush strokes: Paint Normal, Paint Fills, Paint Behind, Paint Selection, and Paint Inside. Used in conjunction with selections, the Brush Modes option yields a broad range of sophisticated paint masking capabilities. True masking is fully described and defined in Chapter 32, "Drawing in Flash."

The following images depict various ways in which the Brush Modes interact with drawn and painted elements. The base image is a solid gray rounded rectangle drawn with a black, hatched outline. Three white lines of various widths are drawn on top of the gray fill of the rectangle.

Paint Normal Mode

Paint Normal Mode, shown in Figure 27-11, applies brush strokes over the top of any lines or fills.

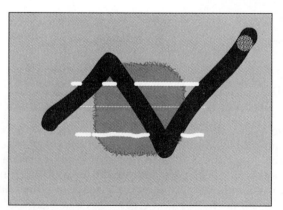

Figure 27-11: In Paint Normal Mode, a black scrawl covers all elements: background, outline, fill, and drawn lines.

Paint Fills Mode

Paint Fills Mode, shown in Figure 27-12, applies brush strokes to replace any fills, but leaves lines untouched.

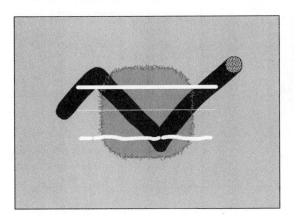

Figure 27-12: In Paint Fills Mode, a black scrawl covers both the gray fill and the background—which, surprisingly, is considered a fill in this case.

Paint Behind Mode

Paint Behind Mode applies brush strokes only to blank areas and leaves all fills, lines or other items untouched. As shown in Figure 27-13, the only parts of the stroke that cover are those over the background. Effectively, the scrawl has gone behind the entire shape. If the stroke had originated within the gray fill, it would have covered the fill and gone behind the drawn white lines.

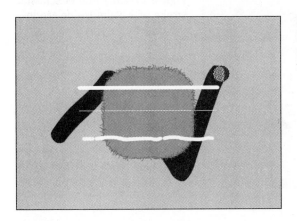

Figure 27-13: Scrawling again in Paint Behind Mode, the only parts of the stroke that cover are those over the background.

Paint Selection Mode

Paint Selection Mode applies brush strokes only to selected fills. In Figure 27-14, a selection was made by shift-clicking both the gray fill and the upper white line.

The same black scrawl has been drawn with the selection described in the previous figure still active, using Paint Selection Mode.

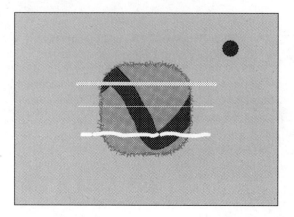

Figure 27-14: Only the selected gray fill has been covered by the brush stroke.

Paint Inside Mode

Paint Inside Mode, shown in Figure 27-15, applies brush strokes only to the singular fill area where the brush stroke was first initiated. As the name implies, Paint Inside never paints over lines. If you initiate painting from an empty area, the brush strokes won't affect any existing fills or lines, which approximates the same effect as the Paint Behind setting.

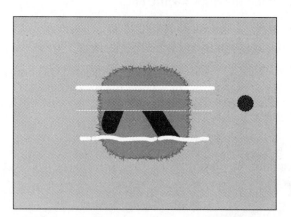

Figure 27-15: Another scrawled stroke with Paint Inside Mode — the only difference between this stroke and the others is that it was initiated over the gray fill.

Using the Brush Size option

The Brush Size option, shown in Figure 27-16, is a simple pop-up menu with a range of ten preset brush sizes. Although the sizes are shown as circles, the diameter size applies to all brush shapes. In the case of an oblong brush, the diameter size refers to the broadest span of the brush. You can combine brush sizes and shapes for a great variety of custom brush tips.

Figure 27-16: The Brush Size drop-down reveals ten well-distributed brush sizes, ranging from pin line to humongous.

 Note

In Flash, the apparent brush size is always related to the Zoom setting. Therefore, identical brush diameters applied at different Zoom settings result in different-sized brush marks.

Using the Brush Shape option

The Brush Shape option, shown in Figure 27-17, is a simple pop-up menu with nine possible brush shapes that are based on the circle, ellipse, square, rectangle, and line shapes. The oval, rectangle, and line shapes are available in several angles. Although no custom brush shapes are available, you can combine these stock brush shapes with the range of brush sizes to generate a variety of nearly custom brush tips. When using shapes other than circles, note that the diameter sizes indicated in the Brush Size drop-down apply to the broadest area of any brush shape.

Figure 27-17: The Brush Shape drop-down is loaded with nine preset brush shapes.

Using the Brush Lock Fill option

The Lock Fill option is a toggle that controls how Flash handles areas filled with a gradient or bitmap fill. Once this button is pressed, all subsequent areas (or shapes) that are painted with the same gradient or bitmap fill appear to be part of a single, continuous filled shape. This option locks the angle, size, and point of origin of the current gradient so that it remains consistent throughout the scene. This capability is useful, for example, if you are creating a gradated sunset sky with gradated clouds, and the clouds must appear to be part of one continuous gradient, while the sky needs to appear to be another.

Cross-Reference   Working with gradient colors is discussed in Chapter 28, "Applying Color."

To demonstrate the distinction between painting with or without the Brush Lock Fill option, as shown in Figure 27-18, on the left, we created five shapes and filled them with a gradient, using the Paint Inside setting — with Lock Fill off. The gradient is noticeably not aligned from one shape to the next. On the right, those same shapes were repainted with that same gradient, still using the Paint Inside setting — but with Lock Fill on. Note how the gradient is now aligned from one shape to the next.

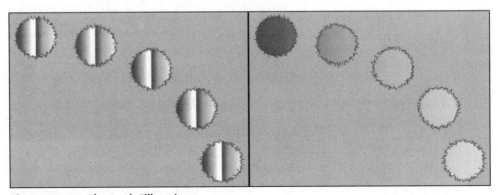

Figure 27-18: The Lock Fill option

Note   When the Dropper Tool is used to pick up a fill or gradient from a scene, the Lock Fill button is automatically engaged.

Using the Brush Pressure option

The Brush Pressure option appears only if you have a pressure-sensitive tablet. This option button is a simple toggle that is used to enable or disable the finer capabilities of a pressure-sensitive tablet. With pressure-sensitivity enabled, the size of the brush stroke increases with increased drawing pressure.

The difference between the Brush Tool and the Pencil Tool

A pencil stroke has no fill, whereas a brush stroke is technically a filled outline of zero thickness. Regardless of the width of a pencil stroke, when viewed as an outline, it will *always* appear as a single vector. Conversely, when viewed as outlines, brush strokes of varied thickness will be exhibited as outlines whose breadth varies according to the thickness of the stroke. Yet the outlines themselves will always be outlines (or vectors) of zero thickness.

Figure 27-19 displays a pencil line and a brush line, each drawn with a Stroke Height of 10, (A) in what is regarded as regular mode (View ⇨ Antialias), and again (B) as outlines (View ⇨ Outlines). The same lines are displayed both above and below. This demonstrates the technical detail that brush strokes are filled vector outlines of zero thickness, while a pencil stroke is a stroked vector of zero thickness.

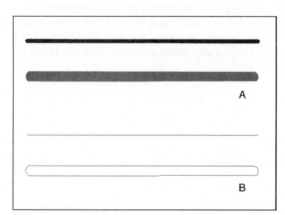

Figure 27-19: Comparing the Brush and Pencil Tools

As shown in Figure 27-20, these differences have demonstrable consequences when pencil strokes and brush strokes are edited with the selection tools: A brush stroke can be pulled out of shape, whereas a pencil stroke can only be bent. The results of each operation are shown at the right.

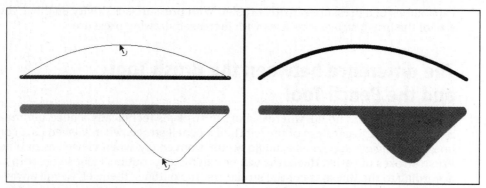

Figure 27-20: A brush stroke (bottom) can be pulled out of shape, whereas a pencil stroke (top) can only be bent.

The Dropper Tool

The Dropper Tool (shown in Figure 27-21), which is found at the bottom of the Toolbox tools, is used to acquire (or copy) the color and style information from existing pencil lines, brush strokes, and fills. The Dropper Tool has no options, but then it doesn't need options. That's because the Flash Dropper Tool performs a function entirely unlike any dropper tool in any other program that we know of.

 — Dropper

Figure 27-21: The Dropper Tool is an amazingly useful "one-trick pony." It has no options.

When the Dropper Tool isn't hovering over a line, fill, or brush stroke, its cursor is similar to the Dropper icon in the Drawing Toolbox. However, the Dropper Tool's cursor changes as follows to indicate when it is over a line or a fill:

✦ When the cursor is over a line, a tiny pencil appears to the lower right of the standard Dropper Tool cursor.

✦ When the cursor is over a fill, a tiny brush appears to the lower right of the standard Dropper Tool cursor.

When the Dropper Tool is over a line, fill, or brush stroke, and the Shift key is pressed, the cursor changes to an inverted U shape. In this mode (that is, when you Shift+Click), use of the Dropper Tool changes the attributes for all editing tools in Flash (for instance, the Pencil, Brush, Ink Bottle, and Text Tools) to match the attributes of the area clicked. That's right! . . . Shift-clicking with the Dropper Tool acquires the attributes of the clicked item and simultaneously changes the color and style settings for the Ink Bottle Tool, as well as the Pencil Tool and the Text Tool.

✦ When the clicked item is a line, the Dropper Tool is automatically swapped for the Ink Bottle Tool, which facilitates the application of the acquired attributes to another line. Similarly, when the clicked item is a fill, the Dropper Tool is automatically swapped for the Paint Bucket Tool. This facilitates the application of acquired fill attributes to another fill.

✦ When the Dropper Tool is used to acquire a fill that is a bitmap, the Dropper Tool is automatically swapped for the Paint Bucket Tool and a thumbnail of the bitmap image appears in place of the Fill Color option in the Color Tray of the Toolbox.

This composite image shown in Figure 27-22 shows all Dropper Tool cursors as they appear when the Dropper is brought to hover over various types of lines and fills. The figure shows the Dropper Tool:

✦ Alone (A)

✦ Over a gradient fill created with the Rectangle Tool (B)

✦ Over a white line created with the Rectangle Tool (C)

✦ Over a line painted with the brush (D)

✦ Over a line drawn with the Pencil Tool (F)

✦ After pressing Shift and clicking to acquire the attributes of the clicked item and simultaneously change the color and style settings for the Ink Bottle Tool, as well as the Pencil Tool and the Text Tool (E)

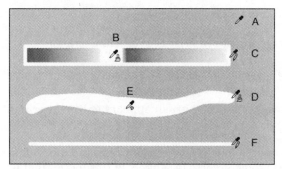

Figure 27-22: The Dropper Tool cursors

 Note

The Dropper Tool can be extremely helpful when changing the attributes of multiple lines. However, the Ink Bottle cannot apply acquired attributes to lines that are grouped. To work around this limitation, you must first ungroup the lines, then apply the attributes to the lines (either individually or as a multiple selection), and then regroup the lines.

The attributes of a group can be acquired using the Dropper Tool if the contents are being edited. For more information on editing groups, please refer to Chapter 30, "Exploring the Timeline."

 New Feature

When used to acquire colors, the Toolbox Dropper Tool is limited to acquiring colors from the Flash interface, which includes not only items created in Flash (that is, on or next to the Stage), but also icons, buttons, and menus of the Flash application. However, the Droppers that are accessed from the Color Palettes of the Mixer, Stroke, Fill, and Character Panels can acquire colors from anywhere on the entire computer interface, such as the system background, items on the desktop, or items that are open in other applications. For more information about this new feat, refer to Chapter 28, "Applying Color."

The Ink Bottle Tool

The Ink Bottle Tool, shown in Figure 27-23, is used to change the color, style, and thickness of existing outlines. It is most often used in conjunction with the Dropper Tool. When the Ink Bottle Tool is in use, attention to three options may be required: The current Stroke Color option on the Toolbox or the Stroke Panel, and both the Line Height and Stroke Style options of the Stroke Panel.

 Note

The Ink Bottle Tool reveals the underlying consistency in the way that Flash "sees" lines. Lines, outlines, and those *lines of zero thickness* that describe strokes of the Brush are all treated as lines by the Ink Bottle Tool.

Figure 27-23: The Ink Bottle Tool has no options on the Toolbox.

Caution When you click a selected line with the Ink Bottle Tool, all other *selected* lines (if any) are changed simultaneously.

The Ink Bottle is especially useful for applying custom line styles to multiple lines. You can build a collection of custom line styles either off-screen, or in a special custom line palette that is saved as a single-frame Flash movie. You can then acquire these line styles whenever necessary.

Caution Depending on the level of zoom, some lines may not appear on the screen — although they will print correctly on a high-resolution printer. Stroke Weight may also be adjusted in the Stroke Style dialog that is accessible by choosing Custom from the Stroke Style option drop-down list (the arrow at the top right of the panel).

The Paint Bucket Tool

The Paint Bucket Tool is used to fill enclosed areas with color, gradients, or bitmap fills. Although the Paint Bucket Tool is a more robust tool than the Ink Bottle, and can be used independently of the Dropper Tool, it's often used in conjunction with the Dropper Tool. That's because, as was discussed earlier in the section on the Dropper Tool, when the Dropper Tool is clicked on a fill, it first acquires the fill attributes of that fill and then automatically swaps to the Paint Bucket Tool. Because this *acquire and swap* function of the Dropper Tool readily facilitates the application of acquired fill attributes to another fill, the Bucket Tool is frequently used in tandem with the Dropper. When the Paint Bucket Tool is active, as shown in Figure 27-24, four options are available from the Toolbox: Lock Fill, Transform Fill, Gap Size, and Fill Color. The Gap Size drop-down, which is shown at the right, offers four settings to control how Flash handles gaps when filling with the Bucket Tool.

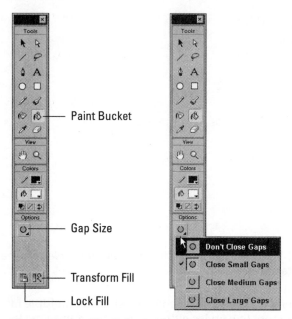

Figure 27-24: The Paint Bucket Tool and its options

When the Dropper Tool is used to acquire a fill that is a broken-apart bitmap, the Dropper Tool is automatically swapped for the Paint Bucket Tool and a thumbnail of the bitmap image appears in place of the Fill Color Option chip. This procedure also automatically engages the Paint Bucket Lock Fill Option. For more information about working with bitmap fills, refer to Chapter 34, "Using Bitmaps and Other Media with Flash."

Caution   Using the Paint Bucket to paint with white (or the background color) is not the same as erasing. Painting with white (or the background color) may appear to accomplish something similar to erasing. However, you are, in fact, creating a filled item that can be selected, moved, deleted, or reshaped. Only erasing erases!

Like the Ink Bottle, the Paint Bucket can be especially useful for applying custom fill styles to multiple items. You can build a collection of custom fill styles either off-screen or in a special, saved, custom-fills-palette, single-frame Flash movie. You can then acquire these fills whenever necessary.

Caution

If you click with the Paint Bucket Tool on one of several selected fills, *all* of the selected fills will be changed with the new fill.

Using the Paint Bucket Gap Size option

As shown in Figure 27-24, the Gap Size option drop-down offers four settings that control how the Paint Bucket Tool treats gaps when filling. These settings are Don't Close Gaps, Close Small Gaps, Close Medium Gaps, and Close Large Gaps. These tolerance settings enable Flash to fill an outline if the end points of the outline aren't completely joined, leaving an open shape. If the gaps are too large, you may have to close them manually.

Note

The level of zoom changes the apparent size of gaps. Although the actual size of gaps is unaffected by zoom, the Paint Bucket's interpretation of the gap is dependent upon the current Zoom setting. Thus, the Paint Bucket's behavior in relation to Gap Size is liable to change with the Zoom setting.

Using the Paint Bucket Lock Fill option

The Paint Bucket's Lock Fill option is the same as the Brush Lock Fill option — it controls how Flash handles areas filled with gradient color or bitmaps. When this button is turned on, all areas (or shapes) that are painted with the same gradient will appear to be part of a single, continuous, filled shape. The Lock Fill option locks the angle, size, and point of origin of the current gradient to remain constant throughout the scene. For further information, please refer to the earlier discussion of the Brush Tool.

Tip

When the Dropper Tool is used to pick up a fill or gradient from the scene, this Lock Fill button is automatically engaged.

Using the Paint Bucket Transform Fill option (a.k.a. the Reshape Arrow cursor)

The Transform Tool option button is used to adjust the size, angle, and center of a gradient or fill, including bitmap fills. When the Transform Tool option is selected, the Paint Bucket Tool automatically becomes a *Reshape Arrow cursor*. (This Reshape Arrow cursor is different from either of the Arrow Tool's Rotate or Scale options.) This is a lot like scooting, rotating, or skewing a larger piece of material so that a different portion is displayed within a smaller frame. To use the Reshape Arrow to transform a fill, first select the Transform Tool option, and then simply click an existing gradient or fill. A set of three or four adjustment handles appears, depending on the type of fill. With this option, three transformations can be performed on a fill: adjusting the fill's center point, rotating the fill, and scaling the fill.

Adjusting the center point with the Reshape Arrow

To adjust the center point, follow these steps:

1. Deselect the fill if it has been previously selected.

2. Choose the Paint Bucket Tool.

3. Choose the Transform Fill option.

4. Click the fill.

5. Bring the Reshape Arrow Cursor to the small circular handle at the center of the fill until it changes to a four-arrow cursor, pointing left and right, up and down like a compass, indicating that this handle can now be used to move the center point in any direction.

6. Drag the center circular handle in any direction you want to move the center of the fill.

Figure 27-25 shows the Reshape Arrow cursor (A). It transforms into a compass point when it's brought near the round center handle of a gradient or fill (B). Click the center handle and drag to move the center point (C).

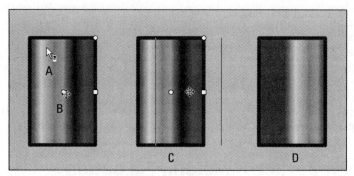

Figure 27-25: Repositioning a gradient fill's center

Rotating a fill with the Reshape Arrow

To rotate a gradient or bitmap fill, find the small circular handle that's at the corner of the fill. (In a radial gradient, choose the middle circular handle.) This circular handle is used for rotating a fill around the center point. Click the handle and four circular arrows appear, indicating that this handle will rotate the fill about the center point.

Figure 27-26 shows how the Reshape Arrow cursor becomes a Rotate cursor when it is brought near the circular handle at the corner of a gradient fill (A). Click the circular handle with the Rotate cursor and rotate the gradient fill (B).

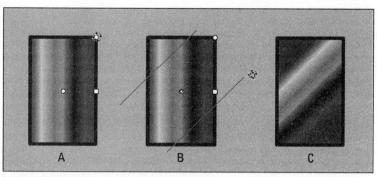

Figure 27-26: Rotating a gradient fill

Reshape Arrow Anomalies

Fills can differ in their characteristics when you use the Reshape Arrow, primarily in the placement of their handles, subject to a number of variables, including whether they are applied horizontally or vertically:

✦ Some fills may not have the full complement of Reshape Arrow cursors available.

✦ For a horizontally applied fill: To rotate the fill, find the small circular handle that is at the *upper right*, at the top of the hatched line. This circular handle is used for rotating a horizontally applied gradient or fill around the center point. Click the handle and four circular arrows appear, indicating that this handle will rotate the fill about the center point.

✦ For a vertically applied fill: To rotate the fill, find the small circular handle that is at the *upper left*, at the end of the hatched line. This circular handle is used for rotating a vertically applied gradient or fill around the center point. Click the handle and four circular arrows appear, indicating that this handle will rotate the fill about the center point.

✦ These general characteristics may differ if a fill (or bitmap fill) has been variously copied, rotated, or pasted in any number of ways. The fundamental rule is this: Round center handle moves the center point; round corner handle rotates; round edge handles skew either vertically or horizontally; square-edge handles scale either vertically or horizontally; and the square-corner handle scales symmetrically.

✦ Skewing and scaling of bitmap fills may have a counterintuitive effect: If the bitmap fill is scaled *smaller*, it will tile to fill the space of the original fill.

✦ Due to their nature, gradient fills don't support skewing; they can only be scaled on the horizontal axis.

Skewing the fill with the Reshape Arrow

To skew a bitmap fill horizontally, find the small round handle at the middle of the right-hand border. This round handle is used to skew the gradient or fill. Click the handle and arrows appear, parallel to the edge of the fill, indicating the directions in which this handle will skew the fill.

Figure 27-27 shows how the Reshape Arrow cursor changes to the Skew Arrow cursor when it is brought near a small round horizontal skew handle (first image). Click and drag the round horizontal skew handle with the Skew Arrow cursor to skew the bitmap fill (second image). Release the skew handle to view the result (third image). Note that the skew procedure is still active, meaning that the skew may be further modified — this behavior is common to all functions of the Reshape Arrow. To skew a bitmap fill vertically, locate the vertical skew handle. Vertical skew is functionally equivalent to skewing horizontally.

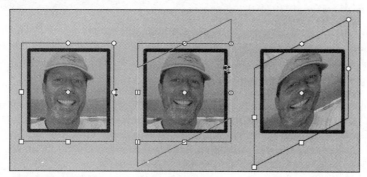

Figure 27-27: Skewing a bitmap fill

Figure 27-28 hones in on radial gradients. A radial gradient has slight variations from a linear gradient, mostly as regards the placement of the handles. So here's a quick tour: The Reshape Arrow cursor (A); Center Point cursor (B); Skew cursor (C) and Skew handle (G); Radius cursor (D, F) and Radius handle (H); and, finally, the Rotate cursor (E) and Rotate handle (I).

Symmetrically adjusting the scale with the Reshape Arrow

To resize a bitmap fill symmetrically, find the small square-corner handle, which is usually located at the lower-left corner of the fill. This square-corner handle is used to resize the fill while retaining the aspect ratio. The Symmetrical Resize cursor, shown in Figure 27-29, has diagonal arrows, and appears when the Reshape Arrow cursor is brought into proximity of this square-corner handle, indicating the direction(s) in which the handle will resize the fill. Click and drag the square-corner handle to scale the fill symmetrically.

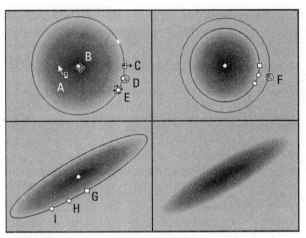

Figure 27-28: Adjusting radial gradients: The final skewed, scaled (with the Radius handle), and rotated gradient is shown in the lower right.

Figure 27-29: The Symmetrical Resize cursor appears when the Reshape Arrow cursor is the square-corner handle.

Asymmetrically adjusting the scale with the Reshape Arrow

To resize a bitmap fill asymmetrically, find a small square handle on either a vertical or a horizontal edge, depending whether you want to affect the width or height of the fill. The Asymmetrical Resize cursor, which has arrows that appear perpendicular to the edge, appears when the Reshape Arrow cursor is brought into proximity of any one of these square-edge handles, indicating the direction in which this handle will resize the fill, as shown in Figure 27-30. Click and drag a handle to reshape the fill.

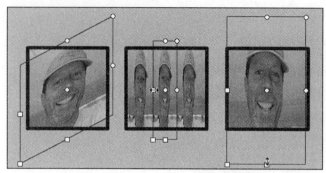

Figure 27-30: The Asymmetrical Resize cursor appears when the Reshape Arrow cursor is brought into proximity of the square-edge handle.

Note   The center of Figure 27-30 is a good example of a situation in which scaling a bitmap fill with the Reshape Arrow cursor may have a counterintuitive effect. When a bitmap fill is scaled in either dimension so that it is *smaller* than the shape that encloses it, this causes it to tile — or repeat — and fill the space of the original fill. As you can see, your author takes a rather narrow view of this feature.

The Eraser Tool

Although the Eraser Tool is neither a Drawing nor a Painting Tool, we feel that it belongs together with the Drawing and Painting Tools rather than orphaned in a category of its own. After all, without the Eraser Tool to complement the Drawing and Painting Tools, the process of Drawing and Painting might get impossibly complex — one mistake and you'd have to start over. The Eraser Tool is used in concert with the Drawing and Painting Tools to obtain final, usable art. As the name implies, the Eraser Tool is primarily used for erasing. When the Eraser Tool is active, three options appear in the Options Tray, as shown in Figure 27-31. The Erase Mode option and the Eraser Shape option are both drop-down menus with multiple options. The third option, the Faucet button, is used to clear enclosed areas of fill.

The only alternative to using the Eraser Tool to remove graphic elements or areas of drawings is to select them and then delete them by pressing either the Delete or the Backspace key.

Caution   As has been mentioned previously, in context with various Drawing and Painting Tools, Drawing or Painting with white (or the current background color) is *not* the equivalent of erasing. Only the Eraser Tool erases! Either use the simple Eraser Tool or harness the power of the Faucet option to take away filled areas and lines. Of all the things that we have repeated about the Flash Tools, if you don't "get" this one, it can really come back to bite you!

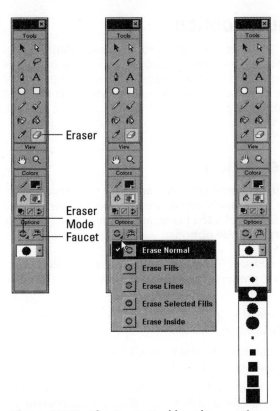

Figure 27-31: The Eraser Tool has three options: the Erase Mode, Eraser Shape, and the Faucet. Both the Mode and Shape options have menus.

 Note The Eraser Tool only erases lines and fills that are in the current frame of the scene. It won't erase groups, symbols, or text. When you need to erase a part of a group, you have two options: Select the group and choose Edit ➪ Edit Selected from the Menu Bar, or select the group and choose Modify ➪ Ungroup from the Menu Bar.

Using the Eraser Shape option

The Eraser Shape option defines both the size and shape of the eraser. As shown in Figure 27-31, it's a simple drop-down menu with ten brushes available in two shapes: circular and square. These are arrayed in two banks of five sizes each, ranging from small to large.

Using the Eraser's Faucet option

The Eraser Tool's Faucet option is Flash's version of selective annihilation — kind of like a neutron bomb. The Faucet option deletes an entire line segment or area of fill with a single click. Using the Faucet option is the equivalent of selecting and deleting an entire line or fill in a single step. Select the Eraser Tool, and then choose the Faucet Option button. Click the offending item to say goodbye. Clicking a selected line or fill erases all selected lines or fills.

Using the Erase Mode option

The Erase Mode option both controls and limits what and how the Eraser Tool erases. As shown in Figure 27-31, the Erase Mode pop-up reveals five options: Erase Normal, Erase Fills, Erase Lines, Erase Selected Lines, and Erase Inside. These function in a similar manner to the Brush Mode options:

✦ **Erase Normal:** With this, the Eraser Tool functions like a normal eraser. It erases all lines and fills that it passes over, as long as they are on the active layer.

✦ **Erase Fills:** In Erase Fills Mode, the Eraser Tool becomes a specialty eraser, erasing only fills and leaving lines unaffected.

✦ **Erase Lines:** When in Erase Lines Mode, the Eraser Tool works by erasing lines only and leaving fills unaffected.

✦ **Erase Selected Fills:** In Erase Selected Fills Mode, the Eraser Tool becomes even more specialized. In this mode, it only erases fills that are currently selected, leaving unselected fills and all lines unaffected.

✦ **Erase Inside:** With Erase Inside Mode, the Eraser Tool only erases the area of fill *on which you initiate erasing*. This is much like the Erase Selected Fills Mode, except that the selection is accomplished with the initial erasure. In this mode, the eraser leaves all other fills and all lines unaffected.

Caution   To quickly erase everything in a scene, double-click the Eraser Tool in the Drawing Toolbox. (Don't click in the scene! You have to double-click the Eraser Tool button in the Drawing Toolbox. Okay?)

Summary

✦ The Flash 5 drawing tools are more robust and more capable than they were in any previous version of Flash.

✦ The process for choosing colors and for editing Stroke Height and Style has been streamlined. Lines drawn with the Pen Tool can be easily modified with the Color options and with the controls on the Stroke Panel.

✦ The Pencil Tool is used to draw expressively with natural ease. A range of options enable a user to fine-tune the manner in which Flash applies shape recognition to lines and shapes drawn with the Pencil Tool.

✦ The Line and the Oval Tools are useful for creating perfect geometric shapes.

✦ The Brush Tool applies strokes of color to Flash artwork. Brush strokes can be applied with a number of mask settings, called Brush Modes, that control how color is applied.

✦ The Dropper Tool is used to acquire color from Flash art so that it may be applied to other items with either the Paint Bucket or Ink Bottle Tools.

✦ The Ink Bottle Tool is used primarily to apply acquired color to lines, outlines, and lines of zero thickness.

✦ The Paint Bucket is used to fill shapes and closed areas of drawings. It can also edit the colors and properties of such fills.

✦ The Eraser Tool is used to erase anything that's been drawn on the Flash Stage. Like the Brush Tool, it has powerful masking capabilities that make it easier to erase specific items without endangering other portions of your Flash art.

✦ ✦ ✦

Applying Color

Before we get into the specifics of applying color with
Flash, we think it's essential to discuss some of the fundamental theory behind working with color that's destined for
display on the Web. In the process, we also introduce some
cool resources that may be helpful to you, both in concert
with Flash and as bona fide Web resources on their own. Then
we look at how the Flash Tools access Flash Color; and we
show you how to work with the new Flash Color Panels to
select, change, mix, and apply both colors and gradients.

Introducing Color Basics

Computer monitors display color by using a method called
RGB color. A monitor screen is a tightly packed array of pixels
arranged in a grid, where each pixel has an address. For example, a pixel that's located 16 rowsdown from the top and 70
columns over from the left might have an address of 70,16.
The computer uses such an address to send a specific color
to each pixel. Because each pixel is composed of a single red,
green, and blue dot, the colors that the monitor displays can
be "mixed" at each pixel by varying the individual intensities
of the red, green, and blue color dots. Each individual dot can
vary in intensity over a range of 256 values: starting with 0
(which is *off*) to a maximum value of 255 (which is *on*). Thus,
if red is *half-on* (a value of 127), while green is *off* (a value of
0), and blue is fully *on* (a value of 255), the pixel appears
reddish-blue.

This is the description for unlimited, full color, which is sometimes referred to as 24-bit color. However, many computer
systems are still incapable of displaying full color. Limited
color displays are either 16-bit or 8-bit displays. Although a
full discussion of bit-depth is beyond the scope of this book,
it is important to note several points:

✦ 24-bit color is required to accurately reproduce photographic images.

✦ Because 8-bit and 16-bit systems are color challenged, they can only display a limited number of colors, and they must dither-down anything that exceeds their gamut, which is their expanse of possible colors. *Dithering* means that, in order to approximate colors that are missing from the palette, two near colors are placed in close proximity to fool the eye into seeing intermediate colors.

✦ Although most color-challenged systems have the capability to adequately handle a few out-of-gamut colors without exceeding their palette, serious problems occur once their palette is exhausted. This means that your Flash site might look okay on a color-challenged system if it's the first site visited when the system is started up. However, the site may look much worse after an hour of browsing the Web.

✦ Some image formats, such as GIF, use a color palette, which limits them to 256 colors. This is called *indexed color*.

✦ Calibration of your monitor is essential for accurate color work. For more information check out www.colorpar.com.

Discussing Web-Safe Color issues

Web-Safe Color is a complex issue but what it boils down to is this: The Mac and PC platforms handle their color palettes differently, thus the browsers don't have the same colors available to them across platforms. This leads to inconsistent, unreliable color — unless one is careful to choose their colors for Web design from the Web-Safe Palette. The Web-Safe Palette is a palette of 216 colors that's consistent on both the Mac and the PC platforms for the Netscape, Explorer, and Mosaic browsers. The Web-Safe Palette contains only 216 of 256 possible indexed colors because 40 colors vary between Macs and PCs. Use the Web-Safe Palette to avoid color shifting and to ensure greater design (color) control.

The Swatches Panel has an option, Web 216, which is accessible from the options triangle at the upper right of the panel. Web 216 restricts the color palette to Web-Safe Colors. However, intermediate colors (meaning any process or effect that generates new colors from two Web-Safe Colors) such as gradients, color tweening, transparent overlays, and alpha transitions, will not be snapped to Web-Safe Colors.

Using hexadecimal values

Any RGB color can be described in hexadecimal (hex) notation. *Hexadecimal notation* is used with HTML code and some scripting languages to specify flat color, which is a continuous area of undifferentiated color. Hex code is used because it describes colors in an efficient manner that HTML and scripting languages can digest. In HTML, hexadecimal is used to specify colored text, lines, background, borders, frame cells, and frame borders.

A hexadecimal color number has six places. It allocates two places for each of the three color channels: R, G, and B. So, in the hexadecimal example 00FFCC, 00 signifies the red channel, FF signifies the green channel, and CC signifies the blue channel. The corresponding values between hexadecimal and customary integer values are as follows:

16 integer values:	0 1 2 3 4 5 6 7 8 9 10 11 12 13 14 15
16 hex values:	0 1 2 3 4 5 6 7 8 9 A B C D E F

Applying ColorSafe and other solutions

There are a couple of valuable tools used to create custom-mixed Web-Safe Colors. They build patterns composed of Web-Safe Colors that fool the eye into seeing a more desirable color. These are essentially blocks of preplanned dithers, built out of the Web-Safe Palette, that augment the usable palette while retaining cross-platform, cross-browser color consistency.

✦ ColorSafe is an Adobe Photoshop plug-in that generates hybrid color swatches with this logic. ColorSafe (Mac and Win) is available directly from BoxTop software at www.boxtopsoft.com. Furthermore, the ColorSafe demo is included in the software folder of the Flash 5 Bible CD-ROM.

✦ ColorMix is an easily used online utility that interactively delivers hybrid color swatches, much like ColorSafe. It is free at www.colormix.com.

Note   Now that we've arrived at the millennium, there's a growing trend among developers to consider the art of designing with Web-Safe Color something like building Web sites for the Ice Age. As Dorian Nisinson remarked, "What can you *do* with that many shades of weird green? Even a lime would be embarrassed." We *are* inclined to agree. It is true, especially in North America and Europe, that even the most inexpensive systems are equipped to display full color. But we also feel compelled to ask: What about the rest of the world? What about the poorer areas of North America — as, for example, most school systems? <soapbox> If we are to survive through this next century, then *inclusion* — no matter how inconvenient for the privileged — needs to become a planetary priority. </soapbox> We urge you to know your audience and design accordingly, but with a dash of generosity.

Expert Tutorial: Using Hybrid Color Swatches in Flash, *by Jon Warren Lentz*

Both ColorSafe and ColorMix can be teamed up with the Flash Dropper Tool to expand the available palette yet retain Web-Safe Color consistency. It takes a little fussing, but once you've built a set of Flash hybrid color swatches they can be reused from the library, and once you get the knack, new swatches are more easily created. (Note: In order to illustrate the principle of hybrid swatches, the images that illustrate this tutorial were created at high zoom levels. In normal practice, the checkered appearance would not be noticeable.)

Whether you use ColorMix online or use the ColorSafe plug-in for Photoshop, the optimal size for your hybrid color swatch is about ten pixels square, as shown in the following figure. Some swatches for this tutorial were saved as TIFFs, others as GIFs. The optimal workflow is to generate all of your swatches first. Then, before proceeding further, open the Photoshop Preferences dialog with File ⇨ Preferences ⇨ General, and make sure that Export Clipboard is enabled. Don't close Photoshop.

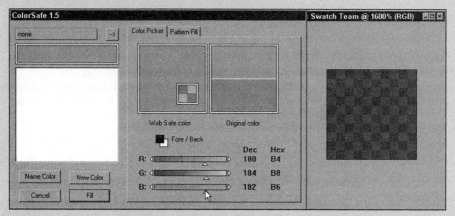

BoxTop Software's ColorSafe Photoshop plug-in creates Web-Safe hybrid color swatches.

Next, open a new Flash document and name it *HybridSwatches.FLA*. Next, turn off Flash's default dithering by unchecking the View ⇨ Fast Toggle, and then save the document. Return to Photoshop and open all of your Hybrid Color Swatches, as seen in the following figure. Working with the topmost swatch, select and then copy the entire swatch as follows: Select ⇨ All and then Edit ⇨ Copy. Now return to Flash and paste the swatch (that you've just copied) into the Hybrid Swatches document with Edit ⇨ Paste. Use the Arrow Tool to position the swatch. Repeat this procedure for each swatch until they've all been pasted into Flash. Save the PhotoShop document as a layered .PSD for possible reuse, and then close Photoshop.

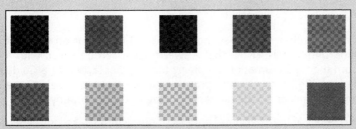

Ten hybrid color swatches were imported into Flash and arranged on the Stage. For convenience, these were moved into the offstage Work Area.

Now for a few examples to show how this works: Add a new layer to your Hybrid Swatches document and use the Rectangle Tool to drag out a rectangle, filled with any color. Return to the Swatches layer and use the Arrow Tool to select a swatch with which to fill the rectangle. When the swatch is selected, break it apart with Modify ⇨ Break Apart. (A bitmap that's broken apart is signified by a fine grid pattern that covers the bitmap.) Then use the Dropper Tool to acquire the bitmap fill of this swatch. When you click the swatch, the Dropper Tool is automatically swapped to the Paint Bucket Tool, as shown here. Click inside the rectangle with the Paint Bucket — the fill has been replaced with the hybrid bitmap fill!

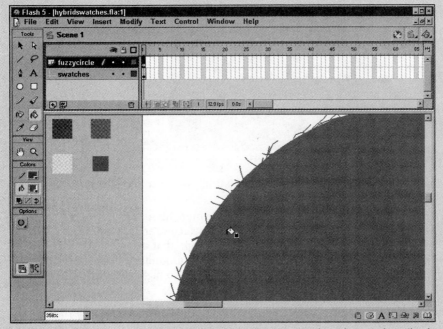

The edge of the shape on stage and to the right is an enclosed area, described by a custom line — it has just been filled with the hybrid swatch.

Continued

Continued

Follow the same procedure to fill other shapes—either on the same layer or on different layers—with Web-Safe hybrid bitmap fills. (Note that a swatch layer can be saved with a project and be excluded from the final animation simply by turning that layer into a Guide layer.) As regards the procedure, the most common problem encountered in acquiring the bitmap fill is either forgetting to break apart the bitmap or failing to do so properly.

The following figure shows a detail of the checkered pattern of our hybrid fill, accompanied by a view of the Library that contains each of our bitmaps.

When bitmaps are brought into Flash, they automatically reside in the Library.

Before we leave our document behind, let's see a little more about the way these imported bitmaps behave. In the following figure, the same fill is selected, and the Fill Panel is shown, with the Bitmap menu open, revealing all of the bitmaps that are currently used in the .FLA—including those offstage. We've drawn a rectangle around the bitmap fill that was originally broken apart and applied to the shape, which is also highlighted above the cursor in the Fill Panel.

With the fill selected on Stage, the second bitmap in the Fill Panel was clicked. This caused the bitmap to become highlighted in the Fill Panel. It also caused this newly activated fill to be swapped in as the fill for our selected shape. This replacement fill is clearly different, as the grid pattern is much larger than the grid of the original swatch.

Furthermore, the second fill has also replaced the original bitmap swatch (around which we drew the rectangle), as shown in the following figure. Note, however, that swapping bitmaps from the Fill Panel only works when the bitmaps are present on the Stage.

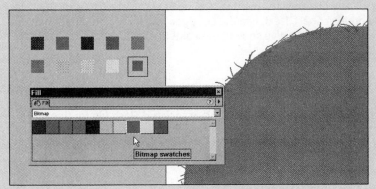

The Fill Panel's Bitmap menu

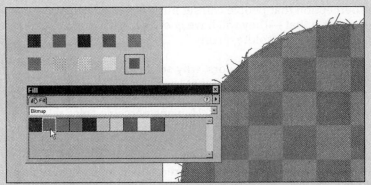

Use the Fill Panel's Bitmap menu to swap one bitmap fill for another.

Finally we need to prepare and save the Hybrid Swatches document so that it can be used as a Library: To do this, add a new layer, leave it blank, and then delete all of the other layers, including the layer into which the swatches were originally pasted, because they aren't on any layer. Or if you've arranged your swatches off stage, you'll need to select and delete them, since they aren't visible on any layer.

How does this work? Well, because imported bitmaps reside in the Library, and because we want this document as a Library, you don't need to keep them on Stage. Save the document and close it. Now you can open a new Flash document and then access the hybrid swatches library with File ➪ Open as Library and use the dialog to locate and open Hybrid Swatches.FLA. As long as you open this file as a Library, all of the bitmap fills saved in HybridSwatches.FLA will be available for use within any new Flash document.

Continued

Continued

With the Library open, to use a hybrid swatch, select the appropriate swatch from the Library and drag the swatch from the Preview window onto the work area, or onto any active layer. If the swatch is not selected, use the Arrow Tool to select it, and then use Modify ⇨ Break Apart to break it apart. Next, use the Dropper Tool to acquire the bitmap fill, which loads the Paint Bucket Tool. As we've shown, the Paint Bucket can now be used to fill any shape with hybrid Web-Safe Color.

If you'd like to see the example swatches and associated Flash file for this tutorial, open the Hybrid Swatches folder located in the ch28 folder of the *Dreamweaver and Flash Bible* CD-ROM.

Using color effectively

According to some developers, the issue of color on the Web has been seriously confused by the misperception that people can set numbers to give them Web-Safe Colors, and that — if they do that — they will have *good* color. It's given a lot of people the idea that color has some absolute quality.

But when there over 16 million possible colors, why settle for a mere 216? Or, if you do settle for 216 colors, you must understand that the value of color in Web design (or any design or art for that matter) has to do with color perception and design issues, and numbers have little to do with that. Humans perceive color relative to the context of other colors in which the color is set.

Most art schools offer at least one course about color. They often start with color experiments that are conducted with pieces of colored paper. An early assignment is to make three colors look like more than three colors — this is done by placing small scraps of the same color on larger pieces of different colors. Students are always amazed to learn how much a person's perception of a single color is tainted by placing it on those different-colored backgrounds. The lesson is that color is *not* an absolute — it never was before computers and never will be. Just step into a computer classroom and note the range of variation between monitors. Do you think it's any different out on the Web?

Perhaps there is one thing that is more important than color: contrast. Here's a good test: Take a colorful design that you admire and render it to grayscale — does it still work? Contrast is a major factor in good color composition. Good design almost doesn't need color because it leverages contrast instead.

So what's the point? Consider your audience. Choose a color strategy that will enable the preponderance of your viewers to view your designs as you intend them.

For example, if your audience is the public schools, then you must seriously consider limiting your work to the Web-Safe Palette. (If you choose this route, then hybrid swatches may enable you to access colors that are technically unavailable, while remaining within the hardware limitations of you audience.) On the other hand, if you are designing an interface for a stock photography firm whose clients are well-equipped art directors, then please use the full gamut. But in either case, understand that no one will see the exact same colors that you see. The variables of hardware, calibration, ambient light, and environmental decor are insurmountable.

Here's the bottom line: To achieve good Web design you'll need to use color — to achieve *great* Web design your colors should leverage contrast as well.

Working with Flash Color

Flash 5 has three levels for working with Flash Color. The first level is Toolbox Color, which is discussed in this chapter and which was briefly introduced in Chapter 27. At the intermediate level are the Stroke and Fill Panels, which can be used to set any predefined color, or immediately capture a color from anywhere on screen with the Eyedropper Tool, or invoke the system color picker. At the third level are the Mixer and Swatches Panels, where Alpha can be set for individual swatches, colors can be mixed and edited, and color sets can be added to, subtracted from, or loaded into the Swatches Panel. For many operations, proceeding from any of these panels, you can use existing swatches or any onscreen color, or set a color without needing to access any other panels. Other more complex operations, such as creating a gradient, require adjustments across several panels.

Using Toolbox Color

Just as there are several ways to approach the subject of color, there are also a number of ways to access the various — but fundamentally similar — color-handling tools in Flash 5. The quickest, and perhaps most convenient route is to approach color from either of the Color buttons located on the Toolbox: the Stroke Color and the Fill Color buttons located in the Color Tray. As we discussed in Chapter 27, these options serve double duty: Although these controls appear to be Color Chips that indicate the current color, they're also buttons. Click either Color button to open the current Swatches pop-up and select a new stroke or fill color. Whenever any Flash drawing or painting tools are activated, the current stroke and fill colors are represented by the Color controls located in the Flash Toolbox. These controls are present regardless of which tool is being used.

As shown in Figure 28-1, clicking either the Stroke or Fill Color button opens the current Swatches pop-up. This pop-up displays the same Swatch set that is currently loaded in the Swatches Panel. It includes a hexadecimal color entry box — which facilitates keyboard entry, as well as cut-and-paste of hex values — and a button that launches the Color Picker. Depending upon the tool selected, the Fill Color pop-up may also display a No Color button. The Swatches pop-up for Fill Color also includes a row of Gradients at the bottom of the solid colors. For all Drawing Tools, elementary color selection is accomplished by clicking either the Stroke or Fill Color buttons, and then choosing a color from the Swatches pop-up. If the color you want is not there, you may opt to invoke the Color Picker by clicking the Color Picker button. Alternatively, you may also open the Mixer Panel to create a new color and add it to the Swatches.

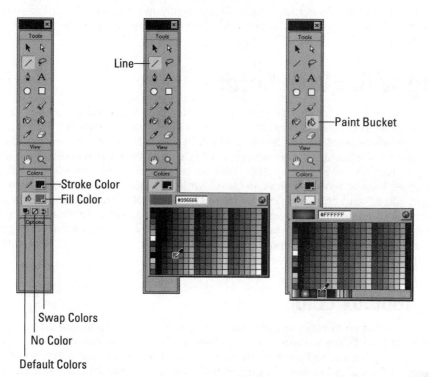

Figure 28-1: The Toolbox Color Tray and the Stroke and Fill Swatches Panels

New Feature

In addition to the basic reorganization of the Toolbox, the Color Controls include three new buttons, arrayed across the bottom of the Color Tray. As shown at the left of Figure 28-1, these are buttons for Default Colors (Stroke and Fill), No Color, and Swap Colors. The Default button sets the stroke to black and the fill to white. The No Color button sets the active control—which may be either the Stroke or the Fill—to apply no color. The Swap button swaps the current colors between the Stroke and Fill controls.

Tools that create a line include the Line Tool, Pencil Tool, Ink Bottle Tool, Pen Tool, and—because they draw outlines around their fills—both the Oval and Rectangle Tools. Each tool relies upon the Stroke Color button, which appears in the Toolbox

Color Tray. Click the Stroke Color button to open the Swatches pop up, which contains all colors in the current color set, including any new colors that have been temporarily added to the set. It is identical for any tool that has a stroke color.

In addition to tools that create lines, there are also fill tools. The fill tools include the Brush, Paint Bucket, Oval, and Rectangle Tools. Each of these tools is accompanied by the Fill Color button, which also resides in the Color Tray of the Toolbox. Clicking the Fill Color button invokes the Swatches pop up. Although the Fill Swatches pop-up is similar to the line pop up, it has one significant difference: It has another row of swatches at the bottom, which are gradient swatches — click one to fill with that gradient. The Fill Swatches pop-up contains all of the colors and gradients in the current color set, including any new colors or gradients that have been temporarily added to the set. It is identical for any tool that has a fill color.

Applying color from the Stroke and Fill Panels

You won't need to keep all of the color panels open to use colors. That's because, for most color operations, the colors are already present in any panel you're using. Flash 5 color works best if you use the Mixer Panel to create new colors, and the Swatches Panel to manipulate the display of colors that are available in the other panels. If you already have a predetermined palette for your project (which is a smart workflow), you may find that you do most of your color work from the Stroke and Fill Panels. The Stroke and Fill Panels each have a single option available from their options triangles: The Stroke option invokes the Line Style dialog, which was discussed in Chapter 27, while the Fill Panel option invokes Add Gradient. In Figure 28-2, the Fill Panel is set for solid colors only. For more information, please see Chapter 27.

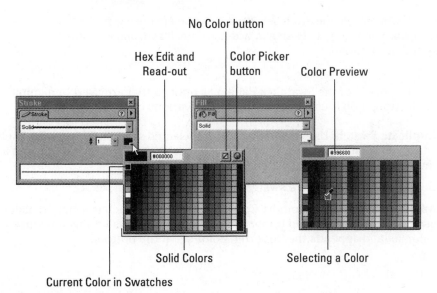

Figure 28-2: The Stroke and Fill Panels

The Fill Panel is also used for working with bitmap fills. This topic is covered in detail in Chapter 34, "Using Bitmaps and Other Media with Flash."

Working with the Swatches Panel

Think of the Swatches Panel (see Figure 28-3) as a way to organize your existing swatches and to manipulate the display of colors that are available in the other panels. Use the Swatches Panel to save color sets, import color sets, and reorder or change selected colors.

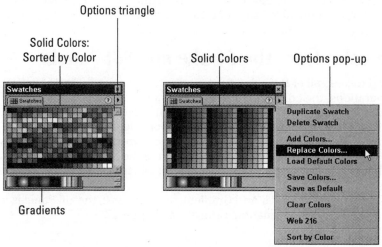

Figure 28-3: On the left, the Swatches Panel is shown after using the Sort by Color option. On the right, it's shown with the default sort, and with the Options pop-up displayed.

The Options pop-up of the Swatches Panel has options that are used to manipulate and administrate individual swatches as well as various color sets:

✦ **Duplicate Swatch:** Use this to duplicate a selected swatch. This can be useful when you want the make a range of related color swatches by duplicating and then editing subsequent swatches from the Mixer Panel.

✦ **Delete Swatch:** Botched a swatch? Select and delete it here.

✦ **Add Colors:** Opens the Import Color Swatch menu, which is a simple dialog used to locate, select, and import color sets. Add Colors retains the current color set and appends the imported color set at the bottom.

✦ **Replace Colors:** Also opens the Import Color Swatch menu. However, Replace Colors drops the current color set when it loads the selected color set. If the current set has not been saved it will be lost.

✦ **Load Default Colors:** Clears the current color set and replaces it with the default Flash color set. Again, if the current set has not been saved it will be lost.

✦ **Save Colors:** Opens the Export Color Swatch Menu, which is used to name and save color sets to a specific location on your hard drive. Color sets may be saved in either the Flash color set — on the PC (.clr), on the Mac (.fclr) — or Color Table (.act) format.

By default, colors are saved *within* your Flash document, rather than as an external file. Using the Add Colors, Replace Colors, and Save Colors menu options, Flash can import and export solid colors from files in the Flash color set (.clr) format. But Flash can also import and export solid colors from files in the Fireworks-savvy Color Table (.act) format, which can be imported by Photoshop, and imported and exported from Fireworks. Flash can also import solid colors from GIF files. If it isn't already obvious, this means greater workflow flexibility, which is a boon to project management because you can save a specific color set for a project and load different color sets as needed. Gradients may only be imported and exported with the Flash color set (.clr) format.

✦ **Save as Default:** Saves the current color set as the default — this action replaces the original default Flash color set.

✦ **Clear Colors:** When Clear Colors is selected, the swatches in the current colors window are removed, leaving only black and white.

✦ **Web 216:** Upon initial installation, this is the default Flash color palette that is displayed in the Swatches Panel. Select this option to replace any current color set with the Web-Safe Palette of 216 colors.

You can override the default Web 216 Palette by switching the Mixer Panel to either the RGB or HSB (Hue, Saturation, Brightness) color spaces. You can then mix your own fresh colors; add them to the Swatches; and save that palette as the default. Another alternative is to locate the Photoshop Color Tables on your hard drive (or download a specialty color table from the Web) and replace the default set with a broader gamut.

✦ **Sort by Color:** Click this button to rearrange an accumulation of custom colors into a palette that is freshly reordered according to color. It sorts by hues, with the values of each are arranged together from light to dark in declining order. However, once you've sorted a palette in this manner there is no toggle to return to the other view — so save your palette before sorting, and then save the sorted palette, too.

Caution   Be careful about creating huge color sets! On some systems (for example, a 17-inch monitor set at 800×600 resolution),the Toolbox Color pop-ups may extend beyond the visible screen and you'll be forced to use the Swatches Panel to choose colors that are hidden offscreen. This can get really bad if you add colors from a GIF image.

Working with the Mixer Panel

The Color Mixer, which is shown in Figure 28-4, enables you to create new colors, working within any of these three color spaces — RGB, HSB (Hue, Saturation Brightness, or hex — using either the interactive Color Bar or the Color Value slider controls. All colors are handled with four channels, which are RGBA (Red, Green, Blue, Alpha). New colors can be added to the current Swatches, which causes a new swatch to appear in the Fill, Stroke, and Character Panels — just select Add Swatch from the Options pop-up. When working with the Mixer Panel, to add a new color just select Add Swatch from the Options pop-up.

Color values (RGB, HSB, or Hex)

Options triangle   Solid Colors   Fill has focus

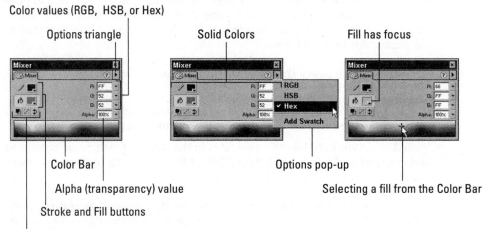

Color Bar   Options pop-up

Alpha (transparency) value   Selecting a fill from the Color Bar

Stroke and Fill buttons

Default Colors, No Color, and Swap Color buttons

Figure 28-4: The Color Mixer gives you precise control over the creation of new colors, including Alpha values.

There are two ways to change the Alpha value for a selected color: Either drag the Alpha Slider until the Alpha readout looks right or enter a numeric value in the Alpha readout. Numeric entry is useful when you already know what level of transparency is required, while the slider is useful for interactive fiddling with transparency to get it just right — as indicated in either the Stroke or Fill Color button. In Figure 28-5, a copy of the Flash icon is donating its orange color to our palette. On the right, this orange is shown with the Alpha — or transparency — of the color set to 30 percent. Before proceeding, this swatch was saved from the Options pop-up by clicking Add Swatch.

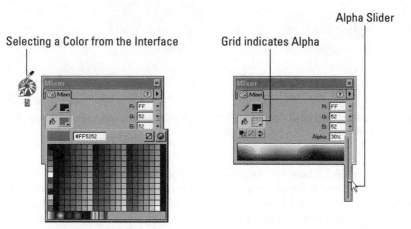

Figure 28-5: When selecting a color from the Swatches pop-up of the Mixer Panel, the Dropper Tool enables you to pluck a color from anywhere in the interface.

 New Feature   When working in the Mixer, Stroke, Fill (including Color Pointers), and Character Panels, the Dropper associated with these panels enables you to pluck color information from anywhere in the interface. Simply click the Color button of any of these three panels, which will cause the mouse to display as a Dropper. Then drag the Dropper over any open application — or panel of the Flash interface itself — and click to acquire the color that's at the end of the Dropper. (Although the Toolbox Dropper doesn't facilitate this move, it does have a unique trick of its own: It adds a new swatch to the Swatches pop-up whenever a color is acquired.)

Figure 28-6 shows the Mixer and Swatches Panels on the left. Previous to this shot, we used the Duplicate Swatch command of the Swatches Panel to duplicate the 30-percent-orange swatch. You can see this duplicate swatch highlighted at the bottom of the Swatches Panel on the left. Using the Mixer, we returned the Alpha of this swatch to 100 percent. Then, as shown on the right in Figure 28-6, we used the Save Colors command to add both swatches to the current color set.

 Tip   If you're working with a color and want to make it just a little darker, HSB color will come to your rescue! You can do this dynamically, too. Here's how: Click the options arrow of the Mixer Panel and choose HSB. Now make sure your color is selected on Stage and hide the selection with Ctrl/Command+H. Then, from the Color values of the Mixer Panel, reduce the B value, which is brightness, either numerically or by dragging the slider.

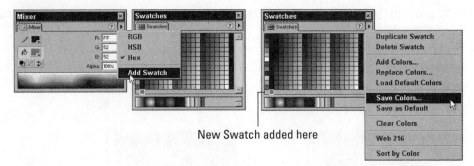

New Swatch added here

Figure 28-6: Use the Mixer and Swatches Panels to add a new color Swatch and then save the new color(s) to the current color set.

As shown in Figure 28-7, the new color — an Orange with an Alpha value of 30 percent — is selected for a ten-point solid line. This same color may also be used as a solid fill. However, to create gradients with new colors, including transparent colors, you need to use the drop-down menu of the Fill Panel, as explained in the next section.

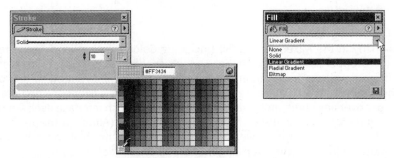

Figure 28-7: A newly created color, with an Alpha value, is selected for a solid line (left). The drop-down menu of the Fill Panel is used to initiate the creation of custom gradient fills (right).

Creating gradient colors

Often you'll find that creating a custom gradient swatch requires that you use several panels. In addition to the Fill Panel, this usually requires the Mixer, and sometimes the Swatches Panel. The drop-down list of the Flash 5 Fill Panel lists two gradient styles: Linear and Radial. When editing or creating a gradient, the current changes can be saved by clicking the Save button at the bottom right of the Panel, which adds another gradient to the Swatches Panel. The gradient shown in Figure 28-8 is being modified from a default black and white linear gradient.

Gradient Editor (or Edit Gradient Range)

Fill Color button

Fill Menu

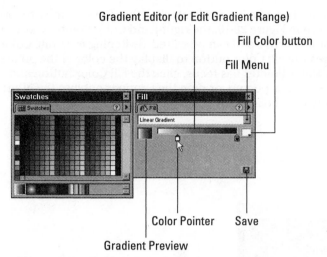

Color Pointer   Save

Gradient Preview

Figure 28-8: The Pointer Color button displays
the color of the active Color Pointer.

 Tip   Working with the tiny default Fill Panel to create or edit a complex gradient can be
tedious. Want a bigger work area? Simply grab any corner of the panel to resize
it — and expand the gradient editor simultaneously.

To change the color of the active pointer, which has focus, click the Pointer Color
button and then select a color from the Swatches pop-up. The Fill Color button is
updated to reflect the change. Note that the Swatches pop-up contains all of the
solid colors in the current color set, including any new colors that may have been
temporarily added to the set. As shown in Figure 28-9, the left-hand pointer is being
changed to a color that has an Alpha value, which is indicated by the grid pattern in
both the Color Preview and, upon release of the pointer, by the Fill Color button.

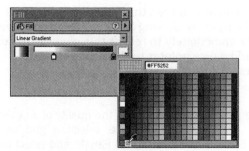

Figure 28-9: Changing the color of the active
pointer for a gradient

To customize another point of an existing gradient, click that Color Pointer to give it focus. In the example shown in Figure 28-10, the right-hand Color Pointer was given *focus* — which means that it is active and can be edited. Switching from one Color Pointer to another changes the Fill Color button to display the color of the pointer that has focus. While the Color Pointer has focus, click the Fill Color button and choose a color from the Swatches pop-up, or drag the Dropper out into the interface to acquire a color from any item onscreen, including any color displayed in any open Flash panel.

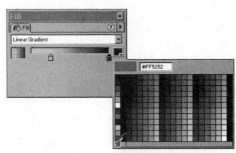

Figure 28-10: Changing the second point
of the gradient

 Note A new color may also be specified in the Mixer Panel by numeric or hex entry in the RGB entry fields.

In Figure 28-11, the gradient from the previous figure was applied to this simple composition of a circle described by a custom, fuzzy stroke. On the layer behind is a black pattern of black lines, which is visible through the transparent portions of the gradient fill that's been applied to the circle on the top layer. Note the active swatch in the Swatches Panel, and the Gradient Preview of the left-hand Color Pointer in the Mixer Panel, which has focus in the Fill Panel.

Figure 28-12 was changed to a radial gradient and then the left-hand Color Pointer of the previous figure was moved to the right by clicking and dragging it to a new position. The Gradient Preview adjusts immediately to reflect this change. To add a new color to a gradient, you need to add a new pointer to the Gradient Editor, by clicking slightly beneath the bar. To remove a pointer, drag it downwards, away from the bar of the Gradient Editor.

 Tip Here's how to obtain an interactive preview while adjusting the quality of an existing gradient fill: First select the fill, and then hide the selection grid with Ctrl/Command+H. Next, open the Swatches, Mixer, and Fill Panels, and select the appropriate gradient in the Swatches Panel. Next, in the Fill Panel, choose a Color Pointer to edit and proceed to edit that color in the Mixer. As each Mixer slider is released, the adjustment will be updated in all relevant Color buttons *and* in the selected fill on the Stage. This same functionality also works with new gradients: Simply make a new single color gradient, apply it as a fill, and then proceed to edit — adding more colors and finessing Alphas to suit.

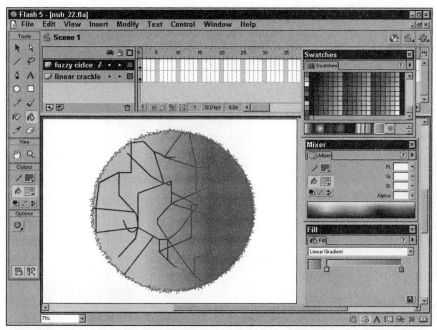

Figure 28-11: Applying a new gradient, with a transparent color, to an object

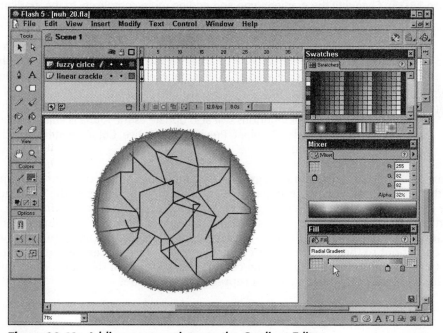

Figure 28-12: Adding a new pointer to the Gradient Editor

As shown in Figure 28-13, more pointers have been added to the gradient. In this figure, the center Color Pointer is active and white is being selected from the Swatches pop-up. Next, the Alpha for this pointer will be reduced to 30 percent by entering this number into the numeric entry field of the Alpha value of the Mixer Panel.

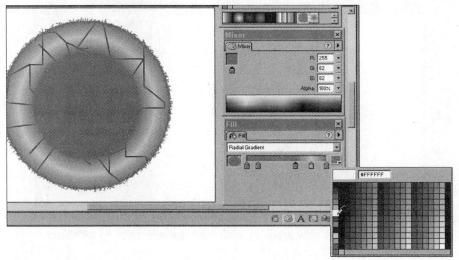

Figure 28-13: Changing the gradient type and adding more complexity to the gradient

Note   The Alpha (or relative opacity, or transparency) of a Color Pointer may be adjusted either by entering a numeric value or by dragging the Alpha Slider. When using the slider, the Alpha value is displayed as a percentage in the numeric entry box. When adjusting Alpha, a visual cue for the level of transparency is the appearance of a faint grid in the Mixer's active Color button (Stroke Color, Fill Color, or Color Proxy). If visible, other related Color buttons will also update as the Alpha is adjusted, particularly in the Fill Panel's Gradient Preview, the active Color Pointer, and the Gradient Fill Color button.

Figure 28-14 shows our final radial gradient, which is opaque at the center and proceeds through variations of transparency and color as it radiates to the outer edge. The procedure for making a radial gradient is similar to those for creating a linear gradient. The only real difference is that the Gradient Editor bar — when used in conjunction with radial gradients — must be considered as a radius, or slice from the center out to the edge, of the circular gradient. Color Pointers at the left end of the Gradient Editor bar represent the center — or inside — of the radial gradient, while Color Pointers at the right end represent the outside.

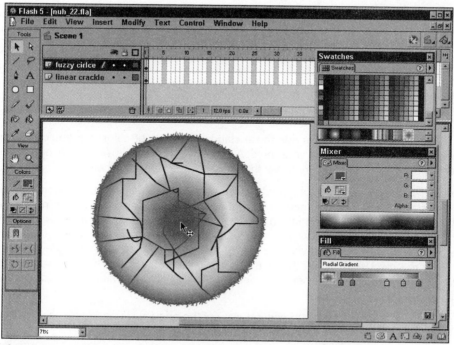

Figure 28-14: The final radial gradient applied to an object in Flash 5

New Feature

When applying a gradient, it's now easy to interactively orient the direction of the gradient as it is applied: Simply click with the Paint Bucket and drag. A direction line is drawn between the click point and the drag point. If you aren't satisfied with the orientation of the gradient, simply repeat the procedure and reorienting the direction arrow as you drag.

Expert Tutorial: Creating Color Schemes, by *Molly E. Holzschlag*

Comparing Adobe LiveMotion to Macromedia Flash is like comparing proverbial apples and oranges. Both offer something special and unique. Maybe you like them both, as I do. Each has features that empower designers seeking to add life to their Web sites. In the realm of color, LiveMotion (LM) offers one tool that is especially intriguing. Part of LM's appeal is that it is used for static as well as motion graphics for the Web, so the application has a lot of color support built-in. One very tasty feature that will serve to inspire you in your color goals is a specialty palette known as the *Color Scheme*. In fact, if you were to use LM for nothing else, you might find that the Color Scheme palette is a worthwhile companion to Flash.

Continued

Continued

Color Scheme palette, Triangle view

Think of a color wheel — you know, those standard wheels of color that you've certainly seen before. With that wheel in your mind: Analogous colors are those that are next to each other. Complementary colors are those that are across from each other.

LM works on the concept of analogous and complementary colors to make schemes, which are especially helpful if you're new to working with color, or for those design newcomers and veterans who need inspiration in terms of setting up a palette for a design. Schemes combine colors in interesting ways, and can really help you get creative. The Color Scheme palette shows off its colors via two views, which are known as *Triangle view* and *Honeycomb view.* Use the view that you like best. Sometimes I switch views. Variety, after all, is the one true spice. Along with the views, there are six combinations of color available in the palette:

✦ **Analogous:** This scheme provides a view of the original (referred to as *base*) color plus any analogous colors.

✦ **Split Complementary:** This scheme shows the base color, its complement, and its complement's analogous colors.

✦ **Complementary Analogous:** Using this scheme shows a base color, its analogous color, and the analogous color's complements.

✦ **Triad:** This is a base color and two equidistant colors.

✦ **Tetrad:** This is a base color and three colors chosen at equal intervals along the color wheel.

✦ **Sextet:** This is the base color plus five colors placed at equal distances from one another along the color wheel.

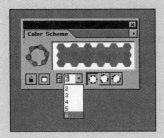
Views and numeric combinations can be employed to create a Color Scheme palette (Honeycomb view).

Getting excited? Great! If you already have LM, open it up because you're about to create your own color scheme. And, if you don't have it, you can download a full-feature, 30-day demo from Adobe. To begin a color scheme, follow me:

1. Select Window ➪ Color Scheme to bring up the Color Scheme palette.

2. Choose a color for your base color. To do this, select the Foreground color box in the Toolbox. Open the Color Palette (Window ➪ Color Palette), and then choose the color you like using the Color Picker.

3. In the Color Scheme palette, choose a number and scheme combo. There are lots of combinations — play around until you find one you really like.

4. As you create your scheme, you'll find that it appears in the Color Scheme portion of the Toolbox. Got a scheme you're happy with? Lock that puppy so that it stays until further commands are given by clicking the Scheme Lock icon on the Color Scheme palette.

5. Got a scheme that you want to use in Flash? Simply open your Color Scheme and make a set of rectangular swatches on the LM stage. Then save it as a .SWF. When you open this .SWF in Flash, you can access those colors with the Dropper and save it out as a Flash color set.

Pretty creative, indeed. But what happens when you don't know much about color and what it represents? Well, here's a little guide I created some time back, and I'm including it here for you to enjoy. Color meanings and perceptions vary, and color meanings are often paradoxical. I've kept this information very basic because getting more detailed would end up taking up a whole, well, book. Instead, use this as a starting point and then put your own savvy to work to come up with fun and interesting colors and color combinations for your designs. For a basic introduction to the psychological responses to various colors, refer to the following table.

Color	*Psychological Response*
Red	Power, energy, warmth, passions, love, aggression, danger
Blue	Trust, conservative, security, technology, cleanliness, order
Green	Nature, healthy, good luck, jealousy ("green with envy"), renewal
Yellow	Optimism, hope, philosophy, dishonesty, cowardice (a coward can be described as "yellow"), betrayal
Purple	Spirituality, mystery, royalty, transformation, cruelty, arrogance
Orange	Energy, balance, warmth
Brown	Earth, reliability, comfort, endurance
Gray	Intellect, futurism, modesty, sadness, decay
White	Purity, cleanliness, precision, innocence, sterility, death
Black	Power, sexuality, sophistication, death, mystery, fear, unhappiness, elegance

Continued

Continued

For a deeper examination of the complex subject of color, especially within the context of World Wide Web design and the variegated impact of color on different cultures, check out my recent article for Web Techniques, *Color My World*, at `www.webtechniques.com/archives/2000/09/desi/`.

Honored as one of the Top 25 Most Influential Women on the Web, Molly Holzschlag was onto Flash from the start. She first encountered it when, "It was Futuresplash, from a little company in San Diego called FutureWave." She's the author of 15 books, including *Teach Yourself Adobe LiveMotion in 24 Hours* (New York: Macmillan, Sam's Publishing 2000). Some of the sites she's worked on include The Microsoft Network, Desert.Net, RedMeat.Com, and, of course, Molly.Com. Here are her answers to other questions: "Born: Brooklyn. Raised: New Jersey. Do you have a problem with that?" And, after tremendous prodding about her last days as a teenager, she reminisced, "If there was anything worth remembering, I don't remember it. Hey, it was the 70s!"

Tip   You can obtain functionality similar to what is available from the Color Scheme Palette of LiveMotion without the expense of owning LiveMotion. It's found in a Photoshop plug-in called Color Harmony. The plug-in is from Hot Door, Inc. — `www.hotdoor.com`. Although currently available only for the Mac, a Windows version is planned for 2001.

Flash Symbols: Tweened Color Effects and Color Objects

Flash Symbols can be tweened so that they will change color over time. Although this involves color, the selection of colors for the keyframes of the tween is merely a rudimentary application of fill and line color, as described in this chapter. For information regarding the tweening and keyframe aspects of Symbols and Tweened Color effects, including the new Negative Alpha, please refer to Chapter 33, "Animating in Flash."

New Feature   One brilliant aspect of the improvements to ActionScript is that Flash 5 now has a new Color object. This means that color is scriptable. As one developer remarked, "Ahhh, the lengths to which we will no longer have to go in order to simulate this effect!" Although beyond the scope of this chapter, some mention of it does belong here. Technically, it means that you can use the methods of the predefined Color object to change the color and transparency of any movie clip. This is covered in detail in Chapter 41, "Controlling Movie Clips."

Summary

✦ The science of color on the computer is far from accurate. There are many variables involved in the presentation of color over the Web. One variable revolves around the issue of Web-Safe Color. When targeting color-challenged audiences, one solution is to use Hybrid Color Swatches.

✦ Toolbox Color is available to every Flash drawing tool. It gives immediate, intuitive access to the currently loaded swatches and all temporary colors. It also permits direct insertion of hexadecimal values.

✦ At their basic level, the Stroke and Fill Panels are used to access deeper features of the Flash Color system. They both permit sampling of color from anywhere in the interface. Additionally, the Fill Panel is used to create and edit gradients.

✦ The Swatches Panel is used to save out color sets, import color sets, and reorder or change selected colors and gradients.

✦ The Color Mixer is used to create new colors, and adjust the Alpha of new or existing colors. It's also used to choose from three color spaces: RGB, HSB, or hex. New colors can be added to the current Swatches, which causes them to appear in the Fill, Stroke, and Character Panels.

✦ Although Flash doesn't directly support Color Schemes, they can be developed outside Flash, imported (as either a .SWF from LiveMotion, or as an .ACT from Color Harmony) and then sampled and saved into a color set with the Swatches Panel.

✦ Advanced Color capabilities of Flash include color tweening, scriptable color, and negative Alpha. These topics are discussed in depth in subsequent chapters.

✦   ✦   ✦

Working with Text

T ype and text are often needed to convey information in a Flash movie. In this chapter, we explain how to create text and avoid font display problems.

Understanding Font Display Problems

TrueType, Type 1 PostScript, and bitmap fonts can be used in Flash. Although Flash exports the system information about the fonts that are used, fonts may still appear incorrectly on other platforms — if the end-user doesn't have the font installed, the font may appear incorrectly (even on the same platform). Often this is a due to the fact that although Flash can display the font within the editor, it does not recognize that particular font's outline and can't export the text. One way to check for this is to momentarily switch your view to View ⇨ Antialias Text. If the text appears jaggy, that's a problem font.

Such problems can be avoided by using the _device fonts (_sans, _serif, and _typewriter fonts), which can be chosen either from the Text ⇨ Font Menu or from the Character Panel. These _device fonts tell the Flash player to use whatever equivalent font is available on the local computer. For example, _sans usually becomes Arial or Helvetica, while _serif becomes Times or Times New Roman, and _typewriter becomes Courier. Because these settings utilize the default fonts on the user's machine, these fonts also make the final movie size smaller, because Flash doesn't have to export their outlines in the .SWF when the movie is exported. Of course, the result of smaller movies is faster downloads.

Characteristics of these _device fonts are that they are always available, always fast, never rotate, and may vary slightly in their metrics from player to player. You can use _device fonts for text fields and areas of text that you don't want *antialiased* (processed for smoother edges).

Tip Another way to avoid system conflicts with fonts is by breaking apart all text, which turns it into shapes instead of fonts. (Breaking apart text is indispensable for creating the text effects explained in Chapter 32, "Drawing in Flash.") However, broken-apart text usually increases the file size considerably, so use it sparingly. Furthermore, text cannot be edited after it's been broken apart — everything must be written correctly before investing the time required to break the text apart and to apply special effects to it.

Because Flash is a vector program, it enables the integration of most fonts within the movie, without fuss. For normal blocks of text, this means that fonts don't have to be rendered into bitmap elements. The .SWF files that Flash publishes (or exports) include all of the necessary information for the font to display properly on every browser.

Problems with fonts on the Mac

Adobe PostScript fonts usually function on the Mac without problems. However, if a font is not properly installed, it may appear to function and display properly within the .FLA, yet falter when the movie is published. Often this is due to the editor using what is called the screen font while you are working in the editor. If, however, the actual font to which the screen font refers cannot be found when the movie is published, that causes problems.

Problems with fonts on the PC

On the PC, it is reported that PostScript fonts that are used with Adobe Type Manager can cause problems when publishing the movie. For this reason, it's often recommended that PC Flash users limit themselves to TrueType fonts. This is especially relevant for block text. But if a text block has been broken apart, this restriction does not apply, because breaking type apart renders it into a vector shapes (or objects) that will ship with the .SWF when the project is published. But the primary disadvantages of breaking text apart are that it may increase the file size considerably, and that once it's broken apart, the text is no longer editable.

Cross-platform issues and codevelopment problems

Sometimes a project from the Mac will open on the PC with the Times font displayed in substitution for all of the text! This isn't anything strange — at least in terms of how Flash is trying to help you — because Flash knows that you don't have the font on your machine.

Resources for Further Study in Typography

Although Flash offers the capability to deliver finely designed typography to 90 percent of the Web-browsing population, too many Flash artists are *typography challenged*. Unfortunately, it shows. If you are unfamiliar with typography, here are two excellent resources:

The Non-Designer's Type Book (Berkeley: Peachpit Press, 1998) by Robin Williams. This is a must-read (and study) for anyone who really wants to take their Flash Web designs to the next level.

The Elements of Typographic Style (Vancover, B.C.: Hartley & Marks, 1997) by Robert Bringhurst. This is a manual of typography and book design that concludes with "appendices of typographic characters and currently available digitized fonts [and] a glossary of terms."

If you select a text block and check you'll most likely see the name of the original font that was used, even though the text is displayed in the Times font. As long as you don't edit the text, Flash will continue to try to use the named font. You may have the same font installed on both the Mac and the PC and notice (now) that there is a slight difference in their names. Usually, there's an extra space or an underscore messing up the font sync.

The Text Tool

The Text Tool is used to create and edit text. Although Flash is neither a drawing program like FreeHand, nor a page-layout program, its text-handling capabilities are well thought-out and implemented. The Text Tool, shown in Figure 29-1, delivers a broad range of control for generating, positioning, tuning, and editing text. Although the basic Text Tool is located in the Flash Toolbox, the controls for working with Text are located in three text panels: the Character, Paragraph, and Text Options Panels.

Tip   Use the Eyedropper Tool to acquire text: Click extant text to acquire all of the formatting and attributes and apply these settings to subsequently entered text.

Note   If your handling of text demands a more robust and thorough environment, you can generate your text in Freehand (or Illustrator) and import that more refined text into Flash.

Flash handles text as a group. This means that when you create type, you can use the Text Tool to edit the individual letters or words inside the text area at any time. But if you click once anywhere on the text, the entire text block is selected.

Figure 29-1: The Text Tool has no options in the Toolbox.

Working with Flash text boxes

Flash now generates three flavors of text in three kinds of text boxes: Label Text (A), Block Text (B), and Editable Text (C), shown in Figure 29-2. The bottom example shows an Editable Text box as it is being resized (D).

Each of the three kinds of text blocks has its own characteristics:

✦ **Label Text:** With Label Text, Flash creates text blocks that widen as you continue to add text. As shown in the top example of Figure 29-2, Label Text has a round handle at the upper-right corner. To create a Label Text box, click once in the movie area with the Text Tool and then commence typing. If you keep typing without making line breaks in Label Text Mode, the Label Text box continues beyond the right edge of the movie area. When this happens, the text is not lost. To regain view of this off-movie text, add line breaks, move the Label Text box, or select View ➪ Work Area from the Menu Bar, to make the off-movie area Label Text box entirely visible.

✦ **Block Text:** Flash creates Block Text when you *drag out* the text box as you create it in the movie area. As shown in the second example in Figure 29-2, a Block Text box has a square handle at the upper-right corner. The Block Text box has a fixed width, and wraps words automatically. You create a Block Text box by simply selecting the Text Tool, clicking, and then dragging out a box of the desired width in the movie area. When you commence typing, the text wraps automatically and the box extends downwards as you add more lines of text.

✦ **Editable Text:** With Editable Text fields, the content is variable. This means that the page viewer can change the contents of an Editable Text field: for example, when used in a password entry box or a form field. As shown in the third and bottom examples in Figure 29-2, an Editable Text box has a square handle at the lower-right corner that can be dragged in or out to resize it. Create Editable Text by choosing either Dynamic or Static Text from the Text Behavior dropdown of the Text Options Panel, and then click in the movie area to drag out and define the text box.

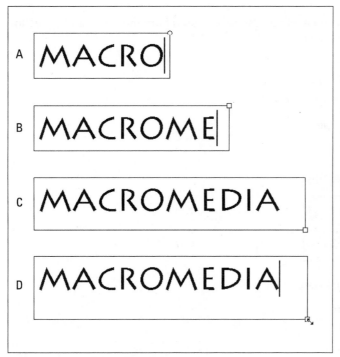

Figure 29-2: Shown here are examples of Flash text in three kinds of text boxes, from top to bottom: Label (or Extending) Text, Block (or Fixed) Text, and Editable (or Dynamic or Input) Text.

A Label Text box can be converted into a Block Text box. Place the cursor over the round text handle at the upper-right corner of the Label Text box. A double-ended arrow appears, indicating that you can modify the Label Text box's width. Drag to reshape the Label Text box. When you release the mouse, the text handle at the upper-right corner will now be square (formerly, it was round), indicating that this is now a Block Text box. To revert back to Label Text, double-click the square text handle.

Tip   Can't tell if it's Label or Block Text? That's because it's not in Edit Mode. To return the text item to Edit Mode, either double-click the item with the Arrow Tool or click it once with the Type Tool.

Using the Character Panel

The Character Panel, shown in Figure 29-3, is readily accessed from the Launcher Bar, or from the Window Menu with Window ➪ Panels ➪ Character. The main feature of this panel is the Font Name drop-down, which is use to select fonts.

Tip   The Character Panel can also be accessed from the keyboard by pressing Ctrl+T/Command+T.

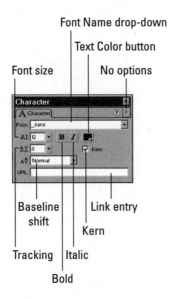

Figure 29-3: The Character Panel is one of three panels used to select and modify manipulated text.

✦ **No options:** There are no options for this panel. The options button here is vestigial.

✦ **Font Name drop-down:** When the Text Tool is active, this displays the name of the current font. Click the button (which is a downward-pointing triangle) to invoke a scrolling menu of available fonts. Choose a font from this scrolling menu to set the font for the next text element that you create. Or, to change the font of existing text, first select the text in the movie area, and then choose a different font from the scrolling menu. When selecting a font from the Character Panel, the currently highlighted font is previewed in its typeface.

Tip

The font of existing text can also be changed from the Menu Bar with Text ➪ Font. The advantage of this method is that the list is more expansive and easier to scan. The disadvantage of this list is that it doesn't preview the fonts in their typefaces.

✦ **Text Color button:** Click this button to invoke the Current Swatches, which — in addition to current and temporary swatches — also enables you to acquire a color from anywhere within the interface.

✦ **Kern Check box:** If the font includes built-in kerning information, which evens out the spaces between letterforms, check this to activate automatic kerning.

✦ **Bold and Italic:** The Bold option is a simple button that toggles selected text between either Normal or Bold. The Italic option is another simple button. It toggles selected text between Normal and Italic.

Note

Many computer programs (including Flash) that deal with type permit you to fake a Bold and/or Italic version of fonts that you do have; this has led to a lot of confusion. Each typeface has a basic or Normal form. The shape of the Bold version of that typeface is not the same as the Normal form. Nor is the Italic simply a slanted version. The shapes and proportions are different. With a well-designed font, the real bold font will always look better than a Normal letter shape thickened with an outline. A real Bold or Italic version of a typeface will be appropriately named and will be selected as a *separate* font.

✦ **Font size:** This is both a pop-up and a text entry field. When the Text Tool is active, it displays the current font size in a text entry field. You can change the font size by entering a specific font size in this text entry field. If you click the arrow to the immediate right of the text entry field, a pop-up displays a slider of available font sizes.

✦ **Tracking:** In addition to the other controls that Flash affords for the arrangement and adjustment of text, text can be manually tracked. *Tracking* is the process of adjusting the space between two or more text characters. To track characters from the Character Panel, first select the characters that you want to adjust, and then either enter a numeric value in the read out, or drag the interactive slider. The Text menu also has its own Tracking menu suboptions. Menu tracking has the additional advantage that it can be applied either: (a) to selected (highlighted) text characters or (b) to the pair of text characters on either side of the cursor:

- **Decrease Spacing by One Half-Pixel:** To decrease text character spacing by one half-pixel, press Ctrl+Alt+Left Arrow (Command+Option+Left Arrow).

- **Decrease Spacing by Two Pixels:** To decrease text character spacing by two pixels, press Ctrl+Shift+Alt+Left Arrow (Command+Shift+Option+Left Arrow).

- **Increase Spacing by One Half-Pixel:** To increase text character spacing by one half-pixel, press Ctrl+Alt+Right Arrow (Command+Option+Right Arrow).

- **Increase Spacing by Two Pixels:** To increase text character spacing by two pixels, press Ctrl+Alt+Right Arrow (Command+Shift+Option+Right Arrow).

- **Reset Spacing to Normal:** To reset text character spacing to normal, press Ctrl+Alt+Up Arrow (Command+Option+Up Arrow).

✦ **Baseline shift:** There are three options in this drop-down menu. Normal resets text to the baseline, while Superscript and Subscript shift the text either above or below the baseline.

✦ **Link entry:** This is used to link selected text as a hyperlink to another URL. To do this, first select a text block on Stage, and then enter the URL in this Link entry field.

Figure 29-4 shows several uses of the Character Panel, such as previewing and selecting fonts, and adjusting the font size. On the left, this composite image shows selected Block Text as the font is being changed from the _sans device font to Lithos Regular. Note that the font preview displays the selected text, rather than the font name, which is the default display when no text is selected. On the right, the point size is being adjusted by dragging the Font size slider. As the text resizes, the Block Text box, which has a constrained width, forces the text to break and stack vertically, leaving only the M visible on stage.

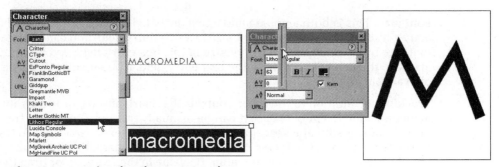

Figure 29-4: Using the Character Panel

Using the Style submenu

Some of the settings of the Character Panel are also available from the Style submenu that appears when you choose Text ➪ Style from the Menu Bar. These include:

✦ Plain — Ctrl(Command)+Shift+P

✦ Bold — Ctrl(Command)+Shift+B

✦ Italic — Ctrl(Command)+Shift+I

✦ Subscript

✦ Superscript

Using the Paragraph Panel

The Paragraph Panel, shown in Figure 29-5, can be directly invoked from the Window Menu with Window ⇨ Panels ⇨ Paragraph. If you use the default panels layout, you can click the Character Panel button on the Launcher Bar and then select the Para-graph tab to bring it forward in the panel stack. This Panel features alignment controls that can be used to align selected text. When entering new text, if you predetermine the alignment settings before text entry, subsequently entered text will be aligned accordingly.

Tip   The keyboard shortcut for the Paragraph Panel is Ctrl/Command+Shift+T.

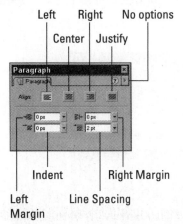

Figure 29-5: The Paragraph Panel is used to set, edit, and adjust the alignment of selected characters and paragraphs.

✦ **No Options:** There are no options for this panel. The options button here is vestigial.

✦ **Alignment Options:** The top area of the panel displays four buttons for the arrangement of text: Left, Center, Right, and Full Justification. When editing, alignment affects the currently selected paragraph(s) only. When entering text, use these options to predetermine the alignment before text entry, and all subsequent text will be aligned accordingly.

✦ **Right Margins:** Use this numeric entry field (or click the arrow button to invoke the interactive slider) to define the space between the text and the right border of the text box. By default, this space is described in pixels.

✦ **Line Spacing:** Use this numeric entry field or associated slider to adjust line spacing. By default, Line Spacing is described in points. Regardless of settings for individual fonts, the largest font on a line will always determine line spacing for that line.

✦ **Indentation:** Use this numeric entry field or associated slider to adjust the indent, also described by default in pixels, of the first line of a paragraph. The indent is relative to the left margin.

✦ **Left Margins:** Use this numeric entry field (or click the arrow button to invoke the interactive slider) to define the space between the text and the left border of the text box. By default, this space is described in pixels.

Figure 29-6 shows how selected text can be realigned, formatted, and edited for size, color, and other attributes. Here, the lower line of text is selected; it's point size reduced; and, as shown, its alignment set to Center.

Figure 29-6: Using the Character and Paragraph Panels to format selected text.

Note

The default units of measurement for both the Margin and Indentation entries of the Paragraph Properties dialog are determined by the Ruler Units for the movie. Ruler Units can be reset in the Movie Properties dialog, which is accessed from the Menu Bar with Modify ⇨ Movie or from the keyboard by pressing Ctrl+M (Command+M).

Using the Alignment submenu

Some of the settings of the Paragraph Panel are also available from the Alignment submenu that appears when you choose Text ⇨ Align from the Menu Bar:

✦ **Align Left:** Ctrl(Command)+Shift+L

✦ **Align Center:** Ctrl(Command)+Shift+C

✦ **Align Right:** Ctrl(Command)+Shift+R

✦ **Justify:** Ctrl(Command)+Shift+J

Using the Text Options Panel

The Text Options Panel can also be directly invoked from the Window menu with Window ➪ Panels ➪ Text Options. Or, if you use the default Panels layout, you can click the Character Panel button on the Launcher Bar and then select the tab to bring Text Options forward in the panel stack. This is the most varied of the text-related panels. Depending upon your choice of Text Behavior, it displays three option sets: Static, Dynamic, or Input Text.

Tip

There is no keyboard shortcut for the Text Options Panel, but you can make one with the new Flash 5 Keyboard Shortcuts dialog, Edit ➪ Keyboard Shortcuts.

As shown in Figure 29-7, when the Text Behavior is set to Static Text, the Text Options Panel has only two options (left). To choose another behavior, click the Text Behavior drop-down (right).

Text Behavior drop-down

Device Fonts   No options

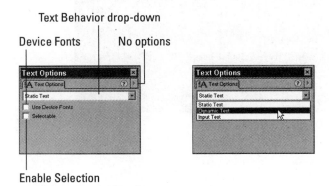

Enable Selection

Figure 29-7: The Text Options Panel

Note

As with the other text-related panels, the Options button is disabled on this panel.

Static (noneditable) text behavior

The default behavior for any text block created in (or pasted into) Flash is static. So, for display text and many of the more ordinary implementations of text in Flash, it's unnecessary to use the Text Options Panel. Nevertheless, you may encounter a situation that requires a text field to display information, but also enables users to select and copy the information. Or you might want to fine-tune the display quality of some text. That's when the Static Text Behavior of the Text Options Panel becomes indispensable:

✦ **Selectable:** Check this box to make selected text, or text that's entered subsequently, selectable when displayed on users' machines.

✦ **Use Device Fonts:** This little check box is the secret to a poorly documented, yet extremely powerful enhancement to the way in which Flash 5 handles text. *It is* not *a substitute for selecting one of the three_ device fonts that appear at the top of the Font Menu.* Rather, it's an innovative way in which Flash enables you to use many common fonts without embedding the characters. It also provides a mechanism that improves text display at small point sizes. For more details refer to the following sidebar.

As shown in the composite Figure 29-8, the chosen font is present on the system. The variations are the result of different settings in the Text Options Panel for Static Text. At the top, Use Device Fonts was unchecked. For the following two examples, Use Device Fonts was checked. However, in the middle example, Global Activation of the Type Manager was on, whereas for the bottom example, Global Activation of the Type Manager was off.

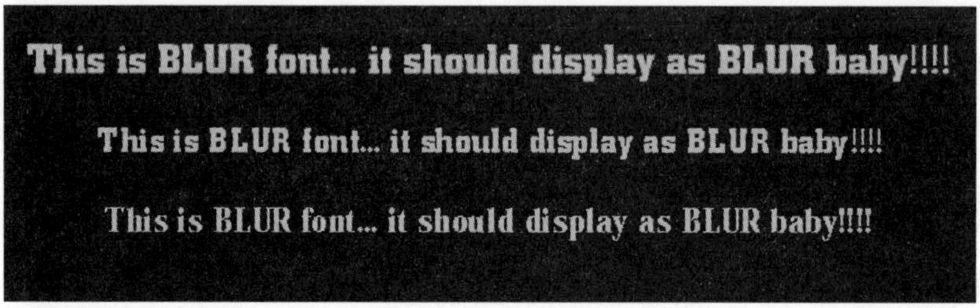

Figure 29-8: Using various Device Font settings

Editable Text fields

All Flash Text is created in text blocks or text boxes. Editable Text is no different except that Editable Text boxes are referred to as text fields, or Input Text boxes — that's probably because they are often used as empty fields in which users can input text, as with a form or a password entry. Think of an Editable Text field as an empty window with a variable — which is a name — attached to it. When text or data is sent to the Flash Movie, it is sent to the variable, which ensures that it will be displayed in the proper window. Flash 5 supports two kinds of editable text fields: Dynamic Text and Input Text. Both of these are introduced in the subsequent sections of this chapter.

Use Device Fonts

When Use Device Fonts is checked, the font is not embedded — only the Font Name, Font family/type (serif/sans serif/monospace), and other information are added to specify the font — which adds no more than 10 or 15 bytes to the .SWF file. This information is used so that the player on the user's system will know if it has the font or not. If the font is not present, it lets the system know whether the substitute font should be serif/sans serif.

Without Use Device Fonts checked, the font metrics for used characters are embedded, which results in a larger file size.

However, even if the user has the font installed, the same test file with Use Device Fonts checked and Use Device Fonts unchecked will not look the same:

✦ A font that is installed but has Use Device Fonts enabled renders better at smaller sizes. That's because there is no antialiasing or smoothing applied to any _device font (including _device fonts), regardless of its existence on your system.

✦ If the font is installed, but does *not* have Use Device Fonts enabled, then the characters from that font are embedded. This means that all text is smoothed (regardless of the fact that the font is available). Smoothed text can be illegible at small point sizes.

Finally, to accurately preview this Use Device Fonts setting on your machine, if you have a font manager (as most Web designers do), then you'll need to make sure you're careful about your font activation settings — make sure Global activation is turned off.

For best results with this specific Use Device Fonts option, we suggest that you limit your font selection to those that most of your audience is likely to have, or which will translate into one of the default _device fonts without disrupting the look of your design. Otherwise, for unusual fonts, we suggest that you either embed the characters (Device Font option unchecked) or, especially for headlines and display text, that you break the text apart.

Dynamic Text fields

Dynamic Text fields are often fed data from a server. Common uses for this are stocks, sports scores, or weather updates. Creative uses might include a daily memo, frequently updated statements, an introduction, journal, or a randomly selected poem. This content can be supplied from a database, read from a server-side application, or be loaded from another movie or another part of the same movie. Figure 29-9 shows the Text Options Panel when Dynamic Text is chosen from the Text Behavior drop-down list.

Text Behavior drop-down

Line Display
drop-down   No options

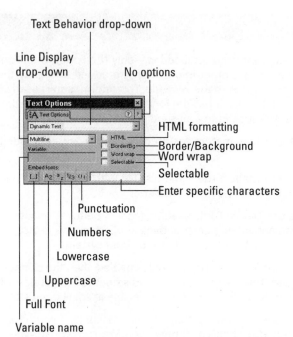

HTML formatting

Border/Background
Word wrap
Selectable

Enter specific characters

Punctuation

Numbers

Lowercase

Uppercase

Full Font

Variable name

Figure 29-9: Dynamic Text fields are used to display
dynamically updating text, such as stocks, sports,
or weather updates.

✦ **Line Display:** Use this drop-down to choose between a Single Line and a
Multiline field.

✦ **HTML:** By enabling this check box, Flash preserves rich text styles when displaying Dynamic Text. This includes font, font style, hyperlink, paragraph, and
other formatting consistent with permissible HTML tags. You can also enable
HTML in Text Options so that the entry field will accept formatting that has
been assigned to it in the Actions Panel.

✦ **Border/Background:** Use this to draw the text field with a border and a
background.

✦ **Word wrap:** With a Multiline text field, Word wrap will break lines at the end
of the box.

✦ **Variable:** This is where you name the text field, so that your dynamic data will
know where it is supposed to go.

✦ **Embed Fonts:** When embedding a font, Flash 5 gives you have control over
how much of the font is actually embedded. Choose one or more character
categories for the font — by clicking buttons for Full Font, Uppercase, Lowercase, Numbers, and/or Punctuation. Or, simply enter specific characters in
the text field.

Permissible HTML tags

You can use the following HTML tags to control the display of Dynamic and Input Text:

`<A>`	`<P>`	`<FONT FACE>`
`<B>`	`<U>`	`<FONT SIZE>`
`<I>`	` `	`<FONT COLOR>`

Caution   The `<B>` and `<I>` tags may cause text to disappear if you've included the font outlines. Apparently this is because the bold and italic variations of fonts are handled as separate fonts by Flash. (Technically, they *are* separate!)

Input Text fields

When users fill out forms and answer Web surveys, or enter a password, they are using Input text fields. Figure 29-10 shows the Text Options Panel when you choose Input Text from the Text Behavior drop-down list.

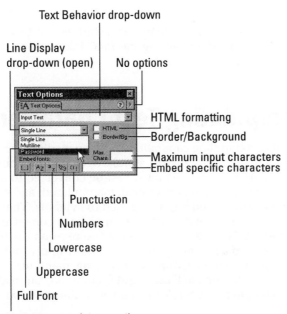

Figure 29-10: The Input Text Behavior has many of the same options as Dynamic Text. In addition to Single Line and Multiline, there is also an option to display the text as a Password.

Here are the options for Input Text fields:

✦ **Line Display:** In addition to Single Line and Multiline, there is also an option to display text as a Password.

✦ **HTML:** By enabling this check box, Flash preserves rich text styles when displaying Dynamic Text. This includes font, font style, hyperlink, paragraph, and other formatting consistent with permissible HTML tags. For specifics, see the explanation of Dynamic Text earlier in this chapter.

✦ **Border/Background:** Use this to draw the text field with a border and a background.

✦ **Maximum Input Characters:** Use this to limit the number of characters that a user can enter in this particular text field. Simply enter the maximum number of characters. This is most common when working with passwords.

✦ **Variable:** This is where you name the text field, so that your dynamic data will know where it is supposed to go.

✦ **Embed Fonts:** When embedding a font, Flash 5 gives you have control over how much of the font is actually embedded. Choose one or more character categories for the font — by clicking buttons for Full Font, Uppercase, Lowercase, Numbers, and/or Punctuation. Or, simply enter specific characters in the text field.

New Feature   Flash 5 enables you to use a Font as a Shared Library item, which means that you can link to the font and use it without embedding the font. This is covered in depth in Chapter 42, "Sharing and Loading Assets."

Reshaping and Manipulating Text Characters

In addition to all of the powerful text-handling capabilities previously discussed, Flash also gives you the ability to reshape and distort standard text to suit your taste (or lack thereof). To manipulate text, the text must first be converted to its component lines and fills. Then it can be reshaped, erased, manipulated, and distorted. Converted text characters can be grouped or changed to symbols. These items can also be animated. However, after text characters have been converted to lines and fills, they can no longer be edited as text. Even if you regroup the text characters and/or convert the text into a symbol, you can no longer apply font, kerning, or paragraph options. For more information on reshaping, manipulating, and animating text, see Chapter 32, "Drawing in Flash," and Chapter 33, "Animating in Flash." But just to get you started, here are a few tips and guidelines for manipulating text in Flash:

✦ To convert text characters to component lines and fills: First, the text characters that you want to convert must be selected, or highlighted. Then choose Modify ➪ Break Apart from the Menu Bar. To undo, choose Edit ➪ Undo from the Menu Bar.

✦ Rotation and Break Apart can only be applied to outline fonts such as TrueType fonts.

✦ On Macs, PostScript fonts can only be broken apart if ATM (Adobe Type Manager) is installed.

✦ Bitmap fonts disappear from the screen if you attempt to break them apart.

✦ Test whether a font is a bitmapped font by choosing View ⇨ Antialias from the Menu Bar. If the text still appears with ragged edges, it is a bitmapped font and will disappear when broken apart.

Summary

✦ Although minor issues may come up when working with text in Flash, it is relatively simple to work cross-platform and deliver high-quality textual presentations to users on both Macs and PCs with many varied configurations.

✦ The Text Tool is used to create and edit text. Flash's text-handling capabilities are robust and well implemented. There are many improvements to the text handling in Flash 5.

✦ The Text Tool delivers a broad range of control for generating, positioning, fine-tuning, and editing text.

✦ The most powerful controls for working with text are located in the Character, Paragraph, and Text Options Panels.

✦ Flash offers three kinds of text fields for use in interactive projects and for delivering dynamic textual content: Editable Text, Dynamic Text, and Input Text.

✦ Although textual characters and words are complex outlines, they can broken apart in Flash so that they can be reshaped, morphed, manipulated, and animated.

✦   ✦   ✦

Creating Flash Graphics

Exploring the Timeline

The timeline is the backbone of Flash. A clear understanding of the timeline is critical to productive work in Flash. As you'll soon learn, one of the most powerful features of the timeline is that a quick glance at the timeline frames provides a lot of information about what is on those frames.

Viewing the Timeline

The timeline graphically orders Flash content across two dimensions: time and depth.

✦ **Time:** The sequence of frames is arranged horizontally, from left to right, as they appear in time. Thus, if your movie is set to 20 frames per second, frame 40 occurs at the 2-second point of your animation.

Note Although they say that time and space are without limits, there are limits to nearly everything, including the number of frames (time) on any one Flash timeline. You get 16,000 frames — which will result in a timeline so unwieldy that it will extend into next Christmas. If that's not enough timeline for you, you should be working with scenes and movie clips.

✦ **Depth:** The timeline layers enable you to separate content on discrete layers. These layers are arranged vertically, from bottom to top. They also enable you to separate content from actions, comments, labels, and sounds. Any items placed on layers above will block out any items in layers beneath them, without otherwise affecting each other. In the editing environment, you can set layer visibility (the eye icon), editability (the lock icon), and the display mode — regular or just outlines (the square icon). Note, however, that these settings do not affect the final movie: All layer content, regardless of visibility or outline settings, is included in the final movie.

At this point, it's worth noting that Flash 5 occasioned several changes to the way the timeline works. These changes were designed to make frame spans more easily recognized and manipulated. (A frame span is the group of frames ranging from one keyframe to, but not including, the next.)

Because the frames between two keyframes do not add any new information to the movie, they really depend on the keyframes preceding them. Thus, in a logical sense, it's reasonable to be able to select them as a singular entity (the keyframe and all of the frames that depend on it), rather than individually. This group selection also makes moving frame spans easier — clicking a frame span turns the cursor into a hand and enables dragging.

Tip   Although some accomplished Flash artists say that they find the new Flash 5 timeline confusing, we recommend that you use the new timeline because it really is better. But, if you've tried and find that you are more comfortable with the Flash 4 timeline, you'll be happy to know that you may revert to some of the Flash 4 functionality. To revert to Flash 4 functionality, Choose Edit ⇨ Preferences ⇨ General, check the Flash 4 Selection Style and Flash 4 Frame Drawing check boxes, and then click OK.

Figure 30-1 shows the many features, options, and controls of the timeline.

As shown in Figure 30-1, the principal parts of the timeline are:

✦ **Title Bar:** This identifies the timeline if the timeline is not docked near the top of the screen.

✦ **Active Layer Toggle:** This is more of an icon, really. To make a layer active, either click the layer's name, or select a frame or group of frames. Then the pencil icon appears, indicating that the layer is now active — that's in addition to this more obvious clue: The Layer Bar of the active layer is black, whereas inactive Layer Bars are gray. Only one layer can be active at a time.

✦ **Show/Hide Layer Toggle:** This is a true toggle. Click the dot beneath the eye icon to hide the contents of this layer from view on the stage. When the layer is hidden, a red X appears over the dot. To return the layer to visibility, click the X.

Caution   Hidden layers export, and any content on stage within a hidden layer will become visible upon export. Even if the content is offstage and not visible, it may add considerably to the file size when a Flash movie is published, so you should save your .FLA and then purge these layers before your final export.

✦ **Lock/Unlock Layer Toggle:** This toggle locks or unlocks the layer to either prevent (or enable) further editing. As with Show/Hide, when the layer is locked, a red X appears over the dot.

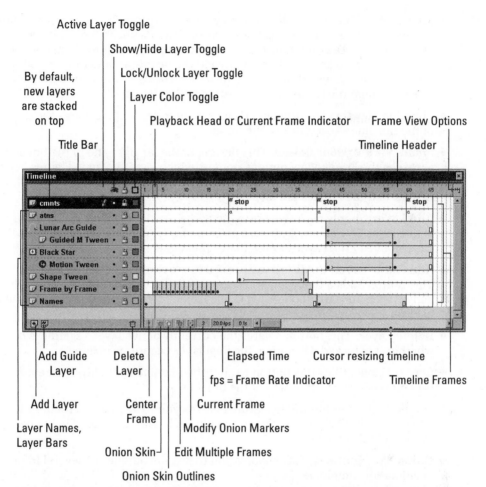

Active Layer Toggle

Show/Hide Layer Toggle

Lock/Unlock Layer Toggle

By default, new layers are stacked on top

Layer Color Toggle

Playback Head or Current Frame Indicator

Frame View Options

Title Bar

Timeline Header

Add Guide Layer

Delete Layer

Elapsed Time

Cursor resizing timeline

fps = Frame Rate Indicator

Timeline Frames

Add Layer

Center Frame

Current Frame

Layer Names, Layer Bars

Modify Onion Markers

Onion Skin

Edit Multiple Frames

Onion Skin Outlines

Figure 30-1: Because animation is the art of making things happen with pictures that change over time, the timeline might be considered the backbone of Flash. The timeline uses layers and frames to organize and control a movie's contents.

✦ **Layer Color Toggle:** This toggles the colored layer outlines on or off. When on, the dot changes into a small square outline of the same color as the outlines for the layer. When on, the items in the layer are displayed only as colored outlines, which can be useful for analyzing and finessing animated effects. The Layer Color can be changed with the Outline Color control of the Layer Properties dialog (shown in Figure 30-7), which is accessed by choosing Modify ➪ Layer.

✦ **Playhead or Current Frame Indicator:** The red rectangle with a line extending down through all layers is the Playhead. The Playhead indicates the current Frame. Drag it left or right along the timeline to move from one area of the timeline to another. Push it beyond the visible area to force-scroll the timeline. You can also drag the Playhead at a consistent rate for a preview of your animation; this is called "scrubbing the timeline."

✦ **Timeline Header:** The Timeline Header is the ruler that measures the time of the timeline — each tick is one frame.

✦ **Frame View options button:** This button, at the far right end of the timeline, accesses the Frame View options pop-up, which — as shown in Figures 30-38 and 30-9 — affords many options for the manner in which both the Timeline Header and the Frames are displayed.

✦ **Add Layer:** Simply click this button to add a new layer above the currently active layer. By default, layers are given numeric names. Double-click the Layer name in the Layer Bar to change the name.

✦ **Add Guide Layer:** Guide layers are used to move elements along a path. This button adds a Guide Layer directly above (and linked to) the currently active layer. To learn about using Guide Layers, refer to Chapter 33, "Animating in Flash."

✦ **Delete Layer:** This button deletes the currently active layer, regardless of whether it is locked. Of course, the final layer cannot be deleted.

✦ **Center Frame:** Click this button to shift the timeline so that the current frame is centered in the visible area of the timeline.

✦ **Onion Skin:** The Onion Skin feature enables you to see several frames of animation simultaneously. (Onion skinning is further described in the next section of this chapter.)

✦ **Onion Skin Outlines:** This enables you to see the outlines of several frames of animation simultaneously.

✦ **Edit Multiple Frames:** Normally, onion skinning only permits you to edit the current frame. Click this button to make each frame between the Onion Skin Markers editable.

✦ **Modify Onion Markers:** Click this button to evoke the Modify Onion Markers pop-up, as shown in Figure 30-15. In addition to manual adjustments, the options are used to control the behavior and range of onion skinning.

✦ **Current Frame:** This indicates the number of the current frame. It's most useful when working with small frame sizes, which, as shown in Figure 30-38, can be specified from the Frame View options.

✦ **Frame Rate Indicator:** This indicates the Frame Rate of the movie, measured in fps, or frames per second. Although the program default is 12 fps, usually 20 fps is a good starting point. The Frame Rate is specified in the Movie Properties dialog, which is accessed by choosing Modify ➪ Movie (Ctrl/Command+M). You can also double-click the Frame Rate Indicator to invoke the Movie Properties dialog.

Note The fps setting is not a constant or absolute — it means maximum frame rate. The actual frame rate is dependent upon a number of variables, including download speed, processor speed, and machine resources — these are variables over which you have no control. However, another factor, over which you do have control, is the intensity of the animation: Complex movement with multiple moving parts is more processor intensive than simple movement. It is *very* important that Frame Rate be established — with a little testing on various machines — early on in your development process.

✦ **Elapsed Time:** This indicates the total movie time, measured in fps, which would elapse from frame 1 to the current frame — provided that the movie is played back at the specified speed.

Manipulating the Timeline

The position, size, and shape of the timeline can be manipulated to better suit your workflow, much like any other Flash window or panel. On a dual monitor system, the timeline can be exiled to the second monitor, together with all the panels — leaving the stage clear and unencumbered for wild creativity.

✦ Move the timeline by dragging it by the Timeline Title Bar, which is the bar at the top that says timeline. If the timeline is docked, click anywhere in the gray area above the layer stack to undock the timeline and reposition it.

✦ If undocked, resize the timeline by dragging on the lower right corner (PC), or the size box (Mac), which is also in the right corner. If docked, drag the bar at the bottom of the timeline that separates the layers from the application window, either up or down.

✦ To resize the name and icon controls (either to accommodate longer names or to apportion more of the timeline to frames), click and drag the bar that separates the name and icon controls from the frames area.

Layer specifics

Knowing how to work with layers makes the Flash creation process flow much more smoothly.

By default, new layers are stacked on top of the currently active layer. To rearrange layers, click in the blank area (between the layer name and the layer toggle icons), and drag the Layer Bar to the desired position in the layer stack and release.

For enhanced functionality and control, as well as to enable reliable interactivity and ActionScripting, it's a good habit to give your layers meaningful names. Simply double-click the layer's name on the Layer Bar and enter a meaningful name.

Timeline specifics

The new Flash 5 timeline still offers you many clues about what's going on with your animation, as shown in Figures 30-2 and 30-3.

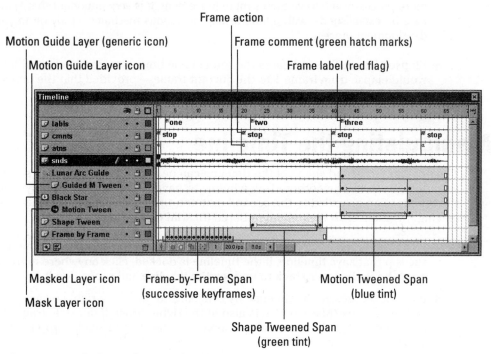

Figure 30-2: Flash 5 Style Layer specifics

✦ **Keyframe:** A keyframe is any frame in which the contents of the frame may differ from the contents of either the previous or subsequent frames. Solid circles designate keyframes with content.

✦ **Keyframe spans:** Keyframe spans — newly designated in Flash 5 — are the sections from one keyframe up to (but not including) the next keyframe, which are separated from each other by vertical lines. Thus, as shown, the span between frames 3 and 6 in the buttons layer is a keyframe span. Note that these spans can now be dragged intact, as a whole, to a different location. This functionality is shown in the selected span between frames 30 and 13 in the buttons layer.

 • **Final keyframe:** The final frame of a keyframe span with content is marked with an empty rectangle (that is, frame 6 of the buttons layer), and a vertical line to the right of the rectangle.

Empty keyframes

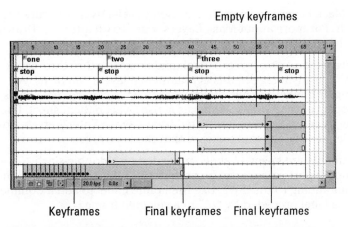

Keyframes   Final keyframes   Final keyframes

Figure 30-3: Here's the same timeline that was shown in Figure 30-2, except that it's cropped to show just the frames area of the timeline, with three varieties of keyframes called out.

- **Intermediate frame(s):** The intermediate frames of a nonempty keyframe span are gray.

- **Empty span(s):** Empty spans are white (for example, the visible portion of the sweep mc layer).

✦ **Frame-by-Frame Animation:** Frame-by-Frame Animation is animation composed entirely of keyframes. In a Frame-by-Frame Animation, the contents of each individual frame differs from both the previous and subsequent frames. For more information on Frame-by-Frame Animation, refer to Chapter 33, "Animating in Flash."

✦ **Tweened Animation:** Tweened Animation is an animation where the movement or change is interpolated, or tweened, over a range of frames that extend between two keyframes. (For more information refer to Chapter 33, "Animating in Flash.") An arrow stretching across a colored keyframe span designates a Tween, of which there are two varieties:

- **Motion Tweens:** Motion Tweens are indicated by a blue tint.

- **Shape Tweens:** Shape Tweens are indicated by a green tint.

✦ **Motion Guide Layer:** A Motion Guide Layer is used to guide an animated item along a path, which can be drawn with either the Pencil or the Line Tool. For more about Motion Guide Layers, refer to Chapter 33, "Animating in Flash."

✦ **Mask Layer:** A Mask Layer is a layer that is used to selectively obscure the layers beneath it. For more about Mask Layers, refer to Chapter 32, "Drawing in Flash," and Chapter 33, "Animating in Flash."

✦ **Label:** Labels are used to give layers meaningful names, rather than using frame numbers. The advantage of this is that named layers can be moved without breaking ActionScript calls assigned to them. Upon export, Labels are included as part of the .SWF, so it makes sense to keep them short. Use the Frame Panel to add a Label to a selected frame. Press Enter/Return after typing a frame label or comment to ensure that the label takes.

✦ **Comment:** Comments are special Labels, preceded by a double-slash "//" — Comments do not export, so you can be verbose (within the confines of the timeline) without adding to the .SWF. Use the Frame Panel to add a Comment, which is merely a label preceded by "//," to a selected frame.

Tip

Jon begins nearly *every* Flash project with the creation of four labeled layers at the top of the layer stack of the new timeline. The consistency of his working methodology ensures clarity and simplicity when returning to edit old files or when sharing files with other contributors. These abbreviations are as follows (it's not important that you adopt *these* conventions, but it is important that you institute some conventional consistency to structure your work): lbls = labels, cmnts = comments, atns = actions, and snds = sounds.

✦ **Waveform:** This squiggly blue line in the snds layer is the waveform of a placed sound.

✦ **Frame Actions:** The small a's in frames 1, 20, 40, and 60 of the atns layer designate the presence of frame actions.

Caution

If you copy multiple frames extending down through multiple layers and paste them into another timeline, you'll usually lose your layer names.

General preferences

The General Tab of the Flash Preferences dialog, which is accessed from the Main Menu by choosing Edit ➪ Preferences, has two sections specifically related to the timeline and its behavior in Flash 5. These are Timeline Options and Highlight Color. For more about the other aspects of the Flash Preferences dialog, refer to Chapter 24, "Exploring the Interface: Panels, Settings, and More." Otherwise, you'll find that the relevant timeline behaviors are discussed in greater detail here.

Timeline options

The Disable Timeline Docking option prevents the timeline from attaching to the application window after it's been deployed as a floating panel.

On both the Mac and PC, to undock the timeline and deploy it as a floating palette as shown in Figure 30-4, click the gray area to the left of the eyeball icon and then, with the mouse still depressed, drag the palette away from the application window. To prevent the timeline from docking, press the Control key while dragging. To permanently disable timeline docking, use Edit ➪ Preferences and, under Timeline Options, check the Disable Timeline Docking check box. As shown in Figure 30-4, the timeline can be dragged away from its docked position by clicking the Timeline Header and dragging the timeline away from the edge of the Flash application.

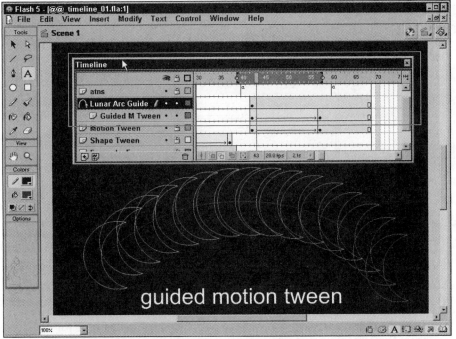

Figure 30-4: The timeline deployed as a floating palette

The next two options in the Preferences dialog let you revert to the Flash 4 timeline style:

✦ **Flash 4 Selection Style:** Flash 5 introduced a new methodology for selecting frames in the timeline. This option toggles that functionality back to Flash 4 Selection Style.

✦ **Flash 4 Frame Drawing:** Flash 5 also introduced a new methodology for drawing frames in the timeline. This option toggles that functionality back to the Flash 4 style.

Figures 30-5 and 30-6 show the difference between the timelines in Flash 5 and Flash 4.

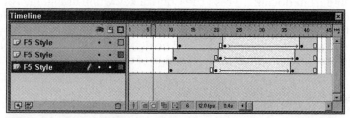

Figure 30-5: Flash 5 frame drawing

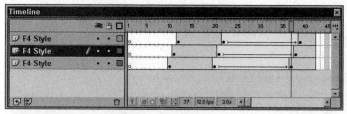

Figure 30-6: Flash 4 frame drawing

Highlight color

The Highlight Color options in the Preferences dialog control which colors are used for selected objects:

+ **Highlight Color:** This preference controls the highlight color for selected groups, symbols, or text — excluding shapes.

+ **Use this color:** Check this option to choose a Highlight Color for selections from the Swatches pop-up.

+ **Use layer color:** Check this option to use the layer color as the Highlight Color for selections. This option enables you to distinguish selected items according to their associated layer color (which you set in the Layer Properties dialog).

Layer Properties

Layer Properties dialog is most readily accessed by Right/Ctrl+clicking any Layer Bar and then choosing Properties from the layer contextual menu. It can also be invoked by choosing Modify ➪ Layer.

The layers contextual menu

As shown in Figure 30-7, the layers contextual menu affords convenient access to a number of layer-specific operations, many of which are duplicated elsewhere.

✦ **Show All:** Shows all layers. If some layers have had their visibility turned off, this makes them all visible.

✦ **Lock Others:** Unlocks the active layer and locks all other layers.

✦ **Hide Others:** Makes the currently active layer visible, if it is not visible, and hides all others.

✦ **Insert Layer:** Inserts a new layer above the currently active layer.

✦ **Delete Layer:** Deletes the active layer.

✦ **Properties:** Invokes the Layer Properties dialog for the currently active layer.

✦ **Guide:** Transforms the current layer into a Guide Layer.

A Guide Layer differs from a Motion Guide Layer. A Motion Guide Layer is linked to a Guided Layer, which usually has a Motion Tweened animated item that follows a path that is drawn on the Guided Layer. A Guide Layer is independent. A Guide Layer is most often used for placing a bitmap design composition, or other items that should not export with the project. Neither a Guide Layer nor a Motion Guide Layer export with the project.

✦ **Add Motion Guide:** Inserts a new Motion Guide Layer directly above the current layer and automatically links the current layer to the Guided Layer.

✦ **Mask:** Transforms the current layer into a Mask Layer.

✦ **Show Masking:** Use this command on either the Mask or the Masked Layer to activate the masking effect — essentially, this command locks both layers simultaneously, which enables the masking effect.

The Layer Properties dialog

The Layer Properties dialog is used to control and edit the properties of the active layer and to facilitate routine layer operations.

✦ **Name:** Use this option to change the name of the layer.

✦ **Show:** With this option checked, the layer is visible; otherwise, it's hidden.

✦ **Lock:** This option enables you to lock or unlock the layer.

✦ **Type:** These options are used to set the type of layer:

• **Normal:** This is the default, used for drawing and animation.

• **Guide:** Guide Layers have two purposes. They can be used either as Motion Guides or as drawing guides. Guide Layers aren't exported, so they aren't visible and they don't add to the exported file size. Guided Layers are linked to a Guide Layer.

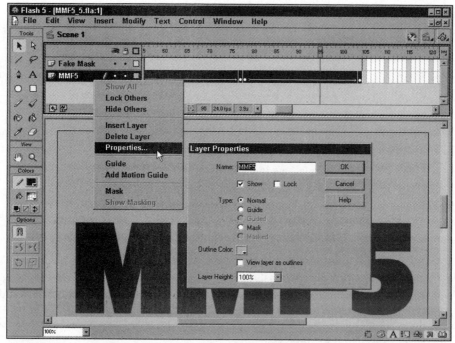

Figure 30-7: This composite screen shot shows the layer contextual menu and ensuing Layer Properties dialog.

Tip

An empty Guide Layer can be used to organize multiple layers of related content for better timeline organization. It can also be used as a repository for custom strokes and fills.

- **Mask:** A Mask Layer is used in conjunction with a Masked Layer to create special effects. The Masked Layer is hidden except beneath filled areas of the Mask Layer that it's linked to.

✦ **Outline Color:** Use this to choose the color of the layer's outlines.

✦ **View layer as outlines:** When this is checked, all items on the layer appear as outlines, according to the color chosen in the previous option. Viewing as outlines speeds the display while editing because all items are shown as thin outlines. As discussed in the previous section regarding General Preferences, this option can be used in conjunction with the Highlight Color options of the General tab of Edit ⇨ Preferences, to either give each layer a unique color, or to employ a global color for all outlines.

✦ **Layer Height:** Use this to increase the height of the *individual* layer. This means that you can have most layers displayed tiny, and yet have others display with more visible content. This is useful if you use the Preview or Preview in Context Timeline options on the Frame View options pop-up. It's also useful when viewing the waveforms of sound files.

Frame View options

As shown in Figure 30-38, the Frame View options pop-up is used to customize the size, color, and style of frames displayed within the timeline. These features can prove very helpful when you are working with cartoon animation, and want to see each frame previewed. Or, if you are working on an extremely long project with a huge timeline, it can be helpful to tweak the size of the individual frames, so that you can see more of the timeline at a single glance.

Figure 30-38: The Frame View options pop-up is used to customize the size, color, and style of frames displayed within the timeline.

When used in conjunction with the Layer Height option of the Layer Properties dialog, you can customize your timeline in myriad ways to better suit your particular project. Your options include:

✦ **Tiny, Small, Normal, Medium, Large:** These options afford a range of sizes for the width of individual frames. When working on extremely long animations, narrower frames facilitate some operations.

✦ **Short:** This option makes the frames shorter in height, permitting more Layer Bars to be visible in the same amount of space. When working with many layers, short layers help squelch the tedium of scrolling through layers of layers.

✦ **Tinted Frames:** This option toggles tinted frames on or off. With Tinted Frames on, the tints are as follows:

• **White:** Empty or unused frames (for any layer). This is the default. The white color of empty or unused frames is unaffected regardless of whether Tinted Frames is on or off.

• **Gray:** There are two kinds of gray frames: (a) The grayed-out gray frames in the default (empty) timeline are a quick visual reference that indicates every fifth frame, like the tick marks on a ruler. These tick frames appear regardless of whether Tinted Frames are enabled. (b) The solid gray color, which appears when Tinted Frames are enabled, indicates that a frame is either filled or otherwise used. Frame usage means that the frame has something in it, which may be either visible or invisible as, for example, an item with an alpha of 0 percent, or a hidden symbol.

• **Blue:** Indicates a Motion Tween span.

• **Green:** Indicates a Shape Tween span.

Note

Regardless of whether Tinted Frames is enabled, Flash displays tween arrows (and keyframe dots) to a tween. However, with Tinted Frames disabled, tweened spans are indicted by a faintly checked gray pattern, and the arrows display in color to the indicate the type of tween:

- **A red arrow:** Indicates a Motion Tween span, when Tinted Frames are off.

- **A green arrow:** Indicates a Shape Tween span, when Tinted Frames are off.

✦ **Preview:** As shown at the top of Figure 30-9, the preview option displays tiny thumbnails that maximize the element in each frame. Thus, the scale of elements is not consistent from frame to frame. (Frame 1 of the animation is shown in Figure 30-9.) In this Frame-by-frame animation, the phases of the moon increase over a span of 15 frames.

✦ **Preview in Context:** As shown at the bottom of Figure 30-9, when previewed in context, the same animation is seen with accurate scale from frame to frame (because elements are not maximized for each frame).

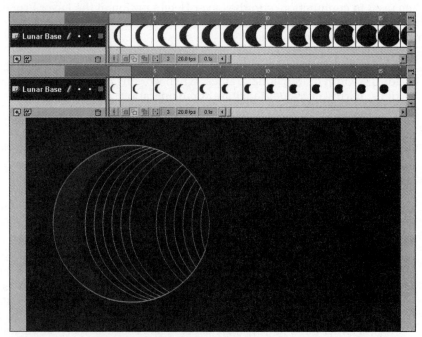

Figure 30-9: In this composite screen shot, the Frames are shown with Preview option (top) and Frames shown with Preview in Context option (middle) for the same animation (bottom).

Scene and Symbol Bar

Nested between the Menu Bar and the top of the timeline is the Scene and Symbol Bar shown in Figure 30-10. This bar is also shown in context in Figure 30-1 and elsewhere in this chapter. The Scene Name button, at the far left, indicates the name of the current scene. When in Symbol Editing Mode, click this button to return to the current scene. To the right is the Edit Scene button, and at the far right is the Edit Symbols button. Click either button to evoke a menu of scenes or symbols that are editable within the current movie.

Cross-Reference For more about Symbols, and the Symbol Editing Mode in particular, refer to Chapter 31, "Checking Out the Library: Symbols and Instances."

Figure 30-10: The Scene and Symbol Bar

Scenes are used to organize a Flash project into logical, manageable parts. By default, on export Flash plays back all of the scenes within the movie in the order in which they are listed in the Scene Panel.

Note Since Flash 4, with the increasingly robust power of ActionScript, there's been a trend among many advanced developers to move away from Scene-based architectures. Although this may require a shift in thinking, it has been shown to result in files that download more efficiently and that are easier to edit due to their modular organization. It's like the difference between one huge ball of all-purpose twine that's the size of a house, and a large drawer filled with manageable spools — sorted neatly according to color and weight.

To navigate to other scenes from within the Movie Editor:

✦ Click the Edit Scene button at the far right of the Scene and Symbol Bar, and then click the desired scene.

✦ Navigate to a specific scene from the View Menu with the View ➪ Go To command.

Use the Scene Panel, shown in Figure 30-11, to manage your scenes. The Scene Panel may be accessed with either of these commands: Modify ➪ Scene or Window ➪ Panels ➪ Scene.

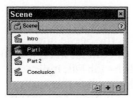

Figure 30-11: The Scene Panel

When your movie is published to .SWF, the scenes play in the order in which they are listed in either the Scene Panel or the Scene pop-up.

✦ To delete a scene, either use the Scene Panel's delete button or, from the Insert menu, use the Insert ➪ Remove Scene command.

✦ To add a scene, either use the Scene Panel's add button or, from the Insert menu, use Insert ➪ Scene.

✦ Use the duplicate button on the Scene Panel to duplicate a scene.

✦ To rename a scene, simply double-click the scene name and type the new name.

✦ To rearrange scene order, simply click and drag a scene to alter its position with in the Scene Panel. You can use actions to force the movie to access scenes outside the default linear order. For more about actions, refer to Part X, "Adding Basic Interactivity to Flash Movies."

Caution

There are several limitations to the use of scenes in more advanced, ActionScript environments. For example, you can't issue a command from within a Movie Clip to go to and play a frame in another scene.

The Timeline/Stage Relationship

So far in this chapter, we have focused on the features of the timeline and we have shown how the timeline offers detailed control of Flash functionality, especially as regards its ordering of time from left to right. Now we are going to look at the manner in which timeline relates to the depth of a Flash movie, or the arrangement of items from the front to the back of the Stage.

Stacking order

Within a single layer, Flash stacks like items in the order in which they are placed or created, with the most recent item on top, subject to the *kind* of item. The rules that control the stacking order of various kinds of items are simple:

✦ Within a layer, ungrouped, drawn lines and shapes are always at the *bottom* level, with the most recently drawn shape or line at the top of that layer's stack. Furthermore, unless you take precautions, drawn items either compound with, or cut into, the drawing beneath them.

✦ Groups and symbols (including bitmaps) stack above lines and shapes in the *overlay* level. To change the stacking order of several drawings, it's often advisable to group them first, as described in the next section of this chapter.

To change the stacking order within a layer, first select the item that you want to move. Then, do one of the following:

✦ Select Modify ⇨ Arrange ⇨ Bring to Front or Send to Back to move the item to the top or bottom of the stacking order.

✦ Select Modify ⇨ Arrange ⇨ Move Ahead or Move Behind to move the item ahead or back one position in the stacking order.

Remember the stacking order rules: You won't be able to bring an ungrouped drawing above a group or symbol—if you need that drawing on top, group it and then move it.

Layers are another factor in the stacking order. To stack an item in a lower layer above an item in a higher layer you simply change the order of the layer among the other layers: First activate the layer, and then drag the Layer Bar to the desired position in the layer stack of the timeline.

Tip

Although having a million layers in your Flash movie might be hard to manage and will, most likely, result in a huge and unwieldy .FLA that requires massive RAM, neither the file size nor the performance of the final .SWF will be adversely impacted because Flash flattens movies upon export to .SWF.

Grouping

Grouping drawings makes them easier to handle. Rather than manipulating a single drawing, group several drawings to work with them as a single item. Grouping also prevents shapes from being altered by other shapes. Furthermore, the stacking of groups is more easily controlled than ungrouped drawings. Here's how to create groups:

1. Use Shift+click to select everything that you want to group—any combination of items: shapes, lines, and symbols—even other groups.

2. Select Modify ⇨ Group (Ctrl+G or Command+G). The selected elements are now grouped.

3. To ungroup everything, select the group then use Modify ⇨ Ungroup (Ctrl+Shift+G or Command+Shift+G).

Caution

Be careful when ungrouping—your newly ungrouped drawings may alter or eliminate drawings below in the same layer.

Editing groups

To edit a group:

1. Either select the group and then choose Edit ➪ Edit Selected, or double-click the group.

2. Everything on stage—except for the parts of the group—is dimmed, indicating that only the group is editable.

3. Make the changes in the same way you would edit any items.

4. To stop editing the group, choose Edit ➪ Edit All (or double-click an empty part of the stage). Items on stage return to normal color.

Editing on the Timeline

After you create your artwork and animations, you may find that you need to edit it. Flash has features that make such edits quick and easy. You can move frames and keyframes, copy and paste frames and keyframes, insert frames and keyframes, delete frames and keyframes, change the sequence of an animation, and edit the contents of a keyframe. You can also use onion skinning to view frames at one time, and you can even edit multiple frames at once.

✦ **Selecting Frames:** The methods for selecting single frames and spans of frames differ slightly. For users of previous versions of Flash, this may take a little getting used to. Overall, however, we find the new methodology is an improvement. Of course, if you aren't happy with the Flash 5 timeline, you can use Edit ➪ Preferences ➪ General, to make your timeline behave more like the familiar Flash 4 timeline (as explained earlier in this chapter).

Tip

If you're comfortable with Flash 4, you need to know this: Selecting multiple frames and then hitting F6 to generate multiple keyframes no longer works. Instead, select your multiple frames and then use this command, Modify ➪ Frames ➪ Convert to Keyframes. If you still want F6 to generate multiple keyframes, then make a custom Keyboard Shortcut with Edit ➪ Keyboard Shortcuts. (For more on Edit ➪ Keyboard Shortcuts, refer to Chapter 24, "Exploring the Interface: Panels, Settings, and More.")

  • **Frame Spans:** To select a span of frames extending between two keyframes, click anywhere between the keyframes. The cursor will switch to a hand and the entire span will be selected.

  • **Single Frames within a Span:** To select a single frame within a span, press the Ctrl/Command key and click a frame. Keyframes at either end of a span can usually be selected with a simple click.

  • **Single Frames not within a Span:** To select a single frame that is not implicated with a span, simply click to select it.

✦ **Moving Frames:** Select the frame(s) that need to be moved, and drag them to the new location.

✦ **Extending the Duration of a Span:** To extend the duration of a span, which is the same result as extending a keyframe, select the keyframe and then drag the keyframe to the position where you want the span to end.

✦ **Copying Frames:** Select the frame(s) that you want to copy. Either Choose Edit ➪ Copy Frames from the menu, or press the Alt/Option key and drag to copy the selected frames to another location in the timeline.

You can select a range of frames that you want to copy and drop them anywhere in the timeline — even if there are no frames in the destination area. Any gaps that might result in the timeline will be automatically filled with static frames. In addition, you can Alt/Option+Drag from one layer to another, or even select frames from multiple layers and drag and drop to multiple layers — provided the destination layers exist prior to the operation!

✦ **Pasting Frames:** Select the frame(s) that you want to paste the copied frame(s) into, and select Edit ➪ Paste Frames from the menu.

✦ **Inserting Frames:** Select the point at which you would like to insert a new frame, and select Insert ➪ Frame (F5) from the menu.

✦ **Inserting Keyframes:** Select the point at which you would like to insert a new keyframe, and select Insert ➪ Keyframe (F6) from the menu. Or, you can Right+Click/Ctrl+Click the frame that you want to make a keyframe and then, in the contextual menu, select Insert Keyframe.

✦ **Inserting Blank Keyframes:** Select the point at which you would like to insert a new blank keyframe, and select Insert ➪ Blank Keyframe (F7) from the menu. Or, you can Right+Click/Ctrl+Click the frame that you want to make a keyframe and then, in the contextual menu, select Insert Blank Keyframe.

If you already have content in the current layer and you insert a keyframe, a new keyframe will be created that duplicates the content of the keyframe immediately prior. But if you insert a blank keyframe, the static content of the prior keyframe will cease and the blank keyframe will, as its name implies, be void of content. For a hands-on example, refer to the keyframes folder within the ch30 folder of the CD-ROM.

Figure 30-12 shows a timeline that illustrates some editing points. The top layer shows the original layer, which has content in the first frame, followed by 19 empty frames. This layer was copied into all three lower layers, with the result that the initial content of all four layers was the same. When a keyframe was inserted at Frame 10 of the Keyframe layer, the content of keyframe 1 was copied into the new keyframe, and the gray color of the subsequent frames indicates the continuity of static content. But, when a blank keyframe was inserted at frame 10 of the Blank Keyframe layer, a blank keyframe was inserted and the continuity of content was stopped, as indicated by the white frames extending from frame 10 to frame 20. The dotted line running through the frames of the bottom layer shows what happens when a tween is missing the final keyframe, which often happens when editing on the timeline.

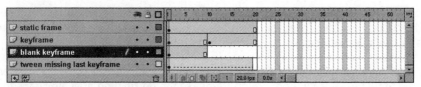

Figure 30-12: Editing on the timeline

✦ **Adding Content from the Library:** To add content from the Library to a selected keyframe, drag an instance of the item from the Library and onto the Stage.

✦ **Deleting Frames (Remove Frames):** Select the frame(s) that you want to delete, and then select Insert ⇨ Remove Frames (Shift+F5), or else Right/Ctrl+click the frame and select Remove Frames from the contextual menu. This no longer works for deleting keyframes; instead, it will remove an intervening frame and scoot the keyframe backward toward frame 1.

✦ **Clearing a Keyframe:** To obliterate a keyframe and its contents, use Clear Keyframe. Select the keyframe and use Insert ⇨ Clear Keyframe (Shift+F6), or use the contextual menu, Right/Ctrl+click, and choose Clear Keyframe. When deleting a keyframe, the deleted keyframe and all of the frames following, up to the next keyframe, are replaced with the static contents of the previous keyframe.

✦ **Reversing Animation:** Select the animation sequence that you would like to reverse, and select Modify ⇨ Frames ⇨ Reverse from the menu. For this to work, you must have keyframes at both the beginning and the end of the selected sequence.

✦ **Editing the Contents of a Keyframe:** Select the keyframe that you want to edit. Then, on the Stage, edit the contents of the keyframe.

Caution

There are several issues regarding single-frame movies, which are movies whose architecture has shifted all content off of the Main Timeline and, via Movie Clips, has planted that content in a single frame on the Main Timeline: (a) Netscape can have a problem loading these movies properly. (b) Because ActionScripts on frames are evoked before the frame itself is drawn, the player can have problems if it has not finished loading all the necessary components before it starts to run the script. The fix for both issues is to delay contents and scripts by placing them at the second frame of the Main Timeline.

Onion Skinning

Onion skinning enables you to view multiple frames at once. When any of the three Onion Skin buttons is clicked, Onion Skin Markers appear on the timeline, centered over the current frame. These markers indicate the range of frames that will be displayed with onion skinning applied. To reposition either of these markers manually, click and drag it to another location on the timeline. Or, you can use the Modify Onion Markers pop-up to manage the manner in which onion skinning displays. By default, the current frame is displayed in full color, while the remaining frames are dimmed out. As shown in Figure 30-13, they appear as if they were each drawn on a sheet of onion skin paper and then stacked in order. (Note how the frames are dimmed with increasing opacity as they move farther away from the current time marker. This is an important visual clue that works both in filled and outline modes.) Only the selected frame can be edited, but this feature is useful because it enables you to see how your edits will affect the flow of the entire selected animation. It's also useful for Frame-by-Frame Animation, because you can see each part of the animation without having to switch back and forth.

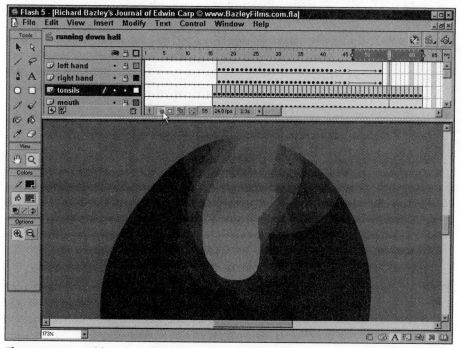

Figure 30-13: With onion skinning turned on, the current frame is shown normally, while the surrounding frames are successively dimmed. The Onion Skin Markers are visible here on the Timeline Header, which surrounds the Playhead.

Figure 30-14 shows how you can view the Onion Skin as Outlines, which is useful for complex animations. (If you have trouble seeing the outlines, remember that the color of the outlines can be changed with the Layer Properties dialog.)

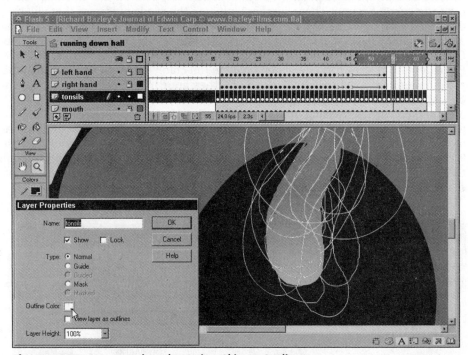

Figure 30-14: You can view the Onion Skin as Outlines.

To set up onion skinning, you first turn onion skinning on, and then adjust the features to suit you, following these steps:

1. Click the Onion Skin button.

2. Move the Start Onion Skin and End Onion Skin markers to contain the frames that you want to view simultaneously.

3. If you'd like to view the Onion Skin as outlines, as shown in Figure 30-14, click the Onion Skin Outlines button.

4. To edit frames between Onion Skin markers, click the Edit Multiple Frames button.

Caution

It has been reported that everything moves, except whatever's on the last frame, if you choose to Edit Multiple Frames, and then set the Start and End Onion Skin Markers to encompass the whole timeline, and then select all and try to nudge everything with the arrow keys. So, we suggest that you first save a copy of your working file. Then, before proceeding after such an adjustment, confirm that this was *not* a problem.

5. Change the display of the Onion Skin Markers by clicking the Modify Onion Markers button. Choose one of the following from the menu:

   • **Always Show Markers:** Check this option to always show the Onion Skin Markers, regardless of whether onion skinning is on or not.

   • **Anchor Onion:** Usually, the Onion Skin Markers follow the position of the current frame. Check this option to anchor the Onion Skin Markers at their current position on the timeline, thus preventing the Onion Skinning effect to move in relation to the position of the current frame pointer.

   • **Onion 2, Onion 5, and Onion all:** These options apply the onion skinning effect as follows: (2) to two frames on either side of the current frame, (5) to five frames on either side of the current frame, or (All) to All frames.

Note

When you enable onion skinning and drag the Onion Markers to display a specific range of frames, the range will migrate in unison with the Playhead. This way, you can always see the same span of frames relative to the current frame, while you are working. If this annoys you, you can click the Anchor Onion Markers to lock the markers at their current position.

In Figure 30-15, the Onion 5 option was clicked. If you compare this figure to the previous figure, you'll note that the range of the Onion Markers has changed accordingly.

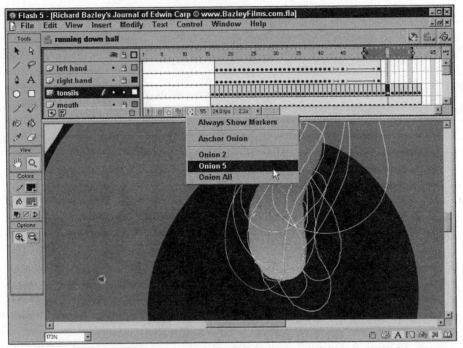

Figure 30-15: In addition to manual adjustments, the Modify Onion Markers pop-up offers several other options for managing Onion Markers.

Summary

✦ The timeline is the backbone of Flash. A clear understanding of both the logic and the many features of the Flash timeline is essential to competency with Flash.

✦ The timeline organizes Flash content with regards to both time and depth.

✦ On the timeline, time is incremented from left to right, while depth is organized in the stacking order of layers, as well as the order of content within each individual layer.

✦ Animations are organized and controlled by using various kinds of frames on the timeline. The characteristics of these frames can be edited, and the frames themselves can be moved, copied, and adjusted on the timeline.

✦ There are three kinds of animation possible in Flash: Frame-by-Frame, Shape Tweened, and Motion Tweened Animation.

✦ The content of the individual frames can be created, edited, manipulated, and otherwise orchestrated on the Stage.

✦ Onion skinning is useful for the manipulation of the content of frames in the context of surrounding frames.

✦   ✦   ✦

Checking Out the Library: Symbols and Instances

Symbols are the key to both the file-size efficiency and the interactive power in Flash. A *symbol* is a reusable element that resides in the current movie's Library, which is accessed with Window ➪ Library. Each time you place a symbol on the stage or inside of another symbol, you're working with an *instance* of that symbol. Unlike using individual graphic elements, you can use many instances of a given symbol, with little or no addition to the file size.

Using symbols helps reduce the file size of your finished movie because Flash only needs to save the symbol once. Each time that symbol is used in the movie, Flash refers to this original profile. Then, to support the variations of an instance, Flash only needs to save information about the differences — such as size, position, proportions, and color effects. If a separate graphic were used for each change, Flash would have to store a complete profile of all the information about that graphic — not only the size and color, but also what the graphic looks like.

Furthermore, symbols can save you a lot of time and trouble, particularly when it comes to editing your movie. That's because changes made to a symbol are reflected in each instance of that symbol throughout the movie. Let's say that your logo changes halfway through production. Without symbols, it might take hours to find and change each copy of the logo. However, if you've used symbol instances, you need only edit the original symbol — the instances are automatically updated throughout the movie.

With the advent of the increasingly robust Flash ActionScript language, symbols can be considered as objects within an object-oriented authoring environment.

In this chapter, you learn to create and edit symbols. You also learn to use symbols, both within the movie and within other symbols, and to modify each instance of a symbol. Flash stores symbols, as well as imported sounds, bitmaps, and QuickTime movies, in the Library. Understanding how to use the Library is crucial to working with symbols — so to start, let's take a tour of the Library itself.

The Library and Its Features

The Library is the repository of all recurring elements, known as symbols, that are placed as Instances within a Flash movie. Imported sounds and bitmaps are automatically placed in the Library. Upon creation, both Buttons and Movie Clips are also stored in the Library. It's a smart practice to make nearly *every* item within a Flash movie a symbol, and to develop every item within a Flash movie from component symbols.

The Library is also a true window, not a panel. As shown in Figure 31-1, the Library Window (left) — Window ⇨ Library — is not the same as the six default asset Libraries (right) that are accessed from the Menu at Window ⇨ Common Libraries. However, they are related. When you choose Window ⇨ Library, you open a Library specific to the current movie, while Common Libraries are available whenever Flash is open.

Choose Window ⇨ Common Libraries to open the submenu of Common Libraries that ship with Flash. The Libraries menu is the one menu over which the user has real control. That's because — in addition to the Library items that are placed there in the process of a default installation of Flash — you can place your own items there, too. The default Libraries contain a selection of buttons and symbols to get you started. These are located in the Libraries folder of the Flash application folder. (And when you're tired of them, you can remove them!) To add your own buttons, symbols, or libraries for specific projects, first save them in a Flash file with a descriptive name, and then place that Flash file in the Libraries folder within the Flash Program folder on your hard drive. Because these default Common Libraries have such obvious names, we won't waste valuable pages to describe them here. They are Buttons, Graphics, Learning Interactions, Movie Clips, Smart Clips, and Sounds.

New Feature

In previous versions of Flash, when working with more than one .FLA movie open at a time, it was easy enough to get confused and start working in the wrong Library. This is no longer possible. Although it's still possible to drag items from the Library of a movie that does not have focus, in Flash 5 that Library is grayed out, indicating that it is not associated with the current movie. Furthermore, double-clicking a symbol within that Library will not transport you to the associated movie.

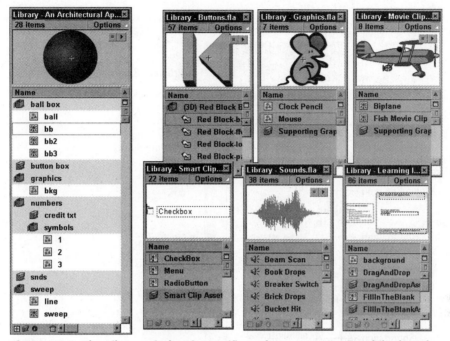

Figure 31-1: The Library window is specific to the current movie, while the other windows, known as the Common Libraries, are available whenever Flash is open.

Working with the Library

Every Flash movie has its own Library, which is used to store and organize symbols, sounds, bitmaps, and other assets such as video files. As shown in Figure 31-2, the item highlighted — or selected — in the *Sort Window* is previewed in the *Preview Window*.

If the item selected in the Library is an animation or sound file, you'll see a controller in the upper-right corner of the Preview window. This Preview Stop/Play controller pops up to facilitate previewing these items. It's almost equivalent to the Play option that's found in the *Options* menu. The Options menu is accessed by clicking the Options triangle, which is located at the upper right of the Library window. As shown in Figure 31-3, the Library options pop-up menu lists a number of features, functions, and controls for organizing and working with items in the Library.

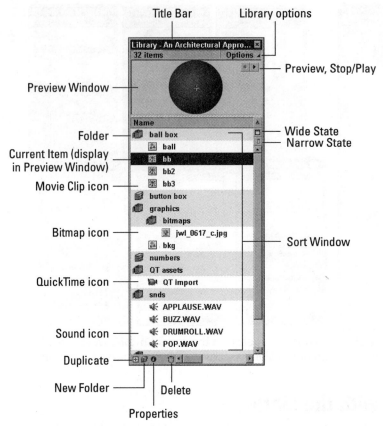

Figure 31-2: The Library window as viewed in Normal state.

✦ **New Symbol:** Choose this item from the Options menu to create a new symbol. When a new symbol is created, it is stored at the root of the Library Sort window. To create a new symbol in a folder, select the desired folder first — the new symbol will be placed in the selected folder.

✦ **New Folder:** Items in the Library can be organized in folders. The New Folder button simply creates a new folder within the Sort window.

✦ **New Font:** Use this option to invoke the Font Symbol Properties dialog, which is the first step in creating a Font Symbol for use within a Shared Library. For more information about Shared Libraries and Font symbols, refer to the end of this chapter, as well as to Chapter 42, "Sharing and Loading Assets."

✦ **Rename:** Use the Rename option to rename an item.

✦ **Move to New Folder:** Use the Move to New Folder to open the New Folder dialog.

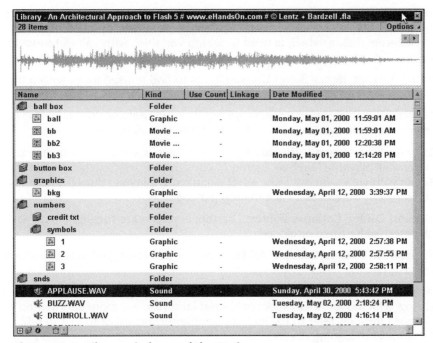

Figure 31-3: Library window and the Options pop-up menu

Note Library items can also be moved between folders by dragging.

✦ **Duplicate, Delete:** Click Duplicate to duplicate an item and Delete to delete an item.

✦ **Edit:** Click Edit to access the selected symbol in Symbol Editing Mode.

Tip Double-clicking a symbol on stage takes you to Edit in Place Mode, which is variant of Symbol Editing Mode.

✦ **Edit With:** Provided that you have appropriate external applications installed, most imported assets (such as sounds, bitmaps, and vectors) will have this command available to jump to the external editing environment.

✦ **Properties:** Click to invoke the related Properties dialog for the particular symbol type — Sound Properties, Bitmap Properties, Symbol Properties, or (for QuickTime) Video Properties.

✦ **Linkage:** Use this command to invoke the Linkage Options menu. Linkage means that you can assign an identifier string to a Font symbol or to a sound so that it can be accessed as an object with ActionScript. This is an aspect of Shared Libraries. For more information about Shared Libraries and Linkage, refer to the end of this chapter, as well as to Chapter 42, "Sharing and Loading Assets."

✦ **Define Clip Parameters:** With Flash 5, you can now assign clip parameters to a movie clip to create a Smart Clip. This control invokes the Define Clip Parameters dialog, which is used to assign variables with values to movie clips.

✦ **Select Unused Items:** Select Unused Items to find unused items within the Library.

✦ **Update:** Use this option if you've edited items subsequent to importing them into Flash. Items will be updated without the bother of reimporting.

✦ **Play (or Stop, if currently playing):** If the selected asset has a timeline or is otherwise playable (such as a sound), click this to preview the asset in the Library Preview window. If the asset is currently playing, this option is updated to Stop—in which case, click to stop playing.

✦ **Expand Folder/Collapse Folder:** Use this command to toggle the currently selected folder open or closed.

✦ **Expand All Folders/Collapse All Folders:** Use this command to toggle all folders open or closed.

✦ **Shared Library Properties:** Use this command to invoke the Shared Properties dialog, which is another aspect of Shared Libraries. For more information about Shared Libraries, refer to the end of this chapter, as well as to Chapter 42, "Sharing and Loading Assets."

✦ **Keep Use Counts Updated:** Use this command to tell Flash to continuously keep track of the usage of each symbol. If you are working with multiple, complex graphics and symbols, this feature generally slows things to a crawl.

✦ **Update Use Counts Now:** Use this option to tell Flash to update the usage of each symbol. This command is a one-time check, and is probably less of a drain on system resources than the previous command, which checks continuously.

As shown in Figure 31-4, the Library can also be expanded. Expand the Library by clicking the Wide State button. When displayed in this manner, all of the column headings are visible in the Sort Window. Click any heading to sort the window by Name, Kind, Usage Count, or Date.

Selecting New Symbol, Duplicate, or Properties from the Options Menu launches the Symbol Properties dialog, shown in Figure 31-5. Use this dialog to give the symbol a unique name and assign it a behavior (as a symbol type—graphic, button, or Movie Clip). However, if the Properties Option is chosen for a sound asset, then the Sound Properties dialog appears. For more information on Sound Properties, refer to Part IX, "Sound Planning."

Tip

If you're having trouble moving elements from the Library to the Stage on the Mac version of Flash, you may have a corrupt folder on your system. This problem is not due to Flash—it seems to be related to Mac OS 31. For more information, refer to the Macromedia technote at www.macromedia.com/support/flash/ts/documents/cantdrag.htm.

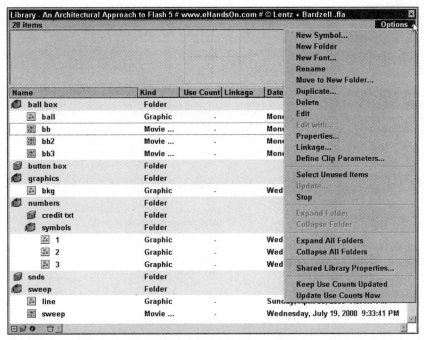

Figure 31-4: The Library deployed in Wide State with the waveform of a sound shown in the Preview window

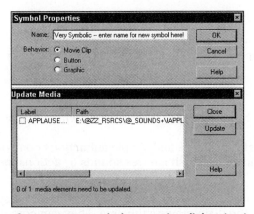

Figure 31-5: Symbol Properties dialog (top), and the Update Media dialog (bottom)

Symbol Types

There are three types of symbols. Each type is unique and suited for a particular purpose. Figure 31-6 illustrates the icons associated with each type of symbol.

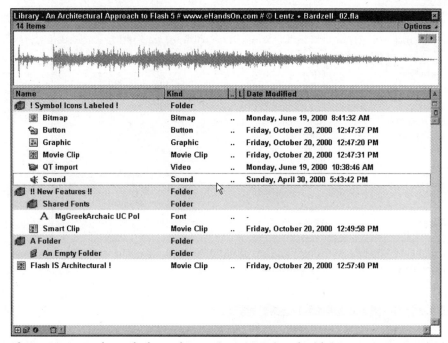

Figure 31-6: Each symbol type has an icon associated with it.

Native symbols

A typical Flash Library may contain these objects that are created within Flash:

✦ **Graphic symbols** are great for static images and simple animations controlled by the main movie's timeline. However, Flash ignores sounds or actions inside a Graphic symbol.

✦ **Movie Clips** are actually like movies within a movie. They're good for animations that run independently of the main movie's timeline. They can contain actions, other symbols, and sounds. Movie Clips can also be placed inside of other symbols and are particularly useful for creating animated buttons.

✦ **Button symbols** are used for creating interactive buttons. Buttons have a specialized timeline with four frames, which are referred to as states. These states are Up, Over, Down, and Hit. Each of these button states can be defined with graphics, symbols, and sounds. After you create a button, you can assign actions to its instances within both the main movie and Movie Clips.

✦ **Shared Fonts** are a new feature of Flash 5. Refer to the end of this chapter as well as to Chapter 42, "Sharing and Loading Assets," for more details.

✦ **Smart Clips** are another new feature of Flash 5.

Imported symbols

A typical Flash library may also contain these imported objects:

✦ **Bitmaps** are handled as symbols. The topic of importing and using bitmaps in Flash is covered in detail in Chapter 34, "Using Bitmaps and Other Media with Flash."

✦ **Sounds** are also handled as symbols. Importing and using sounds effectively is a complex subject. This critical topic is covered in Part IX, "Sound Planning."

Importing sounds, bitmaps, vectors, and QuickTime

When you import a sound, a bitmap, or a QuickTime (QT) asset (which may be either a QT Movie, or a Sound Only QT Movie), Flash stores these assets in the Library. The advantage of this is that you only need one copy of each asset — regardless how many times, or how many different ways, it might be used throughout your movie. Although each of these assets will be covered in greater depth within their own chapters, we introduce them here, in context with the Library.

Sounds

Flash can import (and export) sounds in a range of sound formats. Upon import, these sound files reside in the Library. To use a sound, drag an instance of the sound out of the Library and onto the stage. Export settings for sound files are managed from within the Library by choosing Properties from either the contextual menu or the Library Options menu. For more information about sounds, refer to Part IX, "Sound Planning."

Bitmaps and vectors

Flash can also import (and export) a range of artwork formats, of both vector and bitmap type. Upon import, bitmaps reside in the Library. To use a bitmap asset, drag an instance out of the Library and onto the Stage. Export settings for individual bitmaps are managed in the Bitmap Properties dialog, which is invoked by choosing Properties from either the contextual menu or the Library Options Menu. Bitmaps are discussed in greater detail in Chapter 34, "Using Bitmaps and Other Media with Flash."

Unlike bitmaps, upon import, vectors arrive on the Flash stage as a group, and may be edited or manipulated just like a normal group drawn in Flash. Vectors are discussed in greater detail in Chapter 34, "Using Bitmaps and Other Media with Flash."

Caution   Use care in managing the properties of 8-bit images in the Flash Library. The Smoothing option renders custom predithered hybrid Web colors differently from the original colors.

QuickTime

If you have QuickTime 4 or later, you can import QuickTime assets into Flash in the form of either a QT Movie, or a Sound-only QT Movie. QuickTime assets also reside in the Library.

Graphic Symbols

Graphic symbols are the simplest kind of Flash symbol. Use them for static images, as well as animations. Note, however, that animations within Graphic symbols are tied to the Main Timeline of the movie — when you stop the movie, the animated Graphic symbol stops, too. Furthermore, actions and sounds don't work within Graphic symbols. You can create an empty symbol first and then add the elements to the symbol or you can convert existing elements into a Graphic symbol.

To create an empty symbol, use the following steps:

1. Use Insert ⇨ New Symbol (Ctrl+F8) to initiate a new, empty symbol. This opens the Symbol Properties dialog.

2. Enter a name for your symbol and select a Behavior — Graphic, Button, or Movie Clip. The Behavior setting specifies the default behavior of this symbol as a Graphic, a Button, or a Movie Clip. For this symbol, set the Behavior to Graphic, and then press OK.

3. Click OK. Flash switches to Symbol Editing Mode, in which you can create content for your symbol just as you might normally do in the Movie Editor.

4. When you've finished the symbol and are ready to return to the Stage, use Edit ⇨ Edit Movie (Ctrl+E/Command+E) to exit Symbol Editing Mode.

To create a Graphic symbol from existing elements do the following:

1. Select the element or elements that you want to include in the symbol.

2. Use Insert ⇨ Convert to Symbol (F8) to access the Symbol Properties dialog.

3. As shown in Figure 31-7, type a name and select a Behavior for the symbol. Then click OK. The Behavior setting specifies the default behavior of this symbol as a Graphic, a Button, or a Movie Clip. For this symbol, set the Behavior to Graphic, and then press OK.

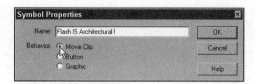

Figure 31-7: Type a name in the Symbol Properties dialog, and then select the Behavior type.

Movie Clips

Movie clips are nested movies inside the main movie. You can add animation, actions, sounds, other symbols, and even other Movie Clips to Movie Clips. Movie Clips have their own timelines, which run independently of the Main Timeline. This can be useful for animations that continue running after the main movie has stopped. Unlike animated Graphic symbols, Movie Clips only need a single keyframe (the initial one) in the timeline of the main movie to play.

Note   A Movie Clip with 40 frames will run to its conclusion, even if it is placed at the first frame of a Main Timeline that has only a single frame.

Creating a Movie Clip using existing animation

You can create a Movie Clip from an empty symbol, as explained in the previous section. However, the simplest way to create a Movie Clip is to use existing animation from the Main Timeline. To do this:

1. Select every frame of every layer of the existing animation that you want to turn into a Movie Clip.

2. Copy the animation by doing one of the following:

    • Right-click or Ctrl+click and select Copy Frames from the pop-up menu.

    • Select Edit ➪ Copy Frames (Option+Command+C or Ctrl+Alt+C) from the Main Menu.

3. Select Insert ➪ New Symbol (Command+F8 or Ctrl+F8) from the Main Menu.

4. Again, as shown previously in Figure 31-7, the Symbol Properties dialog appears. Give the symbol a name and select Movie Clip as the Behavior. Click OK.

5. Now select the first frame of the -timeline in the new symbol that was just created, and paste the frames you copied by doing one of the following:

    • Right-click (Ctrl+click) and select Paste Frames from the pop-up menu.

    • Select Edit ➪ Paste Frames from the Main Menu.

6. Use Edit ➪ Edit Movie (Command+E or Ctrl+E) to return to the main movie.

7. Select the frames from the main movie's timeline (if they aren't still selected from the first step), and delete them with Insert ➪ Delete Frame (Shift+F5).

Expert Tutorial: Graphic Symbols versus Movie Clips, by Robin and Sandy Debreuil

A very important yet often confused aspect of Flash 5 are the different methods, and relative advantages of those methods, for storing information — both graphic images and interactivity. This is especially true about Graphic symbols and Movie Clip symbols. In this tutorial, the Debreuils discuss the general nature of the types of information handled by Flash. They then focus on the advantages and disadvantages of both Graphic symbols and Movie Clip symbols.

Flash Information Types

There are six main types of information created by Flash: raw data, groups, buttons, Graphic symbols, Movie Clips, and loaded movies.

Raw Data — These are the raw shapes that are drawn right on the stage. Each separate keyframe of the Main Timeline can contain and display raw data. Note, however, that every time the Flash player encounters a new piece of raw data, even if that same data was displayed in the previous frame, it will be reloaded across the Internet. That's a no-no. For absolute maximum file efficiency, never (ever) leave raw data in the Main Timeline.

Groups — Groups are very useful, but they are not symbols and they don't have any trimming effect on file size. Why? Because, as commonly implemented, groups are usually just groups of raw data. They are only there for your convenience; unfortunately, they give the illusion of being symbols. Just like raw data, placing groups on the stage of the Main Timeline will cause your file size to swell very quickly. That's no-no number two.

Button symbols — Buttons are a straightforward special case — use them for making buttons! (They are also useful for creating other types of interactivity.) Although buttons are symbols, the optimal practice is to use other symbols as the graphic material to build buttons.

Graphic symbols: *static* — These are collections of data that reside in the Library and that are given a name and ID number. When a Graphic symbol is used, essentially the Flash Player says something like, "get the Contents symbol number 47 from the Library and put it right here."

Graphic symbols: *animated* — These are nearly the same as static Graphic symbols, except that these symbols have more than one frame. Accordingly, now the Flash Player must say, "put the contents of the *n*th frame of symbol 47 right there" — and it must say this for each frame. And that tedious statement gets longer for each frame that has raw data in it. This causes the Flash player to think evil thoughts. Another reason to always use symbols, even as that the components that make up your symbols.

Movie Clip symbols: *static* — Error! By definition, all Movie Clips should animate. If a Movie Clip just contains raw graphic information, it should be a Graphic symbol (although a single frame Movie Clip containing other Movie Clips is fine). The reason for this rule is that Movie Clips require slightly more overhead (bytes) to store and to render because they include a new timeline. Again, placing raw graphics on *any* timeline should make you squeamish, even if the file size is not terribly affected.

Movie Clip symbols: *animated*—These are similar to Graphic symbols, but with a few differences. The big difference is that Movie Clips have their own timeline that runs independently of the Main Timeline. This means the Flash player just says, "Oh, hi, Mr. Movie Clip. I see that you're here, so do what you do." Thus, the Movie Clip does its own thing, in its own sweet time. Because of this -timeline independence, you can give the Movie Clip a name and tell it what to do. This is where ActionScript comes into play with things like:

```
bob.gotoAndPlay(4);
judy._rotation=45;
```

(If you run out of aunt and uncle names, you can use cousins and close friends.) One downside of authoring with Movie Clips is that ActionScript only runs while the .SWF is playing, so it isn't possible to scrub or preview the Main Timeline and view a placed Movie Clip while designing.

Loaded movies—These behave much like Movie Clips, except that (a) they are separate .SWF files and (b) each loaded movie is inserted into a new level, so they can't appear be beneath the Main Timeline. Also, loaded movies have an *obvious* restriction: Because they are loaded from a separate file, there needs to be a mechanism to verify that they *are* loaded before giving them instructions. (It's a big Internet and all kinds of things can happen.) There are other differences, between Movie Clips and loaded movies, but those are the main ones.

Graphic versus Movie Clip

That brings us to the difference between Graphic symbols and Movie Clip symbols: Graphic symbols are a quick and tidy way of placing static information into a timeline, while Movie Clips animate independently on their own timeline. Graphics should be used to hold single frames of raw data, or multiple frames when it is important to preview your work while designing it, as with linear animation. Movie Clips must be used when ActionScript is involved, or when an animation must run regardless of what is happening around it. However, the use of one type of symbol rather than the other may not always involve clear-cut choices, because often either will work. Consequently, to use symbols effectively, it's important to know the pluses, minuses, and absolutes of both Graphic symbols and Movie Clips. Here are some tips to keep in mind:

✦ Instance properties of graphics (height, color, rotation, and so on) are frozen at design time, whereas Movie Clips can have their instance properties set on the fly. This makes Movie Clips essential for programmed content such as games.

✦ Scrubbing (previewing while working) is not possible with Movie Clips, although it is possible with Graphic symbols. This makes Graphic symbols essential for animating cartoons. Eyes open, eyes closed—it's that big of a difference.

✦ Movie Clips can't (easily) be exported to video or other linear medium. This is only significant if you plan to convert your .SWF's to another medium.

Continued

Continued

✦ A Graphic symbol's instance properties are controlled (modified) at design time, in the Effect and Instance Panel. One advantage is that this is simple and sure, because you have an instant preview of what's happening. In addition, this information is embedded right in that particular instance of the Graphic symbol—meaning that, if it is either moved or copied, all of this information comes with it.

✦ A Movie Clip's instance properties are set with ActionScript. This gives it great flexibility, although it's a little more abstract to work with. One advantage is that the actions do not need to be directly linked to the Movie Clip, which has the concurrent disadvantage that care must to be taken when moving Movie Clips.

✦ Graphic symbols that are animated (have more than one frame) and are nested (a.k.a. nested animated graphic symbols) may have problems with synchronization. For example: (a) If you have a pair of eyes that blink at the end of a ten-frame Graphic symbol, and you put the graphic symbol containing those eyes within a five-frame Graphic symbol of a head . . . the eyes will never blink. The Graphic symbol will run from frame 1 to frame 5, and then return to frame 1. (b) If you put them in a 15-frame Graphic symbol, they will blink on the 10th frame, and then every 15 frames. That's ten frames, then blink, and then they loop back to frame 1; however, when reaching frame 5 this time, the movie they are in loops back to frame 1 (it's a 15-frame movie), and thus resets the eyes to frame 1.

✦ Movie Clips do not have the problem/feature described in the preceding bullet point.

✦ When using Graphic symbols, looping actions that occur over long timelines result in larger file sizes. While this may seem trivial, understanding this goes a long way toward understanding the Graphic symbol/Movie Clip issue. To understand why the use of Graphic symbols for looping actions is more file intensive, it helps to visualize what the Flash Player is being told to do. The next section goes over this in some detail.

Now that we've given you some background information on Graphic symbols and Movie Clips, let's put our knowledge into practice!

How Flash Sees the World

The miracle that we know as the .SWF format performs two functions: It stores graphical information, and it displays it.

The majority of the file is consumed with information that both defines the symbol and places it. The definition information describes shapes, fills, bitmap fills, and sounds, while the placement information includes instructions for locating these objects, which includes setting their x,y coordinates, scaling, rotating, skewing, coloring, or otherwise manipulating their properties with ActionScript.

Drawing creates shape information. Try drawing a head—this creates lots of curves, and color information as well. If this drawing is confined to a single frame, Flash will play this frame by saying "curve-curve-color-etc."

However, if, at this point, before making it into a symbol, you animate it in a new keyframe, that new keyframe will be required to *duplicate* (or reload) all the curve and color information again. That is, for each frame, Flash will be required to reiterate, completely, "curve-curve-color-etc." (Don't be fooled by groups; although they look like symbols, they are not symbols — all the information inside the group is duplicated in *each* keyframe in which the group appears.)

However, if you make this drawing a Graphic symbol (press F6), and call it head, and then distribute instances of head in those same frames, something different occurs. Things will look the same, but there has been an important change. Now, instead of that first frame containing "curve-curve-color-etc.," it contains these instructions: "head placed at 37,42." And the "curve-curve-color-etc." data is stored in the Library as the head definition. Consequently, all subsequent appearances of head in another keyframe will only require a few bytes of reference and placement data, not all the shape information.

Flash will only rewrite this information when something changes. Adding a keyframe and changing nothing only adds 2 bytes for the keyframe.

However, if, in this new keyframe, you move head to a new position the reference will now be something like "head placed at 45,51" and this will animate the head. Furthermore, because head is a symbol, you can also scale it ("head placed at 45,51, scaled 110 percent"), rotate it ("head placed at 45,51, scaled 110 percent, rotated 45 degrees") and modify its color instance ("head placed at 45,51, scaled 110 percent, rotated 45 degrees, tinted with light blue 20 percent"). Any of these instructions will add information to the placed instance but this is typically very compact, and not something to worry too much about. The savings in file size, compared to animation without Graphic symbols, is tremendous. If a symbol is just moved, very little new data is added, scaling adds a bit more — about 5 bytes, and once it is rotated, skewed, or colored a matrix function kicks in and 10 bytes are added.

What about symbols inside symbols? Let's make a hat for the head — make it a Graphic symbol called hat. We'll put this hat on the head symbol, and then select both symbols and make them into a third Graphic symbol called hatAndHead. Now the timeline contains a reference to the hatAndHead symbol along with its placement information (rotate, scale, and so on), as well as a reference to the hat symbol, its placement information, and lastly a reference to the head symbol, and its placement information. Whew. That might seem like a lot, but it's really only about 35 bytes of new information.

Now things start to get interesting. Just remember, we're still working with a Graphic symbol. If you insert another keyframe into the hatAndHead symbol and move things around, this new information won't be added to the exported .SWF. That's because the Main Timeline is still only one frame, so only the first frame of the hatAndHead symbol is exported. In fact, the Mona Lisa could be added to frame 2 of hatAndHead, and the exported .SWF would never know about it.

Continued

Continued

However, if you now extend the Main Timeline to 100 frames, Flash would repeat the first frame's data into the Main Timeline 50 times (frames 1, 3, 5, 7 . . .) and would also repeat the Mona Lisa frame's data 50 times (frames 2, 4, 6, 8 . . .). With an average of 35 bytes per frame, that would come to $35 \times 100 = 3500$ bytes, or about 3.4KB (1024 bytes per kilobyte). Although that might seem reasonable enough, note that a simple animation of a person running can easily require 20 symbols, which would be something like 34KB over 100 frames. As you can see, this can get significant.

How can Movie Clips accomplish a smaller file size with these looping Graphic symbols? Well, the only thing that really changes is they have a separate timeline. Imagine, the hatAndHead symbol is now a Movie Clip. It has its own two-frame timeline that runs independently of the Main Timeline, so if the Main Timeline is back to being one frame long, the exported .SWF will contain both frames. This means that, even though the .SWF will just sit on frame one of the Main Timeline, hatAndHead will loop through it's own timeline. It will bounce back and forth between its own two frames, because a Movie Clip's timeline is not affected by what is happening around it, it just plays on its own. Unless told otherwise, a Movie Clip will loop, which is the default setting.

But because it's a Movie Clip, another interesting difference occurs. Even if a stop action is placed on frame one of hatAndHead, so that the Mona Lisa frame will never be displayed, it will still be loaded. This is necessary, because a movie can be told to go to any of its frames by other movies, by button clicks, or even by JavaScript in the browser, so it must be loaded and ready to play.

Finally, even though this seems to be a one-frame movie, there are actually three keyframes here: one in the Main Timeline, and two in the hatAndHead timeline. Consequently, at this point it is slightly bigger than had it been a graphic, because Movie Clips must load all their frames, and because making a new timeline involves an extra overhead. However, it is animating, and equivalent Graphic symbol wouldn't be. So, to compare them properly, the timeline for both examples should be extended by 100 (or more) frames. Now we see that the size of the Movie Clip version only increased by about one or two kilobytes, while the Graphic symbol version has increased by 30 + KB.

Why is the Movie Clip so much more efficient than the Graphic symbol? It's because the Movie Clip only has 3 frames with information in it, while the Graphic symbol has 100.

In the example mentioned previously of an animated runner, if the running animation loop required 6 frames, there would be about 35 bytes in each of the 6 frames inside the runner Movie Clip, and 1 frame in the Main Timeline placing it, so the file size for that animation would be about $(6 \times 35) + (1 \times 5) = 215$ bytes. This is much better than 3500. But the downside is that there is now no preview while you are designing it, so it's hard to determine whether the running feet will be sliding or not. On the other hand, if the Movie Clip were subjected to a tween (especially a Rotating Tween), much of the benefit would be lost. That's because each frame of the tween would need to contain placement information for the Movie Clip. The important thing is to understand how Graphic symbols and Movie Clips differ in size and functionality, and choose accordingly.

The Debreuil brothers, Robin and Sandy, are from Miami, Manitoba, Canada — and they are still there. Understandably, they reported that their favorite thing to do is: Robin, "Not drive a combine," and Sandy, "Not drive a swather." They also confided that they enjoy an occasional rough game of scrub hockey. They discovered Flash in the olden days of Flash 2, through the fabled RealFlash Animation Festival. In the ensuing years, they have worked on "theromp.com, honkworm.com, FoxSports . . . various animation sites." Responding to our attempt to place them chronologically via the memorable pop music and/or film of the year they graduated from high school, they returned, unsurprisingly, "Eh?" Their other interests include, "travel, travel, travel, children, children, children, Flash, Flash, Flash."

Button Symbols

Button symbols have four states, based on the mouse states, which are:

✦ **Up:** The mouse is neither over nor clicking on the button

✦ **Over:** The mouse is over the button

✦ **Down:** The mouse is clicking on the button

✦ **Hit:** This represents the active area of the button

Each button state can present a different image. Buttons can also have actions assigned to them for each of the four mouse states. The images are set inside of the button symbol, while the actions are set in each of the button's instances. Actions cannot be assigned directly to the button symbol itself — only to an instance (or instances) of the symbol. Instances are discussed later in this chapter.

Refer to Chapter 39, "Understanding Actions and Event Handlers," for more about adding actions to button instances.

The timeline for a Button symbol, as illustrated in Figure 31-8, is different from other symbols. It consists of four frames, each one labeled for a mouse state: Up, Over, Down, and Hit. These are the only frames that can be used when creating a button; but you can use as many layers as you like — go ahead, get crazy.

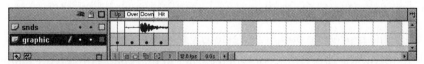

Figure 31-8: The Button symbol timeline always consists of four keyframes labeled Up, Over, Down, and Hit. This button has sounds associated with the Over and the Down states.

The source file for this button discussion is included on the CD-ROM. It's in the button folder of the ch31 folder.

Creating a button

Here are the steps for creating a simple button:

1. Select Insert ➪ New Symbol to create a new (empty) symbol and launch the Symbol Properties dialog. Name the button and set the Behavior to Button. Click OK.

2. A Button Symbol Editing window opens. It displays each of the four states as a separate frame: Up, Over, Down, and Hit. By default, the initial state automatically has a keyframe. Draw a graphic for this initial state of the button — the Up state. Note that a Graphic symbol or imported graphic (including a bitmap) may also be used or pasted into the keyframe for the Up state.

3. Next, insert a keyframe (Insert ➪ Keyframe) in the Over state. This is the frame that appears when the mouse passes over the button. If you'd like your button to do something interesting on mouseover, this is where you make it happen. A Graphic symbol, imported graphic, or bitmap (or even a Movie Clip) may also be used or pasted into this keyframe for the Over state — as well as for the next two states.

4. Insert a keyframe in the Down state. This is the frame that appears when the button is clicked. If you don't want the button to change when it's clicked, just insert a frame here instead of a keyframe.

5. Finally, insert a keyframe in the Hit state. This frame defines the effective hit area of the button. If you're only using text for your button, this is particularly important, because without a Hit state the effective hit area is limited to the letter shapes of the text itself — which makes it very hard to hit the button. So, in this frame, draw a shape to define the hit area. Because the user never sees this state, it doesn't matter what it looks like, as long as it defines a usable hit area. It's good practice to add a Hit state to every button you make — this way you won't forget to add one when it's necessary.

For another pass at creating a button, refer to the button section of the QuickStart, "Flash in a Flash."

Adding animation to a button

To add an animated state to a button:

1. Follow the procedure outlined previously to make a new button.

2. Next, follow the procedures outlined earlier in this chapter to create a Movie Clip for the animated state.

3. Now, open the Library with Window ➪ Library (Ctrl+L or Command+L) and select the button that you've just made, and then open it in Symbol Editing Mode by right-clicking it and then selecting Edit from the contextual menu.

4. For the sake of clarity, add a new layer to the button and name it **MC**, for Movie Clip. Give it four keyframes to match the keyframes of the button states.

5. Select the frame to which you want to add an animated state. This can be the Up, Over, or Down state. (As you already know, the Hit state is *never* seen in the movie, so there's no reason to animate it.)

6. Now, return to the Library with Window ➪ Library (Command+L or Ctrl+L), and select the Movie Clip that you created for the animated state. Then, with the appropriate keyframe active for the desired state, drag the Movie Clip into place, as shown in Figure 31-9.

7. Finally, test your work by selecting Control ➪ Test Movie (Ctrl+Enter or Command+Enter).

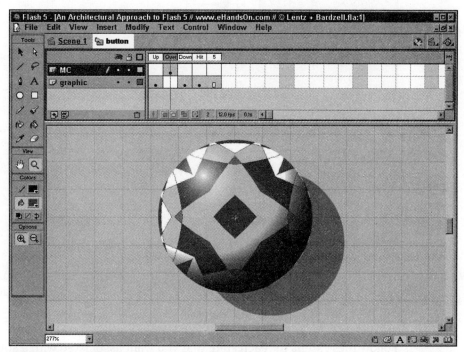

Figure 31-9: This figure illustrates a Movie Clip added to the Over state of a Button symbol.

Adding sound to a button

Here's how to add sound to a button:

1. Make a button with all the necessary states, as described previously, and then add an animated state or two if you want.

2. Now, create a second layer to put your sounds in. Although this isn't absolutely necessary, it's recommended because it keeps the button organized.

3. In the new layer, add a keyframe to each state for which you want a sound.

4. Import the sound(s) that you'd like to add to the button state(s).

5. Add the appropriate sound to each state that requires sound. Figure 31-10 shows a button with a sound in both the Over and Down states. Commonly, the Over and Down states have sounds associated with them, but you can add sound to the Up state too.

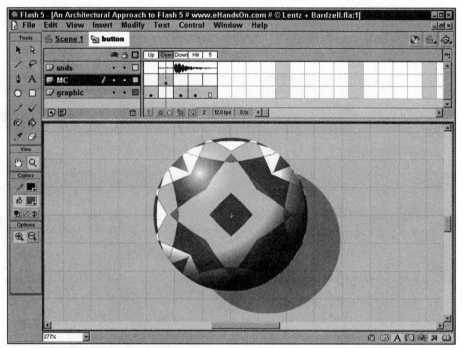

Figure 31-10: This is the Button to which we previously added the animated state. Now, it also has a sound in the Over and Down states.

Follow these steps for each state that you want associated with a sound:

a. Select the keyframe in the sound layer of the desired Button state.

b. Open the Library and drag the sound onto the Stage.

c. Open the Sound Panel (Window ➪ Panels ➪ Sound), select your sound in the Sound drop-down menu, and set the Synch to Event (it's actually the default).

Cross-Reference   Refer to Part IX, "Sound Planning," for more information about importing external sound files.

6. After you've added all your sounds, test the Button (Control ⇨ Test Movie) to see how well it works with the sounds.

Organizing Your Library

When your movies start to become complex, you'll find that the Library gets crowded, and it can be hard to find symbols. When this happens, you'll probably appreciate the capability to create and name folders for your symbols. You can organize your Library folders however you like, but here are a few suggestions for greater productivity:

✦ Create a separate folder for each Scene.

✦ Create folders for certain kinds of symbols, such as Buttons, sounds, or bitmap imports.

When you nest complex symbols with each other — a Graphic symbol on the first frame of a Button symbol, with a text symbol on the layer above it — the Library doesn't indicate this hierarchy. But you can — just put all the associated symbols in a folder! You can even nest folders within other folders. Organizing with folders is easy:

✦ To create a folder, click the folder icon at the bottom-left corner of the Library.

✦ To move a file or folder into another folder, simply drag it over the target folder.

✦ To move a folder that's been nested within another folder back to the top level of the Library, drag the folder until it is just above the Library list and over the word Name and release.

Note   Putting symbols in different folders does not affect the links between them and their instances (in the same way, for example, that moving a graphic file into a new folder will break an existing link on a Web page). Flash tracks and updates all references to Library items whenever they are renamed moved into separate folders.

The new Flash 5 Movie Explorer gives you a view of the nested interrelationship of symbols, Movie Clips, and other items. Refer to the end of this chapter for more on the Movie Explorer.

Caution   There is one Library action for which there is neither undo nor escape: Delete. Any item that is deleted from the Library is gone forever, including all instances throughout the current .FLA editor file.

Adding Symbols to Movies

Now that you've created some symbols, you can use them in movies and modify each instance. Use the Library to put them in a movie. But remember that, in addition to putting symbols on the stage of the main movie, you can also add them to or include them within other symbols as well.

When you add a symbol to the Stage, you are placing an *instance* of the symbol on the Stage rather than the symbol itself. An instance is simply a copy of the original symbol. To put symbols on the stage:

1. Add a Keyframe to the appropriate layer at the point in the timeline where you want the symbol to appear.

2. Use Window ⇨ Library (Command+L or Ctrl+L) to open your Library.

Note   Don't choose Common Library from the Windows menu. Those libraries come with Flash and—unless you've put them there—won't contain your symbols.

3. Use the Library to find and select the symbol that you want to add to the movie.

4. Drag the symbol onto the Stage by dragging either the graphic of the symbol from the Preview window or the symbol's name as it appears in the Sort window.

Editing Symbols

Because every instance of a symbol is a copy of the original, *any* edit applied to that original is applied to every instance. There are several ways to edit a symbol.

Editing a symbol in Symbol Editing Mode

On the Stage, select an instance of the symbol that you want to edit, and then do one of the following:

1. Choose Edit ⇨ Edit Selected from the Edit Menu.

2. Right-click (Ctrl+click) the instance and choose Edit (or Edit in Place) from the contextual pop-up menu.

3. Double-click the instance on stage.

4. Select a symbol from the Library, right-click (Ctrl+click) and choose Properties, and then click the Edit button in the Symbol Properties dialog, as shown in Figure 31-11.

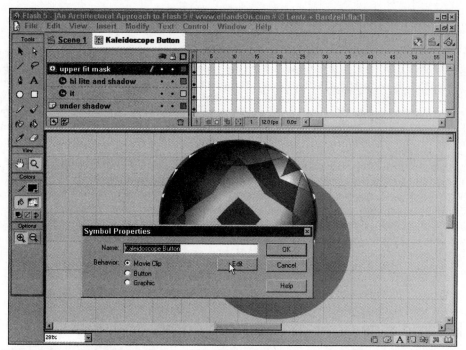

Figure 31-11: Click the Edit button in the Symbol Properties dialog to open Symbol Editing Mode (shown behind).

Editing and Developing

Development in Flash occurs in one of two places: (a) in the Main Timeline and on the Main Stage; or (b) within a symbol, which has its own Stage and a timeline. You can always tell in which mode you are authoring in a couple ways:

The Main Stage (if it is not too large to fill up your screen) is surrounded by a gray area; this is the Work Area, which indicates the edges of the movie, as defined in the Movie Properties. The dimensions of the Main Stage, however, do not limit the symbol Stage. If you make your symbols too large, when you place them on the Main Stage, portions that fall outside of the Main Stage will not appear in the final .SWF. In that event, you can scale the symbol.

Continued

Continued

But how do you know when you are on the Main Stage or when you are in Symbol Editing Mode? Here's one clue: At the upper-left of the timeline is a tab. If you're working on the Main Stage, you will see a single tab with the name of the scene. Unless you name your scenes, this tab should simply say, Scene 1 (or Scene 2). However, in Symbol Editing Mode, a second tab appears to the right of the scene name: This tab displays the name and symbol icon (Movie Clip, Button). If you have nested symbols, more tabs may appear. In this manner, you have convenient access to the hierarchy of your files, no matter how deeply you nest your symbols.

Symbol Editing Mode is much like working on the regular Stage. You can draw with any of the drawing tools; add text, place symbols, import graphics, and sound, and (within limitations) use ActionScript. When you're done working with a symbol, you have an encapsulated element, whether it is a static Graphic, a Movie Clip, or a Button. This element can be placed as many times as needed on your Stage or within other symbols. Each time you place it, the symbol's entire Stage and timeline (if it is a Button or a Movie Clip) will be placed as well, identical to all other instances and the symbol itself.

Editing a symbol in a new window

This method is useful if you want to quickly open a new window to work in. When editing in a new window, the movie remains open and available. You can switch between these windows by choosing from the Window menu. Or, you can divide the workspace between both windows by choosing Window ➪ Arrange All.

1. Select an instance on the Stage of the symbol that you want to edit.

2. Then right-click (Ctrl+click) the instance, and select Edit In New Window from the contextual pop-up menu.

Editing a symbol in place

Edit in Place Mode is very useful. The advantage is that, rather than opening the Symbol Editing Mode, you simply edit your symbol in context with the surrounding movie. Everything else on the stage is visible, but dimmed out. To do this:

1. Select an instance of the symbol that you want to edit.

2. Right-click (Ctrl+click) the instance and select Edit In Place from the contextual pop-up menu.

Editing symbols from the Library

You might not have an instance of your symbol available to select for editing, but you can still edit it. Just edit it from the library.

1. Open your movie's library with Window ➪ Library (Command+L or Ctrl+L) from the Main Menu.

2. Select the symbol that you want to edit and do one of the following:

   • Double-click the symbol.

   • Right-click (Ctrl+click) and select Edit from the contextual pop-up menu.

3. Flash switches to Symbol Editing mode. Edit your symbol any way you want.

Returning to the movie after editing a symbol

After you've edited your symbol, you'll want to go back to the movie to make sure that your changes work properly. Just do one of the following:

✦ Select Edit ➪ Edit Movie (Command+M or Ctrl+M) from the Main Menu.

✦ Select the scene name in the left corner of the timeline as shown in Figure 31-12.

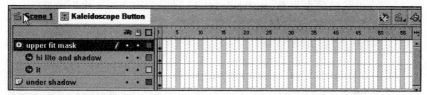

Figure 31-12: Select the scene name to return to editing the movie.

Modifying Instance Properties

Every instance of a symbol has specific properties that can be modified. These properties only apply to the specific instance — not to the original symbol. Properties such as the brightness, tint, alpha (transparency), and behavior can all be modified. An instance can also be scaled, rotated, and skewed. As previously discussed, any changes made to the original symbol will be reflected in each instance — this still holds true even if the instance's properties are modified.

Modifying color effects with symbols

Each instance of a symbol can have a variety of color effects applied to it. The basic effects are changes of brightness, tint, and alpha (transparency). Tint and alpha changes can also be combined for special effects. To apply color effects to a symbol instance:

1. Select the instance that you want to modify.

2. Open the Effect Panel with Window ➪ Panels ➪ Effect.

3. Select one of the options from the drop-down menu. Figure 31-13 shows the Effect Panel drop-down with the Tint option selected.

Figure 31-13: The Effects Panel has several options to choose from. Shown here is the Effect drop-down with the Tint option selected.

The options available from the Effect drop-down are as follows:

- **None:** No effect is applied.

- **Brightness:** Adjusts the relative brightness or darkness of the instance. It ranges from 100 percent (black) to 100 percent (white). Use the slider to change the value or just type a numeric value into the entry field.

- **Tint:** Enables you to change the color of an instance. Either select a hue with the color picker, or enter the RGB values directly. Then, select the percentage of saturation (Tint Amount) by using the slider or by entering the percentage in the entry field. This number ranges from 0 percent (no saturation) to 100 percent (completely saturated).

- **Alpha:** Enables you to modify the transparency of an instance. Select a percentage by using the slider or by entering a number directly. The Alpha percentage ranges from 0 percent (completely transparent) to 100 percent (no transparency).

- **Advanced:** Enables you to adjust the tint and alpha settings of an instance. The controls on the left reduce the tint and alpha values by a specified percentage, while the controls on the right either reduce or increase the tint and alpha values by a constant value. The current values are multiplied by the numbers on the left, and then added to the values on the right.

Note The Advanced option includes the potential for negative alpha values. Potential uses for this capability, together with more information about using the Effects Panel, are detailed in Chapter 33, "Animating in Flash."

Changing the behavior of an instance

You don't need to limit yourself to the native behavior of a symbol. There may be times when you want an animated Graphic symbol to have the behavior of a Movie Clip. You don't have to go through the extra effort of creating a new symbol — just change the behavior of the instance as needed:

1. Select the instance that you want to modify.

2. Open the Instance Panel with Window ➪ Panels ➪ Instance, or click the Instance Button on the Launcher.

3. From the Behavior drop-down, select the desired behavior. As shown in Figure 31-14, you can select Graphic, Button, or Movie Clip, which is the default behavior.

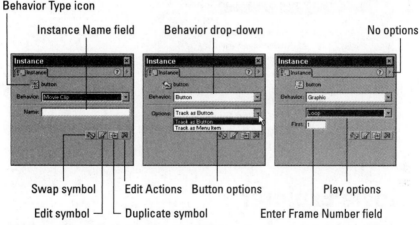

Figure 31-14: As this composite screen shot indicates, you can change the Behavior of an instance from the Instance Panel.

Cross-Reference Working with Symbol Instances is covered in great depth in Part X "Adding Basic Interactivity to Flash Movies."

Switching symbols

There may be times when you need to replace an instance of one symbol with another symbol. You don't have to go through and recreate your entire animation to do this — just use the Switch Symbol feature. This feature only switches the instance of the symbol for an instance of another symbol — all other modifications previously applied to the instance will remain the same. Here's how to switch symbols:

1. Select the instance that you want to switch.

2. Open the Instance Panel with Window ➪ Panels ➪ Instance (or use the Instance Button on the Launcher).

3. Click the Swap Symbol button and, from the ensuing Swap Symbol dialog (shown in Figure 31-15), select the symbol that you want to switch to.

4. Click OK to swap symbols.

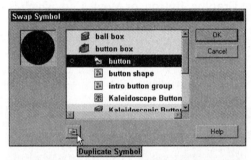

Figure 31-15: Click the Swap Symbol button of the Instance Panel to invoke this Swap Symbol dialog.

The Movie Explorer

The Movie Explorer Panel is a powerful new tool for deciphering movies and finding items within them. It can be opened from the Launcher Bar, or from the Main Menu by choosing Window ➪ Movie Explorer (Ctrl+Alt+M/ Option+Command+M).

New Feature

The Movie Explorer is one of the best new features of Flash 5. It will help you to organize, build, and edit your projects with greater clarity and efficiency. For example, if your client decides to change the font at the last minute, you can use the Movie Explorer to locate and update all occurrences of the original font — without a tedious manual search.

The Movie Explorer is an especially useful tool for getting an overview and for analyzing the structure of a Flash movie. This means that you can now see every element in its relationship to all other elements, and you can see this all in one place.

However, it's also useful for troubleshooting a movie, for finding occurrences of a particular font, and for locating places where you refer to a certain variable name in any script throughout a movie. As an editing tool, you can use it as a shortcut to edit any symbol, for changing the properties of an instance, or even for doing multiple selections and then changing the attributes of the selected items. Furthermore, the Find function is an incredible timesaver.

The new Movie Explorer has so many features that it may be difficult to get used to — however, it's well worth the effort to become familiar with this organizational powerhouse. Figure 31-16 shows the Movie Explorer as well the Movie Explorer Settings dialog, which you can open by clicking the Customize Which Items to Show button in the Movie Explorer.

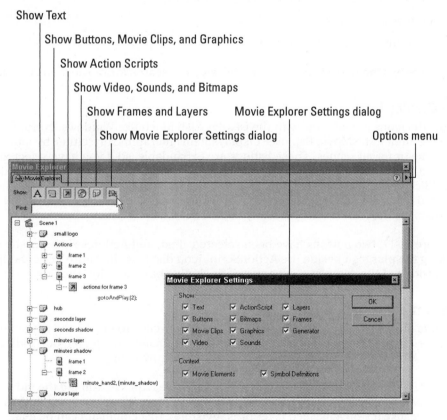

Figure 31-16: The Movie Explorer displays the file structure for Jake Smith's Flash Clock.

Filtering Buttons

As shown in Figure 31-16, there are several icon buttons across the top of the Movie Explorer Panel. These are called Filtering Buttons and they have icons representative of their function. Click any button to toggle the display of those elements in your file. Note, however, that the Movie Explorer's display becomes more crowded as you select more buttons — and that it performs more slowly because it has to sift more data. From left to right, the buttons filter the display of the following kinds of content:

✦ Text

✦ Buttons, Movie Clips, and Graphics (placed instances)

✦ ActionScripts

✦ Video, Sounds, and Bitmaps (placed instances)

✦ Frames and Layers

✦ Customize which Items to Show

Note also the Find entry field, which enables you to search for movie items by name.

The Display List

Below the icons is a window with the Display List. Much like Windows Explorer, or the Mac Finder, the Movie Explorer displays items hierarchically, either by individual scene or for all scenes. These listings are expandable, so if you have selected the Text button, a plus sign will appear beside the name of any Scene that includes text. Clicking the plus sign (or right-pointing arrow on the Mac) displays all of the selected items included in that Scene. At the bottom of the Display List, a status bar displays the Path for the currently selected item.

In Figure 31-17, two buttons have been selected: Text, and ActionScripts. As shown, clicking the plus sign beside the ActionScript icon displays the entire ActionScript. Note, too, that the complete text appears, including basic font information.

The contextual menu

Select an item in Movie Explorer and right-click/Ctrl+click to invoke the contextual menu related to that particular item. Irrelevant commands are grayed-out, indicating that functionality is not available in context with the item.

Figure 31-18 shows the contextual menu of the Movie Explorer. Among the most useful commands is the Goto Location option at the top. When you can't find an item (because it's on a masked layer or is invisible), this command can be a lifesaver.

Next, we cover the Movie Explorer Options menu.

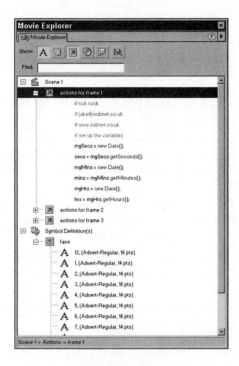

Figure 31-17: The Movie Explorer for one of Jake's Clocks

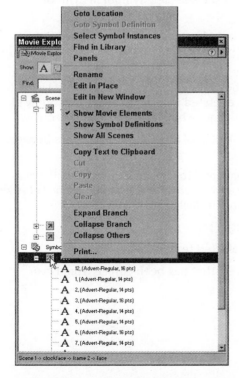

Figure 31-18: The Movie Explorer's contextual menu

The Movie Explorer Options menu

The Options menu is accessed by clicking the Options triangle, which is located in the upper-right corner of the Movie Explorer Panel. These commands are the same as the commands that are found in the Movie Explorer's contextual menus:

✦ **Goto Location:** For a selected item, this transports you to the relevant layer, scene, or frame.

✦ **Goto Symbol Definition:** (For this to work, both Show Movie Elements and Show Symbol Definitions must be toggled on.) This jumps to the symbol definition for the symbol that's selected in the Movie Elements area. *(At the time of this writing, this feature was not functional.)*

✦ **Select Symbol Instances:** Jumps to the scene containing instances of the symbol that is selected in the Symbol Definitions Area. (For this to work, both Show Movie Elements and Show Symbol Definitions must be toggled on.)

✦ **Find in Library:** If the Library Window is not open, this opens the Library and highlights the selected item. Otherwise, it simply highlights the item in the Library.

✦ **Panels:** Click this to open all relevant panels (or panel) for the selected item.

✦ **Rename:** Enables you to easily rename selected items.

✦ **Edit in Place:** Use this to edit the selected symbol in context on the Stage.

✦ **Edit in New Window:** Use this to edit the selected symbol in Symbol Editing Mode.

✦ **Show Movie Elements:** One of two broad categories for how filtered items are viewed in the Display List, Show Movie Elements displays all elements in the movie, organized by scene.

✦ **Show Symbol Definitions:** This is the other category of the Display List, which shows all of the components that are related to each symbol. Both Show Movie Elements and Show Symbol Definitions may be displayed simultaneously.

✦ **Show All Scenes:** This toggles the display of Show Movie Elements between selected scenes, or all scenes.

✦ **Copy Text to Clipboard:** Use this command to copy selected text to the clipboard. Text may then be pasted into a word processor for editing, spell checking and other textual operations not found in Flash.

✦ **Cut:** Use this command to cut selected text.

✦ **Copy:** Use this command to copy selected text.

✦ **Paste:** Use this command to Paste text that has been copied from Flash or another application.

✦ **Clear:** Use this command to clear selected text.

✦ **Expand Branch:** This expands the hierarchical tree at the selected location; it's the menu equivalent of clicking the tiny + sign/right-facing arrow.

✦ **Collapse Branch:** This collapses the hierarchical tree at the selected location; it's the menu equivalent of clicking the tiny – sign/down-facing arrow.

✦ **Collapse Others:** This collapses the hierarchical tree everywhere except at the selected location.

✦ **Print:** The Movie Explorer prints out, with all of the content expanded, displaying all types of content selected.

Make sure to use Movie Explorer! When planning or looking for ways to improve a project, this tool can provide an excellent map to the structure and function of what you've already accomplished. Whenever relevant, print out the Movie Explorer; this document can function as a project file for finished work, providing a reference of all scripting and Movie Clip placement. As such, it can make it much easier to return to a project months later. It can also facilitate collaboration amongst developers, whether they share the same office or are geographically distributed. Finally, for all of the reasons listed previously, the Movie Explorer can also be used as a tool for both learning and teaching.

Shared Library and Shared Fonts

Shared Library is a new feature of Flash 5. The idea behind this is very good. It is intended to enable you to create a Library of assets that can be uploaded to the server and then share those assets with multiple movies. These assets would include any asset that is normally included in a Flash movie, with the inclusion of shared fonts. Furthermore, because an asset file is not added to the movie that references it, this method would enable a developer to trim bandwidth and also obtain a more streamlined authoring procedure.

Unfortunately, *at the time of this writing*, some users have reported that it does not seem to perform consistently in some intensive situations.

Exercise *extreme* care when using any aspect of the Shared Library. If you want to use the Shared Library feature, we suggest that you research the Macromedia site for any technotes on the topic, and that you also search Flash user groups for information, before you commence work.

For more information about Shared Libraries, refer to Chapter 42, "Sharing and Loading Assets."

Summary

✦ Symbols are the building blocks of Flash. They save you time, reduce your file size, and add flexibility to your movies. With the advent of the increasingly robust Flash ActionScript language, symbols can be considered as objects within an Object Oriented authoring environment.

✦ Flash handles imported sounds, bitmaps, and QuickTime assets as symbols. They reside in the Library and instances of these assets are deployed within a Flash project.

✦ In addition to imported assets, there are three other kinds of symbols that can be created within Flash: Graphic symbols, Movie Clips, and Buttons.

✦ The Library can be organized with folders and symbols and assets can be rearranged without breaking their linkage to instances deployed within the project.

✦ Using symbols within a project is as easy as dragging an asset or symbol from the Library and onto the stage, although it's usually best to have a new layer ready and to have the appropriate keyframe selected.

✦ Symbols can be edited in a number of ways. Any edits to a symbol are reflected by all instances of that symbol throughout the project.

✦ The color and transparency of individual instances of a symbol can be modified, via the Instance Panel. Furthermore, specific instances can be switched for other symbol instances by using the Behavior Panel.

✦ The new Flash 5 Movie Explorer is a powerful new tool for deciphering movies and finding items within them.

✦ Shared Libraries and Shared Font symbols are a promising new feature of Flash 5.

✦　　✦　　✦

Drawing in Flash

Flash has a variety of drawing tools that enable you to
create whatever you need for your projects. You should
already know how to use these drawing tools from your reading of Chapter 23, "Understanding the Flash Framework." This
chapter provides a more in-depth look at using these tools —
and several others — when working with your drawings. We
manipulate drawings, create special effects, and more.

Simple Shapes and Items

To learn Flash, it's essential to know how to create simple
shapes and items with the drawing tools, as described in
Part VII, "Mastering the Flash Environment." Drawing simple
shapes with Flash has always been easy, but with the addition
of the Pen Tool in Flash 5, drawing has become even easier.
Individually, these basic drawing tools are quite powerful, but
when used in combination, they enable you to create an endless variety of complex shapes.

Creating shapes

In Flash, it takes little effort to draw most primitive shapes
such as circles or rectangles. But what happened to the
Triangle Tool? And how do you create irregular shapes?

Creating complex shapes requires adding or removing parts.
If you've already been playing around with shapes, you may
have noticed that by joining or overlapping two shapes of the
same color on the same layer, a brand new shape is created.
(To pull the pieces apart you need to use the Undo [Edit ⇨
Undo] command a few times.) This feature is used to create
irregular and complex shapes.

Creating shape combinations

Add a rectangle to a circle of the same color (on the same
layer) and you'll combine them into a new shape (as shown in

Figure 32-1). This can be accomplished by either drawing the second shape directly over the first, or by selecting the second shape elsewhere on the stage and then dropping it over the first shape. If you find that this doesn't seem to work, be sure that you aren't trying to combine shapes that have been grouped. Remember that even single shapes can be grouped, and thereby protected from shape combination.

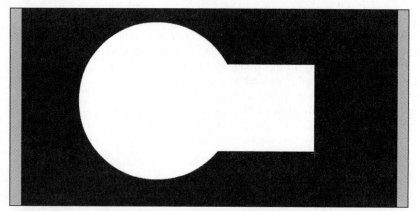

Figure 32-1: Using shape combinations to generate a complex shape from primitive shapes.

Creating shape cutouts

Another effect that can be created by playing around with shapes is a cutout, by combining shapes of different fill colors. For example, add the same circle to a rectangle of a different color, and the circle acts like a cookie cutter, creating another brand-new shape. A similar result is obtained by drawing a shape of a different color directly over the top of an existing shape: the one drawn last (or dropped) acts as the cutter. Drop a collection of selected lines on a rectangle, then deselect, and then reselect and move them away—and you'll create a filigree knockout.

On the
CD-ROM   The Flash resource files for this example are located in the Moon folder of the ch32 folder on the CD-ROM.

As shown in Figures 32-2 through 32-4, a moon shape is achieved by drawing the cutout shape, then dragging it over the top of the background shape, and then deleting the cutout, as follows:

1. Let's begin with a black background, as if it were the night sky. This is accomplished by using Movie Properties (Modify ➪ Movie Properties).

2. Select the Oval Tool, change the fill color to white for the moon, set the stroke color to transparent, and then hold down the Shift key and draw a perfect circle.

3. Now, copy the original circle as follows: Select the circle with the Arrow Tool, and then hold down the Alt/Option key while dragging a copy of the circle off to the side. This second circle will be the shape cutter.

4. Next, with the new circle still selected, change its fill color by choosing a new color (gray) from the Fill Color control of the Toolbox (as shown in Figure 32-2). If you don't change the fill color for this secondary circle, it will merge and become part of the original circle shape (as in the preceding example) in our next step.

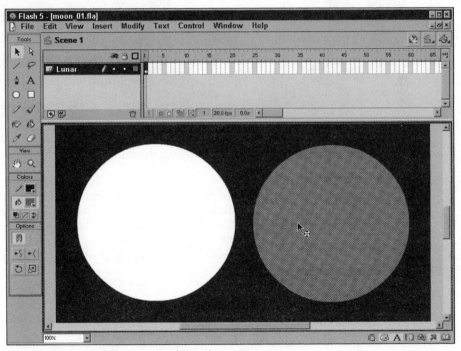

Figure 32-2: The full moon and the shape cutter

5. Use the Arrow Tool to drag the gray circle over the top of the original white circle and position it so that it reveals a sliver of crescent-shaped white (as shown in Figure 32-3). After the gray circle is positioned appropriately, deselect it by clicking off the circle at the edge of the stage.

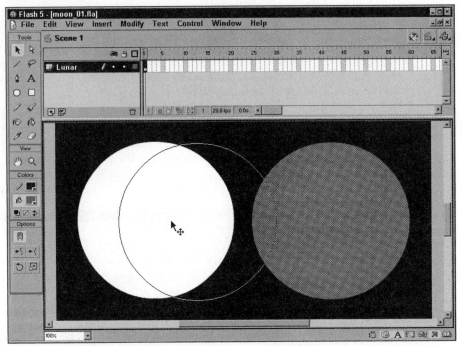

Figure 32-3: Dragging the shape cutter over the full moon

6. Use the Arrow Tool to click the gray shape-cutter circle to select it and drag it away (see Figure 32-4). Then delete the gray circle. What remains? You should now have a sliver of white in the shape of a crescent moon.

You can apply this technique to any number of shapes, limited only by your ingenuity and patience.

Grouping

Here's how to use grouping so that items won't cut out the shapes that occur beneath them.

In the previous example, cutting into the full-moon shape with the gray shape cutter created a sliver of moon. In such cases, there's always a potential for problems if the shape cutter is accidentally deselected. The potential for problems is increased if more than one shape is being used as a cutter. However, if the cutter shape (or shapes) is grouped before it is placed over the shape that's being cut, the problem is eliminated. Furthermore, the group enables you to nudge and align until the cutter is precisely where you want it. And you don't have to decide immediately, either. If you choose the appropriate color for the cutter shape(s), you can wait until later to commit to the cut. When you're ready to make the final cut, simply ungroup the cutter shape(s), and then deselect before selecting and finally deleting them.

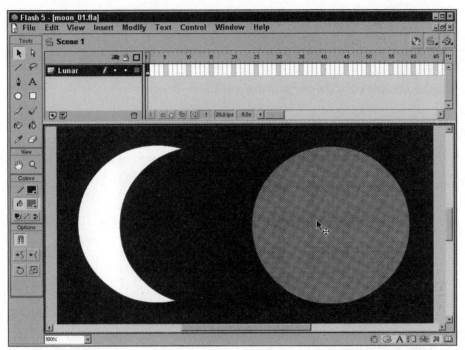

Figure 32-4: With the shape-cutter circle dragged away, the original circle is cut, leaving a crescent moon shape.

Note

Although grouping doesn't usually add significantly to file size, it certainly does not reduce file sizes. Here are a few facts: Although the "grouping" itself requires only a few more bytes, the vectors hidden behind a group do mount up. Because Flash doesn't distinguish between what is in front and behind, it renders everything both within and behind a group. Thus, for the smallest possible files, it makes sense to ungroup most groups before final publication of your project. This will let all of the grouped pieces cookie-cutter themselves down into one unified piece of artwork. Nevertheless, before ungrouping to trim file size, be sure to save an archive of the file with all of the components grouped.

Drawing a triangle

The easiest way to create a triangle is to take the Pencil, draw three lines to outline the shape, and then fill it in. However, you might be interested in drawing a more precise triangle, as follows:

1. Select the Rectangle Tool. Set your Line Color to No Color, and select a fill color. Press the Rounded Rectangle modifier to open the Rectangle Settings dialog, and make sure that the Corner Radius is set to 0 points.

2. Draw a rectangle that's about twice the size of the triangle that you want to create.

3. Choose View ➪ Snap to Objects to turn on object snapping.

4. Use the Line Tool to draw a line from the top-left corner of the rectangle to the bottom-right corner as shown in Figure 32-5.

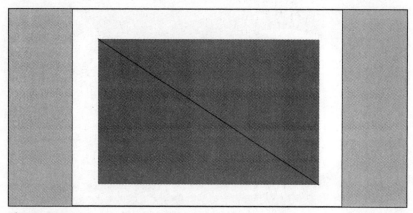

Figure 32-5: Draw a line from the top-left corner of the rectangle to the bottom-right corner.

5. The line has bisected the rectangle into two triangular filled areas. Use the Arrow Tool to select one of the triangular filled areas and drag it away from the rest of the shape. Then select the rest of the shape (the remaining triangle and bisecting line) and delete it. The finished triangle is resting on its side; we discuss how to change that later in this chapter.

Here's how to draw a similar triangle using the Line Tool and the Grid with Snap enabled:

1. From the View Menu, enable both View ➪ Grid ➪ Show Grid and View ➪ Grid ➪ Snap to Grid.

2. Select the Line Tool from the Drawing Toolbox. Choose your line color using the Stroke Color control, and then choose a Stroke Height and Weight from the Stroke Panel.

3. Beginning at one intersection of the Grid, draw a baseline for the triangle, and then draw one of the sides, either by eyeballing the center point above the base line, or by quickly counting grid spaces.

4. Finally, as shown in Figure 32-6, draw the final side of the triangle; the Line Tool will snap to close the shape. When drawing with Snap enabled, a small circle appears adjacent to the cursor whenever snap is active.

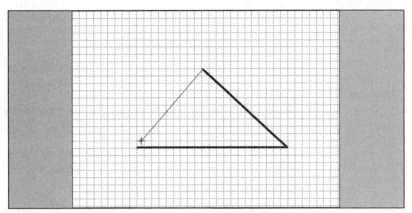

Figure 32-6: This triangle was created with the Line Tool, using Snap to Grid, with the Grid's visibility enabled with View ⇨ Grid ⇨ Show Grid.

Drawing a polygon

A polygon is a flat shape with four or more sides. Polygons are more complicated to make than triangles, but they're not difficult. Figure 32-7 shows a five-sided polygon, drawn directly in Flash.

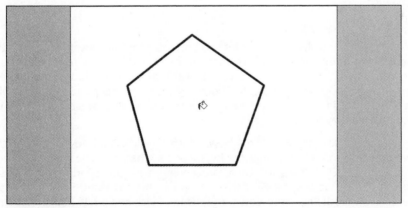

Figure 32-7: This polygon was created with the Line Tool, and is about to be filled with the Paint Bucket.

The simplest way to draw a polygon is to use the Line Tool to draw an outline, and then fill it in with the Paint Bucket Tool. Another method is to draw several rectangles, rotate and adjust them — using the Scale and Rotate Tools — and then place them on top of each other. Yet another method is to draw a rectangle and then chop its corners off by drawing intersecting lines, as demonstrated in the earlier section on Drawing a Triangle. Furthermore, the shape of any polygon can be modified and perfected using:

✦ The Line Processing and Shape Recognition techniques described in Chapter 26, "Working with Selections and the Pen Tool," and Chapter 27, "Working with the Drawing and Painting Tools."

✦ The Pen Tool and Subselect Tool techniques discussed in Chapter 26, "Working with Selections and the Pen Tool," and Chapter 27, "Working with the Drawing and Painting Tools."

✦ The Arrow Tool techniques discussed in Chapter 26, "Working with Selections and the Pen Tool."

On the CD-ROM

The Flash resource files for the following tutorial are located in the Larry D. Larsen folder of the ch32 folder on the CD-ROM.

Expert Tutorial: Pill Technique, *by Larry D. Larsen*

Larry has contributed to many sites, including The Poynter Institute, Flash Foundry (content), Machoman Randy Savage, The Alien Containment Facility, E-Hands on Flash tutorial, and Kung Foo Flash.

Making Pill-Shaped Buttons

Pill-shaped buttons are particularly valuable for text buttons. That's because it can be pretty hard to make circular buttons look good with text on them and because rectangular buttons are just plain boring. It's very easy to create oval buttons in Flash, but pill-shaped buttons take a little bit more work. Thus, the procedures used in this tutorial are valuable not only as a solution to the pill problem, but also for their delivery of an advanced way of *thinking* with the Flash drawing tools.

Start by opening a new Flash file with File ⇨ New, which should default to a single, active layer. We want to create a gradient fill that can be applied so that the circle will look three-dimensional. Select the Oval Tool, and then, proceeding from the Window menu, use Window ⇨ Panels ⇨ Fill to access the Fill Panel (shown in the following figure). Choose Radial Gradient from the Fill Style drop-down. The default black-and-white Radial Gradient should appear. If not, click the Swatches tab and choose the default black-and-white Radial Gradient from the bottom of the panel, and then return to customize this Radial Gradient with the Fill Panel.

Click twice just beneath the Edit Gradient Range to add two new Color Pointers and position them as shown. (If you have any problems with the color terminology or operations, please refer to Chapter 28, "Applying Color," for a complete explanation before proceeding further.) Next, change the colors of the Color Pointers: From left right, change the first Color Pointer to light yellow, the second and fourth to bright orange, and the third to dark red. Finally, click Add Gradient in the option pop-up (which is the triangle near the upper-right corner of the panel) to add this Radial Gradient to the Swatches Panel. Hold down the Shift key and draw a perfect circle, filled with the new gradient color (see the following figure).

If you've drawn a circle with an outline, click to select and then delete the outline. The circle doesn't look very dimensional, does it? The next step is to reapply the same gradient to this circle in a more convincing way.

Choose the Paint Bucket Tool and confirm that the custom gradient is still the fill color. (If not, return to the Swatches Panel and reselect it.) Now, click somewhere in the upper-left corner of the circle. The light yellow highlight of the gradient should appear in the upper left and there should be a dark red shadow in the lower right. The resulting orange ball (shown in the following figure) will be used as the basis from which the pill shape is created.

Continued

Continued

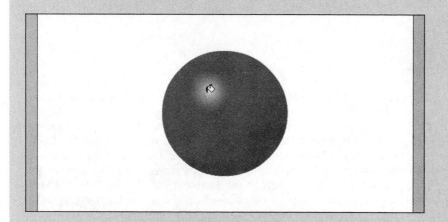

Finally, the dimensional orange ball needs to be centered on the Stage. Select the ball with the Arrow Tool, and then use Edit ⇨ Cut to cut it. Center the stage by double-clicking the Hand Tool. Then, paste the ball back onto the stage using Edit ⇨ Paste. (Don't use the Ctrl+Shift+V (Command+Shift+V) keyboard shortcut because that pastes the ball in its original location!) This process centers the ball.

Create a new layer above Layer 1. (When you create this new layer—Layer 2—Flash will make it the current layer, which is what we want.) Then select the orange ball and copy it with Edit ⇨ Copy. Next, we need to paste a new copy of the orange ball onto Layer 2, directly over the original. This is easily accomplished with Edit ⇨ Paste in Place, which pastes a copy in the same exact position that it was copied from. Now we're going to use a vertical line to bisect the orange ball on Layer 2. To do this, draw a vertical line off to the side of Layer 2 that's taller than the orange ball, as shown in the following figure.

Then, select the line with the Arrow Tool and — as with the ball in the previous step — cut it with File ⇨ Cut. Paste the line back into Layer 2 using Edit ⇨ Paste. This will paste the vertical line in the center of the stage directly over the center of the orange ball, which is also centered on the stage (see the following figure).

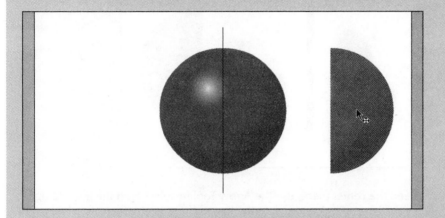

Deselect the vertical line so that it will bisect the ball. Now, select the right side of the orange ball. (Only the right half of the orange ball should be selected.) Hold down the Shift key (to constrain the movement to the horizontal axis) and move this half to the right. Repeat this procedure for the left half of the ball. Then, use the Arrow Tool to select and delete the line (as shown in the following figure).

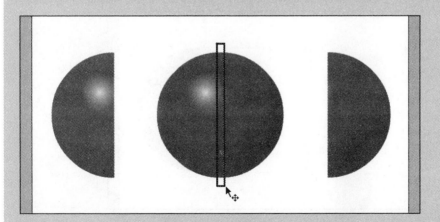

Now, make Layer 1 the current layer. Working off to the side, use the Rectangle Tool — with the fill color set to no fill — to draw a very narrow, empty vertical rectangle, taller than the orange ball. Repeat the procedures used with the line to copy and paste this rectangle over the center of the orange ball on Layer 1. The lines of the vertical rectangle have cut the orange ball into three pieces (as shown in the following figure).

Continued

Continued

Because we only need the center piece, use the Arrow Tool to select both the left and right pieces of the orange ball on Layer 1 and delete them, and then delete the rectangle.

Select the remaining vertical slice of the orange ball on Layer 1 with the Arrow Tool, and then click the Scale option. Now, drag the right-middle handle to the right until it snaps to the left edge of the orange ball half on Layer 2 (as shown in the following figure). Then, repeat the procedure on the left side. Drag the left-middle handle to the left until it snaps to the left edge of the orange ball half on Layer 2.

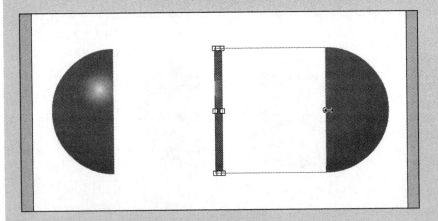

Finally, select all, cut, and then paste into Layer 1. Then delete Layer 2. This will take all of the pieces and put them on the same layer. Group them and you have your pill shape (shown in the following figure).

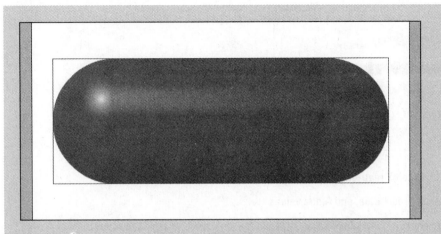

Turn it into a symbol and you won't have to repeat these steps again. (For a discussion of Symbols, refer to Chapter 31, "Checking Out the Library: Symbols and Instances.")

A native of St. Petersburg, Florida, Larry D. Larsen is a true Flash pioneer. This is evident in his claim that "Flash found me." He says that in the year that he graduated from high school, the most memorable media production was the movie *Die Hard*. "I don't know what was on the radio, but I was listening to The Police — "Ghost in the Machine." It was old at the time."

The Drawing Panels

When drawing in Flash, the drawing panels — Info, Transform, and Align — can be your best friends. Use the Info Panel to modify the coordinates and dimensions of an item. Or use the Transform Panel to scale, rotate, and skew an item. Use the Align Panel to align, regularize (match the sizes of), or distribute several items on Stage either relative to each other or to the Stage.

The Info Panel

Use the Info Panel, shown in Figure 32-8, to give precise coordinates and dimensions to your items. Type the numbers in the spaces provided, and your item will be transformed relative to its top-left corner. Or, when working with groups and symbol instances, use the Alignment Grid to apply changes from the center. To open the Info Panel, use Window ➪ Panels ➪ Info.

Symbol type

Alignment Grid

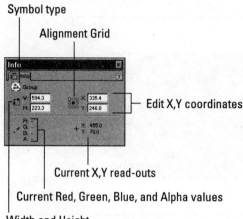

Edit X,Y coordinates

Current X,Y read-outs

Current Red, Green, Blue, and Alpha values

Width and Height

Figure 32-8: Use the Info Panel options to change the location and dimensions of an item.

The Info Panel has these controls:

✦ **Width:** Use this numeric entry field to alter the width of a selected item.

✦ **Height:** Use this numeric entry field to alter the height of a selected item.

Units for both Width and Height are measured in the units (pixels, inches, points, and so on) as set in Ruler Units option of the Movie Properties dialog. Note, however, that upon changing the unit of measurement, the item must be deselected and then reselected in order for these readouts to refresh and display in the current units.

✦ **Alignment Grid:** The alignment grid is located just to the left of the numeric entry fields that are used for adjusting the X and Y location of any selected item. This alignment grid consists of nine small squares. Together, these squares represent an invisible bounding box that encloses the selected item. Every shape created in Flash, even circles, resides within an imaginary rectangular bounding box that includes the extremities of the shape. The alignment grid enables you to position the selected item relative to either the upper-left corner or to the center of its bounding box. Click either square to define which point to use for positioning.

The X (horizontal) and Y (vertical) coordinates are measured from the upper-left corner of the Flash Stage, which is the origin with coordinates 0,0.

✦ **X:** Use this numeric entry field to either read the X coordinate of the item or to reposition the item numerically, relative to the center point on the X (or horizontal) axis.

✦ **Y:** Use this numeric entry field to either read the Y coordinate of the item or to reposition the item numerically, relative to the center point on the Y (or vertical) axis.

✦ **RGBA:** This sector of the Info Panel gives the Red, Green, Blue, and Alpha values or graphic items and groups at the point immediately beneath the cursor. Values for symbols, the background, or interface elements do not register.

✦ **+ X: / + Y:** This sector of the Info Panel gives the X and Y coordinates for the point immediately beneath the cursor — including offstage values. A negative X value is to the left of the Stage, while a negative Y is located above the Stage.

To scale or reposition an item, select the item and then open the Info Panel with Window ➪ Panels ➪ Info, as shown in Figure 32-8:

✦ First you must choose to scale or reposition the item relative to either the center, or to the upper-left corner. (The selected square turns black to indicate that it is selected.)

  • To work relative to the center, select the center square of the Alignment Grid.

  • Or to scale relative to the upper-left corner, click that square of the Alignment Grid.

✦ To scale the item numerically, enter new values in the Width and Height fields, and then click elsewhere or press Enter to effect the change.

✦ To reposition the item numerically, enter new values in the X and Y fields (located in the *upper* half of the panel), and then either press Enter or click elsewhere, outside the panel, to effect the change.

The Transform Panel

This panel gives precise control over scaling, rotation, and skewing of an item. With this panel, instead of using manual techniques — which may be imprecise — numeric values are entered in the appropriate fields and applied directly to the item. However, once transformations are applied to an item, these numbers disappear when it is deselected.

With an item selected, open the Transform Panel with Window ➪ Panels ➪ Transform, as shown in Figure 32-9.

Figure 32-9: Use the Transform Panel to scale, rotate, and skew items.

The Transform Panel has several options that relating to scaling, rotating, and skewing:

✦ **Scale:** Use this to scale the selected item numerically by percentage. Enter a new number in the Scale field and press the Return or Enter key. The shape scales to the specified percentage of its previous scale. To constrain the shape to its current proportions, click the Constrain check box. To restore the shape to its original size, press the Reset button However, once the shape is deselected, it cannot be Reset. The only way to get back your original object's size is to immediately choose Edit ⇨ Undo (probably more than once) or exit your movie without saving your changes (in which case you'll probably lose other work as well).

Tip

When using the Transform Panel with groups and symbol instances, the original settings can be reset even after the item has been deselected.

✦ **Rotate:** Click the radio button and then apply a rotation to the selected item by entering a number in the Rotate field, and then pressing the Return or Enter key.

✦ **Skew:** Items can be skewed (slanted in the horizontal or vertical direction) by clicking the Skew radio button, and then entering values for the horizontal and vertical angles. Click Apply and the item will be skewed to the values entered.

✦ **Copy and Apply Transformation:** Note this Copy button! It's the left button at the bottom-right corner of the panel. Press it and Flash makes a copy of the selected item (including shapes and lines), with all Transform settings applied to it. The copy is pasted in the same location as the original, so select it with the Arrow Tool and scoot it to a new position.

✦ **Reset:** This button, at the bottom-right corner of the panel, removes the transformation you just performed on a selected object. However, once the object is deselected, this button does not work. For simple items, this is really an Undo button, rather than a Reset button. However, you can use the Reset button for instances, groups, or type blocks even after they have been deselected (but not after you save your movie).

The Transform submenu

If you've already mastered Part VII, "Mastering the Flash Environment," you know that the Arrow Tool options enable you to interactively scale, rotate, or skew an item relative to its center point. In conjunction with a watchful eye over either the Transform Panel, or the Info Panel, the Arrow Tool options can be used for a measure of numeric control over these processes. But there's another area of Flash (only briefly mentioned in Part VII) that can be indispensable. It's the Transform submenu, Modify ⇨ Transform, shown in Figure 32-10.

Figure 32-10: The Transform submenu of the Modify menu

The Transform submenu has these items:

✦ **Scale:** Use this command to interactively scale an item, several selected items, or a group.

✦ **Rotate:** Use this command to interactively rotate an item, several selected items, or a group.

✦ **Scale and Rotate:** Use this command to invoke the Scale and Rotate dialog to numerically scale and rotate an item, several selected items, or a group.

✦ **Rotate 90° CW:** Use this command to rotate an item, several selected items, or a group 90° clockwise.

✦ **Rotate 90° CCW:** Use this command to rotate an item, several selected items, or a group 90° counterclockwise.

✦ **Flip Vertical/Flip Horizontal:** Use either Flip command to flip an item, several selected items, or a group on either their vertical or horizontal axis — while leaving the relative position of the item intact, as shown in Figure 32-11.

Figure 32-11: The item on the left is the original. The item in the middle has been flipped vertically, while the item on the right was flipped horizontally.

✦ **Remove Transform:** Use this command to remove previous transformations. Depending on the item transformed, this command remains viable as follows:

- Simple items — until deselected.

- Instances, groups, and type blocks — until the movie is saved.

✦ **Edit Center:** Use this command to relocate the center, or axis, of a group, instance, type block, or bitmap to a position that is off-center. This command does not work on simple graphic shapes.

While nearly all the commands of the Transform submenu are redundant of commands that might be more easily accessed elsewhere in Flash, Edit Center is a unique and powerful command because it enables you to freely decentralize the axis about which an item (a group, instance, type block, or bitmap) will transform — or animate! For example, by moving the center of a grouped rectangle to its lower-right corner, the rectangle could be animated so that it expands from that corner, and then rotates around that same point.

Figure 32-12 shows the same item as in the previous figure, except that the center, as shown on the left, is being edited, so that the new center will be at the lower right. As shown in the middle, this affects the way that it responds to a rotation as well as how it sits when scaled, as at the right.

Figure 32-12: Changing an item's center for rotation and scaling.

The Align Panel

The Align Panel, shown in Figure 32-13, is one of many features for which you'll be grateful every time you use it. It enables you, with pixel-perfect precision, to align items to each other and the Stage and to distribute items evenly on the Stage. To open the Panel, choose Window ➪ Panels ➪ Align (Ctrl+K/Command+K).

Figure 32-13: Use the Align Panel to both size and line up items without fuss.

The Align Panel has five controls. The icons on the buttons are relatively self-explanatory:

✦ **Align:** There are six buttons in this first control. The first group of three buttons is for horizontal alignment, and the second group of three is for vertical alignment. These buttons align two or more items (or one or more items with the Stage) horizontally (top, middle, bottom) or vertically (left, middle, right).

✦ **Distribute:** This control also has six buttons, three for horizontal distribution and three for vertical distribution. These buttons are most useful when you have three or more items that you want to space evenly (such as a set of buttons). These buttons distribute items equally, again vertically or horizontally. The different options enable you to distribute from edge to edge, or from item centers.

✦ **Match Size:** This control enables you to force two or more items of different sizes to become equal in size; match items horizontally, vertically, or both.

✦ **Space:** This option enables you to space items evenly, again, vertically or horizontally. You might wonder how this differs from Distribute. Both are similar in concept, and if your items are all the same size, they will have the same effect. The difference becomes more apparent when the items are of different sizes:

• Distribute evenly distributes the items according to a common reference (top, center, or bottom). For example, if one item is larger than the others, it may be separated from the other items by less space, but the distance between its top edge and the next item's top edge will be consistent with all the selected items.

• Space ensures that the spacing between items is the same; for example, each item might have exactly 36 pixels between it and the next.

✦ **To Stage:** On the right, you will also notice a To Stage button. By clicking this, you include the full Stage in the operation.

To align an item to the exact center of the Stage, do the following:

1. Click to select the item that you wish to center.

2. Click To Stage in the Align Panel.

3. Click the Align horizontal center button.

4. Click the Align vertical center button.

Fill and Stroke Effects

Gradient fills are one kind of important fill effect. They give extra depth and richness to shapes that are drawn in Flash and are commonly used to give a three-dimensional effect to shapes.

Cross-Reference Colors are discussed in great detail in Chapter 28, "Applying Color." Refer to that section to learn more about creating and working with gradient fills.

Spheres

Spheres are very easy to make. To make one, draw a circle on the stage, and then apply a radial gradient fill to it—but don't just stop there! Learn to use the gradient fill to give it some depth by adding highlights and shadows.

As shown in Figure 32-14, starting with a simple sphere (left), a highlight effect is added to the sphere (middle). Then, working with the Radial Gradient drop-down of the Fill Panel, a unique radial fill is generated to apply highlight and shadow effects to the sphere (right).

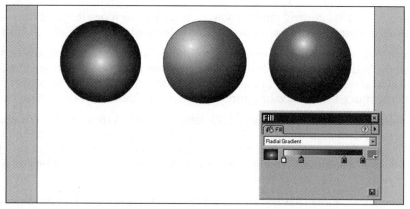

Figure 32-14: Creating highlights and shadows for a 3D effect.

Here's how to make a simple sphere look more realistic.

1. Select the Oval Tool and choose a radial gradient for the fill. (Refer to Chapter 28, "Applying Color," for more about working with fills.)

2. Shift-drag across the stage with the Oval Tool to make a circle, which should look like the sphere shown at the left.

3. To give the sphere a little highlight effect, transform the fill by reapplying it with the Bucket Tool, so that the lightest part is at the top left of the circle, as shown in the middle sphere of the figure.

4. Now play around with the colors in the fill until you get a nice looking sphere, as shown in the figure at the right. Add colors to the radial gradient to tweak the effect of highlight and shadows.

Refer to Chapter 28, "Applying Color," for more information on using fills, as well as modifying gradients. Also, refer to Chapter 27, "Working with the Drawing and Painting Tools," for information about Transform and Lock Fill modifiers, which are useful when modifying fills.

The sphere illustrates a very simple 3D effect created with gradient fills. Although it's not really three-dimensional, it does give the illusion of it. More complex and detailed 3D effects can be created by judiciously combining the power of gradient fills.

Stroke effects

Stroke effects — which are controlled by the Stroke Panel in concert with the Line, Oval, Rectangle, and Pencil Tools — can be used to give more life to lines. One really neat way of using this effect is to apply a stroke style (stipple, hatch, custom) to a line, and then turn the line into a fill (Modify ➪ Shape ➪ Convert Lines to Fills) and apply various effects to the resulting fill. Then you can apply both Gradients and Bitmap Fills to your lines. Beware that overuse of this technique on complex styles can significantly increase .SWF file size and download **time**. On slower machines, it may also cause the animation to drag.

Strokes are discussed in detail in Chapter 27, "Working with the Drawing and Painting Tools." Refer to the "Using the custom stroke styles" section to learn how to control strokes and how to customize their styles.

Expert Tutorial: Using Modify ⇨ Curves, *by Dorian Nisinson*

To see the examples for Dorian's tutorial in a real Flash (.FLA) file, open the DNCurves.fla in the ch32 folder on the CD-ROM.

Lines to Fills

Here are three examples where the Modify ⇨ Shape ⇨ Convert Lines to Fills command is indispensable. The following figure shows an example of using Convert Lines to Fills to create square corners.

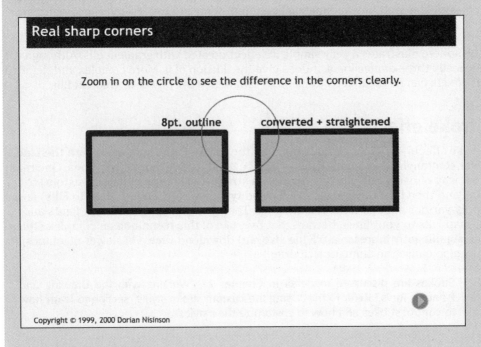

Here's how to get real square corners:

1. First, select the Rectangle Tool and draw a square complete with both an outline and a fill.

2. Then, with the Arrow Tool, double-click the outline to select the entire outline.

3. With only the outline selected, use Modify ⇨ Shape ⇨ Convert Lines to Fills.

4. Now, reselect the converted line with the Arrow Tool and click the Straighten option. The corners will be nice and sharp.

If you create a complex shape, put a line around it, and then use this process, the results are less predictable. Some corners may gain an extra facet or two.

Scalable Lines

What about real scalable lines? In the old days of Flash 3, an item created with lines would look fine at 100 percent view, but if an instance was made of that item (which was constructed of lines) and then reduced to 20 percent, the thin lines would not scale properly. Instead, they looked huge and ugly. And because lines (unlike fills) can never be represented by anything smaller than one whole pixel, reducing the line width in the original would not improve the scaled appearance. Well, here's a solution, shown in the following figure:

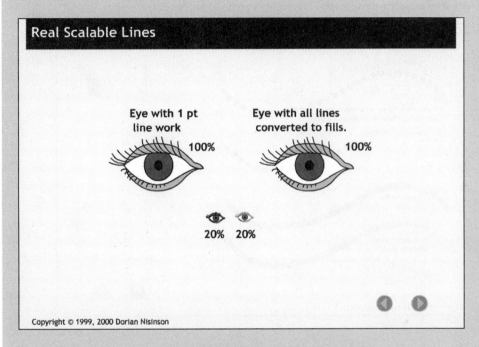

Real Scalable Lines

Eye with 1 pt line work — 100%

Eye with all lines converted to fills. — 100%

20% 20%

Copyright © 1999, 2000 Dorian Nisinson

1. If a symbol will appear at different scales, convert those pesky lines to fills.

2. Then, fill the lines as you choose; they will scale with the artwork!

Converting Styled Lines Retains Style

Now, converting styled lines retains style! That's right, you can convert a dashed or dotted line yet maintain the line style (see the following figure)!

Here's how:

1. Select the Pencil Tool, choose 8 points for the line width, and create a line using the dotted line style. This will draw a line with a row of big dots.

2. Next, use Modify ⇨ Shape ⇨ Convert Lines to Fills. You'll notice that, although you converted the line to fills, the dots are still there.

Continued

Continued

3. Click a single dot; each dot is a separate item that can be filled. But each dot can also be edited much more extensively than if it were a line.

4. So what about lines? As you can see in the example .FLA, even plain lines can be filled with gradients, and even the opacity can be controlled.

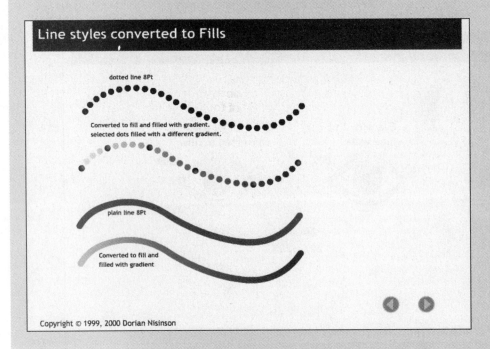

Faux 3D

Now we look at making a slightly 3D rectangle. Here's how to create the effect shown at the left in the following figure:

1. Start with a light gray for the movie background and draw a rectangle with rounded corners set to 10 and no outline.

2. Fill this rectangle with a linear gradient that goes from blue-green to white and back to blue-green.

3. With the Paint Bucket Tool selected, choose the Transform Fill Option. Click the gradient to select it and then rotate it to approximately 45 degrees.

4. Next, expand or contract the gradient so that the full color ends of the gradient are at opposite corners of the filled shape.

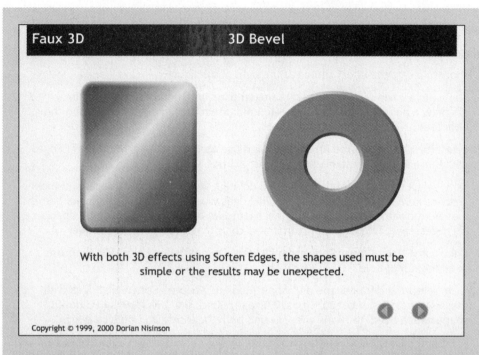

Faux 3D   3D Bevel

With both 3D effects using Soften Edges, the shapes used must be
simple or the results may be unexpected.

5. Now, we're ready to make our 3D effect. To do this, select the rectangle with the
Arrow Tool and use Modify ⇨ Shape ⇨ Soften Fill Edges with the following settings:
Distance: 16, Steps: 6 px, Expand. Click OK to apply.

6. Then, with the Arrow Tool, select the outer band of this softened shape and copy it.
Create a new layer, drag it beneath the first layer, and use Edit ⇨ Paste in Place to
put the outermost band in the same position as the original rectangle (but on the
new layer underneath it).

7. Now, return to the top layer and click the eye icon (in the Layers Panel) of the top
layer to hide it, so that you can see what you're doing to the lower layer in the
next step.

8. Next return to the bottom layer, make it the active layer, and then fill the center of
the pasted shape with a white-to-black opaque gradient.

9. Then edit this lower gradient to a 45-degree angle and squeeze it so that 25 percent
of the filled area is either pure white or pure black. (This can be adjusted later.)

10. When you make the top layer visible again, you'll notice a 3D effect.

Continued

Continued

Making a 3D bevel

Here's how to create the effect shown at the right of the figure:

1. Start with a circle of 150 pixels in diameter filled with an intermediate color. (To draw a perfect circle, remember to hold down the Shift key to constrain the Oval Tool.)

2. Select the circle (with the Arrow Tool) and use Modify ⇨ Shape ⇨ Soften Fill Edges with these settings: Distance: 140, Steps: 2, Inset. Click OK to apply.

3. Now, select the center of the circle and delete it, leaving a donut shape with a perfectly centered hole. Because Soften Fill Edges works by creating a series of bands that are the same color as the original shape, yet of gradually decreasing opacity, it's necessary to fill this donut with a new color that's 100 percent opaque.

4. Choose the Paint Bucket Tool and a fill with a middle value color, and then use it to fill the donut hole.

5. Next, select the donut shape and apply Modify ⇨ Shape ⇨ Soften Fill Edges with these settings: Distance: 20, Steps: 2, Expand. Click OK. This results in a donut shape with a band 10 pixels wide around both the inside and outside edges.

6. Now, in the Linear Gradient drop-down of the Fills Panel, create a linear gradient that goes from white to a darker shade of the original donut color. Use this gradient to fill first the outer and then the inner band of the donut. Take care, as the bands must be filled individually and with the Lock Fill Modifier turned off in order to enable subsequent manipulation of these fills — which will complete the 3D effect.

7. Next, with the Paint Bucket Tool and Transform Fills option, click the outer band and edit the application of the gradient. Assuming a light source from the upper left, rotate the gradient approximately 45 degrees until the outer band is whitest at the upper left edge and darkest color at the lower right.

8. Finally, edit the gradient for the inner band. As a dimensional item, the upper left of the inner band would be in shadow, while lower right would be illuminated — so, rotate this gradient until the inner band to opposes the orientation of the outer band.

9. Now the donut is 3D!

The Settings in the Soften Edges Panel are:

✦ **Distance:** The number of pixels the selected shape will expand or contract

✦ **Number of steps:** The number of bands around the edges of a shape

✦ **Expand or Inset radio buttons:** Tells Flash whether to enlarge or contract the original shape

When working with circular shapes, the width of each band will be equal to the Distance number divided by the number of steps. For example:

✦ If the distance is 10 and the number of steps is 2, then each band will be 5 pixels larger or smaller, depending on whether Expand or Inset is checked. However, the innermost band (the band closest to the original shape) will become the same color as the original shape. (This means that the inner band automatically becomes part of the original shape.)

✦ But with an original circle of 40 pixels in diameter with Expand checked, distance set to 10 and number of steps set to 2, the result will be a circle 45 pixels in diameter with a band of 5 pixels surrounding it—for a total diameter of 50 pixels.

✦ Using those same original numbers but with Inset rather than Expand, the result will be a circle 35 pixels in diameter, with a 5-pixel band—for a total diameter of 40 pixels.

✦ Finally, note that transparency increases successively with each larger band. If Distance is 20 and number of steps is 6, then the inner band will be opaque, while the next smallest band will have 80 percent opacity, the next band will have 60 percent opacity, the next band will have 40 percent opacity. The final band, with the largest diameter, will have an opacity of 20 percent.

When asked how near she lives to New York City, Dorian once replied, "You couldn't get any closer, I was born and raised and live there—right uptown." This was the perfect answer from the woman who perfected the methodology for using the new Flash 5 hitTest method. In the year that she graduated from high school, "the movie [she] remember[s] most from that time was not new—quite old, in fact: Murders of the Rue Morgue with Bela Lugosi, with gorgeous black and white cinematography." She discovered Flash when it was still Future Splash, just before MM bought it. It was love at first sight. Her favorite thing is, "I don't have one favorite. Draw, design, sing, talk, learn, write, creative problem solving." She's the cofounder of www.FlashCentral.com and designed the graphic intro for www.flashability.org. She has her own motion graphics company, Dorian Nisinson Design.

Static Masks

In the real world, a mask is used to selectively obscure items beneath it. In Flash, a Mask layer is used to selectively obscure items on the specific layers beneath it. To create a mask effect, a Mask layer is used in conjunction with a Masked layer, or multiple Masked layers.

When a mask is enabled, everything on the Masked layer is hidden except what's beneath filled areas of the Mask that it's linked to. Almost any content, (excluding lines) may be used to create a mask. Masks may be animated or static. The only limitation is that motion paths cannot be used to animate a mask, nor can layers within buttons be masked. Animated masks are covered in Chapter 33, "Animating in Flash."

Caution Although groups, text, and symbols can be used as a mask, such items fail to mask when they share a masking layer with a simple shape that's also applied as a mask.

The source files for the next three examples are located in the ch32 folder on the CD-ROM, in the Static Masks subfolder. You can also refer to the sample file, 10_Mask Tests, and examine all of the scenes, for more complex examples of the exceptions to masking.

Masking with a graphic

Here's how to create the simplest form of mask:

1. To begin with, the content that will be visible through the mask should be in place on its own layer, with visibility turned on. This is called the Masked layer.

2. Next, create a new layer above the Masked layer.

3. Then, create the aperture through which the contents of the Masked layer will be viewed. This aperture can be any filled item, text, or placed instance of a symbol. The only constraint is that the aperture must be a filled item. (Of course, lines *can* be used as masks if they are first converted to fills with the Modify ➪ Shapes ➪ Convert Lines to Fills command.) This layer is called the Mask layer.

4. Now, situate your Mask over the contents of the Masked layer so that it covers the area that you will want to be visible through the mask.

5. Finally, right-click/Ctrl+Click the layer bar of the Mask layer to invoke the contextual menu, and then choose Mask from the menu.

6. The Masked layer will become subordinated to the Mask layer and both layers will become locked. The contents of the Masked layer are now visible only through the filled portion(s) of the Mask layer (as shown at the left in Figure 32-15.)

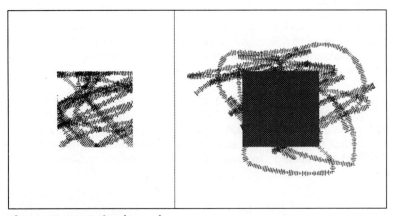

Figure 32-15: A simple mask

7. To reposition the Mask layer, unlock it (as shown at the right in Figure 32-15.)

8. To reactivate masking, lock the Mask layer (and confirm that the Masked layer is locked, too).

Masking with a group

A group can also be used as a mask, as long as it consists of filled shapes and as long as the mask doesn't also include simple ungrouped shapes:

If a mask is composed of multiple items, using a group usually facilitates positioning the mask, as shown in Figure 32-16.

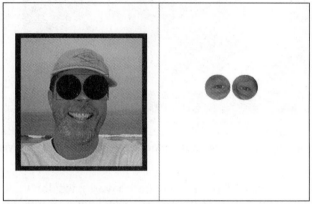

Figure 32-16: Who is that masked man?

Masking with a symbol

Working with symbols is working smart because doing so can help to reduce file size. Because symbols comprised of filled items can be used as masks, there's no reason *not* to use a symbol from your Library to make a mask. Let's return to our moon example from earlier in this chapter and see what we might be able to do with our primitive shapes.

Figure 32-17 shows the original shapes that we used to create a moon shape. The only difference here is that the shape that was used to cut out the bulk of the moon (the gray shape cutter), leaving only a sliver of moon, is now on its own separate layer — and the layers are set up as a Mask layer and a Masked layer.

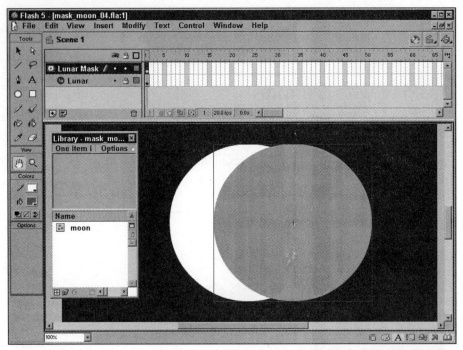

Figure 32-17: Using a circular moon shape for both a Mask layer and a Masked layer

Unfortunately, when we enable masking (by locking both layers), we don't get a sliver of moon. Instead, as seen in Figure 32-18, we get a silly lemon shape! What happened? Well, if you think about it, you'll notice that the upper shape *reveals* the content beneath it. So, as you can see, masking involves a logic that's the opposite of the cookie-cutter interaction that we used to create shapes earlier in this chapter. As you learn in the Chapter 33, "Animating in Flash," a clear understanding of this principle is critical to animating masks.

Masking text

Not only can text be masked, it can also be used to mask. To mask text, simply set up your layers as described in the previous section, with the text to be masked on the Masked layer, and the filled item that you'll use for your aperture on the Mask layer, as shown in Figure 32-19.

The source files for these examples are located in the ch32 folder on the CD-ROM, in the Static Masks subfolder.

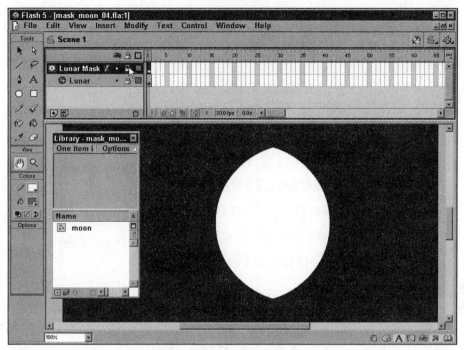

Figure 32-18: The upper circle reveals only the part of the lower circle that it covers.

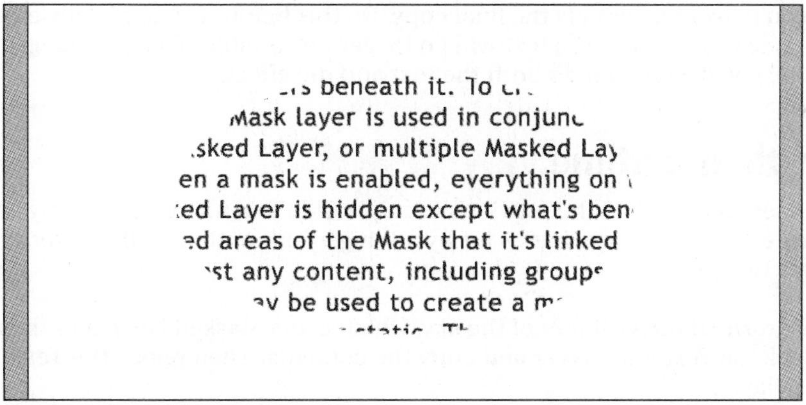

...rs beneath it. To c...
Mask layer is used in conjunc...
.sked Layer, or multiple Masked Lay...
en a mask is enabled, everything on ...
:ed Layer is hidden except what's ben...
ed areas of the Mask that it's linked...
.st any content, including group...
.v be used to create a m...
. static. Th...

Figure 32-19: Masking text

To use text as a mask, the layers should be set up as described previously. In this situation, the text (which goes on the Mask layer) will look as though it were filled by whatever is place on the Masked layer. For this to be effective, a larger point size and fuller, bold letterforms are advised, as shown in Figure 32-20.

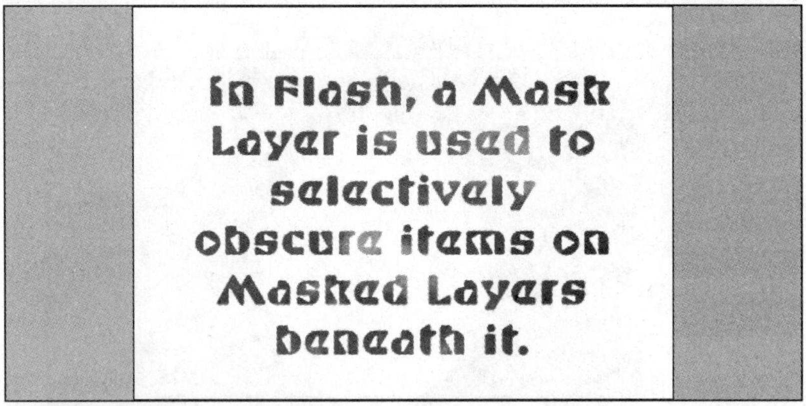

Figure 32-20: Using text as a mask

Creating Type and Text Effects

Whenever you set out to create a Type or Text effect, you'll want to make sure that the text you're working with is the final copy. Do this before you apply any effects, because once you're done, the text will no longer be editable. Thus, if changes need to be made, you'll have to redo both the text and the effect.

Text with an outline

The text used as a mask in the previous example didn't stand out as sharply as it might. The effect could be helped a lot by adding a faint outline to the letters. Here's how to do it:

1. First, turn off the visibility of the sky, which is the Masked layer, and then unlock the Text Mask layer and copy the contents. Then relock the Text Mask layer.

2. Add a new, normal layer beneath the Sky layer. If you inadvertently create a Masked layer, use the contextual menu to access the Properties dialog and assign the layer as a normal layer. Rename the layer Outline. Then paste the copied text in perfect alignment with the Text Mask by using Edit ➪ Paste in Place.

Tip

Do you find that you rely heavily on Paste in Place? Do you wish that this was the default, instead of Paste, for the keyboard shortcut Ctrl/Command+V? You could try using the new Flash 5 keyboard shortcuts (Edit ⇨ Keyboard Shortcuts) to customize your shortcuts. Or did you know that when you right-click/Ctrl+Click anywhere on the Stage, the contextual menu offers both the Paste and Paste in Place commands?

3. Select the text on the Outline layer and then break it apart using Modify ⇨ Break Apart. Then, with the text still selected, choose Modify ⇨ Shape ⇨ Expand Fill. In the ensuing Expand Fill dialog, enter a value of 3 pixels, and check that the Direction is set to Expand. Click OK.

4. Check to ensure that none of your letters have been obliterated by this process; sometimes, if the expand value is too high, the letterforms become corrupt.

5. Reactivate the masking, as previously described. If you've done it right, your letters should now have a thin outline.

Figure 32-21 shows the effect of adding a thin outline to the text that has been used as a mask.

In Flash, a Mask
Layer is used to
selectively
obscure items on
Masked Layers
beneath it.

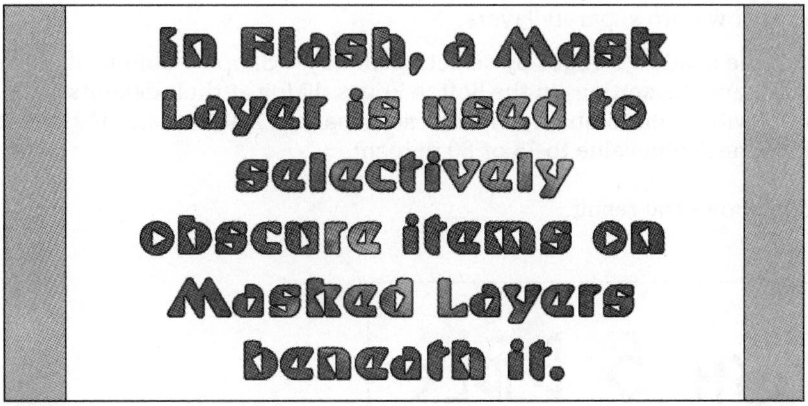

Figure 32-21: Adding a thin outline to text that has been used as a mask helps to sharpen the letters.

On the CD-ROM

The source files for these examples are located in the ch32 folder on the CD-ROM, in the Text Effects subfolder.

Text with drop shadows

Drop shadows are special effects that can be added to text to make the text stand out. There are many ways to achieve such effects. We discuss two of them here.

Type some text. Then, with the text still selected, copy the text with Edit ⇨ Copy.

1. Paste the copied text onto the Stage. Then, select it and change its color to something appropriate for a drop shadow — perhaps dark gray, or something slightly transparent.

2. Now, position the shadow on the Stage, and then send it to the back of the stacking order (behind the original text) with Modify ⇨ Arrange ⇨ Move Behind or Modify ⇨ Arrange ⇨ Move to Back.

3. Finally, select the original text and position it over the shadow text. Move the text and the shadow around until the shadow effect is optimal. To join the shadow and the text, select both and use Modify ⇨ Group.

   But that shadow is too crisp, and it doesn't look convincing. So:

4. For a softer shadow, repeat the preceding steps, and then break apart the shadow text using Modify ⇨ Break Apart.

5. You may find that it's easier to manage Text Effects if you move the Text and the Shadow onto separate layers.

6. Soften the shadow's edges by selecting Modify ⇨ Shape ⇨ Soften Fill Edges. Either leave the settings in the Soften Edges dialog at their defaults, or play around with them to obtain an ideal, soft shadow. Another alternative is to reduce the Alpha value to 75 or 80 percent.

Figure 32-22 shows the result.

Figure 32-22: Drop shadows make text stand out from the page.

Tip   Although a soft drop shadow looks good, it can add a lot to the file size — particularly if the edges are softened with a lot of steps. This may cause long waits during download and slow animations on less-capable processors. So use this effect sparingly!

More text effects

Text effects aren't limited to plain drop shadows. Any of the effects and modifications that have been discussed in this chapter can also be applied to text. You can skew, rotate, and scale text just like any other item. Break text apart and the use the Soften Edges and Expand Shape commands to invent your own effects. Or break text apart to apply fills. Finally, to radically reshape text use the methods discussed in Chapter 27, "Working with the Drawing and Painting Tools," regarding both processing lines and shape recognition.

 Tip
Don't sacrifice readability for cool effects. The special effects listed in this section are great for text that really needs to stand out, such as headings and button labels. However, the effects aren't advisable for large blocks of text. Although the final decision is up to you, consider the impact that your decision will have on the readability of your project.

Glowing text

You can also give text a glowing look with a method similar to the Drop Shadow effect. First, break apart the shadow text. Then apply a light-colored fill to it. Now, soften the edges — just increase the distance in the Soften Edges dialog, and make sure that the Direction is set to Expand. Then, move this modified text squarely behind the original text. Or modify this technique to create an embossed look by using a dark fill for the shadow text.

Gradient fills in text

Adding gradient fills to text can also make it stand out. Here's how:

1. Select the text and then break it apart with Modify ⇨ Break Apart (Ctrl+B or Command+B). The text appears as selected shapes on the stage. Be careful to keep these shapes selected.

2. Choose the Paint Bucket Tool and select a gradient fill from one of the Gradient drop-downs of the Fill Panel.

3. Apply the gradient fill to the selected shapes of the broken-apart text. The gradient will fill the text as if it were one shape. To add the gradient to each text character individually, deselect the text and apply the fill to each character.

4. A similar effect can be accomplished by choosing a Bitmap Fill, instead of a Gradient Fill, from the Fill Panel.

Summary

✦ Once you've mastered the basics of drawing, there are innumerable manipulations, effects, and combinations of them that can be used to develop your drawings.

✦ Using the basic Flash drawing tools, you can create irregular shapes, modify simple and complex strokes and fills, and apply many effects to those strokes and fills.

✦ Nearly anything that you can draw or create in Flash can be masked or even be used as a mask.

✦ Using these same Flash drawing tools, you can also create custom text and apply multiple effects to it.

✦　　✦　　✦

Animating in Flash

In this chapter, we discuss the basic methods and tools used to create animations in Flash. Animation is the process of creating the effect of movement or change over time. Animation can be the movement of an item from one place to another, or it can be a change of color over a period of time. The change can also be a morph, or change in shape, from one shape to another. Any change of either position or appearance that occurs over time is animation. In Flash, changing the contents of successive frames (over a period of time) creates animation. This can include any or all of the changes discussed previously, in any combination. There are two basic methods of Flash animation; frame-by-frame and tweened animation:

+ **Frame-by-frame animation** is achieved by changing the individual contents of each of any number of successive frames.

+ **Tweened animation** is achieved by defining the contents of the end points of an animation, and then allowing Flash to interpolate the contents of the frames in between. As discussed previously, this is often referred to as tweening. There are two kinds of tweening in Flash — shape tweening and motion tweening.

Note   There's a growing trend among many Flash developers to regard animation as a form of programming. After all, computer animation is the art of orchestrating items according to various properties over time. Perhaps this is a shift in thinking occasioned by the increasingly robust implementations of ActionScript that have accompanied these last two releases of Flash? It is worth mentioning, however, that a tremendous amount of animation is possible by using Movie Clips instead of simple groups and graphics. But before you can go *there,* you need to know how to animate on the Main Timeline with those simple groups and graphics.

Frame-by-Frame Animation

The most basic form of animation is frame-by-frame animation. Because frame-by-frame animation employs unique drawings in each frame, it's ideal for complex animations that require subtle changes — for example, facial expression. However, frame-by-frame animation also has its drawbacks. It can be very tedious and time-consuming to draw unique art for each frame of the animation. Moreover, all those unique drawings contribute to a larger file size. In Flash, a frame with unique art is called a *keyframe*. As shown in Figure 33-1, frame-by-frame animation requires a unique drawing in each frame, which makes every frame a keyframe.

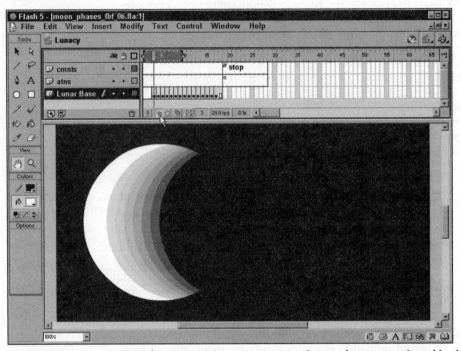

Figure 33-1: You can see the progression across seven frames because onion skinning has been activated. (Note the cursor, having just clicked the Onion Skinning button.)

All of the source files, including the files that were used to generate these shapes for the lunar phases, are included on the CD-ROM — they're in the frame-by-frame folder of the ch33 folder. The timeline shown in Figure 33-1 is from the file named moon_phases_fbf_06.fla. If you examine the files leading to this animation, you'll gain an insight into one process for generating unique drawings. The final .SWF plays like an elapsed time-shot of the moon; 14 days in less than 1 second!

Adding keyframes

To add a keyframe to the timeline, select the frame that you would like to turn into a keyframe. Then, do one of the following:

✦ Right-click or Control+click the keyframe and select Insert Keyframe.

✦ Select Insert ⇨ Keyframe from the main menu.

✦ Press F6 on the keyboard.

Creating frame-by-frame animation

Here are the steps for creating a frame-by-frame animation:

1. To create your own frame-by-frame animation, start by selecting the frame in which you'd like your frame-by-frame animation to begin.

2. If it's not already a keyframe, use Insert ⇨ Keyframe (F6) to make it one.

3. Then, either draw or import the first image for your sequence into this keyframe. Wherever possible, use symbols and flip, rotate, or otherwise manipulate them to economize on file size.

4. Then click the next frame and make it another keyframe. Change the contents of this second keyframe.

5. Continue to add keyframes and change the contents of each keyframe until you've completed the animation. Finally, test your animation by returning to the first keyframe and then selecting Control ⇨ Play from the menu.

Deciphering Flash Source Files

This sidebar is based substantially on content that was developed by Jon Warren Lentz and Jeffrey Bardzell for their interactive Flash curricula at www.Flash-Guru.com. *They've taken a uniquely structural approach to teaching Flash, and the course is titled accordingly:* Flash Five, An Architectural Approach.

There's an old saying, "Give a man a fish, and he'll eat for a day. Teach a man to fish, and he will eat for a lifetime." We think the same concept applies to Flash. There's limited value in delivering linear examples that don't explore the innumerable possibilities for variation at every step — unless you want to duplicate the example precisely, you are headed for unknown territory . . . and you're heading there without a guide.

Beginning with the preceding chapter, we've pointed you toward many source files that are located on the CD-ROM. Many of these source files were designed to lead you from the general example in the book to more particular variations of the same concept. Others are just plain indispensable, because you won't understand the concept until you've seen it in Flash.

Continued

Continued

But examining these Flash source files requires that you decipher them. In a manner of speaking, after you learn how to decipher Flash source files, you are ready to fish with Flash. So, if you aren't familiar with the process of deciphering source files, or if you'd like a few tips, this sidebar is for you.

When you take the time to decipher a Flash file, and persevere until you get the methodology, you'll discover that this process has numerous advantages. Although deciphering source files can be a daunting task for beginners, knowing how to decipher a .FLA is definitely a skill that you want in your Flash repertoire. With this skill, you'll be able to

✦ Understand what your colleagues have done, even if they weren't careful enough to give all symbols and layers meaningful names.

✦ Learn from others, especially by taking advantage of the innumerable online Flash resource sites that offer .FLAs for this purpose.

✦ Engage with Flash architecture by examining a file from a top-down viewpoint, in which you increasingly and systematically discover its functionality.

✦ Explore a file by using the full Flash interface (timeline, Library, Actions Panel, Movie Explorer). This helps you make the kinds of connections among disperse interface elements that will enable you move forward into creative and powerful Flash development.

Preliminary Steps

Start with these steps when preparing to decipher a .FLA file:

1. Open the .FLA file.

2. View the .SWF by choosing Control ➪ Test Movie (Ctrl+Enter/Command+Enter). The best way to understand a .FLA is to know what the final movie looks like!

3. Return to the .FLA and make sure that the timeline and the Library are visible (View ➪ Timeline and Window ➪ Library).

Kinds of Information

When deciphering a .FLA, you seek different kinds of information:

✦ There are three structural axes that organize and structure any Flash architecture: the horizontal timeline; the vertical layers; and the deploying and nesting of symbols:

  • The timeline organizes content, from left to right, according to time.

  • The layers organize content, from front to back, according to space — or depth.

  • Symbols, Movie Clips, and nested symbols and Movie Clips organize reusable content through the magic of instances. Generally, this is the most difficult axis to comprehend and decipher.

✦ An understanding each axis is a prerequisite to a thorough understanding of:

• The functionality of a Flash movie — meaning, how users can interact with it.

• How (or how well) the movie was created.

Deciphering Procedures

In most Flash movies, the information that you seek is found in a few predictable locations of the Flash interface, as schematized in the following table:

Kind of Information	Likely Interface Location
What elements are in the file?	Main Timeline and layers (don't forget to look at all the Scenes, if appropriate)
What is the *structural nature* of the elements in the file?	Library and Symbol Editing Mode
How does the movie *function*?	Actions, Labels, and Comments in the timeline; Actions attached to objects (such as Buttons)
All of the above	Movie Explorer (discussed in depth in Chapter 31)

Tweening

Tweening is great for a couple of reasons. Tweened animation is a huge time-saver because it doesn't require that you draw out your animation frame-by-frame. Instead, you establish endpoints and make drawings for each of those end points. Then you let Flash interpolate, or *tween,* the changes between them. Tweening also minimizes file size because you do not have to save the contents for each frame in the animation. Because you only define the contents of the frames at each end point, Flash only has to save those contents, plus the values for the changes between the end points. Two kinds of tweens can be created in Flash — Shape Tweens and Motion Tweens — each with its own unique characteristics.

The Frames Panel

To work with tweens, you need to become familiar with the Frames Panel, shown in Figure 33-2, which is used for choosing the kind of tween and for assigning the properties for each tween. Additionally, the Frames Panel is used for adding labels and comments to keyframes, which is most often associated with ActionScripting operations.

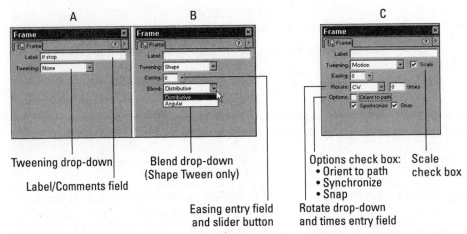

Tweening drop-down

Label/Comments field

Blend drop-down
(Shape Tween only)

Easing entry field
and slider button

Options check box: Scale
• Orient to path   check box
• Synchronize
• Snap

Rotate drop-down
and times entry field

Figure 33-2: The Frames Panel, in three configurations: as a Label maker (A), when used for assigning properties for a Shape Tween (B), and when assigning properties for a Motion Tween (C).

Shape tweening

Shape tweening is useful for morphing basic shapes between end points. Flash can only shape tween shapes, so don't even try to shape tween a group, symbol, or editable text—it won't work. You can shape tween multiple shapes on a layer, but for the sake of organization it's clearer (and advised!) that each shape be put on its own layer. This makes it much easier to return to the animation later and to make changes, because it can be nearly impossible to figure out what's going on if a number of tweens share the same layer. Shape tweening also enables you to tween colors.

In Figure 33-3, you can see the progression across seven frames because onion skinning has been activated. Although this appears similar to the frame-by-frame example as shown in Figure 33-1, the two animations play quite differently.

On the
CD-ROM

The source file for this example is located on the CD-ROM, in the shape tweening folder of the ch33 folder. Take some time to compare this file, and how it plays, to the frame-by-frame previous example.

Here are the steps for creating a Shape Tween:

1. Select the frame in which you'd like to start the animation. If it's not already a keyframe, make it one.

2. Next, before drawing anything, add a second keyframe at the point on the timeline where you want the tween to complete.

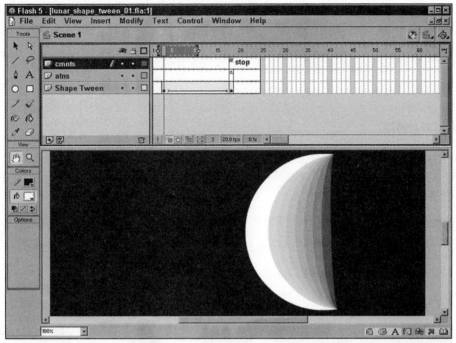

Figure 33-3: Shape tweening enables you to accomplish easy morphing of basic shapes.

3. Now reselect the first keyframe, and then draw your starting image on the stage. Always remember that shape tweening only works with *shapes* — not groups, symbols, or editable text. To shape tween such an element, you first need to break it apart into shapes (Modify ⇨ Break Apart).

4. Next, select the second keyframe and draw your ending image on the stage.

5. Open the Frames Panel by choosing Window ⇨ Panels ⇨ Frames. You can also select a frame between the end points and right-click to invoke the contextual menu. Choose Panels from the menu and then choose Frames from the ensuing submenu.

6. Choose Shape from the Tweening drop-down menu. The panel updates to present several options for modifying the shape tween, as shown in Figure 33-2:

   • Set the Easing slider if necessary. Easing determines the rate of your animation from start to finish. This is useful if you want to create the effect of acceleration or deceleration. If you want your animation to start slowly and progressively speed up, push the slider down. This will cause In to display adjacent to the slider and will also cause a negative number to display in the numeric readout. For an animation that starts out fast, and then progressively slows, push the slider up, causing it to display Out and a positive number in the readout. If you want the rate of your animation to stay constant, leave the slider in the middle. You can also type in a number for the Easing value (−100 to 100).

• Select a Blend Type. Distributive blending creates smoother interpolated shapes, whereas Angular blending creates interpolated shapes with corners and straight lines. If your end points contain shapes with corners and lines, select Angular blending. Otherwise, select Distributive blending, which is the default.

7. Test the animation by selecting Control ⇨ Play (Enter) from the menu.

Shape hints

Shape hints give you more control over complex Shape Tweens. As shown in Figure 33-4, they link corresponding points on each shape at both end points of the Shape Tween. The best way to see why shape hints are so useful is to actually work with them.

When copying a span of frames and then pasting that span of frames elsewhere — into a Movie Clip — Flash 5 drops the shape hints (in addition to dropping any layer names). When pasting is confined to the Main Timeline, hints are retained.

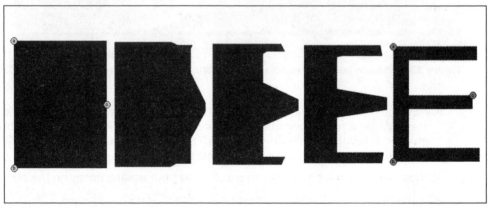

Figure 33-4: Shape hints are small, circled letters at the end points of a Shape Tween.

Using shape hints in a Shape Tween

To use shape hints, follow these steps:

1. Create a more complex Shape Tween using the method described previously — one that would not succeed without a few hints. For example, satisfactorily tweening from the shape of one numeral to another would usually require shape hints.

2. Select the starting frame of your Shape Tween (you can't initiate shape hints from the ending frame). Use Modify ⇨ Transform ⇨ Add Shape Hint, or press Ctrl/Command+Shift+H to add a shape hint. At first, the shape hint will appear as a red circle with a letter inside of it (the letters start with *a* and go to *z*) as shown in Figure 33-4.

3. Move the shape hint to where it's needed — try to visualize points that must correspond from shape to shape over the course of the tween.

4. Now go to the last frame of your tween. You'll see another small red circle with the same letter as your starting shape hint. Move this shape hint to the corresponding point to which the first shape hint will move during the Shape Tween. After you've placed the second hint, the initiating hint turns yellow and the final hint turns green.

5. Play your movie (Control ⇨ Play) to see how the shape hint affects the tweening.

6. Continue adding shape hints until you're satisfied with the results. Remember to match shape hints at the start and end frames — *a* goes with *a*, *b* with *b*, and so on.

   To get a better idea of just what shape hints do, take a look at the sample in the shape hints folder of the ch33 folder on the CD-ROM. A good experiment is to compare the hinted example to the same example with all hints removed. You just might be amazed!

7. After you've added the first hint, you can simply return to the initiating frame and right-click/Control+click the hint to invoke a contextual menu with options for further shape hinting, including Add Hint, Remove Hint, Remove All Hints, and Show Hints — which is a toggle that's on by default. When you want to see the shape hints again, just use this toggle or View ⇨ Show Shape Hints. To remove all the shape hints, you can also use Modify ⇨ Transform ⇨ Remove All Hints.

Surprising and interesting results can be obtained by using Shape Tweens in, ahem, unconventional ways. Although the results can be unpredictable, a certain amount of experimentation will yield shapes that might be difficult to obtain through other means. When encapsulated within a Movie Clip, a specific slice of a tween can be captured, by using the Behavior Options of the Instance Panel, or by attaching a `stop` or using a `gotoAndStop990` action, and used with few limitations. For more information on Actions, refer to Part X, "Adding Basic Interactivity to Flash Movies." For example source files, refer to the weird hinted shape tween folder, within the ch33 folder on the CD-ROM.

Motion tweening

Motion tweening is useful for animating groups, symbols, and editable text; however, it cannot animate regular shapes. As the name suggests, motion tweening is used to move an item from one place to another, but it's capable of much more. Motion tweening can be used to animate the scale, skew, or rotation of items; it can also animate the color and transparency of a symbol.

Motion tweening can only be applied to one item per layer — use multiple layers to motion tween multiple items.

A motion tweened item can be started and stopped as much as you want — simply insert a keyframe for each change of pace. Using the easing controls can further finesse this pacing control of Motion Tweens. Furthermore, the kind of tween can be changed; for example, the symbol can be tweened to rotate in the opposite direction. So, if you use a tween to move a symbol from frame 1 to frame 10 and stop the tween on frame 11, you can have the symbol sit still for 10 frames, and then start a new tween (of this same symbol on same layer) from frames 20 to 30. The possibilities are almost endless.

A Motion Tween, such as the one shown in Figure 33-5, is more efficient because it doesn't require unique content for each frame of animation. Yet it is *not* appropriate for all effects — sometimes you'll need to use either frame-by-frame or shape tweening to accomplish what you have in mind.

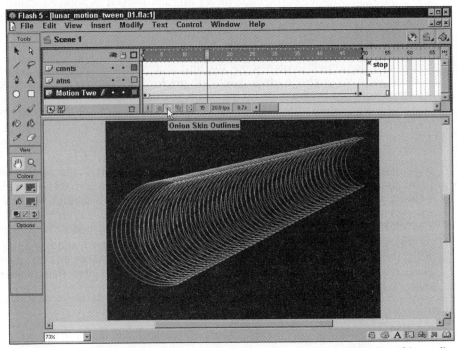

Figure 33-5: The extent of a Motion Tween is revealed here with Onion Skin outlines.

Create a Motion Tween

Here's how to create a Motion Tween:

1. Select the frame in which you'd like to start your animation. If it's not already a keyframe, make it one by selecting Insert ⇨ Keyframe (F6).

2. Draw or import the image that you want to tween. Just remember that you can only motion tween groups, symbols (including imported bitmaps — which are, by default, symbols), and editable text (a text block).

   • If you are using an image, group it or turn it into a symbol (refer to Chapter 31, "Checking Out the Library: Symbols and Instances," for a review of creating symbols).

   • If you already have the image as a symbol in your movie's Library, you can just drag it from the Library onto the stage.

   • If you are using editable text, you don't have to do anything — it's already an item.

3. Select the frame where you want the tween to end and make it a keyframe by selecting Insert ➪ Keyframe (F6).

4. Position your images in the two end points. Remember that you can move tweened elements, as well as scale, skew, and rotate them. If your end point images are symbols, you can also use the Effects Panel to apply color effects to them.

5. Right-click/Control+click a frame between your two end points and select Create Motion Tween. Test your animation by choosing Control ➪ Test Movie.

6. Open the Frames Panel by choosing Window ➪ Panels ➪ Frames. You can also select a frame between the end points and right-click to invoke the contextual menu. Choose Panels from the menu and then choose Frames from the ensuing submenu.

7. Choose Motion to make it a Motion Tween. The animation shown in Figure 33-6 involves both diminishing scale and deceleration to mimic the moon as it moves further away.

   Open the easing source file folder located in the ch33 folder on the CD-ROM. Look inside the Frame Properties dialog, under the Tweening tab. Pay special attention to the Easing option.

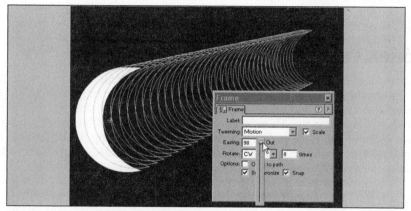

Figure 33-6: Using the Easing option to decelerate animation

- **Rotate:** You can rotate your items using this option. Select a rotation type from the drop-down menu and then type the number of rotations in the entry field. Automatic rotation rotates your item in the direction that requires the least amount of motion, while Clockwise and Counter-clockwise rotate your item in the indicated direction. In both cases, the rotation will be completed as many times as you specify in the entry field. If you type 0 in the entry field, or select None from the drop-down menu, no rotation will occur.

- **Orient to path:** When your item follows a path, turning this selection on forces the item to orient its movement to that path. We discuss paths in the next section of this chapter.

- **Synchronize:** This option ensures that your animation loops properly in the Main Movie. It forces the animation to loop properly even if the sequence is not an even multiple of the number of frames occupied by the symbol in the Main Movie's Timeline. This is only important if your animation is contained within a graphic symbol.

- **Snap:** This option snaps your animated item to a Motion Guide. Motion Guides are discussed later in this chapter.

Tip

Flash 4 added a feature that automatically adds new keyframes between the end points of a Motion Tween. This is very useful if you decide to add a third point to your animation (you aren't stuck with only two!). Just select the frame that you want to turn into an end point, and move the item that it contains to the desired location—a new keyframe appears like magic.

Caution

Tweened Zooms (where an item is initiated at a reduced scale and then tweened to full-scale or larger) and tweened alpha effects can be both CPU and bandwidth intensive—not only do they result in larger files that take longer to download, but they also require more computing horsepower on the user's machine. Our advice: Use such effects judiciously, and always double-check them for performance spikes by using the bandwidth profiler when testing your work. The bandwidth profiler is accessed from the Test Movie player (Control ➪ Test Movie) with View ➪ Bandwidth Profiler. For more discussion about the Bandwidth Profiler, refer to Chapter 42, "Sharing and Loading Assets," and Chapter 43, "Publishing Flash Movies."

Motion Tweened effects

Because symbol instances have properties that can be manipulated separately from their root symbol, it's possible to scale, rotate, and skew an instance. This feature of symbols makes it possible to generate a wide range of animated effects that rely almost entirely upon the file efficiency of Flash symbols. While this is indeed great, it gets even better: There's one more class of instance properties that can be tweaked—these properties are tint, brightness, alpha (or opacity), and advanced combinations of all three.

Using the chromatic options of the Effects Panel in concert with motion tweening gives you great control over the color and opacity of symbol instances in your animations, with good file size economy too. In Figure 33-7, our lunar example has been modified to slowly become the fabled blue moon.

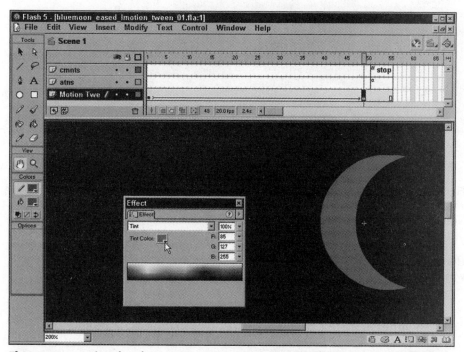

Figure 33-7: Using the chromatic options of the Effects panel along with motion tweening

As shown in Figure 33-8, the Effects Panel enables you to control color and opacity of motion tweened symbol instances. There are five iterations of this panel, each of which is accessed from the Effect drop-down. If you look closely, you'll notice that nearly all of the sliders have the capability to reduce a value by a negative percentage.

On the CD-ROM The source file for the examples discussed in this section can be found in the effects folder, which is located in the ch33 folder on the CD-ROM.

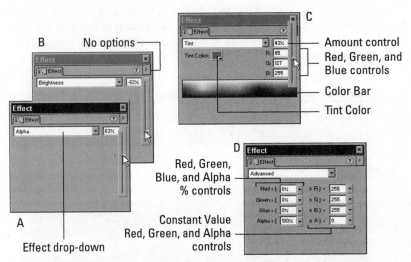

Figure 33-8: The Behavior drop-down of the Effects Panel is shown with four of the five Behaviors and their many options. The fifth behavior, None, has been omitted.

Here's a rundown on the gamut of controls that are available in this colorful workhorse of a panel:

✦ **None:** Use this when you don't want to use this control.

✦ **Brightness:** Use this control to adjust the brightness of the selected instance, on a relative scale that ranges from black to white, which is represented as –100 percent to +100 percent.

✦ **Tint:** Use this control to color (or tint) an instance with a singular color. The tint color that's to be applied can be chosen from the Swatches Panel, which is accessible from the Tint Color button. Alternative methods of choosing the tint color are by entering numeric values in the R, G, B fields, or by adjusting the associated R, G, B sliders. After the tint color is set, the intensity of the tint can be adjusted with the Amount control—which can also be operated as an entry field or as slider.

✦ **Alpha:** Use this control to adjust the alpha, or transparency, of the selected instance on a relative scale that ranges from completely transparent to fully visible, which is represented as 0 percent to 100 percent.

> **Tip**
>
> Alpha effects in Motion Tweens will slow most fps settings. The only way to make sure that the fps is honored, no matter what, is to use a stream sync sound that loops over the course of any critical fps playback. For more on the relationship between streaming sounds and fps rate, see Chapter 38, "Optimizing Flash Sound for Export."

✦ **Advanced:** This truly is the advanced control, and it may take some getting used to. It enables you to adjust the R, G, B, and alpha values independently. The controls on the left are used to adjust values on a *relative* scale — meaning that adjustments are relative to the current colors. The colors on the right are used to adjust values subject to *constant* values — meaning that an absolute value, ranging from 0 to 255, can be assigned for R, G, B, or A. When used independently (that is, without tweaking the other bank of controls) these controls are intuitive. When used in conjunction with each other, they become quite powerful, albeit confusing at first blush. We suggest that you take some time, experiment, and take notes — your effort will be repaid in many colorful instances.

New Feature

Animating with negative alpha: If you take a close look at the Advanced option of the Effect drop-down of the Effects Panel you'll notice that, in this implementation, alpha can be assigned a *negative* value. Huh? Of course, an instance can't get any less visible than invisible. So what's that good for? A little experimentation yielded this one of many possible answers: Suppose you want to make a motion tweened item go from invisible to visible, but that you want it to commence visibility part way through a 100-frame tween. If you set the alpha to negative 100 in frame 1 and then, in frame 100, set the alpha to a positive 100, then the item will *begin* to be visible at frame 50. A similar logic might be employed to cause a tweened item to rotate only one-half rotation — simply make it invisible for the first half of it's rotation. For more information, refer to the examples on the CD-ROM in the negative alpha folder of the ch33 folder. (This same logic applies to negative brightness, which can be applied from the Brightness option of the Effects Panel.)

Guide Layers

Guide layers make it easy to keep the layout of your movie consistent, or to trace images, drawings, or other materials from which you want to develop an item. When employed as Motion Guides, you can use Guide layers to create the complex motion of a frame-by-frame animation with the ease of a tweened animation. Guide layers are not exported with the rest of the movie — they're just guides. So use them as much as you want.

On the CD-ROM

The source file for the examples discussed in this section can be found in the guide layers folder, which is located in the ch33 folder on the CD-ROM.

Using Guide layers for layout

Guide layers are great when you need a little help drawing in Flash. Use them as guides for your layout, as aids for drawing a complex graphic, or for anything else that you might need. To reemphasize, because Guide layers aren't exported with the movie, they do not add to the file size of the final .SWF. As shown in Figure 33-9, Guide layers are marked with unique icons next to the layer name.

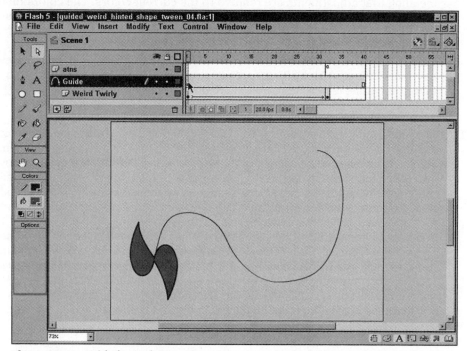

Figure 33-9: Guide layers have unique icons next to the layer name. Shown here is a guided Movie Clip together with its motion path. Note that the motion path is static.

Adding a Guide layer

Here are the steps for adding a Guide layer:

1. Draw or import your guide art into a layer by itself. This can be anything from a hand-drawn sketch of your layout to a full-blown prototype of your design.

2. Open the Layer Properties dialog for this layer by double-clicking the icon to the left of the layer's name.

3. Set the Layer Type to Guide, as shown in Figure 33-10 (using either the Layer Properties or the Contextual Menu, which is accessed with a right-click/ Control+click on the Layer name), and then press OK.

4. Use Control ➪ Test Movie to test the movie. Do you see the guide art in the movie? You shouldn't! Remember, because it's a guide layer, it isn't exported with the rest of the movie.

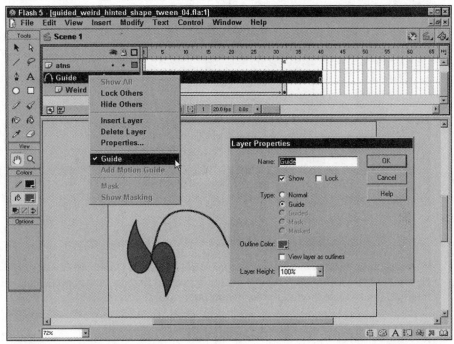

Figure 33-10: This composite screen shot shows how you can choose Guide from the contextual menu, or set the type to Guide in the Layer Properties dialog.

Motion Guides

You already know how to move an item from point A to point B. What if you don't want to move it in a straight line? This is when tweening along a path comes in handy. Motion tweening along a path requires a Motion Guide layer, which defines the path. One or more guided layers that follow the path accompany this Motion Guide layer. The Guide layer does not export with your movie — it's only visible within the editing environment. Figure 33-11 shows an item and its motion path.

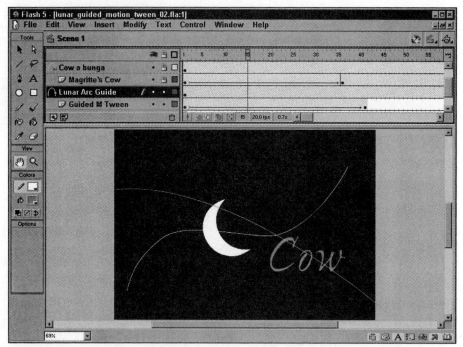

Figure 33-11: Moving items along a path is simple! Just use a Motion Guide. For multiple (as shown) guided items, use multiple Guide layers.

Create a Motion Tween along a path

Follow these steps to create a Motion Tween along a path:

1. Create a Motion Tween as described previously in this chapter.

2. Select the layer containing the tween, and then insert a Guide layer by doing one of the following:

   • Click the Add Guide Layer icon.

   • Right-click or Control+click the layer and select Add Motion Guide from the pop-up menu.

   • Use Insert ➪ Motion Guide from the main menu.

3. Draw a path in the Guide layer. You can use the Line, Pen, Oval, Rectangle, Pencil, or Brush Tools to do this.

4. Snap the center of the items in the end-point keyframes to the path. If you selected Snap to Guide in the Tweening tab of the Frame Properties dialog, it should snap automatically to the item in the starting keyframe.

5. If you want the item to orient itself to the path it's following, select a frame between your Motion Tween's end points, open the Frame Properties dialog, choose the Tweening tab, and make sure that the Orient to path direction option is selected. This forces the item to move so that its center remains parallel to the path.

Tip

If the item ends up oriented sideways or upside down when you orient it to path, simply rotate it and reattach it to the path.

On the CD-ROM

Be sure to look at the Guide layer source files in the ch33 folder on the CD-ROM. They are commented with useful notes to help you understand this process a little better.

Organizational Guides

An empty Guide layer can be used to organize multiple layers of related content for better timeline organization. It can also be used as a repository for custom strokes and fills. To use a Guide layer for organizational purposes:

1. Create an Organizational Guide layer.

2. Give the Guide Layer a meaningful name.

3. Arrange subordinate layers as Guided layers by:

   • Using the Layer Properties dialog; click the Guided radio button to set the layer type to Guided, or

   • Clicking and dragging the layer bar until it hovers just underneath the Guide layer, and then releasing.

Masking Animations

When animating with Flash, a mask can be used either to hide or to reveal elements, with the added complication of movement. As with static masks, an animated mask effect is created by integrating a Mask layer with one or more Masked layers. The Mask and the masked content can be moved at varied rates or in different directions — the possibilities are endless. For more background on static masks, see Chapter 32, "Drawing in Flash."

Some obvious possibilities for masked animations include: spotlights, moonbeams, text that is progressively revealed, a view through a periscope (or binoculars), simulated x-ray vision, navigational devices, and many more. Aside from your imagination, the only limitations upon animated masks are that motion paths cannot be used to animate a mask, and that layers within buttons cannot be masked.

On the CD-ROM

Be sure to look at the masking animation source files in the masking animations folder of the ch33 folder on the CD-ROM. There are several advanced examples that will inspire you to learn this process, as well as to test your facility with the deciphering of source files. In order of complexity, the examples are animated mask, masked moon animation, masked line animation, and kaleidoscopic button animation.

Animated mask text

Here's how to create one of the simplest forms of animated mask:

1. To begin with, we need to make the content that will be visible on its own layer beneath the mask and the mask content. For this example, we mask some text so that it appears to be spot lit. The text we use is MMF5. Create this text on frame 1 and make it big and bold! See Figure 33-12.

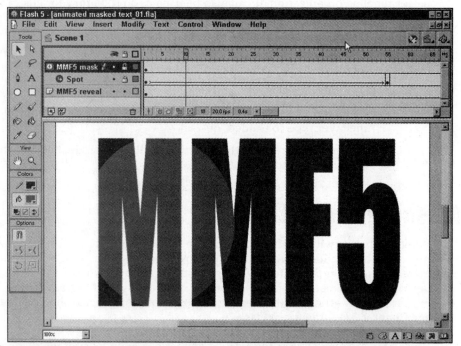

Figure 33-12: This example of animated mask text is among the simplest uses for animated masks.

2. Name this layer **MMF5 reveal**. Then give it about 55 frames, by clicking frame 55 and then hitting the F5 key, to insert a frame.

3. Add another layer above MMF5 reveal, and name it **MMF5 mask**. Make sure that visibility is turned on. Then return to the first layer that you created, MMF5 reveal, and click in the middle of the frame span in order to select all 55 frames.

4. Next, press the Alt/Option key and drag this span of frames up over the MMF5 mask (which is the second layer that you created) to copy the span of frames.

5. Now you're ready to make your masked content, which will be the spotlight. As with static masks, this is called the Masked layer. But first, turn off the visibility for the MMF5 Mask layer.

6. Add a new layer between the two previous layers, and name it **Spot**. Then, with frame 1 selected, use Insert ➪ New Symbol to create a symbol. For this exercise, any behavior and name is fine.

7. Next, use the Oval Tool to draw a red circle. Click the Scene 1 button to return to the Main Timeline. Open the Library (Window ➪ Library) and drag an instance of your symbol onto the Stage. This red circle should be as tall as the text, so adjust its size, if necessary. Position it off to the left, so that it is next to the first M, almost touching, as shown in Figure 33-13.

Figure 33-13: Position the red circle to the left, so that it's next to the first M, almost touching the M.

8. Next, select frame 55 of the Spot layer and press F6 to add a keyframe there.

9. Then select the Arrow Tool to reposition the red circle so that it is on the opposite side of the 5, almost touching the 5. If you use the arrow keys to move the item or press Shift to constrain the movement, you will be assured that the circle will animate in a smooth, straight line.

10. Now click anywhere in the middle of the Spot frame span, and then proceed to the Frame Panel and choose Motion from the Tweening drop-down.

11. Now, return to MMF5 Mask layer, and then right-click/Control+click the layer name and choose Mask (as the layer type) from the ensuing contextual menu. The icons of both this layer and the Spot layer beneath it should update to indicate that they are the Mask and Masked layers, respectively. Both layers should automatically lock.

12. Save your work, and then use Control ➪ Test Movie to preview your work. It should appear as though the Black MMF5 text is being lit by a red spot that moves from left to right.

Now you've probably succeeded with this example, but you might still be wondering how this animated mask text works. Well, here's an explanation.

The first layer that you created, MMF5 reveal, which is at the bottom of the layer stack, is a simple static text layer — it just sits there showing text.

The layer just above MMF5 reveal, which is named Spot, is a simple Motion Tween — the red circle moves from the left of the Stage to the right. Nothing fancy about this, either.

The uppermost layer, MMF5 mask, is the Mask layer, and it's responsible for the effect that you see. As a mask, this layer defines which portions of the Masked layer — which is Spot — will be seen. As Spot moves across the text *beneath* it, the text forms above Spot define where Spot will be seen: only within the shapes of letterforms. So, as Spot moves from left to right, it appears to be illuminating dimensional letterforms, and the "light" falls off the edges where there are no letters.

Masked moon phases

Here's another way in which the phases of the moon might be animated with Flash: by using an animated mask. This is a little more complex because it involves the use of an inverse shape to obtain the desired effect. Consequently, it's a lot less intuitive than the previous example. We strongly urge you to study the sample file on the CD-ROM until you understand why this works.

Figure 33-14 shows the setup for a masked animation of the phases of the moon. The background is black. Shown here are the Masked layer (A), the mask (B), the mask over the Masked layer — but with the layers unlocked and masking consequently disabled (C), and finally, the composite effect with the mask enabled and at frame 30 (D).

Here's the explanation. As shown in Figure 33-14, the Mask layer begins in perfect alignment with the masked shape of the full moon — which is the white circle shown in (A). Because the Mask layer is the inverse of the moon, it covers none of that shape and, consequently, the moon is not revealed. As the mask is moved to the right, a sliver of the mask covers the moon and causes it to be revealed. This continues until the moon is fully masked and, thus, fully revealed. Then the mask is reversed and the moon continues through the other half of its cycle.

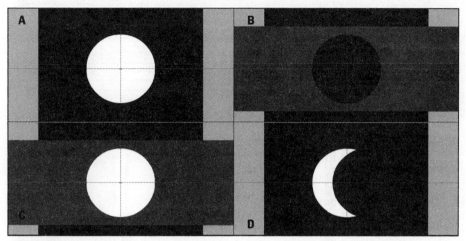

Figure 33-14: The setup for a masked animation of the phases of the moon

Masked line progression

This is a relatively simple effect that's simply repeated to create the effect of a line that appears progressively. Creating such an effect requires either a good bit of clarity before you set to work, or a willingness to tinker and tweak until all of the hiccups are smoothed out. When you decipher this file, and its variations, located in the masking animations folder of the ch33 folder on the CD-ROM, take care to notice how the entire effect was built with multiple instances derived from two symbols.

The animation shown in Figure 33-15 begins with a blank white screen. Starting at the upper-right corner, the first mask moves onscreen from right to left and progressively reveals the hatched line. The effect continues around the screen, until the complete line has been revealed.

This effect is accomplished by creating a stack of four pairs of mask and outline. The first pair is revealed above the others — this mask is Mask 1, together with Outline 1. The only part of Outline 1 that will be revealed is this upper portion.

Next, beginning at frame 25, the left-side portion of Outline 2 is progressively revealed as Mask 2 slides down from the upper offscreen area. Following this, at frame 50, Mask 3 progressively reveals the bottom portion of Outline 3. Finally, the right side of Outline 4 is revealed. Each of these reveals is accomplished with a simple linear Motion Tween.

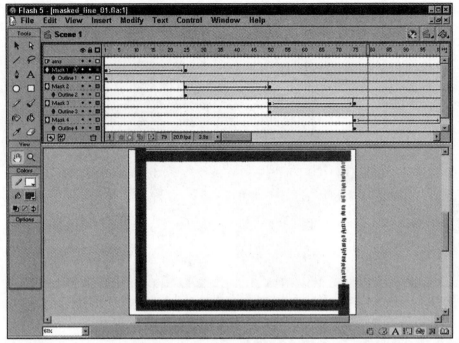

Figure 33-15: Progressively revealing a hatched line

Final notes about animated masks

If you find that these masked animations are a little hard to grasp, don't panic. For most people, the logic of animated masks is slightly inverted. That's because

✦ The mask goes above the item that is revealed by it.

✦ Flash uses an opaque window to reveal items below.

✦ Items that are not covered by the opaque window will not be visible when the mask is enabled by locking the Mask layer together with the Masked layer.

✦ Sometimes mild confusion over the elementary aspects of animation, compounded with the nature of masks, can lead to trouble. If this happens to you, just be patient — separate the animation from the masking. Then, when you've got them both working separately, combine them.

Summary

✦ Animation is an integral part of almost any Flash movie. There are three basic ways to create animated effects, including frame-by-frame animation and two kinds of tweened animation: Shape and Motion Tweens.

✦ More sophisticated animations often involve a combination of all three types of animation. The kind — or combination — that you use will depend on what you're trying to achieve, as demonstrated by the examples in this chapter.

✦ Unless you are working with Shape Tweens, you should always endeavor to work more efficiently by using the Symbols and Instances capability of the Library.

✦ Guide layers can be used in two ways with animations: to organize content and to create Motion Guided Tweens, or motion along a path.

✦ The final ingredient, aside from imagination and creativity, which Flash offers for the creation of animations, is the animated mask.

✦ Combined, these several types of animation, together with guides and masks, can be used to create an endless variety of expressions, effects, and styles. If you have any doubt, just look at the range of Flash animation available for your viewing pleasure on the Web!

✦   ✦   ✦

Using Bitmaps and Other Media with Flash

Although the Flash drawing tools give you a powerful
environment in which to create a variety of graphics,
you don't have to limit yourself to the capabilities of Flash.
That's because Flash also has the capability to import artwork
from a wide range of sources. You can import both vector
and bitmap graphics, and you can use both types in a variety
of ways. In this chapter, we discuss the differences between
vector and bitmap graphics. We also learn how to import
external artwork so that it can be used in a Flash movie,
as well as the Flash features that can be used to handle
imported bitmap images.

Understanding Vector versus Bitmap Images

Flash supports two types of image formats: vector and bitmap.

Vector graphic files consist of an equation that describes the
placement of points and the qualities of the lines between
those points. Using this basic logic, vector graphics tell the
computer how to display the lines and shapes, as well as what
colors to use, how wide to make the lines, where to put it on
the Stage, and at what scale.

Flash is a vector program. Thus, anything that you create
with the Flash drawing tools will be described in vector format.
Vector graphics have some important benefits: They're small in
file size and they scale accurately without distortion. However,
they also have a couple of drawbacks: Highly complex vector
graphics may result in very large file sizes, and vectors aren't
really suitable for creating continuous tones, photographs, or
artistic brushwork.

Bitmap (sometimes also referred to as Raster) files are described as an arrangement of individual pixels which are mapped in a grid like a piece of graph paper with tiny squares. Each square represents a single pixel, and each of these pixels has specific color values assigned to it. So, as the name implies, a bitmap image maps out the placement and color of each pixel on the screen.

Note   Do not be confused by the name bitmap. You might already be familiar with the bitmap format used by Windows, which has the file extension .BMP. Although *bitmap* may refer to that particular image format, it's frequently applied to raster images in general, such as .GIF, .JPEG, .PICT, and .TIFF files, as well as many others.

Although bitmap images aren't created in Flash, they can be used within Flash projects. To do this, you need to use an external bitmap application and then import the bitmaps into Flash. Unlike vector graphics, bitmap images aren't very scalable, as shown in Figure 34-1. Simple bitmap images are often larger in file size than simple vector graphics, but very complex bitmap images, for example a photograph, are often smaller (and display better quality) than comparable vector graphics.

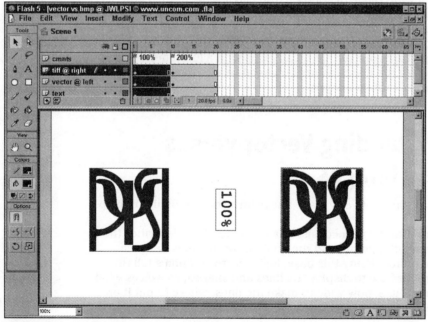

Figure 34-1: Here's JWL's logo—compare the unscaled vector graphic on the left to the unscaled bitmap image on the right. They both look almost equally acceptable, although the vector graphic is sharper.

The rule of thumb is to use scalable, bandwidth-efficient, Flash-compatible vector graphics as much as possible within Flash projects, except for situations in which photographs—or photographic quality, continuous-tone images—are either desired or required.

Figure 34-2 shows the difference between vector and bitmap graphics when scaled.

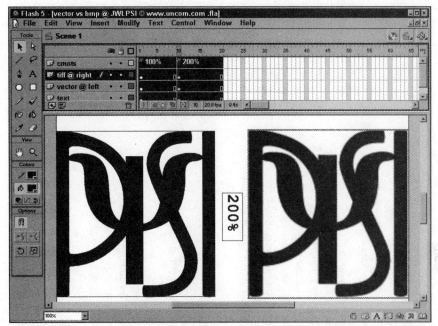

Figure 34-2: Here's JWL's logo again. Now compare the scaled vector graphic on the left to the scaled bitmap image on the right — the vector is *clearly* superior.

 Tip

Most 8-bit raster images are .GIFs, and they are most frequently used for images with large areas of solid color, such as logos and text. Rather than use this image type in Flash, consider re-creating or tracing this artwork with Flash drawing tools. The final .SWF will not only be smaller, it will also look better in Flash.

Importing External Media

Flash can use a variety of external media, including vector graphics and bitmap images. You can import this media directly, or you can copy from another application and paste directly into Flash.

For a complete listing of all importable media supported by Flash 5, refer to section "The File Menu" in Chapter 24, "Exploring the Interface: Panels, Settings, and More." For a full discussion of the importation and handling of sound media, refer to Part IX, "Sound Planning." Take a look at Table 34-1 for image formats for Flash Import.

Table 34-1
Image Formats for Flash Import

File Type	Extension	Description	Win	Mac	QuickTime
Adobe Illustrator	.ai, .eps	Adobe Illustrator files are imported into Flash as vector graphics (unless they contain bitmap images). Flash supports import of files saved as Adobe Illustrator files.	X	X	
AutoCAD DXF	.dxf	.DXF is the original inter-program format for AutoCAD drafting software. It was subsequently used for the original AutoCAD 3D Studio, now known as Kinetix 3DS MAX. This format is used by most other CAD, 3D, and modeling programs for transferring drawings to other programs.	X	X	
Bitmap	.bmp, .dib	Bitmap is a Windows format for bitmap images. Don't be confused by the format name — not all bitmap images are Windows Bitmaps. Can be used with all PC and some Mac applications. Variable bit depths and compression settings with support of alpha channels. Supports lossless compression. Ideal for high-quality graphics work.	X		Mac with QT4
Enhanced Metafile	.emf	Enhanced Metafile is a proprietary Windows format that supports vectors and bitmaps internally. This format is generally used to import vector graphics.	X		

File Type	Extension	Description	Win	Mac	QuickTime
Flash Player	.swf, .spl	Flash player files are exported Flash movies. The movie is flattened into a single layer and scene, and all animation is converted to frame-by-frame animation.	X	X	
FreeHand	.fh7, .fh8, .fh9	This is the vector-based format of Macromedia's FreeHand 7, 8, or 9.	X	X	
GIF Image	.gif	Graphic Interchange Format (.GIF was developed by Compuserve) is a bitmap image type that uses lossless compression. Limited to a 256-color (or less) palette. Not recommended as a high-quality Flash export format, even for Web use. (See Caution.)	X	X	
JPEG Image	.jpg	Joint Photographic Experts Group (JPEG) images are bitmap images that use lossy compression.	X	X	
		Supports 24-bit RGB color. No alpha channel support. Recommended for most high-quality graphics work. Note that this format does throwout color information due to its lossy compression method.			
MacPaint Image	.pntg	This is a legacy format for the old Mac Paint program.			Mac and Win with QT4

Continued

Table 34-1 *(continued)*

File Type	Extension	Description	Win	Mac	QuickTime
PICT Image	.pct, .pict	Can be used with many PC and all Mac applications. Variable bit depths and compression settings with support of alpha channels (when saved with no compression at 32 bits). Supports lossless compression. Can contain vector and raster graphics. Ideal for high-quality graphics work.		X	Win with QT 4
PNG Image	.png	The Portable Network Graphic format (.PNG) is another type of bitmap image. Supports variable bit depth (PNG-8 and PNG-24) and compression settings with alpha channels. Lossless compression schemes make it an ideal candidate for any high-quality graphics work. This is the best media type for imported images with alpha settings.	X	X	
Photoshop 2.5, 3, 5, 5.5, 6 Image	.psd	This is the layered format for most versions of Photoshop – from version 2.5 through version 6. Although it is possible to import .PSD files, it's not the best alternative. If you have the .PSD, open it in Photoshop, optimize it for use in Flash, and then export it as either a .JPEG or a .PNG for ideal import into Flash.			Mac and Win with QT4
QuickTime Image	.qtif	This is the image format created by QuickTime.			Mac and Win with QT4

File Type	Extension	Description	Win	Mac	QuickTime
QuickTime Movie	.mov	QuickTime is a video format created by Apple Computers. Flash imports it with a link to the original file.	X	X	Mac and Win with QT4
Silicon Graphics Image	.sgi	This is an image format specific to SGI machines.			Mac and Win with QT4
TGA Image	.tga	The .TGA, or Targa, format is a 32-bit format that includes an 8-bit alpha channel. It was developed to overlay computer graphics and live video.			Mac and Win with QT4
Tiff Image	.tiff	.TIFF is probably the most widely used image format for photography and printing. It's available across Mac and PC platforms.			Mac and Win with QT4
Windows Metafile	.wmf	Windows Metafile is a proprietary Windows format that supports vectors and bitmaps internally. This format is generally used to import vector graphics.	X		

Caution Although you can use the Publish settings to export to the .GIF format from Flash, this should be considered as a utility for information transfer, as raw .GIFs — and not as a means for creating final .GIF art. For optimal quality and control, Flash-created .GIFs should be brought into Fireworks for fine-tuning and optimization. An even better workflow is to avoid the Flash .GIF entirely by exporting as a .PNG sequence and bringing that into Fireworks for fine-tuning and output to .GIF.

Importing Vector Graphics

Vector graphics from other applications can be easily imported into Flash. These graphics are imported as groups, as illustrated in Figure 34-3 and can be used just like a normal group drawn in Flash.

Most vector graphics are imported as grouped items. FreeHand vectors may be imported as a flattened group or as discrete, aligned, layers. The lovely, craftsman-inspired logo shown in Figure 34-3 is from Nik Scramm's www.industriality.com.

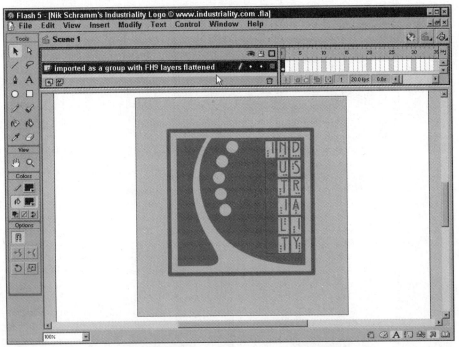

Figure 34-3: Most vector graphics are imported as grouped items.

Cross-Reference Refer to Chapter 30, "Exploring the Timeline," for more information about using grouped items in Flash.

Importing a vector file into Flash

To import a vector file into Flash, follow these steps:

1. Make sure that there's an active, unlocked layer. If no layer is available for placement of the imported item, the Import command will be dimmed and you won't be able to import anything.

2. Select File ➪ Import (Ctrl+R/Command+R).

3. The Import dialog opens, as shown at the left of Figure 34-4. Navigate to the file that you'd like to import, and then select it and click the Open button. If it's a FreeHand file, then—as shown at the right in Figure 34-4—the FreeHand Import dialog opens.

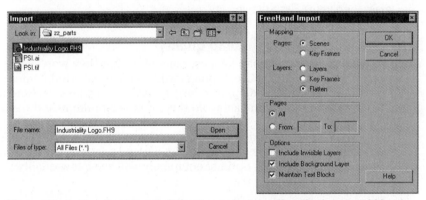

Figure 34-4: Use the Import dialog to navigate to the file that you'd like to import. FreeHand files receive special care upon import.

Preparing Bitmaps for Flash

Flash is a vector-based application, but that shouldn't stop you from using bitmaps when you *need* to use a bitmap. There are many situations in which either the designs or the nature of the client require that photographic images be included in a Flash project. You can import a wide variety of bitmap image types, including .JPEG, .GIF, .BMP, and .PICT using the method described previously in this chapter.

Considering that it's a vector-based program, Flash 5 supports bitmap graphics extraordinarily well. However, because the most common use of Flash movies is for Web presentations, you always need to keep file size in mind — slower Internet connections still dominate the Web. Here's what you can do to offset this problem:

✦ Limit the number of bitmaps used in any one frame of a Flash movie.

✦ Remember that, regardless how many times the bitmap is placed on Stage, the actual bitmap (or its compressed version in the .SWF file) is downloaded during the first occurrence of the bitmap (or its symbol instance).

✦ Try spreading out bitmap usage, or hide a symbol instance of the bitmap in an earlier frame before it is actually needed.

Tip   If you need to include several high-resolution bitmap images in your Flash movie, consider the use of an ActionScript preloader (see Chapter 42, "Sharing and Loading Assets"), or try breaking up the Flash movie into several linked Flash movies. These linked movies could use the Load Movie action to appear in the main (or parent) Flash movie.

Basic tips for preserving bitmap quality

When you choose to use bitmap images, remember that they won't scale as well as vector drawings. Furthermore, bitmaps will become distorted if your movie is resized so that the bitmap is displayed larger than its original size. Here are a few points to consider so that you can avoid this, or at least minimize the effects:

✦ Know your audience and design for the largest screen (at the highest resolution) that your audience may have. (Or, if you deviate from this, know that audience members with optimal equipment will see a low-quality version of your work.)

✦ Measure your hypothetically largest image dimensions in pixels. (One way to determine these dimensions is to take a screen capture of your mockup, and then measure the intended image area in Photoshop. Another way is to use the Info Panel.)

✦ Create or resize your bitmap image to those hypothetical dimensions. If there are any rotations or skews to be applied, do them within your image-editing application — prior to importing into Flash.

✦ Import it into Flash at that size, and then scale it down in Flash to fit into your movie.

The advantage of the previous method, or similar methods, is that the movie can be allowed to scale for larger monitors without causing the bitmap images to degrade. The disadvantage is that it will require sending the same large bitmap to all users. A more sophisticated solution is to use JavaScript to detect browser dimensions and then send the appropriate bitmaps to each user. Other, simpler — albeit partial — solutions might include the following:

✦ Just don't let your movie resize!

✦ Set the bitmap's compression to lossless.

✦ Trace the bitmap to convert it to a vector graphic (covered later in this chapter).

Raster Images: Resolution, Dimensions, and Bit Depth

Resolution refers to the amount of information per a given unit of measurement. Greater resolutions mean better quality (or better resemblance to the original). With respect to raster images, resolution is usually measured in pixels per inch (when viewed on a monitor) or dots per inch (when output on film or paper).

What is Resolution?

The resolution of an original image changes whenever the dimensions of an image are changed, while the pixel dimensions remain fixed. Thus, if an original photograph is scanned at 300 pixels per inch (ppi) with dimensions of 2"×2", subsequently changing the dimensions to 4"×4" will result in a resolution of 150 ppi. Although a 4"×4" image at 300 ppi could be interpolated from the original image, true resolution will be *lost* in such a jump. When an image is enlarged like this, the graphics application simply doubles every pixel, which softens the image considerably. Conversely, reducing the scale of an image has few undesirable side effects — although a smaller version of the original may display reduced (or destroyed) fine details.

Because all raster images consist of pixels, and because resolution simply describes how closely those pixels should be packed, the most accurate way of referencing raster images is by using the absolute pixel width and height of an image. For example, a 4000×5000 pixel image can be printed or displayed at any size with variable resolution. This image could be 4"×5" at 1000 ppi, or it could be 8"×10" at 500 ppi — without any loss of information. Remember that resolution simply describes how much information is shown per unit. When you reduce the pixel width and height of an image, the resolution becomes lower as well. However, once any pixels are thrown out, discarded, or interpolated, they're gone for good.

Bringing Images into Flash

When you want to bring raster images into Flash movies, you should know what portion of the Flash Stage the image occupies. Let's assume that you are working with the default Flash movie size of 550×400 pixels. If you want to use a bitmap as a background image, it won't need to be any larger than 550×440. So, assuming that you are starting with a high-resolution image, you would downscale the image to the largest size at which it will appear in the Flash movie *before* you import it into Flash; for our example, that would be 550×440.

Continued

Continued

Use an image-editing program such as Macromedia Fireworks or Adobe Photoshop to downsize the pixel width and height of your image.

If you mask bitmaps with a Mask layer in the Flash timeline, the entire bitmap is still exported. Consequently, before import you should closely crop all images that will be masked in Flash. For example, if all you need to show is a face, crop the image so that it shows the face with a bare minimum of extraneous detail.

Raster Images: Bit Depth

Bit depth is another factor that influences image quality and file size. Bit depth refers to the amount of information stored for each pixel of an image. The most common bit depths for images are 8-bit and 24-bit, although many others exist. An 8-bit image contains up to 256 colors, while a 24-bit image may contain 16.7 million color values. Depending on their file format, some images can also use an 8-bit alpha channel, which is a multilevel transparency layer. Each addition to an image's bit-depth is reflected in a great file size increase: A 24-bit image contains three times the information per pixel as does an 8-bit image. Mathematically, you can calculate the file size (in bytes) of an image with the following formula (all measurements are in pixels):

```
width×height×(bit depth ÷ 8) = file size
```

Author's Note: You divide bit depth by 8 because there are 8 bits per byte.

The optimal bit depth for us in Flash movies is 24-bit. This is due to the fact that Flashes defaults to 24-bit .JPEG compression for all exported bitmaps. You can, however, import 8-bit images in formats such as .GIF, .BMP, and .PICT. In this circumstance, especially for people viewing your Flash artwork with 8-bit video adapters, you'll have a greater degree of viewing predictability with 8-bit images that use Web-safe color palettes.

More about preparing bitmaps

Before sizing and importing bitmaps, you need to consider how you will set the Dimensions for the Flash movie in the HTML tab of the Publish Settings. You also need to know whether the bitmap is to be scaled in a Motion Tween. If the Flash movie scales beyond its original pixel width and height (or if the bitmap is scaled in a tween), then any placed bitmap images will be resized and appear at a lower resolution with a consequent degradation of image quality. Scaling of Flash movies is discussed in the Publishing sections of Chapter 43, "Publishing Flash Movies," and Chapter 44, "Integrating Flash Content with HTML."

If you are unsure of the final size that you need for a bitmap in Flash, then import a low-resolution version of the image into Flash (being careful not to erase or overwrite your high-resolution version in the process!). Then, make a symbol with a graphic behavior and place the low-resolution bitmap into that symbol. Whenever you need to use the bitmap, place its symbol on the Flash Stage. Then, during final production and testing, after you've determine what pixel size is required for the better quality bitmap, create and import a higher resolution image, as follows:

✦ Double-click the icon of the original low-resolution bitmap in the Flash Library to access the bitmap's properties.

✦ In the Bitmap Properties dialog, click the Import button and select the new, higher resolution version of the bitmap.

✦ Upon reimport, all symbols and symbol instances will update automatically.

Note Although .TIF is now a supported file format for import, it's not a listed file format when you try to use the Import button in the Library properties of a bitmap. To import a .TIF from the Library Properties, you have to switch the file menu to display All Files, instead of All Formats. Consequently, when you select a .TIF and want to import a new .TIF to replace the original image, it only works if All Files is selected.

Be aware that Flash doesn't resize (or resample) an image to its viewed or placed size when the Flash movie (.SWF file) is created. We tested the same source image, resized it into two different pixel dimensions, and placed it in two different Flash movies. In both movies, the image was viewed at 200×300 pixels. The first version of the image had a 400×600 pixel dimension, while the second version had a 200×300 pixel dimension — exactly half the size of the first. In one Flash movie (we'll call it Movie A), the first version was imported and resized (using the Info Panel) to the size of the second. In the other Flash movie (Movie B), the second version was imported and placed as is, occupying the same portion of the Flash Stage as Movie A. Even though both Flash movies contained a bitmap of the same view size on the Flash Stage, the resulting .SWF files, which used the same level of .JPEG compression on export, had drastically different file sizes. Movie A was 44.1KB, whereas Movie B was 14.8KB! Movie A is nearly three times larger than Movie B. However, when a view larger than 100 percent was used within the Flash Player, the difference in resolution was readily apparent in the higher quality of Movie A.

Importing Bitmap Images

There are two ways to bring bitmap images into Flash. You can import bitmap images, as we describe next, or you can copy them from an external application, such as Fireworks, and then paste them directly into Flash. Although the latter process is quick and easy, it doesn't capture any transparency settings, so it may not be the best choice for all of your needs.

When importing bitmaps, Flash 5 supports all of the formats that QuickTime supports — as long as QT4 is installed (refer to Table 34-1). However, the implementation of this reliance upon QuickTime can be confusing. If you attempt to import any previously unsupported format, the following dialog appears: "Flash doesn't recognize the file format of Image.PSD. Would you like to try importing via QuickTime?" If you ignore this dialog and click Yes, the image is imported as a bitmap. According to

Macromedia, you will always get this warning (which you must override in order to complete the import) so that you will be aware that QuickTime is used to complete the import. Other than this rather odd work flow, there are no adverse consequences to importing .PSDs in this manner.

New Feature   With QuickTime support, Flash 5 now enables you to import .TIF images, which is a widely used professional image format in the world of print graphics. .TIFs can also include alpha channels similarly to .PICT and .PNG files. To import a .TIF, you must choose All Files from the Files of type drop-down menu of the Import dialog.

Importing a bitmap file into Flash

To import a bitmap into Flash, follow these steps:

1. Make sure that there's an active, unlocked layer. If no layer is available for placement of the imported item, the Import command is dimmed and you can't import anything.

2. Select File ➪ Import (Ctrl+R or Command+R).

3. The Import dialog opens. Navigate to the file that you'd like to import, select it, and click the Open button.

As shown in Figure 34-5, the Import dialog also appears when importing bitmaps. Note that any file that requires QuickTime support will invoke the dialog shown at the right — in this case, it's OK to click Yes; the file will import properly.

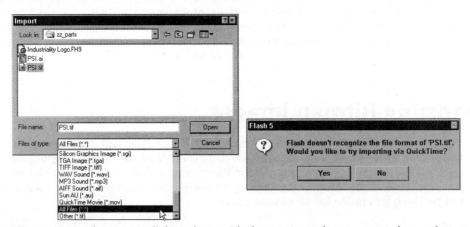

Figure 34-5: The Import dialog, along with the message that you see when trying to import files that require QuickTime support.

If you attempt to open a file that has a number at the end of its name, and there are additional files in the same location with sequential numbers at the ends of their names, Flash prompts you to import the files as a sequence. If that's what you want to do, select Yes when prompted. Flash imports all the files in sequential frames on the timeline. Otherwise, select No, and only the single file that you've selected will be opened.

Copying and pasting a bitmap into Flash

Here's how to use the Clipboard to import a bitmap into Flash:

1. Copy the bitmap from the other application.

2. Return to Flash and make sure that you have an active, unlocked layer that you can paste the bitmap into.

3. Paste the bitmap onto the stage by selecting Edit ⇨ Paste from the menu (Ctrl+E/Command+E). When pasting a selected area from Photoshop, any transparency (alpha channel) is ignored.

Because Flash 5 offers full support for the .PNG image format (including lossless compression and multilevel transparency), .PNG is the ideal format for images that you intend to import into Flash. The .PNG format has two types, PNG-8 and PNG-24. While both provide greater flexibility with compression, only PNG-24 images support 24-bit color and an alpha channel.

Caution   When using a .PNG image with a transparent area masked by an alpha channel, many 16-bit systems may display the background appearing behind the masked area with a faintly dithered variation of the actual background color. For more information, refer to the tech notes at www.macromedia.com/go/13524 and www.macromedia.com/go/13901.

Setting Bitmap Properties

The Bitmap Properties dialog, shown in Figure 34-6, has several options that are used to control the quality of your bitmaps.

Follow these steps to use the Bitmap Properties dialog:

1. Open the movie's library with Window ⇨ Library and select the bitmap.

Smoothing (dither) check box

Preview   Name   Image Path, Date, Dimensions

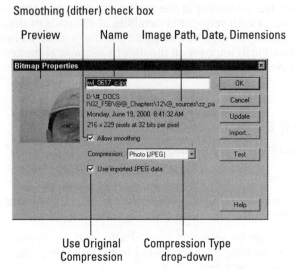

Use Original   Compression Type
Compression   drop-down

Figure 34-6: The Bitmap Properties dialog

2. Double-click the bitmap's icon, or right-click/Ctrl+click the bitmap's name and select Properties to open the Bitmap Properties dialog. You can also select Properties from the Library's Options menu or, with the bitmap highlighted, click the Properties button. Now, set the properties of your bitmap as desired:

   • **Preview Window:** This displays the bitmap according to the current settings.

   • **Name:** This is the name of the bitmap, as indicated in the Library. To rename the bitmap, highlight the name and enter a new one.

   • **Image Path, Date, Dimensions:** Beneath the name Flash lists the local path, dimensions, and date information for the source of the imported image (not available if you pasted the image from the Clipboard).

   • **Update:** This feature enables you to reimport a bitmap if it's been altered outside of Flash. Flash tracks the original location of the imported bitmap and will look for the original file in that location when the Update button is clicked.

   • **Import:** This opens the Import Bitmap dialog. When using this button, the new bitmap will replace the current bitmap (and all instances, if any), while retaining the original's name.

   • **Test:** This button updates the file compression information, which appears at the bottom of the Bitmap Properties dialog. Use this information to compare the compressed file size to the original file size.

- **Compression Type drop-down:** The compression setting enables you to set the bitmap's compression to either Photo (.JPEG) or Lossless (.PNG/ .GIF). Photo is good for very complex bitmap images (photographs for example); Lossless is better for bitmap images with areas of flat color. Play around with these settings to see which works best for each particular image.

- **Use imported .JPEG data/Use document default quality:** If the imported image is a .JPEG, the first option will appear — check this check box to avoid double-JPEG compression. If the image is not a .JPEG, the second option will appear — check this check box to retain the original compression of the image.

- **Allow Smoothing (dither):** Check this check box to enable Flash to attempt to dither, or smooth, the image. Results may vary according to the image. Generally, this is ill advised because it blurs an image. If you've imported and placed a perfectly optimized image, at 100 percent scale, this will noticeably degrade the image quality. It's better to optimize images outside of Flash and then insist that Flash doesn't mess with them.

3. Click OK. All copies of this bitmap used in Flash are updated to the new settings.

Using Bitmaps as Fills

Procedures for working with bitmaps as fills have changed significantly since Flash 4. Upon import, a bitmap appears on the Stage in the current frame of the active layer. However, it also lands in the Library, where it truly resides. In fact, you can delete the bitmap from the Stage without clearing it from the Library. However, you might not have noticed that, on import, the bitmap was also deposited in the Bitmap Swatches drop-down of the Fill Panel, shown in Figure 34-7. Bitmaps that appear in this new Bitmap Swatches are automatically broken apart on import and may be modified with any of the Flash drawing and painting tools.

Figure 34-7: This is the Bitmap Swatches drop-down of the Fill Panel.

New Feature Flash 5 offers improved handling of bitmap fills. Now they live where they are easily accessed, as swatches in the Bitmap Swatches drop-down of the new Fills Panel and are automatically broken apart on import. This means that they don't have to be brought out onto the stage and acquired with the Eyedropper in order to reuse them, as was the case with prior versions of Flash. Nice touch!

Here's how to acquire and apply a bitmap fill (of a bitmap that's already been imported) in Flash 5:

1. Open the Fill Panel and choose Bitmap from the Fill drop-down menu. A display of all imported bitmap swatches appears.

2. Click to select the bitmap swatch that you want from the Bitmap Swatches. (If there is only one, it is automatically selected for you.) The Fill Color button in the Toolbox automatically updates to display the selected bitmap fill.

   • If a fill is currently selected, it is updated with the bitmap you have selected.

   • If no fill is currently selected, choose the Paint Bucket Tool and use it to fill any shape.

3. In either case, as shown in Figure 34-8, the resulting fill contains your bitmap, which can be manipulated with the Paint Bucket Transform Fill modifier, as described in Chapter 27, "Working with the Drawing and Painting Tools."

Figure 34-8: Using a bitmap as a fill can produce some interesting designs.

Caution

If you drag a bitmap from the Library and position it onstage and then attempt to acquire the bitmap fill by first tracing the bitmap and then clicking with the Dropper Tool, you may obtain the following unexpected, undesired results. If the bitmap is still selected, clicking with the Dropper acquires the color immediately beneath the Dropper, and replaces the entire bitmap with a solid fill of the acquired color. If the bitmap is not selected, the Dropper simply acquires the color immediately beneath the Dropper.

Breaking a bitmap apart

Breaking apart a bitmap means that the bitmap image is subsequently seen by Flash as a collection of individual areas of color. After an image is broken apart, it may be modified with any of the Flash drawing and painting tools. You can select individual areas of the broken apart image with any of the selection tools, including the Magic Wand option of the Lasso Tool. (This is not the same as tracing a bitmap, which reduces the vast number of colors in a bitmap to areas of solid color and turns it into vector format.) The command duplicates the new Flash 5 automatic conversion of an imported bitmap as it arrives as a swatch in the Bitmap Swatches of the Fills Panel. You cannot use Modify ➪ Break Apart to generate a variant fill from the same bitmap.

The Magic Wand Option of the Lasso Tool is used to select ranges of a similar color in either a bitmap fill or a bitmap that's been broken apart. After you select areas of the bitmap, you can change their fill color or delete them, without affecting the Bitmap Swatch in the Fills Panel. For more information about the Lasso Tool, refer to Chapter 27, "Working with the Drawing and Painting Tools." Click the Magic Wand option in the Toolbox to invoke the Magic Wand Settings dialog.

The Threshold setting of the Magic Wand

The Threshold setting defines the breadth of adjacent color values that the Magic Wand will include in a selection. Values for the Threshold setting range from 0 to 200 — the higher the setting, the broader the selection of adjacent colors. Conversely, a smaller number results in the Magic Wand making a narrower selection of adjacent colors. To see the threshold settings see Figure 34-9.

A value of zero results in a selection of contiguous pixels that are all the same color as the target pixel. With a value of 20, clicking a red target pixel with a value of 55 will select all contiguous pixels in a range of values extending from red 35 to red 75. (For those of you who are familiar with Photoshop, it's important to note that the Flash Threshold is unlike Photoshop, in which a Threshold setting of 20 will select all contiguous pixels in a range of values extending from red 45 to red 65.)

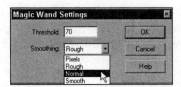

Figure 34-9: The Magic Wand Settings dialog

The Smoothing setting of the Magic Wand option

The Smoothing setting of the Magic Wand option determines to what degree the edge of the selection should be smoothed. This is similar to antialiasing. (Antialiasing dithers the edges of shapes and lines so that they look smoother on screen.) The options are Smooth, Pixels, Rough, and Normal. Assuming that the Threshold setting remains constant, the Smooth settings will differ as follows:

✦ **Smooth:** delivers a selection with more rounded edges

✦ **Pixels:** the selection clings to the rectangular edges of each pixel bordering similar colors

✦ **Rough:** the edges of the selection are even more angular than with Pixels

✦ **Normal:** results in a selection that's somewhere between rough and smooth

Tracing Bitmaps

Trace Bitmap is used to convert a Library image from a bitmap to a native Flash vector graphic with discrete, editable areas of color. This unlinks the image from the original in the Library (and also from the Bitmap Swatch in the Fills Panel). It is possible to create interesting bitmap-based art with this command. However, if your intention is to preserve the look of the original bitmap with maximum fidelity, you will have to work with the settings — and you will most likely find that the original bitmap is less file intensive than its traced cousin. Here's how to trace a bitmap:

1. Use the Arrow Tool to select the bitmap that you want to trace — it should be either a symbol, in Edit Symbol Mode, or on the Stage.

2. Use Modify ⇨ Trace Bitmap to invoke the Trace Bitmap dialog and set the options according to your needs:

    • **Color Threshold:** This option controls the number of colors in your traced bitmap. It limits the number of colors by averaging the colors based on the criteria chosen in Color Threshold and Minimum Area. Color Threshold compares RGB color values of adjacent pixels to the value entered. If the difference is lower than the value entered, then adjacent pixels are considered the same color. By making this computation for each pixel within the bitmap, Flash averages the colors. A lower Color Threshold delivers more colors in the final vector graphic derived from the traced bitmap.

- **Minimum Area:** This value is the radius, measured in pixels, that Color Threshold uses to describe adjacent pixels when comparing pixels to determine what color to assign to the center pixel.

- **Curve Fit:** This value determines how smoothly outlines are drawn. Select Very Tight if the curves in the bitmap have many twists and turns. If the curves are smooth, select Very Smooth.

- **Corner Threshold:** The Corner Threshold is similar to the Curve Fit, but it pertains to the corners in the bitmap image.

3. Click OK. Flash traces the bitmap, and the original bitmap disappears. If the bitmap is complex, this may take a while. The traced bitmap does not look exactly like the original bitmap.

Tip
If your objective is for your traced bitmap to closely resemble the original bitmap, then set a low Color Threshold and a low Minimum Area. You'll also want to set the Curve Fit to Pixels and the Corner Threshold to Many Corners. Be aware that using these settings may drastically slow the tracing process for complex bitmaps and result in larger file sizes. If animated, such bitmaps may also retard the frame rate dramatically. Furthermore, if the image is noisy (grainy) it should be smoothed (despeckled) as much as possible prior to tracing to save time, as well as to reduce file size.

As shown in Figure 34-10, the traced bitmap (right) looks quite different from the original bitmap (left). While you can change the settings in the Trace Bitmap dialog to make a traced bitmap look more like the original, it often requires a lot of work from your computer. This comparison was done with the Trace Bitmap settings at a Color Threshold of 25, Minimum Area of 10 pixels, Curve Fit of Very Smooth, and Corner Threshold of Few Corners.

Figure 34-10: The traced bitmap (right) looks quite different from the original bitmap (left).

Cautionary Notes

Flash retains existing .JPEG compression levels on any imported .JPEG image, but, unless specified otherwise in the Library, it reapplies .JPEG compression when the movie is published or exported. Recompressing an image that has already been compressed usually leads to serious image degradation, due to the introduction of further compression artifacts. When importing .JPEGs (and other bitmaps), you'll note that Use document default quality in the Library is checked by default. This is a feature, not an annoyance. That's because (a) Flash has a relatively generic .JPEG compression engine, which is easily surpassed by both Fireworks and Photoshop, and because (b) as mentioned previously, recompressing a .JPEG is routinely disastrous to image quality.

Tip   If you import .JPEG images, make sure that you either test the results of further .JPEG compression or else choose the Lossless compression setting in Bitmap Properties dialog, which is accessible from the Flash Library.

Apply compression settings to each individual bitmap in the Flash Library to determine the quality that you need before you use the general .JPEG settings in the Export Movie or Publish Settings dialog. You'll find .JPEG export settings for Flash movies (.SWF files) discussed in greater detail in Chapter 43, "Publishing Flash Movies."

Bitmap shift

There is a known problem in Flash that's referred to as *bitmap shift*, which means that colors may shift slightly from one instance to another of the same image. This has been attributed to several reasons. Some developers have reported that turning off compression has, at times, eliminated problems with bitmap shift. Another reported method for eliminating bitmap shift is to make the image a symbol, and then assign it an alpha of 99 percent. Yet the clearest explanation, and related fix, are as follows: Flash renders a bitmap while animating or transforming it, and then rerenders the bitmap as a static image when the motion or transformation ceases. Often, the two don't quite match. From this perspective, the optimal solution is to set the final bitmap's scaling to 99 percent. The advantage of this solution (aside from the fact that it works) is that it's less processor intensive, because any alpha adjustment burdens the processor with computations.

Cross-browser consistency

We've received more than a few queries about image formats and Flash's capability to transcend issues of browser inconsistency, so here's the answer. Many image formats, such as .PNG, are not supported across all browsers. When you import such an image format into Flash and publish or export to the .SWF format, you have accomplished browser independence—because the .SWF is browser independent and because the image has been encapsulated within the .SWF format. (The image is not being sent to the browser in the imported format and then magically empowered to display.) Conversely, if you export any .FLA to .PNG or to any other format that's subject to cross-browser inconsistency, browser independence is lost.

Color Insert: Bitmap Comparisons

To facilitate your deeper exploration into the subject of bitmap settings and their impact upon image quality, we've included the .SWF's that were built to collect and test our sample shots. They are located in the folder titled, BitMap_Comparison_8-SWF's, which is located in the ch34 folder on the CD-ROM. Because this is all about how images look on screen (and print is merely an approximation of this), we encourage you to use the Flash Player's zoom facility to take a good look at these examples. We've chosen to supply these as eight separate .SWF's because this will enable you to open several pages simultaneously for side-by-side comparison.

Generation of comparison images

Before you can make intelligent use of bitmaps in Flash, it's imperative to know about the options for creating bitmaps for use within Flash. That's because all bitmaps are *not* created equal. A bitmap from one program, created with similar settings, can be twice the file size — with no appreciable increase in quality — of a bitmap created in another program. It makes no sense to study optimization constraints within Flash if you ignore your exposure to fatty imports.

To create a set of controlled images that could be used for comparison, we chose a portrait (with a background that shifts contrast) and a landscape (with a broad expanse of graduated color). Both images were derived from high-quality film shots, scanned at a very high resolution, down-sampled to equivalent dimensions and resolution, 227×287 pixels at 96 ppi, and saved as uncompressed .TIFs. These files were used as the source files from which all other variations were derived (with the sole exception of the double-JPEG example, in which an image that had been previously .JPEG'd was used as the source image for the double-JPEG example).

Note

Because the native resolution of most PC monitors is 96 ppi, we used 96 ppi as the originating resolution in order to circumvent the possibility that Flash would need to scale these images in order to display them on the PC. This means that the image is scaled down to display on the Mac, which has a native resolution of 72 ppi. Unfortunately, this procedure also requires a slight bit of extra care when placing images, because Flash has a tendency to import these images ballooned out. Thus, when working with images at 96 ppi, it's advisable to check the Info Panel to ensure that the image dimensions, as measured in inches, has been retained. If the image dimensions haven't been retained, then the image must be scaled down to the image dimensions that correlate with the resolution of 96 ppi.

Our principal comparisons were done with Adobe Photoshop and Macromedia Fireworks, simply to establish a comparison of the quality and degree of compression available from each program. However, when preparing .JPEGs for comparison, we added a choice alternative, BoxTop Software's ProJPEG, which is a Photoshop-compatible plug-in. Because each program offers different options and different combinations of options, it is absolutely impossible to perform a direct one-for-one comparison. As such, our results are necessarily subjective and may not equate with your findings.

Tip   BoxTop Software's ProJPEG plug-in is available for both the Mac and the PC. It may be obtained online from www.BoxTopSoft.com.

The BoxTop interface

As shown in Figure 34-11, the interface for the BoxTop ProJPEG Photoshop-compatible plug-in is roomy and clear. For the purpose of our comparison we retained all settings as shown — except for the Quality setting, which was set at 94, 60, and 30 for the High, Medium, and Low samples.

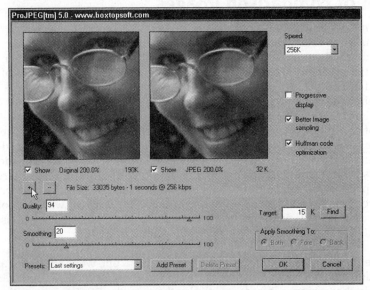

Figure 34-11: Here's the BoxTop ProJPEG interface. Note the check box options at the right for both Better Image Sampling and Huffman code optimization.

The Fireworks interface

As shown in Figure 34-12, Fireworks' Export Preview interface is also roomy and clear. It also provides the option — which we did not use — of comparing the before image with three other previews. Again, for this comparison we retained all settings as shown — except for the Quality setting, which was set at 94, 60, and 30 for the High, Medium, and Low samples. The Fireworks' Export Preview has several options that may have tipped the compression contest in its favor. Note that we used the default, No Smoothing, and that we left the Remove Unused Colors check box activated.

Figure 34-12: The Fireworks Export Preview

The Photoshop interface

The Photoshop Interface that was used for these comparisons is shown in Figure 34-13. In all fairness, it should be noted that Photoshop also sports a roomy interface complete with preview, which is accessed from Photoshop with the File ➪ Save for Web command. (But it should also be noted that, in preliminary testing, the Save for Web interface, in multiple configurations, failed to deliver competitive compressions.) For this comparison we retained all settings as shown — except for the Quality setting, which was set at 11, 9, and 7 for the High, Medium, and Low samples. The deviation in these settings is due to the Quality range of 1 to 12, rather than 1 to 10.

Figure 34-13 shows the familiar Photoshop .JPEG dialog. Note that the Quality range is from 1 to 12, rather than the expected 1 to 10. However, this difference was not the deciding factor in Photoshop's failure to produce competitive compression — we experimented with multiple settings and with the Save for Web dialog. In all cases, Photoshop delivered much heavier .JPEGs than either Fireworks or the BoxTop plug-in ProJPEG.

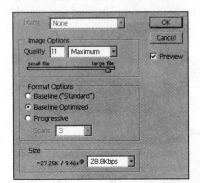

Figure 34-13: The Photoshop .JPEG dialog

Compression Results

To make reasonable sense of the results of our compression tests on the portrait and road images, we assembled the results into Table 34-2.

Table 34-2 Compression Comparison				
Image and Type	*Quality*	*BoxTop*	*Fireworks*	*Photoshop*
Base Tif: Portrait	Uncompressed	–	–	196KB
Base Tif: Road	Uncompressed	–	–	196KB
Jpeg	L (=30%)	7KB	6KB	15KB
Variations: Portrait	M (=60%)	11KB	10KB	19KB
	H (=94%)	33KB	27KB	50KB
Jpeg	L (=30%)	3KB	3KB	10KB
Variations: Road	M (=60%)	5KB	5KB	12KB
	H (=94%)	16KB	13KB	28KB
Png: Portrait	24-bit	–	112KB	128KB
Png: Road	24-bit	–	66KB	76KB

Observations and notes about the results of the settings

When we set out to create this test, we had some preconceptions — based on prior experience — that dissolved in the face of this metrical analysis. In some instances, the results were even counterintuitive, or clearly subject to the specific nature of the bitmap's final use.

As shown in Figure 34-14, in all cases, unless specified otherwise (for smoothing comparisons and to demonstrate double-JPEG corruption), the settings in the Flash Bitmap Properties dialog were maintained to preserve the compression and quality of the imported image. Unless otherwise noted, the .JPEGs and .PNGs were generated with Fireworks from the same Photoshop source .TIF.

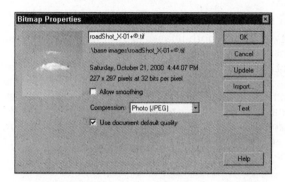

Figure 34-14: Regardless of the kind of image imported, these settings in the Flash Bitmap Properties dialog usually deliver the highest quality image while preserving the imported compression.

Basic image-type comparisons in the color insert

The following is a description of each image in the color section, plate by plate. To see the images discussed, flip to the insert.

Color Plate 1: At the top left, the uncompressed Photoshop .TIF source file is displayed, as rendered by Flash with no compression. In the adjacent panel, this original .TIF is compared to 24-bit .PNGs from both Fireworks and Photoshop; note the slight color shift in the Photoshop .PNG. In subsequent panels, high quality (94 percent) and low quality (30 percent) .JPEGs are compared. Although the quality is nearly the same, on close inspection, at 200 percent zoom (right-click/Ctrl+click), the BoxTop images are slightly less chunky, with less artifacts.

High-quality JPEG smoothing comparisons

Color Plate 2: Here, high-quality .JPEGs are compared when deployed in the Flash Bitmap Properties dialog either with or without smoothing enabled. At 100 percent, the unsmoothed image is superior. However, if you intend to scale the image smoothing may, as shown, improve the quality. The difference is more noticeable with the portrait.

High-quality Fireworks .JPEG scaling comparisons (no smoothing)

Color Plate 3: Here the high-quality .JPEGs of both images are compared to the same image, when scaled to 200 percent. Note how the horizon detail of the landscape is adversely affected by the zoom, while the portrait is chunky but almost acceptable.

Medium-quality Fireworks .JPEG scaling comparisons (no smoothing)

Color Plate 4: Here the medium-quality .JPEGs of both images are compared to the same image, when scaled to 200 percent. At 100 percent, both images are acceptable. But at 200 percent, it's a different story: Here, you'll note that the portrait is too chunky and unacceptable — many areas have a marked checkerboard pattern. Conversely, the zoomed horizon detail of the landscape isn't much worse than the same view of the high-quality version.

Low-quality Fireworks .JPEG scaling comparisons (no smoothing)

Color Plate 5: Here the low-quality .JPEGs of both images are compared to the same image, when scaled to 200 percent. At 100 percent you'll note that the portrait is barely usable — too many areas of soft transition have been chopped and flattened. At 200 percent, the portrait is so corrupted and badly discolored that it's unusable. It's easier to tolerate distortion in landscapes, thus the 100 percent view of the landscape is still usable, although not advisable for anything more than a background or an incidental shot. However, the zoomed horizon detail of the landscape is far worse than the zooms of both the high- and medium-quality versions — note, especially, the shimmer of artifacts both immediately above the horizon and around the clouds.

Medium-quality double-JPEG corruption comparisons (no smoothing)

Color Plate 6: This image was created by first saving a low-quality .JPEG from Photoshop, then opening it in Fireworks, and then saving it as a low-quality .JPEG from Fireworks. Although the portrait faired worse than the landscape, the results weren't nearly as monstrous as we had expected. The double-.JPEGs *are* chunkier and have more artifacts in transition areas, but they aren't as bad as the print world's admonition that precedes them.

Bit depth and color comparisons

Color Plate 7: These images demonstrate the effect of reduced bit depth — or range of color — through a series of three reductions. The 24-bit .PNG is a full-color image, with a range of millions of possible colors. Subsequent images have been reduced to 256, 128, and 64 colors. Note the increased posterization (or clumping of flattened color) in the transition of the cheek from light-to-dark, as well as the blue sky. Also note the successive banding of the accompanying spectrum.

High-quality JPEG rotation comparisons

Color Plate 8: This is perhaps the trickiest comparison to analyze. We had this problem when building our Web site for the *Flash 4 Bible*. When the animation resolved and the book was displayed at a slight, 14-degree angle, it was distorted — and it was distorted regardless of whether it was rotated in Photoshop and imported with the angle, or if it was imported into Flash on the square and subsequently rotated — the manner of the distortion changed, but not the perception of distortion!

✦ When rotated in Flash, hard edges, such as text, may appear choppy — as if they had been cut out with pinking shears. Yet, when zoomed, this effect is less problematic.

✦ When rotated in Photoshop, prior to import into Flash, hard edges are less choppy, although the file will increase (to accommodate the larger overall shape), the background will become a fixed color, and a certain flutter may occur along the edges of the transition between the background and the image. Yet, other straight lines and text will appear smoother and more acceptable. However, at 200 percent zoom, text looks worse than the same image rotated in Flash.

Before rotating a bitmap in Flash, you should perform a few tests to see how your specific bitmap will be affected by the combination of compression, zoom, smoothing, and rotation (either in or out of Flash). Your choices and your decision will certainly vary, subject to the nature of the bitmap and the manner in which it will be used within Flash.

Summary

✦ Flash can use a variety of external media, including vector graphics, bitmap images, and sounds.

✦ Importing external media, such as vector graphics and bitmaps is very easy.

✦ Preparing bitmaps for use within Flash requires considerable forethought and some preliminary design work in order to determine the optimal dimensions. Otherwise, bitmaps may be subjected to unsightly degradation of quality.

✦ A basic understanding of both bitmap resolution and bitmap depth is a prerequisite for the successful implementation of bitmaps within a Flash project.

✦ Bitmap properties are controlled in the Bitmap Properties dialog, which is accessed from the Flash Library.

✦ Bitmaps can be used as fills within vector shapes and drawings. With Flash 5, the new Bitmap Swatches drop-down of the Fills Panel greatly simplifies the application of bitmap fills.

✦ Bitmaps can also be traced to convert them into vector art, although usually with a loss of detail. If a traced bitmap is forced to approximate photographic quality it may incur a larger file size than the original photograph.

✦ The Bitmap Comparisons in the color insert of this *Flash 5 Bible* are dedicated to comparing bitmap quality within Flash at various settings.

✦ ✦ ✦

Designing Interfaces and Interface Elements

Now that you've learned the basic principles behind Flash artwork creation, you probably want to start creating a presentation to put on a Web site. We decided to write a chapter that teaches you how to make a simple interactive Flash movie that has basic navigation and text functionality, before we get into the nitty-gritty of ActionScript in Part X of the book.

The Main Timeline as the Site Layout

Before you can start digging into Flash, you need to know what you're excavating—what is the basic concept of the experience? Is this an all-Flash Web site? Is this a Flash animation that introduces some other type of content (HTML, Shockwave Director movies, and so on)? For the purposes of this chapter, we create a Flash movie for a basic all-Flash Web site.

Creating a plan

Once you know what goals you want to achieve with your Flash content, you should map the ideas on paper (or with your preferred project planning or flowchart software). We create a basic site for a computer parts company that has four areas: main menu (and welcome page), products, services, and contact information. Our organizational chart for this site has four discrete areas, as shown in Figure 35-1.

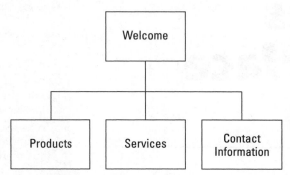

Figure 35-1: Our organizational chart will help us plan our Flash movie architecture.

Determining Flash movie properties

After you've made your organizational chart, you'll want to determine the frame rate, size, and color of the Flash movie. For this example, we use a frame size of 640×400 (a cinematic aspect ratio), a relatively fast frame rate of 20 fps (for smoother animations), and a white background color. These are set in the Movie Properties dialog, shown in Figure 35-2, which is accessed by Modify ➪ Movie (Ctrl+M or Command+M).

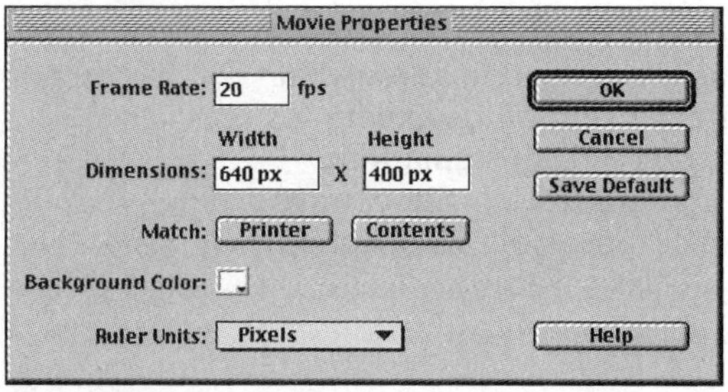

Figure 35-2: The Flash Movie Properties

Mapping site areas to keyframes

After you have set up your Flash movie properties, you can create a Main Timeline structure for the site. Because we have four areas in our site (main menu, products, services, and contact information), we'll have keyframes on the timeline that indicate those sections.

1. Rename Layer 1 to labels, by double-clicking the Layer 1 text in the timeline window.

2. With the Arrow Tool, select frame 10, and press F6. This creates a keyframe on frame 10.

> **Tip** Always leave some empty frame space in front of your "real" Flash content. We can later use these empty frames to add a preloader, as discussed in Chapter 42, "Sharing and Loading Assets."

3. With the keyframe selected, open the Frame Panel (Ctrl+F or Command+F). In the Label field, type **welcome**. After you have typed the text, press Tab (or Enter) to make the name "stick."

4. Repeat Steps 2 and 3 with frames 20, 30, and 40, with the frame labels **products**, **services**, and **contactInfo**, respectively.

5. Select frame 50 of the labels layer, and press F5. This will enable you to read the very last label, contactInfo. Your Main Timeline should resemble Figure 35-3.

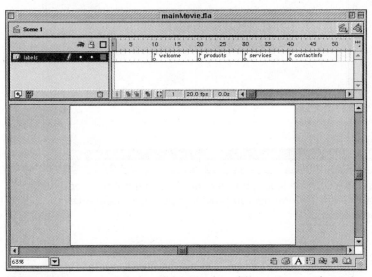

Figure 35-3: Frame labels will be used to differentiate each section of the site.

6. Save your Flash movie as **mainMovie.fla**.

7. Make a new layer, and rename it **actions**. Add a keyframe on frame 10, and open the Frame Actions Panel (Ctrl+Alt+A or Option+Command+A). Make sure the Actions Panel is in Normal Mode by clicking the menu option in the top-right corner and selecting Normal Mode.

8. Click the Basic Actions booklet (located in the left-hand column of the Actions Panel) to expand the actions contained there. Double-click the Stop action. This adds the following code to the Actions list in the right-column of the Actions Panel:

```
stop();
```

9. Close the Actions Panel, and open the Frame Panel. In the Label field, type **//stop**. The // characters assign a frame comment instead of a frame label. Although this step isn't necessary for the functionality of the movie, frame comments can provide quick and easy access to the designer's or programmer's notes. Your Main Timeline should now look like Figure 35-4.

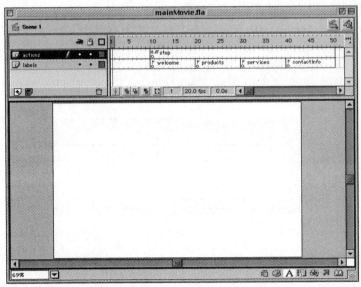

Figure 35-4: Unlike labels, frame comments can not be used in ActionScript. Comments can provide quick visual references for ActionScript code.

10. Save the Flash movie again.

At this point, the Flash movie has a skeleton architecture (a blueprint) for our interactive functionality. Now, let's add some content to each section of the movie.

Main Timeline versus Scene Structure

Arguably, you might be wondering why we are using keyframes to delineate each section, instead of new scenes. There are two reasons to use one scene (in other words, one Main Timeline):

1. We can see the entire layout of our site very easily on one timeline.

2. We can blend interstitials (transitions between each area of the site) over two sections more easily. It's much easier to have one Movie Clip instance span the area between two section keyframes on the Main Timeline.

Ultimately, the decision is yours. Make sure that you determine your Flash architecture well before you start production within the Flash authoring environment. It's not a simple task to rearchitect the layout once production has begun.

Creating content for each area

For the purposes of this example, we add placeholder elements that would be filled in with actual content for live production.

In the ch35 folder of the CD-ROM, you'll find a Flash file called content.fla that contains Graphic symbols of computer parts. Copy this .FLA file to your local hard drive.

1. Using the File ➪ Open as Library command, select your copy of the content.fla file from the CD-ROM. This opens the Library of the content .fla file.

2. Move the playhead in the timeline window of your mainMovie.fla movie to the welcome label (frame 10).

3. Create a layer named **companyLogo**. Add a keyframe at frame 10 of the companyLogo layer.

4. Drag an instance of the companyLogo Graphic symbol from the content.fla Library window to the Stage of your mainMovie.fla movie. Place the symbol instance near the top-left corner of the Stage, as shown in Figure 35-5.

5. Create a new layer named **heading**. Add a keyframe on frame 10 of this layer.

6. On frame 10 of the heading layer, use the Text Tool to add the text **Welcome**. For this example, we use the typeface Verdana at 36 points (using the Character Panel). We place the text near the top-center of the movie Stage, as shown in Figure 35-6.

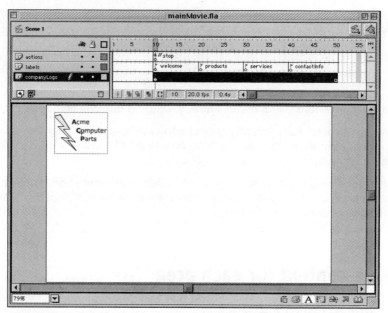

Figure 35-5: The Acme Computer Parts logo should be placed at the top-left corner of the Stage.

Figure 35-6: Use the Text Tool to add a welcome heading to the movie.

7. Add a keyframe at frame 20 of the heading layer. The Welcome text block from the previous keyframe will be copied into this keyframe. Change the text to **Product Catalog**, as shown in Figure 35-7.

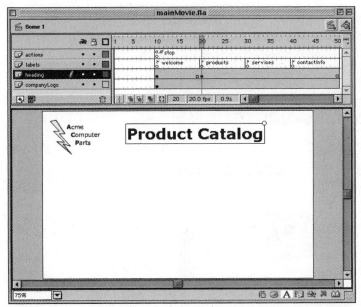

Figure 35-7: Change the text block on frame 20 to indicate the current frame label section.

8. Repeat Step 7 for frames 30 and 40 of the heading layer. Change the text block to indicate the appropriate section of the site (for example, Assembly Services, Contact Information).

    Now lets add a slide show of the computer parts that the company sells. For this, we create a Movie Clip symbol that has each product graphic on a separate keyframe.

9. Create a new symbol using Insert ➪ New Symbol (Ctrl+F8 or Command+F8). Leave the Behavior option at the default Movie Clip setting, and give it a name of **productMovie**.

10. Flash automatically switches to Symbol Editing Mode, on the productMovie timeline. Rename Layer 1 to **products**.

11. Add keyframes to frames 2, 3, 4, 5, and 6 of the products layer. We have six computer parts in the content.fla Library, and each product graphic is put on its own keyframe.

12. Move the playhead to frame 1 of the productMovie timeline, and drag the monitor_1 Graphic symbol from the content.fla Library to the Stage of the productMovie symbol, shown in Figure 35-8.

13. Continue moving the playhead to the next frame, dragging another computer part to the Stage for each frame. When you're finished, press the < and > keys to review your frames. You may want to center each graphic on the Stage using the Align Panel (Ctrl+K or Command+K).

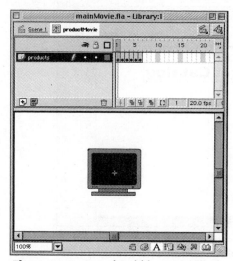

Figure 35-8: You should have six filled keyframes on the products layers of the productMovie timeline.

14. Now we need to insert an actions layer for this Movie Clip symbol. Create a new layer, and rename it **actions**. Select frame 1 of the actions layer, and open the Actions Panel. Add a Stop action:

```
stop();
```

15. Return to the Main Timeline (Scene 1) by clicking the Scene 1 tab in the upper-left corner of the timeline window.

16. Create a new layer, and rename it **productMovie**. Insert a new keyframe on frame 20 of the productMovie layer.

17. Open the mainMovie.fla Library by pressing Ctrl+L or Command+L. Drag the **productMovie** symbol from the Library to the Stage. Place it just left of the center of the Stage, as shown in Figure 35-9.

18. Select frame 30 of the productMovie layer, and press F7. This inserts a blank keyframe. Now, the productMovie instance will only show in the product area of the timeline.

19. Save your .FLA file.

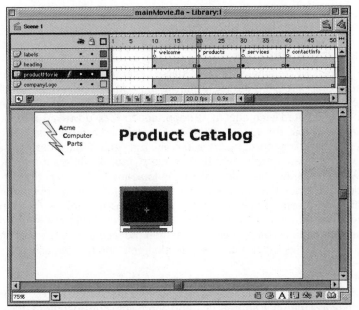

Figure 35-9: The productMovie instance will only be present in the product section of the movie.

Now we have some content in the Flash movie. The following Expert Tutorial provides an excellent overview of the design process for Flash user interfaces. If you want to continue with the demo site, then skip to the next section, "Adding Navigation Elements to the Main Timeline."

Expert Tutorial: Interface Design, *by Eric Jordan*

An important aspect of delivering content on the Web is the method in which it is presented to the audience. In the relatively short period of time since Flash first hit the market, interface design has become an art in and of itself. Now, Flash 5 has empowered designers with the ability to create rich Web-based environments with more interactivity and sophistication than ever before. In the pursuit of attracting attention to information, designers seek to package content within an intuitive *interface*, through which the user can navigate and react with on a new level. Designing a Flash interface is much like designing a product package, as it attempts to represent its contents in the most fashionable way possible. By tapping the new enhancements of the Flash 5 toolsets and property panels, designers now have a much more efficient approach to interface design.

Continued

Continued

Conceptualization and implementation

Whenever I begin the process of creating a Flash interface, I keep in mind one important factor: Once an interface is animated, it is intensely difficult to backtrack if the client should desire a change in the overall design layout. Although the greatest impact of a Flash site normally comes from it's animated elements, it is important to lock down an interface design that pleases the client from the very start. We have developed a process at Design Insites that works very effectively for conceptualizing and finalizing an interface design. This process normally begins with three *roughs*, which are three stylistically different interface concepts envisioned by the designer. These designs vary in look and feel, to give the client an opportunity to settle on a general aesthetic style for the Web site. Then we move onto the next phase, in which we provide three *comprehensive* designs that follow the same aesthetic theme of the chosen rough, yet vary in their execution of the layout structure. After the client has selected the final *comprehensive*, we then proceed to create a working model of the interface that includes the use of animated elements and functionality.

Aesthetic considerations

In my time as a Flash designer, I've developed many different types of interfaces, with a wide range of navigation types, thematic approaches, and bandwidth considerations. Based on the individual requirements of each project I undertake, I attempt to create the most aesthetically pleasing and intuitive interfaces I can, while still maintaining control over the boundaries that have been set forth. Technical requirements aside, the visual appearance of an interface is a creative endeavor that is entirely subjective. It is a matter of one's style. Although my imagination tends to run wild at times, it is a designer's duty to execute a site design that properly delivers it's content based on the branding strategy, corporate mentality, and goals of the client. At Design Insites, our strength lies in our ability to implement interfaces that organize content in a fashionable, yet straightforward manner. To showcase this, we began development of our new site—www.designinsites.com, shown in the following figure—using the enhancements of Flash 5. In doing this, we considered the same design principals that we follow when constructing interfaces for our clients. My implementation of an interface tends to lean toward emulating an operating system, as with www.2advanced.com. The new Design Insites interface uses some of the same concepts, as I have found that draggable panels and drop-down menus provide the user with more interactive navigation and a sense of control over the environment. These elements are by no means a requirement for an interface design; they simply lend themselves to my style of design and layout. The key is to provide the user with straightforward navigation and organized content, and couple it with a visually pleasing environment.

Color is also an indispensable factor for successful interface design. It is an integral part of the visual appeal, and it plays a crucial role in functionality.

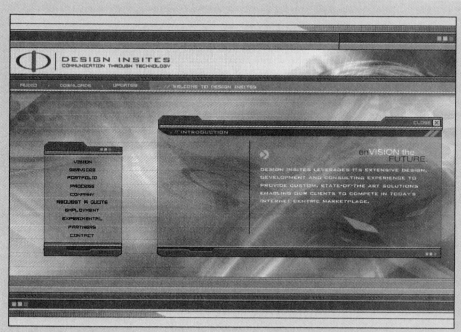

The Design Insites Web site, after the opening animation has completed and the interface has peaked.

The correct colors attract the eye to the most important areas of the interface. They enhance readability and diminish optical exhaustion. Incorrect colors distract the user and decrease the level of comprehension. In all user-interface designs, we concentrate on four issues simultaneously: optical effects, symbolism, aesthetics, and technological components. Paying attention to color theory as it applies to interface design will help you to successfully communicate your message to the audience.

Beginning the design process

Typically, I create my conceptual rough layouts within Flash itself. With the addition of the new Bézier pen tools in Flash 5, sophisticated interfaces can be created easily, without the aid of an illustration program such as Freehand. The new Pen and Sub-Selection Tools enable precise control over strokes, curves, and so on by allowing manipulation of point-to-point drawing. I find that the Flash 5 drawing tools are more than sufficient for creating the overall interface.

Continued

Continued

However, if I choose to implement the use of raster graphics in combination with the vector graphics of Flash, then I have to use a raster-based authoring application such as Photoshop. Then, with feedback from the client, I begin my three rough designs, keeping in mind the various aspects of the decided GUI traits, which include:

✦ Target resolution (640×480, 800×600, and so on)

✦ Color palette support

✦ Navigation (horizontal, vertical, drop-down, draggable, and so on)

✦ Color scheme

✦ Percentage relation of graphics to text

Once these elements have been established, I begin laying out interface concepts using the drawing tools in Flash. However, I continue to pay attention to every factor that may affect the outcome of the final file. The most prominent advantage of using Flash to develop an interactive environment is its combined capability to carry out the construction of graphical layout, content delivery, and functionality, all in one place. This does, however, require careful planning on the part of the designer to ensure that he doesn't back himself into a corner by making a few wrong turns within the complete design process. Without forethought, a Flash site can quickly become an ill-fated nightmare full of unforeseen hurdles such as non-linear navigation and file size limits.

Roughs

Although the three roughs that I create are simply conceptual interfaces, I still maintain constant scrutiny of the file size during the design process. I am well aware that two of the designs are likely to be thrown out, but if I do not pay attention to the optimization of the file from the very start, the chosen rough might have to be redesigned in order to ensure that it makes efficient use of symbols, and other structural elements. While designing the new version of the Design Insites Web site, my main concern was file size. Although this site was a project of our own undertaking, and would not come under the scrutiny of a client, we used the same rough-and-comp approach to ensure that we thoroughly explored the possibilities for our own branding in a similar fashion. As I envisioned the site, the main background of the interface would consist of a large raster graphic that would add a great deal of size to the Flash file. The upper and lower portions of the interface would be built in vector to accommodate navigation and so on. To avoid further bloating the file size, I focused my efforts on using symbols wherever possible. This included reusing simple shapes such as rectangles, lines, and circles within the upper and lower interface bars. Although these areas of the interface appear to consist of 35 gray rectangular shapes, each was derived from a singular symbol. If some rectangles needed to be a different color or size, I didn't draw another. (This is what eventually causes the file size of a Flash movie to inflate.) Instead, I simply used instances of the same symbol, while changing the tint (in the Effect Panel) and size (in the Info or Transform Panel) of the instance. The advantage of this method is that the final movie needs to load only 1 shape during playback, rather than 35 different shapes of various colors and sizes. I used the same technique with lines. Everywhere a line appears, no matter what color or size, it's always an instance of the same symbol. Changes are only made to each particular instance, by using the Effect panel to modify the tint color and by using the Info panel to modify the length. By paying close attention to details such as this, many design headaches can be eliminated from the process. Thus, I end up with three optimized designs that are ready to be refined and built out.

Comprehensives

Once a rough has been chosen, we move onto the comprehensive phase. In this stage, we develop three new designs that have their aesthetic roots based in the stylistic elements of the rough. The only variance is the way in which these elements are structured. Using the symbols that I've already created, I shift the layout around and come up with three distinctly different renditions of the same basic theme. In this phase, we have already locked down the visual feel of the site, and we are developing options to offer the client further choices for the way in which that feel will be executed. A comprehensive can be thought of as the *peak* of the Web site, where animation ceases and the full interface is revealed in all its glory.

The following figure is a view of the source .FLA for the completed Design Insites Web site. Note how many layers appear in the Main Timeline, yet how many more are obscured — as evinced by the scroll bar to the far left of the timeline. In this shot, the playhead is halfway to the peak of the interface animation.

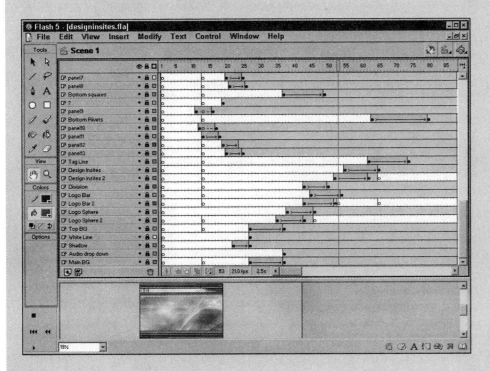

Continued

Continued

I use layers to design the basic levels of the interface elements, so that when it comes time to animate the site, everything is organized on it's own layer and ready for movement and/or functionality. As I add elements to the timeline, each layer is labeled in order to provide clarity for the execution of the animation process. At the end of this phase, I will have a series of layers with one keyframe on each layer. Each keyframe consists of a single symbol that makes up a different part of the interface.

Build out

After our client has chosen one of the three comprehensives, we begin the process of Flashing the interface. In this phase, we add motion and functionality to the site design. Because I've placed each element of the layout on a different layer, it's easy for me to now animate each symbol so that the design will move and manifest into the peak design that I've created. It is almost like deconstructing the interface, so that it may reconstruct itself through animation when played back. I typically insert a set of new keyframes about 100 frames deep in my Flash timeline to be the predetermined peak moment when the site will have achieved its full manifestation. I then proceed to set the properties for the symbol instances at frame 1. This is the very beginning of the animation, where the interface begins to manifest itself. Usually, I set items to have an alpha value of 0, a tint value similar to that of the background, or — if I want the element to slide into place — a position off stage. After I create my Motion Tweens for each animated element of the interface, I set values for easing in the Frame Panel to ensure fluid motion of each symbol. For aggressive and energetic interfaces, I usually have elements ease in and use short Motion Tweens to simulate fast movement. For calmer, more relaxed interfaces, I have elements ease out and use longer Motion Tweens to simulate conservative motion. These techniques are, of course, completely subjective, and each project may follow a different style and/or feel. Of course, some interfaces may not require animation at all, and some interfaces may only use Flash for its implementation of functionality through ActionScripting.

Now that we have a semianimated site, with a key moment in time acting as the peak of the interface, we begin developing content sections either within the main movie (using scenes) or externally for sections that will be loaded into the main movie (using `loadMovie`). The Design Insites interface requires the use of `loadMovie` to introduce additional content into the host Flash movie. Thus, the steps that were pursued during the design and build out process differed from the normal process. The navigation and content windows for the Design Insites Web site were intended to consist of draggable panels, and would be externally loaded into the host movie to avoid bloating it's file size. But rather than design the navigation panel and the content window blindly in a separate movie file, I created them on their own layers within the host movie. This working method enabled me to see how they would appear aesthetically within the main interface. During build out, I simply copied the frames being used by the navigation and content panels and pasted them into their own Flash file, which was then saved out as a separate .SWF file to be externally loaded using button triggers in the main movie. By copying and pasting the frames, I was able to retain all positioning or animation properties they possessed while in the main movie.

After the layout was completed and the file structures established for the externally loaded interface elements (the navigation and content windows), we began ActionScripting to make everything function, such as the navigational elements or the loading of the external .SWF's into the host movie.

Within the upper navigation panels of the main movie, drop-down menus were utilized to control audio, offer downloads, and provide site updates. These are implemented as movie clips that begin with an empty frame on keyframe one of their individual timelines. This allows them to be initially invisible in the interface, and to become visible only when their respective navigation buttons are rolled over. Using drop-down menus is an effective way to organize an interface because they avoid cluttering the main GUI. Considerations such as these are important for providing an intuitive interface that is easily navigable and that doesn't overwhelm the user with too many options at once.

Author's Note: For more information on loading external .SWF files with the `loadMovie` action, see Chapter 42, "Sharing and Loading Assets."

Reflection

Interface design within Flash concerns two factors: (a) how effectively users complete tasks (in other words, comprehend content), and (b) how well-represented the content is aesthetically. Flash 5 has accelerated our ability to create new forms of advanced interactive environments. Without a fundamental understanding of interfaces in general, however, it can be difficult to make these environments become a reality. Our current understanding of interface design, usability, and layout in non-Web–based interfaces can be applied and expanded to maximize the impact and comprehension of information on the Web. To take full advantage of Web efficiency, it is important to explore the use of guidelines, develop new methods of interactivity, and push beyond the existing boundaries of conventional interface design.

"I came across Flash when viewing Gabocorp.com — which was one of the first Flash sites. I set forth to purchase the program and engulf myself in its powerful ability to deliver a new level of interactivity and atmosphere," says Eric Jordan of his indomitable pursuit of Flash. In the year that he graduated from San Clemente High in southern California, Eric says that, "The most memorable movie was *Mission Impossible* — which, through its use of futuristic interfaces, actually greatly influenced my design style." Eric's personal site, 2advanced.com, was nominated for best interface at Flash Forward 2000, featured in the launch issue of CreateOnline Magazine: The Web Designers Bible, and has received various design awards throughout the past year. Other sites that he has worked on include www.centrata.com, www.createlabs.com, and www.cyberspaceguide.com. Eric says that his single most favorite thing is to "turn out the lights, boot up the system, and pursue the creation of the ultimate user experience." This tutorial is a reflection upon the general process that led to the interface design for www.designinsites.com.

Adding Navigation Elements to the Main Timeline

In the last section, we created a Flash movie timeline for a computer parts Web site. We inserted content placeholder for the welcome, services, and contactInfo sections of the timeline, and we made a Movie Clip with product graphics to place in the product section. However, we had no way of actually getting to any section except the welcome frame. In this section, we create a menu that will control the position of the playhead on the Main Timeline.

Creating text buttons for a menu

In this part of the exercise, you make menu buttons that will enable the user to navigate to the different areas of the Flash movie.

1. On the Main Timeline of your mainMovie.fla movie, add a new layer and rename it **menu**. On this layer, we create text buttons to navigate the site.

2. Insert a keyframe on frame 10 of the menu layer. Select the Text Tool, and, with a 16-point Verdana font face, type the word **Home**. Place this text underneath the company logo graphic, on the left-hand side of the Stage (see Figure 35-10 for placement).

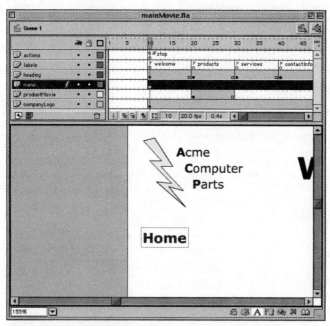

Figure 35-10: The homeButton instance will always take us to the welcome area of the site.

3. With the Arrow Tool, select the Home text block. Press F8 to convert this text into a symbol. In the Symbol Properties dialog, name the symbol **homeButton**. Assign it a Button behavior.

4. Now we need to add a Hit state to the homeButton timeline. By default, Flash will use the last frame of a Button symbol timeline for the Hit state, unless content is added to the Hit state keyframe. Double-click the homeButton instance on the Main Timeline to switch to Symbol Editing Mode.

5. Select the Hit frame of Layer 1 on the homeButton timeline, and press F7 to insert an empty keyframe.

6. Click the Onion Skin Outlines button in the timeline window toolbar. This enables you to view the previous frames of the homeButton timeline, as shown in Figure 35-11.

Figure 35-11: Onion skinning enables you to accurately align the contents of several keyframes.

7. Select the Rectangle Tool, and draw a filled rectangle that covers the same area of the Home text block. You can use any fill color because the user never sees the Hit state. Your button's timeline should resemble the one shown in Figure 35-12.

Figure 35-12: The Hit state defines the "active" area of the Button instance in the movie. If the user's mouse pointer enters this area, then the Over frame of the Button will be displayed.

8. Next, we add an Over state to the homeButton, so that the user knows it's an active button. Select the Over frame of Layer 1, and press F6. This copies the contents of the previous keyframe into the new one. Select the Home text block with the Arrow Tool, and change the fill color to blue. You can also turn off Onion Skin Outlines at this point.

9. Return to the Main Timeline of your movie, and save your Flash movie file. Select Control ➪ Test Movie to test the states of the homeButton.

   You can also use Control ➪ Enable Simple Buttons to preview the graphical states of a Button instance.

10. Now we put an action on the homeButton instance. Select the homeButton instance, and open the Actions Panel. In Normal Mode, double-click the Go To action in the Basic Actions booklet. Flash automatically adds the on(release){} code to store the Go To action, in the right-hand Actions list. In the parameter area of the Actions Panel, uncheck the Go to and Play option. In the Type drop-down menu, select Frame Label. In the Frame drop-down menu (located at the end of the field), select welcome. Your Actions Panel options should match those shown in Figure 35-13.

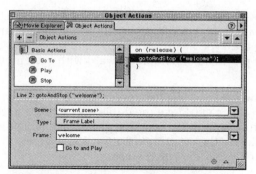

Figure 35-13: With these actions, the homeButton instance will move the Main Timeline playhead to the welcome frame label.

11. If we test our movie at this point, our homeButton won't do anything — our playhead is already on the welcome frame label. Let's add a button for each section on the site. Repeat Steps 2 to 8 for each section name in our movie. You should end up with four buttons: Home, Products, Services, and Contact Us.

12. Repeat Step 10 for each new button instance. For each button instance, change the Frame drop-down menu selection to match the name of the button's area (for example, `gotoAndStop("products");` on the productsButton).

13. Save your Flash movie, and test it (Ctrl+Enter or Command+Enter).

When you test your Flash movie, you should be able to click each button to go to each area of the movie. If a button isn't functioning, double-check the code on the instance. Make sure that each Button instance has a Button behavior in the Instance Panel. In the next section, we add buttons to the productMovie Movie Clip symbol, so that the user can browse the pictures of the computer parts.

Browsing the product catalog

In this section, we go inside the productMovie symbol and add some navigation buttons for our product catalog.

1. From the Main Timeline of our mainMovie.fla, double-click the productMovie instance on frame 20 of the productMovie layer. Flash switches to Symbol Editing Mode.

2. Make a new layer on the productMovie timeline, and rename the layer to **buttons**.

3. Open the Buttons Library (Window ➪ Common Libraries ➪ Buttons). In the Buttons Library window, double-click the (circle) Button Set folder. Drag the Circle with arrow Button symbol to the productMovie Stage. Place the Button instance below and to the right of the monitor_1 Graphic symbol.

4. With the Circle with Arrow instance selected, open the Actions Panel. Double-click the Go To action to add this action to the Actions list. In the parameters area of the panel, change the Type menu option to Next Frame. This action moves the productMovie playhead one frame forward with each mouse click on the Button instance.

5. With the Circle with Arrow instance selected, press Ctrl+D (Command+D) to duplicate the instance on the Stage. Move the duplicate instance to the left of the original arrow button. With the Arrow Tool selected, enable the Rotate modifier in the Toolbar. Rotate the duplicated button 180 degrees. Press the Shift key while rotating, to lock in 45-degree steps.

6. Select both arrow buttons, and align them horizontally to each other, as shown in Figure 35-14, by using the Align Panel.

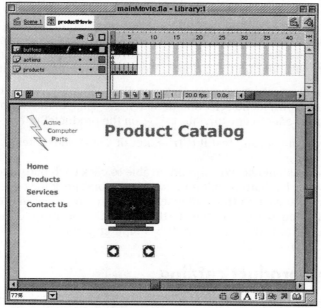

Figure 35-14: Position the arrow Buttons underneath the product graphic.

7. Select the left arrow, and open the Actions Panel. Select the nextFrame(); action in the Actions list. In the parameter area, change the Go To action's Type menu option to Previous Frame.

8. Save your Flash movie, and test it. Click the Products button, and try the new navigation arrows for your product catalog.

You can further enhance your presentation by adding more information in the productMovie Movie Clip symbol. After the following Expert Tutorial, we add a scrolling text window to the catalog that displays text descriptions of the products.

Expert Tutorial: Interface Usability, by *Merien Quintus Kunst*

This tutorial's focus is on the use of Flash as a tool for creating straightforward, serviceable, functioning Web sites. In the past year, Flash design has been under attack by Web usability experts. Although bad interface design is by no means limited to Flash movies, planning and designing interfaces should be a primary concern before building Flash movies.

Looking at Flash

For the last two years I have been running the Quintus Flash Index, which is a rather large collection of links to Flash sites. The reason I started it was simple enough: At the time, there weren't any decent collections of Flash work on the Web. Yet, I wanted to check sites out to see what Flash could do. So I went searching, exploring the world of Flash. As I explored, I decided to bookmark all the Flash sites that I came across. I ended up with a categorized, static list of about 150 links, which I then posted as a Web page, thinking that others might find it useful. Suddenly, I was getting 150 visitors a day to my Web site, which is really not bad for a 1-page site. As part of my internship, my supervisor suggested that I implement the site in ASP, add some ding-dongs, and put it online like that. So I did—and it took off. Today, the QFI has links to over 2,200 Flash sites, and (amazingly) over 12,000 visitor comments.

The comments area was just something I added because I thought it would be a nice feature for people to show their approval or disapproval of a site, which would be very useful for the developers. At first, I posted a lot of comments myself, trying to inspire people to follow my example. I focused mainly on overall impression and user friendliness, not really from an expert point of view, but rather like a regular user. However, the more sites I reviewed, the more I found similar errors and mistakes that would confuse visitors. Over time, many other people at my site also helped the site developers by indicating what elements of the sites were unclear, confusing, or even irritating.

Usability: The user experience

Consequently, I have had the opportunity to learn a lot about Internet usability and interface design. I found that many the site critiques on the Quintus Flash Index could be traced back to basic usability design rules. Not a big surprise, but rather a very clear indication of the value of some of these rules.

Usability may sound mystifying to some people, and some best-selling books may champion the obscurity of this subject, but there's really nothing too complex about it. Usability is the extent to which a system supports its users in completing their tasks efficiently, effectively, and satisfactorily—which may also include the experience of aesthetic pleasure. On the Web, this leads to topics such as navigation, speed, clarity, and readability. The real trick about usability is the horrible task of letting it seep through in your design. Usability extremists call out for Web sites with barely any graphics, using only default browser fonts (and default colors), and certainly no plug-ins.

But the fact is that Flash is one of the best design tools to effectively break most of those extreme rules of usability—and in a very short time. This tutorial attempts to steer both beginning and experienced Flash designers toward a more responsible use of Flash.

Continued

Continued

While this may sound a bit loaded, you should realize that, by now, quite a few sites have banned the use of Flash entirely — simply because they had the unfortunate experience of having Flash implemented on their behalf, but in the *wrong* way. When Flash is used the wrong way, it creates havoc. However, the same can be said of HTML. (The designers should have been blamed, rather than the tool!) So, to help Flash designers avoid making the same errors all over again, I've written out some pointers, highlighting many of the common errors I've encountered when reviewing Flash sites. I hope these hints will be useful to you.

Flash is a tool, not a platform

Flash sites are either sites with Flash elements or 100 percent Flash sites. The latter is a very decent option for small sites such as personal sites or sites that are meant purely for entertainment by animation and sound. But you may want to develop a more elaborate site with features such as a forum, chat room, response forms, user registration, content management, or a search option. While doing this strictly in Flash is certainly a great technical challenge, it's not a very wise decision. The fact is that Flash is just a tool that offers a means for designers to turn their ideas into reality. It is not a platform on which to build a Web site.

The best sites out there combine Flash with other techniques and formats such as DHTML, streaming video, MP3, Java, and the common image formats such as JPEG and GIF, as well as any other medium that will offer the needed content in the most appropriate way to the visitor. The magic rule is to consider every possible medium for each element you want to develop. If you understand the strengths and weaknesses of Flash, you can apply it where it is suitable, or decide when it may not be the best solution.

Button hit area: Number 1 mistake

The single most common error should be mentioned first. When a text button is created, it is essential that the *hit area* frame of the button be filled with a solid shape in roughly the same size as the button text field. The effect of an empty *hit area* frame is a very jerky reaction of the mouse pointer. Often, such buttons require surgical precision to simply use the button. When creating any button, it is best to choose a filled shape that covers the maximum dimensions of your button and put it in the *hit area* frame of the button.

Author's Note: Flash 5 adds a new option for Static Text fields in the Character Panel: URL links. If you need simple text buttons, then you don't need to make a Button symbol — simply specify a URL in the Character Panel. You won't experience hit area problems with this URL-linked Static Text fields. For basic coverage of Button symbols, refer to Chapter 31, "Checking Out the Library: Symbols and Instances."

Font size, font type: Squint, ignore

Designers often choose to use a Flash movie to display textual content in their Web site or presentation. Whenever large pieces of static text are involved, you should question whether Flash is the best medium to present this information to your audience. The downside of embedding large text areas in your Flash movies is mostly an issue of legibility, but there are also concerns about further processing of the information by the viewer.

Often, users aren't prepared to read through pages of small, antialiased text, and usually choose to skip this information—which may be vital information. One technique to solve this problem in Flash 5 is offered in the form of Dynamic Text fields.

Dynamic Text fields are presented as aliased, selectable text that increases the legibility of small fonts while providing a more useful way to present the text. That's because this technique enables users to select an area of text and copy it to the clipboard. This is more user friendly, because it provides better access to the information. Many visitors will want a way to extract specific pieces of information. This technique enables them to store this information wherever they want, exactly like copying text from HTML pages. (For more about Dynamic Text fields, refer to Chapter 29, "Working with Text.")

For large amounts of text, Flash is usually not the best medium, and other media, such as HTML, plain text, Adobe Acrobat, or word processor documents, should be considered. Think twice before you start pasting long passages of text into your Flash movie.

Menu look and feel: Is this a button?

To hang a painting you need a hammer and a nail (and a wall); to water plants you need a hose. How about this one: To find a phone number, you need to start reading each page in the phone book from page one until you reach the page where the wanted name is listed. No? To view your favorite TV show, you zap to the right channel, watch 30 seconds of a creepily familiar introduction video clip, and then the show starts. If you change the channel, but then come back again, you get to watch the introduction all over again. Does that sound right? When you take the elevator, you just press any of the new symbols that are displayed on a huge array of buttons to learn what each does. You keep pressing them, one by one, until you reach the right floor. Oh, and the buttons look like chewing gum stuck to the wall. In fact, some of the buttons aren't even buttons—that *is* gooey chewing gum that you just stuck your finger in! Getting annoyed yet? Well, you're not alone.

Usability is all about offering people something they are looking for. That means offering it quickly, correctly, and with maximum accessibility. On a Web site, accessibility depends on factors such as loading times, user requirements, and navigation. Navigation breaks down into buttons, structure, and guidance. Flash offers wonderful tools to create menus, navigation tricks, and really exotic buttons. Everyone who is working with Flash will think about interfaces such as an interactive phone for a menu, or a tree, a remote control, body parts, cubes, balls, subway maps, giant fruit baskets, planetary models—but remember, no matter how cute or cool or ingenious *your* interface might seem to you, it doesn't work if it doesn't work.

Not many people think, "Gray, square buttons . . ."

Yet, the gray, square buttons are what people know and understand, just like blue, underlined text. Not very exciting, so we need to work out how to merge our galaxy model (or fruit basket) with the user's idea of a menu, and motivate them to navigate through the Web site with it. A solution might be to reconsider your ideas and shape them into a more recognizable menu scheme, making your menu items look a bit more like classic buttons and placing them on the top, side, or bottom of the screen.

Continued

Continued

A less drastic solution might be to have people test your interface. This way, you could see how (or if) they figure out that those thingies are functional buttons, and then make design improvements based on that information.

A menu design can often be improved by adding pointers, like small pop-ups with your buttons, or a help function that delivers a quick explanation. You should expect that Web site visitors aren't very patient, so make sure that a minimal effort is required to *use* your brilliant interface.

Finally, you won't really be testing your navigation with people if you help them, as this will make this a useless test — unless, of course, you also have an ingenious plan to be there to help everyone that visits your site. If you want to design usable Web sites, you must be hard on yourself — because your visitors will certainly be unforgiving of your self-indulgent design lapses.

Some pointers based on problems I often recognize in Flash menus:

✦ Transitions should be short. It doesn't help if the needed segment takes 10 seconds or more to unfold . . . only to show submenu items.

✦ Try to have the current location highlighted in the menu; this visual cue helps people figure out where they are.

✦ Avoid moving or rotating buttons. Even buttons that stop when you move the mouse over them are often very confusing. Slow movement is sometimes acceptable.

✦ Have buttons show their function. Sometimes, buttons don't reveal their function until they're clicked, which is *not* user friendly. If a square shape takes me to the links page, does the triangle shape mean I can send an e-mail? What about the donut? Good practice is to use the right icons, or add text to your buttons.

Skip intro: All the way

If you really want an animated Flash introduction, start it with a SKIP button. In general, don't make intros. They can be interesting for some entertainment sites, or designer agencies, but it's not right to assume that:

✦ The visitor wants to wait for the loading of the intro

✦ The visitor *will* be entertained for 30 seconds

✦ The visitor will *then* wait for the first page to load

✦ The visitor will *stay* long enough to access your information

Intelligent, clear, user-friendly employment of Flash on your Web site is a much better reference than an indulgent intro that takes too long to load. Furthermore, *if* that visitor decides to return to your site, it's not very useful to force them through that intro again.

The only fully justified intro is a light one that entertains the visitor while the main Web site loads. But visitors with fast connections should still be able to skip it—all of it. I could take the next ten pages to tell you the long, long story about how the Flash intro phenomenon started, but that's not very useful, either. However, if I were to tell that story, at least you'd have the mechanism—by turning the page—to move on to the real content. The best advice on this subject is to consider what, if any, added value an intro animation will give to your site.

Finally, here's one option that's not really used often enough. If you really feel driven to create animations that delight and amaze, why not create a separate area of your site for Flash experiments? In such an area, there is no reason to hold back because in that context, your animation *is* the content, rather than an impediment to content.

Browser navigation: Back, Help!

It doesn't seem likely that Flash will ever be well enough integrated into the browsers to eliminate this problem: Using browser navigation buttons is disastrous! When someone's found their way to the information they needed from your Flash site, and then decides to hit the *Back* button to return to the previous segment, they usually end up somewhere unexpected.

A similar annoying result occurs when a visitor attempts to bookmark a particular moment in your Flash movie—the bookmark will only return the visitor back to the start of your Flash movie.

Although a self-made *Back* button can be included in your Flash movie, visitors aren't likely to get used to such features very quickly. Your regular visitors may get the hang of it, but seeing two buttons with the same label (that is, the browser's *Back* button, plus your own *Back* button) may confuse first-timers.

To facilitate bookmarking of specific parts of the Flash content drastic measures would be required: Split your movie into several segments, and distribute them over Web pages that can be individually bookmarked. Usually this effort is worth the extra work, because it has additional advantages. Of course, it saves visitors the drag of navigating back to the point of interest every time they visit the site. However, it also helps improve the speed of your Web site. Plus, if you update just one of the movies, you'll be working on a less complex .FLA. And, finally, when the update is completed, caching can still be used to retrieve the other pages. Only the changed page will have to be reloaded from the server.

Site statistics: Split up your movies or go blind

The method indicated previously to facilitate the bookmarking of your Flash pages could also solve the analysis problem of fully Flashed sites. Because a single movie is grabbed from the Web server, it's virtually impossible to tell what people are doing inside your site. What segments attract most visitors, what are the common exit points, and which pages are never viewed? Web site statistics are a valuable developer tool for Web site improvements and visitor analysis. Complex schemes can solve this problem, involving database logging and/or posting to forms from within your Flash movies, which I do not discuss.

Continued

Continued

The easiest, if somewhat crude, way to generate proper statistics is by splitting your movie into segments that reflect the structure of your site. This enables you to use classic tools to view the statistics of your site, because every segment sits in it's own HTML page. Furthermore, this solution, when coupled with <META> tags, can also ensure that your Flash site is properly represented among the search engines.

Use of sound: Music on demand

With every release, Flash delivers better support for sounds and music. The new support for MP3 import in Flash 5, makes it even easier to balance quality sound with streaming and small file sizes. Sounds can be used to add effects to navigation elements, create cool background music loops, or to offer sound samples to visitors. However, because many people without audio available on their systems view the Internet, the best way to incorporate the sounds with your Web creations is to make the sounds passive. Even if your guests have sound on their system, it may not be turned on. If the experience of your movie depends on the sound effects and music that come with it, tell everybody that they need to turn on their speakers. If you use items such as a background loop, it's thoughtful to make the sound optional *before* your visitor starts loading the (often large) music files into your Flash. That way those with sound-challenged systems won't have to wait for it to download even though they have no way to enjoy it.

Always consider whether Flash is the best way to offer your music items. In many cases, other techniques (or technologies) may have better support. For example, if you want to present a streaming audio clip, then you might want to use RealAudio instead of Flash.

Another setting that deserves mention is the volume of your sound clips. Test the audio elements in a movie with normal system volume, to ensure that it's not too low or doesn't cause hearing discomfort.

It's tempting to use sound bytes as a way to improve navigation. For example, a button that tells you all about it's functionality would be nice to add extra clarity to a menu. However, as useful (and impressive) as this technique might be, don't rely on it too much. As mentioned before, much of the Web population relies purely on the visual part of Web sites.

Print option: Will people understand?

Flash offers a great way to embed specific content into your Flash movie that can be sent directly to a user's printer. A common example for this technique is a small Flash banner that sends a full-page advertisement to the printer when the user hits the print button in the movie. It's a nice way to avoid cluttering Web pages with sundry advertisement details, but it's also a way to offer any single- or multipage document (poster size images, spreadsheets, background details) with the click of a small button. (For more information about Flash printing capabilities, refer to Mike Richards' Expert Tutorial, "Creating Printable Paper Airplanes," in Chapter 41, "Controlling Movie Clips.")

Unfortunately, Flash printing is a functionality that's quite new on the Web, and it's a functionality that can't be properly explained in one or two words. So, if you choose to use this feature, make sure to give a clear indication of its function, with button text similar to "Send the details of this product to my printer" or "Print a full-page version of this image."

Progress indicators: What's going on?

This topic is easily dealt with. It comes down to this: Even though loading bars aren't a pleasant sight to look at (a funny or informational preloader is much better), some movies give no indication of what's happening during download. "Are we there yet?" For modem users, this can be especially frustrating, because there is no way of knowing whether the movie has ended, or the connection was lost, or the last bit is being loaded in the background. (A blank or frozen screen is not very entertaining either.) Progress bars are not the most aesthetic solution. If they are designed properly, they'll at least provide clarity about loading time. Many good tutorials can be found online to help you create a reliable progress indicator.

Obviously, the best loading scheme is one that goes unnoticed. But for heftier movies (or really slow connections) a loading scheme and a progress indicator are needed. A great solution is a small game or animation that also indicates progress (percentage). In case you're wondering, yes, Pong has been done, just like Memory, Simon Says, and Tic-Tac-Toe. But you just can't beat the classics!

Forms: Better let them know

Flash offers reasonable support to embed forms. Many elements, such as drop-down lists and the use of the Tab button, don't respond as they do in classic HTML forms. To get around these problematic defaults, some clever ActionScript is needed.

Another problem worth mentioning is that forms in Flash aren't always easily recognized as *forms*. This is attributable to the two issues: The design of the form is rarely that of a classic Web form, and users are not (yet) used to Flash forms. So, some help is required. Try putting a blinking cursor in the first entry field, or, better yet, something like a big arrow that says *Please Use This Form*, to reduce the chance that people will leave the page mystified.

There are few examples on the Web in which Flash forms really use the specific advantages of the Flash medium. Good examples are chat room applications with interactive characters and interactive games that require keyboard input. One clear advantage of Flash is its capability to make form posts without (re)loading a page. This is a feature that can be exploited in clever ways, but consider the visitors' expectations (based on classic HTML forms): Give clear feedback about post results after submission, or they'll wait forever for a form to submit.

Conclusion: The Flash experience

This tutorial has addressed only a few of the many topics that are relevant to Flash developers who care about the user friendliness of their creations.

Continued

Continued

Although some of the topics may be very obvious, this is no guarantee that they aren't easily overlooked. Flash has become so versatile that it's hard to tell people how they should use it, largely because it is used for so many different goals. The focus of this article has been on the use of Flash as a tool for creating rather straightforward Web sites. These are sites that want to inform, entertain, and maybe educate their visitors.

The most important concept to realize about Flash is that it really is just a tool. If you need to create something, first think about what you want to make; then think about how you're going to realize it afterwards. It's bad practice to assume that Flash is such a cool program that it will be a good way to create anything that you might conjure. If the project has elements that would benefit from the features Flash offers, use it the best way possible. Again, that doesn't mean using all the imaginable tween effects that you can think of; it does mean, however, thinking about the user experience you want to create.

That user experience is dependent on overall impression, entertainment value, ease of navigation, loading times, and the sense of control by the visitor. These criteria pose quite a challenge to the best designers and developers. At times, it may be boring or frustrating to address these criteria, but in the long run, it will make your Flash masterpieces more durable and appreciated.

Online reference

This tutorial wouldn't be complete without some interesting links. To ensure that they remain current, I've added an area to the Quintus Flash Index where you'll find additional information about this subject: `www.quintus.org/use`.

A native of Utrecht, Netherlands, Merien Quintus Kunst wins the prize for the most amazing name. He says that his middle name is an old family tradition. In fact, it's Latin for "fifth," while his last name, Kunst, is Dutch for art. So, we might expect him to know a thing or two about art and design. When he came of age, he was rockin' to Nature Boy by Primus, while the rest of Holland succumbed to Let The Beat Control Your Body, by 2 Unlimited. Merien's single most favorite thing to do is snowboarding. He also enjoys, "inline skating, buying CDs, my girlfriend, renting videos, being online, English and American literature, and modern art." Currently employed at BSUR Concepting & Communications Amsterdam, he's also the man behind QFI, the Quintus Flash Index—`www.quintus.org`—and has worked on many other sites, including `www.sarah.nl` and `www.vastned.nl`. How did Quintus find Flash? "Like half the world, through `www.gabocorp.com`. He introduced Flash to the masses."

The topic of Flash usability has received a lot of press lately, particularly because many Flash interfaces are considered experimental or nonintuitive to the average Web user. In December 2000, Macromedia released a new section to their Web site — Macromedia Flash Usability. You can read their usability tips and view examples of interface design at:

`www.macromedia.com/software/flash/productinfo/usability`

Basic Text Scrolling

Continuing from our previous Flash movie example with the computer parts catalog, we demonstrate basic scrolling text using Motion Tween animation and Button
actions. We demonstrate this technique for one product in the catalog to get you
started.

1. In the mainMovie.fla from the previous section, double-click the productMovie
   instance on the productMovie layer, located on the Main Timeline. Flash
   switches to Symbol Editing Mode.

2. Add a new layer, and rename it **scrollingText**. On frame 1 of the scrollingText
   layer, draw a filled rectangle shape (with any fill color) to the right of the
   product graphic, as shown in Figure 35-15. The size of the rectangle should
   match the size of the text area you wish to display in the scrolling text window. The rectangle shape will become a Mask Layer inside another symbol
   for the text.

3. Select the rectangle shape, and press F8 to convert it into a symbol. Give the
   new symbol the name **scrollingText**, and keep the default Movie Clip behavior.

4. Double-click the instance on the Stage, and Flash switches to Symbol Editing
   Mode. The timeline of the scrollingText symbol will be displayed.

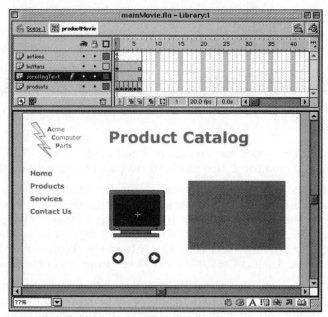

Figure 35-15: This rectangle will be used to mask the text
in our scrolling text window.

5. Rename Layer 1 to **textMask**. Add a new layer, rename it **text**, and move this layer below the textMask layer. Switch the viewing mode of the textMask to Outline Mode by clicking the colored square at the right end of the textMask layer options. Also, lock the textMask layer so that you won't accidentally alter its shape or position. The outline of the shape will indicate where our text should be placed.

6. Select the first frame of the text layer, and, using the Text Tool, insert the text that follows into a Static Text block, as shown in Figure 35-16. You can copy and paste this text from the monitor_1_text symbol in the content.fla Library. Keep the right margin of the text block at the right edge of the outlined rectangle in the textMask layer, and don't worry about the text that extends below the Stage edge:

```
This generic flat-screen CRT 22" monitor is optimal for
intense graphics production, ideal for desktop publishing,
video, and 3D art professionals. With a premium dot pitch and
a large viewable area, this monitor can handle all the
demands of accurate color-calibrated output.

Viewable area:

21"

Dot pitch:

.23 mm

Refresh rates:

640 x 480, 67 Hz
800 x 600, 85 Hz
1024 x 768, 85Hz
1152 x 870, 75 Hz
1280 x 1024. 75Hz
1600 x 1200, 75Hz
```

7. Select the Static Text block you created in Step 6, and press F8. This new symbol will be named monitor_1_text, and will have a Graphic symbol behavior.

8. Now we create a Motion Tween over ten frames. We add buttons that will move the playhead one frame with each click. Therefore, nine clicks will get us to the end of the text. Select frame 10 in both the textMask and text layers, and then press F5. Then, select just the frame 10 of the text layer, and press F6. Right-click (or Ctrl+click on the Mac) any frame between frames 1 and 10 of the text layer, and select Create Motion Tween from the contextual menu.

9. On frame 10 of the text layer, select the monitor_1_text instance, and move the instance toward the top edge of the Stage, until the bottom edge of the text aligns with the bottom edge of the mask outline, as shown in Figure 35-17. For greater accuracy, use the up arrow key (with the Shift key pressed) to move the instance.

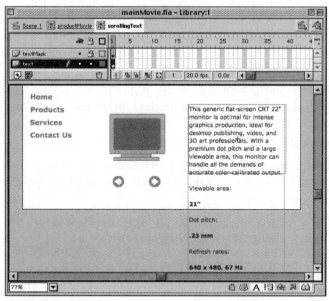

Figure 35-16: The text in Step 6 will be too lengthy to keep within the area of the rectangle outline. Don't worry—we'll be adding scroll buttons that will enable the viewer to see the text outside of the mask.

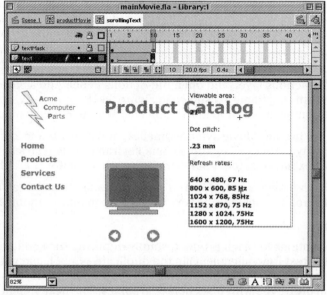

Figure 35-17: By aligning the contents of the end keyframe, you are setting the lower limit of the scrolling window.

10. To complete the masking effect, right-click (or Ctrl+click on the Mac) the label name for the textMask layer. Select Mask from the contextual menu. This automatically nests the text layer with the textMask layer.

11. Now, add two Button instances to this timeline, just like we did in the product Movie symbol. Create a new layer named **buttons**, and place it above the textMask layer. Open the Buttons Library (Window ➪ Common Libraries ➪ Button), and drag an arrow button from the Library on to the scrollingText Stage.

12. If necessary, rotate the arrow instance so that it points upwards.

13. With the arrow instance selected, open the Actions Panel, and add a Go To action, changing the Type to Previous Frame. The Actions list should read:

```
on(release){
      prevFrame();
}
```

14. Select the arrow instance and duplicate it (Ctrl+D or Command+D). Move this instance below the original arrow instance, and rotate the arrow so that it points downward. With the instance selected, open the Actions Panel. Select the prevFrame() action in the Actions list, and, in the parameters area, change the Type menu to Next Frame. The Actions list should now read:

```
on(release){
      nextFrame();
}
```

15. Now we should draw a visual frame from our scrolling text area. Create a new layer, and rename it **frame**. Place this layer underneath the buttons layer, but above the textMask layer. Draw an unfilled rectangle with a 1-point black stroke, just slightly larger than the original rectangle used to create the textMask.

16. Finally, we need to stop this timeline from automatically playing. Add a new layer, and rename it **actions**. Place this layer above the buttons layer. Select frame 1 of the actions layer, and open the Actions Panel. Add a Stop action (stop();) to this keyframe, as shown in Figure 35-18. Optionally, you can add a frame comment of //**stop** in the Label field of the Frame Panel.

17. Go back to the productMovie symbol timeline, and select frame 2 of the scrollingText layer. Press F7 to add a blank keyframe. This restricts the scrollingText layer to the first keyframe, for the monitor_1 graphic.

18. Save your Flash movie, and test it. You should be able to click the Products button, and scroll the description text for the first monitor graphic in the catalog.

To add more descriptions for each product, simply duplicate the scrollingText symbol, change the text (and alignment) in the duplicate symbol, and place it on the corresponding keyframe in the productMovie symbol. Of course, this example is just a functional prototype with placeholder graphics. The next step in real production would be to finesse the artwork, and to add transitional effects between each area of the movie. Perhaps some sound effects would be useful, too. The next chapter introduces Part IX of the *Dreamweaver and Flash 5 Bible*, "Sound Planning."

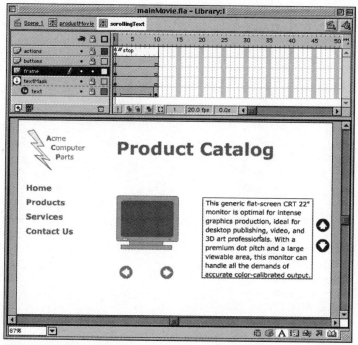

Figure 35-18: The complete scrollingText timeline

Summary

✦ Before you can start to create an interface in Flash, you need to have a plan for your Flash movie timeline. Create an organizational chart outlining the sections of the presentation.

✦ Determine your Flash movie properties (frame size, frame rate, and background color) before you undergo production in Flash.

✦ If you don't have final art for a Flash production, you can still create a functional prototype of the presentation using placeholder graphics. When the final artwork is ready, replace the placeholder graphics with the final artwork.

✦ You can create simple slide shows or product catalogs using sequential keyframes and buttons with nextFrame() and prevFrame() actions.

✦ The Hit area of a text-based Button symbol should always be defined with a solid shape.

✦ Basic nonscripted scrolling can be added to a presentation with simple Motion Tweens and buttons using nextFrame() and prevFrame() actions.

✦　　✦　　✦

Sound Planning

Understanding Sound for Flash

This chapter introduces the basics of digital audio for Flash. Properly implemented, the integration of sound with your Flash project adds dimension to your creation. That's because sound introduces another mode of sensory perception. Coordinated with visual form and motion, sound deepens the impact and can even enhance the ease of use of your Flash creation. With careful planning and attention to technical detail, sound can be leveraged to great advantage. Rather than add sound as an afterthought, we encourage you to create a seamless multisensory experience for your audience. In this chapter, we explain sample rate and bit resolution, and the difference between the two. We also discuss how audio files sizes are calculated, and the audio formats that are supported by Flash.

Basics of Sampling and Quality

Before you begin integrating sound with your Flash project, it's important to understand the basics of digital audio. To help you with this, we've dedicated this chapter to an introduction to sampling, bit resolution, and file size — and the relevance of these topics to sound in Flash 5.

What is sound?

Sound, or hearing, is one of our five principal sensations; it's the sensation that's produced when vibrations in the air strike the aural receptors located within our ears. When we hear a sound, the volume of the sound is determined by the intensity of the vibrations, or sound waves. The pitch that we hear — meaning how high (treble) or low (bass) — is determined by the frequency of those vibrations (waves). The frequency of sound is measured in hertz (which is abbreviated as Hz).

Theoretically, most humans have the ability to hear frequencies that range from 20 to 20,000 Hz. The frequency of the sound is a measure of the range of the sound—from the highest high to the lowest low. It's important to note here that, when starting to work with sound, the most common error is to confuse the frequency of the sound with the recording sample.

What you should know about sound for Flash

When integrating sound with Flash, a number of factors affect the final quality of the sound and the size of the sound file. The quality of the sound is important because it determines the aesthetic experience of the sound, while the file size is important because it determines how quickly (or not) the sound will arrive at the end user's computer. The primary factors that determine the quality and size of a sound file are sample rate and bit resolution.

Sample rate

The sample rate, measured in hertz (Hz), describes the number of times an audio signal is sampled when it is recorded digitally. In the late 1940s, Harry Nyquist and Claude Shannon developed a theorem that determined that, for optimal sound quality, a sampling rate must be twice the value of the highest frequency of a signal. Thus, the higher the sample rate, the better the audio range. Generally, higher sample rates result in a richer, more complete sound. According to Nyquist and Shannon, in order for the audible range of 20 to 20,000 Hz to be sampled correctly, the audio source needs to be sampled at a frequency no lower than 40,000 Hz, or 40 kHz. This explains why CD audio—which closely resembles the source sound—is sampled at 44.1 kHz.

Note   A sound sample refers to one "analysis" of a recorded sound, whereas a sound file refers to the entire collection of samples recorded, which comprise a digital recording.

The less a sound is sampled, the further the recording will deviate from the original sound. However, this tendency toward loss of the original quality of the sound yields one advantage: When the sample rate of a sound file is decreased, the file size drops proportionately. For example, a 300KB, 44.1 kHz sound file would be 150KB when saved as a 22.05 kHz file. See Table 36-1 for more details on how sample rate affects quality.

Table 36-1
Audio Sample Rates and Quality

Sample Rate	Quality Level	Possible Uses
48 kHz	Studio quality	Sound or music recorded to digital medium such as miniDV, DAT, DVCam, and so on
44.1 kHz	CD quality	High-fidelity sound and music

Sample Rate	Quality Level	Possible Uses
32 kHz	Near-CD quality	Professional/consumer digital camcorders
22.05 kHz	FM radio quality	Short, high-quality music clips
11.025 kHz	Acceptable for music	Longer music clips; high-quality voice; sound effects
5 kHz	Acceptable for speech	"Flat" speech; simple button sounds

Because the native playback rate of all audio cards is 44.1 kHz, sound that is destined for playback on any computer should be a multiple of 44.1. Thus, we recommend sample rates of 44.1 kHz, 22.05 kHz, and 11.025 kHz for *any* use on computers. (Although sample rates that deviate from the rule of 44.1 may sound fine on your development platform, and may sound fine on many other computers, some may have problems. This simple rule will go a long ways toward reducing complaints of popping and distorted sound.) This becomes more important with Flash. When Flash imports sounds that are not multiples of 11.025, the sound file is resampled, which causes the sound to play at a lower or higher pitch than the original recording. This same logic applies to sound export, which is discussed later in this chapter. Finally, although Flash menus list sample rates as 11, 22, and 44, these are abbreviations for the truly precise sample rates of 11.025, 22.05, and 44.1 kHz.

Bit resolution

The second key factor that influences audio quality is bit resolution (or bit depth). Bit resolution describes the number of bits used to record each audio sample. Bit resolution is increased exponentially, meaning that an 8-bit sound sample has a range of 2^8, or 256, levels, while a 16-bit sound sample has a range of 2^{16}, or 65,536, levels. Thus, a 16-bit sound is recorded with far more information than an 8-bit sound of equal length. The result of this additional information in a 16-bit sound is that background hiss is minimized, while the sound itself is clearer. The same sound recorded at 8 bits will be noisy and washed out.

Reducing file size

Another point to remember is that the 16-bit sound file is twice the size of the same file saved at 8-bit quality. This is due to the increase in the amount of information taken to record the higher quality file. So, if your sound is too big, what can you do? Well, a sound that's been recorded at a higher bit resolution can be converted to a lower bit resolution, and a sound with a high sample rate can be converted to a lower sample rate. Although a professional studio might perform such conversions with hardware, either of these conversions can also be done with software.

Tip If you're having difficulty understanding the significance of bit depths yet are familiar with the intricacies of scanning photographic images, consider the difference between an 8-bit grayscale image and a 24-bit color image of equivalent dimensions. The file size for the 8-bit grayscale image (such as a black and white photograph) is much smaller than the 24-bit color image (such as a color photograph). The gray scale image doesn't have as much tonal information — only 256 levels of gray — yet the 24-bit color image records a range of 16.7 million colors. Unlike photographs, sound samples don't require anything close to a range of 16.7 million values. Sixteen-bit sound samples deliver a dynamic range of over 64,000 values, which is more than the human ear can detect.

Table 36-2 lists the various bit depths of sound along with their quality level and possible uses.

Table 36-2 Audio Bit Resolution and Quality		
Bit Depth	**Quality Level**	**Possible Uses**
16-bit	CD quality	High-fidelity sound and music
12-bit	Near-CD quality	Professional/consumer digital camcorder audio
8-bit	FM radio quality	Short, high-quality music clips
4-bit	Acceptable for music	Longer music clips; high-quality voice; sound effects

Refer to Figures 36-1 and 36-2 for a comparison of the differences between sounds at different sample rates and bit depths. Both figures show a wave form derived from the same original sound file, differing only in their sample rates and bit depths. The waveform of the 16-bit 44.1 kHz sound has twice as many "points" — or samples of information — as the 8-bit 11.025 kHz sound. Because the 16-bit 44.1 kHz sound has more samples, the gap between each sample isn't as large as the gaps of the 8-bit 11.025 kHz sound. More samples result in a much smoother, cleaner sound.

Tip A common mistake that novices make with sound is the assumption that 8-bit audio is acceptable, especially because it ought to result in a much smaller file size than 16-bit sound. This is wrong for at least two reasons. First, 8-bit is unacceptable because it sounds incredibly worse than 16-bit sound. Second, the horrible sound will not pay for itself in diminished file size because most compression codecs won't work on 8-bit sound.

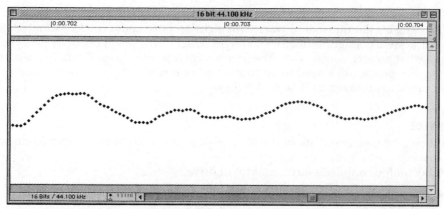

Figure 36-1: This is a waveform of a sound sampled at 44.100 kHz with a 16-bit resolution, as displayed in a high-end sound application.

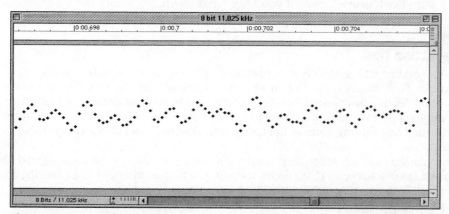

Figure 36-2: Here's the same sound as shown in Figure 36-1, but down sampled to 11.025 kHz with an 8-bit resolution.

Channels

Audio files are either mono (single channel) or stereo (dual channel: left and right). Stereo files are twice the size of mono files because they have twice the information. Most audio-editing applications offer the option to mix the two stereo channels together and either save or export a stereo sound to a one channel mono sound. Most audio applications also have the ability to save the right or left channel of a stereo sound separately as a .WAV or .AIF file.

With the more robust, multitrack-editing applications, such as Deck II, ProTools, or AudioLogic, it's not unusual to work with eight or more audio tracks — limited only by your system configuration. As you might imagine, these applications give the sound artist greater control over the final sound mix. For use in Flash, these multi-track audio project files need to be "bounced" or mixed down to a stereo or mono file in order to be saved as WAV or AIF files.

File size

You should be concerned about the file size of your audio clips for several reasons.

✦ Sound files require a large amount of drive space.

✦ Managing large sound files, and importing them into Flash can be cumbersome and slow.

✦ Download times for large, elaborate sound clips (even when heavily com-pressed upon export from Flash) can be detrimental to the appreciation of your Flash project, even if you have what might be considered a high speed Internet connection.

Production tips

When working with audio clips, it's important to create the shortest audio clips possible. That means trimming off any excess sound that you don't need, especially any blank lead-in or lead-out *handles* (also called in and out points) at the either the beginning or the end of a clip. This procedure is discussed briefly in Chapter 37, "Importing and Editing Sounds in Flash," with reference to Flash's sound tools.

If you plan to have a background music track in your Flash project, it's a good idea to use a small audio clip that can be looped. Looping audio clips are described in Chapter 37, "Importing and Editing Sounds in Flash."

Here is a simple formula to determine the file size, in bytes of a given audio clip:

```
Seconds of audio x sample rate* x # of channels x (bit depth ÷
8**) = file size

*Expressed in hertz, not kilohertz.
**There are eight bits per byte.
```

Thus, a 20-second stereo audio loop at 8 bits, 11 kHz would be calculated like this:

$20 \text{ sec} \times 11,025 \text{ Hz} \times 2 \text{ channels} \times (8 \text{ bits} \div 8 \text{ bits/byte}) = 441,000 \text{ bytes} = 430 \text{ KB}$

There are two schools of thought regarding the ideal quality of sound files for import into Flash. These schools are pretty much divided into those who have high-end sound-editing tools and those who don't. In an effort to delineate the best path for each group, we've noted the following: (a) If you *don't* have high-end sound tools available, then you may be among those who *always* prefer to start with audio source files of the highest possible quality (16 bit, 44.1 kHz is ideal), and then use the Flash sound settings to obtain optimal compression upon export. See Chapter 38, "Optimizing Flash Sound for Export," for detailed information on the Flash sound export settings for .SWF movies. (b) If you *do* have high-end sound tools available, then you may prefer to compose most of 1your clients' music from scratch and that you very rarely work with the MP3 format before importing into Flash. You may also disagree with those who advise that one should bring their sound into Flash at the highest quality before optimizing. This workflow difference may be attributable to the plethora of options that are available to those with high-end sound tools. We know of one sound engineer who converts all of his audio to 16-bit 22.1 kHz mono files, "with major bass reduction," *before* importing into Flash. As with so many things, individual mileage may vary.

Sound File Import Formats

Prior versions of Flash could import several different file formats — but the format you chose depended primarily on the platform you were using to develop your content. Flash still supports those formats and, regardless of whether a sound file was imported on a Mac or PC, the resulting .FLA file can still be edited on either platform. The big news with Flash 5 is that it imports MP3.

New Feature   Flash 5 now supports direct import of MP3 sound files!

Flash supports more than just MP3 files. Here's the entire list:

✦ **MP3 (MPEG-1 Audio Layer 3):** Among the many advantages of MP3 sound files for Flash 5 users, the most obvious is that they are cross-platform. Flash 5 can import MP3 sound on either the PC or the Mac. This single advantage improves Flash workflow in cross platform environment. Other advantages are the efficiency of MP3 compression and the resultant wealth of sound files that are increasingly available in this format. For more information about MP3's please seen the sidebar at the end of the section.

✦ **.WAV (Windows Wave):** Until the recent support for MP3, .WAV files reigned for nearly a decade as the standard for digital audio on Windows PCs. Flash can import .WAV files created in sound applications and editors such as Rebirth, SoundForge, and Acid. The imported .WAV files can be either stereo or mono, and can support varying bit and frequency rates. Unassisted, Flash 5 for Macintosh cannot import this file format. But with QuickTime 4 installed, .WAV files can be imported into Flash 5 on a Mac. Flash 5 recognizes, properly opens, and can edit .FLA files created on a Windows PC that contain .WAV sounds — with the limitation that any previously imported .WAV sound cannot be updated or edited.

✦ **.AIFF or .AIF (Audio Interchange File format):** Much like .WAV on the PC, prior to the success of the MP3 format, the .AIFF format was the most commonly used digital audio format for the Mac. Flash can import .AIFF sounds created in sound applications and editors such as PEAK, DECK II or Rebirth. Like .WAV, .AIFF supports stereo and mono, variable bit, and frequency rates. Unassisted, Flash 5 for PC cannot import this file format. But with QuickTime 4 installed, .AIFF files can be imported into Flash 5 on the PC. Flash 5 recognizes, properly opens, and can edit .FLA files created on the Mac that contain .AIFF sounds — with the limitation that any previously imported .AIFF sound cannot be updated or edited.

✦ **QuickTime:** Unfortunately QuickTime Audio files (.QTA or .MOV files) cannot be imported directly into Flash. However, QuickTime audio files can be prepared for import into Flash by saving them as either .WAV or .AIFF files. This requires that you have QuickTime Pro 4.0 (or greater) installed. QuickTime Pro is available from Apple at `www.apple.com`.

Note

If you're working in a cross-platform environment, unless you're importing MP3 sounds exclusively, it may be important to take a few precautions to ensure that the sound aspect of your .FLA's will be editable on both platforms. Don't rely upon the imported sound that's embedded in the .FLA as your master sound file. Do make sure that the master sound is retained as both a .WAV and as an .AIFF, and that both sound sources are distributed with the .FLA. Of course, this becomes a moot point in environments where QuickTime 4 is installed and maintained on all machines.

MP3s Demystified

MP3 is a noteworthy technology as well as a file format. It excels at the compression of a sound sequence — MP3-compressed files can be reduced to nearly a twelfth of their original size, without destroying sound quality. MP3 was developed under the sponsorship of the Motion Picture Experts Group (MPEG) using the following logic: CD-quality sound is typically sampled at a bit depth of 16 (16-bit) at sample rate 44.1 kHz, which generates approximately 1.4 million bits of data for each second of sound — but that second of sound includes a lot of data for sounds that most humans cannot hear! By devising a compression algorithm that reduces the data linked to imperceptible sounds, the developers of MP3 made it possible to deliver high-quality audio over the Internet without excessive latency (the delay between playing a sound and hearing it back). Another way of describing this is to say that MP3 uses perceptual encoding techniques that reduce the amount of overlapping and redundant information that describe sound. As implemented by Flash 5, MP3 has the added advantage that it streams longer sounds, which means that the sound begins to play before the sound file has been received in its entirety. Shockwave Audio, the default audio compression scheme for Director-based Shockwave movies, is actually MP3 in disguise.

Sound Export Formats Used by Flash

Although the default in Flash 5 is to export all audio as MP3, sound can also be exported in the ADPCM format. You can also decide what export format to use for audio when exporting .FLA project files to .SWF movies. The benefits and drawbacks of each format are noted in the list that follows.

Regardless of the format that you choose for exporting your sounds, you can individually specify a compression scheme for each sound by using the Flash Library. Furthermore, each format has specific options and settings. For more information on the export settings for sound, see Chapter 38, "Optimizing Flash Sound for Export."

✦ **ADPCM (Adaptive Differential Pulse-Code Modulation):** ADPCM is an audio compression scheme that converts sound into binary information. It is primarily used for voice technologies, such as fiber-optic telephone lines, because the audio signal is compressed, enabling it to carry textual information as well. ADPCM works well, because it records only the difference between samples, and adjusts the encoding accordingly, keeping file size low.

Note   ADPCM was the default setting for older versions of Flash, such as Flash 2 and 3. It isn't as efficient as MP3 encoding, but is the best choice for situations in which compatibility is required with *all* older Flash Players.

✦ **MP3 (MPEG-1 Audio Layer 3):** Over the last 18 months, MP3 has become the standard for digital audio distributed on the Internet. Although MP3 compression delivers excellent audio quality with small files, it's much more processor-intensive than other compressors. This means that slower computers may gasp when they encounter a high-bit-rate MP3 audio while simultaneously processing complex animations. As always, it's wise to know your audience, and, when in doubt, to test your Flash movie with MP3 audio on slower computers. As a final note, the Flash Player only supports MP3 at versions 4 and above.

✦ **RAW (Raw PCM):** Flash can export sound to .SWF files in a RAW format. If you use this setting Flash won't recompress any audio. However, uncompressed sound makes very large files that would be useless for Internet-based distribution. Even for those people who develop Flash content for QuickTime, it's more effective to use either Premiere or Final Cut to add uncompressed sound to a Flash animation. The only advantage of exporting RAW sounds might be backward compatibility with earliest versions of Flash.

Table 36-3 shows the compatibility of Flash's audio import formats with various platforms.

Table 36-3 Audio Import Formats in Flash 5				
Import Formats	**Mac Compatibility**	**PC Compatibility**	**Flash 4 Compatibility**	**Comments**
.MP3	Yes	Yes	No	Cross-platform, wealth of available sources
.AIF	Yes	No	Yes	Default sound format for Macintosh
.WAV	No	Yes	Yes	Default sound format for PC

Table 36-4 shows the compatibility of Flash's audio export formats with various platforms.

Table 36-4 Audio Export Formats in Flash 5				
Export Format	**Mac Compatibility**	**PC Compatibility**	**Flash 4 Compatibility**	**Comments**
ADPCM	Yes	Yes	Yes	Good encoding scheme; Flash Player 3 and earlier compatibility
MP3	Yes	Yes	Yes	Best encoding scheme; not compatible with versions 1, 2, and 3 of Flash Player
RAW	Yes	Yes	Yes	No compression; lossless; large file sizes

Summary

✦ The sample rate (or sampling rate) of a sound file describes the number of times the source sound is "analyzed" per second. The higher the sample rate, the better the sound quality.

✦ The bit resolution, or bit depth, of a sound file describes the breadth of information recorded at each sample. The higher the bit depth, the better the sound quality.

✦ Because the unaided human ear can perceive frequencies between 20 and 20,000 Hz, the best sampling rate for sound reproduction is 44.1 kHz. This is the sampling rate that's used for high-fidelity audio, such as CDs.

✦ Sound files with high sampling rates and bit depths result in ideal sound quality, but they also have large file sizes. In order to transmit audio over the Internet effectively, without losing your audience, most sounds need to be down sampled or encoded with processor-intensive audio compression schemes. For this, the MP3 format is ideal.

✦ Flash 5 can now import MP3, the most popular audio format.

✦ Flash can import .WAV files in the Windows version of Flash, and .AIFF files in the Macintosh version. However, after the audio files have been imported, the Flash movie (.FLA files) can be exchanged between platforms with the sounds intact in the Flash Library. In such cases, everything is editable except the previously imported, foreign-platform sounds.

✦ Flash .SWF movies have three types of audio compression: ADPCM, MP3, and RAW. Although ADPCM is compatible with earlier versions of the Flash Player, MP3, which is compatible with versions 4 and 5 of the Flash Player, delivers the best sound quality with the least addition to file size.

✦ ✦ ✦

Importing and Editing Sounds in Flash

Sound can be used in Flash to enhance interactive design with multisensory elements such as buttons, to layer the visitor's experience with a background soundtrack, to add narrative, or for more experimental uses. This chapter focuses on the fundamentals of importing and integrating sound files into your Flash project.

Importing Sounds into Flash

In Chapter 36, we explained the basic principles relevant to the use of digital sound within Flash. We also discussed the various sound formats that Flash can import and export. We championed the inclusion of .MP3 among the sound formats that Flash 5 can import. In addition to our discussion of the merits of .MP3 sound, we also explained the uses of platform specific .AIFF (Mac) and .WAV (PC) audio files. But we didn't delve into the process of importing sound into Flash. So, let's get started.

Note When working with sound, you may encounter some interchangeable terminology. Generally, these terms — sound file, sound clip, or audio file — all refer to the same thing, a single digital file in one of several formats, which contains a digitally encoded sound.

Unlike other imported assets, such as bitmaps or vector art, Flash doesn't automatically insert an imported sound file into the frames of the active layer on the timeline. In fact, you don't have to select a specific layer or frame before you import a sound file. That's because all sounds are sent directly to the Library immediately upon import. At this point, the sound becomes part of the .FLA editor file, which may make the file size balloon significantly if the sound file is large. However, the sound does not become part of the .SWF, nor will it add to the size of the .SWF file unless it is assigned to a keyframe, as an instance. Although this may seem peculiar, it does serve a useful purpose: It helps to ensure that instances of the sound will be employed within your project, rather than duplicates of the same large sound file, which keeps the .SWF file size down. So, to use an imported sound within Flash you must first import the sound, and then assign an instance of that sound to a specific layer and keyframe.

Cross-Reference Refer to Chapter 31, "Checking Out the Library: Symbols and Instances," to learn more about how to organize and access sound assets in the Library, as well as how to work with instances.

To import a sound file into the Flash authoring environment:

1. Choose File ➪ Import.

2. From the Files of Type drop-down, choose All Sound Formats.

3. Select the .MP3, .AIFF, or .WAV file that you want to import.

4. Click Open.

   The selected sound file is imported into your Flash editor document (.FLA) and arrives in the Flash Library with its filename intact. If the Library is closed, you can open it by choosing Window ➪ Library, or by using the keyboard shortcut (Ctrl/Command+L). With the Library open, locate the sound, and click it to highlight the name of the sound file where it appears in the Library Sort Window. The waveform appears in the Library Preview Window, as shown in Figure 37-1. Click the Play button above the waveform to audition the sound.

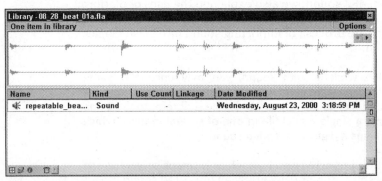

Figure 37-1: This is a stereo sound in the Flash Library.

Cross-Reference Refer to Chapter 38, "Optimizing Flash Sound for Export," for an explanation of how unique compression settings can be specified for each sound in the Flash Library.

Sounds may also be loaded from a shared library. Refer to Chapter 31, "Checking Out the Library: Symbols and Instances," to learn how to assign an identifier string to an asset, such as a sound file, in the Flash Library. Refer to Chapter 42, "Sharing and Loading Assets," to learn how to load an asset, such as a sound, from a shared Library.

Assigning a Sound to a Button

The experience of interactivity is enhanced by the addition of subtle effects. The addition of sounds to correspond with the various states of a button is perhaps the most obvious example. Although this effect can be abused, it's hard to overuse an effect that delivers such meaningful user feedback. Here, we show how different sounds can be added to both the Over (mouseover) and the Down (click) states of a button. For more general information about creating the buttons themselves, see Chapter 31, "Checking Out the Library: Symbols and Instances," and Chapter 35, "Designing Interfaces and the Interface Elements." Because buttons are stored in the Library, and because only instances of a button are deployed within the Flash movie, sounds that are assigned to a button work for all instances of that button. However, if different sounds are required for different buttons, then a new button symbol must be created. You can create a new button symbol from the same graphic symbols as the previous button (provided it was built out of symbols) or duplicate it in the Library using the Duplicate command on the Library's Option menu.

To add a sound to the Down state of a Flash button:

1. From the Common Library, choose a button to which you want to add sound effects. Open it for editing by either double-clicking it, or by choosing Edit from the Library Options menu. Both methods invoke the Symbol Editing mode.

2. Add a new layer to the button's timeline, label the new layer Sound, and then add keyframes to this layer in the Over and Down columns. Your timeline should look similar to Figure 37-2.

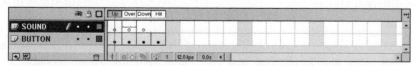

Figure 37-2: The timeline for your button should resemble this timeline.

3. Next, select the frame of the button state where you want to add a sound for interactive feedback (such as a clicking sound for the down state), and then access the Sound Panel by doing one of the following: (a) right-click/Ctrl+click the selected frame, choose Panels from the ensuing contextual pop-up, and then choose Sound; or (b) proceed from the menu with Window ➪ Panels ➪ Sound. An alternative method (with the frame selected) is to simply drag the sound from the Library and onto the stage.

You should now have the new Flash 5 Sound Panel open, as shown in Figure 37-3. For more information about the Flash 5 Panels, refer to Chapter 29, "Working with Text."

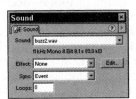

Figure 37-3: The new Flash 5 Sound Panel.

4. Choose the sound clip that you want to use from the Sound drop-down menu. This menu lists all of the sounds that have been imported and that are available in the Library of the current movie.

5. The next step is to use the Sync drop-down menu to choose *how* you want the sound to play. For this lesson, simply use the default, which is the Event option. We defer our exploration of the other options in the Sync pop-up for a later section.

You have now added a sound to your button state. Remember, you're still in Symbol Editing mode, so to test the button, return to the movie editor either by clicking the scene tab at the upper-left of the timeline or by pressing Ctrl+E (Command+E). From the movie editor, choose Control ➪ Enable Simple Buttons, or Control ➪ Test Scene.

To add a sound to the Over state of a Flash button, simply retrace the previous steps, referencing the Over state of the button wherever appropriate. Remember that different sounds can be assigned to the Over, Down, and Hit states of a button.

On the CD-ROM

For a completed example of this button, refer to the Flash movie push_bar_button_01.fla located in the ch37 folder of the *Flash 5 Bible* CD-ROM. This movie has a button with sounds attached and was made with the same technique described in this section.

Adding Sound to the Timeline

In addition to the use of sounds to enhance the interactivity of buttons, another popular use of sound in Flash is to provide a background "score." The simplest way to achieve this is to place the sound within its own layer in the timeline, at the precise frame in which you want the sound to begin. To do this, you must first import the sound (as described earlier in this chapter) and also create a new layer for it.

On the CD-ROM If you don't have access to sounds, you can use the sample sound *counting 123*, or *repeatable beat* to practice. These sounds are in the ch37 folder of the *Flash 5 Bible* CD-ROM. They are available in both .WAV and .AIF formats. There's also a silly example, titled jwl_silly_soundtest, that may help you get started in your work with sounds.

Adding sound files to the timeline is similar to assigning sound to a button. To add sounds to a movie's timeline, follow these steps:

1. Add a new layer to the timeline and label the layer with the name of the sound.

2. Create a keyframe on the sound layer at the frame where you want the sound to begin.

3. With that keyframe selected, either (a) right-click/Ctrl+click the selected frame, choose Panels from the ensuing contextual pop-up, and then choose Sound; or (b) proceed from the menu with Window ⇨ Panels ⇨ Sound.

   You should now have the new Flash 5 Sound Panel open. (See how similar this is to the methodology for adding sound to a button?)

4. If you remembered to import the sound that you want to use, you can now choose that sound clip from the Sound drop-down menu. If you find yourself stuck at this point, review the preceding steps and/or retrace your steps through the methodology for adding sound to a button.

5. From the Event pop-up, choose how the sound should be handled by Flash. The Event pop-up offers several preset effects, plus custom, which invokes the Edit Envelope. For no special effect, choose None. For more about the Event presets and the Edit Envelope, refer to the subsequent section, "Applying Effects from the Effect Pop-up of the Sound Panel."

6. From the Sync pop-up, choose one of four options — Event, Start, Stop, or Stream — to control how you want to the sound to be synchronized. (See the next section for a detailed explanation of Sync options.)

7. Specify how many times you want the sound to loop. To loop indefinitely, enter a high number, such as 999. (For specific information about looping stream sounds, refer to the next section.)

8. Perform any last minute editing or finessing of the sound file (see "Editing Audio in Flash," later in this chapter). Then return to the Main Timeline and save your work.

Your sound is now part of the timeline. Its waveform is visible on the layer to which it was added. Test your sound by pressing Enter on your keyboard, which plays the timeline. Or, for sound with a Sync setting of Stream, manually "scrub" the sound by dragging the Playhead across the timeline. To perform the most accurate test of the sound, use either Control ➪ Test Scene or Control ➪ Test Movie to see and hear it as a .SWF file.

Tip   If you sync a sound to the timeline using the Stream feature, you should test your .SWF movie on various platforms and machines with different processor speeds. What looks and sounds good on the latest Power Mac G4 Cube might be less impressive on an underpowered legacy machine.

Organizing sounds on the timeline

There is no technical limit to the number of sound layers; each layer functions like a separate sound channel, and Flash mixes them on playback. (This capability of Flash might be considered an onboard, economy sound mixer.) There is, however, a practical limit, because each sound layer increases the movie's file size, while the mix of multiple sounds may burden the computer it's being run on.

Tip   If you can't recall the *name* of a particular sound in the timeline, remember that with Tooltips enabled from the Preferences dialog (Edit ➪ Preferences), the file-name of the sound will pop-up whenever the cursor is allowed to settle over the waveform.

Enhanced viewing of sound layers

Because sound is different from other types of Flash content, some users find that increasing the layer height of the sound layers eases working with multiple sounds in the timeline. That's because a taller layer height provides a better visual cue due to the unique waveforms of each sound. To increase the layer height for individual layers:

1. Right-click/Ctrl+click the layer bar, and then choose Properties from the contextual pop-up.

2. At the bottom of the ensuing Layer Properties dialog, change the layer height from the default 100 percent to either 200 or 300 percent.

3. Note that these percentages are relative to the settings chosen in the Frame View Options pop-up. For more information on the intricacies of the timeline, see Chapter 30, "Exploring the Timeline." For an actual example of this, open the file titled, jwl_silly_soundtest.fla, located in the ch37 folder on the CD-ROM in the counting 123 folder.

Tip

Your movie's frame rate, as specified in the Movie Properties dialog, affects the expanse (or number) of frames that a sound occupies on the timeline. For example, at Flash's default setting of 12 frames per seconds (fps), a 30-second sound clip extends across 360 frames of the timeline. At 18 fps, the same 30-second clip expands to 540 frames — but in either case, the time length of the sound is unchanged.

Organizing sound layers with a mask

A helpful trick for organizing sounds is to use a Mask layer. Because Flash doesn't have a utility to group, nest, or collapse multiple sound track layers (or other content, for that matter), a Mask layer (or a Guide layer) can be used to achieve a similar result. Here's how:

1. Create a new empty layer above the sound track layers.

2. From the layer bar, right-click/Ctrl+click to open the Layer Properties dialog. Give it a meaningful name, such as Sound Gang, and change the layer type to Mask. (Leave this Mask layer empty.) Click OK.

3. Drag each of the sound track layers up to the Sound Gang layer. They'll indent beneath the Sound Gang layer, neatly organizing sound content within the timeline.

Cross-Reference

For more information about working with the timeline and Mask layers, refer to Chapter 30, "Exploring the Timeline."

Synchronizing Audio to Animations

In film editor's lingo, to *synchronize*, or *sync*, means to precisely match picture to sound. It's a conjunction of the Greek words *syn*, meaning *with*, and *chronos*, meaning *time*. In Flash, sound is synchronized to the visual content of the timeline. Flash sync affords several options for the manner in which the audio component is related to animation on the timeline. Each of these sync options is appropriate for particular uses, which are discussed in the following section.

Types of sound synchronization in Flash

The Sync options on the Sound Panel control the behavior of sound in Flash, relative to the timeline in which the sound is placed. The Sync option you choose will depend on whether your sound is intended to add dimension to a complex multimedia presentation or to add interactivity in the form of button-triggered sound, or whether it is intended to be the closely timed sound track of an animated cartoon.

✦ **Event:** Event is the default Sync option for all sounds in Flash, so unless you change this default to one of the other options, the sound will automatically behave as an Event sound. Event sounds begin contemporaneously with the keyframe in which they occur, and then play independently of the timeline. If an event sound is longer than the timeline movie, it will continue to play even though the movie has stopped. If an Event sound requires considerable time to load, the movie will pause at that keyframe until the sound has loaded completely. Event sounds are the easiest to implement, and are useful for background soundtracks and other sounds that don't need to be synced. Event is the default Sync setting in Sound Panel.

Event sound can degrade into a disturbing inharmonious round of out-of-tune sound loops. If the movie loops before a sound has completed, the sound may begin again — over the top of the initial sound that has not finished playing. After several loops, this can become intolerable — although in some circles, among the unsound, it may be an esteemed feature. To avoid this effect, use the Start Sync option.

✦ **Start:** The Start Sync option is similar to an Event sound, but with one crucial difference: If it's already playing, a sound that is assigned the Start option will stop and begin over again. A good example of the utility of this option is buttons. Suppose you have three identical buttons that play the same two-second sound on the mouseover. In practice, the sound will begin when any button is moused over. When a second or third button is moused over, the sound will play again with each mouseover.

✦ **Stop:** The Stop Sync option is similar to the Start Sync option, except that the selected sound stops playing when the Sync event occurs. The Stop Sync option can also be used to stop a specific sound.

✦ **Stream:** Stream sounds are similar to a traditional track in a video-editing application. A Stream sound locks to the timeline, and is given priority over visual content. When Stream sound is chosen, the Flash player attempts to pace the animation in sync with the sound. However, when animations either get too complex or are run on slower machines, Flash will skip — or drop — the frames as needed to stay in sync with the Stream sound. A Stream sound will stop once the animation ends (at the end of the timeline) or, more specifically, when the playback head reaches the last frame that includes the waveform of the streamed sound. A Stream sound can be *scrubbed*; by dragging the Playhead along the timeline, the Stream sound will play in direct relationship to the content as it appears, frame by frame. This is especially useful for lip-synch and coordinating the perfect timing of sound effects with visual events.

To use sound effectively, it's important to understand how stream sounds work. When the Sync option for a sound is set to Stream, on export or publish, Flash breaks the sound into chunks that are tied to the timeline. Although this is transparent to you, it is nearly the equivalent of breaking a single sound file into many separate files and adding them to the timeline as individual pieces — but that would be a lot of work. Luckily, Flash does this for you.

Tip When adding sounds to the timeline, no matter how many times you tell a Stream sound to loop, a Stream sound will stop at the end of its timeline. To extend a Stream sound's looping capacity, add as many frames as necessary to a stream sound's layer.

Stopping Sounds

The default behavior of event sounds is for them to play through to the end, regardless of the length of the timeline. However, there's a trick that can be used to stop any sound, including event sounds. Place another instance of the same sound at the keyframe where the sound should stop and assign this instance as a Stop Sync sound. This Stop setting can be on any layer, it will stop all instances of the sound.

Stopping a single instance of a Stream sound

A single instance of a sound can also be stopped, if it's sync option is set to Stream. To do this, simply place an empty keyframe in the sound layer at the point where the sound should stop.

Stopping all sounds

You can stop all sounds that are playing in any timeline (including Movie Clips) at any point by doing the following:

1. If there isn't already an actions layer on your timeline, add a new layer, label it **Actions** (or **atns**), and then select the frame that occurs at the point where you want all sounds to stop. Make this frame into a keyframe.

2. With the keyframe selected, proceed to the Frame Actions panel by either clicking the Show Actions Icon near the far-right end of the Launcher Bar, or by navigating to Window ➪ Actions.

3. From the Basic Actions group in the left side of the Normal Mode (or in Expert Mode, for the Action group) double-click the Stop All Sounds action. The following ActionScript code,

```
stopAllSounds ();
```

appears in the right side of the Frame Actions panel, as shown in Figure 37-4.

4. Return to the Movie Editor, save your work, and then test it with Control ➪ Test Movie.

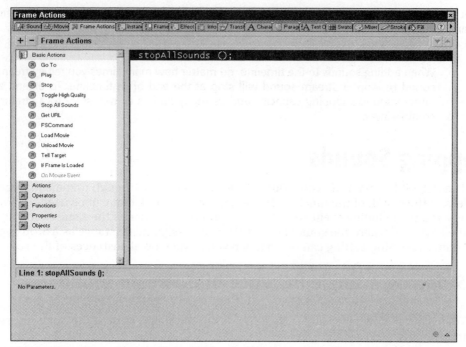

Figure 37-4: Any sound that's currently playing stops when the movie reaches a keyframe with a Stop All Sounds action. Note that all of the panels are ganged here into a mega-panel.

Editing Audio in Flash

Although Flash was never intended to perform as a full-featured sound editor, it does a remarkable job with basic sound editing. If you plan to make extensive use of sound in Flash, we recommend that you consider investing in a more robust sound editor. You'll have fewer limitations and greater control over your work. In Chapter 41, "Controlling Movie Clips," we discuss several popular sound editors that are commonly used in concert with Flash.

Sound editing controls in Flash

Flash has basic sound editing controls in the Editing Envelope control, which is accessed by clicking the Edit button of the Sound panel. (As you may recall from previous sections, you must first select the keyframe containing the sound, and then open the Sound Panel by choosing Window ➪ Panels ➪ Sound.) The Time In control and the Time Out control, or Control Bars, in the Editing Envelope enable you to change the In (start) and Out (end) points of a sound, and the Envelope Handles are used to create custom Fade-in and Fade-out effects.

Note Edits applied to a sound file in the Edit Envelope only affect the specific instance that has been assigned to a keyframe. The original file that resides in the Library is neither changed nor exported.

Setting the In and Out points of a sound

A sound's In point is where the sound starts playing, and a sound's Out point is where the sound finishes. The Time In control and the Time Out control are used for setting or changing a sound's In and Out points. Here's how to do this:

1. Start by selecting the keyframe of the sound you want to edit, and then access the Sound Panel, either from the menu by choosing Window ⇨ Panels ⇨ Sound, or from the contextual menu, with a right-click/Ctrl+click on the keyframe.

2. Open the Edit Envelope dialog, shown in Figure 37-5, by clicking the Edit button of the Sound panel.

3. Drag the Time In control and Time Out control (located in the horizontal strip between the two channels) onto the timeline of the sound's waveform in order to define or restrict which section will play.

4. Use the Envelope Handles to edit the sound volume, by adding handles and dragging them up or down to modulate the volume.

5. Click the Play button to hear the sound as edited before returning to the authoring environment. Then, rework the sound if necessary. When you've finessed the points and are satisfied with the sound, click OK to return to the Sound Panel. Then return to the Movie Editor and save your work.

Applying effects from the Effect pop-up of the Sound Panel

You can apply a handful of preset fades and other effects to a sound by selecting the effect from the Effect pop-up of the Sound Panel. (For many uses, the Flash presets will be more than sufficient, but if you find yourself feeling limited, remember that more subtle effects can be created in an external sound editor.) Flash's preset effects are described in detail here:

✦ **None:** No effect is applied to either of the sound channels.

✦ **Left Channel/Right Channel:** Plays only the right or left channel of a stereo sound.

✦ **Fade Left to Right/Fade Right to Left:** This effect lowers the sound level of one channel while raising the level of the other, creating a Panning effect. This effect occurs over the entire length of the sound.

Edit button (invokes Edit Envelope control)

Envelope handles (left channel)

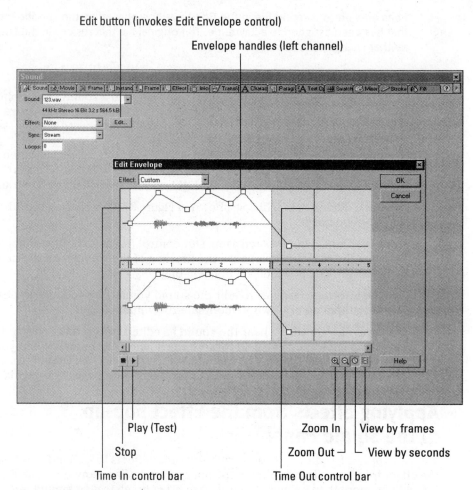

Play (Test)

Stop

Zoom In

Zoom Out

View by frames

View by seconds

Time In control bar

Time Out control bar

Figure 37-5: The sound-editing tools and options of the Edit Envelope, which is accessed from the new Sound panel

✦ **Fade In/Fade Out:** Fade In gradually raises the level of the beginning of a sound clip. Fade Out gradually lowers the level at the end of a sound. The default length for either effect is approximately 25 percent of the length of the clip. We've noticed that even if the size of the selection is edited with the control bars, the duration of the Fade In/Fade Out will remain the same. (Thus, a 35-second sound clip with an original default Fade In time of 9 seconds, still has a 9-second Fade In time even when the selection's length is reduced to, say, 12 seconds.) This problem can be resolved by creating a Custom Fade.

✦ **Custom:** Any time you manually alter the levels or audio handles on this screen, Flash automatically resets the Effect menu to Custom.

Creating a custom Fade In or Fade Out

For maximum sound-editing control within Flash, use the envelope handles to create a custom fade or to lower the audio levels (or amplitude) of a sound. In addition to creating custom fades, the levels can be lowered creatively to create subtle, low-volume background sounds. Here's how:

1. Select the keyframe of the sound you want to edit.

2. Access the Sound Panel by either (a) right-clicking/Ctrl+clicking the selected frame and choosing Panels ⇨ Sound from the ensuing contextual pop-up, or (b) proceeding from the menu with Window ⇨ Panels ⇨ Sound.

3. Click the Edit button of the Sound Panel to open the Edit Envelope control. Click the envelope lines at any point to create new envelope handles.

4. After handles have been created, you can drag them around to create your desired volume and fading effects. The lines indicate the relative volume level of the sound. When you drag an envelope handle down, the line slopes down, indicating a decrease in the volume level, while dragging an envelope handle up has the opposite effect. The Edit Envelope control is limited to eight envelope handles per channel (eight for left and eight for right).

Tip

Envelope handles may be removed by dragging them outside the Edit Envelope.

Other controls in the Edit Envelope control

Other useful tools in the Sound tab warrant mention. See Figure 37-5 for their locations.

✦ **Zoom In/Zoom Out:** These tools either enlarge or shrink the view of the waveform, and are particularly helpful when altering the In or Out points or envelope handles.

✦ **Seconds/Frames:** The default for viewing sound files is to represent time in seconds. But viewing time in frames is advantageous for syncing sound with the Stream option. Toggle between viewing modes by clicking either the Seconds or Frames button at the lower right of the Edit Envelope control.

The Loop control

This control appears on the Sound panel, yet a measure of its functionality occurs in conjunction with the Edit Envelope control. The Loop numeric entry field is used to set the number of times that a sound file will loop (or repeat). A small looping selection, such as a break beat or jazz riff can be used for a background soundtrack. A short ambient noise can also be looped for an interesting effect. To test the quality of a looping selection, click the Edit button, which will take you to the Edit Envelope control where you can click the Play button for a preview of your loop. If the loop isn't perfect, or has hiccups, use the Control Bars and envelope handles to trim or taper off a blank or adversely repeating section.

Tip   Flash links looped sounds and handles them as one long sound file (although it's really one little sound file played repeatedly). Because this linkage is maintained within the editing environment, the entire expanse of a looped sound can be given a custom effect in the Edit Envelope. For example, a simple repeating 2-measure loop can be diminished over 30 loops. This is a subtle effect that performs well, yet is economical as regards file size.

Summary

✦ When sound is imported to a Flash movie, it's added to the Library. You assign sounds from the Library to a keyframe on a timeline.

✦ Different sounds can be assigned to the Over, Down, and Hit states of a Flash button.

✦ The Sync settings control how a sound will play with relation to the rest of the Flash timeline. Event sounds play in their entirety, regardless of the timeline's playback. Stream sounds are frame-exact, meaning that they are locked to the timeline's playback. Start sync initiates a new instance of a sound, and can be useful when the same sound is used on multiple buttons. Stop sync stops an instance of a sound, if it is playing.

✦ Because sounds are measured and played in seconds (not frames), the frame rate of a Flash movie affects a stream sound's apparent duration in the timeline.

✦ Use the Loop setting in the Sound Panel to repeat a soundtrack in the timeline. Because there's no infinite loop setting, use high numbers for extended playback.

✦ Stream sounds force the Flash Player to keep the timeline in pace with the sound. If the Player can't play every frame (especially with faster frame rates), some frames may be dropped from playback to insure that the sound stays in sync.

✦ Use a Stop All Sounds action to stop all sounds that are currently playing in any current timeline. This is useful during transitions between scenes. For more information about using actions to control sounds, refer to Part X, specifically Chapter 41, "Controlling Movie Clips."

✦ The Effect menu of the Sound panel contains useful presets for sound channel playback. Click the Edit button of the Sound Panel to access the Edit Envelope and create a custom effect.

✦ Basic sound editing can be easily done within the Edit Envelope. Sounds can be trimmed with the Time In and Out Control Bars, or faded in or out with the envelope handles.

✦   ✦   ✦

Optimizing Flash Sound for Export

After you have added sound to buttons and timelines in a Flash movie, you need to know how to modify the audio's export settings for optimal sound quality and file size. In this chapter, we discuss the intricacies of controlling audio output, with particular attention to MP3 bit rates. We also discuss how to use the Publish Settings dialog and compare that with the enhanced control that is available for customizing compression from within the Sound Properties dialog of the Flash Library. Finally, we discuss sound export and the methods available for converting Flash sounds into QuickTime sound tracks.

Sound Optimization Overview

There are several considerations to be cognizant of when preparing Flash sound for export. For Web-based delivery, the primary concern is to find an acceptable middle ground between file size and audio quality. But the concept of acceptability is not absolute; it is always relative to the application. Consider, for example, a Flash Web site for a record company. In this example, sound quality is likely to be more important than file size because the audience for a record company will expect quality sound. In any case, consideration of both your audience and your method of delivery will help you to determine the export settings you choose. Luckily, Flash 5 has new capabilities that can enhance the user's experience both by optimizing sounds more efficiently and by providing improved programming features to make download delays less problematic.

There are two ways of optimizing your sound for export. The quickest, simplest way is to use the Publish Settings and apply a one-setting-optimizes-all approach. This works well only if all of your sound files are from the same source. It also will not deliver the highest possible level of optimization.

If you demand that your Flash movie has the smallest possible file size, or if your Flash project includes audio from disparate sources, or uses a combination of audio types—such as button sounds, background music, speech—it's better to fine-tune the audio settings for each sound in the Library. This method gives you much better control over output.

Publish Settings for Audio

Choose File ⇨ Publish Settings to access the Publish Settings and to take a global approach to the control of audio output quality. Then choose the Flash tab of the Publish Settings dialog, shown in Figure 38-1. This dialog has three areas where the audio quality of an entire Flash movie can be controlled *globally*.

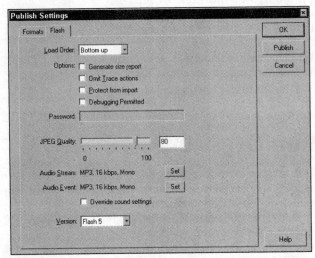

Figure 38-1: The Flash tab of Publish Settings has three options to control audio quality.

The Flash tab of the Publish Settings dialog has three options for controlling audio quality:

✦ **Audio Stream:** Controls the export quality of Stream sounds (see Chapter 37, "Importing and Editing Sounds in Flash," for more information on Stream sounds in Flash.) To customize, click Set. This gives you a number of options, which are described in the section that follows. Flash 5 supports .MP3, which is the optimal streaming format.

✦ **Audio Event:** Controls the export quality of Event sounds. (See Chapter 37, "Importing and Editing Sounds in Flash," for more information on Event sounds in Flash.) To customize, click Set. This gives you a number of options, which are described in the section that follows.

✦ **Override Sound Settings:** If this box is checked, Flash uses the Publish Settings, rather than the individual audio settings that are fine-tuned in the Library. For more information, see the section "Fine-Tuning Sound Settings in the Library," later in this chapter.

The Set options

Audio Stream and Audio Event have individual compression settings, which can be specified by their respective Set button options. If you click ether Set button on the Flash Tab, the same Sound Settings dialog appears — it is identical for both Audio Stream and Audio Event, which means that the same options are offered for both types of sound. The Sound Settings dialog, shown in various permutations in Figure 38-2, displays numerous settings related to the control of audio quality and audio file size. The type of compression chosen governs the specific group of settings that appear.

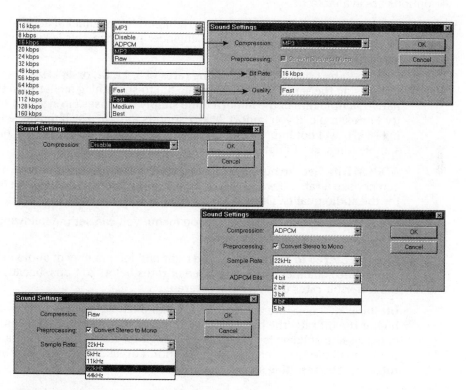

Figure 38-2: The Sound Settings dialogs

Note The impact of individual sound settings may be overridden by another setting. For example, a Bit Rate setting of 380 Kbps will not result in good sound if the Quality is set to Fast. Optimal results require attention to *all* of the settings. This is like a set of interlinked teeter-tooters: A little experimentation will reveal the cumulative or acquired impact of each setting on the others. However, the need to experiment here is hobbled by the lack of a preview mechanism. By contrast, tuning a sound in the Library is much more serviceable, because there's a sound preview button adjacent to the settings controls. For more about this workflow, refer to the following section of this chapter, "Fine-tuning Sound Settings in the Library."

The specific options that are available in the Sound Settings dialogs are always related to the compression, or audio-encoding scheme, selected in the Compression drop-down menu. That's because different compression technologies support different functionalities:

✦ **Disable:** This option turns off all sounds that have been assigned — in the Sound panel — to Sync as either Audio Stream or Audio Event. If this option is selected, no sound of that Sync type will be exported when the .SWF movie is published. There are no further options for this setting.

✦ **ADPCM:** With ADPCM selected in the Compression menu, the following options are available:

  • **Convert Stereo to Mono:** Mixes the right and left channel of audio into one (mono) channel. In sound engineer parlance, this is known as "bouncing down."

  • **Sample Rate:** Choose from sampling rates of 5, 11, 22, or 44 kHz. (Increasing the sample rate of an audio file to something higher than the native sample rate of the imported file simply increases file size, not quality. For example, if you import 22 kHz sounds into the Flash movie, selecting 44 kHz will not improve the sound quality. For more information on sample rates, see Chapter 36, "Understanding Sound for Flash.")

  • **ADPCM Bits:** Set the number of bits that ADPCM uses for encoding. You can choose a rate between 2 and 5. The higher the ADPCM bits, the better the audio quality. Flash's default setting is 4 bits.

✦ **MP3:** If you select MP3 in the Compression menu, you can set the following options:

  • **Convert Stereo to Mono:** Mixes the right and left channel of audio into one (mono) channel. This is disabled at rates below 20 Kbps, because the lower bit rates don't support stereo.

  • **Bit Rate:** MP3 measures compression in kilobits per second (Kbps). The higher the bit rate, the better the audio quality. Because the MP3 audio compression scheme is very efficient, a high bit rate still results in a relatively small file size. Refer to Table 38-1 for a breakdown of specific bit rates and the resulting sound quality.

- **Quality:** Choose Fast, Medium, or Best quality. Fast optimizes the audio file for faster delivery on the Internet, although there's usually a significant loss in quality. The truth about the Fast setting is this: Unless you're only using the sound as a rudimentary button click, or (in conjunction with the 8 Kbps bit rate) as the voice track for a simulated moonwalk, this setting is useless. Medium is a usable setting that delivers acceptable quality but sacrifices some speed in favor of quality. Best is the highest quality setting, chiefly intended for files distributed through broadband connections, intranets, or on CD-ROMs.

✦ **Raw:** When Raw (a.k.a. Raw PCM audio) is selected in the Compression menu, there are two options:

  - **Convert Stereo to Mono:** Mixes the right and left channel of audio into one (mono) channel.

  - **Sample Rate:** This option specifies the sampling rate for the Audio Stream or Audio Events sounds. For more information on sample rate, please refer to Chapter 36, "Understanding Sound for Flash."

Table 38-1
MP3 Bit Rate Quality

Bit Rate	Sound Quality	Good For
8 Kbps	Very bad	Best for simulated moonwalk transmissions. Don't use this unless you want horribly unrecognizable sound.
38 Kbps	Barely acceptable	Extended audio files where quality isn't important, or simple button sounds.
20, 24, 32 Kbps	Acceptable	Speech or voice.
48, 56 Kbps	Acceptable	Large music files; complex button sounds.
64 Kbps	Good	Large music files where good audio quality is required.
112–128 Kbps	Excellent	Near-CD quality.
380 Kbps	Best	Near-CD quality.

As a general rule, if you use the Publish Settings to control audio export globally, we recommend choosing MP3 at 64 Kbps. This will result in moderate to good sound quality (suitable for most Flash projects), and the ratio of file size-to-quality will give reasonable performance.

Supporting the MP3 Player

Although this is becoming less of an issue with the release of Flash 5, it may still be important to consider that MP3 is not supported by Flash 3 (or earlier) players. There may be a number of users in your audience that haven't upgraded their Flash Player plug-in to version 4, much less to version 5. Although, as Flash developers, it would be nice to assume that your audience will eventually upgrade, it's more realistic, and therefore advisable, to consider implementing a transitional solution. For example, you could provide both a Flash 3 movie with ADPCM-encoded audio and a Flash 5 movie with MP3-encoded audio. Include information on the splash page about the benefits of the Flash 5 player: reduced download time and increased audio quality. This is an incentive for you users to upgrade. You'll also want to provide a link to Macromedia to download the new plug-in. Another, more "invisible" solution is to add intelligence to your splash page with a "plug-in detection" script that automatically serves users the movie that corresponds to the version of the Flash Player they have installed.

Cross-Reference
To add plug-in detection to your Flash movies, use one of the HTML templates installed with Flash 5. HTML templates are discussed in the "Using the HTML settings" section of Chapter 43.

Fine-Tuning Sound Settings in the Library

The Publish Settings menu is convenient because it permits you to tweak a minimal set of sound adjustments, whereupon Flash exports all of your "noncustomized" Stream sounds or Event sounds at the same rate. However, if you have many sounds and you are seriously concerned about obtaining the ideal balance of both optimal sound quality and minimum file size, you will need to export them at different rates. Consequently, for the fullest level of control over the way in which Flash compresses sound for delivery, we recommend that each sound should be optimized, individually, in the Library. In fact, it would be impossible for us to overemphasize this bit of sound advice: *We recommend that each sound should be optimized, individually, in the Library.*

Settings for audio in the Library

Audio settings in the Library are similar to those discussed previously for the Publish Settings. These settings appear in the Sound Properties dialog, shown in Figure 38-3. To access these settings, either (a) double-click the icon of the sound in the Library, or (b) select the sound as it appears in the Library and (i) click the Properties button, or (ii) choose Properties from the Library Options popup.

There are four groupings of information and controls in the Sound Properties dialog: Status, Export Settings, Estimated Results, and Buttons.

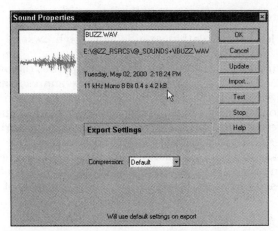

Figure 38-3: The Sound Properties dialog enables you to control the compression settings and to precisely balance all other related settings for each individual sound in the Library.

The top half of the Sound Properties dialog displays status information about the sound file: To the far left is a window with the waveform of the selected audio; to the right of the waveform is an area that displays the name of the file together with its location, date, sample rate, channels, bit depth, duration, and file size.

The lower half of the dialog is titled Export Settings. The first setting is a drop-down menu that is used to select the Compression scheme. The Compression options, and the subsequent compression related options that appear in the other settings, are exactly the same as the sound options of the Publish Settings dialog, discussed earlier in this chapter.

Beneath the Export Settings is where Estimated Results are displayed. Here, the estimated final file size (after compression) of the clip is displayed, together with the compression percentage. This is an extremely important tool that is easily overlooked.

The buttons to the right of the Sound Properties dialog offer the following options:

✦ **Update:** Click this button to have Flash check for an update of the audio file, if the original .MP3, .WAV or .AIFF file has been modified, and update it accordingly. Generally, this only works on the machine the audio file was originally imported to.

✦ **Import:** Enables you to import another audio file into the Flash environment. For more information on importing audio files, see Chapter 37, "Importing and Editing Sounds in Flash."

✦ **Test:** This excellent feature enables you to audition the export quality of the sound based on the options that you've selected from the Compression drop-down list.

✦ **Stop:** Click this button to stop (silence) the sound Test.

✦ **Help:** Launches the Flash Help system within your default Web browser.

There are three benefits to fine-tuning your audio in the Sound Properties dialog of the Library. Foremost of these benefits is the ability to set specific compressions and optimizations for individual each sound. Another benefit is the Test button — this is an excellent way to audition your audio file and to know what it will sound like when it is exported with different compression schemes and bit rates; hearing is believing. Finally, the Estimated Results, which display how each setting will affect the compressed file size, is a powerful tool that helps to obtain the desired balance of quality and file size. In contrast, optimizing sounds with the Publish Settings is more of a blind process — it is not only more global; it's also more of a painful trial-and-error method.

Combining methods for controlling sounds

One of the coolest things about Flash audio is that you can combine the two methods of controlling sounds, using both the Publish Settings and the Library Sound Properties dialog to streamline your work flow while still maintaining a relatively high degree of control over sound quality. (This method works best if you already have some experience with sound behavior in Flash.)

For example, let's assume that you have three different Event sounds in your Flash project. Two of these are simple button sounds. You decide that you won't require optimal sound for buttons, so based on your prior experience of sound behavior in Flash, you go directly to the Publish Settings and set Event sounds to publish as .MP3 at 48 Kbps with Medium Quality. Then, in the Library, by setting the Compression to default, you tell Flash to handle the compression for these sounds with the Publish Settings. But the third sound is a loop of background jazz that you want to be heard at near-CD quality. For this sound, you return to the Sound Properties tab and try a number of combinations — and test each one — until you find a balance between file size and audio quality that pleases your ears. You assign this sound to export as an .MP3, stereo at 112Kbps, with Quality set to Fine.

Expert Tutorial: Sound Clipping on the Flash Player, by William Moschella

William Moschella is a sound engineer with extensive Flash experience. He's provided a number of Expert Tutorials for this edition of the Flash 5 Bible.

If you've spent much time with Flash, you've probably noticed an annoying clipping sound that sometimes occurs with event and stream sounds (especially on Windows PCs) in previous versions of Flash. Well, I've volunteered to report that it's still there.

Here's the reason: Flash Player acts as a preamp to its sounds, which means that the sound becomes a few decibels louder *after* the movie is published. It's important to know this, because it means that what you put in isn't what really comes out. This clipping sound is more noticeable with certain types of sounds and instruments than others. Particular offenders include heavy bass, deep vocals, and ultrahigh twangy sounds. This happens because these sound waves tend to peak above and below the threshold of both the Player and sound cards. When overamplified by the Flash Player, this will even happen with sounds that you may have already have optimized. Although the ultimate fix lies with Macromedia, there are a few workarounds. These solutions apply to projectors, CD-ROMs, and Web browsers.

If your clipping is minimal, you may get good results with a custom setting in the Edit Envelope Control to lower volume (stereo channels have two volumes which must be lowered). Move the envelope handles down evenly for both channels; this acts like a volume knob. By testing and making adjustments, you should be able to minimize, if not eliminate the clipping entirely. For more about the Edit Envelope Control, refer to Chapter 37, "Importing and Editing Sounds in Flash."

When the clipping sound is more pronounced, you might need to take additional steps to optimize your sound. Start by using a third-party sound editor, such as Sound Forge, SoundEdit, or Cool Edit to normalize the sound. By removing the high peaks in the sound wave, you help to reduce clipping.

The previous steps usually help, but they aren't the true solution to the problem. Unfortunately, certain sound cards will clip Flash audio at most settings. This is due to a communication issue between the Flash Player and the sound card. So far, there's no way to prevent this before publishing your movie. However, there is a way that this particular clipping can be eliminated after your movie is published. Unfortunately, it means devising a mechanism for moving the user through another step before they finally enter your movie. The answer lies with the mouse. I've determined two actions that clear the communication path between the Flash player to the sound card. Once either of these mouse actions has been performed, the annoying sound clipping will go away.

While an audio track is playing, the viewer must either execute a right mouse-click over the movie, or else act to either minimize or maximize the screen. Although the first of these options is the most user friendly, it will not work if the movie is viewed full-screen. This "fix" will clear up the clipping problem for the current movie as well as for any other movie that is subsequently loaded into the current projector — but it will not work if you open another projector.

The ultimate solution will come from users who choose not to accept this flaw. Send an e-mail to Macromedia at wish-flash@macromedia.com. Perhaps this problem will be resolved in Flash 6.

The Options pop-up menu of the Library has new sound features. When a sound is selected in the Library, the pop-up displays one or two menu items related to editing the selected sound. These menu items will either directly open the sound in a sound-editing application, or lead to the Select External Editor dialog. One such menu item is Edit With; however, the particular menu items that are available will vary depending on both the platform and the software installed on the host computer.

Publish Settings for QuickTime Sound

Flash 4 introduced a hot new feature: the capability to export your Flash movies as QuickTime Flash (or Windows AVI) movies. With the release of Flash 5, this is an important and growing area of Flash usage. This section offers brief coverage of the audio options available from within Flash for export to the QuickTime (QT) architecture. Note that these options only pertain to a Flash sound that's converted to a QuickTime sound track. The resulting QuickTime sound track is a new sound track — it is *not* merged with preexisting QT sound tracks. When authoring for export to QuickTime, there is no limit to the number of sounds or sound channels. That's because all sounds are combined into a single sound track upon export to QuickTime (or Windows AVI). When exporting to QuickTime, neither the lack of sounds nor the number of sounds has any effect upon the size of the final file. When exporting a Flash movie (or sound track) to QuickTime, you have two choices:

✦ If you want to export Flash sounds (such as background music) to use compression schemes currently unavailable in Flash 5, then you can opt to convert the Flash sound to a QuickTime-supported audio codec such as QDesign Music.

✦ If you are exporting your Flash movie to QuickTime but want to keep the Flash sound embedded with its original Flash media track, you can disable QuickTime sound compression.

To access the QuickTime audio export Settings:

1. Choose File ➪ Publish Settings.

2. In the Formats tab, check the QuickTime option.

3. A QuickTime tab appears. Click the QuickTime tab.

4. Now, at the Streaming Sound setting, check Use QuickTime Compression.

   Finally, click the Settings button. The Sound Settings dialog appears, shown in Figure 38-4, with several options to select your audio compression settings. Depending upon the configuration of your machine, different QuickTime audio-encoding options appear. Depending upon the intended use of your QuickTime movie, you may want to choose different options. Table 38-2 explains some of the popular QuickTime encoding methods and their intended uses. Table 38-3 demystifies alternative formats.

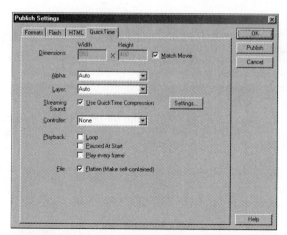

Figure 38-4: The QuickTime tab of Publish Settings has options to control the conversion of Flash sounds into QuickTime audio tracks with the Streaming Sound setting.

Table 38-2 QuickTime Sound Compressors		
Popular Codecs	*Best For*	*Description*
Qdesign Music Codec	Internet	Very good compression ratio, great for music. Downloads progressively.
Qdesign version 2	Internet	Excellent compression ratio, great for music, streaming audio.
Qualcomm PureVoice	Internet	Excellent compression ratio. Very good for voice.
IMA	CD-ROM	Good quality, only encodes 38-bit audio. Inadvisable for low frequencies (booming bass) or Web use.

	Table 38-3 Alternative Formats	
Other Formats	**Description**
24-bit Integer, 32-bit Integer	Increases bit rate to 24- and 32-bit, respectively.
32-bit Floating Point, 64-bit Floating Point	Increases bit rate to 32-bit and 64-bit, respectively. Note that current computer systems generally are only capable of playing back 38-bit sound.
ALaw 2:1	European standard compression scheme. Low quality, not recommended.
MACE 3:1, MACE 6:1	Old Macintosh standards. Low quality, high file size. Forget about using these codecs.
uLaw 2:1	Old Internet standard for Japan and North America. Low quality, high file size.

Final Sound Advice and Pointers

Here are a few final notes about sound and some pointers to more complex sound-related topics that are presented later in the book.

VBR (Variable Bit Rate) MP3

Flash 5 has licensed the Fraunhofer MP3 codec, which supports streaming MP3 with a constant bit rate. However, Flash 5 does not support Variable Bit Rate (VBR), or VBR MP3. VBR MP3 is a variant of MP3 that utilizes specialized algorithms to vary the bit rate according to the kind of sound that is being compressed. For example, a soprano solo would be accorded a higher bit rate than a crashing drum sequence, resulting in a superior ratio of quality to file size. There are a number of sound applications, such as the Xing Audio Catalyst 2.1 codec, that export VBR MP3. If you have access to a sound application that exports VBR MP3, you'll be happy to know that you can import your VBR MP3 sound files, which are (theoretically) optimized for file size and quality beyond the compression capabilities of Flash, and that the compression of such files can be maintained by doing the following:

✦ In the Flash tab of the Publish Settings, leave the option to Override Sound Settings unchecked.

✦ In the Sound Properties dialog, which is accessed from the Library, choose Default for the Compression option in Export Settings.

✦ The Sync Option in the Sound Panel may not be set to Stream.

If you choose to use VBR in your Flash projects, please refer to Table 38-4 for a guide to the optimal use of this format.

Table 38-4
Quick Guide to Common VBR Quality Settings

VBR	CBR Bitrate +/– 10%	Supported Channels	Recommended Use
Low	96kbits/s	Mono Joint Stereo Stereo	Near-CD quality; good choice for portable MP3 Players (smallest file size). Use when storage space is a consideration; when playback is performed with low-end sound equipment and listening environment, such as portable players or car players.
High Frequency	Not supported at this rate	Not supported at this rate	Not supported at this rate.
Low/Normal	112 Kbits/s	Mono Joint Stereo Stereo	CD-quality; best choice for portable MP3 players where file size is limited.
Normal	128 Kbits/s	Mono Joint Stereo Stereo	CD-quality; best choice for most users. Normal use; similar to encoding moderately difficult to difficult content with a CBR of 128 Kbits/s.
Normal/High	380 Kbits/s	Mono Joint Stereo Stereo	Archival quality; for high-end stereo (larger file size). Compromise between Normal and High settings.
High	192 Kbits/s	Mono Joint Stereo Stereo	Archival quality; for highest-end stereo unlimited file size. Use when storage space is not a consideration; when playback is performed with high-end sound equipment and listening environment; and when heavy equalization adjustments might be used on playback.

Continued

Table 38-4 *(continued)*			
VBR	**CBR Bitrate +/− 10%**	**Supported Channels**	**Recommended Use**
Very High	224 Kbits/s	Mono Joint Stereo Stereo	Archival quality; for highest-end stereo unlimited file size.
Ultra High	256 Kbits/s	Mono Joint Stereo Stereo	Archival quality; for highest-end stereo unlimited file size.

Extracting a sound from a .FLA editor file

Sometime you may be handed a .FLA file that has sound embedded within it, and told that the original sounds have either been lost or are no longer available. Here's how to extract a sound from such a file:

Note Unfortunately, an equivalent process does not exist for the Macintosh. However, for users with QuickTime Player Pro, a workaround is to export the movie as a QuickTime Video movie and then use QuickTime Player Pro to extract the audio channel.

1. Back up the file. If the original file is named, Mess.fla, then you might resave it as Mess_Sound_Extraction.Fla.

2. Add a new layer in the timeline, at the top of the layer stack. Label this layer **Sound Extraction**. Add nine empty frames to this layer by selecting frame 10 and then using the keyboard shortcut, which is F5. (If it's a long sound, you'll probably want to add more frames.)

3. Delete all other layers.

4. Open the Library and locate the sound that needs to be extracted from the file. In this case, the sound is named Buzz.wav. Note that any other assets within this file are irrelevant to this process. That's because Flash will only utilize Library items that have been actually used within the movie.

5. Double-click Buzz.wav to invoke the Sound Properties dialog. Set the Compression to default, if it's not that way already. This ensures that the Library won't alter the sound upon export. Note the sound specifications just to the right of the waveform display, as you'll be double-checking for these specifications in only a few steps. See Figure 38-5.

6. Click frame 1 of the Sound Extraction layer to select it. This should now be the only keyframe on the only layer in this file.

7. With frame one selected, drag Buzz.wav onto the Stage. Assuming it's a short sound, the waveform will appear in the timeline across the ten frames of the Sound Extraction layer.

8. Next, on the Flash tab of the Publish Settings dialog, make sure that the Override Sound Settings check box is *not* checked.

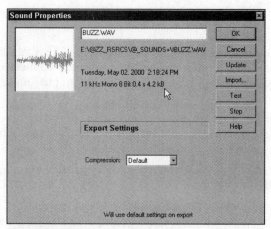

Figure 38-5: The Sound Properties dialog, which is accessed from the Library, includes the original specifications for each sound, located down and to the right of the waveform.

9. Now we're ready to extract Buzz.Wav from this .FLA. We've created a .FLA that will ignore all other assets in the Library except this sound, and we've told Flash to honor all of the original specifications of the sound. Choose File ⇨ Export Movie, and specify a file location, name, and file type — in this case, .WAV — and click Save.

10. The Export Windows WAV dialog appears with those sound specifications. If you've done everything correctly, these should match the original specifications that appeared in the Library Sound Properties dialog. If not, go back and recheck your work.

Several sound-related topics must be deferred until after our discussion of Flash 5's enhanced Action Scripting capabilities. Work your way forward to Chapter 41, "Controlling Movie Clips," for a discussion of the following topics:

✦ How to determine whether a sound is currently playing: Despite powerful enhancements to Flash's scripting capabilities, there is no method to determine whether a sound is currently playing. We've found a simple workaround that fits into the Smart Clip, a new Flash 5 feature.

✦ Using the Flash 5 sound control: The Flash 5 Sound Object supports pan and zoom control. Expert tutor Jay Vanian shows how to make sound fade and move from side to side, with incredible realism as a bouncing basketball follows your mouse from side to side and in and out of a virtual basketball court.

✦ Loading sounds from the Library: By using the power of the Flash Library and Movie Clips, sounds can be preloaded from the Library and started and stopped. Robert's soundLib.fla method provides that any asset will be available when it's required to play.

Summary

✦ Audio compression for Flash movies is controlled on the Flash tab of the Publish Settings dialog. The compression settings here are applied to all sounds used in the Flash movie, unless the sound is given custom settings in the Flash Library.

✦ You can use the Override sound settings check box in the Flash tab of the Publish Settings dialog to cancel the custom settings applied to sounds in the Flash Library.

✦ Flash 5 enables you to compress sound files as MP3-encoded audio. MP3 provides near-CD quality at higher bit rates.

✦ Generally, MP3 bit rates below 20 Kbps produce low-quality audio. Use bit rates between 20 and 32 Kbps for acceptable quality audio with the smallest file-size gains.

✦ While MP3 provides the best sound quality with the smallest file sizes, it is not compatible with Flash 3 Players. You may want to create two versions of your Flash movie: one with ADPCM audio encoding, and another with MP3 audio encoding. Both movies could be available to Web visitors to choose from. Alternatively, a JavaScript plug-in detector could automatically deliver the right movie to the visitor's browser.

✦ Use the Flash Library to customize the audio compression schemes of individual sounds.

✦ The Sound Properties dialog enables you to test different compression settings and to hear the results. Useful file size information is also provided in the Export Settings section of this dialog.

✦ Variable Bit Rate (VBR) MP3 sound files can be brought into Flash and exported without degrading the encoding; however, Flash itself cannot encode using VBR.

✦ Orphaned or lost sound files that are embedded within a .FLA file can be extracted without degrading the original sound file.

✦ Flash sounds can be converted to QuickTime sound tracks in QuickTime Flash movies. If you are creating QuickTime Flash movies, then you can access a wide range of Apple and third-party audio compressors.

✦   ✦   ✦

Adding Basic Interactivity to Flash Movies

Understanding Actions and Event Handlers

CHAPTER

39

Interactivity in a Flash movie can broadly be thought of as the elements that react and respond to a user's activity or input. A user has many ways to give input to a Flash movie, and Flash has even more ways to react. But how does interactivity actually work? It all starts with actions and event handlers.

Actions and Event Handlers

Even the most complex interactivity in Flash is fundamentally composed of two basic parts: (a) the behavior (what happens), and (b) the cause of the behavior (what makes it happen). Here's a simple example: Suppose you have a looping sound-track in a movie and a button that, when clicked, turns the soundtrack off. The *behavior* is the sound turning off, and the *cause* of the behavior is the mouse clicking the button. In Flash, behaviors are referred to as *actions*. The first step in learning how to make interactive movies is becoming familiar with the list of possible actions. However, actions can't act without being told to act *by* something. That something is often the mouse coming in contact with a button, but it can also be a keystroke, or simply a command issued from a keyframe. We refer to any occurrence that can cause an action to happen (such as the button click in the preceding example) as an *event*. The mechanism we use to tell Flash what action to perform when an event occurs is known as an *event handler*.

This cause-and-effect relationship seems obvious, but it is an extremely important concept. For the purposes of creating basic interactivity, the difference between an action and the cause of an action is merely a practical detail. But with

Flash 5's new programmatic actions and the scripting capabilities that they provide, understanding the relationship between actions and the things that cause them can be the key to adding more sophisticated behavior to your movies with traditional programming techniques.

Don't worry, we're taking it one step at a time. First, we set up the new Frame and Object Actions Panel. Then we look at the Basic Actions booklet. Later, we see how to call these actions in various ways with three kinds of event handlers: button manipulation, keyframes, and keystrokes.

What is ActionScript?

Every interactive authoring system uses a language (or code) that enables elements within the system to communicate. Just as there are several languages that people use to speak to one another around the globe, there are hundreds of programming languages in use today. In an effort to make Flash more usable to computer programmers, Flash's scripting language, called ActionScript, has changed much of its formatting to mirror JavaScript, a fundamental component for DHTML and HTML Web pages. Right now, we focus on using the most basic Flash ActionScript.

Cross-Reference   We look at more advanced ActionScript in Chapter 41.

Setting up the Actions Panel

Unlike previous versions, Flash 5 has a new way of adding interactive commands to Flash movies — the Actions Panel. Unlike with previous versions of Flash, you do not have to double-click frames and buttons to access actions. Also, you don't have to use menus to select Actions — you can type them by hand in or out of Flash! To open the Actions Panel, go to Windows ⇨ Actions (Option+Command+A or Ctrl+Alt+A). If you have a frame selected in the timeline, you will see the Actions Panel with the name Frame Actions (see Figure 39-1). If you have a Button or Movie Clip symbol selected on the stage, you'll see the name Object Actions. Don't be confused — there is only one Actions Panel. Flash simply lets you know the event handler to which you are assigning actions.

Most actions have user-definable parameters that can be set in the gray area below the left and right panes of the Actions Panel. You can show or hide this area by clicking the arrow in the lower-right corner of the panel. You can also hide the left pane of the Actions Panel by clicking the arrow on the divider line between the left and right panes.

Note   In the *Flash 5 Bible*, we do not differentiate between the Frame and Object Actions Panel. We simply use the term *Actions Panel*.

Figure 39-1: The new Actions Panel enables you to instantly add, delete, or change Flash interactive commands.

Normal versus Expert Mode

Flash has two authoring modes for actions: Normal and Expert. By default, Flash uses the Normal Mode (Command+N or Ctrl+N when the Actions Panel is active). In this mode, Flash arranges actions in the left pane into six booklets, each booklet containing sets of ActionScript. You can choose actions from any of the sets by double-clicking a specific action. For this chapter, we work entirely within the first booklet, Basic Actions. In Expert Mode (Command+E or Ctrl+E when the Actions Panel is active), Flash eliminates the Basic Actions booklet (they're all included in the Actions booklet), and enables you to type, copy, cut, and paste code at will into the right pane of the Actions Panel. You can change the mode setting by accessing the Actions Panel options, located at the upper-right corner of the panel (see Figure 39-2).

You can add actions by dragging them from the left pane to the right pane, by selecting them from the plus (+) menu button in the upper-left corner of the Actions Panel, or by double-clicking them from an Action booklet. To delete actions, select the action line(s) in the right pane, and press the Delete key on the keyboard. Or you can select the action line(s) and push the minus (–) button in the upper-left corner.

Shortcut to action menus

Deletes selected actions in right pane

Action window options

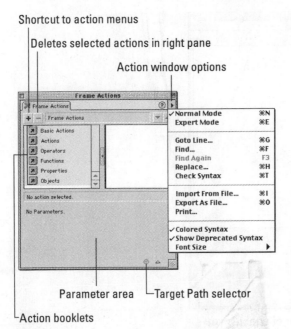

Parameter area   └Target Path selector

└Action booklets

Figure 39-2: You can control the Actions Panel's look and feel by switching between Normal and Expert Modes.

The Basic Actions are listed as unsorted groups according to the functions they can perform. The first group, comprised of Go To, Play, and Stop, control the playback of the movie. The second group, which includes Toggle High Quality and Stop All Sounds, provides global tools for handling sounds and visual quality. The third group — Get URL, FSCommand, and Load/Unload Movie — let movies load external files and communicate with the browser, a Web server, or the standalone player. The fourth group is effectively made up of Tell Target and If Frame Is Loaded. These two actions afford, respectively, communication between Movie Clips and control over the display of movies as they are downloading.

Note   We omit On Mouse Event from the Basic Actions list because it's not an Action in and of itself — it's an event handler for buttons.

The remaining Action booklets primarily offer extended ActionScript programming capabilities. We discuss their use in later chapters.

Deprecated and Incompatible Actions: What Are They?

As the ActionScript language of Flash continues to expand and encompass new functionality, older actions will coexist with newer and better actions (or methods, which we discuss later). While the Flash 5 Player will continue to support older Flash 4 and earlier actions, it's better not to use these older actions, which are called deprecated actions. If your Publish Settings for the Flash format are set to Flash 5, certain actions such as `tellTarget` and `ifFrameLoaded` will be highlighted in green (in all but the Basic Actions booklet), as shown in the following figure. Why shouldn't you use these actions? As we see in more advanced scripting, Flash 5 has introduced new ways of targeting Movie Clips and determining if certain frames have loaded.

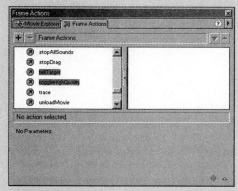

Actions that are highlighted in green should be avoided if possible. However, the Flash 5 Player will support these older actions.

Flash 5 will also let you know if certain actions are not supported with the Player version that is selected in the Flash format's Publish Settings. These actions are highlighted in yellow as shown in the following figure.

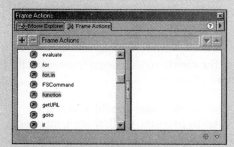

The Flash 4 Player will not support the for...in or function actions (among others), as these actions have been introduced to Flash in Version 5.

Continued

Continued

Finally, Flash will tell you if you have added conflicting actions to one keyframe or object. For example, if you have several Go To actions on one frame or button, Flash will highlight the offending action(s) in red, as shown in the following figure. The red highlighting will only appear in Normal Mode.

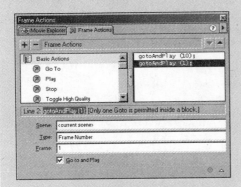

Highlighted actions are in conflict with previously added actions. You must remove or correct the parameters if you want your movie to behave correctly.

Your First Six Actions

So, now that you have a general picture of what actions do, let's look at the first six in detail (the remaining actions are covered in later chapters). At this point, we're only describing the functionality of each action, not how to add an action to your movie. Information on adding an action is covered in the next section, "Making Actions Happen with Event Handlers."

As they appear in the Flash interface, the actions are coincidentally sorted from top to bottom roughly according to their complexity. Let's take it from the top.

Go To

The Go To action changes the current frame of the movie to the target frame specified in the Go To settings. The Go To action has two variations:

✦ **Go to and Stop:** Changes the current frame to the frame specified and then halts playback. Go to and Stop is often used to produce toolbar-style interfaces where the user clicks buttons to view different areas of content in a movie.

✦ **Go to and Play:** Changes the current frame to the frame specified, and then executes a Play Action. Like Go to and Stop, Go to and Play can be used to create toolbar interfaces, but provides the capability to show animated intro sequences as preludes to individual content areas. Go to and Play also gets frequent use in choose-your-own-adventure style animations, in which the user guides an animated character through different paths in a narrative. Note that Go to and Stop is the default type of Go To action. To create a Go to and Play action, you must first add a Go To action, and then check the Go to and Play option in the Parameters area of the Actions Panel.

Each Go To action enables you to jump to certain areas of the Flash movie. The parameters of the Go To actions start with the largest time unit, the Scene, and end with the smallest one, the Frame.

You can specify frames in other scenes as the target of Go To actions with the Scene parameter. In the Scene drop-down menu, you can find a list of all the scenes in your movie, as well as built-in references to <current scene>, <next scene>, and <previous scene>, as shown in Figure 39-3. The Scene drop-down can be used together with the Type and Frame parameters to target a frame in any Scene in a movie.

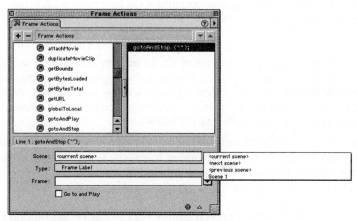

Figure 39-3: Setting the Go To action that targets a specific Scene.

There are five methods of specifying the frame to which the movie should go when it receives a Go To action. You set the method by selecting the appropriate Type and Frame parameters. After you've chosen the method to use to refer to your target frame, enter or select the frame's name or number under that setting's options (see Figure 39-4).

Figure 39-4: Setting the Go To action with a Frame Number type.

The methods for specifying the frame are:

✦ **Number:** Specify the target frame as a number. Frame 1 is the beginning of the movie or scene. Number spans scenes, so if you have a movie with two scenes, each containing 25 frames, and you add a Go to action with Frame Number set to 50, your action advances the movie to the 25th frame of the second scene.

Using frame numbers to specify the targets of Go To actions can lead to serious scalability problems in Flash movies. Adding frames at the beginning or in the middle of a movie's timeline causes the following frames to be renumbered. When those frames are renumbered, all Go to Frame Number actions must be revised to point to the correct new number of their target frames.

In the vast majority of cases, Go To actions that use Label to specify target frames are preferable to Go To actions that use Number to specify target frames. Unlike numbered frame targets, Go To actions with labeled frame targets continue to function properly even if the targeted frame changes position on the timeline.

✦ **Label:** Individual keyframes can be given names via the Label text field in the Frame panel. Once a frame is labeled, a Go To action can target it by name. To specify a label as the target of a Go To action, select Frame Label in the Type drop-down menu. Then either type the name of the frame into the Frame text field, or select it from the automatically generated list of frame labels in the Frame drop-down menu as seen in Figure 39-5.

The automatically generated list of labels that appears in the Label drop-down can include labels from other scenes, but cannot include labels that are inside Movie Clips. To target a label in a Movie Clip, you have to embed the Go To action in a Tell Target action and type the label in manually. However, Flash 5 offers a new way of targeting Movie Clips and their frame labels. For more information, see Chapter 40, "Navigating Flash Timelines."

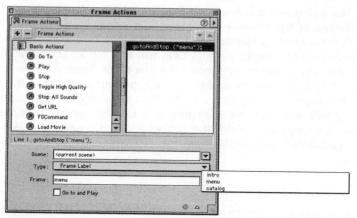

Figure 39-5: Setting the Go To action with a Frame Label.

✦ **Expression:** Specify the target frame as an interpreted ActionScript code segment. Expressions are used to dynamically assign targets of Go To actions.

✦ **Next Frame:** Specify the target frame as the frame after the current frame. Next Frame can be used in conjunction with Previous Frame to quickly set up a slide-show-style walkthrough of content, where each of a series of contiguous keyframes contains the content of one "slide."

✦ **Previous Frame:** Specify the target frame as the frame before the current frame.

Play

This simple action is one of the true foundations of Flash. Play sets a movie or a Movie Clip in motion. When a Play action is executed, Flash starts the sequential display of each frame's contents along the current timeline. The rate at which the frames are displayed is measured as frames per second, or fps. The fps rate can be set from 0.01 to 120 (meaning that the Play Action can cause the display of as little as 1 frame every 100 seconds to as many as 120 frames in 1 second, subject to the limitations of the computer's processing speed). The default fps is 12. Once Play has started, frames continue to be displayed one after the other, until another action interrupts the flow, or the end of the movie or Movie Clip's timeline is reached. If the end of a movie's timeline is reached, the movie either loops (begins playing again at frame 1, scene 1), or stops on the last frame. (Whether a movie loops or not depends on the Publish settings described in Chapter 43, "Publishing Flash Movies.") If the movie is set to loop, once the end of the Movie Clip's timeline is reached, playback loops back to the beginning of the clip, and the clip continues playing. To prevent looping, add a Stop action to the last frame of your Movie Clip.

A single Play action affects only a single timeline, whether that timeline is the main movie timeline or the timeline of a Movie Clip instance on the Main Timeline (Scene 1). For example, a Play action executed inside a Movie Clip does not cause the Main Timeline to begin playing. Likewise, any Go To action on the Main Timeline doesn't migrate to the Movie Clips that reside there. A timeline must be specifically targeted to control it. If there is no specified target, then the action is referring to its own timeline. However, this is not the case for animations within Graphic symbol instances. An animation in a Graphic symbol is controlled by actions on the timeline in which the symbol instance is present — Flash ignores actions on a Graphic symbol's timeline.

Stop

Stop, as you may have guessed, halts the progression of a movie or Movie Clip that is in a Play state. Stop is often used with buttons for user-controlled playback of a movie, or on frames to end an animated sequence.

Movie Clip instances placed on any timeline will begin to play automatically. It's important to remember to add a Stop action on the first frame of a Movie Clip if you don't want it to play right away.

Toggle High Quality

Here's a straightforward action that changes the entire movie's visual rendering quality setting to High if it is currently set at Low, and to Low if it is currently set at High. In High-Quality Mode, the edges of lines and text appear smooth because they are antialiased (or blurred slightly between shifts in color). In Low-Quality Mode, the edges of lines and text appear choppy because they are not antialiased. Low Quality is occasionally set on movies that are played back on slower computers because it causes animation to play back more quickly. See the difference for this toggle setting in Figure 39-6. Toggle High Quality is considered a deprecated action because of the new Flash 5 _quality and _highquality properties. All quality settings are global, which means that every timeline (including Movie Clip timelines) will be affected regardless of where the action is executed.

The Toggle High Quality Action is most frequently used to set the Quality of standalone Flash movies. (On the Web, the quality of a movie can be set with HTML attributes.) If the Quality is not explicitly set to High, it defaults to an automatic mode where the Quality shifts between High and Low depending on how demanding each frame of the movie is on the computer. The effect is rather jarring, so most designers avoid it by simply choosing the often slower, but more attractive High Quality.

Figure 39-6: Low Quality (left) versus High Quality (right)

Stop All Sounds

A simple but powerful action that mutes any sounds playing in the movie at the time the action is executed. Stop All Sounds does not disable sounds permanently — it simply cancels any sounds that happen to be currently playing. It is sometimes used as a quick-and-dirty method of making buttons that shut off background looping soundtracks. Stop All Sounds is not appropriate for controlling whether multiple sounds are played or muted. For information on more accurate control over sounds, please see Chapter 40, "Navigating Flash Timelines," and Chapter 41, "Controlling Movie Clips."

Get URL

Want to link to a Web page from a Flash movie? No problem. That's what Get URL is for. Get URL is simply Flash's method of making a conventional hypertext link. It's nearly exactly the equivalent of an Anchor tag in HTML, except that Flash's Get URL also allows for form submission. Get URL can be used to link to a standard Web page, an ftp site, another Flash movie, an executable, a CGI script, or anything that exists on the Internet or on an accessible local file system. Get URL has three parameters that are familiar to Web builders (the first one, URL, is required for this Action to work):

✦ **URL:** This is the network address of the page, file, script, or resource to which you are linking. Any value is permitted (including ActionScript expressions), but the linked item can only be displayed if the reference to it is correct. URL is directly analogous to the HREF attribute of an HTML Anchor tag. You can use a relative or absolute URL as well. Examples:

```
http://www.yoursite.com/
ftp://ftp.yoursite.com/pub/documents.zip
menu.html
/cgi-bin/processform.cgi
```

Since Flash 4, Get URL can now link to documents on the Web from the standalone Flash player. Execution of a Get URL action in the standalone player causes an external Web browser to launch and load the requested URL (see Figure 39-7).

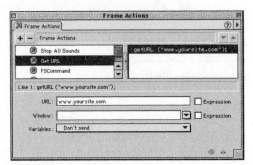

Figure 39-7: Setting the URL of a Get URL action

✦ **Window:** This is the name of the frame or window in which you wish to load the resource specified in the URL setting. Window is directly analogous to the TARGET attribute of an HTML Anchor tag. In addition to enabling the entry of custom frame and window names, Window provides four presets in a drop-down menu:

- **_self:** Loads the URL into the same frame or window as the current movie.

- **_blank:** Creates a new browser window and loads the URL into it.

- **_parent:** Removes the current frameset and loads the URL in its place. Use this option if you have multiple nested framesets, and you want your linked URL to replace only the frameset in which your movie resides.

- **_top:** Loads the URL into the current browser and removes all framesets in the process. Use this option if your movie is in a frame, but you want your linked URL to be loaded normally into the browser, outside the confines of any frames.

 Note   Frame windows and/or JavaScript windows can be assigned names. You can target these names by manually typing the name in the Window field. For example, if you had a frame defined as `<FRAME NAME="main". . .>`, you could load specific URLs into "main" from a Flash movie.

✦ **Variables:** This option enables Get URL to function like an HTML form submission. For normal links, the Variables setting should be left at its default value, Don't Send. But in order to submit values to a server-side script, one of the submission methods (Send Using GET or Send Using POST) must be selected.

Tip Get URL functions in the Test Movie environment. Both the Flash stand-alone player and the Test Movie command give you access to external and/or local URLs.

Although this chapter focuses on using Basic Actions, you should start familiarizing yourself with the ActionScript notation that Flash uses for each action (see Table 39-1). As you use Flash for more advanced interactivity, you'll need to have a firm grasp of code notation.

Table 39-1
Basic Actions and ActionScript Notation

Action	ActionScript Notation	Arguments
Go to and Stop	gotoAndStop(arguments);	Scene Name (Frame Label, Number, or Expression)
Go to and Play	gotoAndPlay(arguments);	Scene Name (Frame Label, Number, or Expression)
Go to Next Frame	nextFrame();	None
Go to Previous Frame	prevFrame();	None
Go to Next Scene	nextScene();	None
Go to Previous Scene	prevScene();	None
Play	play();	None
Stop	stop();	None
Toggle High Quality	toggleHighQuality();	None
Stop All Sounds	stopAllSounds();	None
Get URL	getURL(arguments);	URL, Target frame or window, Variable send method

Making Actions Happen with Event Handlers

The first six Basic Actions — Go To, Play, Stop, Toggle High Quality, Stop All Sounds, and Get URL — provide all the behaviors that you need to make an interesting interactive Flash movie. But those six actions can't make your movies interactive on their own. They need to be told when to happen. To tell Flash when an action should occur, you need event handlers. Event handlers specify the condition(s) under which an action can be made to happen. For instance, you might want to mouse-click a button to initiate a Play action, or you might want a movie to stop when a certain frame in the timeline is reached. Creating interactivity in your movies is simply a matter of deciding what event you want to detect (mouse click, keystroke, and so on), adding the appropriate event handler to detect it, and specifying the action(s) that should be performed when it happens.

Before we describe each event handler in detail, let's see an example of exactly how an event handler merges with an action to form a functioning interactive button.

Combining an action with an event handler to make a functioning button

Imagine that you have a short, endlessly looping movie in which a wire-frame cube rotates. Now imagine that you want to add a button to your movie that, when clicked, stops the cube from rotating by stopping the playback of the looping movie. Here's what you need to do.

For this exercise, you can use the rotatingCube.fla file located in the ch39 folder on the *Flash 5 Bible* CD-ROM. The finished file is named rotatingCube_complete.fla.

1. Open your Flash movie (.FLA file), and make a new layer called **button**.

2. Place a button on the button layer. (You could use Flash 5's sample VCR stop button found in Window ➪ Common Libraries ➪ Buttons, in the (circle) VCR Button Set folder.)

3. Bring up the Instance Panel for the button (as shown in Figure 39-8) by selecting the symbol instance on the Stage and choosing Modify ➪ Instance (Command+I or Ctrl+I). If the Instance Panel was already open, then this command will close the panel. Reapply the command to open it again. With the button selected, make sure that the Behavior menu reads Button. If some other Behavior is shown, then change it to Button.

Selecting buttons and editing button properties can be sometimes be tricky if buttons are enabled in the Flash authoring environment. For easier button manipulation, disable buttons by unchecking Enable Simple Buttons under the Control menu.

4. Open the Actions Panel (Option+Command+A or Ctrl+Alt+A), and then open the Basic Actions booklet in the left pane. A list of all the Basic Actions appears.

5. Double-click the On Mouse Event action, or drag it to the right pane. A list of parameters for On Mouse Event appears on the lower portion of the Actions Panel. This list contains all the event handlers for buttons.

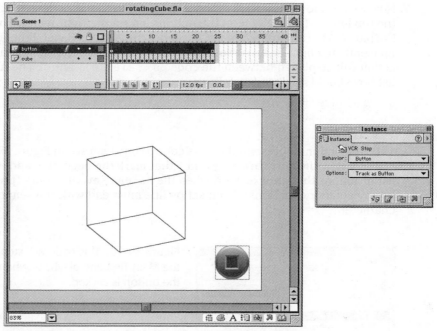

Figure 39-8: The Instance Panel for the VCR Stop button.

6. By default, the Release option of the Event setting (shown in Figure 39-9) is already checked. The Release event handler is one of two kinds of mouse-click handlers (the other is Press; both are described later in this chapter in the section titled "The Flash event handlers"). You should notice that the Actions list in the right pane indicates the event handlers that are selected. You've now told Flash that you want something to happen when the mouse clicks the button. All that's left is to tell it what should happen. In other words, you need to nest another action with the on (release){ and } code.

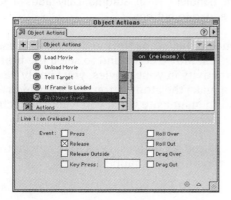

Figure 39-9: Adding a Release event handler

7. Now we try another method for adding an action to the Actions list. Select the top line `on (release){` in the Actions list (in the right pane). Then, click the plus (+) button in the top-left corner of the Actions Panel. From the pop-up menu, highlight Basic Actions, and select Stop from the submenu. A Stop action will be placed between the code `on (release){` and `}`. The Actions list box should now read as follows:

```
on (release){
      stop();
}
```

The Stop action, represented by the code `stop()` shown in Figure 39-10, is contained by the curly braces `{` and `}` that mark the beginning and end of the list of actions that are executed when the `release` event occurs (there could be any number of actions). Each action line must end with the semicolon (`;`) character.

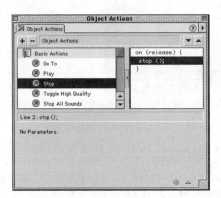

Figure 39-10: This code will stop the Main Timeline playback when the button is clicked.

Tip   In this example we selected the event handler before adding our action. This helped illustrate the individual role that each of those components plays. During real production, however, you may simply drag or add any action to the right pane without first specifying an event handler — Flash automatically adds a Release event handler to actions that are added to buttons.

We now have a button in our Flash movie that stops the movie's playback when it is clicked. You can use the Control ➪ Test Movie command to see if the button is working correctly. To make any interactivity in your movies, you simply have to apply the basic principles we used to make the stop button: Decide which action (or actions) you want to happen, and then indicate when you want that action to happen with an event handler.

In the first part of this chapter, we explored six actions. Let's look now at the list of Event Handlers you can use to make those actions happen.

The Flash event handlers

Three primary event handlers exist in Flash. Those that detect mouse activity on buttons (button manipulation), those that recognize when a key is pressed on the keyboard (key presses), and those that respond to the progression of the timeline (keyframes).

Note   Flash 5 adds some new event handlers such as `onClipEvent` and data-driven events such as `XML.loaded` and `XMLSocket.onConnect`. There is also a new Key Object and methods associated with it (for example, `Key.isDown` and `Key.isToggled`).

Button manipulation

Event handlers that occur based on the user's interaction with a button rely entirely on the location and movement of the mouse pointer. If the mouse pointer comes in contact with a button's Hit area, it changes from an arrow to a hand symbol. At that time the mouse is described as "over" the button. If the mouse pointer is not over a button, it is said to be *out* or *outside* of the button. General movement of the mouse *without* the mouse button depressed is referred to as *rolling*. General movement of the mouse *with* the mouse button depressed is referred to as *dragging*.

New Feature   Event handlers and actions on buttons must be placed only on Button instances on the Stage, not on the four frames in the timeline of the original Button symbol. Flash 5 will not allow you to place actions on any event handlers in the Button symbol timeline.

Here are the mouse-based event handlers for Flash buttons.

Press

A single mouse click can actually be divided into two separate components: the downstroke (the *press*) and the upstroke (the *release*). A Press event occurs when the mouse pointer is over the Hit area of a button *and* the downstroke of a mouse click is detected. Press is best used for control panel-style buttons, especially toggle switches. Press is not recommended for important user moves (such as irreversible decisions or primary navigation) because it does not give users an opportunity to abort their move.

Release

A Release event occurs when the mouse pointer is over the Hit area of a button *and* both the downstroke and the upstroke of a mouse click are detected. Release is the standard button click Event Handler.

Release Outside

A Release Outside event occurs in response to the following series of mouse movements: The mouse pointer moves over a button's Hit area; the mouse button is pressed; the mouse pointer is moved off the button's Hit area; and the mouse button is released. Release Outside can be used to react to an aborted button click.

Roll Over

A Roll Over event occurs when the mouse pointer moves onto the Hit area of a button without the mouse button depressed.

The Roll Over event handler should not be used to make visual changes to a button (such as making it appear "active" with a glow or size increase). Flash has a built-in method of handling strictly visual changes on buttons that is described in Chapter 31, "Checking Out the Library: Symbols and Instances." The Roll Over event handler should only be used to initiate actions.

Roll Out

A Roll Out event occurs when the mouse pointer moves off of the Hit area of a button without the mouse button depressed.

Drag Over

A Drag Over event occurs in response to the following series of mouse movements: The mouse button is pressed while the mouse pointer is over the Hit area of a button; the mouse pointer moves off the Hit area (mouse button still depressed); and the mouse pointer moves back over the Hit area (mouse button still depressed). Drag Over is rather obscure, but could be used for special cases of interactivity such as revealing an Easter egg in a game (for example, when the mouse button is held down and mouse movement occurs over a specific area, then ActionScript can detect the coordinates of the mouse movement and reveal a Movie Clip instance that is otherwise invisible on the Stage).

Drag Out

A Drag Out event occurs in response to the following series of mouse movements: The mouse button is pressed while the mouse pointer is over the Hit area of a button; and the mouse pointer moves off the Hit area (mouse button still depressed).

Key Press (or keystroke)

The Key Press event handler for an On Mouse event action lets you execute an action (or series of actions) when the user presses a key on the keyboard. The implementation method for a Key Press event handler may be confusing: To add a Key Press event handler, you must first place a button onstage at the frame where you want the keyboard to be active. You then attach the keystroke event handler to the button.

If you are only using the button as a container for your keystroke event handler and you do not want the button to appear on Stage, you should make sure that (in Symbol Editing Mode) all the frames of the button are blank.

The Key Press event handler, which was introduced with Flash 4, opens up many possibilities for Flash. Movies can have keyboard-based navigation, buttons can have keyboard shortcuts for convenience and accessibility, and games can have keyboard-controlled objects (such as ships and animated characters). But watch out for some potential "gotchas" to keyboard usage, *specifically with On Mouse event actions*. If you're planning ambitious keyboard-based projects, you may want to check this list of potential issues first:

✦ The Esc key does not work as a key press.

✦ Multiple key combinations are not supported. This rules out diagonals as two-key combinations in the classic four-key game control setup. It also means shortcuts such as Ctrl+S are not available. Uppercase is functional, however.

✦ If presented in a browser, the Flash movie must have "focus" before keystrokes can be recognized. To "focus" the movie, the user must click anywhere in the space it occupies. Keyboard-based movies should include instructions that prompt the user to perform this initial mouse click.

Note When a Flash movie is loaded into a Web browser, Key Presses cannot function until the user has clicked at least once somewhere in the Flash movie.

✦ Because the Enter, less than (<), and greater than (>) keys are used as authoring shortcuts in the Test Movie environment, you may want to avoid using them as control keys in your movies. If you need to use those keys in your movies, make sure that you test the movies in a browser.

✦ Key Press events are case sensitive. For example, an uppercase letter "S" and a lowercase letter "s" can trigger two different actions. No case-insensitive keystroke event handler exists (one that would enable both cases of a letter to trigger the same action). Achieving case-insensitivity would require duplication of event handler and action statements.

Note Flash 5's new Key Object and its methods enable you to do much more with Key Press events than the On Mouse event action does. The Key Object is discussed in the *Macromedia ActionScript Reference Guide* (which ships with the software) on pages 279–288.

Keyframes

The keyframe event handler depends on the playback of the movie itself, not on the user. Any action (except On Mouse event) can be attached to any keyframe on the timeline. An action attached to a keyframe is executed when the playhead enters the keyframe, whether it enters naturally during the linear playback of the movie or as the result of a Go To action. So, for instance, you may place a Stop action on a keyframe to pause the movie at the end of an animation sequence.

In some multimedia applications, keyframe event handlers can differentiate between the playhead *entering* a keyframe and *exiting* a keyframe. Flash has only one kind of keyframe event handler (essentially, on enter). Hence, as an author, you do not need to add keyframe event handlers explicitly — they are a presumed component of any action placed on a keyframe. As mentioned in an earlier note, Flash 5 has a new `onClipEvent` handler, which allows an argument of `enterFrame`. We look at this new handler in Chapter 41, "Controlling Movie Clips."

Tip
Complex movies can have dozens, or even hundreds of actions attached to keyframes. To prevent conflicts between uses of keyframes for animation and uses of keyframes as action containers, it is highly advisable to create an entire layer solely for action keyframes. Name the layer **actions** and keep it on top of all your layers for easy access. Remember not to place any symbol instances, text, or art-work on your actions layer. You can also create a labels layer to hold — you guessed it — frame labels.

Summary

✦ ActionScript is Flash's interactive language. It is a set of actions that enables Flash to communicate with internal elements (timelines, symbols, sounds, and so on) and external Web pages and scripts.

✦ Flash interactivity is based on a relatively simple structure: An event handler waits for something to happen (a playback point being reached or the user providing input), and when that something does happen, it executes one or more actions (which alter the movie's playback, behavior, or properties; loads a file; or executes a script).

✦ There are two authoring modes for adding actions in Flash: Normal and Expert. Normal Mode enables you to add interactivity easily by clicking action names and using menus to set parameters. Expert Mode enables experienced Flash users to type actions directly and to copy text from other applications into Flash.

✦ The Basic Actions booklet contains the fundamental actions for navigating Flash playback through multiple scenes and keyframes, as well as controlling soundtracks and accessing external Web resources such as HTML pages and ftp downloads.

✦ All actions need an event handler to activate them. Event handlers include keyframes on a timeline, button clicks, mouse movements, and key presses.

✦ ✦ ✦

Navigating Flash Timelines

Unlike most multimedia authoring applications, Flash has the capability to use multiple timelines simultaneously. So far, most of the examples in this book have only one timeline and one scene. You've seen how to add basic actions to your movies to make them interactive. Now, we begin exploring the world of multiple movie timelines using the Movie Clip symbol.

Movie Clips: The Key to Self-Contained Playback

A powerful addition to Flash was the Movie Clip symbol, which was introduced in version 3. Movie Clips enabled Flash developers to create complex behaviors by nesting self-contained sequences of animation or interactivity inside each other. These sequences could then be placed as discreet, self-playing modules on the Main Timeline. The key to the power of Movie Clips was their capability to communicate with and control each other via the Tell Target action. In Flash 4, the role of Movie Clips was expanded — they could be used with Action Script. That capability put Movie Clips at the foundation of advanced interactivity in Flash.

How Movie Clips interact within a Flash movie

Previous chapters have dealt with Flash movies as a single sequence of frames arranged along a single timeline. Whether the playback along that timeline was linear (traditional animation) or nonlinear (where the Playhead jumps arbitrarily to any frame), our example movies have normally comprised only the frames of a single timeline. Ostensibly, a single timeline may seem to provide everything you'd need to create any Flash behavior, but as you get more inventive or ambitious, you'll soon find yourself conceiving ideas for animated and interactive segments that are thwarted by the limits of a single timeline.

Suppose you want to create a looping animation of a character's face. You decide that the character's eyes should blink every 2 seconds, and that the character's mouth should yawn every 15 seconds. On a single timeline, you'd have to have a loop of 180 frames for the mouth (assuming a frame rate of 12 frames per second), and repeating keyframes for the closed eye artwork every 24 frames. Although creating your face in that manner would be a bit cumbersome, it wouldn't be impossible — until your character's face had to move around the screen as an integrated whole. Making the mouth and eyes loop while the whole face moved around complex paths for extended periods of time would quickly become impractical, especially if the face were only one part of a larger environment.

Now imagine that you could make your character's face by creating two whole separate movies, one for the eyes and one for the mouth. Could you then place those movies as self-contained animating objects on the timeline of your main movie, just like a graphic or a button? Well, you can — that's what Movie Clips are all about. Movie Clips are independent sequences of frames (timelines) that can be defined outside the context of the main movie timeline and then placed onto it as objects on a single frame. You create Movie Clips the same way you create a Graphic symbol (in the Edit Symbol environment). Unlike a Graphic symbol, a Movie Clip (as the name implies) acts in most cases just like a fully functional .SWF file, meaning, for instance, that frame actions in Movie Clip timelines are functional. After you have created a Movie Clip as a symbol, you drop instances of it into any keyframe of the main movie timeline or any other Movie Clip timeline. The following are some general Movie Clip principles:

✦ During playback, a Movie Clip instance placed on a timeline begins to play as soon as the frame on which it occurs is reached, whether or not the main movie is playing.

✦ A Movie Clip plays back autonomously, meaning that as long as it is present on stage it is not governed by the playing or stopping of the Main Timeline.

✦ Movie Clips can play when the Main Timeline is stopped, or stay halted when the Main Timeline plays.

✦ Like a Graphic or a Button symbol, Movie Clips can be manipulated on the stage — you can size them, skew them, rotate them, place effects such as Alpha blending on them, or tween them, all while the animation within them continues to play.

✦ All timelines play at the frame rate specified by the Modify Movie dialog. However, it is possible to control a timeline's frame rate with ActionScript routines.

In our character face example, the animated eyes and mouth could be looping Movie Clips, and then those movie clips could be grouped and tweened around the Stage on the Main Timeline to make the whole face move. The same principle could be used to move a Movie Clip of a butterfly with flapping wings along a motion path.

One movie, several timelines

Because a Flash movie can have more than one timeline existing in the same space and time, there needs to be away of organizing Movie Clips within the Main Timeline (Scene 1) of your Flash movie. Just like artwork can be placed inside of any symbol, symbol instances can be "nested" within other symbols. If you change the contents of the nested symbol, the parent symbol (the symbol containing the other symbol) will be updated as well. Although this may not seem special, it's of extreme importance to movie clips and Flash interactivity. Because the playback of each Movie Clip timeline is independent from any other timeline, you need to know how to tell Flash which Movie Clip you want to control.

The Flash movie diagram in Figure 40-1 illustrates multiple timelines. This Flash movie has two layers on the Main Timeline, Layer 1 and Layer 2. Layer 1 has a Movie Clip (instance "A") which exists for 19 frames on the Main Timeline. Layer 2 has a Movie Clip (instance "B") which exists for 10 frames on the Main Timeline, but also contains a nested Movie Clip (instance "C").

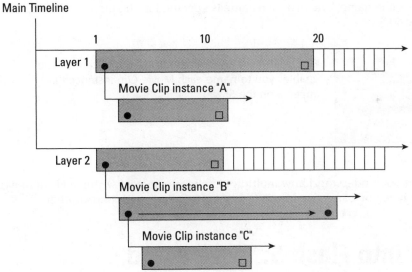

Figure 40-1: This figure shows one method of diagramming Flash timelines.

In Figure 40-1, if the Main Timeline has a Stop action on the first frame, then all three Movie Clips will continue to play unless there are Stop actions on their first frames or they are told to stop by actions targeted to them. If the Main Timeline plays to frame 20, then instance "A" will no longer be on the Stage, regardless of how many frames it may have on its timeline. A more practical diagram of a timeline hierarchy can be found in Figure 40-2.

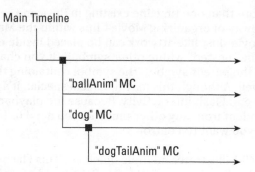

Figure 40-2: Flash movies can be flow-charted in this fashion. This diagram is similar to the new Movie Explorer's method of displaying Flash movie information.

In Figure 40-2, you can see three Movie Clips. Two of them, ballAnim and dog, occupy space on the Main Timeline. The other one, dogTailAnim, is nested within the dog Movie Clip. Each Movie Clip instance on any given timeline needs to have a unique name — you can't have the two Movie Clip instances on the same timeline with the same name. The instance name is specified in the Instance Panel, shown in Figure 40-3.

Figure 40-3: Among other things, the Instance Panel enables you to name each Movie Clip instance that appears on the Stage.

Now that you understand how multiple timelines can exist within a Flash movie, let's see how you can make Movie Clips communicate with one another.

Flash 4 into Flash 5: Targets and Paths Explained

If you already studied Movie Clips in Chapter 31, "Checking Out the Library: Symbols and Instances," you probably know that they provide the solution to our animated face problem. However, you might not have guessed that Movie Clips can also add logic to animation and Flash interfaces. Let's take our animated face example a little further: When people yawn, they generally close their eyes for as long as they are yawning. Our hypothetical character's face may look strange if it is blinking and yawning at the same time. Suppose we wanted to make our character's eyes stay closed during every yawn. We'd have to have some way for the mouth Movie Clip to control the eyes Movie Clip so that we could tell the eyes to go to a "shut" frame when the mouth opens, and then tell them to return to their blink loop again when the mouth closes.

Well, we have a few ways to control the eyes Movie Clip from the mouth Movie Clip. In Flash 3 and 4, the Tell Target action was used to let actions on any timeline (including Movie Clip timelines and the Main Timeline) control what happens on any other timeline. How? Tell Target simply provided a mechanism for extending actions, enabling them to specify (or *target*) the timeline upon which they should be executed. Targets are any Movie Clip instances that are available at any given frame in a Flash movie. In addition to Tell Target, Flash 5 enables you to direct actions to specific timelines by attaching the same actions as methods to the Movie Clip object. If you're new to scripting, please read the "The New and Improved ActionScript" sidebar.

The Tell Target action is a deprecated action; it's still supported in Flash 5, but it's been replaced with more versatile actions and syntax that make its use outdated. For an overview of deprecated actions, see the sidebar in the previous chapter. We show you how to use both Tell Target and Flash 5 methods in this chapter. First, however, you need to understand how targeting works in Flash movies.

The New and Improved ActionScript

Flash 5 has introduced a new method of writing all ActionScripts called *dot syntax*. Earlier versions of Flash used a natural-language scripting environment that was menu-based, in which actions could be read and understood easily and accessed via pop-up menus. While most people prefer easy-to-use scripting environments, the production demands of complex interactive projects are often compromised by such menu-driven scripting environments. Computer programmers prefer to create, edit, and debug scripting with a language that can be accessed and modified easily. Consequently, we see the best of both worlds with Flash 5.

Flash 5 ActionScript adheres closely to the ECMA-262 specification that is based on JavaScript, the universal scripting language used by most browsers for interactive HTML and DHTML documents. Therefore, Flash ActionScript uses a dot syntax. What does that mean? It means that all actions are written within a standard formula that is common with object-oriented programming (OOP) languages:

```
Object.property = value;
```

or

```
Object.method();
```

Continued

Continued

The examples beg four things to be defined: objects, properties, methods, and values. An *object* is any element in a program (in this case, the Flash movie) that has changeable and accessible characteristics. Objects can be user-defined (in other words, you create and name them) or predefined by the programming language. Flash has several predefined Objects, meaning that they're already built into the ActionScript language. We look at both types in more detail in later chapters. An important object (and perhaps the easiest to conceptualize) is the Movie Clip Object. Any Movie Clip instance on the Stage is an object, such as `ballAnim` or `dogTailAnim`. An object has characteristics, or *properties*, that can be updated or changed throughout the movie. An example of a Movie Clip property is scale, which is referred to as `_xscale` and `_yscale`. We look at Movie Clip properties in the next chapter. Properties always have some data accompanying them. This data is called the property's *value*. Using the previous example, at full size, a Movie Clip's `_xscale` is 100 (the scale property uses percent as the unit of measure). For a Movie Clip instance named `ballAnim`, this would be represented in ActionScript syntax as:

```
ballAnim._xscale = 100;
```

Finally, objects can be enacted upon by procedures that do something to or with the object. These procedures are called *methods*. One method for the Movie Clip object is the `gotoAndPlay()` method, which we used as a Basic Action in the previous chapter. In Flash 5, methods can be created for your own objects or predefined for existing Flash objects. Any Basic Action can be attached as a method to any Movie Clip instance, as in:

```
ballAnim.gotoAndPlay("start");
```

The preceding example tells the `ballAnim` Movie Clip to direct its playback head to the frame label `start` on its timeline. This chapter helps you understand how to use the `gotoAndPlay` method for Movie Clips.

Paths: Absolute and relative modes

Earlier in this chapter, you learned how multiple Movie Clip timelines appear on the Flash Stage. It's entirely possible to nest several Movie Clips within another Movie Clip. To understand how Movie Clips communicate with one other by using actions, you need to have a firm grasp on Movie Clip paths. A path is simply that — the route to a destination, an address per se. If you have a Movie Clip instance named dogTailAnim inside a dog Movie Clip instance, how is Flash supposed to know? What if there was one than one dogTailAnim in the entire movie, with others nested in other Movie Clips besides the dog instance? You can specify a Movie Clip's path in an absolute or a relative mode.

An *absolute path* is the full location (or target) information for a given Movie Clip instance from any other location (or target). Just like your postal address has a street name and number and a zip code so that people can find you on a map, all Movie Clips have a point of origin: the Main Timeline (Scene 1). Before Flash 5, the Main Timeline was represented in a Movie Clip path as a starting forward slash (/) character. The absolute path of a Movie Clip instance named dog on the Main Timeline is:

```
/dog
```

Any nested Movie Clips inside of the dog instance would be referenced after that starting path. For example, the absolute path to dogTailAnim, an instance inside the dog Movie Clip instance would be:

```
/dog/dogTailAnim
```

Another / character was put between the two instance names. Think of the / as meaning "from the timeline of," as in dogTailAnim is from the timeline of dog. Use of the / character in Movie Clip paths is known as the *Slashes* notation.

In Flash 5, you can use either the Slashes or *Dots* notation with absolute paths. The Dots notation follows the new ActionScript language conventions. With Dots notation, the Main Timeline becomes:

```
_root
```

Using our previous example, a Movie Clip instance named dog on the Main Timeline (or _root) would have an absolute path of:

```
_root.dog
```

And, following in suit, a Movie Clip instance named dogTailAnim that is nested within the "dog" Movie Clip would have the absolute path of:

```
_root.dog.dogTailAnim
```

Just like Tell Target is considered a deprecated action in Flash 5, the Slashes notation is deprecated syntax. It will still work with the Flash 5 Player, but subsequent versions of the Flash authoring program will be built of the new Dots notation.

A *relative path* is a contextual path to one timeline from another. From a conceptual point of view, think of a relative path as the relationship between the location of your pillow to the rest of your bed. Unless you have an odd sleeping habit, the pillow is located at the head of the bed. You may change the location of the bed within your room or the rooms of a house, but the relationship between the pillow and the bed remains the same.

With Flash, relative Movie Clip paths are useful within movie clips that contain several nested movie clips. That way, you can move the container (or parent) Movie

Clip from one timeline to another, and expect the inner targeting of the nested movie clips to work. As with absolute paths, there are two methods of displaying relative paths: Slashes and Dots notations. To refer to a timeline that is above the current timeline in Slashes notation, use:

```
../
```

The two dots here work just like directory references for files on Web servers; use a pair of .. for each timeline in the hierarchy. You can use relative Slashes notation to refer up and down the hierarchy at the same time. For example, if you have two nested movie clips, such as dogTailAnim and dogPantingAnim, within a larger Movie Clip named dog, you may want to target dogTailAnim from dogPantingAnim. The relative Slashes path for this is:

```
../dogTailAnim
```

This path tells Flash to go up one timeline from dogPantingAnim to the dog timeline, and then look for the instance named dogTailAnim from there.

The relative Dots path for a timeline that is located above the current timeline is:

```
_parent
```

To target one nested Movie Clip from another nested movie clip in the same container Movie Clip instance, you would put the targeted Movie Clip's name after _parent, as in:

```
_parent.dogTailAnim
```

As with absolute paths, we recommend that you become familiar with using the Dots notation for relative paths.

Okay, that's enough theory. We're going to let Colin Moock ease the transition of Flash 4 to Flash 5 targeting by showing how he uses Tell Target and Movie Clips with GWEN!, the star of his online animated series by the same name. (If you want to see more of GWEN! after you've finished the tutorial, you can visit www. moock.org/gwen/.) Note that Colin's material from the previous edition of the Flash Bible has been updated to reflect the Flash 5 look and feel of adding ActionScripts to Movie Clips. We have kept his original procedure intact. In addition to the intrinsic value of his methodology, we're also using this tutorial as an example of one way to migrate Flash 4 content to Flash 5. As you'll see later, though, ActionScript offers new ways to address targets in Flash 5.

On the CD-ROM

To do this tutorial, you need the gwen.fla file in the ch40 folder on the *Flash 5 Bible* CD-ROM. If you want to see the finished product, open gwen-finished.fla located in the same folder.

Expert Tutorial: Making GWEN!'s Eyes Shut When She Yawns, *by Colin Moock*

Colin's tutorial uses the Flash 4–compatible action tellTarget *to enable communication between multiple timelines. If you wish to retain backward compatibility with Flash 4, then you cannot use Dots notation to enable actions of Movie Clips (for example,* _root. mcName.gotoAndStop() *will not work in the Flash 4 Player). While you can use the Dots notation as the path name to a Movie Clip instance, you will need to use* tellTarget *if you're "targeting" a Flash 4 audience.*

GWEN! was born as a Flash 2 animation. In Episode One, she didn't blink much, or yawn at all. By the time Episode Two was nearly finished, Flash 3 had hit the streets, and oh, the joy to GWEN! when she discovered Movie Clips and Tell Target. Now, after much convincing, GWEN! has agreed to be dismantled a little so that you can see how her eyes and mouth work. We're going to show you how to put her back together in this tutorial. Don't worry, GWEN!, this won't hurt a bit.

Begin by opening gwen.fla (it's in the ch40 folder on the *Flash 5 Bible* CD-ROM). Open the Library for gwen.fla by choosing Window ➪ Library. In the Library, are five symbols and one folder: gwen's face, gwen's eyes, gwen's eyes shut, gwen's mouth, gwen's mouth open, and the folder face artwork. Drag a copy of the gwen's face graphic symbol, shown in the following figure, from the Library onto the Stage.

Gwen's face graphic symbol

Next we're going to make a Movie Clip with GWEN!'s eyes blinking. Make a new Movie Clip by choosing Insert ➪ New Symbol. In the Symbol Properties dialog, enter the name **eyes** and keep the Movie Clip option of the Behavior setting, as shown in the following figure. Click OK.

Continued

Continued

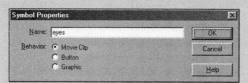

Enter the name of the Symbol and leave
the Behavior option set to Movie Clip.

When you create a new Movie Clip symbol, you are automatically taken into Symbol Editing
Mode where you work on your Movie Clip. Rename Layer 1 to **Eyes Blinking**. Click Frame
24 of the Eyes Blinking layer, and then select Insert ⇨ Frame. While still on Frame 24, select
Insert ⇨ Blank Keyframe. You can add a blank keyframe to frame 24 by selecting it and
pressing the F7 key (see the following figure).

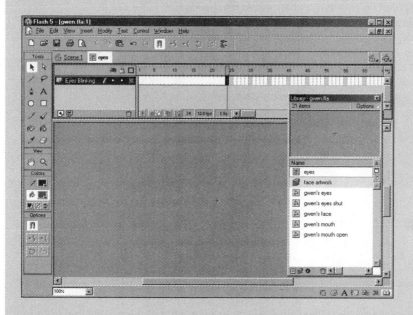

Click Frame 1 and drag the symbol gwen's eyes onto the Stage. Make sure gwen's eyes is
still selected, and then open the Align Panel (Ctrl+K/Command+K). Center the symbol on
the Stage by clicking To Stage, and then clicking the middle button in the left and right sets
of the Align buttons, shown in the following figure.

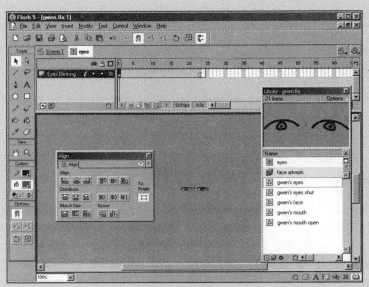

The new Align Panel features a To Stage button, along with the familiar Align Modes.

Click Frame 24 and drag the symbol gwen's eyes shut onto the Stage. Center the symbol on Stage as you did in the previous step.

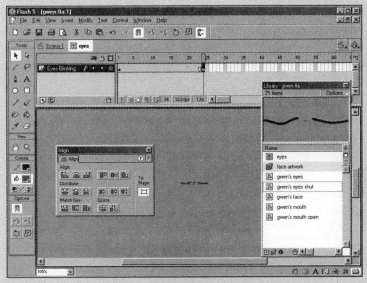

Drag the symbol gwen's eyes shut onto the Stage.

Continued

Continued

Next we need to label our eyes shut frame so that we can move to it whenever GWEN!'s mouth opens. Add a new layer by choosing Insert ➪ Layer. Name the new layer **Labels**. Labels should always be kept on their own layer. Click Frame 24 of the Labels layer, and then select Insert ➪ Blank Keyframe (or press F7). Open the Frame Panel by choosing Modify ➪ Frame (Ctrl+F or Command+F). In the Label text field, type **shut** (as in the following figure). Make sure you press Enter or Return after typing any frame label name to make sure it "sticks" to the current frame.

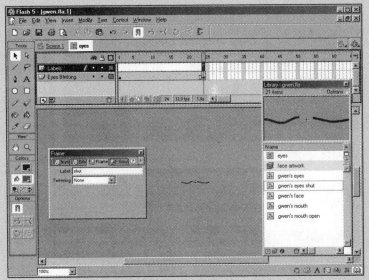

It's better to refer to frame labels (rather than frame numbers) in any Go To actions.

We're done with the eyes, so let's make the mouth. Make a new Movie Clip by choosing Insert ➪ New Symbol. In the Symbol Properties dialog, enter the name **mouth** and select the Movie Clip option of the Behavior setting, as shown in the following figure. Click OK.

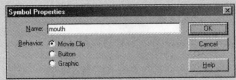

Name the symbol and select the Movie Clip option.

As with the eyes, you are automatically taken into Symbol Editing Mode for your new Movie Clip. Rename Layer 1 to **Mouth Yawning**, as in the following figure. Click Frame 180 of the Mouth Yawning layer, and then select Insert ➪ Frame. Click Frame 160 and select Insert ➪ Blank Keyframe.

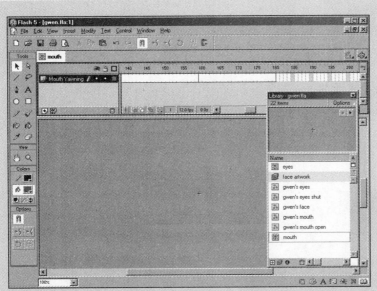

Get in the habit of giving yourself a timeline "workspace" with many frames to prepare your Flash content.

Click Frame 1 and drag the symbol "gwen's mouth" onto the Stage. Make sure "gwen's mouth" is still selected, and then open the Align Panel. Center the symbol on the Stage as you did with previous symbol instances.

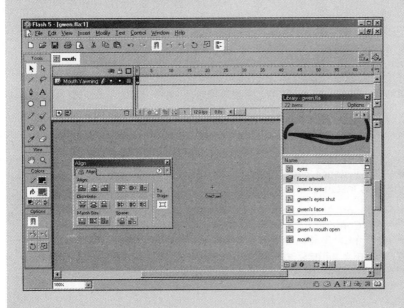

Continued

Continued

Click Frame 160 and drag the symbol. Center the symbol on Stage with the Align Panel, shown in the following figure.

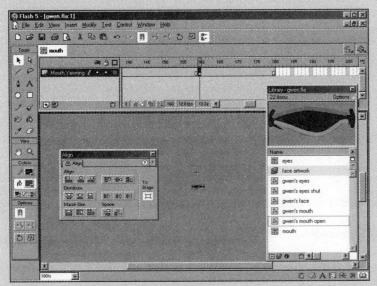

Drag gwen's mouth open onto the Stage and use the Align Panel to center the symbol.

It's time to place our eyes and mouth onto GWEN!'s face. Return to the main stage by choosing Edit ⇨ Edit Movie (Ctrl+E or Command+E). Create two new layers, and name them **eyes** and **mouth**. Drag the newly created Movie Clip symbols, eyes and mouth, out of the Library onto GWEN!'s face, as shown in the following figure. Make sure you select their respective layer before dragging each onto the Stage.

At this point, you have a functional animated girl. If you test your movie now, you'll see that GWEN!'s eyes blink, and her mouth opens for her yawn, but we still have to add the interactivity that lets the mouth tell the eyes when to shut and reopen. To do that, we first have to name the instance of the eyes Movie Clip you created and dragged onto the Stage so that the mouth Movie Clip instance can identify it. Then we have to add the Tell Target actions that control the eyes instance. Hang on GWEN!, we're almost there!

Select the eyes Movie Clip on Stage, and then open the Instance Panel by choosing Modify ⇨ Instance (Ctrl+I or Command+I). In the Instance Panel, you see a text field next to Name (see the following figure). That text field is where we give our Movie Clip instance a unique identification. Instance names are something like serial numbers—they enable actions in the movie to address a specific copy of a Movie Clip. Type **her-eyes** in the Name text field, and then press Enter or Return.

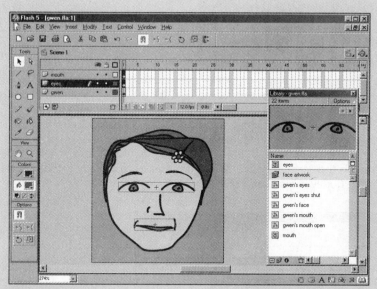

Drag the eyes and mouth symbols out of the Library and onto
GWEN!'s face.

Remember that, like any symbol, a Movie Clip that is placed on Stage is only a reference to
the symbol in the Library. That's why you name the symbol instance on the Stage, rather
than simply referring to the symbol by name in the Library. You could place multiple copies
of GWEN!'s eyes on the Stage and give them all different names so that each could be individually controlled and manipulated without any effect on the others. With eyes, the results
can be a little trippy . . . look at Episode Two of GWEN! at www.moock.org/gwen/.

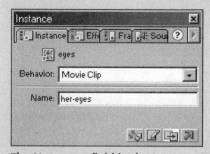

The Name text field in the Instance Panel

Now that the eyes Movie Clip instance is named her-eyes, we can return to the mouth to
add the Tell Targets that control the her-eyes instance. Deselect all selections by clicking in
a blank area of the Stage. Now, select only the mouth symbol. Choose Edit ⇨ Edit Selected
to resume work on the mouth Movie Clip. Add a new layer by choosing Insert ⇨ Layer.
Name the new layer **Actions**. Actions should always be kept on their own layer.

Continued

Continued

Author's Note: You can also deselect all selections by pressing the Esc key.

Click Frame 160 of the Actions layer, and then select Insert ⇨ Blank Keyframe. Open the Frame Actions Panel by double-clicking frame 160 or by right-clicking (Ctrl+clicking on Mac) the frame and selecting Actions from the contextual menu. Click the plus (+) button at the upper left of the Frame Actions Panel, shown in the following figure, select the Basic Actions menu item, and then select Tell Target. In the parameters area of the Actions Panel, find the Target text field and type **/her-eyes**. Now every Action we add between the `tellTarget` (`"/herEyes"`){ line and the } closing line in the Actions list is applied to the Movie Clip instance named her-eyes on the Main Timeline. We're now ready to add the action that controls the playback of the her-eyes instance.

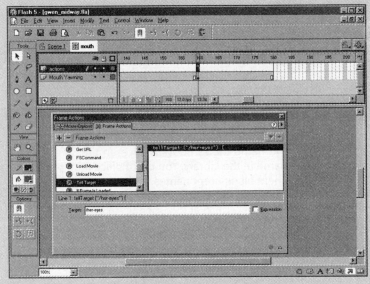

Frame Actions Panel

With the line `tellTarget("/her-eyes"){` highlighted in the actions list, click the plus (+) button, select the Basic Actions menu item, and select Go To. In the parameters area, select the Frame Label option in the Type drop-down menu, and type **shut** in the Frame text field. This makes the her-eyes instance playhead move to the shut frame label and stay there until told otherwise. Make sure that you uncheck the Go to and Play option, as shown in the following figure.

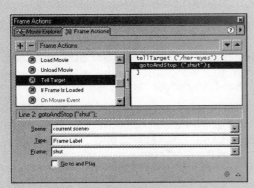

Frame Actions Panel with the parameters area
displayed

The Actions list should now read as follows:

```
tellTarget ("/her-eyes"){
    gotoAndStop ("shut");
}
```

Click Frame 180 of the actions layer, and select Insert ⇨ Blank Keyframe. Again, open the
Frame Actions Panel by double-clicking frame 180. Click the plus (+) button at the upper
left of the Frame Actions Panel, select the Basic Actions menu item, and then select Tell
Target. In the Target text field type **/her-eyes** (as in the following figure). With the line
`tellTarget("/her-eyes"){` highlighted in the Actions list, click the plus (+) button and
select Play from the Basic Actions menu. This will make the eyes resume their two-second
blink loop.

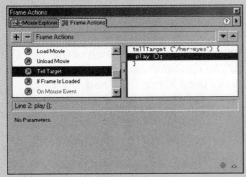

This simple tellTarget action nest will tell the
her-eyes instance to play.

Continued

Continued

That's it. Test your movie with File ⇨ Publish Preview ⇨ Flash, or by using Control ⇨ Test Movie (Ctrl+Enter or Command+Enter). You should now see GWEN!'s eyes close when she yawns. If things aren't working perfectly, compare your work closely with the finished version of GWEN!, called gwen-finished.fla, in the ch40 folder of the *Flash 5 Bible* CD-ROM.

A final hint: Tell Targets can be a little finicky — always be sure to check your target names and instance names to be sure that they match, that they are in the correct location, and that they are referred to correctly. You may make a few mistakes at first, but it won't be long before you'll know where to look to find the cause of the most common problems. Oh, and if you want to play with GWEN! some more, visit her at www.moock.org/gwen/. She's kind of snooty, but you never know . . . she might pay more attention to you now that you've seen how she works. Don't forget to pinch her cheeks.

Although we asked Colin Moock the same questions that we asked the other tutorialists, Colin won the prize for the fewest, most evasive answers. He first encountered Flash when, "Futurewave mailed it to me as a trial while I was working at Softquad (makers of Hotmetal Pro)." When we inquired, what was the most memorable movie or song in the year that he graduated from high school, Colin replied, "Can't remember." When we explained that we are doing a media-date thing this time, rather than spell out the ages of all the contributors, he insisted, "Honestly, I didn't really watch movies or listen to hit songs at the time." So, we have little information to give you about Colin Moock; except that he lives in Toronto, is highly regarded among the Flasheratti, and that he has worked on many Flash sites, most notably: www.moock.org/webdesign/portfolio and www.moock.org/webdesign/flash/sandbox.

Using Tell Target and Movie Clips with interfaces

GWEN! is an example of using Tell Target to create enhanced animation. However, the same technique can also be used to produce interfaces. Interface-based Tell Targets are often implemented on buttons. Just as you used Tell Targets with actions on keyframes in Colin's tutorial, so can you also use Tell Targets with actions on buttons. While working at ICE during the spring of 1999, Colin produced much of the interactive component of McClelland and Stewart's *The Canadian Encyclopedia 1999* CD-ROM in Flash. Most of the interactive pieces used Movie Clips and Tell Targets extensively. A simple but good example of using Tell Targets to enhance an interface comes from the Painting Retrospective in the encyclopedia as seen in Figure 40-4.

Figure 40-4 depicts the Painting Retrospective in action. Painting thumbnails are shown on a carousel that the user moves by clicking the right and left arrows. Below the carousel is a status window that displays the painting title, date, and artist when the user rolls their mouse over a painting. The status window is a Movie Clip that has one frame for each of the painting descriptions. The painting thumbnails in the carousel are all buttons. When the user points to a painting, the button's Roll Over event handler initiates a Tell Target action that makes the status window Movie Clip go to the frame that contains the appropriate painting description. Even when the paintings are moved along the carousel, the status window stays put because it's a separate Movie Clip, not a part of the thumbnail buttons.

Targeting Movie Clips in Flash 5

With Flash 5's new ActionScript syntax comes a new way to target and control movie clips. In the last section, you learned about the difference between the Slashes and Dots notations for absolute and relative paths. In Colin's tutorial, you learned how to use the Slashes notation with the Tell Target action to control movie clips. Now, you'll see how to make Movie Clips interact with one another with the Dots notation and Flash 5 ActionScript.

 Caution   If you want your Flash movies to retain compatibility with the Flash 4 Player, then you need to use Tell Target actions. The methods described in this section will only work with Flash 5 Player and subsequent releases of it.

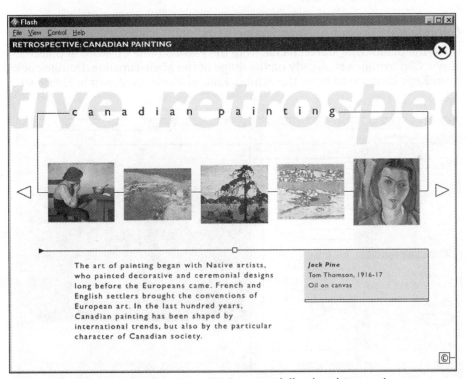

Figure 40-4: The Painting Retrospective from McClelland and Stewart's *The Canadian Encyclopedia 1999*

Using Movie Clips to create Sound Libraries

In Chapters 36 through 38, the ins and outs of sound import and use in Flash movies was discussed. In this chapter, we show you to create sound Movie Clips that are nested within a larger Sound Library Movie Clip. With Sound Library Movie Clips, you can transport sets of sounds easily between timelines and other Flash movies. In this section, you learn the importance of:

✦ Consistent timeline structure

✦ Naming conventions for Movie Clip instances

✦ Nested Movie Clip instances

✦ Streamlining Movie Clip production

These production principles are rather straightforward, and relatively simple to learn.

On the CD-ROM

You'll find sound files (.WAV and .AIFF) in the ch40 folder of the *Flash 5 Bible* CD-ROM. You can use the pianoKeys_starter.fla file or one of your own Flash movies for this exercise.

Overview of the pianoKeys Movie Clip

Open the pianoKeys_starter.fla file from the *Flash 5 Bible* CD-ROM. A pianoKeys Movie Clip instance is already on the Stage of the Main Timeline. Double-click the pianoKeys instance to enter the Symbol Editing Mode, as shown in Figure 40-5.

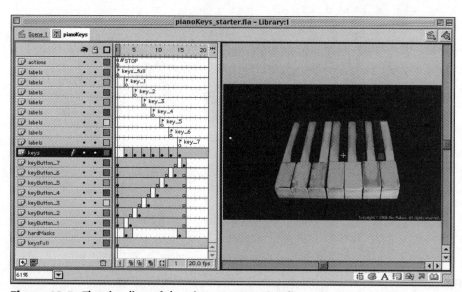

Figure 40-5: The timeline of the pianoKeys Movie Clip

The timeline for pianoKeys has several layers, with Button instances and Label layers. If you test this movie using Control ➪ Test Movie (Ctrl+Enter or Command+Enter), you'll see that the Button instances over each piano key will tell the playback head of the pianoKeys timeline to go to that key's frame label. For the first key on the left, the button on layer keyButton_1 has the following action list:

```
on (press, keyPress "a") {
    gotoAndStop ("key_1");
}
on (rollOver) {
    gotoAndStop ("keys_full");
}
```

These actions don't use any Tell Target actions — they are simple navigation actions that you learned in the last chapter. When the keyButton_1 Button instance is clicked with the mouse, the playback head moves to the key_1 label on the current timeline, which is the pianoKeys timeline. Unless targeting is used, all actions on a Button instance will target the timeline on which the Button exists.

When the timeline goes to the key_1 frame label, a new .PNG bitmap of a "pressed" piano key (key_01.png on the keys layer) appears on top of the pianoKeys_full.png bitmap that is placed on the bottom keysFull layer. Note that the pianoKeys_full.png bitmap is present throughout the entire pianoKeys timeline. Each Button instance in the pianoKeys Movie Clip sends the playback head to the appropriate piano key frame label.

Now that you have an understanding of what's happening in this Movie Clip, let's create some sound Movie Clips that the pianoKeys instance can target.

Making sound Movie Clips

Before we start making new Movie Clip symbols, we need to establish *a naming convention* for our sounds. A naming convention is simply a way of consistently identifying components in any project, in or out of Flash. As a member of a Web production team, the importance of naming conventions can not be overemphasized — everyone involved with the project should know how to give names to images, sounds, symbol names, instance names, and so on. Even if you work by yourself, a naming convention provides a system of integrating elements from project to project, and enables you to identify elements much more easily when you open old files.

1. For each key on the piano, we'll make a unique sound. Each sound will be on its own timeline where it can be targeted to play. Because there are seven keys on the piano, we need to import seven sounds into Flash. Using File ➪ Import, locate the ch40 folder on the *Flash 5 Bible* CD-ROM. Import each of the key sounds (.AIFF or .WAV) into your Flash movie.

Cross-Reference Imported sounds do not show up on the timeline — they go straight into the movie's Library. If you need to know how to import sound files into Flash, refer to Chapter 37, "Importing and Editing Sounds in Flash."

2. Create a new Movie Clip symbol (Insert ⇨ New Symbol) and give it the name **sound_1**, as shown in Figure 40-6. This Movie Clip's timeline will be dedicated to the key_1 sound that you imported in the previous step.

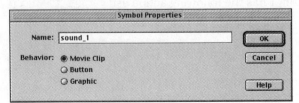

Figure 40-6: The Symbol Properties dialog with the Movie Clip behavior selected

3. Flash will automatically move you into the Symbol Editing Mode for the sound_1 Movie Clip symbol. Rename Layer 1 to **labels** and make a new layer called **sound**. On the labels layer, we need to establish three "states" or positions for the sound: no sound, initiate sound, and mute sound. Why? Remember that all Movie Clips will try to play as soon as they appear on a timeline. So, we need to make sure there's nothing on the first frame (no sound state). For the remaining two states, add two frame labels: one called **start** on frame 3, and another called **mute** on frame 15 (see Figure 40-7). Make sure that you add these labels to unique keyframes — if you try to add a label to a regular frame, the label will be attached to an earlier keyframe. Add an empty frame (F5) on frame 30 for both the labels and sound layers.

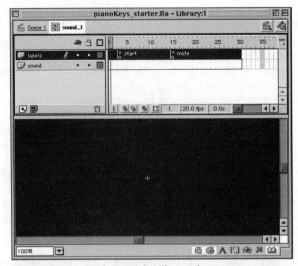

Figure 40-7: Each sound will use the same structure as the sound_1 Movie Clip: an empty first frame and two labels for starting a sound and stopping a sound.

4. Add an empty keyframe (F6) on frame 3 of the sound layer. With that frame selected, open the Sound Panel (Window ➪ Panels ➪ Sound), and select the key_1.aif (or key_1.wav) sound from the Sound drop-down menu. Leave the Sync setting at Event so that multiple instances of the key_1 sound can overlap (play on top of one another). See Figure 40-8 for reference.

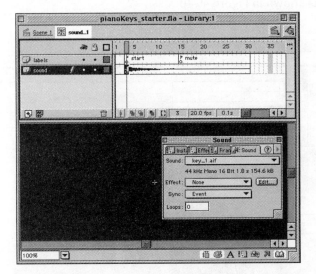

Figure 40-8: When the start label is played on the sound_1 timeline, the key_1 sound will play.

5. Repeat Step 4 for frame 15 on the sound layer. This time, however, change the Sync setting to Stop, as shown in Figure 40-9. When this keyframe is played, all instances of the sound key_1 will stop playing.

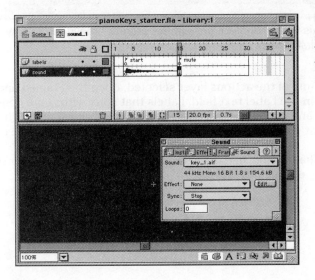

Figure 40-9: Whenever the Stop Sync setting is selected, the sound graphic on the timeline will appear as a short blue line.

6. Now we need to add some Stop actions to the timeline. Because we want each sound Movie Clip to play each time its respective key is pressed, we need to make sure playback from one action doesn't run into the timeline space of other labels. Add a new layer called **actions** and move it above the other two layers. Double-click its first frame to open the Actions Panel. Select the **Stop** action from the Basic Actions booklet, and drag it to the right pane of the Actions Panel, as shown in Figure 40-10.

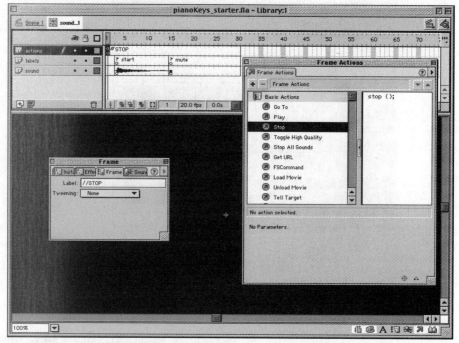

Figure 40-10: This Stop action will prevent the sound's timeline from playing when the Flash movie first loads.

7. With the first frame of the actions layer selected, open the Frame Panel and type **//stop** in the Label text field. Labels that start with // are considered comments and cannot be targeted like ordinary frame labels. The //stop comment gives you a quick indication of what this keyframe does.

Note   Many thanks to Shane Elliott, one of the technical editors of this book, for sharing his //stop frame comment technique.

8. Copy the Stop keyframe on frame 1 by selecting the keyframe and pressing Ctrl+Alt+C (Option+Command+C). You can also right-click (Ctrl+click) the keyframe and select Copy Frames from the contextual menu. Then, select frame 10 of the actions layer and press Ctrl+Alt+V (or Option+Command+V) to paste the Stop keyframe. Repeat for frame 20. The placement of these Stop actions is a bit arbitrary—we only need to stop the playhead from playing into labels that occur later in the timeline. When you're finished with this step, your timeline should resemble the one shown in Figure 40-11.

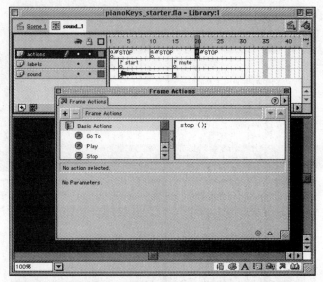

Figure 40-11: These Stop actions will keep each area of the timeline from playing into the others.

9. Next, we add an icon to this Movie Clip so that it can be seen on the Stage. Make a new layer and name it **icon**. On its first frame, draw a white rectangle. Then, use the Text Tool to add the text **Sound** (with a black fill color) on top of the rectangle. Select both items and align them to the center of the Stage using the Align Panel. With both items still selected, choose Insert ⇨ Convert to Symbol (F8). In the Symbol Properties dialog, name the symbol **soundIcon**, and select the **Graphic** Behavior, as shown in Figure 40-12. Click OK.

10. Add keyframes for the soundIcon Graphic instance on frames 3, 10, 15, and 20 of the icon layer, as shown in Figure 40-13.

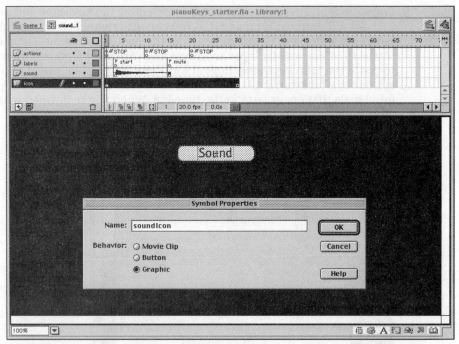

Figure 40-12: The soundIcon will provide a visual representation for this sound on the Stage.

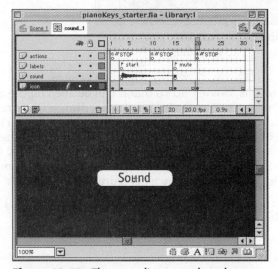

Figure 40-13: The soundIcon needs to have dedicated instances for each state of the sound_1 timeline.

11. Select the instance of soundIcon on frame 3, and open the Effect Panel. Choose the Advanced option from the drop-down menu, and type **255** in the second column text field for the **Green** color channel (see Figure 40-14).

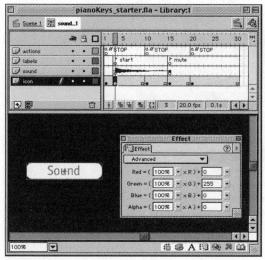

Figure 40-14: When the sound_1 timeline reaches the start label, the soundIcon will turn green.

12. Repeat Step 11 for the instance of soundIcon on frame 15. This time, however, type **255** in the **Red** color channel (see Figure 40-15). This step completes the first sound Movie Clip.

Now, we need to repeat this process for key sounds 2 through 7 — but don't worry! Because we created a coherent structure for the sound_1 timeline, creating the other Movie Clips will be relatively painless.

13. Open the movie's Library (Ctrl+L or Command+L). Right-click (Ctrl+click) the sound_1 Movie Clip and choose Duplicate from the contextual menu (see Figure 40-16).

14. Name the new Movie Clip copy **sound_2**, and make sure that the Movie Clip behavior is selected. Click OK.

15. Double-click the sound_2 Movie Clip in the Library to edit this symbol's time-line. Remember that we're no longer working on the sound_1 timeline.

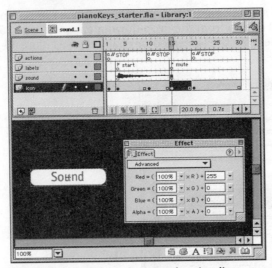

Figure 40-15: When the sound_1 timeline reaches the mute label, the soundIcon will turn red.

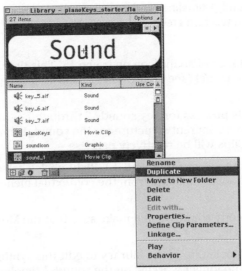

Figure 40-16: You can access many options by right-clicking (Ctrl+clicking) Symbols in the Library.

16. Select frame 3 of the sound layer, and open the Sound Panel (shown in Figure 40-17). Choose key_2.aif (or key_2.wav) from the Sound drop-down menu. Leave all other settings the same.

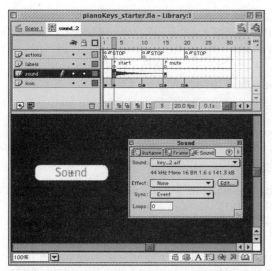

Figure 40-17: In Step 16, you're changing the sound that will be played back on the sound_2 timeline.

17. Repeat Step 16 for frame 15 of the sound layer (see Figure 40-18).

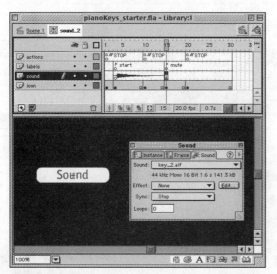

Figure 40-18: In Step 17, you're changing the sound that will be muted to key_2.aif (or key_2.wav).

That's it! You can now easily create the remaining sound Movie Clips (3 through 7) by repeating Steps 13 through 17 and incrementing the Movie Clip's name by one number each time. When you've finished creating all seven sound Movie Clips, you're ready to create a Sound Library Movie Clip.

On the CD-ROM   You can refer to the pianoKeys_starter_sounds.fla file located in the ch40 folder of the *Flash 5 Bible* CD-ROM. This file has the seven sound Movie Clips in the Library, sorted in the keySounds folder.

Nesting sounds into a Sound Library Movie Clip

We have seven sound Movie Clips all ready to go, but we need somewhere to put them on the Stage. It's feasible to place each sound Movie Clip on the Main Timeline's Stage, but your Stage will start to get cluttered if many Symbols populate that space. So, we'll make a Movie Clip container for all those sounds. We refer to a container for sounds as a Sound Library, or soundLib for short.

1. Create a new Symbol by choosing Insert ➪ New Symbol (Ctrl+F8 or Command +F8). Name the symbol **soundLib** and give it a Movie Clip behavior. Click OK. The Stage switches to Symbol Editing Mode for the soundLib Movie Clip timeline.

2. Rename the first layer to **sound_1** and drag an instance of the sound_1 Movie Clip to the Stage. Open the Instance Panel and give the name **sound_1** to the instance, as shown in Figure 40-19.

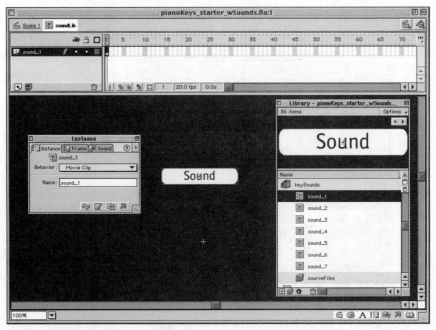

Figure 40-19: The sound_1 instance on the soundLib timeline

Note For consistency, it's not a bad idea to give your instance (and the layer it occupies) the same name as its parent symbol in the Library. If the sound is not going to be replicated on the same timeline more than once, then you won't have any targeting issues. It makes it simpler to match up instances with their symbols in the Library as well.

3. Create six more layers in the soundLib Movie Clip, named **sound_2** through **sound_7**. Drag an instance of each remaining sound Movie Clip onto its respective layer. Make sure that you name each instance after its symbol in the Library, just as you did in Step 2. Place each instance on the Stage from top to bottom, with the sound_1 instance at the top (see Figure 40-20 for reference). Use the Align Panel to center the instances horizontally and to space them evenly.

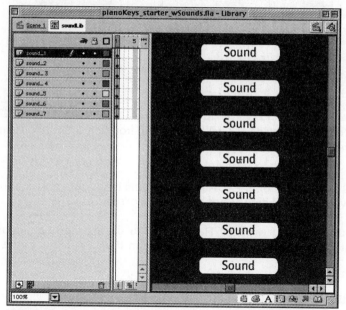

Figure 40-20: The soundLib timeline contains all seven sounds as individual instances.

4. Go to the Scene 1 timeline (the Main Timeline). Create a new layer called **soundLib**. Place an instance of the soundLib Movie Clip on the first frame of the soundLib layer. Give the instance the name **soundLib** in the Instance Panel, as shown in Figure 40-21. You may need to resize the soundLib instance so that it fits on the Stage.

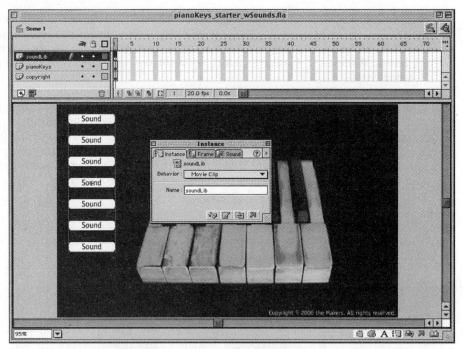

Figure 40-21: The sound Movie Clips will be accessed from the soundLib instance on the Main Timeline.

Our Sound Library is now complete. All that remains is to add actions to our pianoKeys Movie Clip to target the sounds in the correct order.

On the CD-ROM You can compare your working Flash movie to the finished Sound Library in the pianoKeys_starter_soundLib.fla file, located in the ch40 folder of the *Flash 5 Bible*.

Targeting sounds with ActionScript syntax

Now you have a Movie Clip instance called soundLib along with the instance pianoKeys, both located on the Main Timelime. Instead of using the Tell Target action, we show you how to use the Movie Clip Object in ActionScript. You may want to the review the sidebar "The New and Improved ActionScript" earlier in this chapter before you proceed. The remainder of this exercise shows you how to add Flash 5 actions to the pianoKeys timeline that will target the sounds in the Sound Library.

Note There will be more than one actions layer in this timeline. The actions layer in Step 1 is a new layer in addition to the existing actions layer (with the //stop comment).

1. Enter the Symbol Editing Mode by double-clicking the pianoKeys instance in Scene 1. On its timeline, add a new layer and name it **actions**. Move this new actions layer underneath the layer that contains the key_1 frame label, as shown in Figure 40-22.

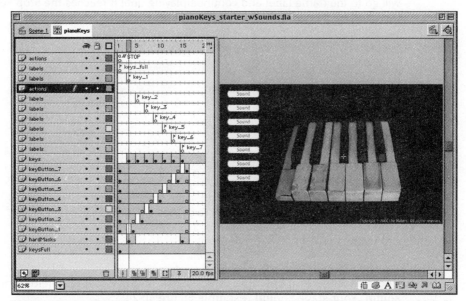

Figure 40-22: Don't be afraid to keep information separated on actions and labels layers. Separating the information will make it much easier for you to access the appropriate sections of your timelines.

2. On frame 3 of the new actions layer, we need to add actions that will play the first sound in our Sound Library. Remember that the button Instances on the pianoKeys timeline already move the playback head to each key's label. Insert a blank keyframe (F7) on frame 3.

3. Double-click the keyframe to open the Actions Panel. In the panel's options menu (located in the right corner), switch to Expert Mode (Ctrl+E or Command+E). Click the Actions list area of the panel (on the right side), and type the following ActionScript:

```
_root.soundLib.sound_1.gotoAndPlay("start");
```

See the Actions Panel in Figure 40-23 for reference. This code looks at the Main Timeline (_root), and then looks for a Movie Clip named soundLib. Then, it tells the timeline of sound_1 instance inside of soundLib to move the playback head from the stopped first frame to the start label keyframe.

Note   For the sound to play more than once, we use the `gotoAndPlay()` action instead of the `gotoAndStop()` action. If a timeline goes to and stops on a keyframe, any other actions that tell the timeline to go to the same keyframe won't work. Why? Because the playback head is already on that frame, it doesn't need to go anywhere. By using `gotoAndPlay()`, the playback head on the sound_1 timeline will go to the frame label and continue playing until it reaches the Stop keyframe just after the frame label.

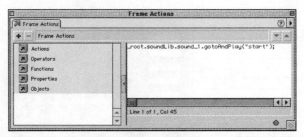

Figure 40-23: This one line of ActionScript is equivalent to the three lines of code using Tell Target (as in, `tellTarget("/soundLib/sound_1"){gotoAndPlay ("start");}`).

4. Click the Stage, and open the Frame Panel. In the Label text field, type **//play sound**. Your stage should resemble Figure 40-24.

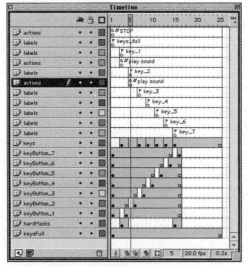

Figure 40-24: The //play sound comment lets you know what the actions on this keyframe do.

At this point, you will want to test your movie to see if the action is finding the target and playing the sound. Save your movie, and use Control ➪ Test Movie to create a .SWF movie. Make sure that the action on the keyframe works, and that you hear a sound. Notice that you'll also see the soundIcon Graphic change to green when you hit the first key.

5. Now, we need to enable all the other sounds in the soundLib instance. Create a new layer and name it **actions**. Place the new layer underneath the label layer that contains the key_2 frame label. Copy the //play sound keyframe from the previous actions layer, using the method described in Step 8 of the "Making Sound Movie Clips" section. Then, paste the copied keyframe to the new actions layer, on frame 5.

6. Double-click the new //play sound keyframe underneath the key_2 frame label layer. In the Actions Panel, we need to change the sound's target to sound_2:

```
_root.soundLib.sound_2.gotoAndPlay("start");
```

See Figure 40-25 for reference.

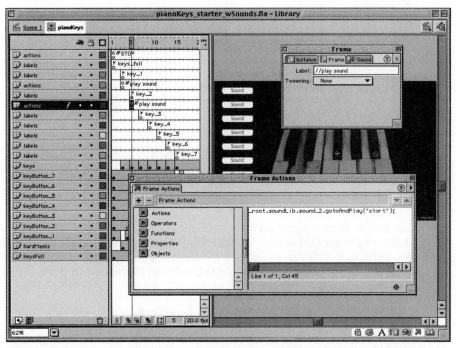

Figure 40-25: This timeline has enabled two sounds from the Sound Library.

7. Repeat Steps 5 and 6, for each key and sound. Each key_ frame label should have its own actions layer with a //play sound keyframe. When you're finished with this task, your pianoKeys timeline should resemble the one shown in Figure 40-26. Test your movie each time you add a new keyframe with Action Script. If a particular key doesn't work, then check two things: the target's name in the ActionScript, and the instance name of the sound in the soundLib Movie Clip. Most errors occur as a result of not naming a Movie Clip instance.

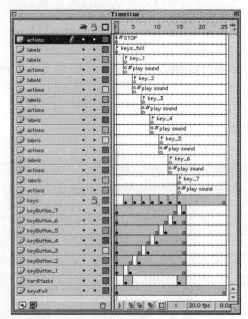

Figure 40-26: The completed pianoKeys timeline

When you've finished adding frame actions for every key, save the movie and test it. After all's been said and done, you should have a functional Flash piano that plays a sound whenever you click a piano key. If you want to change the sounds, you can either update the sound file in the Flash Library or import new ones.

How Movie Clips can add logic to a movie

A not-so-obvious yet significant aspect to Movie Clips is that they do not need to have any content in them. They can be used solely as empty devices that instigate interactive behavior. A Movie Clip can be just a string of empty frames with only Labels and Actions. Tell Targets from other timelines can move the playhead of empty Movie Clips in order to achieve basic levels of memory and logic in a Flash movie. We refer to these empty Movie Clips as *Logical Movie Clips*. An example of interactivity with a Logical Movie Clip is keeping score in a simple game.

Suppose you have a movie consisting of three true-or-false questions with a true button and a false button for each question. The user answers each question by clicking one or the other button. You also have a Logical Movie Clip with four keyframes. The first frame has a Stop action on it. The last frame has a Tell Target action on it that tells the main movie timeline to go to a keyframe that has a congratulations message. Finally, all the "correct" answer buttons have Tell Target actions that tell the Logical Movie Clip to go to the next frame. Here's what happens when the user plays and gets all the questions right: question one, the user clicks the correct button, and the Logical Movie Clip moves to frame 2; question two, the user clicks the correct button, and the Logical Movie Clip moves to frame 3 and so on. When the user gets to frame 4, the last frame of the Logical Movie Clip, it tells the Main Timeline to go to the congratulations frame, which says, "Congratulations, you got a perfect score!" So, what happens if the user gets a question wrong? Well, when the user gets any of the questions wrong, the Logical Movie Clip does not advance, so by the end of the game, the playhead never reaches frame 4, and the Tell Target action that causes the congratulations message to be displayed is not executed.

Tricks such as the score keeper were common tools for Flash 3 developers. Using Logical Movie Clips, inventive developers produced impressive results — even a primitive version of Pac Man exists as a Flash 3 movie (see www.spookyand thebandit.com/ for the game and to download the free .FLA file). However, now that Flash 4 and 5 movies support variables and scriptable Movie Clip properties, those kinds of Movie Clip uses are less important. Nevertheless, conceptually, it's useful to understand that Movie Clips can serve as more than just devices for embedded animation. They can also serve as containers for meta-information stored in movies.

Summary

✦ Movie Clips are the key to Flash interactivity. Each Movie Clip has its own independent timeline and playback.

✦ Each Movie Clip instance needs a unique name on any given timeline. You cannot reuse the same name on other movie clips on a timeline. You can, however, use the same instance name on different timelines.

✦ There are two types of target paths for Movie Clips: absolute and relative. Absolute paths start from the Main Timeline and end with the targeted instance name. Relative paths start from the timelines that's issuing the action(s) and end with the targeted instance name.

✦ The Slashes and Dots notations are formats for writing either absolute or relative paths. The Slashes notation is considered deprecated, and should be avoided unless you are authoring for Flash 4 or earlier players. The Dots notation is new to Flash 5 and has a more complete syntax for programming in ActionScript.

✦ The Tell Target action can be used to control Movie Clip playback in all Flash Players, while the Movie Clip Object method introduced with the new version of ActionScript works only in Flash 5 or later players.

✦ All movie clips and Flash movie elements should adhere to a naming convention.

✦ The use of a Sound Library Movie Clip enables you to store sounds in one area, and target them from others. Sounds used in a Sound Library can be updated easily, and reused in other Flash movies.

✦   ✦   ✦

Controlling
Movie Clips

In the previous chapter, we established the key role that
Movie Clips have within the Flash movie structure. By
having a timeline that plays separately from other timelines,
Movie Clips enable multiple events to occur — independently
or as part of an interaction with other Movie Clips. This chapter explores how to manipulate movie clips beyond navigation
actions such as `gotoAndPlay` or `stop`.

Movie Clips: The Object Overview

Flash 5's implementation of ActionScript mirrors true object-
oriented programming languages. Much like JavaScript, each
element in a Flash movie has a data type. A data type is simply a category to which an element belongs. According to the
Flash 5 documentation, there are five data types available:
Boolean, number, string, object, and Movie Clip. For our purposes, the Movie Clip *is* an object, and we'll refer to it as such
throughout the remainder of the book. An object is any element in Flash 5 that has changeable and accessible characteristics *through ActionScript*. Objects can be user-defined (you
create and name them) or predefined by the programming language. The Movie Clip Object is a predefined object, meaning
that all of its characteristics are already described in the
ActionScript language.

Cross-Reference For a brief overview of object-oriented programming con-
cepts, please review the sidebar titled *The New and
Improved ActionScript* located in Chapter 40, "Navigating
Flash Timelines."

A Movie Clip Object is the same Movie Clip instance we've seen in previous chapters. Any instance of a Movie Clip is a unique object in ActionScript. However, we haven't treated it like an object in our scripting. Before we can proceed with a discussion of Movie Clips as Flash movie assets, you need to understand what predefined characteristics are available in the Movie Clip Object. See Figure 41-1 for more information.

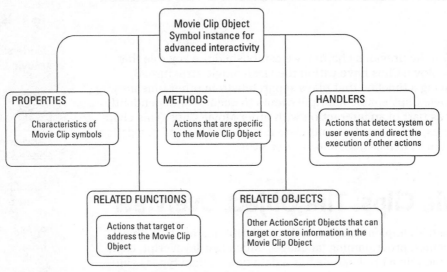

Figure 41-1: An overview of the Movie Clip Object

Movie Clip properties

Each Movie Clip instance has definable properties, or attributes, that control its appearance, size, and position. For example, you can move a Movie Clip instance to a new position on the Stage by changing the value of its X or Y coordinate. This property in ActionScript is denoted as _x or _y, respectively. Some properties have values that are read-only, meaning that these values can't be altered. One read-only property is _url, the value of which indicates the download location of the Movie Clip (or .SWF file) such as http://www.yourserver.com/swf/background.swf. Figure 41-2 is a summary of the properties of the Movie Clip Object. For more information on each property, please refer to Table 41-1.

All properties are preceded by the underscore (_) character. In Table 41-1, each property has an "R" (as in "read") and/or "W" (as in "write") designation. All properties can be read, which means that you can retrieve that property's current value. In Flash 4, these properties were retrieved using the getProperty action. The values of some properties can also be changed, through ActionScript. The table represents these properties with the "W" designation.

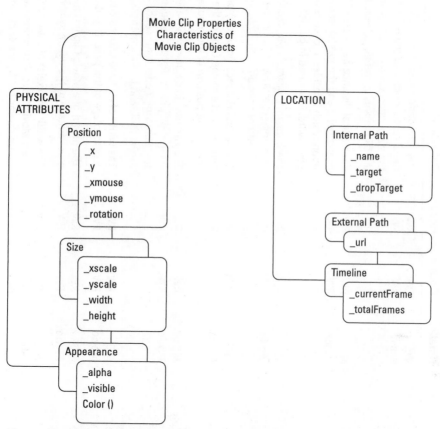

Figure 41-2: Properties of the Movie Clip Object

Use the propInspector Movie Clip in the Library of the property_inspector.fla file on the *Flash 5 Bible* CD-ROM to see the values of Movie Clip or Movie properties.

Table 41-1
Flash Movie and Movie Clip Properties

Category	Property	Timeline	Flash 4	Flash 5	Definition
Position	_x	MC Movie	RW RW	RW RW	The horizontal distance between a Movie Clip's center point and the top-left corner of the stage upon which it resides. Increases as the clip moves to the right. Measured in pixels.
	_y	MC Movie	RW RW	RW RW	The vertical distance between a Movie Clip's center point and the top-left corner of the stage upon which it resides. Increases as the clip moves downward. Measured in pixels.
	_xmouse	MC Movie	N/A N/A	R R	The horizontal distance (in pixels) between the zero point of a Movie Clip (or the Movie) and the current position of the mouse pointer.
	_ymouse	MC Movie	N/A N/A	R R	The vertical distance (in pixels) between the zero point of a Movie Clip (or the Movie) and the current position of the mouse pointer.
	_rotation	MC Movie	RW RW	RW RW	The amount (in degrees) that a Movie Clip is rotated off plumb. Returns values set both by the Transform Panel (or Rotation modifier of the Arrow Tool) and by ActionScript.
Size	_xscale	MC Movie	RW RW	RW RW	The width of a Movie Clip instance (or Movie) as a percentage of the parent symbol's actual size.
	_yscale	MC Movie	RW RW	RW RW	The height of a Movie Clip instance (or Movie) as a percentage of the parent symbol's actual size.
	_width	MC Movie	R R	RW R	The width (in pixels) of a Movie Clip or the main Movie Stage. Determined not by the width of the canvas but by the width of the space occupied by elements on the Stage (meaning it can be less or greater than the canvas width set in Movie Properties).

R = Read property (cannot be modified); W = Write property (can be modified)

Category	Property	Timeline	Flash 4	Flash 5	Definition
Size	_height	MC Movie	R R	RW R	The height (in pixels) of a movie clip or the main movie stage. Determined not by the height of the canvas but by the height of the space occupied by elements on the Stage.
Appearance	_alpha	MC Movie	RW RW	RW RW	The amount of transparency of a Movie Clip or Movie. Measured as a percentage: 100 percent is completely opaque, 0 percent is completely transparent.
	_visible	MC Movie	RW RW	RW RW	A Boolean value that indicates whether a Movie Clip instance is shown or hidden. Set to 1 (or true) to show; 0 (or false) to hide. Buttons in "hidden" movies are not active.
	Color()*	MC Movie	N/A N/A	RW RW	Color() is a Flash Object, not a property of the Movie Clip Object. Because Movie Clips can be specified as the target of the Color Object, color values of a Movie Clip can be treated as a user-definable property.
Internal Path	_name	MC Movie	RW R	RW R	Returns or reassigns the Movie Clip instance's name (as listed under the Instance Panel).
	_target	MC Movie	R R	R R	Returns the exact string in Slashes notation that you'd use to refer to the Movie Clip instance. To retrieve the Dots notation, use eval(_target).
Internal Path	_droptarget	MC Movie	R R	R R	Returns the name (in Slashes notation) of the last Movie Clip upon which a draggable Movie Clip was dropped. To retrieve the Dots notation, use eval(_droptarget). For usage, see "Creating Draggable Movie Clips" in this chapter.
External Path	_url	MC Movie	R R	R R	Returns the complete path to the .SWF file in which the Action is executed, including the name of the .SWF itself. Could be used to prevent a movie from being viewed if not on a particular server.

R = Read property (cannot be modified); W = Write property (can be modified)

Continued

Table 41-1 (continued)

Category	Property	Timeline	Flash 4	Flash 5	Definition
Timeline	`_currentframe`	MC	R	R	Returns the number of the current frame (for example, the frame on which the playhead currently resides) of the Movie or a Movie Clip instance.
		Movie	R	R	
	`_totalframes`	MC	R	R	Returns the number of total frames in a Movie or Movie Clip instance's timeline.
		Movie	R	R	
	`_framesloaded`	MC	R	R	Returns the number of frames that have downloaded over the network.
		Movie	R	R	
Global	`_highquality`	Movie	W	W	The visual quality setting of the Movie. 0=Low, 1=High, 2=Best. For details, see "Toggle High Quality" in Chapter 39. This is considered deprecated syntax in Flash 5.
	`_quality`	Movie	N/A	RW	The visual quality of the Movie. The value is a string equal to: "LOW" (no antialiasing, no bitmap smoothing), "MEDIUM" (antialiasing on a 2 × 2 grid, no bitmap smoothing), "HIGH" (antialiasing on a 4×4 grid, bitmap smoothing on static frames), "BEST" (antialiasing on a 4×4 grid, bitmap smoothing on all frames)
	`_focusrect`	Movie	W	W	A Boolean value that indicates whether a yellow rectangle is shown around buttons when accessed via the Tab key. Default is to show. When set to 0, the Up state of the button is shown instead of the yellow rectangle.
	`_soundbuftime`	Movie	W	W	The number of seconds a sound should preload before it begins playing. Default is 5 seconds.

R = Read property (cannot be modified); W = Write property (can be modified)

Movie Clip methods

Although the name might sound intimidating, don't be scared. Methods are simply actions that are attached to objects. As you well know, Movie Clips qualify as objects in Flash. A method looks like a regular action except that it doesn't (and in most cases, can't) operate without a Dots notation reference to a target or an object:

Action: gotoAndPlay("start");

becomes

Method: _root.gotoAndPlay("start");

As actions, interactive commands are executed from the timeline on which they are written. As methods, interactive commands are tied to specific (or dynamic) targets. Figure 41-3 lists the methods and Table 41-2 reviews every method associated with the Movie Clip Object. Some methods can be used with Movie Clip instances and with the entire Flash movie (_root, _level0, and so on), while others can only be used with Movie Clip instances. The "Flash 4" column indicates if the method (when used as an action) is compatible in the Flash 4 Player. Some commands need to be written in Dots notation, as a method (designated as "M" in the table) of a timeline or Movie Clip Object. Other commands can be used as actions (designed as "A" in the table), meaning that the Movie Clip Object name need not precede the command.

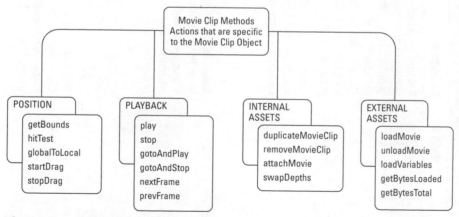

Figure 41-3: Methods of the Movie Clip Object

onClipEvent: The Movie Clip Object handler

Yet another exciting addition to Flash 5 ActionScript is the `onClipEvent` handler. In previous versions of Flash, our only event handlers were keyframes and Button instances. Now, we can add Actions to the wrapper of a Movie Clip instance — meaning that these actions are not added to keyframes on the Movie Clip's timeline. Nine events can be used with the `onClipEvent` handler. Refer to Table 41-3 for a summary of these events.

Table 41-2
Flash Movie and Movie Clip Methods

Category	Method	Flash 4	Definition	Usage

Position	getBounds M	No	Returns an object containing the minimum and maximum X and Y coordinates, as properties of that object: xMin, xMax, yMin, and yMax. These values can be used to compare the positions of two or more Movie Clips.	*timeline.getBounds(target space);*
				
				 `myBounds = myMovieClip.¬`
				 `  getBounds(_root);`
				 `current_xMin = myBounds.xMin;`

	hitTest M	No	Returns a `true` value if the Movie Clip touches or overlaps a specified coordinate space or target.	*timeline.hitTest(x, y, shapeFlag);*
				 timeline.hitTest(target space);
				
				 `var isTouching = myMC.¬`
				 `  hitTest(otherMC);`
				 `trace("isTouching is " + ¬`
				 `  isTouching);`

	globalToLocal M	No	Translates coordinates from the Main Timeline's stage to a specified Movie Clip's stage. Requires the creation of a new Object with X and Y properties.	*timeline.globalToLocal(object reference);*
				
				 `_root.myPoint = new Object();`
				 `_root.myPoint.x = _root.¬`
				 `  _xmouse;`
				 `_root.myPoint.y = _root.¬`
				 `  _ymouse;`
				 `_myMC.globalToLocal(_root.¬`
				 `  myPoint);`

	localToGlobal M	No	Translates coordinates from a Movie Clip's stage to the Main Timeline's stage. Same requirements as `globalToLocal`.	*timeline.localToGlobal(object reference);*
				
				 `myMC.myPoint = new Object();`
				 `myMC.myPoint.x = myMC._x;`
				 `myMC.myPoint.y = myMC._y;`
				 `myMC.localToGlobal(myMC.¬`
				 `  myPoint);`

Note: Throughout this table the ¬ character indicates continuation of the same line of code.

M = Method, A = Action

Category	Method	Flash 4	Definition	Usage

Position	`startDrag`
	M, A
		Yes	Enables the user to move a Movie Clip instance on the Stage. The Movie Clip moves (or drags) in tandem with the movements of the mouse. You can specify whether the mouse pointer locks to the center of the Movie Clip instance and if the drag area is constrained to a range of X and Y coordinates (in the parent symbol or timeline space). Constraining the drag area is useful for slider controls.	*timeline.startDrag(lock, min X, min Y, max X, max Y);*
				`myMC.startDrag(false, ¬`
				`   200,0,200,200);`

	`stopDrag` M, A	Yes	Stops any `startDrag` action currently in progress. No target needs to be specified with this action.	*timeline.stopDrag();* `myMC.stopDrag();`

Playback	`play`
	M, A
		Yes	Starts playback from the current position of the playhead on a specified timeline.	*timeline.play();*
				`// plays the Main Timeline`
				`_root.play();`
				`// plays myMC`
				`_root.myMC.play();`

	`stop`
	M, A
		Yes	Stops playback on a specified timeline.	*timeline.stop();*
				`// stops the Main Timeline`
				`_root.stop();`
				`// stops myMC`
				`_root.myMC.stop();`

	`gotoAndPlay`
	M, A
		Yes	Jumps the playhead of a specified timeline to a label, frame number, or expression, and starts playing from there.	*timeline.gotoAndPlay(position);*
				`// plays from the "start"`
				`// label of the myMC timeline`
				`_root.myMC.gotoAndPlay ¬`
				`   ("start");`

Continued

Note: Throughout this table the ¬ character indicates continuation of the same line of code.

M = Method, A = Action

Table 41-2 *(continued)*

Category	Method	Flash 4	Definition	Usage

Playback	gotoAndStop M, A	Yes	Jumps the playhead of a specified timeline to a label, frame number, or expression, and stops playback.	*timeline.gotoAndStop(position);*
				`// stops playback on the`
				`// "mute" label of myMC`
				`_root.myMC.gotoAndStop¬`
				`("mute");`

	nextFrame M, A	Yes	Moves the playhead of the specified timeline to the next frame.	*timeline.nextFrame();* `_root.myMC.nextFrame();`
	prevFrame M, A	Yes	Moves the playhead of the specified timeline to the previous frame.	*timeline.prevFrame();* `_root.myMC.prevFrame();`

Internal Assets	duplicate MovieClip M, A	Yes	Makes a copy of a Movie Clip instance on the Stage (or nested in another Movie Clip). The new copy is placed directly above the parent instance, at a specified depth. Higher depth numbers appear above lower depth numbers (for example, a Movie Clip at depth 2 is stacked above a Movie Clip at depth 1).	*timeline.duplicateMovieClip (new name*, depth);*
				`myMC.duplicateMovieClip¬`
				`("myMC_2", 20);`
				`myMC_2._x = 200;`
				*You should not specify a new path for the copy. It will be located from the same root as the parent MC instance.

	removeMovieClip M, A	Yes	Deletes a previously duplicated Movie Clip instance. When used as a method, you do not need to specify a target. You can not remove a Movie Clip instance that is manually inserted on any timeline frame from the Library.	*timeline.removeMovieClip();* `myMC_2.removeMovieClip();`

	attachMovie M	No	Places an instance of a Movie Clip symbol from the Library into the specified timeline. Each attached instance requires a unique name and depth. Attached Movie Clip instances can be deleted with `removeMovieClip`.	*timeline.attachMovie(ID*, new name, depth);*
				`_root.attachMovie("eye", ¬`
				`"eye_1", 1);`
				*You need to specify a unique identifier to attached MC symbols in the Library, using the Linkage Properties.

Note: Throughout this table the ¬ character indicates continuation of the same line of code.

Category	Method	Flash 4	Definition	Usage
Internal Assets	swapDepths M	No	Switches the depth placement of two duplicated or attached Movie Clips. This method is useful for placing one Movie Clip instance in front of (or behind) another instance.	*timeline.swapDepths(depth);* *timeline.swapDepths(target);* ` // depth` ` eye_1.swapDepths(10);` ` // target` ` eye_1.swapDepths(eye_2);`
External Assets	loadMovie M, A	Yes	Loads an external .SWF file into the main movie .SWF. As one of the most powerful features of Flash, this method enables you to break up your Flash movie into several smaller components, and load them as needed. This method can load .SWF files into Movie Clip targets.	*timeline.loadMovie(path, send variables*);* `myMC.loadMovie("menu.swf");` **You can also send Flash variables to the newly loaded .SWF file with an optional "GET" or "POST" parameter.*
	loadMovieNum M, A	Yes	Same functionality as loadMovie. This method can load .SWF files into Levels instead of Movie Clip targets.	*timeline.loadMovieNum(path, send variables*);* `_level1.loadMovieNum-` `  ("menu.swf");` **See note in loadMovie.*
	unloadMovie M, A	Yes	Removes an externally loaded .SWF file from the main movie .SWF. This method enables you to dump .SWF assets when they are no longer needed. Use this method for assets loaded into Movie Clip targets.	*timeline.unloadMovie();* `myMC.unloadMovie();`
	unloadMovieNum M, A	Yes	Same functionality as unloadMovie. This method is used to remove externally loaded .SWFs that exist in Levels, not Movie Clips.	*timeline.unloadMovieNum();* `_level1.unloadMovieNum();`

Continued

Note: Throughout this table the ¬ character indicates continuation of the same line of code.

M = Method, A = Action

Table 41-2 (continued)

Category	Method	Flash 4	Definition	Usage
External Assets	loadVariables M, A	Yes	Loads external text-based data into the main movie .SWF. This method enables you to access data (in the form of variable name/value pairs) from server-side scripts or text files, and place it in a Movie Clip target.	*timeline.loadVariables(path, send variables*)*; myMC.loadVariables¬ ("info.txt"); *See note in loadMovie.
	loadVariablesNum M, A	Yes	Same as loadVariables, except that this method is used to load data into Levels, not Movie Clips.	*timeline.loadVariablesNum(path, send variables*)*; _level1.loadVariablesNum¬ ("info.txt"); *See note in loadMovie.
	getBytesLoaded M	No	Returns the number of bytes that have streamed into the Flash Player for a specified Movie Clip (or main movie).	*timeline.getBytesLoaded();* loadBytes = ¬ myMC.getBytesLoaded();

	getBytesTotal
	M
		No	Returns the total file size (in bytes) for a loading movie or Movie Clip. Combined with getBytesLoaded(), you can use this method to calculate the movie's loaded percentage.	*timeline.getBytesTotal();*
				totalBytes = ¬
				  myMC.getBytesTotal();
				loadBytes = ¬
				  myMC.getBytesLoaded();
				newPercent = (loadBytes/¬
				  totalBytes)*100;

Note: Throughout this table the ¬ character indicates continuation of the same line of code.

M = Method, A = Action

Table 41-3
onClipEvent Handler for Movie Clip Objects

Category	Event	Definition	Usage

Playback	load	This event is triggered when (a) a Movie Clip instance first appears on the Stage; (b) a new instance is added with attachMovie or duplicateMovieClip; or (c) an external .SWF is loaded into a Movie Clip target.	`onClipEvent(load){`
			`trace( _name + " has loaded.");`
			`}`

	unload	This event occurs when (a) a Movie Clip instance exits the Stage (just after the last frame has played on the Main Timeline), or (b) an external .SWF is unloaded from a Movie Clip target. Actions within this handler type will be executed *before* any actions in the keyframe immediately after the Movie Clip's departure keyframe.	`onClipEvent(unload){`
			`trace( _name + " has unloaded.");`
			`}`

	enterFrame	This event executes when each frame on a Movie Clip instance's timeline is played. The actions within this event handler will be processed *after* any actions that exist on the keyframes of the Movie Clip timeline. Note that enterFrame events will execute repeatedly (at the same rate as the movie's frame rate), regardless of whether any timelines within the movie are actually playing frames.	`onClipEvent(enterFrame){`
			`trace( _name + " is playing.");`
			`}`

User Input	mouseMove	This event is triggered each time the mouse moves, anywhere on the Stage. Combined with the hitTest method, this event can be used to detect mouse movements over Movie Clip instances. All Movie Clip instances with this event handler receive this event.	`onClipEvent(mouseMove){`
			`myX = _root._xmouse;`
			`myY = _root._ymouse;`
			`if(this.hitTest(myX, myY, ¬`
			`true) == true){`
			`trace("Mouse move over MC.");`
			`}`
			`}`

Continued

Note: Throughout this table the ¬ character indicates continuation of the same line of code.

Table 41-3 (continued)

Category	Event	Definition	Usage
User Input	mouseDown	This event occurs each time the left mouse button is pressed (or down) anywhere on the Stage. All Movie Clip instances with this event handler receive this event.	```onClipEvent(mouseDown){` ` myX = _root._xmouse;` ` myY = _root._ymouse;` ` if(this.hitTest(myX, myY, true) ==` ` true){` ` trace("Mouse press on MC.");` ` }` `}```
	mouseUp	Each time the left mouse button is released (when the user lets up on the mouse button), this event is triggered. All Movie Clip instances with this handler receive this event.	```onClipEvent(mouseUp){` ` myX = _root._xmouse;` ` myY = _root._ymouse;` ` if(this.hitTest(myX, myY, true)` ` == true){` ` trace("Mouse release on MC.");` ` }` `}```
	keyDown	When the user presses a key, this event occurs. Combined with the Key.getCode method, you can use this event handler to detect unique key presses.	```onClipEvent(keyDown){` ` newKey = Key.getCode();` ` myKey = Key.UP;` ` if(newKey == myKey){` ` trace("UP arrow is pressed.");` ` }` `}```

Note: Throughout this table the ¬ character indicates continuation of the same line of code.

Category	Event	Definition	Usage
User Input	keyUp	This event happens when the user releases a key (when the finger leaves the key). Same functionality as the keyDown event.	```onClipEvent(keyUp){ newKey = Key.getCode(); myKey = Key.LEFT; if(newKey == myKey){ trace("LEFT arrow released."); } }```
External Input	data	This event is triggered when (a) the loadMovie action retrieves an external .SWF and puts it in a Movie Clip target, or (b) the data from a file or script with the loadVariables action (targeted at a Movie Clip instance) is finished loading.	```onClipEvent(data){ trace("New data received."); }```

Note: Throughout this table the ¬ character indicates continuation of the same line of code.

Other objects that can use the Movie Clip Object

Movie Clips can be used with other ActionScript objects to control appearance and sounds, and to manipulate data.

Color Object

This object requires a Movie Clip as a target. After a new object is created with the `Color()` action, you can control the color effects of the targeted Movie Clip. We'll look at the Color Object more closely in this chapter.

Sound Object

With this object, you can create virtual sound instances on a Movie Clip timeline, and target them for later use. We'll explore this object later in the chapter as well.

Mouse Object

This object controls the appearance of the mouse pointer within the Flash movie Stage. After the Mouse Object is hidden, you can attach a Movie Clip Object to the X and Y coordinates of the mouse pointer.

XML Object

If you're working with XML (Extensible Markup Language) data from a server-side script or file, then you can store the output within a Movie Clip instance for better data management.

Related functions that target the Movie Clip Object

Some ActionScript functions work directly with Movie Clip instances for printing and targeting. Refer to Table 41-4 for a summary of these functions.

Table 41-4
Related Functions with a Movie Clip Target

Function	Definition	Options
print() printNum()	This action prints a frame (or series of frames) in the targeted timeline. The printNum function is used when targeting Levels. Each frame prints to one piece of paper. Use this function to print high-quality artwork. Note that alpha and color effects do not print reliably with this method. We discuss this function later in the chapter.	*print(target, ["bmovie"," bmax", or "bframe"]);* where: *target* is the path to Movie Clip instance. Each frame of the Movie Clip is printed unless you designate printable frames with a #p frame label. and one of the following options: "bMovie" assigns a cropping area for printing, by placing artwork sized to the printable area on a keyframe with the label #b "bmax" uses the frame with the largest-sized artwork to determine the printable area. "bframe" prints each frame at its largest size to fill the paper width.
printAsBitmp() printAsBitmapNum()	Same functionality as the print() function. Use this action to print artwork that employs alpha or color instance settings. We discuss this function later in the chapter.	*print(target, ["bmovie","bmax", or "bframe"];* See the print() function earlier in this table for descriptions of options.

targetPath()	This function is an advanced substitute for the Flash 4 tellTarget action. Actions within the curly braces are targeted at the Movie Clip instance.	*targetPath(path to Movie Clip instance){ [actions here] }*
		targetPath(_root.myMC){
		  stop();
		}

tellTarget()	This Flash 4 action can direct actions to a specific Movie Clip timeline. To be compatible with Flash 4, you need to use Slash notation for the target path.	*tellTarget(path{ [actions here] }*
		tellTarget("/myMC"){
		  stop();
		}

with()	This function enables you to avoid needless replication of object references and paths. By specifying a target for the with function, you can omit the path from nested actions.	*with(path to Object){ [actions here] }*
		with(_root.myMC){
		  stop();
		}

Working with Movie Clip Properties

Now that you have a sense of what a Movie Clip can do (or be told to do), let's get some practical experience with the Movie Clip properties. This section shows you how to access Movie Clip appearance properties that control position, scale, and rotation.

Note   The following exercises use Button Symbols from the prebuilt Common Libraries that ship with Flash 5. To access buttons from the Common Libraries, use Window ⇨ Common Libraries ⇨ Buttons to open the .FLA library file, and drag an instance of any button into your Flash movie.

Positioning Movie Clips

You can change the location of Movie Clip instances on-the-fly with position properties such as _x and _y. How is this useful? If you want to create multiple Movie Clip instances that move randomly (or predictively) across the Stage, then you can save yourself the trouble of manually tweening them by writing a few lines of Action-Script code on the object instance:

1. Create a new movie file (Ctrl+N or Command+N).

2. Draw a simple shape such as a circle. Select the shape and press F8 to convert it into a symbol. Accept the default Movie Clip behavior in the Symbol Properties dialog, and give the new Movie Clip symbol a unique name such as **circle**.

3. With the Movie Clip instance selected on the Stage, open the Actions Panel (Ctrl+Alt+A or Option+Command+A). Turn on Expert mode (Ctrl+E) and type the following code:

```
onClipEvent(enterFrame){
    this._x += 5;
}
```

4. Save your movie as a new .FLA file, and test the movie (Ctrl+Enter or Command+Enter). The Movie Clip instance moves across the Stage.

How does this code work? In step 3, you specified that the onClipEvent (enterFrame) handler should be assigned to the Movie Clip instance. Because this particular Movie Clip has only one frame (with no stop() action in it), the enterFrame event is triggered continuously. Therefore, any actions nested within the handler will be executed repeatedly.

Our nest contains one action: this._x += 5. On the left side of the action, this refers to the object instance to which this handler and code has been applied. In our case, this refers to our circle Movie Clip instance. Immediately after this is the property for X position, _x. By adding the property _x to the object this, Flash knows that we want to change the value of this property.

On the right side of the action are the operators += and the value 5. By combining the + and = operators, we've created a shortcut to adding the value of 5 to the current X position of the circle Movie Clip instance. Each time the enterFrame event occurs, the circle Object moves 5 pixels to the right.

To show how quickly you can replicate this action on multiple Movie Clips, select the instance of the circle Movie Clip on the Stage, and duplicate it (Ctrl+D or Command+D) as many times as you wish. When you test your movie, each instance moves independently across the Stage.

Tip   To move the instance diagonally across the Stage, add the action this._y += 5 to the onClipEvent handler nest. This moves the instance down 5 pixels each time the handler is processed.

Scaling Movie Clips

In the last example, you learned how to access the _x and _y properties of the Movie Clip Object. The next example shows you how to use a Button symbol to enlarge or reduce the size of a Movie Clip on the Stage.

1. Create a new movie file (Ctrl+N or Command+N).

2. Draw a shape (or multiple shapes), select the shape(s), and press F8 to convert the artwork into a symbol. Give the Movie Clip symbol a distinct name to identify it in the Library.

3. Select the instance of the Movie Clip on the Stage, and open the Instance Panel. Give the Movie Clip a unique name. In this example, we've named the instance **circle**.

4. From the Button Library, drag an instance of a button onto the Stage.

5. Now we create an ActionScript that will enlarge our circle Movie Clip instance. Select the Button instance on the Stage, and open the Actions Panel. In Expert mode, type the following code:

```
on (release){
     with (circle){
          _xscale += 10;
          _yscale += 10;
     }
}
```

This code uses the with() function to target the circle Movie Clip instance with a nested group of actions. In this case, we've increased the values of the _xscale and _yscale properties by 10 percent. With each release event on the Button symbol, the scale properties of the circle instance will be changed.

6. Save your movie as a new .FLA file, and test the movie (Ctrl+Enter or Command+ Enter). Each time you click the Button instance, your circle Movie Clip instance enlarges by 10 percent.

7. Duplicate the Button instance (Ctrl+D or Command+D). With the new copy of the Button instance selected, change the code in the Actions Panel so that it reads:

```
on (release){
    with (circle){
        _xscale -= 10;
        _yscale -= 10;
    }
}
```

By changing the += operator to -=, each click on this Button instance will reduce (shrink) the circle Movie Clip instance by 10 percent.

8. Resave your Flash file and test the movie again. Make sure that each Button instance behaves appropriately. If one doesn't work (or works in an unexpected manner), go back to the Flash movie file and check the code on both Button instances.

Caution   In this simple exercise, we haven't placed any limits on the how much the Movie Clip can be reduced or enlarged. If you click the reduce button enough times, the Movie Clip instance will actually start enlarging again.

Rotating Movie Clips

Let's move along to the rotation property, _rotation, which is used to control the angle at which our Movie Clip is shown. In this sample, we'll use the same .FLA file that we created in the previous section.

Note   If you had drawn a perfect circle in past exercises for the Movie Clip Object, then you will want to edit your Movie Clip symbol to include some additional artwork that provides an indication of orientation and rotation. If you try to rotate a perfect circle, you won't see any visual difference on the Stage. Because the value of the rotation property is determined from the center point of the Movie Clip, you can also move the contents of the Movie Clip (in Symbol Editing Mode) off-center to see updates in the _rotation value.

1. Select the Button instance we used to enlarge the circle Movie Clip instance. Change the button's ActionScript in the Actions Panel to:

```
on (release){
    circle._rotation += 10;
}
```

2. Now, select the Button instance we used to shrink the circle Movie Clip instance. Change the button's ActionScript in the Actions Panel to:

```
on (release){
    circle._rotation -= 10;
}
```

3. Save your movie as a new .FLA file, and test the movie. Each button should rotate the circle Movie Clip instance accordingly.

At this point, you should have a general knowledge of how to access a Movie Clip's properties. Repeat these examples using other properties that can be modified, such as _width and _height. Try combining all the properties into one Button instance or one onClipEvent handler.

Manipulating Color Attributes

The new Color Object in Flash 5 gives you unprecedented control of your Movie Clip Objects. By controlling the color (and transparency) of your artwork with ActionScript's Color Object, you can:

✦ Create on-the-fly color schemes or "skins" for Flash interfaces.

✦ Enable users to select and view color preferences for showcased products on an e-commerce site.

✦ Instantly change the color attributes of a Flash design-in-progress for a client.

Because color is controlled through the Color Object, we'll quickly review the unique methods available to this object. Refer to Table 41-5 for more information. Note that this table is organized by order of practical use.

Table 41-5
Methods for the Color Object

Method	Definition	Options
setRGB	Changes the RGB offset for the specified Color Object (and targeted Movie Clip). This method changes all colors in the targeted instance to one solid RGB color.	*colorReference.setRGB(0xRRGGBB);* where: *colorReference* is the name of the Color Object. We'll discuss the creation of Color Objects in this section. *RR, GG* and *BB* are the offset values (in hexadecimal) for the Red, Green, and Blue channels, respectively.
getRGB	Retrieves the values established with the last setRGB execution. If you want to reapply RGB offsets to a new Color Object, use this method.	*colorReference.getRGB();* No options or arguments for this method.
setTransform	Changes the RGB offset and percentage values for the specified Color Object (and targeted Movie Clip). This method produces visual results that resemble both left- and right-hand color controls in the Advanced section of the Effect Panel.	*colorReference.setTransform(colorTransformObject);* where: *colorTransformObject* is the name of a Object that has percentage and offset properties for Red, Green, Blue, and Alpha channels. We'll discuss the intricacies of these properties in the following sections.
getTransform	Retrieves the values established with the last setTransform execution. Use this method to reapply color transforms to new Color Objects.	*colorReference.getTransform();* No options or arguments for this method.

Creating a Color Object

To manipulate the color attributes of a Movie Clip instance, you need to create a new Color Object that references the Movie Clip instance. In the following steps, you learn to use the constructor for the Color Object.

On the
CD-ROM

For the exercises with the Color Object, use the dog.fla movie in the ch41 folder of the *Flash 5 Bible* CD-ROM. Thank you, Sandro Corsaro of spanktoons.com, for supplying the artwork of the dog!

1. Select the instance of the dog graphic on the Stage. Open the Instance Panel and name this Movie Clip instance **dog**.

2. Open the Button library (Window ➪ Common Libraries ➪ Buttons) and drag an instance of a Button symbol onto the Stage. In this example, we used the Grey button-stop in the (rectangle) Button Set.

3. Select the Button instance on the Stage, and open the Actions Panel. In Expert Mode, type the following actions:

```
on(release){
redSolid = new Color(_root.dog);
redSolid.setRGB(0xFF0000);
}
```

With the `on(release)` handler, this Button instance's actions create a new Color Object called `redSolid`, which refers to the `_root.dog` Movie Clip instance we made in step 1. Once the `redSolid` Object is initiated, we can access methods of the Color Object, such as `setRGB`. In this example, we changed the color of the Movie Clip instance to pure red, designated by FF in hexadecimal.

4. Save the movie as a new .FLA file, and test the movie. Click the Button instance on the Stage. The color of the dog Movie Clip should change to bright red. Close the test .SWF, and return to the Flash authoring environment.

5. To see the `getRGB` method in action, let's create some `trace` messages for the Output window. Select the Button instance on the Stage, and open the Actions Panel. Add the following line of code to the end of the nest of actions inside the `on(release)` handler:

```
trace("redSolid's RGB numeric value = " + redSolid.getRGB());
```

6. Save the .FLA file and test the movie. When you click the button, the Output window should open and display the following text:

```
redSolid's RGB numeric value = 16711680
```

7. To change this value back to the hexadecimal value that we entered in the setRGB method, we need to convert the value to base 16. Add the following action to the on(release) action nest:

```
trace("redSolid's RGB hex value = " +
redSolid.getRGB().toString(16));
```

8. Save the .FLA file and test the movie. When you click the button, the Output window should open and display the new value:

```
redSolid's RGB numeric value = 16711680
redSolid's RGB hex value = ff0000
```

9. However, you won't need to convert getRGB's native return value to set another Color Object equal to a previous setRGB value. Duplicate the dog Movie Clip instance on the Stage, and name the new instance **dog2**. Duplicate the Button instance on the Stage. Change the new Button instance actions to:

```
on (release) {
    redSolid2 = new Color(_root.dog2);
    redSolid2.setRGB(redSolid.getRGB());
}
```

10. Save the FLA file and test the movie. When you click the first button, the dog Movie Clip instance turns red. When you click the second button, the dog2 Movie Clip instance turns red.

Note If you click the second button first, the dog2 Movie Clip instance will turn black. Why? Because the first button's actions were not executed, there was no previous setRGB method execution for the getRGB method to refer to. Moreover, there was no redSolid Object either. Consequently, Flash returns a zero or null value for the getRGB method. In hexadecimal color, zero is equivalent to black.

Now that you've had some experience with the Color Object's setRGB and getRGB methods, let's move on to the more complex colorTransformObject. We'll use the .FLA file from this exercise, so keep the dogs on the Stage!

Creating a Transform Object

The two remaining methods of the Color Object, setTransform and getTransform, require a more thorough understanding of RGB color space. Before the setTransform method can be used with a Color Object, we need to create a generic object using the object constructor. This generic object will become a colorTransformObject once we have assigned color properties to the generic object.

The properties of the colorTransformObject are:

✦ **ra**, the Red channel percentage

✦ **rb**, the Red Channel offset

✦ **ga**, the Green channel percentage

✦ **gb**, the Green channel offset

✦ **ba**, the Blue channel percentage

✦ **bb**, the Blue channel offset

✦ **aa**, the Alpha channel percentage

✦ **ab**, the Alpha channel offset

The *a* properties are percentage-based, ranging in value from –100 to 100. The *b* properties are offset-based, ranging from –255 to 255 (derived from 24-bit RGB color space, in which each 8-bit color channel can have a range of 256 values).

While these properties and values may seem complex, refer to the Advanced options of the Effect Panel for guidance. With the Advanced option chosen in the Effect Panel drop-down menu, the left-hand color controls are percentage-based, while the right-hand controls are offset-based. Admittedly, color is difficult to visualize from numbers. To accurately predict the color changes with setTransform, we'll use the Effect Panel to help us out.

1. Using the same .FLA file from the previous exercise, select the original dog Movie Clip instance on the Stage. Open the Effect Panel (Window ➪ Panels ➪ Effect), and select the Advanced option in the drop-down menu. Enter the following value on the left-hand side: **–100% Blue**. On the right-hand side, enter these values: **37 G** and **255 B**. With these values, the dog instance should be a monochrome blue with yellow eyes. Normally, you would want to write these values down so that you had them to use later. Because you have them printed here, erase them by choosing None from the Effect Panel drop-down menu.

2. Duplicate one of the existing Button instances on the Stage. On this new instance, we'll create some code that will initiate a new Color Object, and a new colorTransformObject. The colorTransformObject will be given properties that have the same values as those determined in Step 1. Then, we'll execute the setTransform method for the Color Object, using the colorTransformObject's data for the color change. Select the new Button instance, and add the following code in the Actions Panel:

```
on (release) {
    dogColor = new Color(_root.dog);
    rabidLook = new Object();
    rabidLook.ba = -100;
    rabidLook.bb = 255;
    rabidLook.gb = 37;
    dogColor.setTransform(rabidLook);
}
```

In the preceding code, we created two objects: `dogColor` and `rabidLook`. `rapidLook` is assigned the `ba`, `bb`, and `gb` `colorTransformObject` proper-ties. Each of these properties is given the values we determined in Step 1. Then, we specified that the `rabidLook` Object be used as the target for `dogColor`'s `setTransform` method.

3. Save the Flash movie file, and test the movie. Click the new Button instance that you added in Step 2. The colors of the dog Movie Clip instance should change to match those we saw in Step 1. Close the .SWF file, and return to the Flash authoring environment.

4. Now let's create a button that restores the original look of the dog Movie Clip instance. The code structure resembles that of Step 2, but we use a different way to assign color properties to the `colorTransformObject`. Duplicate the button created in Step 2, open the Actions Panel, and change the ActionScript code to:

```
on (release) {
    dogColor = new Color(_root.dog);
    restoreLook = new Object();
    restoreLook = {
        ra: '100',
        rb: '0',
        ga: '100',
        gb: '0',
        ba: '100',
        bb: '0',
        aa: '100',
        ab: '0'
    }
    dogColor.setTransform(restoreLook);
}
```

In the `restoreLook` Object, we defined all the default properties using name/value pairs separated by the colon character (:). Notice that all the properties of the `restoreLook` Object can be declared and given values within a { } nesting.

5. Save the .FLA file, and test the movie. Click the Button instance you created in Step 2. After the dog Movie Clip instance changes color, click the Button instance you created in Step 4. Voila! The dog Movie Clip instance reverts to its original color. Click the first Button instance that you created in the previ-ous section. This Button instance (which uses the `setRGB` method) changes the appearance of the dog Movie Clip instance to a solid red color. Now click the Button instance with the `restoreLook` Object — the dog Movie Clip instance reverts to its original look!

While the setRGB method can alter basic color properties of Movie Clip Objects, the setTransform method is the color-control powerhouse. Any look that you can accomplish with the Effect Panel, you can reproduce with the setTransform method and the colorTransformObject.

Tip   Just as the getRGB method can retrieve the values of a past setRGB method, you can transfer past setTransform values using the getTransform method.

Enabling Sound with ActionScript

Flash 5 offers many new object types, and one of the most exciting objects to use is the Sound Object. Like most objects, the Sound Object has predefined methods that you can use to control each new Sound Object. Table 41-6 provides an overview of the Sound Object and its methods.

Reasons for using Sound Objects over traditional Sound Movie Clips or keyframe sounds:

✦ Dynamic event sounds that play in a random or user-defined order.

✦ Precise control over volume and panning.

✦ The ability to dump (or erase) a Sound Object when the sound is no longer needed.

Note   All Sound Objects are treated as Event sounds. You can not use Sound Objects for Stream sounds. For more information on Synch modes for sound, please refer to Chapter 37, "Importing and Editing Sounds in Flash."

Unlike the Color Object that uses Movie Clips as targets, the Sound Object uses sounds directly from the movie's Library. You cannot use the Sound Object to control sounds that are specified in the Sound Panel for any given keyframes.

The next section shows you how to create Sound Objects, using the object constructor with the attachSound and start methods.

Table 41-6
Methods for the Sound Object

Method	Definition	Options
attachSound	Creates a new instance of a sound file (.AIF or .WAV) available in the Library. The new instance becomes a part of the Sound Object and can be targeted with Sound Object methods. Unlike attached Movie Clips, attached sounds do not require a depth number.	*soundObject.attachSound(libraryID);* where: *soundObject* refers to the sound Object's name *libraryID* is the name of the sound in the Symbol Linkage properties (available in the Library)
start	Plays the targeted Sound Object. A sound must be attached to the Sound Object before it can play.	*soundObject.start(inPoint, loopFactor);* where: *inPoint* is the time (in seconds) in the sound where playback should begin. *loopFactor* is the number of times the sound should be repeated. Both of these parameters are optional and can be omitted.
stop	Stops playback of the targeted Sound Object. If no target is specified, then all sounds will be stopped. Note that this is not equivalent to pausing a sound. If a stopped sound is played later, it will start at the beginning (or at the *inPoint*).	*soundObject.stop(libraryID);* where: *libraryID* is the name of the sound in the Symbol Linkage properties (available in the Library)
setVolume	Changes the overall volume of the specified Sound Object. This method accepts values between 0 and100 (in percentage units). You can not enter percentages greater than 100 percent to increase sound output beyond its original recording level.	*soundObject.setVolume(volume);* where: *volume* is a number between 0 and 100

Method	Definition	Options
getVolume	Retrieves the values established with the last setVolume execution. If you want to reapply RGB offsets to a new Color Object, use this method.	soundObject.getVolume(); No options or arguments for this method.
setPan	Changes the offset of sound output from both the left and right channels.	soundObject.setPan(panValue); where: panValue is a value between –100 (full left-speaker output) and 100 (full right-speaker output). Use a value of 0 to balance sound output evenly.
getPan	Retrieves the values created with a previous setPan execution. Use this method to apply Pan settings consistently to multiple Objects, or to store a Pan setting.	soundObject.getPan(); No options or arguments for this method.
setTransform	Changes the volume for each channel of the specified Sound Object. This method also enables you to play the right channel in the left channel and vice versa.	soundObject.setTransform(soundTransformObject); where: soundTransformObject is the name of an object that has percentage properties for left and right output for the left channel, and left and right output for the right channels.
getTransform	Retrieves the values established with the last setTransform execution. Use this method to reapply sound transforms to new Sounds Objects, or to store setTransform values.	soundObject.getTransform(); No options or arguments for this method.

Creating sound libraries with ActionScript

In the previous chapter, you learned how to create a sound library Movie Clip that stored several individual sound Movie Clip instances. You learned how to target these sounds in order to play them (or mute them). From a conceptual point of view, manually creating each sound Movie Clip enabled you to see each sound "object" on the Stage very easily. However, we can produce the sounds for a sound library much more quickly using ActionScript.

In this section, we start with the soundLibrary Movie Clip that you made in the previous chapter. You can also open the pianoKeys_complete.fla file from the ch40 folder of the *Flash 5 Bible* CD-ROM.

1. Using the Open as Library command in the File menu, select the pianoKeys.fla file that you made in the previous chapter. Opening a Flash file as a Library enables you to access symbols and media in that file.

Caution

Do not use the Open as Shared Library command in Step 1. This is a special option that we explore in the next chapter.

2. If you don't have a new untitled Flash document open, then create a new Flash file (Ctrl+N or Command+N). Drag the soundLib Movie Clip from the pianoKeys Library onto the Stage of your new movie. If you open the Library for your new movie, you'll see that all the elements contained within the soundLib Movie Clip have been imported into your new movie. Close the pianoKeys Library window, and save your new Flash movie as **soundLib_ActionScript.fla**.

3. Select the soundLib instance on the Stage, and open the Instance Panel. Give the instance the name **soundLib**. Press the Return or Tab key to make the name "stick."

4. Double-click the soundLib instance on the Stage. In Symbol Editing Mode, create a new blank layer and delete all of the sound layers. (You always need to have at least one layer in a Movie Clip.) On the empty layer, draw an icon representing the soundLib Movie Clip. In this example, we made a white-filled rounded rectangle with soundLib black text. Center the icon elements to the Movie Clip Stage.

5. Go back to the Main Timeline (click the Scene 1 tab in the upper right, or choose Edit ➪ Movie). Before we can attach sounds to the soundLib instance, each sound in the Library needs to be given a unique ID name in order for ActionScript to see it. Open the Library (Ctrl+L or Command+L), and select key_1.aif (or key_1.wav). Right-click (or Contrl+click on the Mac) the highlighted item, and choose Linkage in the contextual menu. In the Symbol Linkage Properties dialog, check the Export this symbol option and type **sound_1** in the Identifier text field, as shown in Figure 41-4. Click OK.

6. Repeat the naming routine from Step 4 on each sound in the Library. Increase the number that you append to the end of sound_ for each new sound (for example, sound_2 for key_2.aif, sound_3 for key_3.aif, and so on).

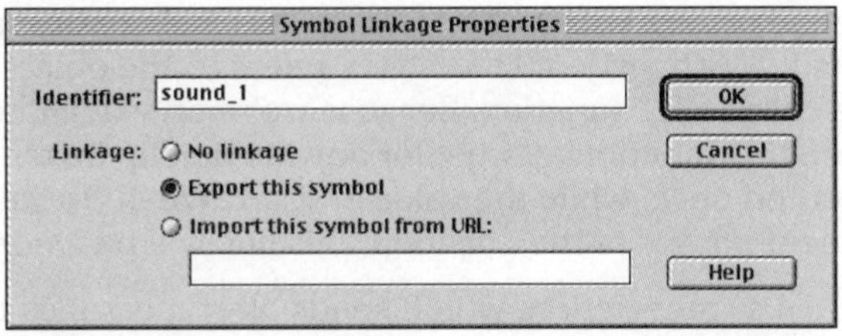

Symbol Linkage Properties

Identifier: sound_1

Linkage: ○ No linkage
      ● Export this symbol
      ○ Import this symbol from URL:

OK

Cancel

Help

Figure 41-4: The attachSound method can only use sounds that have been set to export with the Flash .SWF file.

7. Now, we need to add the ActionScript code that will create our Sound Object. We will construct a function that, when executed will form a list of sound instances. Create a new layer named actions and double-click its first keyframe. This will open the Actions Panel. With Expert Mode turned on, type the following code:

```
function createLib(num){
    for(i=1;i<=num;i++){
```

These first lines establish the name of our function, createLib. We will want to dynamically change the number of sounds we create with this function. Therefore, we assign an optional parameter (called an argument) num that will be passed to the nested actions within the function.

The second line starts a for loop that cycles its nested actions until the condition i<=num is no longer true. i starts (or initializes) with a value of 1, and the syntax i++ tells i to increase by 1 with each pass of the for loop.

In the next step, we want the for loop to (a) create an array to store a reference to each sound instance; (b) create a new instance of the Sound Object for each sound in the Library; and (c) attach each sound in the Library to its new instance.

Note

We do not discuss the overall structure and purpose of functions, arrays, and logic in this exercise. We do, however, use these mechanisms in this exercise.

8. In the Actions Panel, add the following ActionScript to the code from Step 6:

```
if(i==1){
    this.snd = new Array();
    trace("new array created.");
}
trace("this="+this);
this.snd[i] = new Sound(this);
this.snd[i].attachSound("sound_"+i);
    }
}
```

The first line of code in Step 7 checks whether i's current value is 1. During the first pass in the for loop, this will be true. So, the contents of the if nest will be executed.

The second line of code occurs within the if nest. This line creates a new Array named snd and is made a property of this. this refers to the object that targets (or evokes) the createLib function. Because we're only defining our function, we haven't made this function a target for any Movie Clip instance. This line will only be executed once, while the value of i is 1. When i's value increases in subsequent passes of the for loop, this line will be ignored.

The third line executes a trace action, which sends alert messages to the Output window (in the Test Movie environment). The trace action in the third line will tell us that the actions in the if nest have been executed by sending new Array created to the Output window.

The fourth line is also a trace action that tells us what object is evoking (or executing) the createLib function.

The fifth line makes a new element in the snd array. The new element is a new Sound Object that is targeted at the this timeline. Ultimately, our Sound Objects will be tied to the soundLib Movie Clip instance, which you'll see later. Each element in an array has a number indicating its position in the array. Because the value of i increases with each pass of the for loop, each Sound Object will have a unique position within the snd array.

The sixth line uses the attachSound method to take a sound element in the Library and attach it to the Sound Object in the snd array. The target for the attachSound method is specified as "sound_" + i. On each pass of the for loop, this expression will return "sound_1", "sound_2", and so on until our limit prescribed by the num argument is reached.

The complete block of code on the first keyframe of the actions layer should look like this:

```
function createLib(num){
    for(i=1;i<=num;i++){
        if(i==1){
            this.snd = new Array();
            trace("new array created.");
        }

        trace("this="+this);

        this.snd[i] = new Sound(this);

        this.snd[i].attachSound("sound_"+i);
    }
}
```

9. Now that we have a function defined to create all the Sound Objects on a this Object (or timeline), we need to have an object (for this to refer to) that uses the createLib function. In the Actions list for frame 1 of the Actions layer, type the following code after the function createLib:

```
soundLib.createLib = createLib;
soundLib.createLib(7);
```

The first line of code defines a *method* called `createLib` that used the function `createLib` as a value. Because `createLib` is a function, the `createLib` method of soundLib will execute the `createLib` function whenever the method is evoked.

The second line of code evokes the `createLib` method—the use of ( ) after the method name indicates that the method is being executed, *not* defined. In addition to executing the `createLib` method, we're also sending the function the number **7** as the num argument. Therefore, seven Sound Objects will be created.

10. Save the Flash movie file and test it (Ctrl+Enter or Command+Enter). The Output window should open and display the trace statements:

```
new array created.
this = _level0.soundLib
```

11. Close the Test Movie window and return to the authoring environment. Double-click frame 1 of the actions layer, and add this last bit of code to the Actions list:

```
soundLib.snd[1].start();
soundLib.snd[2].start();
```

The first line of code targets the first declared element, 1, of the snd array, and tells it to begin playback with the start method. Remember that element 1 in the array is a Sound Object, which references the sound_1 ID in the Library.

The second line of code targets the second declared element, 2, of the snd array, and tells it to start.

12. Save the Flash movie and test it. Both lines of code will execute simultaneously. So, you will hear sound_1 (which is key_1.aif or key_1.wav) and sound_2 (key_2. aif or key_2.wav) play together.

Now you should practice targeting these Sound Objects with Button instances and other keyframes. To access a different sound, simply change the number in the array brackets. In the next chapter, you'll learn to load a Flash movie (a .SWF file) into another Flash movie. You can use the `loadMovie` action to place this sound library file into another movie.

On the CD-ROM

You can view the completed sound library movie, soundLib_AS.fla, located in the ch41 folder of the *Flash 5 Bible* CD-ROM.

The next tutorial introduces the pan methods of the Sound Object, and shows you how to use Sound Objects with interactive projects.

Caution

During our testing of Flash 5 and the Sound Object methods, we learned that you should only attach one sound per timeline (or Movie Clip instance). While you can create more than one Sound Object instance on a timeline, you can not use the setVolume to control each individual sound—the volume will be set for all Sound Object instances on the targeted timeline.

Expert Tutorial: Sound Control, *by Jay Vanian*

Jay's tutorial introduces the setPan *method, and provides a compelling use of Sound Objects with draggable Movie Clips, which are discussed in more detail near the end of this chapter. Note that Jay's tutorial uses some Flash 4 syntax for Slash notation and property usage. As such, the tutorial will help those making the transition from Flash 4 Actions to Flash 5 ActionScript.*

Sound is one of the most powerful tools available to a designer with which to enhance a Flash project, yet it's probably been the most overlooked aspect of Flash. I think this will change with the introduction of Flash 5's new sound controls. But to use these controls (and to begin this tutorial), you first need a compelling reason to adjust either the volume or the left-to-right pan of Flash sound. Randomly setting the audio to go wild in your Flash movie won't endear you to anyone, and isn't likely to encourage repeat visits to your site. So, for this tutorial, I've chosen to use a bouncing basketball to create an interactive design situation that demonstrates this control appropriately.

For the first time, Flash 5 delivers the means to dynamically adjust the sound levels of movies by using the new sound object to control both the volume and to alter the left-to-right pan of a sound.

1. Before we get started, I'd like to offer a little bit of advice: Always determine the dimensions of your movie before you do anything else. Set these dimensions in the Movie Properties dialog. You might eventually learn this the hard way, but once you've had to resize an entire movie, you won't readily repeat the mistake. For this project, set the movie dimensions to 500×300. Also, be sure to save frequently as you work through these steps!

2. With the file size set, the first task is to import the background image, floor.jpg, position it on the default layer, and then rename this layer as **Floor**.

3. Next, import the vector basketball, gfx_basketball.ai, convert it to a graphic symbol and name it **gfx_basketball**. Follow the same procedure for the shadow, gfx_shadow. Now create a movie clip and name it **mov_basketball**; then drag an instance of gfx_basketball into the movie clip, and animate the basketball (along with a shadow) with a Motion Tween so that it bounces up and down. Be sure to use the easing controls for a more realistic bounce. (For more information on animating a bouncing ball, refer to the introductory Quick Start section of the book, "Flash in a Flash.")

   Author's Note: You'll find the source .FLA and related assets for this tutorial in the ch41 folder on the accompanying CD-ROM.

4. The last asset to be imported is the ball-bounce sound; name this **ballbounce**. In the Library, double-click the ballbounce icon to access the Sound Properties Panel, where the properties for this sound can be adjusted and tested until an acceptable balance between quality and file size is achieved. Click OK and return to the Library. Now, right-click the sound and choose Linkage from the pop-up menu. In the ensuing Symbol Linkage Properties dialog, type **ballbounce** in the Identifier box, and under Linkage options choose the radio button for Export this symbol.

5. Still working within the basketball movie clip, add a keyframe on the sixth frame. The bounce sound needs to be in synch with the bounce animation. For our sound, the sixth frame is the appropriate synchronized frame. With that keyframe selected, open the Actions Panel (Ctrl+Alt+A/Commnad+Option+A). There, we'll add actions to link this keyframe to the sound that was identified in the previous step as `ballbounce`.

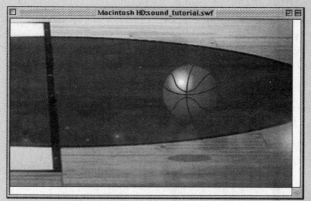

As the basketball bounces and follows the cursor, the sound mimics the change in space: The sound fades or rises as the ball moves backward and forward, and moves from left to right in synch with the position of the ball.

6. For the first action, in Normal Mode, under the Objects ⇨ Sound menu of the left pane of the Actions panel, set the value for the variable `s` to `new Sound`.

7. Still, within the same menu (Objects ⇨ Sound), double-click `attachSound` and enter **ballbounce** as the idName, and then scroll back to add **s** to the beginning of this action.

8. For the last action in this menu, click `start`, and then delete both `secondsOffset` and `loops` from inside the brackets. Finally, scroll back again and add **s** to the beginning of this action. The actions for the sixth frame of the basketball movie clip should now look like this:

```
s = new Sound();
s.attachSound("ballbounce");
s.start();
```

9. Now return to the Main Timeline and drag an instance of this basketball Movie Clip onto the stage and center it by using the Align Panel (Ctrl+K/Command+K). Name this instance, **basketball**. Save your work!

Continued

Continued

10. To make the basketball respond to mouse movements, we're going to make it into a draggable object. To do this, select the first frame of the top layer (labeled A for actions) and add a `startdrag` action from the Objects ⇨ Movie Clip menu, located within the Actions Panel. The target will be the basketball Movie Clip, /basketball. Both options, `Constrain to rectangle` and `Lock mouse to center` must be checked at the bottom of the panel. Coordinates for the `Constrain to rectangle` options should be Left: 10, Top: 10, Right: 490, Bottom: 200. These settings lock the Movie Clip to the center of any mouse movement, while constraining it to remain within an area of the Stage, as defined by the coordinates. The actions for the first frame of the Main Timeline now look like this:

```
startDrag ("/basketball", true, 10, 10, 490, 200);
```

Author's Note: Because this movie uses Flash 5-specific ActionScript, you may opt to use Dots notation for target names. In Step 10, /basketball would be _root.basketball.

11. On the second frame of the Actions layer, add the following actions:

```
basketball.s.getVolume();
basketball.s.getPan();
```

These actions are used to get (and then store) the volume and pan properties for the sound inside of the movie clip, basketball.

12. Next, set the variable n to equal the _y position of the basketball Movie Clip. This variable is used to scale the basketball with relationship to the mouse as it moves forwards and backwards. But because the basketball shouldn't be allowed to scale down too small, an `If (n<=50)` statement is used to set the variable n back to 50 if it is recognized as being any value less than 50. The code is as follows:

```
n = getProperty("/basketball", _y);
if (n<=25) {
     n = 25;
}
```

Author's Note: The value for n in Step 12 could also be written as `n = _root. basketball._y;` (in Flash 5 Dots notation).

13. With n set, the `_xscale` and `_yscale` properties of /basketball must now be set to equal n. When setting these properties, it's important to check the Expression box for the value n; otherwise, the movie attempts to set these properties to equal the name n instead of to the value derived from the mouse's _y position (which is what n is set to be). Here's the code:

```
setProperty ("/basketball", _xscale, n);
setProperty ("/basketball", _yscale, n);
```

Author's Note: You can change property values with the following Dots notation: `_root.basketball._xscale = n;` and `_root.basketball._yscale = n;`.

14. (If you still haven't saved the .FLA, you are courting disaster.) For the volume to be dynamic, the sound must change with the movement of the viewer's mouse. The mechanism for this is much like the scaling of the basketball, shown previously. Because n has already been set to equal the value of the _y position, this can also be used to set the volume. All that's needed is to set the pan. To do this, a variable is assigned to get the _x position of the basketball Movie Clip:

```
s1 = (getProperty ("/basketball", _x));
```

Author's Note: *In Flash 5 ActionScript, the preceding code could be written as* `s1 = _root.basketball._x;`.

15. This variable, which equals the _x position of the viewer's mouse, is used to set the variable that returns the value for the left-to-right pan. Before setting this value, it's important to understand the sliding scale for the pan. The pan is controlled by a scale of values that range from −100 to 100, with 0 being equal balance. This works fine, on a one-to-one relationship for movies that are precisely 200 pixels wide. But for movies where the range of possible value for the _x position exceeds 200, there will be a discrepancy between the possible values of the _x position and the scale of 200 units that is used for controlling the sliding pan. Thus, if a movie is anything other than 200 pixels wide, an adjustment has to be made for the difference. A magic number must be conjured that, when multiplied by 200, will equal the width of the movie. For this particular movie, we divide the width of our movie by 200. Because the width of this movie is 500, the magic number is 2.5.

16. Now, to set s2, which will be the final value of the pan, divide the value of s1 (which is the _x position of the mouse) by the magic number, 2.5. This equation scales the width of the movie to synch with the pan scale of 200. For example, if the _x position of the mouse is 350 (in our 500-pixel-wide movie), we divide by 2.5 to get a value of 140. We always subtract 100, because our scale goes from −100 (full left) to 100 (full right). This delivers a final value of 40 for s2; in other words, 40 percent full right pan. If the _x position is 50 (in a 500-pixel-wide movie), the value for s2 is 80 percent full left pan ((50/2.5 = 20) − 100) = −80. Thus:

```
s2 = ((s1/2.5)-100);
```

If your movie were less than 200 pixels wide, you would substitute multiplication for division. In other words, if your movie was 100 pixels wide and the _x position of the viewer's mouse was at 50, you would multiply 50 × 2 (which is the number that, when multiplied by the width of your movie, gives you 200), and then subtract 100 — giving you a final value of 0, or equal left-right balance.

Continued

Continued

17. Next, to keep the value of the pan between −100 and 100 without any slop in either direction, an `if` statement is added to ensure that `s2` will not be greater than 100 or less than −100:

```
if (s2<=-100) {
    s2 = -100;
}
if (s2>=100) {
            s2 = 100;
        }
```

18. Finally for the last actions in this keyframe, the volume of `/basketball` is assigned to the value of `n`, and the pan to the value of `s2`. As follows:

```
basketball.s.setVolume(n);
basketball.s.setPan(s2);
```

19. In the third and final keyframe, an action is added to continuously return the movie to the second frame, whereupon the variables are reevaluated and the properties are reset:

```
gotoAndPlay (2);
```

20. The scripting is done. Have you saved your movie yet? If not, save it, and then publish the movie and bounce on!

_____

Jay Vanian's single most favorite thing to do is actually three things, foremost of which is "taking pictures of buildings." He's also prone to "plan world strategies." Jay also enjoys Krav Maga, practice of which includes frequent visits to the emergency room. Perhaps these interests explain why he has no memories of popular culture from the year (4192) that he graduated high school, in his home town of Newport Beach, CA. Jay is billed as a multimedia artist with Pixelpushers, Inc. He was inspired to learn Flash because he "saw two sites that really stood out—Balthaser's and Shiny Entertainment's." He's worked on a number of sites, including: 11th Hour (www.hourtogo.com), THQ/Evil Dead (www.evildeadgame.com), Rhythmcraft (www.rhythmcraft.com), Crave Entertainment (www.cravegames.com), 2thebiz (www.2thebiz.com), Irvine Barclay Theatre (www.thebarclay.org), Ghosts (www.vanian.com/ghosts), and Alien Dog (www.alien-dog.com).

You can also use the `getPan` method to store values of the `setPan` method. In the tutorial example, you could create a hovering object that follows the basketball wherever you drag it. Instead of duplicating the value of the `setPan`, you could use `getPan` to retrieve the current Pan value of the sound of the basketball. The next section provides an overview of the ultimate sound control methods, `setTransform` and `getTransform`.

Creating a soundTransformObject

The two remaining methods of the Sound Object, `setTransform` and `getTransform`, work in the same manner as the transform methods of the Color Object. You need to create a generic object using the object constructor before the `setTransform` method can be used with a Sound Object. This generic object will become a `sound TransformObject` once we have assigned sound channel properties to the generic Object.

Luckily, the `soundTransformObject` doesn't have as many properties as the `colorTransformObject`, and they're much simpler to predict with trial and error testing. The properties of the `soundTransformObject` are:

✦ **ll**, the percentage of left channel output in the left speaker

✦ **lr**, the percentage of right channel output in the left speaker

✦ **rr**, the percentage of right channel output in the right speaker

✦ **rl**, the percentage of left channel output in the right speaker

The first letter of each property determines which physical speaker is being affected. The second letter determines which channel's output (or its volume) is played in that speaker. Each property can have a value between –100 and 100.

The steps to produce and incorporate a `soundTransformObject` are nearly the same as the `colorTransformObject`. The only difference is that you specify paths to Sound Objects rather than Movie Clip Objects for the `setTransform` and `get Transform` methods. Refer to the steps described earlier in this chapter for `colorTransform` Objects.

Tip Use the soundTransformObject to vary the output of the sounds in the soundLib example you created in this section. Just like the setTransform example for the Color Object, create buttons that create and execute unique transform settings.

Creating Draggable Movie Clips

Flash 4 introduced the drag'n'drop feature, which enables the user to pick up objects with the mouse pointer and move them around the movie stage. Flash 5 has added some new ways to use drag'n'drop with the new `onClipEvent` Movie Clip handler. Drag'n'drop in Flash is based entirely on Movie Clips. The only objects that can be moved with the mouse are Movie Clip instances. So, if you want a drawing of a triangle to be moveable by the user, you have to first put that triangle into a Movie Clip, and then place a named instance of that clip onto the Stage. Flash's drag'n'drop support is fairly broad, but more-complex drag'n'drop behaviors require some ActionScript knowledge. We'll cover building drag'n'drop Movie Clips in two parts: "Drag'n'Drop Basics" and "Advanced Drag'n'Drop."

Drag'n'drop basics

In mouse-based computer interfaces, the most common form of drag'n'drop goes like this: A user points to an element with the mouse pointer, clicks the element to begin moving it, and then releases the mouse button to stop moving it. In Flash 4, drag'n'drop functionality could only be achieved with the use of a nested Button instance in a Movie Clip symbol. Why? The Button symbol was the only Flash symbol that responded to mouse clicks. Furthermore, because Buttons couldn't be targeted like Movie Clips, a Button instance needed to exist within a Movie Clip in order for it be draggable. Then, a Drag Movie Clip Action (in Flash 4) was added to that Button instance. This method still works in Flash 5 (with the `startDrag` method or action), and uses the least amount of ActionScript to enable drag behavior. Here's how:

1. Start a new movie. Create a new Movie Clip named **dragObject**.

2. Create a simple button and place it on Frame 1, Layer 1 of the dragObject Movie Clip.

3. Return to the main stage by choosing Edit ➪ Edit Movie (Ctrl+E or Command+E). Place a copy of the dragObject Movie Clip on Stage and, with it still selected, open the Instance Panel (Ctrl+I or Command+I). Type **dragObject** in the Name text field, and then press the Enter or Tab. This names our Movie Clip instance so that it can be referred to by the `startDrag` action.

4. Return to the Symbol Editing Mode for the dragObject Movie Clip by double-clicking the instance. Select the Button instance on the Stage, and open the Actions Panel. In the upper right-hand corner of the Actions Panel, make sure Normal Mode is selected in the options menu.

5. Click the plus (+) button in the top-left corner of the Actions Panel and select Actions ➪ startDrag. In the parameter area of the Actions Panel, type **_root.dragObject** in the Target text field. The Target option specifies which Movie Clip should begin dragging when the `startDrag` action is executed. Note that though our `startDrag` action will be applied to the same Movie Clip that houses our button, a `startDrag` action can target any Movie Clip from any button, or from any keyframe.

Note You can also specify an empty string (in other words, leave the Target field blank) to refer to the current timeline on which the Button instance exists. Another way of specifying the current timeline (or Movie Clip Object) is to use the term `this`.

6. Now remember that we want to make our Movie Clip start moving as soon as the user presses the mouse button. So, change the button's Event Handler from `on (release)` to `on (press)` by selecting the `on (release)` line in the Actions list, unchecking the Release option of the Event setting, and then checking Press.

7. At this point, our button, when clicked, causes the dragObject Movie Clip instance to start following the mouse pointer. Now we have to tell the Movie Clip to stop following the pointer when the mouse button is released. With the last curly brace (}) highlighted in the Actions list, click the plus (+) button and select Actions ⇨ stopDrag. The default Event Handler added is on (release), which is what we want, so that's all we have to do. The stopDrag action stops any current dragging Movie Clip from following the mouse pointer.

Caution

It is possible to use a button that is not contained in the draggable Movie Clip to stop the dragging Action. If you use a button like that, remember that when your only Event Handler is on (release), your Action will not be executed if the mouse button is released when it is no longer over the button (which is likely to happen when the user is dragging things around). You should also add an on (releaseOutside) event handler to capture all Release events.

8. Test your movie with File ⇨ Publish Preview ⇨ Flash or Control ⇨ Test Movie (Ctrl+Enter or Command+Enter).

Did it work? Great! Now we can tell you about the other basic settings for the startDrag action.

Constrain to rectangle

Check this setting in order to specify the limits of the rectangular region within which a draggable Movie Clip instance can be dragged. After you've checked Constrain to Rectangle, enter the pixel locations of the four corners of the rectangle. The pixel coordinates are set relative to the top-left corner of the Stage upon which the draggable Movie Clip instance resides. For example startDrag ("drag-me", false, 0, 0, 300, 300) would constrain the draggable Movie Clip instance named drag-me to a 300-pixel square region in the top-left corner of the Main Timeline's Stage.

Note

If the draggable Movie Clip instance is located outside of the defined drag region when the Drag Movie Clip action occurs, then the instance is automatically moved into the closest portion of the drag region.

Lock mouse to center

This setting makes the dragged Movie Clip instance center itself under the mouse pointer for the duration of the drag. If the dragged Movie Clip instance is not already under the mouse pointer when the Drag Movie Clip action occurs, the instance will automatically be moved under the pointer, providing that the pointer is not outside the region defined by Constrain to Rectangle. When checked, this setting will add a Boolean value of true just after the specified instance name in the startDrag action.

Detecting the drop position: Using _dropTarget

In "Drag'n'Drop Basics," we showed you how to make Movie Clip instances that the user can move around. But what if we wanted to force the user to move a Movie Clip Object into a certain location before we let them drop it? For instance, consider a child's shape-matching game in which a small circle, square, and triangle should be dragged onto corresponding larger shapes. If the child drops the small circle onto the large square or large triangle, the circle returns to its original location. If, on the other hand, the child drops the small circle onto the large circle, the small circle should stay where it is dropped, and the child should receive a "Correct!" message. That kind of game is quite possible in Flash, but it requires some understanding of Movie Clip properties.

Here's how it works—we'll use the circle as an example. First, create a draggable instance of the little circle Movie Clip just as you did earlier in the "Drag'n'Drop Basics" section (put a button in a Movie Clip, put a named instance of that clip on stage, and then add the startDrag and stopDrag actions to the button). Then, you create a large circle graphic Symbol, put it into a Movie Clip, and place an instance of that Movie Clip onto the Main Timeline's Stage. Name the large circle Movie Clip **circleBig**. Here's where the Movie Clip properties come in: When the user drops any Movie Clip instance, the instance's _droptarget property is updated. The _droptarget property specifies the name of the Movie Clip instance upon which the dragged Movie Clip instance was last dropped. So if the user dropped the little circle Movie Clip instance onto the large circle instance, the _droptarget property for the little circle instance would be set to /circleBig. Knowing that, we can add an if . . . else condition to check whether the little circle was dropped onto the big circle. If it was, we simply let the little circle stay dropped, and we display a "Correct" message by targeting a Movie Clip to update a status-message contained within it. If the little circle wasn't dropped onto the big circle, we return the little circle to its place of origin by setting the X and Y coordinate properties of the little circle instance. Here's what the code on the little circle button would look like (note that the stopDrag action must occur before we check the _droptarget property):

```
on (press){
     startDrag ("_root.circle")
}
on (release){
     stopDrag();
     if (_root.circle._droptarget ) eq "/circleBig"){
          _root.status.gotoAndPlay ("correct");
     } else {
          _root.circle._x = 112;
          _root.circle._y = 316;
     }
}
```

For further study, we've included this basic child's drag'n'drop game as a sample movie called dragndrop.fla on the *Flash 5 Bible* CD-ROM in the ch41 folder.

Making alpha and scale sliders

A compelling use of a draggable Movie Clip is a slider that can alter the properties of another object. By checking the position of a Movie Clip, you can use the position's X or Y coordinate value to alter the value of another Movie Clip. In this section, we create two sliders (one for alpha and another for scale) that will dynamically change the transparency and size of a Movie Clip instance on the Stage. Many thanks to Sandro Corsaro of spanktoons.com for supplying the artwork of Robert's dog Stella and the park sign.

You need to copy the slider_basic_starter.fla file from the ch41 folder of the *Flash 5 Bible* CD-ROM. You'll use premade artwork to understand the functionality of startDrag, stopDrag, duplicateMovieClip, **and the** colorTransform Object.

Assembling the parts

In this section, we set up the basic composition of the Stage, using elements from the slider_basic_starter.fla Library. You will add artwork of a dog and a park sign to the movie. The dog artwork will be duplicated using the duplicateMovieClip method, and the duplicate instance will be manipulated by the sliders that we create in the next section. The park sign will be used to remove the duplicate instance using the _dropTarget property and the removeMovieClip method.

1. Open your copy of the slider_basic_starter.fla. Rename Layer 1 to **dog_1**.

2. Access the movie's Library by pressing Ctrl+L (Command+L). Open the dogElements folder, and drag the dog Movie Clip symbol onto the Stage. Place the instance in the upper-left corner of the Stage.

3. With the dog instance selected, open the Instance Panel. In the Name field, type **dog_1**, as shown in Figure 41-5.

4. Using the Text Tool, add the words **Original Dog** under the dog_1 instance. You don't need to make a new layer for this artwork.

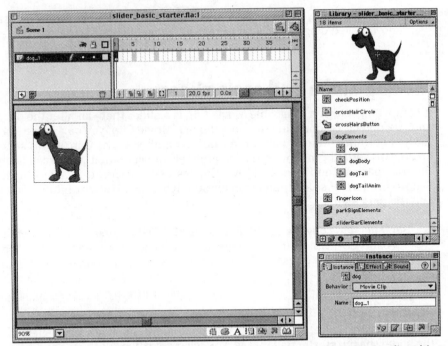

Figure 41-5: The dog_1 instance will be used as our reference Movie Clip Object. The scale and transparency of this dog instance will not be changed.

5. Create a new layer and name it **parkSign**. Move this layer below the dog_1 layer. Drag the parkSign Movie Clip symbol, located in the parkSignElements folder in the Library, to the lower-right corner of the Stage. In the Instance Panel, assign the instance the name **parkSign**. In the Transform Panel, reduce the size of the parkSign instance to **50.0%**, as shown in Figure 41-6.

6. Create a new layer called **actions**, and place it above all the other layers. Double-click the first keyframe of this layer. In the Actions Panel (in Expert Mode), add the following actions:

```
_root.dog_1.duplicateMovieClip ("dog_2", 1);
_root.dog_2._x = 350;
_root.dog_2._y = 175;
```

The first line of code duplicates the instance dog_1, names the new instance dog_2 and places it on the first depth layer of the _root timeline.

The second and third lines of code position the dog_2 instance at the X coordinate of 350 (350 pixels from the left corner of the Main Timeline Stage) and the Y coordinate of 175 (175 pixels down from the left corner).

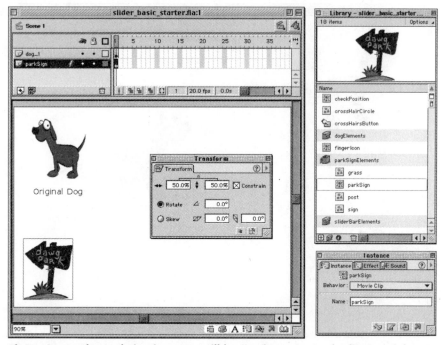

Figure 41-6: The parkSign instance will be used to remove duplicates of the dog_1 Movie Clip instance.

7. Save your movie as a new .FLA file, and test the movie (Ctrl+Enter or Command+Enter). You should see a new instance of the dog_1 Movie Clip appear on the right side of the Stage (see Figure 41-7).

Now that we have some artwork on the Stage, we can manipulate the duplicated Movie Clip with a pair of dynamic sliders.

Building the sliders

In this section, you'll create two sliders: one for scale, and one for transparency. We'll only need to make one slider Movie Clip symbol, and use a new instance for each slider. The basic "problems" of a dynamic slider are to (a) retrieve the position value of an object on the slider (we'll call this the **slider bar**), and (b) set the value of another object equal to (or some factor of) the position value of the slider bar. Finding the position of a slider bar is relatively straightforward. The difficulty lies in creating the value scale for the slider.

Figure 41-7: The duplicateMovieClip method creates a new instance of a Movie Clip Object. Unless you alter the new instance's X and Y position, it will appear directly above the parent instance.

Because we have already determined the properties that will be altered (scale and transparency) we need to establish a range of values that each property can use. Luckily, both scale (as _xscale and _yscale in ActionScript) and transparency (as _alpha) use percentage units. However, scale can be any value that's greater than 0 percent and less than 3200 percent. Alpha has a range of 0 to 100 percent. If we want to use the same parent slider for each property slider, then we need to manipulate the position values of the slider bar differently for each property. Let's start with building the basic slider.

1. Create a new Movie Clip symbol (Ctrl+F8 or Command+F8) and name it **slider**. In Symbol Editing Mode, rename the first layer **sliderRule**. On this layer, drag an instance of the sliderRule Graphic symbol (located in the sliderElements folder of the Library) onto the Movie Clip Stage.

Note   The sliderRule artwork contains a line that is 200 pixels long, bound with a circle on each end. The length of this line determines the position range for the slider bar. Therefore, our absolute range is between 0 and 200.

2. With the sliderRule Graphic selected, open the Info Panel. On the right side of the Info Panel (on the diagram of the square bounding box), make sure that the registration point is set to the top-left corner of the selection's bounding box. Then, enter the values **–28.4** for the X coordinate and **–12.4** for the Y coordinate, as shown in Figure 41-8.

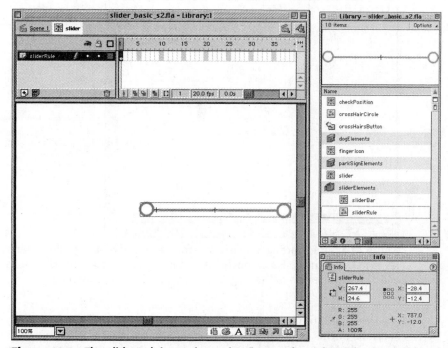

Figure 41-8: The sliderRule's starting point (just to the right of the first left-hand circle) needs to be at the slider Movie Clip's zero X coordinate.

3. Create another layer for the slider Movie Clip and name it **position**. Drag an instance of the sliderBar Movie Clip (located in the sliderElements folder of the Library) to the slider Movie Clip Stage.

4. With the sliderBar instance selected, open the Transform Panel. Type **90** in the Rotate field, and press Enter. In the Info Panel, click the center registration point in the bounding box diagram (on the right side), and enter **100** for the X coordinate and **–0.3** for the Y coordinate.

5. To see the position of the sliderBar instance, we need to assign a unique instance name. Select the sliderBar instance and type **position** in the Name field of the Instance Panel, as shown in Figure 41-9.

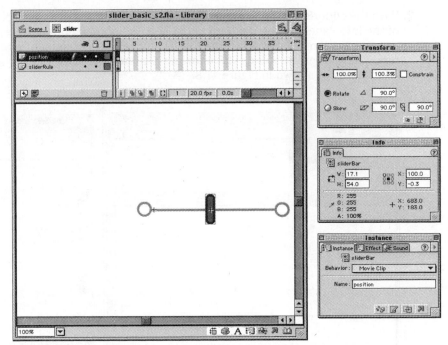

Figure 41-9: The starting X coordinate for the position Movie Clip instance is set to 100. When the Flash movie starts, this value will be applied to the scale and alpha properties of the dog_2 instance on the Main Timeline.

6. Now we need to make the position Movie Clip instance draggable. In earlier sections of this chapter, you saw how to embed an invisible button in the draggable Movie Clip in order to receive mouseDown and mouseUp events. In this example, we're going to make a button-free draggable Movie Clip instance, using the new onClipEvent handler for Movie Clip Objects. Select the position Movie Clip instance and open the Actions Panel. Add the following code to the Actions list:

```
onClipEvent (mouseDown) {
    if(this.hitTest(_root._xmouse,_root._ymouse, true)){
        this.startDrag (true, 10, 0, 200, 0);
        _root.state = "down";
    }
}
```

To make the position instance draggable, we need to detect the mouseDown event. Any Movie Clip that has the onClipEvent(mouseDown) handler will receive any and all mouse clicks on the Stage. Because this is the case, we need to determine whether the mouse click occurs within the space that the position instance occupies on the Main Timeline Stage.

The first line of code uses the `onClipEvent` handler to detect the `mouseDown` event (the act of pressing down on the left mouse button). When a mouse click occurs, the actions nested within the `onClipEvent` action will be executed.

The second line of code uses an `if` action to test whether the mouse click occurs on the position instance. The `hitTest` method can test the overlap of spaces in one of two ways: (a) by comparing a specific X and Y coordinate to an instance's occupied space, or (b) by comparing one Movie Clip instance's occupied space to another Movie Clip instance's space. If the `hitTest` method is used in the first way, then you can also check whether the X and Y coordinate intersects with the bounding box of the instance (`false`) or the entire shape of the instance (`true`). In this example, we use the `hitTest` method to retrieve the current X and Y coordinates of the mouse pointer (`_root._xmouse` and `_root._ymouse`) and compare them to the occupied space of `this`, which is a reference to the current instance of the position Movie Clip. If the mouse pointer is over the position instance on a mouse click, then the `hitTest` method will return a `true` condition, and execute the nested `if` actions.

Caution   Don't confuse the `true` argument of the `hitTest` method with the return value of the `hitTest` method. In this example, we have omitted the condition to check for `hitTest`. By doing this, ActionScript knows to infer a `true` comparison, meaning that the actions below the `if` action will only occur if `hitTest` returns a `true` value.

The third line of code will execute only if the `if` condition on the second line is `true`. Here, we enable the dragging behavior of the position instance by using the `startDrag` method on `this`. Because it's used as a method and not as an action, we don't need to specify a target instance in the arguments. The arguments prescribed here lock the mouse to the center of the object and constrain the draggable region to a bounding box defined by 10, 0 and 200, 0. This effectively keeps the position instance confined to the line of our sliderRule Graphic.

Note   We've limited the left end of the `startDrag` to the X coordinate of 10. This keeps the scale properties from going below 10 percent. If you try to assign a value of 0 or less to the scale properties, Flash will start scaling the instance back up to positive values in an unpredictable manner.

The fourth line of code sets a variable called `state` on the Main Timeline (`_root`) to the value of `down`. Because we'll be using two instances of the slider Movie Clip symbol, we need to know whether any instance has received the `mouseDown` event. We'll see why we need this code in later steps.

7. Now we need to be able to stop dragging the position Object when the left mouse button is released. Again, we'll use the `onClipEvent` handler to define our actions. Open the Actions Panel for the position instance:

```
onClipEvent (mouseUp) {
  if(this.hitTest(_root._xmouse,_root._ymouse, true)){
    this.stopDrag ();
    _root.state = "up";
  }
}
```

This block of code performs in the same manner that our code in Step 6 did. Once a `mouseUp` event (the act of releasing the left mouse button) is detected (line 1), we check whether the event occurred over the space of the position instance (line 2). If it did, then we stop the dragging of the position instance initiated in Step 6 (line 3). Finally, we set the `state` variable on the Main Timeline (_root) to `up`.

Next, we'll create two instances of the slider Movie Clip symbol on the Main Timeline Stage: one for scale, and one for alpha.

8. Exit the Symbol Editing Mode, and return to the Scene 1 timeline (the Main Timeline). Create a new layer called **scaleSlider**. Open the Library and drag an instance of the slider Movie Clip to the Stage. Name this instance **scaleSlider** in the Instance Panel.

9. Rotate the scaleSlider instance **180°**, so that the registration point is on the right side of the slider. Move the scaleSlider instance to the lower right of the Stage.

10. Create another layer called **alphaSlider**. Drag another instance of the slider Movie Clip on to the Stage, and name the instance **alphaSlider**. Rotate this instance **–90°**. Place the instance near the right edge of the Stage, as shown in Figure 41-10.

11. Save your Flash movie file and test it. You should be able to drag the position instances on both sliders.

Checking the positions of the sliders

Once we have a slider bar that is draggable, we need to access the new values of the position instance and apply the values to the properties of the dog_2 instance. To do this, we need to have a Movie Clip whose sole job is to check the X coordinate of the position instance. In this section, you'll learn how to make a Movie Clip that uses the `onClipEvent(enterFrame)` handler.

1. Create a new layer on the Main Timeline, and name it **checkPosition**. In the Library, you'll find a Movie Clip symbol with the same name. If you double-click this symbol in the Library, you'll find that there's nothing inside of this symbol except some artwork indicating the symbol's name on a single keyframe.

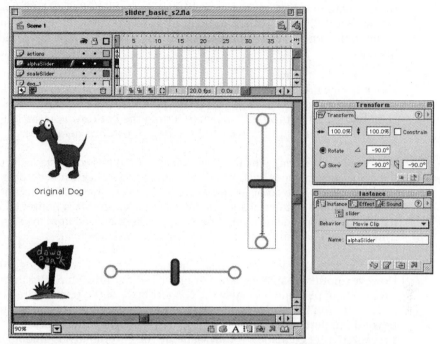

Figure 41-10: At this point, your Flash movie Stage should contain the dog and parkSign artwork, as well as two instances of the slider Movie Clip symbol.

2. Name the new instance **checkPosition** in the Instance Panel. Select the instance, and open the Actions Panel. In the Actions list, type the following code:

```
onClipEvent(enterFrame){
    _root.dog_2._xscale = _root.scaleSlider.position._x;
    _root.dog_2._yscale = _root.scaleSlider.position._x;
    _root.dog_2._alpha = _root.alphaSlider.position._x;
}
```

Because the event `enterFrame` is specified for the `onClipEvent` handler, this block of code will execute continuously in our Flash movie. Why? Any timeline will continuously enter a frame for playback, even if a `stop()` action is applied to all timelines. The speed at which the `enterFrame` event occurs is determined by the frame rate of the Flash movie (as defined by the Modify ⇨ Movie dialog). The frame rate of 20 fps was already set in the sample file before you opened it. Therefore, this block will execute 20 times each second.

What happens on each execution of the `enterFrame` event? The second and third lines of code set the X and Y scale properties of the dog_2 instance to the value returned by the current X coordinate of the position instance (relative to the coordinates within the slider Movie Clip symbol).

Notice that the target path for the position instance is the scaleSlider instance in lines 2 and 3. The fourth line sets the alpha property of the dog_2 instance equal to the X coordinate of the position instance within the alphaSlider instance.

3. Save your Flash movie, and test it. When you drag the bar on the bottom scale slider, notice how the *size* of the dog_2 instance increases as you drag it to the left. Remember that we rotated this instance 180°, so it increases from right to left, not left to right. When you drag the bar down on the left alpha slider, you'll see that the *opacity* of the dog_2 instance decreases.

Note

You may be wondering why the X coordinate of the position instance is used for the alphaSlider instance, instead of the Y coordinate. Indeed, you do drag the bar on a vertical axis instead of a horizontal one. However, the position instance exists within the space of the slider Movie Clip symbol, which has a horizontal orientation in the Symbol Editing Mode. The X coordinate is derived from the stage of the Symbol Editing Mode, regardless of the instance's orientation.

Okay, we have the sliders changing the size and opacity of the dog_2 instance. However, nothing happens as we drag the bar on the alphaSlider instance toward its upper limit. Because the X coordinate of the position instance starts at 100, we won't see any visual effect to the alpha property as it increases beyond 100 percent. The lower limit of the alpha slider is 10 percent — it's prevented from going below that value by the coordinate arguments of the startDrag method. Therefore, it would be better to have the alphaScale slider convert the X coordinate of the position instance to a true 0 to 100 range of values.

To do this, we need to develop an equation that will do the work of automatically remapping values to a 0–100 scale. We know that the lowest X coordinate of the position instance is 10, and that the highest X coordinate is 200. If we want the highest position of the bar to provide 100 percent opacity, then we need to divide 200 by a number that will give us 100. Dividing 200 by 2 gives us 100. How does that work for the low end? If the X coordinate returns the lowest value of 10, then our lowest opacity value will be 5.

4. Open the Actions Panel for the checkPosition instance, and modify the fourth line to read:

```
_root.dog_2._alpha = (_root.alphaSlider.position._x)/2;
```

5. Save your movie and test it. Now, as you drag up with the bar for the alphaSlider, the opacity increases. As you drag down, it decreases.

So far, so good. However, it would be useful if the alphaSlider's position instance started with an X coordinate of 200. This would initialize the dog_2 instance with an opacity of 100 percent. We could physically move the position instance within the slider symbol to an X coordinate of 200, but that would increase the scale of the dog_2 instance to 200 percent at the start. To change only the alphaSlider's position instance at the start of the movie, we'll add an onClip Event(load) handler to the position instance in the slider Movie Clip symbol.

`load` events will be triggered as soon as a Movie Clip Object appears on the Stage. Within the `onClipEvent` action, we'll check whether the position instance is within the alphaSlider instance. If it is, then we'll move the position instance to an X coordinate of 200; otherwise, nothing will happen to the position instance.

6. In the Library, double-click the slider Movie Clip symbol. In Symbol Editing Mode, select the position instance. Open the Actions Panel and add the following code to the Actions list:

```
onClipEvent (load){
     if(_parent._name == "alphaSlider"){
        this._x = 200;
     }
}
```

This block of code will execute once, when the position instance (a Movie Clip Object) first appears (or loads) on the Stage. Remember that the position instance occurs twice: once inside scaleSlider, and again inside alphaSlider. The second line of code checks which slider instance is executing this code. We use the `_parent` target to access the properties of the outer Movie Clip containing the position instance. Then, we access its name property (`_name`) to see if its name is alphaSlider. If it is, then, in line 3, we'll change the X coordinate (`_x`) of `this` (which is the position instance) to 200.

7. Save the Flash movie and test it. This time, the alphaSlider's bar (its position instance) will immediately start at the upper limit.

Removing Movie Clips

At this point in the chapter, you have two sliders that dynamically control the scale and alpha of the dog_2 Movie Clip instance on the Stage. What if you wanted to get rid the dog_2 instance? How would you delete it? The only way to remove a duplicated Movie Clip instance is to use the `removeMovieClip` method or action. In this section, we show you how to use the `_dropTarget` property and the `remove MovieClip` method of the Movie Clip Object.

1. Select the dog_1 instance in the upper-left corner of the Stage, and open the Actions Panel. Type the following code into the Actions list:

```
onClipEvent (mouseDown) {
     if(this.hitTest(_root._xmouse,_root._ymouse, true) ¬
&& this._name != "dog_1"){
          this.startDrag (true, 0, 0, 550, 400);
     }
}
onClipEvent (mouseUp) {
     if(this.hitTest(_root._xmouse,_root._ymouse, true)){
          this.stopDrag ();
     }
     if(eval(this._dropTarget) == _root.parkSign){
          this.removeMovieClip();
     }
}
```

Most of this code is already familiar to you. Here we want to make only our duplicate dog instance (dog_2) draggable. We don't want to be able to remove our original dog. Even if we wanted to, we couldn't delete the dog_1 instance, as it is physically placed on the Stage of the Flash movie. Only duplicated Movie Clip instances can be removed with ActionScript.

When a `mouseDown` event is detected, this code uses the `hitTest` method to see if the mouse pointer is over the current dog instance (`this`) and if the current dog instance (`this`) is *not* named dog_1. If both of these conditions are `true`, then the `startDrag` method of the current dog instance (`this`) will be enabled and constrained to the dimensions of the Flash movie Stage.

When a `mouseUp` event is detected over the dog instance, then the `stopDrag` method will be executed. The last `if` statement checks whether the `_drop Target` property of the current dog instance is equal to the target path of the parkSign instance. If the dog instance is over the parkSign instance on the Stage when the dragging stops, then the current dog instance is removed.

Note   We use the `eval()` action on the `_dropTarget` property because `_dropTarget` returns the path of the target in Slashes notation (for Flash 4 compatibility). If we use `eval()` on the `_dropTarget` property, then Flash will return the target path in Dots notation.

2. Save your Flash movie and test it. When you drag the dog_2 instance over the parkSign instance, it disappears.

Duplicating Movie Clips with new colors

What do we do after we've removed the dog_2 instance? How do we get more dog instances to use in the movie? This next section explores using the `duplicate MovieClip` method on a Button symbol. Not only will we duplicate the dog instance, but we'll also change its color attributes using the `colorTransformObject`.

Cross-Reference   Please see the Color Object coverage earlier in this chapter for details on the `colorTransformObject`.

1. On the Main Timeline, create a new layer and name it **duplicateButton**. Drag the crossHairsButton symbol from the Library onto the Stage. Place it in the lower-right corner, between the two sliders, as shown in Figure 41-11.

2. With the crossHairsButton instance selected, open the Actions Panel and type the following code:

```
on (release) {
    _root.dog_1.duplicateMovieClip ("dog_2", 1);
    _root.dog_2._x = 350;
    _root.dog_2._y = 175;
    dogColor = new Color(_root.dog_2);
    colorTransform = new Object();
```

```
colorTransform = {
    ra: randomPercent(),
    rb: randomOffset(),
    ga: randomPercent(),
    gb: randomOffset(),
    ba: randomPercent(),
    bb: randomOffset()
}
dogColor.setTransform(colorTransform);
}
```

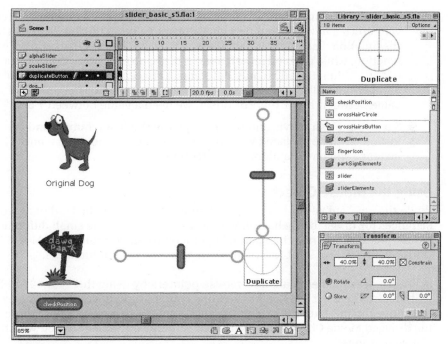

Figure 41-11: The crossHairsButton will contain actions that duplicate the dog_1 instance and apply different color attributes to the new instance.

Because we already covered the `colorTransformObject` earlier in this chapter, we won't explain its use here. However, we will describe the use of two new user-defined functions, `randomPercent()` and `randomOffset()`. These functions will be added to the Main Timeline (_root) in the next step. Instead of assigning fixed values to the color attributes, we supply new random values each time this button is clicked.

3. Return to the Main Timeline and select the first keyframe in the actions layer. Open the Actions Panel, and add the following code to create the `randomPercent()` and the `randomOffset()` functions:

```
function randomPercent(){
    newPercent = Math.round(Math.random()*100 + 1);
    return newPercent;
}
function randomOffset(){
    newOffset = Math.round(Math.random()*255 + 1);
    return newOffset;
}
```

Both of these functions work the same way. When each function is evoked, it will return a new random percent or offset value to the line of code that called the function. Each percent attribute (ra, ga, ba) evokes the `randomPercent()` function, while each offset attribute (rb, gb, bb) accesses the `random Offset()` function. The only difference between the two functions is the number multiplied to the `Math.random()` method. For percent, we need a value between 1 and 100. For offset, we need a value between 1 and 255.

4. Save your Flash movie and test it. Click the Duplicate button and the dog_2 instance will be replaced with another instance of the same name. The new instance will have random color attributes.

Using the Mouse Object

While the `onClipEvent(mouseDown)` handler can be used instead of nested Button instances for draggable behavior, you may have noticed one small difference: The mouse pointer does not change the finger icon when you rollover a Movie Clip Object with `onClipEvent(mouseDown` or `mouseUp)` event handlers.

In Flash 4, we could emulate new mouse pointers by using the `startDrag` behavior (with lock to center `true`) on Movie Clips containing icon graphics. However, this technique did not hide the original mouse pointer — it would appear directly above the dragged Movie Clip instance. In Flash 5, there is a Mouse Object, which has two simple methods:

✦ `show()`: This method reveals the mouse pointer. By default, the mouse pointer will appear at the start of a movie.

✦ `hide()`: This method turns off the mouse pointer's visibility. To reveal the mouse pointer again, execute the `show()` method.

Once the Mouse Object (the mouse pointer) is hidden, you can lock a Movie Clip Object (containing a new icon graphic) to the position of the mouse pointer. If you have only one Movie Clip Object that works like a Button symbol, then attaching a new Movie Clip instance to the mouse pointer is relatively straightforward. However, in our slider example, we have two different sliders with draggable bars. If we want to enable a custom icon, we need to know which bar is being moused over, and which bar isn't.

1. On the Main Timeline, select the checkPosition Movie Clip instance. Open the Actions Panel, and add the following code to the Actions list:

```
onClipEvent(load){
     overSlider = false;
}

onClipEvent(mouseMove){
   scaleSliderOver = _root.scaleSlider.position.hitTest ¬
     (_root._xmouse,_root._ymouse,true);
   alphaSliderOver = _root.alphaSlider.position.hitTest ¬
     (_root._xmouse,_root._ymouse,true);
   if (scaleSliderOver == true || alphaSliderOver == true){
     if (overSlider != true){
       _root.attachMovie("fingerIcon","fingerIcon",2);
       Mouse.hide();
       overSlider = true;
     }
     _root.fingerIcon._x = _root._xmouse;
     _root.fingerIcon._y = _root._ymouse;
   } else {
     if(_root.state != "down"){
       Mouse.show();
       _root.fingerIcon.removeMovieClip();
       overSlider = false;
       } else {
         _root.fingerIcon._x = _root._xmouse;
         _root.fingerIcon._y = _root._ymouse;
       }
   }
}
```

The first `onClipEvent` handler detects the `load` event. Remember that the `load` event happens when a Movie Clip instance first appears on the Stage. When the Movie Clip instance checkPosition appears on the Stage, the variable `overSlider` will equal `false`. This variable remembers if we're currently mousing within one of the position instances.

The second `onClipEvent` handler detects any mouse movements on the Stage with the `mouseMove` event. The two variables, `scaleSliderOver` and `alphaSliderOver`, will be either `true` or `false`, depending on the return of the `hitTest` method for the mouse pointer and the position instances.

The first `if` statement checks to see if either `hitTest` returned a `true` value. The `||` operator indicates that only one `hitTest` needs to return a `true` value for the nested actions after the `if` statement to execute.

If the mouse is over either slider, then the next `if` statement checks whether `overSlider` is *not* equal to `true`. When the checkPosition instance first loads, `overSlider` is equal to `false`. Therefore, the actions in this second `if` statement will execute.

If overSlider is false, then the attachMovie method will be executed from the Main Timeline (_root). In this example, we are attaching the fingerIcon Movie Clip from the Library to a new instance of the same name. This new fingerIcon instance is a child of the _root timeline, and is located on its second depth layer — the dog_2 instance occupies the first depth layer. After the fingerIcon is attached to the _root timeline, we need to hide the mouse pointer. The code line Mouse.hide(); does just that. Then, we set overSlider to equal true so that these nested actions are not repeated until we leave a position instance and reenter its space.

Note

To use attachMovie on Movie Clip symbols in the Library, you need to assign a unique identifier to the symbol. You can assign an identifier to a symbol by right-clicking the symbol in the Library and choosing Linkage. In our example, the identifier fingerIcon was already assigned as the identifier. We discuss Linkage Properties in more detail in Chapter 42, "Sharing and Loading Assets."

Then, we need to change its X and Y coordinates to match the position of the mouse pointer — we can still track its position even if it's hidden. The next two lines of code set the X and Y coordinates of the fingerIcon to the X and Y coordinates of the mouse pointer.

If the mouse pointer is *not* over either of the sliders, then the else condition tells Flash what to do on mouseMove events: If the mouse isn't currently dragging a slider's bar (_root.state != "down"), then show the mouse pointer, remove the fingerIcon Movie Clip instance, and set overSlider back to false. If the mouse has clicked a position instance *and* is overdragging the area of the position instance (see the following Tip), we still want the fingerIcon to move with the hidden mouse pointer.

Tip

Why do we need to check the state variable if the mouse isn't over the position instance in either slider? If you start to drag the position on a slider, your mouse pointer might move ahead (or beyond) the entire slider as you drag. If the mouse is dragging a position instance, we don't want to see the mouse pointer — only the fingerIcon instance should show.

2. Save the Flash movie, and test it. When you mouse over the bar of each slider, you should see the fingerIcon instance appear instead of the mouse pointer.

That might have seemed like a lot of work to hide a mouse pointer, but in the process, you learned how to attach your own icons to the mouse pointer. If you want more than two Movie Clip instances to use the fingerIcon instance, you would add them to the first if statement that checks hitTest with the mouse pointer.

Printing with ActionScript

Table 41-4, earlier in this chapter, summarizes the printing functions of ActionScript. Using the `print` and `printAsBitmap` functions, you can enable your Flash movies to output Flash artwork, text and bitmaps. With these actions, you can:

✦ **Create Flash ads that have printable specifications for e-commerce merchandise.** Imagine if the next car ad you saw on your favorite Web site automatically printed dealer locations and maps without having going to the car manufacturer's Web site?

✦ **Make Flash coupons.** You could design printable coupons for e-tailers on the Web that can be printed and redeemed at their brick-and-mortar stores.

✦ **Automate dynamic Web-generated invoices and receipts at e-commerce sites.** With Flash 5, you can format ordered items and add dynamic data to printable sheets.

✦ **Print rich vector illustrations or photorealistic bitmaps from a Web site.** Design Flash portfolio sites that print samples of stock images, or create personalized vector artwork that can be print unique images for each visitor.

✦ **E-mail printable Flash artwork to clients.** The next time you have proof of concepts or finished artwork that needs final approval, you can e-mail your clients the Flash artwork in a standalone projector or .SWF file.

✦ **Design custom contact information pages.** Sick of HTML tables that won't print your nice row-and-column–formatted pages of information consistently from browser to browser? Printable Flash frames will print beautifully each time. You could even add a visitor's contact information to a dynamic database and print it.

Although we can't describe how to do all these tasks in the space of this chapter, we will show you how to get started with the last idea. The following Expert Tutorial by Mike Richards shows you how to add `print` and `printAsBitmap` functions to his cool Flash paper airplane creator.

Note Because Flash natively uses vector artwork, it translates best when output to a PostScript printer. Nevertheless, both `print` and `printAsBitmap` actions will produce high-quality output to both PostScript and non-PostScript printers.

Expert Tutorial: Creating Printable Paper Airplanes, by Mike Richards

Mike's tutorial provides a great example of distributing interesting printable content on the Web. Instead of formatting and printing text and standard layouts, this tutorial shows you how to print Mike's paper planes. He has already prepared a paperplane_starter.fla file that you can find in the ch41 folder of the Flash 5 Bible CD-ROM. We invite you to review this file's contents and timeline structure, and copy the file to your hard drive before you start this tutorial.

This tutorial focuses on printing using the `print` and `printAsBitmap` actions, which can print frames in any timeline within the Flash movie. These actions become a powerful tool for creating printable content for the Web.

Using the print action to print content in the Main Timeline

When completed, this first section will demonstrate how to print content located on the Main Timeline using the basic `print` action. Additionally, we will control the printable area using the Flash movie's bounding box option in conjunction with the frame labels #b and #p.

1. First we set the printing boundary box for the paper wing folding instructions. Open your copy of paperplane_starter.fla and select frame 54 on the layer print content.

2. With frame 54 of the layer print content selected, drag the Graphic symbol named bounding box from the Library to the Stage. In the Frame Panel, enter **#b** for its label name.

3. Next, we specify the frame to be printed. With frame 55 of the layer print content selected, drag paper wing to the Stage. In the Frame Panel, enter **#p** for it's label. It is important to note that all frames on the Main Timeline will print if #p is not used to designate printable content.

4. Because we will specify a bounding box to define the printable area, it is necessary to horizontally and vertically center the two symbol instances. At the bottom of the timeline window, click the Edit Multiple Frames icon and select the two symbols that we previously placed on the Stage. With both symbols selected, align the horizontal and vertical centers to the Stage using the Align Panel. When finished aligning to center, be certain to click again on the Edit Multiple Frames icon to disable its function.

5. Now we are ready to add the `print` action to the button in our movie. Move the playhead on the timeline to frame 65 and select the printer button in the lower-right corner of the Stage. Choose Window ➪ Actions to add actions to the Button instance. With the Actions Panel open, click the Actions booklet on the left-hand side of the panel. Double-click print to place the `print` action in the Actions list on the right side, as shown in the following figure. Because there are no alpha effects to preserve in the printed material, choose As vectors in the Print drop-down menu. Because our content resides on the Main Timeline, select Target for the Location option and enter **_root** in the field. Finally, because we specified a bounding box on the Main Timeline, select Movie for the Bounding box option.

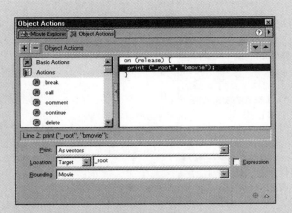

6. Save your Flash movie file and select Control ⇨ Test Movie to view the results. In Test Movie mode, select standard wing and click the printer icon in the lower-right corner to print the one page of wing folding instructions.

Using the printAsBitmap action with content in a Movie Clip instance

This next section demonstrates how to print content residing in a Movie Clip using the printAsBitmap action. The print area is controlled by using the Frame bounding box option. The Frame bounding box option scales the print area for each frame of content, thus ensuring that every page is printed at its maximum printable size. Note that Movie Clip instances can use either print or printAsBitmap actions, depending on the contents of the Movie Clip symbol. For purposes of demonstration, we use the printAsBitmap action.

1. With frame 27 of the layer print content selected, drag the Movie Clip symbol named paper shuttle from the Library to the work area located to the right of the Stage. With the instance still selected, enter **shuttle** in the Name field of the Instance Panel. It is not necessary to designate printable frames with #p in the Movie Clip Symbol timeline because we intend to print all frames within this timeline.

2. Now we are ready to assign actions to our print button. Move the playhead on the Main Timeline to frame 27 and select the printer button in the lower-right corner of the Stage. With the Actions Panel open, click the Actions booklet at the left side. Double-click print to place the print action in the Actions list on the right side. For the Print option, choose As bitmap because the Movie Clip symbol contains alpha effects on the second frame artwork. For the Location option, choose Target. Our printable content resides in the shuttle instance on the Main Timeline. Therefore, we enter **_root.shuttle** to correctly target the movie, as shown in the following figure. Finally, we choose Frame for our Bounding box option because we want to scale each page of printable content to it maximum size.

Continued

Continued

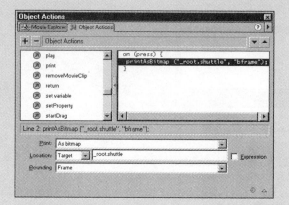

3. Save your Flash movie and select Control ➪ Test Movie to view the results. In Test Movie mode, select the first plane and customize the paper plane with art and text. To print the plane and instructions, press the printer icon in the lower-right corner of the Stage.

Printing a loaded .SWF file

For this last example, we walk through the basics of printing Flash content that is loaded into a target. This method is optimal if the content that you intend on printing is significant in size. The *Flash 5 Bible* discusses loading .SWF files in Chapter 42, "Sharing and Loading Assets."

1. Move the playhead on the Main Timeline to frame 47 and select the printer button in the lower-right corner of the Stage. Choose Window ➪ Actions to view the Actions list for the Button instance. In this example, the loadMovie action is used to load a two-frame .SWF file, classic_instructions.swf.

2. Next, with the Actions Panel open, select the word Placeholder, which is located just outside the top-right corner of the Stage. The onClipEvent(load) handler, along with this._visible = 0, is used to make the content invisible during playback. Even though it is hidden, this Movie Clip instance is still printable. Because content needs to be completely loaded to print, the clip event data is used in conjunction with the methods getBytesTotal and getBytesLoaded to confirm the completion of load before printing. For the Print option, As vectors was chosen because the printable content does not contain alpha effects. For Location, Target was chosen. The printable content will load into this Movie Clip with an instance name of classic_placeholder. Therefore, _root.classic_placeholder was entered to correctly target the movie, as shown in the following figure. Finally, the Bounding box option of Frame was chosen because we want to scale each page to its maximum printable size.

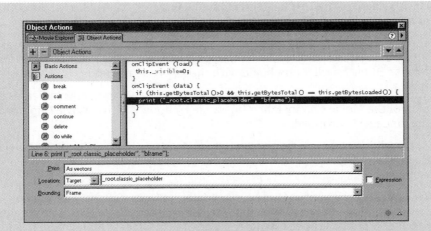

3. Save the Flash movie and select Control ➪ Test Movie to view the results. In Test Movie mode, select the center plane and customize the paper plane with art and text. Press the printer icon in the lower-right corner of the Stage to print the plane and instructions.

Mike Richards claims that his most favorite thing to do is, "Using Flash." Perhaps that explains why he relocated to San Francisco last year to work for Macromedia. Prior to that move, he worked for American Greetings (american greetings.com) creating animated flash cards and games. It was there that he discovered Flash, "when we were looking for an alternative to Macromedia Director that artists could easily learn and use." From the year that he graduated from High School in Cleveland, Ohio, Mike deems the Chocolate War as the most memorable movie. In addition to his work for Macromedia, Mike's current site development is devoted to www.hipid.com.

Summary

✦ The Movie Clip Object has unique properties, methods, and handlers. Using Dots notation, you can access these characteristics of the Movie Clip Object.

✦ You can change a Movie Clip instance's position, scale, and rotation using ActionScript. Most physical attributes are accessed by specifying the Movie Clip's path followed by the property name, as in _root.myMCinstance._rotation.

✦ The Color Object can store new color values and apply them to Movie Clip instances using the setRGB and setTransform methods.

✦ Sound libraries can be created in less time by using ActionScript and the Sound Object. Sound Objects are created by using Linkage identifiers for sound files in the movie's Library.

✦ Flash 5 enables you to change the volume and pan values of any Sound Object at any point in your Flash movie.

✦ You can add mouse drag behaviors to your Movie Clip symbols in two ways: (a) by using nested Button instances; or (b) by using the new `onClipEvent` `(mouseDown)` handler combined with the `hitTest` method.

✦ The `_dropTarget` property of Movie Clip instance (instance A) indicates the path of the Movie Clip instance (instance B) upon which a Movie Clip instance (instance A) is dropped.

✦ As the sliders example demonstrated, you can use the values of one Movie Clip instance's properties to change the property values of another Movie Clip instance.

✦ The `onClipEvent(mouseMove)` event handler does not give any visible representation of a `mouseOver` on Movie Clip instances with `onClipEvent` `(mouseUp` or `mouseDown)` handlers. The Mouse Object can be hidden, and a custom Movie Clip instance can be attached to the coordinates of the mouse pointer.

✦ By using the `print` and `printAsBitmap` functions, you can output high-quality artwork to a PostScript or non-PostScript printer.

✦   ✦   ✦

Sharing and Loading Assets

Because most Flash movies are downloaded and viewed over the Web, Flash 5 has a number of advanced actions that are dedicated solely to controlling the download and display of movies and Library assets. Actions that check movie frame counts and file size properties let developers prevent a movie from playing before a specified portion of it has finished loading. The `loadMovie` and `unloadMovie` actions enable movies to be broken into small pieces or assets that are downloaded only if required by user choice.

Managing Smooth Movie Download and Display

When Flash movies are played back over the Internet, they *stream*, meaning that the plug-in shows as much of the movie as it can during download, even if the whole file has not been transferred to the user's system or browser cache. The benefit of this feature is that users start seeing content without having to wait for the entire movie to finish downloading.

Nevertheless, streaming has potential drawbacks. First, during streamed playback, the movie may unexpectedly halt at arbitrary points on the timeline because a required portion of the movie has not yet downloaded. Second, ActionScript code is ignored when it refers to segments of the movie that have not downloaded. These drawbacks can lead to unpredictable and often undesired playback results.

Thankfully, there's a solution. You can regulate the playback of the movie by using ActionScript code to prevent the movie from playing until a specified portion of it has downloaded. This technique is often referred to as *preloading*. A common preload sequence, or *preloader* involves displaying only a short message, such as "Loading . . . Please Wait," while the movie loads. Once the appropriate amount of the movie has been retrieved, the movie is allowed to play. Flash 5 provides basic and advanced methods of producing a preloader. This section of the chapter shows you how to use three different actions (or methods) to check the download status of a Flash movie:

✦ `If Frame is Loaded` **or** `ifFrameLoaded`: This action has been around since Flash 3, and enables you to check whether a specified frame label in the Flash movie has been downloaded by the plug-in. This is the simplest action to use to check a movie's download progress.

✦ `_framesLoaded` **and** `_totalFrames`: Introduced with Flash 4, these properties can be checked on a Movie Clip timeline or the main movie timeline (Scene 1, Scene 2, and so on). `_framesLoaded` returns the current number of frames that have downloaded into the plug-in, while `_totalFrames` returns the number of frames that exist on the specified target timeline.

✦ `getBytesLoaded()` **and** `getBytesTotal()`: These methods are new to Flash 5 ActionScript. The most accurate way to check the progress of a Flash movie download is to use these methods with other ActionScript code.

The following examples show you how to use each of these actions to monitor the download of a Flash movie over the Web.

Note   Technically, Flash movies are a progressive download file format, similar to original QuickTime 3 video movies. A progressive download is one that can be viewed before the entire file has been received by the browser. Streaming file formats are never saved as actual files in the browser cache. You can't save a streaming file, but you can typically save a shortcut or link to the file's location on the Web.

Building a basic preloader with ifFrameLoaded

In this example, we explain how to create a preloader for a 100-frame movie, where the movie doesn't begin playing until all 100 frames have been downloaded. For this exercise, make sure the Actions Panel is in Normal Mode.

1. Create a new movie with 100 frames. Rename Layer 1 to **actions**.

2. Create a new layer and name it **labels**. On the labels layer, create a blank keyframe on frames 2, 5, and 100. Label those frames **preload_loop**, **begin_movie**, and **minimum_loadpoint**, respectively.

3. Create a new layer and name it **content**. Create blank keyframes at frame 5 and frame 100. On each of those keyframes, place a large symbol such as a complex vector shape or a bitmap (you need some content in order to see the load sequence working in Test Movie Mode). See Figure 42-1 for reference.

Figure 42-1: Add content to the Main Timeline that will be preloaded.

4. On frame 1 of the Content layer, use the Text Tool to type the words **Loading . . . Please Wait**.

5. On the actions layer, create a blank keyframe at frames 3, 4, and 100.

6. Edit the actions of frame 3 by double-clicking it in the timeline. This opens the Actions Panel. Click the plus (+) button in the top-left corner of the panel and select Basic Actions ➪ If Frame is Loaded. Choose the Frame Label option in the Type setting, and select minimum_loadpoint from the Frame drop-down menu.

7. With the line ifFrameLoaded ("minimum_loadpoint"){ highlighted in the Actions listbox, click the plus (+) button and select Basic Actions ➪ Go To. Choose the Frame Label option of the Type setting, and then select begin_ movie from the Frame drop-down menu. Then check the Go to and Play option at the bottom of the parameter area. This Go To action, which starts playback of the real movie, will only be executed if the frame labeled minimum_loadpoint has been downloaded.

The `ifFrameLoaded` action is a one-time check. If the frame specified in `ifFrameLoaded` action has already downloaded, then the action(s) contained within the `ifFrameLoaded` statement are executed. If, on the other hand, the frame specified has not yet downloaded, then the action(s) contained are not executed, and the movie simply continues playing. In most cases, however, you won't want the movie to carry on playing until your desired frame has been downloaded, so you have to force the movie to perform the `ifFrameLoaded` check repeatedly until the specified frame is loaded.

8. To loop the `ifFrameLoaded` action, edit the frame actions of frame 4 on the actions layer by double-clicking the frame in the timeline. In the Actions Panel, add a `Go To` action to the Actions list. Choose Frame Label from the Type menu, and select preload_loop from the Frame drop-down menu. Then check the Go to and Play option.

9. Finally, add a `stop()` action on frame 100 of the actions layer. Now you're ready to test your movie and see the preloader work its magic. Choose Control ➪ Test Movie (Command+Enter or Ctrl+Enter). Once in Test Movie Mode, you'll have to configure the environment a bit to watch the simulated download. Enable the Bandwidth Profiler by checking View ➪ Bandwidth Profiler. Click frame 1 in the Profiler timeline. Select View ➪ Frame by Frame Graph. Choose Control ➪ 28.8 (2.3KB/s) (this simulates a 28.8-baud modem). To watch your movie playback as it would over the Web, choose Control ➪ Show Streaming. You'll see the playhead in the timeline looping around your `ifFrameLoaded` action while it waits for the movie to download. The green bar in the timeline indicates how much of the movie has downloaded.

On the CD-ROM   For further study, we've included this basic preloader movie as a sample movie called preloader_1.fla on the Flash 5 Bible CD-ROM in the ch42 folder.

There are some general guidelines to keep in mind when you make a preloader. First, preloaders do not work inside Movie Clips. You cannot preload individual portions of a Movie Clip. If a Movie Clip instance is placed on a frame, the frame is not considered loaded until the entire instance has finished loading. Second, you don't need to preload the entire movie when using preloaders. In our previous example, you could move the `minimum_loadpoint` keyframe to any point in the movie after frame 5. By using the streaming emulator in Test Movie Mode, you can determine approximately how much of your movie should be loaded before you allow it to play. Also, by using more than one preloader you can show the first part of a movie and then reenter a loading state before showing any subsequent parts.

Preloading with _framesLoaded and _totalFrames

In Flash 3, the only tool developers had to create preloaders was the `If Frame is Loaded` action. Using multiple preloaders, developers attempted to simulate a percentage-loaded feature that told the user how much of the movie had been downloaded. Although they demonstrated the ingenuity of the developers, these percentage-loaded indicators were mostly inaccurate. With the introduction of ActionScript in Flash 4, developers had a way to precisely determine the percentage of *frames* that have been downloaded to the user's system. In this section, we convert the preloading mechanism of the preloader_1.fla movie to the _framesLoaded and _totalFrames method.

1. Open the preloader_1.fla that you created in the last section. If you didn't do that exercise, then open a copy of the same file from the *Flash 5 Bible* CD-ROM.

2. On frame 3 of the actions layer, remove the ifFrameLoaded and Go To actions.

3. On frame 4 of the actions layer, remove any existing actions and add the following ActionScript in the Actions list (in Expert Mode):

```
loadedFrames = _root._framesloaded;
totalFrames = _root._totalframes;
if (loadedFrames < totalFrames){
    percentageOutput = int((loadedFrames / totalFrames)ù
        * 100);
    gotoAndPlay("preload_loop");
else{
    gotoAndPlay("begin_movie");
}
```

4. Create a new layer called **textField**. On this layer, create keyframes on frames 2 and 5. On frame 2 of the textField layer, create a text block with the Text Tool. In the Text Options Panel, change the text type to Dynamic Text, as shown in Figure 42-2. In the Variable field, enter the name **percentageOutput**. Uncheck the Selectable option.

5. Save your Flash movie as **preloader_2.fla** and test the movie.

When the playhead reaches frame 4, Flash executes the script. If, at that time, it finds that the number of frames downloaded is fewer than the number of total frames in the movie, it sends the playhead back to the preload_loop keyframe. Then it updates the percentageOutput variable to show, as a percentage, how many frames have loaded relative to the total number of frames in the movie. If, on the other hand, the number of frames loaded is not less than the total number of frames in the movie (in other words, if all the frames have loaded), then the playhead is moved to the begin_movie keyframe, and the movie proper starts playing.

An interesting variation on this advanced style of preloading is a graphical preload bar. A preload bar would simply be a small Movie Clip that contains a rectangle shape. Once placed on stage, the width of the bar would be set using the _xscale property to adjust the width percentage of the rectangle Movie Clip instance. The following steps show you how to do this.

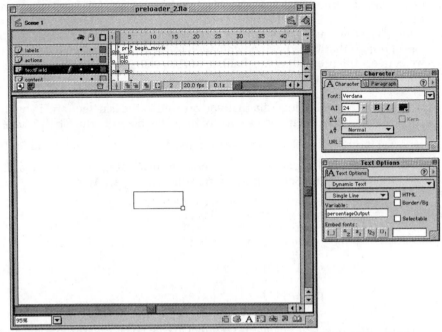

Figure 42-2: Make sure you change the text block into a dynamic text field.

6. Create new layer called **loaderBar**. Create keyframes on frames 2 and 5 of the loaderBar layer. On frame 2, draw a long rectangle, as you want it to be appear when the movie has finished loading. Select the rectangle, and press the F8 key. Call this Movie Clip symbol **loaderBar**.

7. With the loaderBar instance selected on the Stage, open the Instance Panel and name the instance loaderBar. Double-click the instance to enter the Symbol Editing Mode, and position the rectangle shape so that the left edge is at the zero X coordinate, as shown in Figure 42-3.

8. Go back to the Main Timeline, and reposition the loaderBar instance so that it's centered on the Stage.

9. Double-click frame 4 of the actions layer, and change the ActionScript to the match the following code block:

```
loadedFrames = _root._framesloaded;
totalFrames = _root._totalframes;
if (loadedFrames < totalFrames){
    percentageOutput = int((loadedFrames / totalFrames)ù
        * 100);
    _root.loaderBar._xscale = percentageOutput;
    gotoAndPlay("preload_loop");
}
else{
    gotoAndPlay("begin_movie");
}
```

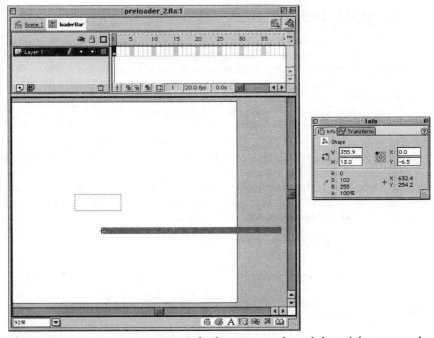

Figure 42-3: Because we want to the bar to grow from left to right, we need to make sure that the registration point is on the left edge of the rectangle.

10. Save your Flash movie, and test it.

On the CD-ROM

You can examine the finished Flash movie, preloader_2.fla, located in the ch42 folder of the Flash 5 Bible CD-ROM.

Both the text-based and graphical preloaders are not accurate measurements of downloaded file size. They measure only the number of frames that have been downloaded. So, if the content of your movie is distributed evenly over the frames of the timeline, the frames-based percentage values will closely match the real file-size transfer percentage.

If, however, your heaviest content occurs only on sporadic frames (as our examples have demonstrated), then the frames-based percentage values may appear imprecise to the user. When such a movie is streamed, the progress bar will jump to discrete sizes regardless of connection speed or duration. Our next example demonstrates a new Flash 5 method for measuring the load progress of a Flash movie.

Using getBytesLoaded() and getBytesTotal() in Flash 5

By far the most accurate way to check the loading progress of a streaming Flash movie is to use the new Flash 5 methods getBytesLoaded() and getBytesTotal(). As their names indicate, you can now access the actual number of bytes that have downloaded to the browser or stand-alone player. With these new methods, we don't need to try to disperse content evenly over frames on the Main Timeline—we can simply place our content where and when we want it.

We continue with the preloader_2.fla that we created in the last exercise. If you want to open a fresh file, use a copy of the preloader_2.fla file from the Flash 5 Bible.

1. Double-click frame 4 on the actions layer. In the Actions Panel, change the Actions list to match the following code block. Pay particular attention to the new variable names we've assigned:

```
loadedBytes = _root.getBytesLoaded();
totalBytes = _root.getBytesTotal();
if (loadedBytes < totalBytes){
    percentageOutput = int((loadedBytes / totalBytes)ù
        * 100);
    _root.loaderBar._xscale = percentageOutput;
    gotoAndPlay("preload_loop");
}
else{
    gotoAndPlay("begin_movie");
}
```

In Step 1, we've changed loadedFrames to loadedBytes, and more importantly, we've made the value of loadedBytes equal the current number of bytes of the main movie file (_root) that have loaded into the Flash Player. Likewise, we've switched totalFrames to totalBytes, and made its value equal to the total number of bytes for the main movie file. Make sure you've also changed the if condition to indicate the new variable names, as well as the math expression for the percentageOutput variable.

2. Save your Flash movie as **preloader_3.fla**, and test it. Make sure the Bandwidth Profiler is in Show Streaming Mode.

After you've tested your movie, you'll see that the loaderBar displays the true loading progress of the Flash movie. Not only can you check the progress of the Main Timeline, but you can also use getBytesLoaded() and getBytesTotal() on loaded .SWF movies. The following Expert Tutorial by Gareth Pursehouse shows you how to check the progress of .SWF files that are loaded into the main movie .SWF. We discuss the actual process of loading external .SWF files later in this chapter.

Expert Tutorial: Preloading Audio .SWF Files, by *Gareth Pursehouse*

Gareth's tutorial demonstrates the new `getBytesTotal()` *and* `getBytesLoaded()` *methods of the Movie Clip Object. He also uses the* `loadMovie` *action, which is discussed in more detail in the next section of this chapter. Gareth's ActionScript code uses a combination of Flash 4 and 5 syntax. You will want to make a copy of the music_preloader.fla and stream.swf files located in the ch42 folder of the Flash 5 Bible CD-ROM.*

Ever need to play and control music in a Flash movie? Unfortunately, it's not as easy as just dropping a song on to the Stage, with a prebuilt interface or control bar that Web visitors can access to control the sound. You need a loading display, a progress display for playback, and playback controls. Otherwise, your Flash movie might end up on worstsites.com, in which case, you're out of a job and your kids never get braces. Luckily you bought this book because we're going to show you how to control your external music .SWF files.

This example focuses on several new Movie Clip Object methods such as `getBytesTotal()` and `getBytesLoaded()`. You learn to create a loop to evaluate properties of an external .SWF file that is loaded into a target, how to display loading and playblack progress on a display bar, and how to create play control buttons for .SWF files that use Stream audio synch modes.

Concept overview

Open a copy of the music_preloader.fla file located in the ch42 folder of the *Flash 5 Bible* CD-ROM. You'll see three top layers on the Main Timeline, named !song, _song and song. The instances !song and _song use the same Movie Clip symbol, `load checker`, found in the Library. We will use this Movie Clip symbol to show the loading status and the playback status. In order to let the ActionScript routine know which status to display, we name the instance with either an _ or a ! as the first character.

A simple check of the first character of the instance's _name value will tell the script inside of `load checker` which routine to run:

```
if (substring(_name, 1, 1) eq "_") {
    // insert actions for playback status display...
} else if (substring(_name, 1, 1) eq "!") {
    // insert actions for loading status display...
}
```

Because the whole idea of programming is to make code as flexible and dynamic as possible, we will have the routine check the _name of the instance to define whether to display the loading progress, or the playback progress.

After the initial _ or ! character, the word *song* is used in the name of both instances. We'll use this suffix to also indicate the Movie Clip instance that is being targeted with a `loadMovie` action (which we'll see later).

Continued

Continued

The Movie Clip instance that will display the playback progress will be called _song, and the instance that will display the loading progress on the display bar !song. These names will also direct our ActionScript code to check the loading or playing status of the Movie Clip instance named song.

The load checker Movie Clip symbol, which has two unique instances on the Stage, will continuously check the progress of the loading .SWF file, targeted at the instance song. Because we don't want the ActionScript code to display status information before the Movie Clip has been loaded, we put a variable in the first frame of the song Movie Clip instance (which is the load placeholder symbol in the Library) to define that the load has not yet begun:

```
loading = false;
```

In our load checker Movie Clip symbol, we start the ActionScript routine on frame 2 with an if statement that checks for that variable:

```
if (_parent[substring(_name, 2, -1)].loading != false) {
```

By referring to a substring (a particular section) of the current instance's name, we can access a completely different instance nested outside of the current instance. This method of addressing Movie Clip instances allows easier alterations to the code and display mechanisms, so that you can reuse the load checker in different sections of your .SWF movie.

This advanced syntax for addressing Movie Clip objects is discussed in Chapter 40, "Navigating Flash Timelines" and Chapter 41, "Controlling Movie Clips."

Building the progress bar

To display the results of the ActionScript code within the load checker symbol, some other Movie Clips are needed. One of the Movie Clips, which we call msize, will be the background for the loading and playback display bars. This Movie Clip must be the exact size of the full display bar, as its width is used within the routine to determine placement and length of the marker Movie Clip. With an instance of the display bar named msize in the load checker symbol, we set a variable called mw that stores the width value (in pixels) of the display bar:

```
mw = msize._width;
```

This line of code occurs on the first frame of the load checker Movie Clip symbol.

The marker Movie Clip will be our second Movie Clip for the display bars. In this example, we use a simple rectangle. Because it will be continually stretched (or moved, depending upon the instance) along the background msize Movie Clip, its size shouldn't interfere with any artwork or design on it.

Initiating the loadMovie action

On the `loadButton` layer of the Main Timeline, we have a Button instance with the text Load. If you select this instance and open the Actions Panel, you'll see the following code:

```
on (release) {
    loadMovie (loadfile, "song");
    song._visible = 0;
}
```

When a user clicks the button, a `loadMovie` action will execute. It will load a .SWF file, whose name will be determined by the `loadfile` variable, into the `song` Movie Clip instance. The `loadfile` variable, in our example, is actually the text field located on the loadfile layer of the Main Timeline. You'll see that the text field already contains the text stream.swf. Therefore, the stream.swf file will be loaded into the `song` Movie Clip instance.

The second action on the Button instance will set the `_visible` property of the `song` Movie Clip instance to 0, which makes it hidden on the Stage.

Once the stream.swf file starts to load into the song instance, the `!song` instance will start to monitor the loading progress.

Loading progress display

Once the `loadMovie` action has been initiated, the loading variable in the `song` Movie Clip instance will no longer exist. Therefore, the first `if` statement on the second frame of the `!song` and `_song` instances will no longer prevent the remaining `if . . . else` statements from executing. The `!song` instance, which monitors our loading progress, will execute the code within the

```
} else if (substring(_name, 1, 1) eq "!") {
```

nest. The first line of code after the `else . . . if` statement will set a variable named `check` to the path of the song instance on the Main Timeline:

```
check = eval("_parent." + substring(_name, 2, -1));
```

Then, we get to use the new `getBytesLoaded()` and `getBytesLoaded()` methods now available in Flash 5. The `getBytesLoaded()` method will evaluate what percentage of the .SWF has loaded:

```
loaded = check.getBytesLoaded();
total = check.getBytesTotal();
percentage = int(loaded/total)*100;
currentKB = int(loaded/1024);
totalKB = int(total/1024);
```

Continued

Continued

After the loaded and total variables are determined, we can find the current percent loaded by dividing the current loaded amount by the total amount, and then multiplying by 100, to return a true percent. By using the `int` function, we get the whole-number integer of the percent in order to cut off any trailing decimals.

We also use the `loaded` variable to determine the kilobyte equivalent of `getBytesLoaded()`, by declaring another variable named `currentKB` which divides the value of `loaded` by 1024—there are 1024 bytes to 1 kilobyte. We establish another variable called `totalKB`, whose value is equal to the total size (in bytes) divided by 1024.

Then, our ActionScript will display the percent that has loaded into the main movie by (a) putting the `percentage`, `totalKB` and `currentKB` variables into our text field named `disp` within the `!song` instance, and (b) stretching the width of the `marker` Movie Clip instance to the same width as the `msize` Movie Clip instance. As the `stream.swf` file loads into the `song` instance, the `marker` Movie Clip instance will extend itself over the width of the `msize` instance:

```
disp = percentage + "% of " + totalKB + "kb ù
    loaded.(" + currentKB + " kb)";
marker._x =0;
marker._width = mw*(percentage/100);
```

Playback progress display

When the `stream.swf` file has fully loaded into the `song` instance, then the `_song` instance will start to execute its portion of the ActionScript code in the `loader check` Movie Clip symbol. Because there is no `stop()` action on the timeline of the stream.swf file, the contents of stream.swf will begin play automatically.

Because stream.swf has just one sound set to Stream Synch Mode, the timeline has as many frames as required to play the sound on its timeline. That means that there is a playhead whose position we can check. Using `_totalframes` and `_currentframe` properties, we can retrieve the playhead's position in the audio clip currently being played:

```
total = check._totalframes;
current = check._currentframe;
percentage = int((current/total)*100);
```

Using the `percentage` variable, we can display what percent of the audio clip has played, and also change the position of our `marker` Movie Clip, compared to the `msize` width, to display a graphic representation of the songs progress:

```
disp = "at " + percentage + "% of " + total + ù
    " frames. (frame " + current + ")";
marker._x = (mw-10) * (percentage/100);
marker._width = 10;
```

Audio control buttons

To achieve the playback control over the audio clip in our `song` instance, a variable is established to know whether the audio is playing or has been stopped.

The first example of this type of variable will be used in the Rewind button. Just like in programs such as Winamp, or hardware such as your car CD player, the Rewind and Fast Forward buttons scan through the music and begin playing as soon as you release the mouse button. To correctly gauge how each control button should work, we need to know whether the song timeline is playing. We'll use a variable named `play` on the Main Timeline (_root). If play is equal to a Boolean value of `false`, then we know playback is paused or stopped. If it's equal to `true`, then we know the timeline is playing. Let's start with the Rewind button.

The Rewind button code looks like this:

```
on (press, keyPress "<Left>") {
    if (_root.play == false) {
        song.gotoAndStop(song._currentframe-5);
    } else {
        song.gotoAndPlay(song._currentframe-5);
    }
}
```

If the song timeline is currently stopped, then a `gotoAndStop` method is used. If the timeline is playing, then a `gotoAndPlay` method is used.

With the Play button, two outcomes are possible: (a) If the Play button is pressed while the audio is playing, then the song will start over at the beginning; or (b) if the audio is in a paused state, then the playback will resume from the current frame. The Play button code contains the following ActionScript:

```
on (press, keyPress "x") {
    if (play == false) {
        song.play();
    } else {
        song.gotoAndPlay(1);
    }
    play = true;
}
```

The Pause button uses the following code:

```
on (press, keyPress "c") {
    play = false;
    song.stop();
}
```

Continued

Continued

The remaining buttons use similar ActionScript to fast forward or stop the audio clip. Select the remaining Button instances to see their code in the Actions Panel.

That wraps up this tutorial on preloading and controlling playback of streamed audio in Flash movies. For further enjoyment, you might want to try adding ActionScript that enables you to drag'n'drop the marker Movie Clip instance to your desired playback position.

Hanging out in San Diego, California, Gareth Pursehouse's single most favorite thing to do is practice Capoeira, which is considered, by some, a type of martial art. Capoeira blends dance, music, rituals, acrobatics, and fighting. This blend originates in Brazil, where it is played like a game. We wouldn't be surprised if Gareth conquered Flash ActionScript with the help of some good mojo from Capoeira. He earned his Flash recognition with one of his first Flash sites, `www.infinovation.com`.

Loading Flash Movies

Long sequences of animation in Flash naturally require the preloading described in the previous section to guarantee smooth playback. But traditional information-based Web sites done in Flash require a different kind of download management. Suppose you're building a Web site with three sections: products, staff, and company history. Each section is roughly 100KB in size. In a normal Flash movie, you'd place those sections in a sequential order on the main movie timeline. The last section you place on the timeline would, of course, be the last section to download. Might sound fine so far, but here's the problem: What if the section that appears last on the timeline happens to be the first and only section the user wants to see? They'd have to wait for the other two sections to download before they could view the one they want—but they don't even want to see the other two sections, so really they're waiting for nothing. The solution to this problem is the `loadMovie` action.

`loadMovie` provides a means of inserting one or more external .SWF files into a Flash movie (whether that movie resides in a browser or on its own in the stand-alone player). `loadMovie` can be used to replace the current movie with a different movie or to display multiple movies simultaneously. It can also be used, as in our company Web site example, to enable a parent movie to retrieve and display content kept in independent .SWF files on a need-to-retrieve basis (similar to the way a frame in an HTML frameset can call external pages into different frames).

Basic overview of Flash site architecture

There are two primary ways to produce and distribute straight Flash content on the Web: (a) create several small .SWF files, each one living within a standard HTML page on a Web site; or (b) create one HTML page that hosts one main .SWF file that loads additional content through the Flash Player plug-in. Figure 42-4 illustrates these alternatives.

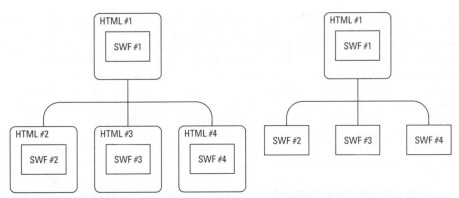

Figure 42-4: The diagram on the left illustrates a Web site that uses multiple HTML pages, each with an individual .SWF file. The diagram on the right shows a Web site that uses one HTML page (or frameset) that has one primary .SWF file, which loads other .SWF files as needed.

If you decide to break up your Flash movies across several HTML pages, your Web visitors will experience:

✦ Short download times for each page

✦ Easier bookmarking of discrete sections of your Web site

✦ Abrupt transitions between each section of the Web site

However, if you use one primary Flash movie in one HTML page (or frameset), your visitors will benefit from:

✦ Short download times for each .SWF file (download times vary with file size)

✦ Seamless integration of new Flash content

✦ Controllable transitions between .SWF asset changes

Which method should you use for your Flash projects? The answer depends on the specifics of each Web project. You may decide to use a combination of both methods, especially for larger sites that use several Web technologies (QuickTime, Flash, RealPlayer, Windows Media, and so on). In either scenario, you can use the loadMovie action to manage Flash content more easily.

Where are the multiple movies stored?

You may already be wondering how these newly loaded movies are managed relative to the original movie. Flash uses the metaphor of *levels* to describe where the movies are kept. Levels are something like drawers in a cabinet; they are stacked on top of each other, and can contain things; you can place things in any drawer you like, but once a drawer is full you have to take its contents out before you can put anything else in. Initially, the bottom level, referred to as `_level0` ("Level 0"), contains the original movie. All movies subsequently loaded into the Flash Player must be placed explicitly into a target Level. If a movie is loaded into Level 1 or higher, it appears visually on top of the original movie in the Player. If a movie is loaded into Level 0, it replaces the original movie, removing all movies stored on Levels above it in the process. When a loaded movie replaces the original movie, it does not change the frame rate, movie dimensions, or movie background color of the original Flash stage. Those properties are permanently determined by the original movie and cannot be changed.

Tip   You can effectively change the background color of the stage when you load a new movie by creating a rectangle shape of your desired color on the lowest layer of the movie you are loading.

Loading an external .SWF file into a movie

A new movie is imported onto the main movie Stage when a `loadMovie` action is executed. Here's how to make a button click load an external movie named movie2.swf:

1. Place a Button instance on the Stage of your main movie. Bring up the Actions Panel for the Button by selecting the instance and pressing Ctrl+Alt+A (PC) or Option+Command+A (Mac). Make sure the Actions Panel is in Normal Mode (see Figure 42-5).

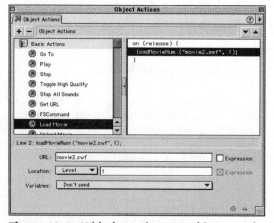

Figure 42-5: With the Actions Panel in Normal Mode, you can clearly see the options and settings of the loadMovie action.

2. Click the plus (+) button in the top-left corner of the Actions Panel, and select Basic Actions ⇨ Load Movie. Type **movie2.swf** (or your external .SWF file name) into the URL text field. The URL text field contains the network path to the movie file that you want to load. That path must be specified relative to the location of the page that contains your main movie, not relative to the location of the movie itself.

3. Select the Level option in the Location menu, and type **1** into the Location text field. This instructs Flash to load movie2.swf into _level1. If there had already been a movie loaded into _level1, it would automatically have been replaced by movie2.swf.

4. Click OK.

Caution Internet Explorer 4.5 (or earlier) for the Macintosh does not resolve paths correctly. For more information, please see Macromedia's tech note at: www.macromedia. com/support/flash/ts/documents/mac_ie_issues.htm

Note When a movie is loaded above any other movie (including the main movie), the Buttons in the movies on lower levels will continue to be active, even though they may not be visible. To prevent this undesired behavior, you need to send movies on lower levels to an idle or blank frame where no buttons are present. Do that by adding a Go To action before your loadMovie action that sends the current movie to the idle frame. This technique is known as "parking" the movie. If you have to park multiple movies, you'll need to know how to communicate between movies on different levels. This will be discussed shortly.

_level0 or _root: What's the Difference?

Until now, we have referred to the Main Timeline as _root in ActionScript. If you don't employ Levels in a Flash movie, then _root will always refer to the Main Timeline of the Flash movie that is loaded into a browser. However, if you start to use Levels to load external .SWF files, _root will be relative to the Level that's executing actions.

For example, if the main movie uses a _root reference in an action, such as:

```
_root.gotoAndStop(10);
```

then the Main Timeline playhead will go to frame 10 and stop.

If a loaded Movie has the same action within its timeline, then it will go to frame 10 on its timeline and stop.

While this works with movies that are loaded into Level locations, it will not work with Movie Clip instance targets. As you'll see in the following sections, a movie that is loaded into a Movie Clip target becomes an instance located within Level 0. Therefore, _root will still refer to the main movie's timeline (the Scene 1 timeline).

How Flash handles loaded movies of differing sizes

A movie loaded onto Level 1 or above that is smaller than the Level 0 movie is positioned in the top-left corner of the Stage. In this situation, elements on the Level 1 movie's Stage are displayed even when they go beyond the bottom and right dimensions of the Level 1 movie. To prevent objects from being displayed off Stage you would have to create a curtain layer above all the other layers in the Level 1 movie that covers up the work area (the space outside the movie's Stage).

Movies loaded onto Level 0 that are smaller than the original Level 0 movie are automatically centered and scaled up to fit the size of the original movie (the manner in which they are scaled depends on the Scale setting in the Publish settings).

Movies loaded onto Level 0 that are larger than the original Level 0 movie are cropped at the right and bottom boundaries defined by the original movie dimensions.

Placing, scaling, and rotating externally loaded .SWF files

Especially when your movies are different sizes, it's not very convenient to have newly loaded movies dropped ingloriously in the top-left corner of the Stage. To give you more flexibility with the placement, rotation, and scale of your loaded movies, Flash provides the capability to load a movie into a Movie Clip instance. So far, this may not make a whole lot of sense. Loading a movie into a Movie Clip instance seems like a strange feature at first, until you find out what it can do — then it seems indispensable. The easiest way to understand what happens when you load a movie into a Movie Clip is to think of the `loadMovie` action as a Convert Loaded Movie-to-Movie Clip action.

When a movie is loaded into a Movie Clip instance, many attributes of the original Movie Clip instance are applied to the newly loaded movie:

✦ The timeline of the loaded movie completely replaces the original instance's timeline. Nothing inside the original Movie Clip (including actions on keyframes) remains.

✦ The loaded movie assumes the following Properties from the original Movie Clip instance:

- Name
- Scale percentage
- Color effects, including alpha
- Rotation degree
- Placement (X and Y position)
- Visibility (with respect to the `_visible` property)

✦ Any `onClipEvent` handlers (and actions within them) that are written for the original Movie Clip instance will still be available (and executing) on the loaded Movie.

We like to refer to Movie Clips that are used to load other movies as Movie Clip holders. Usually, you will load movies into empty Movie Clips that don't have any artwork or actions. However, because you'll need a physical reference to the actual area your loaded movie will occupy on the Stage, it's useful to create temporary guides or artwork that indicate this area. The following steps show you how to create a Movie Clip holder, and how to load an external .SWF file into it.

1. Create a new Movie Clip symbol (Ctrl+F8 or Command+F8) that contains a square or rectangle. This shape can be drawn with the Rectangle Tool. The shape should have the same dimensions as the external .SWF movie's Stage, as defined in the Movie Properties dialog.

2. Place the shape so that its top-left corner is at the 0,0 X,Y coordinate. To do this, select the shape and open the Info Panel. Click the top-left corner of the bounding box diagram, and type 0 in the X and Y fields. Make sure that you press Enter after you type each zero.

3. Go back to the Main Timeline (Scene 1), and place an instance of this Movie Clip on the Stage. In the Instance Panel, give this Movie Clip instance the name **movieHolder**. Position it where you want the external .SWF movie to appear. At this point, you can also tween, scale, or apply color effect to the instance as well.

4. Add a `loadMovie` action to a Button instance or keyframe.

5. Specify the loaded movie's network path and filename in the URL field. Select the Target option in the Location menu. Type **movieHolder** into the Location field. The field specifies the name of the Movie Clip instance into which you want to load your external .SWF file.

Note   The instance must be resident on Stage at the time the `loadMovie` action occurs. Any instance can either be manually placed on the timeline, or created with ActionScript code, such as the `duplicateMovieClip` or `attachMovie` method. If any specification of the `loadMovie` action is incorrect, then the movie will fail to load. Flash will *not* start a request for an external .SWF file if the Movie Clip instance target is invalid.

6. Save the Flash movie file and test it. Your .SWF file's top-left corner will match the top-left corner of the original Movie Clip instance.

7. You may have noticed that there was a quick flash of the original Movie Clip's rectangle artwork before the external .SWF loaded into it. To avoid this, go into the Movie Clip symbol for movieHolder and turn the layer containing the rectangle artwork into a Guide Layer. Guide Layers will not export with the .SWF file.

loadMovie versus loadMovieNum

You may have noticed that a `loadMovie` action will be shown as `loadMovieNum` when a Level location is chosen. Because you can specify variables (that point to dynamic targets) as a Location value, Flash ActionScript needs a way to distinguish a numeric Level location from a Movie Clip instance.

Consequently, if you choose a Level location for a `loadMovie` action (in Normal Mode), then the action will show as:

```
loadMovie("external_1.swf", "movieHolder");
```

which specifies that the file `external_1.swf` be loaded into Level 1.

If you specify the Movie Clip target as `movieHolder` for the `loadMovie` action, then the action will appear as:

```
loadMovie ("external_1.swf", "movieHolder");
```

If you need to add functionality to the loaded movie, then use ActionScript to control the new loaded movie instance. The next section shows you how to communicate with loaded movies.

On the
CD-ROM

For further study, we've included a `loadMovie` example as a group of files on the *Flash 5 Bible* CD-ROM in the ch42 folder. Open movie1.html in a browser to view the files in action.

Communicating between multiple movies on different levels

After a movie or two are loaded onto different levels, you may want each timeline to control the other, just as Movie Clips can control each other. To communicate between different Levels, you simply need to address actions to the proper Level. The method for addressing a Level that controls a timeline on a different Level is identical to the method for addressing a Movie Clip target that controls the timeline of another Movie Clip instance, except for one small change. You have to indicate the name of the Level you want target rather than the name of the Movie Clip. Level names are constructed like this: First, there's an underscore (_), then there's the word *level,* and then there's the number of the Level that you want your Action to occur on.

This tells the movie loaded onto Level 1 to go to frame 50:

```
_level1.gotoAndStop(50);
```

This tells the main movie timeline to go to frame 50:

```
_level0.gotoAndStop(50);
```

You can also target Movie Clips that reside on the timelines of movies on other levels. Here's an example:

```
_level3.products.play();
```

This sends a `play()` action to the Movie Clip named `products` on the timeline of the movie loaded onto Level 3.

Unloading movies

Even though a movie loaded into an occupied Level (one that already contains a loaded movie) will automatically be removed before the new movie is displayed, the transition can be choppy. To ensure a smooth transition between movies, or to lighten the memory required by the Flash player, you can explicitly unload movies in any Level or Movie Clip target by using the `unloadMovie` action. The only option for `unloadMovie` is the path to the desired location (for example, `_level1`, `_root.instanceName`).

Loading External Files through Proxy Servers

If you are creating Flash movies that will be loaded through proxy servers on the Internet, then you'll need to know how to trick them into loading "fresh" .SWF files every time a user visits your site. What is a proxy server? With the growth of high speed Internet connections such as DSL and cable, many Internet service providers (ISPs) will process all outgoing HTTP requests through a go-between computer that caches previous requests to the same URL. Anytime you type a Web site URL into a browser, you're making an HTTP request. If that computer, called a proxy server, sees a request that was made previously (within a certain time frame), then it will serve its cached content to the end user, instead of downloading the actual content from the remote server.

Similarly, when a Flash movie makes an HTTP request with a `loadMovie` action, then a proxy server may serve the cached .SWF file instead of the one that actually exists on your server. Why is this a problem? If you are updating that .SWF file frequently, or if you want precise Web usage statistics for your Flash movies and content, then you'll want users to download the actual .SWF file on your server each time a request is made.

Continued

Continued

The question remains: How do you trick a proxy server into serving the real .SWF file instead of its cached one? The proxy server knows what's in its cache by the URL for each cached item. So, if you change the name of the loaded Flash movie each time you make a request for it, then the proxy server won't ever see an identical match with its cached content.

To change the name of a loaded Flash movie, simply add a random number to the end of the movie's name in the `loadMovie` action. This random number won't actually be part of the movie's filename. Rather, it will appear as a query at the end of the filename. Place the following actions on a Button instance that initiates a `loadMovie` action:

```
on(release){
       randomNum = Math.round(Math.random()*9999999999);
       loadMovie("external_1.swf?" + randomNum, "movieHolder");
}
```

In the preceding example, a variable called `randomNum` is established and given a random value, a number in the range of 0 to 9999999998. Each time a user presses this button, a different number is appended to the filename of the loaded movie. The proxy server will think that each request is a different, and route the request to your Web server.

Not only does this method prevent a proxy server from server a cached Flash movie file, but it also prevents most browsers from caching the loaded movie in the user's local cache folder.

loadMovie as a method or action for Movie Clip targets

Both `loadMovie` and `unloadMovie` can be used as either an ActionScript method or action for Movie Clip targets. What does this mean? You can apply actions in Flash 5 in two ways: as methods of a Movie Clip Object (or some other ActionScript Object), or as a stand-alone action.

As an action, `loadMovie` and `unloadMovie` start the ActionScript line of code. When you use actions in this manner, the target of the action is specified as an argument (option) within the action. In the following example, the file external_1.swf is loaded into Level 1:

```
loadMovie ("external_1.swf", "movieHolder");
```

As a method, actions are written as an extension of the object using the action. Therefore, the target is already specified before the action is typed. The same example shown previously could be rewritten as a method of the movieHolder Movie Clip Object:

```
movieHolder.loadMovie("external_1.swf");
```

or

```
_root.movieHolder.loadMovie("external_1.swf");
```

Because we have specifically referenced the movieHolder instance as an object, the loadMovie action (now a method) knows where to direct the loading of external_1.swf.

Expert Tutorial: Keeping Content Fresh and Dynamic Using the Load/Unload Movie Action, *by Derek Franklin*

Derek's tutorial shows you how to randomize the external files that load into a Flash. He provides some examples of interesting uses of the loadMovie action for creative projects.

A quick way to lose visitors who are returning to your Web site is for them to realize that every time they visit your site, nothing has changed. The graphics are always the same, the text is always the same, and — after only two visits — they feel that another visit to your site is an utter waste of time. This is known as boredom, and we all know that it's sacrilege to mix the term boredom with Flash site, but it happens.

There are numerous reasons why a Flash developer might not want to update or revise a completed project. One reason is fear of messing up something that already works, especially if it has a complex structure. Or, it could be just the drudgery of having to refamiliarize themselves with a movie's structure, which is often no small task.

To combat the issue of stale Flash content, Macromedia developed Generator. Generator creates dynamic Flash movies on the fly, complete with custom text and graphics. While Generator is a very cool development tool for keeping Flash content fresh, it's not for everyone. Generator involves learning new concepts, and the price of the software may be prohibitive to a lot of Flash. Luckily, there's a functionality already built into Flash that gives you power to deliver dynamic, Generator-like presentations with very little extra effort. It's the loadMovie action, which is part of the Flash 5 ActionScript arsenal. Due its power to enable you to keep content fresh and exciting, I think of this action as the "pseudo-Generator" action. How does it do this?

Continued

Continued

How loadMovie works

The `loadMovie` action enables you to compartmentalize different elements of your movie by enabling you to separate them into separate .SWF's that can be loaded at any time into the main movie. While the `loadMovie` action is commonly used for loading .SWF's that are complete productions in themselves, you can just as easily use it to load:

✦ Navigational controls

✦ The movie's soundtrack

✦ A background image

✦ Any single image

✦ Any text content

✦ An ActionScript functionality

The significance of this is twofold:

First, updating and keeping content fresh becomes much easier. For example, you could create a separate .SWF file for the text content that first displays on your site. You could name this movie text.swf and then place a `loadMovie` action in your main movie that loads text.swf into level 1 (the main movie is always Level 0). Then, whenever you want to edit or update the text content, you wouldn't have to go through the hassle of reopening the main authoring file, finding the text on the timeline, changing the text, making sure you don't mess anything up, testing, and then finally reexporting and uploading the entire movie again. Instead, by using the `loadMovie` action, you could simply open and edit the text.swf, reexport it to the same name (`text.swf`), and then upload the updated .SWF to your server. When the main movie plays again and text.swf gets loaded, it will reflect the updated text. You can just as easily use this trick for updating a graphic or even a sound-track in your movie. By making your movie modular, updating or changing content becomes less of a hassle.

The second functionality that `loadMovie` offers is to make your movie truly dynamic — each time a visitor returns to your site! Believe me, after learning this trick, you'll never look at Flash construction the same way.

Imagine how unique and fresh a user's experience would be if you could randomly play 1 of 10 different soundtracks each time a visitor stops by; or, if you could pack 24 different bitmaps, 1 for each hour in the day, and have the proper one displayed depending on the hour of the day a user visits. I know what you're thinking, "That sound's great, but with that much content in a single movie, the user would have to wait a week for the whole movie to download." Think again! Using the `loadMovie` action along with some additional, yet very simple, ActionScripting you can accomplish amazing feats of dynamism without adding any more download time to your users' experience than if you'd placed a single soundtrack or bitmap inside a single movie. Let me show you how:

A random soundtrack

The first step in building a movie that contains a randomly generated soundtrack is to create ten different .SWF files (could be more or less for your purposes). Each .SWF will contain a single frame with a looping soundtrack in that single frame. Export these soundtrack .SWF's as soundtrack0.swf, soundtrack1.swf, soundtrack2.swf, and so on. Save them in the same directory in which the main .SWF will be placed. Next, in your main movie, place the following ActionScript wherever you would like the music to begin:

```
randomNum = random(10);
loadMovie ("soundtrack" + randomNum + ".swf", 1);
```

Note that the preceding code is derived from Flash 4. Ideally, you should use the recommended Flash 5 version of the script, which requires a bit more code to generate a random number:

```
randomNum = Math.Round(Math.random () * 10);
loadMovie ("soundtrack" + randomNum + ".swf", 1);
```

When this script is run is a random number is generated between 0 and 9 (not 0 and 10, as you might suspect, because 0 is one of the possible numbers generated) and placed in the variable randomNum. Next, using an expression, the loadMovie action uses the randomNum variable to load one of the soundtrack movies into Level 1. This delivers a randomly generated soundtrack each time someone visits the site, yet download is not increased any more than if you had given them only a single choice.

Placing your soundtrack in it's own Level is an easy way to facilitate sound on/off functionality. That's because turning the music on or off simply involves loading/unloading it from that Level.

A time-based image

The first step in building a Flash movie that will load 1 of 24 images at the appropriate hour, is to create 24 different .SWF files: Each .SWF should contain a single bitmap graphic, placed on frame 1. (There are 24 .SWF's to represent each hour of the day.) The graphic can be any size that your design requires. Export the .SWF's with meaningful file names, such as: hour0.swf, hour1.swf, and so on. Save these into the same directory in which the main .SWF will be placed. Then, in your main movie, place the following ActionScript in the appropriate frame, wherever you would like the picture to appear:

```
myDate = new Date()
currentHour = myDate.getHours();
loadMovie ("hour" + currentHour + ".swf", 1);
```

This script first creates a Date Object that is named myDate. Next, using the getHours method of the Date Object, Flash determines the current hour on the user's system and places a number representing that hour into the variable currentHour (0 = 12 a.m., 23 = 11 p.m.). Then, using an expression, the loadMovie action uses the currentHour variable to load the appropriate .SWF, which represents the particular hour, into Level 1 of the main movie.

Continued

Continued

If you want the image in the loaded .SWF to appear in particular place in the movie window, add the following code to the end of the previous script:

```
setProperty (_level1, _x, 100);
setProperty (_level1, _y, 100);
```

(This particular code example will cause the top-left corner of the loaded movie to be placed 100 pixels from the top and 100 pixels from the left of the main movie's top-left corner.)

And that's the joy of authoring Flash with pseudo-Generator! Harness the power and flexibility of this command by creating separate .SWF's for different parts of your movie, and you'll find many ways to keep your site fresh and dynamic. Whatever you do, have *loads* of fun with the `loadMovie` action.

The .SWF file format that's used with the `loadMovie` action has become a standard file format in its own right. This means that you have even more tools to help you make your movie modular with separate .SWF files. For example, there are a growing number of tools that enable you to export content directly from them to the .SWF format, including:

✦ **Macromedia Fireworks:** Fireworks 3 allows you to export bitmaps created within its environment as .SWF files. This enables you to easily update individual bitmap graphics in your movie.

✦ **Macromedia FreeHand:** FreeHand 9 not enables you to create vector graphics, as well as simple animations that can be exported to the .SWF format.

✦ **Adobe LiveMotion:** LiveMotion is Adobe's entry into the Web animation market. Although it's interactive capabilities don't compete with Flash, its interface is fabulous and it enables you to quickly create beautiful graphics or animations that can be exported as .SWF files.

✦ **Adobe Illustrator:** Illustrator 9 enables you to create vector graphics as well as simple animations, along the same lines as FreeHand, and then export them to the .SWF format.

✦ **Swift 3D:** Want to add 3D elements to your project? This great software creates 3D objects, complete with animation, that can be exported as .SWF files. You can find it at www.swift3d.com.

✦ **SWisH:** Very cool text effects are what SWisH is all about. SWisH provides an amazing assortment of effects that are all configurable and that are easily exported to the .SWF format. You can find it at www.swishzone.com.

Derek Franklin is the coauthor of *"Flash 5!" Creative Web Animation,* (Berkeley: Peachpit Press, 4200) one of the most authoritative and usable books on the subject. Born in Illinois and raised in Bloomington, Indiana, he recently moved back to Bloomington. He recalls Kenny Loggin's "Footloose" as the most memorable tune from his last year of high school. Derek claims to have found Flash "by accident really. At first glance (Flash 2), I wasn't all that impressed. But when I saw what people were doing with it, there was no turning back." He says his favorite pastime is "either playing my drums or being the life of the party—they kind of go hand-in-hand."

Accessing Items in Shared Libraries

Flash 5 adds an exciting new feature to asset management in Flash movies: the capability to link external .SWF files (and the symbols, sounds, bitmaps, and font symbols within) to each Flash movie that you use on your Web site. These external .SWF files, called *Shared Libraries*, are different than loaded .SWF files.

A Shared Library .SWF doesn't load into a Level or a Movie Clip instance location. Instead, you set up a the Library of a Flash movie (.FLA file) with assets that you want to use in other Flash movies. This movie is the basis of the Shared Library .SWF file. After you assign an identifier to each asset in the Library, you save the .FLA file, publish a .SWF file, and close the .FLA file. Then, you open another Flash movie .FLA file, and using File ➪ Open as Shared Library, you open the Shared Library .FLA file. Its Library window will open (in a dimmed gray state), and you can drag and drop assets to your new Flash movie file.

Note　　Even though the assets are linked to the external Shared Library .SWF file, the Flash movie will actually store copies of the assets in its .FLA file. However, they will not be exported with the .SWF file that is published.

After you have established a Shared Library file, any changes to the actual contents of the Shared Library .FLA and .SWF files will propagate to any Flash movie that uses the shared assets. In the following sections, you learn how to create a Shared Library file and use it with other Flash movies.

Caution　　At the time of this writing, the Shared Library feature of Flash 5 has proven to work very inconsistently. It is recommended that you use only small (low byte size) elements in your Shared Libraries, to ensure that they are downloaded and available for Flash movies that use them. As with any Web production, make sure that you test early and often before you develop an entire project that fails upon final delivery.

Setting up a Shared Library file

To share assets among several Flash files, you need to establish a Shared Library file (or files) that is available to other Flash movie files. To create a Shared Library file:

1. Open a new Flash movie (Ctrl+N or Command+N).

2. To place Flash artwork into the Library, draw the shapes and other elements (text, lines, gradients, and so on). Select the artwork and convert it to a Flash symbol. Choose a symbol type (for example, Graphic, Button, or Movie Clip) that best suits the nature of your artwork.

3. To place bitmaps and sounds into the Library, import the source files as you normally would, using File ➪ Import (Ctrl+R or Command+R).

4. Delete all artwork that you have placed on the Stage. Every asset that you want to share should be in the Library.

5. To place an entire font (or typeface) into the Library, open the Library (Ctrl+L or Command+L), and choose New Font from the Options menu, located at the top-right corner of the Library window. In the Font Symbol Properties dialog, type a reference name for the font, choose the font face from the Font menu, and select a faux font Style (Bold or Italic) to be applied (optional). (See Figure 42-6.)

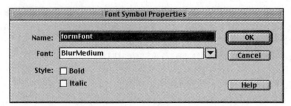

Figure 42-6: Give each embedded font face a descriptive name that indicates its functionality within the Flash movie.

Assigning names to assets

After you have placed each asset into the Library of your starter .FLA file, you'll need to assign a unique identifier to each asset.

1. Select the symbol, bitmap, sound, and font in the Library. Choose Linkage from the Library's Options menu.

2. In the Symbol Linkage Properties dialog, shown in Figure 42-7, choose Export this symbol for the Linkage option. This forces the asset to export with the published .SWF file. Then, type a unique name in the Identifier field. Click OK.

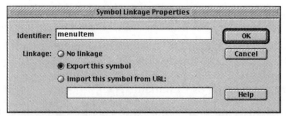

Figure 42-7: Each asset in the Library of the Shared Library .FLA file needs a unique name.

3. Repeat Steps 1 and 2 for each asset in the Library.

Specifying the Shared Library's location

An optional setting for the Shared Library .FLA is the relative or absolute path (as a URL) to the Shared Library .SWF on your Web server. You only need to specify this URL if you plan to store the Shared Library .SWF file within a different directory on the Web server, or on a completely different Web server.

1. In the Options menu in the Library window, choose Shared Library Properties.

2. In the URL field, type the location of the Shared Library .SWF file (or where you intend to publish it on the Web). This location will be preappended to each shared asset's identifier in the movies that use the assets.

Caution Make sure that you specify this URL before you start using the Shared Library .FLA file with other .FLA files. The URL location is stored within the each movie that uses the Shared Library .SWF file, and will not update if you decide to change the URL later in the Shared Library .FLA file.

Publishing the Shared Library .SWF file

After the assets of the .FLA file have been assigned identifiers and the URL of the Shared Library has been set (optional), you need to publish a .SWF version of the .FLA file.

1. Save the .FLA movie. Use a descriptive name that notifies other members of your Web production team that this is a Shared Library file, such as `sharedLib.fla`.

2. Publish the Flash movie as a .SWF file. No other publish formats are necessary. In the Publish Settings (File ➪ Publish Settings), select only the Flash format in the Format tab. Click OK. Choose File ➪ Publish to create a .SWF file from your .FLA file.

3. Close the .FLA file.

Linking to assets from other movies

After the Shared Library .SWF file is published, you can use the shared assets in other Flash movies.

1. Create a new Flash movie, or open an existing one.

2. Using the File ➪ Open as Shared Library command, browse to the folder where your Shared Library .FLA was saved. For testing purposes, you should keep this .FLA file in the same folder as the .FLA files that share it. Select the Shared Library .FLA file, and click Open. A separate grayed-out Library window for the Shared Library .FLA file will open in the Flash authoring environment.

3. Drag the asset(s) that you wish to use into the new Flash movie's Library and onto its Stage. Even though Flash will copy the contents of each shared asset, the asset will load from the separate Shared Library .SWF file.

4. To see whether an asset is native to the Flash movie or from a Shared Library .SWF file, right-click (or Control-click on the Mac) the symbol or asset in the Library. Select Linkage from the contextual menu. The Symbol Linkage Properties dialog, shown in Figure 42-8, will indicate whether the symbol (or asset) will be imported from an external Shared Library .SWF file.

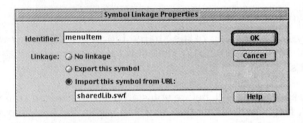

Figure 42-8: If a Shared Library asset is used in another movie, the Symbol Linkage Properties will indicate the name (and path) of the Shared Library .SWF file.

Caution

Do not try to use the Open as Shared Library command when the Shared Library .FLA file is already open. Likewise, you cannot open a Shared Library .FLA file with File ⇨ Open if it's already opened as a Shared Library. Close the grayed-out Library window before you attempt to open the Shared Library .FLA to edit its contents.

When you are done dragging the assets from the Shared Library file, close its Library window. When you publish the new Flash movie(s) that use the Shared Library .SWF file, make sure you put all of the files on your Web server for live testing.

Summary

✦ If you want to make sure that your larger Flash movies don't pause during playback over the Web, then you may want to make a preloader for each Flash movie you make.

✦ Preloaders can use three different ways to test the download progress of the Flash movie .SWF file: `ifFrameLoaded`, `_framesLoaded/_totalFrames`, and `getBytesLoaded()/getBytesTotal`. The most accurate mechanism uses the new Flash 5 `getBytesLoaded()/getBytesTotal()` methods.

✦ You can breakup large Flash projects into several smaller Flash movie components that are loaded into a primary .SWF file when they're needed.

✦ The `loadMovie` action enables you to download .SWF files into Level or Movie Clip instance locations.

✦ Flash 5 offers a new way to share movie assets with the Shared Library feature. As this is a new mechanism to load assets, we recommend that you thoroughly test any Shared Libraries on live production servers before you make the content accessible to the public.

✦   ✦   ✦

Distributing
Flash Movies

Publishing Flash Movies

If you have read the entire book to this point, then you're
probably more than ready to get your Flash movies uploaded
to your Web server to share with your visitors. This chapter
shows you how to create .SWF files from Flash 5 so that your
Flash movies can be played with the Flash Player plug-in for
Web browsers.

Optimizing Flash Movies

Before you create a .SWF file from your Flash movie (.FLA file),
you should read through this section to determine whether
you can optimize your Flash movie. Optimizing can mean finding anything redundant in the final movie — extra points in a
line, repeated artwork, and so on — to breaking apart your
large .FLA file into several smaller .FLA files that will be loaded
into a primary Flash movie. As you should see, symbols are
the key to eliminating unnecessary repetition with Flash artwork. Optimizing can also entail the restricted use of band-
width-heavy items, such as bitmapped artwork or lengthy
sound tracks.

Simplify artwork

Although Flash can do some pretty amazing things with vector
shapes and animation, you don't want to overdo it — at least
not if you want 28.8 Kbps modem users to see your work without too much waiting. Keep the following tips in mind while
creating your Flash artwork or reviewing your final production:

+ Use tweens for animations wherever possible. If you
  need complicated paths for objects to follow, use
  a motion guide layer instead of using a series of
  keyframes — the fewer keyframes, the better.

✦ Custom line types (such as dashed, dotted, ragged, and so on) take up more file space than regular solid lines. Strokes created with the Brush Tool also use more memory than lines created with the Pencil Tool. Artwork created with the Brush Tool is actually a fill — not a stroke. The boundary of a fill is more complex than a simple line or stroke.

✦ Reduce the number of points and/or lines used to create a shape. In Flash, you can use the Modify ⇨ Optimize command, which joins line segments in a line or shape. Note that you need to ungroup any grouped lines to use this command. The Use Multiple Passes option optimizes the selection to the fullest extent possible.

✦ Gradients are more complex than a solid fill for a computer processor to handle. Try to minimize the number of simultaneous gradients shown in any given frame, and avoid any complex animation with gradient shapes or symbols. Gradients add more bytes to a .SWF's file size than does a solid color. See Table 43-1 for a study of gradient color and .SWF file sizes.

✦ Don't use many different fonts (typefaces) or font styles (such as Oblique, Bold, Condensed, and so on) in your Flash movies. Most elegant designs use complementary typefaces that occur in the same typeface family, or use a balanced and restricted number of sans serif or serif fonts. Font characters can require a lot of file space, from 81 bytes to over 191 bytes *per character*. Generally, more elaborate serif fonts (such as Garamond) take up more room per character than sans serif fonts (such as Arial). For text fields, make sure that you embed only what is necessary from a font for the given field. For example, if a text field needs to use only lowercase characters of a font for a login or name field, then specify this in the Text Options Panel for that text field. Ultimately, use device fonts (_sans, _serif, and _typewriter) whenever possible, as they do not need their outlines stored in the .SWF file.

Caution   You cannot use device fonts underneath a Mask layer. Any font that is in a Mask layer nesting needs to be embedded in the .SWF file.

✦ Keep bitmap or raster images to a minimum. Flash's strength is its vector-based technology. Animated bitmap sequences inflate your Flash file sizes. Unless the content you are creating needs to be photorealistic (as in a photographer's portfolio), don't use 24-bit color bitmaps.

✦ Use alpha effects on symbol instances sparingly with Motion Tweens. Alpha options can be found in the Effect Panel. In a sample three-keyframe Motion Tween, adding an alpha effect to a symbol instance on the start keyframe added 85 bytes to the .SWF file size. Adding another alpha effect to a symbol instance on the end keyframe added 175 bytes to the original alpha-free

Motion Tween. Alpha effects can also slow frame rates during complex animated sequences. If you need to fade in or out a symbol, try using the Tint option in the Effect Panel first.

Table 43-1
Effects of Gradient Colors on .SWF File Size

Artwork Type	Colors	.SWF Size	Percent Increase
Circle Shape	1	115 bytes	n/a
Circle Shape	2	130 bytes	13%
Circle Shape	3	134 bytes	16.5%
Circle Shape	4	143 bytes	21.7%
Graphic Symbol	4	143 bytes	21.7%
Graphic Symbols*	4	152 bytes	32.7%
Movie Clip Symbol	4	162 bytes	43.9%
Circle Shapes*	4	225 bytes	95.6%
Graphic Symbols**	4	248 bytes	115.7%
Movie Clip Symbols**	4	272 bytes	136.5%
Circle Shapes**	4	923 bytes	702.6%

*Two instances or shapes with the same gradient fill.

**Ten instances or shapes with the same gradient fill.

Although some of these optimization tips may not seem to have a drastic effect on file size, realize that most Flash movies on the Web don't just use one or two elements, or one or two Motion Tweens. When you start to compound the file size reductions over several Movie Clips or .SWF files, you'll find that you can cut many kilobytes from your Flash .SWF files.

Use symbols

Anything in Flash can be turned into a symbol. When the Flash movie is exported as a .SWF file, the symbol's contents are stored on the first frame that uses that symbol. Symbol instances are similar to <A HREF> tags in HTML: They link data to a given frame, rather than copying or storing it there. After a symbol's contents are downloaded to the Flash player, it is easily available for any subsequent reuse in the Flash movie. After you've completed a Flash movie, you want to review your Flash production and perform the following optimizations:

✦ If any element is used in more than one keyframe or scene, consider making a symbol out of it. Just about every professional Flash designer uses nested symbols: An element is drawn, converted to a symbol, and then used in another symbol such as a Button or Movie Clip. Symbol instances reduce the resource overhead in .SWF files. Unlike grouped shapes, symbols need only refer to the original resource in the .SWF file rather than storing a new resource for every occurrence of it. You can, however, make a grouped shape into a symbol.

✦ If you want to use the same shape in a variety of colors, then make that shape a symbol. For each instance of the symbol, use the Effect Panel to change the color.

✦ The contents of a symbol are downloaded when the Flash Player encounters the first frame that uses the symbol. Given this, put any heavy symbol (for example, a symbol with bitmaps or sounds) in its own Flash movie, and start preloading the .SWF file near the beginning of the main Flash movie.

✦ Avoid using linked symbols from large Shared Library .SWF files (as discussed in Chapter 42, "Sharing and Loading Assets"). Any Flash movie that links to a Shared Library .SWF file will not start to play until the entire Shared Library .SWF has downloaded.

✦ Avoid setting large symbols or assets to be exported as Linked Symbols (to use with `attachSound` or `attachMovie` methods) in the movie's native Library. All Linked Symbols must be downloaded before playback of the .SWF can begin.

✦ If you are streaming your Flash movies (and not preloading them), then streaming playback can be interrupted when the playhead reaches a frame with a large symbol. Flash will not play a frame until the entire contents of any symbol on that frame are fully downloaded.

Cross-Reference You can preload movies into a browser by using either the `ifFrameLoaded`, `_framesLoaded`/`_totalFrames` or the `getBytesLoaded()`/`getTotalBytes()` method. See Chapter 42, "Sharing and Loading Assets," for more information.

Manage assets in the Flash Library

Bitmaps and sound files that have been imported into Flash automatically become items stored in the Flash Library. As later sections of this chapter show you, you can specify the sound quality of audio events and streams in the Export Movie or Publish Settings dialog. However, these settings control the audio quality for the entire movie unless a specific encoding scheme is specified for individual sound clips in the Flash Library. Use the Library to assign specific compression methods to any given media element. For audio, Flash's MP3 encoding provides the best compression-to-quality ratio available. Specify MP3 compression on as many sounds in the Flash Library as possible.

Cross-Reference Check out Chapter 34, "Using Bitmaps and Other Media with Flash," and Chapter 38, "Optimizing Flash Sound for Export," for detailed information regarding compression of Flash media in the Library.

Testing Flash Movies

You have three ways to test your Flash movies: in the authoring environment of Flash 5 using the Test Movie and Scene commands, in a browser using the Publish Preview command, or in the standalone Flash Player using Flash files (.SWF) made with the Export Movie command. There are several reasons why you should test your Flash movie before you transfer Flash movies to your Web server (or to the intended delivery medium):

✦ Flash .FLA files have much larger file sizes than their .SWF file counterparts. To accurately foretell the network bandwidth that a Flash movie requires, you need to know how large the final Flash movie will be. If the download demand is too overwhelming for your desired Internet connection speed (for example, a 28.8 Kbps modem), then you can go back and optimize your Flash movie.

✦ The Control ➪ Play command in the Flash authoring environment does not provide any streaming information. When you use the Test Movie or Scene command, you can view the byte size of each frame, and how long it will take to download the .SWF from the Web server.

✦ Movie Clip animations and actions targeting Movie Clip instances cannot be previewed using the standard Control ➪ Play command (or the Play button on the Controller) in the Flash authoring environment.

Tip You can temporarily preview Movie Clip symbol instances within the Flash authoring environment (for example, the Timeline window) by changing the Symbol instance behavior to Graphic instead of Movie Clip. Do this by selecting the instance, opening the Instance Panel and choosing Graphic in the Behavior drop-down menu. However, when you switch the behavior back to Movie Clip, you will have lost the original instance name of the Movie Clip.

✦ Most scripting done with Flash 5 actions, such as `loadMovie`, `loadVariables`, and `startDrag`, cannot be previewed with the Play command. Enabling Frame Actions or Buttons in the Control menu has no effect with new scripting actions. You need to use Test Movie to try out most interactive functions in a Flash movie.

Any actions that require the use of remote CGI (Common Gateway Interface) scripts to load variables, movies, or XML data, will now work in the Test Movie environment. You do not need to view your .SWF files in a browser to test these actions.

✦ Accurate frame rates cannot be previewed with the Play command (Control ⇨ Play) in the authoring environment. Most complex animations appear jerky, pausing or skipping frames when the Play command is used.

Using the Test Scene or Movie command

You can test your Flash movies directly within the Flash 5 interface by using the Control ⇨ Test Movie or Test Scene command. When you choose one of these commands, Flash opens your Flash movie in a new window *as a Flash .SWF movie*. Even though you are only "testing" a Flash movie, a new .SWF file is actually created and stored in the same location as the Flash .FLA file. For this reason, it is a good idea to always save your Flash file before you begin testing it.

If your movie is currently titled Untitled1, Untitled2, and so on in the application title bar, then it has not yet been saved. Make sure you give your Flash movie a distinct name before testing it.

Before you use the Test Scene or Movie command, you need to specify the settings of the resulting Flash .SWF movie. The Test Scene or Movie command uses the specifications outlined in the Publish Settings dialog to generate .SWF files. The Publish Settings dialog is discussed later in this chapter. For the time being, we can use the Flash 5 default settings to explore the Test Scene and Movie commands.

Test Movie

When you choose Control ⇨ Test Movie (Command+Enter or Ctrl+Enter), Flash 5 generates a .SWF file of the entire Flash .FLA file that is currently open. If you have more than one Flash movie open, Flash creates a .SWF file for the one that is currently in the foreground and that has "focus."

Test Scene

If you are working on a lengthy Flash movie with multiple scenes, you want to test your scenes individually. You can do this by using Control ⇨ Test Scene (Option+ Command+Enter or Ctrl+Alt+Enter). The process of exporting entire movies via Test Movie may require many minutes to complete, whereas exporting one scene will require a significantly smaller amount of time. As is shown in the next section, you can analyze each tested scene (or movie) with the Bandwidth Profiler.

Tip
You can use the Test Scene command while you are in Symbol Editing Mode to export a .SWF file that contains the current symbol timeline. The .SWF will not contain anything else from your Flash movie. Note that the symbol's center point will become the top-left corner of the playback stage.

How to use the Bandwidth Profiler

Do you want to know how long it will take for a 28.8 Kbps modem to download your Flash movie or scene? How about a 36.6 Kbps modem? Or a 56 Kbps modem? Or a cable modem? The Bandwidth Profiler enables you to simulate any download speed.

On the CD-ROM
In the ch43 folder of the CD-ROM is a .FLA file called bandwidth.fla. We use that Flash movie for this section.

To use the Bandwidth Profiler, you first need to create a test movie or scene. When you create a .SWF file with the Control ➪ Test Movie or Scene commands, Flash opens the .SWF file in its own Player window.

One Reason to Use Imported .MP3 Files

If you have imported raw audio files (.WAV or .AIFF files) into your Flash movie, you may notice lengthy wait times to use the Test Movie or Publish commands in Flash 5. Why? The MP3 encoding process consumes much of the computer processor's power and time.

Flash has three MP3 compression qualities: Fast, Medium, or Best. Fast is the default MP3 quality setting—this is by far the fastest method of encoding MP3 sound. Because MP3 uses perceptual encoding, it compares a range of samples to determine how best to compress the sound. Fast compares over a smaller range of samples than either Medium or Best. As you increase quality, the sampling range increases.

This process is similar to building 256-color palettes for video files; it's best to look at all the frames of the video (instead of just the first frame) when you're trying to build a palette that's representative of all the colors used in the video. While MP3 doesn't quite work in this fashion, the analogy is appropriate. So, at Best quality, the MP3 encoding scans more of the waveform to look for similarities and differences. However, it's also more time intensive.

If you want to avoid the wait for Flash to publish .SWF files that use MP3 compression, we recommend that you compress your source audio files to the MP3 format (including the newly supported VBR—Variable Bit Rate—compression in Flash 5) and import those .MP3 files into Flash 5. Unless the .MP3 sound file is used for Stream Synch audio, Flash 5 will export the audio in its original MP3 compressed format.

View menu

The Test Movie or Scene viewing environment changes the View and Control menus. The first four commands in the View menu are the same as those of the Flash Player plug-in viewing controls:

✦ **Zoom In:** Selecting this option enlarges the Flash movie.

✦ **Zoom Out:** Selecting this option shrinks the Flash movie.

✦ **Magnification:** This submenu enables you to change the zoom factor of the movie. The .SWF movie is displayed at the original pixel size specified in the Modify ➪ Movie dialog when 100 percent (Ctrl+1 or Command+1) is the setting. For example, if the movie size is 500×300 pixels, it takes up 500×300 pixels on your monitor. If you change the size of the viewing window, the movie may be cropped. The lower section of this submenu enables you to change the viewable area of the Flash movie. Show Frame (Ctrl+2 or Command+2) will show only the frame boundary area in the Player window. Show All (Ctrl+3 or Command+3) shrinks or enlarges the Flash movie so that you can view all the artwork in the Flash movie, including elements off stage.

✦ **Bandwidth Profiler:** To view the Bandwidth Profiler in this new window, use View ➪ Bandwidth Profiler (Ctrl+B or Command+B). The .SWF movie shrinks to accommodate the Bandwidth Profiler.

 • The left side of the profiler displays three sections: Movie, Settings, and State. Movie indicates the dimensions, frame rate, size (in KB and bytes), duration and preload (in number of frames and seconds). Settings displays the current selected connection speed (which is set in the Debug menu). State shows you the current frame playing and its byte requirements, as well as the loaded percent of the movie.

 • The larger right section of the profiler shows the timeline header and graph. The lower red line beneath the timeline header indicates whether a given frame streams in real-time with the current modem speed specified in the Control menu. For a 28.8 Kbps modem, any frame above 200 bytes may cause delays in streaming for a 12 fps movie. Note that the byte limit for each frame is dependent on frame rate. For example, a 24 fps movie has a limit of 120 bytes per frame (for a 28.8 Kbps modem connection).

 • When the Bandwidth Profiler is enabled, two other commands are available in the View menu: Streaming Graph (Ctrl+G or Command+G) and Frame-By-Frame Graph (Ctrl+F or Command+F).

✦ **Show Streaming:** When Show Streaming is enabled, the Bandwidth Profiler emulates the chosen modem speed (in the Control menu) when playing the Flash movie. The Bandwidth Profiler counts the bytes downloaded (displayed in the Loaded subsection of the State heading), and shows the download/play progress via a green bar in the timeline header.

✦ **Streaming Graph:** By default, Flash opens the Bandwidth Profiler in Streaming Graph mode. This mode indicates how the Flash movie streams into a browser (see Figure 43-1). Alternating light and dark gray blocks represent each frame. The size of each block indicates its relative byte size. For our bandwidth.swf example, all the frames will have loaded by the time our playhead reaches frame 22.

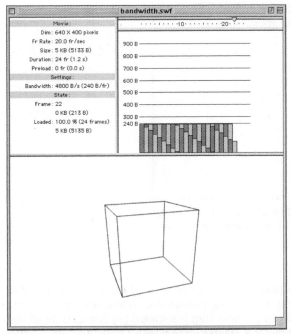

Figure 43-1: The Streaming Graph indicates how a movie will download over a given modem connection. Shown here is our bandwidth.swf as it would download over a 56 Kbps modem.

✦ **Frame-By-Frame Graph:** This second mode available to the Bandwidth Profiler lays each frame side by side under the timeline header (see Figure 43-2). Although the Streaming Graph enables you to see the real-time performance of a .SWF movie, the Frame-By-Frame Graph enables you to more easily detect which frames are contributing to streaming delays. If any frame block goes beyond the red line of the graph (for a given connection speed), then the Flash Player halts playback until the entire frame downloads. In the bandwidth.swf example, frame 1 is the only frame that may cause a very slight delay in streaming. The remaining frames are right around 200 bytes each — below our threshold of 243 bytes per frame for a 56 Kbps modem connection playing a 20 fps Flash movie.

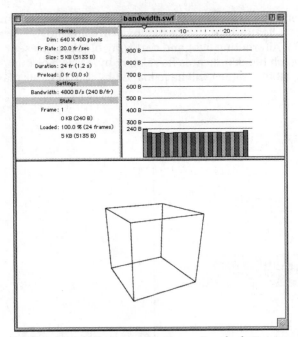

Figure 43-2: The Frame-By-Frame Graph shows you the byte demand of each frame in the Flash movie.

Control menu

Use the Control menu to play (Return) or rewind (Option+Command+R or Ctrl+Alt+R) the test movie. Rewinding pauses the bandwidth.swf movie on the first frame. Use the Step Forward (>) and Step Backward (<) commands to view the Flash movie frame by frame. If a Flash movie doesn't have a stop() action on the last frame, the Loop command forces the player to infinitely repeat the Flash movie.

Debug menu

The Debug menu also features commands that work in tandem with the Streaming and Frame-By-Frame Graphs:

> ✦ **14.4, 28.8, 56K:** These settings determine what speed the Bandwidth Profiler uses to calculate estimated download times and frame byte limitations. Notice that these settings use more practical expectations of these modem speeds. For example, a 28.8 modem can theoretically download 3.5 kilobytes per second (KB/sec), but a more realistic download rate for this modem speed is 2.3KB/sec.

> ✦ **User Settings 4, 5, and 6:** These are user-definable speed settings. By default, they are all 2.3KB/sec.

✦ **Customize:** To change the settings for any of the modem speeds listed previously, use the Customize command to input the new value(s).

Note The Control menu also contains List Objects and List Variables commands. List Objects can be used to show the names of Movie Clip instances or ActionScript Objects in the Output window, while the List Variables command displays the names and values of any currently loaded variables, ActionScript Objects, and XML Data.

Using the size report

Flash also lets you view a text-file summary of movie elements, frames, and fonts called a size report. In addition to viewing Frame-By-Frame Graphs of a Flash movie with the Bandwidth Profiler, you can inspect this size report for other "hidden" byte additions such as font character outlines. This report can only be generated when using the Export Movie or Publish commands.

On the CD-ROM A sample size report, called bandwidth_report.txt, is included in the ch43 folder of the *Dreamweaver and Flash Bible* CD-ROM.

Publishing Your Flash Movies

After you've made a dazzling Flash movie complete with Motion Tweens, 3D simulations and ActionScripted interactivity, you need to make the Flash movie usable for the intended delivery medium — the Web, a CD-ROM (or floppy disk), a template for Macromedia Generator, a QuickTime Flash movie or a RealPlayer presentation, to name a few. As we mentioned in the introduction to this book, you need the Flash 5 application to open .FLA files. Because the majority of your intended audience won't have the full Flash 5 application, you need to export or publish your .FLA movie in a format that your audience can use.

A Word about the Export Movie Command

Even though Flash 5 has incredibly streamlined the process of creating .SWF movies with the Publish commands (discussed in the next section), it is worth mentioning that the File ⇨ Export Movie command provides another route to creating a simple .SWF file. Although the Publish command is the quickest way to create HTML-ready Flash movies, the Export Movie command can be used to create updated .SWF files that have already been placed in HTML documents, or Flash movies that you intend to import into Macromedia Director movies.

You can convert your Flash movie (.FLA) files to .SWF files by using either the File ➪ Export Movie or File ➪ Publish/Publish Settings commands. The latter command is Flash's Publish feature. You can specify just about all file format properties in one step using the File ➪ Publish Settings command. After you've entered the settings, the File ➪ Publish command exports any and all file formats with your specified parameters in one step — all from the Flash 5 application.

Three commands are available with the Publish feature: Publish Settings, Publish Preview, and Publish. Each of these commands is discussed in the following sections.

Publish Settings

The Publish Settings command (File ➪ Publish Settings) is used to determine which file formats are exported when the File ➪ Publish command is invoked. By default, Flash 5 ships with Publish Settings that will export a Flash (.SWF) file and an HTML file with the proper markup tags to utilize the Flash plug-in or ActiveX control. If you want to customize the settings of the exported file types, you should familiarize yourself with the Publish Settings before you attempt to use the Publish command.

Selecting formats

Select File ➪ Publish Settings to access the Publish Settings dialog, which is nearly identical for both PC and Mac. The dialog opens to the Formats tab, which has checkboxes to select the formats in which your Flash movie will be published (see Figure 43-3). For each Type that is checked, a tab appears in the Publish Settings dialog. Click each type's tab to specify settings to control the particulars of the movie or file that will be generated in that format.

The Use default names checkbox either enables or disables default names (disabled means that the Filename entry boxes are unavailable or grayed out). For example, if your movie is named intro.fla, then, if Use default names is selected, this is the base from which the names are generated in publishing. Thus, `intro.swf`, `intro.html`, `intro.gif`, and so on would result.

Tip

By unchecking Use default names, you can enter non-version–specific filenames for .FLA files that you incrementally save as you work. For example, if you have a .FLA file named main_100.fla, uncheck Use default names and set the Flash .SWF filename to main.swf, then every new .FLA version you save (for example, main_101.fla, main_102.fla, and so on) will still produce a main.swf file. This way, you can consistently refer to one .SWF file in your HTML code and incrementally save your Flash movies.

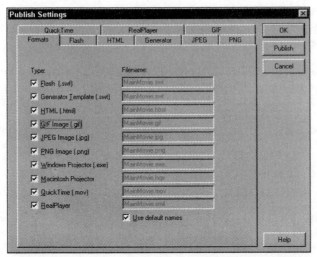

Figure 43-3: The Formats tab of the Publish Settings dialog enables you to select the published file formats and to use default or custom names for these published files.

Using the Flash settings

The primary and default publishing format of Flash 5 movies is the Flash (.SWF) format. Only .SWF movies retain full support for Flash actions and animations.

Here are your options in the Flash tab:

✦ **Load Order:** This option determines how Flash will draw the first frame of the Flash movie as it is downloaded to the plug-in or player. When Bottom up (the default) is chosen, the layers load in ascending order: The lowest layer displays first, then the second lowest, and so on, until all of the layers for the first frame have been displayed. When Top down is selected, the layers load in descending order: the top-most layer displays first, then the layer underneath it, and so on. Again, this option only affects the display of the first frame of a Flash movie. If the content of the first frame is downloaded or streamed quickly, you probably won't notice the Load Order's effect.

✦ **Generate size report:** As discussed earlier in this chapter, the size report for a Flash movie can be very useful in pinpointing problematic bandwidth-intensive elements, such as font characters. When this option is checked, the Publish command exports a SimpleText (Mac) or TXT file (PC) to view separately in a text-editor application.

✦ **Omit Trace Actions:** When this option is selected, the Flash player ignores any trace actions used in Flash ActionScripting. Trace actions will open the Flash Output window for debugging purposes. In general, if you used Trace actions, you will want to omit them from the final .SWF file — they can't be viewed in the Flash Player anyway.

✦ **Protect from import:** This option safeguards your Flash .SWF files on the Internet. When enabled, the .SWF file cannot be imported back into the Flash 5 authoring environment, or altered in any way.

Caution

The Protect from import option will *not* prevent a Web browser from caching your .SWF files. Also, Macromedia Director can import and use protected .SWF files. Hacking utilities called *swiffers,* can break into any .SWF file and extract artwork, sounds, and ActionScripted code. Even Notepad can open .SWF files and see variable names and values. For this reason, you should always use CGI scripts to verify password entries in Flash movies, rather than internal ActionScripted password checking with if . . . else conditions. Don't store sensitive information such as passwords in your source files!

✦ **Debugging Permitted:** If this option is checked, then you can access the Debugger Panel from in the Debug Movie environment, or from a Web browser that is using the Flash Debug Player plug-in or ActiveX control.

Note

To install the Flash Debug Player plug-in or ActiveX control, go to the Players folder in your Macromedia Flash 5 application folder. There, you will find a Debug folder. Run the Flash 5 Player Installer file (Netscape for Mac and/or Internet Explorer for Mac), the flash32.exe file (Netscape for Windows), or the InstallAXFlash.exe (Internet Explorer for Windows) file located there.

✦ **Password:** If you checked the Debugging Permitted option, you can enter a password to access the Debugger Panel. Because you can now debug movies over a live Internet connection, you should always enter a password here if you intend to debug a remote Flash .SWF file. If you leave this field empty and check the Debugging Permitted option, Flash will still ask you for a password when you attempt to access the Debugger Panel remotely. Simply press the Enter key if you left this field blank.

✦ **JPEG Quality:** This slider and text-field option specifies the level of JPEG compression applied to bitmapped artwork in the Flash movie. The value can be any value between (and including) 0 to 100. Higher values apply less compression and preserve more information of the original bitmap, whereas lower values apply more compression and keep less information. The value entered here applies to all bitmaps that enable the Use document default quality option, found in the Bitmap Properties dialog for each bitmap in the Flash Library. Unlike the audio settings discussed in a moment, no "override" option exists to disregard settings in the Flash Library.

✦ **Audio Stream:** This option displays the current audio compression scheme for Stream audio. By clicking the Set button (see Figure 43-4), you can control the compression applied to any sounds that use the Stream Sync setting in the Sound tab of the Frame Properties dialog. Like the JPEG Quality option discussed previously, this compression value is applied to any Stream sounds that use the Default compression in the Export Settings section of each audio file's Sound Properties dialog in the Flash Library. See Chapters 36 through 38 for more information on using Stream sounds and audio compression schemes.

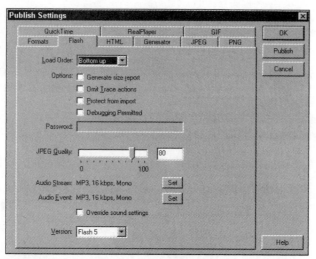

Figure 43-4: The Flash tab of the Publish Settings dialog controls the settings for a movie published in the Flash format.

✦ **Audio Event:** This setting behaves exactly the same as the Audio Stream option, except that this compression setting applies to Default compression-enabled Event sounds. See Chapter 37, "Importing and Editing Sounds in Flash," for more information on Event sounds.

New Feature

Flash 5 now supports imported MP3 audio that uses VBR (Variable Bit Rate) compression. However, Flash 5 cannot compress native sounds in VBR. If you use any imported MP3 audio for Stream Sync audio, Flash will recompress the MP3 audio on export.

✦ **Override sound settings:** If you want the settings for Audio Stream and Audio Event to apply to all Stream and Event sounds, respectively, and to disregard any unique compression schemes specified in the Flash Library, then check this option. This is useful for creating multiple .SWF versions of the Flash movie (hi-fi, lo-fi, and so on) and enabling the Web visitor to decide which one to download. See Figure 43-5.

✦ **Version:** This drop-down menu provides the option to publish movies in any of the Flash .SWF formats. To ensure complete compatibility with all of the new Flash 5 features, select Flash 5. If you haven't used any new Flash 5 ActionScript commands or Dots notation, then you can use Flash 4. Flash 1 and 2 support only basic animation and interactive functions. Flash 3 will support just about all animation and artwork created in Flash 5, but it doesn't recognize any of the ActionScripts introduced with either Flash 4 or 5, editable text fields (such as form elements), or MP3 audio. If in doubt, you should test your choice of version in that version's Flash Player.

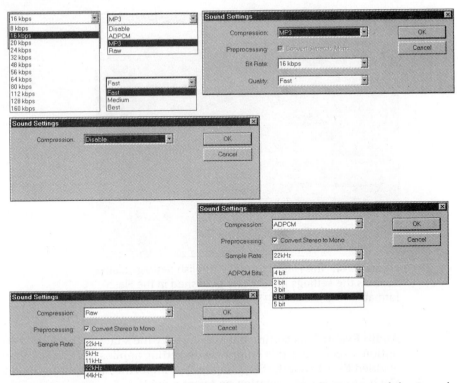

Figure 43-5: Click the Set button for Audio Stream or Audio Event, and the Sound Settings dialog appears.

Tip

You can download older versions of the Flash Player from the Macromedia site at: www.macromedia.com/support/flash/ts/documents/oldplayers.htm

When you are finished entering the settings for the .SWF movie, you can proceed to other file-type settings in the Publish Settings dialog. Or, you can click OK to return to the authoring environment of Flash 5 so that you can use the newly entered settings in the Test Movie or Scene environment. You can also export a .SWF file (and other file formats currently selected in Publish Settings) by clicking the Publish button in the Publish Settings dialog.

Using the HTML settings

HTML is the language in which the layout of most Web pages is written. The HTML tab of the Publish Settings dialog (see Figure 43-6) has a number of settings that control the way in which Flash will publish a movie into a complete Web page with the HTML format.

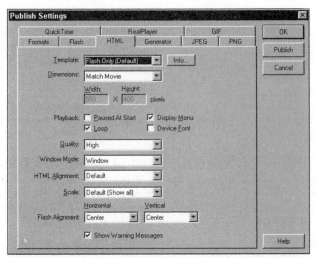

Figure 43-6: The HTML settings tab controls flexible Flash movie options — you can change this options without permanently affecting the Flash .SWF movie.

The settings available in the HTML tab include:

✦ **Template:** Perhaps the most important (and versatile) feature of all Publish Settings, the Template setting enables you to select a predefined set of HTML tags to display your Flash movies. To view the description of each template, click the Info button to the right of the drop-down list (shown in Figure 43-6). All templates use the same options listed in the HTML dialog — the template simply places the values of those settings into HTML tags scripted in the template. You can also create your own custom templates for your own unique implementation of Flash movies. Figure 43-7 shows the description for the Flash Only (Default) template.

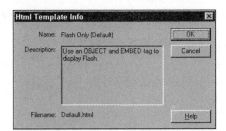

Figure 43-7: Clicking the Info button shown in Figure 43-6 summons a brief description of the HTML template that has been specified in the Template drop-down list.

Tip

You can view the "source" of each template in the HTML folder of the Flash 5 application folder. Although these template files have.html extensions, use Notepad (PC) or SimpleText (Mac) to view the files. All of the preinstalled templates include HTML tags to create an entire Web page, complete with <HEAD>, <TITLE>, and <BODY> tags.

- **Ad 3 Banner:** With this template, Flash creates an HTML document that checks for the Flash 3 Player plug-in. If JavaScript or VBScript detects the plug-in, then the Flash .SWF file will be served. If there is no Flash Player, then a GIF or JPEG will be loaded into the page. You must choose either the GIF or JPEG option in the Format tab of the Publish Settings dialog. As the name of the template implies, this template is useful for serving Flash ad banners. You can, however, use any of the Ad templates for any Flash movie version checking. Make sure that you have selected Flash 3 as the .SWF version in the Flash tab.

- **Ad 4 Banner:** Same as the Ad 3 Banner, except that the JavaScript and VBScript check for the Flash 4 Player plug-in. You need to change the .SWF Version option to Flash 4 in the Flash tab of the Publish Settings. Use this template only if you are using Flash 4-specific ActionScripts, such as variable declarations or loadVariable actions.

- **Ad 5 Banner:** Same as the Ad 3 Banner, except that the JavaScript and VBScript check for the Flash 5 Player plug-in. Change the .SWF version option to Flash 5 in the Flash tab of the Publish Settings dialog. If you are serving Flash ad banners, you may not want to serve the Flash 5 format. Unless your Flash 5 movies use Flash 5-specific ActionScripts (Dots notation, XML data, and so on), choose one of the previous Banner templates.

- **Ad Any Banner:** This template checks whether the Flash 3, 4, or 5 Player plug-in is installed. If any of these players is installed, then the published .SWF file will load into the HTML document. Otherwise, the published JPEG or GIF will be served. Use this option only if you are publishing Flash 3-compatible .SWF files, and want to serve a .SWF file to everyone who has a Flash 3, 4, or 5 Player plug-in.

- **Flash Only (Default):** This template simply inserts the <OBJECT> and <EMBED> tags for a Flash 5 movie. It does not perform any browser or plug-in detection.

- **Flash with FSCommand:** Use this template if you are using the FSCommand action in your Flash movies to communicate with JavaScript in the HTML page. The FSCommand is discussed in the next chapter. The necessary <OBJECT> and <EMBED> tags from the Flash Only (Default) template are also included.

- **Generator Ad Any Banner:** This template is similar to the Ad Any Banner template. If you have used Generator Objects or Generator Environment variables to your Flash movie, then this template will create an HTML that checks for the Flash 3, 4, or 5 Player plug-in. If any of those versions are installed, then a request will be made for a dynamic .SWF file (?type=swf) from the Generator template (.SWT file). Otherwise, a JPEG, GIF, or PNG image will be made from the Generator template. You need to specify an image format (JPEG, GIF, or PNG) in the Formats tab for this template. However, you will not need to upload the published image file — the Generator Server is responsible for creating the static image on the fly.

- **Generator Image Output:** This template creates a simple <IMG> tag with a SRC attribute that contains the template's filename and the desired image format, as in <IMG SRC="templateFile.swt?type=gif">, which will tell the Generator Server to create a GIF image from the templateFile.swt file. You need to check the desired image format in the Formats tab of the Publish Settings dialog. As with the Generator Ad Any Banner template, you will not need to upload the published image file.

- **Generator Only (Default):** This template makes an HTML document that is similar to the Flash Only (Default) template. It will include <OBJECT> and <EMBED> tags that refer to the Generator template file (.SWT file) and a Flash output format (?type=swf).

- **Generator QuickTime:** The HTML document published with this template will create an <EMBED> tag that references the Generator template file (.SWT file) and a QuickTime Flash output format, as in <EMBED SRC= "template.swt?type=mov" . . . .>. Note that this output format will require the QuickTime 4 (or higher) Player plug-in.

- **Image Map:** This template does not use or display any .SWF movie. Instead, it uses a GIF, JPEG, or PNG image (as specified in the Publish Settings' Format tab) as a client-side image map, via an <IMG> tag with a USEMAP attribute. Use a frame label of #map in the Flash editor document (.FLA file) to designate which frame is used as the map image. See "Using the GIF settings" later in this chapter for more details.

- **Java Player:** Instead of using the Flash Player or an image map, this template creates the necessary <APPLET> tags to use the Flash Java Player. To use this player, you must select the Publish Settings' Flash tab and specify a version 2 .SWF format. The Flash Java Player needs to access Java class files (found in the Players folder of the Flash 4 application folder). Make sure that you have uploaded the class files to your Web server. You may need to add a CODEBASE=[URL of class files] to the <APPLET> tag created by this template.

- **QuickTime:** This template creates an `<EMBED>` tag to display QuickTime Flash movies. You need to enable the QuickTime file type in the Publish Settings' Format tab. A QuickTime Flash movie is a special type of QuickTime movie, playable with QuickTime 4 or higher. QuickTime 4 can only recognize Flash 3 features. You must choose Flash 3 as the Version option in the Flash tab. Depending on the options selected in the QuickTime tab of Publish Settings, the Flash movie may or may not be stored within the QuickTime movie file.

Note   At the time of this writing, the QuickTime 5 Public Preview had been released. This version of QuickTime supports Flash 4 ActionScripts.

- **User Choice:** Often the scripter's testing tool, this template creates an HTML document with Flash 5 plug-in detection and a JavaScript cookie that enables you to choose three loading options for the Flash .SWF file: automatic plug-in detection, standard plug-in usage (via direct non-JavaScript–written `<OBJECT>` or `<EMBED>` tags), or substitute image (for example, GIF, JPEG, or PNG).

✦ **Dimensions:** This setting controls the `WIDTH` and `HEIGHT` values of the `<OBJECT>` and `<EMBED>` tags. The dimension settings here do not change the original .SWF movie, they simply create the viewport through which your Flash movie is viewed on the Web page. The way that the Flash movie "fits" into this viewport is determined with the Scale option (discussed later). Three input areas exist: a drop-down menu and two text fields for width andheight.

- **Match Movie:** If you want to keep the same width and height that you specified in the Modify ⇨ Movie dialog, then use this option in the drop-down menu.

- **Pixels:** You can change the viewing size (in pixel units) of the Flash movie window by selecting this option and entering new values in the Width and Height text fields.

- **Percent:** By far one of the most popular options with Flash movies, Percent scales the movie to the size of the browser window — or a portion of it. Using a value of 100 on both Width and Height expands the Flash movie to fit the entire browser window. If Percent is used with the proper Scale setting (see the description of the Scale setting later in this chapter), then the aspect ratio of your Flash movie will not be distorted.

- **Width and Height:** Enter the values for the Flash movie width and height here. If Match Movie is selected, you shouldn't be able to enter any values. The unit of measurement is determined by selecting either Pixels or Percent from the drop-down menu.

✦ **Playback:** These options control how the Flash movie plays when it is downloaded to the browser. Each of these options has an `<OBJECT>` and `<EMBED>` attribute if you want to control them outside of Publish Settings. Note that these attributes are not viewable within the Publish Settings dialog — you need to load the published HTML document into a text editor to see the attributes.

- **Paused at Start:** This is equivalent to adding a Stop action on the first frame of the first scene in the Flash movie. By default, this option is off — movies play as soon as they stream into the player. A button with a Play action can start the movie, or the Play command can be executed from the Flash Player shortcut menu (by right-clicking or Control+clicking the movie). Attribute: PLAY=true or false. If PLAY=true, the movie will play as soon as it is loaded.

- **Loop:** This option causes the Flash movie to repeat an infinite number of times. By default, this option is on. If it is not checked, the Flash movie stops on the last frame unless some other ActionScripted event is initiated on the last frame. Attribute: LOOP=true or false.

- **Display Menu:** This option controls whether the person viewing the Flash movie in the Flash Player environment can access the shortcut menu via a right-click (PC) or Ctrl+click (Mac) anywhere within the movie area. If this option is checked, then the visitor can select Zoom In/Out, 100 percent, Show All, High Quality, Play, Loop, Rewind, Forward, and Back from the menu. If this option is not checked, then the visitor can only select About Flash Player from the menu. Attribute: MENU=true or false.

- **Device Font:** This option only applies to Flash movie played in the Windows version of the Flash Player. When enabled, this option replaces fonts that are not installed on the Player's system with antialiased system fonts. Attribute: DEVICEFONT=true or false.

✦ **Quality:** This menu determines how the Flash artwork in a movie will render. While it would be ideal to play all Flash movies at high quality, slower processors may not be able to redraw antialiased artwork and keep up with the frame rate.

- **Low:** This setting forces the Flash Player to turn off antialiasing (smooth edges) completely. On slower processors, this may improve playback performance. Attribute: QUALITY=LOW.

- **Auto Low:** This setting starts in Low quality mode (no antialiasing), but will switch to High quality if the computer's processor can handle the playback speed. Attribute: QUALITY=AUTOLOW.

- **Auto High:** This setting is the opposite of Auto Low. The Flash Player starts playing the movie in High quality mode, but, if the processor cannot handle the playback demands, then it switches to Low quality mode. For most Web sites, this is the optimal setting to use because it favors higher quality first. Attribute: QUALITY=AUTOHIGH.

- **Medium:** This quality produces antialiased vector graphics on a 2×2 grid (in other words, it will smooth edges over a 4-pixel square area), but does not smooth bitmap images. Artwork will appear slightly better than the Low quality, but not as smooth as the High setting. Attribute: QUALITY=MEDIUM.

New Feature The Medium quality option is new to Flash 5. You can now specify this intermediate quality in order to achieve smoother playback and smoother graphics quality.

- **High:** When this setting is used, the Flash Player dedicates more of the computer's processor to rendering graphics (instead of playback). All vector artwork is antialiased on a 4×4 grid (16-pixel square area). Bitmaps are smoothed unless they are contained within an animation sequence such as a Motion Tween. By default, this setting is selected in the HTML tab of the Publish Settings dialog. Attribute: QUALITY=HIGH.

- **Best:** This mode does everything that High quality does, with the addition of smoothing all bitmaps — regardless of whether they are in Motion Tweens. This mode is the most processor-intensive. Attribute: QUALITY=BEST.

✦ **Window Mode:** The Window Mode setting only works with the Flash ActiveX control. Therefore, it only applies to 32-bit Windows versions of Internet Explorer. If you intend to deliver to this browser, then you can animate Flash content on top of DHTML content. Attribute: WMODE=WINDOW, or OPAQUE, or TRANSPARENT.

✦ **HTML Alignment:** This setting works much like the ALIGN attribute of <IMG> tags in HTML documents, but it's used with the ALIGN attribute of the <OBJECT> and <EMBED> tags for the Flash movie. Note that these settings may not have any effect when used within a table cell (<TD> tag) or a DHTML layer (<DIV> or <LAYER> tag).

- **Default:** This option horizontally or vertically centers the Flash movie in the browser window. If the browser window is smaller than a Flash movie that uses a Pixel or Match Movie dimensions setting (see Dimensions setting earlier in this section), then the Flash movie will be cropped.

- **Left, Right, Top, and Bottom:** These options align the Flash movie along the left, right, top, or bottom edge of the browser window, respectively.

✦ **Scale:** This setting works in tandem with the Dimensions setting discussed earlier in this section, and determines how the Flash movie displays on the HTML page. Just as big screen movies must be cropped to fit the aspect ratio of a TV screen, Flash movies may need to be modified to fit the area prescribed by the Dimensions setting.

- **Default (Show all):** This option fits the entire Flash movie into the area defined by the Dimensions setting without distorting the original aspect ratio of the Flash movie. However, borders may appear on two sides of the Flash movie. For example, if a 300×300-pixel window is specified in Dimensions and the Flash movie has an aspect ratio of 1.33:1 (for example, 430×300 pixels), then a border fills the remaining areas on top of and below the Flash movie. This is similar to the "letterbox" effect on widescreen video rentals. Attribute: SCALE=SHOWALL.

- **No border:** This option forces the Flash movie to fill the area defined by the Dimensions setting without leaving borders. The Flash movie's aspect ratio is not distorted or stretched. However, this may crop two sides of the Flash movie. Using the same example from Show All, the left and right sides of the Flash movie are cropped when No Border is selected. Attribute: `SCALE=NOBORDER`.

- **Exact fit:** This option stretches a Flash movie to fill the entire area defined by the Dimensions setting. Using the same example from Show All, the 430×300 Flash movie is scrunched to fit a 300×300 window. If the original movie showed a perfect circle, it now appears as an oval. Attribute: `SCALE=EXACTFIT`.

✦ **Flash Alignment:** This setting adjusts the `SALIGN` attribute of the `<OBJECT>` and `<EMBED>` tags for the Flash movie. In contrast to the HTML Alignment setting, Flash Alignment works in conjunction with the Scale and Dimensions settings, and determines how a Flash movie is aligned within the Player window.

- **Horizontal:** These options — Left, Center, and Right — determine whether the Flash movie is horizontally aligned to the left, center, or right of the Dimensions area, respectively. Using the same example from the Scale setting, a 430×300-pixel Flash movie (fit into a 300×300 Dimension window with `SCALE=NOBORDER`) with a Flash Horizontal Alignment setting of Left crops only the right side of the Flash movie.

- **Vertical:** These options — Top, Center, and Bottom — determine whether the Flash movie is vertically aligned to the top, center, or bottom of the Dimensions area, respectively. If the previous example used a Show All Scale setting and had a Flash Vertical Alignment setting of Top, then the border only occurs below the bottom edge of the Flash movie.

✦ **Show Warning Messages:** This useful feature alerts you to errors during the actual Publish process. For example, if you selected the Image Map template and didn't specify a static GIF, JPEG, or PNG file in the Formats tab, then Flash returns an error. By default, this option is enabled. If it is disabled, then Flash suppresses any warnings during the Publish process.

Using the GIF settings

The GIF (Graphics Interchange File) format, developed by CompuServe, defined the first generation of Web graphics, and is still quite popular today, despite its 256-color limitation. In the context of the Flash Publish Settings, the GIF format is used to export a static or animated image that can be used in place of the Flash movie if the Flash Player or plug-in is not installed. Although the Flash and HTML tabs are specific to Flash movie display and playback, the settings of the GIF tab (see Figure 43-8) control the characteristics of a GIF animation (or still image) that Flash will publish.

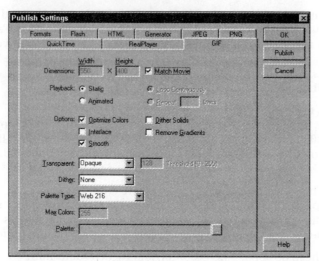

Figure 43-8: Every subtle aspect of a GIF animation or still image can be finessed with these settings of the GIF tab of the Publish Settings dialog.

The settings in the GIF tab include the following:

✦ **Dimensions:** This setting has three options: Width, Height, and Match Movie. As you might surmise, Width and Height control the dimensions of the GIF image. These fields are enabled only when the Match Movie checkbox is unchecked. With Match Movie checked, the dimensions of the GIF match those of the Flash Movie that is being published.

✦ **Playback:** These radio buttons control what type of GIF image is created and how it plays (if Animated is chosen).

• **Static:** If this button is selected, then Flash exports the first frame of the Flash movie as a single still image in the GIF format. If you want to use a different frame other than the first frame, use a frame label of #Static on the desired frame. Alternatively, you could use the File ➪ Export Image command to export a GIF image from whatever frame the Current Frame Indicator is positioned over.

• **Animated:** If this button is selected, then Flash exports the entire Flash movie as an animated GIF file (in the GIF89a format). If you don't want to export the entire movie as an animated GIF (indeed, a GIF file for a Flash movie with over 100 frames would be most likely too large to download easily over the Web), you can designate a range of frames to export. Use a frame label of #First on the beginning frame of a given range of frames. Next, add a frame label of #Last to the ending frame of the desired sequence of frames. Flash actually does a pretty good at optimizing animated GIFs by only saving areas that change over time in each frame — instead of the entire frame.

- **Loop Continuously:** When the Animated radio button is selected, you can specify that the animated GIF repeats an infinite number of times by selecting the Loop Continuously radio button.

- **Repeat __ times:** This option can be used to set up an animated GIF that repeats a given number of times. If you don't want the animated GIF to repeat continuously, then enter the number of repetitions here.

✦ **Options:** The options in the Options settings control the creation of the GIF's color table and how the browser displays the GIF.

- **Optimize Colors:** When you are using any palette type other than Adaptive, this option removes any colors preexisting in the Web 216 or custom palettes that are not used by the GIF image. Enabling this option can only save you precious bytes used in file overhead — it has no effect on the actual quality of the image. Most images do not use all 216 colors of the Web palette. For example, a black and white picture can only use between 3 and 10 colors from the 216-color palette.

- **Interlace:** This option makes the GIF image download in incrementing resolutions. As the image downloads, the image becomes sharper with each successive "scan." Use of this option is usually personal preference. Some people like to use it for image maps that can provide basic navigation information before the entire image downloads.

- **Smooth:** This option antialiases the Flash artwork as it exports to the GIF image. Text may look better when it is antialiased, but may want to test this option for your particular use. If you need to make a transparent GIF, then smoothing may produce unsightly edges.

- **Dither Solids:** This option determines if solid areas of color (such as fills) are dithered. In this context, this type of dithering would create a two-color pattern to mimic a solid color that doesn't occur in the GIF's color palette. See the discussion of dithering later in this section.

- **Remove Gradients:** Flash gradients do not translate or display very well in 256 or less colors. Use this option to convert all Flash gradients to solid colors. The solid color is determined by the first color prescribed in the gradient. Unless you developed your gradients with this effect in mind, this option may produce undesirable results.

✦ **Transparent:** This setting controls the appearance of the Flash movie background, as well as any Flash artwork that uses alpha settings. Because GIF images only support one level of transparency (that is, the transparent area cannot be antialiased), you need to exercise caution when using this setting. The Threshold option is only available if Alpha is selected.

- **Opaque:** This option produces a GIF image with a solid background. The image has a rectangular shape.

- **Transparent:** This option makes the Flash movie background appear transparent. If the Smooth option in the Options setting is enabled, then Flash artwork may display halos over the background HTML color.

- **Alpha and Threshold:** When the Alpha option is selected in the drop-down menu, you can control at what alpha level Flash artwork becomes transparent by entering a value in the Threshold text field. For example, if you enter 128, then all alphas at 50 percent become completely transparent. If you are considering an animated GIF that has Flash artwork fading in or out, then you probably want to use the Opaque transparent option. If Alpha and Threshold were used, then the fade effect would be lost.

✦ **Dither:** Dithering is the process of emulating a color by juxtaposing two colors in a pattern arrangement. Because GIF images are limited to 256 colors (or less), dithering can often produce better-looking images for continuous tone artwork such as gradients. However, Flash's dithering seems to work best with the Web 216 palette. Dithering can increase the file size of a GIF image.

  - **None:** This option does not apply any dithering to the GIF image.

  - **Ordered:** This option applies an intermediate level of dithering with minimal file size overhead.

  - **Diffusion:** This option applies the best level of dithering to the GIF image, but with larger file size overhead. Diffusion dithering only has a noticeable effect when the Web 216 palette is chosen in Palette Type.

✦ **Palette Type:** As mentioned earlier in this section, GIF images are limited to 256 or less colors. However, this grouping of 256 is arbitrary: Any set of 256 (or less) colors can be used for a given GIF image. This setting enables you to select predefined sets of colors to use on the GIF image. See Chapter 24, "Exploring the Interface: Panels, Settings, and More," for more information on the Web color palette.

  - **Web 216:** When this option is selected, the GIF image only uses colors from the limited 216 Web-color palette. For most Flash artwork, this should produce acceptable results. However, it may not render Flash gradients or photographic bitmaps very well.

  - **Adaptive:** With this option selected, Flash creates a unique set of 256 colors (or fewer, if specified in the Max Colors setting) for the GIF image. However, these adapted colors fall outside of the Web-Safe Color Palette. File sizes for adaptive GIFs are larger than Web 216 GIFs, unless few colors are chosen in the Max Colors setting. Adaptive GIFs look much better than Web 216 GIFs, but may not display very well with 8-bit video cards and monitors.

  - **Web Snap Adaptive:** This option tries to give the GIF image the best of both worlds. Flash converts any colors close to the 216 Web palette to Web-safe colors and uses adaptive colors for the rest. This palette produces better results than the Adaptive palette for older display systems that used 8-bit video cards.

  - **Custom:** When this option is selected, you can specify a palette that uses the .ACT file format to be used as the GIF image's palette. Macromedia Fireworks and Adobe Photoshop can export color palettes (or color look-up tables) as .ACT files.

✦ **Max Colors:** With this setting, you can specify exactly how many colors are in the GIF's color table. This numeric entry field is only enabled when Adaptive or Web Snap Adaptive is selected in the Palette Type drop-down menu.

✦ **Palette:** This text field and the ". . ." browse button are only enabled when Custom is selected in the Palette Type drop-down menu. When enabled, this dialog is used to locate and load a palette file from the hard drive.

Using the JPEG settings

The JPEG (Joint Photographic Experts Group) format is just as popular as the GIF format on the Web. Unlike GIF images, though, JPEG images can use much more than 256 colors. In fact, JPEG files must be 24-bit color (or full-color RGB) images. Although GIF files use lossless compression (within the actual file itself), JPEG images use lossy compression, which means that color information is discarded in order to save file space. However, JPEG compression is very good. Even at its lowest quality settings, JPEG images can preserve quite a bit of detail in photographic images.

Another significant difference between GIF and JPEG is that GIF images do not require nearly as much memory (for equivalent image dimensions) as JPEG images do. You need to remember that JPEG images "uncompress" when they are downloaded to your computer. While the file sizes may be small initially, they still open as full-color images in the computer's memory. For example, even though you may get the file size of a 430×300-pixel JPEG image down to 10KB, it still requires nearly 352KB in memory when it is opened or displayed.

Flash publishes the first frame of the Flash movie as the JPEG image, unless a #Static frame label is given to another frame in the Flash movie. The limited settings of the JPEG tab of the Publish Settings dialog (see Figure 43-9) control the few variables of this still photoquality image format:

✦ **Dimensions:** This setting behaves the same as the GIF Dimensions setting. Width and Height control the dimensions of the movie. But these fields are enabled only when the Match Movie checkbox is unchecked. With Match Movie checked, the dimensions of the JPEG match those of the Flash Movie.

✦ **Quality:** This slider and text field work exactly the same way as the JPEG Quality setting in the Flash tab of Publish Settings. Higher values apply less compression and result in better quality, but create images with larger file sizes.

✦ **Progressive:** This option is similar to the Interlaced option for GIF images. When enabled, the JPEG image loads in successive scans, becoming sharper with each pass.

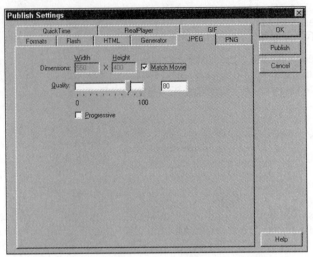

Figure 43-9: The settings of the JPEG tab are limited because JPEGs are still images with relatively few variables to be addressed.

Using the PNG settings

The PNG (Portable Network Graphic) format is another still-image format. It was developed quite recently and is an improvement over both the GIF and JPEG formats in several ways. Much like JPEG, it is excellent for transmission of photographic quality images. The primary advantages of PNG are variable bit-depths (images can be 256 colors or millions of colors), multilevel transparency, and lossless compression. However, most browsers do not offer full support for all PNG options without some kind of additional plug-in. When in doubt, test your PNG images in your preferred browser.

The settings of the PNG tab (see Figure 43-10) control the characteristics of the PNG image that Flash will publish.

The PNG tab options are:

✦ **Dimensions:** This setting works just like the GIF and JPEG equivalents. When Match Movie is checked, you cannot alter the Width and Height of the PNG image.

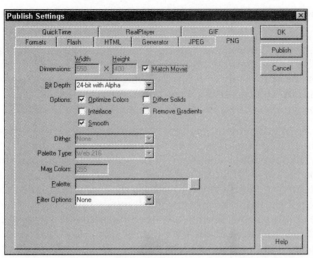

Figure 43-10: The settings found on the PNG tab closely resemble those on the GIF tab. The PNG was engineered to have many of the advantages of both the GIF and JPEG formats.

✦ **Bit Depth:** This setting controls how many colors are created in the PNG image:

- **8-bit:** In this mode, the PNG image has a maximum color palette of 256 colors, similar to the palette function of GIF images. When this option is selected, the Options, Dither, Palette Type, Max Colors, and Palette settings can be altered.

- **24-bit:** When this option is selected, the PNG image can display any of the 16.7 million RGB colors. This option produces larger files than 8-bit PNG images, but renders the Flash artwork most faithfully.

- **24-bit with Alpha:** This option adds another 8-bit channel to the 24-bit PNG image for multilevel transparency support. This means that Flash will treat the Flash movie background as a transparent area, so that information behind the PNG image (such as HTML background colors) shows through. Note that, with proper browser support, PNG can render antialiased edges on top of other elements, such as HTML background images!

Caution

Flash's PNG export or publish settings do not reflect the full range of PNG options available. PNG can support transparency in both 8-bit and 24-bit flavors, but Flash only enables transparency in 24-bit with Alpha images.

✦ **Options:** These options behave the same as the equivalent GIF Publish Settings.

✦ **Dither, Palette Type, Max Colors,** and **Palette:** These settings work the same as the equivalent GIF Publish Settings. Because PNG images can be either 8- or 24-bit, these options are only apply to 8-bit PNG images. If anything other than 8-bit is selected in the Bit Depth setting, then these options are disabled. Please refer to the previous section for more information.

✦ **Filter Options:** This drop-down menu controls what type of compression sampling or algorithm the PNG image uses. Note that this does not apply an art or graphic "filter effect" like the filters in Adobe Photoshop do, nor does it throw away any image information — all filters are lossless. It simply enables you to be the judge of what kind of compression to use on the image. You need to experiment with each of these filters on your Flash movie image to find the best filter-to-file size combination. Technically, the filters do not actually look at the pixel data. Rather, they look at the byte data of each pixel. Results vary depending on the image content, but here are some guidelines to keep in mind:

- **None:** When this option is selected, no filtering is applied to the image. When no filter is applied, you usually have unnecessarily large file sizes.

- **Sub:** This filter works best on images that have repeated information along the horizontal axis. For example, the stripes of a horizontal American flag filter nicely with the sub filter.

- **Up:** The opposite of the sub filter, this filter works by looking for repeated information along the vertical axis. The stripes of a vertical American flag filter well with the up filter.

- **Average:** Use this option when a mixture of vertical and horizontal information exists. When in doubt, try this filter first.

- **Paeth:** This filter works like an advanced average filter. When in doubt, try this filter after you have experimented with the average filter.

Creating Windows and Macintosh projectors

To export a Mac standalone projector, check the Macintosh Projector option in the Formats tab. To publish a PC standalone projector, check the Windows Projector option in the Formats tab.

Using the QuickTime settings

Now that QuickTime 4 (and the forthcoming QuickTime 5) includes built-in support for Flash tracks and .SWF files, you may want to publish QuickTime 4 movies (.MOV files) in addition to your Flash movies (.SWF files). If you want to enable QuickTime movie output via the Publish command, make sure that it is selected in the Formats tab of the Publish Settings dialog.

Producing RealPlayer presentations

Flash 5 can now automatically create tuned .SWF files and RealAudio files from your Stream Sync audio used in your Flash movie file. To create the tuned .SWF, RealAudio, and .SMIL files necessary for playback in RealPlayer, check the RealPlayer option in the Formats tab of the Publish Settings dialog.

Publish Preview and Publish Commands

After you have entered the file format types and specifications for each in the Publish Settings dialog, you can proceed to preview and publish the file types you selected.

Using Publish Preview

The Publish Preview submenu (accessible from File ➪ Publish Preview) lists all of the file types currently enabled in the Publish Settings dialog.* By default, HTML is the first file type available for preview. In general, the first item enabled in the Formats tab of Publish Settings is the first item in the submenu, and can be executed by pressing F12. Selecting a file type in the Publish Preview menu launches your preferred browser and inserts the selected file type(s) into the browser window.

Note

When you use Publish Preview, Flash 5 actually creates real files in the same location as the saved Flash movie. In a sense, previewing is the same as running the Publish command, except that Publish Preview will save you the steps of opening the browser and loading the files manually.

Using Publish

When you want Flash to export the file type(s) selected in the Publish Settings, choose File ➪ Publish (Shift+F12). Flash creates the new files wherever the Flash movie was last saved. If you have selected an HTML template in the HTML tab of Publish Settings, then you may receive a warning or error message if any other necessary files were not specified. That's it! After you've tested the files for the delivery browser and/or platforms of your choice, you can upload the files to your Web server.

---

*RealPlayer files cannot be previewed from this menu.

Summary

✦ To achieve the smallest possible file size for quick download over the Internet, make sure that you have optimized your Flash movie. Reducing the use of bitmapped artwork and the number of points in a line or shape, and using nested symbols, can help reduce wasted space in a Flash movie.

✦ For audio, we recommend that you use Flash's MP3 encoding. MP3 provides the best sound quality with the smallest byte requirements. However, you will want to experiment with different audio codecs, depending on your source audio.

✦ Test your Flash movies and scenes within the Flash authoring environment. The Bandwidth Profiler can provide vital information about frame byte requirements, and can help you find problematic streaming areas of the Flash movie.

✦ The size report that can be generated from the Export Movie or Publish commands for .SWF movies lists detailed information regarding any and all Flash elements, such as audio, fonts and frame byte size.

✦ The Publish Settings dialog box enables you to pick any number of file formats to export at one time. You can control just about every setting imaginable for each file type, and use HTML templates to automate the insertion of Flash movies into your Web pages.

✦ Publish Preview will automatically launch your preferred browser and load the selected publish file(s) into the browser window.

✦   ✦   ✦

Integrating Flash Content with HTML

If you're not one for automated HTML production using templates, then this chapter is for you. This chapter teaches you the ins and outs of the `<OBJECT>` and `<EMBED>` tags, as well as some secrets to using `<FRAMESET>` tags to display Flash movies. At the end of this chapter, we examine how Flash movies can interact with JavaScript and DHTML by using `FSCommand` actions from Flash.

Writing Markup for Flash Movies

In Chapter 43, you learned how to use the new Publish feature, which included automated HTML templates. These templates created the necessary HTML tags to display Flash movies on Web pages. This section discusses the use of Flash movies in your handwritten HTML documents. You can also use this knowledge to alter HTML documents created by the Publish feature.

> **Note** In the following code examples, we use an asterisk (*) when displaying optional parameters that are not in the default setting of the Flash Only (Default) HTML template.

Two tags can be used to place Flash movies on a Web page (such as an HTML document): `<OBJECT>` and `<EMBED>`. You need to include both of these plug-in tags in HTML documents, as each tag is specific to a browser: `<OBJECT>` for Internet Explorer on Windows, and `<EMBED>` for Netscape on Windows and Mac (and Internet Explorer on Mac). Each tag works similarly to the other, with some slight differences in attribute names and organization. Remember that if both sets of tags are included with the HTML, only one set of tags is actually read by the browser, depending on which browser is used to view the Web page. Without these tags, Flash movies cannot be displayed with other HTML elements such as images and text.

Tip

You can, however, directly link to .SWF files as an alternative method for displaying Flash content. That method, however, precludes the use of parameters to control the look and playback of the Flash movie — it would be the same as loading the .SWF movie straight into the standalone Flash Player. See Colin Moock's tutorial later in this chapter for more information on direct linking.

Using the <OBJECT> tag

Microsoft Internet Explorer for Windows uses this tag exclusively to enable the Flash ActiveX control. When the Flash Only (Default) HTML template is used in Publish Settings, the HTML document that is published uses the <OBJECT> tag in the following way:

```
A.  <OBJECT
B.        classid="clsid:D27CDB6E-AE6D-11cf-96B8-
          444553540000"
C.        codebase="http://download.macromedia.com/pub/
          shockwave/cabs/flash/swflash.cab#version=5,0,0,0"
D.        ID=home
E.        WIDTH=550 HEIGHT=400>
F.        <PARAM NAME=movie VALUE="home.swf">
G.        <PARAM NAME=quality VALUE=high>
H.        <PARAM NAME=bgcolor VALUE=#FFFFFF>
I.*       <PARAM NAME=scale VALUE=noborder>
J.*       <PARAM NAME=play VALUE=false>
K.  </OBJECT>
```

A. <OBJECT: This is the opening tag containing the ID code and locations of the ActiveX control for Flash. Note that this opening tag includes the attributes lettered B through E.

B. classid: This lengthy string is the unique ActiveX identification code. If you are inserting the <OBJECT> tag by hand in a text editor, make sure that you copy this ID string exactly.

C. codebase: Like the codebase attribute of Java <APPLET> tags, this attribute of the <OBJECT> tag specifies the location of the ActiveX control installer as a URL. Notice that the #version=5,0,0,0 portion of the URL indicates that the Flash Player version 5 should be used. You can also specify specific minor releases, such as #version=5,0,29,0, which would install the Flash 5.0 r29 ActiveX control. If the visitor doesn't have the ActiveX control already installed, then Internet Explorer automatically downloads the control from this URL.

D. `ID`: This attribute of the `<OBJECT>` tag assigns a JavaScript/VBScript identifier to the Flash movie, so that it can be controlled by HTML JavaScript/VBScript functions. By default, this attribute's value is the name of the actual of .SWF file, without the .SWF extension. Each element on an HTML page should have a unique `ID` or `NAME` attribute. The `NAME` attribute is discussed in the next section.

E. `WIDTH` **and** `HEIGHT>`: These attributes control the actual width and height of the Flash movie, as it appears on the Web page. If no unit of measurement is specified, then these values are in pixels. If the % character is added to the end of each value, then the attribute adjusts the Flash movie to the corresponding percent of the browser window. For example, if 100 percent was the value for both `WIDTH` and `HEIGHT`, then the Flash movie fills the entire browser, except for the browser gutter. See Colin Moock's tutorial later in this chapter to learn how to minimize this gutter thickness.

F. `<PARAM NAME=movie VALUE="home.swf">`: This is the first set of `<PARAM>` subtags within the `<OBJECT></OBJECT>` tags. Each parameter tag has a unique `NAME=` setting, not to be confused with JavaScript `NAME`'s or `ID`'s. This parameter's `NAME` setting `movie` specifies the filename of the Flash movie as the `VALUE` attribute.

G. `<PARAM NAME=quality VALUE=high>`: This parameter has a `NAME` attribute-setting quality that controls how the Flash movie's artwork renders within the browser window. The VALUE can be `low`, `autolow`, `autohigh`, `high`, or `best`. Most Flash movies on the Web use the `autohigh` value, as this forces the Flash Player to try rendering the movie elements antialiased. If the processor of the machine can't keep up with the Flash movie using antialiased elements, then it turns off antialiasing by switching to a `low` quality. For a full description of each of the `quality` settings, please refer to the section "Using the HTML settings" in Chapter 43.

H. `<PARAM NAME=bgcolor VALUE=#FFFFFF>`: This last parameter name, `bgcolor`, controls the background color of the Flash movie. If you published an HTML document via the Publish command, then the `VALUE` is automatically set to the background color specified by the Modify ⇨ Movie command in Flash. However, you can override the Movie setting by entering a different value in this parameter tag. Note that this parameter, like all HTML tags and attributes concerning color, uses hexadecimal code to describe the color. For more information on color, see Chapter 28, "Applying Color."

I. `<PARAM NAME=scale VALUE=noborder>`: This optional parameter controls how the Flash movie scales in the window defined by the `WIDTH` and `HEIGHT` attributes of the opening `<OBJECT>` tag. Its value can be `showall`, `noborder`, or `exactfit`. If this entire subtag is omitted, then the Flash Player treats the movie as if the `showall` default setting was specified. The `showall` setting fits the Flash movie within the boundaries of the `WIDTH` and `HEIGHT` dimensions without any distortion to the original aspect ratio of the Flash movie. Again, refer to "Using the HTML Settings" section of Chapter 43 for a complete description of the `scale` settings and how they work within the dimensions of a Flash movie.

J. <PARAM NAME=play VALUE=false>: This optional parameter tells the Flash Player whether or not it should start playing the Flash movie as it downloads. If the VALUE equals false, the Flash movie loads in a "paused" state, just as if a "stop" action was placed on the first frame. If the VALUE equals true, Flash starts playing the movie as soon as it starts to stream into the browser.

K. </OBJECT>: This is the closing tag for the starting <OBJECT> tag. As is shown later in this chapter, you can put other HTML tags between the last <PARAM> tag and the closing </OBJECT> tag for non-ActiveX–enabled browsers, such as Netscape. Because Internet Explorer is the only browser that currently recognizes <OBJECT> tags, other browsers simply skip the <OBJECT> tag (as well as its <PARAM> tags) and only read the tags between the last <PARAM> and </OBJECT> tags.

Tip
The <OBJECT> tag can use other parameter tag names such as WMODE. This parameter only works on 32-bit versions of Windows 95/98/NT Internet Explorer.

Using the <EMBED> tag

Netscape Communicator (or Navigator) uses the <EMBED> tag to display non-browser native file formats that require a plug-in, such as Macromedia Flash and Shockwave Director or Apple QuickTime.

```
A.  <EMBED
B.        src="home.swf"
C.        quality=high
D.*       scale=noborder
E.*       play=false
F.        bgcolor=#FFFFFF
G.        WIDTH=550 HEIGHT=400
H.*       swLiveConnect=false
I.        TYPE="application/x-shockwave-flash"
J.        PLUGINSPAGE="http://www.macromedia.com/shockwave/
          download/index.cgi?P1_Prod_Version=ShockwaveFlash">
K.  </EMBED>
```

A. <EMBED: This is the opening <EMBED> tag. Note that lines B through H are attributes of the opening <EMBED> tag, which is why you won't see the > character at the end of line A.

B. src: This stands for "source," and indicates the filename of the Shockwave Flash movie. This attribute of <EMBED> works exactly like the <PARAM NAME= movie VALUE="home.swf"> subtag of the <OBJECT> tag.

C. quality: This attribute controls how the Flash movie's artwork will display in the browser window. Like the equivalent <PARAM NAME=quality> subtag of the <OBJECT> tag, its value can be low, autolow, autohigh, high, or best.

D. `scale:` This attribute of `<EMBED>` controls how the Flash movie fits within the browser window and/or the dimensions specified by `WIDTH` and `HEIGHT` (F). Its value can be `showall` (default if attribute is omitted), `noborder`, or `exactfit`.

E. `play:` This attribute controls the playback of the Flash movie. If set to `false`, the Flash movie does not automatically play until a Flash action tells the movie to play (such as a Flash button or frame action). If set to `true`, then the Flash movie plays as soon as it starts to stream into the browser.

F. `bgcolor:` This setting controls the Flash movie's background color. Again, this attribute behaves identically to the equivalent `<PARAM>` subtag of the `<OBJECT>` tag. See that tag's description in the previous section.

G. `WIDTH` and `HEIGHT:` These attributes control the dimensions of the Flash movie as it appears on the Web page. Refer to the `WIDTH` and `HEIGHT` descriptions of the `<OBJECT>` tag for more information.

H. `swLiveConnect:` This is one attribute that you can't find in the `<OBJECT>` tag. This unique tag enables Netscape's LiveConnect feature, which enables plug-ins and Java applets to communicate with JavaScript. By default, this attribute is set to `false`. If it is enabled (for example, the attribute is set to `true`), the Web page may experience a short delay during loading. The latest versions of Netscape don't start the Java engine during a browsing session until a Web page containing a Java applet (or a Java-enabled plug-in such as Flash) is loaded. Unless you use FSCommands in your Flash movies, it's best to leave these attribute set to `false`.

I. `TYPE="application/x-shockwave-flash":` This attribute tells Netscape what MIME (Multipurpose Internet Mail Extension) content-type the embedded file is. Each file type (.TIF, .JPG, .GIF, .DOC, .TXT, and so on) has a unique MIME content-type header, describing what its content is. For Flash movies, the content-type is `application/x-shockwave-flash`. Any program (or operating system) that uses files over the Internet handles MIME content-types according to a reference chart that links each MIME content-type to its appropriate parent application or plug-in. Without this attribute, Netscape may not understand what type of file the Flash movie is. As a result, it may display the broken plug-in icon when the Flash movie downloads to the browser.

J. `PLUGINSPAGE:` Literally "plug-in's page," this attribute tells Netscape where to go to find the appropriate plug-in installer if it doesn't have the Flash plug-in already installed. This is not equivalent to a JavaScript-enabled autoinstaller. It simply redirects the browser to the URL of the Web page where the appropriate software can be downloaded.

K. `</EMBED>:` This is the closing tag for the original `<EMBED>` tag in line A. Some older or text-based browsers such as Lynx are incapable of displaying `<EMBED>` tags. You can insert alternate HTML (such as a static or animated .GIF with the `<IMG>` tag) between the `<EMBED>` `</EMBED>` tags for these browsers.

Caution   You may be surprised to learn that all versions of Internet Explorer (IE) for the Macintosh cannot read `<OBJECT>` tags. Rather, IE for Mac uses a Netscape plug-in emulator to read `<EMBED>` tags. However, this emulator does not interpret all `<EMBED>` tags with the same level of support as Netscape. As a result, the `swLiveConnect` attribute does not function on IE for Mac browsers. This means that FSCommands are not supported on these browsers.

Expert Tutorial: Filling the Browser Window by Using the `<FRAMESET>` Tag, *by Colin Moock*

Colin's biographical information can be found in his expert tutorial, Making GWEN!'s Eyes Shut When She Yawns, *located in Chapter 40, "Navigating Flash Timelines." Perhaps one of Colin's most famous (and often read) tutorials is this* `<FRAMESET>` *technique that forces the Flash movie to fill nearly all of the browser window.*

Filling the Gap

Many Flash designers have experienced the problem that Flash movies don't default to fill the entire viewing space of a browser window. This results in wasted screen space, or, what's worse, an unsightly gutter, or gap, between the edge of the Flash movie and the edges of the browser.

In the following figure, the browser on the left sports an unsightly white gutter around a Flash Movie. On the right, the same movie is displayed with a minimal gutter around a framed Flash Movie. For designers who prefer the effect shown on the right, two options work with most browsers. One solution depends on the use of frames, and is therefore limited to frames-capable browsers. The other solution requires that the Flash Player plug-in be detected before serving pages built with this method—so it's not appropriate for a splash page.

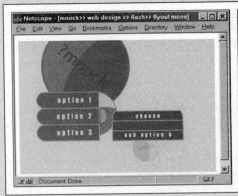
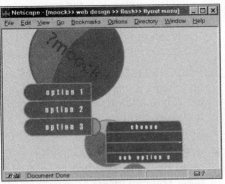

Single-frame frameset

With the attributes a frameset set correctly, framed Flash content can stretch to within one or two pixels (depending on the browser) of the edge of the browser window. To do this, first make the page (yourmovie.html) in which your movie is embedded. Then when embedding the movie, set the width, height, and scale for the desired effect. The SCALE parameter has three options:

✦ **HEIGHT="100%" WIDTH="100%" SCALE="EXACTFIT":** This combination forces every edge of your movie to the edge of the browser, and distorts your movie to fit the aspect ratio (proportion of height to width) of the browser.

✦ **HEIGHT="100%" WIDTH="100%" SCALE="SHOWALL":** This combination fits the width or height of your movie to the smaller of either the width or height of the browser. Your movie is not cropped or skewed to fit the browser window, but there are borders on either the top and bottom or right and left of your movie.

✦ **HEIGHT="100%" WIDTH="100%" SCALE="NOBORDER":** This combination adjusts either the height or width of your movie to the larger of either the width or height of the browser. When the dimensions of your movie do not match the dimensions of the browser, your movie is matted with additional background space on either the vertical or horizontal axis.

Your embedded movie code will look something like this. (The ¬ symbol indicates a continuation of the same line of code. Do not insert this character in your actual code.)

```
<OBJECT
CLASSID="clsid:D27CDB6E-AE6D-11cf-96B8-444553540000"
CODEBASE="http://download.macromedia.com/pub/ ¬
   shockwave/cabs/flash/swflash.cab#version=5,0,0,0"
WIDTH="100%"
HEIGHT="100%">
<PARAM NAME="MOVIE" VALUE="moviename.swf">
<PARAM NAME="PLAY" VALUE="true">
<PARAM NAME="LOOP" VALUE="true">
<PARAM NAME="QUALITY" VALUE="high">
<PARAM NAME="SCALE" VALUE="SHOWALL">

<EMBED SRC="yourmovie.swf"
       WIDTH="100%"
       HEIGHT="100%"
       PLAY="true"
       LOOP="true"
       QUALITY="high"
       SCALE="SHOWALL"
       PLUGINSPAGE="http://www.macromedia.com/shockwave/¬
          download/index.cgi?P1_Prod_Version=ShockwaveFlash">
</EMBED>
</OBJECT>
```

Continued

Continued

Now you're ready to make the single-frame frameset. Actually, it's a two-frame frameset, but you only use one of the frames for displaying your page. The first frame is allotted 100 percent of the browser area, and the second frame is allotted "*" (meaning whatever is left, which is nothing). The SRC of the first frame of the frameset will be the page (yourmovie.html) with your Flash Movie, while the SRC of the second frame will be an empty HTML page with a matching BGCOLOR. Then real trick is to specify the attributes of the frameset and frames so that the Flash movie will extend to the edges of the browser. Here's an example of code with the correct settings:

```
<HTML><HEAD><TITLE>Your Flash Movie Title</TITLE></HEAD>

<FRAMESET ROWS="100%,*"
          FRAMESPACING="0"
          FRAMEBORDER="NO"
          BORDER="0">

  <FRAME NAME="top"
         SRC="yourmovie.html"
         FRAMEBORDER="0"
         BORDER="0"
         MARGINWIDTH="0"
         MARGINHEIGHT="0"
         SCROLLING="NO">

  <FRAME NAME="hidden"
         SRC="empty.html"
         FRAMEBORDER="0"
         BORDER="0"
         MARGINWIDTH="0"
         MARGINHEIGHT="0"
         SCROLLING="NO">

</FRAMESET>
</HTML>
```

Now let's look at some of the code in detail:

✦ As an attribute of <FRAMESET>, FRAMEBORDER is either true or false, but as an attribute of <FRAME>, FRAMEBORDER is a pixel value for setting the width of the space between the browser edge and the page content.

✦ On <FRAMESET>, BORDER refers to the number of pixels between frames, while on <FRAME>, BORDER is simply a now-obsolete version of FRAMEBORDER.

✦ The SCROLLING attribute must be set to NO, otherwise, if the content is not larger than the browser window, a gap will appear on the right and bottom of the frame where the scroll bars would normally appear.

As a final option, to reduce the gutter as much as possible in Internet Explorer 4 (or higher) and Netscape Communicator 4 (or higher), you can set the margin values on the movie page (yourmovie.html). To accomplish this, Netscape 4 or higher uses MARGINHEIGHT and MARGINWIDTH, while Internet Explorer 4 or higher uses TOPMARGIN, BOTTOMMARGIN, LEFTMARGIN, and RIGHTMARGIN. So, to accommodate both browsers, use these values:

```
<BODY MARGINWIDTH="0" MARGINHEIGHT="0" LEFTMARGIN="0"
RIGHTMARGIN="0" TOPMARGIN="0" BOTTOMMARGIN="0">
```

Directly Linking to the Flash Movie (.SWF File)

An alternate method to the single-frame frameset described previously is to link directly to the Flash movie and let the browser display it inline. So, if your movie mymovie.swf is normally embedded in mymovie.html, then:

```
<A HREF="mymovie.html">View my movie</A>
```

would be changed to:

```
<A HREF="mymovie.swf">View my movie</A>
```

This method is easier to implement than the frames method, but should only be used after Flash has been successfully detected, because the browser won't have access to any of the HTML instructions that would normally tell it where to get the plug-in if the plug-in is not present. Thus, this method should not be used for a splash page.

If you use the Direct Link method, it's also important to remember to set the QUALITY of your movie to "high" from inside your movie using the Toggle High Quality action (Flash 3+ only). To do this, select your first keyframe, open the Actions Panel (in Normal Mode), and then add a toggleHighQuality action.

If you'd like to learn more about Colin Moock, please see his bio in Chapter 40, "Navigating Flash Timelines."

Detecting the Flash Player

What good is an awesome Flash experience if no one can see your Flash movies? Because most Flash content is viewed with a Web browser, it's extremely important to make sure that your HTML pages check for the existence of the Flash Player plug-in before you start pushing Flash content to the browser. There are a variety of ways to check for the Flash Player, and this section provides an overview of the available methods.

Plug-in versus ActiveX: Forcing content without a check

The Flash Player is available for Web browsers in two forms: the Flash Player plug-in (as a Netscape-compatible plug-in) and the Flash Player ActiveX Control (for use only with Microsoft Internet Explorer on Windows 95/98/NT/2000).

If you directly insert a Flash movie into a Web page with the <EMBED> tag (for Netscape browsers), then one of two scenarios will happen:

1. The browser has the Flash Player plug-in and will load the Flash movie.

2. The browser does not have the Flash Player plug-in, and displays a broken plug-in icon.

If scenario 2 occurs and the PLUGINSPAGE attribute of the <EMBED> tag is defined, the user can click the broken plug-in icon and go to the Macromedia site to download the Flash Player plug-in. If no PLUGINSPAGE attribute is specified, then clicking the broken plug-in icon will take you to a generic Netscape plug-in page.

If you insert a Flash movie into a HTML document with the <OBJECT> tag (for Internet Explorer on Windows only), then one of two scenarios will happen:

1. The browser has the Flash Player ActiveX Control and will load the Flash movie.

2. The browser does not have the Flash Player ActiveX Control, and will autodownload and install the ActiveX Control file from the Macromedia site.

The ActiveX Control will only autodownload and install if the classid and codebase attributes of the Flash movie's <OBJECT> tag are correctly specified. Depending on the user's security settings, the user needs to grant permission to a Security Warning dialog (shown in Figure 44-1) in order to commence the download and install process.

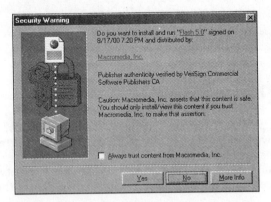

Figure 44-1: The Flash 5 Player ActiveX Control will automatically download if Microsoft Internet Explorer for Windows encounters an HTML page with Flash content.

Although using the <OBJECT> and <EMBED> tags by themselves is by far the simplest method for integrating Flash content into a Web page, it's not the most user-friendly method of ensuring that the majority of your Web visitors can view the Flash content. The most common way to detect Flash movies is by using JavaScript and VBScript, as we see in the next section.

JavaScript and VBScript player detection

The use of scripts written into an HTML document is very popular for Flash Player detection. If you're getting familiar with Flash 5's new ActionScript syntax, then you'll find that JavaScript detection code isn't all that complex. JavaScript is a universal scripting language that most 3.0 or higher Web browsers can employ to some capacity. Microsoft's implementation of JavaScript, called JScript, isn't exactly the same as Netscape's JavaScript. For this reason, you can translate some JavaScript functionality into Microsoft's proprietary Web-scripting language, VBScript.

 You'll find the HTML, .FLA, .SWF, and .GIF files for this section in the ch44 folder of the CD-ROM.

In this section, we look at how to create an HTML document that checks for the presence of the Flash Player plug-in with JavaScript, and the Flash ActiveX Control with VBScript. We use two images of a traffic light — one .SWF image with a green light on, and one .GIF image with a red light on — to display the results of our plug-in and ActiveX detection. Many Web sites employ a similar mechanism: Before an HTML page with Flash content can be accessed, the visitor will be presented with a screen telling them if they have the Flash Player installed. If they don't have it, then they can click a link to get the plug-in or ActiveX Control.

 The Flash Player can be detected with most JavaScript-enabled Web browsers, by using the JavaScript array `navigator.mimeTypes`. The value for this array is always empty for Internet Explorer browsers, including IE 4.5 on Macintosh. IE 5.0 for Macintosh now supports this array. While we can use VBScript to detect for IE on Windows, there is no script plug-in detection available for IE 4.5 on Macintosh. You can however, use the Flash Sniffer method, discussed in the next heading, to detect Flash on IE 4.5 on Macintosh.

Detecting the plug-in with JavaScript

By rearranging the JavaScript code that is created by the Ad 5 Banner template in the Publish Settings, we can set up a testing mechanism that delivers one of two graphics to the visitor's Web browser. Copy the `scriptDetection.html` document located in the ch44 folder of the *Dreamweaver and Flash Bible* CD-ROM, and open it in your preferred text editor (SimpleText, Notepad, BBEdit, and so on). Look at lines 10 to 15 (The ¬ indicates a continuation of the same line of code. It should not be written in the actual JavaScript code in the HTML document.):

```
10. var plugin = 0;
11. var activeX = 0;
12. var plugin = (navigator.mimeTypes && ¬
    navigator.mimeTypes["application/x-shockwave-flash"]) ¬
    ? navigator.mimeTypes["application/x-shockwave- ¬
    flash"].enabledPlugin : 0;
13. if ( plugin ) {
14.   plugin = parseInt(plugin.description.substring ¬
      (plugin.description.indexOf(".")-1)) >= 5;
15. }
```

Line 10 initializes a variable `plugin` to indicate the presence of the Flash 5 Player plug-in on Netscape (or IE 5.0 Mac). Line 11 initializes a variable called `activeX` to indicate the presence of the Flash 5 Player ActiveX Control. At this point, we create them with a value of 0, meaning that the plug-in and ActiveX Control are not installed.

Line 12 is borrowed from the Ad 5 Banner HTML template output. It uses the `mimeTypes` array of the navigator JavaScript Object to determine whether the Flash Player (in any version) is installed. If the Flash Player plug-in is installed, then the variable `plugin` is now equal to the value `[object Plugin]`. If this is `true`, then lines 13 and 14 will execute. Using the `description` property of the Plugin Object, we can determine whether the Flash Player is the correct version. In this example, we check whether it's greater than or equal to 5. Notice that we can use a comparison as the value of the `plugin` variable. If the Flash 5 Player (or higher) is installed, then `plugin` will equal `true` (or 1); if a lower version is installed, then `plugin` will equal `false` (or 0).

Creating a test object in VBScript

At this point, if the visitor is using Netscape (on any operating system) or Internet Explorer on the Macintosh, then the variable `plugin` will have a value of either 0 or 1. However, we still need to check for the ActiveX Control, if the visitor is using Internet Explorer for Windows. Line 11 already initialized a variable called `activeX`. Lines 16-21 check to see if VBScript can create a Flash Object in the document (The ¬ indicates a continuation of the same line of code. It should not be written in the actual JavaScript code in the HTML document.):

```
16. else if (navigator.userAgent && ¬
       navigator.userAgent.indexOf("MSIE")>=0 && ¬
       (navigator.userAgent.indexOf("Windows 95")>=0 || ¬
       navigator.userAgent.indexOf("Windows 98")>=0 || ¬
       navigator.userAgent.indexOf("Windows NT")>=0)) {
17.    document.write('<SCRIPT LANGUAGE=VBScript\> \n');
18.    document.write('on error resume next \n');
19.    document.write('activeX = ( IsObject(CreateObject ¬
       ("ShockwaveFlash.ShockwaveFlash.5")))\n');
20.    document.write('<' + '/SCRIPT>');
21. }
```

Line 16 determines whether the visitor is using Internet Explorer on Windows 95, 98, or NT. If that's the browser they're using, then lines 17 to 21 will execute. These lines of code create the VBScript that is necessary to check for the existence of the Flash 5 Player ActiveX Control. Using the `IsObject` and `CreateObject` methods, VBScript can determine whether the ActiveX Control is installed. If it is installed, then the variable `activeX` will equal `true` (or 1). Note that this variable is available to both JavaScript and VBScript. This section of code is also borrowed from the Ad 5 Banner HTML template.

Inserting the graphics

After the variables plugin and activeX have been set appropriately, we can use these variables to either display a Flash .SWF graphic or a .GIF image graphic. In the body of the HTML document, we can reuse the plugin and activeX variables to insert either the Flash or .GIF graphics. Lines 31 to 36 of the HTML document will write the tags to display the .SWF or .GIF image for Netscape (on any platform) or IE on the Mac (The ¬ indicates a continuation of the same line of code. It should not be written in the actual JavaScript code in the HTML document.):

```
31. if ( plugin ) {
32.    document.write('<EMBED SRC="trafficLightGreen.swf" ¬
       WIDTH="105" HEIGHT="185" SWLIVECONNECT="FALSE" ¬
       QUALITY="HIGH"></EMBED><BR><FONT ¬
       FACE="Verdana,Arial,Geneva" SIZE=2>Flash 5 ¬
       Player<BR>Plug-in detected.</FONT>');
33. } else if (!(navigator.appName && ¬
       navigator.appName.indexOf("Netscape")>=0 && ¬
       navigator.appVersion.indexOf("2.")>=0)){
34.    document.write('<A HREF="http://www.macromedia.com ¬
       /shockwave/download/index.cgi ¬
       P1_Prod_Version=ShockwaveFlash">');
35.    document.write('<IMG SRC="trafficLightRed.gif" ¬
       WIDTH="105" HEIGHT="185" BORDER="0"></A><BR> ¬
       <FONT FACE="Verdana,Arial,Geneva" SIZE=2>Flash ¬
       5 Player<BR>Plug-in not installed.</FONT>');
36. }
```

If the plugin variable is not equal to false (line 31), then line 32 will execute. Line 32 uses the <EMBED> tag to insert a Flash .SWF file, depicting a green light that animates to a full green color, and the HTML text "Flash 5 Player Plug-in detected." If the plugin variable is equal to false and the browser is Netscape 2.0 or higher (line 33), then lines 34 and 35 will create <A HREF> and <IMG> tags, depicting a static .GIF image of a red traffic light that links to the Macromedia download area. Then, JavaScript will create the HTML text "Flash 5 Player Plug-in not installed."

Lines 43 to 52 perform the same functionality for Internet Explorer for Windows. If the activeX variable is true, then an <OBJECT> tag is written and a green traffic light will animate on. If it's not installed, then a static .GIF image of a red traffic light will be displayed.

Finally, we should do two more things:

1. Tell IE 4.5 (or earlier) Mac users that we can't detect the Flash 5 Player plug-in.

2. Tell other users that they can either (a) proceed to the main Flash site, or (b) click the appropriate traffic light to download the plug-in or ActiveX Control.

Lines 59 to 62 tell IE 4.5 (or earlier) Mac users that we can't detect their plug-in settings. We can either leave it to them to decide whether they should download the plug-in, or we could direct them to a sniffer movie (discussed in the next section) to determine if the plug-in is installed.

Lines 63 to 65 check whether either the plug-in or the ActiveX Control is installed. If it is, then we tell the visitor to proceed to the main Flash site. Note that you would want to insert more JavaScript code here that includes a link to your Flash content.

Lines 66 to 74 check whether the plug-in and the ActiveX Control are both absent. If neither is installed, then we tell them which traffic light (lines 67 to 74) to click.

Although you'll most likely want to spruce up the look and feel of this page to suit your particular site, you can use this scripting layout to inform your visitors about their plug-in or ActiveX Control settings.

Using a Flash Swiffer movie

If you would prefer to avoid JavaScript and VBScript, then you can also use small Flash movies known as *swiffers* to detect the Flash Player. Swiffers are virtually hidden from the visitor, and direct the HTML page to a new location (using a `getURL` action) where the real Flash content (or site) exists. If the Player is not installed, then the movie won't be able to play and direct the HTML page to a new location. If this happens, then a special `<META>` tag in the `<HEAD>` of the HTML document will direct the browser location to a screen that informs the visitor to download the plug-in or ActiveX Control.

Making the Swiffer movie

The Swiffer movie is a small Flash movie that has the same background color as the HTML document. We do not need any artwork or symbols in this movie.

1. Open Flash 5, and in a new Flash movie document (.FLA file), rename Layer 1 to **actions**.

2. Add a keyframe on frame 2 of the actions layer. Double-click this new keyframe to open the Actions Panel.

3. In the Actions Panel, we create some ActionScript that checks for Flash 3 (or earlier), 4, and 5 Player versions. We can direct each version of the Player to a unique URL. The basic principle of this ActionScript is to use Flash version-specific actions to determine which Player is displaying the movie:

```
// create a Flash variable, whose value is equal to the
// $version environment variable in Flash 4 or 5. This
// action line will not be read by Flash 3 (or earlier)
// Players.
```

```
player = eval("$version");

/* The $version value will be in the format:

   abc 1,2,3,4

   where abc is the operating system (e.g. WIN, MAC)
   and 1 and 2 are the major version designations
   (e.g. 4.0, 5.0, etc.) and 3 and 4 are the minor
   version designations (e.g. r20, r27, etc.)

   By default, Flash 5 ships with a Player version equal
   to WIN 5,0,30,0 or MAC 5,0,30,0

   We just need the major version designation, at
   placeholder 1. Using substring(), we can extract this
   number. The major version starts at the 5th character
   of the version value. The Flash 3 Player will
   disregard this line.
*/

player = substring(player, 5, 1);

// player will be equal to either 4 or 5 in Flash 4 or 5
Player, respectively.

if (player eq ""){

    // Flash 3 Player will execute this code
    // automatically, because it will need interpret the
    // if action.

    getURL("flash3.html");

} else if (player eq "4"){

    // Flash 4 Player will execute this code.

    getURL("flash4.html");

} else if (player eq "5"){

   // Flash 5 Player will execute this code.

    getURL("flash5.html");
}

// We will prevent the movie from accidentally looping.

stop();
```

4. Change the size of the movie frame to **18 px×18 px**, in the Modify ⇨ Movie dialog. This is the smallest size a Flash movie can have. Change the background color of the movie to match the background color of the HTML document. Click OK.

5. Save the Flash movie as **swiffer.fla**.

6. Open the Publish Settings dialog (File ⇨ Publish Settings). Check the Flash and HTML options in the Formats tab. Uncheck the Use default names option, and rename the HTML file to swiffer_start.html.

7. In the Flash tab, select Flash 4 in the Version drop-down menu.

We are using the Flash 4 format because the Flash 3 Player will ignore all Flash 4 or higher actions, and the Flash 4 Player will recognize the formatting of the variable and ActionScript structures. Flash 5 .SWF files restructure variables and ActionScript (even Flash 4–compatible code) in a manner that doesn't work consistently in the Flash 4 Player.

8. In the HTML tab, select the Flash Only (Default) template. Click the Publish button located on the right side of the Publish Settings dialog.

9. When the files have been published, click OK to close the Publish Settings dialog. Save your movie again.

You now have swiffer.html and swiffer.swf files in the same folder as your swiffer.fla file. In the next section, we add some additional HTML tags to the swiffer.html document.

Integrating the Swiffer movie into an HTML document

After you have made the swiffer.swf and the swiffer.html files, you can modify the HTML document to guide the browser to a unique URL where plug-in information and download screen will be shown. Remember that the ¬ indicates a continuation of the same line of code. Do not insert this character into your HTML document.

1. Open the swiffer.html file in your preferred HTML document editor. Macromedia Dreamweaver, Notepad (PC), SimpleText (Mac), or BBEdit will do just fine.

2. Somewhere between the <HEAD> </HEAD> tags, insert the following HTML <META> tag:

```
<META http-equiv="Refresh" content="5; ¬
URL=download.html">
```

This <META> tag has two attributes, http-equiv and content. The http-equiv attribute instructs the hosting Web server to add the value of http-equiv as a discrete name in the MIME header of the HTML document. The value of the `content` attribute becomes the value of the MIME entry. Here, the Web browser will interpret the META tag as:

```
Refresh: 5; URL=download.html
```

in the MIME header. This name/value pair tells the browser to reload the browser window in five seconds, with the file `download.html`. After testing, you may decide to increase the time the browser waits before reloading a new URL. On slower connections (or during peak Internet hours), you may find that five seconds is not long enough for the Flash movie to initiate its `getURL` actions.

Caution

Some older browsers may require an absolute URL in the content attribute. This means that you may need to insert a full path to your HTML document, such as `http://www.yourserver.com/download.html`, as the URL in the content attribute.

3. Save the HTML file. At this point, you need to create a download.html file. As a temporary measure, you can use the scriptDetection.html file from the previous detection method. You also need to create flash3.html, flash4.html, and flash5.html files for the `getURL` actions in the swiffer.swf movie.

On the CD-ROM

We have included sample flash3.html, flash4.html, and flash5.html files on the CD-ROM. These are simple placeholder documents that do not contain any Flash movie URLs.

When you have your HTML documents ready, you can load the swiffer.html document into a browser. If the Flash Player is not installed, then the META tag should transport the browser location to the download.html URL. If the Flash Player is installed, then the Flash ActionScript will direct the browser to the appropriate page.

Expert Tutorial: Flash Player Detection (a.k.a. the moock fpi), *by Colin Moock*

While there are several ways to check for the existence of the Flash Player plug-in, no one has developed as comprehensive a strategy as Colin's strategy. We are pleased to present an introduction to his moock fpi.

Producers of Flash content live with an undeniable, often frustrating truth: Flash content is not always immediately viewable by the audience for which it is intended. Because Flash is normally viewed as a secondary application to a Web browser, a user attempting to view a Flash site may not have the Flash player installed in his or her browser, or may have an older version of the Flash player that won't allow the user to view the site.

Continued

Continued

The first time I dealt directly with the accessibility (or inaccessibility) of Flash content was in 1997, when I embarked on my first large-scale production in Flash — the Levi's Canada Web site. Throughout the project, the issue of accessibility was a matter of great concern for both the client, Levi's, and the agency producing the site, ICE (where I work). How should the site handle visitors without Flash installed in their browser? Should it simply tell everyone to get Flash? Should it only tell visitors without Flash to get Flash? What if a visitor had never heard of Flash?

After various discussions, it was decided that the best approach was to use JavaScript to automatically detect the presence of Flash in the user's browser. If the user had Flash, we sent the user to the Flash content. If not, we sent the user to equivalent non-Flash content. If detection failed, we sent the user to a page describing Flash, and offering installation instructions.

Since the Levi's project, I have yet to encounter a project that did not revisit the issue of Flash accessibility, deployment, and detection in some way. The factors have changed somewhat over the years, but the issue is always there. After countless hours of testing, thinking, and meeting, I have come to a single conclusion: No matter what the script or publication model, a site must never, ever cause its audience to feel lost.

Thus, with that single philosophy in mind, I decided to build a standard system for detecting and publishing Flash content: the moock fLASH pLAYER iNSPECTOR (a.k.a. the moock fpi). The moock fpi is a scripted system for detecting Flash. The use of a scripted detection system offers users with Flash-enabled browsers seamless access to our content, and users with non-Flash browsers a controlled and customized experience.

The behavior of the moock fpi is simple: Supply the user with Flash content if appropriate, and with alternate content if not. This premise translates to the following scripted behavior:

✦ If we can undeniably detect that a user has the correct version of Flash installed, we deploy Flash content.

✦ If we can undeniably detect that the user has an old version of Flash installed, we either ask the user to upgrade, or simply deploy non-Flash content.

✦ If we can undeniably detect that a user does not have Flash, or if our attempt to detect Flash fails, we deploy non-Flash content.

By following these three rules, the moock fpi should, in theory, never strand a user, and will always provide a user with the smoothest path to a site's content. Luckily, with the help of heavy testing by the Internet community, the theory seems to be working so far.

The moock fpi is posted for public use at: `www.moock.org/webdesign/flash/detection/moockfpi/`.

My research notes and thoughts on detection and publishing Flash content are posted at: `www.moock.org/webdesign/lectures/ff2knyc/`

If you'd like to learn more about Colin Moock, please see his bio in Chapter 40, "Navigating Flash Timelines."

Using Flash Movies with JavaScript and DHTML

The new ActionScripting features in Flash 5 have greatly increased the range of inter-active and dynamic possibilities for Flash movies on the Web. In previous releases of Flash, Flash movies could only interact with external HTML or scripts through the FSCommand action. This meant mapping commands and variables to JavaScript, which, in turn, passed information to the document object model of DHTML, Java applets, or CGI (Common Gateway Interface) scripts. Now that Flash movies can directly send and receive data to server-side CGI scripts, just about anything can be done within the Flash movie. However, if you want to directly communicate with the Web browser or the HTML document, you need to use FSCommands or getURL actions with javascript: statements. Because all JavaScript-capable browsers do not support these methods, we're limiting our discussion to FSCommands and JavaScript-controllable Flash movie properties.

A word of caution to Web developers

This section covers FSCommands, which, when used in Flash movies on Web pages, are only supported by a handful of browsers. Currently, not one version of Internet Explorer for Macintosh (up to version 5.0) can interpret FSCommands (see the Caution note in "The <EMBED> Tag" section earlier in this chapter). Only Netscape 3.0 (or higher) offers cross-platform support for FSCommands. Internet Explorer 3 and higher for Windows 95/98/NT also support FSCommands. Our coverage of the FSCommand assumes that you have basic knowledge of JavaScript and Flash ActionScript. If you don't know how to add Actions to frames or buttons, please read Chapter 39, "Understanding Actions and Event Handlers." If you don't know JavaScript, you can still follow the steps to the tutorials and create a fully functional Flash-JavaScript movie. However, because this isn't a book on JavaScript, we don't explain how JavaScript syntax or functions work.

How Flash movies work with JavaScript

As mentioned earlier, Flash has an action called fscommand. FSCommands are used to send a command (and an optional argument string) from a Flash movie to its hosting environment (such as a Web browser or standalone Flash Player). What does this mean for interactivity? The FSCommand offers the capability to have any Flash event (Button instance, onClipEvent, or frame actions) initiate an event in JavaScript. Although this may not sound too exciting, you can use FSCommands to trigger anything that you would have used JavaScript alone to do in the past, such as updating HTML-form text fields, changing the visibility of HTML elements, or switching HTML background colors on the fly. Most Flash-to-JavaScript interactivity works best with dynamic HTML (DHTML) browsers such as Netscape 4 or higher and Internet Explorer 4 or higher. We look at these effects in the next section.

Flash movie communication with JavaScript is not a one-way street. You can also monitor and control Flash movies with JavaScript. Just as JavaScript treats an HTML document as an object and its elements as properties of that object, JavaScript treats Flash movies as it would any other element on a Web page. Therefore, you can use JavaScript functions and HTML hyperlinks (<A HREF> tags) to control Flash movie playback. At the end of this chapter, we show you how to make an HTML form menu that can jump to various scenes of a Flash movie.

Note   In order for JavaScript to receive Flash FSCommands, you need to make sure that the attribute swLiveConnect for the <EMBED> tag is set to true. By default, most Flash HTML templates have this settings set to false.

Changing HTML attributes

In this section, we show you how to dynamically change the BGCOLOR attribute of the <BODY> tag with an FSCommand from a Flash movie while it is playing in the browser window. In fact, we change the background color a few times. Then, once that has been accomplished, we show you how to update the text field of a <FORM> tag to display what percent of the Flash movie has been loaded.

On the CD-ROM   Open the Flash movie countdown.fla located in the ch44 folder of the *Dreamweaver and Flash Bible* CD-ROM. This is quite a large .FLA file (over 14MB) as it uses many imported bitmap images and sounds to demonstrate slow-loading movie. If you are using the Mac version of Flash 5, you may want to increase the memory allocation for the Flash 5 application file to 64MB or higher.

Adding FSCommands to a Flash movie

Open a copy of the countdown.fla Flash movie from the *Dreamweaver and Flash Bible* CD-ROM, and use Control ➪ Test Movie to play the Flash .SWF version. You should notice that the filmstrip countdown fades to white, and then to near-black, and then back to its original gray color. This countdown contains to loop until the entire first scene has loaded into the Flash Player. When the first scene has loaded, playback will skip to a Movie Clip of two dogs (in "negative") and a title sequence. There's more to the Flash movie, but for now, that's all we need to deal with.

Our goal for this section of the tutorial is to add FSCommand frame actions to specific keyframes in the countdown.fla Flash demonstration movie. When the Flash Player plays the frame with the FSCommand action, the Player sends a command and argument string to JavaScript. JavaScript then calls a function that changes the background color to the value specified in the argument string of the FSCommand (see Figure 44-2). To be more exact, you add an FSCommand to the frames where the color fades to white, black, and gray. When the Flash movie changes to these colors, so will the HTML background colors.

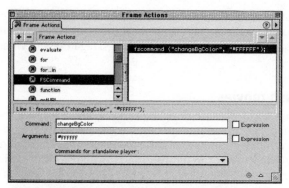

Figure 44-2: Frame 16: FSCommand of
changeBgColor with an argument of #FFFFFF
(the hexadecimal code for the color white)

Here's the process:

1. On frame 16 of the Introduction scene, add a keyframe on the actions layer. With the keyframe selected, open the Actions Panel. Make sure the Panel is in Normal Mode. Add an FSCommand action from the + pop-up menu (located in the top-left corner of the panel). In the Command field, type **changeBgColor**. In the Arguments field, type **#FFFFFF**. The command changeBgColor is mapped to a JavaScript function called changeBgColor later in this tutorial. The argument string #FFFFFF is passed to that function, changing the HTML background color to white.

2. On frame 20, add another FSCommand action to the corresponding keyframe on the actions layer. Again, insert **changeBgColor** in the Command text box. In the Arguments text box, type **#333333**. This argument changes the HTML background color to a dark gray.

3. On frame 21 of the actions layer, follow the same instructions for Step 2, except use **#9E9E9E** for the argument string. This changes the HTML background color to the same color as the Flash movie countdown graphic.

4. On frame 66 of the actions layer, add another changeBgColor FSCommand action to the empty keyframe. This time, use an argument string of **#000000**, which changes the HTML background color to black.

5. Now that we've added several FSCommands, let's try them out in the browser. Save the countdown.fla Flash movie to a folder on your hard drive, and open the Publish Settings dialog (for more information on Publish Settings, refer to Chapter 43, "Publishing Flash Movies"). In the HTML tab, select the template Flash with FSCommand. Click OK to close the Publish Settings dialog. Select the File ⇨ Publish command to export the Flash .SWF movie and HTML document.

Next, we look at the automated JavaScript code that the HTML template created. While the basic code structure has been set up, we need to make some alterations and additions to the JavaScript in order for our FSCommands to work.

Note You may have noticed that some FSCommands have already been entered on other keyframes of the countdown.fla movie. These have been placed to ensure that the background color stays consistent with other settings, regardless of where playback occurs.

Enabling JavaScript for Flash movies

Although the Flash with FSCommand template does a lot of the JavaScripting for you, it doesn't automatically map out the commands and arguments (args) to JavaScript-defined functions. In this section, we add the necessary JavaScript to make the FSCommands work in the browser. What follows is the JavaScript code that Flash 5 generates.

Note Any numbered line of code marked with an asterisk (*) is custom JavaScript code that Flash 4 does not create. Also, remember that the ¬ indicates a continuation of the same line of code. Do not insert this character into your HTML document.

```
1.   <SCRIPT LANGUAGE=JavaScript>
2.   <!--
3.   var InternetExplorer = ¬
     navigator.appName.indexOf("Microsoft") != -1;
4.*  var stringFlash = "";
5.   // Handle all the FSCommand messages in a Flash movie
6.       function countdown_DoFSCommand(command,args){
7.           var countdownObj = InternetExplorer ¬
               ? countdown : document.countdown;
8.*          stringFlash = stringFlash + args;
9.*          if(command=="changeBgColor"){
               changeBgColor();
             }
         }
10.*     function changeBgColor(){
11.*         document.bgColor = stringFlash;
12.*         stringFlash = "";
         }
13.   // Hook for Internet Explorer
        if (navigator.appName && ¬
          navigator.appName.indexOf("Microsoft") != -1 ¬
          && navigator.userAgent.indexOf("Windows") != -1 ¬
          && navigator.userAgent.indexOf("Windows 3.1") ¬
          == -1){
        document.write('<SCRIPT LANGUAGE=VBScript\> \n');
        document.write('on error resume next \n');
        document.write('Sub countdown_FSCommand(ByVal ¬
          command, ByVal args)\n');
        document.write('  call ¬
          countdown_DoFSCommand(command,args)\n');
        document.write('end sub\n');
        document.write('</SCRIPT\> \n');
        }
      //-->
14.   </SCRIPT>
```

The following is a line-by-line explanation of the code:

1. This HTML tag initializes the JavaScript code.

2. This string of characters is standard HTML comment code. By adding this after the opening `<SCRIPT>` tag, non-JavaScript browsers ignore the code. If this string wasn't included, text-based browsers such as Lynx might display JavaScript code as HTML text.

3. This variable simply condenses the JavaScript code that detects Internet Explorer into a single term, `InternetExplorer`.

4. We added this line of code to declare a variable called `stringFlash`. Its value is set to nothing by putting two straight quote characters together. This variable is necessary for FSCommand arguments to pass cleanly into JavaScript functions on both Netscape and Internet Explorer.

5. This is comment code added by the Macromedia team to let us know that the following JavaScript code is designed to catch the FSCommands from a Flash movie.

6. This is the initial JavaScript function that works exclusively with Flash FSCommands. The function's name is the value of the `NAME` attribute of the `<EMBED>` tag (or the value of the `ID` attribute of the `<OBJECT>` tag) followed by a underscore and `DoFSCommand(command,args){`. In this sample, the Flash movie `NAME` is `countdown`. Notice that the command and arguments that were specified in Flash are passed to this function as `(command,args)`, respectively.

7. This is a handy optional variable that the Flash with FSCommand template created. Strangely, it is not necessary unless you need to refer to the differing document object models between Internet Explorer and Netscape. Instead of testing for either browser, you can insert the `countdownObj` variable in your own JavaScript code. For this example, though, it is not needed.

8. This code makes the `stringFlash` variable called in line 4 equal to the argument string (`args`) from the Flash FSCommand. Because stringFlash was equal to nothing (`""`), `stringFlash` is now the same as the original argument string. This isn't necessary for Internet Explorer, but Netscape doesn't recognize arguments straight from Flash without it.

9. This compares the passed command string from the Flash FSCommand to the string `changeBgColor`. If they're the same, then JavaScript executes the code contained within the `if` statement. Because we only made one unique command in Flash for this sample, we only have to map the Flash FSCommand `changeBgColor` to the JavaScript function `changeBgColor()`.

10. This is where the function `changeBgColor()` is defined. Remember that line 9 maps the Flash FSCommand `changeBgColor` to this JavaScript function.

11. This line of code passes the variable `stringFlash` to the `document.bgColor` property, which controls the HTML background color. When the Flash FSCommand sends the command `changeBgColor`, the JavaScript `change Bgcolor()` function is invoked, which passes the argument string from the Flash FSCommand to `document.bgColor`.

12. This resets the variable `stringFlash` back to nothing (`""`), so that future invocations of the FSCommand don't use the same argument from the previous execution.

13. This section of code detects the presence of Internet Explorer for Windows and maps the JavaScript functions to VBScript (which is used exclusively by Windows-only versions of Internet Explorer).

14. The closing `</SCRIPT>` tag ends this portion of JavaScript code.

Caution

For some reason, the Flash with FSCommand template omits the `NAME` attribute for the `<EMBED>` tag. Make sure that you add this attribute to the `<EMBED>` tag. Set its value equal to the name of the Flash .SWF movie, without the .SWF file extension. For example, in the sample used for this section, the `<EMBED>` tag should have a `NAME` attribute equal to `countdown`.

That's it! Once you've manually added the custom lines of JavaScript code, you can load the HTML document into either Internet Explorer or Netscape (see the caveats mentioned at the beginning of this section). When the Flash Player comes to the frames with FSCommands, the HTML background should change along with the Flash movie. Next, we add a `<FORM>` element that displays the percentage of the Flash movie that has loaded into the browser window.

On the CD-ROM

You can find the completed version of the countdown.fla movie on the CD-ROM. It is called countdown_complete.fla and is located in the ch44 folder. You will also find countdown_complete.swf and a fully JavaScripted HTML document called countdown_complete.html. The JavaScript and HTML reflect the usage of the countdown_complete filename.

Using the PercentLoaded() method

JavaScript can control several Flash movie properties. It's beyond the scope of this book to describe each JavaScript method for Flash movies. If you want to see a complete list of Flash JavaScript methods, see the Macromedia Flash tech support page (The ¬ indicates a continuation in the URL. Do not type this character into the browser location field.):

```
http://www.macromedia.com/support/flash/ts/documents/¬
tn4460.html
```

In this section, we use the `PercentLoaded()` method to display the Flash movie's loading progress update as a text field of a `<FORM>` element. First, we add the necessary FSCommand to the Flash movie. HTML `<FORM>` elements, and then we add the appropriate JavaScript.

1. Open the countdown.fla movie that you used in the previous section. There should already be an empty keyframe present on frame 1 of the percentLoaded actions layer. Add an `FSCommand` action to this keyframe. Insert **PercentLoaded** in the Command field. This command has no arguments. Add the same FSCommand to the keyframes on frames 10, 20, 30, 40, 50, 60, and 67 of the percentLoaded actions layer. Export a Flash .SWF movie called countdown.swf with the File ⇨ Export Movie command. Make sure you place the new .SWF file in the same folder as the HTML document that we were using in the previous section.

2. In a text editor such as Notepad or SimpleText, open the HTML document showing the countdown.swf Flash movie.

3. Add the following HTML after the `<OBJECT>` and `<EMBED>` tags:

```
<FORM METHOD="post" ACTION="" NAME="flashPercent"
STYLE="display:show">
  <INPUT TYPE="text" NAME="textfield" SIZE="5" STYLE =
"display:show">
</FORM>
```

The code in Step 3 uses two `NAME` attributes so that JavaScript can recognize them. Also, the DHTML `STYLE` attribute assigns a `display:show` value to the both the `<FORM>` and `<INPUT>` tags.

Caution

Netscape 4's implementation of the document object model (DOM) doesn't allow styles to be updated on the fly unless the page is reformatted (for example, the user resizes the window). It could be possible to write more JavaScript code that would insert JavaScript styles for the `<FORM>` elements, but that's beyond the scope of this section.

4. Now we need to map the `PercentLoaded` FSCommand to a JavaScript function. Add the following JavaScript to the `if` statement(s) in the `function countdown_DoFSCommand` of the HTML document:

```
if(command=="percentLoaded"){
        moviePercentLoaded();
}
```

5. Add the following JavaScript after the `function changeBgColor()` section. This function tells the browser to update the `<FORM>` text field with the percent of the Flash movie currently loaded. When the value is greater than or equal to 99, then the text field reads 100 percent and disappears after 2 seconds. As mentioned earlier, Netscape is unable to change the `style` of the

<FORM> elements on the fly. (The ¬ indicates a continuation in the URL. Do not type this character into the browser location field.)

```
function moviePercentLoaded(){
     var m = InternetExplorer ? countdown_complete : ¬
       document.countdown_complete;
     var Percent = m.PercentLoaded();
     var temp = 0;
     if(Percent >= 99 ){
      document.flashPercent.textfield.value="100 %";
      if (navigator.appName.indexOf("Microsoft") != -1){
        setTimeout("document.flashPercent.¬
          textfield.style.display = 'none'",2000);
        setTimeout("document.flashPercent.style.¬
          display = 'none'",2000);
          }
     }
     else {
         temp = Percent;
         document.flashPercent.textfield.value = temp ¬
           + " %" ;
     }
}
```

6. Save the HTML document and load it into a browser. If you run into errors, check your JavaScript syntax carefully. A misplaced ; or } can set off the entire script. If you continue to run into errors, compare your document to the countdown_complete.html document on the *Dreamweaver and Flash Bible* CD-ROM.

Okay, that wasn't the easiest task in the world, and, admittedly, the effects might not have been as spectacular as you may have thought. However, now that you know the basics of Flash and JavaScript interactivity, you can take your Flash movie interactivity one step further.

Expert Tutorial: Java Script and FSCommands, *by Christian Honselaar*

Flash has changed the way we see and experience the Web; and with the increased power and functionality of Flash 5, this trend will only continue. Yet one underutilized capability is Flash's capability to talk with HTML to coordinate an interface. That is, Flash is capable of sending data and instructions to HTML by means of FSCommands. Similarly, JavaScript in the HTML document can be used both to get and to set Flash variables as well as perform operations in Flash. To facilitate this, Macromedia developed JavaScript methods for Flash objects. In this tutorial, you learn how to use both communication paths in one Web page.

The .FLA source file for this Flash project is on the CD-ROM in the ch44 folder. So, before we get started, please locate and open this example file, bothways.FLA.

Looking at the Main Timeline, you'll see two keyframes with ActionScripts in each one. Plus, there's a third ActionScript that is hidden from view.

The first ActionScript is located in frame 1:

```
var goalNumber=0, i=0;
fscommand("flashloaded","true");
```

The first line of code initializes the variables, goalNumber and i, and sets their value at zero. The second line issues a fscommand "flashloaded" to the JavaScript and VBScript of the HTML page.

The second script, located in the last frame looks like this:

```
if ((i==1)&&(goalNumber==0)) fscommand ( "ballGone", "dfgf");

if (i<=goalNumber){
    surface.attachMovie( "cBall", "Ball_"+i, i );
    setProperty ( "surface.Ball_"+i, _yscale, i*10 );
    setProperty ( "surface.Ball_"+i, _xscale, i*10 );
    i++;} else goalNumber=0;
gotoAndPlay (2);
```

This script uses an if statement to check whether a limit defined by the variable goalNumber hasn't yet been reached. If goalNumber hasn't been reached, then the script copies a Movie Clip instance (the ball symbol) to the Stage. You should notice that goalNumber is not assigned a proper value anywhere in this script. That's because goalNumber will be set externally, by the Web page! Also note that the other variable i tracks the current number of balls. Both of these variables were initialized in the first frame script.

There's just one more script to discuss:

```
This.removeMovieClip();
_root.i--;
if (_root.i==0) fscommand ( "ballGone" );
```

This script is in the last frame of the Movie Clip, ballAnim. The first line of this script deletes the ballAnim Movie Clip instance. With the next two lines, the script checks whether any balls are left. If not, the fscommand is evoked, sending a message to the Web browser that hosts the Flash Player.

Here's how an fscommand is constructed: The first parameter of the fscommand is the command name itself, while the second parameter can contain any arguments. Both are strings that you can pick arbitrarily. The fscommand sends a message to the Web browser, which, in turn, passes it to JavaScript or VBScript in the document. A special event handler in the script then processes the fscommand. Let's see how to do it for our example.

Continued

Continued

Open the finished HTML document that is located in the ch44 folder of the *Flash 5 Bible* CD-ROM. The JavaScript/VBScript is broken into four sections:

Section 1: Internet Explorer automatically links any `fscommand` from the Flash movie to a VBScript procedure with a specific name, which must look like this: the name (`ID`) you gave it in the `<OBJECT>` tag, with `_FSCommand` appended to it. The parameters are equal to those in the Flash movie `fscommand`. Not that we do anything with them. Our sole purpose here is to reveal the `<DIV>` or `<LAYER>` element containing our message. We create these tags in the next section.

This setup works fine on Internet Explorer 3.0 and up, on PC and MAC platforms. To make it work with Netscape 3.0+, you create a JavaScript function to receive the `FSCommand`. Its name is a little different: replace `_FSCommand` with `_DoFSCommand`. In addition, you need to add two attributes to the `<EMBED>` tag, found after the `<BODY>` tag:

```
NAME=flash and SWLIVECONNECT=true
```

That's right, Flash is controlling the HTML!

Section 2: Because each browser has its own way of using DHTML layers, we write code that will create the appropriate HTML tag for each browser. Internet Explorer will use a `<DIV>` tag, and Netscape will use a `<LAYER>` tag. This element will display the text "Flash to control center: no balls!"

Section 3: A function called `hideMessage` will be executed when the user clicks the Form button. This function will change the visibility of the `<DIV>` and `<LAYER>` tags to `false`.

Section 4: The `showMessage` function will execute when the Flash movie sends an `fscommand` to the HTML document. This will occur when the last remaining ballAnim symbol is removed from the Flash movie.

HTML can control the Flash movie by invoking JavaScript methods of the Flash object. We added a text box where the user can input the desired number of balls, and a button that will send this input to the Flash Movie. Here's the text box:

```
number of balls:<input id="nBalls" name="nBalls" value=20
type="text"></input>
```

`nBalls` now contains the desired number. By making use of the Flash method `SetVariable`, we set the variable `goalNumber` in the Flash movie to this value. But first we hide the "no balls" message. The following `<INPUT>` tag will execute the `hideMessage` function (in Section 3), which will use the `nBalls` value for the `goalNumber` value:

```
<input type="button" value="Allright Flash, do a ball trick!"
onmouseup="hideMessage(); "></input>
```

The following figure shows the form fields, as they appear beneath the Flash movie.

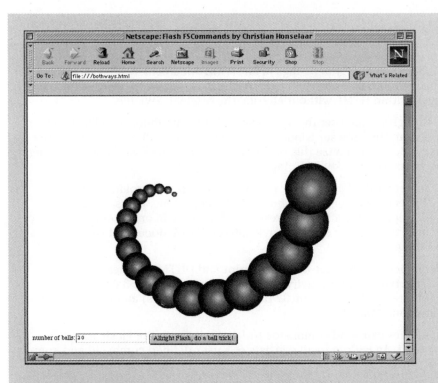

Now, when the button is pressed, the `nBalls` value is sent to Flash, updating the variable `goalNumber`, which Flash checks to see if it should create any more balls! This was just a simple example of Flash methods. In real-world situations, you'll probably find Flash methods/FSCommands most useful for synchronization purposes, such as updating navigation bars. In fact, there are many more Flash methods, and you can find documentation on them at: `www.macromedia.com/support/flash/publishexport/scriptingwithflash`.

Summary

✦ You can customize many Flash movie attributes by adjusting the attributes of the <OBJECT> and <EMBED> tags in an HTML document. Scaling, size, quality, and background color are just a few of the Flash movie properties that can be changed within HTML without altering the original .SWF file.

✦ Even though you can set the WIDTH and HEIGHT attributes of a Flash movie to 100 percent, the browser window will still show a small border around the Flash movie. To minimize this border effect, place the Flash movie in a single frame within the <FRAMESET> tag.

✦ You can detect the Flash Player plug-in or ActiveX Control in a variety of ways: by using the <OBJECT> and <EMBED> tags alone, by using JavaScript and VBScript to check for the presence of the plug-in or the ActiveX Control, or by inserting a Flash swiffer movie into an HTML document with a special <META> tag.

✦ Flash movies can interact with JavaScript and DHTML elements on a Web page. This type of interactivity, however, is limited to the 3.0 or higher versions of Internet Explorer (on 32-bit Windows versions) and Netscape (on Windows and Macintosh).

✦ Flash movies can send commands to JavaScript with the Flash action, fscommand. An FSCommand consists of a user-defined command and argument string.

✦ Although the Flash with FSCommand HTML template will set up the initial JavaScript to enable FSCommand support, it won't find the FSCommands you specified in the Flash and map them to JavaScript functions. You have to do this manually.

✦ FSCommands can be used to change HTML document attributes or styles.

✦ The Flash Player plug-in has JavaScript-specific methods that can be used to send or receive information to a Flash movie. For example, JavaScript can query a Flash movie to determine how much of it has downloaded to the browser.

✦ ✦ ✦

What's on the CD-ROM?

The CD-ROM that accompanies the *Dreamweaver and Flash Bible* contains the following:

✦ Fully functioning trial versions of Dreamweaver 4, Flash 5, Dreamweaver UltraDev 4, Fireworks 4, Director 8.5, Generator 2 (Developer Edition), and FreeHand 10.

✦ Additional programs useful in creating Web pages and Flash movies such as Sound Forge 5.0 and SWISH 1.51.

✦ Code and other examples used in the book including just about every .FLA and .SWF file discussed in the Flash chapters, including those in the Expert Tutorials.

Also included are hundreds of Dreamweaver extensions from the leaders in the Dreamweaver community, designed to make your work more productive:

✦ Behaviors

✦ Objects

✦ Commands

✦ Browser profiles

✦ Inspectors

✦ Floaters

Using the Accompanying CD-ROM

The CD-ROM is what is known as a *hybrid CD-ROM*, which means it contains files that run on more than one computer platform — in this case, both Windows and Macintosh computers.

Several files, primarily the Macromedia trial programs and the other external programs, are compressed. Double-click these files to begin the installation procedure. Most other files on the CD-ROM are uncompressed and you can simply copy them to your system by using your file manager. A few of the Dreamweaver extensions with files that must be placed in different folders are also compressed.

In the Configuration folder, the file structure replicates the structure that Dreamweaver sets up when it is installed. For example, objects found in the Dreamweaver\Configuration\Objects folder should be in that location for both the CD-ROM, and the installed program. One slight variation: In the Additional Extensions folder, you'll find the various behaviors, objects, and so on, filed under their author's name.

Files and Programs on the CD-ROM

The *Dreamweaver and Flash Bible* contains a host of programs and auxiliary files to assist your exploration of Dreamweaver, as well as your Web page design work in general. The following is a description of the files and programs on the CD-ROM that comes with this book.

Macromedia demos

If you haven't had a chance to work with Dreamweaver (or Fireworks or Flash), the CD-ROM offers fully functioning trial versions of key Macromedia programs for both Macintosh and Windows systems. Each of the demos will run for 30 days; they cannot be reinstalled in order to gain additional time. The trial programs are:

✦ Dreamweaver 4

✦ Flash 5

✦ Dreamweaver UltraDev 4

✦ Fireworks 4

✦ Director 8.5

✦ FreeHand 10

✦ Generator 2, Developer Edition

To install any of the programs, just double-click the program icon in the main folder of the CD-ROM where the programs are located and follow the installation instructions on your screen.

Caution The trial versions of Macromedia programs are very sensitive to system date changes. If you alter your computer's date, the programs will time-out and no longer function. It is a good idea to check your system's date and time before installing them. Moreover, if you've previously run the trial version of the same program from another source (such as downloading it from the Internet), you won't be able to run the trial version again.

Dreamweaver extensions

Dreamweaver is amazingly extendible, and the Dreamweaver community has built some amazing extensions. In the Additional Extensions folders of the CD-ROM, you'll find hundreds of behaviors, objects, commands, inspectors, and more. The extensions are grouped according to author, and within each author's folder they are organized by function. Almost all of these extensions were written prior to the availability of the Extension Manager and do not require that program for installation. Extensions that contain files that must be placed in different folders, such as the Commands and Inspectors directories, are compressed in a Zip format.

Note Within the Additional Extensions folder, all behaviors are stored in the Behaviors folder to make it easy to access them. When installing, make sure to put them in the Configuration\Behaviors\Action folder on your system and not just the Behaviors folder.

You'll find a ReadMe.htm file in each author's folder, with links to the author's Web site and more information about their creations.

Following is a partial list of extension authors featured on the CD-ROM (alphabetized by first word to match how you'll see them on the disc):

✦ Brendan Dawes

✦ Eddie Traversa

✦ Hal Pawluk

✦ Jaro von Flocken

✦ Lucas Lopatin

✦ Marijan Milicevic

✦ Massimo Foti

✦ Olle Karneman

✦ Project Seven Development

✦ Robert Sherman — SnR Graphics

✦ Simon White — Derren Whiteman

✦ Subnet Ltd.

✦ Webmonkey

Dreamweaver Bible extensions

The majority of the following extensions were built specifically for this book. You can find these extensions in the Configuration folder on the CD-ROM.

Note   Where available, extensions are packaged in an .mxp file, which can easily be installed using the Extension Manager. To run the Extension Manager from Dreamweaver, choose Commands⇨Manage Extensions. Then choose File⇨Install Extension and browse to the location of the extension's .mxp file. Other extensions need to be installed by copying the required files to your Dreamweaver\ Configuration folder as described below.

Behaviors

Dreamweaver behaviors automate many functions that previously required extensive JavaScript programming. The behaviors included on the CD-ROM are in addition to the standard set of behaviors included with Dreamweaver and discussed in Chapter 19. The behaviors on the CD-ROM are stored in the Configuration\Behaviors\Actions folder. Copy the behaviors to the similarly named folder in your system installation of Dreamweaver, and restart Dreamweaver to access the new behaviors.

Objects

Much of Dreamweaver's power is derived from its extensibility. Each of the standard Dreamweaver objects is based on an HTML file. The CD-ROM contains various Dreamweaver objects designed to help you create your Web pages faster and more efficiently.

Each Dreamweaver object consists of two files, an HTML file and a GIF file with the same name that is used to create the button on the Objects Palette. For example, the Character Entities object comprises the two files char_entities.htm and char_entities.gif.

To install the Dreamweaver objects, go to Dreamweaver\Configuration\Objects and copy any pair of files from the subfolders Common, Forms, Invisibles, Media, and New to similarly named folders in your system installation of Dreamweaver. (The Media and New folders are not included in the standard release of Dreamweaver and must be created on your system.) Restart Dreamweaver to access the new objects.

Commands

Commands are proving to be the real workhorses of Dreamweaver extensibility. Not only can they do pretty much everything that behaviors and objects do, but they also have their own capabilities as well. Command files come in many shapes and sizes — from a single file to five or more files split across multiple folders. The commands found in the Configuration\Commands folder on the CD-ROM go into the equivalent Dreamweaver folder on your system. The commands are as follows:

✦ **Repeat History:** Repeats any selected actions in the History palette any number of times. This command requires the Extension Manager to install.

✦ **Replicator:** Duplicates any selected object, any number of times. Be sure to copy both Replicator.htm and Replicator.js into the Commands folder.

✦ **Install Shockwave HTML:** Reads an HTML file generated by Director to insert a Shockwave object, complete with proper dimensions and other needed parameters.

✦ **Change Case:** Converts the case of the selected text to uppercase or lowercase.

Browser profiles

Dreamweaver recognizes the proliferation of browsers on the market today and makes it easy for you to check your Web page creations against specific browser types. The browser targeting capability is available through the use of browser profiles. In addition to the standard profiles that come with Dreamweaver, the CD-ROM contains several browser profiles for checking various implementations of HTML, including the following:

✦ HTML 2.0

✦ HTML 3.2

✦ HTML 4.0

✦ Opera 3.0

✦ Pocket Internet Explorer 1.0 (for Windows CE 1.0)

✦ Pocket Internet Explorer 1.1 (for Windows CE 1.0)

✦ Pocket Internet Explorer 2.0 (for Windows CE 2.0)

Each additional browser profile is contained in the Dreamweaver\Configuration\ BrowserProfiles folder of the CD-ROM. To install the browser profiles, the files must be copied to a similarly named folder in your system installation of Dreamweaver. Restart Dreamweaver to access the new browser profiles.

Dreamweaver and Flash Bible code examples

You can find example code used in the *Dreamweaver and Flash Bible* in the Code folder of the CD-ROM. Virtually all the example Flash movies and their source can be found in the Flash chapter files. You can easily view the files through Dreamweaver or Flash without transferring the files to your system. If you do wish to transfer the files, it's best to copy the entire folder over to your system.

Dreamweaver style sheets

Dreamweaver makes using a Cascading Style Sheets (CSS) a point-and-click operation. One of the great features of CSS is the capability to link your Web site to external style sheets. The CD-ROM contains several external style sheets that you can customize for your Web sites. Each external style sheet comes with an example HTML file that you can view in your browser.

To incorporate the external style sheets in your Web sites, copy files with .css extensions into your local site's root folder. Then follow the instructions in the "Linking to an External Style Sheet" section found in Chapter 27.

Web resource directory

The World Wide Web is a vital resource for any Web designer, whether a seasoned professional or a beginner. The CD-ROM contains an HTML page with a series of links to resources on the Web; the series contains general as well as Dreamweaver-specific references.

Dreamweaver 4 Bible and Flash 5 Bible in PDF Format

Can't find the exact reference that you know you read earlier? Search for it in the Dreamweaver 4 Bible or Flash 5 Bible in PDF format located on the CD-ROM. You'll need Adobe Acrobat Reader to view the PDF files; if you don't have it installed on your system, you'll find it on the CD-ROM also.

✦   ✦   ✦

Index

S

<s> tag, 242, 293
\S wildcard character, 281
\s wildcard character, 281
salign attribute, 546–547
    <EMBED> tag, 1295
    <OBJECT> tag, 1295
<samp> tag, 242, 293, 586
sample rate, 1076–1077, 1104, 1105
sans serif fonts, 1274
saturation, 303, 305, 853, 854, 855
Save All Frames command, 83, 447
Save As command, 83, 447, 698, 743
Save as Default option, Swatches Panel, 853
Save as Shockwave Movie in Director command, 539
Save As Template command, 83, 688, 698
Save Colors, 853, 855
Save command, 83, 743
Save Copy As, 321
Save Default button, 763
Save dialog box, 188
Save Files Before Putting option, 134
Save Frameset As command, 83, 447
Save Frameset command, 83, 447
Save Log button, 211
Save on Launch option, 124
Save Panel Layout command, 771
Save Query, 274
Save Site Map as JPEG command, 223
Save Site Map as PICT command, 223
Save Site Map command, 223
Save Spacer Image File As dialog box, 127
saving pages, 188
scalable lines, 969
Scale
    Arrow Tool option, 794–795
    parameter, Flash, 545–546
    Publish Settings field, 1294–1295
    Transform menu command, 963
    Transform Panel field, 962
Scale and Rotate command, Transform menu, 963
Scale and Rotate dialog, 794
scale attribute, <EMBED> tag, 1309, 1311
scaleSliderOver variable, 1233
scaling Movie Clips, 1195–1196
Scene
    command, 761
    Go To action parameter, 1125
    panel, 771, 901–902
scene
    adding, 902
    deleting, 902
    duplicating, 902
    movie, 725
    order, rearranging, 902
    renaming, 902
Scene and Symbol Bar, 901–902
Scene Name button, 901
Scene Properties dialog, 761
Scramm, Nik, 1016

screen size, 46–48
script preferences, 116
<script> tag, 694, 1327
    noformat keyword, 154
Scripts category, Assets panel, 71
scroll, 451–452
SCROLLING attribute, <frame> tag, 1312
scrolling list
    in forms, 424–426
    height and width, 425–426
    inserting, 424
scrolling text, 1067–1071
scrubbing, 925
Search button, 161
search engine
    aiding with Keywords and Description objects,
      236–237
    frames and, 457
    refresh tag and, 239
Search For option button, 275, 276, 278
searching. *See also* Find and Replace
    filters for, 277
    Help files, 160–162
    with regular expressions, 280–284
Security Warning dialog, 1314
Select All command, 85, 373, 749
Select Browser dialog box, 135
Select Child command, 85
Select Child Tag command, 254
Select External Editor dialog, 1109
Select File dialog box, 352, 691, 698
    link modification and, 218
    linking to existing files, 217
Select First Item After URL Change option, 428
Select Image Source dialog box, 320, 325, 642
Select Newer Local option, 205
Select Newer Remote option, 205
Select Parent Tag command, 85, 254
Select Symbol Instances command, Movie Explorer, 944
Select Table command, 373
Select Template dialog box, 692
Select the Files That Use option, 713
Select Unused Items option, Library, 918
<select> tag, 422
Selected Local Files Only option, 210
selecting
    cells, 375
    layer, 626–627
    rows and columns, 373–375
    table, entire, 373, 374
    table elements, 372–375
    text, 264
Selection Made in List Validation behavior, 573
Selection Options, Flash Preferences, 750
Selection Properties command, 92
selection style, 75, 296
selection tools
    Arrow Tool (A), 788–797
    Lasso Tool (L), 785–788
    Subselect Tool, 802–803

Hungry Minds, Inc.
End-User License Agreement

READ THIS. You should carefully read these terms and conditions before opening the software packet(s) included with this book ("Book"). This is a license agreement ("Agreement") between you and Hungry Minds, Inc. ("HMI"). By opening the accompanying software packet(s), you acknowledge that you have read and accept the following terms and conditions. If you do not agree and do not want to be bound by such terms and conditions, promptly return the Book and the unopened software packet(s) to the place you obtained them for a full refund.

1. **License Grant.** HMI grants to you (either an individual or entity) a nonexclusive license to use one copy of the enclosed software program(s) (collectively, the "Software") solely for your own personal or business purposes on a single computer (whether a standard computer or a workstation component of a multi-user network). The Software is in use on a computer when it is loaded into temporary memory (RAM) or installed into permanent memory (hard disk, CD-ROM, or other storage device). HMI reserves all rights not expressly granted herein.

2. **Ownership.** HMI is the owner of all right, title, and interest, including copyright, in and to the compilation of the Software recorded on the disk(s) or CD-ROM ("Software Media"). Copyright to the individual programs recorded on the Software Media is owned by the author or other authorized copyright owner of each program. Ownership of the Software and all proprietary rights relating thereto remain with HMI and its licensers.

3. **Restrictions On Use and Transfer.**

   (a) You may only (i) make one copy of the Software for backup or archival purposes, or (ii) transfer the Software to a single hard disk, provided that you keep the original for backup or archival purposes. You may not (i) rent or lease the Software, (ii) copy or reproduce the Software through a LAN or other network system or through any computer subscriber system or bulletin-board system, or (iii) modify, adapt, or create derivative works based on the Software.

   (b) You may not reverse engineer, decompile, or disassemble the Software. You may transfer the Software and user documentation on a permanent basis, provided that the transferee agrees to accept the terms and conditions of this Agreement and you retain no copies. If the Software is an update or has been updated, any transfer must include the most recent update and all prior versions.

4. **Restrictions on Use of Individual Programs.** You must follow the individual requirements and restrictions detailed for each individual program in the Appendix of this Book. These limitations are also contained in the individual license agreements recorded on the Software Media. These limitations may

include a requirement that after using the program for a specified period of time, the user must pay a registration fee or discontinue use. By opening the Software packet(s), you will be agreeing to abide by the licenses and restrictions for these individual programs that are detailed in the Appendix and on the Software Media. None of the material on this Software Media or listed in this Book may ever be redistributed, in original or modified form, for commercial purposes.

5. Limited Warranty.

   (a) HMI warrants that the Software and Software Media are free from defects in materials and workmanship under normal use for a period of sixty (60) days from the date of purchase of this Book. If HMI receives notification within the warranty period of defects in materials or workmanship, HMI will replace the defective Software Media.

   (b) **HMI AND THE AUTHOR OF THE BOOK DISCLAIM ALL OTHER WARRANTIES, EXPRESS OR IMPLIED, INCLUDING WITHOUT LIMITATION IMPLIED WARRANTIES OF MERCHANTABILITY AND FITNESS FOR A PARTICULAR PURPOSE, WITH RESPECT TO THE SOFTWARE, THE PROGRAMS, THE SOURCE CODE CONTAINED THEREIN, AND/OR THE TECHNIQUES DESCRIBED IN THIS BOOK. HMI DOES NOT WARRANT THAT THE FUNCTIONS CONTAINED IN THE SOFTWARE WILL MEET YOUR REQUIREMENTS OR THAT THE OPERATION OF THE SOFTWARE WILL BE ERROR FREE.**

   (c) This limited warranty gives you specific legal rights, and you may have other rights that vary from jurisdiction to jurisdiction.

6. Remedies.

   (a) HMI's entire liability and your exclusive remedy for defects in materials and workmanship shall be limited to replacement of the Software Media, which may be returned to HMI with a copy of your receipt at the following address: Software Media Fulfillment Department, Attn.: *Dreamweaver and Flash Bible*, Hungry Minds, Inc., 10475 Crosspoint Blvd., Indianapolis, IN 46256, or call 1-800-762-2974. Please allow four to six weeks for delivery. This Limited Warranty is void if failure of the Software Media has resulted from accident, abuse, or misapplication. Any replacement Software Media will be warranted for the remainder of the original warranty period or thirty (30) days, whichever is longer.

   (b) In no event shall HMI or the author be liable for any damages whatsoever (including without limitation damages for loss of business profits, business interruption, loss of business information, or any other pecuniary loss) arising from the use of or inability to use the Book or the Software, even if HMI has been advised of the possibility of such damages.

   (c) Because some jurisdictions do not allow the exclusion or limitation of liability for consequential or incidental damages, the above limitation or exclusion may not apply to you.

7. **U.S. Government Restricted Rights.** Use, duplication, or disclosure of the Software for or on behalf of the United States of America, its agencies and/or instrumentalities (the "U.S. Government") is subject to restrictions as stated in paragraph (c)(1)(ii) of the Rights in Technical Data and Computer Software clause of DFARS 252.227-7013, or subparagraphs (c) (1) and (2) of the Commercial Computer Software - Restricted Rights clause at FAR 52.227-19, and in similar clauses in the NASA FAR supplement, as applicable.

8. **General.** This Agreement constitutes the entire understanding of the parties and revokes and supersedes all prior agreements, oral or written, between them and may not be modified or amended except in a writing signed by both parties hereto that specifically refers to this Agreement. This Agreement shall take precedence over any other documents that may be in conflict herewith. If any one or more provisions contained in this Agreement are held by any court or tribunal to be invalid, illegal, or otherwise unenforceable, each and every other provision shall remain in full force and effect.

CD-ROM Installation Instructions

The *Dreamweaver and Flash Bible* CD-ROM contains trial versions of Dreamweaver 4, Flash 5, Dreamweaver UltraDev 4, Fireworks 4, Director 8.5, Generator 2 (Developer Edition), and FreeHand 10, in addition to a host of extensions, objects, commands, and code from this book. The CD-ROM is also packed with tutorials from almost all of the .FLA and .SWF files that are discussed in this book. For more information on installing and using the programs on the CD-ROM, please refer to the Appendix.

Accessing the Programs on the CD-ROM

The CD-ROM is what is known as a *hybrid CD-ROM*, which means it contains files that run on more than one computer platform — in this case, both Windows and Macintosh computers.

Several files, primarily the Macromedia trial programs and the other external programs, are compressed. Double-click these files to begin the installation procedure. Most other files on the CD-ROM are uncompressed and you can simply copy them to your system by using your file manager. A few of the Dreamweaver extensions with files that must be placed in different folders are also compressed.

In the Configuration folder, the file structure replicates the structure that Dreamweaver sets up when it is installed. For example, objects found in the Dreamweaver\Configuration\Objects folder should be in that location for both the CD-ROM, and the installed program. One slight variation: In the Additional Extensions folder, you'll find the various behaviors, objects, and so on, filed under their author's name.

Installing Dreamweaver and Flash

To install Dreamweaver and Flash on your Windows system, follow these steps:

1. Insert the *Dreamweaver and Flash Bible* CD-ROM into your CD-ROM drive.

2. Double-click the .exe file to unpack it and begin the installation process.

3. Follow the onscreen instructions. Accept the default options for program location.

Changing the Windows read-only attribute

You may not be able to access files on the CD-ROMs after you copy the files to your computer. After you copy or move the entire contents of the CD-ROMs to your hard disk or another storage medium (such as a Zip disk), you may get the following error message when you attempt to open a file with its associated application:

```
[Application] is unable to open the [file]. Please make sure
the drive and file are writable.
```

Windows sees all files on a CD-ROM drive as read-only. This normally makes sense because a CD-ROM is a read-only medium — that is, you can't write data back to the CD-ROM. However, when you copy a file from a CD-ROM to your hard disk or to a Zip disk, Windows doesn't automatically change the file attribute from read-only to writable.

Installation software normally takes care of this chore for you, but in this case, because the files are intended to be manually copied to your disk, you have to change the file attribute yourself. Luckily, it's easy — just follow these steps:

1. Click the Start menu button.

2. Select Programs.

3. Choose Windows Explorer.

4. Highlight the file name(s) on the hard disk or Zip disk.

5. Right-click the highlighted file name(s) to display a pop-up menu.

6. Select Properties to display the Properties dialog box.

7. Click the Read-only option so that it is no longer checked.

8. Click the OK button.

You should now be able to use the file(s) with the specific application without getting the annoying error message.